Financial
Valuation

Founded in 1807, John Wiley & Sons is the oldest independent publishing company in the United States. With offices in North America, Europe, Australia, and Asia, Wiley is globally committed to developing and marketing print and electronic products and services for our customers' professional and personal knowledge and understanding.

The Wiley Finance series contains books written specifically for finance and investment professionals as well as sophisticated individual investors and their financial advisors. Book topics range from portfolio management to e-commerce, risk management, financial engineering, valuation, and financial instrument analysis, as well as much more.

For a list of available titles, please visit our Web site at www.WileyFinance.com.

Financial Valuation

Applications and Models

**Third Edition
with Website**

JAMES R. HITCHNER

WILEY

John Wiley & Sons, Inc.

Published by John Wiley & Sons, Inc., Hoboken, New Jersey.

Published simultaneously in Canada.

For general information on our other products and services or for technical support, please contact our Customer Care Department within the United States at (800) 762-2974, outside the United States at (317) 572-3993 or fax (317) 572-4002.

Wiley also publishes its books in a variety of electronic formats. Some content that appears in print may not be available in electronic books. For more information about Wiley products, visit our web site at *www.wiley.com*.

Library of Congress Cataloging-in-Publication Data

Hitchner, James R.
   Financial valuation : applications and models / James R. Hitchner. – 3rd ed.
     p. cm. – (Wiley finance series)
   Includes index.
     ISBN 978-0-470-50687-5 (hardback); ISBN 978-0-470-91522-6;
     ISBN 978-0-470-91523-3; ISBN 978-0-470-91524-0
   1. Corporations–Valuation. I. Title.
   HG4028.V3H583 2011
   658.15–dc22

                                             2010048924

Printed in the United States of America

10 9 8 7 6 5 4 3

To my greatest champion, my dad, Earle R. Hitchner, Jr. Thank you for instilling in me a work ethic and tenacity that keeps me going. I miss you. To his sister and my godmother, Aunt Thelma. You are simply the best and a true inspiration to all who know and love you.

To the authors: It has truly been one of the highlights of my career to work with such a wonderful group of professionals. Thank you for your perseverance in helping to advance the business valuation profession.

To my mother, Virginia M. Hitchner, who passed away during the final days of editing this book. Thank you for sticking by me, always. I miss you.

Contents

James R. Hitchner, CPA/ABV/CFF, ASA, is the managing director of Financial Valuation Advisors, Inc. (www.finvaluation.com) in Ventnor City, New Jersey. He is also president of the Financial Consulting Group, LLC (www.gofcg.org), a national association of professional services firms dedicated to excellence in valuation, financial, and litigation consulting. He is CEO of Valuation Products and Services, LLC (www.valuationproducts.com), a company dedicated to developing educational resources for valuation analysts and fraud/forensics practitioners. He holds the American Institute of Certified Public Accountants (AICPA) specialty designations of Accredited in Business Valuation (ABV) and Certified in Financial Forensics (CFF) and is an Accredited Senior Appraiser (ASA) with the American Society of Appraisers. Mr. Hitchner has over 30 years' experience in valuation services. He has often testified as a qualified expert witness on valuations in federal and state courts across the country. He has also been involved in hundreds of intangible asset valuations and was an ad hoc advisor to the Financial Accounting Standards Board (FASB) on its deliberations concerning fair value, presenting two sessions to the FASB on valuing and lifing intangible assets.

He has coauthored 20 courses, taught over 60 courses, published over 80 articles, and made over 180 conference presentations. He was with Phillips Hitchner Group, Inc. for seven years and was also partner-in-charge of valuation services for the southern region of Coopers & Lybrand (currently PricewaterhouseCoopers), where he spent more than nine years. He was also employed as a senior appraiser with the national appraisal firm American Appraisal Associates, in both the financial and industrial valuation groups.

Mr. Hitchner is coauthor of the book *Valuation for Financial Reporting, Fair Value Measurements and Reporting: Intangible Assets, Goodwill, and Impairment*; editor/coauthor of the book *Financial Valuation Applications and Models (FVAM)*; and coauthor of the book *Financial Valuation Workbook (FVW)*—all published by John Wiley & Sons. He is coauthor, along with Shannon Pratt and Jay Fishman (fellow coauthors of *FVAM*), of *PPC's Guide to Business Valuations*, published by Thomson Reuters. *FVAM* and *FVW* have been adopted by the AICPA for its five-day National Business Valuation School courses and by the National Association of Certified Valuation Analysts (NACVA) for its three-day Advanced Business Valuation courses. He is editor in chief of *Financial Valuation and Litigation Expert*, a bimonthly journal that presents views and tools from some of the leading experts in valuation, forensics/fraud, and litigation services.

He has also been a faculty member teaching valuation courses for judges for the National Judicial College and the Flaschner Judicial Institute. He is an inductee in the AICPA Business Valuation Hall of Fame and a two-time recipient of the AICPA's Business Valuation Volunteer of the Year award. He was one of only four members of the original AICPA Business Valuation Standards Writing Task Force and served for the entire six years up to the June 2007 official release of the standards.

Mr. Hitchner is past chairman of the Business Valuation Committee of the Georgia Society of CPAs, past member of the AICPA Business Valuation Subcommittee, past member of the AICPA ABV exam committee, past chairman of the ABV exam review course committee, and contributing editor of the AICPA *CPA Expert* newsletter. He has a bachelor of science degree in engineering from the University of Pittsburgh and master of business administration degree from Rider University.

Mel H. Abraham, CPA/ABV, ASA, CVA, is a successful entrepreneur with multiple businesses. He is a forensic expert in financial and valuation issues and a nationally recognized, award-winning speaker, having addressed professional conferences on a local, state, and national level. He has been part of various training and mentoring programs from people like Anthony Robbins, Gavin de Becker, Keith Cunningham, and Marshall Sylver. His book *Valuation Issues and Case Law Update—A Reference Guide* is in its fifth edition. He is coauthor of one of the business valuation industry's best-selling books, *Financial Valuation: Applications and Models*, and two additional books, *A Healthier You* (with Deepak Chopra and Billy Blanks) released in 2005, and *Masters on Success* (with Ken Blanchard, Jack Canfield, and John Christensen) released in 2005. Mr. Abraham holds the AICPA designation of Accredited in Business Valuation (ABV), and is an Accredited Senior Appraiser (ASA) with the American Society of Appraisers, a Certified Valuation Analyst (CVA) with the National Association of Certified Valuation Analysts, and a member of the National Speakers Association. He has a bachelor of science degree from California State University, Northridge.

R. James Alerding, CPA/ABV/CFF, ASA, CVA, is partner in the Valuation and Forensic Services Client Service Center for Clifton Gunderson, LLP. He holds the AICPA specialty designation of Accredited in Business Valuation (ABV) as well as the Certified in Financial Forensics (CFF) designation, is an Accredited Senior Appraiser (ASA) with the American Society of Appraisers, and is a Certified Valuation Analyst (CVA) with the National Association of Certified Valuation Analysts (NACVA). Mr. Alerding has over 43 years of financial/accounting/investment experience, including over 30 years of business valuation experience. He has taught over 40 valuation courses, published numerous articles, and made over 100 business valuation presentations. He has been recognized as an expert witness in several states across the United States and has testified approximately 500 times in depositions and trials. Mr. Alerding was a member of the writing task force for the AICPA Statement on Standards for Valuation Services No. 1 (SSVS), and is a member of the Indiana CPA society, a past member of the AICPA Business Valuation Subcommittee, and an AICPA Business Valuation Hall of Fame member. He is a summa cum laude graduate of Xavier University with a bachelor's degree in accounting.

Neil J. Beaton, CPA/ABV, CFA, ASA, is the national partner in charge of Grant Thornton LLP's valuation services. He has over 25 years' experience analyzing both closely and publicly held companies. He has appeared as an expert witness across the country and in international tribunals, is an instructor for the AICPA's business valuation courses, and speaks nationally on business valuation with a special emphasis on early-stage and high-technology companies. He has published two books and written many articles on early-stage company valuations as well. He has served on the AICPA's National Accreditation Commission and the Financial Accounting Standards Board Valuation Resource Group. Mr. Beaton has a bachelor of arts degree in economics from Stanford University and a master of business

administration in finance from National University. In addition to his formal education, he is a Certified Public Accountant, Accredited in Business Valuation, a Chartered Financial Analyst, and an Accredited Senior Appraiser in business valuation
from the American Society of Appraisers.

Marcie D. Bour, CPA/ABV, CVA, CFE, BVAL, CFFA, is president of the Florida
Business Valuation Group and a member of the American Business Appraisers
National Network. She provides business appraisal, forensic accounting, and litigation consulting services and has over 25 years of professional experience. Ms. Bour
currently serves on the Board of Governors of the Institute of Business Appraisers.
She is an instructor in the area of economic damages, leading a team to develop the
NACVA's workshop *Business Interruption Losses and Claims.* She has spoken at
valuation conferences on lost profits damages and valuation issues. Ms. Bour has testified at depositions or trials in damage, shareholder dispute, usury, and criminal
sentencing cases. Her valuation and litigation experience covers a variety of industries. Ms. Bour graduated from Emory University with a BBA, earning distinction in
accounting. Her business valuation credentials include Accredited in Business Valuation (ABV) from the AICPA and Certified Valuation Analyst (CVA) from the
NACVA. She is a Certified Fraud Examiner (CFE), Business Valuator Accredited for
Litigation (BVAL), and Certified Forensic Financial Analyst (CFFA).

Stacy Preston Collins, CPA/ABV, CFF, is a managing director at Financial
Research Associates. In this role, she is responsible for financial analysis, economic
and industry analysis, forensic accounting, economic damages, and valuation of privately held and publicly traded businesses and professional practices. She has provided expert witness testimony on forensic accounting and business valuation issues
in several states. Ms. Collins has been actively engaged in performing business valuations, litigation support, and related services since 1993, and was in public accounting for a national firm for several years. Her experience includes matters related to
marital dissolution, shareholder disputes, estate and gift taxes, and transactions. She
has coauthored courses on business appraisal issues and has presented valuation seminars and courses to financial professionals, attorneys, and judges in a variety of
forums, including the AICPA, state CPA societies and institutes, the ASA, and various
national, state, and city legal and bar associations and institutes. She has also served
as instructor on several valuation courses sponsored by the AICPA. Ms. Collins has
been a faculty member at the American Bar Association's Family Law Advocacy Institute from 2003 to 2005 and from 2007 to 2009, and has been active in the Institute's
annual mock trial since 2000. She has participated as an instructor/mentor at the
American Academy of Matrimonial Lawyers' Institute for Training Family Law Associates each year since 2006. Ms. Collins is a member of the AICPA, PICPA, and
NJSCPA. She holds the Accredited in Business Valuation (ABV) and Certified in
Financial Forensics (CFF) designations from the AICPA and is a member of the
AICPA's Family Law Task Force and its Forensic and Litigation Services Committee.
Ms. Collins is also a candidate of the American Society of Appraisers.

Larry R. Cook, CPA/ABV/CFF, CBA, is the owner of Larry R. Cook & Associates, PC, a financial services firm located in Houston, Texas, that focuses on business
strategies, business valuations, transitions, and solution planning and implementation. Mr. Cook is a founding member and former president of the Financial Consulting Group, LLC. He holds the AICPA specialty designation of Accredited in
Business Valuation (ABV) and Certified in Financial Forensics (CFF). Mr. Cook also
holds the designation of Certified Business Appraiser (CBA) from the Institute of

Business Appraisers and has taught countless seminars on a wide range of subjects for groups such as the AICPA, TSCPA, the Institute of Business Appraisers, and FCG. He has over 30 years of business valuation and financial experience and has been recognized in state and federal courts as an expert witness in finance. Mr. Cook is the author of *Financial Valuation of Employee Stock Ownership Plan Shares* and a coauthor in all three editions of *Financial Valuation Applications and Models*. He has served as chair of the ABV Credential Committee for the AICPA and as a board member for the Texas Society of CPAs and for the Business Valuation Standards for Professional Practice Committee of the Institute of Business Appraisers. Mr. Cook graduated from Sam Houston State University in its first class of accounting majors.

Don M. Drysdale, CPA/ABV, ASA, is the managing member of Drysdale Valuation, PLLC, with offices in Tucson, Arizona, and Centerville, Utah. He holds the AICPA specialty designation of Accredited in Business Valuation (ABV), is an Accredited Senior Appraiser (ASA) with the American Society of Appraisers, and is a member of the Appraisal Issues Task Force. Mr. Drysdale has more than 20 years financial and accounting experience with more than 15 years providing business valuation services. He has considerable experience in lecturing to academic and professional organizations, including the University of Arizona, the American Institute of Certified Public Accountants, the National Association of Certified Valuation Analysts, the Institute of Business Appraisers, the Arizona Society of CPAs, the Utah Association of CPAs, and others. He has a bachelor of arts degree in accounting from Weber State University.

Robert E. Duffy, CPA/ABV, ASA, CFA, is a partner with Grant Thornton. He holds the AICPA specialty designation of Accredited in Business Valuation (ABV), is an Accredited Senior Appraiser (ASA) with the American Society of Appraisers, and is a Chartered Financial Analyst (CFA). He has over 25 years' experience in valuation services and has appeared as an expert witness in state, federal, and bankruptcy courts. Mr. Duffy is a charter panelist on the Technical Advisory Panel for the AICPA's *ABV E-Alert*, a contributing editor of the AICPA publication *CPA Expert*, and a member of the AICPA's Business Valuation Hall of Fame. He has a bachelor of arts degree from Western Washington University and a master of business administration from Pacific Lutheran University.

Edward J. Dupke, CPA/ABV/CFF, ASA, is a senior consultant in valuation and forensic services at Clifton Gunderson LLP based in the firm's Phoenix, Arizona office. He holds the AICPA specialty designations of Accredited in Business Valuation (ABV) and Certified in Financial Forensics (CFF). He also holds the Accredited Senior Appraiser (ASA) designation from the American Society of Appraisers. Mr. Dupke is a former chairman of the AICPA Business Valuation Committee and a former chairman of the Michigan Association of CPAs. He has over 35 years of professional experience in public accounting and business valuation practice. He has been qualified as an expert witness in both state and federal courts and is a regular instructor in business valuation at both the state and national level. Mr. Dupke is a former member of the AICPA Board of Directors and recently chaired the AICPA task force writing the first business valuation standard for AICPA members. He is a member of the AICPA Business Valuation Hall of Fame. He is the recipient of special recognition awards from both the AICPA and the Michigan Association of CPAs for his work on business valuation standards. He is coauthor *of Financial Valuation Applications and Models* and a contributing author to other valuation specialty texts. He is a member of the panel of experts of the *Financial Valuation and Litigation Expert*. In 2008, he was named by *Accounting Today* magazine as one of the 100 most influential CPAs. He holds a bachelor of science degree in business administration from Wayne State University.

Jay E. Fishman, FASA, is a managing director of Financial Research Associates and has been actively engaged in the appraisal profession since 1974. He specializes in the valuations of business enterprises and their intangible assets. Mr. Fishman has coauthored several books, including the highly acclaimed *Guide to Business Valuations* (with Shannon Pratt and Jim Hitchner) and *Standards of Value* (with Shannon Pratt and William Morrison). He has also written numerous articles on business valuations as well as qualifying as an expert witness and providing testimony in 12 states. He has taught courses on business valuation to the Internal Revenue Service, the National Judicial College, the Hong Kong Society of Accountants, and on behalf of the World Bank in St. Petersburg, Russia. He recently taught courses in Moscow, Russia, for Kwinto Management. He holds bachelor's and master's degrees from Temple University as well as an MBA from LaSalle University. Mr. Fishman is a Fellow of the American Society of Appraisers, a Fellow of the Royal Institution of Chartered Surveyors, a former chairman of the Business Valuation Committee of the American Society of Appraisers, former editor of the *Business Valuation Review*, chair of ASA's Government Relations Committee, a former trustee of the Appraisal Foundation, and a member of the Appraisal Standards Board of the Appraisal Foundation.

Chris Hamilton, CPA, CFE, CVA, DABFA, is a Certified Public Accountant, Certified Fraud Examiner, Certified Valuation Analyst, and Diplomate with the American Board of Forensic Accounting. He is a founder and principal of Arxis Financial in Simi Valley, California. Most of his professional time is spent in the areas of business valuation, fraud, forensic accounting, and other litigation-related engagements. He has served as an expert in civil, criminal, probate, and family court matters. He has also presented courses at national conferences, training institutes, and seminars on topics including fraud, business appraisal, and forensic accounting. He is a member of the team teaching the Advanced Business Valuation courses around the country for the National Association of Certified Valuation Analysts. He is the author and presenter of two courses, Capitalization and Discount Rates: Assessing the Differences and Advanced Case Law Update, offered by the NACVA. The NACVA has recognized him as an Instructor of Exceptional Distinction. Mr. Hamilton is regularly asked by civic and business groups to speak on a variety of topics related to his experience and expertise. His articles on a variety of topics have been published in several periodicals, including the *Forensic Examiner*, the *Valuation Examiner*, *Los Angeles Lawyer*, *Valuation Strategies*, and the *Journal of Forensic Accounting*. He currently serves on the editorial board of *Insights on Valuation*. He has a bachelor of science degree in business administration and accounting from California State University, Northridge.

Thomas E. Hilton, MS, CPA/ABV/CFF, ASA, CVA, is director of the Forensic & Valuation Services Group at Anders Minkler & Diehl LLP in St. Louis and is licensed to practice in Missouri, Illinois, and Florida. He has testified regarding forensic accounting and valuation matters in a variety of venues in Missouri, Florida, Arkansas, and Illinois. Mr. Hilton is chair of the AICPA Forensic and Valuation Services Executive Committee. He also currently serves as a member of AICPA Governing Council. In 2005 and 2006, Mr. Hilton was named one of the Top 100 Most Influential Practitioners by *CPA Magazine*. He was inducted into the AICPA

Business Valuation Hall of Fame in 2004. In 2003, Mr. Hilton was named a CPA All-Star in the Business Valuation Discipline by *CPA Magazine*. He has a bachelor of science degree in business administration from the University of Missouri–St. Louis, and a master of finance degree from St. Louis University.

James R. Hitchner, CPA/ABV/CFF, ASA, is the managing director of Financial Valuation Advisors in Ventnor City, New Jersey. He is also president of the Financial Consulting Group, LLC, a national association of professional services firms dedicated to excellence in valuation, financial, and litigation consulting. He is president of Valuation Products and Services, LLC, a company dedicated to developing educational resources for valuation analysts and fraud/forensics practitioners. He holds the AICPA specialty designations of Accredited in Business Valuation (ABV) and Certified in Financial Forensics (CFF) and is an Accredited Senior Appraiser (ASA) with the American Society of Appraisers. Mr. Hitchner has over 30 years experience in valuation services. He has often testified as a qualified expert witness on valuations in federal and state courts in numerous states. He has coauthored 20 courses, taught over 60 courses, published over 80 articles, and made over 180 conference presentations. Mr. Hitchner is coauthor of the book *Valuation for Financial Reporting, Fair Value Measurements and Reporting: Intangible Assets, Goodwill, and Impairment*; editor/coauthor of the book *Financial Valuation Applications and Models (FVAM)*; and coauthor of the book *Financial Valuation Workbook (FVW)*— all published by John Wiley & Sons. He is coauthor, along with Shannon Pratt and Jay Fishman (fellow coauthors of *FVAM*), of *PPC's Guide to Business Valuations*, published by Thomson Reuters. He is editor in chief of *Financial Valuation and Litigation Expert*, a bimonthly journal that presents views and tools from some of the leading experts in valuation, forensics/fraud, and litigation services. He is an inductee in the AICPA Business Valuation Hall of Fame and a two-time recipient of the AICPA's Business Valuation Volunteer of the Year award. He was also one of only four members of the original AICPA Business Valuation Standards Writing Task Force and served for the entire six years up to the June 2007 official release of the standards. Mr. Hitchner is past chairman of the Business Valuation Committee of the Georgia Society of CPAs, past member of the AICPA Business Valuation Subcommittee, past member of the AICPA ABV exam committee, and past chairman of the ABV exam review course committee.

Steven D. Hyden, CPA/ABV, ASA, is a managing director of the Financial Valuation Group of Florida, Inc. (www.fvgfl.com), a valuation and litigation services firm located in Tampa, Florida, and president of Hyden Capital, Inc. He holds the AICPA specialty designation of Accredited in Business Valuation (ABV) and is an Accredited Senior Appraiser (ASA) with the American Society of Appraisers. Mr. Hyden has over 20 years of professional business valuation and mergers and acquisitions (M&A) experience, including 10 years with Merrill Lynch in Chicago. He is a coauthor of *Valuation for Financial Reporting: Fair Value Measurements and Reporting, Intangible Assets, Goodwill, and Impairment*, published by John Wiley & Sons. He runs the firm's corporate finance department, including all financial reporting analyses. Mr. Hyden currently is a member of the Appraisal Issues Task Force, which monitors issues related to valuation for financial reporting. He holds a bachelor of science degree in marketing from Syracuse University and a master of business administration degree from Pace University.

Gregory S. Koonsman, CFA, is cofounder and senior partner in VMG Health. VMG Health is a valuation and financial advisory firm that specializes exclusively in the healthcare services sector. VMG was founded in 1995 and has offices in Dallas, Texas, and Nashville, Tennessee. Mr. Koonsman was also cofounder and director in Practice Performance, Inc., a business outsourcing provider to surgical specialists. Practice Performance, Inc., was sold to MedSynergies, Inc., in September 2006. Prior to founding VMG Health, Mr. Koonsman began his healthcare financial advisory career with Ernst & Young. He serves as a member of the board of directors of IntraOp Medical Corporation, a publicly traded manufacturer of radiation therapy technology, and speaks frequently on the subject of healthcare business valuation and transactions. Mr. Koonsman is a Chartered Financial Analyst and a member of the American Society of Appraisers, and was coauthor of *Financial Valuation Applications and Models*. He received a master's degree in business administration from the University of Dallas in 1990 and a bachelor of science degree in aerospace engineering from Texas A&M University in 1986.

Mark G. Kucik, CPA, CVA, CM&AA, is founder of the Kucik Valuation Group, LLC, of Chicago, Illinois, specializing in business valuations of family-owned and closely held securities for use in estate tax planning, financial statement reporting, estate tax returns, gift tax returns, buy/sell agreements, purchase/sale transactions, employee stock ownership plans (ESOPs), economic damages, and matrimonial and shareholder disputes. He is an instructor in the NACVA's Training Development Team. He was awarded the NACVA's Outstanding Member award, NACVA's Circle of Light Award, NACVA's Outstanding Instructor award, and Instructor of Great Distinction award. Mr. Kucik teaches NACVA's *Business Valuations: Fundamentals, Techniques & Theory, Applications and Calculations of the Income and Asset Approaches, Advanced Valuation: Applications and Models*, and business valuation standards courses around the country. He also presents valuation seminars throughout the Chicago area. He is a member of the International Glossary Task Force. He serves on NACVA's Executive Advisory Board and NACVA's Standards Committee. He is a Certified Valuation Analyst (CVA), and a member of the American Institute of Certified Public Accountants (AICPA) and the Illinois CPA Society (ICPAS). Mr. Kucik is a graduate of Loyola University of Chicago.

Eva M. Lang, CPA/ABV, ASA, is the executive director of the Financial Consulting Group, LLC, a nationwide alliance of business valuation and consulting firms (www.gofcg.org), and the president of Valuation Products and Services, LLC (www.valuationproducts.com). She is an Accredited Senior Appraiser (ASA) with the American Society of Appraisers and holds the Accredited in Business Valuation (ABV) credential from the AICPA. Ms. Lang has over 15 years of business valuation experience. She is a nationally recognized expert on internet research for business valuation and litigation services. She has published numerous articles, is a frequent speaker to national groups on technology issues, is a contributing editor for the AICPA's *CPA Expert*, and was coauthor or contributing author to six books, including *The Best Websites for Financial Professionals, Business Appraisers, and Accountants*. Ms. Lang has served as a member of the Business Valuations Subcommittee of the AICPA and on CPA committees at the state level in the areas of estate planning, litigation services, and management consulting. She has a bachelor of science degree in business administration from Northwestern State University.

Derald L. Lyons, MT, CPA, CVA, is president of Lyons & Seacrest, PC, CPAs. He has been a practicing CPA for over 30 years and has specialized in business valuations for much of that time. His valuation specialties include marital dissolution (including separate property tracing); tax (gift, estate, income tax, purchase price allocations, and S elections); dissenting shareholder actions; economic loss calculations; and mergers and acquisitions. He has been qualified as an expert witness and provided testimony regarding valuations and other financial matters on numerous occasions. He is one of the primary instructors for the National Association of Certified Valuation Analysts and part of NACVA's Training Development Team. Mr. Lyons was the recipient of the NACVA's 2003 Circle of Light award (NACVA's highest instructor distinction), the Instructor of the Year award, Instructor of Exceptional Distinction (1999–2005), Instructor of Great Distinction, and NACVA's Outstanding Member award. He is a past president of the Colorado Society of Certified Public Accountants and a council member for the American Institute of Certified Public Accountants (1996–2000). He has also been named in "Who's Who in Professional Services" in the Denver accounting profession by the *Denver Business Journal*.

Michael J. Mard, CPA/ABV, ASA, is a managing director of the Financial Valuation Group of Florida, Inc. (www.fvgfl.com), and was founding president of the Financial Consulting Group, today the nation's largest organization of independently owned business valuation, forensics, and financial services firms. He has received the AICPA Business Valuation Volunteer of the Year award and has been inducted into the AICPA Business Valuation Hall of Fame. For over 21 years, he has served as an expert witness and over that span has testified on the public record more than 300 times. Mr. Mard has testified in Federal District Court, Tax Court, and throughout the state of Florida. His subjects of testimony include eminent domain (jury trials), divorce, shareholder disputes, and damages to intellectual property, including trade names and trademarks. Mr. Mard is marking 12 years of serving the Financial Accounting Standards Board, originally as a resource for the development of FAS 141 and FAS 142 and now as a member of the FASB's Valuation Resource Group.

Harold G. Martin, Jr., CPA/ABV/CFF, ASA, CFE, is the principal-in-charge of the Business Valuation, Forensic, and Litigation Services Group for Keiter, Stephens, Hurst, Gary & Shreaves, PC, in Richmond, Virginia. He holds the AICPA specialty designations of Accredited in Business Valuation (CPA/ABV) and Certified in Financial Forensics (CPA/CFF), is an Accredited Senior Appraiser (ASA) with the American Society of Appraisers, and is a Certified Fraud Examiner (CFE) with the Association of Fraud Examiners. He has over 25 years of experience and has appeared as an expert witness in federal and state courts, served as a court-appointed neutral, and also served as a court-appointed accountant for receiverships. He is an adjunct faculty member of the College of William and Mary Mason Graduate School of Business and teaches in the Master of Accounting program. He is a contributing author to *Cost of Capital: Estimation and Applications*, 4th edition. He is an instructor for the AICPA's National Business Valuation School and ABV Examination Review Course, and was an editorial advisor and contributing author for the AICPA's *CPA Expert*. He is a former member of the AICPA Business Valuation Committee, former editor of the AICPA's *ABV e-Alert*, and a two-time recipient of the AICPA Business Valuation Volunteer of the Year award. Mr. Martin received his bachelor of arts degree in English from the College of William and Mary and has a master of business administration degree from Virginia Commonwealth University.

Edward F. Moran, Jr., MBA, CVA, CBA, ABAR, recently retired partner from Horne, LLP, has been advising restaurant businesses and franchises on accounting and valuation issues for almost 35 years. Mr. Moran has valued or participated in hundreds of industry sales, mergers, purchases, exchanges, and estate and gift planning engagements. He has been quoted in the *Wall Street Journal* and is published in the *Valuation Examiner, CPA Expert, Valuation Strategies,* and *Franchise News,* among others. He is the author of *BVR's Guide to Restaurant Valuations,* 2010 Edition. He is currently a Certified Valuation Analyst (CVA) from the National Association of Certified Valuation Analysts, as well as a Certified Business Appraiser (CBA) and Accredited in Business Appraisal Review (ABAR) from the Institute of Business Appraisers. Mr. Moran recently retired as a Certified Public Accountant (CPA) Accredited in Business Valuation (ABV) from the AICPA. In addition to a master of business administration degree from the University of Pittsburgh, Mr. Moran holds a bachelor of arts degree in economics (with a minor in statistics) from Georgetown University and a bachelor of science degree in business administration (with a major in accounting) from the University of Arizona.

Raymond E. Moran, ASA, MRICS, serves as senior vice president for American Appraisal Associates and works in its New York City office. Mr. Moran has over 30 years of valuation experience and is an Accredited Senior Appraiser (ASA) with the American Society of Appraisers and a member of the Royal Institute of Chartered Surveyors. Prior to his return to the United States, Mr. Moran was posted to China on behalf of his company and has spoken on global valuation issues in Shanghai, Guangzhou, Hong Kong, and Tokyo, in addition to presentations throughout Europe and North America. He has testified before the U.S. Bankruptcy Court in Houston and Los Angeles and is the author of several articles on the valuation industry. Mr. Moran has a bachelor of arts degree in valuation sciences from Hofstra University.

Patricia A. Perzel, CPA, CVA, CFFA, CFF, is the founder of Perzel & Lara Forensic CPA's, PA, and has more than 30 years of experience testifying in both criminal and civil matters in state and federal courts, serving as an expert witness/consultant in various types of cases. She currently teaches and was also a contributing author for the development of the following publications and educational courses for the National Association of Certified Valuation Analysts (NACVA): "The Fundamentals, Techniques & Theory of Business Valuations," "Training Course—Forensic Accounting Investigation Methodology," "Training Academy—Fraud Prevention & Detection Training Course," and "Business Interruption & Damage Claims Training Course." Ms. Perzel lectures nationally and internationally in the areas of business valuations, forensic investigation techniques, and damage quantifications. She also participates as a speaker in continuing education courses for attorneys and CPAs.

Shannon P. Pratt, CFA, FASA, ARM, MCBA, ABAR, CM&AA, is the chairman and CEO of Shannon Pratt Valuations, Inc., a nationally recognized business valuation firm headquartered in Portland, Oregon. He is also the founder and editor emeritus of Business Valuation Resources, LLC. He has earned a doctorate of business administration, finance, from Indiana University and a bachelor of arts, business administration, from the University of Washington. Dr. Pratt is an Accredited Senior Appraiser and Fellow (FASA) of the American Society of Appraisers and is also accredited in Appraisal Review and Management (ARM). He is a Chartered Financial Analyst (CFA) and a Master Certified Business Appraiser (MCBA), and is Accredited in Business Appraisal Review (ABAR) by the Institute of Business Appraisers. He is also a Master Certified Business Counselor (MCBC), and is Certified in Mergers and Acquisitions (CM&AA) with the Alliance of Merger and Acquisition Advisors.

Dr. Pratt is a life member of the American Society of Appraisers and its Business Valuation Committee, a lifetime member emeritus of the Advisory Committee on Valuations of the ESOP Association, and the first life member of the Institute of Business

Appraisers. He is a recipient of the magna cum laude award of the National Association of Certified Valuation Analysts for service to the business valuation profession. Dr. Pratt is a past trustee of the Appraisal Foundation and is currently an outside director of Paulson Capital Corporation.

Dr. Pratt is the author of *Valuing a Business: The Analysis and Appraisal of Closely Held Companies*, 5th edition (McGraw-Hill, 2008); coauthor, *Valuing Small Businesses and Professional Practices*, 3rd edition (McGraw-Hill, 1998); coauthor, *Guide to Business Valuations*, 20th edition (Practitioners Publishing Company, 2010); coauthor of the following Wiley books: *Standards of Value* (2007) and *Business Valuation and Taxes: Procedure, Law, and Perspective*, 2nd edition, with Judge David Laro (2010); and author of the following Wiley books: *Business Valuation Discounts and Premiums*, 2nd edition (2008); *Business Valuation Body of Knowledge: Exam Review and Professional Reference*, 2nd edition (2003); and *The Market Approach to Valuing Businesses*, 2nd edition (2005). He is the author of *The Lawyer's Business Valuation Handbook*, 2nd edition (American Bar Association, 2010). He has also published nearly 200 articles on business valuation topics.

Ronald L. Seigneur, CPA/ABV/CFF, ASA, CVA, is a partner in Seigneur Gustafson LLP, a CPA firm located in Lakewood, Colorado. He holds the AICPA specialty designations of Accredited in Business Valuation (ABV) and Certified in Financial Forensics (CFF), is an Accredited Senior Appraiser (ASA) with the American Society of Appraisers, and is a Certified Valuation Analyst (CVA) with the National Association of Certified Valuation Analysts. Mr. Seigneur has over 25 years of experience working with complex valuation and litigation support matters. He has published over 100 articles on business valuation and related subjects and has developed and taught a number of intermediate and advanced business valuation courses for the AICPA, NACVA, and state bar associations. He is a past chair of the AICPA ABV Credential Committee and has been a member of the AICPA BV Committee and the AICPA Consulting Services Executive Committee. Mr. Seigneur was the 2009–2010 chair of the Colorado Society of CPAs. He is a Fellow of the College of Law Practice Management and is an adjunct professor at the University of Denver College of Law, where he teaches financial, management and leadership courses. He holds a bachelor of arts degree in hotel, restaurant, and institutional management from Michigan State University and a master of business administration degree in corporate policy and finance from the University of Michigan.

Robin E. Taylor, CPA/ABV, CBA, CFE, CVA, is a partner in the Birmingham, Alabama, office of Dixon Hughes PLLC, a regional accounting firm, and is a founding member and past president of the Financial Consulting Group, LLC. He holds the AICPA specialty designation of Accredited in Business Valuation (ABV). He is a Certified Business Appraiser (CBA) from the Institute of Business Appraisers, a Certified Fraud Examiner (CFE) with the Association of Fraud Examiners and a Certified Valuation Analyst (CVA) with the National Association of Certified Valuation Analysts. Mr. Taylor has provided expert witness testimony in the area of business valuations and has testified in other areas, including government contracts and damages quantification. His articles have been published in various professional journals, including the *CPA Expert*, the *White Paper*, and the *CPA Litigation Service Counselor*, and he has spoken to national conferences on a number of valuation issues. He is also an AICPA instructor for its valuation curriculum, including the AICPA National Business Valuation School and the ABV Examination Review Course, has chaired and served on the AICPA Business Valuation Committee, and has served on several AICPA valuation task forces. He is an honors graduate from the University of Alabama and holds a master of arts degree in accounting.

Linda B. Trugman, CPA/ABV, ASA, MCBA, MBA, is the vice president of Trugman Valuation Associates and specializes in business valuation and litigation services. She holds the AICPA specialty designation of Accredited in Business Valuation (ABV), is a Master Certified Business Appraiser (MCBA) from the Institute of Business Appraisers, and is an Accredited Senior Appraiser (ASA) with the American Society of Appraisers. Ms. Trugman has over 15 years of professional experience. She has been qualified as an expert witness in state courts in New Jersey, instructed numerous courses on business valuation, authored and coauthored two courses on valuation, and received the Instructor of the Year award from the Institute of Business Appraisers. Ms. Trugman was chair of the 2002 AICPA Business Valuation conference, has served as editor of the professional journal *Business Appraisal Practice* (published by the IBA), and has served on the AICPA Business Valuation Committee and the BV/FLS Executive Committee. She is secretary of the ASA's BV Committee as well as cochair of its BV Education Committee. Ms. Trugman was inducted into the AICPA BV Hall of Fame in 2009. She has a bachelor of science degree from the University of North Carolina and a master's degree in business administration from Fairleigh Dickinson University.

Samuel Y. Wessinger is managing director of Peachtree Valuation LLC in Atlanta, Georgia. He has 22 years of professional experience, including 18 years of valuation and financial advisory experience. Mr. Wessinger has valued securities and assets for hundreds of businesses in many different industries, and has provided valuation and related services in a wide range of matters for many different purposes. He has qualified as an expert witness in state and federal court and has testified in several states. Mr. Wessinger has written articles on valuation and related subjects appearing in professional publications, and has spoken on valuation topics to valuation professionals seeking continuing education, CPAs, and attorneys. He received his master's degree in business administration from the Colgate Darden Graduate School of Business Administration at the University of Virginia and a bachelor of arts degree, with distinction, in political and social thought from the University of Virginia.

Donald P. Wisehart, ASA, CPA/ABV/CFF, CVA, MST, is the owner of Wisehart Inc., a CPA/consulting firm located in Kingston, Rhode Island, and a founding member of the Financial Consulting Group, LLC. He is an Accredited Senior Appraiser (ASA), holds two AICPA specialty designations of Accredited in Business Valuation (ABV) and Certified in Financial Forensics (CFF), and is a Certified Valuation Analyst (CVA) with the National Association of Certified Valuation Analysts (NACVA). Mr. Wisehart has over 35 years of professional experience, including 20 years of business valuation experience. He has lectured extensively on business valuation topics, and developed and taught many business valuation courses, two of which were required courses for the NACVA certification program. He has testified as an expert witness in valuation litigation cases, and has served as the chairman of the Education Board for the NACVA and as a member of the AICPA ABV Credential Committee. He has taught at several colleges and universities and served as the first president of the Rhode Island Business Appraisal Group. He received a bachelor's degree from Kent State University and a master of taxation degree from Bryant College.

Kevin R. Yeanoplos, CPA/ABV/CFF, ASA, is the Director of Valuation Services for Brueggeman and Johnson Yeanoplos, PC, a firm with offices in Seattle, Phoenix, and Tucson, that specializes in the areas of business and intellectual property valuation.

Mr. Yeanoplos is a CPA Accredited in Business Valuation and Certified in Financial Forensics (CPA/ABV/CFF) and an Accredited Senior Appraiser (ASA) for the American Society of Appraisers. He has 17 years of valuation experience. He was one of the original coauthors of the AICPA's *Accredited in Business Valuation Exam Review Course*, was contributing author to the 2001 and 2008 *Supplement to Valuing Professional Practices & Licenses*, and was a contributing author to the 2004 *Forensic Accounting in Matrimonial Divorce* supplement to the *Journal of Forensic Accounting*. Mr. Yeanoplos is currently serving as a commissioner on the AICPA's National Accreditation Commission. He is immediate past chair of the AICPA's ABV Credential Committee and a former member of the Business Valuation Subcommittee. He is a two-time past chair of the Arizona Society of CPAs' Business Valuation Committee and was the founding chair of the Utah Association of CPAs' Business Valuation Committee. Mr. Yeanoplos graduated magna cum laude from the University of Utah in 1983, where he received his bachelor of science degree in accounting.

Contributing Authors: The following people provided valuable insight and knowledge to the authors and assisted in the preparation of parts of this text and/or addendums:

Dr. Ashok Abbott	Business Valuation
Farhad Aghdami	Williams Mullen
Terry Allen	Financial Valuation Group
Jeff Balcombe	BVA Group
Don Barbo	Ernst & Young
Scott Beauchene	Grant Thornton
Melinda Brandan	Food Industry Consultants
Michael L. Brandan	Food Industry Consultants
Steve Campana	Doyle & Keenan
Adrian Campelo	Eisner LLP
Derick O. Champagne	Huron Consulting Group
Adrian Ciocoi	Riedel Research Group
Brenda M. Clarke	Seigneur Gustafson
J. Richard Claywell	J. Richard Claywell
Darren Cordier	FV Specialists
David Dufendach	Grant Thornton
David Ellner	Peachtree Valuation
Nancy Fannon	Fannon Valuation Group
Carl-Henry Geschwind	Cocke, Szpanka & Taylor
John Gilbert	Financial Valuation Group
Roger Grabowski	Duff & Phelps
Robert Grossman	Grossman Yanak & Ford
Lance Hall	FMV Opinions
William A. Hanlin, Jr.	Hanlin Moss
James Harrington	Duff & Phelps
Jeremy T. Hess	Keiter Stephens Hurst, Gary & Shreaves
John Hill	Clifton Gunderson
Laura Kelley	Mendon Capital Advisors
David King	Mesirow Financial Consulting
Robert Kleeman	OnPointe Valuation
M. Mark Lee	Eisner LLP

Scott M. LeMay	LeMay-Lang Consulting
Gil Matthews	Sutter Securities Inc.
Michael Mattson	Financial Valuation Group
Simon C. Mazumdar	LECG, University of California–Berkeley
Chris Mercer	Mercer Capital
Katherine Morris	American Appraisal Associates
William Morrison	Morrison & Company
Deanna Muraki	Financial Valuation Group of Florida
Deborah Patry	
Michelle Patterson	Sutter Securities Inc.
Brian K. Pearson	Valuation Advisors
Laura Pfeiffenberger	Fannon Valuation Group
Charles M. Phillips	Acuitas
Rob Raney	Grant Thornton
Jim Rigby	In memoriam (1946–2009)
Jerry Ross	Famous Sam's franchisor
Scott Saltzman	Saltzman LLC
Dr. Donald Shannon	DePaul University
Leonard Sliwoski	Minnesota State University–Moorhead
Brent Sloan	Grant Thornton
Peter N. Thacker, Jr.	Keiter Stephens Hurst, Gary & Shreaves
Chris Treharne	Gibraltar Business Appraisals
Dan Van Vleet	Stout Risius Ross
Marc Vianello	Vianello Forensic Consulting
Paul Vogt	Grant Thornton

ACKNOWLEDGMENTS

At John Wiley & Sons, I would like to thank John DeRemigis and Judy Howarth for their encouragement, direction, and tough love to keep me on track.

For the third edition, I would like to thank Karen Warner of Valuation Products and Services, LLC, and Janet Kern of Financial Valuation Advisors, Inc., for working with the coauthors, editing, and proofreading.

I thank all of the following prominent valuation practitioners for their insightful comments in reviewing either the entire book or certain chapters in the first, second, and/or third editions of this book.

> Parnell Black, National Association of Certified Valuation Analysts, Salt Lake City, Utah
> Mark Dietrich, Dietrich & Wilson, PC, Framingham, Massachusetts
> Christopher Mercer, Mercer Capital, Memphis, Tennessee
> Shannon Pratt, Shannon Pratt Valuations, Portland, Oregon
> Scott Saltzman, Saltzman, LLC, National Association of Certified Valuation Analysts, Denver, Colorado
> Gary Trugman, Trugman Valuation Associates, Plantation, Florida

> I would also like to thank the following organizations or sources for the use of certain information:

John Wiley & Sons, Inc.
Mercer Capital
Morningstar
Financial Valuation Group
Appraisal Foundation
Risk Management Association
Beckmill Research
Brookings Institution
Financial Consulting Group
Financial Accounting Standards Board
American Institute of Certified Public Accountants
Internal Revenue Service
Partnership Profiles, Inc.
Trugman Valuation Associates
National Center for Employee Ownership
Business Valuation Resources, LLC
Duff & Phelps, LLC
Investopedia, Inc.
Shannon Pratt Valuations
Institute of Business Appraisers
National Association of Certified Valuation Analysts

American Society of Appraisers
Standard & Poor's
McGraw-Hill, Inc.
Journal of Corporation Law
Capital Ideas
American Business Review
Valuation Strategies/Warren, Gorham & Lamont of RIA
Business Valuation Review
FVG Holdings, Inc.
FVG California Partnership
Financial Valuation Solutions, LLC
Valuation Products and Services, LLC

Preface

It's hard to believe that almost five years have passed in the journey to publish the third edition of *Financial Valuation: Applications and Models* (*FVAM*). When I started this book, it was my intention to design it to accomplish two main goals. The first and most obvious one was to gather a group of respected valuation practitioners from all over the country and from the various valuation and appraisal associations to coauthor a text on valuation and to have a consensus view and presentation. Given the strong personalities of the authors, this was no easy task. As one of my coauthors said to me in the beginning, "Jim, what you are doing is equivalent to trying to herd cats." Well, he was right. However, I believe we met this goal in all three editions, and I credit my coauthors in their willingness to be open-minded and to change their opinions when a better way was presented.

My second goal was to use this text and the companion *Financial Valuation Workbook* for business valuation education. Both texts are the foundation for the American Institute of Certified Public Accountants (AICPA) five-day National Business Valuation School, which is offered around the country, and the National Association of Certified Valuation Analysts (NACVA) three-day Advanced Valuation: Applications and Models course, also offered around the country. I want to thank all the instructors and staff of both organizations. What a wonderful group of people to work and consult with.

FVAM is an all-encompassing valuation text that presents the application of financial valuation theory in an easily understood manner. Although valuation theory is thoroughly discussed, the focus is on applications, models, and methods. *FVAM* contains numerous examples and methods that will assist the reader in navigating a valuation project, along with hundreds of short, easily understandable "ValTips." These ValTips alert the reader to important and often controversial issues.

We have assembled 30 highly visible and well-respected valuation professionals to discuss and agree upon the proper methods of valuation and to collectively present the group's views and positions on business valuation concepts and, most important, applications. Each author is the coauthor of the entire book. The authors come from all over the United States and are members of many professional valuation and financial associations, including the American Institute of Certified Public Accountants (AICPA), the American Society of Appraisers (ASA), the CFA Institute, the Institute of Business Appraisers (IBA), and the National Association of Certified Valuation Analysts (NACVA). Many hold multiple designations or certifications:

- 20 Accredited in Business Valuation (ABV) with the AICPA
- 19 Accredited Senior Appraisers (ASA) with the ASA
- 5 Certified Business Appraisers (CBA) with the IBA
- 4 Chartered Financial Analysts (CFA) with the CFA Institute
- 4 Certified Fraud Examiners (CFE) with the ACFE
- 9 Certified in Financial Forensics (CFF) with the AICPA

- 24 Certified Public Accountants (CPA)
- 12 Certified Valuation Analysts (CVA) with the NACVA

Collectively, they have several hundred years of valuation and related financial experience. This text is the first time such a large group of diverse valuation practitioners has been assembled to agree on the application of valuation principles and methods. Given the often judgmental nature of valuation and the strong opinions that seem to go with being a valuation analyst, this was no easy task. We hope we continue to advance the profession by providing our agreed-upon views. We invite other practitioners to comment on this edition and/or assist in future editions of this book. We will never gain consensus in everything in the valuation profession; however, we do hope to shorten the long list of controversies and disagreements. This text represents the state-of-the-art in the business valuation profession as it evolves. This book includes basic, intermediate, and advanced topics, including:

- Shareholder disputes
- Mergers and acquisitions
- S corporations
- Advanced company risk analysis
- Income, estate, and gift taxes
- Marital dissolution
- Employee stock ownership plans (ESOPs)
- Financial reporting
- Discounts and premiums
- Family limited partnerships
- Healthcare and other industries
- Intellectual property
- Commercial damages
- High-tech issues

FVAM is targeted to the following professionals and groups, who are typically exposed to financial valuation issues:

- Appraisal associations and societies
- Appraisers
- Actuaries
- Attorneys
- Bankers
- Business brokers
- Business executives, including CEOs, CFOs, and tax directors
- Business owners
- CPAs
- Estate and gift planners
- Financial analysts
- Government agencies, including the IRS, SEC, DOL, OIG, and DOJ
- Insurance agents
- Investment advisors
- Investment bankers
- Judges
- Pension administrators

- Professors
- Stockbrokers

Some chapter highlights include:

Chapter 2, Standards of Value, is a completely new chapter that delves deeply into the various standards of value and how they affect value.

Chapter 6, Cost of Capital/Rates of Return has been greatly expanded and includes new thinking and research on risk premiums, beta, and data sources.

Chapter 7, Market Approach, has been rewritten and includes new thoughts on the use of transaction databases.

Chapter 9, Valuation Discounts and Premiums, expands on discounts, including new quantitative models for discounts for lack of marketability.

Chapter 10, Report Writing, has been updated to include the new AICPA business valuation standards (SSVS No. 1).

Chapter 11, Business Valuation Standards, has been updated to include the new AICPA business valuation standards and changes to other standards.

Chapter 19, Valuation Issues in Small Businesses, has been rewritten and expanded.

Chapter 20, Valuation Issues in Professional Practices, has been rewritten and expanded.

This book also includes a companion website, which can be found at www.wiley.com/go/FVAM3E. The website includes additional chapter addendums referenced throughout the book.

Financial valuations are very much affected by specific facts and circumstances. Consequently, the views expressed in these written materials do not necessarily reflect the professional opinions or positions that the authors would take in every business valuation assignment or in providing business valuation services in connection with an actual litigation matter. Every situation is unique, and differing facts and circumstances may result in variations of the applied methodologies. Furthermore, valuation theory, applications, and methods are continually evolving and at a later date may be different than what is presented here. Nothing contained in these written materials shall be construed as the rendering of valuation advice, the rendering of a valuation opinion, the rendering of an opinion of a particular valuation position, or the rendering of any other professional opinion or service. Business valuation services are necessarily fact-sensitive, particularly in a litigation context. Therefore, the authors urge readers to apply their expertise to particular valuation fact patterns that they encounter, or to seek competent professional assistance as warranted in the circumstances. *Mel Abraham, Jim Alerding, Neil Beaton, Marcie Bour, Stacy Collins, Larry Cook, Don Drysdale, Bob Duffy, Ed Dupke, Jay Fishman, Chris Hamilton, Tom Hilton, Jim Hitchner, Steve Hyden, Greg Koonsman, Mark Kucik, Eva Lang, Derald Lyons, Mike Mard, Harold Martin, Ed Moran, Ray Moran, Pat Perzel, Shannon Pratt, Ron Seigneur, Robin Taylor, Linda Trugman, Sam Wessinger, Don Wisehart, Kevin Yeanoplos.*

CHAPTER 1

Introduction to Financial Valuation

There is an ever-increasing need for financial valuation services pertaining to ownership interests and assets in non-public companies/entities and subsidiaries, divisions, or segments of public companies. Many textbooks discuss valuation issues pertaining to public companies and their stock prices. Much of that information also can be used to value nonpublic companies. However, over the past 30 years or so, specific techniques, methods, applications, and models applicable to nonpublic entities and assets have emerged and grown. This text addresses this body of knowledge.

Valuation has many judgmental factors, and this leads to many differences of opinion. This book presents the consensus view of 30 of the leading valuation analysts in the country.

Much of the notation system used in this text is that used by Dr. Shannon P. Pratt (a coauthor of this book) in his various publications,[1] a system adopted by the American Institute of Certified Public Accountants (AICPA), the National Association of Certified Valuation Analysts (NACVA), the American Society of Appraisers (ASA), and the Institute of Business Appraisers (IBA) in their business valuation courses.

As a quick reference guide to important factors and concepts, numerous "ValTips" are found throughout the volume. These ValTips are intended to provide guidance and insight on handling key issues as well as to provide practice ideas.

WHO VALUES BUSINESSES?

Many providers and/or users of business valuation services exist. The AICPA unofficially estimates that tens of thousands of Certified Public Accountants (CPAs) perform business valuations on at least a part-time basis. Many of these are also full-time valuation practitioners. Several of the national accounting firms also have valuation services groups. There are also analysts and appraisers who practice out of various types of organizations, including appraisal companies, valuation boutiques, and consulting firms. Valuations are also performed by investment bankers, usually as part of a transaction. Owners and financial executives also participate in valuations of their companies or segments of their companies. This book attempts to provide a sound understanding of financial valuation for all users and providers of valuation services and to advance consensus views on some of the more troublesome aspects of valuation science.

---

[1] Shannon P. Pratt and Roger J. Grabowski, *Cost of Capital: Estimation and Applications, Third Edition* (New York: John Wiley & Sons, 2008), pp. xxix–xxxviii.

PURPOSE OF A VALUATION

Businesses or their assets are valued for a variety of reasons. Some of the more common purposes for valuation are:

- Mergers and acquisitions
- Litigation and ownership disputes
- Estate, gift, and income tax
- Marital dissolution
- Dissenters' rights cases
- Shareholder oppression cases
- Employee Stock Ownership Plans (ESOPs)
- Financial reporting
- Allocation of purchase price
- Goodwill impairment
- Buy/sell agreements
- Family limited partnerships
- Reorganizations and bankruptcies
- Recapitalizations
- Business planning
- Stock option plans
- Compensation

Various types of businesses can be valued:

- C corporations
- S corporations
- Limited liability companies
- Limited liability partnerships
- Limited partnerships
- General partnerships
- Trusts
- Sole proprietorships
- Undivided interests

The types of interest within each of the organizational structures can vary as well. The types of interest that can be valued include:

- 100 percent controlling interest
- Majority interests that possess control
- Majority interests that do not possess control
- 50 percent interest
- Dominant minority interest
- Nondominant minority interest

The individual ownership characteristics of any interest in a company being valued must also be evaluated. As such, it is important for an analyst to review corporate documents, including articles of incorporation, by-laws, buy/sell agreements, restrictive agreements, and the like. A review of these documents, along with an understanding of state rights, will indicate any particular rights that the interest enjoys.

PROFESSIONAL VALUATION ORGANIZATIONS

Four U.S. professional organizations, listed alphabetically below, provide assistance to their members in valuing businesses, particularly closely held business interests:

1. American Institute of Certified Public Accountants (AICPA)
2. American Society of Appraisers (ASA)
3. Institute of Business Appraisers (IBA)
4. National Association of Certified Valuation Analysts (NACVA)

Each of these organizations is briefly described in Chapter 11.

Canada has a very active group devoted to business valuation as well: the Canadian Institute of Chartered Business Valuators (CICBV), www.cicbv.ca.

STANDARDS OF VALUE

Before analysts can attempt to value a business, they must fully understand the standard of value that applies (see Chapter 2).

Relying on the wrong standard of value can result in a very different value, and in a dispute setting, the possible dismissal of the value altogether.

There are five main standards of value:

1. Fair market value (FMV)
2. Investment value
3. Intrinsic value
4. Fair value (state rights)
5. Fair value (financial reporting)

FAIR MARKET VALUE

The U.S. Treasury regulations define fair market value as "the price at which the property would change hands between a willing buyer and a willing seller, neither being under any compulsion to buy or to sell and both having reasonable knowledge of relevant facts."[2]

---

[2] Treasury Regulation 20.2031-1.

Fair market value for tax purposes also assumes a hypothetical willing buyer and a hypothetical willing seller. This is in contrast to investment value, which identifies a particular buyer or seller and the attributes that buyer or seller brings to a transaction. Fair market value also assumes an arm's-length deal and that the buyer and seller are able and willing. This is not the same as the definition of market value, an often-used real estate term. For example, the Uniform Standards of Professional Appraisal Practice (USPAP) defines market value as "a type of value, stated as an opinion, that presumes the transfer of a property (i.e., a right of ownership or a bundle of such rights), as of a certain date, under specific conditions set forth in the definition of the term identified by the appraiser as applicable in an appraisal."[3]

Internal Revenue Service Revenue Ruling 59-60 (see Addendum 1 to this chapter for a checklist summary for Revenue Ruling 59-60) defines fair market value as "the price at which the property would change hands between a willing buyer and a willing seller when the former is not under any compulsion to buy and the latter is not under any compulsion to sell, both parties having reasonable knowledge of relevant facts. Court decisions frequently state in addition that the hypothetical buyer and seller are assumed to be able, as well as willing, to trade and to be well informed about the property and concerning the market for such property."[4]

> Although many states use the term "fair market value" in their marital dissolution cases, the definition of fair market value may vary from state to state and will not necessarily be the same definition as in the tax area.

The *International Glossary of Business Valuation Terms (International Glossary)* represents the collective wisdom of the American Institute of Certified Public Accountants, American Society of Appraisers, Canadian Institute of Chartered Business Valuators, National Association of Certified Valuation Analysts, and the Institute of Business Appraisers. See Addendum 2 to this chapter for the complete *International Glossary*. Its definition of fair market value reads: "The price, expressed in terms of cash equivalents, at which property would change hands between a hypothetical willing and able buyer and a hypothetical willing and able seller, acting at arm's-length in an open and unrestricted market, where neither is under compulsion to buy or sell and when both have reasonable knowledge of the relevant facts."

This is obviously very similar to the definition of fair market value in the tax area. Fair market value is used most often in tax situations. It is also used in many buy/sell agreements and marital dissolution situations. Unless otherwise noted, the standard of value discussed throughout this text is fair market value.

---

[3] USPAP 2010–2011 Edition, P.U-3, The Appraisal Foundation.
[4] Rev. Rul. 59-60,159-1 CB 237.

INVESTMENT VALUE

The *International Glossary* defines investment value as "the value to a particular investor based on individual investment requirements and expectations." Investment value is the value to a particular investor, which reflects the particular and specific attributes of that investor. The best example would be an auction setting for a company in which there are five different bidders attempting to purchase the company. More than likely each of the bidders will offer a different price because the prices are based on the individual outlook and synergies that each bidder brings to the transaction. Investment value may also reflect more of the risk of a particular investor than the market consensus of the risk of the investment.

INTRINSIC VALUE

Intrinsic value is based on fundamental analyses of companies, particularly publicly traded companies. It is often what is taught in university financial courses and presented in finance textbooks. Jeffrey C. Hooke, in his text *Security Analysis on Wall Street: A Comprehensive Guide to Today's Valuation Methods,* states that "Under the intrinsic value method, future dividends are derived from earnings forecasts and then discounted to the present, thereby establishing a present value for the stock. If the stock is trading at a price lower than this calculation, it is a 'buy'; if the market price is higher than the intrinsic value, the stock is a 'sell.'"[5]

Others define intrinsic value as the "true" or "real" worth of an item, based on an evaluation of available facts. It is sometimes called *fundamental value.* It is an analytical judgment of value based on perceived *characteristics inherent in the investment* (not characteristic peculiar to any one investor). Intrinsic value is not applied often in valuations of nonpublic companies.

FAIR VALUE (STATE RIGHTS)

The common definition of fair value is that from the Uniform Business Corporation Act, which defines it as "the value of the shares immediately before the effectuation of the corporate action to which the dissenter objects, excluding any appreciation or depreciation in anticipation of the corporate action."[6] Fair value is the standard of value for state actions, including dissenting rights cases and shareholder oppression cases. Its definition and application can vary from state to state. As such, the definition of fair value in one state may be quite different from the definition of fair value in another state. Analysts must understand both the definition and the application of fair value in the particular state in which the action is taking place. A discussion with an attorney familiar with a state's statutes and case law is very helpful.

FAIR VALUE (FINANCIAL REPORTING)

Fair value has been the standard of value for financial reporting for many years. It is the standard of value in many Statements of Financial Accounting Standards (SFAS) (now Accounting Standard Codification [ASC] as issued by the Financial Accounting

---

[5] Jeffrey C. Hooke, *Security Analysis on Wall Street: A Comprehensive Guide to Today's Valuation Methods* (New York: John Wiley & Sons, 1998), p. 14.
[6] Georgia Dissenters Right Statute.

Standards Board (FASB). The older definition of fair value is from SFAS 141 and 142: "The amount at which an asset (or liability) could be bought (or incurred) or sold (or settled) in a current transaction between willing parties, that is, other than in a forced or liquidation sale."[7]

The later definition from SFAS 157 (now ASC 820) is: "Fair value is the price that would be received to sell an asset or paid to transfer a liability in an orderly transaction between market participants at the measurement date."[8]

Fair value for financial reporting purposes often has been equated with fair market value. However, in certain situations, e.g., purchase of a business, fair value for a company or a segment of a company would include synergies within a transaction, if present. As such, in those situations, the purchase price may have more aspects of investment value than fair market value or fair value. In other situations, such as the value of certain individual assets, synergies may not be included, and fair value would be more similar to fair market value. It is important for the analyst to look for guidance from FASB and the Securities and Exchange Commission (SEC) in terms of their views on fair value and its applications.

PREMISE OF VALUE

There are two main premises of value in a business valuation, going-concern value and liquidation value. The *International Glossary* defines premise of value as "an assumption regarding the most likely set of transactional circumstances that may be applicable to the subject valuation, e.g., going concern, liquidation." It defines going-concern value as "the value of a business enterprise that is expected to continue to operate into the future. The intangible elements of going-concern value result from factors such as having a trained work force, an operational plant, and the necessary licenses, systems, and procedures in place."

> Some companies are worth more dead than alive. It is important for the analyst, particularly when valuing an entire company, to determine if the going-concern value exceeds the liquidation value. For a minority interest, there are situations where the going-concern value is less than the liquidation value. However, the minority shareholder cannot force a liquidation if the controlling shareholder desires to continue the business as a going concern.

There are two types of liquidation value, orderly liquidation and forced liquidation. The *International Glossary* defines orderly liquidation value as "liquidation

---

[7] Statement of Financial Accounting Standards No. 142, "Goodwill and Other Intangible Assets," Financial Accounting Standards Board of the Financial Accounting Foundation, June 2001, p. 117.

[8] Statement of Financial Accounting Standards No. 157, "Fair Value Measurements," Financial Accounting Standards Board of the Financial Accounting Foundation, September 2006, p. 2, now ASC 820, "Fair Value Measurements and Disclosures."

value at which the asset or assets are sold over a reasonable period of time to maximize proceeds received." It defines forced liquidation value as "liquidation value at which the asset or assets are sold as quickly as possible, such as at an auction." It also defines liquidation value as "the net amount that can be realized if the business is terminated and the assets are sold piecemeal. Liquidation can be either 'orderly' or 'forced.'"

PRINCIPLES OF APPRAISAL PRACTICE

The modern financial valuation body of knowledge is based to some extent on the evolution of appraisal practices. The ASA's seminal text, *Appraisal Principles and Procedures,* discusses the general characteristic of value.

> It is a characteristic of value, in the sense that the word is understood in appraisal practice, that it is expressible in terms of a single lump sum of money considered as payable or expended at a particular point in time in exchange for property, i.e., the right to receive future benefits as at that particular timepoint. The amount of the lump sum of money, in any particular instance, is exactly equivalent to the right to receive the particular future benefits encompassed in the property under consideration. In this, value differs from price or cost. Price and cost refer to an amount of money asked or actually paid for a property, and this may be more or less than its value.[9]

> Price and cost *can* equal value but don't necessarily *have to* equal value. Furthermore, value is future-looking. Although historical information can be used to set a value, the expectation of future economic benefits is the primary value driver. Investors buy tomorrow's cash flow, not yesterday's or even today's.

DATES

All valuations are done as of a single date. It is important that the users of valuations understand this fact. The *International Glossary* defines the valuation date as "the specific point in time as of which the valuator's opinion of value applies (also referred to as 'Effective Date' or 'Appraisal Date')."

---

[9] Henry A. Babcock, *Appraisal Principles and Procedures* (Washington, DC: American Society of Appraisers, 1994), p. 95.

APPROACHES TO VALUE

There are only three approaches to value any asset, business, or business interest:

1. The income approach
2. The market approach
3. The asset approach

There are no other approaches to value. However, there are numerous methods within each one of the approaches that the analyst may consider in performing a valuation. For example, under the income approach, the analyst can use a discounted cash flow method or a capitalized cash flow method. Each of these methods also can be prepared on a direct equity method or an invested capital method. In the market approach, the analyst can apply guideline public company multiples or multiples derived from transactions both public and private. In the asset approach, the analyst often must choose between valuing just tangible assets, individual intangible assets, or all intangible assets as a collective group. Various methodologies exist for each one of these choices.

All three approaches should be considered in each valuation. However, it is not common to use all three approaches in each valuation. For example, the asset approach is used less often in valuing operating companies, since the time and cost involved in performing valuations of intangible assets do not warrant the increased level of accuracy, if any, provided by the cost approach. Specific intangible asset values are often excluded due to the fact that intangible asset values are captured in the proper application of the income and market approaches, which would provide, in most circumstances, the aggregate intangible asset values.

VALUATION PROCEDURES

Numerous procedures and factors must be considered in performing a business valuation. However, they can generally be classified into the following areas:

- Understand the purpose of the engagement
- Understand who the client is
- Understand the client's use of the valuation
- Determine the standard of value and its definition
- Determine the premise of value
- Determine the users of the value
- Determine the interest or assets to be valued
- Ascertain whether discounts and/or premiums are to be considered
- Analyze the company's financial information
- Gather information about the company or assets
- Gather information about the industry and economy
- Consider all approaches of value and select the most appropriate
- Apply the approaches to value through the various methodologies
- Reconcile the values
- Apply discounts and premiums if applicable
- Write the report if applicable
- Ensure compliance with professional standards, if applicable

All of these steps are discussed throughout the book.

SUMMARY

Valuation, by its very nature, contains many controversial issues. We address many of these issues throughout this book, highlighting them through the ValTips. These issues are further addressed in Chapter 27, which presents these issues as "Valuation Views" (VV) in the sequence of an actual abbreviated report.

The valuation of business enterprises and business assets is well founded in academic publications and empirical studies. The use of public company information has provided the foundation for the analysis of business valuation. The biggest difference between valuing investments in public companies and nonpublic businesses is the level of available information. The application of recognized valuation methodologies combined with rigorous analysis of the private entity provides the foundation for business valuation. This book presents state-of-the-art methods for the valuation of closely held businesses, nonpublic entities and other assets as they have evolved.

ADDENDUM 1—VALUATION CHECKLIST/READY REFERENCE (REVENUE RULING 59-60)

Introduction

Revenue rulings provide useful guidance in various valuation situations. Revenue Ruling 59-60 is applicable to many types of valuation engagements. Revenue Ruling 77-287 applies to restricted securities, such as private placements, investment letter stock, control stock, or unregistered securities. Revenue Ruling 93-12 applies to valuing minority interests in closely held companies for intrafamily transfers. See Chapter 13 for checklists for Revenue Rulings 77-287 and 93-12.

A valuation checklist/ready reference has been created for each of these revenue rulings to assist in a quick review of their key points as well as for the practical application of these rulings to an actual valuation.

Although Revenue Ruling 59-60 and others provide excellent guidance, they are often cumbersome to apply. The checklists are designed to make it easier to apply these rulings.

Keep in mind that many valuation analysts disagree with various components of the revenue rulings. However, a thorough understanding of these revenue rulings is essential to prepare valuations for tax and other purposes. See Chapter 13 for a detailed discussion of these revenue rulings.

Revenue Ruling 59-60

Revenue Ruling 59-60 contains a wealth of information. It has also stood the test of time and is often quoted in various valuation situations. However, many analysts feel that it is poorly organized and hard to follow. This checklist presents the ruling in an easy-to-follow format.

The primary information concerning discounts and premiums is highlighted by an asterisk (*).

1. *Purpose*

_____ Estate tax

_____ Gift tax

_____ Income tax (as amplified by Revenue Ruling 65-192)

_____ *Value of closely held corporations

_____ *Value of thinly traded stock

_____ Value of other business entities such as partnerships, proprietorships, etc. (as amplified by Revenue Ruling 65-192)

2. *Background Definitions*

Dates of Valuation

_____ Date of death

_____ Alternate date (6 months after date of death)

Definition of Fair Market Value

_____ "The price at which the property would change hands between a willing buyer and a willing seller when the former is not under any compulsion to buy and the latter is not under any compulsion to sell, both parties having reasonable knowledge of relevant facts."

_____ "The hypothetical buyer and seller are assumed to be able, as well as willing, to trade and to be well informed about the property and concerning the market for such property."

3. *Approach to Valuation*

_____ Facts and circumstances

_____ No general formula applicable

_____ Wide difference of opinion as to fair market value

_____ Valuation is not an exact science

_____ Sound valuation:

    _____ Relevant facts

    _____ Common sense

    _____ Informed judgment

    _____ Reasonableness

_____ Future outlook:

    _____ Value varies as general economic conditions change

    _____ Optimism versus pessimism

    _____ Uncertainty as to the stability or continuity of future income

    _____ Risk of loss of earnings and value

    _____ Highly speculative value to very uncertain future prospects

    _____ Valuation is a prophecy as to the future

_____ Use of guideline public companies

4. *Factors to Consider*

Nature of the Business and History of the Enterprise from Inception

_____ Past stability or instability

_____ Growth or lack of growth

_____ *Diversity or lack of diversity of its operations

_____ *Degree of risk in the business

_____ Study of gross and net income

_____ *Dividends history

_____ Nature of the business

_____ Products or services

_____ Operating and investment assets

_____ *Capital structure

_____ Plant facilities

_____ Sales records

_____ *Management

_____ Due regard for recent significant changes

_____ Discount events of the past that are unlikely to recur in the future

_____ Value has a close relation to future expectancy

_____ Recent events are of greatest help in predicting the future

Economic Outlook in General and Condition and Outlook of the Specific Industry in Particular

_____ Current and prospective economic conditions

_____ National economy

_____ Industry or industries

_____ More or less successful than its competitors; stable with competitors

_____ Ability of industry to compete with other industries

_____ Prospective competition

_____ Price trends in the markets for commodities and securities

_____ *Possible effects of a key person or thin management/lack of succession

_____ Effect of the loss of the manager on the future expectancy of the business

_____ *Key person life insurance could be partially offsetting

Book Value of the Stock and the Financial Condition of the Business

_____ Two historical fiscal year-end balance sheets

_____ Balance sheet as of the end of the month preceding the valuation date

_____ *Liquid position (ratio of current assets to current liabilities)

_____ Gross and net book value of principal classes of fixed assets

_____ Working capital

_____ Long-term indebtedness

_____ *Capital structure

_____ Net worth

_____ *Revalued nonoperating assets (i.e., investments in securities and real estate) on the basis of their market price

_____ Generally, nonoperating assets command lower rates of return

_____ Acquisitions of production facilities or subsidiaries

_____ Improvements in financial position

_____ *Recapitalizations

_____ *Changes in capital structure

_____ *Classes of stock

_____ *Examination of charter or certificate of incorporation for rights and privileges of the various stock issues including:

    _____ Voting powers

    _____ Preference as to dividends

    _____ Preference as to assets in the event of liquidation

The Earning Capacity of the Company

_____ Preferably five or more years of detailed profit and loss statements

_____ Gross income by principal items

_____ Deductions from gross income:

    _____ Operating expenses

    _____ Interest and other expense on each item of long-term debt

    _____ Depreciation and depletion

    _____ *Officers' salaries in total if reasonable and in detail if they appear excessive

    _____ Contributions based on nature of business and its community position

    _____ Taxes

_____ *Net income available for dividends

_____ *Rates and amounts of dividends paid on each class of stock

_____ Remaining amount carried to surplus

_____ Adjustments to, and reconciliation with, surplus as stated on the balance sheet

_____ Separate recurrent from nonrecurrent items of income and expense

_____ *Distinguish between operating income and investment income

_____ Ascertain whether or not any line of business is operating consistently at a loss and might be abandoned with benefit to the company

_____ *Note percentage of earnings retained for business expansion when considering dividend-paying capacity

_____ Secure all information concerning past income that will be helpful in predicting the future (potential future income is a major factor in many valuations)

_____ Prior earnings records are usually the most reliable guide as to future earnings expectancy

_____ The use of arbitrary five- or ten-year averages without regard to current trends or future prospects will not produce a realistic valuation

_____ If a record of progressively increasing or decreasing net income is found, consider according greater weight to the most recent years' profits in estimating earning power

_____ Look at margins and percentages of sales to assess risk:

      _____ Consumption of raw materials and supplies for manufacturers, processors, and fabricators

      _____ Cost of purchased merchandise for merchants

      _____ Utility services

      _____ Insurance

      _____ Taxes

      _____ Depreciation and depletion

      _____ Interest

Dividend-Paying Capacity

_____ *Primary consideration to dividend-paying capacity rather than dividends actually paid

_____ *Recognition of the necessity of retaining a reasonable portion of profits to meet competition

_____ *When valuing a controlling interest, the dividend factor is not a material element, since the payment of such dividends is discretionary with the controlling stockholders

_____ *The individual or group in control can substitute salaries and bonuses for dividends, thus reducing net income and understating the dividend-paying capacity of the company

_____ *Dividends are a less reliable factor for valuation than dividend-paying capacity

Whether the Enterprise Has Goodwill or Other Intangible Value

_____ Goodwill is based on earning capacity

_____ Goodwill value is based on the excess of net earnings over and above a fair return on the net tangible assets

_____ Factors to consider to support intangible value:

      _____ Prestige and renown of the business

      _____ Trade or brand name

      _____ Record of success over a prolonged period in a particular locality

_____ Sometimes it may not be possible to make a separate valuation of tangible and intangible assets

_____ Intangible value can be measured by the amount that the value of the tangible assets exceeds the net book value of such assets

Sales of the Stock and the Size of the Block of Stock to be Valued

_____ Prior sales should be arm's length

_____ Forced or distressed sales do not reflect fair market value

_____ Isolated sales in small amounts may not control as a measure of value

_____ *Blockage is not an issue since the stock is not publicly traded

_____ *Size of the block of stock is a relevant factor

_____ *A minority interest in an unlisted corporation's stock is more difficult to sell than a similar block of listed stock

_____ *Control of a corporation, either actual or in effect, may justify a higher value for a specific block of stock since it is an added element of value

Market Price of Stocks of Corporations Engaged in the Same or a Similar Line of Business Having Their Stocks Actively Traded in a Free and Open Market, Either on an Exchange or Over-the-Counter

_____ *Must be evidence of an active free public market for the stock as of the valuation date to be used as a comparable company

_____ Use only comparable companies

_____ The lines of business should be the same or similar

_____ A comparable with one or more issues of preferred stock, bonds, or debentures in addition to its common stock should not be considered to be directly comparable to one having only common stock outstanding

_____ A comparable with a declining business and decreasing markets is not comparable to one with a record of current progress and market expansion

5. Weight to Be Accorded Various Factors

_____ Certain factors carry more weight than others because of the nature of the company's business

_____ Earnings may be the most important criterion of value in some cases, whereas asset value will receive primary consideration in others

_____ Give primary consideration to earnings when valuing stocks of companies that sell products or services to the public

_____ Give greatest weight to the assets underlying the security to be valued for investment or holding-type companies

_____ Closely held investment or real estate holding company:

      _____ Value is closely related to the value of the assets underlying the stock

      _____ The appraiser should determine the fair market values of the assets of the company

      _____ *Operating expenses of such a company and the cost of liquidating it, if any, merit consideration

      _____ The market values of the assets give due weight to potential earnings and dividends of the particular items of property underlying the stock, capitalized at rates deemed proper by the investing public at the valuation date

      _____ Adjusted net worth should be accorded greater weight in valuing the stock of a closely held investment or real estate holding company, whether or not it is family owned, than any of the other customary yardsticks of appraisal, such as earnings and dividend-paying capacity

6. Capitalization Rates

_____ Capitalize the average or current results at some appropriate rate

_____ One of the most difficult problems in valuation

_____ No ready or simple solution will become apparent by a cursory check of the rates of return and dividend yields in terms of the selling price of corporate shares listed on the major exchanges

_____ Wide variations will be found even for companies in the same industry

_____ The ratio will fluctuate from year to year depending upon economic conditions

_____ No standard tables of capitalization rates applicable to closely held corporations can be formulated

_____ Important factors to consider:

      _____ Nature of the business

      _____ Risk

      _____ Stability or irregularity of earnings

7. *Average of Factors*

_____ Valuations cannot be made on the basis of a prescribed formula

_____ There is no means whereby the various applicable factors in a particular case can be assigned mathematical weights to derive the fair market value

_____ No useful purpose is served by taking an average of several factors (e.g., book value, capitalized earnings, and capitalized dividends) and basing the valuation on the result

_____ Such a process excludes active consideration of other pertinent factors, and the end result cannot be supported by a realistic application of the significant facts in the case except by mere chance

8. *Restrictive Agreements*

_____ *Where shares of stock were acquired by a decedent subject to an option reserved by the issuing corporation to repurchase at a certain price, the option price usually is accepted as the fair market value for estate tax purposes

_____ *The option price is not determinative of fair market value for gift tax purposes

_____ *Where the option or buy and sell agreement is the result of voluntary action by the stockholders and is binding during the life as well as at the death of the stockholders, such agreement may or may not, depending on the circumstances of each case, fix the value for estate tax purposes

_____ *Such restrictive agreements are a factor to be considered, with other relevant factors, in determining fair market value

_____ *Where the stockholder is free to dispose of his shares during life and the option is to become effective only upon his or her death, the fair market value is not limited to the option price

_____ *Determine whether the agreement represents a bona fide business arrangement or is a device to pass the decedent's shares for less than an adequate and full consideration in money or money's worth:

_____ Relationship of the parties

_____ Relative number of shares held by the decedent

_____ Other material facts

ADDENDUM 2—INTERNATIONAL GLOSSARY OF BUSINESS VALUATION TERMS

To enhance and sustain the quality of business valuations for the benefit of the profession and its clientele, the below-identified societies and organizations have adopted the definitions for the terms included in this glossary.

The performance of business valuation services requires a high degree of skill and imposes upon the valuation professional a duty to communicate the valuation process and conclusion in a manner that is clear and not misleading. This duty is advanced through the use of terms whose meanings are clearly established and consistently applied throughout the profession.

If, in the opinion of the business valuation professional, one or more of these terms needs to be used in a manner that materially departs from the enclosed definitions, it is recommended that the term be defined as used within that valuation engagement.

This glossary has been developed to provide guidance to business valuation practitioners by further memorializing the body of knowledge that constitutes the competent and careful determination of value and, more particularly, the communication of how that value was determined.

Departure from this glossary is not intended to provide a basis for civil liability and should not be presumed to create evidence that any duty has been breached.

American Institute of Certified Public Accountants
American Society of Appraisers
Canadian Institute of Chartered Business Valuators
National Association of Certified Valuation Analysts
The Institute of Business Appraisers

Adjusted Book Value Method—a method within the asset approach whereby all assets and liabilities (including off-balance sheet, intangible, and contingent) are adjusted to their fair market values (*Note:* In Canada on a going-concern basis).

Adjusted Net Asset Method—see **Adjusted Book Value Method.**

Appraisal—see **Valuation.**

Appraisal Approach—see **Valuation Approach.**

Appraisal Date—see **Valuation Date.**

Appraisal Method—see **Valuation Method.**

Appraisal Procedure—see **Valuation Procedure.**

Arbitrage Pricing Theory—a multivariate model for estimating the cost of equity capital, which incorporates several systematic risk factors.

Asset (Asset-Based) Approach—a general way of determining a value indication of a business, business ownership interest, or security using one or more methods based on the value of the assets net of liabilities.

Beta—a measure of systematic risk of a stock; the tendency of a stock's price to correlate with changes in a specific index.

Blockage Discount—an amount or percentage deducted from the current market price of a publicly traded stock to reflect the decrease in the per share value of a block of stock that is of a size that could not be sold in a reasonable period of time given normal trading volume.

Book Value—see **Net Book Value.**

Business—see **Business Enterprise.**

Business Enterprise—a commercial, industrial, service, or investment entity (or a combination thereof) pursuing an economic activity.

Business Risk—the degree of uncertainty of realizing expected future returns of the business resulting from factors other than financial leverage. See **Financial Risk.**

Business Valuation—the act or process of determining the value of a business enterprise or ownership interest therein.

Capital Asset Pricing Model (CAPM)—a model in which the cost of capital for any stock or portfolio of stocks equals a risk-free rate plus a risk premium that is proportionate to the systematic risk of the stock or portfolio.

Capitalization—a conversion of a single period of economic benefits into value.

Capitalization Factor—any multiple or divisor used to convert anticipated economic benefits of a single period into value.

Capitalization of Earnings Method—a method within the income approach whereby economic benefits for a representative single period are converted to value through division by a capitalization rate.

Capitalization Rate—any divisor (usually expressed as a percentage) used to convert anticipated economic benefits of a single period into value.

Capital Structure—the composition of the invested capital of a business enterprise: the mix of debt and equity financing.

Cash Flow—cash that is generated over a period of time by an asset, group of assets, or business enterprise. It may be used in a general sense to encompass various levels of specifically defined cash flows. When the term is used, it should be supplemented by a qualifier (for example, "discretionary" or "operating") and a specific definition in the given valuation context.

Common Size Statements—financial statements in which each line is expressed as a percentage of the total. On the balance sheet, each line item is shown as a percentage of total assets, and on the income statement, each item is expressed as a percentage of sales.

Control—the power to direct the management and policies of a business enterprise.

Control Premium—an amount or a percentage by which the pro rata value of a controlling interest exceeds the pro rata value of a noncontrolling interest in a business enterprise, to reflect the power of control.

Cost Approach—a general way of determining a value indication of an individual asset by quantifying the amount of money required to replace the future service capability of that asset.

Cost of Capital—the expected rate of return that the market requires in order to attract funds to a particular investment.

Debt-Free—*we discourage the use of this term.* See **Invested Capital.**

Discount for Lack of Control—an amount or percentage deducted from the pro rata share of value of 100 percent of an equity interest in a business to reflect the absence of some or all of the powers of control.

Discount for Lack of Marketability—an amount or percentage deducted from the value of an ownership interest to reflect the relative absence of marketability.

Discount for Lack of Voting Rights—an amount or percentage deducted from the per share value of a minority interest voting share to reflect the absence of voting rights.

Discount Rate—a rate of return used to convert a future monetary sum into present value.

Discounted Cash Flow Method—a method within the income approach whereby the present value of future expected net cash flows is calculated using a discount rate.

Discounted Future Earnings Method—a method within the income approach whereby the present value of future expected economic benefits is calculated using a discount rate.

Economic Benefits—inflows such as revenues, net income, net cash flows, and so forth.

Economic Life—the period of time over which property may generate economic benefits.

Effective Date—see **Valuation Date.**

Enterprise—see **Business Enterprise.**

Equity—the owner's interest in property after deduction of all liabilities.

Equity Net Cash Flows—those cash flows available to pay out to equity holders (in the form of dividends) after funding operations of the business enterprise, making necessary capital investments, and increasing or decreasing debt financing.

Equity Risk Premium—a rate of return added to a risk-free rate to reflect the additional risk of equity instruments over risk-free instruments (a component of the cost of equity capital or equity discount rate).

Excess Earnings—that amount of anticipated economic benefits that exceeds an appropriate rate of return on the value of a selected asset base (often net tangible assets) used to generate those anticipated economic benefits.

Excess Earnings Method—a specific way of determining a value indication of a business, business ownership interest, or security determined as the sum of a) the value of the assets derived by capitalizing excess earnings and b) the value of the selected asset base. Also frequently used to value intangible assets. See **Excess Earnings.**

Fair Market Value—the price, expressed in terms of cash equivalents, at which property would change hands between a hypothetical willing and able buyer and a hypothetical willing and able seller, acting at arm's length in an open and unrestricted market, when neither is under compulsion to buy or sell and when both have reasonable knowledge of the relevant facts. (*Note:* In Canada, the term "price" should be replaced with the term "highest price.")

Fairness Opinion—an opinion as to whether or not the consideration in a transaction is fair from a financial point of view.

Financial Risk—the degree of uncertainty of realizing expected future returns of the business resulting from financial leverage. See **Business Risk**.

Forced Liquidation Value—liquidation value at which the asset or assets are sold as quickly as possible, such as at an auction.

Free Cash Flows—*we discourage the use of this term*. See **Net Cash Flows**.

Going Concern—an ongoing operating business enterprise.

Going-Concern Value—the value of a business enterprise that is expected to continue to operate into the future. The intangible elements of Going-Concern Value result from factors such as having a trained work force, an operational plant, and the necessary licenses, systems, and procedures in place.

Goodwill—that intangible asset arising as a result of name, reputation, customer loyalty, location, products, and similar factors not separately identified.

Goodwill Value—the value attributable to goodwill.

Guideline Public Company Method—a method within the market approach whereby market multiples are derived from market prices of stocks of companies that are engaged in the same or similar lines of business, and that are actively traded on a free and open market.

Income (Income-Based) Approach—a general way of determining a value indication of a business, business ownership interest, security, or intangible asset using one or more methods that convert anticipated economic benefits into a present single amount.

Intangible Assets—nonphysical assets such as franchises, trademarks, patents, copyrights, goodwill, equities, mineral rights, securities, and contracts (as distinguished from physical assets) that grant rights and privileges, and have value for the owner.

Internal Rate of Return—a discount rate at which the present value of the future cash flows of the investment equals the cost of the investment.

Intrinsic Value—the value that an investor considers, on the basis of an evaluation or available facts, to be the "true" or "real" value that will become the market value when other investors reach the same conclusion. When the term applies to options, it is the difference between the exercise price or strike price of an option and the market value of the underlying security.

Invested Capital—the sum of equity and debt in a business enterprise. Debt is typically a) all interest-bearing debt or b) long-term interest-bearing debt. When the term is used, it should be supplemented by a specific definition in the given valuation context.

Invested Capital Net Cash Flows—those cash flows available to pay out to equity holders (in the form of dividends) and debt investors (in the form of principal and interest) after funding operations of the business enterprise and making necessary capital investments.

Investment Risk—the degree of uncertainty as to the realization of expected returns.

Investment Value—the value to a particular investor based on individual investment requirements and expectations. (*Note:* In Canada, the term used is "Value to the Owner.")

Key Person Discount—an amount or percentage deducted from the value of an ownership interest to reflect the reduction in value resulting from the actual or potential loss of a key person in a business enterprise.

Levered Beta—the beta reflecting a capital structure that includes debt.

Limited Appraisal—the act or process of determining the value of a business, business ownership interest, security, or intangible asset with limitations in analyses, procedures, or scope.

Liquidity—the ability to quickly convert property to cash or pay a liability.

Liquidation Value—the net amount that would be realized if the business is terminated and the assets are sold piecemeal. Liquidation can be either "orderly" or "forced."

Majority Control—the degree of control provided by a majority position.

Majority Interest—an ownership interest greater than 50 percent of the voting interest in a business enterprise.

Market (Market-Based) Approach—a general way of determining a value indication of a business, business ownership interest, security, or intangible asset by using one or more methods that compare the subject to similar businesses, business ownership interests, securities, or intangible assets that have been sold.

Market Capitalization of Equity—the share price of a publicly traded stock multiplied by the number of shares outstanding.

Market Capitalization of Invested Capital—the market capitalization of equity plus the market value of the debt component of invested capital.

Market Multiple—the market value of a company's stock or invested capital divided by a company measure (such as economic benefits, number of customers).

Marketability—the ability to quickly convert property to cash at minimal cost.

Marketability Discount—see **Discount for Lack of Marketability**.

Merger and Acquisition Method—a method within the market approach whereby pricing multiples are derived from transactions of significant interests in companies engaged in the same or similar lines of business.

Mid-Year Discounting—a convention used in the Discounted Future Earnings Method that reflects economic benefits being generated at mid-year approximating the effect of economic benefits being generated evenly throughout the year.

Minority Discount—a discount for lack of control applicable to a minority interest.

Minority Interest—an ownership interest less than 50 percent of the voting interest in a business enterprise.

Multiple—the inverse of the capitalization rate.

Net Book Value—with respect to a business enterprise, the difference between total assets (net of accumulated depreciation, depletion, and amortization) and total liabilities as they appear on the balance sheet (synonymous with Shareholder's Equity). With respect to a specific asset, the capitalized cost less accumulated amortization or depreciation as it appears on the books of account of the business enterprise.

Net Cash Flows—when the term is used, it should be supplemented by a qualifier. See **Equity Net Cash Flows** and **Invested Capital Net Cash Flows**.

Net Present Value—the value, as of a specified date, of future cash inflows less all cash outflows (including the cost of investment) calculated using an appropriate discount rate.

Net Tangible Asset Value—the value of the business enterprise's tangible assets (excluding excess assets and nonoperating assets) minus the value of its liabilities.

Nonoperating Assets—assets not necessary to ongoing operations of the business enterprise. (*Note:* In Canada, the term used is "Redundant Assets.")

Normalized Earnings—economic benefits adjusted for nonrecurring, noneconomic, or other unusual items to eliminate anomalies and/or facilitate comparisons.

Normalized Financial Statements—financial statements adjusted for nonoperating assets and liabilities and/or for nonrecurring, noneconomic, or other unusual items to eliminate anomalies and/or facilitate comparisons.

Orderly Liquidation Value—liquidation value at which the asset or assets are sold over a reasonable period of time to maximize proceeds received.

Premise of Value—an assumption regarding the most likely set of transactional circumstances that may be applicable to the subject valuation; e.g., going concern, liquidation.

Present Value—the value, as of a specified date, of future economic benefits and/or proceeds from sale, calculated using an appropriate discount rate.

Portfolio Discount—an amount or percentage deducted from the value of a business enterprise to reflect the fact that it owns dissimilar operations or assets that do not fit well together.

Price/Earnings Multiple—the price of a share of stock divided by its earnings per share.

Rate of Return—an amount of income (loss) and/or change in value realized or anticipated on an investment, expressed as a percentage of that investment.

Redundant Assets—see **Nonoperating Assets**.

Report Date—the date conclusions are transmitted to the client.

Replacement Cost New—the current cost of a similar new property having the nearest equivalent utility to the property being valued.

Reproduction Cost New—the current cost of an identical new property.

Required Rate of Return—the minimum rate of return acceptable by investors before they will commit money to an investment at a given level of risk.

Residual Value—the value as of the end of the discrete projection period in a discounted future earnings model.

Return on Equity—the amount, expressed as a percentage, earned on a company's common equity for a given period.

Return on Investment—see **Return on Invested Capital** and **Return on Equity**.

Return on Invested Capital—the amount, expressed as a percentage, earned on a company's total capital for a given period.

Risk-Free Rate—the rate of return available in the market on an investment free of default risk.

Risk Premium—a rate of return added to a risk-free rate to reflect risk.

Rule of Thumb—a mathematical formula developed from the relationship between price and certain variables based on experience, observation, hearsay, or a combination of these; usually industry specific.

Special Interest Purchasers—acquirers who believe they can enjoy post-acquisition economies of scale, synergies, or strategic advantages by combining the acquired business interest with their own.

Standard of Value—the identification of the type of value being used in a specific engagement; e.g., fair market value, fair value, investment value.

Sustaining Capital Reinvestment—the periodic capital outlay required to maintain operations at existing levels, net of the tax shield available from such outlays.

Systematic Risk—the risk that is common to all risky securities and cannot be eliminated through diversification. The measure of systematic risk in stocks is the beta coefficient.

Tangible Assets—physical assets (such as cash, accounts receivable, inventory, property, plant and equipment, etc.).

Terminal Value—see **Residual Value**.

Transaction Method—see **Merger and Acquisition Method**.

Unlevered Beta—the beta reflecting a capital structure without debt.

Unsystematic Risk—the risk specific to an individual security that can be avoided through diversification.

Valuation—the act or process of determining the value of a business, business ownership interest, security, or intangible asset.

Valuation Approach—a general way of determining a value indication of a business, business ownership interest, security, or intangible asset using one or more valuation methods.

Valuation Date—the specific point in time as of which the valuator's opinion of value applies (also referred to as "Effective Date" or "Appraisal Date").

Valuation Method—within approaches, a specific way to determine value.

Valuation Procedure—the act, manner, and technique of performing the steps of an appraisal method.

Valuation Ratio—a fraction in which a value or price serves as the numerator and financial, operating, or physical data serves as the denominator.

Value to the Owner—see **Investment Value.**

Voting Control—*de jure* control of a business enterprise.

Weighted Average Cost of Capital (WACC)—the cost of capital (discount rate) determined by the weighted average, at market value, of the cost of all financing sources in the business enterprise's capital structure.

CHAPTER 2

Standards of Value

In Chapter 1 of this text, there is a brief discussion of the standards of value commonly used by analysts. The chapter contains definitions of the five most frequently used standards of value: fair market value, investment value, intrinsic value, fair value (state rights), and fair value (financial reporting). There is also a brief discussion concerning the relationship between standards of value and premises of value. While this discussion is extremely useful as an introduction, in this chapter we discuss these concepts in greater depth. Selection and application of the appropriate standard of value is critical in providing valuation services that are useful and relevant.

INTRODUCTION[1]

From a practical point of view, the appraisal process can be viewed as no more than answering the question: "What is the value?" That question is often followed by another question: "What do you mean by value?" These questions highlight the importance of selecting, understanding, and applying the correct standard of value. The identification of the type of value being sought is known as the standard of value. Each standard of value contains numerous assumptions that represent the underpinnings of the type of value being utilized in a specific engagement. Even if a standard of value is specified, there is no guarantee that all would agree on its underlying assumptions. As James C. Bonbright wrote in his pioneering book, *Valuation of Property:*

> When one reads the conventional value definitions critically, one finds, in the first place, that they themselves contain serious ambiguities, and in the second place, that they invoke concepts of value acceptable only for certain purposes and quite unacceptable for other purposes.[2]

It has been our observation that Bonbright's 1937 quote still applies today. This chapter addresses some of the ambiguities referenced by Bonbright and discusses the contexts in which various standards are applied.

---

[1] Portions of this chapter appeared in *Standards of Value: Theory and Applications,* Jay E. Fishman, Shannon P. Pratt, and William J. Morrison (Hoboken, NJ: John Wiley & Sons, 2007).
[2] James C. Bonbright, *Valuation of Property* (Charlottesville, VA: Michie Company, 1937), p. 11.

Defining a Standard of Value

In 1989, the College of Fellows of the American Society of Appraisers published an opinion on defining standards of value. In that opinion, the college recognized the importance of defining the standard of value, including:

> the necessity to identify and define the applicable standard of value as a critical part of any appraisal report or appraisal engagement. It also recognizes that there legitimately can be different definitions of the same appraisal term and different contexts based either on widely accepted usage or legal definitions through statutes, regulations, case law and/or legally binding documents.[3]

With regard to business valuation, the College of Fellows asserts that "every appraisal report or engagement should identify the applicable standard of value."[4] In addition, the Uniform Standards of Professional Appraisal Practice and all of the National Business Valuation Standards mandate identification of the standard of value in every appraisal.[5]

> While selecting a standard of value in a valuation assignment seems like a straightforward concept, different standards may have different meanings in different contexts. Therefore, defining *value* and adhering to the assumptions inherent in a particular standard of value, especially in connection with a valuation for tax, judicial, or regulatory purposes, is often not an easy task.

In this chapter, we discuss, in detail, five of the most commonly used standards of value and their application in four distinct contexts: estate and gift taxation, shareholder dissent and oppression, divorce, and financial reporting. Our discussion of these standards of value is in the context of their application in judicial, regulatory, and financial reporting assignments. Our review of case law, statutes, and varying legal analyses is approached from a valuation analyst's perspective and should not be viewed as legal advice.

Every Appraisal Is Unique

In preparing an appraisal on a judicial matter, whether for federal estate or gift tax or for a state court matter pertaining to stockholders or divorcing spouses, the analyst must be sensitive to the facts and circumstances of the case at hand. The analyst must realize that the standard of value previously used in court cases may not apply across all cases. The specific fact pattern of a previous case might distinguish it from the case at hand.

---

[3] "Defining Standards of Value," Opinion of the College of Fellows, *Valuation*, vol. 34, no. 2 (June 1989), 19.
[4] "Defining Standards of Value," Opinion of the College of Fellows, *Valuation*, vol. 34, no. 2 (June 1989), 19.
[5] *Uniform Standards of Professional Appraisal Practice*, 2010–2011, Standards Rule 10-2 a(vi): appraisal report must "state the standard (type) and definition of value and the premise of value and cite the source of the definition."

The valuation analyst must also be aware that, in prior case law, the terminology used and the ultimate outcome of the valuation may not be in sync. Additionally, jurisdictional differences may exist, and the way a certain standard of value is used in one jurisdiction may differ from other states and federal jurisdictions.[6]

As mentioned previously, the standard of value is a definition of the type of value being sought. The premise of value is an assumption as to the actual or hypothetical set of circumstances applicable to the subject valuation. Later in this chapter, we introduce the standards and premises of value that are critical to understanding valuation in the judicial, regulatory, and financial reporting contexts.

HOW STANDARD OF VALUE CAN AFFECT THE FINAL "NUMBER"

As mentioned previously, the standard of value defines for the analyst the type of value being sought[7] and drives both the theoretical and practical aspects of the valuation assignment. In some circumstances, the applicable standard of value is clear. In federal tax cases, fair market value is applied in accordance with the definition set forth in the Treasury Regulations and the guidance provided in IRS Revenue Rulings and Tax Court cases. There may still be controversies over such issues as the size of discounts allowed, but essentially, the definition is consistent and provides fairly clear guidance.

In other types of valuation, the applicable standard of value is not as clear. While the statutory application of fair value is nearly ubiquitous among the 50 states in dissenter's rights and oppression cases, the term is rarely meaningfully defined by those statutes. Over the past century, the courts, law associations, and state legislatures have weighed in on the appropriate definition of *fair value* to clarify its application.

Even less clear, in divorce, the standard of value is rarely explicitly established by case law, and even less frequently by statute. The valuation analyst has to have a discussion with the attorney for the spouse to sort through various aspects of case law, such as the application of discounts, in order to determine how a given state's courts view the standard of value. In some instances, application of the standard of value may differ by county.

We all know that the value of a business is the present worth of the future benefits of ownership, which could even be represented by a range of values at a given time,[8] and a value expressed as a dollar amount will change for the same asset as premises and standards of value change.

The standard of value can have a substantial effect on the final valuation. To better illustrate this concept, we can walk through an example of the value that would be arrived at using different standards for different purposes. We will use, as an example, an accounting practice/corporation owned equally by three accountants.

For the estate tax valuation upon the death of one of the owners, the business would be valued as a minority interest in a closely held corporation. The standard would be fair market value; the decedent's share of the assets of the business, including its tangible and intangible assets, is valued as if it was to be sold. Discounts would most likely be reflected or applied at the shareholder level for the lack of control and marketability.

---

[6] David Laro and Shannon P. Pratt, *Business Valuation and Taxes* (Hoboken, NJ: John Wiley & Sons, 2005), 5.

[7] Shannon P. Pratt, *Valuing a Business,* 5th ed. (New York: McGraw Hill, 2008), p. 41.

[8] Shannon P. Pratt, *Valuing a Business,* 5th ed. (New York: McGraw Hill, 2008), pp. 30, 41.

Alternatively, should two of the shareholders oppress the third, the wronged party could allege oppression and the remaining shareholders could choose to exercise their buyout option. Under the fair value buyout remedy in his or her state's dissolution statute, the oppressed shareholder could be paid the fair value of his or her interest. In this case, in the majority of states (and as prescribed by the guidelines set by the American Bar Association [ABA] and the American Law Institute [ALI]), the entity would be valued as a whole, with the departing shareholder most likely entitled to a pro rata share of that value based on percentage of ownership. Generally, no shareholder level discounts would be applied.

Upon divorce, a whole range of values could arise, based on the differing premises and standards of value. Depending on the statutes, case law, and public policy in a given state, the standard of value might be fair market value, as defined in estate or gift tax matters, or at an even more rigid application of fair market value that could eliminate goodwill altogether. On the other hand, the business might be valued at fair value at the enterprise level without the application of discounts. Then again, it might be valued at investment value, including the nonsalable personal goodwill of the individual CPA.

PREMISES OF VALUE

Throughout this chapter, we discuss two overarching valuation premises: *value in exchange* and *value to the holder*.[9] These premises affect the applicable standard of value. The premise chosen establishes the "value to whom?"

- *Value in exchange.* Value in exchange is the value assuming the business or business interest is changing hands, in a real or hypothetical sale. The buyer exchanges the interest for cash or cash equivalents. Accordingly, shareholder level discounts, including those for lack of control and lack of marketability, are considered in order to estimate the value of the property in exchange. The fair market value standard and, to some extent, the fair value standard, as applied in dissenting stockholder, stockholder oppression, and financial reporting matters, usually fall under the value in exchange premise.
- *Value to the holder.* The value to the holder premise represents the value of a property that is not being sold but instead is being maintained in its present form by its present owner. The property does not necessarily have to be marketable to be valuable. One often overlooked aspect of the value to the holder premise is that the result may be more or less than the value in exchange. The standard of investment value falls under the premise of value to the holder, as does, in certain cases, fair value.

These two premises represent the theoretical underpinnings of each standard of value. In other words, they represent the framework under which all other assumptions follow.

---

[9] Valuation premises relate to the assumptions underlying the standard of value. This is differentiated from operational premises, which relate to how the business is viewed operationally. See Chapter 1 for a discussion of going concern versus liquidation.

COMMON STANDARDS OF VALUE

In many situations, the choice of the appropriate standard of value is dictated by circumstance, intended use of the appraisal, contract, operation of law, or other factors. However, in other instances, the choice of the standard of value may be clear, but the meaning of that standard of value is less clear. To the valuation analyst, the application of a specific standard of value has significant implications regarding the assumptions, methodologies, and techniques that should be used in a valuation.

In a judicial context, the standard of value is generally set by regulations (as in estate or gift tax), by statute (as in dissent and oppression), by case law (as either stated or implied by divorce cases in most states), or by some combination of these. In financial reporting, the standard is set by the Statements of Financial Accounting Standards (now Accounting Standards Codification [ASC]) as promulgated by the Financial Accounting Standards Board. The following discusses five of the most frequently used standards of value.

Fair Market Value

ValTip

> *Fair market value* is perhaps the most well-known standard of value and is commonly applied in judicial and regulatory matters. Fair market value applies to virtually all federal and state tax matters, including estate, gift, inheritance, income, and ad valorem taxes, as well as many other valuation situations.[10]

The Treasury Regulations give the most common valuation definition of fair market value:

> The fair market value is the price at which the property would change hands between a willing buyer and a willing seller, neither being under any compulsion to buy or to sell and both having reasonable knowledge of relevant facts.[11]

Black's Law Dictionary defines fair market value as "the price that a seller is willing to accept and a buyer is willing to pay on the open market and in an arm's length transaction; the point at which supply and demand intersect."[12]

The willing buyer and willing seller deal at arm's length; they are independent third parties, not specific individuals, and therefore the price arrived at will generally not be influenced by any special motivations or synergies available only to a specific

---

[10] Shannon P. Pratt, *Valuing a Business*, 5th ed. (New York: McGraw Hill, 2008), p. 41.
[11] Treasury Regulation 20.2031-1.
[12] Bryan A. Garner, ed., *Black's Law Dictionary*, 6th ed. (New York: West Publishing, 1991), p. 1587.

buyer.[13] Fair market value implies a market in which the buyer and seller transact, and it assumes current economic conditions as of the date of the valuation.

Under fair market value, shareholder level discounts may be applied to shares of a closely held company if they lack all or some of the prerogatives of control over the corporation or lack marketability. Additionally, the property being valued is under the value in exchange premise and therefore assumes a sale regardless of whether the property actually will be sold.

Estate and gift tax cases applying fair market value provide the most frequent interpretation of the definition and application of its principles. Using these principles, fair market value may be applied in other areas. Indeed, when used in other contexts, the terms of fair market value are discussed only when they depart from the interpretation in estate and gift tax matters, in other words, how a particular standard of value differs from fair market value.[14]

Fair market value is the espoused standard of value used in a number of states for valuations in connection with divorce. While definitions and applications can differ state by state, generally only assets that can be sold are considered under a fair market value standard. In these cases, only the elements of a company's assets, including certain types of goodwill that are salable, will be included in the valuation. In addition, shareholder level discounts for lack of control or lack of marketability are usually considered.

Fair Value

Fair value may be the applicable standard of value in a number of different situations, including financial reporting, valuation of a company going private, shareholder dissent and oppression matters, corporate dissolution, and divorce.

The definition of fair value depends on its context. For financial reporting, fair value is defined in relevant accounting literature and is closely akin to but not the same as fair market value. The definition of fair value from the Financial Accounting Standards Board for financial reporting purposes is:

> The price that would be received to sell an asset or paid to transfer a liability in an orderly transaction between market participants at the measurement date.[15]

> In judicial appraisals, *fair value* is a legally mandated standard that applies to specific transactions and is commonly used in matters involving dissenter's rights and shareholder oppression.

---

[13] There are some circumstances when strategic synergies are considered. Often this is when the market is populated mostly or entirely by strategic buyers.

[14] For example, there is considerable discussion in dissenting shareholder cases as to how fair value differs from fair market value. There is also discussion of these differences in SFAS 157 as applied to valuation for financial reporting.

[15] Statement of Financial Accounting Standards No. 157: Fair Value Measurements, p. 2.

This definition is fairly similar to the one used in estate and gift tax regulations. While the parties are required to be uncompelled under the Treasury Regulations, fair value for financial reporting purposes dictates that transactions be ordered.

Until recently, there was no clear consensus on the definition of fair value in judicial valuations, but prevailing precedents have suggested that use of the term *fair value* distinguishes it from fair market value and the assumptions that underlie its application. While not clearly defined until the last 20 years or so, the most recent applications of fair value have established it, absent special circumstances, as the value of the shares on a pro rata enterprise basis.

Investment Value

Investment value, in the nomenclature of business valuation, means the value of an asset or business to a specific or prospective owner. Accordingly, this type of value considers the owner's (or prospective owner's) knowledge, abilities, expectation of risks and earning potential, and other factors.[16] Investment value often considers synergies available to a specific purchaser.

For example, for some companies, investment value may reflect the added value of vertical or horizontal integration to that company. For a manufacturer, it may reflect the added value of a distributor in order to control the channel of distribution of the manufacturer's particular products. For other companies, it may reflect the added value to acquire a competitor in order to achieve the cost savings of combined operations and possibly eliminate some price competition. For an individual, investment value considers value to the owner and typically includes a person's reputation, unique skills, and other attributes.

Investment value crops up often in the context of marital dissolutions,[17] whether the court calls it by that name or not. It is not uncommon to have a family law court's opinion refer to a standard of value by name, but upon reading the text of the opinion, one may find that the court considered some aspects of what the business appraisal community would view as a different standard of value, often investment value. In this context, investment value usually considers the value of property not to a hypothetical buyer or seller, but to its current owner. From a business valuation perspective, when a divorce court uses investment value in this manner, the particular buyer is the current owner, and the application of value to that particular buyer translates to an investment value. Hence, *investment value is often used synonymously with value to the holder.*

Investment value can be measured, for example, as the discounted net cash flow that a particular investor would expect a company to earn, in the way that particular (owner) investor would operate it.

---

[16] David Laro and Shannon P. Pratt, *Business Valuation and Taxes* (Hoboken, NJ: John Wiley & Sons, 2005), pp. 201–209.

[17] That is in the context of judicial valuations. Investment value is often considered in the purchase or sale of a business enterprise.

For a potential corporate acquirer, for example, investment value could be measured as the stand-alone value of the subject company plus any revenue increases or cost savings that the buyer would expect to achieve as a result of the synergies between the companies.

Investment value considers value from these perspectives of the potential sellers and buyers:[18]

- Respective economic needs and abilities of the parties to the transaction
- Risk aversion or tolerance
- Motivation of the parties
- Business strategies and business plans
- Synergies and relationships
- Strengths and weaknesses of the target business
- Form of organization of target business

Intrinsic Value

Intrinsic value is the value considered to be inherent in the property itself. Intrinsic value is defined by *Webster's Dictionary* as "being desirable or desired for its own sake without regard to anything else"[19] and by *Black's Law Dictionary* as "the inherent value of a thing, without any special features that might alter its market value. The intrinsic value of a silver coin, for instance, is the value of the silver within it."[20]

Intrinsic value is not the legal standard of value in any federal or state statute. Nevertheless, the phrase *intrinsic value* is found in many judicial opinions regarding business valuation, particularly in family law cases and dissenting stockholder or oppressed stockholder cases. Because it connotes the inherent value of a thing, the term *intrinsic value* has often been used synonymously with the value to the holder premise.

The concept of intrinsic value arises out of the literature and practice of security analysis. In fact, the most widely sold book ever on security analysis, *Graham and Dodd's Security Analysis,* has an entire chapter on intrinsic value.[21] Graham and Dodd define intrinsic value as *"the value which is justified by assets, earnings, dividends, definite prospects, and the factor of management"* (emphasis original).[22]

According to Graham and Dodd, these four factors are the major components of the intrinsic value of a going concern:

1. Level of normal earning power and profitability in the employment of assets as distinguished from the reported earnings, which may be, and frequently are, distorted by transient influences

[18] David Laro and Shannon P. Pratt, *Business Valuation and Taxes* (Hoboken, NJ: John Wiley & Sons, 2005), p. 1587.
[19] *Webster's Third New International Dictionary* (Springfield, MA: G&G Merriam Company, 1966).
[20] Bryan A. Garner, ed., *Black's Law Dictionary*, 6th ed. (New York: West Publishing, 1991), p. 1587.
[21] Sidney Cottle, Roger Murray, and Frank Block, *Graham and Dodd's Security Analysis*, 5th ed. (New York: McGraw-Hill, 1988).
[22] Sidney Cottle, Roger Murray, and Frank Block, *Graham and Dodd's Security Analysis*, 5th ed. (New York: McGraw-Hill, 1988), p. 41.

2. Dividends actually paid or the capacity to pay such dividends currently and in the future
3. A realistic expectation about the trend line growth of earning power
4. Stability and predictability of these quantitative and qualitative projections of the future economic value of the enterprise

In general, investment practitioners now concede the existence of an intrinsic value that differs from price. Otherwise, the merit of substantial expenditures by both Wall Street and investment management organizations for the development of value estimates on broad lists of common stocks would be highly questionable.[23]

In other words, when a security analyst says something like "XYZ stock is selling at $30 per share, but on the basis of its fundamentals, it is worth $40 per share," the $40 value is that analyst's estimate of the stock's intrinsic value, but the trading price on that date is $30 per share. If the analyst is right, the stock price may make it to $40 per share, in which case the intrinsic value would be equal to the trading price.

Graham and Dodd say that "perhaps a more descriptive title for this estimated value is central value . . . intrinsic value is in essence the central tendency[24] in price."[25]

However, as mentioned, the term *intrinsic value* has not been restricted to securities analysis. It has been used in connection with valuations for other purposes.

Here is a representative example from a divorce case:

> The value of an item of marital property is its intrinsic worth to the parties; the worth to the husband and wife, the value to the marital partnership that the court is dissolving.
> (Howell v. Howell, *31 Va. App. 332, 523 S.E.2d 514* [2000])

ValTip

Intrinsic value and investment value may seem like similar concepts, but they differ in that *intrinsic value* represents an estimate of value based on the perceived characteristics adhering to the investment itself, while *investment value* is more reliant on characteristics adhering to a particular purchaser or owner.[26]

While using the language of "intrinsic worth," the court applied a standard of value more closely associated with fair value, as treated in dissenting and oppressed stockholder matters.

---

[23] Sidney Cottle, Roger Murray, and Frank Block, *Graham and Dodd's Security Analysis*, 5th ed. (New York: McGraw-Hill, 1988), p. 43.

[24] Central tendency of a data set is a measure of the "middle" or "expected" value of the data set. There are many different descriptive statistics that can be chosen as the central tendency of the data items; arithmetic, geometric, and harmonic means are examples, as are median and mode.

[25] Sidney Cottle, Roger Murray, and Frank Block, *Graham and Dodd's Security Analysis*, 5th ed. (New York: McGraw-Hill, 1988), p. 43.

[26] Shannon P. Pratt, *Valuing a Business*, 5th ed. (New York: McGraw Hill, 2008), p. 44.

Following is another representative example from a dissenting stockholder case:

> In Robbins v. Beatty, 246 Iowa 80, 91, 67 N.W.2d 12C, 18, we define "real value" as the "intrinsic value, determined from a consideration of every relevant factor bearing on the question of value," including "the rate of dividends paid, the security afforded that dividends will be regularly paid, possibility that dividends will be increased or diminished, the size of the accumulated surplus applicable to payment of dividends, record of the corporation, its prospects for the future, selling price of stocks of like character, value of its assets, book values, market conditions, and reputation of the corporation. It is unwise to attempt to state every factor that may bear on value of stock in a particular case."
>
> Woodward v. Quigley, *257 Iowa 1077; 133 N.W.2d 38;*
> *1965 Iowa Sup. LEXIS 599*

As can be seen, courts may use the term *intrinsic value* rather liberally. Because of this, if practitioners are requested to determine the intrinsic value of a company or a fractional interest in a company, they should seek further clarification of what type of value is being sought.[27]

COMMON OPERATIONAL PREMISES UNDERLYING THE STANDARD OF VALUE

While value in exchange and value to the holder are valuation premises under which the standards of value fall, operational premises further refine the assumptions that should be made under a given standard of value. For instance, in finding fair market value (a standard falling under a value in exchange premise), typically the valuation professional is looking to establish a value of a company either as a going concern or, when appropriate, upon liquidation. This operational premise of value may have a substantial effect on the value of property.

These operational premises impact the amount that will be paid upon the exchange of a business. For example, most businesses are valued under the premise that they will continue operating as going concerns. However, when valuing a controlling interest, there are times when the amount realized upon the liquidation of the assets and extinguishment of all liabilities is more appropriate. Either could be higher, depending on the nature of a business and the composition of its balance sheet. An accounting practice might have a high going-concern value but a low liquidation value. A golf driving range, however, might be worth more if the land could be zoned for property development and sold in liquidation.

Going Concern

Most judicial valuations look to determine the value of a company as a going concern. *Black's Law Dictionary* defines *going-concern value* as "the value of a commercial enterprise's assets or of the enterprise itself as an active business with future

---

[27] Jay E. Fishman, Shannon P. Pratt, J. Clifford Griffith, and James R. Hitchner, *PPC's Guide to Business Valuations* (Fort Worth, TX: Thompson PPC, 2009), at 201.11.

earning power as opposed to the liquidation value of the business or of the assets."[28]

In judicial valuations, it is often assumed that a company will continue functioning as it had been prior to, during, and after the valuation. The circumstances of a business may be different because of an event necessitating or triggering the valuation, such as the death of a shareholder or key person or the departure of a dissenting or oppressed shareholder. In other cases, the business may continue as usual, as in the case of a valuation upon divorce.

Liquidation Value

Black's Law Dictionary defines *liquidation value* as "the value of a business or of an asset when it is sold in liquidation, as opposed to being sold in the ordinary course of business."[29] This definition broadly encompasses the idea of liquidation value, that is, that assets and liabilities are valued individually. However, there may be additional refinements to the assumptions under liquidation value, mostly dealing with the time and circumstances surrounding the disposal of the assets and extinguishment of liabilities. Methodologically, liquidation value not only considers the proceeds from selling the assets of a business but also takes into consideration any associated expenses.[30]

The liquidation value of a business is most relevant in the case of an unrestricted 100 percent control interest.[31] There are different levels of liquidation. In the valuation of machinery and equipment, these levels are fairly well developed; there is orderly liquidation, liquidation value in place, liquidation in a forced sale, and so forth (see Chapter 8). As discussed, each level deals with the time and circumstances surrounding the disposition of the machinery and equipment. Pratt has attempted to apply these definitions to valuing a business.[32]

- *Value as an orderly disposition is a value in exchange on a piecemeal basis.* A value in exchange that contemplates the price at which the assets of a business will be sold with normal exposure to their appropriate secondary markets.
- *Value as a forced liquidation.* A value in exchange that contemplates the price at which assets will be sold on a piecemeal basis, but instead of normal exposure to the market, these assets will have less than normal exposure.
- *Value as an assemblage of assets.* A value in exchange, consisting of the value of the assets in place, but not in their current use in the production of income and not as a going-concern business enterprise.

---

[28] Bryan A. Garner, ed., *Black's Law Dictionary*, 6th ed. (New York: West Publishing, 1991), p. 1587.

[29] Ibid.

[30] Jay E. Fishman, Shannon P. Pratt, J. Clifford Griffith, and James R. Hitchner, *PPC's Guide to Business Valuations* (Fort Worth, TX: Thompson PPC, 2009), at 210.12.

[31] Michael J. Bolotsky, "Valuation of Common Equity Securities When Asset Liquidation Is an Alternative" in *Financial Valuation: Business and Business Interests*, ed. James Warren Zukin (New York: Warren Gorham and Lamont, 1990).

[32] Shannon P. Pratt, *Valuing a Business,* 5th ed. (New York: McGraw Hill, 2008), p. 47.

APPLICATION OF SPECIFIC STANDARDS OF VALUE

Fair Market Value in Estate and Gift Tax Valuations

In the federal tax arena, fair market value is an established standard with a generally uniform interpretation. The most common definition of fair market value comes from the Estate Tax definition 20.2031-1, as follows:[33]

> The Fair Market Value is the price at which the property would change hands between a willing buyer and a willing seller, neither being under any compulsion to buy or to sell and both having reasonable knowledge of relevant facts.[34]

By this definition, assets are valued under a premise of value in exchange under the fair market value standard. While there are many issues that must be decided in each case under the fair market value standard, appraisers can generally rely on the assumption that the property to be valued is that which the shareholder holds (as they themselves or their estate holds it), whether that be a minority or a majority share of a given asset.

Through case law, IRS rulings, and valuation literature, there is an established body of law and theory that frames the issues dealt with on an ongoing basis by the federal tax court. We have reviewed a sample of the major federal tax court cases to provide clarity on the legal framework of appraisal. We also explain the elements of fair market value so that later we can see the characteristics that distinguish other valuation standards like fair value from fair market value.

Fair market value is a hypothetical standard that assumes a sale. It is not a measure for one or even several transactions, but hypothetical as opposed to an actual transaction. Moreover, when the definition of fair market value is decomposed, there are five constituent parts:

1. Price at which a property would change hands
2. The willing buyer
3. The willing seller
4. Neither being under any compulsion
5. Both having reasonable knowledge of relevant facts[35]

Price

In determining price, the analyst must first determine the premise of value to understand exactly how the business should be valued. The value in exchange is estimated whether the property is actually up for sale or not; it is presumed to be for sale in a hypothetical transaction at a point where there is a meeting of the minds. Furthermore, under a value in exchange premise, a business can be viewed as a going concern or upon liquidation. In *Estate of Watts v. Commissioner,*[36] the value of the

---

[33] Gift Tax Regulation 25.2512-1 defines the term similarly.

[34] Estate Tax Regulation § 20.2031-1.

[35] IRS Rev. Rul. 59-60. The valuation date and use of subsequent events is also an important consideration.

[36] 823 F.2d 483; 1987 U.S. app. LEXIS 10281; 87-2 U.S. tax Cas. (CCH) P13, 726; 60 A.F.T.R.2d (RIA) 6117.

lumber company in the decedent's estate was valued at $2.5 million as a going concern and was valued in liquidation at over $20 million; therefore, the price varied greatly, depending on whether the business was in liquidation or a going concern. The court of appeals held that as a minority shareholder, the estate's shares did not come with the rights to liquidate; therefore, the value of the shares should be valued on a going-concern basis.

Price implies cash or cash equivalents; therefore, the present value of future benefits is reduced to their cash equivalents. This is an important distinction in that many actual transactions take place in stock-for-stock deals that may either be more or less valuable than a cash transaction,[37] or as earnouts where the exact consideration is not known until the end of the earnout period. Financial terms may also not be at market. Therefore, it is important to consider how, in what form, and when the payments will be made.

Willing Buyer

By definition, fair market value will be the price a hypothetical willing buyer and a hypothetical willing seller arrive at after successfully negotiating a sale of the property or asset in question.[38] As stated by a 1923 case in the Third Circuit, *Walter v. Duffy*,[39] the existence of a market suggests the existence of both supply and demand for a property. Offers to sell without buyers to buy are not evidence of fair market value, and neither are offers to buy without anyone willing to sell. Additionally, the willing buyers need not be a particular class of buyers, as in *Estate of Meuller v. Commissioner*,[40] or can be considered as a class of buyers, as in *Estate of Winkler v. Commissioner*.[41] Even in a hypothetical transaction, courts have been known to, nonetheless, consider in some way the actual owners and the particular facts and circumstances of a given case. The court's view of who constitutes a willing buyer appears to be greatly influenced by the facts and circumstances of each individual case.

Willing Seller

Like a willing buyer, the willing seller considers certain information before deciding to engage in a transaction, including liquidity, alternate uses for the investment, future cash flows, and risk.[42] The case *Mandelbaum v. Commissioner*[43] points out that consideration of a willing buyer is not enough. In *Mandelbaum*, based on the family nature of the company, the willing buyer seeking stock in the company would be likely to demand a large discount on its value; however, if the shareholders of the

---

[37] Black and Kraakman, "Delaware's Takeover Law: The Uncertain Search for Hidden Value," *Northwestern University Law Review* 96 (Winter 2002), 521.

[38] John A. Bogdanski, *Federal Tax Valuation*, ThomsonReuters/Warren Gorham & Lamont, Valhalla, NY, at 2.02 [2] [a] 1996.

[39] 287 F.41, 45 (3rd Cir. 1923).

[40] Tax Ct. Memo 1992-284 at 1415, 63 TCM 3027-17.

[41] Tax Ct. Memo 1989-231; 1989 Tax Ct. Memo LEXIS 231; 57 T.C.M. (CCH) 373; T.C.M. (RIA) 8923.

[42] Z. Christopher Mercer, *Quantifying Marketability Discounts* (Memphis, TN: Peabody Publishing, LP, 2001), 178.

[43] Tax Ct. Memo 1995-255; 1995 Tax Ct. Memo LEXIS 256; 69 T.C.M. (CCH) 2852.

company were willing to sell, that might lead to a substantially different value. Without any compulsion to sell, the seller wants to receive the highest possible price. By deciding not to sell, the shareholder decides to continue to own the property because it's more valuable to him or her. Accordingly, the existence of a willing seller is an important element in determining fair market value. The valuation analyst needs to consider what price the seller would accept, not only what price the buyer would offer.

Compulsion

In the real world, the parties involved in a transaction may be compelled to buy or sell based on involvement in bankruptcy or insolvency, a need for immediate liquidity, the need of an immediate sale for charitable purposes, or a variety of other factors.[44] The fact that there is no compulsion to sell also suggests that the company be valued with ample exposure to an appropriate market, rather than in a forced liquidation.[45] In the previously cited case of *Walter v. Duffy,*[46] the taxpayer sold shares of stock at $455 per share. There was no proof as to what the stock originally cost.[47] However, the court ordered all shares to be valued as of a specified valuation date, March 1, 1913.[48] The IRS based the incremental increase on the difference between $455 per share and $262.50 per share. The basis of $262.50 per share stems from an unrelated sale of the same stock on March 1, 1913. However the Tax Court held that the value of $262.50 was improper because the shares in that transaction were purchased below market price, as the seller was compelled to sell the stock to satisfy creditors.[49]

Reasonable Knowledge

Fair market value requires that both the willing buyer and the willing seller be reasonably informed of the relevant facts affecting the property in question. It is also clear that reasonable knowledge does not mean perfect knowledge. A valuation at fair market value should include information that is known by any party to the transaction, as well as any information that may not be apparent at the valuation date but would have been known or knowable at the time by the parties involved.[50] *Estate of Tully v. United States*[51] is an example where knowable information that may not be known by the owner can affect the determination of value. Here, the decedent was unaware that company officials had been rigging bids until four years after the valuation date. The court determined that through accounting procedures the wrongdoing could have been discovered. The court discounted the value by 30 percent due to the information that could have been discovered on the valuation date with proper investigation.[52]

---

[44] John A. Bogdanski, *Federal Tax Valuation*, ThomsonReuters/Warren Gorham & Lamont, Valhalla, NY, at 2.02 [2] [a] 1996.
[45] Jay Fishman and Bonnie O-Rourke, "Value: More than a Superficial Understanding Is Required," *Journal of the American Academy of Matrimonial Lawyers* 15, No. 2 (1998).
[46] 287 F. 41, 42 (3rd cir. 1923).
[47] 287 F. 41, 42 (3rd cir. 1923), p. 43.
[48] 287 F. 41, 42 (3rd cir. 1923).
[49] 287 F. 41, 42 (3rd cir. 1923), p. 45.
[50] John A. Bogdanski, *Federal Tax Valuation*, ThomsonReuters/Warren Gorham & Lamont, Valhalla, NY, at 2.02 [2] [a] 1996.
[51] 41 AFTR.2d 1477 (ct. Cl. Tr. Div. 1978) (not officially reported) at 1490.
[52] See *Estate of Tully,* 41 AFTR.2d 1477.

Subsequent Events

Although analysts are required to reach their conclusions based on information that is known or knowable at the valuation date, subsequent events that were foreseeable at the valuation date may be considered in a valuation.[53] If an event was completely unforeseen and dealt with factors affecting value at the date of valuation, it is generally not considered. However, events that are reasonably foreseeable at the date of valuation should be considered.[54] In *Ridgely v. U.S.*,[55] the decedent owned land that, just prior to his death, he could not sell at an offer price of $1,000. Five months after his death, General Foods purchased the land for $2,700 an acre. While the IRS claimed the transaction was worth $2,700 per acre, the court did not consider the General Foods transaction as an indicator of value, as no one could have foreseen the purchase at the time of death.

Although not an estate or gift tax case, an application of the aforementioned elements of fair market value can be observed in the dissolution of a partnership ruled on by the Supreme Court of South Dakota, *In re: Dissolution of Midnight Star Enterprises, L.P. ex rel. Midnight Star*.[56] Midnight Star Enterprises, L.P. (Midnight Star) was a limited partnership that operated a gaming, on-site liquor, and restaurant business in Deadwood, South Dakota.[57] The owners included the actor Kevin Costner (Costner), the majority owner, and Francis and Carla Caneva (Canevas), the minority owners, who also managed Midnight Star. The buyout provision in the partnership agreement called for a buyout to be at fair market value.

Ultimately, the Canevas brought a petition for dissolution and determined the fair market value of Midnight Star to be $6.2 million, based on a previous offer to purchase Midnight Star. Midnight Star determined the fair market value of the same to be $3.1 million, based on an appraisal using the fair market value standard of value.[58] The trial court held that fair market value was the actual offer price of $6.2 million.

The issue before the Supreme Court of South Dakota was whether the actual offer price of $6.2 million or the fair market value of $3.1 million should be used in determining the value of the entity. The court remanded the case, reasoning that the appropriate standard was the hypothetical transaction and not the actual offer. The court held the hypothetical transaction should control, as it removes the irrationalities, strategies, and emotions from the analysis.[59] As Chris Mercer and Terry Brown have noted:

> The world of fair market value is a special world in which participants are expected to act in specific and predictable ways. It is a world of hypothetical willing buyers and sellers engaging in hypothetical transactions.[60]

---

[53] In estate and gift tax matters, there have been exceptions when subsequent events providing evidence of value have been considered. See, for example, *Estate of Mildred Herschede Jung v. Commissioner*, 101 TC No 412 (1993) or *Estate of Arthur G. Scanlan v. Commissioner* (TC Memo 1996-331 (1996) and Reconsideration denied in TC Memo 1996-414 (1996).

[54] *Couzens v. Commissioner*, 11 B.T.A. 1040; 1928 BTA LEXIS 3663.

[55] 20 AFTR 2d 5946 (1967).

[56] 724 N.W.2d 334 (2006).

[57] Ibid., p. 335.

[58] Ibid., pp. 335–336.

[59] Ibid., p. 339.

[60] Z. Christopher Mercer and Terry S. Brown, *Fair Market Value v. the Real World*, 2 Valuation Strategies 6, 1999 WL 33327233.

FAIR VALUE IN SHAREHOLDER DISSENT AND OPPRESSION

Because modern corporations function under a system of majority rule, minority shareholders are vulnerable to exclusion or abuse by those with a controlling interest. As a special protection, minority shareholders are granted limited rights in dissent and oppression statutes as a check against majority rule. However, there remains ambiguity in the statutory language, which lends itself to varying interpretations of exactly what the shareholder will receive as compensation in those cases.

Although dissent and oppression are addressed under separate statutes, cases in both areas reference each other in their common use of fair value. Most states define fair value only in their dissent statutes. The model corporate business statutes set forth by the ABA's Revised Model Business Corporation Act (RMBCA) and the ALI's Principles of Corporate Governance also provide guidance as to procedural requirements of both oppression and dissent, as well as in setting guidelines for the determination of fair value.

In a 1950 Delaware dissent case, *Tri-continental Corp v. Battye*,[61] the court established a concept of fair value that would be widely referenced in the future:

> The basic concept of value under the appraisal statute is that the stockholder is entitled to be paid for that which has been taken from him, viz., his proportionate interest in a going concern. By value of the stockholder's proportionate interest in the corporate enterprise is meant the true or intrinsic value of his stock which has been taken by the merger. In determining what figure represents this true or intrinsic value, the appraiser and the courts must take into consideration all factors and elements which reasonably might enter into fixing the value.

Shareholders are generally entitled to the fair value of their shares when they dissent from particular actions defined by statute or they petition for the dissolution of a corporation because of the alleged abuse at the hands of majority shareholders. Dissenter's rights proceedings generally involve a minority shareholder who disagrees with the direction the board of directors is taking the company. A disagreement will generally involve a merger, share exchange, disposition of assets, amendment to the articles of incorporation that creates fractional shares, or any other amendment to the articles from which shareholders may dissent.

Oppression cases often include more egregious actions than do dissent cases. Oppressed shareholders are those who believe they have been treated unfairly or prejudicially by the majority shareholders or the board of directors. Those cases often involve shareholder-employees. Oppression cases can involve termination of dividends, compensation, or employment or a siphoning of corporate assets for the benefit of the majority at the expense of the minority. In some states, shareholders may petition to dissolve the corporation in order to regain what was taken from them. Instead of dissolving, the corporation may elect to buy their shares at fair value, or the courts may order the buyout, if provided for in the individual state's statute.

The major issue addressed in the determination of fair value in these matters is whether shareholder level minority and lack of marketability discounts should be applied. The trend over the past 25 years, as guided by the ABA and the ALI and

---

[61] 74 A.2d 71, 72 (Del. 1950).

precedential case law, has been to generally not apply these discounts. Many courts (and much of the modern commentary and scholarship) direct the minority shareholder's value to be determined as a pro rata share of the equity value of a corporation, without the application of shareholder level discounts for lack of control and lack of marketability.

In the Delaware case of *Cavalier Oil v. Harnett*,[62] the corporation argued that the minimal interest that the shareholder maintained in the corporation, 1.5 percent of the outstanding common stock, was a "relevant factor" to be considered in the valuation for the purposes of the proceeding. The vice chancellor concluded (and the Delaware Supreme Court affirmed) that the objective of the appraisal outlined by the statute was to value the corporation itself, rather than a specific fraction of shares in the hands of one shareholder; therefore, no shareholder level discounts should be applied.

CONTROL PREMIUMS

Although many analysts believe that there is little support for adding a premium to values determined through the use of the guideline public company method, there are instances in these types of judicial matters where there has been explicit consideration of such premiums. Accordingly, when ascertaining the value of a corporation for the purposes of an appraisal proceeding, a control premium, if warranted, may be allowed.

> While allowed in some jurisdictions, this is a controversial area. When it is already reflected in the cash figures, many analysts do not believe in applying a control premium, as they believe this is a double count. This creates a potential problem when a court believes it should be applied. See the addendum to Chapter 16, "Testing for an Implied Minority Discount in Guideline Company Prices" by Gilbert E. Matthews, CFA, *Financial Valuation and Litigation Expert* journal, Issue 19, at www.wiley.com/go/FVAM3E.

New Jersey's *Case v. Brennan*[63] acknowledged the need for an entity-level control premium, as the court believed that an embedded or inherent minority discount existed when valuing shares using the guideline public company method. In this case, the court rejected minority and marketability discounts and acknowledged the need for a control premium to reflect market realities and arrive at the value of the company as a whole.

The ABA and the ALI definitions of fair value have suggested clarification in reference to the application of shareholder level discounts. The 1984 fair value definition from the RMBCA reads as follows:

> The value of the shares immediately before the effectuation of the corporate action to which the dissenter objects, excluding any appreciation or depreciation in anticipation of the corporate action unless exclusion would be inequitable.

---

[62] 564 a.2d 1137; 1989 Del. LEXIS 325.
[63] 344 N.J. super. 83; 780 A.d 553; 2001 N.J. Super. LEXIS 331.

IMMEDIATELY BEFORE

This portion of the definition suggests a time frame for the valuation. It instructs the court to set a valuation date immediately prior to the corporate action from which the shareholder dissents. This time frame tries to ensure that the shareholder does not suffer or benefit from the effects of the transaction he or she dissents from, including benefits from synergies arising from the prospective transaction.

For example, in the case of *Pittsburgh Terminal Corporation v. The Baltimore and Ohio Railroad,*[64] minority shareholders in PTC objected to a merger that would effectively cash out their interest in the corporation. They argued that the consideration they received was considerably less than an outsider would bid for a controlling interest in the corporation. Upon review, the court found that the controlling parties had effective control even before the merger, and therefore it would not be appropriate to place a premium on the share price in consideration of the merger.

UNLESS EXCLUSION WOULD BE INEQUITABLE

This portion of the definition requires valuing the company as if the corporate action did not take place, so as not to unfairly benefit either of the parties from the result of the action. However, this definition also suggests that postmerger information could be considered to the extent that it reflects appreciation unrelated to the merger.[65] Primarily, appreciation in value due to the normal course of business can be included, but the exclusion provision suggests that if the action was unfair or self-dealing by the majority, having enriched themselves at the expense of the dissenter, those acts may be considered in the determination of fair value.

The ABA removed "excluding any appreciation or depreciation in anticipation of the corporate action unless exclusion would be inequitable" from the fair value definition in the 1999 RMBCA, discussed later. The ABA's commentary on the removal indicates that the provisions have not been susceptible to significant judicial interpretation and that their exclusion would allow for the broadening of the concept of fair value. Instead of using these lines, the ABA follows the ALI in recommending the use of customary and current techniques to keep up with evolving economic concepts.[66]

In 1992, the ALI's Principles of Corporate Governance established the following definition:

> The value of the eligible holder's proportionate interest in the corporation, without any discount for minority status or, absent extraordinary circumstances, lack of marketability. Fair Value should be determined using the customary valuation concepts and techniques generally employed in the relevant securities and financial markets for similar businesses in the context of the transaction giving rise to appraisal.

---

[64] 875 f.2d 549; 1989 U.S. App. LEXIS 6910. Applying Maryland Law.

[65] Wertheimer, Barry M., "The Shareholders' Appraisal Remedy and How Courts Determine Fair Value," Duke L.J. 613, 636-37 (1998).

[66] American Bar Association, Report of the Committee on Corporate Laws, "Changes in the Revised Model Business Corporation Act."

EXTRAORDINARY CIRCUMSTANCES

The ALI suggests that fair value should be the value of the eligible holder's pro rata share of the enterprise value, without any discount for minority status or, absent extraordinary circumstances, lack of marketability. These so-called extraordinary circumstances require more than just lack of public market for shares. Instead, the court usually applies a discount only if merited by the circumstances of the case. The ALI offers the example of a dissenting shareholder withholding approval of a merger in an attempt to exploit the appraisal-triggering transaction in order to divert value to himself or herself at the expense of the other shareholders. In that case, the court may make an equitable adjustment.[67]

Devio v. Devio,[68] a Connecticut case, and *Advanced Communication Design, Inc. v. Follet* in Minnesota found that the company would not be able to achieve the liquidity needed to compensate the departing shareholder, so the court applied a marketability discount in order to be fair to the parties involved.

CURRENT AND CUSTOMARY TECHNIQUES

In 1983, the Delaware Supreme Court established the foundation for the current and customary valuation techniques used by the financial community in their decision in *Weinberger v. UOP, Inc.*[69] In this landmark decision regarding the determination of value in a shareholder dissent case, the court's opinion affirmed the concept that a company could be valued using alternative methods, rather than relying solely on the Delaware block method[70] as the courts had before. In this case, the court implemented the discounted cash flow method after considering all the relevant factors of the case.

Weinberger did not entirely do away with the use of the Delaware block method; instead, it allowed the possibility for a widely accepted alternative valuation procedure to be used, as well as industry-appropriate valuation techniques. The appropriate valuation method is not the same in every case. But it is likely that a court will use the most relevant evidence presented to it to determine value. For instance, the asset approach would typically be used to value a real estate company. As current and customary techniques evolve, so will the case law.

In 1999, the ABA followed the ALI in recommending that discounts not be applied. The RMBCA was revised so that the definition of fair value states:

> The value of the shares immediately before the effectuation of the corpo-
> rate action to which the shareholder objects using customary and current
> valuation concepts and techniques generally employed for similar busi-
> nesses in the context of the transaction requiring appraisal, and without

---

[67] American Law Institute, *Principles of Governance,* p. 325.

[68] 2001 Conn. Super. LEXIS 1285.

[69] 457 A.2d 701; 1983 Del. LEXIS 371.

[70] The Delaware block method weights *investment value* (based on earnings and dividends), *market value* (usually based on its public trading price, guideline public company informa-
tion, or guideline transaction information), and *asset value* (usually the net asset value based on current value of the underlying assets). These individual values are then assigned a selected weight to compute the fair value. See Jay E. Fishman, Shannon P. Pratt, J. Clifford Griffith, and James R. Hitchner, *PPC's Guide to Business Valuations* (Fort Worth, TX: Thompson PPC, 2009), pp. 1502.21–27.

discounting for lack of marketability or minority status except, if appropriate, for amendments to the certificate of incorporation pursuant to section 13.02(a)(5).

According to the American Bar Association, Committee on Corporate Laws, "Revised Model Business Corporation Act" (1999), Section 13.02(a)(5) states that "any other amendment to the articles of incorporation, merger, share exchange or disposition of assets to the *extent provided by the articles of incorporation, bylaws, or a resolution of the board of directors* [emphasis added]"; the official comment to the 1999 RMBCA states that if the corporation grants special appraisal rights voluntarily for certain transactions that do not affect the entire corporation, the court can use its discretion in applying discounts.

While these definitions are established by these scholarly associations, the state legislatures have the opportunity to establish their own definitions, with or without referral to these suggested guidelines. We have seen statutes and case law moving toward the latter definition.

In this section, we have addressed the special nature of fair value in dissent and oppression matters. However, the valuation analyst may be called upon to render an opinion of value in the breakup of a company where there is no dissenting or oppressed shareholder. The official comment to the 1999 changes to the RMBCA's definition of fair value asserts:

> In cases where there is dissension but no evidence of wrongful conduct, fair value should be determined with reference to what the petitioner would likely receive in a voluntary sale of shares to a third party, taking into account his minority status. If the parties have previously entered into a shareholder's agreement that defines or provides a method for determining the fair value of shares to be sold, the court should look to such definition or method unless the court decides it would be unjust or inequitable to do so in light of the facts and circumstances of the particular case.[71]

In re: Dissolution of Midnight Star Enterprises, which we cited at the end of our discussion of the fair market value standard for estate and gift taxes, was a partnership dissolution matter in which no oppression was alleged. In its decision, the court ruled that the buyout should be determined in accordance with the partnership agreement, which called for a buyout at fair market value.

Therefore, in dissent and oppression matters, the valuation analyst will typically use current and customary methods to value a minority owner's interest in a business on a pro rata basis (usually without shareholder level minority and marketability discounts). However, the analyst should seek legal guidance for the proper application of fair value, given the particular facts and circumstances of the case at hand.

STANDARD OF VALUE IN DIVORCE

When valuing a business for estate and gift tax purposes, the purpose of the valuation is to determine the tax to be paid on the portion of the business included in an estate or upon gift. In dissent and oppression matters, the purpose of the valuation is to

---

[71] American Bar Association, a Report of the Committee on Corporate Laws, "Changes in the Revised Model Business Corporation Act-Appraisal Rights," *Business Lawyer* 54 (1998), 209.

determine the buyout price to be paid to a dissenting or oppressed shareholder. In a divorce, the purpose of valuing a business acquired during marriage is so that it can be distributed. The fundamental issue is: What constitutes property acquired during a marriage? The individual state statutes offer little guidance. For example, the statutory definitions of marital property in Arizona and Pennsylvania reveal that although the word *property* appears in the respective statutes, its meaning is not clearly defined.

Community property states, typified by the statute in Arizona, define community property as:

> All property acquired by either husband or wife during the marriage, except that which is acquired by gift, devise or descent is the Community Property of the husband and wife.[72]

Alternatively, an equitable distribution state, such as Pennsylvania, defines marital property as:

> (a) all property acquired by either party during the marriage; (b) including the increase in value, until the day of final separation of non-marital property acquired by gift, bequest, devise or descent; and (c) the increase in value of property owned prior to the marriage or property acquired in exchange for property owned prior to the marriage until the date of final separation.[73]

In a divorce valuation, a professional practice may have a much higher value in the state of Washington, where a value to the holder premise appears to be used, than it would in Virginia, where a value in exchange premise appears to be used. The difference would be the inclusion of goodwill that adheres to the professional personally. Washington includes this goodwill, whereas Virginia does not.

The value in Virginia would be higher still than in Pennsylvania, where a fair market value standard is used. Personal goodwill would still be excluded, but shareholder level discounts would be applied, decreasing the overall value. The business would be worth even less in states where fair market value is also used, but because a different set of assumptions applies in these states, even the enterprise goodwill of the business would be excluded.

We find no consistent pattern as to why the states are divergent in their application of standards of value. It appears that the application of standards of value in the 50 states developed independently, and these laws are continually evolving. Moreover, a court can name one standard of value and apply another. In *Hamby v. Hamby*,[74] a North Carolina case, the court looked to determine fair market value but used an expert's testimony of value that looked at the going-concern value of the business to the owner, an investment value standard. Recently, some states have had cases of first impression dealing with the standards of value by which businesses are valued, and in these cases, the courts have performed an analysis of nationwide case law to guide their decisions. However, there does not appear to be an overwhelming trend in divorce scholarship to centralize the standards of value across the states, as the ABA and the ALI have done in dissent and oppression matters.

---

[72] Arizona Statute 25-11.

[73] Pennsylvania Divorce Code Section 3501.

[74] 143 N.C. App. 635, 547 S.E.2d 110 (2001).

Through our survey of case law, annotated statutes, and legal and valuation publications, we have attempted to discuss states based on their interpretation and use of various issues and methodologies to reveal the standard of value generally applied in the state.[75] We have grouped states according to the premise of value and the standards of value either stated in their statutes or stated or implied in their case law. With this analysis, we hope to give practitioners a framework as to the type of value used by courts in certain states.

For instance, if marital property is only something that can be sold, a value in exchange premise would be appropriate. If the state considers the value that inures to the benefit of an owner even if the asset cannot be transferred, a value to the holder premise would apply.

> Because states view property differently, there is no one consistent business valuation model that can be used across the nation. States treat various issues such as professional goodwill, buy-sell agreements, and shareholder level discounts differently.

In reviewing these issues, we have found that there is a continuum over which the standard of value may fall, and the individual states fall on a different place on that continuum, depending on their treatment of these issues.

The basic levels of this continuum can be viewed using two premises of value, namely, value in exchange and value to the holder, and three standards of value: fair market value, fair value, and investment value.

In order to place states on this continuum of value, we looked first at whether the individual state statute addressed the standard of value. Only two states, Arkansas and Louisiana, define standards of value in statutes. The Arkansas statute says:

§ 9-12-315.(4) When stocks, bonds, or other securities issued by a corporation, association, or government entity make up part of the marital property, the court shall designate in its final order or judgment the specific property in securities to which each party is entitled, or after determining the fair market value of the securities, may order and adjudge that the securities be distributed into one (1) party on condition that one-half (1/2) the fair market value of the securities in money or other property be set aside and distributed to the other party in lieu of division and distribution of the securities.

The Louisiana statute more generally applies the fair market value standard:

§ 9:2801-(1) (a) Within forty-five days of service of a motion by either party, each party shall file a sworn detailed descriptive list of all community property, the fair market value and location of each asset, and all community liabilities.

---

[75] We remind the reader that this information will change as statutes and case law changes.

Second, we reconsidered whether the state defined a standard of value in the case law. While Arkansas uses a fair market value standard cited by statute[76] and case law,[77] states such as Connecticut,[78] Florida,[79] Hawaii,[80] Kansas,[81] Missouri,[82] Nebraska,[83] New York,[84] South Carolina,[85] and Wisconsin[86] use a fair market value standard as defined by their case law. Louisiana[87] uses a fair market value standard set forth by statute. Additionally, Minnesota[88] uses a market value standard.

For the other states, we looked at the manner in which the courts treated personal versus enterprise goodwill, shareholder level discounts, and buy-sell agreements.

Personal Goodwill

Personal goodwill is goodwill that adheres to an individual. It consists of the personal attributes of a practitioner, including relationships, skill, reputation, and various other factors. It is usually not transferable. A useful working definition of personal goodwill is "[the] part of increased earning capacity that results from the reputation, knowledge and skills of individual people, and is nontransferable and unmarketable."[89] Enterprise goodwill is the goodwill of the business. Therefore, it generally is a transferable asset, and it almost always is included in the valuation of the enterprise, even in those states that adhere to the narrowest interpretation of fair market value.[90]

California's *In re: Marriage of Lopez*[91] is an example of an early case where the court suggested a list of factors to be considered in valuing goodwill. Those five factors pertain to the individual and address personal goodwill:

1. The age and health of the professional
2. The professional's demonstrated earning power
3. The professional's reputation in the community for judgment, skill, and knowledge
4. The professional's comparative professional success
5. The nature and duration of the professional's practice, either as a sole proprietor or as a contributing member of a partnership or professional corporation

---

[76] Arkansas Statute § 9-12-315 (4).
[77] *Totorich v. Totorich*, 902 S.W.2d 247 (Ark. App. 1995).
[78] *Dahill v. Dahill*, 1998 Conn. Super. LEXIS 846 (Conn. Super. Ct. Mar. 30 1998).
[79] *Christians v. Christians*, 732 So. 2d 47; 1999 Fla. App. LEXIS 6687; 24 Fla. L. Weekly D 1218.
[80] *Antolik v. Harvey*, 7 Haw. App. 313; 761 P.2d 305; 1998.
[81] *Bohl v. Bohl*, 232 Kan. 557; 657 P.2d 1106; 1983 Kan. LEXIS 236.
[82] 738 S.W.2d 429 (Mo. 1987).
[83] *Taylor v. Taylor*, 386 N.W.2d 851 (Neb. 1986).
[84] *Beckerman v. Beckerman*, 126 A.D.2d 591; 511 N.Y.S.2d 33; 1987 N.Y. App. Div. LEXIS 41733. New York also follows an investment value standard of value, as evidenced by *O'Brien v. O'Brien*, 66 N.Y.2d 576; 489 N.E.2d 712; 498 N.Y.S.2d 743; 1985; and *Moll v. Moll*, 187 Misc. 2d 770, 722 N.Y.S.2d 732 (2001).
[85] *Hickum v. Hickum*, 463 S.E.2d 321 (S.C. Ct. App. 1995).
[86] *Sommerfeld v. Sommerfeld*, 454 N.W.2d 321 (S.C. Ct. App. 1995).
[87] La. R.S. 9:2801.
[88] *Bateman v. Bateman*, 382 N.W.2d 240; 1986 Minn. App. LEXIS 4017.
[89] Helga White, "Professional Goodwill: Is It a Settled Question or Is There 'Value' in Discussing It?" *Journal of the American Academy of Matrimonial Lawyers*, vol. 15, no. 495 (1988), 499.
[90] Enterprise goodwill in a professional practice may be treated differently because of the reliance on a particular power.
[91] 113 Cal. Rptr. 58, 38 Cal. App.3d 1044 (1974).

Since *Lopez* discusses attributes specific to the owner, one can infer that California would be considered an investment value state following a value to the holder premise. In *Dugan v. Dugan,*[92] the New Jersey Supreme Court found that the goodwill of a sole proprietor attorney could have value as a marital asset, even though he was ethically prohibited from selling his goodwill at that time. Therefore, one could infer New Jersey is an example of a state that allows for a value to the holder premise and an investment value standard of value.

Enterprise Goodwill

On the other hand, in *Thompson v. Thompson,*[93] the Florida Appellate Court found that if Mr. Thompson could not sell the goodwill of his law practice, it had no value as a marital asset.

Similarly, in *May v. May,*[94] the West Virginia Court distinguished between the business's enterprise goodwill, which was marital property, and the husband's personal goodwill, which was not subject to equitable distribution.

Moreover, in Florida, goodwill is measured based on its walk-away value. Under this narrower view of fair market value, the assumption is that the seller could and would compete with the buyer, thereby eliminating nearly all of the otherwise transferable goodwill. *Held v. Held*[95] demonstrates the concept of walk-away value where the trial court relied on the opinion of one expert who claimed that a nonsolicitation agreement was part of enterprise goodwill.

Shareholder Level Discounts

In some matrimonial courts, it appears that the intention to sell can be an issue in determining what stream of income the individual can expect to receive and whether shareholder-level discounts should be applied. The Oregon case *Tofte v. Tofte*[96] directly addresses this point. Here, the wife argued that discounts should not be included in the calculation of the husband's stock value as he had no intention to sell his share of the company. The court found that intention to sell did not matter in the determination of value of a close family corporation, and discounts should therefore be applied. This view is consistent with a typical application of the fair market value standard.

The Virginia case *Howell v. Howell*[97] addresses the applicability of shareholder level discounts while excluding any personal goodwill by virtue of an individual's reputation. In this case, the court indicated that the value of goodwill can have two components: (1) professional goodwill, also designated as individual, personal, or separate goodwill, which is attributable to the individual and is categorized as separate property, and (2) practice goodwill, also designated as business or commercial goodwill, which is attributable to the business entity, the professional firm, and may be marital property.

The New Jersey case *Brown v. Brown*[98] addresses the valuation of a wholesale flower distributor in a marital dissolution case in terms resembling those normally

---

[92] 92 N.J. 423; 457 A.2d 1; 1983 N.J. LEXIS 2351.
[93] 576 So.2d 267; (1991).
[94] 214 W. Va. 394; 589 S.E.2d 536; 2003 W. Va. LEXIS 118.
[95] 2005 Fla. App. LEXIS 14138 (September 7, 2005).
[96] 134 Ore. App. 449; 895 P.2d 1387; 1995 Ore. App. LEXIS 772.
[97] 46 Va. Cir. 339; 1998 Va. Cir. LEXIS 256.
[98] 348 N.J. super. 466; 792 A.2d 463, 2002.

found in fair value in dissenter and oppression rights matters. In this case, no distinction was made as to personal or enterprise goodwill, and the issue at hand between the valuation experts was whether the lack of intention to sell the business should control whether discounts should be applied or not; ultimately no shareholder level discounts were applied.

Shareholder Agreements

Many times, especially in a professional practice, there are agreements in place between shareholders or partners that provide for the treatment of a shareholder or partner buyout upon death, retirement, or other manner of withdrawal. In a divorce proceeding, many states view such agreements as indicia of value but not necessarily as presumptive of value. Still other states view the existence of such an agreement, if timely, arm's length, and acted upon, as the sole indicator of value.

Logically, states that more closely adhere to a fair market value standard may be inclined to rely more heavily on such an agreement if it meets the previously mentioned criteria. States that closely adhere to an investment value standard may assign little, if any, weight to these agreements because no sale is intended.

Connecticut adheres to a fair market value standard. In the case of *Dahill v. Dahill*,[99] the court stated that it was its duty to find the fair market value rather than the book value or "in hand value." Accordingly, the court rejected the buy-sell agreement in *Dahill v. Dahill*[100] because the buy-sell agreement did not provide for the fair market value of the business.

On the other hand, the Colorado Supreme Court came to a similar conclusion but from a much different point of view. In the case *In re: Huff,*[101] it rejected a valuation based on the partnership agreement because the husband intended to stay with the firm. The argument put forth was that the buyout provision in the stockholder agreement was not relevant because there was no intention to sell, and the proper valuation should be in accordance with investment value, because this standard allowed the court to determine the value of the partnership interest in use.

To summarize, standards of value in divorce are determined on a state-by-state basis. We began with two distinct premises, namely, value in exchange and value to the holder, and three basic standards of value: fair market value, fair value, and investment value. We first looked at statutes and case law for specific guidance on the standard of value. When there was none, we then looked at the treatment of goodwill, shareholder level discounts, and the weight accorded buy-sell agreements as indicia of the premise and standard of value implied by various states. Our conclusion is that one can look at a continuum of value as a way to conceptualize the intersection of valuation theory and case law and use this continuum toward a standard of value classification system in divorce. While we think our suggested classification system may be a useful way of interpreting how the standards of value have been used by courts, it is likely that the courts will continue to identify, value, and distribute marital property in ways they deem equitable and not feel constrained by valuation theory.

---

[99] 1998 Conn. Super. LEXIS 846 (Conn. Super. Ct. Mar. 30 1998).
[100] Ibid.
[101] 834 P2d 244 (Colo. 1992).

FAIR VALUE IN FINANCIAL ACCOUNTING

Fair value is the standard of value used in valuations performed for accounting purposes. The terminology comes from accounting literature, including generally accepted accounting principles (GAAP) and the Securities and Exchange Commission (SEC). In 2006, the Financial Accounting Standards Board issued SFAS 157 (now ASC 820), which defines fair value, establishes a framework for measuring fair value in GAAP, and expands disclosures about fair value measurements.[102] The intent of clarifying the definition of fair value in SFAS 157 is that a single definition of fair value, together with a framework for measuring fair value, should result in increased consistency and comparability of financial measurements.[103] SFAS 157 is effective for financial statements issued for fiscal years beginning after November 15, 2007, and interim periods within those fiscal years.

MEASUREMENT

As mentioned previously, fair value is defined as:

> The price that would be received to sell an asset or paid to transfer a liability in an orderly transaction between market participants at the measurement date.[104]

The following sections discuss the various components of the definition.

The Asset or Liability

Fair value is measured for a particular asset or liability and therefore considers attributes specific to the asset and/or liability. Examples include the condition of the asset or liability and restrictions on sale or use of these assets and/or liabilities.

The Price

The objective of a fair value measurement is to determine the price that would be received to sell the asset or paid to transfer the liability at the measurement date.[105] Accordingly, the statement does not discuss price in terms of cash or cash equivalents, but the exit price considered from the point of view of a market participant (seller) who holds the asset or liability.

The Principal (or Most Advantageous) Market

The exit price is measured assuming a transaction that occurs in the principal market for the asset or liability. The market with the greatest level of activity and volume

---

[102] Statement of Financial Accounting Standards No. 157: Fair Value Measurements, Summary.
[103] Ibid.
[104] Ibid., p. 2
[105] Ibid., p. 3.

is considered the principal market, while the most advantageous market is the market where the reporting entity would maximize the amount that would be received for the asset or minimize the amount that would be paid to extinguish the liability. The fair value of the asset or liability shall be determined based on the assumptions that market participants would use in pricing the asset or liability.[106]

Market Participants

Market participants are buyers and sellers in the principal or most advantageous market. The characteristics of these market participants include:

- Independence from the reporting entity
- A reasonable understanding about the asset or liability based on all available information
- The ability and motivation to transact for the asset or liability[107]

Input Levels

In measuring the fair value of assets and liabilities, emphasis is clearly placed on the concept of market participants, market information, and market inputs. SFAS 157 (now ASC 820) establishes a fair value measurement hierarchy, which relates to a preference for using observable market data in measuring fair value, when market data are available. There are three levels of inputs:

> Level 1 inputs are observable market inputs that reflect quoted prices for identical assets or liabilities in active markets that the reporting entity has the ability to access at the measurement date.[108]
>
> Level 2 inputs are observable market inputs but for assets that are similar but not identical. Assets that will typically be valued using Level 1 and Level 2 estimates are financial instruments. Examples of financial instruments include investments such as marketable securities.[109]
>
> Level 3 inputs are unobservable market inputs and may consider assumptions about market participant inputs that are estimated by the management of an entity. However, management assumptions should not include factors specific to that entity if such factors do not also reflect the assumptions of market participants. For business combination purposes, the valuation of most nonfinancial assets often uses Level 3 inputs.[110]

Estimates of fair value are determined using one or more of the multiple valuation techniques consistent with the market, income, and cost (asset-based) approaches to valuation. Judgment is required in the selection and application of relevant techniques and inputs.

---

[106] Ibid., p. 4.

[107] Ibid., p. 4.

[108] Ibid., p. 10.

[109] Ibid., p. 11.

[110] Ibid., p. 11.

Summary

Valuation analysts have an opportunity to participate in the growing emphasis on fair value measurement in financial reporting, and the need for valuation analysts in financial reporting will probably increase. However, it is incumbent upon valuation analysts to help the accounting profession determine consistent and appropriate valuation methodologies for financial reporting valuations, which will help the accounting profession achieve its stated goal of improving the reliability and consistency of fair value determinations in accounting statements.

CONCLUSION

As you can see, an understanding of standards of value is not as easy as you may think. This understanding must be repeated for every engagement to ensure that it lines up with the purpose and use of the valuation, including consideration of levels of value and, if applicable, discounts or premiums.

CHAPTER 3

Research and Its Presentation

A significant part of the valuation process involves identifying and incorporating both internal and external material into the valuation report. Internal information is generated by the subject company and includes items such as budgets, marketing plans, and projections. Information gathered and prepared by an outside firm specifically for and about the company is also considered to be internal information. This information may include financial statements, audit reports, and market analyses. External information is generated by sources outside the subject company, such as trade associations, newspapers, and magazines. An example of external information would be a trade journal article about trends in the subject company's industry.

OBTAINING INTERNAL INFORMATION

Most valuation engagements begin with the collection of data from the subject company. Typically, analysts gather information on the company by reviewing documents, by visiting all or some of the company's operations, and by interviewing management.

> Because of the complexity of the data-assembling process, many professionals use checklists that detail the types of information they are seeking. Addendum 1 presents a sample list of documents requested and questions to be asked in the course of a valuation engagement. Addendum 2 is a sample management interview questionnaire. Both addenda are at the end of this chapter. Using these tools can help ensure that the valuation analyst covers the necessary bases in gathering internal information.

A DIRECTIVE FROM THE INTERNAL REVENUE SERVICE

Why do we need to consider external information? Why not just base the valuation on internal information generated by the company's management? Besides the obvious need to consider outside influences on a company, another reason is because the

Internal Revenue Service (IRS) has specifically instructed valuation analysts to examine external information as part of the valuation process.

In Revenue Ruling 59-60, the IRS lays out eight factors to consider when performing a valuation for estate and gift taxes. Factor 2 and Factor 8 deal specifically with external information.

Factor 2 instructs the valuation analyst to consider "the economic outlook in general and the condition and outlook of the specific industry in particular." Revenue Ruling 59-60 goes on to say that:

> A sound appraisal of a closely held stock must consider current and prospective economic conditions as of the date of appraisal, both in the national economy and in the industry or industries with which the corporation is allied. It is important to know that the company is more or less successful than its competitors in the same industry, or that it is maintaining a stable position with respect to competitors. Equal or greater significance may attach to the ability of the industry with which the company is allied to compete with other industries. Prospective competition which has not been a factor in prior years should be given careful attention.

Factor 8 focuses on the necessity of comparing the subject company to similar companies: "The market price of stocks of corporations engaged in the same or a similar line of business having their stocks actively traded in a free and open market, either on an exchange or over the counter." Revenue Ruling 59-60 goes into some detail on this issue:

> In valuing unlisted securities the value of stock or securities of corporations engaged in the same or a similar line of business which are listed on an exchange should be taken into consideration along with all other factors. An important consideration is that the corporations to be used for comparisons have capital stocks, which are actively traded by the public. . . . stocks listed on an exchange are to be considered first. However, if sufficient comparable companies whose stocks are listed on an exchange cannot be found, other comparable companies which have stocks actively traded on the over-the-counter market also may be used. The essential factor is that. . . . there is evidence of an active, free public market for the stock as of the valuation date. In selecting corporations for comparative purposes, care should be taken to use only comparable companies. . . . consideration must be given to other relevant factors in order that the most valid comparison possible will be obtained.

Following the outline of Revenue Ruling 59-60, most external data used in a closely held company valuation falls into three areas:

1. *Economic Data.* Economic data includes information on national economic conditions and local market conditions. It encompasses the entire macroeconomic environment, including demographic and social trends, technological issues, and the political/regulatory environment.
2. *Industry Data.* Industry data should focus on the competitive structure of the industry and its prospects for growth. The relative position or market share of

the subject company in the market area and the subject company's financial performance as compared to industry standards are important considerations.

3. *Guideline Publicly Traded Company and Guideline Company Transaction Data.* Guideline information, if available, can be important to understanding the subject company's relative performance. Collecting guideline information involves identifying companies similar to the subject company, locating pricing and financial data, and identifying, if appropriate, transactions involving the sales of controlling interests in similar companies. The analysis of guideline publicly traded company information and guideline company transaction data is covered in detail in Chapter 7.

The remainder of this chapter focuses on techniques that will help the valuation analyst locate and analyze information in these three areas and identifies some specific sources of economic, industry, and guideline company data.

RESEARCH TECHNIQUES AND PLANNING THE SEARCH

Researching external information for inclusion in a valuation report has become easier with the advent of the Internet and other electronic resources. However, the proliferation of resources makes it all the more important to have good search skills to prevent spending unnecessary time in unproductive searches.

Before looking for information, valuation analysts should have a plan.

The few minutes it takes to plan a search can save hours and can greatly enhance its effectiveness. Four considerations will help analysts develop the search plan:

1. *Determine what information is needed.* Define the topic. Consider the goals to be reached and how much information is needed to achieve them. Is a projection of growth in the restaurant industry for the next few years the only item needed, or is there also a need for a detailed analysis of current issues in the industry? Knowing what you hope to accomplish will keep you from pursuing tangential issues.

    To begin analyzing a topic, start by identifying the key words or central concepts in the research question. Write down a number of key terms related to the topic, including synonyms and words describing related topics. Because there are so many ways to express any idea, the trick is to find terms that are consistent with the way databases organize information.

    For example, if you are valuing a company that collects and disposes of residential garbage, you might consider a key phrase to be "garbage collection." However, many databases classify articles about this type of company under the heading "waste haulers."

Develop a standard research form to use as you define a search strategy. Addendum 4 at the end of this chapter contains a sample Industry Research Form. An industry research form might include the following headings:

- *Industry Name.* Be as specific as possible in naming the industry described to you by the subject company's management. "The wholesale home appliance industry, primarily laundry appliances" is more meaningful than "the appliance industry."
- *Industry Codes.* Identify the Standard Industrial Classification (SIC) code and/or the North American Industry Classification System (NAICS) code. (Consult a copy of the SIC Code and NAICS Code manual at a local library or search the manuals on the Internet at www.osha.gov/oshstats/sicser.html and www.naics.com/search.htm respectively.)
- *Key Words.* Brainstorm possible key terms. Ask management at the subject company to assist you in learning industry terms. Supplement this list as you locate other resources that contain new or unfamiliar terms.

2. *Determine where you are going to look.* Consider who might produce the type of information you have defined in step 1. While this may seem simple, it requires an understanding of the information industry and the types of publications and resources that are available. This type of knowledge is developed over time.

Many valuation analysts start their research with an Internet search. Depending on the skill level of the researcher, this can be either a productive exercise or a waste of time. Many reputable data providers now post information on the Internet that was previously available only in print publications or in proprietary databases. There is a trend toward more free information on the Internet, so an Internet search using a search engine such as Google or Bing could turn up a report or document for free that may have been previously available only for purchase.

If you are looking for information on a particular industry, a trade association may be a good place to start. If you are looking for information on valuation multiples for sales of waste haulers, a business broker specializing in waste haulers can be a great source.

Would the information you are seeking be a likely topic for an article in a newspaper or magazine? If so, consider using a periodicals database.

Databases that index periodicals include Lexis-Nexis, Dialog, Factiva, and Proquest, all of which are accessible on the Internet for a fee. These databases, which index articles from thousands of newswires, magazines, newsletters, and trade journals, are discussed in more detail later in this chapter. Check with the reference desk at your local library or business school to see if they make these or similar databases available free of charge to patrons or alumni. Other information sources include:

- *Trade Associations.* Determine if there are trade associations for the industry you are researching. Most libraries have trade association directories such as the three-volume *Encyclopedia of Associations* published by Gale Research, Inc., which contains information on more than 24,000 U.S. associations. A less comprehensive but more convenient source is the online Gateway to

Associations search engine on the American Society of Association Executives' website at http:asaecenter.org/Directories/AssociationSearch.cfm. Be sure to ask the management of the subject company if they belong to a trade association and if they have any association materials that you can review.

- *Trade Publications.* Are there trade journals or specialty publications targeted at this industry? For example, *Appliance Magazine* is the journal of global appliance manufacturers, and *Engineering News Record* is a source for information on engineering firms. Identify these publications by asking the management of the subject company about the periodicals they read, by searching the aforementioned periodical databases, and by reviewing lists of journals in a directory such as MediaFinder (www.mediafinder.com) or the business journal library of *Entrepreneur Magazine* at http:entrepreneur.com/tradejournals/index.html.
- *Other Resources.* Can you identify industry analysts at major brokerage firms? Which are the large public companies in the industry?

VaITip

The 10-Ks of public companies often have detailed analyses of the industry.

Industry profiles prepared by industry analysts and available for purchase can be some of the most useful sources. They are discussed in more detail later in this chapter. The *Standard & Poor's Industry Surveys* publication is available at most larger libraries and contains industry information and economic trends on 52 major U.S. industries. First Research reports are available online at www.firstresearch.com and cover more than 900 industry segments with detailed strengths/weaknesses/opportunities/threats (SWOT) analyses and links to sources and additional information. Other providers of industry data include IBIS (www.ibisworld.com) and Hoover's (www.hoovers.com/free/ind/fr/list.xhtml).

3. *Develop a search strategy.* Now that you have defined your search and identified some sources of information, how can you most efficiently find the information you need? A number of printed documents still are great sources for business valuation research, so do not rule out local libraries or nearby universities, or your firm's in-house library.

Using the Internet to search for business valuation information is potentially one of the most efficient ways, depending on the skill of the researcher. Understanding the basic elements of search logic common to most systems enables analysts to greatly enhance their ability to find information on the Internet and within electronic databases.

Planning how you will look for information can save you time and effort. The more care and thought you put into your search strategy, the more relevant your search results will be.

Once you have decided on your search strategy, there are a number of tips that can make your search more efficient. Here are some tips for using a search engine such as Google:

- *Phrase Searching.* If you are looking for a phrase and want to be sure that your results contain all of the search terms in a specific order, then place your search terms in quotes. Example: "Discount for Lack of Marketability."
- *Exclude Search Terms.* Let's say you want to search for content about Internet marketing, but you want to exclude any results that contain the term *advertising*. To do this, simply use the "-" sign (hyphen) in front of the word you want to exclude. Example: Internet marketing -advertising.
- *Site-Specific Search.* Often it is beneficial to limit your search to a single web site. Even if the site doesn't support a built-in search feature, you can use Google to search the site for your term by using the "site:somesite.com" modifier. Example: "damages calculations" site: www.aicpa.org.
- *Similar Words and Synonyms.* You may want to expand your search to include results that contain similar words or synonyms. To do this, use the "~" sign in front of the word. Example: ~medical.
- *Specific Document Types.* If you're looking to find results that are of a specific type, you can use the modifier "filetype:". For example, you might want to find only PowerPoint presentations related to marketability discounts. Example: "marketability discount" filetype:ppt.

4. *Evaluate information.* The amount of information available on the Internet is staggering, and it varies widely in its accuracy, reliability, and value. Anyone can place a page on the Internet. Unlike most traditional media, no one has to approve the content before it is made public. It is up to the researcher to evaluate information found on the Internet.

Sometimes evaluating information is fairly easy. Official data from government and public corporate sites are generally reliable. Many government agencies digitize their printed reports so that you may access online the same information you could get from the print version of the document. If you are dealing with less familiar sources, determining whether the information is legitimate can require more analysis.

Ask the following questions to determine if the information found is reliable:

- *Who authored this information?* Is the author's name and affiliation disclosed? Is there an e-mail address so that you can inquire further? Is the author the creator or the compiler of the information?
- *Who is publishing this information?* Can the producer be identified and contacted? Is it a professional organization? Does the organization have a particular bias? Who is the intended audience?
- *What can you determine about the content?* How complete is the information? Is it an abstract of the complete text? Are the references documented, current, and relevant?

Warning signs include:

- Numbers or statistics presented without an identified source
- Information you cannot corroborate with other sources

- Extremist language or sweeping generalizations
- Undated information or old dates on information known to change rapidly

INFORMATION SOURCES: BUSINESS FINANCIAL DATABASES

> The major information services provide one-stop sources for business and financial data. These services, which include Dialog, Lexis-Nexis, Factiva, OneSource, Proquest, and Bloomberg, offer extensive collections of periodicals, legal information, and financial data.

Business databases offer a wealth of information. Most include data on industry conditions, public company filings, and articles from major business publications. You can access these databases online with a subscription. Many now offer special pricing packages or pay-as-you-go options. Also be sure to check your local library. Most local or university libraries subscribe to one or more of these services.

- *Bloomberg.* Bloomberg is the premier financial data provider catering primarily to professional brokers and institutional investors. Bloomberg offers a continuous data feed delivering real-time, historical, and descriptive data. Users can import financial data into spreadsheets. Information includes quotes, company information, information on warrants, options, and convertibles, historical prices/yields, fundamentals, and earnings analysis. The Bloomberg site provides far more information than is necessary for most valuations; however, certain practitioners swear by the extensive database of downloadable financial information, news stories, and industry information.
- *Dialog.* The Dialog Corporation, PLC, a leading provider of information to the corporate market, provides access to information on 14 million U.S. and international companies. Dialog's market research information covers market share and sales figures, competitive intelligence, corporate finance, business directories, and financials. Dialog has contracts with content providers such as Dun & Bradstreet, Information Access Corporation, and Standard & Poor's. Access to Dialog's collection of more than 600 databases is available on the Internet at www.dialog.com.
- *Factiva.* Factiva.com gives subscribers direct access to a collection of more than 28,000 leading sources from 157 countries in 23 languages, including local and global newspapers, newswires, trade journals, newsletters, magazines, and transcripts. Financial data is available on thousands of global companies.
- *Lexis-Nexis.* Lexis-Nexis (www.lexisnexis.com) is one of the world's largest providers of information products. Nexis is a news and business online information service offering comprehensive company, country, financial, demographic, market research, and industry reports. Nexis provides access to thousands of

worldwide newspapers, magazines, trade journals, and industry newsletters. It also provides tax and accounting information, financial data, public records, legislative records, and data on companies and their executives. The IRS uses the Lexis-Nexis information service extensively.

- *OneSource Information Services.* OneSource provides access to corporate, industry, and market intelligence information at www.onesource.com. The Business Browser product line includes business and financial information on millions of public and private companies and their executives, drawing on more than 2,500 data sources. These sources include both textual information, such as news, trade press, executive biographies, and analyst reports, and numeric information, such as company financial results, stock quotes, and industry statistics.

- *Alacra* (www.alacra.com). Alacra is an online service designed for users of business information and built around the concept of offering data that can easily be downloaded onto a spreadsheet. Over the years, Alacra expanded to offer more databases and additional formats. The 100+ databases accessible on Alacra contain not just financial information but also economic data, business news, and investment and market research from providers such as Mergerstat, I/B/E/S Analyst Estimates, Barra Beta Books, Edgar, Media General, and Freedonia Market Research. A unique Alacra feature is the ability of users to select content from a variety of sources (financial, market research, and industry data, for example) and create a nicely formatted PDF "book" of the selected data. Alacra is available by subscription or on a pay-per-view basis.

- *Thomson Reuters.* Thomson Reuters is the largest data services company and has an extensive collection. The Thomson One Product bundles a number of databases (http://thomsonreuters.com/products_services/financial/).

    In addition to these information services, there are a number of individual website sources for business valuation information. Much of the remainder of this chapter is devoted to descriptions of these resources.

    Before starting the economic and industry data research using the sources presented here, the valuation analyst should be familiar with the quantitative analysis models that use these economic and industry inputs. The Porter Model, the McKinsey 7-S Model, and the Macroenvironmental Analysis Model are covered in other chapters.

ECONOMIC RESEARCH

The purpose of economic research is to understand the effects of economic conditions on the subject company at both the national level and the company's market level. These macroeconomic forces are factors over which the company has no control.

ValTip

Analysts consider the key external factors that affect value, such as interest rates, inflation, technological changes, dependence on natural resources, and legislation.

It is important to identify trends that may be particularly favorable or unfavorable to the subject company. For example, low home mortgage rates are favorable if the subject company is a residential contractor. Low unemployment may be a negative factor if the subject company is heavily dependent on labor resources.

Issues to consider when analyzing a local economy include:

- Whether the local economy is dependent on a single employer or industry
- The extent and condition of the area's infrastructure
- Announcements of major plant openings or closings
- Income levels and poverty rates
- Attitudes of local officials toward attracting new employers
- Population growth

SELECTED SOURCES OF ECONOMIC INFORMATION

The specific sources detailed below will provide basic information on economic conditions. The information obtained from these sites can be supplemented with information from the services listed previously, your local or university library, and discussions with experts knowledgeable about the market area.

- *Conference Board.* The Conference Board collects and publishes a variety of information on the U.S. economy, including the monthly Consumer Confidence Survey and other research publications based principally on original survey research and extensive executive interviews. Conference Board publications cover such issues as workforce diversity, the role of the board of directors in strategic assessment, the measurement of companies' community involvement, performance enhancement, organizational structure and strategy, and leadership. The Conference Board also publishes ongoing series on top executives' and directors' compensation, institutional investment, and the contributions budgets of U.S. corporations. Information is available at www.conference-board.org.
- *Economy.com.* Economy.com, owned by Moody's, is a provider of economic, financial, country, and industry research. There are a number of related economic data sites owned by Economy.com, Inc., including the Dismal Scientist, FreeLunch, and DataBuffet. Information available includes country analysis, financial markets, industrial markets, and regional markets. These databases contain more than 190 million economic, financial, and demographic time series covering more than 180 countries and their subregions.
- *Federal Reserve System.* The Federal Reserve publishes data on the economies of the 12 Federal Reserve Districts. *The Summary of Commentary on Current Economic Conditions by Federal Reserve District,* commonly known as the Beige Book, is published eight times each year (www.minneapolisfed.org/bb/).
- *National Economic Reviews.* Several firms, including Mercer Capital Management (www.bizval.com), JT Research (www.jtresearch.com), Business Valuation Resources (www.bvlibrary.com), Valusource's Keyvalue data (www.keyvaluedata.com), and Terry Allen (www.valuationproducts.com) produce quarterly economic overviews. These typically include an economic narrative covering major economic variables, stock market trends, interest rates, and economic indicators.

- *STAT-USA.* The U.S. Department of Commerce developed STAT-USA as a clearinghouse to disseminate economic, business, and international trade information produced by the U.S. government. The information collected by STAT-USA is produced by hundreds of separate offices and divisions of the government. STAT-USA (www.stat-usa.gov) has an extensive collection of domestic and international economic statistics available to users on a subscription or as-needed basis.

    Another entry point for government information is www.firstgov.gov. FirstGov.gov is an interagency initiative administered by the U.S. General Services Administration and serves as a gateway to a vast amount of information published by the U.S. government on a variety of topics.

- *The U.S. Census Bureau.* American FactFinder, the interactive database engine developed by the Census Bureau, allows users to browse the bureau's data warehouse and then to search, view, print, and download statistical reports and summary tables. Users may even cross-tabulate data to come up with their own customized statistics. The American FactFinder (http://factfinder.census.gov) is the Census Bureau's primary vehicle for distributing the 2000 Census data.

Other information collected by the Census Bureau is available at www.census.gov, including retail sales, housing starts, durable goods orders, factory orders, trade balances, and inventories. Numerous print publications are available from the bureau, including *Census of Retail Trade, Census of Manufacturers,* and the annual volume of the *Statistical Abstract of the United States.*

> The Beige Book contains information on current economic conditions in each district gathered through reports from interviews with key business professionals, economists, and market experts.

INDUSTRY RESEARCH

The industry analysis can provide a picture of where the industry is going and how the subject company fits in. Look at historical and projected growth in the industry, the number and respective market shares of competitors, if available, and prospects for consolidation. These questions can help in the preparation of an industry analysis:

- What are the prospects for growth?
- What are the industry's dominant economic traits?
- What competitive forces are at work in the industry and how strong are they?
- What are the drivers of change in the industry and what effect will they have?
- Which companies are in the strongest/weakest competitive positions?
- What key factors will determine competitive success or failure?
- How attractive is the industry in terms of its prospects for above-average profitability?

- How large is the industry?
- Is the industry dominated by a few large companies?
- Are there many public companies in this industry?
- How much merger and acquisition activity is occurring?
- What are the barriers to entry?
- Is it a regulated industry?
- Who are the customers? Is that base growing?

SELECTED SOURCES OF INDUSTRY INFORMATION

The specific sources detailed here provide information on industry conditions. The information obtained from these sites can be supplemented with information from the data services listed earlier in this chapter, your local or university library, and discussions with experts knowledgeable about the industry conditions.

- *American Society of Association Executives.* The website of the American Society of Association Executives (ASAE) (www.asaecenter.org/directories/association search.cfm) is an excellent starting place for locating other trade associations. The ASAE has compiled on its site a "gateway" to a searchable index of thousands of trade associations. From this gateway you can type in a key word describing your industry, and the ASAE search engine will return a list of associations whose names contain that key word.
- *First Research Industry Profiles.* First Research (www.firstresearch.com) publishes summary industry analyses on a wide variety of industries. The reports focus on understanding industry dynamics relative to suppliers, customers, and competitors. The reports are, on average, about eight pages long and cover industry trends, challenges, and opportunities, and provide links to industry-related sites.
- *Integra Information Benchmarking Data.* Industry Benchmarking Data reports describe the normative financial performance of privately held businesses in more than 900 industry sectors and 13 sales ranges. The Microbilt Integra Data Product (www.microbilt.com/financial-benchmarking.aspx) is a benchmarking tool with comparative statistical information similar to the Annual Statement Studies published by the Risk Management Association (formerly Robert Morris Associates), but more extensive. The Comparative Profiler also allows users to upload summary financial statements for a subject company, and then, using SIC codes, select an industry to produce a report showing side-by-side comparisons between the company and its industry.
- *MarketResearch.com.* MarketResearch.com provides access to more than 250,000 market research reports from more than 650 leading global publishers. If you need in-depth data on a particular product or market segment, these market research reports at www.marketresearch.com may be the answer.
- *Standard & Poor's Industry Surveys.* Industry Surveys profiles more than 50 industries in detail. Coverage is extensive with a focus on the current situation and outlook for each industry. Summary data on major companies and a section on how to analyze a company are included for each industry. Printed volumes are published quarterly with each industry being updated twice a year. Industry Surveys are available online as part of the Standard & Poor's Marketscope Advisor or Net Advantage, OneSource service, and Alacra.

- *IBIS World* (www.ibisworld.com). IBIS World provides industry overviews on more than 700 industries. Each report is 25 to 30 pages in length and is updated regularly. There are pay-as-you-go and subscription plans. Reports are archived. Search the site by SIC, NAICS, or key word.

GUIDELINE COMPANY AND TRANSACTION RESEARCH

A search for guideline public companies begins with an understanding of the operations and markets of the subject company. Choosing the right guideline companies and transactions is an involved process that is discussed at length in Chapter 7. The sources below, along with the information services discussed earlier, will provide the information necessary for analysts to choose guideline public companies and transactions for valuation analysis.

SOURCES FOR PUBLICLY TRADED COMPANY DATA

- *Alacra.* Alacra offers business information, such as financial, economic, demographic, industry, country, and market-specific data. Alacra provides a single point of access to more than 100 commercial business databases. Alacra includes information on more than 45,000 public and 350,000 private companies. Content

| ValTip |

> The EDGAR database contains information on thousands of public companies.

categories include Investment Research, Deal Information, Credit Research, Earnings Estimates, Economic Data, News, Ownership, and Executive Data.
- *EDGAR (Electronic Data Gathering, Analysis, and Retrieval).* The EDGAR system was established by the Securities and Exchange Commission to allow public access to the filings of public companies. EDGAR filings can be downloaded at no charge from the SEC site at www.sec.gov. Private vendors have found a niche offering enhancements to the basic EDGAR information offered by the SEC. The web site 10-K Wizard (www.10kwizard.com), which is now a part of Morningstar, allows users a variety of search options, including full-text and SIC code searching. Similar services are available from other vendors, including EDGAR Online and LiveEDGAR, now a part of Westlaw Business.
- *Mergent Online.* Available online at www.mergentonline.com, this data service evolved from the *Moody's Manual of Industrial and Miscellaneous Securities,* the first guide available to U.S. public companies. Today the service offers access to a fully searchable database of more than 25,000 U.S. public companies (active and inactive) listed on the NYSE, AMEX, and NASDAQ exchanges. Other information includes annual reports, company fact sheets, and country profiles.
- *Thomson Reuters.* The Thomson Reuters financial databases (http://thomson reuters.com/products_services/financial/) mentioned earlier in this chapter cover a broad spectrum of information. Products like Thomson One Banker and

Thomson One Corporate Finance have publicly traded guideline company data, including SEC filings, insider trading filings and analysis, state and federal agency documents, criminal and civil filings, and bankruptcy filings for thousands of companies traded on the major U.S. stock exchanges.

- *Standard & Poor's.* The Standard & Poor's Capital IQ/CompuStat database (www.compustat.com) includes fundamental and market data on 98 percent of the world's market capitalization with data on more than 90,000 global securities. It also includes information on market indices and financial ratios, including dividends, growth rates, profitability, and relative market performance.
- *Hoover's Online.* The Hoover's Online site at www.hoovers.com provides extensive company, industry, and market intelligence information. The Hoover's database of more than 65 million companies includes both publicly traded and privately held companies. Information includes detailed descriptive data such as company background, financials, and current news.
- *One Source.* The Business Browser by One Source (www.onesource.com) provides information on millions of U.S. and Canadian public and private companies, the executive decision makers, and hundreds of industry sectors. The Analysis Pack feature provides comparative financial reports, including public company financial statements, ratios, valuations, and growth rates for in-depth financial analysis, peer-to-peer comparisons, and peer-to-industry norms comparisons.
- *Morningstar.* Custom Peer Group Builder (www.Morningstar.com) is part of Morningstar's cost of capital resource center with more than 10,000 U.S. companies. You can screen by various characteristics and also calculate the cost of capital for a custom group of companies.

GUIDELINE TRANSACTION DATABASES

There is additional information on these transaction databases in Chapter 7.

- *Bizcomps.* Bizcomps is compiled by Jack R. Sanders of Asset Business Appraisal and is distributed by Business Valuation Resources at www.bvmarketdata.com. It contains information on thousands of small business sales. The database is updated and expanded every year. Deals are sorted by industry, and each record reflects revenue and cash flow multiples.
- *Done Deals Database.* The Done Deals Database (www.donedeals.com) contains information on transactions of private and public midmarket companies sold for purchase prices between $1 million and $1 billion. The more than 8,600 reported transactions cover approximately 30 industries. The data include sale prices, terms, and ratios. The Done Deals database is part of Practitioners Publishing Company, which is owned by Thomson Reuters.
- *Pratt's Stats.* Pratt's Stats is a database of more than 13,000 private company transactions compiled by Business Valuation Resources. This database provides a large number of data items for each transaction, including financials, ratios, and some company background information. Transaction data are obtained from the International Association of Business Brokers and some public filings. Pratt's Stats is accessible online at www.bvmarketdata.com.
- *IBA Database.* The Institute of Business Appraisers database (www.go–iba.org) contains information on more than 34,000 small business transactions, the majority of which are priced below $1 million.

- *SDC Platinum.* The SDC Platinum product is part of Thomson Reuters and available in several of the databases listed earlier in this chapter. Completed-transaction data are searchable on a wide range of parameters, including SIC code, time frame, and transaction size. Updated daily, the data go back to 1979 and cover hundreds of thousands of transactions. Output options include more than 1,400 detailed information elements, including target and acquirer profiles, deal terms, deal value, and stock premiums.
- *Mergerstat.* More transaction data is available in the Mergerstat BVR Control Premium study available from Business Valuation Resources (www.bvmarketdata.com). This web-based tool is used by some analysts to quantify minority discounts and control premiums in the business valuation, business appraisal, venture capital, and merger and acquisition professions.

PRESENTING RESEARCH IN A REPORT

Once you have used the sources presented here to gather information, that information can be analyzed and prepared for inclusion in the valuation report. The relevant economic and industry information presented in the report should relate to the valuation conclusion.

Some analysts add the industry and economic data as an afterthought to the report, without taking time to make sure the appropriate data is fully integrated into the engagement. It is not uncommon to find, for example, a report where the economic outlook may be for recession and the industry shrinking, but the valuation conclusion implies a brisk rate of growth and low level of risk. Analysts may also find the following sites that focus directly on business valuation to be of interest.

> A common mistake by inexperienced valuation analysts is to wait until the last minute to do the industry and economic analysis and then to drop it into the text without any discussion of how it relates to the valuation conclusion.

OTHER SOURCES OF INFORMATION

BVLibrary.com

This site from Business Valuation Resources has a wealth of business valuation information. It contains the full text and abstracts of all important federal and state court cases involving business valuation; IRS materials including revenue rulings, preliminary loss reports (PLRs), technical advice memorandums (TAMs), and Internal Revenue Code sections relevant to business valuation; conference papers; and other articles not published elsewhere. You can also subscribe or purchase single articles featured in Business Valuation Update and access related publications. All documents are key word searchable.

Mercer Capital

The website for Mercer Capital Management at http://mercercapital.com has the full text of dozens of articles on business valuation topics. You can also register for several free business valuation newsletters, download a selection of free e-books, or purchase a book written by a Mercer Capital author.

Willamette Management Associates

The Willamette site at www.willamette.com has an online library with articles from *Insights* magazine, presentations, and information on the many books published by WMA authors.

Valuation Products and Services, L.L.C.

This site, owned by Jim Hitchner, at www.valuationproducts.com, offers a number of resources to assist the business appraiser in financial valuation, forensic/fraud, and litigation services. In addition to the journal *Financial Valuation and Litigation Expert*, it offers webinars, guides, and tool kits produced by the top leaders in the valuation profession.

Valuation Resources

There are hundreds of links to valuation resources at www.valuationresources.com.

Dr. Aswath Damodaran of the Stern School of New York University has a comprehensive site with papers and presentations on valuation issues (www.stern.nyu.edu/~adamodar/).

There are also data and research resources at www.keyvaluedata.com.

SUMMARY

While every attempt has been made to provide up-to-date information in this chapter, the nature of this rapidly changing information industry makes that virtually impossible. Some of the specific sources mentioned may no longer be available or may have changed content. Before attempting to access any of the information sources discussed, check with the vendor for the most current pricing and access information.

A properly conducted search for information will yield very reliable information that will support valuation analyses and enhance the presentation of a valuation in a report. For further information on information gathering, refer to *The Best Websites for Financial Professionals, Business Appraisers, and Accountants,* 2nd ed., by Eva M. Lang and Jan Davis Tudor (New York: John Wiley & Sons, 2003).

ADDENDUM 1—VALUATION INFORMATION REQUEST (VIR) GENERAL

Business Name: _____

Valuation Date: _____

This is a generalized information request. Some items may not pertain to your company, and some items may not be readily available to you. In such cases, indicate N/A or notify us if other arrangements can be made to obtain the data. Items already provided are indicated.

Provided

N/A

Financial Information

❑	❑	1.	Financial statements for fiscal years ending FIVE YEARS (order of preference: audited, reviewed, compiled, and internal).
❑	❑	2.	Interim financial statements for the month-end DATE OF VALUATION and one year prior.
❑	❑	3.	Financial projections, if any, for the current year and the next three years. Include any prepared budgets and/or business plans.
❑	❑	4.	Federal and State Corporate Income Tax Returns and supporting schedules for fiscal years ending FIVE YEARS.
❑	❑	5.	Explanation of significant nonrecurring and/or nonoperating items appearing on the financial statements in any fiscal year if not detailed in footnotes.
❑	❑	6.	Accounts payable aging schedule or summary as of DATE OF VALUATION.
❑	❑	7.	Accounts receivable aging schedule or summary and management's general evaluation of quality and credit risk as of DATE OF VALUATION.
❑	❑	8.	Restatement of inventories and cost of goods sold on a FIFO basis for each of the past five fiscal years if LIFO accounting is used for inventory reporting purposes.
❑	❑	9.	Fixed asset and depreciation schedule as of DATE OF VALUATION.
❑	❑	10.	Amortization schedules of mortgages and notes payable; and terms of bank notes, credit lines, and/or debt agreements as of DATE OF VALUATION.
❑	❑	11.	Current financial statements for any ESOP, profit-sharing, pension, or other employee benefit trust at DATE OF VALUATION.
❑	❑	12.	Current level of over- (under-) funding for any defined benefit plan at DATE OF VALUATION.
❑	❑	13.	Description of any compensation, salaries, dividends, or distributions received by persons not active in the operations of the business, including the year and respective compensation.
❑	❑	14.	Estimated total revenue, gross profit, and net income for the current fiscal year.
❑	❑	15.	Explanation of fluctuations, growth, or decline in revenue of the business during the past five years.
❑	❑	16.	Explanation of expected failure of the business to meet this year's budget based on the year-to-date financial data, if applicable.
❑	❑	17.	Description of any anticipated significant rate increases in the cost of labor or materials.

❑ ❑ 18. Estimate of revenues, gross profits, and earnings before interest and tax (EBIT) for the next five years if revenue growth, gross margins, or net margins are expected to be significantly different as compared to the past five years.

❑ ❑ 19. Explanation of expected changes in the amount of capital expenditures during the next five years if expectations differ from those incurred during the past five years, including the anticipated new levels of capital expenditures.

❑ ❑ 20. Average borrowing rate for the business and financial ratios that must be maintained to comply with lenders' credit terms.

❑ ❑ 21. Description of any assets with stated net book value on the balance sheet that differ significantly from the fair market value that could be realized if the business were liquidated (i.e., appreciated real estate, obsolete inventory, or equipment).

❑ ❑ 22. Description of any assets owned by the business that are not being used in the operations of the business (i.e., excess land, investments, excess cash, unused equipment, etc.).

Products and Markets

❑ ❑ 1. List of the major products, services, or product lines of the business and copies of marketing materials, including sales brochures, catalogs, or other descriptive sales materials.

❑ ❑ 2. Sales and profit contributions analysis by product, product line, service category, customer, subsidiary, and/or location (whichever is applicable).

❑ ❑ 3. Unit volume analyses for existing product lines for the past five years.

❑ ❑ 4. Description of major products or services added in the last two years (or anticipated) and current expectations as to sales potential.

❑ ❑ 5. Description of the features, if any, that distinguish the business's products or services from the competition.

❑ ❑ 6. Causes for the cost of products and services supplied to your business to fluctuate, and list of alternative suppliers available at similar rates, if any.

❑ ❑ 7. Description of new products under development with expectations as to potential.

❑ ❑ 8. List of the top 10 customers of the business, indicating sales (or sales on which commissions were earned) and unit volumes for each of the past three fiscal years if customers are consolidated.

❑ ❑ 9. Summary of major accounts gained (lost) in the last year indicating actual sales in the current year and beyond.

❑ ❑ 10. List of major competitors (full name, location, size, and estimated market share of each).

❑ ❑ 11. List of trade association memberships and industry publications of interest to management.

❑ ❑ 12. Classification of the business's industry (SIC No. or NAICS No.).

❑ ❑ 13. Description of any significant business operations that have been discontinued in recent years or are expected to be discontinued in the future (i.e., sale of facility or business line, closed-out product line, etc.), including date of discontinuation and impact on revenues and profits.

❑ ❑ 14. Description of any significant business operations that have been added in recent years or are expected to be added in the near future (i.e., purchase of facility, business acquisition, introduction of new product line, etc.), including date of addition and financial impact.

❑ ❑ 15. List of the names of all principal suppliers accounting for over 10 percent of total purchases.

❑ ❑ 16. Summary of terms of any existing purchase agreements with principal suppliers.

Provided

N/A

Products and Markets (*continued*)

- ❑ ❑ 17. Summary of importance of research and development to the success of the business.
- ❑ ❑ 18. Characteristics of customers (i.e., industries served, demographics).
- ❑ ❑ 19. Approximate number of customers that the business has and percentage that are repeat clientele.
- ❑ ❑ 20. Approximate time the average customer has been purchasing from the business.
- ❑ ❑ 21. Description of customers that account for over 10 percent of annual revenue or gross profit of the business.
- ❑ ❑ 22. Summary of any contractual agreements with customers and/or distributors.
- ❑ ❑ 23. Description of any contracts or agreements with customers, suppliers, or distributors that would be nontransferable if the business were sold.
- ❑ ❑ 24. Number of clients that would discontinue relations with the business if the business were sold, including reason(s) and the estimated impact on revenues.
- ❑ ❑ 25. Summary of factors that stimulate demand for the business's products or services.
- ❑ ❑ 26. Description of seasonal or cyclical factors, if any.
- ❑ ❑ 27. Reason for increases or decreases of major competitors during the past five years, including their respective market share.
- ❑ ❑ 28. Approximate percentage of the market the subject business holds.
- ❑ ❑ 29. Description of level of difficulty to enter into the market or industry by potential competitors.
- ❑ ❑ 30. Description of the differences of the subject business from its competitors, including price, quality, strengths, and weaknesses.
- ❑ ❑ 31. List any publicly held companies or subsidiaries known to operate in your industry.
- ❑ ❑ 32. Name, address, and phone number of contact at industry organization that assists with market data, if any.

Operations

- ❑ ❑ 1. In a paragraph or so, complete this statement: "Our company is in the business of . . ."
- ❑ ❑ 2. Name and description of the operations of all major operating entities, whether divisions, subsidiaries, or departments.
- ❑ ❑ 3. List of the top 10 suppliers (or all accounting for 5 percent or more of total purchases) and the level of purchases in each of the past two years (include total purchases by the business in each year).
- ❑ ❑ 4. List of product(s) on which the business is single-sourced or suppliers on which the business is otherwise dependent.
- ❑ ❑ 5. Dividend policy, dividend history, and prospect for future dividends.
- ❑ ❑ 6. Copy of any existing employee stock ownership plan (ESOP).
- ❑ ❑ 7. Copies of all other stock option plans or option agreements, or any other plan providing vested benefits in business stock. Also list number of options granted and to whom, and the stated exercise price(s) and expiration date(s).

❏   ❏   8. Basis for business contributions (contribution policy), contributions in each of the past five years, and projection for future contributions to the ESOP, pension plan, and/or profit-sharing plan.

❏   ❏   9. The most recent projection of emerging ESOP repurchase liability. If no study has been done, list known ESOP liquidity requirements during the next three years (e.g., known retirements during period).

❏   ❏   10. Description of any services performed for, or by, a related party or business, including services provided, dollar amounts, nonmonetary benefits, and if transactions are at market rates.

Facilities

❏   ❏   1. Location, age, and approximate size of each facility. Provide or estimate business volume by major facility.

❏   ❏   2. Ownership of each facility and other major fixed assets. If leased, include name of lessor and lease terms or agreements. If owned by the business, include:

- Date purchased;
- Purchase price;
- Recent appraisals;
- Insurance coverage; and
- Book values.

❏   ❏   3. Estimated depreciation of all assets on a straight-line depreciation basis if accelerated depreciation is used for financial statement purposes.

❏   ❏   4. Copies of any appraisals of real estate or personal property owned by the business.

❏   ❏   5. Copies of any appraisals of any company-owned real property or personal property performed during the last three years.

❏   ❏   6. Comparison of rates of leases to market rates if facilities are rented from a related party.

❏   ❏   7. Description of the terms of the real estate lease including date of expiration, anticipated lease rate changes, and whether it is renewable.

❏   ❏   8. Estimate of the cost to relocate business operations including lost profits from business interruption.

❏   ❏   9. Percentage of total capacity (expressed as percentage of total revenue) of the current business operations.

❏   ❏   10. Description of changes in total operating capacity during the past five years (i.e., physical expansion, technological improvement), including related expenditures.

❏   ❏   11. Based on future expected growth, description of when additional facilities or expansion (if foreseeable) will be needed, including approximate cost.

❏   ❏   12. Approximate current and historical backlog (in revenues) or waiting list (number of customers).

Personnel

❏   ❏   1. Current organization chart.

❏   ❏   2. Number of employees (distinguish full-time and part-time) at year-end for the last six years including current employee classifications, general wage scales, and approximate rate.

Provided   **N/A**

Personnel *(continued)*

❑ ❑   3. List all union relationships including name of union, date of current agreement, workers and facilities covered.

❑ ❑   4. Number of part-time and full-time business-employed salespersons including compensation arrangements or schedules. If there are none, describe how sales are obtained and by whom.

❑ ❑   5. Description of the management team, including current title, age, length of service, background, annual salary, and bonus for the current year and each of the last two years.

❑ ❑   6. Full names of the board of directors, including occupation of outside members.

❑ ❑   7. Summary of employee turnover (i.e., below average, average, or above average) compared to your industry.

❑ ❑   8. Adequacy of supply of labor.

❑ ❑   9. Summary of employee compensation (i.e., below average, average, or above average) compared to your industry.

❑ ❑   10. Description of any significant staffing changes or increases anticipated during the next three to five years.

❑ ❑   11. Description of terms of any contracts with personnel, such as noncompete agreements or employment contracts.

❑ ❑   12. Description of significant adverse effect on the operating performance of the business due to the loss of a key employee or manager, including potential revenue losses.

❑ ❑   13. Specify succession of management, if determined.

❑ ❑   14. Description of staff members who would not be retained if the business were sold, including their respective current compensation and position with the business.

Corporate Documents and Records

❑ ❑   1. Corporate charter, articles of incorporation, and/or bylaws.

❑ ❑   2. Minutes of board of directors and shareholders' meetings for the most recent three years (may be reviewed by us on-site).

❑ ❑   3. Summary of major covenants or agreements binding on the business (e.g., union contracts, capital leases, employment contracts, service contracts, product warranties, etc.).

❑ ❑   4. Description of any pending litigation including parties involved, date of filing, description and nature of the lawsuit or claim, current status, expected outcome, and financial impact.

❑ ❑   5. List of all subsidiary companies and the percentage ownership in each.

❑ ❑   6. Name of any "related" companies (common ownership, common shareholders, etc.) and brief description of the relationship(s).

❑ ❑   7. Stock ledger.

❑ ❑   8. All closing statements and purchase agreements related to all purchases of the business's stock over the history of the business.

❑ ❑   9. All closing statements and purchase agreements related to all mergers or acquisitions by the business up to the valuation date.

❑ ❑   10. Copies of any appraisals of the stock or assets of the business made during the last three years.

❑ ❑   11. State(s) and year of incorporation or registration.

❑ ❑   12. Form of ownership (C corporation, S corporation, general partnership, limited partnership, sole proprietorship).

❏   ❏   13. List of the largest ownership interests in the business including name of owner, percentage of shares held and position with business or inactive in business, total shares authorized, total shares issued, and total shares outstanding.

❏   ❏   14. Description of any unusual stock features (i.e., voting or nonvoting, preferred or convertible, class A and class B).

❏   ❏   15. Description of any restrictions on the sale or transfer of ownership interests (buy-sell agreement, lettered stock option to buy, stock options, etc.).

❏   ❏   16. Description of familial or other relationships among owners.

❏   ❏   17. Description of sales or transfers of any ownership interests in the business in the past five years, including how the price or value was determined.

❏   ❏   18. Description of any bona fide offers to purchase the business during the past five years.

❏   ❏   19. Analysis of adequacy of the current business insurance.

❏   ❏   20. Description of any subsidiaries, joint ventures, or investments of a material nature in other companies.

Disclaimer Excluding Any Warranties: This checklist is designed to provide guidance to analysts, auditors, and management but is not to be used as a substitute for professional judgment. These procedures must be altered to fit each assignment. The practitioner takes sole responsibility for implementation of this guide. The implied warranties of merchantability and fitness of purpose and all other warranties, whether expressed or implied, are excluded from this transaction and shall not apply to this guide. The Financial Valuation Group shall not be liable for any indirect, special, or consequential damages.

ADDENDUM 2—MANAGEMENT INTERVIEW–OPERATIONS

Exact Business Name _____ Date of Valuation _____

Address _____ Phone _____

_____

Analyst/Interviewer _____ Date of Interview _____

The objective of this management interview is to provide us with operational information that will aid us in the valuation of your business. We will keep the information confidential. Describe the following to the best of your ability. If necessary, use a separate sheet of paper, with reference to each item number. If some items are not applicable, please indicate N/A. Items already provided are indicated.

Provided   **N/A**

Interviewee(s)

❑ ❑ 1. Name   Title

   _____   _____

   _____   _____

   _____   _____

Purpose and Objective of the Valuation

❑ ❑ 2. The activity or transaction giving rise to the valuation.

Other Information Regarding the Transaction

❑ ❑ 3. Number of shares being valued (each class).
❑ ❑ 4. Total number of shares issued (each class).
❑ ❑ 5. Total number of shares outstanding (each class).
❑ ❑ 6. Date of the valuation.
❑ ❑ 7. State of incorporation.
❑ ❑ 8. Standard of value.

Corporate Information

❑ ❑ 9. Name, address, and telephone number of the business attorney.
❑ ❑ 10. Name, address, and telephone number of the business accountant or bookkeeper.

Description of the Business

❑ ❑ 11. Type of business.
❑ ❑ 12. Products/services sold.
❑ ❑ 13. Type of customers/clients.
❑ ❑ 14. Location of sales/services.
❑ ❑ 15. Business code (see tax return).
❑ ❑ 16. SIC number or NAICS number.

❑ ❑ 17. Type of industry(ies).
❑ ❑ 18. Important industry trends.
❑ ❑ 19. Date business started.
❑ ❑ 20. Fiscal year-end date.
❑ ❑ 21. Factors you consider most important to your business's success.

History of the Business

❑ ❑ 22. From founding to the present, history including people, date, places, new products, markets, and physical facilities.

Ownership

❑ ❑ 23. Shareholder list as of the date of valuation.
❑ ❑ 24. Transactions in the common stock and basis for price (parties, dates, shares, and prices).
❑ ❑ 25. Offers to purchase the company, if any. Discuss price, dates, terms, and current status of negotiations.
❑ ❑ 26. Prior appraisals.

Management

❑ ❑ 27. Current organizational chart.
❑ ❑ 28. List key management personnel with title, length of service, age, and annual compensation.
❑ ❑ 29. Key management positions open at this time.
❑ ❑ 30. Plans for succession if key-man dependency exists.
❑ ❑ 31. Adverse impact on business if sudden loss or withdrawal of any key employee.
❑ ❑ 32. Amount and description of key-person life insurance policy, if any.

Products and Services

❑ ❑ 33. Business mix.
❑ ❑ 34. Changes in business mix.
❑ ❑ 35. New products/services.
❑ ❑ 36. Development procedure(s) of new products/services.
❑ ❑ 37. Expected performance of new products/services.
❑ ❑ 38. Percent of output manufactured by company.
❑ ❑ 39. Percentage of manufactured products for resale.
❑ ❑ 40. Proportion of sales that are replacement parts.
❑ ❑ 41. Note any important differences in profit margins by product line.

Markets and the Economy

❑ ❑ 42. Market area.
❑ ❑ 43. Determination of market area by market segment, geography, or customer type.
❑ ❑ 44. Important characteristics of the relevant economic base (obtain information from local Chamber of Commerce if needed).
❑ ❑ 45. Business sensitivity to economic cycles or seasonal influences.
❑ ❑ 46. Industry(ies) of market concentration.
❑ ❑ 47. Approximate percentage of foreign sales, and, if any, total dollar amount of foreign sales.
❑ ❑ 48. Difference in profit margins of foreign sales to domestic sales, if any.
❑ ❑ 49. New product lines or services under consideration.

Provided   N/A

Customers

☐   ☐   50. Major customers and the annual sales to each.
☐   ☐   51. Length of relationships and customer turnover.
☐   ☐   52. Company dependency, if any, on small group of large customers or large group of small customers.

Marketing Strategy

☐   ☐   53. Sales and marketing strategy.
☐   ☐   54. Sales procedures.
☐   ☐   55. Sales personnel.
☐   ☐   56. Basis of sales personnel compensation.
☐   ☐   57. Risks of obsolescence or replacement by new or similar products.

Operations

☐   ☐   58. Corporate organization structure (divisions, departments, etc.).
☐   ☐   59. Flow of operations that produce the product or service.

Production

☐   ☐   60. Operating leverage of business (high or low level).
☐   ☐   61. Relationship of variable costs and fixed costs to total revenue.
☐   ☐   62. Difficulty obtaining liability insurance, if any.
☐   ☐   63. Insurance rates.
☐   ☐   64. OSHA or EPS concerns in the work environment, if any, including the prospective cost of compliance.
☐   ☐   65. Concerns over environmental hazards due to location or previous uses of land or facility.
☐   ☐   66. Dependency in the production process on patents, licenses, or other contracts not controlled by the company.
☐   ☐   67. Major suppliers and for what production inputs.
☐   ☐   68. Raw material suppliers that are manufacturers.
☐   ☐   69. Raw material suppliers that are wholesalers.
☐   ☐   70. Dependency for critical components of the product or service on any one supplier.
☐   ☐   71. Name of union, if any.
☐   ☐   72. Status of union contract or future organizing activities.
☐   ☐   73. Number of past union strikes.
☐   ☐   74. Number of full- and part-time employees.
☐   ☐   75. Number of employees by division or department.
☐   ☐   76. General experience, skill, and compensation levels of employees.

Real Property

☐   ☐   77. List real estate and equipment used by the company including name of owner, affiliated parties (if leased), and market terms (if leased).
☐   ☐   78. Size, age, condition, and capacity of the facilities.
☐   ☐   79. Adequacy of facilities or plans for future expansion.

❑   ❑   80. Plant/office facilities, including:
- Owners;
- Real estate taxes;
- Land:
  - Acreage;
  - Cost;
  - Assessed value; and
  - Fair market value, if known.
- Buildings:
  - Type of construction;
  - Age and condition;
  - Location on the property;
  - Assessed value;
  - Fair market value, if known;
  - Fire insurance amount; and
  - Square feet.
- Machinery and equipment:
  - Description;
  - Age and condition;
  - Efficiency utilization (older equipment or state of the art); and
  - Future plant, machinery, and equipment requirements, including estimated repairs.

❑   ❑   81. Current value of the real estate and equipment.

❑   ❑   82. Appraisals of real estate and equipment, or estimates.

Description of the Capital Structure

❑   ❑   83. Classes of securities.

❑   ❑   84. Common stock restrictions (such as a buy-sell agreement or charter restrictions), if any.

❑   ❑   85. Preferred stock terms of issue and protective covenants.

❑   ❑   86. Subordinated debt terms of issue and protective covenants.

❑   ❑   87. Outstanding stock options or warrants.

❑   ❑   88. Obtain and attach copies of the option agreement.

Other

❑   ❑   89. Dividend policy and dividend history.

❑   ❑   90. Anticipated future dividend payments.

❑   ❑   91. Pending litigation and potential impact on the company.

❑   ❑   92. Existing buy-sell or other restrictive agreements.

❑   ❑   93. Prenuptial agreement, if any.

❑   ❑   94. Profit-sharing, ESOP, or other retirement plans.

❑   ❑   95. Copy of the ESOP plan, if not already provided.

❑   ❑   96. Copies of provisions related to shareholder liquidity in the plan.

❑   ❑   97. Company's regulators (e.g., public service commissions, bank regulators).

❑   ❑   98. Copies of regulatory orders, if any.

❑   ❑   99. General outlook (if not covered elsewhere).

❑   ❑   100. Other pertinent information about the business.

Disclaimer Excluding Any Warranties: This checklist is designed to provide guidance to analysts, auditors, and management but is not to be used as a substitute for professional judgment. These procedures must be altered to fit each assignment. The practitioner takes sole responsibility for implementation of this guide. The implied warranties of merchantability and fitness of purpose and all other warranties, whether expressed or implied, are excluded from this transaction and shall not apply to this guide. The Financial Valuation Group shall not be liable for any indirect, special, or consequential damages.

ADDENDUM 3—MANAGEMENT INTERVIEW–FINANCIAL REVIEW

Exact Business Name _____   Date of Valuation _____

Address _____   Phone _____

_____

Analyst/Interviewer _____   Date of Interview _____

The objective of this management interview is to provide us with financial information that will aid us in the valuation of your business. We will keep the information confidential. Describe the following to the best of your ability. If necessary, use a separate sheet of paper, with reference to each item number. If some items are not applicable, please indicate N/A. Items already provided are indicated.

Remember that the objective of the interview is not only to identify changes in numbers but also to *ascertain the reasons* for the changes.

Provided   **N/A**

Interviewee(s)

❑   ❑   1. Name   Title

_____   _____

_____   _____

_____   _____

Financial Statement Review

❑   ❑   2. Quality of the financial statements.
❑   ❑   3. Reason(s) for qualifications of audited and qualified statements, if applicable.
❑   ❑   4. Consistency of accounting principles of company-prepared interim statements with accountant-prepared statements.

Balance Sheet Review

❑   ❑   5. Approximate total asset book value.
❑   ❑   6. Approximate net book value.
❑   ❑   7. Cash.
❑   ❑   8. Minimum level of cash required to operate the company.
❑   ❑   9. Accounts receivable:
   • Normal terms of sale;
   • Comparison of collection period to industry norms and history;
   • History of bad debts; and
   • Receivables concentration by customer.
❑   ❑   10. Inventory:
   • Accounting method used to calculate inventories;
   • Trend in level of inventories and turnover rate; and
   • Obsolete inventory and the amount paid for it.

❏ ❏ 11. Other current assets:
  - List of current assets; and
  - Current assets not related to the business, if any.

❏ ❏ 12. Fixed assets:
  - Major fixed assets;
  - Depreciation calculations for book and tax purposes;
  - Capital budget for the coming years;
  - Types of fixed assets needed in the future; and
  - List of excess assets.

❏ ❏ 13. Notes receivable:
  - Names and terms (if due from officers and affiliates, comparison of terms to market rates).

❏ ❏ 14. Other assets:
  - Long-term.

❏ ❏ 15. Notes payable:
  - Names and terms of vendors.

❏ ❏ 16. Accounts payable:
  - General terms of purchase of goods and services; and
  - Trend in payables and turnover ratios.

❏ ❏ 17. Taxes payable and deferred taxes.
❏ ❏ 18. Other accrued expenses.
❏ ❏ 19. Long-term debt:
  - Names and terms (if secured, state asset[s] used as security).

❏ ❏ 20. Mortgage notes payable:
  - Terms and collateral.

❏ ❏ 21. Any contingent liabilities.

Income Statement

❏ ❏ 22. Approximate annual sales volume.
❏ ❏ 23. Sales:
  - Reason for changes in sales over the past five years;
  - Attribution of growth in sales:
    - Unit volume; and
    - Inflation.
  - Comparison of growth rate in sales to other items on the income statement;
  - Projections for the current year and beyond; and
  - Basis for projections.

❏ ❏ 24. Costs of goods sold:
  - Key factors that affect cost of goods sold; and
  - Changes in accounting procedures, if any.

❏ ❏ 25. Gross profit margin (GPM):
  - Changes in GPM for the last five years (price increases, cost increases, inventory write-downs, etc.).

❏ ❏ 26. General and administrative expenses:
  - Major expense items of the company;
  - Fluctuations in expenses over the last five years; and
  - Nonrecurring expenses included in the totals.

❏ ❏ 27. Other income/expense:
  - Sources.

❏ ❏ 28. Taxes:
  - Federal tax rate; and
  - State tax rate.

❏ ❏ 29. Hidden or intangible assets, such as:
  - Patents;
  - Favorable leases;

Provided

N/A

Income Statement *(continued)*

- Favorable financing arrangements;
- Number of recurring, stable customers;
- Employment contracts;
- Copyrights;
- Long-term customers' contracts;
- Trademark;
- Unique research and development;
- Highly trained staff in place; and
- Undervalued securities or other investments.

❏ ❏ 30. Key liabilities
- Commitments for new buildings or machinery; and
- Long-term loans outstanding and terms.

ADDENDUM 4—INDUSTRY RESEARCH FORM

Industry Name: _____

_____

Industry SIC CODE: _____   NAICS CODE: _____

Trade Associations in This Industry: _____

_____

Key Words, Industry Terms, Jargon:

_____

_____

Leading Public Companies in This Industry:

_____

_____

____ Checked 10-K for industry discussion ____ Checked for analysts reports

Trade Publications in This Industry _____

_____

____ Checked periodical databases for relevant articles

____ Checked publications by industry analysts (First Research, Standard &
    Poor's, etc.)

CHAPTER 4

Financial Statement and Company Risk Analysis

The power of the Internet dramatically enhanced our ability to obtain, harness, and disseminate information. Information that was once privately owned or perhaps available only to experts is now widely accessible, almost instantaneously. The availability and accessibility of all this data provides the analyst with an expanded tool set by which to gain a deeper insight into the strengths, weaknesses, opportunities, and threats of a given company or industry.

Due to the enormously expanded amount of data available, analysts must go beyond simply measuring the economic income of a given enterprise. Analysts also must attempt to determine what factors give rise to the ability (or inability) of the enterprise to generate required returns for the foreseeable future; that is, they must make in-depth enterprise risk assessments. Consequently, a well-reasoned valuation analysis includes certain critical elements:

- An estimation of the amount of future economic benefits (normalization and projection of future cash flows)
- An assessment of the probability or risk that the projected future economic benefits will be realized and will be sustainable over the long run

This chapter (also see Chapter 5) discusses the methods generally used to evaluate a business in this way. It also focuses on the mechanics of the process of financial statement analysis, generally considered to be five steps:

1. *Spreading* historical financial statements in columnar format
2. *Normalizing* historical financial statements
3. *Common-sizing* normalized historical financial statements
4. *Performing* ratio analysis on the normalized historical financial statements
5. Subjecting normalized historical financial statements to *industry comparison*

HISTORICAL FINANCIAL STATEMENT ANALYSIS

A company's historical financial statements generally provide the most reliable information for estimating future performance and risk assessment. Audited financial statements are preferred. Reviewed statements, while not providing the level of assurance of an audit, nonetheless are generally reliable since they are prepared in accordance with

Generally Accepted Accounting Principles (GAAP) and contain footnote disclosure and supplemental schedules. However, since the financial statements of many closely held businesses are neither audited nor reviewed, the analyst may have to rely on compiled financial statements that provide no level of assurance and may not contain footnote disclosure. In other cases, the analyst may have to rely on corporate income tax returns or internally generated financial statements, the quality of which may be an issue for purposes of proper financial statement analysis. If applicable or appropriate, analysts may wish to review the paper or electronic "books" of original entry.

> The CPA-analyst must take special care to set expectations in both the engagement letter and the valuation report regarding the degree of responsibility assumed regarding financial statements presented within the report because of accounting standards for attestations, reviews, and compilations.

LENGTH OF FINANCIAL HISTORY TO BE USED

An analysis of five years of historical financial statements is generally considered sufficient to identify trends occurring in the business. This five-year period is suggested in Revenue Ruling 59-60 for income statements (two years for balance sheets) and is commonly used. However, financial statements may be necessary for more or fewer than five years if the subject company's business cycle does not coincide with a five-year time frame or if certain earlier years are not relevant or available.

SPREADING FINANCIAL STATEMENTS IN COLUMNAR FORMAT

Generally, the balance sheets and income statements for the period selected are laid side by side in columnar fashion. This format allows the analyst to compare the business to itself over the period and to spot trends or to identify unusual items requiring further investigation and analysis. This format also allows the analyst to match the subject company data to comparative data.

Exhibits 4.1 and 4.2 demonstrate the results of spreading the historical balance sheets and income statements of a fictitious company, Ale's Distributing Company, Inc., for the five-year period ended December 31, 20X5. These exhibits represent one of many possible presentations.

ADJUSTMENTS TO FINANCIAL STATEMENTS

One of the objectives of financial statement analysis is to ensure that the historical financial statements, which can provide the basis for any forward-looking estimates, reliably reflect the true operating performance of the enterprise. Therefore, the historical financial statements may need to be adjusted (modified) for certain items that, in the analyst's judgment, distort the true operating performance of the business.

Exhibit 4.1 Ale's Distributing Company, Inc.—Historical Balance Sheets

	12/31/X5	12/31/X4	12/31/X3	12/31/X2	12/31/X1
Assets					
Current Assets					
Cash	$ 1,391,500	$1,314,600	$1,278,300	$ 920,800	$1,031,300
Accounts Receivable	2,027,100	1,599,500	1,194,900	1,000,700	762,600
Inventory	2,317,200	1,958,300	1,735,600	1,643,400	1,137,000
Other Current Assets					
Prepaid Expenses	56,600	90,100	145,600	117,200	177,900
Total Other Current Assets	56,600	90,100	145,600	117,200	177,900
Total Current Assets	5,792,400	4,962,500	4,354,400	3,682,100	3,108,800
Fixed Assets - Net					
Fixed Assets - Cost	8,256,500	8,165,800	7,854,200	7,526,400	7,157,000
Accumulated Depreciation	(5,435,100)	(5,236,700)	(5,012,400)	(4,892,300)	(4,526,100)
Total Fixed Assets - Net	2,821,400	2,929,100	2,841,800	2,634,100	2,630,900
Other Assets					
Marketable Securities	1,400,000	1,200,000	1,100,000	1,000,000	900,000
Total Other Assets	1,400,000	1,200,000	1,100,000	1,000,000	900,000
Total Assets	$10,013,800	$ 9,091,600	$8,296,200	$7,316,200	$6,639,700
Liabilities and Equity					
Liabilities					
Current Liabilities					
Accounts Payable	$ 237,400	$ 154,500	$ 228,100	$ 131,100	$ 226,300
Other Current Liabilities					
Customer Deposits	178,100	157,300	150,400	185,800	167,000
Accrued Expenses	465,600	463,200	439,800	395,600	310,600
Total Other Current Liabilities	643,700	620,500	590,200	581,400	477,600
Total Current Liabilities	881,100	775,000	818,300	712,500	703,900
Long-Term Liabilities	3,000,000	2,750,000	2,500,000	2,250,000	2,000,000
Total Liabilities	3,881,100	3,525,000	3,318,300	2,962,500	2,703,900
Equity					
Common Stock	50,000	50,000	50,000	50,000	50,000
Additional Paid-In Capital	150,000	150,000	150,000	150,000	150,000
Retained Earnings	5,932,700	5,366,600	4,777,900	4,153,700	3,735,800
Total Equity	6,132,700	5,566,600	4,977,900	4,353,700	3,935,800
Total Liabilities and Equity	$10,013,800	$9,091,600	$8,296,200	$7,316,200	$6,639,700

Financial statement adjustments are made for a variety of reasons, some of which are:

- To develop historical earnings from which to predict future earnings
- To present historical financial information on a normalized basis, that is, under normal operating conditions
- To adjust for accounting practices that are a departure from industry or GAAP standards

Exhibit 4.2   Ale's Distributing Company, Inc.—Historical Income Statements

	12/31/X5	12/31/X4	12/31/X3	12/31/X2	12/31/X1
Revenues	$38,054,800	$35,497,100	$35,201,800	$34,627,900	$32,979,800
Cost of Goods Sold	28,323,200	26,389,800	26,246,500	25,779,000	24,355,800
Gross Profit	9,731,600	9,107,300	8,955,300	8,848,900	8,624,000
Operating Expenses					
Advertising	63,700	47,100	58,100	80,800	54,500
Bad Debts	6,400	10,800	7,800	13,900	2,600
Contributions	21,900	25,600	55,700	85,300	33,500
Gas & Oil Expense	96,700	89,700	85,200	86,900	75,900
Employee Benefits	483,900	463,200	451,300	470,200	433,900
Insurance	164,300	124,300	144,500	147,600	134,800
Legal & Accounting	397,500	168,900	173,900	181,300	165,600
Meals & Entertainment	49,300	61,000	59,100	75,700	57,600
Office Expense	120,400	117,900	124,400	129,300	97,600
Other Deductions	28,800	19,900	21,300	24,300	18,700
Pension/Profit-Sharing	160,000	155,000	150,000	145,000	140,000
Promotional Expenses	203,200	191,600	219,600	261,300	202,400
Payroll Taxes	447,700	429,600	486,600	451,900	473,100
Rent	165,000	165,000	13,700	0	0
Repairs and Maintenance	126,300	157,000	158,100	177,400	176,300
Salaries	3,380,400	3,374,400	3,314,200	3,299,000	2,932,700
Taxes & Licenses	124,400	119,700	116,200	140,600	109,800
Utilities & Telephone	156,700	146,800	145,900	167,200	130,100
Total Operating Expenses	6,196,600	5,867,500	5,785,600	5,937,700	5,239,100
Officers' Compensation	2,224,600	1,876,600	1,832,400	1,732,600	2,008,300
Operating EBITDA	1,310,400	1,363,200	1,337,300	1,178,600	1,376,600
Depreciation and Amortization	429,800	474,700	498,700	508,200	507,700
Operating Income/(Loss) - EBIT	880,600	888,500	838,600	670,400	868,900
MIscellaneous Income					
Interest Income	153,200	148,100	128,800	101,700	94,300
Dividend Income	18,600	17,800	16,500	14,200	12,100
Gain/Loss on Sale of Fixed Assets	20,800	22,300	124,700	5,600	11,200
Gain/Loss on Sale of Securities	10,300	20,400	21,500	8,700	25,700
Other Income	5,600	5,100	5,300	3,800	2,500
Total Miscellaneous Income	208,500	213,700	296,800	134,000	145,800
Interest Expense	231,400	210,300	189,600	171,200	151,200
Pretax Income	857,700	891,900	945,800	633,200	863,500
Less: Income Taxes	291,600	303,200	321,600	215,300	293,600
Net Income/(Loss)	$ 566,100	$ 588,700	$ 624,200	$ 417,900	$ 569,900

- To facilitate a comparison of a given company to itself, to other companies within the same industry, or to an accepted industry standard
- To compare the debt and/or capital structure of the company to that of its competition or peers
- To compare compensation with industry norms

An adjustment to historical financial statements should be made if the effect of the adjustment will present more accurately the true operating performance of the enterprise. Therefore, all appropriate adjustments should be made, regardless of whether they reflect positively on the company. Since adjustments that are appropriate for one valuation may be inappropriate for another, it is important to disclose the key assumptions underlying the adjustments.

NORMALIZATION OF HISTORICAL FINANCIAL STATEMENTS

To facilitate proper analysis and interpretation of a company's financial statements, these statements should first be adjusted to reflect the economic realities of "normal" operating conditions. The objective of normalizing historical financial statements is to present the data on a basis more comparable to that of other companies in the industry, thereby allowing the analyst to form conclusions as to the strength or weakness of the subject company relative to its peers. It can also reflect what a willing buyer would expect the operating results to be.

Normalization generally involves adjusting for a number of broad categories:

- Unusual items
- Nonrecurring items
- Extraordinary items (both unusual and nonrecurring, per Accounting Principles Board [APB] Opinion #30)
- Nonoperating items
- Changes in accounting principle
- Nonconformance with GAAP
- Degree of ownership interest, including whether the interest has control

UNUSUAL, NONRECURRING, AND EXTRAORDINARY ITEMS

Although APB 30 was not specifically targeted to business valuation, it does provide useful definitions of unusual, nonrecurring, and extraordinary items.

Unusual items. Events or transactions that possess a high degree of abnormality and are of a type clearly unrelated to, or only incidentally related to, the ordinary and typical activities of the entity, taking into account the environment in which the entity operates.

Nonrecurring items. Events or transactions that are not reasonably expected to recur in the foreseeable future, taking into account the environment in which the entity operates.

Extraordinary items. Events or transactions that are distinguished by their unusual nature and by the infrequency of their occurrence. Thus, for an item to be classified as an extraordinary item, the item must be *both* an unusual item and a nonrecurring item.

Revenues or expenses that are unusual, nonrecurring, or extraordinary usually are removed from the historical data because they can distort the picture of the ongoing earning power of the business. Caution is advised, however, in that items that might be deemed unusual and infrequent in one industry might not be deemed so in another. Items representative of the type of adjustments made to historical financial statements for unusual, nonrecurring, and extraordinary items include:

- Strikes and other types of work stoppages (unless common for the industry)
- Litigation expenses or recoveries
- Uninsured losses due to unforeseen disasters such as fire or flood
- One-time realization of revenues or expenses due to nonrecurring contracts
- Gain or loss on the sale of a business unit or business assets
- Discontinuation of operations
- Insurance proceeds received on the life of a key person or from a property or casualty claim

NONOPERATING ITEMS

To achieve a clear picture of true operating performance, the analyst may wish to remove nonoperating assets and liabilities and their related earnings and/or expenses from the subject's historical financial statements. This assumes they are not used, or only partially used, in the business. Common examples of nonoperating items include:

- Excess cash
- Marketable securities (if in excess of reasonable needs of the business)
- Real estate (if not used in business operations, or, in some situations, if the business could operate in rented facilities)
- Private planes, entertainment or sports facilities (hunting lodge, transferable season ticket contracts, skyboxes, etc.)
- Antiques, private collections, etc.

CHANGES IN ACCOUNTING PRINCIPLE

Analysts often find financial statements with a change in accounting principle. APB 20 states that a change in accounting principle results from the adoption of a generally accepted accounting principle different from the one used previously for financial reporting purposes. The term "principle" includes not only principles and practices but also methods of applying them. Thus, an analyst must understand the effect that a change in accounting principles has on a company's financial statements. Some common examples of changes in accounting principles are:

- A change in the method of pricing inventory, such as LIFO (last in, first out) to FIFO (first in, first out) or FIFO to LIFO
- A change in the method of depreciating previously recorded assets, such as from straight-line method to accelerated method or from accelerated method to straight-line method

- A change in the method of accounting for long-term construction-type contracts
- A change to or from the full-cost method of accounting in the extractive industries

NONCONFORMANCE WITH GAAP

Where appropriate, public companies tend to choose accounting treatments that please shareholders with higher reported earnings. Most closely held business owners tend to elect an accounting treatment that minimizes earnings and, hence, the corporate tax burden. These choices may mean that, if the financial statements of a private company have not been audited or reviewed, the accounting practices adopted by management may not be in compliance with GAAP. The analyst may choose to make adjustments to bring them into or closer to GAAP compliance so that the subject's financial results can be compared to the financial results of its publicly held industry counterparts, if available and applicable. Adjustments may also be made to calculate cash flow.

Examples of commonly encountered areas of nonconformance with GAAP are:

- Financial statements prepared on a tax or cash accounting basis
- Unrecorded revenue in cash businesses
- Inadequate bad debt reserve (or use of specific write-off method)
- Understated amounts of inventory, failure to write off obsolete or slow-moving inventory, and other inventory accounting issues
- Unrecorded liabilities such as capital lease obligations, workforce-related costs (wages, sick/vacation pay, etc.), deferred income taxes
- Capitalization/expense policies for fixed assets and prepaid expenses
- Fixed asset write-off policies
- Depreciation methods
- Accounting for investments in subsidiaries or affiliated entities
- Timing of revenue/expense recognition for contract accounting, installment sales, warranties, subscriptions, and the like

TAX AFFECTING THE EARNINGS OF SUBCHAPTER S CORPORATIONS AND OTHER ADJUSTMENTS

One of the more highly debated issues in business valuation is the treatment of income taxes in valuing S corporations.

The tax code specifically grants a tax advantage to S corporations because the taxable income of an S corporation is not taxed at the corporate level but is "passed through" to its shareholders to be taxed at the individual level. Due to the absence of a corporate-level tax, all other things being equal, an S corporation will possess more postcorporate tax cash flow than a C corporation. Ignoring all other factors, two otherwise identical companies will appear to have different values if one is a C corporation and one is an S corporation and their earnings streams are being valued (see Exhibit 4.3).

Exhibit 4.3   Net Income Comparison—C Corp. vs. S Corp. (Illustration Only)

C Corporation		S Corporation	
Revenue	$ 1,000	Revenue	$ 1,000
Expenses	800	Expenses	800
Taxable Income	200	Taxable Income	200
Taxes @ 40%	80	Taxes @ 0%	0
Net Income	$ 120	Net Income	$ 200

Consequently, much has been written and presented on this topic with respect to the valuation of both controlling and noncontrolling interests in S corporations. At the end of the day, the facts and circumstances of a given valuation situation must be carefully examined by the analyst prior to making a determination of whether various adjustments should be made.

The arguments on the subject are interesting but too extensive to present here. Consequently, the reader is encouraged to consult Chapter 12, "Valuation of Pass-Through Entities," which contains a detailed analysis of the various theories that address this issue and provides necessary guidance to assist the analyst in making an informed determination when faced with the question of normalization of the financial statements of an S corporation.

DEGREE OF OWNERSHIP INTEREST

The appropriateness of certain financial statement adjustments is dependent on whether the subject size of the ownership interest is controlling or noncontrolling. Except for in states with super majority provisions (generally $66\frac{2}{3}$ percent or greater), a controlling ownership interest is generally considered to be a voting interest of greater than 50 percent that allows the control owner to make decisions unilaterally that directly affect the earnings, assets, or capital structure of the business. Certain adjustments are normally made only in the valuation of a controlling interest unless evidence exists that the subject ownership interest may become a controlling interest in the immediate future. Unadjusted financial statements reflect the lack of ability of a noncontrolling ownership interest to affect the financial results, distributions, or destiny of the company in any way.

Examples of commonly encountered control adjustments are:

- Smoothing of excess or deficient compensation or perquisites
- Elimination of discretionary expenses and operating inefficiencies
- Removal of transactions with family or other insiders such as salary, benefits, or nonmarket transactions
- Implementation of changes in capital structure that could be executed by the controlling interest

NORMALIZATION ADJUSTMENTS

Exhibits 4.4, 4.4A, and 4.5 provide detailed normalization adjustments to both the balance sheets and income statements of Ale's Distributing Company, Inc., for some

Exhibit 4.4 Ale's Distributing Company, Inc.—Balance Sheet Normalization Adjustments

	12/31/X5	12/31/X4	12/31/X3	12/31/X2	12/31/X1
Assets					
Current Assets					
Cash	$ 0	$ 0	$ 0	$ 0	$ 0
Accounts Receivable	0	0	0	0	0
Inventory[2]	(100,000)	(100,000)	(100,000)	(100,000)	(100,000)
Other Current Assets					
Prepaid Expenses	0	0	0	0	0
Total Other Current Assets	0	0	0	0	0
Total Current Assets	(100,000)	(100,000)	(100,000)	(100,000)	(100,000)
Fixed Assets—Net					
Fixed Assets—Cost	0	0	0	0	0
Accumulated Depreciation	0	0	0	0	0
Total Fixed Assets—Net	0	0	0	0	0
Other Assets					
Marketable Securities[1]	(1,400,000)	(1,200,000)	(1,100,000)	(1,000,000)	(900,000)
Total Other Assets	(1,400,000)	(1,200,000)	(1,100,000)	(1,000,000)	(900,000)
Total Assets	$(1,500,000)	$(1,300,000)	$(1,200,000)	$(1,100,000)	$(1,000,000)
Liabilities and Equity					
Liabilities					
Current Liabilities					
Accounts Payable	$ 0	$ 0	$ 0	$ 0	$ 0
Other Current Liabilities					
Customer Deposits	0	0	0	0	0
Accrued Expenses	0	0	0	0	0
Total Other Current Liabilities	0	0	0	0	0
Total Current Liabilities	0	0	0	0	0
Long-Term Liabilities	0	0	0	0	0
Total Liabilities	0	0	0	0	0
Equity					
Common Stock	0	0	0	0	0
Additional Paid-In Capital	0	0	0	0	0
Retained Earnings	(1,500,000)	(1,300,000)	(1,200,000)	(1,100,000)	(1,000,000)
Total Equity	(1,500,000)	(1,300,000)	(1,200,000)	(1,100,000)	(1,000,000)
Total Liabilities and Equity	(1,500,000)	$(1,300,000)	$(1,200,000)	$(1,100,000)	$(1,000,000)

items commonly encountered by the analyst, many of which have been described in the preceding paragraphs. Exhibits 4.6, 4.6A, and 4.7 provide normalized balance sheets and income statements for the five-year period analyzed.

Exhibits 4.4 and 4.4A, and Exhibits 4.6 and 4.6A differ only in that Exhibits 4.4A and 4.6A include a normalization adjustment restating the fixed assets to fair market value. Exhibits 4.4 and 4.6 do not include this adjustment. Many analysts do

Exhibit 4.4A   Ale's Distributing Company, Inc.—Balance Sheet Normalization Adjustments

	12/31/X5	12/31/X4	12/31/X3	12/31/X2	12/31/X1
Assets					
Current Assets					
Cash	$ 0	$ 0	$ 0	$ 0	$ 0
Accounts Receivable	0	0	0	0	0
Inventory[2]	(100,000)	(100,000)	(100,000)	(100,000)	(100,000)
Other Current Assets					
Prepaid Expenses	0	0	0	0	0
Total Other Current Assets	0	0	0	0	0
Total Current Assets	(100,000)	(100,000)	(100,000)	(100,000)	(100,000)
Fixed Assets—FMV					
Fixed Assets—Cost[3]	2,178,600	1,970,900	1,958,200	2,065,900	1,969,100
Accumulated Depreciation	0	0	0	0	0
Total Fixed Assets—Net	2,178,600	1,970,900	1,958,200	2,065,900	1,969,100
Other Assets					
Marketable Securities[1]	(1,400,000)	(1,200,000)	(1,100,000)	(1,000,000)	(900,000)
Total Other Assets	(1,400,000)	(1,200,000)	(1,100,000)	(1,000,000)	(900,000)
Total Assets	$ 678,600	$ 670,900	$ 758,200	$ 965,900	$ 969,100
Liabilities and Equity					
Liabilities					
Current Liabilities					
Accounts Payable	$ 0	$ 0	$ 0	$ 0	$ 0
Other Current Liabilities					
Customer Deposits	0	0	0	0	0
Accrued Expenses	0	0	0	0	0
Total Other Current Liabilities	0	0	0	0	0
Total Current Liabilities	0	0	0	0	0
Long-Term Liabilities	0	0	0	0	0
Total Liabilities	0	0	0	0	0
Equity					
Common Stock	0	0	0	0	0
Additional Paid-In Capital	0	0	0	0	0
Retained Earnings	678,600	670,900	758,200	965,900	969,100
Total Equity	678,600	670,900	758,200	965,900	969,100
Total Liabilities and Equity	$ 678,600	$ 670,900	$ 758,200	$ 965,900	$ 969,100

Exhibits 4.4 & 4.4A—FOOTNOTES

Normalization Adjustments—Balance Sheet:

- Unusual and Nonrecurring Items
    None
- Nonoperating Items
    Adjustment #1—Based upon analytical review, including comparisons to financial ratio benchmark data, it was determined that the company has excess marketable securities that exceed the company's working capital requirements.
- Nonconformance with GAAP
    Adjustment #2—Based upon discussions with management, it was discovered that the company has not properly written off obsolete inventory.
- Control Adjustment
    Adjustment #3—Based upon appraisals of the company's land, buildings, and fixed assets, an adjustment has been made to restate the company's fixed assets to reflect their fair market value. *Note:* Some analysts do not make this adjustment for comparison purposes since the benchmark data that subject companies are compared to do not usually have this adjustment made. This is a decision each analyst must make. Also, some analysts make tax adjustments to the asset values.

Exhibit 4.5 Ale's Distributing Company, Inc.—Income Statement Normalization Adjustments

	12/31/X5	12/31/X4	12/31/X3	12/31/X2	12/31/X1
Revenues	$ 0	$ 0	$ 0	$ 0	$ 0
Cost of Goods Sold	0	0	0	0	0
Gross Profit	0	0	0	0	0
Operating Expenses					
Advertising	0	0	0	0	0
Bad Debts	0	0	0	0	0
Contributions	0	0	0	0	0
Gas & Oil Expense[3]	(6,000)	(6,000)	(6,000)	(6,000)	(6,000)
Employee Benefits	0	0	0	0	0
Insurance	0	0	0	0	0
Legal & Accounting[1]	(200,000)	0	0	0	0
Meals & Entertainment[4]	(7,500)	(7,500)	(7,500)	(7,500)	(7,500)
Office Expense	0	0	0	0	0
Other Deductions	0	0	0	0	0
Pension/Profit-Sharing	0	0	0	0	0
Promotional Expenses	0	0	0	0	0
Payroll Taxes[5]	(23,700)	(9,900)	(15,000)	(15,000)	(49,200)
Rent[6]	(45,000)	(45,000)	(3,700)	0	0
Repairs and Maintenance	0	0	0	0	0
Salaries[5]	(30,000)	(30,000)	(30,000)	(30,000)	(30,000)
Taxes & Licenses	0	0	0	0	0
Utilities & Telephone	0	0	0	0	0
Total Operating Expenses	(312,200)	(98,400)	(62,200)	(58,500)	(92,700)
Officers' Compensation[5]	(224,600)	(76,600)	(132,400)	(132,600)	(508,300)
Operating EBITDA	536,800	175,000	194,600	191,100	601,000
Depreciation and Amortization	0	0	0	0	0
Operating Income/(Loss)—EBIT	536,800	175,000	194,600	191,100	601,000
Miscellaneous Income/ (Expense)					
Interest Income[2]	0	0	0	0	0
Dividend Income[2]	(18,600)	(17,800)	(16,500)	(14,200)	(12,100)
Gain/Loss on Sale of Fixed Assets	0	0	0	0	0
Gain/Loss on Sale of Securities[2]	(10,300)	(20,400)	(21,500)	(8,700)	(25,700)
Other Income	0	0	0	0	0
Total Miscellaneous Income	(28,900)	(38,200)	(38,000)	(22,900)	(37,800)
Interest Expense	0	0	0	0	0
Pretax Income	507,900	136,800	156,600	168,200	563,200
Less: Income Taxes	172,700	46,500	53,200	57,200	191,500
Net Income/(Loss)	$ 335,200	$ 90,300	$ 103,400	$ 111,000	$ 371,700

(continues)

Exhibit 4.5 *continued*

FOOTNOTES

Normalization Adjustment—Income Statement:

- Unusual and Nonrecurring Items
  Adjustment #1—Based upon discussions with management, it was discovered that the Company was involved in a lawsuit in 20X5 that was determined to be nonrecurring in nature.
- Nonoperating Items
  Adjustment #2—Based upon analytical review, it was determined that the Company has excess marketable securities that exceed the Company's working capital requirements. Income and gains/losses attributable to the excess marketable securities have been removed from the income statement.
- Nonconformance With GAAP
  None
- Control Adjustments
  Adjustment #3—Based upon discussions with management, it was discovered that family members of the Company's owner were using Company gas cards for the purchase and use of gas in their personal vehicles for nonbusiness related travel.
  Adjustment #4—Based upon discussions with management, it was discovered that country club dues for the company's owner were being paid by the Company, even though no business meetings were ever conducted at the country club.
  Adjustment #5—Based upon analytical review and discussions with management, adjustments were made to officers' compensation, salaries, and payroll taxes in order to (1) provide for a reasonable level of compensation for officers, (2) remove payroll received by the family members of the Company's owner who performed no services for the Company, and (3) remove the payroll taxes associated with such adjustments.
  Adjustment #6—Based upon analytical review and discussions with management, it was determined that above market rent was being paid by the Company for the rental of a building owned by a related party.

---

not make this adjustment since industry or guideline company benchmark data do not usually have this adjustment, thus making comparisons to the subject company more difficult. Others think that making the adjustment results in a better comparison over the historical period analyzed. This is a decision each analyst must make. Both methods are presented here.

COMMON SIZING NORMALIZED FINANCIAL STATEMENTS

Once financial data has been normalized, analysts commonly employ an analytical methodology to identify operational trends—"common sizing" the financial statements. Common sizing involves expressing each item on the financial statements as a percentage of some base number and is performed on both the normalized balance sheet and the normalized income statement for each period under consideration. On the balance sheet, each item is expressed as a percentage of total assets, and on the income statement, each item is expressed as a percentage of sales.

Common-sized financial analysis provides insight into the company's historical operating performance, facilitates an assessment of relationships between and among certain accounts, identifies certain trends or unusual items, and can be used to compare the operating performance of the subject company to its industry or to specific guideline companies. This analysis is sometimes useful before making normalization adjustments in order to identify other potential adjustments, with a second normalization process then conducted. Exhibits 4.8, 4.8A, and 4.9 present common-size balance sheets and income statements of Ale's Distributing for the five-year period analyzed. Exhibit 4.8A includes the adjustment restating the fixed assets to fair market value.

Exhibit 4.6   Ale's Distributing Company, Inc.—Normalized Historical Balance Sheets

	12/31/X5	12/31/X4	12/31/X3	12/31/X2	12/31/X1
Assets					
Current Assets					
Cash	$1,391,500	$1,314,600	$1,278,300	$ 920,800	$1,031,300
Accounts Receivable	2,027,100	1,599,500	1,194,900	1,000,700	762,600
Inventory	2,217,200	1,858,300	1,635,600	1,543,400	1,037,000
Other Current Assets					
Prepaid Expenses	56,600	90,100	145,600	117,200	177,900
Total Other Current Assets	56,600	90,100	145,600	117,200	177,900
Total Current Assets	5,692,400	4,862,500	4,254,400	3,582,100	3,008,800
Fixed Assets—Net					
Fixed Assets—Cost	8,256,500	8,165,800	7,854,200	7,526,400	7,157,000
Accumulated Depreciation	(5,435,100)	(5,236,700)	(5,012,400)	(4,892,300)	(4,526,100)
Total Fixed Assets—Net	2,821,400	2,929,100	2,841,800	2,634,100	2,630,900
Other Assets					
Marketable Securities	0	0	0	0	0
Total Other Assets	0	0	0	0	0
Total Assets	$8,513,800	$7,791,600	$7,096,200	$6,216,200	$5,639,700
Liabilities and Equity					
Liabilities					
Current Liabilities					
Accounts Payable	$ 237,400	$ 154,500	$ 228,100	$131,100	$226,300
Other Current Liabilities					
Customer Deposits	178,100	157,300	150,400	185,800	167,000
Accrued Expenses	465,600	463,200	439,800	395,600	310,600
Total Other Current Liabilities	643,700	620,500	590,200	581,400	477,600
Total Current Liabilities	881,100	775,000	818,300	712,500	703,900
Long-Term Liabilities	3,000,000	2,750,000	2,500,000	2,250,000	2,000,000
Total Liabilities	3,881,100	3,525,000	3,318,300	2,962,500	2,703,900
Equity					
Common Stock	50,000	50,000	50,000	50,000	50,000
Additional Paid-In Capital	150,000	150,000	150,000	150,000	150,000
Retained Earnings	4,432,700	4,066,600	3,577,900	3,053,700	2,735,800
Total Equity	4,632,700	4,266,600	3,777,900	3,253,700	2,935,800
Total Liabilities and Equity	$8,513,800	$7,791,600	$7,096,200	$6,216,200	$5,639,700

Exhibit 4.6A Ale's Distributing Company, Inc.—Normalized Historical Balance Sheets

	12/31/X5	12/31/X4	12/31/X3	12/31/X2	12/31/X1
Assets					
Current Assets					
Cash	$ 1,391,500	$ 1,314,600	$1,278,300	$ 920,800	$1,031,300
Accounts Receivable	2,027,100	1,599,500	1,194,900	1,000,700	762,600
Inventory	2,217,200	1,858,300	1,635,600	1,543,400	1,037,000
Other Current Assets					
Prepaid Expenses	56,600	90,100	145,600	117,200	177,900
Total Other Current Assets	56,600	90,100	145,600	117,200	177,900
Total Current Assets	5,692,400	4,862,500	4,254,400	3,582,100	3,008,800
Fixed Assets—FMV					
Fixed Assets—Cost	10,435,100	10,136,700	9,812,400	9,592,300	9,126,100
Accumulated Depreciation	(5,435,100)	(5,236,700)	(5,012,400)	(4,892,300)	(4,526,100)
Total Fixed Assets—Net	5,000,000	4,900,000	4,800,000	4,700,000	4,600,000
Other Assets					
Marketable Securities	0	0	0	0	0
Total Other Assets	0	0	0	0	0
Total Assets	$10,692,400	$ 9,762,500	$9,054,400	$8,282,100	$7,608,800
Liabilities and Equity					
Liabilities					
Current Liabilities					
Accounts Payable	$ 237,400	$ 154,500	$ 228,100	$ 131,100	$ 226,300
Other Current Liabilities					
Customer Deposits	178,100	157,300	150,400	185,800	167,000
Accrued Expenses	465,600	463,200	439,800	395,600	310,600
Total Other Current Liabilities	643,700	620,500	590,200	581,400	477,600
Total Current Liabilities	881,100	775,000	818,300	712,500	703,900
Long-Term Liabilities	3,000,000	2,750,000	2,500,000	2,250,000	2,000,000
Total Liabilities	3,881,100	3,525,000	3,318,300	2,962,500	2,703,900
Equity					
Common Stock	50,000	50,000	50,000	50,000	50,000
Additional Paid-In Capital	150,000	150,000	150,000	150,000	150,000
Retained Earnings	6,611,300	6,037,500	5,536,100	5,119,600	4,704,900
Total Equity	6,811,300	6,237,500	5,736,100	5,319,600	4,904,900
Total Liabilities and Equity	$10,692,400	$ 9,762,500	$9,054,400	$8,282,100	$7,608,800

Exhibit 4.7 Ale's Distributing Company, Inc.—Normalized Historical Income Statements

	12/31/X5	12/31/X4	12/31/X3	12/31/X2	12/31/X1
Revenues	$38,054,800	$35,497,100	$35,201,800	$34,627,900	$32,979,800
Cost of Goods Sold	28,323,200	26,389,800	26,246,500	25,779,000	24,355,800
Gross Profit	9,731,600	9,107,300	8,955,300	8,848,900	8,624,000
Operating Expenses					
Advertising	63,700	47,100	58,100	80,800	54,500
Bad Debts	6,400	10,800	7,800	13,900	2,600
Contributions	21,900	25,600	55,700	85,300	33,500
Gas & Oil Expense	90,700	83,700	79,200	80,900	69,900
Employee Benefits	483,900	463,200	451,300	470,200	433,900
Insurance	164,300	124,300	144,500	147,600	134,800
Legal & Accounting	197,500	168,900	173,900	181,300	165,600
Meals & Entertainment	41,800	53,500	51,600	68,200	50,100
Office Expense	120,400	117,900	124,400	129,300	97,600
Other Deductions	28,800	19,900	21,300	24,300	18,700
Pension/Profit-Sharing	160,000	155,000	150,000	145,000	140,000
Promotional Expenses	203,200	191,600	219,600	261,300	202,400
Payroll Taxes	424,000	419,700	471,600	436,900	423,900
Rent	120,000	120,000	10,000	0	0
Repairs and Maintenance	126,300	157,000	158,100	177,400	176,300
Salaries	3,350,400	3,344,400	3,284,200	3,269,000	2,902,700
Taxes & Licenses	124,400	119,700	116,200	140,600	109,800
Utilities & Telephone	156,700	146,800	145,900	167,200	130,100
Total Operating Expenses	5,884,400	5,769,100	5,723,400	5,879,200	5,146,400
Officers' Compensation	2,000,000	1,800,000	1,700,000	1,600,000	1,500,000
Operating EBITDA	1,847,200	1,538,200	1,531,900	1,369,700	1,977,600
Depreciation and Amortization	429,800	474,700	498,700	508,200	507,700
Operating Income/ (Loss)—EBIT	1,417,400	1,063,500	1,033,200	861,500	1,469,900
Miscellaneous Income/ (Expense)					
Interest Income	153,200	148,100	128,800	101,700	94,300
Dividend Income	0	0	0	0	0
Gain/Loss on Sale of Fixed Assets	20,800	22,300	124,700	5,600	11,200
Gain/Loss on Sale of Securities	0	0	0	0	0
Other Income	5,600	5,100	5,300	3,800	2,500
Total Miscellaneous Income	179,600	175,500	258,800	111,100	108,000
Interest Expense	231,400	210,300	189,600	171,200	151,200
Pretax Income	1,365,600	1,028,700	1,102,400	801,400	1,426,700
Less: Income Taxes	464,300	349,700	374,800	272,500	485,100
Net Income/(Loss)	$ 901,300	$ 679,000	$ 727,600	$ 528,900	$ 941,600

Exhibit 4.8   Ale's Distributing Company, Inc.—Normalized Historical Balance Sheets—
Common Size

	12/31/X5	12/31/X4	12/31/X3	12/31/X2	12/31/X1
Assets					
Current Assets					
Cash	16.3%	16.9%	18.0%	14.8%	18.3%
Accounts Receivable	23.8%	20.5%	16.8%	16.1%	13.5%
Inventory	26.0%	23.9%	23.0%	24.8%	18.4%
Other Current Assets					
Prepaid Expenses	0.7%	1.2%	2.1%	1.9%	3.2%
Total Other Current Assets	0.7%	1.2%	2.1%	1.9%	3.2%
Total Current Assets	66.9%	62.4%	60.0%	57.6%	53.4%
Fixed Assets—Net					
Fixed Assets—Cost	97.0%	104.8%	110.7%	121.1%	126.9%
Accumulated Depreciation	−63.8%	−67.2%	−70.6%	−78.7%	−80.3%
Total Fixed Assets—Net	33.1%	37.6%	40.0%	42.4%	46.6%
Other Assets					
Marketable Securities	0%	0%	0%	0%	0%
Total Other Assets	0%	0%	0%	0%	0%
Total Assets	100.0%	100.0%	100.0%	100.0%	100.0%
Liabilities and Equity					
Liabilities					
Current Liabilities					
Accounts Payable	2.8%	2.0%	3.2%	2.1%	4.0%
Other Current Liabilities					
Customer Deposits	2.1%	2.0%	2.1%	3.0%	3.0%
Accrued Expenses	5.5%	5.9%	6.2%	6.4%	5.5%
Total Other Current Liabilities	7.6%	8.0%	8.3%	9.4%	8.5%
Total Current Liabilities	10.3%	9.9%	11.5%	11.5%	12.5%
Long-Term Liabilities	35.2%	35.3%	35.2%	36.2%	35.5%
Total Liabilities	45.6%	45.2%	46.8%	47.7%	47.9%
Equity					
Common Stock	0.6%	0.6%	0.7%	0.8%	0.9%
Additional Paid-In Capital	1.8%	1.9%	2.1%	2.4%	2.7%
Retained Earnings	52.1%	52.2%	50.4%	49.1%	48.5%
Total Equity	54.4%	54.8%	53.2%	52.3%	52.1%
Total Liabilities and Equity	100.0%	100.0%	100.0%	100.0%	100.0%

Exhibit 4.8A Ale's Distributing Company, Inc.—Normalized Historical Balance Sheets—
Common Size

	12/31/X5	12/31/X4	12/31/X3	12/31/X2	12/31/X1
Assets					
Current Assets					
Cash	13.0%	13.5%	14.1%	11.1%	13.6%
Accounts Receivable	19.0%	16.4%	13.2%	12.1%	10.0%
Inventory	20.7%	19.0%	18.1%	18.6%	13.6%
Other Current Assets					
Prepaid Expenses	0.5%	0.9%	1.6%	1.4%	2.3%
Total Other Current Assets	0.5%	0.9%	1.6%	1.4%	2.3%
Total Current Assets	53.2%	49.8%	47.0%	43.3%	39.5%
Fixed Assets—FMV					
Fixed Assets—Cost	97.6%	103.8%	108.4%	115.8%	119.9%
Accumulated Depreciation	−50.8%	−53.6%	−55.4%	−59.1%	−59.5%
Total Fixed Assets—Net	46.8%	50.2%	53.0%	56.7%	60.5%
Other Assets					
Marketable Securities	0%	0%	0%	0%	0%
Total Other Assets	0%	0%	0%	0%	0%
Total Assets	100.0%	100.0%	100.0%	100.0%	100.0%
Liabilities and Equity					
Liabilities					
Current Liabilities					
Accounts Payable	2.2%	1.6%	2.5%	1.6%	3.0%
Other Current Liabilities					
Customer Deposits	1.7%	1.6%	1.7%	2.2%	2.2%
Accrued Expenses	4.4%	4.7%	4.9%	4.8%	4.1%
Total Other Current Liabilities	6.0%	6.4%	6.5%	7.0%	6.3%
Total Current Liabilities	8.2%	7.9%	9.0%	8.6%	9.3%
Long-Term Liabilities	28.1%	28.2%	27.6%	27.2%	26.3%
Total Liabilities	36.3%	36.1%	36.6%	35.8%	35.5%
Equity					
Common Stock	0.5%	0.5%	0.6%	0.6%	0.7%
Additional Paid-In Capital	1.4%	1.5%	1.7%	1.8%	2.0%
Retained Earnings	61.8%	61.8%	61.1%	61.8%	61.8%
Total Equity	63.7%	63.9%	63.4%	64.2%	64.5%
Total Liabilities and Equity	100.0%	100.0%	100.0%	100.0%	100.0%

Exhibit 4.9   Ale's Distributing Company, Inc.—Normalized Historical Income Statements—
Common Size

	12/31/X5	12/31/X4	12/31/X3	12/31/X2	12/31/X1
Revenues	100.0%	100.0%	100.0%	100.0%	100.0%
Cost of Goods Sold	74.4%	74.3%	74.6%	74.4%	73.9%
Gross Profit	25.6%	25.7%	25.4%	25.6%	26.1%
Operating Expenses					
Advertising	0.2%	0.1%	0.2%	0.2%	0.2%
Bad Debts	0.0%	0.0%	0.0%	0.0%	0.0%
Contributions	0.1%	0.1%	0.2%	0.2%	0.1%
Gas & Oil Expense	0.2%	0.2%	0.2%	0.2%	0.2%
Employee Benefits	1.3%	1.3%	1.3%	1.4%	1.3%
Insurance	0.4%	0.4%	0.4%	0.4%	0.4%
Legal & Accounting	0.5%	0.5%	0.5%	0.5%	0.5%
Meals & Entertainment	0.1%	0.2%	0.1%	0.2%	0.2%
Office Expense	0.3%	0.3%	0.4%	0.4%	0.3%
Other Deductions	0.1%	0.1%	0.1%	0.1%	0.1%
Pension / Profit-Sharing	0.4%	0.4%	0.4%	0.4%	0.4%
Promotional Expenses	0.5%	0.5%	0.6%	0.8%	0.6%
Payroll Taxes	1.1%	1.2%	1.3%	1.3%	1.3%
Rent	0.3%	0.3%	0.0%	0.0%	0.0%
Repairs and Maintenance	0.3%	0.4%	0.4%	0.5%	0.5%
Salaries	8.8%	9.4%	9.3%	9.4%	8.8%
Taxes & Licenses	0.3%	0.3%	0.3%	0.4%	0.3%
Utilities & Telephone	0.4%	0.4%	0.4%	0.5%	0.4%
Total Operating Expenses	15.5%	16.3%	16.3%	17.0%	15.6%
Officers' Compensation	5.3%	5.1%	4.8%	4.6%	4.5%
Operating EBITDA	4.9%	4.3%	4.4%	4.0%	6.0%
Depreciation and Amortization	1.1%	1.3%	1.4%	1.5%	1.5%
Operating Income/(Loss)—EBIT	3.7%	3.0%	2.9%	2.5%	4.5%
Miscellaneous Income/(Expense)					
Interest Income	0.4%	0.4%	0.4%	0.3%	0.3%
Dividend Income	0.0%	0.0%	0.0%	0.0%	0.0%
Gain/Loss on Sale of Fixed Assets	0.1%	0.1%	0.4%	0.0%	0.0%
Gain/Loss on Sale of Securities	0.0%	0.0%	0.0%	0.0%	0.0%
Other Income	0.0%	0.0%	0.0%	0.0%	0.0%
Total Miscellaneous Income	0.5%	0.5%	0.7%	0.3%	0.3%
Interest Expense	0.6%	0.6%	0.5%	0.5%	0.5%
Pretax Income	3.6%	2.9%	3.1%	2.3%	4.3%
Less: Income Taxes	1.2%	1.0%	1.1%	0.8%	1.5%
Net Income/(Loss)	2.4%	1.9%	2.1%	1.5%	2.9%

RATIO ANALYSIS (QUANTITATIVE ANALYSIS)

Ratio analysis is perhaps the most commonly used tool in financial analysis. Financial ratios allow the analyst to assess and analyze the strengths and weaknesses of a given company with regard to such measures as liquidity, performance, profitability, leverage, and growth on an absolute basis and by comparison to other companies in its industry or to an industry standard. Common financial ratios, a discussion of their use, and the application to Ale's Distributing may be found in the addendum at the end of this chapter.

Two common types of ratio analyses exist: time series analysis and cross-sectional analysis. Time series analysis (commonly known as trend analysis) compares the company's ratios over a specified historical time period and identifies trends that might indicate financial performance improvement or deterioration.

Cross-sectional analysis compares a specified company's ratios to other companies or to industry standards/norms. It is most useful when the companies analyzed are reasonably comparable, that is, business type, revenue size, product mix, degree of diversification, asset size, capital structure, markets served, geographic location, and the use of similar accounting methods. When some of these items are unknown, some analysts will still make general comparisons. It is important to exercise professional judgment in determining which ratios to select in analyzing a given company.

Most finance textbooks calculate activity ratios and rate of return ratios based on average beginning- and ending-year balances. However, some benchmark data, including Risk Management Association (RMA), report ratios based only on a year-end balance.

> The valuation report should provide reasonable commentary regarding methods and ratios chosen and results of the analysis.

Exhibit 4.10 presents ratios prepared with average balance sheet data with fixed assets at historical costs. Exhibit 4.10A includes a comparison to RMA data; thus Ale's ratios are computed year-end, again using historical costs for the fixed assets. Exhibit 4.10A is used in the detailed ratio analysis appended to this chapter. Exhibit 4.10B presents the ratios using average balance sheet amounts with the adjustment restating the fixed assets to fair market value.

> Analysts should not mix year-end data with beginning- and ending-year average data when preparing comparisons of the subject company to industry benchmark data and ratios.

Exhibit 4.10   Ale's Distributing Company, Inc.—Comparative Ratio Analysis

	12/31/X5	12/31/X4	12/31/X3	12/31/X2	12/31/X1
Liquidity Ratios					
Current Ratio	6.5	6.3	5.2	5.0	4.3
Quick (Acid-Test) Ratio	3.9	3.8	3.0	2.7	2.5
Activity Ratios					
Accounts Receivable Turnover	21.0	25.4	32.1	39.3	N/A
Days Outstanding in A/R	17.4	14.4	11.4	9.3	N/A
Inventory Turnover	13.9	15.1	16.5	20.0	N/A
Sales to Net Working Capital	8.6	9.4	11.2	13.4	N/A
Total Asset Turnover	4.7	4.8	5.3	5.8	N/A
Fixed Asset Turnover	13.2	12.3	12.9	13.2	N/A
Leverage Ratios					
Total Debt to Total Assets	0.5	0.5	0.5	0.5	0.5
Total Equity to Total Assets	0.5	0.5	0.5	0.5	0.5
Long-Term Debt to Equity	0.6	0.6	0.6	0.7	0.7
Total Debt to Equity	0.8	0.8	0.9	0.9	0.9
Profitability Ratios					
Gross Profit Margin	25.6%	25.7%	25.4%	25.6%	26.1%
Operating Profit Margin	3.7%	3.0%	2.9%	2.5%	4.5%
Rate of Return Ratios					
Return on Average Equity	20.3%	16.9%	20.7%	17.1%	N/A
Return on Average Investment	14.4%	12.3%	14.5%	12.3%	N/A
Return on Average Total Assets	12.9%	11.0%	12.8%	10.8%	N/A
Growth Rates (Cumulative)					
Sales—Avg. Growth	3.68%	2.50%	3.33%	5.00%	N/A
Sales—CAGR	3.64%	2.48%	3.31%	5.00%	N/A
Gross Profit—Avg. Growth	3.09%	1.84%	1.90%	2.61%	N/A
Gross Profit—CAGR	3.07%	1.83%	1.90%	2.61%	N/A
Operating Profit—Avg. Growth	3.69%	-6.18%	-10.73%	-41.39%	N/A
Operating Profit—CAGR	-0.91%	-10.23%	-16.16%	-41.39%	N/A

Financial Ratios based on Normalized Historical Balance Sheets and Normalized Historical Income Statements. Activity and Rate of Return Ratios are calculated using average end of year balance sheet values and historical fixed asset values.

COMPARATIVE ANALYSIS

Comparative analysis is a valuable tool for highlighting differences between the subject company's historical performance and industry averages, pointing out relative operating strengths and weaknesses of the subject company as compared to its peers, assessing management effectiveness, and identifying areas where the company is outperforming or underperforming the industry.

Comparative analysis is performed by comparing the ratios of the subject company to industry ratios taken from commonly accepted sources of comparative financial data.

Exhibit 4.10A   Ale's Distributing Company, Inc.—Comparative Ratio Analysis

	RMA	12/31/X5	12/31/X4	12/31/X3	12/31/X2	12/31/X1
Liquidity Ratios						
Current Ratio	1.4	6.5	6.3	5.2	5.0	4.3
Quick (Acid-Test) Ratio	0.6	3.9	3.8	3.0	2.7	2.5
Activity Ratios						
Accounts Receivable Turnover	86.5	18.8	22.2	29.5	34.6	43.2
Days Outstanding in A/R	4.2	19.4	16.4	12.4	10.5	8.4
Inventory Turnover	18.0	12.8	14.2	16.0	16.7	23.5
Sales to Net Working Capital	37.6	7.9	8.7	10.2	12.1	14.3
Total Asset Turnover	3.9	4.5	4.6	5.0	5.6	5.8
Fixed Asset Turnover	21.5	13.5	12.1	12.4	13.1	12.5
Leverage Ratios						
Total Debt to Total Assets	0.6	0.5	0.5	0.5	0.5	0.5
Total Equity to Total Assets	0.4	0.5	0.5	0.5	0.5	0.5
Long-Term Debt to Equity	0.7	0.6	0.6	0.6	0.7	0.7
Total Debt to Equity	1.5	0.8	0.8	0.9	0.9	0.9
Profitability Ratios						
Gross Profit Margin	24.0%	25.6%	25.7%	25.4%	25.6%	26.1%
Operating Profit Margin	3.7%	3.7%	3.0%	2.9%	2.5%	4.5%
Rate of Return Ratios	NOTE 1					
Pretax Return on Equity	35.7%	29.5%	24.1%	29.2%	24.6%	48.6%
Pretax Return on Total Assets	10.3%	16.0%	13.2%	15.5%	12.9%	25.3%
Growth Rates (Cumulative)						
Sales—Avg. Growth	NOTE 2	3.68%	2.50%	3.33%	5.00%	N/A
Sales—CAGR	NOTE 2	3.64%	2.48%	3.31%	5.00%	N/A
Gross Profit—Avg. Growth	NOTE 2	3.09%	1.84%	1.90%	2.61%	N/A
Gross Profit—CAGR	NOTE 2	3.07%	1.83%	1.90%	2.61%	N/A
Operating Profit—Avg. Growth	NOTE 2	3.69%	-6.18%	-10.73%	-41.39%	N/A
Operating Profit—CAGR	NOTE 2	-0.91%	-10.23%	-16.16%	-41.39%	N/A

Financial Ratios based on Normalized Historical Balance Sheets and Normalized Historical Income Statements.
Ratios are calculated using end of year balance sheet values and historical fixed asset values.
Subject SIC Code = 5181 (Beer & Ale).
RMA Code = 5181 (Beer & Ale)—$25MM and Over Sales Median Ratios.
Risk Management Association, Philadelphia, PA, 2001 (used with permission). © 2002 by RMA—The Risk
Management Association. All rights reserved. No part of this table may be reproduced or utilized in any form or by
any means, electronic or mechanical, including photocopying, recording or by any information storage and retrieval
system without permission in writing from RMA—The Risk Management Association. Please refer to
www.rmahq.org for further warranty, copyright and use of data information.
Note 1—RMA does not provide data in regard to After-Tax Returns on Equity, Investment, or Total Assets.
Note 2—RMA does not provide Average Annual Growth Rates or Compounded Annual Growth Rates (CAGR).

Exhibit 4.10B   Ale's Distributing Company, Inc.—Comparative Ratio Analysis

	12/31/X5	12/31/X4	12/31/X3	12/31/X2	12/31/X1
Liquidity Ratios					
Current Ratio	6.5	6.3	5.2	5.0	4.3
Quick (Acid-Test) Ratio	3.9	3.8	3.0	2.7	2.5
Activity Ratios					
Accounts Receivable Turnover	21.0	25.4	32.1	39.3	N/A
Days Outstanding in A/R	17.4	14.4	11.4	9.3	N/A
Inventory Turnover	13.9	15.1	16.5	20.0	N/A
Sales to Net Working Capital	8.6	9.4	11.2	13.4	N/A
Total Asset Turnover	3.7	3.8	4.1	4.4	N/A
Fixed Asset Turnover	7.7	7.3	7.4	7.4	N/A
Leverage Ratios					
Total Debt to Total Assets	0.4	0.4	0.4	0.4	0.4
Total Equity to Total Assets	0.6	0.6	0.6	0.6	0.6
Long-Term Debt to Equity	0.4	0.4	0.4	0.4	0.4
Total Debt to Equity	0.6	0.6	0.6	0.6	0.6
Profitability Ratios					
Gross Profit Margin	25.6%	25.7%	25.4%	25.6%	26.1%
Operating Profit Margin	3.7%	3.0%	2.9%	2.5%	4.5%
Rate of Return Ratios					
Return on Average Equity	13.8%	11.3%	13.2%	10.3%	N/A
Return on Average Investment	11.2%	9.5%	10.8%	8.9%	N/A
Return on Average Total Assets	10.3%	8.7%	9.8%	8.1%	N/A
Growth Rates (Cumulative)					
Sales—Avg. Growth	3.68%	2.50%	3.33%	5.00%	N/A
Sales—CAGR	3.64%	2.48%	3.31%	5.00%	N/A
Gross Profit—Avg. Growth	3.09%	1.84%	1.90%	2.61%	N/A
Gross Profit—CAGR	3.07%	1.83%	1.90%	2.61%	N/A
Operating Profit—Avg. Growth	3.69%	−6.18%	−10.73%	−41.39%	N/A
Operating Profit—CAGR	−0.91%	−10.23%	−16.16%	−41.39%	N/A

Financial Ratios based on Normalized Historical Balance Sheets and Normalized Historical Income Statements.
Activity and Rate of Return Ratios are calculated using average balance sheet values and adjusted fixed asset values.

Widely used sources for comparative financial data include:

- Almanac of Business and Industrial Financial Ratios (www.prenhall.com)
- BizMiner (www.bizminer.com)
- IRS Corporate Financial Ratios (www.valuationresources.com)
- IRS Corporate Ratios and IRS-CALC (www.saibooks.com/fin.html)
- Risk Management Association (RMA) Annual Statement Studies (www.rmahq.org)

The above publications vary in the depth and breadth of data provided. However, most of the sample data is extracted from corporate federal tax filings. RMA obtains its data from financial statements provided to member banks by loan customers. *Financial Studies of the Small Business* obtains small-company financial statements from certified public accounting firms nationwide.

To use benchmark industry ratios appropriately, analysts must be familiar with their scope and limitations as well as with the differences among them regarding data presentation and computation methods.

Exhibits 4.11, 4.11A, and 4.12 present comparative balance sheets and income statements for the same five-year period. Exhibit 4.11A includes the restatement of the fixed assets to fair market value.

RISK ANALYSIS (QUALITATIVE ANALYSIS)

Ratio and other quantitative analyses provide the analyst with information about the company relative to its peers. However, ratios do not inform the analyst as to why the observed results occurred, knowledge that is important to the understanding of business risk and the general probability that a company's estimated future economic benefits will be realized.

As a company operates on a day-to-day basis, it and its competitors are affected by external forces that require both management and the analyst to conduct thorough risk analyses. The disciplines of strategic management and organizational theory provide useful models by which to conduct such risk analyses.

Industry Structure Analysis—The Porter Model

Michael Porter of Harvard Business School developed an analytical approach known as The Porter Model by which to analyze and assess company risk associated with industry structure.[1] Porter divides industry structure into five forces:

1. Rivalry between current incumbents
2. Threat of new entrants
3. Bargaining power of customers
4. Bargaining power of suppliers
5. The threat of substitute products

This model, used thoughtfully in a valuation analysis, can provide valuable information regarding the relative risk of the future profitability for the subject company.

The following is a brief example of the five forces of the Porter Model as applied to Ale's Distributing:

1. *Rivalry among current incumbents.* The industry is segmented by distributorships affiliated with one or more of the three major domestic manufacturers. As a result, competition among distributorships within a given region or sales territory is intense.

---

[1] "How Competitive Forces Shape Strategy," *Harvard Business Review* (May–June 1979), pp. 137–145.

Exhibit 4.11 Ale's Distributing Company, Inc.—Comparative Balance Sheets

	RMA	12/31/X5	12/31/X4	12/31/X3	12/31/X2	12/31/X1
Assets						
Current Assets						
Cash & Equivalents	11.6%	16.3%	16.9%	18.0%	14.8%	18.3%
Accounts Receivable	10.9%	23.8%	20.5%	16.8%	16.1%	13.5%
Inventory	19.7%	26.0%	23.9%	23.0%	24.8%	18.4%
Other Current Assets	2.7%	0.7%	1.2%	2.1%	1.9%	3.2%
Total Current Assets	44.9%	66.8%	62.5%	59.9%	57.6%	53.4%
Fixed Assets (Cost)—Net	23.8%	33.1%	37.6%	40.0%	42.4%	46.6%
Intangibles—Net	20.4%	0.0%	0.0%	0.0%	0.0%	0.0%
Other Non-Current Assets	10.9%	0.0%	0.0%	0.0%	0.0%	0.0%
Total Assets	100.0%	100.0%	100.0%	100.0%	100.0%	100.0%
Liabilities and Equity						
Liabilities						
Current Liabilities						
Accounts Payable	10.9%	2.8%	2.0%	3.2%	2.1%	4.0%
Short Term Notes Payable	7.4%	0.0%	0.0%	0.0%	0.0%	0.0%
Current Maturity LT Debt	4.4%	0.0%	0.0%	0.0%	0.0%	0.0%
Other Current Liabilities	8.4%	7.6%	8.0%	8.3%	9.4%	8.5%
Total Current Liabilities	31.1%	10.3%	9.9%	11.5%	11.5%	12.5%
Long-Term Liabilities	25.8%	35.2%	35.3%	35.2%	36.2%	35.5%
Other Non-Current Liabilities	3.7%	0.0%	0.0%	0.0%	0.0%	0.0%
Total Liabilities	60.6%	45.6%	45.2%	46.8%	47.7%	47.9%
Total Equity	39.4%	54.4%	54.8%	53.2%	52.3%	52.1%
Total Liabilities and Equity	100.0%	100.0%	100.0%	100.0%	100.0%	100.0%

Percentages based on Normalized Historical Balance Sheets.
Subject SIC Code = 5181 (Beer & Ale).
RMA Code = 5181 (Beer & Ale)—$25MM and Over Sales Median Ratios.

2. *Threat of new entrants.* Since all distributorships operate under agreements with one or more of the three dominant domestic manufacturers and are assigned defined sales territories, the threat of new entrants into the marketplace is minimal.
3. *Bargaining power of customers.* Due to the intensely competitive nature of the business, customers tend to possess significant bargaining power. Customers in the on-premise segment of the market require high service levels and on-site displays (bar signage, etc.). Off-premise customers also require high service levels, including assistance in product placement and point-of-sale displays to obtain higher product turn in exchange for greater shelf space.

Exhibit 4.11A Ale's Distributing Company, Inc.—Comparative Balance Sheets

	RMA	12/31/X5	12/31/X4	12/31/X3	12/31/X2	12/31/X1
Assets						
Current Assets						
Cash & Equivalents	11.6%	13.0%	13.5%	14.1%	11.1%	13.6%
Accounts Receivable	10.9%	19.0%	16.4%	13.2%	12.1%	10.0%
Inventory	19.7%	20.7%	19.0%	18.1%	18.6%	13.6%
Other Current Assets	2.7%	0.5%	0.9%	1.6%	1.4%	2.3%
Total Current Assets	44.9%	53.2%	49.8%	47.0%	43.2%	39.5%
Fixed Assets—Net*	23.8%	46.8%	50.2%	53.0%	56.7%	60.5%
Intangibles—Net	20.4%	0.0%	0.0%	0.0%	0.0%	0.0%
Other Non-Current Assets	10.9%	0.0%	0.0%	0.0%	0.0%	0.0%
Total Assets	100.0%	100.0%	100.0%	100.0%	100.0%	100.0%
Liabilities and Equity						
Liabilities						
Current Liabilities						
Accounts Payable	10.9%	2.2%	1.6%	2.5%	1.6%	3.0%
Short Term Notes Payable	7.4%	0.0%	0.0%	0.0%	0.0%	0.0%
Current Maturity LT Debt	4.4%	0.0%	0.0%	0.0%	0.0%	0.0%
Other Current Liabilities	8.4%	6.0%	6.4%	6.5%	7.0%	6.3%
Total Current Liabilities	31.1%	8.2%	7.9%	9.0%	8.6%	9.3%
Long-Term Liabilities	25.8%	28.1%	28.2%	27.6%	27.2%	26.3%
Other Non-Current Liabilities	3.7%	0.0%	0.0%	0.0%	0.0%	0.0%
Total Liabilities	60.6%	36.3%	36.1%	36.6%	35.8%	35.5%
Total Equity	39.4%	63.7%	63.9%	63.4%	64.2%	64.5%
Total Liabilities and Equity	100.0%	100.0%	100.0%	100.0%	100.0%	100.0%

4. *Bargaining power of suppliers.* Distribution agreements with all manufacturers are extremely restrictive. The manufacturer sets product pricing, and distributor inventories are determined by the manufacturer's need to move product, given its short shelf life.
5. *Threat of substitute products.* After decades of decline, the hard liquor industry has begun to experience growth in the United States. The introduction of flavored liquors, combined with sophisticated product presentation to young adult customers, as well as the success of local micro-breweries, poses a potential threat to future unit sales (on a case-equivalent basis of domestic distributors).

Exhibit 4.12   Ale's Distributing Company, Inc.—Comparative Income Statements

	RMA	12/31/X5	12/31/X4	12/31/X3	12/31/X2	12/31/X1
Revenues	100.0%	100.0%	100.0%	100.0%	100.0%	100.0%
Cost of Goods Sold	76.0%	74.4%	74.3%	74.6%	74.4%	73.9%
Gross Profit	24.0%	25.6%	25.7%	25.4%	25.6%	26.1%
Operating Expenses	20.2%	21.9%	22.7%	22.5%	23.1%	21.6%
Operating Profit	3.8%	3.7%	3.0%	2.9%	2.5%	4.5%
Other Income/(Expenses)—Net	−0.5%	−0.1%	−0.1%	0.2%	−0.2%	−0.2%
Pretax Profit	3.3%	3.6%	2.9%	3.1%	2.3%	4.3%

Percentages based on Normalized Historical Income Statements.
Subject SIC Code = 5181 (Beer & Ale).
RMA Code = 5181 (Beer & Ale)—$25MM and Over Sales Median Ratios.
Risk Management Association, Philadelphia, PA, 2001 (used with permission). © 2002 by RMA—The Risk Management Association. All rights reserved. No part of this table may be reproduced or utilized in any form or by any means, electronic or mechanical, including photocopying, recording or by any information storage and retrieval system without permission in writing from RMA—The Risk Management Association. Please refer to www.rmahq.org for further warranty, copyright and use of data information.

Industry Conduct—The McKinsey 7-S Model

Industry conduct and its impact on a given company also can be analyzed and assessed using models such as McKinsey and Company's 7-S framework,[2] which analyze competitors using seven categories:

1. Strategy
2. Structure
3. Systems
4. Skills
5. Staff
6. Style
7. Superordinate goals

The following is a brief example analyzing Ale's Distributing's ability to remain flexible and to adapt to change in the seven categories:

1. *Strategy.* In response to the competitive nature of the industry and profit pressure exerted by the manufacturer by the transferring of certain expenses to distributors, Ale's is looking seriously into acquiring neighboring distributorships (wholesaler consolidation), a strategy encouraged by the manufacturer.
2. *Structure.* As a sales-focused company, Ale's has decentralized the sales process, training its drivers as well as its on-premise and off-premise sales staff to create

[2] Robert H. Waterman, Jr., Thomas J. Peters, and Julien R. Phillips, "Structure Is Not Organization," *Business Horizons* (June 1980), pp. 14–26.

unique value to the customer by consulting with the customer on product placement, point-of-sale strategy, and inventory management.

3. *Systems.* Ale's possesses sophisticated sales training systems, including its involvement as a beta test site for the manufacturer's nationwide interactive satellite sales network, making it one of the more technologically advanced distributorships in the wholesaler network.

4. *Skills.* Ale's possesses the most experienced sales and warehousing staff of any distributor within a 75-mile radius, giving the company an enormous competitive advantage.

5. *Staff.* Ale's personnel exhibit great pride in their product, to the point of identifying closely with the manufacturer and its national advertising presence, with a deep conviction that they market the finest product in the industry.

6. *Style.* Top management exudes teamwork in everything it does, a feeling that pervades the entire organization, resulting in a remarkably cohesive and satisfied workforce.

7. *Superordinate goals.* Ale's operates on the fundamental principle that is best expressed in its president's motto: "Ensuring our customer's success will ensure our success." The company, therefore, looks beyond the sales mentality to focus on providing value to the customer that sets it apart from its competition.

The DuPont Model

Key areas of interest in the financial review of a business enterprise include profitability, effective asset management, liquidity, solvency, and shareholder returns. One framework that has been successfully developed to evaluate these factors is the DuPont Model, so named for the company in which it was developed. The major advantage of this model is that it highlights the important interplay between effective asset management and firm profitability, which also assists the analyst as an additional tool in risk assessment.

The DuPont Model's primary advantage is that it is easy to compute and relatively easy to interpret. The model recognizes a fact that many investors don't: Two companies can have the same return on equity, yet one can be a better-run and more attractive business to a potential buyer. The DuPont Model can be expressed as follows:

$$\text{Return on Common Equity (ROE)} = \text{ROA} \times \text{EM},$$

where

$$\text{Return on Assets (ROA)} = \frac{\text{Net Income to Common Shareholders}}{\text{Total Assets}}$$

and

$$\text{Equity Multiplier (EM)} = \frac{\text{Total Assets}}{\text{Common Equity}}$$

This is generally referred to as the *two-ratio approach* as it focuses on an evaluation of a company's earnings and its investment in assets.

In applying the Dupont Model to Ale's utilizing normalized data at December 31, 20X5, return on assets of 16 percent is multiplied by the equity multiplier of 1.57 to provide a return on common equity of 25.12 percent. This suggests that 16 percent of the return on equity was due to profit margins and sales and 9.12 percent was due to asset management in the business. How would this fact be used in valuation? If an analyst found a company at a comparable valuation with the same return on equity, yet a higher percentage arose from internally generated sales, it may be more attractive.

An extension of the DuPont Model has been developed, which is known as the *ROE Model,* or the *return on shareholders' equity model.* The strength of the ROE Model is that it properly integrates the five key areas of financial analysis mentioned here *and* is premised on the widely held thought that the principal goal of management is to maximize shareholder wealth. The ROE Model can be presented as follows:

$$\text{ROE} = \text{Profitability} \times \text{Financial Leverage}$$

$$= \frac{\text{Net Income}}{\text{Average Total Assets}} \times \frac{\text{Average Total Assets}}{\text{Average Common Shareholder Equity}}$$

Notice that the first component of ROE is simply the company's ROA, the cornerstone of the DuPont Model. The second component provides insight into how management has financed the asset base of the business. Comparisons can then be made between the subject company and others to identify factors that differentiate it (positively or negatively) from its industry peers.

An expanded version, including income margin and sales turnover, is as follows:

$$\text{ROE} = \frac{\text{Net Income}}{\text{Sales}} \times \frac{\text{Sales}}{\text{Average Total Assets}} \times \frac{\text{Average Total Assets}}{\text{Average Common Shareholder Equity}}$$

S.W.O.T. Analysis

Most often employed by strategic business consultants in the framework of organizational strategic planning, S.W.O.T. Analysis (Strengths, Weaknesses, Opportunities, and Threats) provides a framework for the identification of issues that are critical to the business being analyzed. The issues identified are those that must be addressed by the business within a one- to four-year time period. This analysis contains both an internal and external dimension.

Strengths are *positive* aspects that are *internal* to the entity. Through proper identification, an organization's strengths can be leveraged to obtain or maintain competitive advantage. Weaknesses are *negative* aspects that are *internal* to the entity. The analyst can measure the resources (human, economic, etc.) of the enterprise to determine the ability of the business to overcome its inherent weaknesses, and if it can't, how these weaknesses might increase the risk of an investment in the business.

Opportunities are *positive* aspects *external* to the entity. By close consideration of the extent to which an enterprise might be able to seize existing opportunities in a timely fashion, the analyst can gauge the degree to which the company might better its position in the marketplace. Threats are *negative* aspects *external* to the entity. Proper identification of a company's threats is critical to a thorough analysis of the risk facing the company.

In applying a very general S.W.O.T. Analysis to Ale's, the management team identified the following:

1. *Strengths.* The company has a 60-year track record of outstanding performance and is well respected by the manufacturer. The company has a competent and cohesive senior management team that together possesses more than 125 years of beer industry experience.
2. *Weaknesses.* The company's president is 62 years old, and a successor has not been identified. In fact, the company's senior management team does not include an individual possessing a CEO skill set.
3. *Opportunities.* The company's territory is surrounded by smaller wholesalers that could be acquired to create a mega-wholesaler operation and spread fixed costs over a significantly higher number of case equivalents.
4. *Threats.* The recent acquisition of the manufacturer by an international competitor with a differing philosophy of distribution is of serious concern to the ownership of the company.

Interestingly, S.W.O.T. Analysis complements the Porter Model, as many of the opportunities and threats (external factors) are also measured in the Porter Model, but in a different way.

Other Company Risk Analysis Considerations

When analyzing the subject company, analysts often give consideration to the industry in which the company operates for clues about factors impacting the risk of an investment in the subject company. Industry structure can provide the analyst with key insight into both the industry and the subject company's ability to efficiently operate within the constraints of the industry. For example, in applying this concept to Ale's, the analyst recognizes that the beer industry has long operated under what is known as the *three-tier system,* whereby, under state liquor laws of all 50 states, a wholesale distributor acts as an independent intermediary between the manufacturer and the retailer. The longevity of this system has had a stabilizing influence on the beer industry.

Under this structure, the manufacturer determines both the wholesale and the retail price of its product, thus retaining all pricing power and exerting considerable influence over the cost structure of its wholesale distributors. In return, the wholesale distributor realizes the benefit of the national advertising campaign of the manufacturer and focuses its efforts on local promotions within its respective sales territory.

Recent challenges to the three-tier system by large direct shippers (Costco, etc.), which are intended to eliminate the wholesale distributor and favor volume buying, have caused significant unrest in the beer industry. The outcome of litigation in several states could have a significant impact on the long-term structure of the beer industry.

Clearly, it is important that analysts research the industry structure to properly assess its impact on a given company.

MACROENVIRONMENTAL ANALYSIS

Further removed from the subject company than industry forces but still affecting it significantly are five macroenvironmental sources of risk:[3]

1. Technological risk
2. Sociocultural risk
3. Demographic risk
4. Political risk
5. Global risk

   While the company has little or no influence on these risk factors, an assessment of them can be critical in determining the company's (and industry's) future profitability. Shifts in one or more of these risk factors can (and often do) have a material effect on an industry or a company's future fortunes. Therefore, it is prudent for analysts to provide a thorough analysis of such factors and include it in the body of the valuation report.

   Our analysis of the impact of five macroenvironmental risk factors on Ale's revealed:

1. *Technological risk.* The company is recognized as a cutting-edge distributor by its competition and its supplier. It has harnessed new technology to track all delivery vehicles at all times, to maximize route organization, and to ensure productivity.
2. *Sociocultural risk.* Consumer trends toward flavored liquor pose a potential risk to the company's product as these gain a stronger foothold in the domestic market.
3. *Demographic risk.* The company's territory is composed of three mature counties that possess an aging population with little future growth prospects. Since the company's product is preferred by younger consumers, this is a threat to the company's ability to maintain its past earnings stream.
4. *Political risk.* The alcohol industry watched the federal legal action against the tobacco industry with interest, and fears of future regulation or judicial action exist.
5. *Global risk.* The three major domestic manufacturers are fighting to make inroads into the global marketplace, with European counterparts looking to the U.S. marketplace to claim market share from existing competitors.

---

[3] Adapted from Liam Fahey and V. K. Narayanan, *Macroenvironmental Analysis for Strategic Management* (St. Paul: West Publishing Co., 1986), p. 29; and Michael A. Hitt, R. Duane Ireland, and Robert E. Hoskisson, *Strategic Management: Competitiveness and Globalization,* 3rd ed. (Cincinnati: South Western Publishing Co., 1999), pp. 50–60.

ADDENDUM 1—COMMONLY USED FINANCIAL RATIOS: APPLICATION TO ALE'S DISTRIBUTING

This section is neither a comprehensive presentation of all available ratios nor a list of ratios that must be utilized on every valuation engagement. The analyst must use informed judgment to determine which ratios are appropriate for a given valuation engagement. These are examples of some of the more common ratios.

Many analysts recommend the use of beginning-year and ending-year averages when computing the denominator of such ratios as inventory turnover, sales to net working capital, and sales to total assets. That is how these ratios are presented and explained below. In the analysis of Ale's, we also have used year-end balance sheet amounts, since that is how the comparative data, RMA, is presented.

Liquidity Ratios

Liquidity ratios measure a company's ability to meet short-term obligations with short-term assets. These ratios also help identify an excess or shortfall of current assets necessary to meet operating expenses.

Current Ratio

$$\frac{\text{Current Assets}}{\text{Current Liabilities}}$$

The current ratio is the most commonly used liquidity ratio. Normally, the current ratio of the subject company is compared to industry averages to gain insight into the company's ability to cover its current obligations with its current asset base.

Quick (Acid-Test) Ratio

$$\frac{\text{Cash} + \text{Cash Equivalents} + \text{Short-term Investments} + \text{Accounts Receivable}}{\text{Current Liabilities}}$$

The quick ratio is a more conservative ratio in that it measures the company's ability to meet current obligations with only those assets that can be readily liquidated. As with the current ratio, industry norms generally serve as the base for drawing analytical conclusions.

Application to Ale's   The liquidity ratios for Ale's have been steadily increasing during the five-year period analyzed. Ale's current ratio has increased from 4.3 at December 31, 20X1, to 6.5 at December 31, 20X5. Ale's quick ratio has increased from 2.5 at December 31, 20X1, to 3.9 at December 31, 20X5. The median current and quick ratios for comparable companies within the industry were 1.4 and 0.6, respectively. Thus, it appears the company is in a much stronger financial position to meet its current obligations as compared to its industry peers. It also indicates that Ale's is less leveraged (current liabilities) than its peer group.

Activity Ratios

Activity ratios, also known as efficiency ratios, provide an indication as to how efficiently the company is using its assets. More efficient asset utilization indicates strong management and generally results in higher value to equity owners of the business. Additionally, activity ratios describe the relationship between the company's level of operations and the assets needed to sustain the activity.

Accounts Receivable Turnover

$$\frac{\text{Annual Sales}}{\text{Average Accounts Receivable}}$$

Accounts receivable turnover measures the efficiency with which the company manages the collection side of the cash cycle.

Days Outstanding in Accounts Receivables

$$\frac{365}{\text{A/R Turnover}}$$

The average number of days outstanding of credit sales measures the effectiveness of the company's credit extension and collection policies.

Inventory Turnover

$$\frac{\text{Cost of Goods Sold}}{\text{Average Inventory}}$$

Inventory turnover measures the efficiency with which the company manages the investment / inventory side of the cash cycle. A higher number of turnovers indicates the company is converting inventory into accounts receivable at a faster pace, thereby shortening the cash cycle and increasing the cash flow available for shareholder returns.

Sales to Net Working Capital

$$\frac{\text{Sales}}{\text{Average Net Working Capital}}$$

Sales to net working capital measures the ability of company management to drive sales with minimal net current asset employment. A higher measure indicates efficient management of the company's net working capital without sacrificing sales volume to obtain it.

Total Asset Turnover

$$\frac{\text{Sales}}{\text{Average Total Assets}}$$

Total asset turnover measures the ability of company management to efficiently utilize the total asset base of the company to drive sales volume.

Fixed Asset Turnover

$$\frac{\text{Sales}}{\text{Average Fixed Assets}}$$

Sales to fixed assets measures the ability of company management to generate sales volume from the company's fixed asset base.

Application to Ale's   Four of the five activity ratios for Ale's have steadily declined during the five-year period analyzed. The only activity ratio to increase during the five-year period was Ale's fixed asset turnover.

Ale's accounts receivable turnover has declined from 43.2 turns at December 31, 20X1, to 18.8 turns at December 31, 20X5. This decline in accounts receivable turnover has resulted in an increase in the average collection period of accounts receivable from 8.4 days at December 31, 20X1, to 19.4 days at December 31, 20X5. Ale's inventory turnover has declined from 23.5 turns at December 31, 20X1, to 12.8 turns at December 31, 20X5. The declines in accounts receivable turnover and inventory turnover indicate that Ale's management of these critical assets has slipped considerably during the period analyzed. The median accounts receivable turnover and inventory turnover for comparable companies within the industry were 86.5 turns and 18.0 turns, respectively. Consequently, Ale's has clearly fallen below its industry peers in its management of major working capital components. If this trend continues, Ale's working capital could become significantly strained and become an obstacle to future growth.

Ale's sales to net working capital turnover has declined from 14.3 turns at December 31, 20X1, to 7.9 turns at December 31, 20X5. The median sales to net working capital turnover for comparable companies within the industry was 37.6 turns. This decline mirrors the problems in accounts receivable and inventory.

A review of the Ale's total asset turnover indicates a decline from 5.8 turns at December 31, 20X1, to 4.5 turns at December 31, 20X5. The industry-comparable total asset turnover was 3.9 turns. Ale's fixed asset turnover actually has increased from 12.5 turns at December 31, 20X1, to 13.5 turns at December 31, 20X5. However, Ale's fixed asset turnover of 13.5 turns at December 31, 20X5, is far below the median fixed asset turnover for comparable companies within the industry of 21.5 turns. These activity ratios suggest an increase in the risk associated with an investment in Ale's common stock. Additional due diligence is necessary to determine the cause of these potential problems.

Leverage Ratios

Leverage ratios, which are for the most part balance sheet ratios, assist the analyst in determining the solvency of a company. They provide an indication of a company's ability to sustain itself in the face of economic downturns.

Leverage ratios also measure the exposure of the creditors relative to the shareholders of a given company. Consequently, they provide valuable insight into the relative risk of the company's stock as an investment.

Total Debt to Total Assets

$$\frac{\text{Total Debt}}{\text{Total Assets}}$$

This ratio measures the total amount of assets funded by all sources of debt capital.

Total Equity to Total Assets

$$\frac{\text{Total Equity}}{\text{Total Assets}}$$

This ratio measures the total amount of assets funded by all sources of equity capital. It can also be computed as one minus the total debt to total assets ratio.

Long-term Debt to Equity

$$\frac{\text{Long-Term Debt}}{\text{Total Equity}}$$

This ratio expresses the relationship between long-term, interest-bearing debt and equity. Since interest-bearing debt is a claim on future cash flow that would otherwise be available for distribution to shareholders, this ratio measures the risk that future dividends or distributions will or will not occur.

Total Debt to Equity

$$\frac{\text{Total Debt}}{\text{Total Equity}}$$

This ratio measures the degree to which the company has balanced the funding of its operations and asset base between debt and equity sources. In attempting to lower the cost of capital, a company generally may increase its debt burden and hence its risk.

Application to Ale's   The leverage ratios for Ale's have remained fairly steady during the five-year period analyzed. Ale's total debt to total asset ratio has remained at 0.5 for all five years. Ale's total equity to total asset ratio has also remained stable at 0.5 for all five years. The median total debt to total asset ratio for comparable companies within the industry was 0.6. Ale's total debt to equity ratio has been 0.9 to 0.8 historically, well below the industry average of 1.5. This indicates that the company tends to finance growth with more equity than debt.

Profitability Ratios

Profitability ratios measure the ability of a company to generate returns for its shareholders. Profitability ratios also measure financial performance and management strength.

Gross Profit Margin

$$\frac{\text{Gross Profit}}{\text{Net Sales}}$$

This ratio measures the ability of the company to generate an acceptable markup on its product in the face of competition. It is most useful when compared to a similarly computed ratio for comparable companies or to an industry standard.

Operating Profit Margin

$$\frac{\text{Operating Profit}}{\text{Net Sales}}$$

This ratio measures the ability of the company to generate profits to cover and to exceed the cost of operations. It is also most useful when compared to comparable companies or to an industry standard.

Application to Ale's   The profitability ratios for Ale's have declined during the five-year period analyzed. Ale's gross profit margin has declined from 26.1 percent at December 31, 20X1, to 25.6 percent at December 31, 20X5. The median gross profit margin for comparable companies within the industry was 24.0 percent. Thus, although Ale's gross profit margin has declined during the five-year period analyzed, the company has been able to maintain higher margins on its products than that of its industry peers.

Ale's operating profit margin has declined from 4.5 percent at December 31, 20X1, to 3.7 percent at December 31, 20X5. The median operating profit margin for comparable companies within the industry was 3.7 percent, indicating that the company's competitive advantage may be adversely affected by a less focused management team or by some external forces affecting the company.

Rate of Return Ratios

Since the capital structure of most companies includes both debt capital and equity capital, it is important to measure the return to each of the capital providers.

Return on Equity

$$\frac{\text{Net Income}}{\text{Average Common Stockholder's Equity}}$$

This ratio measures the after-tax return on investment to the equity capital providers of the company.

Return on Investment

$$\frac{\text{Net Income} + \text{Interest } (1 - \text{Tax Rate})}{\text{Average (Stockholder's Equity} + \text{Long-Term Debt)}}$$

This ratio measures the return to all capital providers of the company. Interest (net of tax) is added back since it also involves a return to debt capital providers.

Return on Total Assets

$$\frac{\text{Net Income} + \text{Interest} \, (1 - \text{Tax Rate})}{\text{Average Total Assets}}$$

This ratio measures the return on the assets employed in the business. In effect, it measures management's performance in the utilization of the company's asset base.

Application to Ale's   Since RMA reports only pretax returns, that is how Ale's ratios were computed for this exhibit only. Ale's rate of return ratios have fluctuated significantly over the five-year period analyzed. Its return on equity and return on total assets have been very inconsistent in spite of fairly steady sales activity. However, Ale's most recent return on total assets of 16.0 percent is above the industry average of 10.3 percent. Ale's recent return on equity of 29.5 percent is dramatically below the industry average of 35.7 percent. This may have to do with Ale's leverage being so much lower than that of its peer groups, since optimal use of leverage can magnify equity returns. Again, this is cause for further analysis.

Growth Ratios   Growth ratios measure a company's percentage increase or decrease for a particular line item on the financial statements. These ratios can be calculated as a straight annual average or as a compounded annual growth rate (CAGR) measuring growth on a compounded basis over a specific time period. Although it is possible to calculate growth rates on every line item on the financial statements, growth rates typically are calculated on such key financial statement items as sales, gross margin, operating income, and EBITDA. These are calculated through use of the following formulas.

Average Annual Sales Growth

$$\{\text{Sum of all Periods } [(\text{Current Year Sales / Prior Year Sales}) - 1] \, / \\ \text{\# of Periods Analyzed}\} \times 100$$

Compound Annual Sales Growth

$$\{[(\text{Current Year Sales / Base Year Sales})^{(1 \, / \, \text{\# of Periods Analyzed})}] - 1\} \times 100$$

Average and compounded annual growth measures for gross margin, operating income, and EBITDA are computed in the same manner.

Note: Analysts often spread five years of financial statements. When calculating growth rates on financial statements spread over five years, the analyst should be careful to obtain growth rates over the four growth periods analyzed. In other words, periods = number of years − 1.

Application to Ale's   Ale's sales growth on a compounded basis is slightly above the rate of inflation (3 percent), suggesting that the company's unit volume (on a case-equivalent basis) is relatively flat. The operating profit of Ale's decreased over the period, further evidence of a flattening in operating performance. However, Ale's showed a dramatic increase in operating profit within the past year, possibly indicating a rebound.

CHAPTER 5

Income Approach

Perhaps the most widely recognized approach to valuing an interest in a privately held enterprise is the income approach. As with both the market and asset approaches, several valuation methodologies exist within the income approach to develop an indication of value. This chapter explores the fundamental theory behind the approach and its numerous applications.

This chapter will discuss three methods of the income approach: the capitalized cash flow (CCF) method, the discounted cash flow (DCF) method, and the excess cash flow (ECF) method. These methods are sometimes identified by other names. For example, the capitalized cash flow method has been referred to in other publications as the "single period earnings" method, and the excess cash flow method has traditionally been referred to as the "excess earnings method." This chapter will also discuss the economic benefit stream of a privately held entity. Valuation analysts use a number of terms, such as *economic benefits, economic income,* and *net income.* These terms are used interchangeably throughout this chapter. This text identifies each method as "cash flow" (CF), which is an industry standard. In discussing CF, we will address two types of cash flow: "cash flow to equity" (CF-Eq) and "cash flow to invested capital" (CF-IC).

FUNDAMENTAL THEORY

Equity Interests Are Investments

An equity interest in a privately held enterprise is an investment that can be evaluated in the same basic manner as any other investment that the investor might choose to make. An investment is:

> *the current commitment of dollars for a period of time to derive future payments that will compensate the investor for*
>
> - *the time the funds are committed,*
> - *the expected rate of inflation, and*
> - *the uncertainty of the future payments.*[1]

Investments and Business Valuations Involve the "Forward-Looking" Premise

An investment requires a commitment of dollars that the investor currently holds in exchange for an expectation that the investor will receive some greater amount of

---

[1] Frank K. Reilly and Keith C. Brown, *Investment Analysis and Portfolio Management,* 5th ed. (The Dryden Press, Harcourt Brace College Publishers, 1996), p. 5.

dollars at some point in the future. This is one of the most basic premises of business valuation: Value is forward-looking. This "forward-looking" premise is basic to all investment decisions and business valuations. "Value today always equals future cash flow discounted at the opportunity cost of capital."[2]

The income approach to business valuation embraces this forward-looking premise by calculating value based on the assumption that the value of an ownership interest is equal to the sum of the present values of the expected future benefits of owning that interest. No other valuation approach so directly incorporates this fundamental premise in its calculation of value.

BASICS OF INCOME APPROACH—"A FRACTION"

Overview

The income approach is a mathematical fraction consisting of a numerator and a denominator. The numerator represents the future payments of an investment, and the denominator represents a quantification of the associated risk and uncertainty of those future payments.

The Numerator

The *numerator* represents the "future payments" or the "future economic benefit stream." In valuing private businesses, we generally think of these future benefit streams as expected future cash flows. As indicated throughout this chapter and Chapter 6, empirical data are based upon cash flows (after entity-level income taxes, both federal and state). However, it is not uncommon to see net income instead of cash flow as the numerator. Also, the net income may be on a pretax or after-tax basis, or the numerator may be operating income, etc. The list goes on. Furthermore, the beneficiary of the future payments must be clearly defined; that is, a clear understanding must be made as to whether the future payment is going to all the stakeholders—both equity holders and debt holders—or just to the equity holders. When referring to equity holders, we must define whether the beneficiaries are both controlling and noncontrolling shareholders or just controlling or just minority shareholders.

Therefore, whichever "future economic benefit stream" is used as the *proxy* for the "future payments," it *must*:

- Be an appropriate future benefit for the subject company being valued.
- Match the characteristics of the denominator. For example, if the numerator is "after-tax cash flows to equity," then the denominator must be an "after-tax cash flow risk or discount rate to equity."
- Be appropriate for the stakeholders defined.

The Denominator

The second element, the *denominator,* is the rate of return required for the particular interest represented by the cash flow in the numerator. The denominator reflects

---

[2] Richard A. Brealey and Stewart C. Myers, *Capital Investment and Valuation.* (New York: McGraw-Hill, Inc., 2003), p. 67.

opportunity cost, or the "cost of capital." In other words, it is the rate of return that investors require to draw them to a particular investment rather than an alternative investment.

This rate of return incorporates certain investor expectations relating to the future economic benefit stream:

- The "real" rate of return—the amount investors expect to obtain in exchange for letting someone else use their money on a riskless basis
- Expected inflation—the expected depreciation in purchasing power during the period when the money is tied up
- Risk—the uncertainty as to when and how much cash flow or other economic income will be received[3]

The first item is essentially rent. Any investor forgoing current consumption and allowing another party to use his or her funds would require a rental payment. The second item is required due to the time value of money and the decreased purchasing power associated with invested funds being spent later rather than sooner. The third item captures investor expectations about the risks inherent in the specific equity instrument. Generally, this risk assessment is developed through analysis of the future economic benefit and the uncertainty related to the timing and quantity of that benefit. See Chapter 6 for additional detail on rates of return.

INCOME APPROACH METHODOLOGIES

The business valuation profession commonly uses three primary methods within the income approach to value privately held business interests. These include:

1. Discounted cash flow (DCF) method
2. Capitalized cash flow (CCF) method
3. Excess cash flow (ECF) method

Each method requires the determination of a "future benefit stream," a numerator, and a rate of return (risk), a denominator. The CCF method utilizes just one numerator and denominator, whereas the DCF utilizes a series of fractions. The ECF method is really a hybrid method, combining elements of both the asset and the income approaches.

Each method depends on the present value of an enterprise's future cash flows, often based on historical financial data. Preferably, the financial data is in compliance with generally accepted accounting principles (GAAP). Valuation analysts, including CPA-analysts, are not responsible for attesting or verifying financial information or certifying GAAP statements when providing valuations. Often they are given non-GAAP financial information as a starting point to derive income or cash flow; this information is often acceptable. However, analysts still should do their best to make appropriate adjustments to income statements and/or balance sheets within the scope of their engagement. The development of these adjustments is referred to as the normalization process.

---

[3] Shannon P. Pratt, *Cost of Capital: Estimation and Application,* 2nd ed. (Hoboken, NJ: John Wiley & Sons, 2002), p. 5. (Used with permission.)

NORMALIZATION PROCESS

If the value of any investment is equal to the present value of its future benefits, determining the appropriate future benefit stream (cash flow) is of primary importance. Therefore, items that are not representative of the appropriate future cash flow must be either eliminated or adjusted in some manner. The process begins with the collection of historical financial data and includes a detailed review of that data to determine what, if any, adjustments are required.

> Failure to develop the appropriate normalizing adjustments may result in a significant overstatement or understatement of value.

"Big Five"

The normalization process involves the restatement of the historical financial statements to "value" financial statements; i.e., statements that can be used in the valuation process. Normalization generally involves five categories of adjustments:

1. For ownership characteristics (control versus minority)
2. For GAAP departures and extraordinary, nonrecurring, and/or unusual items
3. For nonoperating assets and liabilities and related income and expenses
4. For taxes
5. For synergies from mergers and acquisitions, if applicable

Generally, the second, third, and fourth categories of normalization adjustments are made in all valuations, whether the ownership interest being valued is a minority or a control interest. The first category of normalization adjustments is not always necessary if the ownership interest being valued is a minority interest. The fifth category is most often used to derive investment value.

ADJUSTMENTS FOR OWNERSHIP CHARACTERISTICS

Controlling interest holders are able to extract personal financial benefits beyond fair market amounts in a number of ways. For instance, in a privately held enterprise, it is not unusual for the controlling shareholder to take compensation in excess of going market rates that might be paid for the same services. Since the "willing buyer" of a control ownership interest could reduce compensation to market levels, often it is appropriate to add back excess compensation to cash flow to reflect the additional economic benefits that would be available to the "willing buyer."

By choosing to make certain adjustments to the future economic benefit (i.e., the numerator), the analyst can develop a control or noncontrol value.

Other examples of common control adjustments include:[4]

- Excess fringe benefits including healthcare and retirement
- Excess employee perquisites
- Excess rental payments to shareholders
- Excess intercompany fees and payments to a commonly controlled sister company
- Payroll-related taxes
- Reimbursed expenses
- Nonbusiness travel and entertainment of shareholders and/or key individuals
- Related-party transactions (i.e., leases between shareholder and entity)
- Sales/purchases to/from related entities
- Capital structure
- Excess or insufficient interest on loans to/from shareholders

Normalization adjustments affect the pretax income or cash flow of the entity being valued. Consequently, the control adjustments will result in a corresponding modification in the income tax of the entity, if applicable.

The content of the numerator drives the type of value (control or minority) produced. As such, if the numerator includes adjustments related to control, the value conclusion will be a control value. By excluding adjustments related to control, the value conclusion is a minority value. If control adjustments are included in the normalization and the resulting value is a control value, a minority interest discount may be used to adjust from control to minority value. There are often situations where no control adjustments are necessary and the company's control owners run the company to the benefit of all the owners. In this situation, the value might be the same for minority and control. However, some analysts still apply a minority discount to reflect the risk of a potential change in the control owner or his or her management philosophy. See Chapter 27 for various views on the subject.

---

[4] See Chapters 7 and 9 for other views on control adjustments.

> Adjustments to the income and cash flow of a company are the primary determinants of whether the capitalized value is minority or control.

Example

Assume a control shareholder's salary is in excess of market value by $300,000 per year and the capitalized cash flow method is used to value the net cash flow of the company.

NCF = $700,000 (on a noncontrol basis)

Excess Compensation = $300,000 (assume tax-affected)

$k_e - g$ = 20% (discount rate − growth = capitalization rate)

Under these assumptions, the computation of value is:

$$\text{FMV} = \frac{\text{NCF}}{k_e - g} = \frac{\$700,000}{20\%} = \underline{\$3,500,000}$$

Thus $3.5 million is the value of the entity on a noncontrolling basis.

Assuming that a normalization adjustment would add back the $300,000 of excess compensation to cash flow, the outcome would clearly differ, as illustrated below:

$$\text{FMV} = \frac{\text{NCF}}{k_e - g} = \frac{\$1,000,000}{20\%} = \underline{\$5,000,000}$$

Here, $5 million is the value of the entity on a control basis. The difference in the two conclusions is entirely attributable to those portions of a control benefit stream taken out of the company as excess compensation.

If the analyst chooses to make the control normalization adjustment, a minority interest value still could be determined by utilizing a discount for lack of control.

	Noncontrol	Control
NCF	$ 700,000	$1,000,000
$k_e - g$	20%	20%
FMV	3,500,000	5,000,000
Minority discount at 30%*	0	(1,500,000)
	$3,500,000	$3,500,000

*Example only, discounts are discussed in Chapter 9.

When there are controlling interest influences in the benefit stream or operations of the entity and a minority interest is being valued, it may be preferable to provide a minority value directly by not making adjustments. Doing this will avoid the problems related to determining and defending the application of a more general level of minority discount.

The debate as to whether to make these control adjustments in a minority valuation is ongoing. Some analysts prefer to make the adjustments, then apply a minority discount. They argue that by *not* making these adjustments, one could:

- Understate value
- Overstate the minority discount
- Possibly "double count" the minority discount

Those who believe one should not make control adjustments, that is, leave the cash flows on a minority basis, say that:

- Minority interests have no say in compensation and perquisites to controlling shareholders and cash flows must reflect this fact.
- The amount of these adjustments may be difficult to justify or verify.
- Almost all of the difference in control versus minority value in the income approach is found in the numerator—the expected income—rather than in the denominator—the discount or capitalization rate.

ADJUSTMENTS FOR GAAP DEPARTURES AND EXTRAORDINARY, NONRECURRING, AND/OR UNUSUAL ITEMS

In analyzing historical financial statements, it is important to "smooth" the financial data by removing all items that would not be indicative of future operating performance. The goal is to present a normal operating picture to project earnings into the future. Because conclusions of value are based on future return expectations, and because most analysts use historical financial information as the starting point for estimating future returns, it would be appropriate to consider the following adjustments:

- Departures from GAAP
- Extraordinary items
- Nonrecurring items
- Unusual items

Depending on the situation, statements prepared on a "tax basis" or "cash basis" may have to be adjusted to be closer to GAAP and/or normalized cash flow.

One-time advertising expenditures or unusually high equipment repairs in a single year are just two simple examples of the types of items that might be considered nonrecurring or not part of a normal operating cycle. Other examples include the effects of catastrophic events such as a plant fire, hurricane damage, labor strikes, and/or insurance proceed collections due to such events as the death of a key executive.

Other adjustment items also can be found in historical balance sheet and cash flow accounts. For example, if a company purchased a level of fixed assets far beyond its historical norm and funded the purchases from cash flow from operations, it may be necessary to "smooth" the depreciation and corresponding cash flow to reflect a more normal pattern.

VaITip

As with the control-oriented adjustments, extraordinary, nonrecurring, or unusual item adjustments affect the profit or loss accounts of a company on a pretax basis. Therefore, certain income tax-related adjustments may be necessary.

See Chapter 4 for greater detail and examples on financial statement adjustments.

ADJUSTMENTS FOR NONOPERATING ASSETS AND LIABILITIES AND RELATED INCOME AND EXPENSES

The application of most commonly accepted income approach methodologies results in a valuation of the company's operating assets, both tangible and intangible. Therefore, it is often necessary to remove all nonoperating items from the company's balance sheet and income statement. After the value of the operating assets has been determined, the net nonoperating assets generally are added back at their respective values as of the valuation date.

Examples of nonoperating assets and liabilities might include airplanes, unsold plant facilities that have been replaced, significant investments in unrelated companies, equity investments, excess cash or working capital, and loans to support any of these.

The interest, dividends, and rental income, as well as any related expenses (loan interest, depreciation, and other carrying costs) associated with these nonoperating assets must be removed from the operating benefit stream. Once again, these types of adjustments will alter the pretax operating income.

Methodologies for the valuation of nonoperating assets and liabilities will vary depending on the nature of the asset or liability. Usually more significant fixed assets, such as an airplane or building, are separately appraised. Investments in privately held enterprises may require a separate entity valuation. In many cases, the nonoperating assets will have appreciated since acquisition and may require a consideration of the potential tax implications of any gain associated with this appreciation. If nonoperating assets exist and are to be added to the operating assets, they must be adjusted to their respective fair market values, including an adjustment for discounts if applicable.

When valuing a minority interest, some experts do not add back nonoperating assets since minority shareholders have little or no control over the assets. However, this often results in a very large implied discount on the nonoperating assets, particularly those with low income or high expenses.

ValTip

Specialists in the valuation of particular nonoperating assets may need to be hired. Engagement letters should clearly set out these responsibilities and the related appraisal expenses.

ADJUSTMENTS FOR TAXES

The question of whether to tax-affect or not tax-affect income in pass-through entities is a highly debated issue in business valuation (see Chapters 4 and 12). However, the selection of tax rates can also be an issue.

Income tax expenditures represent a very real use of cash flow and must be considered carefully. If both federal and state taxes are to be reflected, they should be based on the future income that was determined in the valuation process, including the appropriate tax rate(s) to use.

Tax Rate or Rates to Use

Determining the tax on future income can incorporate the:

- Actual tax rate
- Highest marginal tax rate
- Average tax rate

For example, on $1 million of pretax cash flows, the resulting capitalized value would vary depending on the tax rates, as shown in Exhibit 5.1.

Exhibit 5.1 Taxes and Value

	Actual Tax Liability	Average Tax Rate of 35%	Highest Marginal Rate of 39%
Before-tax income	$1,000,000	$1,000,000	$1,000,000
Tax on the taxable income	222,500	350,000	390,000
After-tax cash flows	777,500	650,000	610,000
Capitalized value 20%	$3,887,500	$3,250,000	$3,050,000

The lowest value, which uses the highest marginal rate, is almost 22 percent below the highest value, which uses the actual tax liability. This is a significant difference. Taxes can vary from year to year for a variety of reasons. As such, undue reliance on one year may lead to a faulty valuation.

The tax issue becomes even more controversial when the entities involved are pass-through entities such as S corporations and partnerships. Since these entities have little or no federal and state tax liability, applying after-tax discount and capitalization ("cap") rates to pretax income would result in a higher value for the pass-through entity, all other things being equal (see Exhibit 5.2). See Chapters 4 and 12 for more detail on this important and complicated issue.

Exhibit 5.2 Applying After-tax Cap Rate to Pretax Cash Flow

	Pass-Through Entity	"C" Corporation
Before-tax cash flow	$1,000,000	$1,000,000
Tax on the taxable income	0	350,000
After-tax cash flows	$1,000,000	650,000
Capitalized value 20%	$5,000,000	$3,250,000

ADJUSTMENTS FOR SYNERGIES FROM MERGERS AND ACQUISITIONS

Synergistic adjustments may be needed in mergers and acquisitions engagements. These adjustments will vary in complexity. For example, synergy adjustments could be as simple as adjusting for savings in "office rent" due to the consolidation of office facilities. Synergy adjustments also can include the results of in-depth analyses of increased sales, decreased production costs, decreased sales and marketing costs, and other improvements due to anticipated economies of scale.

ValTip

Synergistic value is investment value, which may not be fair market value.

DETERMINATION OF FUTURE BENEFIT STREAM (CASH FLOWS)

Under the capitalized cash flow method, a single measure of the "expected" annual future economic benefit is used as a proxy for all future benefits. Under a discounted cash flow methodology, discrete "expected" future economic benefits are projected for a specified number of years in the future and then a single measure of economic benefit is selected for use into perpetuity after the specified period, which is referred to as the terminal value.

Both the cap rate and the discount rate are intended to encompass investor expectations regarding the risk of receiving the future economic benefits in the amounts and at the times assumed in the models. Given the forward-looking nature of these methodologies, the valuation analyst will want to properly assess potential future economic benefits to produce a valuation conclusion that is accurate and supportable.

DEFINING THE BENEFIT STREAM

Both single-period benefit streams (CCF) and multiperiod benefit streams (DCF) can be defined in a variety of ways, depending on what definition is most appropriate in a given circumstance. The most common definitions of future economic benefits are net income and net cash flow.

Net Income

Net income is the measure of an entity's operating performance and typically is defined as revenue from operations less direct and indirect operating expenses. Its usefulness as a measure of economic benefit for valuation purposes lies in its familiarity through financial statements. It can be either before or after tax. The problem with using net income as the economic benefit is that it is more difficult to develop discount and cap rates relative to net income; cash flow rates of return are more readily available using traditional cost of capital techniques.

ValTip

In many small companies, income and cash flow can be the same or similar.

Net Cash Flow

In recent years, net cash flow has become the most often-used measure of future economic benefit, because it generally represents the cash that can be distributed to equity owners without threatening or interfering with future operations.

Net cash flow is akin to dividend-paying capacity and as such can be seen as a proxy for return on investment. Finally, it is the measure on which most commonly accepted empirical data on rates of return are based.

DEFINING NET CASH FLOW

Net cash flow is defined differently depending on the method of the income approach selected. As stated earlier, the characteristics of the beneficiary or recipient of the expected cash flows are critical to analysts. Over the years, finance and business valuation analysts alike have segregated cash flows into two groups: (1) *cash flows to the equity* shareholders and (2) *cash flows to invested capital,* which represents cash flows to equity shareholders *and* holders of interest-bearing debt. We refer to these two groups, respectively, as the *direct equity method* and the *invested capital method.* Whether using a DCF or a CCF, the analyst can elect to rely on the direct equity method or the invested capital method. The next sections present the components of net cash flow.

> Cash flows for financial statement purposes are generally not used in business valuations. Because cash flows are normalized to estimate cash flows into perpetuity, specific changes in current assets and liabilities, specific purchases, and specific borrowings and repayments are ignored.

Cash Flow Direct to Equity (Direct Equity Method)

Net income after tax
Plus: depreciation, amortization, and other noncash changes[5]
Less: incremental working capital needs (can be plus)
Less: incremental capital expenditure needs
Plus: new debt principal in
Less: repayment of debt principal
Equals: net cash flow direct to equity

The cash flows here are "direct to equity" because debt has been serviced by the inclusion of interest expense and debt repayment, and what is left is available to equity owners only. This is a debt-inclusive model.

The direct equity method requires that an appropriate discount rate to cash flows to equity be applied to those cash flows. No other discount rate is applicable.

Cash Flow to Invested Capital (Invested Capital Method)

Net income after tax
Plus: interest expense (tax affected)

---

[5] Changes in deferred taxes may be considered if book depreciation and amortization are used instead of tax depreciation and amortization.

Exhibit 5.3   Four Types of Analyses of Income Approach

	Direct Equity	**Invested Capital**
CCF	1	2
DCF	3	4

Plus: depreciation, amortization, and other noncash changes[6]
Less: incremental "debt-free" working capital needs (can be plus)
Less: incremental capital expenditure needs
Equals: net cash flow to invested capital

    The cash flows here are those available to service invested capital, i.e., equity and interest-bearing debt. Cash flow to invested capital is often referred to as "free cash flow." The cash flows exclude interest expense and debt principle payment. It is a debt-free model in the sense that all interest and related debt capital is removed. The value determined by this method is invested capital, which is typically interest-bearing debt, capital leases, and equity. To derive equity value using this method, the analyst subtracts the actual debt of the subject company.

    The invested capital method requires that an appropriate discount rate to cash flows to invested capital be applied to those cash flows. No other discount rate is applicable.

ValTip

> There are only four general types of analyses for application of the income approach.

    See Exhibit 5.3 for the four types of analyses for applying the income approach. See Addendum 1 at the end of this chapter for a comparison of the various models.

---

[6] Ibid.

USE OF HISTORICAL INFORMATION

Once the benefit stream has been defined and adjustments have been made, the analyst will want to analyze historical financial information since it often serves as the foundation from which estimates of future projected benefits are made.

The historical period under analysis usually encompasses an operating cycle of the entity's industry, often a five-year period. Beyond five years, data can become "stale." There are five commonly used methodologies by which to estimate future economic benefits from historical data:

1. The current earnings method
2. The simple average method
3. The weighted average method
4. The trend line-static method
5. The formal projection method

The first four methods are most often used in the CCF method of the income approach or as the starting point for the DCF method. The fifth method is the basis for the DCF method. The CCF and DCF methods are explained in greater detail later in this chapter. All of these methods can be used in either the direct equity or the invested capital method of the income approach.

Current Earnings Method

The current year's income is sometimes the best proxy for the following year and future years in many closely held companies. Management insights will be helpful in deciding whether current cash flows are likely to be replicated in the ensuing years. If management indicates that next year will be very similar to last year, then current earnings and cash flow may be used as the basis to value the company. It is also possible that next year's cash flow will be different from the past but still grow into perpetuity at an average constant rate. Any such projection must be supported with sound underlying assumptions.

> Regardless of the method employed, dialogue with or information from management can provide insight into future projections.

Simple Average Method

The simple average method uses the arithmetic mean of the historical data during the analysis period. The simple average method can be illustrated by the following example:

ACE Corporation—Historical Cash Flow*

20X1	$100,000
20X2	90,000
20X3	160,000
20X4	170,000
20X5	180,000
	$700,000

$$\div\ 5 = 140,000\ \text{(Simple Average)}$$

*After normalization adjustments

A simple average is used most often in developing the numerator for the capitalization of cash flow method when historical normalized information does not discern an identifiable trend. If the historical analysis period encompasses a full industry operating cycle, the use of a simple average also may provide a realistic estimate of expected future performance. However, it may not accurately reflect changes in company growth or other trends that are expected to continue.

In this example, the simple averaging method may not work well in estimating future cash flows. The last three years' results may be more indicative of the company's performance when the company has been growing consistently and 20X2 was perhaps an anomaly. A cursory glance would tell you that the next year's cash flow probably would be expected to be somewhat higher than $180,000, providing that the historical data are representative of the business's direction and mirror management's expectations.

Weighted Average Method

When the historical financial information yields a discernible trend, a weighted average method may yield a better indication of the future economic benefit stream, since weighting provides greater flexibility in interpreting trends. In fact, under certain circumstances, specific years may be eliminated altogether, that is, have zero weight.

The computation of the weighted average requires the summation of a set of results that are the products of assigned weights times annual historical economic benefit streams. It can be illustrated by the following example:

ACE Corporation Normalized Historical Cash Flow

20X1	$100,000
20X2	90,000
20X3	160,000
20X4	170,000
20X5	180,000
	$700,000

Application of Weights

100,000 × 1	=	$	100,000
90,000 × 2	=		180,000
160,000 × 3	=		480,000
170,000 × 4	=		680,000
180,000 × 5	=		900,000
15			$2,340,000

Weighted Average $2,340,000 ÷ 15 = $ 156,000

In this example, the analyst has identified a trend that requires greater weight be applied to the most recent operating periods.

In deciding upon a weighting scheme, the analyst should attempt to model future expected economic benefits accurately. Any weights can apply to any of the years. For example:

Application of Weights

100,000 × 0	=	$	0
90,000 × 0	=		0
160,000 × 1	=		160,000
170,000 × 2	=		340,000
180,000 × 3	=		540,000
6			$1,040,000

Weighted Average $1,040,000 ÷ 6 = $ 173,333

In this specific example, the weighted average method still may not reflect anticipated cash flow correctly. As with the simple average method, the resulting value in this example tends to be conservative and may understate value when future performance is expected to exceed the prior year. Care must be exercised in using weighted averages including the weights and the years.

Trend Line-Static Method

The trend line static method is a statistical application of the least squares formula. The method generally is considered most useful when the company's past earnings have been relatively consistent (either positive or negative) and are expected to continue at similar levels in the future. At least five years of data is suggested.

$$y = a + bx$$

Where:

y = predicted value of y variable for selected x variable

a = y intercept (estimated value of y when x = 0)

b = slope of line (average change in y for each amount of change in x)

x = independent variable

$$a = \frac{\Sigma Y}{N} - \frac{b\Sigma X}{N} \text{ or } \overline{Y} - b\overline{X}$$

Where:

X = value of independent variable

Y = value of dependent variable

N = number of items in sample

$\overline{X}$ = mean of independent variable

$\overline{Y}$ = mean of dependent variable

$$b = \frac{N(\Sigma XY) - (\Sigma X)(\Sigma Y)}{N(\Sigma X^2) - (\Sigma X)^2}$$

The computation can be illustrated as follows:

ACE Corporation—Historical Cash Flow

X	Y	XY	X²
1	$100,000	$ 100,000	1
2	90,000	180,000	4
3	160,000	480,000	9
4	170,000	680,000	16
5	180,000	900,000	25
15	$700,000	$2,340,000	55

The next step requires solving the equations for variables a and b. Because variable b is integrated into the formula for variable a, the value of b must first be determined.

$$b = \frac{[5\ (\$2{,}340{,}000)] - [15\ (\$700{,}000)]}{5\ (55) - (15)^2}$$

$$b = \frac{\$11{,}700{,}000 - \$10{,}500{,}000}{275 - 225}$$

$$b = \frac{\$1{,}200{,}000}{50}$$

$$b = \$24{,}000$$

Solving further for variable *a*,

$$a = \frac{\$700{,}000 - [\$24{,}000\ (15)]}{5}$$

$$a = \frac{\$340{,}000}{5}$$

$$a = \$68{,}000$$

Finally, solving the original least square formula,

$$y = a + bx$$
$$y = \$68,000 + (\$24,000 \times 5)$$
$$y = \underline{\$188,000}$$

As can be seen, the trend line-static method places the greatest weight on the most recent periods, even more so than the weighted average method. Depending on the facts, this may produce a more accurate picture of future cash flows, particularly when growth is expected to continue. There are various statistical measures that can also be used to test the reliability of the results derived from this method.

Formal Projection Method (Detailed Cash Flow Projections)

The formal projection method uses projections of cash flows or other economic benefits for a specified number of future years (generally three to five) referred to as the "explicit," "discreet," or "forecast" period. This method is used to determine future economic benefit streams when using the DCF method. This method has been widely accepted due to the flexibility it allows when estimating year-by-year benefit streams over the explicit period.

ValTip

Theoretically, the length of the explicit period is determined by identifying the year when all the following years will change at a constant rate. Practically, however, performance and financial position after three to five years often are difficult to estimate for many closely held companies. Lesser periods are sometimes used as well.

With exceptions, three to five years is the standard length of the explicit period. One such exception is for start-up and early-stage companies whose profitability often is not projected until several additional years out. The period following the explicit period is called the "continuing value" or "terminal" period.

Projections often are determined by reference to historical financial information that has been normalized. Used as a foundation for future expectations, normalized financial statements may include both balance sheet and income statement adjustments.

Once the analyst has normalized the historical data, when applicable, it may be necessary to review all elements of revenue and expenses to ensure that future operating projections reflect as closely as possible the trends identified in the analysis of historical financial information. These trends can be discussed with management and related to future expectations and economic and industry research undertaken by the business analyst in conjunction with the engagement.

> In some circumstances, the past is not indicative of the future. Analysts must exercise care in analyzing projected performance in these situations. Adequate support must exist for the assumptions that the projections are based upon.

If the value measure selected is net cash flow, it is necessary to establish projections of working capital needs, capital expenditures, depreciation, and, if using a direct equity method, borrowings, and repayments of debt. Each of these items may restrict or provide free cash flow, affecting the return on equity.

A question sometimes arises as to why analysts may need future balance sheets and statements of cash flow when they are using a DCF model. The interactive nature of the balance sheet, income statement, and statement of cash flows operates to ensure that all aspects of future cash flow have been addressed and that assumptions utilized in the projection of the income statement work properly through the balance sheet. This is not always necessary or available.

> The valuation analyst uses normalized historical data, management insights, and trend analysis to analyze formal projections for the explicit period. These projections take into account balance sheet and income statement items that affect the defined benefit stream and involve not only projected income statements but also may include projected balance sheets and statements of cash flow.

THE CAPITALIZED CASH FLOW METHOD

Introduction

The capitalized cash flow method (CCF) is an abbreviated version of the discounted cash flow method where both growth (g) and the discount rate (k) are assumed to remain constant into perpetuity. The CCF is also the *dividend discount model,* also known as the "Gordon Growth Model." Professor Myron J. Gordon brought this model to the forefront in his 1962 book, *The Investment, Financing and Valuation of the Corporation.* Since then, the model has appeared in virtually every valuation and finance treatise, as well as being a widely accepted methodology for determining the "terminal value" of the discounted cash flow (DCF) method discussed later in this chapter.

The CCF Formula

$$PV = \frac{NCF_1}{k - g}$$

Where:

PV = Present value

NCF_1 = Expected economic income in the full period immediately following the effective valuation date realized at the end of the period

k = Present value discount rate (i.e., the cost of capital)

g = Expected long-term growth rate into perpetuity

The CCF formula includes the assumption that the NCF_1 can be "distributable" to the owners of the enterprise.

Other than this constancy of growth and risk, the same theory and assumptions hold true for the CCF method as for the DCF method with regard to economic benefit stream, measurement of risk, the effects of growth, and so forth.

End-of-Year Convention for CCF

The future economic benefit selected for the CCF model is the expected cash flow (or its equivalent) in the period following the valuation date. For example, if NCF is $100,000 and the valuation date is December 31, 2005, and the expected growth rate is 4 percent, then CF_1, expected on December 31, 2006, is $104,000, as shown in Exhibit 5.4.

Exhibit 5.4 Expected Cash Flow

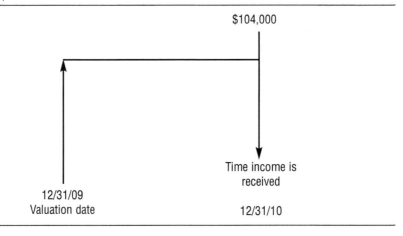

Midyear Convention for CCF Method

Like the DCF discussed later in this chapter, the CCF also can reflect cash flows being received evenly throughout the year with the following midyear convention formula. Midyear theory and application are discussed in detail in the DCF section.

$$PV = \frac{NCF_1(1 + k)^{0.5}}{k - g}$$

Where:

PV $\quad$ = $\quad$ Present value

NCF_1 $\quad$ = $\quad$ Expected economic income in the full period immediately following the effective valuation date

k $\quad$ = $\quad$ Present value discount rate (i.e., the cost of capital)

g $\quad$ = $\quad$ Expected long-term growth rate into perpetuity

11 Common Mistakes

This method is, without a doubt, the most commonly used of all business valuation methods. Its simplicity, however, often masks what the valuation analyst is saying about the business being valued. That is, that the

- Growth of the business, on average, will be X percent . . . *forever*
- Net cash flows will, on average, grow at X percent . . . *forever*
- Risk rate will remain the same . . . *forever*
- Debt to equity ratio will remain the same . . . *forever*

Unfortunately, its simplicity has not reduced the number of misuses or mistakes. We have identified 11 common mistakes often found in the application of this method.

1. *Understating or overstating growth rates.* The growth rate used in the CCF method is intended to reflect a long-term average growth rate. This long-term growth rate is also intended to be the average growth rate into perpetuity. Over the past 80 years or so, inflation and gross domestic product have each grown on average approximately 2.5 to 3.0 percent and 3.0 to 3.5 percent, respectively. Therefore, a company with a long-term growth rate of lower than 2.5 to 3 percent will not keep up with inflation. Alternatively, the company with growth greater than 6 to 6.5 percent will outperform the economy, again on a long-term basis.
2. *Failure to convert to the capitalization rate.* This common mistake is clearly straightforward. The long-term growth rate must be subtracted from the discount rate to arrive at the capitalization rate. Failure to reduce the discount rate will substantially understate value.
3. *Failure to properly normalize earnings.* This common mistake applies to all valuation approaches but tends to be more prevalent with the CCF method. As discussed later in this chapter, future expected earnings must be normalized, including nonrecurring, nonoperating, GAAP adjustments (where appropriate), and those overstated or understated from the norm.
4. *Identifying control versus noncontrol cash flows.* Failure to properly differentiate control versus noncontrol cash flows can cause unreliable valuations, depending on the application of relevant adjustments.

5. *Using beginning rather than ending cash flows.* The CCF formula, as shown in Exhibit 5.4, is based on the mathematical fact that the numerator is the first year's future economic benefit after the valuation date and is received by the investor at the last day of that year. This is often overlooked. For example, if the analyst bases future earnings on the subject company's current year's earnings, then the analyst must add the next year's estimated future growth in earnings to the current year's earnings.

6. *Applying a discount rate inconsistent with estimated future cash flows.* Mismatching the discount rate with the estimated future cash flows is an error found in the use of other methods in addition to the CCF method. For example, an analyst may mistakenly apply a discount rate for "equity cash flows" to "cash flows to invested capital" or apply an after-tax discount rate to pretax earnings.

7. *Not applying midyear convention.* For a given discount rate, the midyear convention produces a present value that is the same percentage greater than the present value produced in the year-end convention, regardless of what average long-term growth rate is used. If the investor of the interest ownership is receiving cash flows evenly throughout the year, the added value as a result of receiving those benefits sooner will not be properly reflected unless the midyear convention is used. Too often, however, it is not. The one exception may take place with seasonal businesses. Some analysts also prefer a simplified presentation.

8. *Not adding or properly adjusting for nonoperating assets.* Certain nonoperating assets should be considered. For example, excess cash and/or marketable securities are often ignored. The analyst may go to great lengths to attest to the company's high, substantial current ratio or quick ratio but stop short of considering whether it's really due to "nonoperating excess cash." Another example may be found in the case of the company's underutilization of the company's plant facilities or its possession of idle plant facilities.

9. *Working capital deficiency.* Economic theory, as well as many business owners, espouse that additional, *permanent* working capital is required to accommodate company growth. Too often, however, analysts reflect the ever-increasing cash flows but fail to reduce those cash flows for the permanent increases in needed working capital.

10. *Nonreconciliation of capital expenditures and depreciation.* Net cash flows in particular require that future estimated noncash items, such as depreciation and amortization, be added, while future estimated annual capital expenditures are subtracted. Many analysts prefer a simple assumption that future estimated annual depreciation and amortization equal future estimated capital expenditures, thus offsetting each other. Other analysts, however, attest that in a growing business, long-term annual estimated capital expenditures exceed annual depreciation, primarily due to inflation. Careful consideration of the facts and circumstances in each valuation must be exercised to address this issue.

11. *Using cash flows to equity over cash flows to invested capital (or vice versa).* In some valuation engagements where interest-bearing debt exists, using cash flows to equity rather than cash flows to invested capital can produce a value that does not reflect the company's true FMV. This distortion can be significant. Examples are presented in Exhibits 5.32A to 5.32E (Addendum 1). This error may be dramatically compounded when debt proceeds, payments, or interest are included in the cash flows to equity and therefore are assumed to continue forever.

THE DISCOUNTED CASH FLOW METHOD

Definition and Overview

The discounted cash flow (DCF) method is similar to the capitalized cash flow method. Although the model might appear more complicated, its theoretical precept is the same:

The value of any operating asset/investment is equal to the present value of its expected future economic benefit stream.

> All other things being equal, the more certain the future streams of cash flow are, the more valuable the asset or entity is.

The reliability of actually receiving future economic benefit streams is different from asset to asset and from entity to entity. Asset or entity risk is assessed and measured in the form of a rate referred to as a "discount rate," a "rate or return," or the "cost of capital." These terms are used interchangeably throughout this book and are covered in detail in Chapter 6.

DCF Model

The basic DCF model is as follows:[7]

$$PV = \sum_{i=1}^{n} \frac{E_i}{(1 + k)^i}$$

Where:

PV = Present value

Σ = Sum of

n = The last period for which economic income is expected; n may equal infinity (i.e., ∞) if the economic income is expected to continue in perpetuity

E_i = Expected future economic income in the ith period in the future (paid at the end of the period)

k = Discount rate (the cost of capital, e.g., the expected rate of return available in the market for other investments of comparable risk and other investment characteristics)

i = The period (usually stated as a number of years) in the future over which the prospective economic income is expected to be received

---

[7] Shannon P. Pratt, *Valuing a Business: The Analysis and Appraisal of Closely Held Companies,* 5th ed. (New York: McGraw-Hill, 2008), p. 177.

The expansion of this formula is:[8]

$$PV = \frac{E_1}{(1+k)^1} + \frac{E_2}{(1+k)^2} + \ldots + \frac{E_n}{(1+k)^n}$$

Where:

PV = Present value

E_n = Expected future economic income in the nth or last period in which an element of income is expected. $E_{1,2, \text{ etc.}}$ is the first, second, third, and so on expected future economic income for each period before the $_n$th period (or year).

k = Discount rate

The basic formula for the DCF using net cash flow (direct equity or invested capital) and a terminal period is shown in Exhibit 5.5.

Exhibit 5.5   Basic DCF Formula

Present Value of NCF's during **Explicit Period**	Present Value of the **Terminal Period**
$\dfrac{NCF_1}{(1+k)^1} + \dfrac{NCF_2}{(1+k)^2} + \ldots + \dfrac{NCF_n}{(1+k)^n} +$	$\dfrac{\dfrac{NCF_n \times (1+g)}{(k-g)}}{(1+k)^n}$

Where:

NCF = E, expected future economic income, but now more specifically net cash flow

The following type of chart (Exhibit 5.6) often will be used to project bottom-line net cash flow. For example, assume current year cash flow is $10,000 with anticipated growth and discount rate as follows:

Exhibit 5.6   Cash Flow and Growth

Current Year Earnings	Discount Rate to Equity	Year	Growth Rates
$10,000	26%		
		1	33%
		2	23%
		3	16%
		4	12%
		5	8%
	Long-Term Sustainable Growth Rate	Perpetuity	6%

---

[8] Ibid., p. 177.

This can be modeled and presented as in Exhibit 5.7.

Exhibit 5.7   DCF with Terminal Year

END of	Further Reduces To		Further Reduces To		Further Reduces To		Final
Period 1	$\dfrac{NCF_1}{(1 + k)^1}$	=	$\dfrac{\$10,000 \times (1 + 33\%)}{(1 + .26)^1}$	=	$\dfrac{\$13,300}{1.26}$	=	$10,556
	+		+		+		+
Period 2	$\dfrac{NCF_2}{(1 + k)^2}$	=	$\dfrac{\$13,300 \times (1 + 23\%)}{(1 + .26)^2}$	=	$\dfrac{\$16,359}{1.5876}$	=	$10,304
	+		+		+		+
Period 3	$\dfrac{NCF_3}{(1 + k)^3}$	=	$\dfrac{\$16,359 \times (1 + 16\%)}{(1 + .26)^3}$	=	$\dfrac{\$18,976}{2.0004}$	=	$ 9,486
	+		+		+		+
Period 4	$\dfrac{NCF_4}{(1 + k)^4}$	=	$\dfrac{\$18,976 \times (1 + 12\%)}{(1 + .26)^4}$	=	$\dfrac{\$21,254}{2.5205}$	=	$ 8,432
	+		+		+		+
Period 5	$\dfrac{NCF_5}{(1 + k)^5}$	=	$\dfrac{\$21,254 \times (1 + 8\%)}{(1 + .26)^5}$	=	$\dfrac{\$22,954}{3.1758}$	=	$ 7,228
	+		+		+		+
	Terminal Value $\dfrac{\dfrac{NCF_5 \times (1 + g)}{(k - g)}}{(1 + k)^5}$	=	Terminal Value $\dfrac{\dfrac{\$22,954 \times (1 + 6\%)}{(.26 - .06)}}{(1 + .26)^5}$	=	Terminal Value $\dfrac{\dfrac{\$24,331}{0.20}}{3.1758}$	=	$38,307

The Sum of the Present Values of Expected Future Cash Flows Using the Gordon Growth Model to Calculate the Terminal Value $84,313

End-of-Year and Midyear Conventions

Some DCF models calculate the present value of the future cash flows as if all periodic cash flows will be received on the last day of each forecast period (see Exhibit 5.8). This is obviously not the case with most companies.

Although some models are based on continuous cash flows through the year, a shortcut method has been developed called the midyear convention. The midyear convention DCF model treats periodic cash flows as if they will be received in the middle of the year. This is accomplished by starting the first forecast period (n) at midperiod (.5n). Each successive forecast period is calculated from midperiod to midperiod (.5n + 1).

Exhibit 5.8   End-of-Year Convention

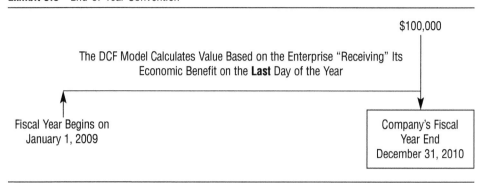

However, this only applies where the valuation date is at the beginning or end of the projection periods (i.e., 1/1 or 12/31 with calendar year projections). For other valuation dates, see the following ValTip:

> When using the mid-term convention for a partial year, the first- and second-year factors are treated a bit differently. For example, if projections begin with calendar year 2009 through 2013 (five years) and the valuation date is 3/31/09, the first-year factor is 0.375 (9/12 × 0.5) and the second year is 1.25 (0.375 × 2 + 0.5). "1" is added to the third, fourth, and fifth years, or 2.25 (3rd), 3.25 (4th), and 4.25 (5th). As usual, the terminal year is equal to the last year of the explicit period of 4.25.

Comparative Example

Assume that a company receives cash flow equal to $100 per month or $1,200 per year (see Exhibit 5.9). Using a 6 percent interest factor, we could compute the present value of the first $100 received by dividing it by $(1 + .06/12)^1$, dividing the second $100 by $(1 + .06/12)^2$, and so on for 12 months, with the total present value equaling $1,161.88.

Assuming the same total received during the year is $1,200, and dividing by $(1 + .06)^{1/2}$ (a midyear convention), the present value equals $1,165.54, a difference of only $3.66.

If it appears that the subject entity is receiving cash flows on a fairly even basis, then the midyear convention is a reasonable approximation.

For further illustration, assume the $1,200 was cash flow received at the end of the year. The present value would be equal to $1,132.08, a difference of $29.80 from the value derived by recognizing $100 per month. As such, the midyear convention

Exhibit 5.9   Midyear Convention Model Compared to a Monthly Model

$$PV \quad = \quad \frac{\$1,200}{(1 + .06)^{1/2}} \quad = \quad \frac{\$1,200}{1.029563} \quad = \quad \underline{\underline{\$1,165.54}}$$

Month	Amount	6.00% Discount Factor Half-Year	Monthly	Present Value
1	100		1.005	99.50
2	100		1.010	99.01
3	100		1.015	98.51
4	100		1.020	98.02
5	100		1.025	97.54
6	100	1.029563	1.030	97.05
7	100		1.036	96.57
8	100		1.041	96.09
9	100		1.046	95.61
10	100		1.051	95.13
11	100		1.056	94.66
12	100		1.062	94.19
	1,200			1,161.88
	1,200		1.029563	1,165.54

more closely resembles how a typical company receives its cash flow. This may differ for seasonal businesses. Distribution policies and timing also can affect the selection of the timing convention.

The midyear convention DCF model (5 years) now looks like Exhibit 5.10, where n = 1 year.

It is important to note that the terminal year begins at 4.5, *not* 5.

Exhibit 5.10   Midyear Convention DCF Model

Present Value of NCF's during **Explicit Period**	**Terminal Value**

$$PV \quad = \quad \frac{NCF_1}{(1 + k)^{n=.5}} \quad + \quad \frac{NCF_2}{(1 + k)^{n=1.5}} \quad + \quad \cdots \quad + \quad \frac{NCF_n}{(1 + k)^{n=4.5}} \quad + \quad \frac{\dfrac{NCF_n \times (1+g)}{(k - g)}}{(1 + k)^{n=4.5}}$$

Adjusting the DCF for a Specific Valuation Date

Since the date of valuation is often *not* the entity's fiscal year end, adjustments to the present value calculations may be needed to reflect the "other than year-end" date.

In the scenario shown in Exhibit 5.11, the valuation date is August 31, 2009, with projections for the first projection year ending in four months, at December 31, 2009. Assuming equal distribution of earnings over the months, then 8/12ths has already been taken into consideration with the August 31, 2009, period. Assuming that the DCF model is the proper valuation tool to use, the present value of the

Exhibit 5.11   Illustration of Specific Valuation Date

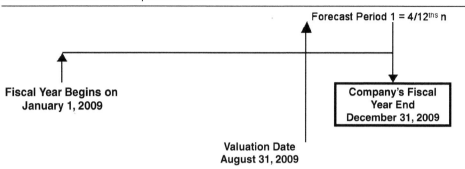

Assumptions:

NCF = $100,000
n = 1

Cash flows have been distributed equally over fiscal year 2009.

g = 7%
k_e = 20%

first-year projection deals *only* with 4/12ths of $100,000, or $33,333. If the second-year projection showed cash flows of $107,000, or a 7 percent increase, then at August 31, 2009, the discount period of the $107,000 is 4/12ths *plus* one year.

For example, let us assume that you are calculating the present value of the $100,000 and the $107,000 referenced above. Exhibit 5.12 presents the schematic view for year 2009. Exhibit 5.13 presents another view.

Exhibit 5.12   Schematic View for Year 2009 (End of Year Example)

1st Forecast Period (4/12ths of 2009)
Partial Period Factor = .3333

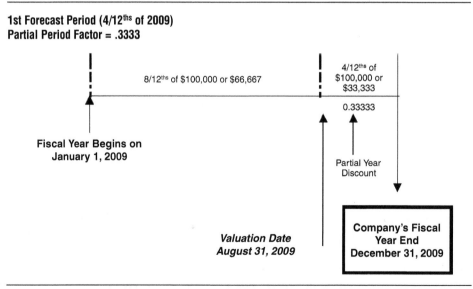

(*continued*)

Exhibit 5.12 *(Continued)*

2nd Forecast Period (2010)

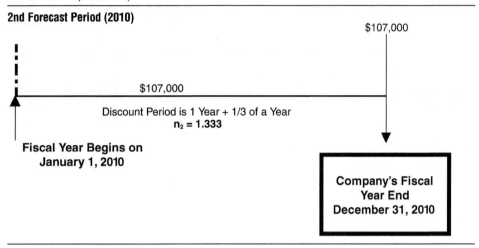

Multistage Explicit Periods

It is possible to have more than one explicit period in a DCF calculation. For example, a start-up might be expected to experience four years of substantial growth, followed by five years of high growth and another four years of growth at rates still in excess of the norm (see Exhibit 5.14). Some analysts also apply different discount rates to the different explicit growth periods to reflect different levels of risk, although this practice is not universally accepted. Most valuations do not include different discount rates.

The formula for multistage models is shown in Exhibit 5.15.

Exhibit 5.13 Another View (End of Year Example)

		Fiscal Year Ending December 31	
		2009	**2010**
NCF		100,000	107,000
Times: Partial Period Factor		0.3333	N/A
Times: Present Value Factor	$k_e = 20\%$	0.9410	0.7842
		↑	↑
		$ 31,364	$ 83,909
		+ 83,909	
Total Present Value at August 31, 2009		$115,273	

TERMINAL VALUE[9]

Definition and Overview

The final component of value in the DCF is the terminal value, sometimes referred to as the continuing value. The terminal value is the value of the business after the explicit or forecast period.

---

[9] "Terminal value" is generally synonymous with residual value, reversionary value, continuing value, and future value.

Exhibit 5.14 Multistage Explicit Periods

Time Periods	Year	Cash Flow to Equity	Average Growth Rates	Equity Discount Rate	End of Year PV Factor	Present Value of Cash Flows
	1	$ 10,000	N/A	26%	0.794	$ 7,940
1st Explicit	2	16,000	60%	26%	0.630	10,080
Period	3	22,400	40%	26%	0.500	11,200
	4	29,120	30%	26%	0.397	11,560
	5	34,944	20%	26%	0.315	11,010
2nd Explicit	6	41,933	20%	26%	0.250	10,480
Period	7	50,319	20%	26%	0.198	9,960
	8	60,383	20%	26%	0.157	9,480
	9	72,460	20%	26%	0.125	9,060
	10	81,155	12%	26%	0.099	8,030
3rd Explicit	11	90,894	12%	26%	0.079	7,180
Period	12	101,801	12%	26%	0.062	6,310
	13	114,017	12%	26%	0.050	5,700
Terminal Value		120,858	6%	26%	0.050	30,210
Total Value of Common "Equity"						$148,200

Exhibit 5.15 Formula for Multistage Models

$$PV = \sum_{i=1}^{n_1} \frac{NCF_0 (1 + g_1)^i}{(1 + k)^i}$$

$$+$$

$$\sum_{i=n_1+1}^{n_2} \frac{NCF_{n1} (1 + g_2)^i}{(1 + k)^i}$$

$$+$$

$$\frac{\dfrac{NCF_{n2} (1 + g_3)}{(k - g_3)}}{(1 + k)^{n2}}$$

Where:

k = the cost of capital
PV = present value
i = a measure of time (in this example the unit of measure is a year)
n_1 = the number of years in the first stage of growth
n_2 = the number of years in the second stage of growth
NCF_0 = cash flow in year 0
NCF_{n1} = cash flow in year n_1
NCF_{n2} = cash flow in year n_2
g_1 = growth rate from year 1 to year n_1
g_2 = growth rate from year $(n_1 + 1)$ to year n_2
g_3 = growth rate starting in year $(n_2 + 1)$

> The terminal value is critically important as it often represents a substantial portion of the total value of an entity.

The example in Exhibit 5.16 shows that the present value of the terminal value could actually be greater than the sum of the interim cash flows (explicit period) as well as the total value of the common equity. This is not an uncommon occurrence.

Exhibit 5.16 DCF Value (Invested Capital Method)

Year	Cash Flow to Invested Capital	Discount Rates to Invested Capital	PV Factor	Present Value of Cash Flows
1	$ 10,000	16%	.862	$ 8,621
2	10,600	16%	.743	7,878
3	11,236	16%	.641	7,198
4	11,910	16%	.552	6,578
5	12,625	16%	.476	6,011
Terminal Value	133,823		.476	63,715

Total Value of "Invested" Capital	100,000
Less: Fair Market Value of Interest-Bearing Debt	(40,000)
Fair Market Value of Equity	$60,000

Growth Rate = 6%

Calculation of the Terminal Value

In a DCF, the terminal value is the value of the company at the beginning of year n + 1. This value often is calculated by using the Gordon Growth Model (GGM), which is the same math that is used in the capitalization of cash flow method. It is as shown in Exhibit 5.17.

Exhibit 5.17 Gordon Growth Model (GGM) for Terminal Year

$$\underbrace{\frac{NCF_1}{(1+k)^1} + \frac{NCF_2}{(1+k)^2} + \cdots + \frac{NCF_n}{(1+k)^n}}_{\text{Present Value of NCFs during \textbf{Explicit Period}}} + \underbrace{\frac{NCF_n \times (1+g)}{(k-g)}}_{\substack{\text{Gordon Growth}^* \\ \text{Terminal Value}}}$$

Where:

NCF = Net cash flow commensurate with k, the required rate of return

k = Required rate of return or discount rate commensurate with the net cash flow

g = Long-term sustainable growth rate

n = Number of periods in the explicit forecast period

*This amount would also be present valued at $1/(1+k)^n$

Because making accurate forecasts of expected cash flows after the explicit period is difficult, the analyst usually assumes that cash flows (or proxies for cash flows) stabilize and can be capitalized into perpetuity. This is an average of future growth rates, not one expected to occur every year into perpetuity. In some years growth will be higher or lower, but the expectation is that future growth will average the long-term growth assumption. As stated above, the GGM and the CCF methods are the same. Therefore, the GGM is susceptible to the kind of common mistakes enumerated in "11 Common Mistakes" discussed earlier.

Other Terminal Value Calculations

The Gordon Growth Model is easy to use, considered theoretically sound, and universally applied. However, other terminal year models sometimes are used. We will look briefly at the Exit Multiple Model, the "H" Model, and the Value Driver Model.

Exit Multiple Model

One alternative method for determining the amount of the terminal value is to use a multiplier of an income parameter such as net income, earnings before interest and taxes (EBIT), earnings before interest, taxes, depreciation, and amortization (EBITDA), etc. This multiple, which is often used by investment bankers, is generally determined from guideline company market data and is referred to as an "exit multiple." It is applied to one of the income parameters at the end of the explicit period. Because it is sometimes difficult to support the use of a market approach within an income approach, this method is not used as much as the Gordon Growth Model. However, it can be used effectively as a reasonableness check on other models.

"H" Model[10]

The "H" Model assumes that growth during the terminal period starts at a higher rate and declines in a linear manner over a specified transition period toward a stable-growth rate that can be used into perpetuity. The "H" Model calculates a terminal value in two stages. The first stage quantifies value attributable to extraordinary growth of the company during the forecast period. The second stage assumes stable growth and uses a traditional Gordon Growth formula (see Exhibit 5.18).

Value Driver Model[11]

The value of continuing cash flows also can be calculated using the Value Driver Model. In the Gordon Growth Model (invested capital), the analyst must estimate continuing incremental investment (capital expenditures and working capital) in order to determine the continuing free cash flow of the company. The free (net) cash flow is then discounted at the weighted average cost of capital (WACC) less the

---

[10] For further information on the H Model see Aswath Damodaran, *Damodaran on Valuation: Security Analysis for Investment and Corporate Finance* (New York: John Wiley & Sons, 1994), p. 387.

[11] Tom Copeland, Tim Koller, and Jack Murrin, *Valuation: Measuring and Managing the Value of Companies,* 4th ed. (Hoboken, NJ: John Wiley & Sons, 2005), pp. 271–290.

Exhibit 5.18 H Model

Stable Growth Value	=	$\dfrac{CF_{(0)} \times (1 + g_s)}{k - g_s}$
	Plus	
Extraordinary Growth Value	=	$\dfrac{CF_{(0)} \times h \times (g_i - g_s)}{k - g_s}$

Where:

CF_0 = Cash Flow (Initial Cash Flow)
 k = Discount Rate
 h = Midpoint of high growth (transition period/2)
 g_i = Growth rate in the "initial high growth period"
 g_s = Growth rate in the "stable period"

growth rate to determine the value of the continuing operating cash flows of the entity. The Value Driver Model, on the other hand, discounts or capitalizes the adjusted net income of the company directly by the cost of capital. The analyst does not have to estimate the level of incremental investment of the entity. This method also eliminates the uncertainty surrounding the estimation of perpetual growth that is a major influence on the value using the Gordon Growth Model.

"For many companies in competitive industries, the return on net new investment can be expected to eventually converge to the cost of capital as all the excess profits are competed away. In other words, the return on incremental invested capital equals the cost of capital."[12] When this occurs, the resulting valuation model is known as the Value Driver (convergence) Model and is defined as:

$$\text{Continuing Value (CV)} = \frac{\text{NOPLAT}_{T+1}}{\text{WACC}}$$

Where:

NOPLAT = Net operating profit less applicable taxes
WACC = Weighted average cost of capital
T + 1 = First year after explicit forecast period

NOPLAT is often equal to debt-free net income, which is net income after tax plus tax-affected interest expense. It is also normalized EBIT times one minus the tax rate. When using the Value Driver Model, NOPLAT is divided by the cost of capital. By contrast, in the Gordon Growth Model, cash flow is divided by the company's cost of capital minus its perpetuity growth rate. The Value Driver

---

[12] Ibid., p. 284. See this work for further information on the Value Driver Model.

Model assumes that the company's return on capital and cost of capital are the same regardless of the growth rate. There is no subtraction of a long-term growth rate.

The growth term has disappeared from the equation. This does not mean that the nominal growth in NOPLAT will be zero. It means that growth will add nothing to value, because the return associated with growth just equals the cost of capital. This formula is sometimes interpreted as implying zero growth (not even with inflation), even though this is clearly not the case. The average return on invested capital moves toward the weighted average cost of capital (WACC) as new capital becomes a larger portion of the total capital base.[13]

The expanded value driver formula is:

$$\text{Continuing Value} = \frac{\text{NOPLAT}_{T+1}\,(1 - g\,/\,\text{ROIC})}{\text{WACC} - g}$$

Where:

NOPLAT_{T+1} = Normalized level of NOPLAT in the first year after explicit forecast period

g = Expected growth rate in NOPLAT in perpetuity

ROIC = Expected rate of return on net new investment

When ROIC is equal to the WACC, then the convergence formula, previously displayed, is the result.

In certain circumstances, the Value Driver Model can be used to test the implicit return on net new investment (ROIC) that is within the Gordon Growth Model. The following equations for continuing value illustrate this.

<table>
<tr><td align="center">Gordon Growth</td><td></td><td align="center">Value Driver</td></tr>
<tr><td>$CV = \dfrac{CF_1}{\text{WACC} - g}$</td><td>$CV =$</td><td>$\dfrac{\text{NOPLAT}_{T+1}\,(1 - g\,/\,\text{ROIC})}{\text{WACC} - g}$</td></tr>
<tr><td>$\dfrac{CF_1}{\text{WACC} - g}$</td><td>$=$</td><td>$\dfrac{\text{NOPLAT}_{T+1}\,(1 - g\,/\,\text{ROIC})}{\text{WACC} - g}$</td></tr>
<tr><td>CF_1</td><td>$=$</td><td>$\text{NOPLAT}_{T+1}\,(1 - g\,/\,\text{ROIC})$</td></tr>
<tr><td>ROIC</td><td>$=$</td><td>$\dfrac{g}{1 - \dfrac{CF_1}{\text{NOPLAT}_{T+1}}}$</td></tr>
</table>

This formula can assist the analyst in determining whether the assumed return on net new investment (capital) is above, below, or at the cost of capital.

---

[13] Ibid., pp. 284–285.

The Value Driver Model can result in a lower terminal value than the Gordon Growth Model.

Advanced Growth Model (AGM)

Mike Adhikari, owner of Illinois Corporate Investments, Inc., and Business ValueXpress, has developed the Advanced Growth Model (AGM), which is, in essence, an expansion of the GGM (Gordon Growth Model). The AGM will adjust the terminal value for changes in capital structure, whereas the GGM does not (see Exhibit 5.19). That is, the GGM assumes a constant debt to equity ratio into perpetuity, where the AGM will segregate the portion of interest-bearing debt (IBD) that is being amortized (over a certain [p] period of time) from the debt that will remain constant (i.e., a revolving line of credit). Said another way, AGM splits the enterprise's cash flow to debt holders from cash flow to equity holders (CF-Eq). As a result of these additional inputs, the terminal value will be lower than if determined by the GGM, other things being equal. The overstatements could be significant, as shown in Addendum 2 at the end of this chapter.

Exhibit 5.19 Advanced Growth Model

$$V_0 = \frac{Z_1 \cdot r_e}{r_e - g} \cdot \frac{R_1 - G}{kR_1 - r_eG + w_d(r_e - r_{dt})\left[1 + \frac{w_{td}}{p} \cdot (R_2 - n)\right]}$$

Z_1 = Unlevered FCF a.k.a. NCF_{ic}

$Z_1 = (1 - t)E_1 - \Delta W_1 - C_1 + t \cdot DA_1$

Where:

E_1 = EBITDA

ΔW_1 = Change in Working Capital

C_1 = Capital Expenditure

DA_1 = Depreciation and Amortization

g = the perpetual growth rate of Z1

t = corporate tax rate

r_e = cost of equity

r_d = cost of debt

r_{dt} = after-tax cost of debt

n = the period when the business is liquidated, or deemed to have been liquidated

p = the debt amortization period

$R_1 = (1 + r_e)^n$

$G = (1 + g)^n$

$R_2 = (R_1 - 1)/r_e$

k = Conventional after-tax WACC

w_{ad} = % amortized debt

p = Debt Amortization period

n = Holding period

Basic Variable Inputs

There are two critical assumptions to point out. First, the cost of equity (r_e) should be developed with the debt to equity ratio existing at the beginning of the terminal period. That is, consider the effect of levering an unlevered beta with the debt to equity ratio immediately following the last day of the discrete period. This will establish the buyer's IRR (internal rate of return) commensurate with risk associated with the debt to equity ratio. The IRR will then remain constant as required by the buyer. Second, the AGM, like the GGM, assumes that the value of the enterprise will increase annually by the constant growth factor, an assumption that is consistent with corporate finance theory when an enterprise's performance has stabilized.

It is important to note that the AGM also assumes that:

- Debt payments have priority over dividends.
- CF-Eq, which is the excess cash flow to equity after debt service and after funding working capital and capital expenditure, is distributed.
- EBITDA, depreciation, capital expenditures, and increases in working capital are a fixed percentage of sales.
- The debt service will be serviced by the business or, in the event of a shortfall, the owners.
- The enterprise is sold or revalued at the end of the holding period (n), which needs to be less than the debt amortization period (p).

Additional assumptions by the AGM, which are found in the GGM as well, are that the growth, the tax rate, and the cost of debt will remain fixed into perpetuity. The AGM, like the GGM, is not limited to computing the terminal value, as both could be the valuation method given the fact patterns. The AGM could be used in place of the CCF method where IBD exists. Mr. Adhikari recommends the AGM when a business would meet the criteria for the CCF method but for the existence of debt. The AGM will adjust value to account for amortization of IBD.

ValTip

> The Advanced Growth Model is shown here for informational purposes only. Currently, it does not have widespread use in the valuation community.

CAPITALIZED CASH FLOW METHOD (REVISITED)

The capitalized cash flow method of the income approach is an abbreviated version of the discounted cash flow method where growth (g) and the discount rate (k) are both assumed to remain constant into perpetuity.

Its formula is:

$$\frac{NCF_1}{(k - g)}$$

Where:

NCF_1 = Net cash flow in year 1
   k = Discount rate
   g = Growth rate into perpetuity

     Other than this constancy of growth and risk, the same theory and assumptions hold true for the CCF method as for the DCF method with regard to the economic benefit stream, measurement of risk, the effects of growth, and so forth. See the beginning of this chapter for additional details.

Relationship of Discounted Cash Flow Method to Capitalized Cash Flow Method

The CCF method formula above works if the numerator, that is, the net cash flow, at the end of the first year divided by the capitalization rate $(k - g)$ in the Gordon Growth Model equals the product of the DCF model with constant growth. Assume a constant growth rate of 6 percent and initial cash flow of \$10,000. The "proof" would look something like Exhibit 5.20.

     Since the CCF method is an abbreviated form of the DCF method, the theory that assets are worth the present value of their future economic income streams holds true with the CCF method. Moreover, as stated in the DCF method section, the economic income stream is a generalized term for any type of economic income (E), including but not necessarily limited to various types of cash flows, dividends, net income, earnings before taxes, and so on. Obviously, the more assured one is of receiving that future cash flow, the higher the value. The detail on determining the appropriate cash flow to be capitalized is discussed elsewhere in this chapter.

     The present value factor for the denominator in the CCF method is called a capitalization rate and is made up of two components, the discount rate (k) and the long-term sustainable growth rate (g).

Where:

k = Discount rate commensurate with the future economic income
g = Long-term sustainable growth rate

     The future economic benefit selected for the CCF model is the expected cash flow (or its equivalent) in the period following the valuation date. For example, if CF is \$100,000 and the valuation date is December 31, 2009, then CF_1 is expected on December 31, 2010, as shown in Exhibit 5.21.

EXCESS CASH FLOW METHOD

History of the Method

The excess cash flow method, referred to in many texts as the "excess earnings method," the "Treasury method," and the "formula method," is a blend of the asset and income approaches. It was introduced to estimate the intangible value of breweries and distilleries lost as a result of Prohibition in the 1920s. This method first appeared in a 1920 publication by the Treasury Department, *Appeals and Review*

Exhibit 5.20   Relationship of DCF to CCF

END of

Period 1	$\dfrac{NCF_1}{(1 + k)^1}$	$=$	$\dfrac{\$10,000 (1 + \mathbf{6}\%)}{(1 + .26)^1}$	$=$	$\dfrac{\$10,600}{1.2600}$	$=$	$\$8,413$
	$+$		$+$		$+$		$+$
Period 2	$\dfrac{NCF_2}{(1 + k)^2}$	$=$	$\dfrac{\$10,600 (1 + \mathbf{6}\%)}{(1 + .26)^2}$	$=$	$\dfrac{\$11,236}{1.5876}$	$=$	$\$7,077$
	$+$		$+$		$+$		$+$
Period 3	$\dfrac{NCF_3}{(1 + k)^3}$	$=$	$\dfrac{\$11,236 (1 + \mathbf{6}\%)}{(1 + .26)^3}$	$=$	$\dfrac{\$11,910}{2.0004}$	$=$	$\$5,954$
	$+$		$+$		$+$		$+$
Period 4	$\dfrac{NCF_4}{(1 + k)^4}$	$=$	$\dfrac{\$11,910 (1 + \mathbf{6}\%)}{(1 + .26)^4}$	$=$	$\dfrac{\$12,625}{2.5205}$	$=$	$\$5,009$
	$+$		$+$		$+$		$+$
Period 5	$\dfrac{NCF_5}{(1 + k)^5}$	$=$	$\dfrac{\$12,625 (1 + \mathbf{6}\%)}{(1 + .26)^5}$	$=$	$\dfrac{\$13,382}{3.1758}$	$=$	$\$4,214$
	$+$		$+$		$+$		$+$

Terminal Value

$$\dfrac{\dfrac{NCF_5 (1 + g)}{(k - g)}}{(1 + k)^5} = \dfrac{\dfrac{\$13,382 (1 + \mathbf{6}\%)}{(.26 - \mathbf{.06})}}{(1 + .26)^5} = \dfrac{\dfrac{\$14,185}{0.20}}{3.1758} = \$22,333$$

The Sum of the Present Values of Expected Future Cash Flows Using the Gordon Growth Model to Calculate the Terminal Value $\$53,000$

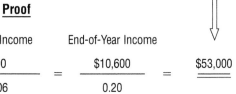

Proof

End-of-Year Income		End-of-Year Income		End-of-Year Income		
$\dfrac{\$10,000 (1 + 6\%)}{(k - g)}$	$=$	$\dfrac{\$10,600}{.26 - .06}$	$=$	$\dfrac{\$10,600}{0.20}$	$=$	$\$53,000$
Capitalization Rate		Capitalization Rate		Capitalization Rate		

Exhibit 5.21 Expected Cash Flow

$100,000

12/31/09
Valuation Date

Time Cash Flow is received
12/31/10

Memorandum Number 34 (ARM 34), but was later updated and restated in Revenue Ruling 68-609.

Over the years, this method has become popular in valuing businesses for divorce cases, especially in jurisdictions where goodwill is considered a nonmarital asset and is therefore segregated. In addition, this method is sometimes used for corporate C to S conversions, financial reporting and other scenarios where there is a need to isolate certain intangible assets. Its popularity was somewhat surprising, however, in light of the very first sentence of Revenue Ruling 68-609: "The 'formula' approach may be used in determining the fair market value of intangible assets of a business *only if there is no better basis available for making the determination*" (emphasis added).

Revenue Ruling 68-609 and ARM 34 discuss using the ECF to estimate the value of the intangible assets of a business rather than the total business assets. The ruling is often misread. Of particular concern is the ruling's reference to various percentage returns. The ruling states:

> A percentage return on the average annual value of the tangible assets used in a business is determined, using a period of years (preferably not less than five) immediately prior to the valuation date. The amount of the percentage return on tangible assets, thus determined, is deducted from the average earnings of the business for such period and the remainder, if any, is considered to be the amount of the average annual earnings from the intangible assets of the business for the period. This amount (considered as the average annual earnings from intangibles), capitalized at a percentage of, say, 15 to 20 percent, is the value of the intangible assets of the business determined under the "formula" approach.
>
> The percentage of return on the average annual value of the tangible assets used should be the percentage prevailing in the industry involved at the date of valuation, or (when the industry percentage is not available) a percentage of 8 to 10 percent may be used.
>
> The 8 percent rate of return and the 15 percent rate of capitalization are applied to tangibles and intangibles, respectively, of businesses with a small risk factor and stable and regular earnings; the 10 percent rate of return and 20 percent rate of capitalization are applied to businesses in which the hazards of business are relatively high.
>
> The above rates are used as examples and are not appropriate in all cases. In applying the "formula" approach, the average earnings period and the capitalization rates are dependent upon the facts pertinent thereto in each case.

The ruling is very clear, however, that these rates are merely suggested rates and should not be used without one's own analysis of risk/reward.

The ECF method can be prepared using either equity or invested capital returns and cash flows. The procedures, using an invested capital method, are shown in Exhibit 5.22.

Exhibit 5.22 Procedures for ECF

Step No.	Procedure
1	Determine the fair market value of the "net tangible assets."
2	Develop normalized cash flows.
3	Determine an appropriate return (WACC) for the net tangible assets.
4	Determine the "normalized" cash flows attributable to "net tangible asset" values.
5	Subtract cash flows attributable to net tangible assets from total cash flows to determine cash flows attributable to intangible assets.
6	Determine an appropriate rate of return for intangible asset(s).
7	Determine the fair market value of the intangible asset(s) by capitalizing the cash flows attributable to the intangible asset(s) by an appropriate capitalization rate determined in step 6.
8	Add the fair market value of the net tangible assets to the FMV of the intangible assets.
9	Subtract any interest-bearing debt to arrive at a value conclusion for equity.
10	Observe the overall capitalization rate for reasonableness.

Returns—Discount or Capitalization?

The difficulty of the ECF method is exacerbated by the inconsistent use of discount and capitalization rates. Although some analysts would disagree, it is our view that the return on tangible assets is, indeed, a discount rate. This appears to be the intent of the original Revenue Ruling 68–609 and is certainly consistent with the IPR&D Task Force of the AICPA, which states that the "*after-tax cash flows of each intangible asset are charged after-tax amounts representing a return of and a return on these contributory assets based on the fair value of such contributory assets.*"[14] The intangible rates of return, again consistent with the AICPA Task Force, are a rate over the life of the asset, including perpetuity, and, accordingly, should represent a capitalization rate that incorporates such growth.

An example of the steps for a control value, mathematically, would look like Exhibit 5.23.

This method actually blends two rates of return, which is fairly similar to our WACC calculation, where the return on debt is blended with the rate of return on

---

[14] AICPA Practice Aid Series, *Assets Acquired in a Business Combination to Be Used in Research and Development Activities: A Focus on Software, Electronic Devices, and Pharmaceutical Industries,* Copyright © 2001 by the American Institute of Certified Public Accountants, Inc., New York, NY 10036-8775, p. 85, 5.3.55.

Exhibit 5.23 Mathematical Steps for ECF

1. Determine the net tangible asset value. $40,000,000

   Careful determination of the fair market value of the tangible assets (less operating liabilities) →

2. Determine normalized cash flows to invested capital.   Normalized Cash Flows $10,500,000

   Adjustments would include those relating to normalizing annual earnings and control

4. Determine the cash flows attributable to the net tangible asset value.   (6,400,000)

   $40,000,000 × 16% =   Cash Flows Attributable to Net Tangible Assets

3. *Careful determination of an appropriate rate of return of the net tangible assets based upon relative risk factors.* ↙

5. Determine the cash flows in excess of the cash flows attributable to the net tangible assets (determined above). =   Excess Cash Flows Attributable to the Intangible Asset(s) → $ 4,100,000

   Subtract the cash flows attributable to the net tangible assets from the total normalized cash flows

7. Using the capitalized cash flow method, determine the fair market value of the intangible asset(s) by dividing the excess cash flows by a capitalization rate commensurate with the intangible asset(s).

$$\frac{4,100,000}{30\%} = \quad \$13,666,667$$

6. *Careful determination of an appropriate rate of return of the net intangible assets based on relative risk factors* ↙

8. Add back the value of the net tangible assets.   40,000,000

                         Value of Invested Capital   53,666,667

9. Deduct long-term debt.   (10,000,000)

                         Value of Equity Capital $43,666,667

equity. In our example, the "blended rate" can be determined by simply dividing the total "nominal cash flows" by the total indicated value, or $10,500,000/$53,646,400 = 19.6 percent. This 19.6 percent appears fairly reasonable at a cursory glance. However, if the result was 10 percent or 40 percent, the reasonableness of the result would be subject to question. All in all, the ECF method can be used as a "sanity test."

The following procedures are typically followed in the application of the ECF method.

Step 1. Determine the Fair Market Value of Net Tangible Assets

IRS Private Letter Ruling 79-05013 states that Rev. Rul. 68-609 addresses the determination of fair market value of intangible assets by the formula approach, and for this reason it is proper that all terms used in the formula be consistent. The formula uses value in terms of fair market value, so the term "value of the tangible assets used in a business," in the formula, should be in terms of fair market values, as defined in Rev. Rul. 59-60. Most analysts use the fair market value standard of value as well as the going-concern premise for the ECF method.

What are "net tangible assets"? There seems to be a general consensus that net tangible assets are composed of all current assets plus plant, property, and equipment plus other operating assets less current liabilities (debt-free for invested capital method). It can also be net equity or net invested capital (depending on the model used) without intangible assets. What is important is to match the rate of return to the selected definition of net tangible assets.

Property (i.e., real estate) also may be segregated from tangible assets at the outset and added back in separately later on. Rent expense can be substituted for real estate-related expenses.

The GAAP book values of cash, receivables, and, to some extent, inventories can serve as good proxies for their respective fair market values. Real estate, plant, and equipment may require independent appraisals since their book values are usually not equivalent to FMV. The need for independent appraisals requires additional time, money, and effort, making it tempting to use "book values." However, since the book values of many operating assets are rarely equivalent to their fair market values, any valuation that uses only book values may not be appropriate.

Normally, all intangible assets are excluded from "net tangible assets." However, some analysts include goodwill or other specific identifiable intangible assets acquired in prior purchases. Including these assets is problematic for two reasons:

1. Like all assets, intangibles must be stated at their respective fair market values, which usually is not an easy task.
2. The excess cash flow method uses a rate of return for net tangible assets commensurate with the particular bundle of tangible assets in the subject company's industry. The intangible assets may require a significantly different rate of return than the return on the tangible assets.

Step 2. Develop "Normalized" Cash Flow

Many analysts agree that "cash flow" is the best proxy for a company's benefit stream. However, other benefit streams, such as net income, are often used. The analyst must remain cognizant of the need to properly match the capitalization rates with the benefit streams selected.

Previous sections have discussed adjustments required to normalize cash flows. Whether to include "control"-related adjustments generally depends on whether a minority or controlling interest is being valued. As presented here, the excess cash flows method yields a control value. Therefore, control-related adjustments as well as the other normalizing adjustments must be made to the benefit stream used in the excess cash flow method. These adjustments include normalization of owner's compensation.

ValTip

> If the control excess cash flow method is used and a minority value is the interest that is being valued, if appropriate, a discount for lack of control may be determined and applied.

The debate over whether S corporation cash flows should be adjusted for income taxes due to S corporation status is discussed in Chapters 4 and 12. As with all valuation methods, any "nonoperating" assets and liabilities must be identified and segregated from the company's operating assets.

Step 3. Determine an Appropriate Blended Rate for Net Tangible Assets

There is general consensus that the rate of return for net tangible assets is based on the company's bundle of assets. The company's ability to borrow against this bundle, its cost of debt, and its cost of equity are the other factors used in developing a rate of return on net tangible assets. Although some analysts may look at historical industry rates of return, these rates may not be a good representation of what will occur in the future. It is preferable, particularly for smaller companies, to build up a rate of return using the risk-free rate, large- and small-company equity risk premiums, and the company's specific risk factors. See Chapter 6.

ValTip

> Assets that are normally considered operating assets may in reality be nonoperating. For example, excess cash and cash equivalents are actually nonoperating assets and can be isolated from the operating assets during normalization.

The debt portion of the blended rate is calculated by using those portions of the FMV of net tangible assets against which a lender would lend money. What cannot be financed with debt is financed with equity, as shown in Exhibit 5.24.

Exhibit 5.24   Rate for Net Tangible Assets (Illustration Only)

Asset Mix	Asset Values	Financing Percentage	Lending Amount	Estimated Interest Rate
Cash and cash equivalents	$ 4,000,000	0%*	$ —	—
Receivables	12,000,000	70%	8,400,000	—
Inventories	13,000,000	50%	6,500,000	—
Prepaids	250,000	0%	—	—
Equipment, fixtures, etc.	23,000,000	40%	9,200,000	—
	$52,250,000		**$24,100,000**	9.0%
Current liabilities	(12,250,000)	0%	—	NA
(Non-Interest-Bearing				
Net Tangible Assets)	**$40,000,000**			

Assumptions	Before Tax		After Tax	
Company's Borrowing Rate	9.0%	× (1−35%)	5.9%	
(Weighted Average)				
Company's Return on Equity			25.0%	
Company's Tax Rate	35.0%			

Calculation of Rate of Return

Debt Portion

$$\frac{\$24,100,000}{\$52,250,000} \quad \times \quad 5.9\% \quad = \quad 2.7\%$$

Equity Portion

$$\frac{\$28,150,000}{\$52,250,000} \quad \times \quad 25.0\% \quad = \quad 13.5\%$$

Weighted average required rate of return on net tangible assets	16.2%
Rounded	16%

*Assumes unrestricted and distributable

Both the borrowing rate of interest and the financing percentages shown in Exhibit 5.24 will vary from company to company as well as from asset to asset. For example, 40 percent financing percentage of equipment, fixtures, etc., is a composite of varying financing percentages of each asset. Also, the financing percentage of real estate may be as high as 75 to 80 percent, while used office furniture may be as low as 0 to 20 percent. The borrowing rate of interest of 9 percent is a composite as well. Lenders charge varying interest rates depending upon the level of security of the particular asset.

The debt portion calculated in Exhibit 5.24, therefore, is hypothetical and is not intended to be the actual interest-bearing debt of the company at the date of valuation. However, the composite rate of interest, as weighted, should approximate the company's borrowing capabilities, given its overall creditworthiness.

ValTip

The company's lending rates may be different if personal guarantees are required from the company's owners/officers and depending on the types of assets.

Step 4. Determine the Normalized Cash Flows Attributable to Net Tangible Assets (See Exhibit 5.25)

The cash flows attributable to net tangible assets would be equal to the sum of the FMVs of those assets times the blended rate for the bundle of assets.

Exhibit 5.25   Step 4

Determine the cash flows attributable to the net tangible asset value.	$40,000,000 × 16% =	(6,400,000)	

Careful determination of an appropriate rate of return of the net tangible assets based on relative risk factors ——————→ *Cash Flows Attributable to Net Tangible Assets*

ValTip

Whatever rate of return is used for goodwill, the aggregate return on all net assets should approximate the weighted average cost of invested capital for the entity.

Step 5. Subtract Cash Flows Attributable to Net Tangible Assets from Total Cash Flows to Determine Cash Flows Attributable to Intangible Assets (See Exhibit 5.26)

Exhibit 5.26   Step 5

Determine normalized cash flows to invested capital. ——————→ Normalized Cash Flows $10,500,000

Adjustments would include those relating to normalizing annual earnings and control

Determine the cash flows attributable to the net tangible asset value. $40,000,000 × 16% = (6,400,000)

Careful determination of an appropriate rate of return of the net tangible assets based on relative risk factors —————— Cash Flows Attributable to Net Tangible Assets

Determine the cash flows in excess of the cash flows attributable to the net tangible assets (determined above). = Excess Cash Flows Attributable to Intangible Assets ——————→ $ 4,100,000

Step 6. Determine an Appropriate Rate of Return for Intangible Assets (See Exhibit 5.27)

To better understand developing the required rate of return on intangible assets, the model shown in Exhibit 5.27 was developed.

Exhibit 5.27 Step 6

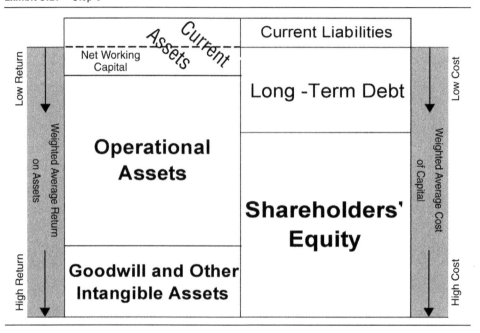

As this model shows, the sum of the individual weighted average returns on assets (including net working capital) equals the weighted average cost of capital for the entity. The more liquid and secure the assets, the lower the return that is required. Therefore, goodwill and other intangibles require higher returns.

Step 7. Determine the Fair Market Value of the Intangible Assets by Capitalizing the Cash Flows Attributable to Them by an Appropriate Capitalization Rate (See Exhibit 5.28)

Exhibit 5.28 Step 7

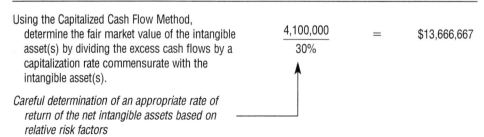

Using the Capitalized Cash Flow Method, determine the fair market value of the intangible asset(s) by dividing the excess cash flows by a capitalization rate commensurate with the intangible asset(s).

$$\frac{4,100,000}{30\%} = \$13,666,667$$

Careful determination of an appropriate rate of return of the net intangible assets based on relative risk factors

Note: The capitalization rate of 30% was estimated for purposes of example presentation. Most analysts would use some adaptation of a build-up method, increasing the subjective risk premium to account for the risk on the intangible assets (see Chapter 21).

Step 8. Add Back the Fair Market Value of the Net Tangible Assets (See Exhibit 5.29)

Exhibit 5.29 Step 8

Using the Capitalized Cash Flow Method, determine the fair market value of the intangible asset(s) by dividing the excess cash flows by a capitalization rate commensurate with the intangible asset(s).	$\dfrac{4{,}100{,}000}{30\%}$	=	$13,666,667
Careful determination of an appropriate rate of return of the net intangible assets based on relative risk factors			
Add back the value of the net tangible assets.			40,000,000
	Value of Invested Capital		53,666,667

Step 9. Subtract Any Interest-Bearing Debt (See Exhibit 5.30)

Exhibit 5.30 Step 9

	Value of Invested Capital	53,666,667
Deduct Interest-Bearing Debt		(10,000,000)
	Value of Equity Capital	$43,666,667

Step 10. Reasonableness Test

$$\frac{\$10{,}500{,}000}{\$53{,}666{,}667} = 19.6\%$$

As can be seen from the calculation, the overall rate of return is 19.6 percent. This appears to be a reasonable capitalization rate on invested capital.

Conclusion

The excess cash flow method is often misused and misunderstood. Analysts must be sure that other methodologies would not be more appropriate. However, in many state courts, this method traditionally is widely accepted. Such acceptance may be a significant consideration in many valuations.

CONCLUSION

The income approach is probably the most widely recognized and utilized approach to valuing an entity. This chapter has discussed in detail the various methodologies that make up this approach. Anyone performing business valuations must have a thorough understanding of the complexities of this approach. However, these complexities mark the approach's flexibility. The income approach offers the analyst the opportunity to customize the calculations to the subject entity in many ways. Due to this flexibility, the income approach is often one of the best approaches to valuing an entity or ownership interest.

ADDENDUM 1—APPLICATION OF THE DIRECT EQUITY METHOD (DEM) AND THE INVESTED CAPITAL METHOD (ICM)

Overview

Applying each method depends upon the facts and circumstances of each valuation engagement. However, misapplication can significantly understate or overstate value. This invariably happens when a company has a relatively healthy level of interest-bearing debt (IBD), but the analyst does not reflect that in the company's overall cost of debt, which generally is far lower than its cost of equity. Simply put, equity holders require a much greater return than IBD holders and by *blending* the higher equity cost of capital with lower IBD cost of capital, the total company's invested value is higher. Looking left to right, Exhibit 5.31 is an example that demonstrates that as the percentage of interest-bearing debt rises, the overall equity risk—that is, the cost of equity—slowly rises. However, as the ratio of interest-bearing debt rises to 50 to 60 percent or more, the equity risk accelerates rapidly.

Exhibit 5.31   Ratios of Debt and Equity to Total Invested Capital and Equity Risk

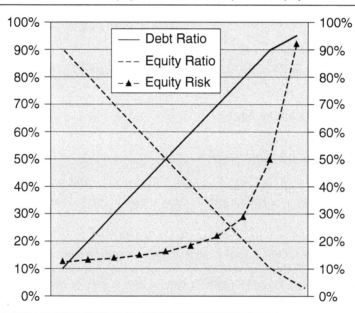

However, where debt is below or near an optimum ratio to total capital, the company's weighted average cost of capital (WACC—see Chapter 6) declines and the company's overall FMV of invested capital increases.

Exhibits 5.32A, B, C, and D show the application of DEM and ICM. These exhibits are intended to illustrate:

- The calculation of the cash flows to either equity or invested capital methods
- The calculation of the discount rate to either *cash flows to equity* or *cash flows to invested capital* (utilizing the build-up method discussed in detail in Chapter 6)

Exhibit 5.32A Presentation of Both Direct Equity and Invested Capital Methods with Variance for ABC Corp.

ABC Corp.

Line #		Direct Equity Method (DEM)		Invested Capital Method (ICM)		Item	Explanation
		% of Value	Amounts	% of Value	Amounts		
	Value Calculations						
1 a	Cash Flows to Equity		$ 1,388,000			1 a	Net Cash Flow to Equity
1 b	Cash Flows to Invested Capital (IC)				$ 1,580,000	1 b	Net Cash Flow to Invested Capital
2	Capitalization Rate		16.0%		11.4%	2	Capitalization Rate (see line 39)
3	Value of Invested Capital (IC)	100.0%	12,675,000	100.0%	13,919,969	3	Line 1 divided by line 2-ICM; line 1 divided by line 2 (see 5a) plus line 4-DEM
4	Value of Interest-Bearing Debt (IBD)	-31.6%	(4,000,000)	-28.7%	(4,000,000)	4	Line 22
5 a	Value of Equity	68.4%	$ 8,675,000	71.3%	$ 9,919,969	5 a	DEM = line 1 divided by line 2
5 b					$1,244,969	5 b	ICM = line 3 minus line 4; Variance in value of equity
	Cost of Equity Capital (Build-Up Method) (See Chapter 6)						
6	Safe rate		5.0%		5.0%	6	Fact
7	Large equity risk premium		7.0%		7.0%	7	Fact
8	Small equity risk premium		6.0%		6.0%	8	Fact
9	Subjective risk premium		3.0%		3.0%	9	Fact
10	Total equity rate		21.0%		21.0%	10	Lines 6, 7, 8, 9
	Cost of Interest-Bearing Debt (IBD)			Rate			
11	After-Tax Interest			8.0%	*Less taxes*	11	Cost of interest-bearing debt is the overall weighted cost of the company's interest, reduced by the company's effective tax rate.
	WACC			Rate	%		
12	Cost of Debt (IBD)			4.8% X	28.7% = 1.4%	12	Cost of debt (after tax), line 11, weighted in the proportion that the total *market* value of debt, line 4, bears to total *market* value of capital, line 3
13	Cost of Equity			21.0% X	71.3% = 15.0%	13	Cost of equity, line 10, weighted in the proportion that that total *market* value of equity, line 5, bears to the total *market* value of capital, line 3
14					16.4%	14	Total Weighted Average Cost of Capital
	WACC (Capitalization Rate)						
14	Cost of Capital		21.0%		16.4%	14	k = Discount rate
15	Growth rate		-5.0%		-5.0%	15	g = Assumed long-term sustainable growth rate
16	Capitalization Rate		16.0%		11.4%	16	Capitalization Rate (k – g)

Exhibit 5.32B Presentation of Financial Information for ABC Corp.

Financial Information — ABC Corp.

Balance Sheet

		Amount	Line #	Explanation
Assets				
Current Assets		$ 2,000,000	17	Fact
PP&E		10,000,000	18	Fact
Total Assets		$ 12,000,000	19	Add lines 17 and 18
Liabilities & Equity			20	
Current Liabilities		$ 3,000,000	21	Fact
Interest-Bearing Debt @	8%	4,000,000	22	Fact
Total Liabilities		7,000,000	23	Add lines 21 and 22
Shareholders' Equity		5,000,000	24	Fact
Total Liabilities and Equity		$ 12,000,000	25	Add lines 23 and 24

Income Statement

		Equity	Invested Capital	Line #	Explanation
Revenues		$ 11,000,000	$ 11,000,000	26	Operating revenues
Operating expenses		(8,000,000)	(8,000,000)	27	All expenses other than interest and depreciation
EBITDA		3,000,000	3,000,000	28	Line 26 minus line 27
Depreciation and amortization (D&A)		(200,000)	(200,000)	29	Depreciation
EBIT		2,800,000	2,800,000	30	Earnings before interest and taxes (line 28 minus line 29)
Interest		(320,000)	(320,000)	31	Interest-bearing debt ($4,000,000 times 8%)
EBT		2,480,000	2,480,000	32	Earnings before taxes (line 30 minus 31)
Income taxes — Effective Rate 40%		(992,000)	(992,000)	33	EBT times income tax rate (federal and state)
Net income		1,488,000	1,488,000	34	Line 32 minus line 33
Interest X (1-tax rate)		NA	192,000	35	Add back interest – net of taxes on interest ($320,000 times (1 – 40%))
Debt-free net income		1,488,000	1,680,000	36	Line 14 plus line 15 (Traditionally referred to as debt-free net income [DFNI])
Add: Noncash items — D&A		200,000	200,000	37	Add back noncash items (generally D&A)
Debt-free cash flow		1,688,000	1,880,000	38	Line 16 plus line 17 (Traditionally referred to as debt-free cash flow [DFCF])
Subtract: Capital expenditures		(200,000)	(200,000)	39	Subtract estimated annual capital expenditures (Often equal to depreciation).
Subtract: Increases in working capital		(100,000)	(100,000)	40	Subtract cash necessary to fund annual increases in working capital
Net cash flow to equity/invested capital		$ 1,388,000	$ 1,580,000	41	Line 18 minus lines 19 and 20

Exhibit 5.32C Presentation of the Iteration Process Required to Equalize Weighted Average Cost of Capital with Ending Ratios of Debt and Equity to Total Invested Capital of ABC Corp.

ABC Corp.		Book Value		Iteration #1				Iteration #2				Iteration 3				Iteration #4			
Item		% of Value	Amounts	% of Value			Amounts	% of Value			Amounts	% of Value			Amounts	% of Value			Amounts
	Value Calculations																		
1	Cash Flows to Invested Capital (IC)					$	1,580,000			$	1,580,000			$	1,580,000			$	1,580,000
2	Capitalization Rate						9.5%				12.0%				11.1%				11.4%
3	Value of Invested Capital (IC)	100.0%	9,000,000	100.0%			16,596,639	100.0%			13,221,757	100.0%			14,183,124	100.0%			13,919,969
4	Value of Interest-Bearing Debt (IBD)	**44.4%**	(4,000,000)	**24.1%**			(4,000,000)	**30.3%**			(4,000,000)	**28.2%**			(4,000,000)	**28.7%**			(4,000,000)
5	Value of Equity	55.6%	$ 5,000,000	75.9%		$	12,596,639	69.7%		$	9,221,757	71.8%		$	10,183,124	71.3%		$	9,919,969
	Cost of Equity Capital (Build-Up Method) (see Chapter 6)																		
6	Safe rate						5.0%				5.0%				5.0%				5.0%
7	Large equity risk premium			After 1st Iter.		24.1%	7.0%	After 2nd Iter.		30.3%	7.0%	After 3rd Iter.		28.2%	7.0%	After 4th Iter.		28.7%	7.0%
8	Small equity risk premium			1st Estimate		40.0%	6.0%	2nd Estimate		25.0%	6.0%	3rd Estimate		30.0%	6.0%	Final Estimate		28.7%	6.0%
9	Subjective risk premium			Variance		-15.9%	3.0%	Variance		5.3%	3.0%	Variance		-1.8%	3.0%	Variance		0.0%	3.0%
10	Total equity rate						21.0%				21.0%				21.0%				21.0%
	Cost of Interest-Bearing Debt			Rate				Rate				Rate				Rate			
11	After-tax Interest			8.0%	*Less taxes*		4.8%	8.0%	*Less taxes*		4.8%	8.0%	*Less taxes*		4.8%	8.0%	*Less taxes*		4.8%
	WACC			Rate		%	WACC	Rate		%	WACC	Rate		%	WACC	Rate		%	WACC
						1st Estimate				2nd Estimate				3rd Estimate				Final Estimate	
12	Cost of Debt			4.8%	X	**40.0%**	1.9%	4.8%	X	**25.0%**	1.2%	4.8%	X	**30.0%**	1.4%	4.8%	X	**28.7%**	1.4%
13	Cost of Equity			21.0%	X	60.0%	12.6%	21.0%	X	75.0%	15.8%	21.0%	X	70.0%	14.7%	21.0%	X	71.3%	15.0%
14							14.5%				17.0%				16.1%				16.4%
	WACC (Capitalization Rate)																		
14	Cost of Capital						14.5%				17.0%				16.1%				16.4%
15	Growth Rate						-5.0%				-5.0%				-5.0%				-5.0%
16	Capitalization Rate						9.5%				12.0%				11.1%				11.4%

Exhibit 5.32D Iteration Process Required for ICM-MCAPM

Value Calculations

	Book Value % of Value	Book Value Amounts	Iteration #1 % of Value	Iteration #1 Amounts	Iteration #2 % of Value	Iteration #2 Amounts	Iteration 3 % of Value	Iteration 3 Amounts	Iteration #4 % of Value	Iteration #4 Amounts
Cash Flows to Invested Capital (IC)				1,580,000		1,580,000		1,580,000		1,580,000
Capitalization Rate				10.5%		12.0%		11.6%		11.6%
Value of Invested Capital (IC)	100.0%	9,000,000	100.0%	15,014,444	100.0%	13,158,991	100.0%	13,607,411	100.0%	13,642,277
Value of Interest-Bearing Debt (IBD)	44.4%	(4,000,000)	26.6%	(4,000,000)	30.4%	(4,000,000)	29.4%	(4,000,000)	29.3%	(4,000,000)
Value of Equity	55.6%	5,000,000	73.4%	11,014,444	69.6%	9,158,991	70.6%	9,607,411	70.7%	9,642,277

Cost of Equity Capital (Build-up Method) (see Chapter 6)

	Iteration #1	Iteration #2	Iteration 3	Iteration #4
Safe rate	5.0%	5.0%	5.0%	5.0%
Large equity risk premium times "RE-Levered" Beta	$7.0\% \times 1.596 = 11.2\%$	$7.0\% \times 1.368 = 9.6\%$	$7.0\% \times 1.419 = 9.9\%$	$7.0\% \times 1.423 = 10.0\%$
(subtotal)	16.2%	14.6%	14.9%	15.0%
Small equity risk premium (beta adjusted)	3.5%	3.5%	3.5%	3.5%
Subjective risk premium	3.0%	3.0%	3.0%	3.0%
Total equity rate	22.7%	21.1%	21.4%	21.5%

Estimate boxes:
- Iteration #1 — After 1st Iter. / 1st Estimate: 26.6% | 40.0% | Variance −13.4%
- Iteration #2 — After 2nd Iter. / 2nd Estimate: 30.4% | 25.0% | Variance 5.4%
- Iteration 3 — After 3rd Iter. / 3rd Estimate: 29.4% | 29.0% | Variance 0.4%
- Iteration #4 — After 3rd Iter. / Final Estimate: 29.3% | 29.3% | Variance 0.0%

Cost of Interest-bearing Debt

	Iteration #1	Iteration #2	Iteration 3	Iteration #4
After-tax Interest (Rate 8.0%, Less taxes → WACC)	4.8%	4.8%	4.8%	4.8%

WACC

	Rate	%	WACC
Iteration #1 — Cost of Debt	4.8%	40.0%	1.9%
Iteration #1 — Cost of Equity	22.7%	60.0%	13.6%
Iteration #2 — Cost of Debt	4.8%	25.0%	1.2%
Iteration #2 — Cost of Equity	21.1%	75.0%	15.8%
Iteration 3 — Cost of Debt	4.8%	29.0%	1.4%
Iteration 3 — Cost of Equity	21.4%	71.0%	15.2%
Iteration #4 — Cost of Debt	4.8%	29.3%	1.4%
Iteration #4 — Cost of Equity	21.5%	70.7%	15.2%

Estimate weights: 1st Estimate 40.0% / 60.0%; 2nd Estimate 25.0% / 75.0%; 3rd Estimate 29.0% / 71.0%; Final Estimate 29.3% / 70.7%

WACC (Capitalization Rate)

	Iteration #1	Iteration #2	Iteration 3	Iteration #4
Cost of Capital	15.5%	17.0%	16.6%	16.6%
Growth Rate	−5.0%	−5.0%	−5.0%	−5.0%
Capitalization Rate	10.5%	12.0%	11.6%	11.6%

Beta Calculations

$$\beta_L = \beta_U \times \left[1 + \frac{DC\%}{EC\%}\,(1-t_m)\right]$$

β_L = Levered Beta
β_U = Unlevered Beta

	Iteration #1	Iteration #2	Iteration 3	Iteration #4
$\beta_L = \beta_U \times [1 + \tfrac{DC\%}{EC\%}\times(1-t_m)]$	$1.14 \times [1 + \tfrac{40.0\%}{60.0\%}\times(1-t_m)]$	$1.14 \times [1 + \tfrac{25.0\%}{75.0\%}\times(1-t_m)]$	$1.14 \times [1 + \tfrac{29.0\%}{71.0\%}\times(1-t_m)]$	$1.14 \times [1 + \tfrac{29.3\%}{70.7\%}\times(1-t_m)]$
bracket	1.400	1.200	1.245	1.249
β_L =	1.596	1.368	1.419	1.423

TEST:

Line		Iteration #1	Iteration #2	Iteration 3	Iteration #4
4	Overall Debt of Company	26.6% ≠	30.4% ≠	29.4% ≠	29.3% =
12	Debt % Used in WACC	40.0% =	25.0% =	29.0% =	29.0% =
7	Debt % Used in Beta Calc.	40.0%	25.0%	29.0%	29.0%

$DC\%$ = Debt of Company (Expressed as % to Total Invested Capital)
$EC\%$ = Market Equity of Company (Expressed as % to Total Invested Capital)
t_m = Marginal Tax Rate of Company

Exhibit 5.32E   Iteration Process for Perpetual Relationship of Computed WACC, Levered Beta, and FMV Conclusion of Value

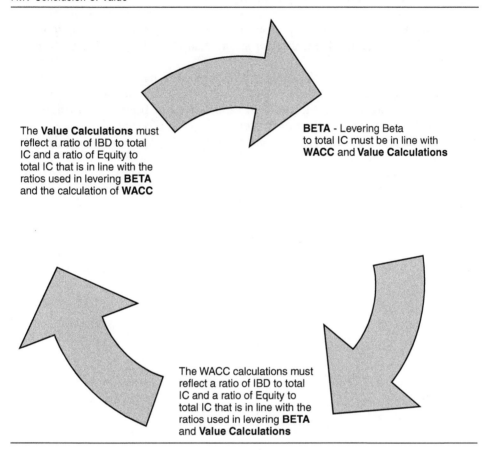

The **Value Calculations** must reflect a ratio of IBD to total IC and a ratio of Equity to total IC that is in line with the ratios used in levering **BETA** and the calculation of **WACC**

BETA - Levering Beta to total IC must be in line with **WACC** and **Value Calculations**

The WACC calculations must reflect a ratio of IBD to total IC and a ratio of Equity to total IC that is in line with the ratios used in levering **BETA** and **Value Calculations**

- The multiple "tries" or estimates needed to arrive at the final blend of interest-bearing debt and equity
- The difference in value that may exist between the DEM and the ICM

It is critical to note that there is a key assumption in the following exhibits; that is, the amount of IBD ($4 million), as well as its interest rate, remains fixed.

Exhibit 5.32A presents the components necessary to calculate both the direct equity method (DEM) and the invested capital method (ICM), and the difference in their corresponding results. As demonstrated, DEM's concluded value of equity is $8,675,000, whereas ICM's concluded value of equity is $9,919,969, a difference of $1,244,969. Also note that lines 3, 4, 5a, and 5b are all intended to be FMV rather than book value.

Exhibit 5.32B presents the basic balance and income statement of ABC Corp. However, both net cash flows to equity and invested capital are calculated starting with line 34, net income.

The application of ICM in Exhibit 5.32A shows a final ratio of IBD *at its fair market value* of 28.7 percent of the company's total cost of capital *at fair market value*. However, it is important that the final ratio of IBD to invested capital be similar to the ratio used in the WACC calculation, keeping in mind that all values are at *fair market value*. So, how do you get these to equal? The process starts out with some educated guesses to finally arrive at the appropriate equilibrium. Although Exhibit 5.32C shows only four iterations, this process may take more than four. Fortunately, there are some spreadsheet programs that can automatically perform the iterations.

The application of ICM in Exhibit 5.32C shows an iteration process using the build-up method. Using the same facts, Exhibit 5.32D illustrates the iteration process using modified CAPM. The final ratio of interest-bearing debt (IBD) *at its fair market value* is 29.3 percent of the company's total invested capital *at fair market value*. Because beta changes after each iteration, the IBD ratio is slightly different from the final ratio in the DEM of 28.7 percent.

Again, it is important that the final ratio of IBD to invested capital (IC) be similar to the ratio used in the WACC. The beta calculation must also agree in order to arrive at the correct cost of capital to equity. Furthermore, the calculated percentages of the total invested capital components are *all* at *fair market value*. So, how do you get these to equal? The iteration process here also starts out with some educated guesses to finally arrive at the appropriate equilibrium. Exhibit 5.32E illustrates the perpetual relationship of the computed WACC, levered BETA, and FMV conclusion of value.

ADDENDUM 2—DEALING WITH DEBT

Overview

The capital structure of an enterprise refers to the means by which the enterprise finances its assets. That is, the capital structure is the sum of capital received from common or preferred shareholders (equity) and/or from borrowings (debt). The extent to which an enterprise borrows to purchase assets is commonly referred to as leveraging, and hence, we refer to a levered enterprise as an enterprise with interest-bearing debt (IBD). An enterprise without debt, not surprisingly, is referred to as an unlevered enterprise. Over the years, much has been written on capital structure, optimum leveraging, and other corporate finance issues. Franco Modigliani and Merton Miller, in their 1958 article, "The Cost of Capital, Corporation Finance, and the Theory of Investment" (*American Economic Review,* vol. 48, no. 3) took corporate finance to a whole new level. Known today as the M&M theorems, their relevant propositions regarding capital structure were that (1) in certain situations, the value of an enterprise is independent of the ratio of debt to equity; (2) the enterprise leverage has no effect on its weighted average cost of capital; and (3) in the presence of taxes, value increases by way of the interest tax deduction. In other words, the value remains the same regardless of the debt to equity ratio because the WACC remains constant regardless of the debt to equity ratio. The components of WACC, the cost of equity (COE), and the cost of debt (net of tax) will change, with the COE rising as debt increases and declining as debt decreases. Finally, there is value added to the enterprise by taking on an optimal level of debt. These postulates, however, are based on an unrealistic perfect market without transaction costs and free of any default risks and taxation. In spite of these unrealistic market assumptions, the M&M theorems paved the way for many of the propositions we use today in modern finance. That said, many later articles have been written to expand on the M&M theorems with the primary aim of determining the enterprise's optimum capital structure. In "An Analytical Process for Generating the WACC Curve and Locating the Optimal Capital Structure" (*Wilmott* magazine, November 2004), Ruben D. Cohen states, "The major breakthrough in capital structuring theory came with the Modigliani and Miller's [M&M] propositions." Although the validity of M&M's theorems in the real world is beyond the scope of this chapter, the selection of the appropriate valuation income method, its applicable cash flow, and discount rate is well within our scope.

Understanding the dynamics of an enterprise's capital structure is, therefore, important to determining its value under the income approach. Choosing the wrong method when "dealing with debt" could result in a value far different from reality. To show the magnitude of differences that could occur, we calculated the cash flow to equity (CF-Eq) and cash flow to invested capital (CF-IC) using both the CCF and the DCF methods. In so doing, we used a hypothetical scenario of an enterprise, XYZ Corp, which has $1,000 in IBD (8 percent interest-bearing debt) to be paid off in five equal annual installments. Furthermore, we assumed that Year 1's EBITDA of XYZ Corp is $500, increasing at a constant growth rate of 3 percent (see Exhibit 5.33). Note: Working capital is ignored here only.

Depending upon the methods selected—that is, DCF or CCF with either cash flow to equity (CF-Eq) or cash flow to invested capital (CF-IC)—the indicated values of equity ranged from $182 to $1,880. Such large differences in calculated values demonstrate that a thorough analysis of the enterprise's capital structure, both current and future, is important to the successful determination of value.

Exhibit 5.33   EBITDA of XYZ Corporation

			Yr 1	Yr 2	Yr 3	Yr 4	Yr 5	Term'l
25%	Discount rate				Beginning Debt Balance			$ 1,000
3%	Constant Long-term growth							
EBITDA of XYZ Corp.			$ 500	$ 515	$ 530	$ 546	$ 562	$ 579
Depreciation			(20)	(21)	(22)	(23)	(24)	(25)
Interest		8.0%	(80)	(64)	(48)	(32)	(16)	-
EBT			400	430	460	491	522	554
Tax rate		40.0%	(160)	(172)	(184)	(196)	(209)	(222)
Net Income			240	258	276	295	313	332
Annual debt payments			(200)	(200)	(200)	(200)	(200)	-
CapX			(20)	(21)	(22)	(23)	(24)	(25)
Add: Depreciation			20	21	22	23	24	25
Cash flow to equity (CF-Eq)			$ 40	$ 58	$ 76	$ 95	$ 113	$ 332
Cash flow to equity (CF-Eq)			$ 40	$ 58	$ 76	$ 95	$ 113	$ 332
Add: Debt payments			200	200	200	200	200	-
Add: Tax effected interest			48	38	29	19	10	-
Cash flow to Invested Capital (CF-IC)			$ 288	$ 296	$ 305	$ 314	$ 323	$ 332

			Yr 1	Yr 2	Yr 3	Yr 4	Yr 5	Term'l
DCF Applied to CF-Eq								
Cash flow to equity (CF-Eq)			$ 40	$ 58	$ 76	$ 95	$ 113	$ 332
Multiplier			1.0	1.0	1.0	1.0	1.0	4.5
PV factors on 25%			0.8000	0.6400	0.5120	0.4096	0.3277	0.3277
Total indicated equity value	$	678	$ 32	$ 37	$ 39	$ 39	$ 37	$ 494
Current debt balance		1,000						
Total indicated investment value	$	1,678						

			Yr 1	Yr 2	Yr 3	Yr 4	Yr 5	Term'l
DCF Applied to CF-IC			288	296	305	314	323	332
PV factors on 13% (Estimated WACC)			0.8850	0.7831	0.6931	0.6133	0.5428	0.5428
Multiplier			1.0	1.0	1.0	1.0	1.0	10.0
Total indicated investment value	$	2,868	$ 255	$ 232	$ 211	$ 193	$ 175	$ 1,802
Less: Debt	$	(1,000)						
Total indicated equity value	$	1,868						

CCF Methods Applied To:	CF-Eq	CF-IC
Cash flows	$ 40	$ 288
Capitalization rates	22%	10%
Multiplier (1 ÷ capitalization rate)	4.5	10.0
Indicated Values (CCF ÷ (1 - capitalizationrate)	$ 182	$ 2,880
Less current debt balance	-	(1,000)
Indicated equity values	$ 182	$ 1,880

Debt and CCF

The analyst should identify the existence of any short- or long-term interest-bearing debt (IBD), at the onset of the valuation engagement. The existence of IBD can be a factor in whether cash flow to equity (CF-Eq) or cash flow to invested capital (CF-IC) is used.

Care needs to be exercised when the CCF method is being used *and* the subject entity has debt. For the CCF method to work properly, two future conditions must exist, in addition to the constant growth rate and the constant risk rate. For the CCF method applied to CF-Eq, these conditions are that (1) the future annual net difference between the debt proceeds and payments (which could be positive or negative) will increase or decrease at the constant annual growth rate forever and (2) the interest rate will remain fixed at its current rate forever.[1] Said in another way, the ratio of

---

[1] A change in debt balances from year to year is likely to affect value more than a change in interest rates from year to year.

debt to equity must remain constant; that is, if equity increases by 3 percent, debt also must increase by 3 percent, while the interest rate remains fixed forever. It is, of course, possible that debt could increase continuously, as with a revolving line of credit, but certainly not decrease forever.

For the CCF method applied to CF-IC, the additional conditions are that (1) the interest rate will remain fixed at its current rate forever and (2) the ratio of debt to equity will remain constant forever. In the latter instance, the CCF applied to CF-IC would be appropriate for an enterprise that requires a revolving credit line, which is constant relative to the value of equity and for whom changes in interest rates, if any, would not necessarily change the entity's weighted average cost of capital (WACC).

> The CCF method (also the Gordon Growth Model) is applicable when IBD is in the form of a line of credit that grows at the same constant growth rate applied.

Unfortunately, this constant growth in debt may not happen in valuing many privately held businesses. IBD may be decreasing or increasing at an amount that changes the debt to equity ratio each year. Although there are, indeed, companies that maintain a constant ratio of debt to equity, the interest rates often change year to year. It is also likely that an enterprise will have a certain amount of IBD that remains constant to equity while having other IBD that is being amortized over a period of time. More times than not, IBD is being paid down while the value of the equity increases, or IBD is paid down for a period of time and the company then refinances in some fashion. Therefore, if the CCF method is applied to cash flows to equity and it is believed that IBD will decrease over a period of time, the result will likely reflect a material understatement of value. Why? Because, as mentioned earlier, the decrease of IBD stops when there is no IBD balance and therefore does not continue into perpetuity. If the CCF method is applied to the cash flows to invested capital and, again, IBD is believed to decrease over a period of time, the result will likely result in a material overstatement of value. Why? Because the decrease in IBD indicates that the capital structure has been (and will be) changing and the average weighted cost of capital (WACC) is, however, increasing as equity holders are taking on more and more of the business risk.

Mike Adhikari, who developed the Advanced Growth Model (AGM) shown in Chapter 5, provides support of the limitations of the CCF or GGM in his article "Advanced Growth Model Reduces the Risk of Overvaluing from 'Constant WACC' Assumptions."[2] He computes the likely overstatement in value when the CCF or GGM is applied to cash flow to invested capital and the IBD is being amortized over a period of time.

---

[2] *Business Valuation Update* 15, no. 6, June 2009, Business Valuation Resources, LLC.

The following overstatements of value are limited to the scenario where debt is declining. In this scenario, according to Mr. Adhikari, the conventional CCF or GGM will overstate value.

Exhibit 5.34 AGM and GGM

The outputs of the AGM and the GGM indicate that the GGM could overstate values by the percentages shown in Exhibit 5.34 when assuming the factors shown.

Input Variables								Output Price Multiple		
Traditional					New			$= V_0/Z_0$, where $Z_1 = Z_0*(1+g)$		
r_e	r_d	W_d	g	t	n	p	W_{ad}	GGM	AGM	Overvaluation
						$p >= n$				
30%	10%	50%	0%	0%	5	5	100%	5.00	4.351	14.9%
30%	10%	50%	0%	40%	5	5	100%	3.33	2.781	19.9%
30%	10%	50%	5%	40%	5	5	100%	4.85	3.666	32.2%
30%	10%	75%	0%	0%	5	5	100%	6.67	5.136	29.8%
30%	10%	75%	0%	40%	5	5	100%	5.00	3.455	44.7%
30%	10%	75%	5%	40%	5	5	100%	9.00	4.745	89.7%

g = the perpetual growth rate of Z_1
p = the debt amortization period
n = the period when the business is liquidated, or deemed to have been liquidated
V_0 = business enterprise value

t = corporate tax rate
r_e = cost of equity
r_d = cost of debt
r_{dt} = after-tax cost of debt
z_0 = EBITDA

In summary, the CCF method will generally distort value when IBD exists and it is changing differently than the growth rate of the company. The greater the year-to-year changes in the debt balances and, to a lesser degree, changes in interest rates, the greater the discrepancies.

Debt and DCF (Discounted Cash Flow)

As previously mentioned in this chapter, determining the existence of either short- or long-term interest-bearing debt (IBD) is important to valuation. In the previous section, the limitations of using the CCF were discussed. The DCF has limitations as well; however, it is the method of choice over the CCF when the subject company has IBD and when the discrete period reflects projected payments of interest and principal as well as projected debt proceeds. In other words, the calculated value (that is, the net present value of the future cash flows) determined by the DCF method applied to the CF-Eq (cash flow to equity) will reflect the changes in debt and interest rates in the discrete periods.

Although the changes in the debt balances and interest payments of the subject company's CF-Eq during the discrete period are incorporated into the DCF calculations, the method does not reflect the annual reduction in the cost of equity (COE) that is the result of declining debt. [As mentioned earlier, COE, the rate used to discount the CF-Eq, decreases as IBD decreases. Not only is this supported in modern finance, it is mathematically demonstrated in the capital asset pricing model (CAPM) when the equity risk premium (ERP) is multiplied by a levered beta (see Chapter 6). As levered beta increases, a function of a higher debt to equity ratio, COE, increases.] One way to handle this would be to change the COE for each year in the discrete period. This, unfortunately, can be difficult, and most analysts use the same discount rate for each period in the discrete period and when determining the terminal value. However, an adjustment to the single COE may be appropriate in these situations.

The terminal value of a DCF is yet another matter of concern when IBD will continue to change after the discrete period. As discussed earlier in this chapter, the terminal value often used the GGM or other models that, unfortunately, do not reflect changes in debt beyond the discrete period. At this point in time, the analyst often makes at least one of the following errors in determining the terminal value. First, in spite of the changes in debt or changes in interest rates, the analyst will use CF-IC, the cash flow that ignores the changes in the debt balances and interest payments. (The application of CF-IC is discussed in the following paragraph.) Second, in spite of the analyst's superb job in reflecting all the changes in debt balances and interest payments of the CF-Eq in each of the discrete periods, the analyst ignores the reality of changes in debt and interest beyond the discrete period and thus calculates the terminal period by using a model, like the GGM, that will not reflect these continued debt changes. As mentioned in Chapter 5, the terminal value may represent the greatest portion of the company's value, and accordingly, the greatest portion of the entire value may be incorrect here. If the terminal year is properly normalized and the debt to equity ratio is to be constant, the GGM will result in a reasonable value.

In engagements where the enterprise's debt to equity ratio has been and will be relatively constant, then the DCF method, as well as the CCF method, applied to CF-IC is preferable. In addition, the long-term interest rates should be viewed as relatively constant in order that the overall WACC remain constant.

In summary, the DCF method can be the preferred method over the CCF method where changing IBD exists. The applicability of CF-Eq or CF-IC depends primarily on the changes in the IBD balances from year to year and the ratio of debt to equity and, secondarily, to changes in interest rates. That is, the value will be less affected by a change in interest rates from 5 percent to 6 percent than by the change in the amortization of IBD from 10 to 8 years, for example. In those cases where the debt to equity ratio is constant, CF-IC discounted by WACC is preferable over CF-Eq. Where the debt to equity ratio is changing year to year, CF-Eq is preferable over CF-IC.

The following decision tree in Exhibit 5.35 is intended to assist the analyst in determining which income method is appropriate or preferable where IBD exists and with other things the same.

Exhibit 5.35   Decision Tree

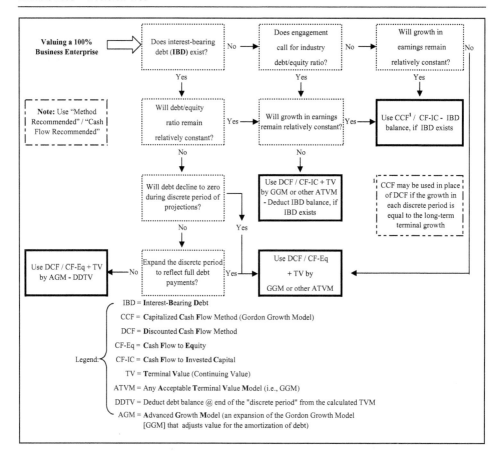

IBD = **I**nterest-**B**earing **D**ebt

CCF = **C**apitalized **C**ash **F**low Method (Gordon Growth Model)

DCF = **D**iscounted **C**ash **F**low Method

CF-Eq = **C**ash **F**low to **Eq**uity

Legend: CF-IC = **C**ash **F**low to **I**nvested **C**apital

TV = **T**erminal **V**alue (Continuing Value)

ATVM = **A**ny **A**cceptable **T**erminal **V**alue **M**odel (i.e., GGM)

DDTV = **D**educt **d**ebt balance @ end of the "discrete period" from the calculated TVM

AGM = **A**dvanced **G**rowth **M**odel (an expansion of the Gordon Growth Model [GGM] that adjusts value for the amortization of debt)

CHAPTER **6**

Cost of Capital/Rates of Return

This chapter focuses on the cost of capital or rates of return for equity and for invested capital (which includes interest-bearing debt). Both of these are explicitly used in the income approach through the application of discount and capitalization (cap) rates to an appropriate economic benefit stream. These same concepts are also implicitly used via price earnings (P/E) multiples in the market approach because a P/E multiple is the reciprocal of an earnings capitalization rate applicable to earnings under the income approach. These sources of cost of capital will be discussed here. Addendum 1 to this chapter contains three articles that analyze each component of the cost of capital in great detail. On the website www.wiley.com/go/FVAM3E, there are seven additional addendums to this chapter. Addendum 2 is an article from *Financial Valuation and Litigation Expert* (*FVLE*) on Ibbotson industry risk premiums. Addendum 3 is an article from *FVLE* on total betas, and Addendum 4 is an article from *FVLE* on cost of equity capital. Addenda 5 and 6 explain Duff & Phelps, LLC 2009 and 2010 Risk Premium Reports. Addendum 7 presents the Risk Rate Component Model. Addendum 8 is an update article from *FVLE* on cost of equity.

THREE VARIABLES

In the income approach, the value of the company is a function of three variables:

1. The economic benefit stream, typically cash flow
2. The growth potential of the company being valued, both short- and long-term
3. The risk involved in receiving the benefits in the proper amounts and time frames anticipated (i.e., the discount rate)

The value of any enterprise will vary directly with its expected level of economic benefit and the expected growth of such benefits. The value will vary inversely with the riskiness of that anticipated economic benefit stream because the increase in risk demands a higher rate of return. Often a business enterprise, particularly in the small and midsize markets, is focused on the benefit stream and growth potential variables while too often the risk is left to chance. Assuming no change in the first two variables, reducing the risk attributes of a business will increase its value.

> Identifying the value drivers of an enterprise and developing action steps to limit or reduce controllable (e.g., internally oriented versus external) risks can be of great benefit to many closely held businesses in terms of their increasing value.

CHARACTERISTICS OF COST OF CAPITAL[1]

The cost of capital for an enterprise represents the economic cost of attracting and retaining capital in a competitive environment where investors carefully analyze and compare all investment opportunities. Some basic concepts follow:

- The cost of capital is the *expected rate of return* that the market requires to attract funds to a particular investment. It is based on investor expectations. Actual past returns are relevant to an estimate of cost of capital only to the extent that they are believed to be representative of future expectations.
- The cost of capital depends on the investment, *not* the investor—that is, it depends on the *riskiness of the investment* rather than the risk characteristics of the investor.
- In economic terms, the cost of capital is an *opportunity cost*—that is, the cost of forgoing the next best alternative investment (equivalent risk at higher expected return or lowered risk at same expected return).
- The cost of capital concept is based on the *principle of substitution*—an investor will not invest in a particular asset if there is a more attractive substitute.
- The cost of capital is *market driven*—it is the competitive rate of return available in the market on a comparable investment (i.e., an investment with equivalent riskiness).
- The most important component of comparability is *risk*, which is the degree of certainty (or lack of it) that the investor will realize the expected returns at the times specified. Since risk cannot always be observed directly, analysts have developed several ways to estimate it using available market data (generally based on some past period of time).
- Each component of a company's capital structure (e.g., debt and equity) has a cost of capital.

INVESTOR EXPECTATIONS AS QUANTIFIED BY THE COST OF CAPITAL[2]

Three basic components of investor expectations are captured in the cost of capital:

1. The "real" rate of return—the amount that investors expect to obtain in exchange for letting someone else use their money on a risk-less basis

---

[1] Shannon P. Pratt, *Cost of Capital: Estimation and Applications, Second Edition.* (New York: John Wiley & Sons, 2002), p. 5. (Used with permission.) A fourth edition, with Shannon Pratt and Roger Grabowski, is now available.
[2] Ibid.

2. Expected inflation—the expected depreciation in purchasing power while the money is tied up
3. Risk—the uncertainty about when and how much cash flow or other economic benefit will be received

The combination of the first two expectations is sometimes referred to as the "time value of money." This can vary for different investors, although the market tends to form a consensus regarding a particular investment or category of investments. That consensus forms the cost of capital for investments of varying levels of risk.

COST OF CAPITAL EQUALS DISCOUNT RATE

The cost of capital is also referred to as the discount rate. It equals the total expected rate of return for the investment, that is, dividends or withdrawals, plus expected capital appreciation over the life of the investment. This rate, when applied to the appropriate income or cash flow stream of a company, will give an estimate of the company's value.

ValTip
The value of a company can be expressed as the present fair market value of all of the future economic benefits that are expected to be generated by the company.

COST-OF-CAPITAL METHODS

Several methods are available to calculate the cost of capital or discount/cap rate for a specific investment. Some of the more common methods include:

- Build-Up method (BUM)
- Capital asset pricing model (CAPM) method
- Modified capital asset pricing model (MCAPM) method
- Weighted average cost of capital (WACC) method
- Price/earnings method

Each of these methods is discussed in detail later in this chapter. We also briefly discuss growth, arbitrage pricing theory (APT), and certain aspects of the excess cash flow (ECF) method as it relates to cost-of-capital determinations.

MORE ON THE BASIC CONCEPTS

The value of an interest in a closely held business typically is considered to be the present value of the future economic benefit stream, typically cash flow. This economic benefit is discounted at an appropriate discount rate to reflect the risks associated with the certainty of receiving such future economic benefits.

No one buys a business or other property simply because of what it has accomplished in the past or even what it consists of at present. Although these may be important considerations in determining what the business or other property is likely to do in the future, it is the anticipated future performance of a business that gives it economic value.

Values are reflections of the future, not the past nor even the present.

DISCOUNT RATE, CAPITALIZATION RATE, AND ANTICIPATED GROWTH

A discount rate is used to calculate the present value of future projections of a benefit stream when growth will vary from year to year. The projections reflect the growth of the business. However, if growth is estimated to remain level throughout the future life of the investment, a capitalization rate is often used. In its most elementary form, the relationship between a discount and a capitalization rate can be summarized as:

$$\text{Capitalization rate} = \text{Discount rate} - \text{Growth}$$

The application of the discounted cash flow (DCF) method with constant growth will result in the same value as the capitalization of cash flow (CCF) method. This is illustrated by the following example (Exhibits 6.1 and 6.2). In Exhibit 6.1 the application of the traditional DCF method with a terminal year value determined by the Gordon Growth Model results in exactly the same value as the CCF method. This is corroborated in Exhibit 6.2, which shows the cash flows going out 50 years resulting in almost the same value ($499,918.17 versus $500,000). It also illustrates how small the present value factors are beyond 15 years or so. For example, the present value over just 15 years is only about 7 percent less than the value into perpetuity.

GROWTH

One of the critical areas where analysts are required to exercise their professional judgment is the assessment of future growth prospects for the subject entity. Over the past decade or two, the public markets have witnessed many companies that have experienced high short-term growth rates. For example, in December 1998 analysts announced that the projected growth rates for CISCO Systems, Inc., would taper off from 55 percent in 1998 to 25 percent to 30 percent for the next five years.[3] Very few

---

[3] Paul Larson, "Cisco Bear's Den," *The Motley Fool* (December 16, 1998).

Exhibit 6.1   An Example of the Relationship Between Discount Rates, Cap Rates, and Growth

<u>Discounted Cash Flow Method</u>

Assumptions: Year 1 normalized cash flow is $100,000
Growth rate is 5%
Discount rate is 25%

	Forecasted Cash Flow	**Present Value Factor for 25% Discount Rate**	**Present Value**
Year 1	100,000	.8	80,000
Year 2	105,000	.64	67,200
Year 3	110,250	.512	56,448
Year 4	115,763	.4096	47,416
Year 5	121,551	.32768	39,830
Terminal Value	*638,141	.32768	209,106
Value Estimate—Discounted			$500,000

*Terminal Value:

Year 5 cash flow		$121,551
Growth factor	×	1.05
Year 6 cash flow	=	127,628
Cap Rate (25% − 5%)	÷	.20
	=	$638,141

<u>Capitalization of Cash Flow Method</u>

Year 1 cash flow/cap rate = Value estimate
$100,000/(25% − 5%) = $500,000

companies, if any, can sustain such high growth rates forever. This creates a need for longer-term growth assumptions. However, usually no long-term growth rates are forecasted. Since most companies are valued into perpetuity, short-term growth rates are helpful but incomplete. The meteoric rise and fall of short-term growth rates for whole market sectors has created problematic valuation data and circumstances. There is often a need to identify companies capable of "sustainable growth," that is, a level of continued growth that the enterprise can reasonably be expected to sustain over the long term.

ValTip

In valuing a company, analysts need to estimate sustainable growth into perpetuity, not just short-term growth.

Exhibit 6.2 Discount Rates and Growth (Growth / Year = 5%, ke = 25%)

No.	End of Yr	CF	Discount Rate	PV
1	1	100,000.00	0.8000	80,000.00
2	2	105,000.00	0.6400	67,200.00
3	3	110,250.00	0.5120	56,448.00
4	4	115,762.50	0.4096	47,416.32
5	5	121,550.63	0.3277	39,829.71
6	6	127,628.16	0.2621	33,456.96
7	7	134,009.56	0.2097	28,103.84
8	8	140,710.04	0.1678	23,607.23
9	9	147,745.54	0.1342	19,830.07
10	10	155,132.82	0.1074	16,657.26
11	11	162,889.46	0.0859	13,992.10
12	12	171,033.94	0.0687	11,753.36
13	13	179,585.63	0.0550	9,872.82
14	14	188,564.91	0.0440	8,293.17
15	15	197,993.16	0.0352	6,966.27
16	16	207,892.82	0.0281	5,851.66
17	17	218,287.46	0.0225	4,915.40
18	18	229,201.83	0.0180	4,128.93
19	19	240,661.92	0.0144	3,468.30
20	20	252,695.02	0.0115	2,913.38
21	21	265,329.77	0.0092	2,447.24
22	22	278,596.26	0.0074	2,055.68
23	23	292,526.07	0.0059	1,726.77
24	24	307,152.38	0.0047	1,450.49
25	25	322,509.99	0.0038	1,218.41
26	26	338,635.49	0.0030	1,023.46
27	27	355,567.27	0.0024	859.71
28	28	373,345.63	0.0019	722.16
29	29	392,012.91	0.0015	606.61
30	30	411,613.56	0.0012	509.55
31	31	432,194.24	0.0010	428.02
32	32	453,803.95	0.0008	359.54
33	33	476,494.15	0.0006	302.01
34	34	500,318.85	0.0005	253.69
35	35	525,334.80	0.0004	213.10
36	36	551,601.54	0.0003	179.00
37	37	579,181.61	0.0003	150.36
38	38	608,140.69	0.0002	126.31
39	39	638,547.73	0.0002	106.10
40	40	670,475.12	0.0001	89.12
41	41	703,998.87	0.0001	74.86
42	42	739,198.81	0.0001	62.88
43	43	776,158.76	0.0001	52.82
44	44	814,966.69	0.0001	44.37
45	45	855,715.03	0.0000	37.27
46	46	898,500.78	0.0000	31.31
47	47	943,425.82	0.0000	26.30
48	48	990,597.11	0.0000	22.09
49	49	1,040,126.96	0.0000	18.56
50	50	1,092,133.31	0.0000	15.59
			Total	499,918.17
			Rounded	500,000.00

Valuation analysts regularly value entities whose growth is either highly erratic or currently advancing at a much higher rate than can be sustained into perpetuity. In both instances, it is likely that analysts will select a discount rate by which to value such "abnormal" benefit streams during a limited future period and then use a terminal year capitalization rate to value the perpetual benefit stream once true sustainable growth can be achieved. This can be achieved by using the DCF method of the income approach, which is explained in Chapter 5. The challenge is to determine the appropriate adjustment for long-term sustainable growth and to convert the discount rate used during the abnormal period to a capitalization rate to be used into perpetuity once the economic benefit stream has been stabilized.

ValTip

Since 1926, the U.S. economy has been able to sustain a nominal growth rate of approximately 6 to 6.5 percent over time. This is a combination of the real growth rate and inflation.

Some analysts believe that in a capitalistic society, it is reasonable to assume that any business entity's growth, regardless of short-term prospects, will eventually plateau at the 6 to 6.5 percent long-term level of growth for the economy. This change in average economic growth is due to competition, which initially is attracted to higher-growth industries putting pressure on profit margins and growth.

A thorough evaluation of the subject company's historical growth can be utilized to assist in this growth determination. Published estimates of industry growth rates, such as those compiled by Ibbotson, can also be relevant analytical tools. Currently, many analysts use a long-term sustainable growth rate between 3 percent and 6 to 6.5 percent, depending on the underlying characteristics of the subject entity, its industry, and its future prospects. Some analysts use the anticipated inflation rate, which has historically averaged approximately 3 percent. This rate assumes no real growth in the underlying business.

ValTip

Overall, the deciding factor in determining how to reflect growth in the rates of return still must be informed professional judgment.

The relationship between risk and growth is illustrated in Exhibits 6.3 to 6.6. Exhibit 6.3 presents various values in a matrix based on varying growth rates and discount rates. Exhibits 6.4 to 6.6 show similar matrices but compare changes in profit margins to changes in growth rates at discount rates of 18, 20, and 22 percent. These charts illustrate the sensitivity of these factors and the effect on value.

Exhibit 6.7 is a chart showing values (using CCF) with growth rates from 0 to 10 percent and discount rates from 10 to 30 percent. This can be used as a ready tool to

Exhibit 6.3 Discount Rate versus Growth Rate

Values ($000)
$$PV = CF_1 / (k_e - g); CF_1 = \$100,000$$

		Growth Rate				
		2%	**4%**	**6%**	**8%**	**10%**
Discount Rate	16%	714	833	1,000	1,250	1,667
	18%	625	714	833	1,000	1,250
	20%	556	625	714	833	1,000
	22%	500	556	625	714	833
	24%	455	500	556	625	714

Exhibit 6.4 Growth Rate versus Margin ($k_e = 18\%$)

Values ($000)
$$PV = CF_1 / (k_e - g)$$
6% Margin = $100,000; $k_e = 18\%$

		Growth Rate				
		2%	**4%**	**6%**	**8%**	**10%**
Margin	2%	208	238	278	333	417
	4%	417	476	556	667	833
	6%	625	714	833	1,000	1,250
	8%	833	952	1,111	1,333	1,667
	10%	1,042	1,190	1,389	1,667	2,083

Exhibit 6.5 Growth Rate versus Margin ($k_e = 20\%$)

Values ($000)
$$PV = CF_1 / (k_e - g)$$
6% Margin = $100,000; $k_e = 20\%$

		Growth Rate				
		2%	**4%**	**6%**	**8%**	**10%**
Margin	2%	185	208	238	278	333
	4%	370	417	476	556	667
	6%	556	625	714	833	1,000
	8%	741	833	952	1,111	1,333
	10%	926	1,042	1,190	1,389	1,667

Exhibit 6.6   Growth Rate versus Margin (k_e = 22%)

Values ($000)
$$PV = CF_1 / (k_e - g)$$
6% Margin = $100,000; k_e = 22%

		Growth Rate				
		2%	**4%**	**6%**	**8%**	**10%**
Margin	2%	167	185	208	238	278
	4%	333	370	417	476	556
	6%	500	556	625	714	833
	8%	667	741	833	952	1,111
	10%	833	926	1,042	1,190	1,389

Exhibit 6.7   Capitalized Value (PV)

$$PV = CF_1 / (k_e - g)$$

	Growth Rate (g)										
	0%	**1%**	**2%**	**3%**	**4%**	**5%**	**6%**	**7%**	**8%**	**9%**	**10%**
10%	10.00	11.11	12.50	14.29	16.67	20.00	25.00	33.33	50.00	100.00	N/A
11%	9.09	10.00	11.11	12.50	14.29	16.67	20.00	25.00	33.33	50.00	100.00
12%	8.33	9.09	10.00	11.11	12.50	14.29	16.67	20.00	25.00	33.33	50.00
13%	7.69	8.33	9.09	10.00	11.11	12.50	14.29	16.67	20.00	25.00	33.33
14%	7.14	7.69	8.33	9.09	10.00	11.11	12.50	14.29	16.67	20.00	25.00
15%	6.67	7.14	7.69	8.33	9.09	10.00	11.11	12.50	14.29	16.67	20.00
16%	6.25	6.67	7.14	7.69	8.33	9.09	10.00	11.11	12.50	14.29	16.67
17%	5.88	6.25	6.67	7.14	7.69	8.33	9.09	10.00	11.11	12.50	14.29
18%	5.56	5.88	6.25	6.67	7.14	7.69	8.33	9.09	10.00	11.11	12.50
19%	5.26	5.56	5.88	6.25	6.67	7.14	7.69	8.33	9.09	10.00	11.11
20%	5.00	5.26	5.56	5.88	6.25	6.67	7.14	7.69	8.33	9.09	10.00
21%	4.76	5.00	5.26	5.56	5.88	6.25	6.67	7.14	7.69	8.33	9.09
22%	4.55	4.76	5.00	5.26	5.56	5.88	6.25	6.67	7.14	7.69	8.33
23%	4.35	4.55	4.76	5.00	5.26	5.56	5.88	6.25	6.67	7.14	7.69
24%	4.17	4.35	4.55	4.76	5.00	5.26	5.56	5.88	6.25	6.67	7.14
25%	4.00	4.17	4.35	4.55	4.76	5.00	5.26	5.56	5.88	6.25	6.67
26%	3.85	4.00	4.17	4.35	4.55	4.76	5.00	5.26	5.56	5.88	6.25
27%	3.70	3.85	4.00	4.17	4.35	4.55	4.76	5.00	5.26	5.56	5.88
28%	3.57	3.70	3.85	4.00	4.17	4.35	4.55	4.76	5.00	5.26	5.56
29%	3.45	3.57	3.70	3.85	4.00	4.17	4.35	4.55	4.76	5.00	5.26
30%	3.33	3.45	3.57	3.70	3.85	4.00	4.17	4.35	4.55	4.76	5.00

Discount Rate (k_e)

derive value by multiplying next year's cash flow (CF_1) of the company being valued by the factor in the table. It is also a tool to test the sensitivity of important assumptions.

RELATIONSHIP BETWEEN RISK AND COST OF CAPITAL

Defining Risk[4]

Financial economics divides risk into three major categories: maturity, systematic, and unsystematic. Maturity risk is the reflection of changes in interest rates over the term of the investment. "Stated in non-technical terms, *market risk* or *systematic risk* (also known as undiversifiable risk) is the uncertainty of future returns owing to the sensitivity of the return on the subject investment to variability in the returns for a composite measure of marketable investments. *Unique* or *unsystematic risk* (also known as diversifiable risk, residual risk, or specific risk) is a function of the characteristics of the industry, the individual company, and the type of investment interest and is unrelated to variation of returns in the market as a whole."[5]

Maturity Risk

Maturity risk (also called horizon risk or interest rate risk) is the risk that the value of the investment may increase or decrease because of changes in the general level of interest rates. The longer the term of an investment, the greater the maturity risk. For example, market prices of long-term bonds fluctuate much more in response to changes in levels of interest rates than do short-term bonds or notes. When we refer to the yields of U.S. Government bonds as *risk-free rates,* we mean that we regard them as free from the prospect of default, but we recognize that they do incorporate maturity risk . . . the longer the maturity, the greater the susceptibility to change in market price in response to changes in market rates of interest.[6]

Systematic Risk

Systematic risk can be defined as the uncertainty of future returns due to uncontrollable movements in the market as a whole. This type of risk generally arises from external, macroeconomic factors that affect all economic assets within the economy as a whole. Diversifiable risk, on the other hand, is based on firm-specific factors.

Defining Beta

Beta is the factor by which the excess market return (in excess of the risk-free rate) is multiplied, with the product then added to the risk-free rate to estimate the cost of equity capital for that company. That cost is in its purest form with no adjustment for

---

[4] Portions of this section have been taken with permission from "Unsystematic Risk and Valuation" (Part I), 1999, by Warren Miller. AICPA, *CPA Expert.*
[5] Shannon P. Pratt and Roger J. Grabowski, *Cost of Capital: Estimation and Applications,* 3rd ed. (Hoboken, NJ: John Wiley & Sons, 2002), p. 80. (Used with permission.)
[6] Ibid, p. 45.

unsystematic risk. That is because one of the underlying assumptions of portfolio management theory is that unsystematic risk does not exist because rational investors diversify it away. Variability in an entity's rate of return—[dividends + capital appreciation]/its stock price—is compared to variability in the rate of return on an underlying market index. The Standard & Poor's (S&P) 500 and the New York Stock Exchange (NYSE) indexes are the two most common benchmarks. The result is a proxy for systematic risk referred to as the beta for that specific enterprise. By definition, the beta of the market (i.e., underlying index) as a whole is equal to a value of 1.0. A stock with a beta greater than 1 will evidence greater volatility in its rates of return than the market, and a stock with a beta less than 1 will evidence less volatility in its rates of return than the market. Stocks with betas of 1 have rates of return whose movements match the movement of the market.

For publicly held companies, systematic risk is captured by a measurement referred to as the *beta* of the enterprise.

Privately held company ownership interests also demonstrate systematic risk (i.e., sensitivity to the movement of market rates of return). However, it is more difficult to develop betas to measure their level of systematic risk.

It is common to assume a privately held company's beta as 1.0 and develop separate risk factors to include in its overall rate of return calculations or to use a beta for an industry group or from guideline public companies.

Unsystematic Risk

Unsystematic risk is the uncertainty of future returns as a function of something other than movements in market rates of return, such as the characteristics of an industry, enterprise, or type of investment. Examples of circumstances that can create or increase unsystematic risk include high product or technological obsolescence, unforeseen loss of management expertise, and negative changes in labor relations.

Classical financial theory, formulated in the Capital Asset Pricing Model (CAPM, described later), assumes that rational investors will eliminate their exposure to unsystematic risk through maintaining fully diversified portfolios. However, this assumption is based on the existence of other interlocking assumptions, the absence of which, in a privately held company setting, creates the need for the valuation analyst to identify and quantify unsystematic risk as a part of an overall rate of return. Some of these assumptions include:

- Investors have access to perfect information for decision-making purposes.
- There are no taxes to be considered.
- The decision maker is fully rational.

> The estimation of unsystematic risk is one of the more difficult aspects of calculating rates of return.

Types of Unsystematic Risk

Unsystematic risk has four primary sources: the size of the firm, its macroenvironment, its industry (or strategic group), and specific company attributes.

1. *Size.* Two ongoing studies[7] monitor the impact of the size effect on rates of return. Although they use different methodologies and overlapping sampling populations, their general conclusion is identical: the smaller the company, the greater the risk.
2. *Macroenvironment.* The macroenvironment comprises six forces (economic, technological, sociocultural, demographic, international, and political) with subforces beneath each.[8] Most companies monitor these forces to minimize the negative impact of sudden macroenvironmental changes. Except for technological innovation, the ability of companies to influence these forces is minimal.
3. *Industry.* According to Michael E. Porter, a noted economist and one of the leading theorists and researchers on strategic thinking, the *industry*-related risk is made up of five forces: the threat of new entrants, bargaining power of suppliers, bargaining power of customers, threat of substitutes, and rivalry.[9] Unlike macroenvironmental forces, industry factors can be influenced by the purposeful actions of insightful managers. For companies that do not compete industry-wide (which includes many closely held businesses), the term "strategic group" describes their "industry." There can be many strategic groups within an industry. However, Porter's five forces remain

---

[7] *Ibbotson SBBI Valuation Yearbook,* Morningstar, Chicago; and *Duff & Phelps Risk Premium Report,* by Roger Grabowski.

[8] Liam Fahey and V. K. Narayanan, *Macroenvironmental Analysis for Strategic Management* (St. Paul: West Publishing Company, 1986), p. 29; and Michael A. Hitt, R. Duane Ireland, and Robert E. Hoskisson, *Strategic Management: Competitiveness and Globalization,* 3rd ed. (Cincinnati: South-Western Publishing Company, 1999), pp. 50–60.

[9] Michael E. Porter, "How Competitive Forces Shape Strategy," *Harvard Business Review* (May-June 1979), pp. 137–145. The follow-up book appeared in 1980, *Competitive Strategy: Techniques for Analyzing Industries and Competitors* (New York: The Free Press). In 1998, Porter wrote a new introduction for this landmark book.

the same, whether for an industry or for a strategic group. This concept of strategic groups is also discussed briefly a bit further into this chapter within the discussion of the recent Ibbotson industry risk premia. (Also see Chapter 4.)

4. *Specific Company Attributes.* Companies need to constantly monitor change and have the resolve and the resources to act. Many times companies must modify their corporate culture to adapt to change.

TYPES OF RISK—ANOTHER VIEW

Ten other types of risk can be examined in conjunction with business valuation assignments[10]:

1. *Economic Risks.* The analyst must determine how the subject company will be affected by changes in the economic environment within which it operates. For example, what effect will anticipated changes in interest rates have on the company and industry?

2. *Business Risks.* The analyst can analyze the company in terms of the risk associated with factors such as sales and growth volatility.

3. *Operating Risks.* The analyst can analyze the subject company to determine how much risk the company is exposed to as a result of the commitments and costs associated with its operations. This assessment includes an analysis of fixed versus variable costs.

4. *Financial Risks.* The financial risks associated with a company pertain to the amount of leverage the company uses and the company's ability to cover its debt payments. The analyst can analyze the capital structure of similar companies to compare the subject company and its risk profile.

5. *Asset Risks.* These risks relate to the age and condition of the company's assets. Older assets represent a higher degree of risk for a company in terms of higher maintenance costs, lower productivity, and functional and technological obsolescence.

6. *Product Risks.* Product risks relate to diversification in a company's product line, including product lines that may become extinct with the introduction of newer products by competitors.

7. *Market Risks.* This type of risk relates to how well the company is geographically diversified. If the company operates within a local marketplace, changes in the local area can greatly affect it. A more diversified geographical market can reduce the risk associated with a company.

8. *Technological Risks.* New technology can adversely affect a company if it does not have the ability to keep up with the other companies in its industry.

9. *Regulatory Risks.* Regulatory agencies can adversely affect a business. Environmental regulations are probably one of the best examples of regulatory risk.

10. *Legal Risks.* The cost of litigation can cause the end of a successful business. Even if successful, litigation can create such a financial burden on a business that it can no longer function as a going concern.

---

[10] Gary Trugman, *Understanding Business Valuation: A Practical Guide to Valuing Small to Medium-Sized Companies,* 3rd ed. (American Institute of Certified Public Accountants, 2008), pp. 232–233. (Reprinted with permission, copyright © 2008 by American Institute of Certified Public Accountants, Inc.)

Every business enterprise will have its own unique attributes and risks, which can be incorporated into the rate of return.

RISKS IN A SMALL BUSINESS

Small businesses have their own set of risk attributes that will need careful attention to ensure they have been included in cost-of-capital calculations. Some of the questions the analyst will want to ask are:

- How much additional risk is associated with the small size of the subject company?
- How much additional risk is associated with the one or two key employees who are the driving force in the company and are generating the benefits to the owners? Could they be replaced in case of death or departure from the company, and what would the effects be on the economic benefit stream of the company? Is there an employment/ noncompete agreement in place in case they decide to leave the company?
- Are there any concentrations or dependencies of customers, suppliers, marketing, technology, and so on, that could indicate higher risk?
- How much additional risk is associated with the company's access to additional financing? Can it finance its growth and at what cost? What effect does this have on the company's leverage? What role do the key persons play in obtaining the financing such as personal guarantees and use of personal wealth?

Typically, the concentration of an investment into one closely held company entails higher risk than investing in the stock market, where diversification can reduce or eliminate specific company risk. In many smaller, closely held companies this means higher risk, higher returns, and lower value. Small business risk is explained in greater detail later in this chapter.

METHODS FOR DEVELOPING COST OF CAPITAL

Build-Up Method (BUM)

The build-up method (BUM) is often used by analysts who work with small and medium-size businesses. In a build-up method, the discount rate is calculated by adding together the analyst's assessment of the systematic and unsystematic risks associated with a particular subject company or ownership interest. The most widely used methodology for deriving a rate under this approach uses four or five basic elements to derive an indication of a discount rate with at least one element being based on empirical evidence compiled by Ibbotson or Duff & Phelps. The rest of this section deals with the use of Ibbotson data for calculation of a rate of return derived by the build-up method. Duff & Phelps data is discussed in a separate section.

The basic formula for the traditional build-up model is:

$$E(R_i) = R_f + RP_m + RP_s + RP_u$$

Where:

$E(R_1)$ = Expected (market required) rate of return on a security

R_f = Rate of return for a risk-free security as of the valuation date

RP_m = Equity risk premium for the "market"

RP_s = Risk premium for small size

RP_u = Risk premium for specific company, where u stands for unsystematic risk

Some analysts also add in RP_i, which is the industry risk premium from Ibbotson. When using Duff & Phelps risk premium data, analysts may choose to rely on risk premiums for size in excess of R_f, which consolidates RP_m and RP_s into one risk premium.

Risk-Free Rate (R_f)

The first component of the discount rate is the risk-free rate of return R_f. This is often referred to as the safe rate or the cost of money and is the rate available on investments that are considered to have no risk of default. The most commonly used source for the risk-free rate of return is the 20-year U.S. Treasury bond. It is widely used because Ibbotson and Duff & Phelps data (to be explained later) used to derive the equity risk premium have been calculated based on this 20-year Treasury bond benchmark for all periods from 1926 (1963 for Duff & Phelps) to present. It also reflects a long-term investment, an assumption used in most closely held business valuations.

ValTip

> There is no direct source for returns on 20-year Treasury bonds going back to 1926 for all years. Analysts can consult the *Wall Street Journal* to find the quoted market yields on 30-year bonds with approximately 20 years of maturity left. Another source for this data is the St. Louis branch of the Federal Reserve Bank, which maintains an extensive inventory of historical yield rates on all types of government securities, including a continuing proxy for the 20-year constant maturity Treasury bond.

It should be noted that the U.S. government has not issued 20-year Treasury bills or notes for many years, so business analysts look to the current market yields on 30-year Treasury bonds with 20 years of maturity remaining, as quoted in sources such as the *Wall Street Journal*, or alternatively, a proxy for a 20-year effective yield can be obtained in roughly weekly intervals directly from the Federal Reserve Bank website.[11]

---

[11] http://research.stlouisfed.org/fred2/categories/115.

In recent years, arguments have been raised with respect to the propriety of the use of a 20-year time horizon for a risk-free rate as compared to shorter time horizons as an assumed holding period to apply when developing rates for the valuation of closely held businesses. While there is merit to this line of thinking, most within the valuation community believe it is more important to stay consistent with the risk-free rates used to develop the underlying risk premia associated with the equity risk and size risk, as utilized with both the Ibbotson and Duff & Phelps data, which continue to use the 20-year horizon benchmark in the development of their respective empirical evidence.

Another emerging issue worthy of discussion is the relatively dramatic changes in the risk-free rate in recent years, due to what many consider to be exigent circumstances related to the government's economic stimulus initiatives and related factors. The 20-year Treasury note rate had decreased roughly 200 basis points from an approximate 5 percent rate (say plus or minus 50 basis points) in place for many years to a rate that was close to only 3 percent in December 2008, before rebounding to a rate slightly above 4 percent in late 2009. The issue here is how to take into account such a relatively extreme change in this risk-free component used in rate development models. Note the following list that highlights these trends:

Yield on 20-Year (Constant Maturity) T-Bonds

2004	Average for 12 months	5.01%
2005	Average for 12 months	4.62%
2006	Average for 12 months	4.98%
2007	Average for 12 months	4.87%
2008	Average—first 8 months	4.52%
2008	September 30	4.43%
2008	October 31	4.78%
2008	November 30	3.72%
2008	December 31	3.03%

It is also interesting to make note of the variances that have developed between long- and short-term government bond rates as evidenced by the following list, as well as the partial rebound of the 20-year rate as of September 2009.

Change in Rate Spread

The interest rate spread between short-term and long-term Treasury bonds is widening; so is the spread from T-bonds to corporate bonds.

	1-Year	10-Year	20-Year	BAA
12/95	5.31%	5.71%	6.12%	7.49%
12/00	5.60%	5.24%	5.64%	8.02%
12/05	4.35%	4.47%	4.73%	6.32%
12/08	0.49%	2.42%	3.18%	8.43%
09/09	0.43%	3.38%	4.14%	6.58%

Source: www.federalreserve.gov.

The key issue here is whether to use a risk-free rate effective as of the valuation date versus a smoothed rate, such as an average of the risk-free benchmark being considered over one more year to moderate the effect of possible short-term aberrations such as the current extreme amount of liquidity the government has added to the economy as a stimulus measure, together with what many have viewed as a flight to quality that has driven the bond rates down to historically low levels in the recent past.

Many analysts believe it is important to stay the course and use the currently quoted indication, and then adjust the overall rate indication elsewhere, primarily within the unsystematic risk component, to get to a final rate indication that is right for the specific application. One significant factor to consider here is what will be appropriate to maintain consistency in how we develop our capitalization and discount rates if our economy experiences significant inflationary forces in the years ahead and the risk-free rates prevailing in these periods are viewed as unusually high, such as in the early 1970s when these rates were approaching double digits.

Equity Risk Premium (RP$_m$)

The next component is the equity risk premium or risk premium for the market (RP$_m$), the premium that investors must receive to entice them to invest in the public equity markets instead of long-term government securities. Most business analysts use a long-term investment horizon with the S&P 500 as a benchmark for this component.

The ERP is forward-looking and represents the anticipated incremental return on common stocks over the investment horizon. There are primarily two schools of thought on how this ERP should be calculated when using Ibbotson data. Both are based on historical excess returns of stocks over the long-term government bond income returns. The major premise of calculating the ERP using these methods is that past ERPs are a reasonable proxy for a future ERP. The first method is called the historical ERP, and the second method is called the supply-side ERP.

The decision on which method to use in calculating the ERP is solely up to the valuation analyst. However, in making this choice, the valuation analyst should be cognizant that the historical ERP is based on data that are already known and easily calculated, but runs the risk that historical results are not always indicative of future results.

Ibbotson provides historical ERP data in its annual publication *Market Results for Stocks, Bonds, Bills, and Inflation (Ibbotson SBBI Valuation Yearbook)*.[12] The data are computed by first finding the total "excess" returns for the public markets over the income returns on annual 20-year government bond rates for a specific period of time, usually 1926 to present, and then taking either an arithmetic or a geometric mean average return for that period.

While these average values are calculated using both geometric and arithmetic mean averages, Ibbotson recommends use of the arithmetic mean as the best indication of the equity risk premium. The arithmetic calculation gives the best indication of what will occur next, assuming past history is the correct proxy.

Supply-Side ERP

In June 2001 Roger Ibbotson and Peng Chen, both then of Ibbotson Associates, Inc., produced a white paper for the Yale International Center for Finance titled *The*

---

[12] Published by Morningstar, Inc.

Supply of Stock Market Returns, which detailed their study of estimating a forward-looking, long-term equity risk premium using a combination of the historical and supply-side approaches. The paper was updated with the July 2002 white paper titled *Stock Market Returns in the Long Run: Participating in the Real Economy.*[13]

Their studies started with the 1926 to 2000 historical equity returns for which their company is well known and decomposed this data into supply-side factors, including inflation, earnings, dividends, price-to-earnings ratio, dividend payout ratio, book value, return on equity, and GDP per capita. Each of these distinct factors was reviewed with respect to its relationship to the long-term supply-side framework.

Using the identified factors, Ibbotson and Chen forecasted the equity risk premium through supply-side models. Their findings validated a lower long-term supply-side forecasted equity risk premium, but only slightly lower than the comparable equity risk premium derived using a purely historical return estimate. Their resulting conclusion of a long-term equity risk premium using this supply-side model was estimated to be about 6 percent arithmetically and 4 percent geometrically. At the time of their 2001 paper, the recognized equity risk premium using purely historical data was about 1.25 percent higher (0.9% *SBBI 2008 Yearbook and 0.8% in the SBBI 2009 Yearbook*).[14]

While this difference has been viewed by some as significant, it is important to recognize that this difference is substantially *less than has been identified by others* in the academic arena, especially when considering the more recently published smaller differences in Ibbotson. (Note: In the 2010 edition it was 1.5%.) Some have concluded a forward-looking equity risk premium of as little as 0 percent to 2 percent.[15] Subsequent to the Ibbotson/Chen study, Dr. Shannon Pratt published an Editor's Column in the November 2003 *Business Valuation Update* newsletter, recommending that all closely held business appraisers reduce their historical equity risk premium by 1.25 percent.

The takeaway point here is that if business appraisers are to utilize a supply-side theory in their rate development, they need to not only be mindful of the theoretical underpinning of how the supply-side rate is developed but also be sure to use the current indication that has moderated from the point in time that Pratt made his November 2003 recommendation.

Since the publication of Dr. Pratt's recommendation, there has been some controversy in the valuation community regarding this adjustment to the historical data that many rely on within the Ibbotson SBBI publications. To better understand these choices, one must comprehend the factors within the forward-looking supply-side

---

[13] Also see Roger G. Ibbotson, and Chen, Peng, "Long-Run Stock Returns: Participating in the Real Economy," *Financial Analysts Journal*, 59, no. 1 (January/February 2003).

[14] The supply-side equity risk premium may not affect returns where a size premium (RP_s) is applied since much, if not all, is eliminated if a supply-side RP_s is calculated. Ibbotson was considering reports on RP_s "in excess of CAPM" with a supply-side RP_m, which may result in a greater size premium. At the time of this writing, a whitepaper had been prepared. However, Ibbotson has not published a supply-side RP_s in its 2009 and 2010 editions. Many analysts are comfortable using a supply-side ERP and a historical based size premium. See Addendum 8 to this chapter at www.wiley.com/go/FVAM3E.

[15] Robert D. Arnott, Peter L. Bernstein V, "What Premium Is Normal?," *Journal of Portfolio Management* (January 2002).

Exhibit 6.8 S&P 500 as a Function of EPS and P/E Ratio Left-Hand Scale: EPS and P/E Ratios Right-Hand Scale: S&P 500 Index Value

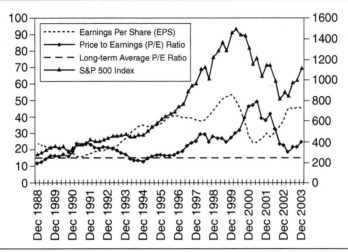

model that cause the difference. An earnings-based model says that the expected return is equal to the earnings yield. A review of the 15-year history of the S&P 500 Index, ending on December 31, 2003, conveys relevant trends (see Exhibit 6.8).

Splitting the S&P 500 Index (triangle data points) into two components—earnings per share (dotted line) and the P/E multiple (solid square data points)—allows for better comprehension of these trends. At each data point, the EPS can be multiplied by the P/E multiple to get the index value. For example, as of the end of December 2003, the S&P Index reached 1112. As of that date, the EPS of the combined companies was $45.20 and the P/E multiple, therefore, was 24.6× ($45.20 × 24.6 = 1112).

As the index finished the year with a P/E of almost 25, the earnings yield was 4 percent (1 ÷ 25 = 4%). According to the earnings-based approach, the expected real return before inflation was this 4 percent return. The underlying intuitive concept is "mean reversion": the theory that P/E multiples cannot get too high or too low before they revert back to the historical trend line. Ibbotson and Chen studied these same P/E multiples over the same period that they used for their traditional equity risk premium calculations beginning in 1926, which indicates a continued run-up of P/E ratios from the early 1970s to the current date. Consequently, a high P/E implies lower future returns and a low P/E implies higher future returns.

This information confirms why some academics have warned that near-term future equity returns will not keep pace with the double-digit returns of the 1990s. Consider the 10-year period from 1988 to 1998, omitting the even more acute bubble that occurred at the end of the decade. EPS grew at an annualized rate of 6.4 percent, but the S&P Index grew at an amazing 16 percent pace. The difference from this so-called "multiple expansion" resulted in an increase in the P/E multiple for this period from about 12× to 28× over this same period. This is precisely what drives the issue upon which many academics have recently focused. Starting from a base P/E multiple of about 25× at the end of 2003 for the overall market, continued expansion of the P/E multiple is required to realize increased long-term returns that outpace earnings growth.

The two leading supply-side approaches start with either dividends or earnings. The dividend-based approach says that returns are a function of dividends and their

Exhibit 6.9 Dividends and Earnings Example

	Start Dividend at $3 and Grow at 5%		Stock Price (Div. Payout + Yield)
	Payout	Div. Yield	
Initial Stock Price (Year 0)			$100.00
Year 1	$3.15	3%	$105.00
Year 2	3.31	3%	110.25
Year 3	3.47	3%	115.76
Year 4	3.65	3%	121.55
Year 5	3.83	3%	127.63
Total at End of Year 5			
Paid Dividends	$17.41		
Reinvested Dividends	19.14		
Total Proceeds (Yr 5 Price + Dividends)			$146.77
Total Annualized Return			8.0%

future growth. Consider an example with a single stock that today is priced at $100, pays a constant 3 percent dividend yield (dividend per share divided by stock price), but for which we also expect the dividend—in dollar terms—to grow at 5 percent per year.

In the example in Exhibit 6.9, you can see that if we grow the dividend at 5 percent per year and insist on a constant dividend yield, the stock price must go up 5 percent per year, too. The key assumption is that the stock price is fixed as a multiple of the dividend. If you like to think in terms of P/E ratios, it is equivalent to assuming that 5 percent earnings growth and a fixed P/E multiple must push the stock price up 5 percent per year. At the end of five years, our 3 percent dividend yield naturally gives us a 3 percent return ($19.14 if the dividends are reinvested). The growth in dividends has pushed the stock price to $127.63, which gives us an additional 5 percent return. Together, we get a total return of 8 percent.

That's the idea behind the dividend-based approach: the dividend yield (%) plus the expected growth in dividends (%) equals the expected total return (%). In formulaic terms, it is just a reworking of the Gordon Growth Model, which says that the fair price of a stock ($\underline{P}$) is a function of the dividend per share ($\underline{D}$), growth in the dividend ($\underline{g}$), and the required or expected rate of return ($\underline{k}$) (see Exhibit 6.10).

Another approach looks at the price-to-earnings (P/E) ratio and its reciprocal: the earnings yield (earnings per share ÷ stock price). The idea is that the market's expected long-run real return is equal to the current earnings yield. For example, at the end of 2003, the P/E for the S&P 500 was almost 25. This theory says that the expected return is equal to the earnings yield of 4 percent ($1 \div 25 = 4\%$). If that seems low, remember it's a real return. Add a rate of inflation to get a nominal return.

Exhibit 6.11 shows the math that gets you the earnings-based approach.[16]

---

[16] Significant portions of this discussion (pp. 166–168) are taken from the two-part Internet article by David Harper, Editor in Chief of Investopedia Advisor, titled "The Equity Risk Premium—Parts 1 and 2," January and February 2004 (www.investopedia.com/articles/04/012104.asp and www.investopedia.com/articles/04/020404.asp), copyright © 1999–2006 Investopedia Inc., www.investopedia.com.

Exhibit 6.10 Gordon Growth Model

Gordon Growth Model	Rearranged to solve for the expected return (k)
$$P = \frac{D}{k - g}$$ Where: **P** = stock price **D** = dividend dollars **k** = the expected return (%) **g** = growth rate (%)	$$k = \frac{D}{P} + g$$ **k** = dividend yield + dividend growth

Other Emerging ERP-Related Resources

Merrill Lynch Quantitative Profiles

This is a monthly publication by Merrill Lynch that uses expected return projections from its own analysts to provide expected return estimates. Using these expected return estimates, an analyst can calculate an implied forecasted ERP.

Greenwich Associates

Greenwich Associates conducts an annual survey of pension-plan administrators where they provide their estimates of annual rates of return expected on individual asset classes for the next five years.

Exhibit 6.11 Derivation of Earnings-Based Approach

Step	Formula	Note
(1) Start with Gordon Growth Model	$$P = \frac{D}{k - g}$$	(P) = Stock price (D) = Dividend per share (k) = Expected return (G) = Growth in dividends
(2) Introduce Earnings Per Share (E) and Retention Ratio (R)	$$P = \frac{E \times (1 - R)}{k - (k \times R)}$$	Replace Dividends (D) with: Earnings Per Share (E) times the payout ratio (i.e., 1 − retention rate) Replace Growth (G) with: expected return (k) multiplied by retention ratio (r). The assumption: that retained earnings are re-invested at the expected rate of return
(3) Solve for Stock Price (P)	$$\frac{E \times (1 - R)}{k \times (1 - R)} \quad - \quad P =$$	$$= \frac{E}{k}$$
(4) Rearrange to solve for expected return (*k*)	$$k = \frac{E}{P}$$	Expected Return (k) equals earnings yield (or 1 ÷ P/E ratio)

Duke/CFO Magazine Global Business Outlook Survey

Duke University's Fuqua School of Business and *CFO* magazine conduct a quarterly survey of CFOs of companies and subscribers of *CFO* magazine around the world whereby respondents provide their estimates of the average total return for the S&P 500 Index over the next 10 years. John R. Graham and Campbell R. Harvey prepare results in periodic white papers.

Dr. Aswath Damodaran

Dr. Aswath Damodaran of the Stern School at New York University also presents ERP data.

Size Premium (RP$_s$)

The size premium (RP$_s$) often is added when valuing smaller, closely held businesses. Empirical evidence demonstrates that as the size of a company decreases, the risk to that company increases. Therefore, a smaller company may have to pay an additional premium to attract funds.

The terms "small-stock premium" and "size premium" are both used to describe the size effect noted above, but each is based on a different set of assumptions and can be used differently in practice. Empirical data points are provided in the Ibbotson SBBI books (*Classic* and *Valuation* editions) for both premiums since both are used regularly by the different markets served by the SBBI data. This discussion focuses mostly on the *Valuation Edition, 2009 Yearbook*.

Small-Stock Premium

Security analysts use small-stock premiums in constructing an expected return for a small-stock benchmark used in forecasting applications. It is reflected in the *SBBI* books as the arithmetic difference between the S&P 500 stock returns and the small-stock segment of the market. According to the studies by Ibbotson (2009 Yearbook), the smaller public stocks that make up the microcap segment of the market have "outperformed" their larger counterparts by 4.8 percent over the last 83 years.

SIZE PREMIUMS

Size premiums, which are used more often by valuation analysts, are presented for each of the 10 deciles of the public securities market. The size premium, which relies on the CAPM model, entails a more complex measurement process.[17] The specific size premium figures reflect the excess returns required on smaller securities after adjusting for the systematic risks captured in the beta adjustment. In other words, the size premia data presented by Ibbotson that are most widely used by valuation analysts today have been adjusted for all other systematic influences, except size.

Does Size Matter?

There is continuing debate over which size premia should be used. Some analysts even have argued against including a size premia adjustment for smaller companies

---

[17] Actual return minus the expected return (CAPM); also called in excess of CAPM.

altogether. Recent studies have been used to advance both sides of this argument, but most analysts agree that some adjustment should be made to account for the fact that, over time, smaller entities in the public markets have demanded higher rates of returns, generally speaking, than their larger counterparts. Both Michael W. Barad[18] of Ibbotson at that time and Dr. Shannon P. Pratt[19] have been featured in articles highlighting the need for a size premium adjustment when using the traditional build-up model to derive rates for use in valuing smaller, closely held businesses.

In a presentation called "The Small Company Risk Premium: Does It Really Exist?" Jeffery S. Tarbell[20] presented a list of factors that typically reflect the increased risks of smaller companies:

- Difficult to raise financing
- Lack of product, industry, and geographic diversification
- Inability to expand into new markets
- Key person management risk
- Lack of management expertise
- Higher sensitivity to economic movements
- Lack of dividend history
- Higher sensitivity to business risks, supply squeezes, and demand lulls
- Inability to control or influence regulatory and union activity
- Lack of economies of scale or cost disadvantages
- Lack of access to distribution channels
- Lack of relationships with suppliers and customers
- Lack of product differentiation or brand name recognition
- Lack of deep pockets necessary for staying power
- Lack of externally generated information, including analyst coverage, resulting in a lack of forecasts
- Lack of adequate press coverage and other avenues to disseminate company-generated information
- Lack of internal controls
- Lack of infrastructure
- Possible lack of internal reporting
- Smaller-capitalization companies are viewed as riskier by the credit markets, resulting in:
  - Higher interest rate spreads
  - Lower multiples of EBITDA for financing
  - Lower collateralization rates
  - More restrictive covenants
  - Less use of stock as security interest

---

[18] Michael W. Barad, "Technical Analysis of the Size Premium," *CCH Business Valuation Alert* (September 2001).

[19] Shannon P. Pratt, "Small Stock Risk Premium No Myth: Size Does Matter," *Business Valuation Update* (September 2001).

[20] Jeffrey S. Tarbell, "The Small Company Risk Premium: Does It Really Exist?" American Society of Appraisers, 18th Annual Advanced Business Valuation Conference, New Orleans, Louisiana, October 1999.

> Lists of small-company risk factors can be used to analyze the attributes of a specific subject company and to select the level of adjustment for size and unsystematic risk. It is important, however, to avoid a "double counting" since adjustments for size may implicitly include adjustments for other operating attributes.

Size Premium Choices

Ibbotson presents data segmented into the 10 deciles of the New York Stock Exchange, with each decile having the same number of companies.[21] Ibbotson then adds similar-size companies from the American Stock Exchange and the NASDAQ. Within the empirical data, there are several possible market segment choices to draw from to adjust for size. Two choices are:

1. *Ibbotson micro-cap size premium.* This is a measure of the extra returns on the public companies making up the 9th and 10th deciles of the market with a mean average market capitalization of $139.0 million and a range of $1.6 million to $453.3 million. Some analysts favor using this benchmark due to the significant breadth of the market covered by this combined strata (2,229 companies in the most recent year).
2. *Tenth decile of the Ibbotson studies.* This benchmark size premium exhibits the additional returns enjoyed historically by companies making up the smallest 10th of the public market. The most recent year of data includes 1,626 companies. These entities range roughly between $1.6 and $218.5 million in market capitalization, with a mean average of $79.2 million.

A significant gap still exists in the market value of these public companies and many of the smaller closely held companies that analysts value. In response, Ibbotson has further broken down the 10th decile by size in the *2009 SBBI Valuation Yearbook.*[22] The entries in the 10a strata range in market capitalization from $136.5 million to $218.5 million; 10b strata companies range between $1.6 million and $136.5 million.

The 10b group of publicly traded stocks exhibits a size premium that is more than double the size of the 10a strata. Besides a smaller sample size, other issues that can create less reliable small-stock premia data include the:

- Impact of transaction costs on small stocks in relation to the value of the underlying shares
- Biases due to infrequent trading of small-company shares and the impact on their betas

---

[21] Morningstar, Inc., *2009 Ibbotson SBBI Valuation Yearbook,* p. 90. (Used with permission. All rights reserved.)
[22] Ibid., p. 95. Note: In the 2010 *Ibbotson SBBI Valuation Yearbook,* decile 10 has been separated into quarters: 10w, 10x, 10y, and 10z.

- Larger bid-ask spread
- "Delisting bias" found in the lower segment of the public markets

Beta Criteria

Once a choice is made between these differing benchmarks, the analyst must determine what set of criteria is appropriate to use. The Ibbotson size premia are all derived by reference to the CAPM model. The various charts provided in the *SBBI* book use different measures of beta coefficients to make the underlying calculations. The analyst must choose from the different sets.

The chart in Exhibit 6.12 illustrates the choices analysts can make in selecting a size premium. All of the following premia are based on returns in excess of CAPM.[23]

Exhibit 6.12   Equity Size Premiums (%) (2009)

			Deciles	
Category	Micro-Cap*	10	10a	10b
S&P 500 (Monthly Beta)	3.74	5.81	4.11	9.53
NYSE (Monthly Beta)	4.21	6.33	N/A	N/A
S&P 500 (Sum Beta)	2.18	3.87	N/A	N/A
S&P 500 (Annual Beta)	2.83	4.43	N/A	N/A

* 9th & 10th Deciles

The range is quite large, 2.18 to 9.53 percent. Some analysts prefer using micro-cap premiums since there is a larger number of companies in the sample size. However, this premium data includes larger companies, diminishing the impact of size. Many analysts use the S&P 500 (Monthly Beta) 10th decile risk premium of 5.81 percent. This premium has become more meaningful since Ibbotson increased the number of companies from 185 companies in the *2000 Yearbook* to 1,626 companies with the publication of its *2009 Yearbook*.

Liquidity and Size

In 2006, Morningstar, Inc., acquired Ibbotson Associates. Morningstar states it is committed to improving and augmenting *SBBI* to increase its usefulness as a resource for valuation professionals. In 2009 *SBBI* included a new section written by Zhiwu Chen and Roger Ibbotson that suggests capitalization is not necessarily the direct underlying cause of higher returns for small companies. The *2009 SBBI book* presents a white paper by Chen and Ibbotson that demonstrates that liquidity strongly predicts stock returns. However, there is still a relationship between size and liquidity.

Also, Ibbotson is introducing a new online application that allows users to identify companies with similar characteristics and then calculates a custom cost of equity and weighted average cost of capital along with other financial ratios for the selected peer group.

---

[23] Ibid., pp. 135–143.

New Ibbotson Data

Ibbotson has also released additional resources in the *2010 Valuation Yearbook* that further segregate the risk premia captured within the 10th decile into four quadrants, identified as 10w, 10x, 10y, and 10z, as opposed to the upper and lower segregation accomplished with their split between what they have referred to as 10a and 10b. This will further allow analysts to evaluate and quantify an appropriate size premium for application to smaller entity valuation engagements, although this further segregation will require the analyst to also evaluate the propriety of the empirical evidence given the smaller sample sizes that will exist within each quadrant of the 10th decile.

Ibbotson has also introduced a new model to identify distressed companies using what they have labeled a Distance to Default framework (based on the option pricing models developed by Black and Scholes and Merton), and further builds on the academic work of Edward Altman in the 1960s and his Altman Z-Score model that has been widely used to predict an enterprise's exposure to insolvency and potential bankruptcy. This model was applied to the market data used and published by Ibbotson to effectively strip out the distressed companies in the data to, in turn, then allow the production of a cleaner set of size and risk premia without the impact of the segregated entities deemed to be in distress. For example, if the distressed companies that many identify with the lower end of the public markets could be sufficiently identified and segregated, the ability to rely on the 10th decile data along with the 10a/b and 10w/x/y/z categories, may be enhanced. In the Ibbotson *2010 Valuation Yearbook*, the distance to default framework was applied. The conclusion was that distressed companies do not have a material impact on the results. Readers are urged to keep an eye and ear out for the application of these resources.[24]

Company-Specific Risk Premium (RP$_u$)

The final component of the discount rate is the risk specific (RP$_u$) to the company being valued and/or the industry in which it operates. This is one of the most judgmental areas of business valuation. Company-specific risk includes risk associated with the particular industry in which the subject company operates in relation to the economy as a whole as well as the risks associated with the internal workings of the subject company, including such things as management, leverage, and dependence on specific suppliers, customers, markets, etc.

Using the Ibbotson Industry Risk Premia

The Ibbotson industry risk premia draw on empirically supported studies of the risk associated with specific industries using a concept called full-information betas. Full-information betas calculate a weighted average beta for an industry segment by segregating the proportion of each publicly traded enterprise within a specific industry based on gross revenues. The result is an indication of the beta coefficient for an industry as a whole in relation to an overall market beta of 1.0.

The 2000 edition of *SBBI* listed estimates of industry premia for over 60 general SIC codes. These estimates are shown as percentage adjustments ranging from –12.59

---

[24] See "A Timely New Study of Bankruptcy Prediction Models from Morningstar," *Business Valuation Update* 15, no. 10 (October 2009), 1–6.

to +7.41 percent. The 2009 edition of *SBBI* expanded this industry risk information to 463 SIC codes with an indication of premia ranging from –6.16 to +11.0 percent. Conceptually, the emergence of this new empirically supported data means that the traditional model utilized to develop rates can be adjusted in certain situations:

Traditional Application of the Build-Up Approach

	Risk-free rate
+	Equity risk premium
+	Size premium
+	Specific company risk
=	Cost-of-capital discount rate

Application of the Build-Up Approach Using Ibbotson Industry Risk Premia

	Risk-free rate
+	Equity risk premium
+	Size premium
+/–	Industry risk premium
+	Specific company risk
=	Cost-of-capital discount rate

As indicated above, Ibbotson calculates industry risk premia using full information betas. This method estimates industry risk by incorporating data from all companies participating within an identified industry. The purpose of this process is to capture the overall risk characteristics of the industry as compared to the overall market risk. The formula used by Ibbotson for calculating the industry risk premia is:

$$IRP_i = (RI_i \times ERP) - ERP$$

Where:

IRP_i = the expected industry risk premium for industry i, or the amount by which investors expect the future return of the industry to exceed that of the market as a whole

RI_i = the risk index (full information beta) for industry i

ERP = the expected equity risk premium (RP_m)

Similar to beta estimation concepts, an industry with a risk index equal to the market, or 1, will have a risk premium of 0; for those industries with a risk index greater than 1, the industry risk premium will be positive; and for those with a risk index less than 1, it will be negative. As an example, if the full information beta (RI_i) for the Miscellaneous Home Furnishings Stores (SIC 5719) is 1.1, and the current ERP is 6.5 percent, the industry risk premium is calculated as follows:

$$IRP_i = (1.1 \times 6.5) - 6.5$$
$$= 0.65\%$$

While the traditional view of the build-up model of rate determination has been viewed as an additive model, it is important to note that the distribution of the industry risk premia, as calculated by Ibbotson using the methodology outlined here, provides data points that are both additive and subtractive from the overall BUM calculation. This is to be expected, given that these risk measures are in relation to the risk associated with the overall market from which they are derived, just like the beta estimation methodology with a distribution both above and below 1.

In the 2009 *SBBI Valuation Yearbook,* Ibbotson provides 463 indications of industry risk premiums with many now extending to the three- and four-digit SIC code level, as compared to prior editions where only a much narrower selection of two-digit SIC code risk premiums were published in the SBBI Yearbook. This trend to expand both the number of data points and the depth thereof by calculating those three- and four-digit industries where sufficient data is available makes this information more useful from a practical application perspective.

Where the calculation references the same number of companies for the risk index for two- and three-digit SIC codes and three- and four-digit SIC codes, the extended SIC code has been eliminated. For example, SIC code 491 and 4911 utilize the same number of companies, and therefore, the calculation for SIC 4911 has been eliminated, as it would be the same as SIC 491 for purposes of this calculation. For a full list of the specific companies that make up each calculation, download the Industry Premia Company List Report at http://corporate.morningstar.com/irp.

An important practice point is to use the *beta-adjusted* size premium found in Table 7-5 or Appendix C of the *SBBI* when using the industry risk premiums as part of the build-up method, as opposed to using the simple difference in returns between large- and small-company stocks, as this latter approach can overstate the cost of equity. The simple difference between large- and small-stock returns makes the assumption that the systematic risk of the company is the same as the risk of the small-company portfolio. Ibbotson argues that the industry risk premium as presented in the SBBI, when used in this manner, is a better measure of the appropriate systematic risk to apply to the BUM.

ValTip

> The authors note that the Ibbotson industry risk data for specific industries, as presented in Chapter 3 of the *SBBI,* appears to change significantly between annual editions, and therefore, caution that the direct application of an added or subtracted component to the BUM for industry risk remains questionable and is affected by the type and detail of the data. An alternate approach is to evaluate the risk premia provided for SIC codes related to the valuation target under consideration and then use such information inferentially to adjust the unsystematic risk component under the premise that industry risk is an element thereof. This is also an important distinction, as well, because when using the industry data directly, it is important to eliminate any consideration of industry risks within the unsystematic adjustment.

This new framework is another step toward helping close the gap between risk factors that can be empirically justified and those that must be selected based on judgment. However, it should be noted that the number of companies included in all SIC codes (Standard Industrial Classification) can range from as few as 5 (the minimum allowed) to over 600. Since the industry risk premia provided is still somewhat limited in terms of the number of companies per industry, the number of industries represented, and the broad definitions of industry categories, the selection of appropriate adjustments for industry risk will continue to be often judgmental. Therefore, the analyst still will need to evaluate industry-related factors not captured by this new premia information. Nonetheless, these data can assist practitioners in certain assignments where a strong relationship between available industry data and the subject entity can be made.

For purposes of assessing enterprise risk, an argument can also be made to focus on strategic groups of business interests, as opposed to industry concentrations alone. This is a major thrust of the work of Michael Porter's research. Overly simplified, the underlying theory with this concept is that the profitability of many business enterprises will be subject more to the economic impacts and performance of those enterprises within their strategic group, than those that simply operate within their same industry. The relevant strategic group often encompasses those customers and suppliers who are aligned vertically with the business, as opposed to competitors on the horizontal plane.

> While the amount of industry risk premia data available from Ibbotson Associates is expected to grow over time, many analysts in the valuation community are not yet comfortable with the direct application of industry risk premia adjustments. However, analysts can consider this new empirical evidence where the subject falls within one of the Ibbotson-defined industries, there are a sufficient number of companies and there is, hopefully, a four-digit SIC code, and there is a need to assess industry risk that may not be captured in the build-up method.

Addendum 2 of this chapter is a front-page article, "Ibbotson Industry Risk Premium Data: If You Use It, Use It with Knowledge," from *Financial Valuation and Litigation Expert*, Issue 17, February/March 2009, which presents some potential problems with the IRP data use. It is based on information in the *Ibbotson 2008 Valuation Yearbook*.[25]

METHODS TO ARTICULATE UNSYSTEMATIC RISK

Frank C. Evans, principal in Evans and Associates, made a presentation at an August 1999 ASA conference that covered the use of a matrix to detail adjustments for company-specific risk factors. An example of this matrix concept was published in the "How Do You Handle It?" column of the September 1999 *Business Valuation Review* newsletter, shown in Exhibit 6.13.

---

[25] See Addendum 2 at www.wiley.com/go/FVAM3E for a more in-depth discussion on when to use the industry risk premium data.

Exhibit 6.13 Specific Company Risk Factors

	Incremental Risk (Ex. only)
Specific Company Risk Factors for XYZ Corporation	
1. Operating history, volatility of revenues and earnings	3.5
2. Lack of management depth	1.0
3. Lack of access to capital resources	0.5
4. Over-reliance on key persons	1.0
5. Lack of size and geographic diversification	0.5
6. Lack of customer diversification	0.0
7. Lack of marketing resources in light of competition	0.5
8. Lack of purchasing power and other economies of scale	0.0
9. Lack of product and market development resources	0.5
10. Over-reliance on vendors/suppliers	0.0
11. Limitations on distribution system	0.0
12. Limitations on financial reporting and controls	0.5
Positive Attributes	
1. Long-term contracts with customers or unique product or market niche	0.0
2. Patents, copyrights, franchise rights, proprietary products	(1.0)
Net increase to discount rate	**7.0**

The above sample chart displays several interesting aspects. First, it is worth noting that the factors outlined in this analysis are similar to the size factors listed by Tarbell, as discussed in the size premia adjustment section earlier in this chapter. Second, the sample lists some positive attributes, which can reduce the adjustment to the discount rate for operating attributes that reduce risk.

Exhibit 6.14 is another example of a format that can be utilized to assist in the measurement of unsystematic risks of an enterprise. It must be emphasized, however, that the use of such tools is judgmental in nature without a direct formula or correlation table to quantify the required adjustment to capture the additional returns required for such risks. In the following example, the first item within each category has a sample of what might be included within the context of a specific assignment with similar descriptions for each listed category utilized for the specific assignment.

ValTip

Analysts must use caution when working with a methodology that assigns specific numerical adjustments to the build-up or CAPM rate. Due to the subjective nature of the numerical assignments for each category, the analyst may be asked if it is reasonable for each of the factors to be, say, a half percent higher or lower, thereby in summation causing a significant change in the resulting capitalization or discount rate being developed. These numerical adjustments are not as exact as they appear and are not based on any empirical data. Also, these lists may not be all inclusive.

Exhibit 6.14 Unsystematic Risk Analysis for a Professional Law Practice—Business Characteristics and Risk Factors: Summary

Risk Ratings can be "High," Medium," or "Low" and are subjective assessments of factors in the professional practice being valued. A numeric scale may also be used, although it is important to emphasize that the results of such an approach cannot be converted directly into a final measure of unsystematic risk.

<u>Risk</u>

I.   Practice Makeup

1.   Range of Services Provided: HIGH
     The practice is not well diversified since it focuses entirely on bankruptcy. Its limited focus not only prevents it from meeting the needs of a broad range of clientele, but also hinders its ability to respond to changing external conditions.

2.   Years in Business:

3.   Stability, change:

4.   Key Personnel Dependence:

5.   Staff Stability:

6.   Availability of New Staff:

7.   Relative Size of Practice:

8.   Ease of Competitive Entry:

9.   Client Loyalty and Dependency:

10. Office and Equipment:

11. Name Recognition of Firm:

12. Reputation of Professionals:

13. Marketing Methods/Strengths:

14. Location:

15. Growth Potential:

II.   Financial Risk: Current Status and Historical Trends

1.   Current and Quick Ratios: LOW
     A current ratio analysis of the enterprise over the past three years shows the following:

	12/31/x1	12/31/x2	12/31/x3
Current Ratio	2.55×	2.32×	2.88×

The current ratio of the enterprise has remained stable over the period analyzed, based on normalized figures. Roughly 90% of the current asset base included in the ratio consists of accounts receivables due from clients. Only the current portion of such receivables (less than 120 days outstanding) has been included in the calculations and the practice appears to have adequate internal controls in place to monitor and address billing and collections. The ratios compare favorably with industry statistics.

2.   Profitability Ratios:

3.   Realization Ratios:

(continues)

Exhibit 6.14 *continued*

<u>Risk</u>

4.   Utilization Ratios:

5.   Debt/Worth Ratio:

6.   Books/Records, Quality, History:

7.   Historical Trends:

III.   Management   LOW

1.   Management Experience:
     The practice is managed by a traditional law firm model, consisting of a managing partner, executive committee, department heads, and a qualified legal administrator. During the period ending 12/31/xx, the firm changed its appointment process to allow for the managing partner to serve for successive periods as opposed to an annual change in this leadership position. The current managing partner is well skilled in management concepts and dedicates a significant portion of her time to the day-to-day management needs of the enterprise. The executive committee was also revamped to allow appointments of the six spots on a basis of three-year terms with two individuals being appointed each year, occurring at the firm's annual owner's retreat. Department heads are appointed by the owner and most have been with the firm for a number of years. The legal administrator, who holds the CLM designation from the Association of Legal Administrators, is a CPA with significant experience in law firm operations.

2.   Depth of Management:

3.   Business Plan: Status:

4.   Management Philosophy and Systems:

5.   Succession Plans and Systems:

Such an analytical framework is only a diagnostic tool to assist the practitioner in the exercise of professional judgment. No formulas, guidelines, or rules of thumb can be relied on consistently to derive indications of unsystematic risk for a specific enterprise. It is based on the analyst's professional judgment.

The format and content of an analytical framework for analyzing unsystematic risk will vary considerably depending on the nature of the assignment and the depth of analysis required. However, the articulation of the analyst's thought process by use of diagnostic tools can be a means of competitive differentiation, whether the tools are included in the final report or only in engagement work papers.

Based on the analysis (Exhibit 6.14), together with our overall assessment of the unsystematic risk associated with the subject interest, we conclude that an additional 6 percent (example only) should be added.

Another useful perspective or framework for analyzing unsystematic risk is incorporated within the work of Warren Miller in his seven-part series of articles on unsystematic risk, which are being published in the AICPA's *CPA Expert* newsletter. Exhibits 6.15 to 6.16, taken with permission from Miller's work, and Exhibit 6.17 help to convey some of the key aspects that an analyst should consider in conjunction with an assessment and quantification of these risks.

Exhibit 6.15   Analyzing Unsystematic Risk 1

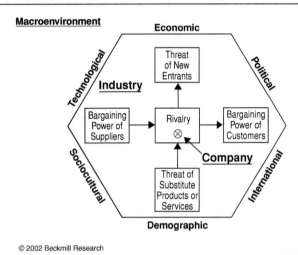

© 2002 Beckmill Research

Exhibit 6.16   Analyzing Unsystematic Risk 2

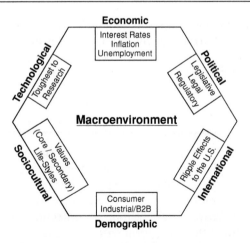

© 2002 Beckmill Research

Adapted from *Microenvironmental Analysis for Strategic Management* by Liam Fahey and V.K. Naraganan (St. Paul: West Publishing Company, 1986), p. 29, and *Strategic Management: Competitiveness and Globalization* (3rd Ed.) by Michael A. Hitt, R. Duane Ireland, and Robert E. Hoskisson (Cincinnati: South Western Publishing Company, 1999), pp. 50–60. Also *Competitive Strategy: Techniques for Analyzing Industries and Competitors* by Michael E. Porter (New York: The Free Press, 1998).

Exhibit 6.17 Analyzing Unsystematic Risk 3

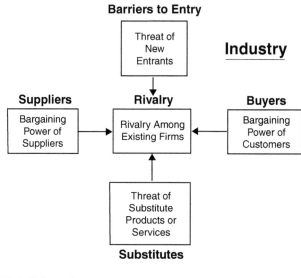

© 2002 Beckmill Research

Source: *Competitive Strategy: Techniques for Analyzing Industries and Competitors* by Michael E. Porter (New York: The Free Press, 1998).

Specific Company Risk and the Total Beta Model

The basic premise of what is referred to as the total beta model (TBM) or Butler/Pinkerton Calculator (BPC), which was made visible to the valuation community by Peter Butler and Keith Pinkerton, remains controversial for assistance in determining specific company risk. However, the model itself is not as controversial as some have tried to make it. It says that beta, which captures the systematic or market risk, doesn't capture all the risk associated with a public company, nor does it capture all the risk associated with a private company. So how do people who value small, closely held businesses use the total beta model to get useful information?

When using the modified CAPM formula, they may use a concept of total beta, which some analysts believe captures both company-specific or idiosyncratic risk and market risk. Put that in place of the typical data. Put a total beta in the same formula as a plain beta. By doing this, some analysts believe you can capture that associated risk and narrow your judgment gap, because that's what all of these models are trying to help us do—narrow our application of professional judgment.

There is a simple, straightforward formula to calculate total beta from beta. Even better, there is the calculator—the BPC. For a fee, you can go online to www.bvresources.com and add in your selection of public guideline companies, and it will calculate the total beta for you and actually calculate estimates of your rate of return and the specific company risk premium. How does this work in practice? First, you have to find supportable guideline public companies, which does, in turn, require an appropriate analytical mindset and application of professional judgment.

Think of it as a market approach, sort of wrapped up as an income approach. You need to calculate the total return for each company, again either using the formula or going to the calculator. You compute the traditional CAPM or build-up return and subtract this from the total return. The BPC does all of this for you, producing an estimate of the company-specific risk for each public guideline company identified. From here you can identify the company-specific risk factors present in that industry or in those companies and explain why guideline company A has a different company-specific risk from guideline company B (and so on). This puts the result in context with the company-specific risk for your subject company.

TBM—Income versus Market Approach

This is still controversial, but some analysts use it as a starting point and as a confirming element to an area that has long been viewed as overly dependent on professional judgment with sometimes wide variations between analysts on the same subject interest being valued. However, there is still indeed a degree of professional judgment involved in getting the information from the calculator to your private company. One practical limitation to the total beta model is that, again, you have to find public guideline companies. If you found public guideline companies, you'd probably use a market approach. So if you have used a market approach and an income approach, just from a pure presentation standpoint, do you want to get your cost of equity—one of the major two components in the income approach—from the same source you used for your market approach? If you did, you'd be opening both of your approaches to additional scrutiny, as opposed to just one of them. However, this is not really that much different from using betas from guideline companies used in the market approach in the modified CAPM.

Summary of TBM

The basic premise underlying the TBM is not controversial on a stand-alone basis. When guideline public companies exist, some analysts believe the model provides a framework from which to analyze and place in context the specific-company risk premium. Access to the model (i.e., the calculator) is priced such that it is affordable to use as appropriate. Limitations exist (such as the need for supportable publicly traded guideline companies), which limit its usefulness in many engagements. It should also be noted that there has been some lively debate and a high degree of criticism over the propriety of the TBM that will likely continue as analysts evaluate the applicability of this resource to help calculate unsystematic risk.

See Addendum 3 at www.wiley.com/go/FVAM3E for the article "Boston's Battle of the Beta," written by Don Wisehart, CPA/ABV, ASA, MST, in *Financial Valuation and Litigation Expert*, Issue 22, December 2009/January 2010, Valuation Products and Services, LLC. Many of the criticisms of total beta are presented there.

Duff & Phelps RP Report

An important alternative to the traditional build-up method using Ibbotson SBBI risk premia data is the Duff & Phelps Risk Premium Report (D&P RP Report). This resource originated in 1990 based on research conducted by Roger Grabowski and David King when the two were at PriceWaterhouseCoopers. The D&P RP Report utilizes historical data similar to Ibbotson *SBBI* data but differs in that the period covered is from 1963 to the present rather than from 1926 to the present, as used by Ibbotson.

The D&P RP Report provides data on the equity risk premium based on alternative measures of size. The same data used by Ibbotson in its calculations of the equity risk premia are divided in the D&P RP Report into 25 different size groups based on the following eight criteria:

- Market Value of Equity
- Book Value of Equity
- 5-Year Average Net Income
- Market Value of Invested Capital

- Total Assets
- 5-Year Average EBITDA
- Sales
- Number of Employees

It is relevant to further define some of these criteria as used in the D&P RP Report studies:

- Book Value of Equity is prior to any add-back of a deferred tax balance
- Average Net Income is net income before extraordinary items
- Number of Employees is either a year-end or yearly average, including part-time and seasonal workers and excluding contract workers and employees in unconsolidated subsidiaries

The companies used in the D&P RP Report come from the intersection of the companies found in both the Compustat and the University of Chicago's Center of Research in Security Prices (CRSP) for rate of return data. Financial Services sector companies (SIC code 6) are excluded, as are nonoperating holding companies and American Depository Receipts (ADRs). Companies must have been publicly traded for at least five years and have an established history of sales[26] and a positive five-year average EBITDA.

The approach taken by Grabowski and King isolates distressed companies by also excluding any companies that have a history of losses, have negative book values, have high leverage, or are in bankruptcy. High leverage is considered to be any company that has debt to MVIC of greater than 80 percent. These companies are placed into a High Financial Risk portfolio. It is interesting to note that this group of candidates now represents about 25 percent of the data set in recent years, while it accounted for less than 5 percent in 1963, meaning that there are now over four times as many "high risk" companies than in 1963 based on the definitions of financial distress used in the D&P RP Report studies.[27]

The remaining companies are sorted into 25 portfolios based on historical returns from 1963, which is the first year Compustat began collecting its data.[28] Returns are calculated based on annual holding periods with returns equal to price

---

[26] Companies with sales below $1 million in any of the previous five years are excluded.

[27] It is also interesting to note that the authors of the D&P RP Report have run their calculations without excluding any nonfinancial entities for these definitions of High Financial Risk and report in the study that the results are substantially similar in terms of the otherwise reported size effect.

[28] Compustat actually has data going back to the 1950s, but it is selective and incomplete, and this is the reason Grabowski and King decided to use 1963 as their base year.

appreciation, plus dividends. The equity risk premiums are calculated in the same manner that Ibbotson calculates its risk premiums in terms of it being based on the return in excess of a long-term Treasury bond income return. A separate and complete set of schedules is produced each year to also reflect the size premiums over CAPM based on the same eight measures of company size.

The benefits of ranking the returns by the criteria that are not based on equity market values is that the circular rationale for determining the size effect is substantially reduced if the discount rate can be based on a size measure that is independent of the value conclusion itself. It is recognized that companies of vastly different sizes in terms of operational characteristics can have the same market capitalization, such as a large multinational enterprise like United Airlines having the same relative market capitalization as some of the smaller start-up public companies.

The D&P RP Report has consistently found a size/return relationship in all published studies since the original release of data in 1995,[29] which used all companies in the NYSE. Grabowski and King published an article in the *ASA Business Valuation Review* journal in September 1996,[30] added NASDAQ and AMEX companies, and excluded companies with a history of poor financial performance. An article published in March 1997[31] further excluded the SIC 6 financial services sector, again with similar results. The 1998 D&P RP Report continued with these attributes and added corrections for the "delisting bias" of the smaller segment of the public market. The 2001 D&P ERP Report introduced a three-month lag between the annual portfolio rebalancing based on the eight size criteria and fiscal-year-end data used in the portfolio selection, again with similar results as compared to the prior studies.

Many business appraisers encounter valuation targets for closely held businesses that are often significantly smaller than entities found within the public markets. The approach taken by Grabowski and King in their studies is helpful in that the lower end (25th strata) more closely parallels the size parameters encountered in the closely held business arena. As an example, the 2009 D&P RP Report presents average size criteria for the 25th strata as follows:

- Market Value of Equity $111 million
- Book Value of Equity $60 million
- 5-Year Average Net Income $3 million
- Market Value of Invested Capital $145 million
- Total Assets $125 million
- 5-Year Average EBITDA $12 million
- Sales $112 million
- Number of Employees   246

While these averages are still significantly higher than a great many closely held business valuation targets, the averages for these expanded size criteria are more closely aligned than what has been heretofore available from the use of the Ibbotson *SBBI* data set.

---

[29] "The Size Effect and Equity Returns," *Business Valuation Review* (June 1995).
[30] "New Evidence on Size Effects and Equity Returns," *Business Valuation Review* (*September* 1996).
[31] "Size Effects and Equity Returns: An Update," *Business Valuation Review* (March 1997).

As an example (illustration only) of how the D&P RP Report data can be used for building up a discount rate for a target company, assume the following operating characteristics:[32]

	Size	Portfolio	Smoother Average Risk Premium Over Risk-Free Rate
Book equity	$40 mill	25	10.88%
Average net income	$3 mill	25	11.74%
Assets	$150 mill	24	9.97%
Average EBITDA	$20 mill	24	10.19%
Sales	$170 mill	24	9.58%
Employees	1,050	23	10.64%
	Average Premium		10.50%
	plus: Riskless rate		4.50%
	Cost of Equity		15.00%

Based on 2009 D & P Risk Premium Report, Arithmetic ERP.

In addition, equity risk premiums are calculated based on three distinct measures of entity risk:

- Operating Margin (the lower the operating margin, the greater the risk)
- Coefficient of Variation in Operating Margin (the greater the coefficient of variation, the greater the risk)
- Coefficient of Variation in Return on Equity (the greater the coefficient of variation, the greater the risk)

As a reminder, the Coefficient of Variation is the standard deviation divided by the mean. It measures volatility relative to the average value of the variable under consideration. This normalizes for differences in the magnitude of the subject variables. The results of the D&P RP Report studies document the correlation between company size and these measures of risk in that the more risky the enterprise, the smaller it will normally be. According to Grabowski and King, this also suggests a positive relationship between the greater risk as measured by the historical accounting information and the greater rate of return earned by equity investors.

The D&P RP Report is segregated into two parts. In Part I, companies are sorted by size, breaking the NYSE universe into the 25 size-ranked portfolios and adding AMEX and NASDAQ companies. Part II presents two varieties of data. First, the correlation between company size and three measures of company risk is documented based on accounting information. Next, the relationship among these three risk measures and historical rates of return is documented. Companies are sorted by the applicable measure of risk, breaking the universe into the 25 risk-ranked portfolios.

[32] D&P also presents "smoothed" premiums based on regression analysis with accompanying statistical data. They suggest that the smoothed premiums may be more appropriate for the smallest size category. See Addendums 5 and 6, "Duff and Phelps LLC Risk Premium Report Excerpts 2009 and 2010", at www.wiley.com/go/FVAM3E.

The D&P RP Report is updated annually and is available at http://corporate. morningstar.com/ib/asp or www.bvresources.com for download in Adobe .pdf format for a fee. The most recent update differs from some previously published versions in a few significant ways:

- It includes an extensive example illustrating how the data can be used in estimating a required rate of return on equity.
- It includes tables of equity premiums over the Capital Asset Pricing Model (CAPM).
- It includes a correction for the "delisting bias" in the CRSP database.
- It includes unlevered average risk premiums and betas.
- It adds explanatory text.
- The 2010 edition has information on high-financial-risk companies.

Reconciling Duff & Phelps and Ibbotson

Using a combination of historical ERPs such as Duff & Phelps as well as Ibbotson to determine an appropriate size-adjusted ERP has become increasingly popular among analysts. To reconcile these two approaches to determining an appropriate equity risk premium, the analyst must first make the necessary adjustments to each method. For Duff & Phelps, the analyst must choose the appropriate size portfolios along with the corresponding premium over the risk-free rate. Next, the analyst chooses the appropriate overall premium over the risk-free rate by either using an average or some other determination. For Ibbotson, the analyst chooses the appropriate equity risk premium and corresponding size adjustment to arrive at a size-adjusted equity risk premium. Since the Duff & Phelps data is already presented based on different metrics for size, a size adjustment is not necessary for the Duff & Phelps equity risk premium in the BUM.

Upon determining the appropriate size-adjusted equity risk premium for each of the two methods, the analyst can use an average or weighting scheme to develop an overall equity risk premium that is applicable to the subject company. Exhibit 6.18 illustrates a cost of equity development utilizing both the Duff & Phelps and Ibbotson data.

This example is for the build-up model. Other data from Ibbotson and Duff & Phelps can also be used for the modified CAPM. See Addendum 4 at www.wiley.com/go/FVAM3E for the article "Cost of Equity Capital: Straight, No Chaser," from the front page of *Financial Valuation and Litigation Expert*, Issue 24, April/May 2010, Valuation Products and Services, LLC. Addendum 8 at www.wiley.com/go/FVAM3E is the article "Cost of Equity Capital: Straight with a Chaser," from Issue 25, June/July 2010; and is an update of Addendum 4.

OTHER ISSUES

Selection of Reporting Period for Ibbotson Data

Ibbotson reports risk premiums based on averages from any reporting period since 1926. Most analysts use the data based on this period of time. However, studies of more recent time periods suggest that size premia may not be as evident in the public marketplace as the longer period data implies. For example, the average risk premium for micro-cap stocks from 1990 to 2000 was –0.7 percent, indicating small companies were less risky over that time period. If you go back to 1980 and 1970, the average risk premium for those periods to 2000 is –2.8 and –0.5 percent, respectively. It is interesting to note that in the first edition of *Financial Valuation Applications and*

Exhibit 6.18 Duff & Phelps and Ibbotson Equity Risk and Size Premium Build-Up Model Reconciliation[5] (illustration only using unadjusted data)

Duff & Phelps—Equity Risk Premium

Characteristic	Company Size	Implied Portfolio	Premium over Risk-Free Rate
Book Value of Equity—(a)	< $60 Mil	25	10.88%
5-Year Average Net Income—(a)	< $3 Mil	25	11.74%
Total Assets—(a)	< $125 Mil	25	11.21%
5-Year Average EBITDA—(a)	< $12 Mil	25	11.42%
Sales—(a)	< $112 Mil	25	10.46%
Number of Employees—(a)	< 246	25	10.64%
		Min	10.46%
		Mean	11.06%
		Median	11.05%
		Max	11.74%

Indicated Duff & Phelps Size Adjusted Equity Risk Premium   **11.05%**

Ibbotson—Equity Risk Premium

Equity Risk Premium—(b)	6.50%
Size Risk Premium—(b)	5.81%
Indicated Ibbotson Size Adjusted Equity Risk Premium	**12.31%**

Cost of Equity and Capitalization Rate Calculation

Risk-Free Rate—(c)		4.29%
Equity Risk Premium		
Duff & Phelps	11.05%	
Ibbotson	12.31%	
Average		11.68%
Company Specific Risk Premium—(d)		3.00%
Cost of Equity		**18.97%**

(a) Morningstar Inc., Duff & Phelps, LLC Risk Premium Report, 2009, 25th size categories
(b) Morningstar/Ibbotson, 2009 *SBBI Yearbook—Valuation Edition*, 10th decile size premium, historical ERP
(c) 20 year T-Bill rate @ 7/31/2009
(d) based on analyst judgment

Models, only a limited number of years from 1970 to 2000 resulted in positive average risk premiums under the micro-cap category: 1971 to 1977, 1991, and 1992, while all other data points from 1970 to 2000 yielded negative risk premiums for this period.

We agree with Ibbotson that a longer-term view is a consideration and that an adjustment for size may be warranted in most situations when the valuation target is a small, closely held enterprise.

After-Tax Cash Flow

Once the build-up rate has been completed, it is important to understand what type of rate the result represents. It is well recognized that the rate is an after-entity-level tax rate, meaning that the major components of the rate (Ibbotson) are derived from publicly traded companies' cash flows after allowing for entity-level taxes. It is also commonly accepted that the rate derived under this method is a cash-flow rate, meaning that it is based on empirical data from studies of cash flow returns of the public markets as opposed to reported earnings or some other measure of economic benefit stream. The definition of cash flows for this purpose includes not only reported dividends but increases in share values, since such capital appreciation represents accessible cash to the shareholders because they can liquidate their holdings at any moment in time.

Minority or Control

Another contentious issue is whether the resultant rate represents a minority or controlling interest return. Given that the underlying data used by Ibbotson in its empirical studies represents minority interest returns in publicly traded companies, many analysts have concluded that the resulting rates derived from the use of this method already incorporate the attributes of minority ownership. Ibbotson, however, argues that the rates derived from its data are neutral and incorporate neither control nor minority characteristics. The rationale is that most publicly traded companies optimize shareholder returns as a key corporate strategy and that the arrival of a new controlling owner would not be able to improve such returns unless that owner were a strategic buyer (which then may shift the standard of value away from FMV). There is no proof that such a control position could improve the shareholder returns. This issue was further discussed in an article by Eric Vander Linden in the December 1998 *Business Valuation Review* quarterly newsletter, titled "Cost of Capital Derived from Ibbotson Data Equals Minority Value?" Vander Linden concludes, after reference to several other recognized sources, that adjustments for control versus minority attributes are done through the numerator (cash flow) and not the denominator (rate of return). This view is also presented by the American Institute of Certified Public Accountants, the American Society of Appraisers, the Institute of Business Appraisers, and the National Association of Certified Valuation Analysts in their business valuation courses.

CAPITAL ASSET PRICING MODEL METHOD

History of CAPM

In 1952 economist Harry Markowitz developed the modern portfolio theory, which presented the efficient frontier of optimal investment. Markowitz promoted a diversified portfolio to reduce risk. However, it was not until the 1960s that the research of William Sharpe was used to develop a means by which to measure this risk.

William Sharpe, a student at the University of California, was searching for a topic for his dissertation. He took the initiative to speak with Markowitz about his earlier work. Markowitz suggested that he explore the portfolio theory.

Sharpe studied the theory and modified it by connecting each portfolio with a single risk factor. He placed these risks into two categories, systematic risk and unsystematic risk. Systematic risk, referred to as beta, is the risk of being in the market. This type of risk cannot be diversified. Once you enter the market, you take on this risk. Unsystematic risk is risk that is specific to each individual company. Sharpe concluded that by diversifying one's portfolio, one could reduce or eliminate unsystematic risk. Therefore, the return of the portfolio would rest entirely on its correlation to the market.

Together, Markowitz and Sharpe received the Nobel Prize in 1990 for their work on this model, which presented a standardized measure for the risk of an asset with respect to the market.

Capital Asset Pricing Model

The CAPM is derived from the capital markets. It attempts to provide a measure of market relationships based on the theory of expected returns *if* investors behave in the manner prescribed by portfolio theory.

Risk, in the context of this application, is defined conceptually as the degree of uncertainty as to the realization of expected future returns and, as previously discussed, can be divided into three segments: maturity risk, systematic risk, and unsystematic risk. As discussed earlier, the capital market divides risk beyond simple maturity risks into two types:

1. *Systematic Risk.* The uncertainty of future returns due to the sensitivity of the return on the subject investment to movements in the return for the investment market as a whole.
2. *Unsystematic Risk.* The uncertainty of future returns as a function of the characteristics of the industry, enterprise, and type of investment interest. Examples of circumstances that can impact unsystematic risk include operating in an industry subject to high obsolescence (e.g., technology), management expertise, labor relations, and the like. Also refer to the detailed discussion earlier in this chapter on types of unsystematic risks and the methods to evaluate them.

The CAPM model is based solely on quantifying systematic risk because it assumes that prudent investors will eliminate unsystematic risk by holding large, well-diversified portfolios. The unsystematic risk attaching to a particular company's stock is eliminated through diversification. The capital asset theory is then extended out in the Modified Capital Asset Pricing Model (MCAPM) to capture unsystematic risk through adjustment for size effects and the specific company risk in order to derive a rate applicable to a specific valuation target.

The traditional formula for CAPM is:

$$E(R_i) = R_f + B(RP_m)$$

Note: See definitions of variables on next page.

However, valuation analysts have modified this formula for application to smaller companies by including size and unsystematic/specific company risk. R_f, B, and RP_m are the same for both CAPM and MCAPM. (The only difference between the build-up method and CAPM is the addition of beta.)

Modified Capital Asset Pricing Model

The basic formula for MCAPM is expressed as follows:

$$E(R_i) = R_f + B(RP_m) + RP_s + RP_u$$

Where:

$E(R_1)$ = Expected (market required) rate of return on the security

R_f = Rate of return for a risk-free security as of the valuation date

B = Subject company's beta coefficient

RP_m = Equity risk premium for the "market"

RP_s = Risk premium for small size

RP_u = Risk premium for specific company, where u stands for unsystematic risk

Note: For detailed information on the components of MCAPM (other than beta), see the section in this chapter on the build-up method.

Understanding Betas

To measure systematic risk, the equity risk premium is adjusted by beta for the anticipated future return of the specific security and that of the market as a whole. It represents the overall risk of a company as it relates to investing in a large market, such as the Standard & Poor's 500 or the New York Stock Exchange. Each public company has a beta. The stock market as a whole is assigned a beta of 1.0. Betas measure the volatility of the excess return on those individual securities relative to that of the market as a whole. Securities with a beta of more than 1.0 are considered more risky and those with betas of less than 1.0 are more conservative investments with systematic risks lower than the market. Furthermore, a portfolio that has a beta of 0.5 will tend to participate in broad market moves, but only half as much as the market overall. A portfolio with a beta of 2.0 will tend to benefit or suffer from broad market moves twice as much as the market overall.

The formula for beta can be expressed as follows:

$$B = COV\ (R_s\ R_m)\ /\ VAR\ (R_m)$$

Where:

B = Subject company's beta coefficient

COV = Covariance of returns between the subject company (R_s) and the market (R_m)

VAR = Variance of the returns on the market

Published Sources of Betas

Published sources of beta information on publicly traded companies include Value Line Investment Survey,[33] Standard & Poor's Compustat and Stock Reports,[34] Merrill Lynch,[35] and Barra[36].

> The betas published by different sources can display different results due to differing time periods, methodologies, and adjustments. Therefore, the valuation analyst should be careful using betas from more than one source in any given valuation.

Another source for beta information is the Ibbotson semiannual *Beta Book*. Individual company betas for over 5,000 companies can be obtained directly from the Cost of Capital center at http://corporate.morningstar.com/ib/asp. Ibbotson beta information is updated regularly and includes the traditional ordinary least squares method calculation, three-factor Fama French calculated betas, and sum beta calculations.

A review of the beta for Bristol Myers Squibb Co. from various sources shows the differences that can occur (see Exhibit 6.19).

Exhibit 6.19 Beta Sources

	Market Proxy	Period and Frequency of Data	Adjustment Factors	Beta for Bristol Meyers Squibb Co.
Bloomberg	Over 20 domestic series	Adjustable, daily, weekly, monthly or annually	$(0.66 \times$ unadjusted beta$) + (0.33 \times 1.0)$	1.05*
Compustat	S&P 500	5 years, monthly	None	1.198
Ibbotson	S&P 500	5 years, monthly	Adjusted toward peer group beta weighted by statistical significance	1.04
Merrill Lynch	S&P 500	5 years, monthly	$0.33743 + 0.66257 \times$ (unadjusted beta)	1.14
Value Line	NYSE Composite	5 years, weekly	$0.35 + 0.67 \times$ (unadjusted beta)	0.95

*using 60 months of monthly data and the S&P 500

[33] Value Line Investment Survey, 220 East 42nd Street, 6th Floor, New York, NY 10017, (212) 907-1524.
[34] Standard & Poor's Corporation, 55 Water St., New York, NY 10041, (800) 523-4534.
[35] Merrill Lynch, 4 World Financial Center, New York, NY 10080, (212) 449-1000.
[36] Barra, Inc., 2100 Milvia St., Berkeley, CA 94704, (510) 548-5442.

Once the appropriate source of betas has been identified, the next step is to determine precisely what beta(s) should be used for a particular subject. This may be accomplished by analyzing the similarities between the subject and public companies to find entities that are sufficiently similar or by using an industry beta. In addition, the type of beta will need to be selected. The types include ordinary least squares betas (often referred to as the standard beta), a lagged or sum beta, and an adjusted beta. See Addendum 1 at the end of this chapter for further details on types of betas.

Unlevering and Relevering Betas

Published betas for publicly traded companies reflect the actual capital structure of the related entity and are referred to as levered betas. Once an appropriate beta has been identified for application to a specific subject company, it can be adjusted for differences in capital structure between the companies supplying the beta and the subject. This process is complex and requires three steps:

1. The guideline companies' betas are recalculated on an unlevered basis assuming a capital structure constructed of equity only.
2. The risk-adjusted unlevered beta is relevered based on the assumed capital structure for the subject entity.
3. The relevered beta is used in the MCAPM.

The Hamada formula named after Professor Robert Hamada for unlevering a beta is:

$$Bu = Bl / [1 + (1 - t)(Wd / We)]$$

Where:

Bu = Beta unlevered

Bl = Beta levered

t = Tax rate for the company

Wd = Percentage of debt in the capital structure (at market value)

We = Percentage of equity in the capital structure (at market value)

Example: Assume for guideline company A:

- Published levered beta: 1.4
- Tax rate: 40 percent
- Market value capital structure: 35 percent debt, 65 percent equity

$$
\begin{aligned}
Bu &= 1.4 / [1 + (1 - .40)(.35 / .65)] \\
&= 1.4 / 1 + .60(.538) \\
&= 1.4 / 1.323 \\
&= 1.06
\end{aligned}
$$

The formula for relevering a beta is:

$$Bl = Bu [1 + (1 - t)(Wd / We)]$$

where the definitions of the variables are the same as in the formula for computing unlevered betas.

Example: Using the unlevered beta decided above, let us assume that the subject company decided to operate with only 20 percent debt and:

- Unlevered beta from above: 1.06
- Tax rate: 40 percent
- Market value capital structure: 20 percent debt, 80 percent equity

$$
\begin{aligned}
Bl &= 1.06[1 + (1 - .40)(.20\,/.80)] \\
&= 1.06[1 + (.60)(.25)] \\
&= 1.06[1 + .15] \\
&= (1.06)(1.15) \\
&= 1.22
\end{aligned}
$$

Some analysts have questioned the use of the Hamada formula, particularly with increasing debt.

The Hamada formulas are consistent with the theory that:

- The discount rate used to calculate the tax shield equals the cost of debt capital (i.e., the tax shield has the same risk as debt).
- Debt capital has negligible risk that interest payments and principal repayments will not be made when owed, which implies that tax deductions on the interest expense will be realized in the period in which the interest is paid (i.e., beta of debt capital equals zero).
- Value of the tax shield is proportionate to the value of the market value of debt capital (i.e., value of tax shield $= t \times W_d$).

But the Hamada formulas are based upon Modigliani and Miller's formulation of the tax shield values for constant debt. The formulas are not correct if the assumption is that debt capital remains at a constant percentage of equity capital (equivalent to debt increasing in proportion to net cash flow to the firm in every period).[37]

The formulas are equivalent to assuming a steadily decreasing ratio of debt to equity value if the company's cash flows are increasing. The formulas are often wrongly assumed to hold in general.[38]

An alternate method for unlevering and relevering betas is through the use of Miles-Ezzell formulas, presented by James A. Miles and John R. Ezzell.[39] These formulas

---

[37] Enrique R. Arzac and Lawrence R. Glosten, "A Reconsideration of Tax Shield Valuation," *European Financial Management* (2005), 453–461.

[38] Shannon Pratt and Roger Grabowski, *Cost of Capital: Applications and Examples*, 3rd ed. (John Wiley & Sons, 2008), 144. Note: The fourth edition is now available.

[39] J. A. Miles and J. R. Ezzell, "The Weighted Average Cost of Capital, Perfect Capital Markets, and Project Life: A Clarification," *Journal of Financial and Quantitative Analysis* (September 1980), 719–730.

introduce the concept of betas for debt capital. The formulas for this model are as follows:

$$B_U = \frac{M_e \times B_L + M_d \times B_d[1 - (t \times k_{d(pt)})/(1 + k_{d(pt)})]}{M_e + M_d[1 - (t \times k_{d(pt)})/(1 + k_{d(pt)})]}$$

$$B_L = B_U + \frac{W_d}{W_e}(B_U - B_d)\left[1 - \frac{(t \times k_{d(pt)})}{(1 + k_{d(pt)})}\right]$$

Where:

B_U = Unlevered beta of equity capital

B_L = Levered beta of equity capital

M_e = Market value of equity capital (stock)

M_d = Market value of debt capital

B_d = Beta of debt capital

t = Tax rate for the company

$k_{d(pt)}$ = Cost of debt prior to tax effect

W_d = Percentage of debt in the capital structure (at market value)

W_e = Percentage of equity in the capital structure (at market value)[40]

Some analysts believe that the Miles-Ezzell formulas are a better fit.

The Miles-Ezzell formulas are consistent with the theory that:

- The discount rate used to calculate the tax shield equals the cost of debt capital (i.e., the tax shield has same risk as debt) during the first year and the discount rate used to calculate the tax shield thereafter equals the cost of equity calculated using the asset beta of the firm (i.e., the risk of the tax shield after the first year is comparable to the risk of the operating cash flows). That is, the risk of realizing the tax deductions is greater than assumed in the Hamada formulas.
- Debt capital bears the risk of variability of operating net cash flow in that interest payments and principal repayments may not be made when owed, which implies that tax deductions on the interest expense may not be realized in the period in which the interest is paid (i.e., beta of debt capital may be greater than zero).
- Market value of debt capital remains at a constant percentage of equity capital, which is equivalent to saying that debt increases in proportion to the net cash flow of the firm (net cash flow to invested capital) in every period.[41]

In *Cost of Capital: Applications and Examples*, 3rd ed., Pratt and Grabowski present two examples of relevering a beta to a subject company capital structure of

[40] Pratt and Grabowski, *Cost of Capital*, 144.
[41] Ibid., 145–146.

60 percent debt and 40 percent equity. The relevered beta from the Hamada formulas is 1.85. The relevered beta from the Miles-Ezzell formulas is 1.92.[42]

DEVELOPMENT OF THE WEIGHTED AVERAGE COST OF CAPITAL

To compute a proper cost of capital, it is common first to examine the capital structure of the business entity being valued. Three types of capital form the capital structure of most business entities:

1. Common equity
2. Preferred equity
3. Long-term debt

Each of these components has a cost associated with it. The definition of the Weighted Average Cost of Capital (WACC) is the blended cost of the company's capital structure components, each weighted by the market value of that capital component. The use of a WACC method to determine value can be appropriate when the objective is to value the entire capital structure of the enterprise or invested capital, such as in an acquisition where the buyer believes the current capital structure may not be optimal or where he or she intends to change it. In this situation, a WACC can be developed for several capital structure scenarios (more debt, less debt, debt of different types with different rates, etc.) as a way for the buyer to try out different approaches to enterprise financing.

Steps for Calculating the Weighted Average Cost of Capital

A company's WACC is calculated in three steps:

1. Determine the proportionate weighting of each source of capital financing based on their market values.
2. Calculate the after-tax rate of return (cost) of each source.
3. Calculate the weighted average cost of all sources.

The traditional formula used to develop a WACC is:

$$\text{WACC} = (k_e \times W_e) + (k_p \times W_p) + (k_{d/(pt)} [1 - t] \times W_d)$$

Where:

WACC	=	Weighted average cost of capital
k_e	=	Cost of common equity capital
W_e	=	Percentage of common equity in the capital structure, at market value
k_p	=	Cost of preferred equity
W_p	=	Percentage of preferred equity in the capital structure, at market value
$k_{d/(pt)}$	=	Cost of debt (pretax)
t	=	Tax rate
W_d	=	Percentage of debt in the capital structure, at market value

---

[42] Ibid., 145–146.

This same WACC formula can be conveyed in a tabular format. See the example in Exhibit 6.20.

Exhibit 6.20   Example of WACC Formula in Tabular Format

Capital Component	% Component in Capital Structure[a]	Cost		Weighted Cost of Capital Component
Debt	.40	.08 − .032[b]	=	.019
Preferred Equity	.15	.10	=	.015
Common Equity	.45	.18	=	.081
	1.00			
	Weighted average cost of capital		=	.115
			=	11.5%

[a] at market rates
[b] assuming a 40% tax rate

The difficulty arises when a WACC needs to be developed for a privately held company. Since no market exists for a private company's securities, market values must be estimated to assign weights to the capital structure components. To do this, the analyst may start with an initial estimate for capital structure weightings and plug these weights and accompanying estimated costs of capital into the WACC formula. Using this initial WACC to calculate the market value of total invested capital and subtracting the value of debt gives the first estimation of the market value of equity and a second (desired) capital structure.[43] This iterative process can be repeated until a reasonable WACC and accompanying capital structure are derived. This process is greatly simplified by use of electronic spreadsheets. Proxy capital structures from public company data also can be useful in determining the weight of debt and equity. (See Chapter 6.)

Cost of Debt

The actual rate a business entity pays on interest-bearing debt is the pretax cost of debt, assuming the enterprise is borrowing at market rates. When there is long-term debt involved, the rates being paid may differ from the prevailing market, due to changes in required yields on debt of comparable risk because of changes in market influences. Current available rates can be checked against the company's actual rate.

Since the interest paid on debt instruments is tax deductible, the cost to the enterprise is derived by multiplying the interest rate of the subject debt times 1 minus the entity's tax rate. The after-tax cost to the enterprise represents its effective rate, possibly subject to adjustments for other costs as detailed below.

Examples of hidden costs include:

- Loan origination fees
- Loan covenants, such as the need to maintain compensating balances or certain financial ratios, such as a current ratio requirement
- Guarantees or pledges of collateral

---

[43] This assumes the current amount of debt and its percentage of the capital structure is the desired amount.

- Fees for unused lines of credit (e.g., some banks charge a small percentage fee for amounts available but not utilized on available borrowings)

These additional costs can be considered when assessing the true cost of debt financing, especially in situations where these costs are significant relative to the principal. This may be the case with many smaller companies. The analyst can factor these costs into the calculation of the true cost of debt capital when appropriate.

Minority versus Control Considerations When Developing a Weighted Average Cost of Capital

When valuing a minority interest, it is often appropriate to use the actual capital structure of the enterprise for the weighting of the WACC components because a minority owner is not able to bring about any changes in the company's capital structure.

When valuing a controlling interest, an argument can be made for using an industry-based capital structure, under the premise that a control buyer normally will attempt to optimize the capital structure of the enterprise. The overall capital structure exhibited by companies operating within the same industry as, and demonstrating similarity to, the subject can serve as a reasonable proxy for the subject's optimal capital structure. If the control owners of the business intend to operate at a different capital structure, then the WACC based on that structure may be appropriate.

A good source of information for determining industry capital structures can be found in the Morningstar Ibbotson *Cost of Capital* publications. If the guideline public company method is being used, the public companies can be a source of capital structure components.

PRICE/EARNINGS METHOD

Relationship Among Cap Rates, Discount Rates, and the Price/Earnings Multiple

A true and mathematical relationship exists between the earnings capitalization rate and the price/earnings (P/E) multiple that is part of the market approach.

Since traditionally derived discount and capitalization rates are cash flow rates, and not earnings rates, an upward subjective adjustment would typically have to be made to convert the rate.

The direct relationship between the P/E multiple and the earnings capitalization rate equals the difference between the discount rate (risk) and long-term sustainable growth. This relationship can be presented mathematically, as shown in Exhibits 6.21 to 6.23.

Exhibit 6.21   Relationship Between the P/E Multiple and the Earnings Cap Rate

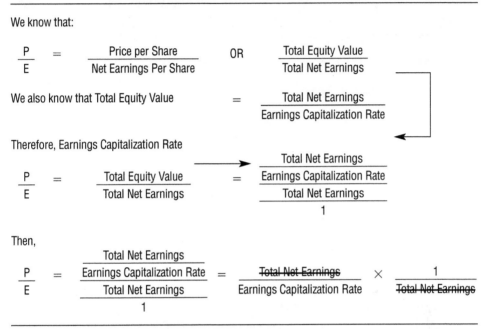

We know that:

$$\frac{P}{E} = \frac{\text{Price per Share}}{\text{Net Earnings Per Share}} \quad \text{OR} \quad \frac{\text{Total Equity Value}}{\text{Total Net Earnings}}$$

We also know that Total Equity Value $= \dfrac{\text{Total Net Earnings}}{\text{Earnings Capitalization Rate}}$

Therefore, Earnings Capitalization Rate

$$\frac{P}{E} = \frac{\text{Total Equity Value}}{\text{Total Net Earnings}} = \frac{\dfrac{\text{Total Net Earnings}}{\text{Earnings Capitalization Rate}}}{\dfrac{\text{Total Net Earnings}}{1}}$$

Then,

$$\frac{P}{E} = \frac{\dfrac{\text{Total Net Earnings}}{\text{Earnings Capitalization Rate}}}{\dfrac{\text{Total Net Earnings}}{1}} = \frac{\text{Total Net Earnings}}{\text{Earnings Capitalization Rate}} \times \frac{1}{\text{Total Net Earnings}}$$

Exhibit 6.22   Relationship between the Earnings Cap Rate and the Discount Rate

We also know that:

Capitalization Rate $=$ Discount Rate $-$ Long-Term Sustainable Growth Rate

Therefore,

$$\frac{P}{E} = \frac{1}{\text{Capitalization Rate}} = \frac{1}{R_k - g}$$

Where:

$R_k =$ Discount Rate associated with the particular income stream or earnings
$g =$ Long-term sustainable growth rate

or

$$\frac{P}{E} = \frac{1}{\text{Earnings Capitalization Rate}}$$

Exhibits 6.23 Components of Both Risk and Growth

$$\frac{P}{E} = \frac{1}{\text{Components of } R_k - \text{Components of } g}$$

	Adjusted Long-Term (In Perpetuity) Rate
Riskless Rate	Inflation Growth Rate
+ Equity risk premia	+ Real growth rate
+ Small-stock size risk premia	
+ Unsystematic / Specific Company Risk	
+ Adjustment to convert from cash flow rate to an earnings rate	

Market-Derived Price/Earnings Multiples

Overview

Understanding how market-derived P/E multiples interplay with risk and growth is important to making appropriate "adjustments" that reflect the risk and growth of a closely held company being valued. Using market multiple(s)[44] can be important for a number of reasons:

- Many analysts believe the public market for securities has an impact on the value of a closely held company's stock.
- Actual market transactions represent compelling empirical evidence of fair market value. There are literally thousands and thousands of "very informed and scrutinized"[45] market transactions daily that are at arm's length and therefore could very well be the best proxy for the definition of the willing buyer and seller.
- Revenue Ruling 59-60 states that the valuation specialist should consider "the market price of stocks of corporations engaged in the same or a similar line of business having their stock actively traded in a free and open market, either on an exchange or over-the-counter."
- The U.S. Federal Tax Court has based decisions on the guideline public company method.

ADJUSTMENTS TO THE PRICE/EARNINGS RATIO

Public Company Adjustments

Adjustments for extraordinary items, nonrecurring items, and income tax of publicly traded companies may be required in addition to adjustments that are specific to the

---

[44] In addition to P/E multiples, multiples to EBIT, EBITDA, tangible assets, and so on, apply as well.

[45] The Securities and Exchange Commission scrutinizes market transactions as well as ensuring timely and accurate reporting information.

closely held company that is being valued. Accordingly, there are two "baskets" of adjustments, one to calculate the multiple itself and one to adjust for specific company factors. See Chapter 7 for more information on calculating multiples.

It is important to recognize the increasingly "noisy" nature of public company-reported valuation multiples including P/E. As indicated in the August 21, 2001, *Wall Street Journal*,[46] many public companies have moved away from using GAAP earnings for the E of the P/E to utilize other earnings measures, such as "operating" earnings before extraordinary items, "core" earnings, and even "pro forma" earnings. Each of these revised definitions of earnings allows reporting entities to exclude certain one-time, exceptional, special, or noncash expenses; in turn, the net income of the enterprise is higher. According to the article, more than 300 of the 500 entities making up the S&P 500 now exclude some ordinary expenses as defined by GAAP from the operating earnings numbers provided to investors and analysts.

Company-Specific Adjustments

Determining the earnings capitalization rate of a publicly held company should be straightforward. However, potential problems in applying that capitalization rate/ multiple exist when the company being valued is different in size, anticipated growth, and other specific risk factors. Certain adjustments may be warranted.

Growth and Size Factors

The growth rates and size of the closely held company are material components of price multiple adjustments. In general, typically downward adjustments are made, resulting in lower price multiples applied to private companies. Public market data observations since 1926 show that smaller companies are generally riskier and therefore require a higher rate of return. In other words, smaller companies sell at lower price multiples. This relationship between size and price multiples has been demonstrated in various studies.

Jerry O. Peters, when analyzing ratios published by *Mergerstat Review*, found that the price paid for "a dollar of earnings varies directly with the total market value of the company. For example, the median price/earnings ratio paid for all companies valued at less than $25 million has averaged 25.9 percent less than that paid for companies valued at $100 million or more over the last five years."[47] Since those

---

[46] Jonathan Weil, "What's the P/E Ratio? Well, Depends on What Is Meant by Earnings," *The Wall Street Journal* (August 21, 2001).

[47] Jerry O. Peters, "Adjusting Price/Earnings Ratios for Differences in Company Size," *Business Valuation Review* (March 1992), p. 3.

transactions were predominantly controlling interests, Peters also looked at publicly traded minority interests and found similar results: "According to my analysis, the median price/earnings ratio for a minority interest in companies valued at less than $25 million has generally been 30 percent less than the median price/earnings ratio for companies valued at $100 million or more."

Peters also quoted the IRS's own research on this:

> There may be some question as to why the value of a company per dollar of earnings should increase in proportion to corporate size. This tendency seems to be quite logical, however, in view of the practical considerations which most investors follow when making their buy and sell decisions. For one thing, the most successful companies gradually become the largest companies and in many cases become the leaders in their particular industry. Their very success and consequent size is ample evidence to the investing public that each of these enterprises has the ability to grow either from internal expansion of its plants and products or by means of mergers. High quality management is ordinarily a prime requisite in such firms and, with such, the investing public is likely to place a greater confidence in these corporations. Certainly, the securities of such corporations are better known to the public and, by the same fact, become more marketable. Any of these reasons could account for the greater interest, popularity, and consequent higher ratio of price to earnings. Regardless of the underlying causes, however, it is apparent that a genuine and easily discernible trend exists with respect to the size of the corporate enterprise and the price-earnings ratio, which it displays.

Peters has since updated his study with similar results. In his September 1995 article in *Business Valuation Review*, the percentages changed from 25.9 to 27.1 percent and 30 to 25.8 percent for the controlling and minority interests, respectively. In the June 1999 edition of *Business Valuation Resources,* he presented another study on size with an emphasis on similar growth expectations.

Size and Company-Specific Risk Adjustments

Example: Assume that the discount rate component of the cap rate must be increased by two points for size and two points for company-specific risk (thin management, limited markets, etc.). Keep in mind that industry risk is already included in the guideline multiple.

1. Convert observed guideline company's pricing multiples to earnings cap rates.

     P/E = Price/net earnings
     IC = Invested capital
     EBIT = Earnings before interest and taxes

Valuation Multiple	Observed Pricing Multiple	Conversion to Capitalization Rate	Capitalization Rate
P/E	15.1	1/15.1	6.6%
IC to EBIT	8.7	1/8.7	11.5%

2. Increase earnings cap rates by the excess expected increase in risk.

Valuation Multiple	Capitalization Rate	Excess Risk	Adjusted Capitalization Rate
P/E	6.6%	4.0%	10.6%
IC to EBIT	11.5%	4.0%	15.5%

3. Convert adjusted earnings cap rates to pricing multiples.

Valuation Ratio	Adjusted Capitalization Rate	Conversion to Pricing Multiple	Adjusted Pricing Multiple
P/E	10.6%	1/.106	9.4
IC to EBIT	15.5%	1/.155	6.5

See Chapter 7 for further information on adjusting multiples for application to closely held companies.

ARBITRAGE PRICING THEORY

While CAPM only recognizes systematic risk relative to a market index, Arbitrage Pricing Theory (APT) extends the concept of CAPM through the recognition of a series of risk factors, with just one of these factors being systematic, or "market timing," risk.

The initial model for APT was developed by Stephen Ross to estimate and monitor the risk of an asset allocation strategy or to estimate the likely response of a portfolio to economic developments. The APT model for predicting the behavior and performance of a financial instrument or portfolio is based on the proposition that if the returns of a portfolio of assets can be quantified and described by a factor-based structure or model, the expected return of each asset in the portfolio can be described by a linear combination of the factors of the returns of the assets within the portfolio group. The resulting factor model can be used to create portfolios that track a market index, to estimate and monitor the risk of an asset allocation strategy, or to estimate the likely response of a portfolio to economic developments.

The APT model formula is:

$$E(R_i) = R_f + (B_{/1}K_{/1}) + (B_{/2}K_{/2}) + \ldots + (B_{/n}K_{/n})$$

Where:

$E(R_i)$ = Expected rate of return on the subject security

R_f = Rate of return on a risk-free security

$K_{/1} K_{/n}$ = Risk premium associated with factor K for the average asset in the market (general macroeconomic factors, i.e., changes in investor confidence, inflation, etc.)

$B_{/1} B_{/n}$ = Sensitivity of the security i to each risk factor relative to the market average sensitivity to that factor

The general risk factors considered in building a rate through APT, in addition to systematic or market risk, include:[48]

- *Confidence Risk.* The unanticipated changes in an investor's willingness to undertake relatively risky investments. It is measured as the difference between the rate of return on relatively risky corporate bonds and the rate of return on government bonds, both with 20-year maturities.
- *Time Horizon Risk.* The unanticipated changes in an investor's desired time to payout. It is measured as the difference between the return on 20-year government bonds and 30-day Treasury bills.
- *Inflation Risk.* A combination of the unexpected components of short- and long-run inflation rates.
- *Business Cycle Risk.* Represents unanticipated changes in the level of real business activity. This component measures whether economic cycles are in the upswing or downswing with each, respectively, adding a positive or negative adjustment to the overall required rate of return.

APT is not widely used in business valuation assignments for cost-of-capital determinations due to the unavailability of usable data for the components of the model.

RISK RATE COMPONENT MODEL FKA BUILD-UP SUMMATION MODEL

Another method to derive capitalization and discount rates has emerged based on a model introduced in 1991 by Parnell Black and Robert Green, the founders of the National Association of Certified Valuation Analysts (NACVA). Known for years as the Black-Green Method, the underlying model, now known as the risk rate component model, was revised and expanded by J. Richard Claywell and William A. Hanlin Jr. in a NACVA course book titled *Capitalization and Discount Rates: The Value of Risk.* This approach uses a series of factors taken from four basic categories to rate various operating attributes of the subject entity:

1. Competition
2. Financial Strength
3. Management Ability and Depth
4. Profitability and Stability of Earnings

Significant emphasis is placed on a detailed financial analysis of the subject enterprise, including financial ratios and comparisons to historical trends and industry benchmarks.

---

[48] Based on a presentation by Edwin Burmeister, Richard Roll, and Stephen A. Ross and in an exhibit prepared by Burmeister, "Controlling Risks Using Arbitrage Pricing Techniques."

Once the subject has been analyzed using these categories and a series of factors has been developed, weights are assigned based on professional judgment. This weighting process leads to the selection of a rate adjustment for each category. Both the original model and the revised work by Claywell and Hanlin provide a suggested range of the rate adjustments (0 to 10 percent) for each category, for a maximum total rate of 40 percent. The selection of the build-up percentages is based on the analysts' determination of whether each factor within a category adds no risk (+0.0 percent), low risk (+1.0 percent), medium-low risk (+2.5 percent), medium risk (+5.0 percent), medium-high risk (+7.5 percent), or high risk (+10.0 percent) to that category. The risk adjustments for the four categories then are summed together, and additional adjustments are considered for environmental and national and local economic considerations. The final sum is the rate of return for the subject company.

ValTip

There has been much debate over the merits of the Risk Rate Component Build-Up Summation model. Many analysts have suggested that some of the rate adjustments are not empirically grounded and can be misleading with regard to the percentage of accuracy of the presentation. However, the detailed list of questions for the various factors can be very useful as an analytical tool and for work paper support.

For additional information, see website Addendum 7 at www.wiley.com/go/FVAM3E. This addendum is authored by Messrs. Hanlin and Claywell, who are major supporters of the model. The authors of this book have not endorsed the model but present it for informational purposes only.

COST-OF-CAPITAL ISSUES RELATED TO USE OF THE EXCESS CASH FLOW METHOD

An approach sometimes used in valuation assignments of certain types of closely held businesses or professional practices involves a method referred to as the excess cash flow (ECF) method. Often referred to as the excess earnings method,[49] it requires cost-of-capital determinations. The U.S. government first used ECF to measure the intangible value of distillers and breweries when Prohibition was enacted in the 1920s. The ECF method is widely used and abused. However, it is important to know and understand it, especially when valuing professional practices for divorce purposes, as some judges and other triers of fact have become accustomed to seeing it.

Overly simplified, the excess cash flow method requires the analyst first to determine a return on the net tangible asset base of the enterprise and then to use this return to determine if there are "excess earnings" that can be attributed to the

---

[49] The excess earnings method was recognized in Revenue Ruling 68-609.

intangible asset base of the enterprise.[50] In applying this approach, the analyst must derive two cost-of-capital rates, one to be applied to the tangible assets and another to be applied to the excess earnings, if any.

The proper rate to apply to the tangible asset base is lower than that used for the intangibles because the income attributable to tangible assets is less risky. In theory, the weighted average rate of these two components should approximate the subject company's overall rate of return or capitalization rate.

> The value from the excess cash flow method should be similar to that derived from the capitalization of cash flow method since the two rates used in the ECF method should reasonably tie to the rate used in the CCF method.

The rate typically applied to the total tangible asset base is derived from the required rates of return on those assets. In some instances, this rate might approximate the borrowing rates that could be achieved if the assets were used as collateral for a business loan. In other instances, the rate might be closer to what would be derived using a traditional build-up approach. This issue itself is what makes the use of the excess earnings method susceptible to scrutiny, because minor variances in the rate of return applied to the tangible asset base can create large swings in the indicated amounts of excess earnings and, in turn, large variances in the resulting indications of calculated aggregate intangible and goodwill value.

The rates of return applied to the intangible asset base often are calculated by adding a judgmentally derived premium to the tangible asset base rate to compensate for the fact that intangible assets are considered to be more risky than the tangible assets. There is no formula or consensus on how to derive this rate component, a fact that also contributes to the wide variations in results when using this method. This method is discussed in detail in Chapter 5.

Additional Information

Addendum 1 at the end of this chapter presents a three-part article (October 2004, January 2005, and May 2005) from Shannon Pratt's *Business Valuation Update,* "Cost of Capital Controversies: It's Time to Look Behind the Curtain," by James Hitchner and Katherine Morris of American Appraisal Associates and Paul Vogt of Grant Thornton. Business Valuation Resources, LLC, granted permission for inclusion in this book.

---

[50] A derivative of this method has the analyst evaluating the amounts of excess earnings of a professional or professional practice above the average returns for a peer group person or practice as the measure of whether there are any excess earnings to be capitalized as an indication of goodwill value. Again, this is a complex topic that warrants further study outside of the rates discussion provided here.

Addendums 2–8 can be found at www.wiley.com/go/FVAM3E.

Addendum 2 is the article "Ibbotson Industry Risk Premium Data: If You Use It, Use It with Knowledge" from *Financial Valuation and Litigation Expert*, Issue 17, February/March 2009, Valuation Products and Services LLC.

See Addendum 3 for the article "Boston's Battle of the Beta," written by Don Wisehart, CPA/ABV, ASA, CVA, MST, in *Financial Valuation and Litigation Expert*, Issue 22, December 2009/January 2010, Valuation Products and Services, LLC.

See Addendum 4 for the article "Cost of Equity Capital: Straight, No Chaser," from the front page of *Financial Valuation and Litigation Expert*, Issue 24, April/May 2010, Valuation Products and Services, LLC.

Addenda 5 and 6 give a detailed explanation of the Duff & Phelps LLC Risk Premium Report 2009 and 2010. They also include exhibits presenting some of the data.

Addendum 7 presents the Risk Rate Component Model by William A. Hanlin Jr. and J. Richard Claywell.

Addendum 8 is an update article, "Cost of Equity Capital: Straight with a Chaser," from the front page of *Financial Valuation and Litigation Expert*, Issue 25, June/July 2010, Valuation Products and Services, LLC.

All addendums are reproduced with permission and without author comment.

ADDENDUM 1—COST OF CAPITAL CONTROVERSIES: IT'S TIME TO LOOK BEHIND THE CURTAIN

By James R. Hitchner, CPA/ABV, ASA, and Katherine E. Morris[51]

The estimation of the cost of capital for a closely held business is fraught with controversy. Many valuation analysts believe there is safety and comfort in using data sources that are widely recognized. These data sources are indeed helpful, but analysts should thoroughly understand how the data are derived, what choices there are in selecting such data, and what the strengths and weaknesses of the data are. This is Part One of a three-part article that takes an in-depth look at all the components of the Weighted Average Cost of Capital (WACC) and provides guidance for choosing the right components in any given valuation. On the surface, the WACC calculations seem straightforward and familiar, but a closer look—a look behind the curtain, as it were—reveals numerous choices and approaches. It's time to look behind the curtain.

Choices, Choices, and More Choices

In calculating the WACC of a closely held company, the analyst must make choices in five major categories that correspond to the variables of the basic WACC formula. See Exhibit 6.24 for definitions of these and other variables used in calculating WACC. We know that the WACC formula, excluding preferred stock, is as follows:

$$WACC = W_d \times k_{dpt}(1 - \text{tax rate}) + W_e \times k_e$$

We also know that k_e (cost of equity capital) for a small to medium-sized closely held company is usually derived by using either the Modified Capital Asset Pricing Model (MCAPM) or the Build-Up Model (BUM). Let's focus on MCAPM first. When MCAPM is used, the WACC equation is expanded as follows:

$$WACC = [W_d \times k_{dpt}(1 - \text{tax rate})] + [W_e \times (R_f + B(RP_m) + RP_s + RP_u)]$$

For the BUM we have:

$$WACC = [W_d \times k_{dpt}(1 - \text{tax rate})] + [W_e \times (R_f + RP_m + RP_s + RP_u + RP_i)]$$

Under both equations, the analyst must make decisions on nine categories that have a direct influence on the WACC and thus value. The difference is that beta is used in the MCAPM, and some analysts use an industry risk premium in the BUM. There is nothing new here in terms of the categories. However, there is plenty new in the choices to determine the amount that goes into each category. Those choices are the main focus of this article. Again, look at Exhibit 6.24 for definitions of these WACC categories.

---

[51] James R. Hitchner, CPA/ABV, ASA, and Katherine E. Morris are with The Financial Valuation Group, Atlanta. Mr. Hitchner is now with Financial Valuation Advisors, Inc. Ms. Morris is now with American Appraisal Associates. Mr. Hitchner is editor and coauthor of *Financial Valuation Application and Models,* and coauthor of the *Financial Valuation Workbook* and *Valuation for Financial Reporting,* published by John Wiley & Sons.

Exhibit 6.24 Definitions of WACC Formula Variables

W_d	Weight of debt in the capital structure at fair market value
k_{dpt}	Pretax cost of debt
Tax rate	Company-specific tax rate
W_e	Weight of common equity in the capital structure at fair market value
k_e	Cost of equity capital
R_f	Risk-free rate of return
Beta	Measure of risk using volatility
RP_m	Risk premium in the marketplace (ERP or equity risk premium)
RP_s	Risk premium adjusted for size (size premium)
RP_u	Risk premium for unsystematic risk (specific company risk)
RP_i	Risk premium for the industry

These equations and the categories that make them up are fairly simple to use. However, as often is the case in valuation, the devil is in the details.

Equity market risk premiums based on historical stock market return data are widely accepted and relied upon by the valuation community. The most prominent publisher of such data is Ibbotson Associates.[52] Standard & Poor's [now Duff & Phelps] also prepares a well-known analysis that relies on historical data to calculate the small-company risk premiums that it publishes in its Risk Premium Report.[53] Ibbotson and Chen have developed a supply-side analysis of equity risk premium based on fundamental market data.[54] We will address the differences between the use of Ibbotson's and Standard & Poor's data for RP_m and RP_s, the new supply-side equity risk premium, and taxes in Part Two of this article. In Part Three we will focus on beta, the cost of debt, specific company risk, and the weights in the WACC. For now, we continue with an analysis of Ibbotson data as they pertain to R_f, RP_s, and RP_i.

Horizons and Returns

First we'll look at an easy category, R_f. Most analysts use the return on a U.S. 20-year Treasury bond, which is a 30-year bond with 20 years remaining till maturity. Why 20 years instead of, say, 5 years or even 30 days? Twenty years is what Ibbotson Associates, in their annual *Valuation Edition Yearbook,* use to calculate the long-horizon equity risk premium, RP_m. Analysts prefer to stay consistent with Ibbotson's use of the data. Furthermore, the 20-year investment term is the most similar to the long-term investment horizon of a closely held company. Remember, under fair market value, the horizon may be that of the investment, not the investor.

Does it make a difference whether we use an $\underline{R}_f$ for 20 years (long-term), 5 years (intermediate-term), or 30 days (short-term)? Let's take a look. Consider the following calculations that use Treasury rates as of May 3, 2004. The equity risk premiums for long, intermediate, and short horizon risk premiums, presented in Exhibit 6.25,

---

[52] Ibbotson Associates, *Stocks, Bonds, Bills, and Inflation, Valuation Edition 2004 Yearbook* (Chicago: Ibbotson Associates, 2004).

[53] Standard & Poor's, *Standard & Poor's Corporate Value Consulting Group Risk Premium Report 2003* (New York: Standard & Poor's Corporate Value Consulting, 2003).

[54] Roger G. Ibbotson and Peng Chen, "Long-Run Stock Returns: Participating in the Real Economy," *Financial Analysts Journal* 59, no. 1, (January/February 2003).

are from the last page of Ibbotson Associates' *SBBI Valuation Edition 2004 Yearbook.*

We have heard from some analysts that the time period doesn't matter because, while the 5-year bond and the 30-day bill have lower yield rates than a 20-year bond, it is offset by a higher historical RP_m. As can be seen in Exhibit 6.25, this is only partially true. Currently, there are much larger differences in the Treasury yield rates for the three different horizon periods than the values for RP_m for those same periods. This is due to the yield curve on Treasury securities and the impact of investor horizon risk on the 5-year and 20-year bonds versus the 30-day bill.

Exhibit 6.25 Differences in Equity Risk Premiums Based on Length of Investment

	Twenty-Year Bond	Five-Year Bond	Thirty-Day Bill
Treasury rate	5.30%	3.60%	0.80%
RP_m	7.20%	7.60%	8.60%
Assumed Beta	1.2	1.2	1.2
Assumed Beta	0.8	0.8	0.8
BUM return	12.50%	11.20%	9.40%
CAPM return (1.2)	13.90%	12.80%	11.20%
CAPM return (0.8)	11.10%	9.70%	7.70%

The returns shown in Exhibit 6.25, using BUM or CAPM with a beta of 1.2 or .8, indicate that the differences due to the selection of the time horizon can have an impact. For example, the returns using a 20-year bond rate and risk premium are 1.1 percent to 1.4 percent higher than the returns using a 5-year bond rate and risk premium and 1.6 percent to 2.0 percent higher than the returns using a 30-day bill rate and risk premium. We believe this example illustrates the importance of using long-term risk-free rates and the 20-year long horizon risk premium using Ibbotson data.

Size Risk Premiums

Now let's look at a more difficult category, RP_s. Did you know that there are 10 primary choices here? And that the range of those choices is approximately 2 percent to 10 percent?[55] With such a range of potential choices, an analyst must be able to explain and support his or her selected assumption. The choices for RP_s are all "in excess of CAPM" rate differentials as defined by Ibbotson. This means that they believe that the difference between the predicted return using CAPM and the actual return must be attributable to differences in size. The size premium is different from the small-stock risk premium, which is not beta-adjusted and is simply the arithmetic return on small stocks less the arithmetic return on the market.

---

[55] Ibbotson Associates, *Stocks, Bonds, Bills, and Inflation, Valuation Edition 2004 Yearbook,* (Chicago: Ibbotson Associates, 2004), 129–137.

EXHIBIT 6.26   Ten Choices for RP_s Size Premium

1. 10th decile monthly beta S&P
2. 10th decile annual beta S&P
3. 10th decile sum beta S&P
4. 10A monthly beta S&P
5. 10B monthly beta S&P
6. Micro-cap annual beta S&P
7. Micro-cap monthly beta S&P
8. Micro-cap sum beta S&P
9. 10th decile monthly beta NYSE
10. Micro-cap monthly beta NYSE[56]

The size premium can be adjusted to reflect the type of beta calculation for the underlying portfolio of companies. The question then becomes over what period is beta best approximated? Ibbotson provides data for betas calculated on an annual basis and on a monthly basis. Ibbotson also calculates betas that reflect the lag of market events on smaller company stocks (sum betas).

Assuming you agree that a beta-adjusted method is correct, the 10 choices for the size premium (RP_s) are those presented in Exhibit 6.26.

So, which one do you use? Well, unfortunately, the answer is "it depends." First we explain what each one is; then we narrow down the choices to four and present their strengths and weaknesses. Ultimately, we leave the decision to you.

EXHIBIT 6.27   Number of Companies in the 10th Decile by Specific Year/Decade

Year	Tenth Decile Companies
1926	52
1930	72
1940	78
1950	100
1960	109
1970	865
1980	685
1990	1,814
2000	1,927
2003	1,724

Tenth decile annual beta means that the expected return is calculated with an annual beta. The 10th decile monthly beta is based on monthly betas. Sum beta is a lagged beta, which reflects the theory that the impact of events on smaller companies may lag the marketplace as a whole. As such, the beta in the expected return is adjusted accordingly. If a sum beta RP_s is used, then sum betas may need to be used in the CAPM, and these are not always readily available. Given this fact, as well as the fact that monthly betas are more readily available than annual betas, we'll eliminate annual betas and sum betas.

---

[56] Ibid.

Eight of the possible choices for RP$_s$ are based on data from S&P. Only two choices are based on data from the NYSE. However, the differences are not that material. For the 10th decile monthly beta and the micro-cap monthly beta, the NYSE based size premiums are only 0.42 and 0.41 percentage points higher, respectively, than the S&P based size premiums. As a percentage difference, the NYSE based risk premiums are only 6.6 percent and 10.2 percent higher, respectively.

And Then There Were Four (Size Premium Choices)

That leaves us with just four choices based on data from S&P: 10th decile monthly beta, microcap quintile, 10A, and 10B.

1. NYSE Deciles

Ibbotson slices the New York Stock Exchange (NYSE) into 10 deciles. In the past, this was the extent of the database and included around 180 to 190 companies in each decile for current periods. In 2001, they started to include companies of similar size from the American Stock Exchange (AMEX) and the National Association of Securities Dealers Automated Quotation System (NASDAQ). This raised the number of companies in the 10th decile to 1,724 in 2003.[57] Obviously, the other deciles increased as well, but there was a greater impact on the 10th decile, which is the area many valuation analysts view as aligned more with the closely held companies they value.

2. Microcap Quintile

Before this increase in the number of companies in the 10th decile, many analysts used the microcap quintile, which is just a fancy term for the 9th and 10th deciles combined. The rationale was that the microcap quintile had more companies—thus more data points, and greater reliability. We've also heard analysts say they used the microcap quintile because of "fallen angels," which are companies that were larger in the past or are still fairly large but have fallen on hard times and dropped into the 10th decile. With the addition of the AMEX and NASDAQ companies in 2001, many analysts shifted to the 10th decile, which now had greater reliability that resulted from such a tremendous increase in the number of companies.

3. 10A and 10B

In 2001, Ibbotson went to 10A and 10B. The *2004 Yearbook* indicates that there are 1,158 companies in the 10B decile and 554 companies in the 10A decile for the period ending 2003.[58] This caused quite a commotion in the valuation community. Were we in Emerald City?

Not so fast! Again, let's look behind the curtain. Sure, there were 1,724 companies in the 10th decile in 2003.[59] However, let's look at Exhibit 5A.4, which shows the total number of companies in the 10th decile by a specific year by decade going back to 1926, the starting point for Ibbotson's calculation of the long-term equity risk premium.[60]

---

[57] Ibid., 132.

[58] Ibid., 130.

[59] There is no explanation of why 1,724 companies are listed on page 132 and 1,712 companies on page 130 of Ibbotson Associates' *Stocks, Bonds, Bills, and Inflation, Valuation Edition 2004 Yearbook*.

[60] *Stocks, Bonds, Bills, and Inflation, Valuation Edition 2004 Yearbook*, 132.

If there were only 52 companies in the 10th decile in 1926, this means that if you split the decile in half, there were approximately 26 companies in 10B.

Let's see. It does get better, but not by much. In 1930 there were 72 companies in the 10th decile and 36 in 10B, assuming an even split. Jumping ahead to 1960, the numbers are 109 and 54. Is this enough to give comfort? The bottom line here is that it may not be until 1970 that we get enough companies to find the comfort we are seeking. By the way, we are not going to address the topic of whether you should look at returns from 1926 or a shorter period, say 1960 or so. That's a topic for another part of this article.

Do you still want to rely upon 10B? Maybe not. However, is 10A, 10B, or just 10 much better? Is the starting point of 52 companies for 10 so much better than 26 companies for 10B? Each analyst must decide this and choose what he or she can best defend. Obviously, using the microcap or 10A size group will increase the number of companies, but will also put you in a size category that may be too large as compared to the closely held company being valued. If you use 10B, the companies may be more similar in size, but you have the potential problem of fewer data in the earlier years and less reliability. Well, at least we narrowed it down to four choices. Good luck.

Using Ibbotson Industry Risk Premiums—CAPM in a Build-Up Wrapper

You can't ignore the man behind the curtain since his name is not the Wizard but beta. First and most importantly, you cannot blindly apply the industry risk premiums (RP_i) as published in Ibbotson's *SBBI Valuation Edition Yearbook*. When we use the industry risk premium information, we must use it with care. Its use is based on answering several questions, including:

1. How many observations are there?
2. What's the validity of the SIC code?
3. Does it make sense?
4. Is it CAPM in a Build-Up wrapper?

Ibbotson's criteria for inclusion as a separate industry risk premium are that there must be five or more observations. Many industries only have a few observations; others have hundreds. Obviously, all other things being equal, the greater the number of observations, the greater the reliability of the data.

Currently there are risk premiums for two- and three-digit SIC codes, but not four digits [this has changed]. The number of digits in the SIC code can result in large variations. For example, the difference between the RP_i for SIC 17, Construction–Special Trade Contractors, and SIC 171, Plumbing, Heating and Air-Conditioning is almost 7 percent. Also, one is positive and one is negative.

The most important criterion is whether it makes sense or not. Some values for RP_i just look strange. Let's take the restaurant industry. The Ibbotson data shows that this industry is less risky than the market as a whole. Well, maybe that's true for larger chains, but many local or regional restaurants we have been involved with were pretty risky. I doubt that a local or regional restaurant is less risky than the market as a whole. A single restaurant would also probably have a different risk profile than the companies that make up the SIC code in the Ibbotson data.

The use of Ibbotson industry risk premiums is nothing more than a form of CAPM disguised as Build-Up Model. The RP_i is calculated as follows: $RP_i = (RI_i \times ERP) - ERP$ where ERP is the equity risk premium of the market as a whole, the same ERP we use in CAPM. The RI_i is the risk index for a specific industry and is based on betas. As such, using the RP_i means relying on betas. One of the reasons often given by practitioners for using the Build-Up Model vs. the CAPM is that they cannot find relevant betas or they don't believe in beta. Those who take that position need to be aware that they are still relying on beta when using the RP_i in the build-up method for calculating discount rates. Again, it is a form of CAPM in a Build-Up wrapper.

We will continue the discussion of cost of capital categories and controversies in Part Two of this three-part article.

Cost of Capital Controversies: It's Time to Look Behind the Curtain

By James R. Hitchner, CPA/ABV, ASA, and Katherine E. Morris[61]

Welcome back. In the October issue, we presented Part One of this three-part series. In summary, the discount rate for a particular company reflects the risk an 'investor perceives in the company's ability to achieve its projected cash flows. Valuation analysts typically rely on two alternative models to calculate the discount rate: the Modified Capital Asset Pricing Model (MCAPM) and its simplified relation, the Build-Up Model (BUM). At the valuation analyst's discretion, critical decisions must be made with regard to the selection of the risk-free rate, risk premiums, beta, cost of debt, taxes, and capital structure.

In Part One, we discussed Ibbotson's calculation of, and alternatives for, the risk-free rate, size premium, and the industry risk premium, and presented some recommendations and considerations for the selection process. In this Part Two, we discuss the sources for size risk premium data, the new supply-side equity risk premium and tax rate assumptions. Part Three will wrap up our discussion with information on beta, the cost of debt, specific company risk, and selection of capital structure.

Risk Premiums

The development of the discount rate is a forward-looking exercise. Analysts try to identify the risk of a subject company at a certain point in time based on expectations for the company in the future. In practice, valuation analysts rarely rely on predictive models to forecast equity risk premiums.

Risk premium components based directly on historical stock market return data are widely accepted and relied upon by the valuation community. The primary sources of such data are Ibbotson Associates through its publication of the *SBBI®️ Valuation Edition Yearbook* ("*Valuation Yearbook*") and the *Standard & Poor's Corporate Value Consulting Risk Premium Report* ("*Standard & Poor's*," formerly published by PriceWaterhouseCoopers [currently Duff & Phelps]).

---

[61] James R. Hitchner, CPA/ABV, ASA, and Katherine E. Morris were with The Financial Valuation Group, Atlanta. Mr. Hitchner is now with Financial Valuation Advisors, Inc. Ms. Morris is now with American Appraisal Associates. Mr. Hitchner is editor and coauthor of *Financial Valuation Applications and Models* and coauthor of *Valuation for Financial Reporting* and *Financial Valuation Workbook*, published by John Wiley & Sons.

Ibbotson Market Equity Risk Premium

To calculate the market equity risk premium, Ibbotson presents annual return data for three different stock market benchmarks: (1) the S&P 500, (2) the NYSE value weighted, and (3) the NYSE Decile 1–2 over the period from 1926 through the present. Ibbotson provides analysts with a choice with regard to the time horizon over which the equity risk premium can be calculated. Ibbotson presents index-based returns weighted on the market capitalization of each stock.

Size Premium—Ibbotson vs. Standard & Poor's

The primary difference between the size premiums presented in the *Valuation Yearbook* and *Standard & Poor's* is the criteria for measurement of the size of the company. *Valuation Yearbook* presents index-based returns weighted on the equity market capitalization of each stock.[62] The *Standard & Poor's Report* is an enhancement of the methodology presented in the *Valuation Yearbook*.[63] Whereas the *Valuation Yearbook* ranks public companies by market value of equity into deciles, *Standard & Poor's* categorizes public companies into 25 size-ranked portfolios for eight different measures of size:

- Market value of common equity
- Book value of common equity
- 5-year average net income
- Market value of invested capital
- Total assets
- 5-year average EBITDA
- Net sales
- Number of employees

Standard & Poor's contends that risk is not necessarily dependent on size of equity, but that the value of equity is dependent on the investor's required rate of return associated with the risk of that stock. By using alternative measures of size, *Standard & Poor's* believes that it will "isolate the effects that are purely due to small size."[64] Furthermore, *Standard & Poor's* points out that ranking solely on market value of equity disregards the potentially significant effect of leverage on size of invested capital.

In the following section, we explain the criteria used by the studies to select data and the methodology used to calculate the size premiums. Then, we discuss the results derived from each study based on the size criteria.

Study Data Selection Criteria

Although the *Standard & Poor's* study contains more size categories, it is more restrictive in terms of historical data than the *Valuation Yearbook* study. While *Valuation*

---

[62] Based on discussion provided in Ibbotson Associates, *Stocks, Bonds, Bills and Inflation Valuation Edition 2004 Yearbook* (Chicago: Ibbotson Associates, 2004).
[63] Based on description provided in Standard & Poor's, *Standard & Poor's Corporate Value Consulting Risk Premium Report 2004* (New York: Standard & Poor's Corporate Value Consulting, 2004).
[64] Ibid., 4.

Yearbook relies on public company data from the Center for Research in Security Prices (CRSP) at the Graduate School of Business at the University of Chicago, which provides data from 1926 to the present, *Standard & Poor's* restricts its analysis to companies included in both the CRSP and Compustat® databases, which effectively limits historical data to the period beginning 1963 to present.

Let's stop here for a minute. Does it matter whether we use data back to 1963 or 1926? Why pick 1926? Ibbotson explains that 1926 was around the time that quality financial data were available. Ibbotson also wanted to include a full business cycle before the 1929 market crash and to include this period of ". . . extreme market volatility from the twenties and early thirties . . ."[65]

Ibbotson states that the longer period is preferred because it better withstands aberrations in individual years. A shorter period is more affected by such aberrations. Ibbotson uses the example of the 1973 and 1974 bear market that was a consequence, in large part, of the oil embargo. "The equity risk premium for these years alone was –21 and –34 percent, respectively."[66]

The *Standard & Poor's* study may only go back to 1963, but it contains much more information to allow analysts to prepare more refined comparisons to the subject company being valued.

Construction of the S&P and SBBI Studies

The studies begin with portfolios based on ranking stocks in the NYSE by selected measurements of size. Companies listed on the NASDAQ and Amex are then allocated to each of the size-based portfolios. *Standard & Poor's* excludes American Depository Receipts, nonoperating holding companies, and financial companies from the study. *Valuation Yearbook* excludes closed-end funds, REITs, foreign stocks, and American trusts.

The *Standard & Poor's* study excludes "companies lacking 5 years of publicly traded price history; companies with sales below $1 million in any of the previous five fiscal years; and companies with a negative 5-year-average EBITDA"[67] to eliminate potential upward bias to small company returns associated with inclusion of riskier technology or venture capital type companies. For similar reasons, *Standard & Poor's* also creates a separate portfolio of companies identified as having "high financial risk" due to recent poor performance.

Standard & Poor's calculates rates of return for individual companies based on dividend income and capital appreciation. The annual rate of return for each portfolio is calculated using a straight average of the individual company returns, whereas the weighted average calculation is presented in *Valuation Yearbook*. *Standard & Poor's* adjusts the returns on delisted stocks to include a 30 percent loss of stock value subsequent to delisting for performance reasons. *Standard & Poor's* bases the adjustment on a third-party study of delisted stocks, but acknowledges that the percentage loss factor to each stock may in actuality be less.

Standard & Poor's Makeup

Standard & Poor's calculates the annual returns on each of its 25 size portfolios for each of the eight criteria. Returns are presented in excess of the riskless rate and in

---

[65] *SBBI,* 74.
[66] *SBBI,* 80.
[67] *Standard & Poor's,* 5.

excess of CAPM. For returns in excess of the riskless rate, *Standard & Poor's* compares the "average rate of return for each portfolio over [the] sample period [to the] average income return earned on long-term Treasury bonds over the same period."[68]

The indicated premiums were plotted by *Standard & Poor's* in a regression line. *Standard & Poor's* recommends that the smoothed premiums be applied by the user in a build-up approach to rate of return, especially for portfolios of smaller size companies. For larger size companies, the smoothed premium may not be appropriate.

For returns in excess of CAPM, *Standard & Poor's* compares the small company returns to the CAPM, "calculated as the beta of the portfolio multiplied by the average market risk premium since 1963 (measured as the difference between Ibbotson's Large Stock total returns and Ibbotson's income returns on long-term Treasury bonds)."[69]

Standard & Poor's further tests the correlation between financial risk and company size. In a supplemental analysis, *Standard & Poor's* ranks the companies of its size study using alternative measures of risk: operating margin, coefficient of variation in operating margin, and coefficient of variation in return on book value of equity. The resulting portfolios were compared based on their historical returns. Overall, the analysis indicates that the identified measures of risk were meaningful.

Impact of Size on Rate of Return—Using the Two Studies in Tandem

Standard & Poor's presents two alternative methods for calculating the risk premium for stocks based on size and operating performance risk. Based on its analysis, *Standard & Poor's* concludes, "the premiums for the smallest companies are often 100–200 basis points lower [than *Valuation Yearbook*] when one sorts by criteria other than market value."[70]

Standard & Poor's and the *Valuation Yearbook* study concur that small company betas applied in the CAPM do not reconcile to the value implied by historical analysis of returns of small company stocks. Both studies confirm that rates of return increase as size decreases.

The advantage of having more portfolios is that an analyst may identify a portfolio with size characteristics that are similar to those of the subject company. So, what do we do? Well, many analysts are using both studies. They are using the Ibbotson data going back to 1926 to select the equity risk premium. They then pick the appropriate size premium (see Part One for the many choices) based on the same data. Ultimately, they use the data in *Standard & Poor's* for size premiums, compare it to the Ibbotson size data, and make a judgment as to the selection of the size premium.

Supply-Side Risk Premiums—Are We in Kansas Anymore?

As mentioned previously, analysts generally assume that historical behavior of stock returns can be used to predict investors' expected returns on stock. Ibbotson and Chen[71] present an alternative model that uses historical economic and market data

---

[68] Ibid., 17.

[69] Ibid., 9.

[70] *Standards & Poor's 2003,* 8.

[71] Roger G. Ibbotson and Peng Chen, "Long-Run Stock Returns: Participating in the Real Economy," *Financial Analysts Journal,* 59, no. 1, (January/February 2003), Internet version, p. 12.

to forecast the equity risk premium. They identify factors that are independent variables upon which equity returns are dependent: inflation, real risk-free rate, equity risk premium, capital gain, earnings, dividends, price-to-earnings ratio, dividend-payout ratio, book value, return on equity, and GDP per capita. These factors are readily observed through historical analysis of the economy and stock market.

Ibbotson and Chen Models

By analyzing these factors over the time period from 1926–2000, Ibbotson and Chen developed six models to explain the historical equity return. The models are differentiated by their use of various combinations of the identified independent variables. Two of the models are "based entirely on historical returns. The other four methods are models of the supply side."[72]

Ibbotson and Chen rely on the models to forecast the equity risk premium, reflecting investors' expectations for the future. They conclude that "the long-term supply of equity risk premium is only slightly lower than the straight historical estimate. The equity risk premium is estimated to be . . . 5.90 pps [%] on an arithmetic basis. These estimates are about 1.25 pps lower than the historical estimates."[73] In essence, this analysis removes the effect of the high growth in P/E ratios from 1926 to 2000. The P/E ratios increased 2.5 times for an average increase of 1.25 percent per year. This effect is removed from the return under the assumption that it cannot continue.[74]

Some analysts are now reducing the Ibbotson equity risk premium by 1.25 percent to adjust to the supply-side model. Others are reluctant to follow this yellow brick road, particularly given the rather flat endorsement in the *2004 Valuation Yearbook*. "This section has briefly reviewed some of the more common arguments that seek to reduce the equity risk premium. While some of these theories are compelling in an academic framework, most do little to prove that the equity risk premium is too high."[75]

Many analysts were expecting Ibbotson to endorse the supply-side adjustment as compared to the traditional equity risk premium. That didn't happen. Currently, *Valuation Yearbook* explains both methods and leaves it to the analyst to decide.

Industry debate continues on the sources for the equity risk premium and small company premiums. Ultimately, the results and application of these models must be tempered by reason, experience, and knowledge of the relevant facts and circumstances.

Taxes, Taxes, and More Darn Taxes

Some analysts question why we don't tax-affect the risk-free rate to have uniformity with the after-tax equity risk premiums and the after-tax discount rate. *SBBI* calculates its long-term equity risk premium by comparing average stock market returns to the average long-term U.S. Treasury bond income yield. The risk-free rate of the Treasury bond is pretax to the individual investor. A discount rate derived from CAPM

---

[72] Ibid., 3.

[73] Ibid., 12.

[74] Ibid., 5.

[75] *SBBI*, 91.

and BUM, including the equity risk premium component, may be after-tax to the corporation but is also pretax to the individual investor. As such, both the risk-free rate and the discount rate are pretax to the individual investor. This is consistent.

The risk-free rate is just a benchmark to make a comparison of additional returns demanded by investors for an investment in a riskier asset such as public stock. As long as the risk-free rate as of the valuation date is derived consistently with its use in estimating the historical average equity risk premium, analysts are on solid ground. As such, the use of a pretax risk-free rate to an investor is "apples to apples" to the pretax risk-free rate used in the equity risk premium component of a discount rate.

Ibbotson Returns Are After-Tax

Now, let's talk about why the discount rate derived by CAPM or BUM and using Ibbotson data is after-tax. It is after-tax to the corporation but, as noted previously, it is pretax to an investor. It is after-tax to the corporation because returns are derived from dividends and capital appreciation. Dividends are paid after corporate tax. Capital appreciation is driven by retained earnings, which are also after-tax. As such, Ibbotson returns are after corporate taxes.

The next question is which tax rate to use. Some analysts always use the highest applicable marginal rate. Others argue that is inconsistent with Ibbotson data since many of the public companies used to derive Ibbotson returns pay substantially less than the highest marginal rate. Ibbotson presents research by John Graham and states, "Under the current tax code, 59 percent of firms can expect to pay substantially less than the marginal rate (tax rates under 10 percent)."[76]

Consistency Is Key

The bottom line is to be consistent and apply after-tax rates of return to after-tax cash flows. Many analysts simply use the expected effective tax rate anticipated to be incurred by the subject company being valued, regardless of the tax rates incurred by the public companies used in the Ibbotson data. Some companies are less profitable than others and some pay lower taxes. In most situations, the bottom line is to make sure after-tax returns are applied to after-tax cash flows.

In part three of this article we will discuss betas, specific company risk premiums, weights in the WACC, and debt. See you then.

Cost of Capital Controversies: It's Time to Look Behind the Curtain

By James R. Hitchner, CPA/ABV, ASA, and Paul J. Vogt[77]

In this third and final part of our article, we discuss some of our favorite topics, including unsystematic/specific company risk (RP_u), as well as beta, weights in the

---

[76] Ibid.

[77] James R. Hitchner is with The Financial Valuation Group, Atlanta, now Financial Valuation Advisors, Inc., and Paul J. Vogt is with Grant Thornton. Mr. Hitchner is editor and coauthor of *Financial Valuation Applications and Models* and coauthor of *Valuation for Financial Reporting* and *Financial Valuation Workbook,* published by John Wiley & Sons, Inc.

WACC (Weighted Average Cost of Capital), and debt. In Part One (October 2004 *BVU*) we discussed the risk-free rate (R_f), the many choices for the size premium (RP_s), and the industry risk premium (RP_i). In Part Two (January 2005 *BVU*) we presented and contrasted the Ibbotson equity risk premium studies to the Standard & Poor's [now Duff & Phelps] study, the new supply-side equity risk premium, and the effect and use of taxes. Okay, on to our finale.

Specific Company Risk (RP$_u$)

No, we have not come up with a revolutionary algorithm for calculating RP_u. It still does not exist. If we were Dorothy, the Tin Man, the Scarecrow, or the Lion, this is what we would have asked the Wizard for—a mathematical formula. This is definitely better than Dorothy's request to go back to Kansas. Don't get us wrong, we like Kansas, but this elusive formula would have been a better request.

Now, let's get back to the real world. The only current way to determine RP_u is through a subjective analysis of the subject company being valued. However, before we get into the potential components of RP_u (Exhibit 6.31), let's talk about methods and presentations. There are three main types of presentations, each with its strengths and weaknesses.

- Component Detail Method
- Component Observation Method
- Component Summary Method

Component Detail Method

This method presents a list of RP_u components, assigns a specific risk premium to each component, and then adds those individual component risk premiums for the concluded RP_u. The resulting RP_u is then added to a Build-Up Model (BUM) or a Modified Capital Asset Pricing Model (MCAPM). Exhibit 6.28 is a brief example of this method.

Exhibit 6.28   Component Detail Method (Illustrative Example)

Component	Specific Risk (%)
Small company	0.5
Management depth	1.0
Access to capital	0.5
Customer concentration	(0.5)
Customer pricing leverage	(0.5)
Supplier concentration	0.0
Supplier pricing leverage	0.5
Product or service diversification	1.0
Geographical distribution	1.0
Volatility of earnings or cash flow	0.5
Technology life cycle	0.5
Potential new competitors	0.0
Life cycle of current products or services	0.0
Availability of labor	0.5
Total RP$_u$	**5.0%**

Looks good, doesn't it? That's its strength—it looks good and enables the reader of a report or analysis to fully understand what components the analyst thought were important and the exact weight assigned to that component. However, it can also be misleading. That's its weakness. There is no empirical foundation for the individual assignments of specific risk percentages. It's not as accurate as it looks. It can also be attacked. Think about this line of questioning to an analyst defending his or her work:

Question: Mr./Ms. Analyst, I notice that you have assigned exact percentages to each component, correct?

Answer: Yes.

Question: Is there any empirical evidence or studies you can cite that indicate such an exact procedure for applying such exact percentages?

Answer: No.

Question: The assignment of a risk percentage to each component is subjective and based solely on your professional judgment, correct?

Answer: Yes.

Question: Could each of your specific risk percentages have been 0.5 percent higher? Would that be within an analyst's range of reasonableness?

Answer: Yes, it could have been 0.5 percent lower, too.

Question: If you increased each specific risk percentage by 0.5 percent, which you just said is within a reasonable range, what would the total specific company risk be?

Answer: It would increase to 12 percent.

Question: So your equity capitalization rate would go up by 7 percent, correct?

Answer: Yes.

Question: Wouldn't that have a dramatic downward effect on the value derived from your income approach?

Answer: Yes.

As you can see, this method, while appealing, is not the pot of gold at the end of the rainbow. Let's go on.

Component Observation Method

This method is the same as the Component Detail Method with a slight twist. Instead of assigning exact specific risk weights, this method presents the analyst's observations about whether the risk factors increase risk (+), decrease risk (−), or are neutral with no change (nc). Exhibit 6.29 is a brief example of this method.

So, where did the 5 percent in Exhibit 6.29 come from? Well, it's still subjective, but the analyst has indicated, through his or her own observations and analysis, the direction of the adjustment for each component.

The strength of this method is, again, that it looks good and still enables a reader of the analysis and report to have some detailed understanding of how the RP_u was derived. Its weakness is that it appears to assign equal weight to each component. It can also be attacked in a similar manner as the previous method.

Someone could ask the analyst to add the pluses and minuses to derive a premium. In the Exhibit 6.29 example, this would result in nine pluses, two negatives and three

Exhibit 6.29 Component Observation Method (Illustrative Example)

Component	Specific Risk (%)
Small company	+
Management depth	+
Access to capital	+
Customer concentration	−
Customer pricing leverage	−
Supplier concentration	nc
Supplier pricing leverage	+
Product or service diversification	+
Geographical distribution	+
Volatility of earnings or cash flow	+
Technology life cycle	+
Potential new competitors	nc
Life cycle of current products or services	nc
Availability of labor	+
Total RP$_u$	**5.0%**

no-changes for a total of 7 percent versus the 5 percent determined by the analyst. This attack assumes that all specific risk components are equal. This is usually not the case, and the analyst has presented that by selecting 5 percent versus 7 percent.

Component Summary Method

This method presents the same categories but concludes only to a summary conclusion of RP$_u$. Exhibit 6.30 is a brief example of this method.

Exhibit 6.30 Component Summary Method (Illustrative Example)

Component	Specific Risk (%)
Small company	
Management depth	
Access to capital	
Customer concentration	
Customer pricing leverage	
Supplier concentration	
Supplier pricing leverage	
Product or service diversification	
Geographical distribution	
Volatility of earnings or cash flow	
Technology life cycle	
Potential new competitors	
Life cycle of current products or services	
Availability of labor	
Total RP$_u$	**5%**

Okay, let's apply to the Exhibit 6.30 example the line of questioning we used with Exhibit 6.28.

Question: Mr./Ms. Analyst, I notice that you have assigned an exact percentage to the conclusion of specific company risk, correct?

Answer: Yes.

Question: Is there any empirical evidence or studies you can cite that indicate such an exact procedure for applying such an exact percentage?

Answer: No.

Question: The assignment of a risk percentage for specific company risk is subjective and based solely on your professional judgment, correct?

Answer: Yes.

Question: Could your specific risk percentage have been 0.5 percent higher? Would that be within an analyst's range of reasonableness?

Answer: Yes, it could have been 0.5 percent lower, too.

Now, look at the difference. In this line of questioning, the range of reasonableness implied is 4.5 percent to 5.5 percent. In the Component Detail Method, the range of reasonableness implied is –2 percent to 12 percent. The first question then becomes "Which method is more accurate?" Well, we believe all three have similar accuracy. The first two methods may appear more accurate, but they really are not significantly different. The last question is "What is easier to defend?" We believe that the Component Summary Method is easier to defend, does not mislead as to accuracy, and is not much more subjective than the other two methods.

As usual, it is up to each analyst to choose the method with which he or she is most comfortable. Properly prepared, we believe the conclusion would be the same regardless of which method is selected. Some analysts are more comfortable with presenting the detail and going through a process of assigning weights. That's okay, as long as the analyst understands that it may be more difficult to defend and the conclusion would not change if a Component Summary Method is used. That's enough about unsystematic risk—on to systematic risk and beta.

Beta—Simple Yet Complex

As previously mentioned, unsystematic risk refers to the risk particular to a specific company. Systematic risk refers to the risk that is common to all stocks or what can be considered market-wide risk.

Beta is an estimate of the systematic risk of a security. Beta measures the sensitivity or volatility of the return of a security relative to movements or the return of the market as a whole as measured by an index, such as the Standard & Poor's 500 Index (S&P 500). By definition, the market index has a beta of one. A security with a beta greater than one would be considered more risky, whereas one with a beta lower than one is considered less risky than the market. That's the simple part. Now on to the complex part.

Calculation of Beta

The formula for beta can be expressed as follows:[78]

$$B = COV(R_sR_m)/VAR(R_m)$$

[78] James R. Hitchner, *Financial Valuation Applications and Models* (Hoboken, NJ: John Wiley & Sons, 2003), p. 153.

Where:

   B = Company's beta coefficient

   COV = Covariance of returns between the subject company (R_s) and the market (R_m)

   VAR = Variance of the returns on the market

   Most analysts do not go to the trouble of calculating their own betas; they rely upon computed company beta sources.

Betas of Closely Held Companies

Since there are no published betas for closely held companies, an analyst using the MCAPM to estimate the cost of equity must develop an alternative. The alternatives, in most instances, are usually an average beta for that closely held company's industry or a beta calculated based on an analysis of selected guideline publicly traded companies.

   As in Oz, things are not always what they appear to be. Be careful of aggregated industry beta averages, particularly where you cannot find individual guideline public company betas. The individual companies that were rejected may be included in the industry average. However, this is sometimes all we have.

   Various data sources estimate and publish betas of publicly traded companies, including Bloomberg, Value Line, Standard & Poor's Compustat, Barra, and Ibbotson Associates.

   The knowledge and understanding of what is behind the numbers or behind the curtain, if you will, is what is important. For example, the sources mentioned above use anywhere from a two- to five-year period to measure beta, with the five-year period being the most common. Similarly, the frequency of the data measurements varies, with monthly data being the most common, although some sources use weekly data. In addition, most of these sources apply different methodologies and adjustments in their beta calculation, including consideration of a peer group beta.

   It is important to remember that a single publicly traded company can possibly have as many different betas as the number of sources obtained. Therefore, analysts should use caution when using betas from more than one source.

Capital Structure

Similar to the difficulties in developing a beta for a closely held company, the development of a WACC for a closely held company poses the same complication—no public market exists for the subject company's equity. Market values must be estimated to determine the appropriate weights of the company's capital structure.

   Because the market values are unknown, an analyst can begin with an initial estimate of market value weights and apply these weights and accompanying estimated costs of capital into the WACC formula. The subsequent WACC that is developed is used to calculate the market value of total invested capital. Subtracting the estimated market value of debt provides the first approximated value of common equity, and accordingly, a second computation of the capital structure weights to be applied.

   Obviously, the change in the debt weights affects the equity returns. This becomes a repeating process or an *iterative process,* which is continuously applied until the computed market value weights are reasonably close to the weights used in calculating the WACC.

Alternatively, capital structures from publicly traded guideline companies can be helpful in determining the weights of a closely held company's debt and equity. However, many closely held companies lack the access to capital that many public companies enjoy. Furthermore, there is often no real "industry" capital structure. Some analysts average selected guideline public companies' capital weights and call that the industry capital structure. However, it is not uncommon to have, say, six different guideline public company capital structures. Would this average be the industry standard? Maybe not, but sometimes there is no alternative.

Exhibit 6.31   Possible Specific Company Risk Components

Small company	Fixed vs. variable costs
Management depth	Demographics
Management expertise	Availability of labor
Access to capital	Economic factors
Leverage	IT systems
Customer concentration	Industry and government regulations
Customer pricing leverage	Fixed assets age and condition
Level of current competition	Strength of intangible assets
Customer loyalty and stability	Legal/litigation issues
Potential new competitors	Technology life cycle
Supplier concentration	Internal controls
Supplier pricing leverage	Employee stability
Product or service diversification	Location
Life cycle of current products or services	Internal and external culture
Geographical distribution	Distribution system
Volatility of earnings or cash flow	Political factors

Cost of Debt

Because interest paid on debt instruments is tax deductible, the cost of debt to a business enterprise is usually equivalent to its interest rate, tax-affected. If the business enterprise is paying a rate that is not at current market rates, the analyst should consider applying what a current market rate would be. Standard & Poor's publishes the *Standard & Poor's Bond Guide* along with debt-rating criteria that can assist an analyst in estimating the appropriate current market rate for the debt component of the capital structure. Simply calling a banker often works as well.

Some loans may contain covenants that require the company to maintain certain asset balances or financial ratios, or some debt may be secured by personal guarantees or pledges of collateral. These additional costs may justify an upward adjustment in the company's cost of debt.

Bank Loans

Lenders will typically provide loans that are collateralized or backed by the tangible assets of the company, such as cash, accounts receivables, inventories, equipment, and real estate. These lenders rely on the value of the underlying collateral to minimize the loan's credit risk. In the event the company should default, these assets can be sold, thereby mitigating any potential loss to the lender. Typically, banks or finance companies will lend a certain percentage of the value of each asset. How much can depend on the liquidity of the asset, e.g., accounts receivables are typically more liquid than equipment.

Conclusion

Well, this is it. It may not be "over the rainbow" or the end of the "yellow brick road"; however, we hope we opened the curtain enough to present the many options in selecting and presenting the various components that make up the cost of capital.

CHAPTER 7

Market Approach

OVERVIEW

The idea behind the market approach is that the value of a business can be determined by reference to sales of reasonably comparable guideline companies (also referred to here as "comparables" or "comps") that have taken place in either the public or the private marketplace. The value may be known either because the companies are publicly traded or because they were recently sold and the terms of the transaction were disclosed. Based on the economic principle of substitution, a rational financial buyer will not pay more for a company than the current price for a comparable company.

There are three methodologies under the market approach that use transactions as indications of the market value:

1. *Guideline Public Company Method*—based on reasonably comparable publicly traded companies.
2. *Guideline Company Transaction Method*—based on transactions of reasonably comparable private companies reported in various databases.
3. *Direct Market Data Method (DMDM)*—based on a significant number of private transactions reported in various databases that purport to represent the market.

Data sources provide financial and other information, which can be used to determine whether the companies are suitable as guideline companies. This information can also be used to understand industry norms. The market approach is the most common approach employed by real estate appraisers, referred to as the sales comparison approach in real estate appraisals. Real estate appraisers, particularly those who specialize in residential real estate, are fortunate in that they generally have tens or even hundreds of comps from which to choose. The Multiple Listing Service (MLS) provides information with standardized data points that are usually sufficient to determine comparability for residential real estate appraisals. For a business valuation professional, there is no standardized reporting among data sets and often the best set of comps may include only half a dozen transactions.

Quantitative and Qualitative Factors

As with other valuation approaches, the market approach does not exempt the valuation analyst from having to exercise professional judgment. The use of guideline companies is a starting point in that they provide analysts with some objective, quantitative guidance; these value indications must, however, be tempered with consideration of qualitative factors, such as product services, depth and breadth of management, risk, and growth—factors that can be ascertained from an understanding of the subject company and the experience of the analyst. However, depending on the method, this information may not be available for the guideline companies.

Questions to Consider

In selecting a methodology under the market approach, the analyst needs to consider the sufficiency of the information to answer basic questions. The analyst may use one or all three of the market methods. Often the availability of information may indicate which methodology can be applied and the level of reliance, if any. In determining whether there are a sufficient number of transactions to use under the DMDM approach, some of the same questions are asked as are asked for the guideline methods. Under DMDM, the analyst is not determining comparability of each company, but rather of a group of companies that purport to act as a proxy for the market.

Comparable companies and markets are not necessarily the same as the subject company. An overall assessment of the potential guideline companies considers factors such as:

- Size measurements:
  - Sales
  - Profits
  - Assets
  - Market capitalization
- Operating efficiencies and financial risk measured by financial ratios
- Geographic diversification and areas of operation
- Similarity in lines of business

Analysts need to decide what factors should be given the most consideration in making the determination of whether a company or industry market is suitable to be used under the market approach. The analyst's inquiry is not over once the guideline companies or industry market is selected. There are still more questions to consider.

What are the differences between the subject and the comps, and how does one incorporate them into the analysis? If all of the guideline companies and industry markets were identical to one another and the subject company were identical to them, then the subject company's value would be equal to the values of the guideline companies (all of which would have values identical to one another) and the industry market. Since this is never the case, the analyst has to identify the important differences and determine what adjustments need to be made to arrive at a reasonable estimate of value for the subject. It gets down to degrees of comparability and the availability of data to determine that comparability.

The analyst must also determine the key value indicators to use for the subject company. What do buyers of these kinds of businesses look at when determining what they will pay? On what types of factors do investors in publicly traded companies focus: revenues, income, cash flow, number of clicks, or assets? Should certain indicators of value be ruled out based on insufficient information? After the analyst has arrived at a value under the market approach, it is still necessary to determine how much weight should be placed on the market approach in the overall valuation. The market approach is one of three approaches used in a valuation analysis. The valuation analyst must decide how much importance the value derived from market approach methods will have in the overall assessment of value. This judgment normally is based on the quantity and quality of the data. Sometimes the value from market approach methods might be used simply as a sanity check on the other values and is not explicitly included in the final assessment.

Market Approach Is Forward Looking

Some people contend that the market approach, unlike other valuation approaches, is not forward looking (e.g., forecasts in an income approach). This is incorrect. The value of a business is not a function of how it performed last year or the year before; rather it is a function of its perceived future prospects. Historical balance sheet and income statements, from which many of the multiples used to value companies have been developed, can help tell where a business has been. More important from a valuation perspective, they provide the necessary foundations from which forecasts can be developed. Yet these are only some of the many pieces of information investors consider when establishing a price. For example, biotechnology start-ups, which may have no sales and negative earnings, can have positive market values simply because investors believe that firms will show positive earnings and cash flows in the future.

The prices paid for businesses and business interests reflect investor expectations. Consequently, any valuation methods that use stock or sales prices of businesses, including the market approach, must necessarily be prospective in nature.

TYPE OF VALUE OBTAINED

The value obtained using the market approach is a function of the type of methodology used. When sales transactions are the basis of the value, this value generally represents a controlling, marketable value. It is controlling because it is based on acquisitions of entire companies, and it is relatively marketable because the transactions represent sales of private entities for which there may be a buyer, but for which no immediate and ready market exists (as compared to the liquidity of public stocks). It is marketable relative to how long it takes to sell the company as compared to a peer group of transactions. The value obtained using publicly traded companies often is considered a noncontrolling liquid value. It is noncontrolling because most of the trades are of minority blocks of stock,[1] and it is liquid because the stocks of publicly

---

[1] Many analysts contend that when public guideline multiples are applied to closely held companies, the resulting value does not only represent a minority position but also a control position, since many public companies are run efficiently and a control buyer would not pay any more for the business unless he or she could realize synergies; thus minority and control values are equal. Also, control or the lack of control is usually reflected in the cash flows of the subject company. As such, if a public company valuation multiple, for example P/E, is applied to control cash flows of a private company, this may result in a control value. If synergistic value is paid, that may be more investment value than fair market value.

traded companies can be bought and sold quickly without significant transaction costs (relative to what is involved in the sale of a private company).

The value indications, however, may be different from those given above if, for example, there has been some modification to the subject company's financial information. These issues will be discussed in more detail later.

> Transactions of companies represent only the companies that have sold. The entire market also includes companies that were never sold or were sold in transactions not reported in the databases. Adjustments for lack of marketability or liquidity depend on the facts and circumstances related to the subject company valuation and for the industry.

ADVANTAGES AND DISADVANTAGES OF THE MARKET APPROACH

As with any valuation approach, the market approach has its advantages and disadvantages, whether perceived or actual.

Advantages

- *It is fairly simple to understand.* Companies with similar product, geographic, and/or business risk and/or financial characteristics should have similar pricing characteristics. People outside of business can understand this logic.
- *It uses actual data.* The estimates of value are based on actual stock prices or transaction prices, not estimates based on a number of assumptions or judgments.
- *It is relatively simple to apply.* The income approach requires the creation of a mathematical model. The market approach derives estimates of value from relatively simple financial ratios, drawn from a group of similar companies. The most complicated mathematics involved is multiplication.
- *It includes the value of all of a business's operating assets.* The income approach also has this advantage. Using the asset approach, all of a business's assets and liabilities must be identified and valued—both tangible and intangible assets and liabilities. Many of the intangible assets may not appear on the balance sheet (e.g., customer lists, trade names, and goodwill). This is one of the reasons the asset approach is often not used to value ongoing businesses, but rather businesses on a liquidation basis, where the value of these intangible assets might be small or zero.

> The values derived from both the market and income approaches implicitly include the value of all operating assets, both tangible and intangible.

- *It does not rely on explicit forecasts.* The income approach requires a set of assumptions used in developing the projected/forecasted cash flows. The market approach does not require as many assumptions.

Disadvantages

- *No good guideline companies exist.* This may be the biggest reason the approach is not used in a valuation; the analyst may not be able to find guideline companies that are sufficiently similar to the subject. Some companies are so unusual or so diversified that there are no other similar companies.
- *An insufficient number of data points or guideline companies exist.* While there may be some information, it is not enough to form an opinion.
- *Most of the important assumptions are hidden.* Among the most important assumptions in a guideline price multiple is the company's expected growth in sales or earnings.

Unlike in the income approach, where the short-term and perpetual growth rates are listed as assumptions, there is no explicit assumption (in the multiple) about the subject company's growth. Consequently, the implicit subject company growth will be a function of the growth rates built into the prices of the guideline companies, on which the value of the subject is based. Other important assumptions such as expected risk and margins, are not explicitly given.

> Implicit in the prices of publicly traded companies and transactions is some assumption about growth. Generally, the higher the expected growth, the higher the value, all else being equal.

- *It is not as flexible or adaptable as other approaches.* Unlike the income approach, in the market approach it is sometimes difficult to include unique operating characteristics of the firm in the value it produces. For example, a shifting product mix, resulting in higher future margins, may not be easily incorporated into a market approach analysis because there may be no other guideline company whose product mix is expected to change in a similar fashion. Likewise, subject company synergies cannot be easily factored directly into the analysis. To estimate the value of these two types of situations, either a combination of the market and income approaches is necessary, or the analyst will have to use professional judgment to adjust the value outside of the parameters suggested by the guideline companies. Furthermore, the market approach typically cannot be used to value a number of specific intangible assets (e.g., customer lists, mortgage servicing rights, and noncompete agreements).

CHOOSING GUIDELINE COMPANIES

The first step in performing any valuation analysis is to understand the business of the subject company.

Understanding the Subject Company

This step includes the company's main products, clients, markets served, modes of distribution, and so forth. Of equal importance is an understanding of its plans, risk, expected growth, and other factors pertaining to the future. Analysts also look at lines of business and how important each of the business segments is to the overall company in terms of assets, sales, or profits. A common difficulty in analyzing larger companies is the presence of more than one distinct line of business. If the subject has one major line of business and a number of other relatively small ones, the value of the overall company will be driven by the major business segment. If, however, the subject comprises numerous business segments that are relatively close in size, then its value is really that of a composite company. Finding comparable companies with similar business lines can be tricky. The valuation analyst can try to find companies engaged primarily in the main business of the subject—sometimes referred to as pure-play companies. In the case where companies have multiple lines of business, it is unlikely that other companies could be found with the same business lines as the subject. Therefore, pure-play companies in all of the subject's lines of business may have to be considered, whether separately or in aggregate.

Sources of Information about Potential Guideline Companies

Finding a good set of potential guideline companies is one of the most important yet most time-consuming aspects of implementing the market approach. There are several ways to identify such companies, but no single way that is best for all valuations.

Industry Classifications

Since there are so many private transactions and publicly traded companies from which to choose, the analyst must develop some way of quickly reducing the set of potential comparable companies. One of the most common ways is to choose companies in the same line(s) of business (or industry) as the subject. Presumably these companies will be affected by many of the same economic and business/industry factors as the subject, and their prices will reflect these influences. This line-of-business criterion is just one way of attempting to incorporate the subject company's outlook as well as its business, industry, and financial risks into its price. Of course, other characteristics influence price. However, similar business lines is the characteristic that typically is used in the initial screening for potential guideline comparable companies.

A number of data providers categorize the companies on which they carry information by industry. Some have developed their own industry categories; almost all, however, categorize potential companies or transactions by Standard Industrial Classification (SIC) or North American Industry Classification System (NAICS) codes. The advantage of categorizing potential companies or transactions by these codes is that they are widely used and more uniform than industry assignments made by the vendors.

There are several problems to be aware of when relying on a particular data vendor's classification of companies in an industry.

- Some companies (even relatively small ones) are diversified such that the sales or profits in their listed industry are only a fraction of their overall business. These companies are not pure plays and, unless their mix of business is largely similar to the subject's, they may not be appropriate for the guideline company set.

- While a company may have most of its business in one industry, it may have been classified incorrectly. This could be due to simple misclassification by the data provider. One common situation involves confusing distribution with manufacturing. For example, some companies that are actually distributors are classified as manufacturers because the data provider has focused on the product being distributed rather than the company's activity.
- Different data providers may place the same company into different industry classifications.

Examining detailed business descriptions of the possible guideline companies is an essential step in the analysis. Some data vendors provide good descriptions of a company's business(es); however, they are never more detailed than the data found in a company's 10-K filing.

One challenge involved with showing a list of guideline public companies to management is that often managers believe their company is "truly unique," and thus, they view none of the publicly traded companies as comparable. It is unlikely that the market niche into which the subject company fits really appreciates some of the nuances that make the subject "truly unique." Unless these nuances result in prospects for the subject that are substantially different from those of the potential guideline companies, those companies usually can be used. On the other end of the spectrum, management may insist that a particular publicly traded company is comparable because it is a competitor, but the division that offers a product or service similar to the subject company's may be just one of many larger lines of business.

Subject Company Management

The management of the subject company can be a good starting point to identify the appropriate industry and potential guideline companies. Often management knows its competition intimately and may be willing and able to supply insider financial and pricing information on them. It also may be useful to present the list of publicly traded companies in the industry to the subject company's management to obtain their input on which of these companies might be comparable.

Other Sources

Professionals who work with the subject company (e.g., accountants and attorneys) and industry experts (who can be contacted through trade associations, commercial banks, or brokerage firms) can also be good sources of information about the subject company and its competitors. Industry publications or web sites can be good sources of information about potential guideline companies as well.

BASIC IMPLEMENTATION

As discussed earlier, one of the advantages to the market approach is the apparent simplicity in implementing it. At its simplest, it requires only multiplication and perhaps some subtraction, depending on the multiple selected. The basic format is:

$$\text{Value}_{\text{Subject}} = \left[\left(\frac{\text{Price}}{\text{Parameter}} \right)_{\text{comps}} \times \text{Parameter}_{\text{Subject}} \right] - \text{Debt}_{\text{Subject}}^{*}$$

*Invested Capital Multiples

"Parameter" might be sales, net income, book value, and the like. The Price/ Parameter multiple is the appropriate pricing multiple based on that parameter (e.g., price/net income, price/book value) and taken from the guideline companies or DMDM data. In some cases (invested capital multiples) the debt of the subject company may have to be subtracted.

SOURCES AND CHARACTERISTICS OF GUIDELINE COMPANY DATA AND DMDM DATA

> Guideline company information can be drawn from two distinct pools.
>
> 1. Guideline company transactions
> 2. Guideline publicly traded companies
>
> Understanding the value implications of using these different types of data is crucial in properly applying the market approach.

Guideline Company Transactions and DMDM

Guideline company transactions refers to acquisitions and sales of entire companies, divisions, or large blocks of stock of either private or publicly traded firms. DMDM attempts to use transaction data as a proxy for the subject company's market considering comparability of transactions only when there is a large data set to allow for segmentation.

INFORMATION SOURCES

A number of publications collect and disseminate information on transactions. Most publications make their databases accessible on the Internet for a fee. Among the most widely used are:

- BIZCOMPS®
- DoneDeals
- Institute of Business Appraisers (IBA) database
- Mergerstat
- *Pratt's Stats*™

The IBA and BIZCOMPS® databases cover transactions of relatively small companies. As of July 2009, the BIZCOMPS® database had over 11,200 transactions, with a median selling price of $156,000. The median revenue of the companies included was $393,000. There were over 34,000 transactions in the IBA database in 785 SIC codes.

In 2009, *Pratt's Stats*™ included over 13,700 transactions (46% below $1 million in value). The companies covered tend to be larger, with a median revenue of $1.0 million and a median selling price of $595,000. It reported transactions in 745 SIC and 820 NAICS codes, respectively. Deal prices range from under $1 million to over $500 million. The information provided for each transaction is much more detailed than it is for either the BIZCOMPS® or IBA databases.

The DoneDeals® and Mergerstat data sets generally include transactions where one of the companies is/was publicly traded. (*Pratt's Stats*™ also include many publicly traded transactions.) As a consequence, readily available financial statements (8-Ks or 10-Ks) may be used to find additional information about these transactions, if needed.

DoneDeals® (Thomson) had approximately 8,800 transactions as of 2009. The deal prices range from $1 million to $1 billion with 75 percent of the companies sold being privately owned. One-half of the prices were under $15 million. Most of the data comes from SEC filings. As with the other databases covering actual transactions, the range of observations is very large.

MORE INFORMATION ON TRANSACTION DATABASES

The following are brief discussions of some of these databases. For more detailed information, the reader should contact the vendors.

IBA

Raymond Miles, the founder of the Institute of Business Appraisers (IBA), is responsible for the DMDM method based on the concept that a sufficient number of private transactions are representative of the industry market for the subject company.

The IBA database provides the smallest number of concepts for each transaction, but has the largest number of transactions of any of these databases. The information in the database is obtained primarily from business brokers. For each transaction, the concepts include business type; SIC code; reported annual gross revenues; reported annual earnings before owner's compensation, interest, and taxes; reported owner's compensation; total reported consideration (or price) excluding real estate; date of sale; and a couple of pricing multiples. There are additional pieces of information on each transaction that are collected by IBA.

The reported asset sale transaction price is presumed to include fixed assets, inventory, and goodwill, except for real estate. It also includes employment contracts and noncompete agreements but does not indicate which transactions include them. When using this information for valuation, the user will need to add real estate and working capital (less inventory) to the resulting value, assuming it is part of the business, and other assets and liabilities to obtain equity value.

> The Institute of Business Appraisers (IBA) cautions users to take into consideration that the P/E ratios in the database are "of only marginal utility given the quality of small business financial statements" and "different interpretations by persons who furnish the data as to what constitutes earnings."

BIZCOMPS®

The BIZCOMPS® database includes some of the same concepts as the IBA database as well as some additional ones. The data are collected from business brokers and transaction intermediaries. These are SIC code, NAICS code, seller's discretionary earnings, asking price, sales price, inventory amount, amount of fixed assets, rent as a percentage of sales, franchise royalty (if any), number of employees, and terms of the sale.

The reported transaction price is that of an asset sale. In particular, the sales price is equal to the business's goodwill plus its fixed assets. Thus, in order to compute an equity value using pricing ratios developed from these data, the user must add real estate and all other assets and subtract all liabilities. It should be noted that inventories are not included in the sales prices in BIZCOMPS®.

Pratt's Stats™

Pratt's Stats™ is an extensive data set that covers up to 88 concepts per transaction. Detailed information is available on the business, its latest financial information, any lease attributes, owner's compensation, the type of entity, the terms of the transaction (including whether it is an equity or asset sale and noncompete information), and the broker. Not every transaction has all of these data—some are not applicable, but others are simply not reported.

DoneDeals®

While the DoneDeals® database does not contain as many concepts as *Pratt's Stats*™, details on most of the transactions can be found in public filings—in particular, 8-Ks and 8-K/As. This allows the user to construct any series of performance or pricing ratios. It also provides important backup for each transaction. Approximately three-quarters of DoneDeals® transactions represent stock sales and one-quarter represent asset sales. For asset sales, the deal price is the amount paid for the net assets purchased plus the value of any liabilities assumed by the buyer.

Advantages and Disadvantages of the Direct Market Data Method

The DMDM is a simple method, which may be its greatest advantage. For smaller businesses, the DMDM may reflect the behavior of buyers and sellers more accurately than a guideline company method. This is because many smaller companies do not report sufficient information to use a guideline company transaction method, and public companies are too dissimilar to be comparable.

The disadvantages to using the DMDM approach include:

- Some industries have undergone changes resulting in a change in the pricing of companies, resulting in limited current data to replicate the market.
- There is generally no way to verify or clarify the data.
- The P/E multiples may generally be unreliable.
- Not all industries have enough transactions to replicate a market.

Use caution when applying the DMDM approach for valuation dates after 2007. During the period of the recession, business brokers observed transaction multiples for small businesses that were lower than prior to the recession. Whereas in the past, multiples may not have changed over time, the recession may have caused fundamental changes in the marketplace.

ADVANTAGES AND DISADVANTAGES OF THE GUIDELINE COMPANY TRANSACTION METHOD

Guideline company transaction information can be useful in the case of a contemplated sale or purchase, or where the ownership characteristics of the subject match those of these transactions—typically controlling and marketable.

When using the market approach to value a very small business, and with the right data, the guideline company transaction method can be a better method than guideline publicly traded company analysis. Some transaction information is often available for very small businesses, but even the smallest guideline publicly traded company may be much larger than the subject.

The application of these data to the subject company is complex because of the difficulty determining whether a transaction is truly comparable given the limited information available in the databases. This is one of the major disadvantages of using guideline company transaction information.

Some examples of information difficulties are as follows: Were there any expected synergies in the price paid for a particular business, or was the buyer a financial buyer? Was there a noncompete agreement, employment contract, promises of perquisites, terms, or other aspects to the transaction that would affect the actual price paid for the business? While some databases contain this type of information, it may not be sufficiently detailed to compute a "true" purchase price.

> The lack of detailed information on comparable transactions is the major disadvantage of this approach. It is difficult to know the structure of the transactions or the motivation of the buyer or seller.

> Detailed financial statements of the acquired company are usually not available, so it is impossible to make certain adjustments to the data underlying the pricing multiples, assuming such adjustments are necessary.

Most of the transaction databases exclude pertinent information. This often leads to the decision to not use the transaction method as a primary method or, depending on the information, a rejection of the method.

See Addendum 1, "Transaction Databases: Useful or Useless" at www.wiley.com/go/FVAM3E from the *Financial Valuation and Litigation Expert* journal, Issue 21, October/November 2009.

PUBLICLY TRADED COMPANIES

Publicly traded companies are those whose securities are traded on any of the major exchanges: New York Stock Exchange (NYSE), American Stock Exchange (AMEX), or National Association of Securities Dealers Automated Quotation System (NASDAQ). As currently more than 10,000 such companies exist, they provide a rich source of information for valuations.

Information Sources for Financial Statement Data of Publicly Traded Companies

Publicly traded companies are required to file their financial statements electronically with the Securities and Exchange Commission (SEC). These filings, made under the Electronic Data Gathering, Analysis, and Retrieval (EDGAR) program are public information and are available on the SEC website at www.sec.gov.

EDGAR documents can also be obtained from a number of commercial vendors, who add value by allowing the user to extract selected items (i.e., the balance sheet, income statement, etc.) or to search all filings for those meeting certain criteria. In addition, vendors put the data for most or all publicly traded companies in a standardized format. A partial list of those vendors who reformat the data into standardized formats includes:

- Alacra
- Compustat
- Disclosure
- Reuters
- Mergent Company Data Direct
- OneSource
- Fetch XL
- IOK Wizard

Each database contains currently operating U.S. companies. In addition to standardizing data across companies, these vendors also allow the user to screen for companies using both descriptive and financial variables. Descriptive data include business descriptions, Standard Industrial Classification (SIC) and/or North American Industry Classification System (NAICS) codes, and/or industry descriptions. Standardized financial data are provided both quarterly and annually, for periods ranging from 5 to 20 or more years.

Standardization of Data

Standardization of the data in the publicly traded company's financial statements is beneficial for the analyst because most financial concepts are uniform across all companies. One of the trade-offs of data standardization across companies is the loss of detail. For example, operating profit for IBM is composed of the same subaccounts as it is for Dell; however, the detail of what is in these subaccounts is usually not available in these databases.

The valuation analyst may have to consult with the publicly traded companies' filings with the SEC for the underlying detail. The amounts in these electronic databases are good starting points, but the data may have to be adjusted to consistently reflect the financial position and performance across the companies analyzed.

In some cases, the data vendor must make judgments about how to compute the numbers to present certain concepts. These may not be the same judgments the analyst would make if presented with the same information. Last, because parameter definitions differ across databases, one data set is often used for all portions of the analysis to lessen the likelihood of glaring inconsistencies.

Restatement of Data

Another issue to consider when using a standardized, publicly traded company financial statement database is how the restatements are treated. The financial statements provided by Compustat, OneSource, and Reuters are restated; restated financial statements replace the originally issued ones. Mergent, Disclosure, and Fetch XL provide the statements as they were originally issued, without any restatements. Restated financials are important when the valuation date is current and comparisons are being made across time for each of the guideline companies. They can be problematic, however, if the valuation date is in the past and financials known as of that date are required.

Periodicity of Data

Finally, the dates in these financial statement databases are a function of the companies' reporting periods and how quickly they release their financial results after the financial reporting period. The latest quarter, or the latest fiscal year may represent different time periods for any two companies. For example, Company A's latest available quarter might end on February 28, 2009, while Company B's might be as of November 30, 2008. If the analyst were to compare results for the latest available quarters, in this case, he or she would actually be comparing data three months apart. Finally, there is a lag time between when the financial statements are released (in 10-K or 10-Q SEC filings) and when they are updated in these data sets.

INFORMATION SOURCES FOR INDUSTRY "COMPS"

Other vendors provide information that can be useful in identifying publicly traded companies in the same industry as the subject. A partial list of such vendors includes:

- Hoover's Online
- Yahoo Finance
- Morningstar Ibbotson's *Cost of Capital Yearbook*

Hoover and Yahoo Finance provide a list of companies that they consider to be similar to one another. The *Cost of Capital Yearbook* has a list of pure-play companies by SIC code in its appendix.[2]

STOCK PRICES AND NUMBERS OF SHARES OUTSTANDING

Sources for publicly traded stock prices are generally different from those for financial statement data. The main reason for this is that the analyst usually relies on the stock prices for the guideline companies on or close to the valuation date, whereas the financial information used might be months prior to the valuation date.[3]

---

[2] Ibbotson considers a pure-play company to be one for which 75 percent of its sales fall within a particular one-, two-, three-, or four-digit SIC code.
[3] This difference in dates is not a problem from a valuation perspective. The market only has this financial data when it prices companies; therefore, the prices do reflect the information available at the time.

The number of shares used to compute the market value of equity for guideline companies (and for the subject company) should be the number of common shares outstanding net of any Treasury shares on a date nearest the valuation date. Therefore, information on number of shares outstanding can be taken directly from one of the publicly traded company's filings, since the reporting date for the number of shares outstanding may be closer to the valuation date than it is to the company's quarter or year end.[4]

ADVANTAGES/DISADVANTAGES OF PUBLIC COMPANY DATA

Because of disclosure laws, the universe of publicly traded companies provides a wealth of information on a very large scale. This means:

- The availability of larger potential samples than those from transaction data
- Readily available, detailed financial statement and pricing data
- Fairly consistent data across companies (i.e., in accordance with GAAP)
- Accurate depictions of the financial condition of the firms

VaITip

> Some analysts believe that publicly traded companies are much too large to be used as comps in many situations. While this may be true for the smallest of subject companies, such as mom-and-pop operations, small professional practices, or sole proprietorships, there is usually enough size variation among publicly traded companies that they should at least be considered for most other valuations.

CHARACTERISTICS OF PUBLICLY TRADED COMPANIES

Exhibit 7.1 provides various summary measures for publicly traded companies, demonstrating the wide variety of companies from which to draw data.[5]

Note the small size of most publicly traded companies. In particular, the median (the halfway point) is $139 million in sales; this means that one-half of publicly traded companies have sales of less than $139 million. However, many of these are not actively traded.

Exhibit 7.2 shows the distribution of public companies by size and broad industry classifications.

---

[4] The first page of the 10-K or 10-Q has the number of shares outstanding (usually net of Treasury shares) as of a later date than the quarter or year end. This later date may be closer to the valuation date.

[5] The data for Exhibits 7.1 and 7.2 were obtained from One Source representing publicly traded companies based on reported information through August 4, 2009.

Exhibit 7.1   Summary Measures for Publicly Traded Companies (2009 Data)

Range (in Millions)	Sales	Assets	Market Cap.
Under $1	6.7%	3.4%	9.8%
$1 to $10	10.6%	8.3%	13.2%
$10 to $25	9.2%	6.3%	10.2%
$25 to $50	9.3%	6.2%	8.6%
$50 to $100	9.7%	6.8%	7.1%
$100 to $250	13.0%	14.2%	11.3%
$250 to $500	9.1%	12.3%	9.8%
$500 to $1,000	9.2%	12.2%	8.2%
$1,000 to $10,000	18.8%	23.6%	17.8%
$10,000 to $100,000	4.2%	6.5%	3.6%
Over $100,000	0.3%	0.1%	0.4%

Summary Statistics (in Millions)
Table

	Sales	Assets	Market Cap.
10th Percentile	$ 2.9	$ 6.6	$ 1.1
25th Percentile	$ 81.0	$ 22.3	$ 47.2
Median	$ 139.3	$ 355.2	$ 109.5
75th Percentile	$ 858.0	$1,601.5	$ 756.6
90th Percentile	$3,582.8	$6,433.9	$3,107.2

Exhibit 7.2   Distribution of Public Companies by Size and Broad Industry Classifications (2009 Data)

Sales Range (in Millions)	SIC Divisions: A	B	C	D	E	F	G	H	I	Totals
Under $1	4	37	4	140	32	10	12	53	103	**395**
$1 to $10	2	40	6	197	39	17	21	122	181	**625**
$10 to $25	3	14	5	170	32	9	5	187	118	**543**
$25 to $50	2	13	9	155	26	9	20	233	85	**552**
$50 to $100	2	17	2	175	31	11	25	200	114	**577**
$100 to $250	3	31	1	259	57	14	25	208	174	**772**
$250 to $500	0	12	6	196	47	23	35	115	107	**541**
$500 to $1,000	2	35	12	203	37	20	42	103	95	**549**
$1,000 to $10,000	1	69	25	391	148	53	113	146	170	**1,116**
$10,000 to $100,000	0	9	2	100	53	13	28	31	13	**249**
over $100,000	0	0	0	8	1	1	1	4	1	**16**
Totals	**19**	**277**	**72**	**1,994**	**503**	**180**	**327**	**1,402**	**1,161**	**5,935**

These divisions, as taken from the 1987 *Standard Industrial Classification Manual*, are:
A. Agriculture, forestry, and fishing
B. Mining
C. Construction
D. Manufacturing
E. Transportation, communications, electric, gas, and sanitary services
F. Wholesale trade
G. Retail trade
H. Finance, insurance, and real estate
I. Services

With the exception of those divisions where there are few companies in total (A and C), there are reasonably large groups of companies of most sizes, including the "$10 million and under" category.

Seventeen percent of all publicly held companies had sales of $10 million or less in the period studied.

Twelve percent of all publicly traded companies have assets of $10 million or less.

One-quarter of all publicly traded companies have market capitalizations of $47 million or less.

Exhibit 7.3 Four-Digit SIC Codes with Market Capitalization (2005 Data)[6]

SIC	Description	Market Cap.	#	Total	Min.	Max.
2834	Pharmaceutical Preparations	212,650.8	242	1,616,971.2	0.3	212,650.8
6021	National Commercial Banks	247,311.5	167	1,434,175.0	1.6	247,311.5
2911	Petroleum Refining	382,708.0	26	1,318,279.4	3.2	382,708.0
4813	Telephone Communications (No Radiotelephone)	62,727.6	126	1,162,751.7	0.2	96,684.8
1311	Crude Petroleum & Natural Gas	124,298.4	174	804,679.0	0.5	124,298.4
7372	Services-Prepackaged Software	270,541.0	295	597,977.6	0.1	270,541.0
3674	Semiconductors & Related Devices	167,411.8	164	524,325.0	0.5	167,411.8
6331	Fire, Marine, & Casualty Insurance	44,293.4	80	433,918.4	1.8	128,588.2
4812	Radiotelephone Communications	169,789.7	52	403,437.3	0.6	169,789.7
6311	Life Insurance	46,624.6	46	403,314.0	0.6	61,448.0

---

[6] Exhibits 7.3 to 7.7 are based on One Source data for the quarter ending June 2005 (minimum market cap of $100,000). This is a different data sort than that used in Exhibits 7.1 and 7.2.

Exhibit 7.4   Top 10 SIC Codes with Market Capitalization (2005 Data)

SIC	Description	Market Cap	#	Total	Min.	Max.
7372	Services-Prepackaged Software	270,541.00	295	597,977.6	0.1	270,541.0
6022	State Commercial Banks	22,906.00	250	212,504.7	7.9	22,906.0
2834	Pharmaceutical Preparations	212,650.80	242	1,616,971.2	0.3	212,650.8
6798	Real Estate Investment Trusts	13,734.60	187	284,648.8	0.4	15,991.9
1311	Crude Petroleum & Natural Gas	124,298.40	174	804,679.0	0.5	124,298.4
6021	National Commercial Banks	247,311.50	167	1,434,175.0	1.6	247,311.5
3674	Semiconductors & Related Devices	167,411.80	164	524,325.0	0.5	167,411.8
6035	Savings Institution, Federally Chartered	49,212.70	155	136,511.3	4.3	49,212.7
7389	Services-Business Services, NEC	50,670.30	151	93,513.7	0.1	50,670.3
4813	Telephone Communications (No Radiotelephone)	62,727.60	126	1,162,751.7	0.2	96,684.8

Exhibit 7.5   Net Income Margins (2005 Data)

Net Income Margin	Percentage of Companies
Losses	32.3%
0% to 5%	21.9%
5% to 10%	16.1%
10% to 15%	9.4%
15% to 20%	6.4%
20% to 50%	11.4%
Over 50%	2.6%
4.1%	(Median)

ValTip

Almost one-third of all publicly traded companies lost money for the last 12 months on a net income (after-tax) basis. Only about 30 percent of all U.S. companies had net income profit margins of more than 10 percent (see Exhibit 7.5).

Exhibit 7.6   P/E Multiples (2005 Data)

Price/ Net Income	Percentage of Companies
Under 5	4.0%
5 to 10	7.8%
10 to 15	18.1%
15 to 20	20.5%
20 to 25	14.2%
25 to 30	9.5%
30 to 50	13.3%
50 to 100	7.4%
Over 100	5.1%
19.9	(Median)

Exhibit 7.7   Median P/E Multiples by SIC (2005 Data)

SIC Division	Median P/E	# of Companies
A	17.6	25
B	23.0	363
C	12.5	67
D	21.4	2,737
E	18.9	659
F	18.9	242
G	20.7	355
H	17.0	1,483
I	26.1	1,453
All	**19.9**	**7,384**

FINANCIAL AND OTHER INDICATORS

Much of the time spent in identifying guideline companies revolves around finding firms engaged in the same or similar line of business as the subject. Other factors, however, also should be considered in the initial identification process, which are also intended to help identify potential guideline companies with similar future prospects and business and financial risk characteristics.

ValTip

> One of the most important indicators of comparability is size. Size can be expressed in terms of sales, total assets, or market capitalization. Numerous studies have indicated that, on average, smaller companies have lower pricing multiples than larger companies. The main reason for this is that smaller companies typically have more business and financial risk than large companies.[7]

Size

While there have been no detailed studies to specifically identify specific size-related risk factors, some of the more important ones might be:

- Concentrations in products, markets, customers, suppliers, or marketing geographic areas
- Lack of depth in the management team

---

[7] More risk means investors will require a higher rate of return on their investment; and the way to get this is by lowering the price.

There are many issues to be considered if size will be used to establish comparability. In particular, the size measure to use is often a function of the industry in which the company operates. For service businesses, total revenue is probably the best measure of size. For manufacturing concerns, size might be captured in the level of total assets as well.

How close must guideline or subject sizes be to be comparable? This will be a matter of judgment and, again, a function of the environment in which the company operates. A $10 million company might not be a good guideline company to use for a $500,000 business; however, it may work well for a $2 million company.

Growth

Growth is another very important factor in comparability. It is inextricably connected to value, since expected growth is imputed in the price of a stock. This relationship is difficult to observe since it is hard to find an "accurate" measure of expected long-term growth for any company (at least as the market perceives it at one point in time).

There is usually a positive relationship between P/E multiple and expected growth. The fact that this relationship is positive is illuminating, given companies from a variety of industries, of different sizes, and with other disparate characteristics. The relationship between P/E multiple and historical growth is not as strong.

Expected growth is a more important factor in the determination of value than is historical growth. Fortunately, this is consistent with valuation theory.

Other Factors

Profitability, both historical and prospective, of the companies can also be considered when selecting guideline companies. For example, potential guideline companies with high gross margins may not be as comparable to a subject company with a low gross margin without adjustments.

Another factor that can affect value is the length of time the business has been operating. Generally, businesses with longer histories tend to have higher pricing multiples than younger companies, because younger companies are generally more risky than more established ones since their prospects are more uncertain.[8]

> Many analysts believe that valuation multiples should not be adjusted for differences in profit margins between the guideline public companies and the subject company. They believe that there may be a double effect by adjusting the multiple downward to reflect the lower margins of the subject company and then applying those lower multiples to that lower profit. They believe the more important criterion is the anticipated growth of those profits.

---

[8] An exception may be high tech companies with high growth prospects but low current earnings resulting in a higher multiple.

SAMPLE SIZE MATTERS

A larger group of comparables will reduce the importance of any single guideline company. Since at least one company in any group may be anomalous, having a larger group reduces the effect of this potential anomaly. Furthermore, companies are complex. No one- or two-guideline company(ies) can approximate all of the characteristics of a complex subject company. Having a larger group of comparables increases the likelihood that more of the subject's characteristics can be captured.

Also at issue is whether trading in a guideline company's stock is sufficiently active to give meaningful and realistic values for that company. While companies with low trading volumes may be very similar to the subject in terms of business and financial characteristics, infrequent trades may not reflect the actual value of the stock so there is no point in using valuation multiples based on these prices.

ValTip

Valuation analysts may have to choose between a very small group of companies whose business descriptions are quite similar to that of the subject or a larger group of companies, some of whose business descriptions are not as good a match.

Even within groups of companies whose business descriptions are nearly identical to the subject's, there can be large variations in pricing measures. In certain cases it may be better to choose guideline companies that are close to the subject in size, growth, and anticipated profitability but less related in terms of business description than companies that have very similar business descriptions but may differ substantially in terms of size, growth, and so on. This is often based on the availability of data.[9]

COMPARABLE COMPANIES' INFORMATION DATES

After identifying companies in similar lines of business, the analyst must also perform a financial analysis of these companies to determine whether they are good comparables from a financial point of view. To do this properly for valuation purposes, all information used must be as of the valuation date. For example, if the valuation date is June 30, 2009, all of the financial statement data, stock prices, and the like is usually for a period ended no later than this date. Gathering these data can be more difficult for older valuation dates, since some data vendors have only the most current data.

---

[9] Analysts do the best they can with the guideline public companies differences and may apply fundamental adjustments to the multiples to address those differences.

BASIC FINANCIAL INDICATORS

Some financial measures that should be included in an analysis for both guideline and subject companies include:

- *Size Measures.* These include the magnitude of sales, profits, total assets, market capitalization, and total invested capital. Given how size may affect value, at least one, and maybe several, of these should be included.
- *Historical Growth Rates.* Consider growth in sales, profits, assets, or equity. The time period over which to measure this growth is important and is discussed later.
- *Activity and Other Ratios.* Examples are the total assets and inventory turnover ratios. Depending on the type of business being analyzed, other ratios also may be important.
- *Measures of Profitability and Cash Flow.* Consider the four most common measures:

  1. Earnings before interest, taxes, depreciation, and amortization (EBITDA)
  2. Earnings before interest and taxes (EBIT)
  3. Net income
  4. Cash flow

  Using concepts such as EBIT and EBITDA can be useful because they can reflect the economics of the business better than net income and cash flow, which are very much influenced by the company's tax planning, its choice of capital structure, and the age of its capital assets.

- *Profit Margins.* The current level of profits is probably less important than the ratio of profits relative to some base item—usually sales, assets, or equity.
- *Capital Structure.* It is essential to use some measures derived from the current capital structure. The most common measures are the values of outstanding total debt, preferred stock (if it exists), and the market value of common equity, since book equity generally has very little to do with how stock investors view their relative position with a company. The ratio of debt to market value of equity can be included since this represents the true leverage of the company.

> The debt number used should be its market value; however, on a practical basis, most analysts simply use the book value of the debt as a proxy for market value.

- *Other Measures.* These will be a function of what is important in the industry in which the subject company operates. For example, value drivers for retailers are inventory turnover; for banks, loan/deposit ratios; and for hospitals, revenue per bed and length of stay.

DISPLAYING THE INFORMATION

Once the key items have been chosen, the next step is to put the information into a usable format. The goal should be to display these data in a way that makes comparisons easy. So that comparisons are meaningful, the concepts must be consistent across companies. Furthermore, the financial information for the subject company should be shown in a consistent format. One of the advantages of getting the data from electronic providers is that they try to standardize concepts across companies.

Exhibit 7.8 (next pages) is an example of what such a presentation of standard financial indicators might look like for guideline public companies.

Several things in this example of a guideline company analysis make establishing comparability easier.

- The income data are for the latest 12 months (LTM) prior to the valuation date (most recent four quarters) and the balance sheet data are for the most recent quarter prior to the valuation date.
- A number of size measures are shown; however, only one or two are really necessary to help establish comparability. The others are used to develop valuation ratios.
- The remaining measures are independent of size, making them meaningful to compare across companies.
- There are summary statistics for each data series. In this case the 25th, Median, and 75th percentiles are shown.[10] Other summary measures that could be used include different percentiles (such as the 10th and the 90th), as well as a simple average of the companies and a composite of the companies.

Using percentiles rather than simple averages or composites provides a range of values and helps protect the information from the effects of outliers.

- Outliers could indicate an anomalous situation for an industry or company. These apparent anomalies can be analyzed because they may contain important information about trends in an industry.
- Profitability ratios are computed using both the most recent data and information over the last five years here.
- The last part of the table gives other operating ratios and indications of the capital structure.

---

[10] The 25th percentile is the value below which are 25 percent of the values in the group. For example, using the above information, 25 percent, or two, of the companies have latest returns on EBIT as a percent of sales of less than or equal to 5.9 percent. The median is simply the 50th percentile; half of the values for that concept are above the median and half are below.

Exhibit 7.8 Presentation of Standard Financial Indicators

	$ Millions					Amounts in $ Millions				
Guideline Company	Tangible Assets	Total Assets	Employees	Sales	Gross Profit	EBITDA	EBIT	Pretax Income	Net Income
Company 1	72.4	74.0	315.0	64.8	33.5	4.5	3.8	4.0	2.5
Company 2	40.2	51.5	353.0	62.0	42.4	9.5	7.0	5.8	3.3
Company 3	35.2	47.4	246.0	55.5	27.3	4.5	3.8	0.8	0.5
Company 4	44.4	52.0	361.0	54.3	26.5	6.0	4.5	4.7	3.1
Company 5	33.4	36.8	121.0	36.7	22.9	12.1	10.7	4.9	2.9
Company 6	25.5	36.3	206.0	31.0	10.7	1.4	0.9	0.1	(0.1)
Company 7	20.7	20.7	134.0	27.5	17.3	1.3	0.8	1.0	1.1
Company 8	26.5	29.8	100.0	21.3	8.0	4.2	1.9	2.3	1.2
Company 9	12.3	13.3	117.0	17.1	7.3	1.7	1.2	0.9	0.5
25th Percentile	25.5	29.8	121.0	27.5	10.7	1.7	1.2	0.9	0.5
Median	33.4	36.8	206.0	36.7	22.9	4.5	3.8	2.3	1.2
75th Percentile	40.2	51.5	315.0	55.5	27.3	6.0	4.5	4.7	2.9
Subject Company	**3.6**	**4.1**	**29.0**	**5.2**	**2.5**	**0.5**	**0.4**	**0.4**	**0.3**

Long-Term Growth

Company	Sales	Gross Profit	EBITDA	EBIT	Pretax Income	Net Income	Assets	Shrhld. Equity
Company 1	17.9%	21.3%	36.0%	40.6%	51.6%	58.4%	32.2%	46.6%
Company 2	18.6%	18.7%	34.4%	36.9%	58.5%	33.7%	18.3%	8.2%
Company 3	17.0%	14.2%	-0.9%	4.9%	-0.4%	-36.6%	15.8%	11.2%
Company 4	10.5%	10.8%	22.8%	23.6%	28.4%	28.6%	17.3%	25.4%
Company 5	49.1%	55.1%	66.4%	67.2%	76.2%	75.2%	42.7%	47.0%
Company 6	40.3%	35.2%	31.0%	32.9%	25.8%	23.0%	28.1%	21.5%

Company 7	13.3%	12.6%	–4.9%	–7.8%	–4.1%	5.3%	9.3%	8.5%
Company 8	5.2%	–2.7%	–5.5%	–12.1%	16.0%	13.1%	4.0%	5.0%
Company 9	18.7%	18.1%	14.9%	14.6%	26.8%	13.9%	11.1%	11.4%
25th Percentile	13.3%	12.6%	–0.9%	4.9%	16.0%	13.1%	11.1%	8.5%
Median	17.9%	18.1%	22.8%	23.6%	26.8%	23.0%	17.3%	11.4%
75th Percentile	18.7%	21.3%	34.4%	36.9%	51.6%	33.7%	28.1%	25.4%
Subject Company	**4.4%**	**2.2%**	**19.2%**	**20.0%**	**25.0%**	**16.7%**	**–2.2%**	**–2.6%**

	Latest 12 Months Margins (% of Sales)					Long-Term Margins (% of Sales)				
Company	**Gross Profit**	**EBITDA**	**EBIT**	**Pretax Income**	**Net Income**	**Gross Profit**	**EBITDA**	**EBIT**	**Pretax Income**	**Net Income**
Company 1	51.7%	6.9%	5.9%	6.2%	3.9%	52.4%	12.5%	11.2%	10.5%	7.5%
Company 2	68.4%	15.3%	11.3%	9.4%	5.3%	69.0%	12.9%	9.7%	5.9%	4.0%
Company 3	49.2%	8.1%	6.8%	1.4%	0.9%	55.5%	12.2%	10.1%	6.5%	6.6%
Company 4	48.8%	11.0%	8.3%	8.7%	5.7%	48.9%	11.2%	9.0%	9.2%	6.2%
Company 5	62.4%	33.0%	29.2%	13.4%	7.9%	55.6%	0.0%	0.0%	10.8%	6.4%
Company 6	34.5%	4.5%	2.9%	0.3%	–0.3%	40.5%	9.6%	7.6%	8.0%	4.6%
Company 7	62.9%	4.7%	2.9%	3.6%	4.0%	66.8%	7.1%	5.1%	6.1%	4.7%
Company 8	37.6%	19.7%	8.9%	10.8%	5.6%	50.4%	33.9%	25.6%	19.7%	11.8%
Company 9	42.7%	9.9%	7.0%	5.3%	2.9%	42.5%	9.4%	6.8%	4.6%	3.0%
25th Percentile	42.7%	6.9%	5.9%	3.6%	2.9%	48.9%	9.6%	7.4%	6.1%	4.6%
Median	49.2%	9.9%	7.0%	6.2%	4.0%	52.4%	11.7%	9.4%	8.0%	6.2%
75th Percentile	62.4%	15.3%	8.9%	9.4%	5.6%	55.6%	12.6%	10.4%	10.5%	6.6%
Subject Company	**48.1%**	**9.6%**	**7.7%**	**7.7%**	**5.8%**	**46.9%**	**9.0%**	**7.3%**	**7.1%**	**5.5%**

(continues)

Exhibit 7.8 *continued*

Company	Sales/ Assets	Curr. Ratio	Quick Ratio	W/C / Sales	Inv. Turn.	Total Debt ($ Mil.)	Comm. Equity ($ Mil.)	Debt/ Equity
Company 1	0.9	2.9	2.4	0.7	3.4	3.1	47.0	0.1
Company 2	1.2	2.8	1.6	0.4	2.5	12.8	28.5	0.4
Company 3	1.2	2.4	1.4	0.3	2.4	8.6	32.2	0.3
Company 4	1.0	5.9	3.9	0.6	2.8	1.8	43.7	0.0
Company 5	1.0	2.9	2.2	0.3	3.8	3.7	19.9	0.2
Company 6	0.9	1.7	0.8	0.2	2.2	7.3	21.1	0.3
Company 7	1.3	4.0	2.6	0.5	2.9	0.1	16.1	0.0
Company 8	0.7	7.6	4.4	0.7	2.2	—	26.2	—
Company 9	1.3	2.2	1.0	0.3	2.5	4.2	7.1	0.6
25th Percentile	0.9	2.4	1.4	0.3	2.4	1.8	19.9	0.0
Median	1.0	2.9	2.2	0.4	2.5	3.7	26.2	0.2
75th Percentile	1.2	4.0	2.6	0.6	2.9	7.3	32.2	0.3
Subject Company	**1.3**	**3.9**	**3.1**	**0.6**	**2.0**	**—**	**3.8**	**—**

Typical periods for which short-term and long-term ratios are computed include:

- Latest 12 months (LTM) prior to the valuation date
- Latest fiscal year prior to the valuation date
- Latest three to five years prior to the valuation date
- A complete business cycle

One of the problems with using either the latest 12 months' or latest fiscal year's data is that, if not adjusted, the results can be significantly affected by a one-time, nonrecurring event (e.g., a large but temporary increase in the price of raw materials that cannot be passed on to customers). Computing ratios over a longer period of time, such as three to five years, reduces the importance of these types of events. However, since the focus of the valuation analysis is prospective, they should not be overemphasized if they are not expected to recur.

ValTip

Market multiples capture investment expectations of the likelihood of these types of conditions continuing into the future. Inappropriate adjustments could cause the multiple to less accurately reflect expectations of the actual earnings base.

To the extent that the company's business is cyclical, a three- to five-year period may pick up only the upward or downward portion of that cycle and give an incorrect indication of what is likely to happen in the future. However, if the guideline companies and the subject are/were affected similarly during that time, it may yield reasonable results.

Usually data for multiple periods are shown alongside one another. In establishing comparability, longer-term measures can be as important as shorter-term measures, although long-term ratios (e.g., pricing multiples based on average earnings over a three- or five-year period) are sometimes given less weight. It is based on the analyst's judgment and the availability of relevant information.

ValTip

When preparing an analysis of controlling guideline company transactions, there is usually much less data available. In particular, usually there are no data on which to compute growth rates or long-term margins. This lack of information might limit the confidence in the results obtained from this method.

ADJUSTMENTS TO THE GUIDELINE AND SUBJECT COMPANIES

Before actually comparing the companies, some adjustments to the data may have to be made. Publicly traded companies tend to need fewer of these adjustments than privately held firms. To the extent that there are certain accounting changes or nonrecurring events reflected in the companies' numbers, or the companies use different accounting methods, the financial data will need to be adjusted so all company financial data is analyzed on a similar basis.

INCOME ADJUSTMENTS

A number of adjustments may have to be made to the subject company's income statement. While not exhaustive, the following discussion covers some of the more common adjustments.

Nonoperating Income/Expense

Nonoperating income or expense items should be removed from the financial statements of the subject company because publicly traded guideline companies typically will not have a large number of nonoperating items.

Nonoperating income or expenses can arise in several ways, including investments in unrelated businesses and assets, and income on excess working capital. Usually the most accurate way to handle this is to subtract the income or expense from the overall income of the subject company, apply the appropriate ratios, and add the value of the asset or liability that is giving rise to the nonoperating income or expense. If the nonoperating income comes from marketable securities, this is a very simple process. If it comes from real estate or another operating entity, a separate appraisal may have to be performed to determine the market value of the assets.

Example: A privately held company manufactures electronic medical instruments. It has a significant amount of excess working capital that it has invested in high-grade corporate bonds. The risk characteristics of the company's main business are much different from those of the corporate bonds. To apply pricing ratios derived from guideline companies holding small amounts of excess cash to the overall income of the subject would misstate its value.

Assumptions:

Nonoperating portfolio of high-grade corporate bonds = $10,000,000 (par and market)
Coupon rate of bonds = 5 percent
Company's pretax income (excluding the interest payments on the bonds) = $1,000,000
Guideline companies' average pretax price-to-earnings ratio = 12

Value of Subject Including Bond Income of $500,000

Total Pretax Income	$ 1,500,000
Price/Pretax Earnings	× 12
Value of Subject	$18,000,000

Value of Subject Excluding Nonoperating Bond Income

Total Pretax Income	$ 1,000,000
× Price/Pretax Earnings	× 12
= Operating Value	$12,000,000
+ Value of Bonds	$10,000,000
= Value of Subject	$22,000,000

These calculations result in substantially different values. There should be no doubt that the first of these is incorrect. The required rate of return implied by the valuation multiple is too high for the operating business and the nonoperating assets (the low risk corporate bond); therefore, the first of these two calculations understates the overall value of this company.

Different assets, including different business operations within a company, may have different rates of return. When a company operates in different business segments or industries, it may be necessary to segregate operations and value them separately.

Owners' Compensation

It is not uncommon in small, privately held companies that owners receive compensation in excess of what their duties would command in larger, publicly traded firms or if they were employees. This "excess" compensation is really not compensation; rather, it can be viewed as a return of or on capital. In publicly traded companies, this return of or on capital comes in the form of a dividend or an increase in the value of the stock, and the income-based stock multiples of publicly traded companies reflect this. For the closely held company to be reported and analyzed on the same basis as the publicly traded guideline companies, this "excess" compensation can be removed from its costs and treated the same way it is in publicly traded companies. The same theory holds if an owner's compensation is less than what his or her duties would command in a publicly traded company; the additional compensation (needed to bring the owner's pay up to a "market level") could be added to the subject company's costs. This concept applies to a controlling interest. Many valuation analysts, when valuing a minority interest, do not make these compensation adjustments since the minority shareholder cannot change the compensation policy in the company. However, it is possible a minority shareholder could sue to force a reduction of the controlling shareholders' compensation.

Of course, determining what is "excess" compensation can be difficult. Salary surveys can be used; yet many owners perform multiple duties, making direct comparisons with managers of publicly traded companies difficult. In addition, some of an owner's compensation may come in the form of perquisites whose values might be difficult to quantify.

One option is to consult with one or more recruiters to assist you in determining the qualifications for a particular position and market compensation. Recruiters understand the market and the available pool of applicants. This information may help you assess how many positions will be necessary to replace an owner and the market level of compensation. Another source of data for executive compensation is the proxy statements for your public company comparables. Executive compensation with benefits is reported annually.

Income Taxes

Another common difference between publicly traded companies and closely held firms is that many times the latter do not pay income taxes at the corporate level because they are partnerships or S corporations. This tax difference is reflected in net income and cash flow that appears higher than that of their tax-paying, publicly traded counterparts.

Most practitioners agree that the facts and circumstances indicate whether a flow-through entity is worth more than taxpaying entities. There are a number of models that can be used to calculate the difference in value resulting from the flow-through status. Most of the models are designed to apply to the income approach, leaving the analyst to formulate an adjustment, if appropriate, for the market approach.

When using private transactions as comparable companies, some databases report the type of entity, making it possible to analyze flow-through entities separately from taxable entities.

Nonrecurring Items

The issues associated with nonrecurring items are similar to those of nonoperating items, and they will need to be similarly eliminated from consideration. This area is likely to affect publicly traded companies as well as privately held ones. If possible, the analyst can evaluate whether nonrecurring items in public company comparables have significantly impacted their value (share price) in analyzing the companies.

BALANCE SHEET ADJUSTMENTS

Unlike the income statement, the balance sheet usually requires fewer adjustments. Since most valuation multiples are based on income or cash flows, these adjustments usually are less crucial to the overall value.

Nonoperating Assets/Liabilities

The balance sheet should be adjusted to remove the nonoperating assets and liabilities and will require a commensurate adjustment on the income statement.

Inventories

Inventories of the guideline companies and of the subject should be reported using the same accounting method: either LIFO or FIFO. As more companies demand just-in-time inventories, or have high inventory turnover, this may be less of an issue.

Debt and Working Capital

Adjustments for debt and working capital are perhaps the most difficult and important adjustments the analyst must make to the balance sheet. Two issues must be addressed here:

1. Actual level of "long-term" debt
2. Whether the company has sufficient or excess working capital

Long-Term versus Short-Term Debt

The term "long-term" debt refers to debt that is part of the capital structure, that is, the permanent long-term funding of the company. What is listed as "long-term debt" on the balance sheet may be only a small portion of this permanent funding. For a number of reasons, a business may choose short-term or floating-rate debt rather than long-term, fixed-rate debt. This may be a choice based on the company's belief that rates will remain stable or fall in the future. Since short-term funding can be cheaper than longer-term debt, it can save a company substantial money. Or it may be based on the company's inability to obtain long-term funding. Either way, this type of short-term debt is often treated as part of the capital structure.

An indication that short-term debt is really part of the capital structure can be obtained from company management or by reviewing changes in short- and long-term debt over time. For example, if long-term debt is being replaced by short-term debt and the overall level of debt is not falling, then this new debt is probably long-term debt disguised as short-term funding. If long-term assets (e.g., property, plant, and equipment) are increasing and this increase is being matched by an increase in short-term debt, then this new debt probably is going to be permanent and should be treated as such. If working capital is negative or low relative to that of the guideline companies, this fact may indicate that some of the short-term debt is not being used to support working capital needs and should be considered permanent funding.

Shareholder loans may be more properly classified as equity than debt. The terms of the loan, whether it is evidenced by a note, whether it bears interest, and whether repayment has been or will be made should all be considered in determining if it is appropriate to treat a shareholder loan as debt or equity.

Excess versus Sufficient Working Capital

The level of working capital can require adjustment as well. Normally one assumes that the publicly traded guideline companies do not have excessive levels of working capital, since investors tend to frown on this.[11] However, it is not uncommon for privately held companies to have either high levels of cash, marketable securities, or other short-term liquid investments or to be thinly capitalized.

> Excess working capital can be identified by comparing the working capital ratio of the subject to those of the guideline companies or by comparisons to industry norms.

Income related to any excess can be eliminated from the subject company's financial statements, and the market value of the assets can be added to the indication of value obtained from applying the guideline company valuation multiples. For example, in the case of cash, there is very little income from it, but the excess amount must be added to the value of the subject company simply because the guideline company multiples may not anticipate that level of cash.

In addition, the issue of working capital is intimately involved with that of long-term debt. Because of this interdependence, it is often a difficult adjustment to make. While it would be better if there were true working capital "norms" to which the subject company could be compared, this may not be the case. As shown earlier, the ranges of financial ratios for similar publicly traded companies are often wide. Because of this, the analyst will have to exercise judgment in making these adjustments.

EFFECTS OF ADJUSTMENTS ON VALUE

> The analyst should be aware that making certain adjustments can change the character of the resulting value—many times from a noncontrol to a control value.

Numerous analysts believe that adjusting excessive owners' compensation downward and then applying publicly traded company multiples to the resulting income amounts gives a controlling, marketable/liquid value. The obverse of this also justifies such an assertion. That is, *not* making this type of adjustment, when there is an issue of excess compensation, implies a minority position, since a minority shareholder cannot force a change in an owner's compensation. The appraiser must use

---

[11] An exception may be cash available for acquisitions or from recent debt or equity funding that has not been used.

judgment when making these types of adjustments and applying either transaction-based or public company–based multiples.

CONCLUDING REMARKS ON CHOOSING COMPARABLES

The process for choosing guideline companies can be summarized as:

- Using a variety of data sources, compile a list of companies in the same or similar industry as the subject company.
- Review the detailed business descriptions of these companies and eliminate those that are dissimilar to the business of the subject company.
- Eliminate or adjust the multiples of companies whose financial characteristics are not similar to the subject such as size and growth potential.
- Collect detailed financial information (both historical and prospective, if available) about each of the potential guideline companies, placing the data in a format that is consistent across all companies, and include the same information for the subject company.
- Make any necessary adjustments to the guideline companies and the subject company.

> The quality and quantity of the publicly traded company information will affect the confidence one places in the results from the guideline public company method of the market approach.

CALCULATING STANDARD PRICING MULTIPLES

A pricing multiple (also known as pricing ratio, valuation multiple, or valuation ratio, among other terms) relates the value of a company to some balance sheet or, more often, income statement item. It is a way of scaling values, allowing the valuation analyst to use pricing information from companies of different sizes. For example, as of August 2009, both Agree Realty Corp. (ticker: ADC) and Exxon Mobil Corporation (ticker: XOM) had price/earnings ratios of around 12, but Exxon was 9,600 times the size of Agree Realty Corp. in terms of sales.

Pricing multiples provide some insight into what investors are willing to pay for a certain level of sales, income, and assets. For example, a price/earnings multiple of 18 implies that investors are willing to pay 18 times earnings for the stock of the company. Of course, this number incorporates some expectations about future earnings growth, along with a reasonable return on investment.

While all pricing multiples have "price" in their numerators, "price" is not always defined in the same way. The price definition used depends on whether the market value of shareholders' equity (MVEq) or the market value of invested capital (sometimes abbreviated MVIC) is used.

Check definitions used by your sources. Fetch XL defines MVIC as equity value less cash plus interest-bearing debt.

EQUITY VERSUS INVESTED CAPITAL

Equity and invested capital are two different facets of the ownership of a company. The latter is sometimes called the business enterprise value, meaning that it represents all claims on the cash or earnings of the business.

The market value of equity is simply the number of all outstanding common stock multiplied by its market price. If there is more than one class of common stock, equity is the sum of the values of all of the classes. Preferred stock may be added here as well.[12] MVIC is equal to the market value of equity plus the market value of all interest-bearing debt that is part of the capital structure (however that is determined).

One way to incorporate the market value of debt into MVIC is simply to use its book value. This is usually accurate for short-term debt items; it may, however, result in some misstatements on longer-term items. The market value of longer-term debt may be of concern if it represents a significant portion of the capital structure and if current market interest rates on comparable debt (comparable in credit quality, payment characteristics, and maturity) are significantly higher or lower than the rate on the subject debt. Where prices on the traded debt of publicly traded companies cannot be easily obtained, they can be estimated using the information available in the companies' 10-Ks. Nontraded debt also can be estimated using this type of information.

The value of preferred stock may or may not be included here, depending upon whether it is included in equity. Usually preferred stock is such a small part of a public company's capital structure that its treatment is immaterial.

The choice of whether to use MVEq or MVIC is a function of the purpose of the valuation, the capital structures of the subject and guideline companies, and the analyst's preference.

If the purpose of the valuation is to determine a controlling interest value, then MVIC may be the better measure of price since a controlling buyer is interested in the entire business, irrespective of its current capital structure. For minority positions, the

---

[12] Preferred stock can be considered equity-like or debt-like. How it is incorporated is a function of the characteristics of the particular issue(s).

market value of equity can be the price concept. Of course, the choice between price terms based on the purpose of the valuation is often a presentation issue; it is a simple matter to convert MVIC to the MVEq and vice versa. The more important reason an analyst has to choose between them is to reconcile the capital structures of the guideline companies and the subject.

> The term "capital structure" refers to the relationship between the market values of debt and equity, never the book value of equity.

Two common ways to express the capital structure are by using either debt divided by MVEq or debt divided by MVIC. If the capital structures of the guideline companies and that of the subject are similar, then either measure of price can be used. If the capital structures are considerably different, using the valuation ratio based on MVIC might be better.

FINANCIAL STATEMENT MEASURES

The second part of the pricing multiple is the denominator, the financial statement parameter that scales the value of the company. The four general groupings of valuation ratios include those based on:

1. Revenues
2. Profitability or cash flows
3. Book values
4. Some other measure

Some specific common measures include:

- Revenues
- Gross profit
- EBITDA
- EBIT
- Debt-free net income (net income plus after-tax interest expense)
- Debt-free cash flows (debt-free net income plus depreciation/amortization)
- Pretax income
- Net after-tax income
- Cash flows
- Asset related
  - Tangible assets
  - Book value of equity
  - Book value of invested capital (book value of equity plus debt)
  - Tangible book value of invested capital (book value of equity, less intangible assets, plus book value of debt).
- Employees

> In theory, the best denominator to use is based on expectations (i.e., using next year's expected revenues or income). It is an appropriate match with the numerator, since the value of equity or invested capital is a prospective concept, containing the market's best assessment of the prospects for the future.

In practice, the denominator usually is based on the most recent 12 months' or latest fiscal year's historical information prior to the valuation date for income statement–based multiples and the most recent observation prior to the valuation date for the balance sheet–based multiples. Often the presumption in using these recent values is that the near future will be similar to the current period. If, however, the company's performance has been volatile and this latest period is either especially high or low relative to what is expected, then a longer-term (three-, four-, or five-year) average might be appropriate. It also may be appropriate to use a multiple of next year's parameters, which are obtained from analyst forecasts.

The analyst must choose those ratios that are appropriate for that type of business being valued. The advantage of using net income is that it is a very popular measure. Most quoted price/earnings multiples are based on net income. Equity analysts, however, look beyond this widely available statistic. A more useful version of net income is net income before extraordinary items; most investors recognize that extraordinary income or expenses will not recur and price the stock accordingly.

The advantages of using EBIT or EBITDA are that they more closely reflect the operations of the business, and they exclude the nonoperating, financing (capital structure), and tax planning (and depreciation policies for EBITDA) aspects that are part of net income. If the capital structures, tax situations, and nonoperating characteristics of the guideline companies and subject company were similar, then it would probably make little difference whether EBIT, EBITDA, or net income were used in the valuation multiple. But because these things can vary widely among companies, it is important to consider these measures along with, or in many situations, as a replacement for net income.

While it is often tempting to use the same set of multiples to value all companies, doing so is not consistent with the way investors make decisions. There are a number of sources of information on what appropriate multiples might be.

> EBITDA and EBIT multiples tend to be frequently used across many industries.

- *Industry.* Investors within an industry tend to look at similar multiples when making investment decisions and can give the analyst an indication of which value measures are most important. Articles in trade journals and the financial press that discuss recent acquisitions often mention the types of multiples that investors rely upon. For example, many acquisitions of manufacturers are discussed in terms of P/Es or price to some form of cash flows. In bank acquisitions, price/book equity (sometimes referred to as market/book) is very important. In service businesses, prices/sales may be important. Hospitals sometimes are priced on a per-bed basis. It is not unusual for an industry to have more than one key valuation multiple.

- *Subject Company.* The appropriate multiples to use in the valuation analysis may be dictated by the particular situation of the subject company. For example, if the key valuation multiple for the industry appears to be price to earnings (where earnings are net income) and the subject company has not had and is not expected to have positive earnings for the next year or two, valuing it using the standard P/E multiple would result in a nonsensical (negative) value. A better choice might be to use a different definition of earnings or a different valuation measure altogether. Furthermore, if a reading of industry literature does not yield good information on how companies are usually valued, then the management of the subject company may be a good source of guidance.

> While rules of thumb seldom, if ever, should be used as the sole way of valuing a business, they can offer insight into the way investors view the industry.

- *Rules of Thumb.* Most rules of thumb have been developed over time as a result of actual transactions. Rules of thumb are usually quoted as a multiple of some financial measure such as 1.5 times operating cash flow or 2 times revenues. These measures are too broad to be of much use in valuing a company as there is no agreed upon definition for the financial measures used, but they can be helpful in two ways. The financial measure used in the pricing definition (e.g., operating cash flow) is an indicator of the measures that investors look at so the analyst may include it in the calculation of the valuation multiples. Rules of thumb can also serve as a test of the reasonableness of the valuation conclusion. If the rule of thumb in an industry is 2 times earnings and the valuation conclusion is 12 times earnings, the analyst may try to reconcile the two measures.

> Rules of thumb developed for smaller businesses may not provide meaningful information for public company comparisons.

COMPUTATION OF MULTIPLES

The calculations of the various valuation multiples are relatively simple. One takes the price, which is either the market value of equity or of invested capital as of the valuation date, and divides it by the appropriate financial statement parameter, computed over the appropriate time period:

$$\text{Multiple} = \frac{\text{Price}}{\text{Parameter}}$$

One approach is to calculate everything on a per-share basis first and then calculate the valuation ratios. Alternatively, these ratios can be computed on a "gross" basis, using aggregate market values, since the number of shares is eliminated from both the numerator and denominator. For example, price/earnings can be calculated by dividing the price of a share of stock by the most recent earnings per share (the per-share approach) or by dividing the latest market value of equity by the last 12 months' earnings (the gross basis approach).

Negative valuation multiples, which usually arise from losses, are not meaningful and should be ignored.

MATCHING PRICE TO PARAMETER

Conventionally, "price" is matched to the appropriate parameter based on which providers of capital in the numerator will be paid with the monies given in the denominator. For example, in price/EBIT, price is MVIC, since the earnings before interest payments and taxes will be paid to both the debt and equity holders. In price/net income, price is the market value of equity only, since net income is after interest payments to debt holders and represents amounts potentially available to shareholders. Any denominators that exclude interest (e.g., EBIT or EBITDA) should usually be matched with its corresponding numerator (e.g., MVIC).

MVIC is usually the numerator for:

- Revenues
- EBITDA
- EBIT
- Debt-free net income
- Debt-free cash flows
- Assets
- Tangible book value of invested capital

MVEq is usually paired with:

- Pretax income
- Net income
- Cash flow
- Book value of equity

Example: Exhibit 7.9 is the remainder of the example (Exhibit 7.8) shown earlier, giving the market values of equity along with the pricing multiples.

DISPERSION OF PRICING MULTIPLES

The coefficient of variation is a useful statistic for analyzing multiples. It measures the dispersion of the data relative to its average value. The higher the coefficient of variation, the larger the range of pricing multiples. For example, in Exhibit 7.9, MVIC/EBITDA, which ranges from 3.8 to 15.6, has a much lower coefficient of variation than price/net income, with a low of 10.2 and a high of 112.2.

The coefficient of variation is computed by dividing the standard deviation of the set of data by its average value. The coefficient of variation can be used to compare the dispersions of a series of numbers, whether or not they are of similar magnitudes. In the table in Exhibit 7.9, the MVIC/revenue multiples are much lower than the price/net income multiples, yet their coefficients of variation can be compared directly.

If the companies in the guideline group are viewed similarly by the market, then the key valuation indicator(s) used by the market to price their stocks also should be similar. The coefficient of variation can help the analyst to find this (these) key valuation indicator(s). In the table in Exhibit 7.9, the companies' MVIC/sales, MVIC/EBIT, and MVIC/EBITDA are fairly close to one another and have a lower coefficient of variation, suggesting that sales, EBIT, and EBITDA might be better indicators considered by the market when it sets prices for these types of companies. Groups of companies in different industries will have different pricing multiples that are important. This type of analysis could be used in conjunction with a knowledge of what professionals in the industry consider to be important drivers of value. Other statistics may also be used.

APPLYING THE VALUATION MULTIPLES

The final step in guideline company analysis is to apply the valuation multiples to the subject company. At this point, the companies that remain in the guideline company set are usually ones that should be reasonably comparable to the subject.

The table in Exhibit 7.10 shows the equity values (for 100 percent of the equity in the subject) using the pricing multiples given previously and applies them to the appropriate financial variables for the subject company (all amounts are in millions of dollars). Clearly, the range of equity values for the subject is quite large—from $1.2 million to $33.7 million. However, the range of values based on the median pricing multiples is very small—from 4.2 to 5.4.[13]

---

[13] Note that this tight a range is not always the case.

Exhibit 7.9 Pricing Multiples

| | ($ Millions) | | | | MVIC/ | | | MVEq/ | | |
| | Market Value of | | Debt/ | | | | | Pretax | Net | Book |
Company	Equity	Inv. Cap	MVEq	Empl.	Sales	EBITDA	EBIT	Income	Income	Value
Company 1	42.3	45.4	0.1	144	0.7	10.1	11.9	10.6	16.9	0.9
Company 2	33.7	46.5	0.4	132	0.8	4.9	6.6	5.8	10.2	1.2
Company 3	56.1	64.7	0.2	263	1.2	14.4	17.0	70.1	112.2	1.7
Company 4	55.3	57.1	0.0	158	1.1	9.5	12.7	11.8	17.8	1.3
Company 5	64.6	68.3	0.1	565	1.9	5.6	6.4	13.2	22.3	3.2
Company 6	6.7	14.0	1.1	68	0.5	10.0	15.6	67.0	—	0.3
Company 7	20.2	20.3	0.0	152	0.7	15.6	25.4	20.2	18.4	1.3
Company 8	16.0	16.0	—	160	0.8	3.8	8.4	7.0	13.3	0.6
Company 9	10.1	14.3	0.4	122	0.8	8.4	11.9	11.2	20.2	1.4
25th Percentile	16.0	16.0	0.0	132	0.7	5.6	8.4	10.6	16.0	0.9
Median	33.7	45.4	0.1	152	0.8	9.5	11.9	11.8	18.1	1.3
75th Percentile	55.3	57.1	0.4	160	1.1	10.1	15.6	20.2	20.7	1.4
Coefficient of Variation				0.8	0.4	0.4	0.5	1.1	1.2	0.6

Exhibit 7.10 Equity Values ($Millions)

Company	MVIC/			MVEq/		
	Sales	**EBITDA**	**EBIT**	**Pretax Income**	**Net Income**	**Book Value**
Company 1	3.6	5.1	4.8	4.2	5.1	3.4
Company 2	4.2	2.5	2.6	2.3	3.1	4.5
Company 3	6.2	7.2	6.8	28.0	33.7	6.6
Company 4	5.7	4.8	5.1	4.7	5.3	4.8
Company 5	9.9	2.8	2.6	5.3	6.7	12.3
Company 6	2.6	5.0	6.2	26.8	—	1.2
Company 7	3.6	7.8	10.2	8.1	5.5	4.8
Company 8	4.2	1.9	3.4	2.8	4.0	2.3
Company 9	4.2	4.2	4.8	4.5	6.1	5.4
25th Percentile	3.6	2.8	3.4	4.2	4.8	3.4
Median	4.2	4.8	4.8	4.7	5.4	4.8
75th Percentile	5.7	5.1	6.2	8.1	6.2	5.4

For equity values based on MVIC pricing multiples, the calculation is (sales is used here as the concept):

$$\text{Equity Value}_{\text{Subject}} = \left[\left(\frac{\text{MVIC}}{\text{Sales}_{\text{comp}}} \times \text{Sales}_{\text{Subject}}\right) - \text{Debt}_{\text{Subject}}\right]$$

Using the sales multiple from Company 1 (Exhibit 7.9) and applying them to the sales of the subject gives us:

$$\text{Equity Value}_{\text{Subject}} = 0.7 \times 5.2 - 0.0 = 3.6 \text{ (rounded)}$$

For equity values based on the MVEq pricing multiples, the calculation is (net income is used here as the concept):

$$\text{Equity Value}_{\text{Subject}} = \frac{\text{MVEq}}{\text{Net Income}_{\text{comp}}} \times \text{Net Income}_{\text{Subject}}$$

Using the net income multiple from Company 1 (Exhibit 7.9) and applying them to the net income of the subject:

$$\text{Equity Value}_{\text{Subject}} = 16.9 \times 0.3 = 5.1 \text{ (rounded)}$$

Analysts use the factors discussed previously to decide which types of pricing multiple(s) to use.

ValTip

The final determination of which particular pricing multiple(s) to use must be based on an understanding of how the subject compares to the guideline companies in term of the important factors discussed earlier (i.e., growth, size, longevity, profitability, etc.).

While the creation of the tables, including the calculation of the pricing multiples, is a fairly objective process, the final assessment of value is less so. As stated earlier, the use of the type of guideline company analysis shown here does not absolve the analyst from using judgment; it simply provides more targeted information on which to develop a concluded value.

The subject in the last example has some attributes that would place it at the high end of the group and some that place it at the low end:

High End
   Asset turnover (Sale/Assets ratio)
   Leverage[14]
   Quick and current ratios

Neutral
   Profit margins

Low End
   Size[15]
   Historical growth (which in this case reflects expected growth[16])

Because of the size and growth issues, the subject appears to be on the low end of this group of companies, implying that its pricing multiples should be at the low end of this group as well. Based on industry research and the types of statistics discussed earlier, we conclude in this illustration that the most appropriate ratios to use are the MVIC/EBIT and MVIC/EBITDA, equally weighted. Furthermore, the 25th percentile pricing ratios appear to adequately capture the subject's position vis-à-vis this group of guideline companies. The final value is $3.1 million. This example is for illustrative purposes only.

An analysis using guideline company transactions is essentially the same as what is shown here except there is considerably less data available to support its use as a primary method. Furthermore, the application of valuation multiples from each of the databases results in a different type of value, e.g., with or without inventory or working capital.

CONCLUDING THOUGHTS ON VALUE

The market approach should be considered in virtually all valuations. Whether the subject is a large, diversified company or a small operation, sources of data may be

---

[14] Lower leverage (in this case, the subject has no debt) implies lower financial risk, all else being equal.
[15] While the subject is placed on the "low end" for size, the guideline companies are all quite small, so the fact that the subject is so small is probably less important here.
[16] This is simply an assertion for this example.

available to estimate its value. Even if the comparables are not truly like the subject, this approach still may provide a sanity check on the values obtained using other approaches or indications of how the market has changed over a period of time.

USING THE PRICING MULTIPLES FOR GROWTH

As discussed earlier, one of the most important determinants of price is growth—expected growth, not historical growth. Given how important this factor is in determining value, it is sometimes desirable to make adjustments to guideline companies whose growth might differ from the subject's to use their pricing multiples on a more objective basis. In other words, the purpose of this process is to restate the guideline companies' pricing multiples so that they reflect the expected growth of the subject and not those of the guideline companies. Obviously, this adjustment only reflects growth. Other adjustments may still be necessary to reflect other differences. For example, if Company A has a P/E multiple of 20, an expected earnings growth of 7 percent/year, and the subject's expected growth is only expected to be 4 percent/year, how can we adjust this P/E multiple of 20 downward so that it reflects an annual growth rate of only 4 percent while retaining other characteristics of Company A?

Mathematics Behind the Adjustment

The ability to make this adjustment is based on some basic valuation relationships:

$$\text{Value}_{\text{Subject}} = \frac{P}{E} \times \text{Earnings}_{\text{Subject}} = \frac{\text{Earnings}_{\text{Subject}}}{\text{Capitalization Rate (Earnings)}}$$

This equation implies that the price/earnings ratio is the reciprocal of the capitalization rate applicable to earnings (not cash flow), further implying that:

$$\frac{P}{E} = \frac{1}{\text{Capitalization Rate}} = \frac{1}{\text{Discount Rate (Earnings)} - \text{Perpetual Growth Rate}}$$

This equation shows how the price/earnings multiple is related to the discount rate and the perpetual growth rate of the company.

Growth Estimates

The growth that is reflected in pricing multiples is expected perpetual growth; that is, it is *long-term* growth, not just for the next year or the next five years. This fact presents a problem, because most of the growth rates available for individual public companies are for the next three to five years, not forever.[17] These shorter-term growth rates can be obtained from individual equity analysts or some of the consensus reporting services, such as Thompson First Call, I/B/E/S, and Zacks.

---

[17] Even though perpetual growth rates are required, the importance of these rates decreases as the time frame increases.

Note: Some analysts believe that pricing multiples reflect short-term investor expectations much more than long-term. This may depend more on the type of company and the industry.

Three things should be noted about estimates obtained from most consensus reporting services:

1. These growth figures represent annual growth in earnings per share for the next three to five years; these are not long-term growth estimates.
2. The analysts from whom these estimates are obtained may be sell-side analysts, meaning that they may be somewhat optimistic about the prospects for these companies, since they work for firms that want to sell the stock. Also, some of these estimates may be a "consensus" of only one analyst. Smaller companies tend to be followed by fewer analysts.
3. Not all publicly traded companies are covered by these services. In such cases and in cases where only one analyst is following the stock, it might be better to also use industry growth estimates, if they are provided. Of course, the implicit assumption here is that the company's growth is consistent with the industry's.

In using these growth estimates, one must assume that the average annual growth in net income over the three- to five-year period is the same as that for Earnings Per Share (EPS). Furthermore, to use these growth rates for revenues and other measures of earnings (i.e., EBITDA, EBIT, pretax income, and cash flow), one must assume they will all grow at the same rate. These are not necessarily unreasonable assumptions; however, there may be certain cases in which they are not appropriate.

Computing Blended Growth

The adjustment for growth requires that *perpetual* growth be adjusted. Perpetual growth is a growth rate that is not readily available; therefore, it must be computed in such a way that is consistent with this growth adjustment approach. Assuming we use the analysts' consensus growth estimates described above for the next three to five years, we must then find growth rates for subsequent periods (years 4 or 6 and beyond). The objective is to blend these two growth rates together, to obtain a single average annual growth rate that can be used in this adjustment.

The blended growth rate, g_0, that is included in each of the guideline company's pricing ratios must satisfy the following:

$$\text{Value} = \frac{CF_1}{r-g_0} = \frac{CF_1}{(1+r)^1} + \frac{CF_1 \times (1+g_1)}{(1+r)^2} + \cdots + \frac{\dfrac{CF_1 \times (1+g_1)^4 \times (1+g_2)}{r-g_2}}{(1+r)^5}$$

Where:

$g_1 =$ The analysts' growth estimate (assumed to be applicable to a five-year period)

$g_2 =$ The annual EPS growth rate after the first five years

$r =$ The discount rate

$CF_1 =$ Cash flow in year 1

Exhibit 7.11   Blended Perpetual Growth Rates

Discount Rate 20%

Short-Term Growth	Long-Term Growth Rate					
	3%	**4%**	**5%**	**6%**	**7%**	**8%**
3%	3.0%	3.6%	4.1%	4.8%	5.4%	6.1%
5%	3.9%	4.4%	5.0%	5.6%	6.2%	6.9%
10%	5.9%	6.4%	6.9%	7.5%	8.1%	8.7%
15%	7.6%	8.1%	8.6%	9.1%	9.6%	10.2%
20%	9.1%	9.6%	10.0%	10.5%	10.9%	11.4%
25%	10.5%	10.8%	11.2%	11.6%	12.1%	12.5%

Fortunately, computers can perform this analysis fairly easily. The table in Exhibit 7.11 shows the blended, perpetual growth rate for a range of short-term (assumed to be five-year) and long-term growth rates and a discount rate of 20 percent.

As a point of reference, real (before inflation) gross domestic product has grown by about 3 to –3.5 percent per year since the 1920s. Since the discount rate and cash flow assumptions are in nominal terms (i.e., they include inflation), the growth rate also must be nominal. Therefore, a long-term growth rate would include the long-term inflation rate forecast as well as any real growth in earnings. (If long-term inflation were expected to be 3 percent and if the real growth in earnings of a company were expected to be 3 percent, then this long-term rate would be 6 percent.)

Calculating the Adjusted Multiple

The formula for adjusting guideline companies' pricing multiples for growth is:

$$\text{Multiple}_{\text{Adjusted}} = \cfrac{1}{\cfrac{1}{\text{Multiple}_{\text{Original}}} + g_{\text{Original}} - g_{\text{Adjusted}}}$$

Where:

g = Blended expected perpetual growth rates

Multiple = Any of the ones based on income statement parameter.[18]

In making this adjustment to the pricing multiples of the guideline companies, the g_{Original} is the growth rate of the guideline company and g_{Adjusted} is the growth rate of the subject. By making this substitution, one is computing the pricing multiples of the guideline companies as if they all had the same expected growth as the subject.

For example, assume a guideline company has a P/E ratio of 20 and a blended perpetual growth rate of 10.5 percent, and the subject's expected perpetual blended growth rate is 7.5 percent. The adjusted multiple would be:

$$1 / ([1 / 20] + 10.5\% - 7.5\%) = 1 / (0.05 + 0.03) = 12.5$$

---

[18] It is not clear that expected growth is included in pricing multiples such as price/book or price/assets. Consequently, these types of ratios should not be adjusted for growth.

The resulting multiple is considerably lower than the original guideline company P/E of 20. This makes sense because the growth rate of the subject is quite a bit lower than that of the guideline. The 12.5 represents the P/E of a company that is similar to the guideline company except its growth is that of the subject. As such, other adjustments may be appropriate as well, including risk adjustments. Many analysts make a subjective fundamental adjustment to the multiples based on several differences, including growth.

Reconciliation with Income Approach

If the subject's growth is much higher than that of the guideline companies and no adjustment has been made to the pricing multiples for this difference, the income approach will likely result in a much higher value than the market approach. The opposite is true if the subject's expected growth is lower than those of the guideline companies. As discussed earlier, expected growth is one of the hidden assumptions in the market approach. This growth adjustment formula can help reconcile differences between this approach and other valuation approaches. Differences in the measurement of industry risk can be another reconciling factor.

ValTip

Sometimes differences in growth assumptions can explain large differences between values derived from the income approach and those from the market approach.

ADJUSTING THE GUIDELINE MULTIPLES FOR SIZE

Earlier it was noted that smaller companies often have more business and financial risk than large companies. As a result, smaller companies tend to have lower pricing multiples. Therefore, the analyst may attempt to restrict the selection of guideline companies to those that are approximately the same size as the subject company.

Unfortunately, despite these attempts, suitable guideline companies often are a significantly different size from the company being valued. This section shows one method on how guideline company multiples can be adjusted for size differences. The adjusted guideline company multiples reflect the information in the original multiples as if they had been derived from firms of the same size as the subject company. It is important to note that this method is not currently widely used, but is presented to illustrate the concept. Many analysts make a subjective fundamental adjustment for size based on their professional judgment.

The popular *Ibbotson Stocks, Bonds, Bills, and Inflation Valuation Yearbook (SBBI)* published by Morningstar documents the differences in *returns* that have been observed for companies of different size (Chapter 6). For illustration, the 2009 *Yearbook* says the largest NYSE/AMEX/NASDAQ firms (in the first decile of companies) have an arithmetic mean return of 10.75 percent, whereas the smallest firms (in the

10th decile) have an arithmetic mean return of 20.13 percent. The difference is 9.38 percent.

Suppose a larger guideline company is in the 8th decile and the smaller subject company is in the 10th decile. Assume that the arithmetic mean return for the companies in the 8th decile is, on average, 4.18 percentage points lower than the arithmetic mean return for the smaller companies in the 10th decile. Given these conditions, most analysts would agree that the equity *discount* rate for the subject firm could be 4.18 percent larger than the equity discount rate for the guideline company. Using this concept, corollary modifications to multiples will be described.

Two types of *base* guideline company multiples include equity multiples and invested capital multiples. These multiples are related to the commonly used valuation models where:

- The value of equity is found by dividing the expected net cash flow to equity by the equity capitalization rate.
- The value of invested capital is found by dividing the expected net cash flow to invested capital by the invested capital capitalization rate.

After showing how these base guideline company ratios should be adjusted for the effects of size, variant forms of these base multiples are adjusted.

The alterations described in the remainder of this section can be made using the following simple formula:

$$\text{Adjusted Multiple} = \frac{1}{\left(\dfrac{1}{\text{Multiple}}\right) + \left(\alpha\epsilon\theta\right)}$$

Where:
α and ϵ = Multiples formed from guideline company information
θ = The required increase in the equity discount rate

(It is assumed that the guideline company is larger than the subject company.)

Guideline Company Data

Suppose a larger guideline company, from the eighth decile of the NYSE, had the following multiples, before considering any adjustments:

Price/ Earnings	11.111
MVIC/After-Tax EBIT	11.111
Price/ Revenue	1.389
MVIC/Revenue	3.472

Also assume the following information had been assembled for the guideline company data:

Equity Discount Rate	14.00%
Growth Rate	5.00%
Equity Capitalization Rate	9.00%
Revenue/ Earnings	8×
Revenue/ After-Tax EBIT	3.2×
Equity/ MVIC	40.00%

Adjusting Base Multiples

If the smaller subject company is about the size of the firms in the 10th decile of the NYSE, both its equity discount rate and its equity capitalization rate should be $\theta = 4.18$ percent larger than the comparable rates for the guideline company.

Using an equity capitalization rate of 13.18 percent ($= 9.00\% + 4.18\%$) results in an adjusted price/earnings multiple of 7.7587 ($= 1 / 13.18\%$). This same result can be obtained by using the general form mentioned above:

$$\textit{Equation 1: Adjusted Multiple} = \frac{1}{\left(\dfrac{1}{\text{Multiple}}\right) + \theta}$$

$$7.587 = \frac{1}{\left(\dfrac{1}{11.111}\right) + 4.18\%}$$

The lower multiple of 7.587 represents what the guideline company's P/E multiple would be if it were the same size as the subject company.

The adjustment of an invested capital multiple requires the use of one additional piece of guideline company information: $\epsilon = $ Equity/MVIC (the ratio of the market value of equity to the market value of total invested capital). Recall that the value of invested capital is found by dividing the expected net cash flow to invested capital by the invested capital capitalization rate. The invested capital capitalization rate, in turn, is derived from the weighted average cost of capital (WACC). *The WACC is affected by modifications of the equity discount rate only to the extent that equity contributes to the total invested capital of the firm. Therefore, changes in the equity discount rate need to be taken into account only partially.* This is the reason for the addition of the ϵ factor.

In this example, the equity of the guideline company represents 40 percent of its invested capital. Accordingly, the MVIC/*After-Tax* EBIT ratio for the guideline company should be adjusted from 11.111 to 9.370.

$$\textit{Equation 2: Adjusted Multiple} = \frac{1}{\left(\dfrac{1}{\text{Multiple}}\right) + \epsilon\theta}$$

$$9.370 = \frac{1}{\left(\dfrac{1}{11.111}\right) + (40\% \times 4.18\%)}$$

The lower multiple of 9.370 represents what the guideline company's base invested capital multiple would be, adjusted downward for the effects of size.

Adjusting Variations of the Base Multiples

Variations of the base multiples are sometimes used. They are formed from alternative measures of the benefits. For example, the analyst might be interested in using a multiple based on revenues as opposed to earnings.

To convert from the base measure of benefits to a variant measure, a scale factor is used. Here α will represent the multiple required in the conversion. For example, if the guideline company has after-tax earnings of $1 million and revenues of $8 million, the value of α would be 8.

When the benefits are increased by a factor of α, the resultant variation of the base multiple should be reduced by a factor of $1/\alpha$. The first two terms in Equation 3 reflect this fact. Here we identify the base multiple simply as "Multiple" but a variant of the base multiple as "Variant."

$$\textit{Equation 3: } \text{Variant} = \frac{\text{Multiple}}{\alpha} = \frac{1}{\alpha \text{ Cap Rate}}$$

The last term in Equation 3 shows that the variant multiple can be found by increasing the capitalization rate by a factor of α.

In the next example, the guideline company's unadjusted price/revenue is 1.389. The *adjusted* price/revenue multiple can be found from the unadjusted guideline multiple as shown in Equation 4.

$$\textit{Equation 4: } \text{Adjusted Multiple} = \frac{1}{\left(\dfrac{1}{\text{Multiple}}\right) + \alpha\epsilon\theta}$$

$$0.948 = \frac{1}{\left(\dfrac{1}{1.389}\right) + (8 \times 100\% \times 4.18\%)}$$

This equation implies that, after adjusting for size, the variant guideline multiple (in this case, its price/revenue multiple) should be reduced from 1.389 to 0.948.

Notice that ϵ was assigned a value of 100 percent. When working with equity multiples such as price/earnings or variants thereof such as price/revenue, the underlying capitalization rate is derived 100 percent from the equity discount rate.

However, as previously mentioned, when working with invested capital ratios such as MVIC/Earnings or variants thereof, such as MVIC/Revenues, the underlying capitalization rate is derived from the WACC. *Again, since the WACC is only partially affected by modifications of the equity discount rate, the fraction ϵ is required.*

In addition, the value of α is also a bit different. *Instead of being 8 (= Revenues/Net Income), it must be 3.2 (= Revenues/After-Tax EBIT). Here, after-tax EBIT is used as a surrogate for the expected net cash flow to invested capital.*[19]

In the example, the guideline company's unadjusted MVIC/Revenue is 3.472. Equation 4 also can be used to find the *adjusted* MVIC/Revenue.

$$2.928 = \frac{1}{\left(\dfrac{1}{3.472}\right) + (3.2 \times 40\% \times 4.18\%)}$$

---

[19] In general, after-tax EBIT is used to represent the cash flows to both the debt and equity holders. The only major differences between this and net income are interest expense and taxes.

This equation implies that, after adjusting for size, the variant guideline multiple (in this case, its MVIC/Revenue ratio) should be reduced from 3.472 to 2.928.

In some cases it may be necessary to use adjusted numbers to properly compute the α scaling factor. For example, if Revenue/(After-tax EBIT) is high or low for the most recent year, it might be better to use such a ratio for a more typical year for making the size adjustment.

SUMMARY

As stated earlier, the value of an original multiple adjusted for the size effect can be obtained by using the following equation:

$$\text{Adjusted Multiple} \quad = \quad \frac{1}{\left(\dfrac{1}{\text{Multiple}}\right) + \alpha\epsilon\theta}$$

Where:

α = The scale factor, which converts the base measure of the benefits to an alternative measure of the benefits for the guideline companies. (If an alternative measure—that is, something other than price/net income—is not being used, then $\alpha = 1$.)

ϵ = The ratio of the equity value to the total invested capital of the guideline company; should only be used when working with invested capital multiples. (When working with equity multiples, $\epsilon = 1$.)

θ = The difference in the equity discount rates due to size effects.

With the exception of θ, all other factors are computed using the balance sheet and income statement items for the guideline companies, not the subject company. The only point at which consideration of the subject occurs here is in determining θ.

Using this approach, the following multiple modifications were made:

Multiple	Unadjusted	Adjusted
Price/ Earnings	11.111	7.587
MVIC/After-Tax EBIT	11.111	9.370
Price/Revenue	1.389	0.948
MVIC/Revenue	3.472	2.928

See Addendum 2, "Adjusting Market Multiples: The Final Decision Is Still a Matter of Professional Judgment," at www.wiley.com/go/FVAM3E from the *Financial Valuation and Litigation Expert* Journal, Issue 20, August/September 2009. This presents additional information and a different view on these adjustments.

Other Information

For additional information on the market approach, see *The Market Approach to Valuing Businesses,* 2nd ed., by Shannon P. Pratt (Hoboken, NJ: John Wiley & Sons, 2005).

CHAPTER 8

Asset Approach

The asset approach is defined in the *International Glossary of Business Valuation Terms* as "a general way of determining a value indication of a business, business ownership interest, or security using one or more methods based on the value of the assets net of liabilities."[1]

In the valuation of a business or business enterprise, the asset approach presents the value of all the tangible and intangible assets and liabilities of the company. As typically used, this approach starts with a book basis balance sheet as close as possible to the valuation date and restates the assets and liabilities, including those that are unrecorded, to fair value (financial reporting) or fair market value (tax and other purposes). In this chapter, either standard will be referred to by the term "fair market value" (see Chapter 1 for definitions).

On the surface, the asset approach seems to be simple, but deceptively so. The application of this approach introduces a number of complicating factors that must be addressed before a satisfactory analysis is concluded.

FUNDAMENTAL THEORY

Even as we evolve to fair value accounting, accounting is still generally historical cost-based. At any point in time, a company's balance sheet represents a number of accounts stated on the basis of cost. Presenting financial statements on a cost basis brings about a conceptual conflict:

> Traditionally, cost (or more precisely historical cost) is assumed to be the proper basis of accounting for assets acquired, services received and for the interests of creditors and owners of a business entity. Completed transactions are the events to be recognized and made part of the accounting records under the cost principle. At the time of the transaction, the exchange price usually represents the fair market value of the goods or services exchanged, as evidenced by the agreement of an informed buyer or seller. With the passage of time, however, the economic value of an asset such as land or a building may change greatly, particularly in times of inflation, however, the cost principle requires that

---

[1] *International Glossary of Business Valuation Terms,* as subscribed to by the American Institute of Certified Public Accountants, American Society of Appraisers, Canadian Institute of Chartered Business Valuators, National Association of Certified Valuation Analysts, and The Institute of Business Appraisers.

historical cost, rather than a later "fair market value" continue to serve as the basis for values in the accounts and in the financial statements.[2]

Thus, with the possible exception of certain financial institutions, a historically based accounting balance sheet will almost always bear little relationship to value. The balance sheet is useful only as a starting point and requires a series of adjustments to reach fair market value. And, as is discussed later in the chapter, depending on the interest being valued, the value indication thus derived may require further adjustments to properly reflect fair market value relative to the specific subject *interest*.

> Book value, which pertains to cost basis accounting financial statements, is *not* fair market value.

The value of certain assets (on a GAAP basis), such as cash, accounts receivable, and to a lesser extent inventory, may closely approximate book value. Likewise, the value of other reported assets may not approximate book value. The value of other assets, such as property, plant, and equipment, seldom equals book value. Furthermore, internally developed intangible assets as distinguished from those that are purchased individually or as part of a transaction, are usually not recorded on the books.

The asset approach is more commonly used in valuations for financial and tax reporting and for asset-intensive businesses. An example of a business valuation employing the asset approach is presented later in this chapter.

APPLICABILITY

Revenue Ruling 59-60 discusses the use of the asset approach:

> Earnings may be the most important criterion of value in some cases whereas asset value will receive primary consideration in others. In general, the appraiser will accord primary consideration to earnings when valuing stocks of companies which sell products or services to the public; conversely, in the investment or holding type of company, the appraiser may accord the greatest weight to the assets underlying the security to be valued.[3]

Revenue Ruling 59-60 also states that:

> The value of the stock of a closely held investment or real estate holding company, whether or not family owned, is closely related to the value of

---

[2] Meigs, Mosich, Johnson, and Keller, *Intermediate Accounting*, 3rd ed. (New York: McGraw-Hill, Inc., 1974), 16–17.
[3] Rev. Rul. 59-60, 1959-1 CB 237.

the assets underlying the stock. For companies of this type the appraiser should determine the fair market values of the assets of the company. Operating expenses of such a company and the cost of liquidating it, if any, merit consideration when appraising the relative values of the stock and the underlying assets. The market values of the underlying assets give due weight to potential earnings and dividends of the particular items of property underlying the stock, capitalized at rates deemed proper by the investing public at the date of appraisal. A current appraisal by the investing public should be superior to the retrospective opinion of an individual. For these reasons, adjusted net worth should be afforded greater weight in valuing the stock of a closely held investment or real estate holding company, whether or not family owned, than any of the other customary yardsticks of appraisal, such as earnings and dividend-paying capacity.[4]

Revenue Ruling 59-60 states that operating companies (i.e., those that sell products or services to the public) typically should be valued based on earnings (as explained in Chapters 5 and 7, a number of methods are available), as that is how the investing community generally values such companies. And, at least in theory, operating companies that earn a rate of return in excess of a fair return on current and tangible assets will demonstrate market values in excess of book value—the implication being that the company also has an element of intangible value that likely is not recorded or, if recorded, is undervalued in the accounts. Thus, if the asset approach is used to value an operating company as a going concern, the result may be undervaluation, because the value of goodwill and other intangible assets likely is not reflected on the company's balance sheet; if such values are recorded, it is likely the result of a prior acquisition and is probably not reflective of current value. Therefore, the asset approach is typically used to value investment or holding companies and is an often-used method for valuing small practices, family limited partnerships, and certain pass-through entities.[5]

The asset approach also is sometimes used in the valuation of very small businesses and/or professional practices where there is little or no practice goodwill.

---

[4] Ibid.

[5] However, the Tax Court has ruled that a weighting of the income approach may be appropriate in the valuation of a holding-type company in certain circumstances. See, for example, *Estate of Andrews v. Commissioner*, 79 T.C., and *Estate of Helen J. Smith v. Commissioner*, T.C. Memo, 1999-368.

Although the asset approach can be used in almost any valuation, it is seldom used in the valuation of operating companies. The time and costs involved in valuing individual tangible and intangible assets typically is not justified, because there is little, if any, increase in the accuracy of the valuation. The value of all tangible and intangible assets is captured, in aggregate, in the proper application of the income and market approaches. In many valuations there is no real need to break out the amount of value associated with individual assets, including goodwill. However, it is sometimes used as a floor value. Other times it may be a value that is too high if the net asset values do not have income support as a going concern.

PREMISE OF VALUE

It is important to determine the premise of value before constructing any fair market value balance sheets. For an overall business valuation, the two premises of value are going concern and liquidation, both orderly and forced (Chapters 1 and 2). However, in applying premises of value to individual assets, other premises may apply, including fair market value-removal, fair market value in continued use, fair market value–installed, orderly liquidation value, and forced liquidation value. Fair market value in continued use and fair market value–installed usually are used to value assets as part of a going concern, giving consideration to installation and indirect costs. These premises are often used in valuations for mergers and acquisitions and financial and tax reporting. Orderly liquidation value and forced liquidation value reflect value in exchange, with forced liquidation value generally considered to be an auction value. Fair market value-removal reflects the value of the property including consideration of the cost of removal of the property to another location. See Addendum 3 at the end of this chapter for further information on premise of value for individual assets.

CONTROL VERSUS MINORITY

As discussed in some detail in Chapter 9, the degree of control possessed by the subject interest is a critical variable. This is an important consideration in the asset approach, because the value indication derived will usually be at *control* and is known as a *control* indicator. Furthermore, the asset approach typically provides a value indication stated on a *marketable* basis.

If the asset approach is used in valuing a minority interest of a closely held company, the value indication derived usually will have to be adjusted from *control* to *minority* and, depending on the facts and circumstances, from a *marketable* to a *nonmarketable* basis.

To illustrate why minority and lack of marketability adjustments might be required, one must look at the underlying premise of this approach. The asset approach can be a liquidation or quasi-liquidation scenario. Irrespective of the approaches and methods employed to value the individual assets, the asset approach assumes the assets can be sold and that the values reasonably represent values that could be obtained in the market. The sale of liabilities is likewise assumed; thus, the net asset value derived is based on the assumption that all assets and liabilities are sold at the indicated net asset value. This implies that the interest has the power to sell or liquidate the company, a classic control power. Furthermore, application of this approach is founded on the assumption that there is a ready and willing buyer for the interest at the appraised value. In reality, the willing buyer under the commonly referenced standards of value likely would not pay a price equal to a pro rata share of the total net asset value for a *minority* interest in an enterprise valued under the asset approach. The buyer likely would extract, and the willing seller likely would accept, discounts to reflect the lack of control (the asset approach assumes the power to liquidate) and lack of marketability (the asset approach assumes ready sale of the business).

BUILT-IN GAINS

The treatment of built-in gains has been controversial, with taxpayers and the Internal Revenue Service (IRS) historically possessing opposed points of view. As discussed more fully in Addendum 1 of this chapter, web Addendum 5 at www.wiley.com/go/FVAM3E, and also in Chapters 9 and 13, built-in gains arise when the fair market value of assets owned by an entity exceeds tax basis.

Built-in gains generally are not an issue in the valuation of operating companies. As discussed in IRS Revenue Ruling 59-60, asset value is the principal value driver for investment or holding companies.

The controversy with respect to built-in gains occurs in the valuation of such companies. The consideration of how buyer and seller might arrive at an agreement as to the fair market value of an asset requires considering the effect of built-in gain upon pricing of the asset.

On the surface, the calculation of built-in gain is simple. The amount of built-in gain is equal to the fair market value of the asset less the tax basis of that asset. In a C corporation, a capital gains tax has to be paid upon the sale of an appreciated asset or the liquidation of a corporation. Thus, in a C corporation valued using the asset approach, a built-in gains tax is accrued to reduce the fair market value of the asset by the amount of the capital gains tax on the built-in gain. For example, the adjusted fair market value of an asset worth $100,000 with a tax basis of $40,000, assuming a C corporation effective tax rate of 40 percent, is $76,000 {$100,000 − [40% × ($100,000 − $40,000)]}. In presenting this concept within an asset approach, the appraiser creates a liability for the capital gains tax and reduces the fair market value of the asset accordingly.

Built-in gains taxes have been endorsed by the Tax Court in a number of cases, based on the reasoning that a hypothetical buyer will consider the tax liability in computing the fair market value of the stock of a holding company. The cases supporting this position demonstrate different approaches for handling the determination of the amount of tax. For example, in *Estate of Simplot v. Commissioner,* the Tax Court applied a 40 percent tax rate in computing the full amount of built-in gains taxes, while in *Estate of Davis v. Commissioner* the built-in gains tax was accounted for by a 15 percent increase in the discount for lack of marketability. Another divergence of views for those supporting the recognition of the built-in gain is whether the amount should be calculated as the present value of the gain, which requires a holding-period assumption, or the gross amount calculated as of the valuation date, without regard to present value.

Thus, there has been a convergence of opinion among practitioners and the courts toward favoring application of a built-in gains tax on the appreciated assets of C corporations. The question is less clear-cut when the holding company is a pass-through entity such as an S corporation or a partnership.

In considering the appropriateness of a built-in capital gains tax for pass-through entities, one must consider the alternatives available to buyers and sellers. In an S corporation, using the previous example, if the S corporation sold the asset, the $60,000 gain would "pass through" to the shareholder(s) and be taxed at a personal capital gains rate assuming that the $60,000 is a capital gain to the S corporation. A minority shareholder cannot control the timing of corporate asset sales or the liquidation of the corporation and thus may not be able to avoid capital gains taxes. This suggests that a hypothetical buyer would be willing to pay $88,000 ($100,000 − 20% × $60,000) for the asset if owned by an S corporation. There are various assumptions here that will vary case-by-case.

In a partnership, even this level of taxation is avoidable if the partnership makes a §754 election. A §754 election allows a buyer to step up his or her share of the inside basis of partnership assets and thereby eliminate built-in gains. If the §754 election is easy to make, it follows that pass-through gains can more readily be avoided.

The issue of built-in gains in general, and the matter of how such gains might affect the fair market value of assets in C corporations, S corporations, and partnerships, is addressed in three excellent articles, two (see Addendum 1 at the end of this chapter) by Sliwoski and Bader that appeared in *CPA Expert* in 2001[6] and a third (see web Addendum 5) by M. Mark Lee, published in *Financial Valuation and Litigation Expert* in April/May 2008.[7]

The recognition of built-in gains taxes has historically been a controversial topic. Court cases have increasingly supported deductions for such taxes in cases where the subject company is organized as a C corporation. As for S corporations, there appears to be growing support for a discount that is reflective of personal taxes on gains. The same cannot be said of partnerships.

The IRS has repeatedly rejected the application of built-in gains, advancing its argument in 1991 with Technical Advice Memorandum (TAM) 9150001. The TAM concluded, "In determining the value of the decedent's stock in a Subchapter C corporation based on net asset value, no discount should be allowed for potential capital gains taxes that would be incurred if the corporation was liquidated since there is no indication that a liquidation is contemplated."[8]

Taxpayers have argued that, under the fair market value standard, a willing buyer could extract a discount for the tax on a built-in gain. In recent years, decisions by the Tax Court and by the U.S. Court of Appeals have taken the view that reductions are warranted in the value of closely held stock to reflect the potential tax on built-in gains (see Chapters 9 and 15). Furthermore, there have now been cases

---

[6] Leonard Sliwoski, CPA/ABV, PhD, CBA, ASA and Mary B. Bader, CPA, JD, LLM, "Built-in Gains Taxes: Business Valuation Considerations, Part 1 and Part 2," *CPA Expert*, 2001.

[7] M. Mark Lee, CFA, "*Jelke*, Again. The Build-In Capital Gains Tax for a Stock Portfolio held by a C Corporation: A Third Alternative View," *Financial Valuation and Litigation Expert* (April/May 2008), pp. 5–7, Valuation Products and Services, LLC.

[8] Internal Revenue Service, *Technical Advice Memorandum* 9150001, 1991.

where the IRS's valuation expert has made capital gains tax adjustments (see Litchfield V. Commissioner, T.C. Memo, 2009–21, January 29, 2009).

GENERAL STEPS IN THE ASSET APPROACH

Balance Sheet as Starting Point

The first step in using the cost approach is to obtain a balance sheet as close as possible to the valuation date. Again, book value is not fair market value but is the starting point to create a fair market value balance sheet. A company balance sheet includes such items as cash, accounts receivable, marketable securities, inventory, prepaid expenses, land, buildings, furniture, fixtures, and equipment on the asset side, and accounts payable, accrued expenses, and interest-bearing debt plus equity accounts on the liabilities and equity side.

Restate Recorded Assets and Liabilities

Each recorded asset must be examined and adjusted to fair market value. In a proper application of this approach, individual intangible assets should be identified and valued as well. See Chapter 21 for techniques to value intangible assets. Once the asset side of the balance sheet has been restated to fair market value, it is a simple process to subtract all liabilities, again at fair market value, to derive the fair market value of the equity of the business under the asset approach. As a practical matter, analysts typically use book value amounts for liabilities. However, to the extent current financing terms differ from actual rates, an adjustment may be appropriate.

| ValTip |

When notes to the financial statements are included, they often contain useful information concerning contingent liabilities.

Unrecorded Assets and Liabilities

Most off-balance sheet assets are intangible in nature. However, there can be other types of assets, including a pending litigation claim to be paid and assets that have been written off but are still used in the business. Off-balance sheet liabilities include contingent liabilities such as potential environmental problems, pending tax disputes, and unfunded pensions.

Current and Tangible Assets

Cash and accounts receivable and other types of marketable securities are generally not difficult to value. Cash is cash, and accounts receivable should be adjusted for uncollectible amounts. The book value of other items, such as prepaid expenses, often is used as proxy for fair market value. The one asset that may entail some adjustment is inventory. Internal Revenue Service Revenue Procedure (Rev. Proc.) 77-12 (see Addendum 4 at the end of this chapter) provides some guidance for valuing inventory. See Addendum 2, Valuation of Real Estate, and Addendum 3, Valuation of Machinery and Equipment, at the end of this chapter.

Exhibit 8.1 B. Brothers Holding Company, Inc., Asset Based Approach, As of December 31, 20XX

Assets	REPORTED December 31, 20XX	DEBITS		CREDITS	ADJUSTED December 31, 20XX
Cash & Equivalents	$ 5,200,000				$ 5,200,000
Investments in Marketable Securities	4,200,000	3,368,000	(1)		7,568,000
Accounts Receivable-Trade	8,400,000		(2)	95,000	8,305,000
Accounts Receivable-Officer	75,000		(3)	75,000	0
Inventories	5,900,000	600,000	(4)		6,500,000
Prepaid Expenses	2,800,000		(5)	100,000	2,700,000
Total Current Assets	$26,575,000				$30,273,000
Land and Buildings	$ 7,200,000	12,000,000	(6)		$19,200,000
Accumulated Depreciation	(4,800,000)	4,800,000	(6)		0
Machinery and Equipment	23,200,000	1,200,000	(7)		24,400,000
Accumulated Depreciation	(12,700,000)	12,700,000	(7)		0
Net Fixed Assets	$12,900,000				$43,600,000
Intangible Assets (Organization Costs)	295,000		(8)	295,000	0
TOTAL ASSETS	$39,770,000				$73,873,000
Liabilities					
Notes Payable	$ 500,000				$ 500,000
Accounts Payable	6,550,000				6,550,000
Current Portion of Long-Term Debt	1,250,000		(9)	11,800	1,261,800
Accrued Expenses	2,400,000				2,400,000

	Book Value		Debit	Credit	Adjusted Value
Total Current Liabilities	$10,700,000				$10,711,800
Long-Term Debt	$ 5,000,000	(9)		152,300	$ 5,152,300
Deferred Income Taxes	800,000				800,000
Other Long-Term Liabilities	250,000	(10)		300,000	550,000
Built-In Gain Liability	0	(11)		18,876,360	18,876,360
Total Liabilities	$16,750,000				$36,090,460
Shareholders' Equity					
Common Stock	$ 100,000				$ 100,000
Paid-In Capital	2,000,000				2,000,000
Retained Earnings	20,920,000	(12)	19,905,460	34,668,000	35,682,540
Treasury Stock	0				0
Total Shareholders' Equity	$23,020,000				$37,782,540
TOTAL LIABILITIES & EQUITY	$39,770,000				$73,873,000

Adjustments to Balance Sheet

(1) To adjust marketable securities to current market value. See Exhibit 8.2.
(2) To write off two uncollectible accounts and adjust allowance.
(3) To write off advance to officer, which will not be repaid.
(4) To adjust inventory to fair value.
(5) To write off (a) the portion of prepaid insurance which has expired, and (b) a forfeited deposit.
(6) To adjust real estate to fair value, per appraisal by Dick Hartz, MAI.
(7) To adjust personal property to fair value, per appraisal by Joe Ernandi, ASA.
(8) To write off capitalized organization costs, which provide no future economic benefit.
(9) To adjust fair value of debt. See Exhibit 8.3.
(10) To record estimated liability for pending litigation.
(11) To record liability for built-in gain. See Exhibit 8.4.
(12) Net adjustments to equity

VALUATION OF INDIVIDUAL ASSETS AND LIABILITIES EXAMPLE

B. Brothers Holding Company, Inc. (the company), a C corporation, is being valued on a minority interest basis for estate tax purposes as of December 31, 20XX. The company has a significant cash position (which includes a large money market account); owns a portfolio of marketable securities; has receivables, inventory, prepaid expenses, land and buildings, and a significant amount of machinery and equipment. Organization costs also appear on the balance sheet. Liabilities include short-term notes payable, accounts payable, accrued expenses, and long-term debt (that which is due in one year is classified as a current liability). Although in reality an income approach and market approach may be applicable in valuing the company, for purposes of this example only the asset approach (without intangible assets) is shown.

To begin the application of the asset approach, we obtained the company's balance sheet as of December 31, 20XX, which is presented in Exhibit 8.1. A brief discussion of the Company's accounts follows.

Cash

Cash is typically not adjusted in the asset approach. If the company is audited, the analyst may rely on the auditors for adjustments to the accounts (this holds true for many accounts, not just cash). If the company is not audited, the analyst may want to obtain copies of the bank statements as documentation.

Marketable Securities

The company has a portfolio of marketable securities with a book value of $4.2 million. The portfolio consists of investments in 20 equities that must be marked to market as of the valuation date. Calculations are presented in Exhibit 8.2. Each investment is recorded at its current fair market value, the result being that the fair market value of the portfolio as of the valuation date is $7,568,000. An adjustment of $3,368,000 is made to bring the account to fair market value (Adjustment No. 1).

Accounts Receivable

Trade receivables should be examined for collectability. The allowance for doubtful accounts should be reasonable and be reviewed for adequacy. In this example, we learned that a review for doubtful accounts had not been performed for eight months and that there were two accounts totaling $32,000 that were uncollectible. Additionally, after that write-off, the reserve for doubtful accounts required an additional provision of $63,000. Thus, the total adjustment is $95,000 (Adjustment No. 2).

Accounts Receivable—Officer

Early in the year, the company loaned its chief executive officer and majority shareholder $75,000. Although carried on the books as a loan, the officer had no intention to repay the debt and the company had no plans to collect. This receivable was written off in its entirety (Adjustment No. 3). This transaction may have tax consequences, as it may be properly classified as compensation expense to the company and income to the officer.

Inventory

Inventories consist of goods held for sale, partially completed goods that have entered the production process, and raw materials to be used in production. The accounting convention for inventory is that it be recorded at the lower of cost or market. This means that inventory price increases during the period inventory is held for sale are ignored, but price declines are recognized.

The three most common inventory valuation methods are the cost of reproduction method, the comparative sales method, and the income method. The methods are summarized in Revenue Procedure 77-12 (Rev. Proc. 77-12). (See Addendum 4 at the end of this chapter.)

In reality, depending on materiality, an appraiser might accept inventory at book value based on client representations that the book value reasonably approximates fair market value. If this were the case, the appraisal report may disclose the fact that valuation procedures such as described in Rev. Proc. 77-12 were not performed.

In our example, we are assuming the fair market value of the company's inventory is $6.5 million. Thus, an upward adjustment of $600,000 (Adjustment No. 4) is required.

Prepaid Expenses

Prepaid expenses, such as deposits and insurance, must be examined to determine whether their amounts on the books represent future economic benefit. For example, a company may have recorded an amount for a deposit that has since been forfeited. Such an amount would have to be written off to reflect its net realizable value of zero.

Exhibit 8.2   B. Brothers Holding Company, Inc., Marketable Securities (As of December 31, 20XX)

Stock	No. Shares	Avg. Cost /Sh.	Basis	Current Price	Fair Market Value
A	15,000	$24.0000	$ 360,000	$72.5000	$1,087,500
B	20,000	35.0000	700,000	28.0000	560,000
C	25,000	40.0000	1,000,000	43.0000	1,075,000
D	30,000	12.5000	375,000	42.0000	1,260,000
E	12,000	28.5000	342,000	21.5000	258,000
F	25,000	11.5000	287,500	15.0000	375,000
G	5,000	4.0000	20,000	29.5000	147,500
H	9,000	0.7500	6,750	65.0000	585,000
I	10,000	8.0000	80,000	14.0000	140,000
J	8,000	9.5000	76,000	12.5000	100,000
K	6,000	24.0000	144,000	15.5000	93,000
L	12,000	5.0000	60,000	14.5000	174,000
M	1,000	2.2500	2,250	7.0000	7,000
N	5,000	7.5000	37,500	38.0000	190,000
O	16,000	12.0000	192,000	17.5000	280,000
P	5,000	10.0000	50,000	16.0000	80,000
Q	20,000	12.0000	240,000	46.0000	920,000
R	10,000	6.5000	65,000	2.0000	20,000
S	4,000	18.0000	72,000	33.0000	132,000
T	4,000	22.5000	90,000	21.0000	84,000
Total			$4,200,000		$7,568,000

We are assuming that the company had paid deposits (classified in prepaid expenses) totaling $40,000 in connection with the proposed move of its sales department to another facility. The move was cancelled in July and the deposits forfeited. An adjustment is required to write off these deposits. It was also determined that $60,000 of prepaid insurance had expired. The total adjustment (Adjustment No. 5) is $100,000.

Fixed Assets

Real Estate and Real Property

Recorded tangible assets representing land, buildings, improvements, and the like are technically termed real estate. Real estate is defined as ". . . the physical land and appurtenances including structures affixed to the land . . ."[9] The term "real property" is an *intangible* concept and "includes all interests, benefits, and rights inherent in the ownership of physical real estate."[10] The real property rights inherent in an entity's real estate ownership interest are taken into account and affect the appraised value of real estate.

All three approaches to value are used in the valuation of real estate. The *cost approach* estimates the cost to reproduce or replace existing improvements. The *market approach* involves comparing recent sales of property similar to the subject. The *income approach* determines value by capitalizing cash flows a property is expected to produce over a defined holding period (see Addendum 2).

The appraisal of real estate is a complex and often expensive process and is best left to specialists. If an entity's real estate has recently been acquired or is a small percentage of its net asset value, using book values as proxies for fair market values may be acceptable.

In the example, the real estate is material to value, and we obtained real estate appraisals of all the land and buildings from the client's appraiser. The total fair market value is $19.2 million. Adjustments are recorded to the asset and accumulated depreciation accounts to reflect the appraised amounts (Adjustment No. 6).

Machinery and Equipment

As with the appraisal of real estate, the appraisal of machinery and equipment (M&E) is usually best left to M&E appraisers, who are specialists in this discipline. The three classic approaches to value are considered in valuing M&E (see Addendum 3), but the income approach is not used often. The M&E appraisal must reflect the premise of value for the enterprise valuation (i.e., if the business is valued as a going concern, then the premise of value for the M&E should be "continued use"). Unless the amounts are immaterial, it is usually not advisable to use book values as proxies for fair market values. Contradictions between book depreciation and functional and economic obsolescence may lead to a misleading result.

In the example, we obtained appraisals from the client's appraiser of all of the machinery and equipment. The total fair market value is $24.4 million. Adjustments are recorded to the machinery and equipment and accumulated depreciation accounts to reflect the appraised amounts (Adjustment No. 7).

---

[9] American Institute of Real Estate Appraisers, *The Appraisal of Real Estate,* 11th ed. (1996), p. 7.
[10] Ibid.

Recognized Intangible Assets

The financial statements of an enterprise often contain accounts such as organization costs or intangible assets related to acquisitions. Recorded intangible assets generally are one of two types:

1. Those that arise from capitalized historic expenditures for services
2. Those that represent historic payments for intangible assets, which may or may not have value at the valuation date

The former typically have no value and are written off, but the latter may need to be revalued.

The company's balance sheet reflects intangible assets (organization costs) of $295,000. These are historic costs that provide no future benefit and are written off (Adjustment No. 8).

LIABILITIES

On the other side of the balance sheet are the liabilities, which, like assets, must be stated at fair market value.

Accounts Payable

These accounts represent short-term obligations incurred in the ordinary course of business. Accounts payable represent amounts due to creditors (suppliers and service providers) who have provided goods and services to the company. The payables should be examined to determine whether any amounts do not represent bona fide obligations. This account is not often adjusted. In our example, no adjustment is required.

Accrued Liabilities

The term "accrued liabilities" is used to designate obligations that come into existence as a result of past contractual commitments or as a result of tax legislation, such as income, property, and sales tax laws.[11] The analyst should be diligent that such liabilities not be understated (by the failure to properly accrue such amounts) or overstated (by the failure to write off amounts that have been satisfied). No such adjustments are required in our example.

Interest-Bearing Debt

Interest-bearing debt may be short-term or long-term. Such liabilities represent financing arrangements. The distinction between a short-term or a long-term classification rests on whether the debts are to be extinguished within one year or one operating cycle. Examples of long-term liabilities are bonds, notes, mortgages, and capitalized lease obligations. The principal reason why fair market value may differ from book value rests with differences in interest rates. The appraiser may examine market interest rates as of the date of value and compare those rates with the coupon rate of the obligation.

---

[11] Meigs et. al., pp. 255–256.

In our example, the company had interest-bearing debt of $6.25 million at the valuation date. Of this amount, the current portion was $1.25 million and the long-term portion $5 million. The coupon rate of the obligation is 7 percent. At the valuation date, the market yield to maturity was 6 percent. If the coupon rate of a security exceeds its yield, the fair market value of the security is greater than its face value, and vice versa.

The valuation of the loan is presented in Exhibit 8.3. In that schedule we value the current portion and long-term portion separately. The general approach is to discount to present value, at the market rate of return, the actual or coupon-based cash flows, principal, and interest. It should be noted that in year one, total interest is $437,500, of which $87,500 relates to the short-term portion (7 percent coupon rate × the short-term principal of $1.25 million) and $350,000 to the long-term portion (7 percent coupon rate × the long-term principal of $5 million). The cash flows are discounted at the market rate of 6 percent. The year-end convention is observed for cash flows and discount periods. The fair market value of the current portion is $1,261,800 and the fair market value of the long-term portion is $5,152,300 (Adjustment No. 9).

UNRECORDED ASSETS AND LIABILITIES

The appraiser performs some reasonable due diligence to determine whether any assets or liabilities may exist that are not recorded in the accounts. Unrecorded assets may take the form of intangible assets or claims. Unrecorded liabilities may take the form of contingencies, such as pending or threatened litigation. Quantifying such assets and liabilities can be difficult.

In our example, management disclosed two potential contingent liabilities relating to "slip and fall" lawsuits. Upon further examination, these were judged to be immaterial and no adjustment was made.

Management also reported that they have been named as defendants in a breach-of-contract dispute. The plaintiff is claiming damages of $1 million. In discussing this pending litigation with management and counsel, we learned that settlement discussions have been under way with a likely outcome of $300,000 to $400,000. Counsel further opined that if the case went to trial, they believed there was a 25 percent chance of losing at the claimed amount, a probability-adjusted loss of $250,000. Based on the range of possible outcomes, we judged the fair market value of the pending litigation contingent liability to be $300,000 (Adjustment No. 10).

BUILT-IN GAIN

As discussed earlier in this chapter, the application of taxes in the asset approach remains somewhat controversial, although such application has become more acceptable. For presentation purposes, the calculation of the built-in gain liability is presented in Exhibit 8.4. The fair market value of the equity of the company after the above adjustments but before an adjustment for built-in gain is $56,658,900. The basis is $9,468,000. Thus, there is a built-in gain of $47,190,900. Assuming an average estimated tax rate of 40 percent, the tax liability related to the gain is $18,876,360 (Adjustment No. 11). Based on the above adjustments (cumulatively shown in Adjustment No. 12), the fair market value of the company using the asset approach is $37,782,540.

Exhibit 8.3 B. Brothers Holding Company, Inc., Valuation of Debt (As of December 31, 20XX)

Current Portion

Principal	$1,250,000
Coupon Rate—Actual	7.0%
Market Yield to Maturity	6.0%
Year	1
Interest Payments—Actual (1)	$87,500
Principal Payments—Actual	1,250,000
Debt Service—Actual	$1,337,500
Present Value Factor @ 6.0%	0.9434
Fair Value/Fair Market Value (rounded)	$1,261,800

Long-Term Portion

Principal	$5,000,000
Coupon Rate—Actual	7.0%
Market Yield to Maturity	6.0%

(continues)

Exhibit 8.3 *continued*

Year	1	2	3	4	5
Principal Outstanding (assume payments are made at year-end)	$5,000,000	$5,000,000	$3,750,000	$2,500,000	$1,250,000
Interest Payments—Actual (2)	$ 350,000	$ 350,000	$ 262,500	$ 175,000	$ 87,500
Principal Payments—Actual (3)	na	1,250,000	1,250,000	1,250,000	1,250,000
Debt Service—Actual	350,000	1,600,000	1,512,500	1,425,000	1,337,500
Present Value Factor @ 6.0%	0.9434	0.8900	0.8396	0.7921	0.7473
Sum of Present Values	$ 330,190	$1,424,000	$1,269,900	$1,128,740	$ 999,510
Fair Value/Fair Market Value (rounded)	$5,152,300				

(1) Related to Short-Term Portion
(2) Related to Long-Term Portion
(3) Principal Payment in Year 1 relates to short-term portion

Exhibit 8.4 B. Brothers Holding Company, Inc., Calculation of Built-In Gain Liability
(As of December 31, 20XX)

Total Assets	$73,873,000
Less: Liabilities	
Total Current Liabilities	(10,711,800)
Long-Term Debt	(5,152,300)
Deferred Income Taxes	(800,000)
Other Liabilities	(550,000)
Net Asset Value Before Built-In Gain	$56,658,900
Less: Basis	(9,468,000)
Built-In Gain	$47,190,900
Effective Tax Rate	40%
Tax Liability	$18,876,360

CONCLUSION

The company's book basis balance sheet, with the fair market value adjustments to the assets and liabilities accounts as described above, is presented in Exhibit 8.1. The net book value of the company's equity was $23,020,000. After making the above adjustments, we conclude that the fair market value of the company's equity under the asset approach is $37,782,540.[12] As stated earlier, this conclusion is control-based, assuming some marketability. Discounts for lack of control and lack of marketability are usually appropriate under a minority interest closely held premise. (See Chapter 9.)

---

[12] This calculation assumes the built-in gain is determined as of the valuation date and is not present-valued.

ADDENDUM 1A—BUILT-IN GAINS TAXES: BUSINESS VALUATION CONSIDERATIONS, PART I[13]

By Leonard J. Sliwoski, CPA/ABV, PhD, CBA, ASA, and
Mary B. Bader, CPA, JD, LLM

The approach used to value an operating company generally differs from the approach used to value a holding or investment company. The valuer of an operating company assumes a business will continue and generally measures value based on future earnings and resultant cash flow. In contrast, the valuer of a holding company generally assumes value is realized, not from future business earnings and resultant cash flow, but from the sale of business assets.[14] The Tax Reform Act of 1986 repealed the General Utilities doctrine, which held that a C corporation did not recognize gain when it distributed appreciated property to shareholders. After 1986, a built-in gains tax on appreciated corporate assets is unavoidable upon the sale or other disposition of such assets by the C corporation.[15]

The repeal of the General Utilities doctrine coupled with the myriad of business entity structures now available to business owners has created controversy among courts and valuers of operating and holding companies. This addendum focuses on that controversy—the question of whether built-in gains taxes of operating and holding companies should be taken into account in valuing C corporations, S corporations, and partnerships, including family limited partnerships, limited liability companies (LLCs), and limited liability partnerships (LLPs).

Operating Companies

The value of operating companies arises from future earnings and resultant cash flow, not from the sale of business assets as of the appraisal date. Conceptually, built-in gains taxes of operating companies are similar to deferred income tax liabilities. Typically, deferred income tax liabilities are reclassified as equity, because payment may not occur, or payment may occur at a point so far in the future that the present value of such liabilities is minimal. As a result, regardless of whether operating companies are organized as C corporations, S corporations, or partnerships, including family limited partnerships, LLCs, and LLPs, built-in gains taxes are generally not taken into account in valuing them.

When operating companies hold nonoperating assets in addition to operating assets, valuers generally assume nonoperating assets either will be purchased by buyers and sold immediately or will be retained and sold by sellers. In other words, the value of nonoperating assets results from their ultimate sale. Accordingly, in

---

[13] Published in *CPA Expert*, Summer 2001. (Reproduced with permission. Copyright 2001 by AICPA).

[14] Rev. Rul. 59-60, 1959-1 C.B. 237 (1959).

[15] The built-in gains tax discussed in this addendum is a broader concept than the §1374 built-in gains tax that applies to S corporations. In this addendum the term "built-in gains tax" refers to the income taxes associated with appreciated property owned by a business entity.

such cases, a combination of an income approach and an asset approach may be used to value operating companies. (The following discussion, which relates to holding companies, is also applicable to nonoperating assets held by operating companies.)

Holding Companies

To examine the issue of built-in gains taxes of holding companies, a simple example is useful. Assume two unrelated individuals, A and B, organized an entity on January 1, 1991. In exchange for a 50 percent ownership interest, A and B each contributed $10,000 cash. On that same date, the entity purchased a parcel of land for $20,000, which it holds for investment. The land is the only asset owned by the holding company. On January 1, 2001, the fair market value of the land is $100,000. On that date, the entity is valued.

Holding Companies Organized as C Corporations

If A and B organize the holding company as a C corporation, the value of the holding company relates to the land held for investment. In valuing the holding company, the valuer would most likely use an asset approach. In this example, if the corporation sold or otherwise disposed of the land, it would pay tax on the built-in gain of $80,000 ($100,000 fair market value of the land less the adjusted basis of the land to the corporation of $20,000). If the C corporation is in the 34 percent marginal bracket, the built-in gains tax on the land is $27,200 (34 percent of $80,000).

Courts have recognized the need to take built-in gains taxes into account when the valuation is done using an asset approach, because a hypothetical buyer would consider this income tax liability in computing the fair market value of holding company stock.[16] While courts recognize the need to take built-in gains taxes into account in valuing holding companies operated as C corporations, the approaches used by courts to do so have varied significantly.

In *Eisenberg v. Commissioner,* the Second Circuit Court of Appeals recognized the need to take built-in gains taxes into account in valuing the holding company, but remanded the case back to the Tax Court to determine the value of the holding company. Thus, the *Eisenberg* court did not directly address the question of how to reduce corporate net asset value to reflect built-in gains taxes. The IRS acquiesced in part to *Eisenberg* by acknowledging possible recognition of built-in gains taxes in holding companies organized as C corporations, stating that "[w]e acquiesce in this opinion to the extent that it holds that there is no legal prohibition against such a discount. The applicability of such a discount, as well as its amount, will hereafter be treated as factual matters to be determined by competent

---

[16] See, for example *Estate of Welch v. Commissioner,* No. 98-2007, 2000 WL 263309 (6th Cir. March 1, 200); *Eisenberg v. Commissioner,* 155 F.3d 50 (2nd Cir. 1998), acq. In part, 1999-4 I.R.B. 4 (January 25, 1999); *Estate of Borgatello v. Commissioner,* 80 TCM (CCH) 260 (2000); *Estate of Simplot v. Commissioner,* 112 T.C. 130 (1999); *Estate of Jameson v. Commissioner,* 77 T.C.M. (CCH) 1383 (1999); *Estate of Davis v. Commissioner,* 110 T.C. 530 (1998); and *Estate of Dunn v. Commissioner,* 79 T.C.M. (CCH) 1337 (2000).

expert testimony based upon the circumstances of each case and generally applicable valuation principles."

In *Estate of Simplot v. Commissioner,* the Tax Court allowed net asset value of a holding company to be reduced by the full amount of built-in gains taxes (combined state and federal rate of 40 percent). Applying the *Simplot* court's holding to the preceding example would result in a valuation of the C corporation stock of $72,800 ($100,000 fair market value of land less $27,200 of built-in gains taxes).

In *Estate of Jameson v. Commissioner,* the Tax Court determined when the holding company would likely pay built-in gains taxes, calculated the net present value of the future built-in gains taxes, and reduced the net asset value of the holding company by this amount. The primary asset held by the holding company in *Jameson* was timberland. The holding company had an I.R.C. §631 election in effect, which meant it paid income taxes as timber was sold to buyers, who cut and harvested the timber. Based on the timberland management plan used by the holding company, the Tax Court determined that ten years was the likely time period in which the holding company would pay built-in gains taxes on the sale of timber.

In *Estate of Dunn v. Commissioner,* the Tax Court allowed a 5 percent reduction in net asset value to take into account the built-in gains taxes. This was an odd case, in which the subject business was an operating company whose primary business was renting heavy equipment. In this case, the fair market value of the company determined by the "net asset value method" and the "capitalization of income method" were divergent. The Tax Court recognized value of the company based on the weighted average net asset value method and the capitalization of income method. The 5 percent reduction for income taxes, which the Tax Court determined was appropriate because of the limited likelihood the corporation would be liquidated, was applied only to the net asset value valuation conclusion. Therefore, the reduction for built-in gains taxes was less than 5 percent, because the final value was based upon reconciliation of both valuation methods.

Other courts have increased the lack of marketability discount by some percentage to take built-in gains taxes into account. For example, in *Estate of Davis v. Commissioner,* the Tax Court allowed a 15 percent increase in the lack of marketability discount to account for built-in gains taxes. The *Davis* court expressly rejected the notion that a lack of marketability discount equal to the full amount of built-in gains taxes should be applied in the absence of a planned liquidation of the holding company on the valuation date. Similarly, in *Estate of Borgatello v. Commissioner,* the Tax Court allowed a 24 percent increase in the lack of marketability discount to account for built-in gains taxes, but refused to increase the marketability discount to reflect the full amount of built-in gains taxes.

In *Estate of Welch v. Commissioner,* the United States Court of Appeals for the Sixth Circuit reversed the decision of the Tax Court, which denied the estate the right to discount the value of corporate stock to reflect a built-in gains tax liability on corporate real estate. The Sixth Circuit Court of Appeals, in remanding the case back to the Tax Court, stated that "[o]n remand, the petitioners, now aware of the required approach to valuation of the stock in light of *Eisenberg,* would need to present expert testimony to satisfy their burden of proof. They may or may not be able to present such testimony, but they should be given that opportunity."

Two Emerging Schools

These rulings reflect the two emerging schools of thought regarding built-in gains taxes of holding companies: (1) The full amount of the built-in gains taxes should reduce net asset value of the holding company; or (2) the lack of marketability discount should be increased by some percentage to take into account the built-in gains taxes. We believe, however, that the better approach is generally to reduce net asset values in holding companies organized as C corporations by the full amount of the built-in gains taxes.

Returning to the preceding example, assume a buyer wanted to purchase the land held by the C corporation. The buyer could potentially purchase the land from the C corporation or purchase stock held by A and B. If the C corporation sold the land to a buyer for its fair market value of $100,000, the C corporation would pay $27,200 of tax on the $80,000 built-in gain. The buyer would take a $100,000 basis in the land. If the buyer purchased the stock of A and B, a rational buyer would pay only $72,800, which is the fair market value of the land less built-in gains taxes. Although the buyer would have a $100,000 basis in the C corporation stock, if the C corporation sold the land, it would still have to pay $27,200 of tax on $80,000 of built-in gain. A rational buyer would reduce the purchase price of the stock by the built-in gains tax to reflect the economic reality that the land is owned by a C corporation.

As rational sellers, A and B would accept $72,800 as payment for their stock. If A and B sold their stock to the buyers for $72,800, together they would net $62,240 after payment of personal income taxes. (See Exhibit 8.5.) This is the same amount A and B would net after taxes if the C corporation was liquidated, the land was distributed to them, and they sold it to a buyer for $100,000. (See Exhibit 8.6.) As rational sellers, A and B should recognize that $72,800 is a fairly negotiated price for their stock in the C corporation. The example demonstrates why it is appropriate to take into account the full built-in gains taxes in determining the value of stock of a holding company organized as a C corporation.

An argument can be made that as long as the buyer doesn't liquidate corporate stock for a long time period after the purchase, the present value of the built-in gains taxes will be minimal. Therefore, a minimal reduction in the price of holding company stock is warranted. However, this argument fails to consider two factors. The first factor is that the shareholder of a minority stock interest in a holding company

Exhibit 8.5   Calculation of After-Tax Cash Received by C Corporation Stockholders

Sale of Stock	A	B	Combined
Sales price	$36,400	$36,400	$72,800
Adjusted basis of stock	(10,000)	(10,000)	(20,000)
Built-in gain	$26,400	$26,400	$52,800
Capital gain tax rate for individuals	× .20	× .20	× .20
Built-in gains taxes	$ 5,280	$ 5,280	$10,560

After-Tax Cash Received	A	B	Combined
Sales price	$36,400	$36,400	$72,800
Less built-in gains taxes paid	(5,280)	(5,280)	(10,560)
After-tax cash received by A and B	$31,120	$31,120	$62,240

Exhibit 8.6 Calculation of After-Tax Cash Received by Shareholders from C Corporation Liquidation*

Corporate-Level Tax on Liquidation	C Corporation
Fair market value of land on date of distribution	$100,000
Adjusted basis of land	(20,000)
Built-in gain on distribution	$ 80,000
Marginal tax rate of corporation	×.34
Corporate level tax on distribution	$ 27,200

If the corporation's only asset is the land, A and B would each have to contribute $13,600 to the corporation, which would increase their stock basis from $10,000 to $23,800 apiece.

Shareholder-Level Tax on Liquidation	A	B	Combined
Fair market value of distributed land	$50,000	$50,000	$100,000
Adjusted basis of stock	(23,600)	(23,600)	(47,200)
Built-in gain	$26,400	$26,400	$ 52,800
Capital gain tax rate for individuals	×.20	×.20	×.20
Built-in gains taxes at shareholder level	$ 5,280	$ 5,280	$ 10,560

Sale of Land by A and B	A	B	Combined
Sales price	$50,000	$50,000	$100,000
Adjusted basis of land	(50,000)	(50,000)	(100,000)
Recognized gain	$ 0	$ 0	$ 0

After-Tax Cash Received by A and B	A	B	Combined
Sales proceeds from land	$50,000	$50,000	$100,000
Less cash contributed to corporation	(13,600)	(13,600)	(27,200)
Built-in gains taxes paid	(5,280)	(5,280)	(10,560)
After-tax cash received by A and B	$31,120	$31,120	$ 62,240

*Land was distributed to shareholders, and they sold it to buyer.

has no control over the timing of a corporate liquidation. The second factor is that the land will continue to appreciate within the corporation after purchase of the stock. Both prepurchase and postpurchase appreciation will be subject to a corporate-level income tax upon ultimate corporate liquidation.

An Argument for Recognizing Built-in Gains Taxes in Operating Companies

An argument can be made for recognition of built-in gains taxes in operating companies in two circumstances. The first circumstance involves marginally profitable or unprofitable operating companies with significant equity in assets owned. These businesses are often appraised under an asset approach with a liquidation premise of value. If they organized as C corporations, built-in gains taxes should be recognized because the liquidation premise of value assumes assets will be sold, liabilities, including built-in gains taxes, will be paid, and the corporation will cease doing business in the near future. The second circumstance involves small operating companies organized as C corporations. Frequently, these entities are sold with the sale transaction structured as an asset sale, not as a stock sale. Business valuers generally appraise business equity, not assets. If a sale of a small operating company is structured as a stock sale, some reduction in the purchase price typically occurs. This reduction occurs because lower depreciation and amortization income tax deductions are available to the buyer due to a lack of an income tax basis adjustment for assets purchased. For a discussion of the reduction in stock price for small operating companies organized as C corporations, see "Recent Cases and Valuation Model Show 'State of the Art' Built-in Gains Calculation" by John Cooper and Richard Gore, *Valuation Strategies* (January/February 2001), pp. 4–13.

ADDENDUM 1B—BUILT-IN GAINS TAXES: BUSINESS VALUATION CONSIDERATIONS, PART II[17]

By Leonard J. Sliwoski, CPA/ABV, PhD, CBA, ASA, and
Mary B. Bader, CPA, JD, LLM

As we said in Addendum 1A, the approach to valuing an operating company generally differs from the approach to valuing a holding or investment company. The valuer of an operating company assumes a business will continue and generally measures value based on future earnings and resultant cash flow. In contrast, the valuer of a holding company generally assumes value is realized, not from future business earnings and resultant cash flow, but from the sale of business assets.[18] The Tax Reform Act of 1986 repealed the General Utilities doctrine, which held that a C corporation did not recognize gain when it distributed appreciated property to shareholders. After 1986, a built-in gains tax on appreciated corporate assets is unavoidable at the C corporation level upon the sale or other disposition of such assets by the C corporation.[19,20]

The repeal of the General Utilities doctrine coupled with the myriad of business entities now available to business owners has created controversy among courts and valuers of operating and holding companies. Simply put, the controversy centers on whether built-in gains taxes should be taken into account in valuing operating and holding companies. This addendum focuses on the question of whether built-in gains taxes of operating and holding companies should be taken into account in the context of C corporations, S corporations, and partnerships, including family limited partnerships, limited liability companies (LLCs), and limited liability partnerships (LLPs).

In Addendum 1A, we discussed this question in relation to operating companies and holding companies organized as C corporations. We concluded that, with some

---

[17] Published in *CPA Expert,* Fall 2001. Reproduced with permission. Copyright 2001 by AICPA.

[18] Revised Ruling 59-60, 1959-1 C.B. 237 (1959).

[19] The built-in gains tax discussed in this addendum is a broader concept than the §1374 built-in gains tax that applies to S corporations. In this addendum the term "built-in gains tax" refers to the income taxes associated with appreciated property owned by a business entity.

[20] An argument could be made that net asset value should not be reduced by the full amount of built-in gains taxes because a C corporation could void these taxes by making an S election and waiting ten years to dispose of appreciated corporate assets. Rather, built-in gains taxes should be included as part of a discount for lack of marketability, since the ten-year holding period would significantly reduce the marketability of the C corporation's stock.

This argument lacks substance. Although closely held business stock holding periods tend to be of substantial duration, it is difficult to identify a universe of probable, willing buyers who would purchase stock of a C corporation, cause it to make an S election, and wait ten years to dispose of appreciated corporate assets. If a universe of probable, willing buyers can't be identified, it is not rational to assume that a sale of this type would occur. Moreover, the incremental increase to the discount for lack of marketability can't be determined without making assumptions about the relevant time period, discount rate, and income tax rate. These assumptions would be difficult to support.

exceptions, built-in gains taxes can be ignored by a valuer in most operating companies, regardless of how they are structured, and that built-in gains taxes may need to be taken into account if the operating company holding nonoperating assets is organized as a C corporation. Also, we generally believe that the full amount of built-in gains taxes should reduce the net asset value of a holding company organized as a C corporation.

Having discussed operating companies and holding companies organized as C corporations, we now look at the same question in relation to holding companies organized as S corporations and partnerships.

HOLDING COMPANIES ORGANIZED AS S CORPORATIONS

If A and B organize the holding company as an S corporation, it may be necessary to take built-in gains taxes into account in valuing the holding company.[7] Returning to the example we used in Addendum 1A, assume the buyer wanted to purchase the land now held by an S corporation. The buyer could purchase the land from the S corporation or purchase stock held by A and B. If the S corporation sold the land to the buyers for its fair market value of $100,000, the corporation would recognize $80,000 of built-in gain on the land sale. This built-in gain would flow through to A and B personally, who would pay $16,000 of tax (see Exhibit 8.7). The buyer would take a $100,000 basis in the land.

Exhibit 8.7   Calculation of Gain in the S Corporation Scenario

Calculation of Gain at S Corporation Level			S Corporation
Sales price of land			$100,000
Adjusted basis			(20,000)
Built-in gain recognized by S corporation			$ 80,000

Recognition of Gain at Shareholder Level	A's Share	B's Share	Combined
Built-in gain recognized by S corporation	$40,000	$40,000	$80,000
Capital gain tax rate for individuals	× .20	× .20	× .20
Built-in gains tax	$ 8,000	$ 8,000	$16,000

Alternatively, if the buyer purchased the stock of A and B, a rational buyer may or may not pay $100,000, the fair market value of the land not reduced by any built-in gains taxes. The buyer would have a $100,000 basis in the S corporation stock. However, if the S corporation sold the land, the buyer/shareholder might have to pay $16,000 of tax on $80,000 of built-in gain, because the S corporation's basis in the land is $20,000. This circumstance occurs if the S corporation sells the land in one tax year and liquidates in a subsequent tax year. Given this circumstance, a buyer would reduce the purchase price of the stock by some amount of the built-in gains tax (see Exhibit 8.8).

---

[21] The built-in gains tax discussed here should be distinguished from the statutory §1374 built-in gains tax imposed on an S corporation. Under §1374 of the Internal Revenue Code, if a C corporation makes an S election and owns appreciated assets on the day of the election, it may be subject to a corporate-level tax on the built-in gain. The §1374 tax is imposed on an S corporation if it disposes of appreciated assets within ten years after the date on which an S election took effect. The built-in gains tax discussed here is a broader concept, which encompasses all income taxes associated with appreciated property owned by a business entity.

Exhibit 8.8 Calculation of Gain at S Corporation Level from Sale of Land on July 1 of Current Tax Year to Third Party*

	S Corporation
Sales price of land	$ 100,000
Adjusted basis	(20,000)
Built-in gain recognized by S corporation	$ 80,000*

*Assume the buyer paid $100,000 for stock A and B on January 1 of the current year. Assume further that the S corporation sold the land on July 1 of the current year and the S corporation was liquidated on September 1 of the current year.

Recognition of Gain at Shareholder Level†	Buyer's Share
Built-in gain recognized by S corporation	$ 80,000†

†Recognition of the gain increases buyer's basis in S corporation stock from $100,000 to $180,000.

Liquidation of S Corporation on September 1 of Current Tax Year	Buyer/Shareholder
Cash distributed to buyer/shareholder	$ 100,000
Adjusted basis of stock	(180,000)
Capital loss	$ (80,000)‡

‡If the land is sold and the S corporation is liquidated in the same year, the built-in gain and capital loss offset each other. As a result, no reduction for built-in capital gains taxes is necessary if the land sale and corporate liquidation occur in the same year. However, this is not the result if the land sale and the corporate liquidation occur in different tax years. If the S corporation is liquidated in the year following the land sale, the result is significantly different, as the following calculations illustrate.

Calculation of Gain at S Corporation Level from Sale of Land in Current Tax Year to Third Party	S corporation
Sales price	$ 100,000
Adjusted basis	(20,000)
Built-in gain recognized by S corporation	$ 80,000

Recognition of Gain at Shareholder Level	Buyer's Share
Built-in gain recognized by S corporation	$ 80,000§
Capital gain tax rate for individuals	× .20
Built-in gains tax paid by buyer	$ 16,000

§Recognition of this gain increases buyer's basis in S corporation stock from $100,000 to $180,000.

Liquidation of S Corporation in Following Tax Year	Buyer/Shareholder
Cash distributed to buyer/shareholder	$ 100,000
Adjusted basis of stock	(180,000)
Capital loss	$ (80,000)¶

¶Assuming buyer/shareholder is an individual, he or she may use only capital loss to offset capital gain and $3,000 of ordinary income per year until the capital loss is used up. Since the land was sold in the previous tax year by the S corporation, the $80,000 of prior-year built-in gain recognized by buyer/shareholder is not available to absorb the $80,000 of current capital loss. Theoretically, the difference between the $16,000 of built-in gains taxes paid by the buyer/shareholder in the previous tax year and the present value of the future income tax savings arising from the carryforward of $80,000 of capital loss should reduce the $100,000 purchase price of the stock.

Exhibit 8.9 Calculation of After-Tax Cash Received by Shareholders' Sale of S Corporation Stock

Sale of Stock	A	B	Combined
Sales price	$ 50,000	$ 50,000	$ 100,000
Adjusted basis of stock	(10,000)	(10,000)	(20,000)
Built-in gain	$ 40,000	$ 40,000	$ 80,000
Capital gain tax rate for individuals	× .20	× .20	× .20
Built-in gains taxes	$ 8,000	$ 8,000	$ 16,000
After-Tax Cash Received	**A**	**B**	**Combined**
Sales price	$ 50,000	$ 50,000	$ 100,000
Less built-in gains taxes paid	(8,000)	(8,000)	(16,000)
After-tax cash received by A and B	$ 42,000	$ 42,000	$ 84,000

Any reduction in the purchase price for built-in gains taxes seems unlikely if the buyer is purchasing a controlling interest in an S corporation. A shareholder with a controlling interest can determine the timing of asset sales and liquidation of the corporation, and thus avoid any negative tax consequences arising from built-in gains taxes. If the buyer purchases a minority stock interest in an S corporation, it is conceivable that some recognition of built-in gains taxes may be necessary. A minority shareholder cannot control the timing of corporate asset sales or the liquidation of the corporation, and thus may not be able to avoid built-in gains taxes. Other factors that may be important to consider in deciding whether to recognize built-in gains taxes in an S corporation include the number and diversity of assets held by the S corporation, the corporate bylaws, and any shareholder agreements. These factors may affect the timing of when S corporations assets are sold and when a corporate liquidation is effected.

If A and B sold their stock to the buyer for $100,000, together they would net $84,000 after taxes from the sale of their stock to the buyer (see Exhibit 8.9). This is the same amount A and B would net if the S corporation was liquidated, the land was distributed to them, and they sold the land to a buyer for $100,000 (see Exhibit 8.10). As rational sellers, A and B may not be willing to accept less than $100,000 for the stock, particularly if they own a controlling interest in the corporation. If A and B own a minority stock interest in the S corporation, they may accept some reduction in their pro rata share of corporate equity reduced by a minority interest discount due to the built-in gains taxes. Acceptance of this lower stock value could occur for convenience purposes, as these shareholders have no active market for their stock and no ability to effect a corporate liquidation.

Holding Companies Organized as Partnerships

General partnerships, limited partnerships (including family limited partnerships), limited liability companies, and limited liability partnerships—all of these entities are income taxed under Subchapter K of the Internal Revenue Code. The term *partnership* is intended to encompass all of these entities.

If A and B organize a holding company as a partnership, it is generally unnecessary to take built-in gains taxes into account in valuing the holding company because of the

Exhibit 8.10   Calculation of After-Tax Cash Received by Shareholders with S Corporation Liquidation*

Calculation of Gain at S Corporation Level	S Corporation
Fair market value of land on date of distribution	$100,000
Adjusted basis of land	(20,000)
Built-in gain recognized by S corporation on distribution	$ 80,000

*The land was distributed to shareholders, and they sold the land to a buyer.

Recognition of Gain at Shareholder Level	A's Share	B's Share	Combined
Built-in gain recognized by S corporation	$40,000	$40,000	$ 80,000
Capital gain tax rate for individuals	× .20	× .20	× .20
Built-in gains taxes	$ 8,000	$ 8,000	$ 16,000

†Recognition of this gain increases shareholders' basis in their stock from $10,000 each to $50,000 each.

Shareholder-Level Tax on Liquidation	A	B	Combined
Fair market value of distributed land	$ 50,000	$ 50,000	$ 100,000‡
Adjusted basis of stock	(50,000)	(50,000)	(100,000)
Recognized gain	$ 0	$ 0	$ 0

‡A and B would take a basis in the land equal to fair market value, or $100,000.

Sale of Land by A and B	A	B	Combined
Sales price	$ 50,000	$ 50,000	$ 100,000
Adjusted basis of land	(50,000)	(50,000)	(100,000)
Recognized gain	$ 0	$ 0	$ 0

After-Tax Cash Received by A and B	A	B	Combined
Sales proceeds from land	$ 50,000	$50,000	$100,000
Less built-in gains taxes paid on land distribution	(8,000)	(8,000)	(16,000)
After-tax cash received by A and B	$ 42,000	$42,000	$ 84,000

ability of the partnership to make a §754 election.[22] Returning once again to the example, assume two buyers (C and D) wanted to purchase the land now held by a partnership organized by A and B. C and D could purchase the land from the partnership or purchase the partnership interests held by A and B. If the partnership sold the land to C and D for its fair market value of $100,000, the partnership would recognize $80,000 of built-in gain on the sale of the land, which would flow through to A and B personally, who would pay $16,000 of tax (see Exhibit 8.11).

---

[22] Internal Revenue Code §754 allows the partnership to make an optional adjustment election. A §754 election is available only to partnerships, not to either C or S corporations. This election is very useful to a buyer when the fair market value of the partnership interest purchased exceeds the inside bases of the partnership assets. This is exactly the situation with built-in gains. The §754 election allows a buyer to step up his or her share of the inside basis of partnership assets to reflect the purchase price paid by the buyer. In other words, built-in gains are eliminated if the partnership has a §754 election in effect.

Exhibit 8.11 Calculation of Gain in the Partnership Scenario

Calculation of Gain at Partnership Level			Partnership
Sales price of land			$100,000
Adjusted basis			(20,000)
Built-in gain recognized by partnership			$ 80,000

Recognition of Gain at Partner Level	A's Share	B's Share	Combined
Built-in gain recognized by partner	$40,000	$40,000	$80,000
Capital gain tax rate for individuals	× .20	× .20	× .20
Built-in gains tax	$ 8,000	$ 8,000	$16,000

If C and D purchased 100 percent of the partnership interests of A and B, they should be willing to pay $100,000 because, as controlling partners, they could cause the partnership to make a §754 election (see "The §754 Election," later in this section). If a §754 election is in effect for the partnership, C and D would have a basis in their partnership interest of $100,000 ($50,000 each) and their share of the inside basis in the land would also be $100,000 ($50,000 each).[23] If the partnership sold the land for $100,000 to a third party, C and D would not pay income tax. Under §754, the partnership's inside basis in the land is $100,000, which is equal to its fair market value of $100,000. Thus, C and D would report no capital gain on the sale of the land by the partnership. The §754 election ensures that the purchase price paid by buyers of partnership interests is reflected by stepping up their share of the inside bases of the partnership assets. In essence, a §754 election prevents purchasing partners from paying built-in gains taxes associated with partnership assets.

Section 754 is useful to buyers who control a partnership to avoid paying built-in gains taxes on partnership assets. Since §754 is an election made by the partnership and not the individual partners, concerns arise when the buyer is not a controlling partner or is a limited partner, who is not allowed to participate in partnership management decisions. This is particularly true in light of the rise of family limited partnerships after the IRS issued Revenue Ruling 93-12.[24]

The Tax Court addressed some of these concerns in *Estate of Jones v. Commissioner* (116 T.C. 121 (2001)). In *Jones,* the taxpayer formed two family limited partnerships by transferring assets, including real property, in exchange for limited

---

[23] Under IRC §708, if C and D purchase the partnership interests of A and B, the partnership has technically terminated. The terminated partnership is deemed to contribute its assets and liabilities to a new partnership in exchange for an interest in the new partnership. Immediately thereafter, the terminated partnership is deemed to distribute partnership interests in the new partnership to the purchasing partners. See Treas. Reg. §1.708-1(b). As a result of the deemed liquidation, the new partnership would initially take a carryover basis of $20,000 for the land. However, if the new partnership makes an election under §754, C and D are allowed to adjust their share of the inside basis of the land from $10,000 each to $50,000 each, to reflect the purchase price paid by them for their partnership interest.

[24] In Revised Ruling 93-12, 1993-1 C.B. 202 (1993), the IRS ruled that a minority discount could be applied to gifts made by family members. The IRS specifically stated that a minority discount would not be disallowed solely because a transferred interest, when aggregated with other interest held by family members, would be part of a controlling interest.

partnership interests. His children also contributed real property in exchange for general and limited partnership interest. Immediately after formation of the family limited partnerships, the taxpayer gifted 83.08 percent of his limited partnership interest in one family limited partnership to his son, and 16.915 percent of his limited partnership interest to each of his four daughters.

One of the issues before the tax court was whether a discount attributable to built-in gains taxes should be applied to the taxpayer's gifts of his family limited partnership interests. In *Jones*, the partnership agreement did not give the limited partners the ability to make a §754 election, but did allow limited partners owning an aggregate of 51 percent of the partnership to remove a general partner and appoint a successor. If no successor were appointed within 90 days, the partnership would dissolve and liquidate. The Tax Court refused to allow a built-in gains tax discount for either the 83.08 percent or the 16.915 percent gifted limited partnership interest. The Tax Court found that a hypothetical willing seller of the 83.08 percent limited partnership interest has effective control and would influence the general partner to make a §754 election.

The Tax Court acknowledged that a hypothetical willing seller of the 16.915 percent limited partnership interest would not exercise effective control. However, the Tax Court refused to allow a built-in gains discount because "there is no reason why a section 754 election would not be made." The Tax Court stated that a §754 election would not cause any detriment or hardship to the partnership or the other partners. In the court's view, a hypothetical seller and buyer of the minority interest would negotiate with the understanding that an election would be made.

The solution to a minority or limited partner avoiding built-in gains taxes on partnership assets is to require the partnership to have a §754 election in effect when the partnership interest is purchased. This can be accomplished in the purchase agreement. Since a rational buyer of a limited partnership interest would insist on such a clause in the purchase agreement, we believe that built-in gains taxes on partnership assets should not be taken into account in valuing a holding company organized as a partnership.

More Conclusions Drawn

As discussed in both parts of this addendum, built-in gains taxes may need to be taken into account if the operating company holding nonoperating assets is organized as a C or an S corporation, but not if the operating company is organized as a partnership. We also believe that in valuing an S corporation, there is no need to take built-in gains taxes into account when valuing stock of a majority stockholder. If, however, stock of a minority stockholder is being valued, some recognition of built-in gains taxes may be necessary. Finally, we believe that, in most cases, built-in gains taxes can be ignored in a holding company organized as a partnership.

The §754 Election

Usually a partnership does not make a §754 election until a partnership interest is sold. Often with family limited partnerships, no partnership interests have been sold. Therefore, as of the appraisal date (and resultant assumed sale of a limited partnership interest), a §754 election is not in place.

A rational, probable, willing buyer of a limited partnership interest (an assumption associated with the fair market standard of value) would request the partnership to make a §754 election and incorporate the §754 election request as a term of the purchase agreement of the limited partnership interest. A rational, probable, willing seller of a limited partnership interest would not have the authority to cause the partnership to make the §754 election. Typically, the partners with authority to make a §754 election would be set forth in the partnership agreement or rest with partners participating in management decisions.

Even though a rational, probable, willing seller of a limited partnership will not have the authority to make a §754 election, we believe it's probable that partners with this authority to make a §754 election will generally do so when the partnership owns appreciated assets. Basis adjustments under §754 arise when a partnership interest is sold or exchanged (§754[b] adjustment). A §754 election allows the inside basis of partnership property to be adjusted upward to reflect the purchase price paid by a buyer (§754[b]). A §754 election allows the inside basis of partnership property to be adjusted upward to reflect basis adjustments and recognized gains on distribution of partnership property to partners (§754[b]).

The disadvantages associated with making a §754 election include:

- Additional record keeping for the partnership.
- The risk that inside basis of partnership assets may be adjusted downward rather than upward as assets have depreciated or partners recognize losses on the distribution of partnership assets.
- A §754 election may be revoked only with the consent of the IRS District Director of the Internal Revenue District in which the partnership files its tax return. Treasury Regulation §1.754-1(c) sets forth several reasons a request for revocation of a §754 election may be granted.

It is the valuer's obligation to discern the probable result of a negotiation between a hypothetical seller and a hypothetical buyer. We believe that if a partnership owns appreciated assets, it's probable that partners who have the authority to make a §754 election will make the election at the request of a hypothetical willing seller. However, the disadvantages identified here should be kept in mind by a valuer. If a valuer believes a §754 election will not be made in a subject engagement, because of the disadvantages, the valuer will need to reduce the fair market value of the partnership interest being valued to reflect the built-in gains tax liability. Given that the built-in gains tax liability will not be paid immediately, but rather when the partnership disposes of appreciated assets, full recognition of the built-in gains tax liability is inappropriate. In this situation, the valuer most likely will consider the built-in gains tax liability as a component of the discount for lack of marketability.

Unless a valuer believes the disadvantages associated with a §754 election will surface in a subject engagement and result in no §754 election being made, it is rational to assume that a §754 election will be made. The result of a valid §754 election is that a willing buyer of a limited partnership interest will not reduce the purchase price for any potential built-in gains tax liability associated with appreciated partnership property.

ADDENDUM 2—UNDERSTANDING REAL ESTATE APPRAISALS

Introduction

Business valuation analysts often rely upon the work of other professionals during the process of a valuation engagement, including real estate appraisers. Although analysts usually include a disclaiming caveat about their reliance on other professionals, it would be helpful, nonetheless, to possess a basic general understanding of real estate appraisal. This addendum summarizes these factors.

The valuation of real estate, and interests in real estate, is well documented, with many textbooks, journals, and publications available for reference. The valuation of real estate has similarities to, and differences from, business valuation. Also, in certain types of asset-intensive businesses, buyers and sellers may confuse real estate value with business value, for example, nursing homes. Real estate appraisal is highly regulated by the states and is much more regulated than business valuation.

Valuation Standards and Regulations

The Uniform Standards of Professional Appraisal Practice (USPAP) was created by legislation spurred by the failures in the savings and loan industry in the 1980s. USPAP addresses the valuation and reporting of real property, tangible personal property including machinery and equipment, and business valuations and intangible assets. Title XI of the Financial Institution's Reform, Recovery, and Enforcement Act (FIRREA) of 1989 set forth the requirements that real estate appraisers be certified or licensed by the states and adhere to standards of appraisal practice (USPAP) set by the Appraisal Foundation in order to perform real estate appraisals for federally related transactions. Some states have extended this requirement to appraisals of real estate performed for other purposes. The primary standards within USPAP that apply to the appraisal of real estate are Standard 1: Real Property Appraisal, Development and Standard 2: Real Property Appraisal, Reporting.

The state licensing and certification process is strictly adhered to in the United States, and real estate appraisers must meet specific educational requirements for their license renewals. Some states require a permanent license. There is an exception if the assignment is for FIRREA-related financing purposes, where the states must grant a temporary license. The licensing process is controlled by each individual state and not coordinated at a federal level. Most appraisers would prefer a national system to ease the burdensome and costly regulatory process of maintaining licenses in several states.

Types of Reports Under USPAP

Real estate appraisers refer to USPAP when describing the type of report they furnish to the client (Restricted Use, Summary, or Self Contained).

A Restricted Use Appraisal Report is often a brief letter that will "state" most information rather than provide a lengthy discussion. It may not discuss the data, valuation process, or analyses used. A Summary Appraisal Report is required to state certain things and to summarize others, including a description of the property, its location, the data used, and methods employed in the approaches to value.

Generally a Summary Appraisal Report may be up to 60 pages long with supporting exhibits. A Self-Contained Appraisal Report is a comprehensive narrative report, which is required to "discuss" items that are "summarized" in a Summary Appraisal Report. It presents all the data, reasoning and analyses used in the determination of value. Generally, a Self-Contained Report may be 60 to 100 pages plus exhibits.

These same types of reports are appropriate for real estate and tangible personal property under USPAP. Under the business valuation standards in USPAP, there are only two report types: an Appraisal Report and a Restricted Use Appraisal Report.

The current version of USPAP is the 2010–2011 edition, effective January 1, 2010, and incorporating changes regarding ethics, competency, jurisdictional exception rules, and Standard 3: Appraisal Review. Many of these changes were made to improve clarity and transparency, particularly in financial transactions. For example, an appraiser will have to disclose to the client and in the certification whether she or he has provided any services—appraisal or any other capacity—regarding the subject property within the past three years.

How to Find a Real Estate Appaiser

Most real estate valuations in the United States must be performed by state licensed appraisers. If you need to locate qualified real estate appraisers, most professional organizations maintain lists of appraisers. The largest organization in the United States is the Appraisal Institute (www.appraisalinstitute.org), which has 25,000 appraisers in 91 chapters and maintains a searchable list of designated appraisers by geographic area and industry/property expertise, such as commercial real estate, airports, healthcare facilities, or timberland. Other organizations are the American Society of Appraisers (www.appraisers.org), American Society of Farm Managers & Rural Appraisers (www.Agri-associations.org), International Right of Way Association (www.irwa.com), National Association of Independent Fee Appraisers (www.naifa.com), and National Association of Master Appraisers (www.masterappraisers.org).

Outside the United States, the largest valuation organization is The Royal Institute of Chartered Surveyors (www.rics.org). It has over 146,000 members in 146 countries and has extensive membership in Europe, Africa, the Middle East and Asia. It also has search capabilities by geography and specialization worldwide.

The appraisal profession in the United States has been criticized by regulatory authorities such as the SEC and FASB for not having one organization to set standards, professional designations, training, and enforcement. There have been failed attempts at integration among the Appraisal Institute (AI), the American Society of Appraisals (ASA), and American Society of Farm Managers & Rural Appraisers (ASFMRA) to create one organization for appraisers of all disciplines, resulting in new efforts to combine the Royal Institute of Chartered Surveyors (RICS), ASA, and ASFMRA. These attempts to merge organizations become increasingly important as the world adopts International Financial Reporting Standards, and the United States moves toward adoption.

Types of Interests

Ownership interests in real estate are referred to within the bundle of rights theory, where each of the interests can be separated and conveyed apart from the others.

Fee simple estate is typically defined as an absolute ownership, unencumbered by any other interest or estate, subject to the limitations imposed by the governmental powers of taxation, eminent domain, police power, and escheat.

Leased fee estate is typically defined as an ownership interest held by a landlord with the rights of use and occupancy conveyed by lease to others. The rights of the lessor (the leased fee owner) and the leased fee are specified by contract terms contained within the lease.

Leasehold estate is typically defined as the interest held by the lessee (the tenant or renter) through a lease conveying the rights of use and occupancy for a stated term under certain conditions.

Other ownership interests may include subleasehold interests, air rights, easements, and partial interests.

Standard and Premise of Value

The most commonly used standard of value in stand-alone real estate appraisals is market value, which is defined as the most probable price that a property should bring in a competitive and open market under all conditions requisite to a fair sale, the buyer and seller each acting prudently and knowledgeably, and assuming the price is not affected by undue stimulus. Implicit in this definition is the consummation of a sale as of a specified date and the passing of title from seller to buyer under conditions whereby:

- Buyer and seller are typically motivated
- Both parties are well informed or well advised, and acting in what they consider their own best interests
- A reasonable time is allowed for exposure in the open market
- Payment is made in terms of cash in U.S. dollars or in terms of comparable financial arrangements
- The price represents the normal consideration for the property sold unaffected by special or creative financing or sales concessions granted by anyone associated with the sale.[25]

This standard of value recognizes value to a theoretical market, based upon the exposure time required for similar properties. If there are elements of duress, such as a short timeframe for a sale, that must be made known to the real estate appraiser, who otherwise will value the property based on standard exposure time periods for similar properties.

In Use Value reflects the value of real estate to a particular enterprise. For example, a special purpose manufacturing facility may have a Market Value in Use to its organization that is much higher than its value in exchange to an alternate user. A Market Value in Use might be an appropriate standard in a valuation of real and personal property for purchase price allocation purposes.

Investment Value is the value of a property to a particular individual or investor and not necessarily the value in the marketplace.

---

[25] Office of the Comptroller of the Currency under 12 CFR, Part 34, Subpart C-Appraisals, 34.42 Definitions (g).

Going-concern value is defined as "the value of a proven property operation. It includes the incremental value associated with the business concern, which is distinct from the value of the real property. The value of the going concern includes an intangible enhancement of the value of the operating business enterprise, which is produced by the assemblage of land, buildings, labor, equipment, and the marketing operation. This assemblage creates an economically viable business that is expected to continue. The value of the going concern refers to the total value of a property, including both the real property and the intangible personal property attributed to the business value."[26]

Going concern appraisals are typically conducted for operating facilities such as hospitals, surgery centers, nursing homes, continuous care retirement centers, hotels, restaurants, bowling alleys, manufacturing enterprises, and other facilities that are normally bought and sold as going concern operations. The market value definition requires that appraisals of these property types parallel the methodology and expectations of buyers and sellers of these operations. For these types of properties, the physical real estate assets are integral parts of an ongoing business, and the real property is very rarely sold independently of the business, except in sale/leaseback financing arrangements. It may be more difficult to separate the market value of the land and building from the total value of the entire business, but such a division of realty and nonrealty components of value is possible and is often required by federal financing regulations.

Appraisals performed for financial reporting are required to use fair value, and most tangible asset valuation reports discuss the relationship between fair value and going concern with a paragraph such as the following:

> As is typical with this type of valuation, our opinion of value will be prepared on the premise of continued use, which reflects the condition where buyer and seller contemplate retention of the assets as part of current and forecasted operations. However, should we become aware of a situation where the premise of continued use might not be applicable, we will notify you and seek counsel with you, your designee, or your financial accounting advisor(s) to resolve the matter.

The standard of value for the requested valuation analyses performed for financial reporting purposes will be fair value as required by Statement of Financial Standards No. 141R (now ASC 805) and 157 (now ASC 820):

> Fair Value is the price that would be received to sell an asset or paid to transfer a liability in an orderly transaction between market participants at the measurement date.

Many real estate holding companies, REITs, and institutional real estate investors apply Statement of Financial Accounting Standards No. 141R to their acquisition of multitenanted properties. These investors traditionally allocate value to land,

---

[26] *The Appraisal of Real Estate,* 13th ed. (Chicago: Appraisal Institute, 2008), pp. 29–30.

buildings, and tenant improvements. Many publicly traded entities also allocate value to above-, below-, and at-market leases; the in-place lease value, or the lease-up costs of having tenants in place; and customer relationships. While the allocation of value to individual leases is fairly consistent among these entities, the identification, valuation, and reporting of in-place lease values and customer relationships remain inconsistent in the industry among those filing financial statements.

Highest and Best Use

In *The Dictionary of Real Estate Appraisal*, 3rd ed. page 171, *highest and best use* is defined as "the reasonably probable and legal use of vacant land or an improved property, which is physically possible, appropriately supported, financially feasible, and that results in the highest value." The four criteria that must be met for the highest and best use are physical possibility, legal permissibility, financial feasibility, and maximum profitability.

The highest and best use of land that as vacant and available for development may differ from the highest and best use of that same property as improved. This is true when the improvements do not constitute an appropriate use. The existing use will continue unless, or until the land value in its highest and best use, exceeds the value of the entire property in its existing use (plus the cost to remove the improvements). Therefore, the analysis of highest and best use includes consideration of the property under two assumptions: land as if vacant for development and property as presently improved. These two analyses are then correlated into a final estimate of highest and best use.

Three Approaches to Value

In contrast to business valuation or personal property valuation, all three approaches to value are commonly "applied" in real estate appraisals. In every real estate appraisal, market data is used in determining value. Market data can include sales and offerings of similar properties and tracts of vacant land, current prices for construction materials and labor, rentals of similar properties and their operating expenses, and current rates of return on investments and properties. From this data, values may be developed for the land and the property as a whole.

Cost Approach

Estimating value through the cost approach requires an estimate of the cost to reproduce or replace existing improvements. The value of improvements is estimated based upon the principle of substitution which holds that an informed purchaser will pay no more than the total cost to construct a similar building or improvements, less any accumulated depreciation. The method used to derive an indication of value by the cost approach is:

- Estimate the value of the site (land) as though vacant and available to be developed to its highest and best use
- Estimate the reproduction or replacement cost of the structure as of the effective date of appraisal
- Estimate the amount of accrued depreciation in the structure and categorize it into three major types: physical depreciation, functional obsolescence, and external obsolescence

- Deduct appropriate estimated depreciation from the reproduction or replacement cost of the structure to derive an estimate of the structure's contribution to total value
- Add estimated total present value of all improvements to the land value to obtain an indication of value for the subject property

There is additional discussion of the types of property depreciation and obsolescence in Addendum 3 to this chapter on the valuation of machinery and equipment.

The cost approach recognizes that market participants sometimes relate value to cost. Reliance on the principle of substitution, where a purchaser would not pay more for a property than it would cost to construct a new one, allows value parameters to be established under traditional appraisal theory.

Sales Comparison (Market) Approach

The Sales Comparison Approach is an estimate of value based upon a process of comparing recent sales of similar properties in the surrounding or competing areas to the subject property. Inherent in this approach is the principle of substitution, whereby a buyer would not pay more for a property than he or she could purchase a similar property for in the marketplace.

Under this approach the subject property is compared with similar properties of the same general type which have been sold recently or currently are available for sale in competing areas. It should be noted that real estate appraisers frequently include data on asking prices rather than just completed transactions, whereas business appraisers sometimes limit their data to completed transactions. The asking prices used by real estate appraisers may be seen as indicators of the future direction of the market. This comparative process involves judgment as to the similarity of the subject property and the comparable sales or listings with respect to many value factors such as location, size, contract rent levels, quality of construction, reputation and prestige, age, and condition.

Each comparable property is analyzed and adjusted to arrive at a unit rate of value for the subject, such as "per square foot" or "per acre." Vacant land or improved property can be valued in this manner, using adjustment grids.

Income Capitalization (Income) Approach

The theory of the income capitalization approach is based on the premise that value is equal to the present value of the cash flow and reversionary value the property will produce over a reasonable holding (ownership) period.

The direct capitalization method converts one year of income into a value using overall capitalization rates from similar sales. The overall rates take into consideration buyers' assumptions of the market over the long-term.

The discounted cash flow method converts cash flows (including interim cash flows and reversion or terminal value) into a present value using an internal rate of return (or discount rate). The internal rate of return (IRR) is derived from a comparison of alternate investments, a comparative analysis of IRRs used by recent buyers of similar properties, and a review of published industry surveys.

The results of the income capitalization method are usually the primary value indicator for commercial, income producing real estate such as office buildings, retail shopping centers, multi-family apartment buildings, hotels, and multi-tenant distribution centers. Investors expect a reasonable rate of return on their investment based on the ownership risks involved; this approach closely parallels the investment decision process.

The value derived by real estate appraisers is the value of the property itself. In contrast to business valuation, real estate appraisers do not differentiate the invested capital value from the equity value. Real estate appraisal methods do not specifically derive an equity value if there is debt against the property.

Direct Capitalization Analysis

In a direct capitalization analysis, estimates are made of the potential gross income (PGI) that might be expected from rental of the real estate and of rent losses and expenses that might be incurred by an owner/lessor. The resulting net income is then capitalized at an appropriate rate to indicate the value of the property. To develop the PGI, lease data from other properties are gathered and analyzed, providing an unadjusted rent range in terms of dollars per square foot. This data is supplemented through discussions with brokers regarding typical lease terms and rates for similar properties, to develop a market rent rate for the subject property. This estimate provides the adjusted rent per square foot, which is multiplied by the square footage of the property to determine the potential gross income of the property.

Other income, rent concessions, vacancy and collection losses, operating expenses, real estate taxes, insurance, management fees, maintenance, and replacement reserves related to the property are identified.

Subtraction of all vacancy and expenses from PGI, and addition of any other income, results in net operating income (NOI), which is then capitalized into an indication of value. This NOI is for a hypothetical owner for the following year and is not necessarily the NOI of the current owner. The NOI is calculated before interest expense or debt payment and income taxes. Replacement reserves, the expected capital expenditures required to keep up the property, may be subtracted to reach NOI depending, in part, on whether the source of the capitalization rate was derived from cash flows before or after replacement reserves. NOI before replacement reserves is similar to the measure of earnings before interests, taxes, depreciation, and amortization (EBITDA) often used in business valuation.

Discount Rate Determination

In the following example, investment criteria are derived for the subject based upon analysis of comparable sales and a survey of national real estate investors. The following table summarizes the conclusions of these surveys.

National Suburban Office Market
Second Quarter 2005

Category	Range	Average	Average 2nd Qtr 04
Discount Rate (IRR)	7.50%–12.50%	9.90%	10.63%
Overall Cap Rate (OAR)	6.50%–10.50%	8.45%	9.11%
Market Rent Change Rate	−10.00%–3.00%	0.89%	0.43%
Expense Change Rate	2.00%–3.00%	2.92%	2.93%
Residual Cap Rate	7.50%–11.00%	9.07%	9.62%

Investment Criteria

Appropriate investment criteria were derived for the subject based on an analysis of comparable sales and a survey of real estate investors. The following summarizes the findings from comparable data of the Real Estate Research Corporation (RERC) (www.rerc.com) for the most recent period:

Overall Capitalization Rate Based on Comparable Sales

Comp. No.	Sales Date	Occup.	Price/Unit	OAR
I-1	June-07	86%	$40,000	8.36%
I-2	June-07	93%	$38,493	7.20%
I-3	May-07	87%	$28,885	7.58%
I-4	Apr-07	91%	$34,444	7.60%
I-5	Jan-07	92%	$34,831	8.00%
			High	8.36%
			Low	7.20%
			Average	7.75%

Overall Capitalization Rate Based on RERC Report
First Quarter 2008
Third-Tier Investment Properties (Apartment)

CAPITALIZATION RATES

	GOING-IN		TERMINAL	
	Low	High	Low	High
Range	7.00%	9.50%	7.50%	11.00%
Average		8.60%		9.50%

Discount Rate Based on RERC Report
First Quarter 2008
Third-Tier Investment Properties (Apartment)

Discount Rate

	Low	High
Range	8.00%	13.00%
Average		11.00%

Based on this information, we concluded the subject's OAR should be 8.50 percent. The terminal capitalization rate is applied to the NOI estimated for the year following the end of the holding period. Based on the concluded overall capitalization rate, the age of the property, and the surveyed information, we have concluded the subject's terminal capitalization rate to be 9.50 percent. Finally, the subject's discount rate or yield rate is estimated based on the previous investor survey and an examination of returns available on alternative investments in the market. Based on this analysis, the subject's discount rate is estimated to be 10.50 percent.

DISTRESSED MARKETS

Appraising real estate in distressed markets and depressed economic conditions can be difficult, with commercial real estate values down 10 percent to 30 percent, depending on type of asset and locations. There are fewer transactions to gauge the market, little debt available to finance acquisitions, and many sellers unwilling to accept reduced values for their assets, particularly for commercial real estate holdings. Real estate appraisers will compensate for the reduced market data in the sales comparison approach by discussing with local brokers and appraisers likely discounts to apply, what percentage adjustments to apply to older comparable sales for market conditions, and lengthening exposure time, and analyze whether current transactions reflect a willing buyer and a willing seller or a distressed sale. They will also look at current tenant vacancies in the marketplace and compare to the subject property for tenant quality. If the subject has high-quality tenants with little default risk, a discounted cash flow analysis may be more highly weighted than the direct capitalization analysis. If the valuation is being performed for financial reporting, there probably will be fewer Level 1 tiered transactions (identical comparables) and Level 2 transactions (similar comparables) and more reliance placed on Level 3 inputs (unobservable inputs), such as market surveys.

GREEN BUILDINGS

A newer trend in real estate is the emphasis on green buildings that are environmentally friendly from reduced energy usage and/or environmental quality, innovation, and design process. The two largest ratings programs are the Leadership in Energy and Environmental Design (LEED), which is sponsored by the United States Green Building Council (USGBC), and the ENERGY STAR system produced by the U.S. Environmental Protection Agency and the U.S. Department of Energy. ENERGY STAR is focused primarily on reduced energy usage through higher efficiency windows, air-handling systems, and power-management systems, while the LEED rating incorporates other nonenergy factors, such as innovation and design.

Real estate consultants can now obtain LEED certifications, and real estate buildings can be rated as LEED Certified, LEED Certified Silver, LEED Certified Gold, and LEED Certified Platinum. Green buildings typically use resources more efficiently than those constructed to code requirements and can offer cost savings from energy usage, while also improving air and water quality. There is debate at the moment whether the cost of constructing a green building is materially higher than conventional construction, but these costs should be recovered by lesser energy costs. To date, there haven't been enough transactions to identify a significant premium in sales of green buildings, although RICS published a study in April 2009 indicating a 3.3% premium in sales of ENERGY STAR–rated buildings, but no identifiable premium for LEED-rated properties.

ADDENDUM 3—UNDERSTANDING MACHINERY AND EQUIPMENT APPRAISALS

Introduction

The appraisal of machinery and equipment (M&E) is not as widely written about or as regulated as real estate appraisal. M&E appraisals tend to be less location-specific than real estate. M&E appraisers often possess specific expertise about industries or assets, such as aircraft, marine vessels, utilities, or petrochemical and natural resources industries. While some M&E appraisers choose to specialize in one of these niches, others are generalists.

M&E appraisers are not subject to the same state licensing criteria as real estate appraisers, but the issue has been discussed by regulatory authorities and appraisal organizations. The Uniform Standards of Professional Appraisal Practice (USPAP) does include sections on Personal Property Appraisal, Development (Standard 7), and Personal Property Appraisal, Reporting (Standard 8).

Purpose of the Appraisal

The purposes for M&E appraisals may include:

- Allocation of purchase price, either in conjunction with the other assets of a going-concern such as current assets, real estate, intangible assets, and goodwill, or a stand-alone analysis
- Financing, where a lender may wish to know the value of the assets being financed in the open market
- Insurance, whether the terms of a policy are based on actual cash value or a Cost of Replacement or Cost of Reproduction—New
- Litigation, where an expert witness is required
- Leasing, whether for off balance sheet financings or for determining a residual value
- Property tax, where the value of personal property is required for determining the appropriateness of the assessment

How to Find a Machinery and Equipment Appraiser

The two largest personal property organizations are the American Society of Appraisers (ASA), which has a Machinery & Technical Specialties Committee (M&TS), and the Association of Machinery & Equipment Appraisers (AMEA). Both organizations are very active, promote continuing education, and have minimum requirements to receive professional designations. They each have searchable web sites to locate qualified appraisers and require their members to adhere to USPAP.

The M&TS Committee of the ASA has a web site (www.appraisers.org/disciplines/machinery. htm) that discusses educational courses, definitions of value, and information relating to the *M&TS Journal*, which is published four times per year. There are also links to purchase one of the few publications on this area, a textbook titled *Valuing Machinery and Equipment: The Fundamentals of Appraising Machinery and Technical Assets,* 2nd ed. This textbook describes the three approaches to value for machinery and equipment, typical methodologies employed, and examples of calculating loss of value via physical depreciation, functional obsolescence, and economic obsolescence. The requirements to receive an ASA (Accredited Senior

Appraiser) designation include five years of experience, passing technical and ethics examinations, and submitting sample reports to a peer review board.

The AMEA (www.amea.org) differs from ASA by requiring its Accredited Equipment Appraisers (AEA) to be employed by a Machinery Dealers National Association (MDNA) member firm. This requires involvement in the buying, selling, and/or appraising of M&E for the last three years. They must also pass a written ethics examination, and submit sample reports for AMEA and USPAP compliance.

Standard and Premise of Value

The ASA published definitions of value for M&TS are:[27]

Fair Market Value. The estimated amount, expressed in terms of money, that may reasonably be expected for a property in an exchange between a willing buyer and a willing seller, with equity to both, neither under any compulsion to buy or sell, and both fully aware of all relevant facts, as of a specific date.

Fair Market Value—Removal. The estimated amount, expressed in terms of money, that may be reasonably expected for a property, in an exchange between a willing buyer and a willing seller, with equity to both, neither under any compulsion to buy or sell, and both fully aware of all relevant facts, as of a specific date, considering the cost of removal of the property to another location.

Fair Market Value In Continued Use. The estimated amount, expressed in terms of money, that may be reasonably expected for a property in an exchange between a willing buyer and a willing seller, with equity to both, neither under any compulsion to buy or sell, and both fully aware of all relevant facts, including installation, as of a specific date and assuming that the business earnings support the value reported. This amount includes all normal direct and indirect costs, such as installation and other assemblage costs to make the property fully operational.

Fair Market Value—Installed. The estimated amount, expressed in terms of money, that may be reasonably expected for an installed property in an exchange between a willing buyer and a willing seller, with equity to both, neither under any compulsion to buy or sell, and both fully aware of all relevant facts, including installation, as of a specific date. This amount includes all normal direct and indirect costs, such as installation and other assemblage costs, necessary to make the property fully operational.

Orderly Liquidation Value. The estimated gross amount, expressed in terms of money, that could be typically realized from a liquidation sale, given a reasonable period of time to find a purchaser (or purchasers), with the seller being compelled to sell on an as-is, where-is basis, as of a specific date.

Forced Liquidation Value. The estimated gross amount, expressed in terms of money, that could be typically realized from a properly advertised and conducted public auction, with the seller being compelled to sell with a sense of immediacy on an as-is, where-is basis, as of a specific date.

---

[27] American Society of Appraisers, *Valuing Machinery and Equipment: The Fundamentals of Appraising Machinery and Technical Assets,* 2nd ed. (2005), p. 3–4.

The *Fair Market Value In Continued Use* and *Fair Market Value–Installed* concepts consider asset value as part of a going concern, and give consideration to installation and various indirect costs. These two definitions of value are commonly used for mergers and acquisitions, and the prior term takes into consideration whether the earnings of the subject company are adequate to support the concluded values. This usually requires coordination among the business valuation analyst and real and personal property appraisers. This will be discussed in more detail under the assumed earnings portion of this chapter.

Appraisals performed for financial reporting are required to use fair value, and most tangible-asset valuation reports discuss the relationship between fair value and going concern with a paragraph such as:

> The premise of value for the requested valuation analyses performed for financial reporting purposes will be fair value as required by Statement of Financial Accounting Standards No. 157 (now ASC 820).

With this type of valuation, the opinion of value is typically prepared on the premise of *continued use*, where buyer and seller contemplate retention of the assets as part of current and forecasted operations. However, a situation where the premise of *continued use* might not be applicable, the analyst should notify the client and seek information, if necessary in certain situations, to resolve the matter.

The *Orderly Liquidation Value* and *Forced Liquidation Value* premises of value reflect value in comparison, with *Forced Liquidation Value* generally considered to be an auction value, with a relatively short time period to advertise and conduct an auction. An *Orderly Liquidation Value* will consider a longer timeframe to advertise and locate interested parties.

International Accounting Standards and International Financial Reporting Standards are increasingly converging towards improved consistency and transparency with other regulatory organizations. The valuation of tangible assets for IAS/IFRS purposes will be performed under:

IAS 16	Property, Plant, and Equipment
IAS 36	Impairment of Assets
IAS 40	Investment Property
IFRS 3	Business Combinations
IFRS 5	Noncurrent Assets Held for Sale and Discontinued Operations

Standards should be reviewed, in detail, but there are several predominant issues. IAS 16 is required to be applied for all appraisals of property, plant, and equipment, except when another standard permits or requires different accounting treatment, such as IAS 40; PP&E classified as held for resale; biological assets for agricultural activity (IAS 41); and mineral rights and reserves.

Under IAS 16, an entity may choose either the cost model or the revaluation model and apply that to the entire class of PP&E. In the cost model, an item of PP&E shall be carried at its cost less any accumulated depreciation and/or impairment losses. In the revaluation model, PP&E whose fair value can be measured reliably shall be carried at the revalued amount, which is its fair value less any subsequent accumulated depreciation. Revaluations should be made with sufficient regularity, as the regulations acknowledge some PP&E may be more volatile and required to have annual revaluations, while others are less volatile and revalued every three to five years.

IAS 16 also introduces the concept of componentization, where assets must be separately identified and depreciated if they have different depreciation periods, for example, power plants having major components such as boilers, turbines, and generators. This is a significant change for those facilities that were previously depreciated as one lump sum for the entire facility, and there is little guidance on determining what constitutes a material asset, requiring the appraiser to work with the client and auditor to ensure proper groupings of assets by useful life. IAS is also different from U.S. GAAP by allowing reversals of prior impairment charges for tangible assets, when the issue causing impairment no longer exists.

IAS 16 goes on to state the valuation of land and buildings is usually performed with market-based evidence, and normally by professionally qualified valuers. If there is no market-based evidence because of specialized assets, then a cost or income approach may be used. IAS 16 also states if one item is revalued, then the entire class of PP&E should be revalued. Disclosure is also more transparent. Financial statements must disclose:

- If assets are revalued
- The effective date
- Whether an independent analyst did the analysis
- The extent to which market-based evidence was employed
- The carrying amounts of temporarily idle PP&E
- Assets retired but not held for sale

IAS 40 acknowledges that investment properties are typically valued considering present value of future cash flows, and market value is considered appropriate for investment properties using fair value reporting. The regulations state there must be disclosures of methods and significant assumptions applied, a statement whether the fair value was supported by market-evidence, or based on other factors, and whether an independent valuer has recent experience in that market and asset type.

IFRS 5 requires that non current assets classified as "held for sale" be measured at the lower-of-carrying amount and fair value less costs to sell, with depreciation ceasing and be presented separately in the balance sheet. Surplus assets are accounted for at the lower-of-carrying amount and fair value, less cost to sell. Analysts must determine if the surplus assets would be sold individually or in a group and report accordingly.

Identifying and Reporting Assets to Be Appraised

If there is a large number of assets to be appraised, for example machinery and equipment located within a factory, M&E appraisers will ask for direction in determining how to set up the reporting process. Following a client's chart of accounts may be required. This enables the new inventory of assets and values to be uploaded into the client's fixed asset reporting system for financial reporting or tax reporting purposes. If a particular chart of accounts is not specified, the M&E appraiser will typically use a fairly common set of accounts and classifications.

As described in *Valuing Machinery and Equipment: The Fundamentals of Appraising Machinery and Technical Assets*, 2nd ed. "accounts are major groupings of assets that are similar in character. The most basic separation of tangible assets into accounts would be land, buildings (or structures), land improvements, and machinery and equipment. The machinery and equipment account can be further broken down into various 'classes' such as production machinery, general plant equipment, office furniture and fixtures, and other classes."[28]

In some M&E engagements, a client may supply a list of the assets to be appraised, and the appraiser accepts the list without verifying the existence or condition of each asset by physical inspection. Examples of this type of engagement are "desktop" appraisals where there is no physical inspection or engagements using a sampling technique, where only the largest and most valuable assets are inspected. Some engagements, such as in a purchase of a company with multiple locations, require only the inspections of the largest manufacturing facilities. The appraiser will then use furnished information to value minor facilities such as offices and warehouses. These techniques may be appropriate for the purpose of the valuation, but they should be disclosed in the report to avoid misleading the client or other intended user.

Approaches to Value

The three approaches to value are all considered in valuing M&E, although the income approach is not commonly employed in determining the value of an individual piece of machinery and equipment. An income stream can rarely be isolated for a particular piece of machinery. It is used, however, in valuing integrated manufacturing facilities or production lines, or quantifying the after-tax penalties for obsolescence. The cost approach and market approach are widely used.

Cost Approach

The cost approach allows each individual asset to be appraised and is the best determinant of value for a special-purpose asset or one without an active secondary market. The appraiser will determine the *Reproduction Cost New* or *Replacement Cost New*. The reproduction cost new is the cost to create an exact duplicate of the subject, while a replacement cost new is the cost to create one with equal capacity and utility as the subject, but using current technology. The difference between them is the possible existence of excess capital costs, a form of functional obsolescence. Some of the possible methods an appraiser will use in determining the *current cost new* would include:

1. Direct Unit Pricing
2. Trending
3. Cost/Capacity

Direct Unit Pricing Method
In the direct unit pricing method, the M&E appraiser inventories the assets at the facility, and records identifying information such as manufacturer, model and serial number, year manufactured, description, capacity, and drive. This inventory includes comments relating to the machine's installation in the facility such as

---

[28] American Society of Appraisers, *Valuing Machinery and Equipment: The Fundamentals of Appraising Machinery and Technical Assets,* 2nd ed. (2005), p. 24.

foundation, power and utility connections, and indirect factors such as costs of installation and engineering. Each asset is individually identified and valued, unless its value is beneath the client's capitalization policy, where it will be grouped by like-kind and valued as a single line-entry. The Reproduction or Replacement Cost is determined by reviewing a variety of data including published cost information manuals, manufacturers' price lists, databases, and Internet based data.

Trending Method

In the trending method, the M&E appraiser can use the existing accounting records as the basis for the inventory of assets to be valued. An advantage of using the existing records is ease of integrating the "new" values to the old fixed asset listing, allowing a reconciliation of the new values to the historical net book values. The disadvantage of using existing accounting records is the possibility of unrecorded retirements. The presence of such "ghost" assets, that linger on the books years after being physically retired, may result in excess depreciation charges affecting earnings. Two other problems in trending are:

1. Inaccurate historical costs and book values due to purchase accounting treatment in past acquisitions.
2. Duplication of costs incurred for rebuilding or retrofitting recorded when the asset was first placed in service and again at a later date.

To make trending techniques more meaningful, appraisers use a battery limit, or unit of production method, where costs will be known to manufacture an entire facility, or major component of a process plant. This unit of production method results in a check on the sum of the trended individual costs for that facility as a whole, without commenting upon each individual line item.

Cost/Capacity Method

In the Cost/Capacity method, the costs of similar equipment or process plants can vary based on size or capacity, raised to a power.[29] The formula is expressed as:

$$(C_2 / C_1) = (Q_2 / Q_1)^x$$

In this formula, C_2 is the desired cost of capacity Q_2. C_1 is the known cost of capacity Q_1. These costs are scaled using factors typically called the six-tenths factor, where costs can be scaled up or down within reasonable ranges. Examples of this technique may also be found in *Valuing Machinery and Equipment.*[30] This cost capacity approach may also be used in conjunction with a trending approach for facilities that have known construction costs (e.g., petrochemical plants, steel mills, or other integrated facilities). The cost capacity formula is used as a check on the reasonableness of the sum of the trended costs for a facility, in part or in whole.

---

[29] Frederic Jelen and James Black, *Cost and Optimization Engineering,* 2nd ed. (New York: McGraw Hill, Inc., 1983), p. 333.
[30] American Society of Appraisers, *Valuing Machinery and Equipment: The Fundamentals of Appraising Machinery and Technical Assets,* 2nd ed. (2005), p. 61.

Depreciation and Obsolescence

These costs are adjustments to value, accounting for physical deterioration, and functional and economic obsolescence. The ASA defines these three adjustments as follows:

> *Physical deterioration* is the loss in value or usefulness of a property due to the using up or expiration of its useful life caused by wear and tear, deterioration, exposure to various elements, physical stresses, and similar factors.
>
> *Functional obsolescence* is the loss in value or usefulness of a property caused by inefficiencies or inadequacies of the property itself, when compared to a more efficient or less costly replacement property that incorporates new technology. Symptoms suggesting the presence of functional obsolescence are excess operating costs, excess construction costs (excess capital costs), over capacity, inadequacy, lack of utility, or similar conditions.
>
> *Economic obsolescence* (sometimes called "external obsolescence") is the loss in value or usefulness of a property caused by factors external to the property, such as increased cost of raw material, labor, or utilities (without an offsetting increase in product price); reduced demand for the product, increased competition, environmental or other regulations; inflation or high interest rates, or similar factors.[31]

Physical Depreciation

Physical depreciation is commonly applied using an effective age/whole life ("age/life") technique, where the appraiser will make an estimate of the effective age of the machinery and the machinery's whole life. Effective age is commonly defined as the age of an asset, in comparison with a new asset of like kind. It gives consideration to rebuilding and maintenance that will extend a property's service life. Economic life is the estimated total life of an asset and can be estimated by the sum of the effective age of an asset plus the asset's remaining useful life. Remaining useful ("economic") life is the estimated period during which a property of a certain age is expected to continue to be profitably used for the purpose for which it was intended. It can be approximated by deducting the asset's effective age from its economic life.

The formula is:

$$[\text{Effective Age} / (\text{Effective Age} + \text{Remaining Useful Life})] \times 100 = \\ \% \text{ of Physical Deterioration}$$

Appraisers will often use depreciation charts reflecting loss in value for various types of equipment and industries. There are published sources, such as those by Marshall & Swift in the *Marshall Valuation Service,* that have their origins in Bulletin F, published by the Internal Revenue Service in the early 1900s. While useful, it is difficult to determine the source data for these studies; hence their reliability is questionable. Statistical analysis of historical retirement behavior, or survivor curves, is also used in determining the average service life and remaining useful life of similar assets. The best known of these studies are the Iowa curves, published in the 1930s at

---

[31] Ibid., p. 70.

Iowa State University.[32] These are survivor curves, not depreciation curves, and should be used with proper statistical analyses. The best estimate of physical depreciation is often based on a combination of an appraiser's personal inspection of the assets, an age/life analysis, and information obtained from interviews with local site engineers and maintenance management.

Functional Obsolescence

Functional obsolescence (FO) includes an investigation of excess construction and operating costs. Excess construction costs are something that a buyer would be unwilling to pay because of advancements in technology. Examples include obsolete construction materials, an inefficient layout that was built piecemeal over many years in a process plant, technology contained in control systems, or the existence of many smaller production units versus a larger, more efficient one. The best way to identify FO is to ask plant engineering management what they would replace or revise if they could build a new facility of the same capacity and utility.

Excess operating costs occur when the property's design results in operating inefficiencies causing higher costs for the subject being valued in comparison to a modern replacement. This form of functional obsolescence, sometimes called operating obsolescence, is measured by estimating the difference in operating expenses between the subject and the modern replacement. Typical expenses to investigate include labor, materials and supplies, utilities, yield, and taxes. Examples might include excess material movement between portions of a facility, or operating costs for HVAC and utilities in underutilized clean rooms in a pharmaceutical facility. The excess costs of operating the subject asset compared to the modern replacement design is calculated, reduced by the tax rate, and calculated by the present value of the excess operating cost penalty over the remaining life of the penalty.

Example

In underutilized clean rooms, both excess construction costs and excess operating costs may exist. The excess operating costs would be developed based on actual costs for operating the entire facility and allocating a portion of those costs to the unused areas. The primary factors would be utility costs such as heating, ventilating and air-conditioning, chilled water, electrical, dust collection, and maintenance.

An estimate would be made of the remaining life of the property reflecting the time the excess operating costs would continue to exist. The present value of the annual excess operating cost penalty over the probable life expectancy would be determined based on an after-tax rate of return on a constant-dollar basis.

To convert this annual excess operating cost penalty into an indication of obsolescence, it would be necessary to discount the penalty over the remaining life of the cost disadvantage. For the discount rate, a weighted average cost of capital (WACC) of, say, 13 percent could be used based on an analysis of the pharmaceutical industry. Since the operating cost penalties are discounted on a constant-dollar basis and the discount rate includes an amount for anticipated inflation, the effect of anticipated inflation is removed, which is approximately 2.5 percent based on various studies on or around the appraisal date. Therefore, the discount rate

---

[32] Richard Ellsworth, "The Valuation of Industrial Facilities," *The Machinery & Technical Specialties Journal* 15, no. 3, p. 22.

applied for operating cost penalties on a constant-dollar basis is 10.5 percent (13.0 – 2.5 percent). This penalty was calculated using the physical remaining life of 15 years.

An indication of operating obsolescence is developed as follows:

Annual Excess Operating Cost Penalty	$ 327,429
Less Tax Benefit @ 40.9%	133,918
Annual Excess Operating Cost (after-tax)	193,511
Present Value Factor	7.394
Operating Obsolescence	$1,430,820
Rounded	$1,400,000

Economic Obsolescence

Economic obsolescence (EO) is the loss in value resulting from external influences to the subject property. These may be global, national, regional, or local factors, including political and governmental regulations. In determining whether this obsolescence exists, a review is made of the economics of the subject property compared to its industry as of the appraisal date. Typical examples of economic obsolescence include reduced demand for products, overcapacity, increased costs of raw materials, and regulations requiring capital expenditures.

Use of an income approach or sales comparison approach will include the quantification of economic obsolescence, as both approaches include all forms of depreciation and obsolescence. The appraiser may not independently separate an amount for EO. In the cost approach, the quantification of EO can be an important consideration. There are several methods for quantifying economic obsolescence.

Utilization can be used as an indicator of EO by comparing a facility's actual utilization to its design utilization, with the use of the previously described "six-tenths" scale factor. As an example, let's assume a facility is operating at 70 percent utilization due to a lack of demand in the market. The design capacity is 90 percent. The formula for determining the penalty for EO is expressed as follows:

$$
\begin{aligned}
\text{EO} &= [1 - (\text{Demand} \div \text{Capacity})^{0.6}] \times 100 \\
&= [1 - (70 \div 90)^{0.6}] \times 100 \\
&= (1 - .86) \times 100 \\
&= 14\%
\end{aligned}
$$

The reduction in utilization may indicate EO and may be taken as a penalty against the assets being valued. It may be applicable to all the assets of a company, or may be applicable to the manufacturing machinery and not the real estate. If actual utilization is at a normal operating level, that does not necessarily indicate the absence of EO. The earnings can be reviewed and compared to industry norms to quantify it. Foreign competition may be the cause for lower profitability due to lower labor costs, lower levels of regulatory requirements, or government subsidies. Other measures that may help identify a loss of profitability include return on capital, where a mean return on capital for an industry can be compared to the subject industry returns; equity to book, where source data such as Standard & Poor's can result in ratios of stock price to book value; and margin analysis, by reviewing current margins to prior margins. Correlating these indicators results in an estimate of economic obsolescence.[33]

Sales Comparison (Market) Approach

The sales comparison approach includes an analysis of recent sales and current offerings of similar pieces of machinery. It can also be the most supportable approach in terms of market indicators. There are many published and on-line sources of market data for machinery and equipment, and many analysts have large databases of sales to use in the valuation of individual assets. This approach is often used in determining value for financing purposes, where the premise of value would be in exchange to another user; or in an allocation of purchase price, where the market value would be adjusted upwards to consider the costs to install the machine at the subject company.

The strength of the sales comparison approach is the ability of an active marketplace to contemplate all forms of depreciation, whether physical, functional, or economic. The identification of comparable sales and offerings of similar property is similar to that in real estate, although the reporting process is different, as the valuation of large numbers of assets does not permit adjustment grids to be included in a report. Similarities include adjustments for effective age, size (capacity), condition, location, and exposure period.

Once adjustments are made to comparable sales and asking prices, fair market value in continued use can be arrived at by adding allowances for freight, wiring, installation, and all other direct and indirect costs necessary to assemble the property as an integrated, functioning unit. The approach considers some or all of the following market evidence: sales through public auctions, catalogs of similar machine units offered for sale, and discussions with local and national brokers.

Income Approach

The income approach is primarily used in the valuation of integrated production facilities or special-purpose assets, such as railcars, refineries, utilities, landfills, and mineral extraction. It is also used to quantify obsolescence penalties. Personal property appraisal typically includes the finite life of personal property. The concepts of present worth and life factors have their origin in Engineering Value and Depreciation, which describes Retirement Rate Analysis and Expectancy Life Factors.[34]

The use of direct capitalization and discounted cash flow analysis and development of discount rates is discussed elsewhere in the book.

Assumed Earnings

One way of measuring external or economic obsolescence is to test whether the earnings of a business support the value of the assets otherwise concluded. In other words, if all the tangible and intangible assets of a company are appraised and the

---

[33] Michael Remsha, "Economic Obsolescence," *The Machinery & Technical Specialties Journal* 16, no. 1.

[34] Richard Ellsworth, "The Valuation of Industrial Facilities," *The Machinery & Technical Specialties Journal* 15, no. 3.

total value of those assets added together is greater than the overall value of the business, then economic obsolescence is suggested. This type of analysis is usually performed in conjunction with a business valuation analyst. Most M&E appraisers will not test the adequacy of a company's earnings to support the concluded values when valuing machinery that is part of a going concern. If they do not, they will include a paragraph disclaiming that to the reader. For example:

> We did not investigate any financial data pertaining to the present or prospective earning capacity of the operation in which the designated assets are used. It was assumed that prospective earnings would provide a reasonable return on the appraised value of the designated assets, plus the value of any assets not included in the appraisal, and adequate net working capital. If prospective earnings are not adequate to justify ownership of the assets at the appraised levels, then the concluded fair market value as reported here must be reduced accordingly.

Asset value will be affected by the ability of the entity being valued to have sufficient earnings to support concluded values for various components of a going concern as in illustrated in Exhibit 8.12.

If a business enterprise valuation (BEV) has been performed, a test for economic obsolescence can be made by ensuring the working capital, real estate, personal property, and intangible assets fit within the BEV. If the sum of components is in excess of the BEV, then obsolescence exists and values may be reduced accordingly. That obsolescence should be directed first to those assets causing the obsolescence, or if the penalty cannot be identified to one component, it may be spread among the appropriate assets. As a going concern's profitability is reduced, the value of the real and personal property cannot be less than its value in the marketplace. If there are no earnings, the assets may be entered at orderly or forced liquidation value.

Exhibit 8.12   Present Worth of Future Benefits of Ownership

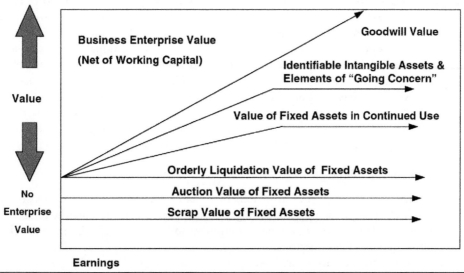

Assets that are nonoperating, and not contributing to the earnings of the operation, may be viewed as excess assets. They are not required for on going operations. Examples might be unused or abandoned buildings and idled production lines. If there are no plans for these assets to be used in future operations, they should be valued using a value in exchange premise, similar to orderly liquidation, as they are not contributing to the earnings of the going concern. If a business valuation is being performed, the value in exchange of the nonoperating assets can be added to the value of the business operations.

Construction in Progress

The construction in progress (CIP) account is often overlooked or improperly reconciled in reviews of real and personal property valuations. This account includes projects not yet completed and costs not capitalized as of the appraisal date. The CIP costs should be analyzed to ensure that the expenditures have not been double-counted or missed. Occasionally, it may be difficult to distinguish between real and personal property accounts. The real estate and M&E appraisers need to communicate with each other regarding how these assets will be treated. CIP should be investigated to determine whether the new construction will increase the value of the plant or just allow it to remain in business. For example, environmental expenditures may be costly to implement, but they do not increase the value of the operating plant on a dollar-for-dollar basis. CIP is either valued on its incremental value to the operating plant or, in some cases, on the basis of actual cost incurred as of the appraisal date. An argument can be made that EO should be applied to CIP in a similar manner as the other assets in the M&E accounts, as appropriate.

SAS 73/101 Real and Personal Property Valuation Review

Statement of Auditing Standards (SAS) No. 73 generally reviews the appropriateness of using a specialist, including qualifications, assessing the relationship of the specialist to the client, and referring to the specialist in the auditors report. SAS No. 101 provides guidance on auditing fair value measurements and disclosures in financial statements. The focus of SFAS 141R and 157 on actions of market participants and Level 1, Level 2, and Level 3 criteria, has led to further research and documentation of market data among market participants by auditors performing these reviews. Level 1 data documenting sales of identical comparable assets are the most reliable, Level 2 data of sales of similar assets are next on the hierarchy, and Level 3 data are the lowest on the hierarchy. The types of questions and issues reviewed will vary based upon the purpose of the valuation, materiality of asset classes, and the nature of the subject company, but for a SFAS—142/142 valuation for business combinations, a fairly typical set of questions for a large multi-location manufacturing company for tangible assests might look something like this:

Valuation Background

1. Provide a description of your firm's experience in valuing assets in similar industries.
2. Provide the professional qualifications of the appraisers conducting the analysis. Please include years of experience, equipment/industry appraised, and any relevant professional designations.
3. Provide the state licenses for those appraisers valuing real property

Valuation Procedures

4. What procedures were conducted to verify the accuracy, completeness, and reliability of the fixed asset data information used as the basis of the valuation? Were the gross and net book values reconciled to consolidating balance sheets? If there were discrepancies, how were these resolved?
5. What is the aggregate net book value of the PP&E assets and how does this compare to the balance sheet as of the date of valuation?
6. For the assets inspected at the non-U.S. locations, what tasks were conducted during the site inspection?
7. For properties visited where you investigated the market for land values, and applied the cost approach for buildings, what market information was investigated for the improvements?
8. What procedures were performed to ensure there is no overlap with appraisals of non capital equipment assets (i.e. real property, internally developed software, identifiable intangibles)?
9. Are any assets held for sale, planned for retirement, abandoned? How were these assets valued? What management documentation/support and reasons are provided that agrees with this disposition or planned course of action?

Valuation Methodology

Cost Approach
10. Describe the methods and sources used to estimate replacement/reproduction cost new. Were the foreign fixed asset listings in the local currency? What adjustments to the calculated reproduction cost were made to consider currency and local inflation fluctuations? If exchange rates were used, what was the source? What differentiation in methodology was made for assets purchased domestically versus from a foreign supplier? If trend or inflation factors were used, what was their source?
11. What normal useful lives were assigned to the assets/asset categories to estimate physical depreciation? What is the average age of the assets within each asset category/classification?
12. Describe the physical depreciation methodology used (i.e., straight-line, Iowa Curve, etc.). If Iowa Curves were used, specify curve (R2, R3, L2, etc.), MTC factor, and inflation rate.
13. Were there any assets that have had major refurbishments affecting its remaining useful life? If so, how was the depreciation adjusted to account for such refurbishments?
14. How were assets valued if the age exceeds the normal useful life assigned?
15. Describe the methods, sources, and calculations used to estimate functional and economic obsolescence penalties. For those facilities operating under capacity, what is the reason? How long will this continue?
16. Please provide a sample of major assets utilizing the cost approach showing the calculations made from original cost to fair value (indirect) or replacement cost to fair value (direct). This list should represent 50 percent of the fair value of assets using the cost approach.
17. Was the life of the leases considered for valuing leasehold improvements? Are there renewal options?

Market Approach

18. Provide a sampling of major assets, market data, and adjustments used to conclude the applicable premise of value. This list should represent 50 percent of the fair value of assets valued using the market approach.
19. Were adjustments made to include the application of costs (i.e., installation, delivery, taxes) consistent with the value premise? Explain how the costs were determined and applied.

Additional Questions

20. Were there any assets that have been allocated, revalued, or reported at net book value as a result of a prior acquisition or transferred from another facility? If so, please identify and describe how these assets were valued.
21. Were any assets purchased used? If so, please identify and describe how these assets were valued.
22. How was construction in progress valued? Does this asset class include assets related to building and improvements? If so, were these already captured in the real property analysis?

ADDENDUM 4—REVENUE PROCEDURE 77-12

1977–1C.B. 569

Sec. 1. Purpose

The purpose of this Revenue Procedure is to set forth guidelines for use by taxpayers and Service personnel in making fair market value determinations in situations where a corporation purchases the assets of a business containing inventory items for a lump sum or where a corporation acquires assets including inventory items by the liquidation of a subsidiary pursuant to the provisions of section 332 of the Internal Revenue Code of 1954 and the basis of the inventory received in liquidation is determined under section 334(b)(2). These guidelines are designed to assist taxpayers and Service personnel in assigning a fair market value to such assets.

Sec. 2. Background

If the assets of a business are purchased for a lump sum, or if the stock of a corporation is purchased and that corporation is liquidated under section 332 of the Code and the basis is determined under section 334(b)(2), the purchase price must be allocated among the assets acquired to determine the basis of each of such assets. In making such determinations, it is necessary to determine the fair market value of any inventory items involved. This Revenue Procedure describes methods that may be used to determine the fair market value of inventory items.

In determining the fair market value of inventory under the situations set forth in this Revenue Procedure, the amount of inventory generally would be different from the amounts usually purchased. In addition, the goods in process and finished goods on hand must be considered in light of what a willing purchaser would pay and a willing seller would accept for the inventory at the various stages of completion, when the former is not under any compulsion to buy and the latter is not under any compulsion to sell, both parties having reasonable knowledge of relevant facts.

Sec. 3. Procedures for Determination of Fair Market Value

Three basic methods an appraiser may use to determine the fair market value of inventory are the cost of reproduction method, the comparative sales method, and the income method. All methods of valuation are based on one or a combination of these three methods.

.01 The cost of reproduction method generally provides a good indication of fair market value if inventory is readily replaceable in a wholesale or retail business, but generally should not be used in establishing the fair market value of the finished goods of a manufacturing concern. In valuing a particular inventory under this method, however, other factors may be relevant. For example, a well balanced inventory available to fill customers' orders in the ordinary course of business may have a fair market value in excess of its cost of reproduction because it provides a continuity of business, whereas an inventory containing obsolete merchandise unsuitable for customers might have a fair market value of less than the cost of reproduction.

.02 The comparative sales method utilizes the actual or expected selling prices of finished goods to customers as a basis of determining fair market values of those finished goods. When the expected selling price is used as a basis for valuing finished goods inventory, consideration should be given to the time that would be required to dispose of this inventory, the expenses that would be expected to be incurred in such disposition, for example, all costs of disposition, applicable discounts (including those for quantity), sales commissions, and freight and shipping charges, and a profit commensurate with the amount of investment and degree of risk. It should also be recognized that the inventory to be valued may represent a larger quantity than the normal trading volume and the expected selling price can be a valid starting point only if customers' orders are filled in the ordinary course of business.

.03 The income method, when applied to fair market value determinations for finished goods, recognizes that finished goods must generally be valued in a profit motivated business. Since the amount of inventory may be large in relation to normal trading volume the highest and best use of the inventory will be to provide for a continuity of the marketing operation of the going business. Additionally, the finished goods inventory will usually provide the only source of revenue of an acquired business during the period it is be being used to fill customers' orders. The historical financial data of an acquired company can be used to determine the amount that could be attributed to finished goods in order to pay all costs of disposition and provide a return on the investment during the period of disposition.

.04 The fair market value of work in process should be based on the same factors used to determine the fair market value of finished goods reduced by the expected costs of completion, including a reasonable profit allowance for the completion and selling effort of the acquiring corporation. In determining the fair market value of raw materials, the current costs of replacing the inventory in the quantities to be valued generally provides the most reliable standard.

Sec. 4. Conclusion

Because valuing inventory is an inherently factual determination, no rigid formulas can be applied. Consequently, the methods outlined above can only serve as guidelines for determining the fair market value of inventories.

CHAPTER 9

Valuation Discounts and Premiums

Two of the fundamental tools used by valuation analysts are discounts, which reduce the value of interests in closely held businesses, and premiums, which increase the value of those interests. The courts have recognized the validity of discounts and premiums at the conceptual level for many years. Tax cases have generally shown an evolving sophistication on the parts of both the courts and the valuation experts as regards the determination and application of discounts and premiums. The usefulness of some established studies for determining discounts and premiums has been questioned in recent years, both in journal articles and in court decisions. There is also the heightened visibility of more quantitative models such as put option models. Analysts will best use available data by remembering that discounts and premiums derive from valuation fundamentals such as timing, risk, and growth of cash flows of businesses and of specific ownership interests. They are really shorthand ways of talking about frequently recurring valuation relationships.

The most common valuation discounts and premiums arise from the basic concepts of control and marketability. A minority shareholder, whether in a publicly held or a privately held company, is often a passive investor with little or no input into how the company is run. In addition, a minority shareholder in a privately held company faces difficulty in finding ready buyers for his or her shares.

This chapter focuses primarily on the most commonly applied discount, the discount for lack of marketability, and the most well known premium, the control premium (or inversely the minority discount). Discounts for lack of control (DLOC)[1] quantify the level of risk assumed by a noncontrolling shareholder. Discounts for lack of marketability (DLOM) quantify the degree to which liquidity is impaired relative to more liquid alternative investments.

The data supporting discounts are covered in some detail later in the chapter, as is the nature of the underlying income streams. The chapter also discusses other discounts, such as the discounts for dependence on a key person, a restrictive agreement, or built-in capital gains. The chapter ends with an analysis of seminal court cases concerning the application of discounts and premiums. For examples on the application of discounts, see Chapters 9, 14, 25, and 27.

---

[1] The discount for lack of control is often referred to as a minority interest discount (MID) and the terms are used interchangeably in this chapter. However, it is important to note that majority shareholders can lack full control.

LEVELS OF VALUE

Discounts and premiums typically are applied near the end of a valuation engagement after the initial analysis is completed. If the initial analysis produces a minority interest value, then depending on the nature of the engagement, a control premium may be added to reach a control value or a marketability discount may be taken to lower the value. However, it is important to note that many analysts now adjust for control and minority in the cash flows of a business as opposed to more subjective applications of control premiums and minority discounts.

To illustrate the concept graphically, the valuation community has historically used a relationship chart (see Exhibit 9.1). This chart, which continues to evolve, shows the various bases to which a premium or discount would be applied.

Exhibit 9.1 Levels of Value (Old View)

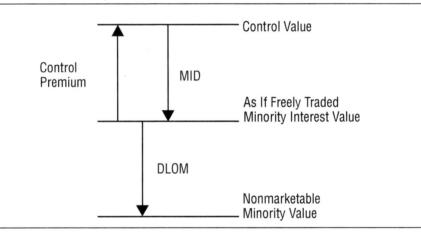

The chart shows the various applications of a control premium (if applicable), a discount for lack of control or minority discount (if applicable), and a discount for lack of marketability (or marketability discount). To understand the chart, start with the horizontal line in the center of the drawing. This level represents a marketable, minority value. To change this to a control value (represented by the horizontal line at the top of the chart), and depending on whether cash flows have been adjusted in certain circumstances, a control premium may be applied. To obtain a nonmarketable minority value (represented by the horizontal line at the bottom of the chart), a discount for lack of marketability is applied to the base marketable minority value.

This interpretation of the chart assumes that the initial valuation analysis has produced a marketable minority value. Obviously, this is not always the case. If the initial analysis produced a control level of value, then the base becomes the top horizontal line. To move this value to the nonmarketable minority value line at the bottom of this chart, two discount calculations may be appropiate, again, depending on whether adjustments have been made to the cash flow. If appropriate, first take a minority discount (the inverse of the control premium) to reach the marketable minority level, and then take a lack of marketability discount.

Note that when applying discounts, the process is multiplicative rather than additive. If, for example, there was a 20 percent minority interest discount and a 20 percent marketability discount, then the total discount is *not* 20 percent + 20 percent = 40 percent; rather, it would be:

$$[1 - (1 - 20\%) \times (1 - 20\%)] = 36\%$$

The traditional version of the levels of value shown as Exhibit 9.1 has generated continuing debate and several proposed refinements to the "levels of value" concept. The chart suggests that no discount for lack of marketability (or liquidity) should be applied to controlling interests, a point on which many analysts disagree. More accepted is the addition of a horizontal line above the control value level to reflect an acquisition or synergistic value. If added, the chart would look more like Exhibit 9.2.

Exhibit 9.2 Levels of Value (New View)

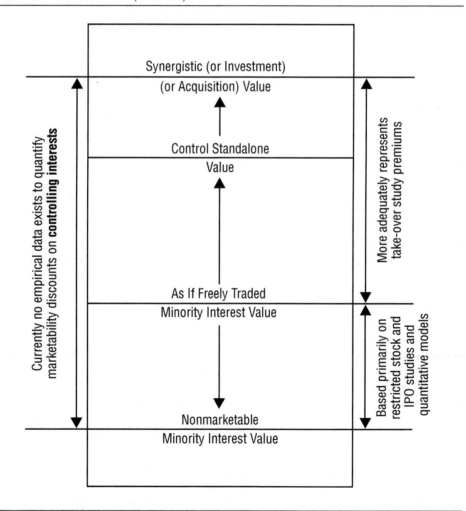

Note that some analysts refer to the "control standalone" value as the "financial control" value and to the "synergistic" value as the "strategic control" value.

The original chart (Exhibit 9.1) also suggested that the control value is always greater than the marketable minority interest value, but there is an exception. If there is no control premium, then the control value and the marketable minority value may be the same. Some analysts believe that the control standalone value and the as-if-freely-traded minority interest value will often be close.

Some analysts believe that the area between the as-if-freely-traded minority interest value and the nonmarketable minority interest value should be subdivided into "restricted [public] stock equivalent" and "private equity" levels of value because of the very long holding periods that are typical of private equity but rare among public restricted stocks.[2] See FMV Opinions restricted stock information later in this chapter for additional information.

Exhibit 9.3 presents another newer view on the interaction of the levels of value based, in part, on the method of valuation and the resultant value.

Exhibit 9.3   Levels of Value (Newer View)

- Control strategic (public or private company)
- Minority/control standalone liquid (public company)
- Control liquid (private company)
- Control standalone (private company)
- Minority nonmarketable (private company)

Control strategic can be for a public and a private company. An example of minority/control standalone liquid is the value resulting from the application of the guideline public company method (Chapter 7). Some analysts believe it is a minority value and some believe it is minority and control. An example of control liquid is the value derived from the application of the income approach (with control cash flows) where the discount or cap rate is based on returns from the public marketplace. Control standalone is the value of a private company after application of the income approach with a discount to reflect the lesser liquidity of a control interest in a private company vs. public stock. Minority nonmarketable is after the application of all discounts. Some of these "levels" of value may be higher or lower than the others depending on the circumstances.

Did you know that *liquidity* and *marketability* are not necessarily the same? Note, first, that anything liquid has to be marketable. However, the reverse is not true. An asset or ownership interest can be marketable, but not liquid.

Let's take two examples. Is an ownership interest in a public stock marketable? Sure it is. Is it liquid? Yes, of course. These days, you can sell public stock almost instantly and receive your cash within three days or so. Now, let's look at a 100 percent controlling interest in a private company. Is it marketable? Although there are exceptions, the answer, generally, is *yes*. Now, is this ownership interest liquid? The answer is, of course, *no*, assuming liquidity means the ability to convert to cash very quickly and easily, that is, public stock. Another example of marketable illiquid is real estate because, generally, it takes time to turn a parcel of real estate into cash by selling it.

---

[2] Espen Robak, "Liquidity and Levels of Value: A New Theoretical Framework," *Shannon Pratt's Business Valuation Update* (October 2004). The proposed method is to determine a restricted stock discount for a subject company by analyzing restricted stocks with similar financial characteristics and to determine a further private equity discount by analysis of large blocks of restricted stock, as most resembling private equity due to liquidation limitations from Rule 144 and from specific securities' trading volumes.

New Labels

We now have a new term for the valuation industry to consider: *marketable illiquid.* Consequently, we now have the following terms:

- Liquid
- Marketable illiquid
- Nonmarketable

Note that we do not include the term *liquid marketable,* since anything liquid has to be marketable. Similarly, we do not use the term *nonmarketable illiquid,* because anything nonmarketable has to be illiquid. Let's now distinguish some common assets and ownership interests:

- Public stock — *Liquid*
- Controlling interest in a private company — *Marketable illiquid*
- Minority interest in a private company — *Nonmarketable*
- Real estate — *Marketable illiquid*
- Machinery and equipment — *Marketable illiquid*

Degree of Marketability

The preceding labels do not, however, definitively address the *degree of marketability or nonmarketability* of the assets. For example, in a hot acquisition marketplace for a certain industry, some private companies may be more marketable than those in an industry that is not so hot. Also, some machinery and equipment may be sold more quickly; examples are vehicles and construction equipment (depending on the market). For a minority interest in a private company, the term *nonmarketable* does not assume that the interest cannot be sold, only that it is usually difficult to do so under normal circumstances.

The distinction drawn nevertheless goes beyond mere semantics by capturing the fact that the underlying valuation methodologies we often use are comparisons to trading prices and rates of return derived from public stocks that, again, can be sold almost instantly and are liquid. We are not advocating taking a liquidity discount in every case; we're just presenting the concept for consideration.[3]

CLASSIFYING DISCOUNTS

ValTip

Discounts and premiums may be classified as "entity level" or "shareholder level" depending on whether the driver for the premium or discount affects the entity as a whole, such as an environmental discount, or whether the driver reflects the characteristics of a specific ownership interest.

---

[3] James R. Hitchner, "In the Know," *CPA Expert* (Fall 2005), AICPA, p. 5.

Entity-Level Discounts

All valuation methodologies discussed in this book lead to value conclusions that are, ideally, based on sound assessments of risk concerning the:

- Subject company
- Industry
- Economy

These factors are referred to collectively as enterprise factors. That is, the value of the company is dependent on our assessment of these enterprise factors. There may be, however, other factors that would affect the company as a whole. Discounts that apply at the company or entity level include:

- Key-person discounts
- Contingent liability discounts (hazardous waste, etc.)
- Contingent litigation discounts
- Small company risks
- Nonhomogeneous assets discounts
- Customer/supplier base discounts (limited customers, loss of suppliers, etc.)
- Blockage and/or market absorption discounts

Some analysts reflect these entity-level discounts by increasing the rate of return (income approach) or by reducing the multiple (market approach).

Shareholder-Level Discounts

Other factors, such as the number of shareholders, the existence of a shareholders' agreement, and the like, would not, at least at this point in the valuation process, affect the value conclusion. This is because the number of shareholders or the existence of a shareholders' agreement are *shareholder-* or *security-specific* factors or attributes rather than *company-specific* factors. Although there may be isolated exceptions, strategic premiums, control premiums, and discounts for either lack of control or lack of marketability account for or measure the degree of these shareholder- or security-specific factors. These discounts and premiums pertain to specific ownership interests.

ValTip

Control premiums *quantify the value of controlling the destiny of the company* and/or the ability to divert cash flows and value to the controlling ownership. Acquisition or strategic premiums *quantify the incremental value of a particular investment as viewed by a specific investor(s)*. There is empirical evidence of the size of combined control and strategic premiums. However, these data do not separate the two types of premiums.

Far too often, control premiums have been overstated by the use of these combined data (control and strategic premiums) as a proxy for control premiums only.

Lack of control and marketability are not unrelated. A majority shareholder may be able to affect marketability in ways that a minority shareholder cannot. Pursuing a sale, a merger, or an initial public offering are examples of such situations. Thus, the two discounts, while separate, should be considered in conjunction with each other.

Controversial Issues

Several undecided issues in the valuation community have either a direct or indirect effect on the discounts and premiums applied to a base of value. Major areas of debate include whether:

- Public companies trade at a control, minority interest, or some other mixed level of value
- There are liquidity discounts that are applicable to control values
- Control-related earnings' adjustments should be made in all valuation engagements
- Restricted stock and initial public offering studies serve as "starting point" proxies for lack of marketability of minority interests
- The use of discounted cash flow (DCF) models or option pricing models is a sound tool for determining marketability discounts of minority interests

Some of these issues are hotly debated in the valuation community while other issues are less controversial. We address these issues throughout this chapter and give the reader, at the very least, viable options to consider. When taking a position on one of these controversial issues, analysts must be prepared to defend their position.

DISCOUNTS FOR LACK OF CONTROL AND CONTROL PREMIUMS

Advantage of Control/Disadvantages of Lack of Control

From the point of view of the minority shareholder, the majority shareholder's ability to control can reduce or eliminate the return on the minority shareholder's investment.

Some examples of the actions the majority shareholder can take to reduce the return on the minority shareholder's investment are:

- *Paying excess compensation and perquisites* to the majority shareholder, to his or her relatives, or to others without giving a proportionate benefit to the minority shareholder. The perks could include paying for trips, meals, autos, retirement plans, medical care, or education expenses. Paying higher compensation and expenses reduces the earnings of the corporation by distributing those funds to the majority shareholder or his or her designee.
- *Having favorable dealings with the corporation.* The majority shareholder could enter into various transactions with the corporation on terms and conditions favorable to him or her. For example, the majority stockholder could:
  - Lease a building to the corporation at higher-than-market rates
  - Borrow funds from the corporation at a lower-than-market interest rate or lend funds to the company at a higher-than-market interest rate
  - Hold corporate meetings in a favorite resort location and reimburse the board of directors but not the minority shareholders for attending
  - Decide to invest in certain opportunities personally rather than on behalf of the corporation
  - Cause the corporation to support charities or make investments of the shareholder's choosing
  - Take some actions to force the minority shareholder out of investment in the corporation
  - Merge the corporation with another corporation, seeking to cash out the minority investor instead of offering that investor the opportunity to continue with his or her investment
  - Sell all or substantially all of the corporate assets, or liquidate and dissolve the corporate entity
  - Have the corporation go through a reverse stock split, thereby reducing the number of shares in the corporation. (For example, a 1-for-10 reverse stock split would reduce a shareholder's nine shares to 9/10 of a share. Under some state laws, such a fractional share may be bought out for fair value.)

In most states, majority control is not absolute. A majority shareholder may have certain duties to other shareholders, including a fiduciary responsibility to manage the company in a way that provides for the benefit of all shareholders. Officers and directors may have a duty of loyalty and, therefore, a duty not to deprive the corporation of favorable business opportunities. States also vary in the way they define control. In some "supermajority" states, certain corporate decisions may require a shareholder vote of just over 50 percent.

Limiting the Risk of the Minority Position

There are various ways to protect a minority shareholder from the full risk of the minority shareholder position, thereby reducing the amount of the discount for lack of control. These break down as follows.

Public Market Liquidity

If the company is a public company, the shareholder can readily liquidate his or her investment in the stock if he or she disagrees with the policies of management. This is a main reason some analysts believe that minority interests in public companies typically trade at or near control standalone value for that public company.

Rights and Restrictions Through Agreements

These may take several forms:

Articles of Incorporation. The articles of incorporation may include allocations of rights, such as creation of multiple classes of stock with each class entitled to elect certain directors. Also, in certain transactions, such as the sale of substantially all of the company's assets or a merger, a majority of each class of stock may be required to approve corporate actions.

Cumulative Voting. Bylaws may provide for cumulative voting that may allow minority shareholders to elect some of the board of directors.

Preemptive Rights. Preemptive rights in the bylaws would allow all shareholders the opportunity to keep their pro rata share upon the issuance of additional stock in the company as opposed to having their interest diluted by the majority shareholder issuing additional shares to him- or herself at an attractive price.

Superior Majority. There could be requirements for a superior majority for certain corporate actions. For example, instead of requiring over 50 percent approval to increase the company president's salary, a 75 percent approval might be required, thereby giving a 30 percent shareholder effective veto power in that situation. Some states have "supermajority vote requirements" for some major corporate actions such as mergers and liquidations.

Shareholder Agreements. Shareholder agreements can set forth the rights and responsibilities of each of the shareholders under various circumstances. For example, a buy-sell agreement could require either the majority shareholder or the corporation to buy back the minority shareholder's stock at a set price or set formula upon the occurrence of some event, such as death or retirement of the shareholder; or a minority shareholder could force the company or the majority shareholder to buy stock at a set price under a "put" option or right.

Employment Agreements. Employment agreements may give further protection to a minority shareholder who also works for the corporation to ensure that he or she will not be discharged and therefore lose the benefits of being an employee.

Right of First Refusal. If the majority shareholder has a right of first refusal, minority shareholders are free to sell their stock to anyone they choose at any price they choose, but the majority shareholder would have the right to match the price and buy the stock as opposed to having a third party buy the stock. However, a buy-sell agreement and right of first refusal also can give the minority shareholder an opportunity to buy out the majority shareholder upon certain events, such as death or disability.

Other Agreements. Other agreements can restrict or combine voting rights. For example, a group of shareholders, typically minority shareholders, may form a voting trust, agreeing to vote their stock as a block and thereby achieving a majority position.

Judicial Remedies

Courts often have found a fiduciary responsibility on the part of a majority shareholder not to operate the company in a way that unreasonably disadvantages the minority shareholders. Sometimes courts will enforce such a duty on a majority shareholder who sells an interest to a third party, but the third party does not purchase the interest of the minority shareholder. Frequently a minority shareholder is discharged as an employee, and that, coupled with a lack of dividends, may precipitate a judicial review. Under the statutes of a majority of the states, noncontrolling stockholders, under certain circumstances, can bring suit to dissolve the corporation.

Appraisal Rights

A merger and certain other transactions involving the stock, including allegations of violation of fiduciary responsibilities, may give the minority shareholder appraisal rights—that is, the right to have the stock appraised and to sell such stock either to the company or to the majority shareholder for fair value. Frequently, exercising these appraisal rights requires very strict adherence to complex procedural rules. Failure to follow the procedural requirements exactly may prevent a minority shareholder from meeting the requirements for judicial enforcement of appraisal rights.

Levels of Noncontrolling Interests

There are varying degrees in ownership from the pure minority interest position to a 100 percent controlling interest. Starting at the highest level of ownership, the ownership pecking order may look something like what is shown in Exhibit 9.4.

Exhibit 9.4   Levels of Ownership

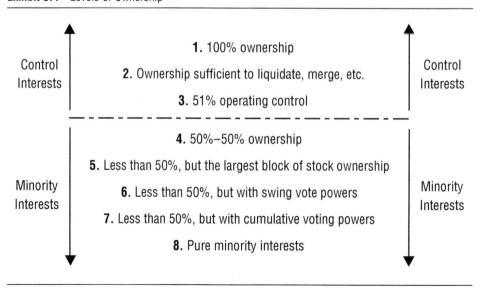

To begin, the level of the noncontrolling interest must be determined. As identified above, levels 3 and 4 represent, respectively, the weakest controlling interest and the strongest noncontrolling interest. Courts generally view any interest greater than 50 percent as a controlling interest, absent factors and/or agreements to the contrary, for example LP interests in an FLP. Interests of exactly 50 percent are common but, unfortunately, raise additional control/noncontrol issues. Although those 50 percent interests lack control, they generally do have veto power. This veto power gives rise to corporate stalemates and, sometimes, corporate dissolution due to disputes between 50-50 shareholders.

The first level of control is one holding a 51 percent or more interest, but less than any "supermajority" qualifying level of interest that may exist in that jurisdiction. As stated earlier, a "greater than 50 percent interest" does not imply, necessarily, the ability to effect liquidation, merger, or any other fundamental change of the company. In some states, as well as in some corporate charters, a two-thirds majority or more is required to liquidate, restructure, or approve a merger. Accordingly, a position of ownership that is insufficient to effect these types of major corporate changes may be assigned a lower value on a per-share basis. The next level of control is for those supermajority interests that have the power of liquidation and merger yet hold less than 100 percent of the stock.

Where there are interests of less than 50 percent representing the largest block, they may be in a quasi-controlling position, while still having little control over their future when compared to true control. An interest of less than 50 percent, but with cumulative voting powers, could secure for a minority shareholder a seat at the board table. A seat on the board of directors could be significant, as it would ensure that a minority shareholder's voice would be heard. Accordingly, such an interest may have a smaller discount for lack of control than an otherwise identical stock without cumulative voting.

Another important issue relative to the position of the minority interests is the ownership of the other interests. *Fragmentation* ownership of the other interests can play an important role on the level of input a minority shareholder will have. For example, a 10 percent shareholder may have more input than any one of the ten 1 percent shareholders would have. The corresponding 90 percent shareholder may tend to be more responsive to the 10 percent minority shareholder than to any, or all, of the ten 1 percent shareholders.

David W. Simpson wrote an article dealing with these issues of ownership. In his article, Simpson illustrated the effects the interests of others might have on one's ownership interest (see Exhibits 9.5 to 9.7).[4]

Exhibit 9.5 Effects of Ownership Interests

	A	B	C
Factors leading to a *smaller* discount for a greater than 50% block.	Equity interest sufficient to liquidate block, merge, or restructure.	Equity interest permits control of the Board of Directors.	Fragmented ownership of the remaining interest in the company.
Factors leading to a *larger* discount for a greater than 50% block.	Equity interest insufficient to liquidate, merge, or restructure.	Cumulative voting: Interest cannot control the entire Board of Directors.	Concentrated ownership of the remaining interest in the company.

[4] David W. Simpson, "Minority Interest and Marketability Discounts: A Perspective: Part I," *Business Valuation Review* (March 1991).

Exhibit 9.6 Effects of Ownership Interests

	A	B	C
Factors leading to a *smaller* discount for a block of less than 50% of the equity.	Equity interest sufficient to suppress a merger, liquidation, or restructure.	Cumulative voting: Interest is sufficient to affect the Board of Directors.	Fragmented ownership of the remaining interest in the company.
Factors leading to a *larger* discount for a block of less than 50% of the equity.	Equity interest insufficient to suppress a merger, liquidation, or restructure.	Interest cannot affect the Board of Directors.	Concentrated ownership of the remaining interest in the company.

Exhibit 9.7 Effects of Ownership Interests

	Ranking
	Least Impaired
Greater than 50% equity interest	
100% Ownership	1
Less than 100% Interest	
Interest sufficient to liquidate, merge, or restructure	2
Interest insufficient to liquidate, merge, or restructure	
Interest permits control of the Board	3
Cumulative voting: Can't control entire board	
Fragmented remainder[a]	4
Concentrated remainder[b]	5
Less than 50% equity interest	
Interest sufficient to suppress merger, liquidation, etc.	
Cumulative voting: Interest can affect Board	
Fragmented remainder	6
Concentrated remainder	7
Interest cannot affect Board	
Fragmented remainder	8
Concentrated remainder	9
Interest insufficient to suppress merger, liquidation, etc.	
Cumulative voting: Interest can affect Board	
Fragmented remainder	10
Concentrated remainder	11
Interest cannot affect Board	
Fragmented remainder	12
Concentrated remainder	13
	Most Impaired

[a] Fragmented ownership of remaining interest in company
[b] Concentrated ownership of remaining interest in company

His article concluded with something similar to the above chart showing 13 levels of ownership interest and control/impairment of control.

It is important to note that ranking number 12, "Interest cannot affect Board, Fragmented remainder," could be less impaired than another interest of another company with a ranking of, say, 6, depending on the behavior of the controlling shareholder toward minority shareholders.

Control Premium Studies

The quantification of the amount of the discount for lack of control (or the minority discount) is difficult due to the lack of empirical evidence in this area.

One of the few sources of data comes from the analysis of acquisitions of public companies. If the price paid for the entire company exceeds the market capitalization of the company prior to announcement of the acquisition, then that difference is a control premium and probably includes an acquisition (i.e., strategic) premium. The *Control Premium Study*, a quarterly publication from FactSet Mergerstat, LLC, www.mergerstat.com tracks premiums for completed transactions involving publicly traded target companies where a controlling interest was acquired.[5] The simple formula below converts the control premium to a minority discount:

$$\text{DLOC} = 1 - \frac{1}{1 + \text{Observed Premium}}$$

Where:

Observed Premium may include both control and strategic components, and DLOC = Discount for lack of control

The Mergerstat data include synergistic and acquisition premiums along with the control premium, and segregation of these premiums is difficult.

Not all analysts view the control premium studies as reflecting both control and strategic premiums. There is a view that the premiums observed in acquisitions are "unrelated to the strategic nature of an acquisition."[6] This view rests primarily on studies showing that expected synergies don't materialize in most

---

[5] FactSet Mergerstat, LLC, also publishes the *Mergerstat Review,* which provides an annual Control Premium Study.
[6] George P. Roach, "Control Premiums and Strategic Mergers, 1989 to 2002," *Business Valuation Review* (March 2003).

acquisitions as well as studies showing that neither the premiums paid nor the acquisitions' success varies, as might be expected, with the degree of relatedness of the industires (as measured by SIC codes) of acquirers and targets. However, at the time of acquisition, premiums are paid by strategic buyers whom we must assume believed that synergies existed to justify the higher purchase price.

Using the Guideline Public Company Method to Arrive at a Minority Value

One common method for obtaining the fair market value of a minority interest in a closely held company is to correlate the various valuation multiples of guideline companies with the closely held company in the market approach technique known as the guideline public company method.

While many analysts accept that the market approach using guideline publicly traded companies yields a minority value, many other experts believe that the guideline public company method may, in fact, not result in just a minority interest value, that is, minority and control in a public company are the same, *even though the market prices are those of minority interests.* According to Eric Nath:

> I have concluded that demonstrable control premiums are rare in public companies, and that, for the most part, statistics on control premiums provide little or no useful information when attempting to estimate the fair market value of a controlling interest in a private company. Therefore, valuation of a private company using a publicly traded comparative should result in a majority interest value.[7]

It is the responsibility of the management and board of directors of a public company to run the company to the benefit of all shareholders regardless of the size of the holding. As such, as the fortunes of the entire company go, so also go the fortunes of minority shareholders. If the company does well, so does the minority interest. If the company does poorly, so does the minority interest. As such, under fair market value, minority and controlling interests in public companies may be so intertwined that they are essentially similar.

Many analysts also believe that the application of public company valuation multiples to control cash flows results in a control value, while their application to non control cash flows results in a minority interest value. Since a multiple is really an inverted cap rate, this position may not be that different from the same concept for the income approach as presented below, which is generally accepted.

Control and the Income Approach

In regard to the income approach to value, Dr. Shannon Pratt states: "First, most, if not all, of the difference between a control value and a minority value in a discounted economic income model results from differences in the projected economic income (the numerator), not from differences in the discount rate."[8]

---

[7] Eric Nath, "Control Premiums and Minority Interest Discounts in Private Companies," *Business Valuation Review* (June 1990). Emphasis added.

[8] Shannon P. Pratt, *Valuing a Business: The Analysis and Appraisal of Closely Held Companies,* 5th ed. (New York: McGraw-Hill, Inc.), p. 228.

> The use of minority cash flows in the income approach produces a minority interest value. As discussed in Chapter 5, minority cash flows are those cash flows *without* any adjustments due to controlling shareholders actions such as excess compensation, rent payments, or perquisites.

When valuing a minority interest, it may be preferable to start work at the minority interest level rather than take on the additional work and risk of error involved in discounting back to a minority value from a control value. Conversely, when valuing a controlling interest, it may be easier to start with a control value than to add a control premium.

However, the argument for making control-related adjustments was made in a September 1992 article in *Business Valuation Review*.[9] The authors stated: "While it is true that the minority shareholder in a privately held company may not be able to control management salaries and other expense items, we feel that by not adjusting the financial statements to market levels the value of the minority interest will be, in most cases, unacceptably low, or in fact zero." They also said: "it is not always the case that a minority shareholder is unable to influence the levels of expenses." Furthermore, they indicate that "we believe that by not adjusting the financial statements there is potential for what would effectively be a double discount."[10] Unfortunately, the authors did not suggest a method for quantifying the discount for lack of control.

Z. Christopher Mercer detailed a related view in his 2004 book, *Valuing Enterprise and Shareholder Cash Flows: The Integrated Theory of Business Valuation*. The "marketable minority level of cash flow is assumed to be 'normalized' for unusual or non recurring events and to have an expense structure that is market-based, at least in terms of owner/key shareholder compensation . . ." he writes, arguing that "the normalization of earnings is not a 'control' process, but one of equating private company earnings to their as-if-public equivalent."[11] Mercer believes that such adjustments are required to correctly use public guideline company multiples in the market approach, and public company rate of return

> Consistency is important. Whether you start with control cash flows or minority cash flows, it is important to apply this methodology consistently throughout your minority value engagements.

---

[9] William C. Herber, Patrick K. Smith, and Robert J. Strachota, "Fairness in Minority Interest Valuation," *Business Valuation Review* (September 1992).

[10] The authors were assuming that one would not consider control adjustments in the first place and then second, apply a discount for lack of control.

[11] Z. Christopher Mercer, *Valuing Enterprise and Shareholder Cash Flows: The Integrated Theory of Business Valuation* (Memphis: Peabody Publishing LP), p. 89, and p. 96.

information in the income approach, and that factors such as excess compensation, perquisites, and favorable corporate dealings by a controlling shareholder should therefore be treated in the discount for lack of marketability, not the minority interest discount. Many analysts disagree and believe that it is not necessary to first perform a control valuation when valuing a minority interest.[12,13]

DISCOUNTS FOR LACK OF MARKETABILITY

The concept of *marketability* deals with the liquidity of the interest—that is, how quickly and certainly it can be converted to cash at the owner's discretion. For this text, we define *marketability* as "the ability to quickly convert property to cash at minimal cost," using the definition provided by the *International Glossary of Business Valuation Terms.*

Marketability expresses the relative ease and promptness with which a security or commodity may be sold when desired, at a representative current price, without material concession in price merely because of the goal of a prompt sale.

The Internal Revenue Service (IRS) speaks to the concept of marketability in Revenue Ruling 77-287, which addresses the valuation of restricted stock. It touches on many important issues regarding general marketability discount theory and practice as well as detailing the IRS's position relative to the marketability of restricted stocks.

With respect to the investment characteristics of assets, the terms "marketability" and "liquidity" are often used interchangeably. The *International Business Valuation Glossary* defines liquidity as "the ability to quickly convert property to cash or pay a liability."

In the context of business valuations, the terms "marketability" and "liquidity" are often loosely used. Most analysts do not make distinctions between liquidity and marketability and capture both elements in the marketability discount applied to closely held companies. However, as previously mentioned, there may be a difference between liquidity and marketability when using rates of return or valuation multiples from public companies and applying these to less liquid controlling interests in a private company.

Other factors being equal, publicly traded securities are more marketable and liquid than the securities of private concerns, and securities with restrictions are generally less marketable than securities without restrictions. David W. Simpson, in the second part of his article on minority interest and marketability discounts, illustrated the factors that would tend to increase or decrease the discount for lack of marketability.[14] The illustration is shown in Exhibit 9.8.

---

[12] See, for example, Samuel Y. Wessinger, "Public Equivalent Value: Are Earnings Adjustments Required in Minority Interest Valuations?" *Valuation Strategies* (July/August 2005).

[13] James R. Hitchner, "Resources Tip of the Month," *ABV E-Alert,* 2005.

[14] David W. Simpson, "Minority Interest and Marketability Discounts: A Perspective: Part II," *Business Valuation Review* (June 1991).

Exhibit 9.8 Factors Affecting Marketability

	A	B	C	D
Factors leading to a *smaller* discount for lack of marketability	Publicly traded	No restrictions on the sale of the securities	Registered securities	Active market relative to the size of the block in question
Factors leading to a *larger* discount for lack of marketability	Closely held	Restrictions on the sale of securities	Unregistered securities	Thin market relative to the size of the block in question

Marketability/Liquidity Discounts for Controlling Interests

There has been an ongoing debate as to whether a discount for lack of marketability/ liquidity should be applied or even considered when valuing a controlling interest. The opponents of marketability discounts are fairly consistent in their arguments that the lack of marketability is included in the pricing of the controlling interest. Proponents of discounts believe some discount should be made over and above the discount rate or price multiple based upon the valuation method employed.

Selling a controlling interest in a privately held company is a difficult task. For that matter, so is selling a controlling interest of a publicly held company. However, a controlling interest in a privately held corporation is certainly "locked in" for a period of time, and it is obviously more than the three days or so that are typically needed to transact a publicly held minority interest and receive your cash.

Annual national surveys showed that the average time required to sell a business during 2000–2002 varied from 172 to 228 days. A 2003 survey indicated that only 6 percent of businesses sold in less than three months, while 34 percent took from three to six months to sell, and 37 percent took from seven to nine months, with 7 percent requiring over a year to sell.[15] The privately held company experiences extra uncertainty not only of the time required for the sale but also of the eventual sales price. In addition, there are typically more costs in preparing for the sale, relative to the size of the

ValTip

While some experts support a discount, there remains no direct empirical evidence to support a discount for the lack of marketability/liquidity for a controlling interest. Remember that all the initial public offering and restricted stock studies deal with minority interests and not controlling interests.

---

[15] Tom West, *The 2005 Business Reference Guide: The Essential Guide to Pricing a Business* (Business Brokerage Press), p. 591.

company, such as business valuation services and accounting and legal costs. To further complicate things, it is quite likely the sale will not transact for cash but will include some deferred payments or notes, assuming the buyer will not back out at the last minute.

Proponents of a DLOM point out that these costs and risks greatly exceed the cost of normal transfers of publicly held stock and that this justifies a marketability discount. They argue that discounts for lack of marketability exist, even in the absence of empirical data. When discounts for lack of marketability or liquidity of controlling interests are taken, they tend to be smaller than discounts for lack of marketability of minority interests. The U.S. Tax Court has recognized discounts for lack of marketability of controlling interests.

As mentioned earlier in this chapter, when comparisons are made to liquid public stocks in the application of a valuation method, that liquidity may be embedded in the private company value.

Many analysts believe that discounts for lack of marketability or liquidity for controlling interests generally range from 0 to 20 percent, depending on the specific facts and circumstances and the prediscount valuation method employed.

ValTip

DLOM studies are usually based on two types of analyses:

1. Studies based on the difference between the initial public offering (IPO) price of a company and transactions in the same company's stock prior to the IPO. These are referred to as IPO studies.
2. Studies that measure the difference between the private price of a restricted security and the publicly traded stock price of the same company. These are referred to as restricted stock studies.

EMPIRICAL EVIDENCE OF MARKETABILITY DISCOUNTS

There is no dissension in the valuation community concerning the applicability of a lack of marketability discount to a minority interest in a privately held company. There are a number of studies and a wealth of empirical evidence supporting such a discount.

Initial Public Offering Studies

Several IPO studies since 1980 have analyzed the stock prices of companies before and after they became public. The Emory studies are without a doubt the most extensive and, over these past 20 years or so, have been relied on by many valuation experts as empirical evidence of marketability discounts. Other studies have followed, some extending Emory's data and others developing data of their own.

Emory Studies[16]

Since 1980, John D. Emory has been researching the value of stocks before and after they became public companies. Emory has published numerous IPO studies starting in January 1980 and ending December 2000. These studies have been published in *Business Valuation Review*, a journal of the Business Valuation Committee of the American Society of Appraisers.

Emory states: "It was my thought that if I could relate the prices at which private transactions took place before the initial public offering to the price at which the stock was offered subsequently to the public I would be able to gauge, in a somewhat objective way, the value of marketability."

In his first eight studies (1/80–4/97) Emory reviewed over 2,200 prospectuses and analyzed 310 transactions. He eliminated development-stage companies, companies with operating losses, and companies with IPO prices less than $5 per share. All of the transactions took place within a five-month period prior to the IPO. In that regard Emory states, "since an initial public offering often takes four or five months from conception to completion, the transactions mentioned in the prospectuses in the study would almost certainly have reflected the likelihood of marketability within the next half year and any other value adjustment associated with being a public company."

According to Emory, companies in the transactions of the study:

> were promising in nature, and their securities had good potential for becoming readily marketable. Why else would investors have bought the unregistered stock and why would a bona fide investment banker pursue a firm underwriting commitment? It should be noted that almost all of the major investment banks are represented as lead underwriters of the IPOs used in this study, as has been the case in the previous studies.

In general, most of the transactions were with promising companies where marketability was probable.

The transactions in the studies were primarily the granting of stock options at the stock's then fair market value. The remaining transactions involved sales of stock. Of the 310 transactions studied, 239, or 77 percent, were stock options.

In defending the stock option prices used by the companies in the studies, Emory states "in most cases, the transactions were stated to have been, or could reasonably be expected to have been, at fair market value. All ultimately would have had to be able to withstand Securities and Exchange Commission [SEC], IRS, or judicial review, particularly in light of the subsequent public offering."

The mean and median discounts for lack of marketability indicated by the aggregate of Emory's first eight studies of transactions that occurred five months prior to an IPO were 44 and 43 percent, respectively. For the more recent of these periods studied, November 1995 to April 1997, the mean discount was 43 percent and the median discount was 42 percent (see Exhibit 9.9). The most recent studies up to 2000 indicate higher discounts.

---

[16] John D. Emory, "The Value of Marketability as Illustrated in Initial Public Offerings of Common Stock (eighth in a series), November 1995 through April 1997," *Business Valuation Review* (September 1997), pp. 123–124.

Exhibit 9.9 Summary of the Emory Studies

Period of Study	Number of Transactions	Mean Discount	Median Discount
May 1997–December 2000[a]	283	50%	52%
May 1997–December 2000[b]	36	48%	44%
May 1997–March 2000[c]	53	54%	54%
November 1995–April 1997	91	43%	42%
January 1994–June 1995	46	45%	45%
February 1992–July 1993	54	45%	44%
August 1990–January 1992	35	42%	40%
February 1989–July 1990	23	45%	40%
August 1987–January 1989	27	45%	45%
January 1985–June 1986	21	43%	43%
January 1980–June 1981	13	60%	66%
Combined Results[d]	593	47%	48%

(a) The Expanded Study
(b) The Limited Study
(c) The Dot.Com Study
(d) To avoid double counting, transactions from the Dot.Com Study and Limited Study are included only as a part of the Expanded Study

The following is a brief explanation of each study:

- *January 1, 1980–June 20, 1981.* Emory reviewed private placements of securities taking place prior to initial public offerings. The difference between the price of a security sold prior to the IPO and the offering price is the discount for lack of marketability. Emory examined 97 prospectuses of securities offered in the period from January 1, 1980, through June 30, 1981. Of the 97 IPOs, he chose 13 that involved "financially sound" companies and transactions that took place no more than five months prior to the IPO. Emory found that the private placements sold at a mean discount of 60 percent and a median of 66 percent.
- *January 1985–June 1986.* Emory analyzed 21 IPOs and the transactions taking place immediately before the offerings. His analysis showed that the mean discount of the securities before the offerings was 43 percent with a median of 43 percent. Emory attributed the difference between the mean of this study (43 percent) and the mean of a similar study he performed in 1980 (60 percent) to the fact that the market for initial public offerings in 1986 was more active.
- *August 1987–January 1989.* Emory reviewed the prospectuses of 98 IPOs, of which 27 met the study criteria of financial soundness, an IPO price greater than $5, and transactions taking place five months before the offering. He found that the mean discount of the securities sold before the initial public offering was 45 percent with a median of 45 percent.
- *February 1989–July 1990.* Emory's analysis of transactions of 23 companies showed that the mean discount for lack of marketability was 45 percent with a median of 40 percent.
- *August 1990–January 1992.* Out of 35 transactions, Emory found that the mean discount on the price of the securities was 42 percent with a median of 40 percent.
- *February 1992–July 1993.* Emory reviewed the transaction data of 54 companies selling securities in IPOs. He found that the average discount on the price of the secu-

rities was 45 percent with a median of 44 percent. Consolidating the results of the six studies, he found the mean discount of the total 173 transactions to be 47 percent.

- *January 1994–June 1995*. Emory evaluated 46 IPO transactions. Both the mean and median discounts on the purchase price of the securities before the IPO were 45 percent. The discounts ranged from 79 to 6 percent. Emory combined the results of all seven studies and found that the mean discount for the 219 transactions to date in all the studies was 45 percent and the median was 43 percent.
- *November 1995–April 1997*. Emory evaluated 91 transactions. The mean and median discounts on these transactions were 43 and 42 percent, respectively. The range of discount was 5 to 85 percent. The combined results of the 310 transactions to date in all the Emory studies indicated a mean discount of 44 percent and a median discount of 43 percent.
- *May 1997–March 2000 (Dot.Com Companies)*. For the first time, Emory included Dot.Com companies in his study, and evaluated 53 transactions. The mean and median discounts on these transactions were 54 percent.
- *May 1997–December 2000*. Emory prepared two studies based on his review of 1,847 IPO prospectuses over this period. In his "limited" study, he analyzed 36 transactions and found a mean discount of 48 percent and a median discount of 44 percent. In his "expanded" study, he broadened his search and did not eliminate companies on the basis of financial strength. The "expanded" study analyzed 283 transactions and found a mean discount of 50 percent and a median discount of 52 percent. Over the entire 11 studies from 1980 to 2000, the 593 transactions analyzed had a mean discount of 47 percent and a median discount of 48 percent.

Emory reviewed all of his studies and underlying data in 2002 in response to certain criticisms that had been made regarding them. He found little impact from the resulting adjustments and corrections of minor errors. "Our adjustments made little difference to the mean and median discounts . . . overall mean and median discounts for all 543 transactions after our adjustments decreased by 1%, to 46% and 47%, respectively."[17]

The adjusted data is as shown in Exhibit 9.10.

Exhibit 9.10 Summary of the Emory Studies (Adjusted 10/10/02)

Period of Study	Number of Transactions	Mean Discount	Median Discount
May 1997–December 2000	266	50%	52%
November 1995–April 1997	84	43%	41%
January 1994–June 1995	45	45%	47%
February 1992–July 1993	49	45%	43%
August 1990–January 1992	30	34%	33%
February 1989–July 1990	17	46%	40%
August 1987–January 1989	21	38%	43%
January 1985–June 1986	19	43%	43%
January 1980–June 1981	12	59%	68%
Total	543	46%	47%

---

[17] John D. Emory Sr., F. R. Dengel III, and John D. Emory Jr., "Discounts for Lack of Marketability Emory Pre-IPO Discount Studies 1980–2000, As Adjusted October 10, 2002," *Business Valuation Review* (December 2002). Excel spreadsheet with the detailed data is available at www.emoryco.com.

Willamette Management Associates Studies[18]

Willamette Management Associates has published the results of more than 20 studies (time periods) that analyze IPO transactions that took place from 1975 to 2000. The premise of the studies was similar to that of the Emory studies; Willamette compared the sale price of stock placed privately before an IPO to the price at IPO to determine the discount for lack of marketability.

The Willamette studies, however, reviewed transactions that took place from 1 to 36 months before the initial public offering, whereas Emory analyzed transactions up to five months prior to IPO. Emory used information provided in the company prospectuses while Willamette used S-1 and S-18 registration statements which disclosed more information. Willamette also compared the price-earnings (P/E) multiple of the security at the time of the private transaction to the P/E multiple at the IPO.

Willamette also made adjustments to reflect differences in market conditions between the dates. To do this, Willamette used an Industry P/E multiple at the time of offering and compared it to the Industry P/E multiple at the time of the private transaction.

Exhibit 9.11 presents the results of the Willamette studies.

Exhibit 9.11   Lack of Marketability Discount

Willamette Management Associates Summary of Discounts for Private Transaction
P/E Multiples Compared to Public Offering
P/E Multiples Adjusted for Changes in Industry P/E Multiples[a]

Period of Study	Median Discount
1975–1978	52.5%
1979	62.7%
1980–1982	56.5%
1983	60.7%
1984	73.1%
1985	42.6%
1986	47.4%
1987	43.8%
1988	51.8%
1989	50.3%
1990	48.5%
1991	31.8%
1992	51.7%
1993	53.3%
1994	42.0%
1995	58.7%
1996	44.3%
1997	35.2%
1998	49.4%[b]
1999	27.7%[b]
2000	31.9%[b]

[a] Shannon P. Pratt, *Business Valuation Discounts and Premiums* (New York: John Wiley & Sons, Inc., 2001), p. 84.
[b] Data from www.willamette.com.

---

[18] Shannon P. Pratt, *Business Valuation Discounts and Premiums* (New York: John Wiley & Sons, 2001), 84.

Summary of the Emory and Willamette Initial Public Offering Studies

The range of discounts associated with both the Emory and Willamette IPO studies is from a low of 32 percent to a high of 73 percent. The majority of the discounts are in the range of 40 to 60 percent. As discussed later, critics of these studies are concerned with the reliability of both the pre-IPO prices and the IPO prices.

Hitchner Study No. 1

James R. Hitchner, CPA/ABV, ASA, and Katherine E. Morris performed an additional analysis on the Emory study data. Emory reported average discounts for companies that had transactions in their stock within five months prior to IPO. Hitchner and Morris analyzed and calculated the discounts on transactions taking place in the fifth, fourth, and third months, respectively, prior to the date of the IPO to see if the discounts were higher for those companies that had transactions farthest from the IPO date. Hitchner and Morris also analyzed the discounts on transactions taking place up to five, four, and three months, respectively, prior to the date of the IPO. They also separately analyzed data on stock options only.

Discounts on transactions occurring between January 1980 and June 1995 were broken into fifth-, fourth-, and third-month analyses up to and including each period.

- *Fifth Month.* The mean and median discounts on the 47 transactions taking place in the fifth month prior to the IPOs were 54 and 50 percent, respectively. For the 219 transactions that took place within five months prior to the IPOs, the mean and median discounts were 45 and 43 percent, respectively.
- *Fourth Month.* The mean and median discounts on the 43 transactions that took place in the fourth month prior to the IPOs were both 51 percent. For the 172 transactions that took place within four months prior to the IPOs, the mean and median discounts were 43 and 42 percent, respectively.
- *Third Month.* The mean and median discounts on the 56 transactions taking place in the third month prior to the initial public offerings were 43 and 42 percent, respectively. For the 129 transactions that took place within three months of the initial public offerings (i.e. transactions at one, two, and three months prior to the initial public offerings), the mean and median discounts were 40 and 39 percent, respectively.

Discounts on transactions occurring between January 1994 and June 1995 also were broken into fifth-, fourth-, and third-month analyses, at only that monthly period.

- *Fifth Month.* For the period, January 1994 to June 1995, the mean and median discounts on the 10 transactions that took place in the fifth month prior to the IPOs were 50 and 46 percent, respectively. The mean and median discounts on the 46 transactions that took place within five months prior to the IPOs were both 45 percent.
- *Fourth Month.* For the January 1994 to June 1995 study period, the mean and median discounts on the 17 transactions that took place in the fourth month prior to the IPOs were 48 and 50 percent, respectively. The mean and median discounts on the 36 transactions that took place within four months prior to the IPOs were 43 and 45 percent, respectively.
- *Third Month.* For the January 1994 to June 1995 study period, the mean and median discounts on the 11 transactions that took place in the third month prior to

the IPOs were 44 and 43 percent, respectively. For the 19 transactions that took place within three months prior to the IPOs, the discounts were 39 and 38 percent, respectively.

Discounts on option transactions occurring between January 1980 and June 1995 were divided into fifth-, fourth-, and third-month analyses.

Most of the transactions included in the Emory study involved options. Hitchner and Morris analyzed the discounts on option transactions that took place in the fifth, fourth, and third months prior to the date of the initial public offerings.

- *Fifth Month.* The mean and median discounts on the 32 option transactions that took place in the fifth month prior to the IPOs for the aggregate Emory studies were 55 and 51 percent, respectively. The mean and median discounts on the 166 option transactions that took place within the five months prior to the IPOs were 44 and 43 percent, respectively.
- *Fourth Month.* The mean and median discounts on the 31 option transactions that took place in the fourth month prior to the IPOs for the aggregated Emory studies were 52 and 51 percent, respectively. The mean and median discounts on the 134 option transactions that took place within four months prior to the IPOS were 42 and 41 percent, respectively.
- *Third Month.* The mean and median discounts on the 45 option transactions that took place in the third month prior to the IPOs for the aggregate Emory studies were 41 and 40 percent, respectively. The mean and median discounts on the 103 option transactions that took place within three months prior to the IPOs were 39 and 37 percent, respectively.

Discounts on option transactions occurring between January 1994 and June 1995 also were divided into fifth-, fourth-, and third-month analyses.

For the Emory study period, January 1994 to June 1995, the mean and median discounts on option transactions were 44 and 43 percent, respectively.

- *Fifth Month.* For the January 1994 to June 1995 study period, the mean and median discounts on the eight option transactions that occurred in the fifth month prior to the IPOs were 53 and 49 percent, respectively. The mean and median discounts on the 33 option transactions that took place within five months prior to the IPOs were 44 and 43 percent, respectively.
- *Fourth Month.* For the January 1994 to June 1995 study period, the mean and median discounts on the 12 option transactions that occurred in the fourth month prior to the IPOs were 47 and 48 percent, respectively. The mean and median discounts on the 25 option transactions that took place within four months prior to the IPOs were 42 and 38 percent, respectively.
- *Third Month.* For the January 1994 to June 1995 study period, the mean and median discounts on the nine option transactions that took place three months prior to the IPOs were both 43 percent. For the 13 option transactions that took place within three months prior to the IPOs, the discounts were 37 and 33 percent, respectively.

Hitchner Study No. 2

Hitchner and Morris performed a second analysis that was very similar to that performed by John Emory in his studies. Hitchner and Morris reviewed the prospectuses of guideline companies from February 1995 to June 1996 in the consulting industry that had gone public. This analysis focused on transactions that had taken place within the companies prior to their IPOs. They found 23 transactions that had taken place among 14 companies within 15 months of their IPO.

The mean and median discounts on the 23 transactions that took place prior (up to 15 months) to the initial public offerings were 51 and 52 percent, respectively.

- *Fifth Month.* The mean and median discounts on the transactions that took place in the fifth month prior to the IPOs were 49 and 53 percent, respectively. The mean and median discounts on the transactions that took place within five months prior to the IPOs were 44 and 36 percent, respectively.
- *Fourth Month.* The mean and median discounts on the transactions that took place in the fourth month prior to the IPOs were 56 and 57 percent, respectively. The mean and median discounts on transactions that took place within four months prior to the initial public offerings were 41 and 36 percent, respectively.
- *Third Month.* The mean and median discounts on the transactions that took place in the third month prior to the IPOs were both 31 percent. The mean and median discounts on the transactions that took place within three months prior to the IPOs were 31 and 35 percent, respectively. Exhibit 9.12 illustrates the analysis of the guideline company transactions.

Recent Criticisms of the IPO Studies

Certain analysts, most prominently Dr. Mukesh Bajaj, have recently raised questions regarding perceived shortcomings in the pre-IPO methodology. (For additional information, see the discussion from Dr. Mazumdar's presentation in Addendum 4 at www.wiley.com/go/FVAM3E. The article is from *Financial Valuation and Litigation Expert,* Issue 15, October/November 2008. This entire issue is devoted to DLOMs. Some of these criticisms have received favorable comment in the U.S. Tax Court (see, for example, the discussion of the *McCord* and *Lappo* cases in Chapter 15).

However, other practitioners have presented the case for the continuing validity and relevance of the pre-IPO studies. Dr. Shannon Pratt wrote a valuable article on this subject, rebutting Dr. Bajaj's criticisms.

Dr. Bajaj suggested that a 50 percent discount for lack of marketability in a transaction occurring six months before an IPO would imply a 200 percent annualized return, which would ". . . appear to be implausibly large."[19]

Dr. Pratt, however, notes that this "implies that investors in pre-IPO stock can gain liquidity at the time of the IPO, which is not generally true. Most underwriters will not register selling shareholder stocks on the IPO. Those that do register it generally have an extended 'lockup' period before the existing shareholders can sell." Dr. Pratt also notes that by annualizing the return, the argument ". . . implies that a comparable investment opportunity will be available to and recognized by the investor immediately. This is almost never true."[20]

Dr. Bajaj suggested that "buyers of shares prior to the IPO are likely to be insiders who provide some sort of service to the firm . . . part of the discount may reflect

---

[19] Mukesh Bajaj, et al., "Firm Value and Marketability Discounts," *Journal of Corporation Law* (October 2001).
[20] Shannon P. Pratt, "Rebuttal to Bajaj: Answers to Criticisms of Pre-IPO Studies," *Shannon Pratt's Business Valuation Update* (June 2004).

Exhibit 9.12 Analysis of Transactions Occurring In Consulting Industry Guideline Companies

Guideline Company		IPO Date	IPO Price ($)	Trans. Date	Trans. Price ($)	Type of Trans.	Disc.	Approx. No. of Mo.
Whittman Hart	(1)	5/3/96	16	12/31/95	6.49	Option	59%	4
Carnegie Group	(2)	12/4/95	8	3/1/95	*4.65	Option	42%	9
Cotelligent Group	(3)	2/14/96	9	9/8/95	2.70	Option	70%	5
Data Processing Res.	(4)	3/6/96	14	1/15/96	9.00	Option	36%	2
Data Processing Res.	(5)	3/6/96	14	6/1/95	2.25	Option	84%	9
Data Processing Res.	(6)	3/6/96	14	3/1/95	*2.25	Purchase	84%	12
Integrated Systems	(7)	4/18/96	5	1/31/95	1.52	Option	70%	15
Integrated Systems	(8)	4/18/96	5	11/17/95	3.33	Option	33%	5
Microware	(9)	4/3/96	10	5/2/95	3.13	Option	69%	11
Registry, Inc.	(10)	6/5/96	17	3/6/96	11.00	Option	35%	3
Registry, Inc.	(11)	6/5/96	17	4/1/96	*11.00	Option	35%	2
Registry, Inc.	(12)	6/5/96	17	5/1/96	*13.00	Option	24%	1
Ultradata	(13)	2/16/96	10	7/31/95	6.00	Option	40%	7
Ultradata	(14)	2/16/96	10	12/1/95	*7.25	Option	28%	3
Sykes	(15)	4/30/96	18	12/31/95	8.67	Option	52%	4
APAC	(16)	10/11/95	16	5/26/95	7.49	Option	53%	5
HCIA	(17)	2/22/95	14	2/1/94	*10.50	Option	25%	13
HCIA	(18)	2/22/95	14	4/1/94	*10.50	Option	25%	11
HCIA	(19)	2/22/95	14	10/1/94	*10.50	Option	25%	5
Idx	(20)	11/17/95	18	2/1/95	4.32	Option	76%	10
Mecon	(21)	12/7/95	13	3/31/95	0.57	Option	96%	8
UUNet	(22)	5/25/95	14	2/1/95	*6.00	Option	57%	4
UUNet	(23)	5/25/95	14	1/1/95	*5.00	Option	64%	5

Discounts	Mean	Median
Overall	51%	52%
At Five Months	49%	53%
Five Months or Less	44%	36%
At Four Months	56%	57%
Four Months or Less	41%	36%
At Three Months	31%	31%
Three Months or Less	31%	35%

*Only month and year of transaction available. Assumed the first of the month because specific day was not available.

equilibrium compensation for these services rather than compensation for the lack of marketability."[21]

On this point Dr. Pratt writes that the "Willamette studies attempt to eliminate insiders. The Emory and Valuation Advisors studies contain a substantial amount of arm's-length transactions, usually with institutional investors, who usually have rights that make their stock *more* valuable than the common stock with which it is compared at the time of the IPO. One-third to one-half of the pre-IPO transactions in recent years are convertible preferred stock, which of course is more valuable than the common stock

---

[21] Mukesh Bajaj, et al., "Firm Value and Marketability Discounts," *Journal of Corporation Law* (October 2001).

with which its price is compared. Also, many of the institutional investors demand 'put' rights. These factors would result in a downward bias in the calculated discounts."[22]

Finally, Dr. Bajaj suggested that ". . . the IPO approach is subject to a serious sample selection problem. Firms will choose to issue shares through an initial public offering when their prospects improve. . . . Once an IPO takes place, this uncertainty is resolved and only the successful (and hence higher valued) firms issue shares."[23]

Dr. Pratt replies that ". . . the effect of this bias is minimal. Only about 20% of companies that file for IPOs fail to have them when scheduled. Some are merely delayed, and others are acquired. Still others remain as viable private companies. Very few actually become worthless."[24]

Restricted Stock Studies

Additional support for the discount for lack of marketability can be found in the study of purchases of restricted securities by investment companies.

Investment companies regularly purchase private placements of restricted securities. Restricted securities may be issued and sold by a publicly traded company without prior registration with the Securities and Exchange Commission. These securities typically cannot be resold for a minimum period under the SEC Rule 144 guidelines.

Because of the restriction on the marketability of the securities, the investment companies purchase the securities at prices lower than the price of a registered security of the same company. The difference between the two prices represents the discount for the lack of marketability.

In the 1970s, the SEC required investment companies to make their transaction records public. The availability of the records made it possible for analysts to directly determine the lack of marketability discount on securities purchased by investment companies and use it as a comparison for the discount on a closely held interest.

Revenue Ruling 77-287

> The IRS, in Revenue Ruling 77-287, dealt with the issue of valuing restricted stocks. It was issued "to provide information and guidance to taxpayers, Internal Revenue Service personnel, and others concerned with the valuation, for Federal tax purposes, of securities that cannot be immediately resold because they are restricted from resale pursuant to Federal securities laws."

---

[22] Shannon P. Pratt, "Rebuttal to Bajaj: Answers to Criticisms of Pre-IPO Studies," *Shannon Pratt's Business Valuation Update* (June 2004).

[23] Mukesh Bajaj, et al., "Firm Value and Marketability Discounts," *Journal of Corporation Law* (October 2001).

[24] Shannon P. Pratt, "Rebuttal to Bajaj: Answers to Criticisms of Pre-IPO Studies," *Shannon Pratt's Business Valuation Update* (June 2004).

The ruling also discusses a study undertaken by the SEC, published in 1971 and covering the period from January 1, 1966, through June 30, 1969.[25] The SEC analyzed the purchases, sales, and holdings of restricted securities held by financial institutions that disclosed the valuation of their holdings. The average discount was about 26 percent for all companies.

In Accounting Release No. 113, the SEC acknowledged discounts for restricted securities.

> Restricted securities are often purchased at a discount, frequently substantial, from the market price of outstanding unrestricted securities of the same class. This reflects the fact that securities which cannot be readily sold in the public market place are less valuable than securities which can be sold, and also the fact that by the direct sale of restricted securities, sellers avoid the expense, time, and public disclosure which registration entails.

Securities and Exchange Institutional Investor Study. Securities and Exchange Commission, "Discounts Involved in Purchases of Common Stock (1966–1969)," *Institutional Investor Study Report of the Securities and Exchange Commission* (Washington, DC: U.S. Government Printing Office, March 10, 1971), Document No. 92-64, Part 5, pp. 2444–2456.

	Period of Study
Mean Discount of 25.8 percent	1966–1969

The Securities and Exchange Commission reviewed purchases of restricted securities by investment companies for the period January 1, 1966 through June 30, 1969. This study was published in March 1971. It compared the prices at which the transactions of restricted securities were made to the prices of publicly traded stocks from the same companies. The study included letter stocks traded on the New York and American Stock Exchange as well as the over-the-counter (OTC) markets. The mean discount for lack of marketability of the letter stocks was 25.8 percent.

The study analyzed discounts both by trading market as well as by sales of the company. Of the OTC nonreporting companies, 56 percent had discounts over 30 percent; 34 percent of the companies had discounts over 40 percent. For companies with sales between $1 million and $5 million, 54 percent had discounts over 30 percent; 34 percent of the companies had discounts over 40 percent.

Other Restricted Stock Studies. Several additional studies since the 1971 Institutional Investor Study have measured the DLOM using similar comparisons between restricted securities and their publicly traded counterparts. The results of these studies have generally averaged between 30 and 35 percent. Many of these studies were conducted during the period when securities were restricted for two years. The more important studies and their results are summarized in Exhibit 9.13.

---

[25] Securities and Exchange Commission, "Discounts Involved in Purchases of Common Stock (1966–1969)," *Institutional Investor Study Report of the Securities and Exchange Commission* (Washington, DC: U.S. Government Printing Office, March 10, 1971), Document No. 92-64, Part 5, pp. 2444–2456.

Exhibit 9.13   Summary of Studies of Restricted Securities Transactions

Study	Period of Study	Discount for Lack of Marketability
Securities Exchange Commission	1966 – 1969	26%
Hall and Polacek	1979 – 1992	23%
Silber	1981 – 1988	33.75%
Stryker and Pittock	1978 – 1982	45%
Maher	1969 – 1973	35%
Gelman	1968 – 1970	33%
Moroney	1969 – 1973[a]	35.6%
Trout	1968 – 1972	33.45%
Arneson	Opinion[b]	50% or greater
Willamette	1981 – 1984	31.2%
Management Planning, Inc.	1980 – 1996	27.1%
FMV Opinions, Inc.	1980 – 1997	22%
Johnson Study	1991 – 1995	20%
Columbia Financial Advisors Inc.	1996 – 1997	21%
Columbia Financial Advisors Inc.[c]	1997 – 1998	13%
Bajaj, et al.	1990 – 1995	22.2%
Management Planning, Inc.[e]	2000 – 2007	14.6%
LiquiStat[d]	2005 – 2006	32.8%
FMV Opinions, Inc.[d]	2002 – 2005	14.6%
FMV Opinions, Inc.[d]	1997 – 2005	21.6%
FMV Opinions, Inc.[d]	1980 – 2005	22.0%
Management Planning, Inc.[e]	1980 – 2000	27.4%
Trugman Valuation Associates, Inc.	2007 – 2008	18.1%

[a] Moroney did not state the exact time period of his study of restricted stocks, but it is within this time frame.
[b] The author used the 35 percent mean discount of the Maher study as a base discount. He then supports a higher discount based upon his analysis of the SEC letter stock study and other SEC studies.
[c] The effect of the SEC Rule 144 change from a two-year waiting period to a one-year waiting period.
[d] Robak, Espen, "Discounts for Illiquid Shares and Warrants: The *LiquiStat* Database of Transactions on the Restricted Securities Trading Network," Pluris Valuation Advisors White Paper Draft (January 22, 2007), pp. 26–27. www.plurisvaluation.com.
[e] MPI, Management Planning, Inc., "Perspectives" newsletter (Winter 2009), pp. 1, 11. www.mpival.com.

Hall and Polacek.   Hall, Lance S., and Polacek, Timothy G., "Strategies for Obtaining the Largest Valuation Discounts," *Estate Planning* (January/February 1994), pp. 38–44.

Mean Discount of 23 percent $\dfrac{\text{Period of Study}}{1979-1992}$

The authors discuss relevant factors for determining the taxable value of an estate. These factors include the criteria outlined by relevant IRS Revenue Rulings as well as the court-allowed discounts for minority interest and lack of marketability. The authors define the purpose for the discounts, evaluate historical trends in court-allowed discounts, and review several methods for determining the appropriate discount for each situation.

The minority interest discount and the lack of marketability discount are separate and distinguishable from each other. The study identifies them as "based upon independent financial principles and analyses."

Silber. Silber, William L., "Discounts of Restricted Stock: The Impact of Illiquidity on Stock Prices," *Financial Analysts Journal* (July–August 1991), 60–64.

Mean Discount of 33.75 percent	Period of Study
	1981–1988

Silber developed a model that describes the relationship of the discount to restricted securities and the factors that affect the discount.

Using data provided by the Securities Data Corporation, the author analyzed reported transactions of restricted stock sales from 1981 to 1988.

Of the 310 private placements of common stock of public companies, Silber chose 69 transactions that carried no "warrants or special provisions." "For each of these 69 companies, we recorded the date of the private placement, the price per share of the restricted stock and the closing price (or the average of the bid and offer prices) for the company's publicly traded shares on the placement date."

Silber compared the securities based on several characteristics, including the "percentage discount on the restricted stock, dollar size of the offering and number of restricted shares as a percentage of all common stock." He also looked at "the earnings of the firm during the previous fiscal year, total revenues during the previous fiscal year and market capitalization prior to the private placement." Analysis of these transactions showed an average price discount of 33.75 percent. The discounts ranged from 84 percent to a premium (negative discount) in one case of 12.7 percent. Further segregation of the data into discounts less than and greater than 35 percent indicates that "firms with higher revenues, earnings, and market capitalizations are associated with lower discounts."

Using the relationships that he found in his analysis, Silber developed a statistical model that described the discount as a function of the:

- Credit worthiness of the issuing company
- Marketability of the shares
- Cash flow
- Special (value-added) concessions to the investor

Silber defined the measurable "proxies" for each of the factors. Earnings and revenues were used to measure creditworthiness. The amount of restricted shares issued as a percent of total shares outstanding was used to measure marketability. Special provisions such as "guarantees of representation on the company's board" or "a customer relationship between investors and issuer," also were included in the model.

Using the least squares statistical model, Silber defined the relationships among the factors. His results indicate that:

- "The size of the price penalty [discount] varies with firm and issue characteristics."
- The size of the block of restricted securities issued affects the size of the discount more than the amount of revenues of the company.
- As the amount of restricted securities issues increases, those securities become less liquid and the issuer will have to sell them at a greater discount.

Silber concludes: "The results indicated that marketing a large block of illiquid securities requires significant prior concessions, even with firms with substantial creditworthiness. Liquidity clearly has a significant impact on the cost of equity capital."

Stryker and Pittock.   Stryker, Charles, and Pittock, William F., "Revenue Ruling 77-287 Revisited," *SRC Quarterly Reports* (Spring 1983), 1–3.

Median Discount of 45 percent   <u>Period of Study</u>
                                            1978–1982

In the manner of the SEC study on letter stock, Standard Research Consultants analyzed 28 restricted stock purchases that occurred from October 1978 through June 1982. Comparing the value of restricted stocks to public stocks issued by the same company, they found the median discount at which the restricted stocks sold to be 45 percent.

According to the authors:

> To be eligible for inclusion in our study, the private placement had to involve the common stock (or the common stock with purchase warrants) of a United States corporation and had to occur as an arm's-length transaction between unrelated parties which did not affect control of the corporation. In addition, the corporation could not be in a state of bankruptcy; nor could it be a financial, insurance, or real estate company.

Other criteria included the fact that the placement price could not be less than a dollar per share and that adequate information had to exist about the placement and the corporation. The discounts ranged from 7 to 91 percent.

The authors also studied the effect on the discount caused by four determinants of discounts that were outlined in Revenue Ruling 77-287:

1. Earnings
2. Sales
3. Trading market
4. Resale agreement provisions

"Profitability in the fiscal year preceding the placement did not seem to influence the discount; the 11 companies showing a profit in that year had a median discount of 45 percent, while the 17 that were unprofitable had a median discount of 46 percent." However, the earnings patterns of the companies did have an effect on the discounts. "On the average, companies that were profitable in each of the five years prior to the date of placement appeared to sell restricted stock at substantially smaller discounts from market than did those with two, three, or four unprofitable years during the five-year period." Companies that were profitable all five of the prior years had a median discount of 34 percent. Those companies with two to four years of profitability had a median discount of 39 percent, whereas those with zero or one year of profitability had a median discount of 46 percent.

The magnitude of revenues for the companies also affected the discount percentages. Those companies with revenues from approximately $30 million to $275 million had a discount of 36 percent whereas those companies that had revenue in the range of $500,000 to $1.6 million had a discount of 48 percent.

The authors concluded that of the 28 companies studied, there was not a significant difference in the magnitude of the discount based on whether they were traded on a major exchange or not. "The fact that there did not seem to be a relationship between the issuer's trading market and discount might be attributable to the development, since 1969, of the NASDAQ trading system."

In terms of resale agreement or registration provisions including trigger or piggyback rights, the authors indicate that:

> the median discount for the ten placements involving resale agreement provisions was 53 percent, versus a median discount for all twenty-eight placements of 45 percent, a result that appears to be at odds with the implications of RR 77-287. It should be noted that the promulgation of Rule 144 in 1972, plus subsequent relaxations of this Rule, have enhanced the marketability of restricted stock and thus made registration rights less important.

The authors also discuss other considerations:

- The length of time the stock was held by the owner and the various factors under Rule 144.
- The length of time it would take to dispose of the restricted stock since "The longer the time needed to dispose of the restricted stock, the greater the discount, ceteris parabis."
- The financial fundamentals of the issuer such that "The sounder the capitalization of an issuer, the lower the discount tends to be."
- The investor's appraisals of the unrestricted stock being traded in the marketplace: "one would analyze the issuer's relative price: earnings multiples, dividend yields, and ratios of market price to tangible book value as compared with those of comparable companies (rational investors require higher discounts from an issuer whose stock they believe is overpriced)."
- The trading volume and volatility of the unrestricted stock: "The greater the company's trading volume, the greater the likelihood that upon expiration of the resale restrictions, the restricted stock can be sold publicly without disrupting the market for the issuer's unrestricted stock. A purchase of restricted stock assumes less additional risk when the market for the issuer's unrestricted stock is stable."

The authors go on to state that "In addition to being probative of discounts in cases involving non controlling restricted common stock interests issued in private placements, these factors are equally important in the valuation of non controlling closely held common stock, qualified option stock, . . . and other forms of restricted ownership interest."

Maher. Maher, Michael J., "Discounts for Lack of Marketability for Closely Held Business Interests," *Taxes* (September 1976), pp. 562–571.

	Period of Study
Mean Discount of 35 percent	1969–1973
Median Discount of 33 percent	1969–1973

The author researched the purchases of restricted securities by investment companies from 1969 to 1973. "The discounts were derived by comparing the cost to the funds to the market value of unrestricted securities of the same class in the same companies on the acquisition date." Maher determined that the mean discount on transactions occurring in this time frame was approximately 35 percent. The range of discounts for the 34 transactions studied was 2.7 to 75.66 percent. Further analysis reveals that 68 percent of the transactions occurred at discounts of 30 percent or more, 35 percent occurred at discounts of 40 percent or higher, and 21 percent occurred at a discount of 50 percent or greater.

Maher acknowledges that the investment companies discounted the purchases to take into account the costs of registering the stocks, but he argues that the applied discounts are considerably higher than the costs that investment companies would incur to register the stock.

Maher justifies the 35 percent discount for lack of marketability by pointing out that investors give up the opportunity to invest in other more marketable instruments and that the investor "would continue to have his investment at the risk of the business until the shares could be offered to the public or another buyer is found."

Gelman. Gelman, Milton, "An Economist-Financial Analyst's Approach to Valuing Stock of a Closely Held Company," *Journal of Taxation* (June 1972), pp. 353–354.

Mean and Median Discount 33 percent $\dfrac{\text{Period of Study}}{1968-1970}$

The author evaluates the purchases of restricted securities by four investment companies from 1968 through 1970. Restricted securities are interests in public corporations that contain covenants limiting the resale of the securities by the investor for periods of up to two years. Investment companies buy the stocks "directly from the company, or, in some instances, from selling stockholders. . . . Since there is a restriction on their transferability, restricted securities are usually purchased at a price substantially below that of the freely-marketable securities of the same class as the company."

Using publicly available financial statements, the author compared the price that the investment companies paid for the restricted securities of a corporation to the market price of publicly traded securities of the same corporation. This study was based on an analysis of publicly traded close-end investment companies that specialized in and reported on restricted securities and letter stocks of public companies. In 1970, the four investment companies "had letter stock investments in the common stocks of 89 public companies." Gelman analyzed these transactions and determined that the mean and median discount of all 89 stock purchases was 33 percent.

It is significant to note that:

- 36 percent of the stocks exhibited discounts greater than 40 percent
- 59 percent of the stocks exhibited discounts greater than 30 percent
- 84 percent of the stocks exhibited discounts greater than 20 percent

Moroney. Moroney, Robert E., "Most Courts Overvalue Closely Held Stocks," *Taxes* (March 1973), 144–156.

	Period of Study
Mean Discount of 35.6 percent,	1969–1973
Median Discount of 33 percent	1969–1973

Public records of the purchases of unregistered securities by investment companies provide a basis for determining the size of the lack of marketability discounts for closely held securities. Because the government restricts the sale of unregistered stocks, they are less marketable than freely traded securities.

Beginning in 1969, the SEC required that registered investment companies make public their internal restricted securities valuation methods and transaction data (SEC Accounting Series Release No. 113, dated October 21, 1969, and Accounting Series Release No. 118, dated December 23, 1970). By the end of 1968, open-end and close-end registered investment companies held over $4.2 billion in restricted equity securities. A review of the prices at which investment companies purchased 146 unregistered and restricted stocks reveals that the actual discount for these securities was sometimes as great as 90 percent.

Moroney also investigated the published financial statements of the companies and reviewed the valuations prepared by the boards of directors of the firms that were required by law to make good-faith estimates of value. Investment companies' boards of directors consider several factors when evaluating the value of their restricted securities holdings for their annual financial statement, including the size of the security block, the size of the issuer, and the issuer's presence in the market.

Of the 146 transactions reviewed, the mean discount based on the original purchase was 35.6 percent. Of further interest is that 64 percent of the transactions occurred at a discount of 30 percent or greater, 40 percent occurred at a discount of 40 percent or greater, and 23 percent occurred at a discount of 50 percent or higher.

Trout. Trout, Robert R., "Estimation of the Discount Associated with the Transfer of Restricted Securities," *Taxes* (June 1977), pp. 381–385.

	Period of Study
Mean Discount of 33.45 percent	1968–1972

To determine the appropriate lack of marketability discount on restricted securities, Trout analyzed 60 historical transactions of investment letter stock purchases by mutual funds in the period from 1968 to 1972. Using multiple regression analysis, he determined the relationship among the factors that influence the size of the discount. These factors are:

- Exchange listing
- Number of shares outstanding
- Percent control, which is the number of shares purchased divided by the shares outstanding
- Size of the purchase
- Value of the purchase

Trout enters actual transaction data for each of the variables and solves for the coefficients of the variables. These coefficients describe the relationship that the variables have to the size of the lack of marketability discount.

- *Exchange Listing.* The exchange listing variable accounts for the fact that stocks traded on larger exchanges are generally more marketable than those that are not, and will have lower discounts. Trout sets the variable to "one if the security is listed on either the New York or the American Stock Exchange, and a value of zero otherwise." Analysis indicates that stocks traded on the above exchanges will have an 8.39 percent lower discount than securities listed on smaller exchanges.
- *Number of Shares Outstanding.* "The number of shares outstanding is a proxy for the marketability of the shares purchased." Securities with a greater number of shares outstanding will be more marketable and therefore have a lower discount. Analysis indicates that "the discount will be about four percentage points smaller for each additional million shares of common stock of the issue which are outstanding."
- *Percent Control.* The amount of control measures both the premium for the privilege of owning a controlling interest in the securities as well as the discount for disposing of a large block of the security. The percent control has a small negative affect on the discount: "the discount should decline by a little less than 1 percentage point for each additional 1 percent of control involved in the purchase."
- *Size of the Purchase.* The size variable "reflects the reduced discount necessary for a purchase of a small number of shares of a restricted security that could easily be sold." The analysis "indicates that small purchases of stock should have a 12.11 percentage point lower discount than purchases that amount to more than 1 percent of the outstanding shares."
- *Value of the Purchase.* The value of purchase discount reflects "the value the shares purchased would have if they were registered or unrestricted." Analysis indicates that "the discount will increase by 4.75 percentage points for each additional million dollars of stock purchased."

In summary, Trout's model has a moderate ability to account for variations in observed discounts. The analysis indicates that the size of the discount is strongly affected by the discussed factors. The model does not explain all of the variations among observed discounts, because other nontangible factors, such as purchase agreements, the bargaining power of the seller, and the lack of an auction market, affect the discount size.

Arneson. Arneson, George S., "Nonmarketability Discounts Should Exceed Fifty Percent," *Taxes* (January 1981), pp. 25–31.

Discount of 50 percent or Greater

Arneson evaluated studies of purchases of letter stock by investment companies. He referred to studies by Maher and Moroney that indicate the appropriate discount for nonmarketability of an interest in a closely held company should be around 35 percent. Arneson agreed with this rate for restricted securities but pointed out that restricted securities of publicly traded companies are different from interests in closely held businesses. He saw enough dissimilarity between the two securities to argue that the discount rates on closely held securities should be above the 35 percent level.

Arneson's support for higher discounts included such factors as:

- Costs of flotation
- Lack of a preestablished market
- Risk
- Inability to market because of company size and history
- Noncash costs of underwriting
- Timing and length of time necessary to go public

He concludes that the discount for lack of marketability for a closely held company should be closer to 50 percent or greater.

- *Costs of Flotation.* Arneson evaluated the cost of flotation and determined that the cost should include compensation to underwriters and other expenses. He found that, on average, the compensation to underwriters was 8.41 percent and other expenses were 4.02 percent of gross proceeds (based on 1,599 offerings to the general public through securities dealers). For companies whose size of issue was between $2 million and $5 million, the underwriters' compensation was 8.19 percent and the other expenses were 3.71 percent. It is important to note that other expenses include federal revenue stamps, state taxes, listing fees, printing costs, and legal and accounting fees.

    Arneson goes on to note that in addition to the other expenses, there was other noncash compensation in the form of warrants or options in many situations. He indicates that such compensation has been prevalent among small equity issues. He feels that "many closely held companies would most likely require such additional consideration, and in appraising the cost to market such securities should be provided for."

    Arneson's information comes from the Securities and Exchange Commission's "Costs of Flotation of Registered Issues, 1971–1972," (December, 1974). He also reviews a related study called "An Empirical Analysis of the Flotation Costs of Corporate Securities," *Journal of Finance* (September 1975) and "Unseasoned Equity Financing," *Journal of Financial and Quantitative Analysis* (June 1975). The extra cost for warrants and options was approximately 12 percent.
- *Preexisting Market.* Using the same studies, Arneson presents evidence concerning the wide difference in compensation paid to underwriters for stocks with no previous market as opposed to stocks that already had established market positions. "On the average this amounted to 3.7 percent but varied with size and listing exchanges." The study also indicated that the discounts were higher for stocks on regional exchanges and OTC compared to the New York Stock Exchange and American Stock Exchange.
- *Risk.* Arneson feels that a thorough analysis of the company and the industry in which it operates is an important element in setting risk. He feels that risk is

affected by the size of the company and that risk affects the costs of securities flotation. Although he did not determine a specific factor, he indicated that risk could be assessed on the basis of "an industry's general market conditions, business risk of a particular company and its financial risk, leverage, margins, and the like."

- *Ability to Market.* "A serious weakness in utilizing flotational basis to determine nonmarketability is that for very small companies, there is almost no possibility that an underwriting could be carried out and a public market created." Arneson quotes in an article by Gerald A. Sears entitled "Public Offerings for Smaller Companies," published in the *Harvard Business Review* (September-October 1968), in which Sears lists the criteria for a company to market its stock successfully: "The company should have a growth rate higher than its industry to attract investors. Owner-managers accustomed to answering to no one in running their businesses must be able to adjust to operating in a sometimes uncomfortable spotlight of attention. The effect of public disclosure must not be to compromise a company's business."

- *Hidden but Real Costs.* "Another cost for a privately-held company going public is an ongoing one of audits, shareholder reports and relations, S.E.C. and state security reports, transfer agent, shareholder meetings, and the like. For a small company, these could represent a sizable additional annual expense."

- *Time and Timing.* "Lettered stock could reasonably expect to become registered and thus freely tradable in two to three years; however, it could take longer for a closely-held company to prepare itself and have its stock marketed." Arneson goes on to talk about the fact that the general condition of the marketplace also could dictate whether a company could go public. Several factors outside a firm will influence its ability to market the equity:

  - General level of business activity
  - Level of interest rates
  - Level of stock prices
  - Availability of funds in the money markets

Willamette Management Associates Study

Median Discount of 31.2 percent	Period of Study
	1981–1984

In a study of 33 transactions involving purchases of restricted securities from 1981 through 1984, Willamette Management compared the prices at which the restricted securities were issued to the prices for comparable publicly traded stocks from the issuing company. It found that the restricted securities sold at a median discount of 31.2 percent.

"The slightly lower average percentage discounts for private placements during this time may be attributable to the somewhat depressed pricing in the public stock market, which in turn reflected the necessary economic conditions prevalent during most of the period of the study."[26]

---

[26] Shannon P. Pratt, Robert F. Reilly, and Robert R. Schweihs, *Valuing a Business: The Analysis and Appraisal of Closely Held Companies,* 4th ed. (New York: McGraw-Hill), p. 400.

Management Planning Restricted Stock Studies.[27]   An independent business appraisal firm, Management Planning, Inc. (MPI), has compiled an analysis of the discounts on restricted stocks as compared to their publicly traded counterparts that includes data from 1980 through 1996. MPI reviewed all reported private placements in that period, choosing transactions that met the following criteria:

- Restricted stock in the transaction had to have a publicly traded and actively held common stock counterpart in the same company with the same rights as the restricted stock.
- Adequate data on the private transaction and company financial information had to be available.
- Publicly traded common stock counterpart had to sell at a price of at least $2 per share.
- Company selling the stock must be domestic.
- The company selling the stock must not be described in disclosure documents as being in a developmental stage.

According to MPI, 231 private placements of restricted stock met the initial criteria. MPI further eliminated any issuer of restricted shares that lost money the year prior to the transaction, any company with revenues less than $3 million (a start-up company), and any transactions of stocks with known registration rights. Only 53 of the original group of companies met the criteria. Exhibit 9.14 summarizes the results of the MPI study.

Exhibit 9.14   Management Planning Inc., Restricted Stock Study—Summary of Transaction Data

	Revenues ($MM)	Earnings ($MM)	Market Cap. ($MM)	Indicated Discount %
Mean	45.6	2.2	78.7	27.1
Median	28.3	0.8	44.1	24.8
Minimum	3.2	0.1	3.4	0.0
Maximum	293.0	24.0	686.5	57.6

To test the relationships between 24 selected factors and the restricted stock discount, MPI divided the transactions into four quartiles. The results of MPI's analysis indicated that some factors had clear explanatory power regarding the restricted stock discount while others had some or no explanatory power regarding the restricted stock discount.

Factors with the Most Explanatory Power.   A number of factors were reviewed in each quartile to confirm whether they appeared to affect the restricted stock discount. The following factors had the most explanatory power:

- Revenues
- Recent earnings

---

[27] Robert F. Reilly and Robert P. Schweihs, eds., *Handbook of Advanced Business Valuation.* (New York: McGraw-Hill, 2000), 97–116.

- Market price/share
- Price stability
- Number of quarters of trading volume
- Rule 144—Dribble-out
- Value of Block

The analysis indicated that revenues and recent earnings had an inverse relationship with the restricted stock discount. Restricted stocks in companies with higher revenues or earnings generally were subject to lower discounts than companies with lower revenues or earnings. Companies whose stock sold at higher prices per share had lower restricted stock discounts. MPI noted the $2 minimum price was set to "eliminate stocks we considered cheap speculative vehicles." MPI measured price stability "on the basis of the standard deviation of the stock-trading price over the 12 months prceding the transaction." The restricted stock discounts are higher for companies with a history of lower price stability. The discount was generally higher the greater the number of quarters required to sell the block based on its weekly trading volume and the longer the time required to sell the block based on Rule 144 limitations. Larger (as measured by value) blocks of stock tended to have higher discounts.

Exhibit 9.15 illustrates the result of MPI's analysis of the above factors. In ranking revenues, earnings, and value of the block, the first quartile represents the higher end and the fourth quartile represents the lower end of the range. For market price/share, the first quartile represents the lowest prices and the fourth quartile the highest. Price stability is also shown across the first to fourth quartiles from lowest stability to highest stability. Number of quarters required to liquidate based on average trading volume and on Rule 144 dribble-out rules are shown with the greatest times required to liquidate in the first quartile and the shortest times in the fourth quartile.

Exhibit 9.15 Management Planning, Inc., Restricted Stock Study—Factors with the Most Explanatory Power Regarding Restricted Stock Discounts[28]

	1st Quartile %	2nd Quartile %	3rd Quartile %	4th Quartile %
Revenues	17.9	24.8	31.4	32.7
Earnings	16.7	23.1	31.6	40.2
Market Price per Share	30.4	24.5	19.6	23.3
Price Stability	31.4	32.5	19.5	18.1
Number of Quarters of Trading Volume	32.5	24.5	29.3	19.2
Rule 144 Dribble-out	28.9	29.3	24.1	21.4
Value of Block	19.4	22.5	30.4	31.0

Note: All discounts shown are median discounts for each quartile.

---

[28] Ibid., p. 110.

Factors with Some Explanatory Power. The following factors showed some explanatory power with regard to the restricted stock discounts:

- Revenue growth rate
- Earnings growth rate
- Revenue stability
- Block size/trading volume
- Block size (number of shares)
- Earnings stability
- Annual trading volume

The analysis indicated that these factors generally followed a predictable pattern. Companies with higher growth rates in revenues or earnings generally have lower discounts. Similarly, companies with more stable earnings and revenues tended to have lower discounts. Discounts tended to be higher the higher the block size as a percentage of annual trading volume and to increase as trading volume decreased. Smaller blocks, whether measured by trading volume or just number of shares, tended to have smaller discounts.

Exhibit 9.16 illustrates the result of MPI's analysis of the above factors. In ranking all seven factors, the first quartile represents the higher end and the fourth quartile represents the lower end of the range.

Exhibit 9.16 Management Planning, Inc., Restricted Stock Study—Factors with Some Explanatory Power Regarding Restricted Stock Discounts[29]

	1st Quartile %	2nd Quartile %	3rd Quartile %	4th Quartile %
Revenue Growth Rate	28.9	19.6	24.1	29.4
Earnings Growth Rate	22.5	16.0	36.6	30.4
Revenue Stability	28.9	18.8	32.5	36.2
Block Size/Trading Volume	32.5	24.5	29.3	19.2
Block Size (Number of Shares)	24.5	29.3	30.4	21.1
Earnings Stability	15.5	30.1	28.9	34.6
Annual Trading Volume	27.5	17.9	24.8	34.3

Note: All discounts shown are median discounts for each quartile.

In applying data from the MPI Study, analysts may wish to consider reviewing the specific transactions and underlying data for applicability to particular engagements. The Tax Court, in the *Lappo* case (see Chapter 15), substantially revised the petitioner's expert's use of MPI Study data, based on the Court's determination that 13 high-technology company transactions in the MPI data used by the petitioner's expert were not comparable to the subject. These companies had relatively high discounts.

---

[29] Ibid., p. 112.

MPI updated their study for the period 1980 to 2000. This included 259 private placement transactions. The mean and median discounts were 27.4 percent and 24.8 percent, respectively.[30]

Their newest DLOM restricted stock study included 1,600 transactions from 2000 to 2007. The average discount was 14.6 percent. For about 100 companies whose privately placed stock was registered, the average discount was 9.5 percent. For the 200 or so companies with unregistered stock, the average discount was 18.7 percent. The rest of the transactions included companies that either had registration rights, had agreed to register, or were registered later. MPI indicated that it was still working on the model and incorporating regression analysis and other statistical techniques.

FMV Opinions Study. FMV Opinions, Inc., reviewed 243 restricted stock transactions from 1980 through April 1997. The initial study was reported in *Valuation Strategies*[31] in 2001 with a follow-up article in *Business Valuation Update.*[32] All transactions were prior to the Rule 144 amendment in 1997 that reduced the holding period from two years to one year. The overall mean (average) discount in the study is 22.1 percent and the median discount is 20.1 percent. The standard deviation of the sample is 16.0 percent. The median discount for exchange-traded securities is 15.3 percent, while the median discount for over-the-counter traded securities is 22.4 percent.

The FMV Study also provides an analysis of the 243 transactions by SIC Code. As there are too few transactions per SIC code to be meaningful, the authors grouped the transactions into SIC code ranges. The study concludes that financial descriptors such as size, risk, profitability, and liquidity are the most important determinants of the discount for the lack of marketability. With two exceptions, FMV Opinions research has indicated that industry is not especially important in determining discounts. Restricted stocks of financial institutions tend to show lower discounts, and those of high-technology companies tend to show higher discounts. Otherwise, business type is generally not important.

Risk had a significant effect on the size of the discounts. The study showed that smaller, less-profitable entities and those with a higher degree of balance sheet risk had the highest discounts. The study also found a correlation between the size of the discount and the stock price. The DLOM increases significantly with decreasing stock prices. Other inferences drawn from the FMV study (including revenue, income, dividend payments, dollar block size, book value, market value, and trading volume) also confirm the relationship between risk and the lack of marketability discount.

The FMV Opinions Study is updated semiannually for purchase. It is also available as a searchable online database. FMV Opinions, Inc., also has studies for the periods 1980–2005, 1997–2005, and 2002–2005. See further discussion later in this chapter and Addendum 1 at www.wiley.com/go/FVAM3E for more detail on this study and database and its suggested use.

---

[30] This information is taken from Management Planning, Inc. (MPI), "Perspectives" newsletter (Winter 2009), pp. 1, 11 (www.mpival.com).
[31] Espen Robak and Lance Hall, "Bringing Sanity to Marketability Discounts: A New Data Source," *Valuation Strategies* 4, no. 6 (July/August 2001).
[32] Espen Robak "FMV Introduces Detailed Restricted Stock Study," *Shannon Pratt's Business Valuation Update* 7, no. 11 (November 2001).

Johnson Study. The Johnson study[33] observed 72 transactions during the years 1991 to 1995. The range of the discounts was from a negative 10 percent (a premium) to 60 percent. The study points to an average discount of 20 percent, which is lower than past studies. The author attributes the decline in the size of the discounts to the increased number of investors who entered the market for restricted stocks in this five-year period following the SEC adoption of Rule 144A, which allowed qualified institutional investors to trade unregistered securities without filing registration statements. The holding period for restricted stocks in this study was two years.

The study also considered the effect of such factors as profitability, size, transaction amount, and the holding period on the amount of the discount for lack of marketability. The average DLOM was 16 percent when the company reported positive earnings compared to 23 percent when the company reported a loss. This spread in the average discount remained constant for each year net income was examined. The relationship between the magnitude of the discount and the size of the company is clearly direct. The average discount was 13 percent for companies with sales greater than $200 million compared to 23.5 percent for companies with sales of less than $10 million.

Columbia Financial Advisors, Inc.   Columbia Financial Advisors, Inc. (CFAI), performed two studies: one examined only private equity placements over the period January 1, 1996, through April 30, 1997, and the other study examined only private common equity placements over the period January 1, 1997, through December 31, 1998. The second study was notable in that it is the first study to consider DLOM after the 1997 Rule 144 change that reduced the holding period for restricted stocks from two years to one.

In the first study, CFAI analyzed 23 transactions and found an average discount of 21 percent. The discounts ranged from 0.8 to 67.5 percent; the median was 14 percent. The study offers this explanation of the decline in the size of DLOM from the earlier studies:

> These discounts are generally lower than the discounts recorded in the earlier studies noted above which generally indicated discounts of approximately 35 percent. The increase in volume of privately placed stock (Rule 144A) in the past several years offers an explanation. As activity in a market increases, more and better information becomes available. In addition, there are now more participants in the market for restricted stocks due to Rule 144A and, therefore, increased liquidity. This would tend to decrease discounts because better information results in less risk and thus a lower required rate of return. The lower discounts in this particular study may also reflect, to some degree, the market's anticipation of the SEC's change in the holding period from two years to one year, although we have no way to verify this. Since June 1995, the SEC proposed amendment to Rule 144 was published for public comment. Therefore, knowledgeable private placement and

---

[33] Bruce Johnson, "Restricted Stock Discounts, 1991–95," *Shannon Pratt's Business Valuation Update* 5, no. 3 (March 1999), pp. 1–3.

Rule 144A market participants were most likely aware of the proposed changes.[34]

The average discount for the second study, after the Rule 144 holding period was shortened to one year, was 13 percent. The range of discounts in the second study, which analyzed 15 transactions, was 0 to 30 percent; the median was 9 percent. According to CFAI, "The lower discounts in this study in all probability reflect the market's reaction to the SEC's change in the holding period from two years to one year."

The CFAI study also noted other market evidence to support declining discounts following the Rule 144 holding period change. Tetra Tech, Inc., a publicly traded environmental engineering firm, is active in industry acquisitions and typically uses its restricted stock for acquisitions. The Tetra Tech Form 10-K for the fiscal year ending September 30, 1999, included the following statement in the footnotes to its September 30, 1999, financial statements: "The Company values stock exchanged in acquisitions based on extended restriction periods and economic factors specific to the Company's circumstances. During fiscal 1998 and 1999, stock exchanged in acquisitions was discounted by 15 percent. During fiscal 1997, the discount on stock exchanged in acquisitions ranged from 16 to 28 percent."

The CFAI study concluded that while discounts for restricted stocks are declining, "the studies conducted after 1990 are not relevant for purposes of determining discounts for lack of marketability for privately held stock, because they reflect the increased liquidity in the market for restricted securities. Such increased liquidity is not present in privately held securities."

LiquiStat. Robak, Espen, "Discounts for Illiquid Shares and Warrants: The LiquiStat Database of Transactions on the Restricted Securities Trading Network," Pluris Valuation Advisors White Paper Draft (January 22, 2007), 22–32 (www.plurisvaluation.com).

	Period of Study
Mean discount of 32.8 percent	2005–2006
Median discount of 34.6 percent	2005–2006

The data for this study came from the LiquiStat database of private sales transactions, which was created by Pluris Valuation Advisors, LLC. The period of the study was April 2005 to December 2006. The transactions were facilitated by Restricted Stock Partners of New York, which created the Restricted Securities Trading Network (RSTN), believed to be the largest trading network for restricted securities, with over 200 institutions and accredited investors as members.

The buyers and sellers in this transaction group tended to be hedge funds, institutions, or other accredited investors. There were 61 all-cash deals. The ownership history was known, allowing for greater precision in estimating the number of days of illiquidity remaining for each stock transacted. The investors were not affiliated

[34] Kathryn F. Aschwald, "Restricted Stock Discounts Decline as Result of 1-Year Holding Period—Studies After 1990 'No Longer Relevant' for Lack of Marketability Discounts," *Shannon Pratt's Business Valuation Update* 6, no. 5 (May 2000), 1–5.

with the issuing company and there were no affiliate sellers, with the assumption of information symmetry between buyer and seller. The mean and median days left to trade in the market were 144 and 120 days, respectively. [*Editor's note:* The actual text says an average of 138 days, but the table says 144 and 120.]

The author makes comparisons to other restricted stock studies. The LiquiStat averages are higher, and he gives various possible explanations. He believes the most convincing one concerns the nature of private investment in public equity (PIPE). "PIPE investments have become highly popular partly because issuers often register the stock shortly after the private placement. When investing, PIPE buyers have fairly strong visibility over how long they will have to wait for the shares to be registered. However, those details are not always available to the authors of private placement studies. Thus, whether or not stock is issued with registration rights, or even a promise of registration very shortly after the placement, may be unknown. This, if true, would tend to overstate the actual expected period of illiquidity for the shares in the studies. . . . In other words, the average 'holding periods' of the private placement studies may be lower than the one- (or two-) year Rule 144 period and might even be lower than the roughly four months of the LiquiStat database."[35]

Trugman Valuation Advisors, Inc. Harris, William, "Trugman Valuation Advisors, Inc. (TVA), Restricted Stock Study," *Business Valuation Review* (Fall 2009), 128–139.

	Period of Study
Mean discount of 18.1 percent	2007–2008
Median discount of 14.4 percent	2007–2008

The author looked at restricted stock discounts from January 2007 to December 2008. This was during a time of high market volatility and uncertainty. Part of the analysis was to determine if the higher volatility led to higher marketability discounts. More than 6,900 8-K filings were looked at and companies were eliminated for such factors as:

- Type of security (e.g., preferred stock, warrants, convertible notes).
- Uncertainty about price being at fair market value (e.g., special contractual arrangements, insiders).
- Unavailability of date and price.
- Average of high and low closing price for the month greater than $1.
- Government Troubled Asset Relief Program (TARP).
- Transaction had to be in cash.
- Stock was traded on a domestic exchange for at least six months.

Eighty transactions met these criteria. The range of discounts was a premium of 1.5 percent to a discount of 73.5 percent. The mean and median were 18.1 percent and 14.4 percent, respectively, with a standard deviation of 15.6 percent. The

[35] Espen Robak, "Discounts for Illiquid Shares and Warrants: The LiquiStat Database of Transactions on the Restricted Securities Trading Network," Pluris Valuation Advisors White Paper Draft (January 22, 2007), 26–27 (www.plurisvaluation.com).

author's conclusion is that his results indicate that the economic environment had no noticeable effect on the size of the discounts, as compared to earlier restricted stock studies.

He also disclosed that his study and analysis differed in some respects from those prior studies, possibly causing a higher or lower discount. A statistical correlation analysis was also performed and presented, as was a quartile analysis.

Recent Criticisms of the Restricted Stock Studies

Dr. Mukesh Bajaj and others have questioned the traditional interpretation and application of the data derived from the restricted stock studies. Lance Hall wrote an article with regard to Dr. Bajaj's view of the restricted stock studies.

Bajaj suggested that the observed discount on restricted stock private placements from the related freely traded public price may represent other factors in addition to lack of marketability. Because some level of discount from the public price is also often observed in private placements of registered unrestricted shares, Bajaj and others argue that factors other than liquidity are at play in the restricted stock studies. The assumption is that such registered shares are liquid: "Registered shares can be transacted freely, and the fact that the firm was publicly traded meant there was a ready market for these shares."[36]

Hall observes, however, that this assumption is faulty: ". . . on average, the registered shares in his [Bajaj's] study were in fact restricted under Rule 144, and had significantly limited marketability. Moreover, the study fails to examine the underlying trading volume of the private placement companies. As private placement companies, in general, are smaller and have less trading volume, it is likely that, even if the registered shares were not subject to the dribble-out provisions of Rule 144, the registered shares would not be as liquid as the typical small block sales that set the public price. In other words, the public price reflects a significantly more liquid security than the registered shares in Bajaj's private placement study."[37]

Hall further notes that all restricted share blocks are not equally illiquid. Given the dribble-out provisions of Rule 144 and a particular security's trading volume, a 30 percent block is significantly less liquid than a 1 percent block, even though the restricted stock investments are in the same publicly traded company. "The discount accorded these two blocks must reflect the differences in their respective relative lack of liquidity."[38] Investments in closely held businesses are typically less liquid than even large blocks of restricted securities.

Bajaj et al. have also opined that part of the discounts in the restricted stock studies are compensation for "(1) assessing the value of the investment, (2) monitoring the investment, (3) a promise of future funding, and (4) management advice to the company," and that ". . . it is often the case that private equity investors commit to provide the issuing firm with advice and oversight following the private placement of equity. Moreover, these investors often commit to providing capital in the future." Citing various academic articles, Bajaj also suggests that ". . . discounts are required . . . to serve

---

[36] Mukesh Bajaj, et al., "Firm Value and Marketability Discounts," *Journal of Corporation Law* (October 2001).

[37] Lance S. Hall, "Counteracting the New and Winning IRS Approach to Determine Discounts for Lack of Marketability," *Valuation Strategies* (March/April 2004).

[38] Ibid.

as compensation for the higher information and monitoring costs associated with the investments."[39]

In reply, Hall states that "the very act of monitoring presupposes one can do something about the investment. In other words, if one monitors a liquid investment, and things change, the investor can decide to sell. . . . However, if one monitors an illiquid investment, and things change, that investor cannot sell the investment and the investor's alternatives are severely limited."[40] Further, Hall notes that a legal promise of future investment is part of the terms of a private placement purchase and should therefore be disclosed and available for analysis. Finally, regarding the idea that part of the discount is a return for advice provided to management, Hall notes that this is speculative and without apparent foundation in the underlying data, adding that ". . . it is interesting to note that this speculation has an interesting flip side. If it is assumed that advice is given by an investor, it also must be assumed that the investor expects the advice to be taken. . . . Advice taken suggests the restricted stock investment carries with it aspects of influence or control. Accordingly, because influence and control are also valuable to an investor—especially in an illiquid investment—the investor will pay more for his or her investment to exercise such influence or control. Therefore, the actual discount for lack of marketability is greater. . . . In other words, because shares with influence and control are more attractive than shares without such rights, the discount for lack of marketability for shares lacking influence and control should be greater than the discounts typically reflected by the restricted stock private placements having influence or control."[41]

Overall Observations of Studies

The following list presents some interesting observations after reviewing these empirical studies:

- The smaller the company (revenues, earnings, market capitalization), the larger was the discount for lack of marketability.
- Issuers of restricted stock may be better credit risks.
- Issuers of restricted stock are publicly traded companies that have an active market for their stock. Owners of stock in a closely held business have no access to an active market for their stock. Closely held businesses are unlikely to ever be publicly traded.
- Many publicly traded companies reflect annual dividends and/or an established record of capital appreciation in their share price. Many closely held businesses cannot offer this.
- Purchasers of restricted stock are institutional investors whose investment goals and criteria are far different from those of the individual purchaser of a closely held business interest.
- Institutional investors have different levels of risk perception and risk tolerance from purchasers of closely held business stock.

---

[39] Mukesh Bajaj, et al., "Firm Value and Marketability Discounts," *Journal of Corporation Law* (October 2001).
[40] Lance S. Hall, "Counteracting the New and Winning IRS Approach to Determine Discounts for Lack of Marketability," *Valuation Strategies* (March/April 2004).
[41] Ibid.

- Purchasers of restricted securities usually intend to market the purchased securities in the future and assume a ready market will exist at that time. Purchasers of stock in closely held companies have little or no expectation to market the stock in the future; if they expect to market the stock, they assume a limited market will exist for them to do so.
- Investments of venture capital companies in OTC nonreporting companies most closely resemble purchases by closely held business owners.
- Venture capital investments are generally of relatively short duration, suggesting even higher discounts for the typically longer positions in closely held business stock.
- When an analyst applies a discount to a closely held company interest that is equal to the discount observed in restricted stock of a publicly traded company, the implication is that the restricted stock is comparable to the closely held stock.
- Blind reliance on empirical studies or discounts allowed by the courts is oversimplistic as each valuation has its own unique facts and circumstances that must be reflected in the selection of discounts.
- Where applicable, analysts may wish to consider analyzing and applying discounts derived from specific selected sets of restricted stock and/or pre-IPO transactions, where underlying data are available.
- Valuation analysts who rely solely on empirical studies without analysis may understate discounts and overstate value.
- Valuation analysts often fail to support discounts with sound reasoning and considered analysis.
- In the valuation of stock in most closely held businesses, the average discounts observed in the restricted stock studies may be considered the *minimum* discount applicable in many situations.

DETAILED STUDIES

FMV Opinions Comparative Analysis with Restricted Stock (CARS) Approach[42]

Ideally, a discount for lack of marketability would utilize data involving two classes of stock in the same company, where the only difference between the two classes was marketability (or lack thereof), and a transaction occurred in both stocks simultaneously. That data exists. It is called restricted stock.

Restricted stock is the term commonly used for the stock of a publicly traded company that is restricted under Rule 144 of the Securities Act of 1933. Currently, Rule 144 prevents the resale of unregistered stock in the public marketplace unless it has been registered or after a holding period.[43] However, Rule 144 allows for a sale of restricted stock to sophisticated private investors at any time, much like private stock. This type of transaction is commonly referred to as a private placement. By measuring the difference between the price of a restricted private placement and its publicly traded counterpart (what a willing buyer will pay and what a willing seller

---

[42] Lance S. Hall, "Is There a 'Best' Lack of Marketability Discount Model?" White paper handout at the University of San Diego School of Law Summit on Lack of Marketability, September 18, 2008. Taken mostly verbatim. (Used with permission.)

[43] Originally the holding period was two years and is now currently six months.

will accept for a limited-liquidity asset), a discount is evidenced that reflects solely the lack of liquidity between the two otherwise identical stocks.

Where the CARS Approach differs from the Benchmark Method is that the appraiser digs through the underlying private placement transaction data to make comparisons based on factors that impact liquidity such as market value, revenue, profitability, and volatility, as well as other factors.

In examining 470 restricted stock transactions, FMV Opinions, Inc. (the author's employer), observed that the discount varied based upon the underlying financial characteristics of the company. FMV found the following relationships:

The magnitude of the observed discount is negatively correlated with:

- The market value of the subject entity.
- The subject entity's revenues.
- The earnings and net profit margin of the subject entity.
- The dividend payout ratio of the subject entity.
- The total assets of the subject entity.
- The book value of shareholders' equity of the subject entity.
- The subject entity's stock price per share.
- The trading volume of the subject entity's stock.
- The size of the block sold (dollar value).

The magnitude of the observed discount is positively correlated with:

- The subject entity's market-to-book ratio (market value divided by book value).
- The subject entity's unrestricted stock price volatility.
- The subject block size relative to the trading volume of the stock.
- The block size, described as a percent of the total ownership.

Exhibit 9.17 examines 197 transactions under the two-year holding period limitations (the most illiquid) of Rule 144 and is divided into quintiles based upon the magnitude of the discount. The discount under a given quintile represents the median discount within that quintile. Financial characteristics of the companies falling within each quintile are then calculated. The concluded number represents the median within that quintile set.

Exhibit 9.17 Two-Year Holding Period (1980-February 1997)*

Quintile	1	2	3	4	5
Discount	**4.8%**	**13.0%**	**21.1%**	**31.2%**	**43.3%**
Market Value ($)	114,206	69,239	63,217	40,137	24,760
Volatility	56.5%	58.1%	72.7%	77.7%	94.9%
Total Assets ($)	45,038	23,558	16,305	10,890	5,941
Revenues ($)	16,801	23,475	11,495	9,721	5,311
Price per Share	$8.75	$8.13	$5.85	$4.00	$4.00

*Registration Rights and Premiums Excluded. 197 Transactions in Sample.

As one can observe, the discount generally increases as the company revenues, market value, and assets decrease. Moreover, discounts are greater for those firms displaying greater price volatility. For a privately held firm where volatility cannot be directly calculated a market-to-book value ratio may be used. Theoretically, the more a company's value is dependent upon intangible assets the greater the investment risk. Overall, we believe that this type of comparative analysis is a superior way to show the relevance of Rule 144 data to the private company equity being valued.

In examining the restricted stock data, FMV also observed that under the dribble-out provisions of Rule 144 some blocks of restricted stock actually had liquidation time frames greater than the holding periods otherwise dictated by Rule 144. For example, a 30 percent block of restricted stock may have a two-year holding period before the investor can begin to sell it in the public marketplace. However, the dribble-out provisions basically limit any such sales to one percent of the total shares outstanding. Accordingly, dribbling out all of the stock would take 7.5 years after the holding period ended. Therefore, large blocks of restricted stock are more illiquid than small blocks of restricted stock even in the same company. Exhibit 9.18 summarizes the results when the restricted stock transaction data is divided by the size of the restricted stock block.

Exhibit 9.18 Summary of Results

	Pct. Shares Placed		Discount
	High	**Low**	**Median**
More than 35%	42.80%	38.88%	48.72%
More than 30%	42.80%	30.42%	44.32%
More than 25%	42.80%	25.01%	39.69%
More than 20%	42.80%	20.48%	37.86%
Less than 20%	19.80%	0.10%	24.41%

While the size of the stock block affects the liquidity of restricted stock, this is not generally the case for private company stock. For a private company, a five percent block of stock is generally just as illiquid as a 20 percent block. Given the fact that private company stock is more illiquid than even the largest blocks of restricted stock, the large block restricted stock data provides a floor to the private company stock discount, regardless of the private company block size.

FMV takes this data and examines the discount in a two-step process. The illustration in Exhibit 9.19 provides a framework for the FMV two-step process.

Exhibit 9.19 FMV Two-Step Process

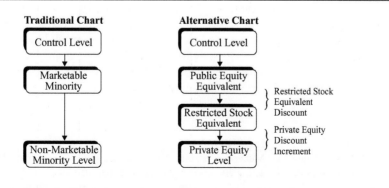

The first step in The FMV Method requires a comparative analysis with the small block restricted stock data to derive an "as if" restricted stock discount for the private company interest. The second step is to develop a set of small-block and large-block data that share similar financial characteristics such that, except for block size, would otherwise share similar discounts. The differential between the "matching sets" for small block discounts and large-block discounts represents the private company discount increment. Exhibit 9.20 illustrates The FMV Method.

Exhibit 9.20   The FMV Method

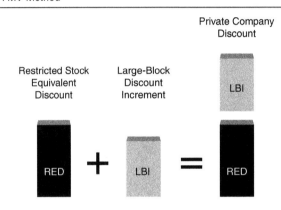

The reason that a direct comparison between the large-block data and the private company interest is not performed is that there remain relatively few large-block transactions to make such a direct comparison as meaningful. Accordingly, a comparison with the plentiful small-block data can be performed to arrive at an "as if" restricted stock discount. Then, a meaningful comparison can be performed between the large-block data and a set of small-block data that share similar financial characteristics to the large-block data. The discount differential between the large-block data and small-block data sharing similar characteristics provides direct evidence for an added incremental discount to reflect the greater illiquidity of the private equity interest.

The advantage to using the two-step FMV Method is that it recognizes that liquidity is a continuum and that, all things being equal, the private equity interest should always have a discount greater than a similarly situated large-block restricted stock interest, regardless of the size of the private company stock block. Further, this analysis is based on empirical, observable data. The data upon which The FMV Method is based was victorious in *Kosman*.[44] The disadvantage of using The FMV Method is that it requires analysis and analysis takes time.[45]

---

[44] *Estate of Kosman* – T.C. Memo. 1996-112.
[45] For more about The FMV Method, see Hall, "New Tactics Required to Prove Discount for Lack of Marketability," *The Value Examiner,* January/February 2007.

Regardless of whether you choose to use The FMV Method, the underlying restricted stock data is available to the appraiser to use as they best see fit.[46]

For additional information on restricted stocks and the FMV Opinions Restricted Stock Study, see Addendum 1, "Determining Discounts for Lack of Marketability, A Companion Guide to the FMV Restricted Stock Study™, Second Edition, 2007" at www.wiley.com/go/FVAM3E.

Valuation Advisors' Lack of Marketability Discount Study[47]

Brian K. Pearson, CPA/PFS/ABV, ASA, of Valuation Advisors, LLC (VAL), has performed studies and created a searchable database on pre-IPO transactions. The source of the data is prospectuses filed with the SEC for companies going public. VAL records transactions in the company's stock prior to the IPO and compare that price with the IPO price. Transactions include stock, stock options, or convertible preferred stock. VAL updates the database monthly. As of 2007 it had over 3,900 pre-IPO transactions fully searchable by:

- Revenues
- Operating income
- Total assets
- SIC or NAICS code
- Company name
- Time period to liquidity
- Type of transaction

The table shown in Exhibit 9.21 presents aggregated discounts for the period 1995 to 2006.

Exhibit 9.21 VAL IPO Discount Study Median Data

VAL IPO Discount Study Median Data					
IPO Year	**0–3 Months**	**4–6 Months**	**7–9 Months**	**10–12 Months**	**1–2 Years**	**Count**
1995	37.82%	28.62%	60.40%	50.33%	60.64%	34
1996	30.83%	52.97%	56.37%	69.38%	71.81%	270
1997	34.18%	50.00%	67.12%	76.01%	80.00%	212
1998	23.35%	46.67%	68.93%	71.41%	71.91%	212
1999	30.77%	53.89%	75.00%	76.92%	82.00%	694
2000	28.70%	45.08%	61.51%	68.92%	76.64%	653
2001	14.74%	33.17%	33.38%	52.06%	51.61%	115
2002	6.15%	17.33%	21.88%	39.51%	55.00%	81
2003	28.77%	22.30%	38.36%	39.71%	61.37%	123
2004	16.67%	22.68%	40.00%	56.25%	57.86%	334
2005	14.75%	26.10%	41.68%	46.11%	45.45%	296
2006	23.47%	20.69%	40.23%	46.51%	56.27%	264
Average	24.18%	34.96%	50.41%	57.76%	64.21%	

---

[46] Espen Robak and Lance S. Hall, "Bringing Sanity to Marketability Discounts — A New Data Source," *Valuation Strategies*, July/August 2001, pp. 7–13, 45, 46. (Warren, Gorham & Lamont)
[47] Valuation Advisors' DLOM Study—August 23, 2007, Business Valuation Resources teleconference (www.bvresources.com; see also www.valuationpros.com). (Used with permission.)

QUANTITATIVE TOOLS

Investor's Discounted Cash Flow Models

John C. Harper, Jr., and J. Peter Lindquist wrote one of the early articles on the use of a "shareholders'" DCF model. In their article they present a straightforward example:[48]

> Let us demonstrate by a simple but realistic example of how this discount is calculated and the impact it can have on today's value of a share of stock. A friend of John Smith is approaching retirement and has offered to sell Smith his 10 percent common stock interest in Acme Services, Inc., which is controlled by members of the William Jones family. What can Smith afford to pay for this stock?
>
> Today's value: Smith analyzes the performance of the company using the Revenue Ruling 59-60 guidelines, and then discusses his opinions with Bill Jones, current president of the company. They agree that $100 per share is a fair value if 100 percent of the stock were to be sold today.

The article also presents that the company will grow 10 percent per year for the next 10 years, at which time Jones is to retire and "may" sell the company. Smith used a 25 percent annual return on investment, given the risks of a private company investment.

If the sale of the company is expected to be in the tenth year, then a buyer should not pay any more than $28, or a 72 percent discount from the original $100. The expected or anticipated year of sale can be most difficult to determine as the controlling shareholder's age, health, mental well-being, and "exit strategy" all affect the decisions to sell.

This example shows that a minority interest with very little market may be near worthless. Furthermore, the discount that we see in this example may be *a combined discount of both lack of control and lack of marketability* because the $100 per share price is an "enterprise" or controlling value, and the present value in the tenth year of $28 may represent "cash equivalent" or marketable minority interest value, thus including both discounts.

For another view, see Addendum 3 at www.wiley.com/go/FVAM3E for an article by John J. Stockdale, ASA, CPA/ABV, "A DLOM Computational Model," which appeared in *Financial Valuation and Litigation Expert,* Issue 11, February/ March 2008, page 5.

Quantitative Marketability Discount Model

In 1997, Z. Christopher Mercer published a book entitled *Quantifying Marketability Discounts* that expanded on the concepts presented in the Harper/Lindquist article. Mercer's book presents a model for analyzing marketability discounts and includes excellent overviews of restricted stock studies, IPO studies, and Tax Court cases.

---

[48] John C. Harper, Jr., and J. Peter Lindquist, "Quantitative Support for Large Minority Discounts in Closely Held Corporations," *The Appraisal Journal* (April 1983).

The quantitative marketability discount model (QMDM) model requires five key inputs:

- Marketable minority value of the stock
- Expected growth rate of a marketable minority shareholder interest
- Expected holding period
- Required rate of return for a nonmarketable minority interest
- Expected dividend payments

The QMDM inputs are analogous to those used in traditional enterprise-level discounted cash flow models. The two sets of assumptions are compared in Exhibit 9.22.

Exhibit 9.22 Comparison of Two Sets of Assumptions

Enterprise-Level DCF Assumptions	Shareholder-Level DCF (QMDM) Assumptions
1. Forecast Period	1. Range of Expected Holding Periods
2. Projected Interim Cash Flows (during forecast period)	2a. Expected Distribution/Dividend Yield
	2b. Expected Growth in Distributions/Dividends
	2c. Timing (Midyear or End of Year)
3. Projected Terminal Value (at end of forecast period)	3a. Growth in Value over Holding Period
	3b. Premium or Discount to Projected Enterprise Value
4. Discount Rate	4. Range of Required Holding Period Returns

Each of the discounted cash flow inputs (from the enterprise model on the left side of Exhibit 9.22) is tailored to the considerations of minority shareholders in private enterprises (on the right side). Although the QMDM directly values the subject nonmarketable minority interest, it is not used in isolation, but rather in conjunction with a contemporaneous valuation of the subject enterprise because the shareholder-level expectations regarding cash flows, risk, and growth are inextricably linked to the corresponding expectations with respect to the enterprise.

The theory behind the QMDM indicates that a marketability discount is defined by the relationship between the value of a company determined at the enterprise level and at the shareholder level. In other words, shareholder-level value is generally less than the value of the enterprise. The reasons can be summarized as follows:

- Cash flow to shareholders is less than cash flow of the enterprise. One of the underpinnings of the QMDM is that there are two potential agency costs that may create a differential between cash flow to shareholders and enterprise cash flows.
  - *Non-pro rata distributions.* Agency costs, perhaps called discretionary expenses, are incurred by minority shareholders when there are non-pro rata distributions to certain shareholders (e.g., controlling shareholders), who take bonuses in excess of normalized compensation. These funds are not available for pro rata distributions, nor are they available for reinvestment, which drives the expected growth in value.
  - Suboptimal reinvestment occurs when the management of an enterprise reinvests funds at less than its cost of capital. It is the reinvestment of earnings that drives the growth of earnings (and value), particularly over defined time

horizons, at rates greater than the long-term expected growth in earnings. Suboptimal reinvestment dampens the expected growth in value and therefore shareholder-level value, implying greater marketability discounts, other things remaining the same.

- Incremental risks faced by minority investors exceed the risks of the enterprise. In developing marketable minority valuation indications (enterprise level), appraisers develop equity discount rates. These discount rates reflect the appraisers' assessments of the risks related to achieving expected cash flows and growth. Those risks are embodied in the enterprise discount rate, and in the enterprise valuation. Minority investors in interests lacking marketability face additional risks, including the uncertainties of the expected holding period (which may be long and uncertain), restrictions on transfer, and, in the case of tax pass-through entities, potential exposure to adverse cash flow (if the entity fails to make tax pass-through distributions).

Any combination of agency costs or incremental shareholder risks contributes to reducing shareholder-level value relative to enterprise value, and therefore to increasing the marketability discount, other things being equal.

For additional information, see articles from the journal *Financial Valuation and Litigation Expert*, Valuation Products and Services, LLC, in web Addendums 2 and 4 at www.wiley.com/go/FVAM3E.

Some analysts have observed that the discount derived in this approach may appear to combine discounts both for lack of control and marketability. As noted earlier, Mercer disagrees. In *Business Valuation, Discounts and Premiums*, he states:

> A number of appraisers have suggested that the QMDM may be capturing elements of the minority interest discount as well as the marketability discount. There has been a recent exchange on this issue in *Shannon Pratt's Business Valuation Update* 7, no. 3 (March 2001) pp. 7–10 and no. 5 (May 2001) pp. 9–10. Assuming, as I do, that it is appropriate for appraisers to make normalizing adjustments in the development of marketable minority valuation indications, the QMDM captures the appropriate marketability discount. The rationale for my position on normalizing adjustments is outlined in Dr. Pratt's book, *Cost of Capital—Estimation and Applications,* in Appendix D which he asked me to write relating to the use of ValuSource PRO Software. Some appraisers assume that such normalizing adjustments for discretionary owner compensation and expenses are inappropriate in minority interest appraisals because they reflect elements of control not available to minority shareholders. They further assume that the diminution of value resulting from the "leakage" of discretionary cash flows reflects elements of a minority interest discount. Under these assumptions, which I do not believe to be correct, the QMDM captures elements of the minority interest discount.[49]

Mercer further outlines the rationale for his position on normalizing adjustments in his 2004 book, *Valuing Enterprise and Shareholder Cash Flows: The Integrated*

---

[49] Shannon P. Pratt, *Business Valuation Discounts and Premiums* (New York: John Wiley & Sons, Inc., 2001), p. 184.

Theory of Business Valuation.[50] In this book, Mercer places the QMDM in a larger setting by developing levels of value framework that he ties firmly to core valuation considerations, all illustrated by the Gordon Model. The framework is gaining some acceptance. Numerous analysts have recognized it as rigorous thinking about the ways in which discounts and premiums arise from valuation fundamentals and merits consideration. See Mercer's comments on its acceptance in web Addendum 2 at www.wiley.com/go/FVAM3E with his article "QMDM: A Long but Important Answer to a Short but Important Question," *Financial Valuation and Litigation Expert,* Issue 11, February/March 2008, pages 13, 18.

> The QMDM represents continued theoretical development of the concept of the marketability discount. This method is gaining in visibility and use, and numerous appraisers have adopted some form of the framework for analyzing discounts that Mercer has presented, but most agree that if used, it should be in conjunction with the use of other discount studies or methods.

Option Pricing Models

In 1993, David B. Chaffe III published an article about his theory that the Black-Scholes pricing model could be used to determine the amount of a marketability discount.[51] Chaffe uncovered relationships in the comparison of his computation of the marketability discount with that of the transaction data. He found that the European option, which is exercisable only at the end of the option period, could be an appropriate model for the SEC Rule 144 holding period of restricted shares. Substituting certain inputs of the model to express conditions of a restricted stock, he was able to produce results similar to those of the restricted stock studies. His analysis was presented in *Business Valuation Review*, December 1993, "Option Pricing as a Proxy for Discount for Lack of Marketability in Private Company Valuations."

Long-Term Equity Anticipation Securities

An article in the Spring 2008 issue of the ASA *Business Valuation Review* entitled "Minimum Marketability Discounts—3rd Edition" by Ronald M. Seaman, ASA, described research on long-term equity anticipation securities (LEAPS) related to discounts for lack of marketability. LEAPS are exchange-listed options that grant the buyer (holder) the right, but not the obligation, to buy, in the case of a call, or to sell,

---

[50] Z. Christopher Mercer, *Valuing Enterprise and Shareholder Cash Flows: The Integrated Theory of Business Valuation,* 2004 (Memphis: Peabody Publishing LP).
[51] David B. Chaffe III, "Option Pricing as a Proxy for Discount for Lack of Marketability in Private Company Valuations," *Business Valuation Review* (December 1993).

in the case of a put, a specified amount of the underlying asset at a predetermined price on or before a given date. During the option term, which ranges from 14 to 26 months, LEAPS are a form of insurance against price fluctuations in publicly traded stocks. Mr. Seaman suggested that LEAPS could be used to quantify a DLOM by representing the cost of a LEAPS put option, expressed as a percentage of the price of the underlying stock, as a measure of the cost of price protection against a loss in value of the stock. He has performed several studies of LEAPS in order to provide evidence of such.

LEAPS are listed on several stock exchanges and are actively traded. They are American-style options that may be exercised at any time prior to the expiration date. LEAPS are issued in September, October, and November each year and expire on the third Saturday of January either two or three years later. For example, you could have purchased a LEAPS put option on Procter & Gamble stock at a certain price in October 2008 that would expire in January 2010 or a longer-term option that would expire in January 2011. As the Chicago Board Options Exchange states, LEAPS put options "provide a medium to long-term insurance or hedge for stock owners in the event of a substantial decline in their stock."

Mr. Seaman's 2008 study was based on the costs of LEAPS put options at the end of November 2008. The total number of LEAPS at that time was about 1,245. He excluded LEAPS on exchange-traded funds (41) and LEAPS on companies whose stock was selling below the $2.50 minimum option limit (approximately 162 companies). The resulting study included the LEAPS put options of 1,036 companies. Not every stock had both one-year and two-year options. A few offered only a 2011 option, but many more offered only the 2010 option.

Sources of data for this study were, in general, the Chicago Board Options Exchange, delayed market quotes, and Yahoo! Finance. The percentage costs of the put options were calculated as the cost of the option divided by the stock price. (A detailed explanation of the sources of information and of the discount calculations is available at www.dlom-info.com, "2009 Study.")

The objective was to determine what factors influenced the costs of price protection or the size of discounts for lack of marketability and to what extent. The analysis was limited to means, medians, and ranges of the middle 50 percent of occurrences. The study indicated the following:

Valuation date. Discounts change over time and are not constant in size.

Industry. Discounts vary by industry. The differences are more pronounced as the definition of the industry becomes more specific or more detailed.

Company size. Company size has a clear and major effect on discounts. The smaller the company, in revenues or assets, the larger the discount.

Company risk. Company risk has a major effect on discounts. The greater the risk, as measured by the company's beta, the greater the discount.

For additional and updated information, see www.dlom-info.com.

Longstaff Upper Bound Lookback Put Option Model

Several other methods involving option pricing have been developed. In the December 1995 issue of the *Journal of Finance*, Francis A. Longstaff published "How Much Can Marketability Affect Security Values?" Like Chaffe, Longstaff utilizes option pricing to attempt to answer the question. However, he suggests using a look-back put option. Unlike a European put option, a lookback put option is path dependent. It assumes that the option holder had perfect hindsight and would exercise the option at the optimal point. The value of a lookback option is therefore greater than a regular option, meaning that it costs more, resulting in a larger DLOM. In the 1995 article, Longstaff posited that volatility and the holding period are the key DLOM factors.

Longstaff's analysis indicates that the marketability discount is not a linear function of time; the greatest risks, and therefore the largest increases in the percentage discount, occur early in the restriction period. Lookback options guarantee the option holder a distribution based on the maximum price the underlying security achieves during the life of the contract. In deriving a lack of marketability discount from a lookback option such as Longstaff's, it appears to be most relevant for strategic investors and/or insiders with asymmetrical information. Empirical evidence indicates that private information enables strategic investors and/or insiders to time the market and realize excess returns. Therefore, for strategic investors and/or insiders, for whom resale restrictions (i.e., SEC Rule 144/lockup provisions) interfere with the investors' ability to exploit their asymmetrical information advantage to time the market, a greater lack of marketability discount may be warranted. For investors with symmetrical information (i.e., rank-and-file employees), however, the Longstaff regression analysis generally provides an upper bound for the lack of marketability indication.

For additional information, see articles from the journal *Financial Valuation and Litigation Expert,* Issue 15, Valuation Products and Services, LLC, in web Addendum 4 at www.wiley.com/go/FVAM3E.

Protective Put Analyses

A protective put on the indicated value would lock in the common shareholder's price by providing protection from downside risk. If the stock price was lower than the indicated value at the liquidity date, the put would protect the investor from this downside risk since the common stockholder would be able to sell the shares at the put strike price. European put options are considered standard contracts; all that matters is the underlying share price at maturity and not how it got there. A European protective put, however, addresses only the downside risk of the common stock price, allowing for upside appreciation in value, which potentially overstates the discount.

Asian put options, however, offer some protection from price manipulations, as the payoffs for these options are not determined by the underlying share price at maturity but by the average underlying price (aka average rate) or the average of the exercise price (aka average strike) over some preset period of time. Generally, the value of an Asian option is lower than a standard contract (i.e., European option) due to the fact that the averaging process reduces the impact of volatility of the stock or exercise price movement over its term (i.e., restriction period). While there are three methods to calculate Asian put options, only two are typically used in practice: geometric average and arithmetic average.

To date, there are no known closed-form analytical solutions to arithmetic average options. As a result, Monte Carlo simulations can be used, whereby underlying assumptions are allowed to vary from their expected values within prescribed limits. There are, however, closed-form analytical solutions to geometric average price options, such as the geometric average rate put model (GARPM). It should be noted that there is no known published study that compares the discounts derived under GARPM to discounts observed empirically. Finally, unlike the protective put models by Chaffe, Longstaff, and Finnerty (whose model is discussed next), GARPM does not share the same framework whereby the discount for lack of marketability is based on the concept that the strike price is compared to the underlying share price at maturity, but instead ignores the underlying share price at maturity and calculates the geometric average rate over the restriction period.

Based on the research by John D. Finnerty,[52] however, the Finnerty model uses an approximate closed-form analytical solution to derive the arithmetic average strike put model (AASPM). The AASPM is consistent with the range of discounts observed empirically in letter-stock private placements that occurred between April 1, 1991, and February 1, 2005, with a one-year restriction period. As the AASPM does not assume that the investor has any special market-timing ability, the Finnerty model appears more appropriate for (unrelated) institutional investors, who are much less likely to have any private information that can be exploited.

Finally, creating a market for a protective put, whether European or Asian, on an illiquid, volatile private company would be expensive, and the banking fees associated with the creation of these derivatives would be high (if it were even possible to create such a security), suggesting that the discounts derived herein may be understated. The theoretical issues discussed here may factor into the weight that is placed on the protective put analyses in discount conclusions.

Measuring the Amount of Discount for Lack of Marketability

Each method of determining a DLOM has strengths and weaknesses. Determining the amount of the marketability discount to be applied to closely held securities by reference to either the various restricted stock, IPO studies, or quantitative models requires careful scrutiny of the studies and models themselves. Some of these studies and models have been challenged as to their applicability to marketability discounts for closely held securities by both the courts and other experts. Accordingly, the reader must understand these particular criticisms before adopting any of these methodologies for determining a discount for lack of marketability.

Factors Influencing Marketability of the Investment

In the landmark *Mandelbaum* case (see web Addendum 5, Tax Court Cases [The Oldies but Goodies] at www.wiley.com/go/FVAM3E for certain case summaries), a number of factors were considered by the court in their analysis of the magnitude of the marketability of the Company. These factors, which are explained in the case summary, included:

- Financial statement analysis
- Dividend policy
- History and nature of the company

---

[52] John D. Finnerty, "The Impact of Transfer Restrictions on Stock Prices," *Financial Management Association International,* 2008 FMA European Conference (revised November 2007). Note: There has been a recent correction of the Finnerty model.

- Management
- Control
- Stock restrictions
- Holding period
- Redemption policy
- Costs of IPO

This was the sole issue at trial. Below is a listing of other factors that may influence marketability and liquidity depending upon the individual circumstances of the engagement. Some of these factors may overlap with issues related to lack of control or may be incorporated in the price multiple or discount rate.

- Accessibility and reliability of financial information
  - Compiled statements are less reliable than audit or review statements.
  - Manual internal accounting systems are generally less reliable and less accessible.
- Number of shareholders
  - Companies with many shareholders may be more likely to enter into a transaction to satisfy diverse owner interests.
- Concentration of control owners
  - Control owners may dominate businesses and operate them to meet their own ends with little consideration for the needs of minority owners.
- Number of potential buyers
  - A large number of interested purchasers may improve the possibility of a transaction.
- Access to capital marketplace
  - Low leverage businesses may be more appealing to prospective purchasers.
- Size of the business
  - Larger businesses may be more easily sold or financed and possess broader appeal than smaller businesses.
- Volume of comparable private transactions
  - Businesses in an industry that is experiencing high merger and acquisition activity may be more marketable.
- Owners with adversarial relationships or an inconsistent business philosophy
  - Owners who are unable to agree may make the business less marketable.
- Desirability of the business
  - Businesses in "hot" industries may be more marketable because they tend to attract interest.
- Existence of restricted stock agreements
  - Shareholder agreements may prevent free transferability and limit marketability of stock.
- Existence of noncompete agreements
  - Businesses that fail to limit the mobility of critical personnel may be less marketable.
- Yield
  - Businesses with a track record of consistent high profitability are usually more easily transferable.
- Liquidity of control owners
  - The existence of other liquid assets on the part of the owners may reduce the desire or need to transfer the business.

- Quality and competence of management team
  - Businesses with competent, experienced management may be more appealing to a broader range of potential purchasers.
- Existence and effect of pending litigation
  - Businesses with potentially costly legal issues (i.e., environmental) are not as desirable in the marketplace.
- Size of block of stock
  - Owners of large blocks may have influence on corporate governance. However, larger blocks may be more difficult to find buyers for.
- Existence and extent of contractual restrictions
  - Financing agreements may limit compensation of control owners or the ability to declare and pay dividends.
- Degree and effect of industry regulations
  - Industry regulation can restrict the control owner where minority shareholders might otherwise be helpless.
- Effects of state law
  - Percentage control required to undertake major corporate actions (i.e., sale of assets) can be more favorable in some states.
- Existence of swing vote attributes
  - Swing votes can lessen the discount in certain situations.
- Relationship between controlling and noncontrolling shareholders
  - Harmonious relationships may reduce discounts, whereas adversarial relationships may increase discounts.
  - Existence of shareholder agreements that grant control to certain shareholders for certain activities (if transferable).

When valuing a closely held company, care, reasonableness, and sound professional judgment must be employed when applying discounts. Furthermore, the particular facts and circumstances of each valuation must be the final determinant of discounts. A thorough understanding of both the subject company and the underlying data used in the discount studies are important for defensible valuation conclusions. The marketability factors as presented should not be considered exhaustive nor are they applicable in each valuation. Any particular closely held company may have a unique discount issue that must be taken into consideration.

Exhibit 9.25 is a summary example of a possible DLOM chart, here using 35 percent, the general average of several restricted stock studies, as the starting point. This is for presentation purposes only.

OTHER DISCOUNTS

ValTip

In addition to the discounts for lack of control and marketability, there are several other potential discounts. Some analysts consider these discounts in the calculation of a discount or capitalization factor while others separately quantify and apply the discounts.

Exhibit 9.25 DLOM Adjustment Example (illustration purposes only)

Marketability Adjustment Factors	Impact on Marketability Discount		
	Warrants an *Above Average* Discount	Warrants an *Average* Discount	Warrants an *Below Average* Discount
Starting Point	35%	35%	35%
History and Outlook	+		−
Financial Factors	+		−
Management	+		−
Holding Period	+		−
Redemption Policy	+		−
Transfer of Control	+		−
Restrictions on Transfer	+	No Change	−
Cash Distribution Policy	+		−
Information Access and Reliability	+		−
Cost of Public Offering	+		−
Other Factor 1	+		−
Other Factor 2	+		−
Other Factor 3, etc.	+		−
Ending Point	**> 35%**	**35%**	**< 35%**

While discounts for lack of control, when appropriate, and lack of marketability may apply to the majority of valuations, the following discounts are taken less frequently as a separately quantified and displayed discount.

Restrictive Agreement Discounts

A review of any buy-sell and/or restrictive agreement within a closely held corporation typically reveals various stockholder rights, including income and dividend preferences, liquidation preferences, voting rights, and limitations of the sale of stock. It also may include an actual stock price or a protocol or method for determining the price.

> Restrictions under certain agreements limit the ability to sell or transfer ownership interests.

In some instances, the sale price is dictated. The effect of these agreements is the difference in price between an unrestricted ownership interest and the restricted interest giving rise to a shareholder level discount. The more severe the restrictions, the higher the discount. The Tax Courts have periodically suggested that restrictive agreements be considered but that they may not necessarily set value. Usually restrictive agreements are of greater importance in an estate tax valuation than a gift tax valuation.

Information Access and Reliability Discount

> In valuing a closely held company, an adjustment for information access and reliability may be in order.

Smaller companies, free of SEC regulations and the restrictions associated with public oversight, can produce scanty and unreliable financial information. An investor considering an investment in such a company would discount any information believed to be suspect or unreliable. If a company being valued is being compared to publicly traded companies, adjustments to the financial statements or valuation multiples (e.g., depreciation, leverage, taxes, nonrecurring items, and non operating assets) may be necessary.

If there is additional risk associated with uncertainty in the underlying data, it may be appropriate to apply a discount. The magnitude of such a discount would depend entirely on the facts and circumstances of each individual situation. Furthermore, if the proper financial adjustments are made, a discount may not be appropriate.

Liquidation Costs Discount

> An ongoing disagreement between the IRS and many tax practitioners revolves around the treatment of the costs related to liquidating the assets in estates.

Certain costs, such as brokers' fees, state and local transfer taxes, and holding period interest, would be incurred to realize the property's fair market value. It has therefore been argued that these costs should be used to reduce the value of the property in the estate; some analysts take a discount.

Trapped Capital Gains Discount

At the very least, a trapped capital gains discount should be considered if liquidation is imminent and the entity holds assets with unrealized appreciation. The IRS outlined its early position in TAM 9150001.[53] In general, the TAM stated that if the

---

[53] IRS TAM 9150001 (August 20, 1991).

immediate liquidation of the subject assets is not contemplated, the capital gains tax cannot be used to reduce the value of the estate. Obviously, many tax practitioners disagree with this assumption. Furthermore the courts have accepted these discounts in several recent cases including *Estate of Artemus Davis,*[54] *Eisenberg v. Commissioner,*[55] and *Dunn v. Commissioner.*[56] When a trapped capital gains discount is taken, practitioners disagree as to whether the entire amount of the tax on the trapped-in gain should be taken or whether the tax on gain should be discounted, perhaps to reflect possible scenarios regarding the timing of its eventual realization. The Tax Court recently endorsed a form of the latter procedure in the *Estate of Jelke,* accepting a reduction for trapped-in gain on appreciated marketable securities, but calculating the discount based on present value of the tax given assumed future sales.[57] This was overturned on appeal in 2007 when the court allowed the estate a dollar-for-dollar reduction.[58] However, a present-value technique was allowed in *Estate of Litchfield,* decided in 2009.[59] See Chapter 8 for additional information.

Key Person/Thin Management Discount

Key person and thin management discounts are based on the premise that the contribution of an individual (or small group of individuals) to a business is so significant that it is almost certain that present and future earnings levels would be adversely affected by their loss. This is not an unusual situation in many smaller closely held companies. Revenue Ruling 59-60 deals with this issue by stating: "The loss of the manager of a so-called one-man business may have a depressing effect upon the value of the stock of such business, particularly if there is a lack of trained personnel capable of succeeding to the management of the enterprise." The selection of a discount to reflect the loss of a key manager or a thin management structure may be tempered by the effects of life insurance policies that are in existence as of the date of the valuation.

ValTip

A key person or thin management entity-level discount would be appropriate in the valuation of a closely held company where an owner or employee is responsible for generating a significant portion of the business's sales or profits. This key person may be a revenue generator, possess technical knowledge, or have close relationships with suppliers, customers, or banks.

---

[54] *Estate of Davis v. Commissioner,* 110 T.C. 530 (1998).

[55] *Estate of Eisenberg v. Commissioner,* 155 F.3d 50 (2d Cir. 1998).

[56] *Estate of Dunn v. Commissioner,* U.S. Court of Appeals, 5th Cir., No. 00-60614, August 1, 2002.

[57] *Estate of Jelke v. Commissioner,* T.C. Memo 2005-131, May 31, 2005.

[58] *Estate of Jelke v. Commissioner,* 05-15549, U.S. Court of Appeals for the 11th Circuit, November 15, 2007.

[59] *Estate of Litchfield v. Commissioner,* T.C. Memo. 2009-21, January 24, 2009.

Investment Company Discount

It is not unusual for investment companies to sell on the basis of their assets (typically real estate and securities) rather than their earnings. Revenue Ruling 59-60 states "the value of the stock of a closely held investment in a real estate holding company, whether or not family owned, is closely related to the value of the assets underlying the stock. For companies of this type, the appraiser should determine the fair market values of the assets of the company."

An analysis of publicly traded investment real estate companies and publicly traded closed-end funds reveals that minority interests in investment companies typically sell at a discount from their respective pro rata share of the firm's net assets restated at fair market value. The application of this entity-level discount would adjust for the shareholders' indirect ownership of these assets and their inability to force the sale, liquidation, or merger of these assets. Investment company discounts range anywhere from 10 to 60 percent, depending on the facts and circumstances of each case.

At first glance, the investment company discount in its purest form may be considered a minority interest discount; however, an investment company discount adjustment has been recognized by the courts for application to a majority interest. In *Estate of Folks*,[60] the court recognized that different investment company discounts might apply to different ownership percentages for the same company. The court opined that a 50 percent discount was allowable for a minority interest and a 40 percent discount was allowable for a majority interest (less than control). Note that the court also allowed an additional marketability discount for the minority interest.

In *Estate of Dougherty*,[61] the court decided that a 35 percent discount was allowable for nonmarketability and operating and liquidation costs. The decedent held a 100 percent beneficial interest in a trust that owned a 100 percent interest in a company that owned primarily real estate and other nonliquid assets.

Blockage Discounts and Market Absorption

Where there is only a limited market for the shares, offering a large block can have a depressing consequence on the value of the shares of stock.

Treasury Regulation Section 20.2031–2 states the following:

> The size of the block of stock to be valued in relation to the number of shares changing hands in sales may be relevant in determining whether selling prices reflect the fair market value of the block to be valued. If the block of stock is so large in relation to the actual sales on the existing market that it could not be liquidated in a reasonable time without depressing the market, the price at which the block could be sold as such outside the usual market, as through an underwriter, may be a more accurate indication of value than market quotations.

---

[60] *Estate of T. John Folks, Jr.*, T.C. Memo 1982–43.
[61] *Estate of Albert L. Dougherty*, T.C. Memo 1990–274.

Blockage discounts are based on the theory that, ordinarily, a large block of publicly traded stock cannot be sold as readily as a few shares of stock.

The following factors, among others, should be considered in determining the blockage discount to be applied to blocks of public stocks:

- Size of the block in relation to the total shares outstanding
- Size of the block in relation to the daily trading volume
- Volatility of the stock
- General, economic, and industry trends
- Alternatives for disposing of the stock
- Length of time necessary to dispose of the stock without affecting the current price

Blockage or market absorption discounts also can be considered when valuing other assets, such as real estate. In the valuation of a closely held real estate investment holding company, a discount for potential market absorption should be considered.

For example, a large block of similar real estate holdings within a single geographical area may create oversupply and may be more difficult to sell over a reasonable period of time than one property. Where there is a limited market for a certain type of property, offering a large block of properties could depress the market and lower the prices that otherwise could have been obtained. It is simply a matter of supply and demand.

The following factors, among others, are considered when valuing a large block of real estate placed on the market on any given day:

- Number of properties and square footage of properties that are being valued
- Geographical concentration
- Type of property (e.g., apartments, office buildings, etc.)
- Total supply of that type of property within the same geographical area
- Length of time to dispose of the real estate without affecting the price
- Whether the market is stagnant or appreciating
- Market and real estate trends

Nonhomogeneous Assets Discount

A nonhomogeneous assets discount may be applicable to an unusually diverse collection of assets or businesses within the subject company being valued. A small company with limited access to capital and a small management team may have difficulty managing such a broad spectrum of assets. The discount will measure underutilization of assets or lack of synergy among assets.

Lack-of-Diversification Discount

A lack-of-diversification discount may be applicable to a niche company. This discount may be used in addition to a small-company discount. Lack of diversification typically is associated with a one or nondiversive product company or with material sales dependent on a fad.

The lack-of-diversification discount is a measure of the risk associated with the niche disappearing and the costs associated with developing a new product segment or possibly liquidation. A thorough understanding of the business's costs relative to its industry is required to quantify a lack-of-diversification discount. Care should be taken with any other approach to value that may already incorporate this discount. For example, this discount could be included implicitly in a capitalization rate or a market multiple.

Although these discounts are most likely included in either the discount rate or market multiple, it may be necessary to make an additional adjustment for a small-company risk discount and a company-specific risk discount.

Small-Company Risk Discount

The degree of comparability among the closely held subject company and its publicly traded counterparts must be evaluated.

Merger, acquisition, and financial data are available that indicate that the prices paid for smaller, closely held companies can be lower than the prices paid for their larger, publicly traded counterparts. Furthermore, studies indicate that rates of return required for investing in small companies can be higher than the rates of return required on much larger, publicly traded, diversified companies. This is important since the higher the rate of return required, the lower the final value. This adjustment is usually made in the discount or cap rate. (See Chapter 6.)

A small-company risk discount may be separate from a marketability discount and a minority discount. Depending on how the discount was determined, this adjustment may incorporate the differences in information access and reliability and lack of adequate succession management.

VaITip

When a smaller closely held company is being compared to a larger publicly traded company, an adjustment for size may be appropriate.

Small companies often have limited access to capital, limited ability to weather a market downturn, limited resources to develop and market new products, and so on. Smaller companies also can have a higher cost of capital than larger companies.

The data from some of these studies are calculated primarily from control valuation multiples from acquisitions of companies. Therefore, a minority discount, if appropriate, may be applied if a minority value were desired. A discount for a key person or thin management may not be applicable because the prices paid for the closely held companies used in the study may have already been reduced to reflect this situation, although this would not be the case in every company. Lack of marketability/liquidity and information access discounts must be carefully considered since prices paid for the companies that make up the studies may have been set and/or adjusted based on some level of due diligence and perception of marketability on the part of the buyer.

Company-Specific Risk Discount

The risk premium for unsystematic risk attributable to the specific company being valued should account for additional risk factors specific to the company that may not be reflected in the comparable companies. This adjustment is usually made in the discount or cap rate. (See Chapter 6.)

Firm-specific risk factors may include:

- Litigation
- Reliance on a few customers
- Limited supply of sources
- Old technology
- Riskier business

Care should be exercised to avoid overlaps or "double discounting" with thin management discounts, small-company risk discounts, lack-of-diversification discounts, or others.

ANALYSIS OF PREMIUMS ACCORDED VOTING VERSUS NON-VOTING STOCK

There is evidence that there is a premium placed on stocks that include special voting rights, as compared with otherwise similar stock without the same voting rights.

However, where the transactions represent only a small minority of the voting class of stock, the premium accorded the shares is comparatively small.

The question considered here is whether the application of a pricing premium is appropriate where there are two classes of shares, identical in every respect, except as to voting rights. The following study presents research into this area. Currently, there are multiple companies listed on the various national exchanges whose stock trades in two classes. Generally, the Class A shares include full voting rights, and a second class of shares is offered either without any voting rights, or with a much more limited voting power (typically 1/10th of a vote per share). Some of the non voting or limited voting shares may have a higher dividend, or a dividend preference (i.e., cumulative dividends, or preference as to dividend distributions). These shares have been eliminated from this research, as the purpose of this research was to isolate the difference in voting rights as the only difference between two classes of shares.

Yearly research by The Financial Valuation Group in Tampa identified nonfinancial and non utility companies whose stock trades in two classes on listed exchanges. The research focused on operational companies and thus excluded the highly regulated financial and utility companies, except where financial or utility data was required as a proxy to fill certain gaps in data. In each case, both the voting and non voting stock were offered, side by side, in their various markets. The list was ultimately reduced to the stock of companies where the only difference between the shares was the voting rights. The dividends were the same, and the shares were equal in all respects, with the exception of voting rights, where the Class A shares generally were granted four to ten times as much voting power per share.

This research seems to indicate that where the shares traded represented only a minority interest, a small added value was placed on the voting shares by the marketplace.

The 12 tables following the summary represent the results of each year's survey. The research was not undertaken for the years 1995 and 1997.

DISCOUNTS AND PREMIUMS SUMMARY

When valuing a closely held company, care, reasonableness, and sound valuation judgment must be employed when applying discounts. The particular facts and circumstances of each valuation must be considered for the final determination of discounts. Experts must understand and properly apply the results of the various studies that they relied on and applied to the subject company. The blind application of discounts, without a thorough understanding of the subject company as compared to the underlying data used for the discounts, can lead to misleading valuation results. For additional information on discounts and premiums see *Business Valuation Discounts and Premiums* by Shannon P. Pratt (New York: John Wiley & Sons, 2001).

STUDY OF VOTING PREMIUMS
AS OF DECEMBER 31, 1992

COMPANY	1992 HIGH	1992 LOW	December 31, 1992 PRICE	December 31, 1992 VOTING PREMIUM	HIGH VOTING PREMIUM	LOW VOTING PREMIUM	AVERAGE HI-LOW VOTING PREMIUM	AVERAGE VOTING SHARES	AVERAGE NO VOTE SHARES
1 ALBERTO-CULVER	$32.000	$21.250	$25.500	6.81%	24.27%	8.28%	17.36%	70.85%	
CLASS A (1/10 VOTE)	$25.750	$19.625	$23.875						29.15%
2 AMERICAN FRUCTOSE A	$26.000	$18.750	$22.875	1.10%	0.00%	4.17%	1.70%	68.80%	
CLASS B (10 VOTES)	$26.000	$18.000	$22.625						31.20%
3 BASE TEN SYS -CL B	$7.500	$2.250	$7.500	3.45%	3.45%	9.09%	4.70%	53.91%	
CLASS A (1/10 VOTE)	$7.250	$2.063	$7.250						46.09%
4 BLOUNT, INC CV B	$14.375	$6.875	$14.250	1.79%	0.00%	5.77%	1.80%	NA	
CLASS A (1/10 VOTE)	$14.375	$6.500	$14.000						NA
5 CHAMBERS DEVELOPMENT	$36.375	$3.500	$7.125	3.64%	(1.69%)	(3.45%)	(1.85%)	56.84%	
CLASS A (1/10 VOTE)	$37.000	$3.625	$6.875						43.16%
6 CHEMICAL BANKING CORP								NA	
CLASS B (1/5 VOTING)	NA	NA	NA						NA
7 COMCAST CL A	$19.750	$13.500	$19.375	6.90%	6.76%	0.93%	4.31%	60.65%	
CLASS A SP (NON-VTG)	$18.500	$13.375	$18.125						39.35%
8 CROWN CENTRAL PETRO A	$26.500	$13.625	$13.625	12.37%	8.72%	21.11%	12.63%	66.22%	
CLASS B (1/10 VOTING)	$24.375	$11.250	$12.125						33.78%
9 DIAGNOSTIC RETR'L CV A	$3.500	$1.500	$3.250	4.00%	0.00%	(7.69%)	(2.44%)	NA	
CLASS B (1/10 VOTING)	$3.500	$1.625	$3.125						NA
10 DICKENSON MINES LTD. B	$4.500	$2.500	$2.625	(12.50%)	2.86%	(4.76%)	0.00%	58.71%	
CLASS A (1/10 VOTING)	$4.375	$2.625	$3.000						41.29%
11 EVEREST/JENNINGS INTL B	$3.375	$1.313	$1.313	(4.51%)	0.00%	23.52%	5.63%	57.38%	
CLASS A LTD VOTING	$3.375	$1.063	$1.375						42.62%
12 FOOD LION INC. B	$18.000	$6.250	$8.125	3.17%	0.70%	4.17%	1.57%	66.46%	
CLASS A NON-VOTING	$17.875	$6.000	$7.875						33.54%
13 McRAE INDUSTRIES CV B	$7.500	$4.500	$6.875	3.77%	(3.23%)	(5.26%)	(4.00%)	NA	
CLASS A (1/10 VOTING)	$7.750	$4.750	$6.625						NA
14 MOOG, INC CL B	$9.250	$5.875	$6.875	14.58%	21.31%	51.61%	31.52%	56.10%	
CLASS A LTD VOTING	$7.625	$3.875	$6.000						43.90%
15 ODETICS, INC CL B	$7.375	$6.000	$7.125	18.75%	(1.67%)	37.14%	12.63%	80.28%	
CLASS A (1/10 VOTING)	$7.500	$4.375	$6.000						19.72%
16 ORIOLE HOMES CV A	$15.125	$8.250	$10.375	3.75%	3.42%	15.79%	7.47%	NA	
CLASS B (1/10 VOTING)	$14.625	$7.125	$10.000						NA
17 PRESIDIO OIL CL B	$4.750	$1.625	$1.625	85.71%	31.03%	188.89%	52.24%	NA	
CLASS A (1/20 VOTING)	$3.625	$0.563	$0.875						NA
18 ROSE'S STORES								NA	
CLASS B NON-VOTING	NA	NA	NA						NA
19 SEQUA CORP CL A	$51.000	$29.000	$31.625	(2.32%)	(12.07%)	(4.13%)	(9.35%)	NA	
CLASS B (1/10 VOTING)	$58.000	$30.250	$32.375						NA
20 SMITH (A.O.) CL A	$37.875	$19.375	$37.875	(0.98%)	(0.98%)	8.39%	2.00%	69.63%	
CLASS B (1/10 VOTING)	$38.250	$17.875	$38.250						30.37%
21 THREE D DEPTS CV B	$2.625	$1.625	$1.625	(7.14%)	10.53%	0.00%	6.25%	NA	
CLASS A (1/10 VOTING)	$2.375	$1.625	$1.750						NA
22 TURNER BROADCASTING CL A	$27.500	$18.625	$21.375	1.18%	0.92%	6.43%	3.07%	61.11%	
CLASS B (1/5 VOTING)	$27.250	$17.500	$21.125						38.89%
23 UNITED FOODS CV B	$2.375	$1.375	$1.750	3.70%	18.75%	0.00%	11.11%	NA	
CLASS A (1/4 VOTING)	$2.000	$1.375	$1.688						NA
24 WATSCO, INC CV B	$13.250	$8.750	$12.125	(1.02%)	2.91%	25.00%	10.69%	NA	
CLASS A (LTD-VOTING)	$12.875	$7.000	$12.250						NA

MEDIAN				3.54%			4.51%		
MEAN				6.65%			7.68%		

STUDY OF VOTING PREMIUMS
AS OF DECEMBER 31, 1993

COMPANY	1993 HIGH	1993 LOW	December 3 1993 PRICE	December 31, 1993 VOTING PREMIUM	HIGH VOTING PREMIUM	LOW VOTING PREMIUM	AVERAGE HI-LOW VOTING PREMIUM	AVERAGE VOTING SHARES	AVERAGE NO VOTE SHARES
1 ALBERTO-CULVER	$28.250	$20.125	$23.125	10.12%	11.88%	18.38%	14.50%	71.04%	
CLASS A (1/10 VOTE)	$25.250	$17.000	$21.000						28.96%
2 AMERICAN MAIZE-PROD B	$24.375	$14.875	$15.375	(1.60%)	3.72%	3.48%	3.63%	14.57%	
CLASS A (LTD VOTING)	$23.500	$14.375	$15.625						85.43%
3 ASSOCIATED COMMUNIC. - A	$34.250	$16.250	$28.500	2.70%	3.01%	3.17%	3.06%	66.06%	
CLASS B (1/25 VOTE)	$33.250	$15.750	$27.750						33.94%
4 BALDWIN & LYONS - A	$16.500	$11.000	$15.000	(7.69%)	1.54%	(1.12%)	0.46%	54.32%	
CLASS B (NON-VOTING)	$16.250	$11.125	$16.250						45.68%
5 BROWN-FORMAN - A	$87.500	$69.625	$87.250	0.00%	(1.41%)	(4.62%)	(2.86%)	27.73%	
CLASS B (NON-VOTING)	$88.750	$73.000	$87.250						72.27%
6 CHAMBERS DEVELOPMENT	$7.375	$3.125	$3.875	(3.13%)	1.72%	0.00%	1.20%	56.83%	
CLASS A (1/10 VOTE)	$7.250	$3.125	$4.000						43.17%
7 COMCAST CL A	$42.250	$17.500	$36.375	1.04%	8.33%	11.11%	9.13%	21.03%	
CLASS A SP (NON-VTG)	$39.000	$15.750	$36.000						78.97%
8 CROWN CENTRAL PETRO A	$18.000	$13.750	$15.250	7.96%	11.63%	14.58%	12.89%	66.22%	
CLASS B (1/10 VOTING)	$16.125	$12.000	$14.125						33.78%
9 DICKENSON MINES LTD. B	$7.250	$2.625	$4.750	(2.56%)	7.41%	0.00%	5.33%	58.61%	
CLASS A (1/10 VOTING)	$6.750	$2.625	$4.875						41.39%
10 FIGGIE INTL - B	$22.000	$12.500	$14.250	4.59%	3.53%	6.38%	4.55%	57.72%	
CLASS A (1/20 VOTING)	$21.250	$11.750	$13.625						42.28%
11 FOOD LION INC. B	$8.500	$5.375	$6.625	1.92%	4.62%	2.38%	3.74%	66.46%	
CLASS A NON-VOTING	$8.125	$5.250	$6.500						33.54%
12 LAIDLAW, INC. - A	$9.375	$5.375	$6.875	0.00%	(1.32%)	0.00%	(0.84%)	14.66%	
CLASS B (NON-VOTING)	$9.500	$5.375	$6.875						85.34%
13 MOOG, INC CL B	$11.125	$6.875	$9.625	14.93%	14.10%	22.22%	17.07%	56.10%	
CLASS A LTD VOTING	$9.750	$5.625	$8.375						43.90%
14 NICHOLS INSTITUTE - A	$8.750	$4.250	$6.125	6.52%	11.11%	3.03%	8.33%	64.99%	
CLASS C (NON-VOTING)	$7.875	$4.125	$5.750						35.01%
15 PLAYBOY ENTERPRISES - A	$11.000	$6.625	$11.000	(15.38%)	(15.38%)	(5.36%)	(11.88%)	56.69%	
CLASS B (NON-VOTING)	$13.000	$7.000	$13.000						43.31%
16 PLYMOUTH RUBBER - A	$9.125	$3.625	$5.875	(2.08%)	21.67%	0.00%	14.61%	66.65%	
CLASS B (NON-VOTING)	$7.500	$3.625	$6.000						33.35%
17 PROVIDENT LIFE AND ACCID - B	$31.875	$25.625	$30.875	11.26%	10.39%	6.77%	8.75%	84.12%	
CLASS A (1/20 VOTING)	$28.875	$24.000	$27.750						15.88%
18 SMUCKER - A	$32.375	$20.250	$22.375	6.55%	10.68%	4.52%	8.23%	66.38%	
CLASS B (NON-VOTING)	$29.250	$19.375	$21.000						33.62%
19 STEVENS GRAPHICS - B	$7.375	$4.500	$7.375	7.27%	(4.84%)	(5.26%)	(5.00%)	20.17%	
CLASS A (1/10 VOTING)	$7.750	$4.750	$6.875						79.83%
20 TURNER BROADCASTING CL A	$29.750	$19.375	$27.250	0.93%	1.28%	1.31%	1.29%	61.04%	
CLASS B (1/5 VOTING)	$29.375	$19.125	$27.000						38.96%
MEDIAN				1.48%			4.14%		
MEAN				2.17%			4.81%		

STUDY OF VOTING PREMIUMS
AS OF DECEMBER 31, 1994

COMPANY	1994 HIGH	1994 LOW	December 31 1994 PRICE	December 31, 1994 VOTING PREMIUM	HIGH VOTING PREMIUM	LOW VOTING PREMIUM	AVERAGE HI-LOW VOTING PREMIUM	AVERAGE VOTING SHARES	AVERAGE NO VOTE SHARES
1 ALBERTO-CULVER CL 'B'	$27.375	$19.375	$27.250	11.22%	10.05%	9.15%	9.68%	71.72%	
CLASS A (1/10 VOTE)	$24.875	$17.750	$24.500						28.28%
2 AMERICAN MAIZE-PROD B	$25.375	$15.500	$25.000	(1.96%)	(2.40%)	(2.36%)	(2.39%)	14.52%	
CLASS A (LTD VOTING)	$26.000·	$15.875	$25.500						85.48%
3 BALDWIN & LYONS - A	$20.500	$14.000	$14.000	(5.08%)	30.16%	1.82%	16.95%	54.50%	
CLASS B (NON-VOTING)	$15.750	$13.750	$14.750						45.50%
4 BROWN-FORMAN - A	$32.250	$26.750	$31.000	1.64%	(0.77%)	2.39%	0.64%	29.58%	
CLASS B (NON-VOTING)	$32.500	$26.125	$30.500						70.42%
5 CHAMBERS DEVELOPMENT	$5.500	$2.000	$3.750	(3.23%)	0.00%	10.34%	2.56%	19.29%	
CLASS A (1/10 VOTE)	$5.500	$1.813	$3.875						80.71%
6 COMCAST CL A	$24.250	$13.750	$15.375	(1.60%)	1.04%	(1.79%)	0.00%	14.03%	
CLASS A SP (NON-VTG)	$24.000	$14.000	$15.625						85.97%
7 COSMETIC CENTER CL 'B' (VTG)	$20.500	$12.500	$13.500	5.88%	(2.38%)	(1.96%)	(2.22%)	61.24%	
CLASS A	$21.000	$12.750	$12.750						38.76%
8 CROWN CENTRAL PETRO A	$24.250	$12.375	$12.750	6.25%	4.86%	6.45%	5.40%	66.29%	
CLASS B (1/10 VOTING)	$23.125	$11.625	$12.000						33.71%
9 FEDDERS CORP.	$7.125	$4.250	$7.125	35.71%	29.55%	6.25%	19.74%	75.00%	
CLASS A (NON-VOTING)	$5.500	$4.000	$5.250						25.00%
10 FOOD LION INC. B	$7.500	$5.125	$5.125	0.00%	1.69%	2.50%	2.02%	66.46%	
CLASS A (NON-VOTING)	$7.375	$5.000	$5.125						33.54%
11 GOLDCORP, INC. 'B'	$6.875	$5.750	$5.875	9.30%	0.00%	17.95%	7.45%	5.11%	
CLASS A (LTD-VOTING)	$6.875	$4.875	$5.375						94.89%
12 HUBBELL, INC 'A' 20 VOTES	$58.000	$49.500	$51.250	(3.76%)	(7.75%)	(5.71%)	(6.83%)	15.81%	
CLASS B	$62.875	$52.500	$53.250						84.19%
13 JONES INTERCABLE	$17.500	$10.750	$11.875	(3.06%)	(2.78%)	(2.27%)	(2.59%)	57.11%	
CLASS A (1/10 VOTING)	$18.000	$11.000	$12.250						42.89%
14 LAIDLAW, INC. - A	$8.250	$5.625	$7.875	0.00%	(2.94%)	2.27%	(0.89%)	14.66%	
CLASS B (NON-VOTING)	$8.500	$5.500	$7.875						85.34%
15 MOLEX, INC.	$36.000	$24.250	$34.500	11.29%	6.67%	0.00%	3.88%	66.78%	
CLASS A (NON-VOTING)	$33.750	$24.250	$31.000						33.22%
16 MOLSON COS CL 'B' (VTG)	$28.250	$18.000	$19.750	(0.63%)	(2.16%)	1.41%	(0.80%)	19.83%	
CLASS A (NON-VOTING)	$28.875	$17.750	$19.875						80.17%
17 MOOG, INC CL B	$15.125	$9.750	$14.625	58.11%	57.14%	39.29%	49.62%	56.09%	
CLASS A (LTD VOTING)	$9.625	$7.000	$9.250						43.91%
18 PLAYBOY ENTERPRISES - A	$11.000	$6.000	$9.500	(9.52%)	(15.38%)	0.00%	(10.53%)	56.68%	
CLASS B (NON-VOTING)	$13.000	$6.000	$10.500						43.32%
19 PLYMOUTH RUBBER - A	$10.625	$5.750	$8.375	0.00%	1.19%	(6.12%)	(1.50%)	66.63%	
CLASS B (NON-VOTING)	$10.500	$6.125	$8.375						33.37%
20 PROVIDENT LIFE AND ACCID - B	$31.875	$21.500	$21.750	4.82%	12.83%	4.88%	9.49%	84.09%	
CLASS A (1/20 VOTING)	$28.250	$20.500	$20.750						15.91%
21 SEQUA CORP 'B' 10 VOTES	$40.250	$21.000	$26.625	2.40%	1.26%	19.15%	6.75%	25.29%	
CLASS A	$39.750	$17.625	$26.000						74.71%
22 SMUCKER - A	$26.000	$20.500	$24.000	9.71%	13.66%	1.86%	8.14%	66.37%	
CLASS B (NON-VOTING)	$22.875	$20.125	$21.875						33.63%
23 STEVENS GRAPHICS - B	$9.000	$6.375	$8.750	4.48%	5.88%	27.50%	13.89%	19.30%	
CLASS A (1/10 VOTING)	$8.500	$5.000	$8.375						80.70%
24 TURNER BROADCASTING CL A	$27.750	$14.500	$16.375	0.00%	0.00%	0.00%	0.00%	59.96%	
CLASS B (1/5 VOTING)	$27.750	$14.500	$16.375						40.04%
MEDIAN				0.82%			2.29%		
MEAN				5.50%			5.35%		

STUDY OF VOTING PREMIUMS
AS OF DECEMBER 31, 1996

COMPANY	1996 HIGH	1996 LOW	December 31, 1996 PRICE	December 31, 1996 VOTING PREMIUM	HIGH VOTING PREMIUM	LOW VOTING PREMIUM	AVERAGE HI-LOW VOTING PREMIUM	AVERAGE VOTING SHARES	AVERAGE NO VOTE SHARES
1 ALBERTO-CULVER CL 'B'	$43.750	$35.500	$38.500	8.07%	12.54%	8.81%	10.84%	71.41%	
CLASS A (1/10 VOTE)	$38.875	$32.625	$35.625						28.59%
2 BALDWIN & LYONS - A	$18.750	$16.750	$16.750	17.54%	15.38%	17.54%	16.39%	54.64%	
CLASS B (NON-VOTING)	$16.250	$14.250	$14.250						45.36%
3 BROWN-FORMAN - A	$41.500	$39.125	$40.250	0.31%	(1.19%)	4.68%	1.57%	29.58%	
CLASS B (NON-VOTING)	$42.000	$37.375	$40.125						70.42%
4 COMCAST CL A	$21.125	$17.000	$17.375	(1.42%)	(1.17%)	(2.86%)	(1.93%)	13.54%	
CLASS A SP (NON-VTG)	$21.375	$17.500	$17.625						86.46%
5 COSMETIC CENTER CL 'B' (VTG)	$5.750	$4.250	$5.500	4.76%	(4.17%)	6.25%	0.00%	61.16%	
CLASS A	$6.000	$4.000	$5.250						38.84%
6 CROWN CENTRAL PETRO A	$19.125	$17.000	$18.000	2.86%	4.08%	3.03%	3.58%	65.96%	
CLASS B (1/10 VOTING)	$18.375	$16.500	$17.500						34.04%
7 E-Z EM, INC CL A	$11.375	$10.000	$11.250	7.14%	4.60%	3.90%	4.27%	64.55%	
CLASS B (NON-VTG)	$10.875	$9.625	$10.500						35.45%
8 ETZ LAVUD LTD CL A (VTG)	$7.125	$5.000	$5.875	(14.55%)	(6.56%)	(18.37%)	(11.82%)	35.15%	
ORD	$7.625	$6.125	$6.875						64.85%
9 FABRI-CENTERS AMER. 'A'	$12.875	$11.500	$11.500	(1.08%)	3.00%	0.00%	1.56%	66.73%	
CLASS B (NON-VOTING)	$12.500	$11.500	$11.625						33.27%
10 FEDDERS CORP.	$7.000	$6.375	$6.500	13.04%	12.00%	15.91%	13.83%	67.97%	
CLASS A (NON-VOTING)	$6.250	$5.500	$5.750						32.03%
11 GOLDCORP, INC. 'B'	$20.000	$18.125	$19.500	(1.89%)	(4.19%)	1.40%	(1.61%)	5.09%	
CLASS A (LTD-VOTING)	$20.875	$17.875	$19.875						94.91%
12 HUBBELL, INC 'A' 20 VOTES	$63.375	$60.750	$61.000	(5.97%)	(5.94%)	(4.33%)	(5.16%)	14.95%	
CLASS B	$67.375	$63.500	$64.875						85.05%
13 JONES INTERCABLE	$17.000	$13.500	$15.625	7.76%	13.33%	0.93%	7.49%	54.49%	
CLASS A (1/10 VOTING)	$15.000	$13.375	$14.500						45.51%
14 LAIDLAW, INC. - A	$10.500	$9.750	$10.500	(1.18%)	(2.33%)	1.30%	(0.61%)	13.94%	
CLASS B (NON-VOTING)	$10.750	$9.625	$10.625						86.06%
15 MOLEX, INC.	$36.000	$33.000	$34.875	8.98%	5.11%	7.32%	6.15%	66.50%	
CLASS A (NON-VOTING)	$34.250	$30.750	$32.000						33.50%
16 MOLSON COS CL 'B' (VTG)	$24.000	$23.000	$24.125	(0.52%)	(1.54%)	0.55%	(0.53%)	20.09%	
CLASS A (NON-VOTING)	$24.375	$22.875	$24.250						79.91%
17 MOOG, INC CL B	$18.875	$18.375	$18.625	3.47%	2.03%	7.30%	4.56%	55.83%	
CLASS A (LTD VOTING)	$18.500	$17.125	$18.000						44.17%
18 PLAYBOY ENTERPRISES - A	$10.875	$10.000	$10.125	0.00%	0.00%	2.56%	1.21%	56.68%	
CLASS B (NON-VOTING)	$10.875	$9.750	$10.125						43.32%
19 PLYMOUTH RUBBER - A	$9.125	$8.750	$9.000	(1.40%)	0.00%	0.00%	0.00%	63.89%	
CLASS B (NON-VOTING)	$9.125	$8.750	$9.128						36.11%
20 SEQUA CORP 'B' 10 VOTES	$41.500	$40.500	$40.375	18.30%	16.49%	21.80%	19.06%	25.24%	
CLASS A	$35.625	$33.250	$34.128						74.76%
21 SMUCKER - A	$22.500	$19.500	$22.250	7.88%	7.78%	4.00%	5.99%	66.37%	
CLASS B (NON-VOTING)	$20.875	$18.750	$20.625						33.63%
22 STEVENS GRAPHICS - B	$3.375	$3.250	$3.250	8.33%	(10.00%)	18.18%	1.92%	18.44%	
CLASS A (1/10 VOTING)	$3.750	$2.750	$3.000						81.56%
23 TURNER BROADCASTING CL A	$29.250	$26.750	$27.125	0.00%	(1.68%)	(0.47%)	(1.10%)	59.92%	
CLASS B (1/5 VOTING)	$29.750	$26.875	$27.125						40.08%
MEDIAN				2.86%			1.57%		
MEAN				3.50%			3.29%		

STUDY OF VOTING PREMIUMS
AS OF JUNE 30, 1998

COMPANY	PER SHARE VOTING RIGHTS	1998 HIGH	1998 LOW	June 30, 1998 PRICE	June 30, 1998 VOTING PREMIUM	HIGH VOTING PREMIUM	LOW VOTING PREMIUM	AVERAGE HI-LOW VOTING PREMIUM	% OF VOTING RIGHTS
1 ALBERTO-CULVER CL B	ONE VOTE	$32.438	$28.250	$29.000	13.17%	13.82%	13.57%	13.70%	96.14%
ALBERTO-CULVER CL A	1/10 VOTE	$28.500	$24.875	$25.625					3.86%
2 BALDWIN & LYONS - CL A	VOTING	$25.125	$19.500	$21.000	(9.68%)	0.75%	(0.95%)	0.00%	100.00%
BALDWIN & LYONS - CL B	NONVOTING	$24.938	$19.688	$23.250					0.00%
3 BANDAG, INC COMMON	ONE VOTE	$59.750	$39.000	$39.000	13.04%	9.89%	13.04%	11.11%	100.00%
BANDAG, INC CL A	NONVOTING	$54.375	$34.500	$34.500					0.00%
4 BROWN-FORMAN CL A	VOTING	$58.250	$49.000	$58.250	(9.34%)	(9.34%)	(5.31%)	(7.54%)	100.00%
BROWN-FORMAN CL B	NONVOTING	$64.250	$51.750	$64.250					0.00%
5 COMCAST CLASS A	VOTING	$43.625	$32.625	$39.750	(2.15%)	(4.38%)	10.59%	1.50%	100.00%
COMCAST CLASS A SPECIAL	NONVOTING	$45.625	$29.500	$40.625					0.00%
6 CRAWFORD & CO CL B	VOTING	$20.625	$17.375	$18.750	0.00%	4.43%	(2.11%)	1.33%	100.00%
CRAWFORD & CO CL A	NONVOTING	$19.750	$17.750	$18.750					0.00%
7 CROWN CENTRAL PETRO A	ONE VOTE	$22.000	$12.500	$12.563	(0.50%)	6.02%	6.38%	6.15%	95.08%
CROWN CENTRAL CL B	1/10 VOTE	$20.750	$11.750	$12.625					4.92%
8 E-Z EM, INC CL A	VOTING	$9.750	$5.875	$6.375	4.08%	8.33%	9.30%	8.70%	100.00%
E-Z EM CL B	NONVOTING	$9.000	$5.375	$6.125					0.00%
9 GRAY COMMUNICATIONS CL A	10 VOTES	$32.625	$24.000	$32.375	4.86%	5.67%	1.59%	3.90%	95.89%
GRAY COMMUNICATIONS CL B	ONE VOTE	$30.875	$23.625	$30.875					4.11%
10 HUBBELL, INC CL A	20 VOTES	$49.063	$43.625	$43.625	4.80%	(6.99%)	5.28%	(1.59%)	76.92%
HUBBELL, INC CL B	ONE VOTE	$52.750	$41.438	$41.625					23.08%
11 JONES INTERCABLE COMMON	ONE VOTE	$26.375	$13.875	$24.750	(1.00%)	(1.86%)	(3.48%)	(2.42%)	91.97%
JONES INTERCABLE CL A	1/10 VOTE	$26.875	$14.375	$25.000					8.03%
12 MOLEX, INC. COMMON	ONE VOTE	$32.125	$23.000	$25.000	6.95%	5.76%	5.75%	5.76%	100.00%
MOLEX, INC. CL A	NONVOTING	$30.375	$21.750	$23.375					0.00%
13 MOOG, INC CL B	ONE VOTE	$45.250	$34.000	$37.625	(1.47%)	(3.98%)	3.82%	(0.78%)	97.55%
MOOG, INC CL A	1/10 VOTE	$47.125	$32.750	$38.188					2.45%
14 PACIFICARE HEALTH CL A	ONE VOTE	$85.875	$46.750	$84.500	(4.38%)	(3.92%)	(4.59%)	(4.16%)	100.00%
PACIFICARE HEALTH CL B	NONVOTING	$89.375	$49.000	$88.375					0.00%
15 PENN ENGR & MFG CL A	ONE VOTE	$26.125	$19.438	$20.500	(18.00%)	(8.33%)	(11.14%)	(9.55%)	100.00%
PENN ENGR COMMON	NONVOTING	$28.500	$21.875	$25.000					0.00%
16 PLAYBOY ENTERPRISES - A	VOTING	$18.375	$13.500	$16.375	(7.75%)	(6.67%)	(7.69%)	(7.10%)	100.00%
PLAYBOY CLASS B	NONVOTING	$19.688	$14.625	$17.750					0.00%
17 PLYMOUTH RUBBER - CL A	VOTING	$7.250	$5.375	$7.000	0.00%	0.00%	19.44%	7.45%	100.00%
PLYMOUTH RUBBER CL B	NONVOTING	$7.250	$4.500	$7.000					0.00%
18 READER'S DIGEST CL B	VOTING	$29.125	$23.500	$27.125	0.00%	(0.21%)	5.03%	2.06%	100.00%
READER'S DIGEST ASSN CL A	NONVOTING	$29.188	$22.375	$27.125					0.00%
19 SEQUA CORP CL B	10 VOTES	$85.750	$73.875	$78.125	17.04%	13.01%	15.66%	14.22%	76.36%
SEQUA CORP CL A	ONE VOTE	$75.875	$63.875	$66.750					23.64%
20 SMUCKER CL A	VOTING	$28.188	$22.750	$24.813	1.79%	1.58%	0.55%	1.12%	100.00%
SMUCKER CL B	NONVOTING	$27.750	$22.625	$24.375					0.00%
MEDIAN					0.00%			1.42%	
MEAN					0.57%			2.19%	

STUDY OF VOTING PREMIUMS
AS OF JUNE 30, 1999

COMPANY	PER SHARE VOTING RIGHTS	1999 HIGH	1999 LOW	June 30, 1999 PRICE	June 30, 1999 VOTING PREMIUM	HIGH VOTING PREMIUM	LOW VOTING PREMIUM	AVERAGE HI-LOW VOTING PREMIUM	% OF VOTING RIGHTS
1 ALBERTO-CULVER CL B	ONE VOTE	$27.875	$21.563	$26.625	17.03%	6.70%	9.18%	7.77%	96.02%
ALBERTO-CULVER CL A	1/10 VOTE	$26.125	$19.750	$22.750					3.98%
2 BALDWIN & LYONS - CL A	VOTING	$25.688	$20.000	$22.250	(6.07%)	(1.20%)	(0.93%)	(1.08%)	100.00%
BALDWIN & LYONS - CL B	NONVOTING	$26.000	$20.188	$23.688					0.00%
3 BANDAG, INC COMMON	ONE VOTE	$41.625	$28.125	$34.688	23.33%	10.26%	20.32%	14.11%	100.00%
BANDAG, INC CL A	NONVOTING	$37.750	$23.375	$28.125					0.00%
4 BROWN-FORMAN CL A	VOTING	$71.000	$52.313	$59.625	(8.53%)	(8.09%)	(7.31%)	(7.76%)	100.00%
BROWN-FORMAN CL B	NONVOTING	$77.250	$56.438	$65.188					0.00%
5 COMCAST CLASS A	VOTING	$40.313	$28.063	$35.813	(6.83%)	(4.73%)	(2.81%)	(3.95%)	100.00%
COMCAST CLASS A SPECIAL	NONVOTING	$42.313	$28.875	$38.438					0.00%
6 CRAWFORD & CO CL B	VOTING	$16.250	$10.125	$16.250	20.37%	15.56%	1.25%	9.61%	100.00%
CRAWFORD & CO CL A	NONVOTING	$14.063	$10.000	$13.500					0.00%
7 CROWN CENTRAL PETRO A	ONE VOTE	$12.375	$7.063	$11.875	7.95%	10.00%	2.73%	7.24%	95.05%
CROWN CENTRAL CL B	1/10 VOTE	$11.250	$6.875	$11.000					4.95%
8 E-Z EM, INC CL A	VOTING	$7.000	$4.875	$5.250	(4.55%)	7.69%	11.43%	9.20%	100.00%
E-Z EM CL B	NONVOTING	$6.500	$4.375	$5.500					0.00%
9 GRAY COMMUNICATIONS CL A	10 VOTES	$20.000	$15.125	$20.000	41.59%	35.02%	23.47%	29.79%	95.90%
GRAY COMMUNICATIONS CL B	ONE VOTE	$14.813	$12.250	$14.125					4.10%
10 HUBBELL, INC CL A	20 VOTES	$45.750	$33.375	$39.875	(12.12%)	(6.99%)	(3.09%)	(5.38%)	76.64%
HUBBELL, INC CL B	ONE VOTE	$49.188	$34.438	$45.375					23.36%
11 JONES INTERCABLE COMMON	ONE VOTE	$58.250	$33.250	$48.000	(2.04%)	(2.92%)	0.00%	(1.88%)	91.96%
JONES INTERCABLE CL A	1/10 VOTE	$60.000	$33.250	$49.000					8.04%
12 MOLEX, INC. COMMON	ONE VOTE	$38.000	$25.500	$37.000	17.46%	18.75%	13.33%	16.51%	100.00%
MOLEX, INC. CL A	NONVOTING	$32.000	$22.500	$31.500					0.00%
13 MOOG, INC CL B	ONE VOTE	$40.750	$35.375	$40.750	18.55%	4.65%	34.12%	16.56%	92.43%
MOOG, INC CL A	1/10 VOTE	$38.938	$26.375	$34.375					7.57%
14 PENN ENGR & MFG CL A	ONE VOTE	$21.000	$17.500	$20.375	(9.44%)	(9.92%)	1.45%	(5.08%)	100.00%
PENN ENGR COMMON	NONVOTING	$23.313	$17.250	$22.500					0.00%
15 PLAYBOY ENTERPRISES - A	VOTING	$32.000	$16.125	$23.500	(11.53%)	(11.42%)	(10.10%)	(10.98%)	100.00%
PLAYBOY CLASS B	NONVOTING	$36.125	$17.938	$26.563					0.00%
16 PLYMOUTH RUBBER - CL A	VOTING	$7.875	$6.063	$7.875	13.51%	12.50%	5.43%	9.31%	100.00%
PLYMOUTH RUBBER CL B	NONVOTING	$7.000	$5.750	$6.938					0.00%
17 READER'S DIGEST CL B	VOTING	$38.000	$23.750	$37.500	(5.66%)	(7.18%)	(4.04%)	(5.99%)	100.00%
READER'S DIGEST ASSN CL A	NONVOTING	$40.938	$24.750	$39.750					0.00%
18 SEQUA CORP CL B	10 VOTES	$73.000	$67.313	$71.500	2.14%	4.29%	52.98%	23.08%	76.28%
SEQUA CORP CL A	ONE VOTE	$70.000	$44.000	$70.000					23.72%
19 SMUCKER CL A	VOTING	$25.688	$20.063	$22.250	17.11%	7.03%	17.15%	11.25%	100.00%
SMUCKER CL B	NONVOTING	$24.000	$17.125	$19.000					0.00%
MEDIAN					2.14%			7.77%	
MEAN					5.91%			5.91%	

STUDY OF VOTING PREMIUMS
AS OF AUGUST 31, 2000

COMPANY	PER SHARE VOTING RIGHTS	2000 HIGH	2000 LOW	August 31, 2000 PRICE	August 31, 2000 VOTING PREMIUM	HIGH VOTING PREMIUM	LOW VOTING PREMIUM	AVERAGE HI-LOW VOTING PREMIUM	% OF VOTING RIGHTS
1 AARON RENTS - CL A	VOTING	$18.625	$14.625	$14.875	8.18%	3.83%	27.17%	12.95%	100.00%
AARON RENTS COMMON	NONVOTING	$17.938	$11.500	$13.750					0.00%
2 ALBERTO-CULVER CL B	ONE VOTE	$31.813	$19.375	$28.313	17.97%	19.48%	6.16%	14.07%	95.98%
ALBERTO-CULVER CL A	1/10 VOTE	$26.625	$18.250	$24.000					4.02%
3 BALDWIN & LYONS - CL A	VOTING	$21.250	$14.875	$18.750	(3.54%)	(3.95%)	(2.46%)	(3.34%)	100.00%
BALDWIN & LYONS - CL B	NONVOTING	$22.125	$15.250	$19.438					0.00%
4 BANDAG, INC COMMON	ONE VOTE	$34.000	$21.875	$32.563	16.29%	15.25%	10.76%	13.45%	100.00%
BANDAG, INC CL A	NONVOTING	$29.500	$19.750	$28.000					0.00%
5 BEL FUSE INC CL A	VOTING	$36.438	$14.813	$34.750	(0.36%)	(0.34%)	(0.42%)	(0.36%)	100.00%
BEL FUSE INC CL B	NONVOTING	$36.563	$14.875	$34.875					0.00%
6 BROWN-FORMAN CL A	VOTING	$57.500	$41.500	$52.750	(0.47%)	(5.93%)	(0.90%)	(3.88%)	100.00%
BROWN-FORMAN CL B	NONVOTING	$61.125	$41.875	$53.000					0.00%
7 COMCAST CLASS A	VOTING	$52.375	$27.938	$36.688	(1.51%)	(5.95%)	0.22%	(3.89%)	100.00%
COMCAST CLASS A SPECIAL	NONVOTING	$55.688	$27.875	$37.250					0.00%
8 CRAWFORD & CO CL B	VOTING	$14.125	$11.000	$12.438	14.37%	18.32%	7.32%	13.24%	100.00%
CRAWFORD & CO CL A	NONVOTING	$11.938	$10.250	$10.875					0.00%
9 CROWN CENTRAL PETRO A	ONE VOTE	$9.875	$5.500	$9.500	2.01%	(2.47%)	4.76%	0.00%	95.04%
CROWN CENTRAL CL B	1/10 VOTE	$10.125	$5.250	$9.313					4.96%
10 DELHAIZE AMERICA CL B	VOTING	$22.375	$14.750	$15.063	0.42%	0.56%	1.72%	1.02%	100.00%
DELHAIZE AMERICA CL A	NONVOTING	$22.250	$14.500	$15.000					0.00%
11 E-Z EM, INC CL A	VOTING	$10.625	$6.000	$8.000	20.75%	(2.30%)	4.35%	0.00%	100.00%
E-Z EM CL B	NONVOTING	$10.875	$5.750	$6.625					0.00%
12 FEDDERS CORP COMMON	VOTING	$6.250	$4.750	$5.188	7.79%	5.26%	7.04%	6.02%	100.00%
FEDDERS CORP CL A	NONVOTING	$5.938	$4.438	$4.813					0.00%
13 GRAY COMMUNICATIONS CL A	10 VOTES	$18.125	$9.750	$11.250	10.43%	32.42%	2.63%	20.22%	94.72%
GRAY COMMUNICATIONS CL B	ONE VOTE	$13.688	$9.500	$10.188					5.28%
14 HUBBELL, INC CL A	20 VOTES	$28.375	$21.750	$25.063	(3.14%)	(1.52%)	0.58%	(0.62%)	76.63%
HUBBELL, INC CL B	ONE VOTE	$28.813	$21.625	$25.875					23.37%
15 JO-ANN STORES CL A	ONE VOTE	$11.688	$6.563	$6.563	(7.89%)	11.31%	9.38%	10.61%	100.00%
JO-ANN STORES CL A	NONVOTING	$10.500	$6.000	$7.125					0.00%
16 MOLEX, INC. COMMON	ONE VOTE	$63.750	$37.313	$52.813	31.62%	34.92%	28.39%	32.43%	100.00%
MOLEX, INC. CL A	NONVOTING	$47.250	$29.063	$40.125					0.00%
17 MOOG, INC CL B	ONE VOTE	$41.250	$40.250	$40.500	24.62%	19.57%	172.88%	65.48%	92.35%
MOOG, INC CL A	1/10 VOTE	$34.500	$14.750	$32.500					7.65%
18 PENN ENGR & MFG CL A	ONE VOTE	$34.125	$20.000	$30.063	(9.76%)	(11.36%)	(7.51%)	(9.98%)	100.00%
PENN ENGR COMMON	NONVOTING	$38.500	$21.625	$33.313					0.00%
19 PLAYBOY ENTERPRISES - A	VOTING	$24.938	$10.250	$13.500	(8.09%)	(15.47%)	(9.89%)	(13.91%)	100.00%
PLAYBOY CLASS B	NONVOTING	$29.500	$11.375	$14.688					0.00%
20 PLYMOUTH RUBBER - CL A	VOTING	$8.250	$3.750	$5.125	70.83%	17.86%	36.36%	23.08%	100.00%
PLYMOUTH RUBBER CL B	NONVOTING	$7.000	$2.750	$3.000					0.00%
21 READER'S DIGEST CL B	VOTING	$38.000	$25.250	$34.750	(9.74%)	(9.25%)	0.00%	(5.77%)	100.00%
READER'S DIGEST ASSN CL A	NONVOTING	$41.875	$25.250	$38.500					0.00%
22 SEQUA CORP CL B	10 VOTES	$61.000	$47.000	$58.875	27.30%	12.83%	55.37%	28.09%	78.22%
SEQUA CORP CL A	ONE VOTE	$54.063	$30.250	$46.250					21.78%
23 VIACOM CLASS A	VOTING	$76.063	$46.063	$67.750	0.65%	0.25%	0.82%	0.46%	100.00%
VIACOM INC CLASS B	NONVOTING	$75.875	$45.688	$67.313					0.00%
MEDIAN					2.01%			1.02%	
MEAN					9.08%			8.67%	

STUDY OF VOTING PREMIUMS
AS OF AUGUST 31, 2001

COMPANY	PER SHARE VOTING RIGHTS	2001 HIGH	2001 LOW	August 31, 2001 PRICE	August 31, 2001 VOTING PREMIUM	HIGH VOTING PREMIUM	LOW VOTING PREMIUM	AVERAGE HI-LOW VOTING PREMIUM	PERCENT OF VOTING RIGHTS
1 AARON RENTS CL A	VOTING	$16.500	$12.120	$15.270	(13.29%)	(15.38%)	(10.55%)	(13.40%)	100.00%
AARON RENTS COMMON	NONVOTING	$19.500	$13.550	$17.610					0.00%
2 ALBERTO-CULVER CL B	ONE VOTE	$46.260	$36.870	$43.070	19.64%	17.11%	20.41%	18.55%	95.98%
ALBERTO-CULVER CL A	1/10 VOTE	$39.500	$30.620	$36.000					4.02%
3 BALDWIN & LYONS CL A	VOTING	$24.900	$18.620	$24.320	9.80%	(13.39%)	(6.90%)	(10.73%)	100.00%
BALDWIN & LYONS CL B	NONVOTING	$28.750	$20.000	$22.150					0.00%
4 BANDAG, INC COMMON	ONE VOTE	$46.750	$25.700	$29.630	16.20%	20.86%	22.97%	21.60%	100.00%
BANDAG, INC CL A	NONVOTING	$38.680	$20.900	$25.500					0.00%
5 BEL FUSE INC CL A	VOTING	$39.750	$19.750	$24.000	0.13%	(0.45%)	(1.25%)	(0.72%)	100.00%
BEL FUSE INC CL B	NONVOTING	$39.930	$20.000	$23.970					0.00%
6 BIO-RAD LABS CL B	ONE VOTE	$54.000	$30.000	$55.000	(1.35%)	(3.57%)	0.84%	(2.04%)	66.57%
BIO-RAD LABS CL A	1/10 VOTE	$56.000	$29.750	$55.750					33.43%
7 BROWN-FORMAN CL A	VOTING	$71.000	$58.000	$65.500	1.55%	(1.39%)	0.61%	(0.50%)	100.00%
BROWN-FORMAN CL B	NONVOTING	$72.000	$57.650	$64.500					0.00%
8 COMCAST CLASS A	VOTING	$45.810	$34.500	$36.490	(0.38%)	(1.08%)	1.35%	(0.05%)	100.00%
COMCAST CLASS A SPECIAL	NONVOTING	$46.310	$34.040	$36.630					0.00%
9 CRAWFORD & CO CL B	VOTING	$18.000	$10.500	$13.050	27.32%	44.00%	17.32%	32.87%	100.00%
CRAWFORD & CO CL A	NONVOTING	$12.500	$8.950	$10.250					0.00%
10 E-Z EM, INC CL A	VOTING	$5.950	$4.610	$4.650	(7.00%)	(2.78%)	15.25%	4.35%	100.00%
E-Z EM, INC CL B	NONVOTING	$6.120	$4.000	$5.000					0.00%
11 FEDDERS CORP COMMON	VOTING	$5.600	$4.060	$4.750	18.75%	11.55%	4.10%	8.30%	100.00%
FEDDERS CORP CL A	NONVOTING	$5.020	$3.900	$4.000					0.00%
12 GRAY COMMUN CL A	10 VOTES	$19.050	$15.270	$16.100	15.25%	7.93%	11.87%	9.65%	94.69%
GRAY COMMUN CL B	ONE VOTE	$17.650	$13.650	$13.970					5.31%
13 HAVERTY FURN CL A	10 VOTES	$15.000	$10.000	$14.200	1.57%	(0.66%)	3.31%	0.89%	70.31%
HAVERTY FURN COMMON	ONE VOTE	$15.100	$9.680	$13.980					29.69%
14 HEICO CORP COMMON	ONE VOTE	$20.900	$11.820	$18.650	15.84%	15.47%	18.20%	16.44%	94.79%
HEICO CORP CL A	1/10 VOTE	$18.100	$10.000	$16.100					5.21%
15 HUBBELL, INC CL A	20 VOTES	$29.750	$23.590	$28.400	(2.51%)	(3.97%)	1.24%	(1.73%)	76.76%
HUBBELL, INC CL B	ONE VOTE	$30.980	$23.300	$29.130					23.24%
16 IDT CORP COMMON & CL A	ONE VOTE	$15.460	$8.620	$12.150	8.58%	3.07%	(13.80%)	(3.68%)	94.98%
IDT CORP CL B	1/10 VOTE	$15.000	$10.000	$11.190					5.02%
17 JO-ANN STORES CL A	ONE VOTE	$6.680	$3.100	$4.800	45.45%	37.73%	82.35%	49.31%	100.00%
JO-ANN STORES CL B	NONVOTING	$4.850	$1.700	$3.300					0.00%
18 LIBERTY MEDIA CL B	10 VOTES	$18.820	$12.500	$16.480	8.42%	4.32%	8.70%	6.03%	45.04%
LIBERTY MEDIA CL A	1 VOTE	$18.040	$11.500	$15.200					54.96%
19 MCDATA CORP CL A	ONE VOTE	$53.570	$11.750	$14.280	(0.83%)	(29.74%)	(3.29%)	(26.11%)	97.47%
MCDATA CORP CL B	1/10 VOTE	$76.250	$12.150	$14.400					2.53%
20 MCRAE IND CL B	ONE VOTE	$5.370	$3.810	$3.750	1.35%	(0.19%)	1.33%	0.44%	76.61%
MCRAE IND CL A	1/10 VOTE	$5.380	$3.760	$3.700					23.39%

Continued

STUDY OF VOTING PREMIUMS
AS OF AUGUST 31, 2001

COMPANY	PER SHARE VOTING RIGHTS	2001 HIGH	2001 LOW	August 31, 2001 PRICE	August 31, 2001 VOTING PREMIUM	HIGH VOTING PREMIUM	LOW VOTING PREMIUM	AVERAGE HI-LOW VOTING PREMIUM	PERCENT OF VOTING RIGHTS
21 MOLEX, INC. COMMON	ONE VOTE	$48.000	$31.490	$31.570	19.95%	37.89%	24.71%	32.35%	100.00%
MOLEX, INC. CL A	NONVOTING	$34.810	$25.250	$26.320					0.00%
22 MOOG, INC CL B	ONE VOTE	$43.000	$40.500	$40.500	13.13%	10.40%	44.03%	24.50%	92.32%
MOOG, INC CL A	1/10 VOTE	$38.950	$28.120	$35.800					7.68%
23 ORIOLE HOMES CL A	ONE VOTE	$3.500	$1.370	$2.350	56.67%	20.69%	47.31%	27.15%	94.37%
ORIOLE HOMES CL B	1/10 VOTE	$2.900	$0.930	$1.500					5.63%
24 PENN ENGR CL A	ONE VOTE	$19.950	$14.700	$16.050	(4.86%)	(9.32%)	3.89%	(4.15%)	100.00%
PENN ENGR COMMON	NONVOTING	$22.000	$14.150	$16.870					0.00%
25 PILGRIM'S PRIDE CL B	20 VOTES	$15.380	$7.560	$14.550	38.44%	39.19%	40.78%	39.71%	98.38%
PILGRIM'S PRIDE CL A	ONE VOTE	$11.050	$5.370	$10.510					1.62%
26 PLAYBOY ENTERPR CL A	VOTING	$16.510	$8.370	$12.900	(5.49%)	(16.41%)	(13.08%)	(15.32%)	100.00%
PLAYBOY ENTERPR CL B	NONVOTING	$19.750	$9.630	$13.650					0.00%
27 PLYMOUTH RUBBER CL A	VOTING	$7.500	$0.800	$1.400	0.00%	163.16%	0.00%	127.40%	100.00%
PLYMOUTH RUBBER CL B	NONVOTING	$2.850	$0.800	$1.400					0.00%
28 READER'S DIGEST CL B	VOTING	$35.250	$18.190	$18.600	(0.53%)	(12.96%)	(0.16%)	(8.99%)	100.00%
READER'S DIGEST CL A	NONVOTING	$40.500	$18.220	$18.700					0.00%
29 SAUCONY CL A	VOTING	$10.500	$5.570	$6.200	0.16%	3.75%	3.15%	3.54%	100.00%
SAUCONY CL B	NONVOTING	$10.120	$5.400	$6.190					0.00%
30 SEQUA CORP CL B	10 VOTES	$63.000	$55.000	$56.000	6.26%	18.62%	62.39%	35.66%	76.23%
SEQUA CORP CL A	ONE VOTE	$53.110	$33.870	$52.700					23.77%
31 VIACOM CLASS A	VOTING	$59.690	$38.400	$42.440	0.09%	0.32%	1.32%	0.71%	100.00%
VIACOM CLASS B	NONVOTING	$59.500	$37.900	$42.400					0.00%
32 WILEY SONS CL B	ONE VOTE	$23.75	$18.05	$20.40	1.24%	(0.59%)	0.84%	0.02%	65.76%
WILEY SONS CL A	1/10 VOTE	$23.89	$17.90	$20.15					34.24%
MEDIAN					**1.56%**			**2.22%**	
MEAN					**9.05%**			**11.63%**	

STUDY OF VOTING PREMIUMS
AS OF AUGUST 31, 2002

COMPANY	PER SHARE VOTING RIGHTS	2002 HIGH	2002 LOW	August 31, 2002 PRICE	August 31, 2002 VOTING PREMIUM	HIGH VOTING PREMIUM	LOW VOTING PREMIUM	AVERAGE HI-LOW VOTING PREMIUM	PERCENT OF VOTING RIGHTS
1 AARON RENTS CL A	VOTING	$27.500	$10.500	$23.250	11.46%	(3.47%)	(27.34%)	(11.50%)	100.00%
AARON RENTS COMMON	NONVOTING	$28.490	$14.450	$20.860					0.00%
2 ADVANTA CORP CL A	VOTING	$14.550	$7.600	$8.350	(0.12%)	3.63%	3.40%	3.55%	100.00%
ADVANTA CL B	NONVOTING	$14.040	$7.350	$8.360					0.00%
3 ALBERTO-CULVER CL B	ONE VOTE	$57.910	$41.550	$49.260	4.92%	11.47%	11.84%	11.63%	95.75%
ALBERTO-CULVER CL A	1/10 VOTE	$51.950	$37.150	$46.950					4.25%
4 BALDWIN & LYONS CL A	VOTING	$25.180	$19.500	$19.780	(4.17%)	(12.69%)	2.25%	(6.74%)	100.00%
BALDWIN & LYONS CL B	NONVOTING	$28.840	$19.070	$20.640					0.00%
5 BANDAG, INC COMMON	ONE VOTE	$39.980	$26.000	$34.960	14.25%	16.87%	13.04%	15.33%	100.00%
BANDAG, INC CL A	NONVOTING	$34.210	$23.000	$30.600					0.00%
6 BEL FUSE INC CL A	VOTING	$26.050	$15.000	$20.920	(11.36%)	(6.29%)	(16.90%)	(10.47%)	100.00%
BEL FUSE INC CL B	NONVOTING	$27.800	$18.050	$23.600					0.00%
7 BIO-RAD LABS CL B	ONE VOTE	$50.250	$27.500	$42.000	0.12%	(1.47%)	0.18%	(0.89%)	65.85%
BIO-RAD LABS CL A	1/10 VOTE	$51.000	$27.450	$41.950					34.15%
8 BROWN-FORMAN CL A	VOTING	$80.500	$58.000	$71.500	1.52%	(0.05%)	(1.18%)	(0.52%)	100.00%
BROWN-FORMAN CL B	NONVOTING	$80.540	$58.690	$70.430					0.00%
9 COMCAST CLASS A	VOTING	$37.550	$17.140	$24.560	3.06%	(0.08%)	4.51%	1.32%	100.00%
COMCAST CLASS A SPECIAL	NONVOTING	$37.580	$16.400	$23.830					0.00%
10 CONSTELLATION CL B	VOTING	$32.500	$21.570	$28.500	0.32%	1.56%	2.47%	1.92%	57.52%
CONSTELLATION BRANDS A	1/10 VOTING	$32.000	$21.050	$28.410					42.48%
11 CRAWFORD & CO CL B	VOTING	$15.000	$6.290	$6.730	24.63%	24.48%	25.80%	24.87%	100.00%
CRAWFORD & CO CL A	NONVOTING	$12.050	$5.000	$5.400					0.00%
12 E-Z EM, INC CL A	VOTING	$14.050	$6.000	$7.250	3.57%	17.08%	12.15%	15.56%	100.00%
E-Z EM, INC CL B	NONVOTING	$12.000	$5.350	$7.000					0.00%
13 FEDERAL AGRICULTURAL MTGE	VOTING	$35.000	$19.750	$21.000	(25.00%)	(28.43%)	(3.89%)	(21.17%)	100.00%
CLASS C	NONVOTING	$48.900	$20.550	$28.000					0.00%
14 GRAY TELEVISION CL A	10 VOTES	$18.150	$12.900	$13.400	14.04%	24.74%	29.65%	26.73%	94.65%
GRAY TELEVISION CL B	ONE VOTE	$14.550	$9.950	$11.750					5.35%
15 HAVERTY FURN CL A	10 VOTES	$21.250	$11.900	$12.930	0.23%	(0.93%)	4.94%	1.10%	67.73%
HAVERTY FURN COMMON	ONE VOTE	$21.450	$11.340	$12.900					32.27%
16 HEICO CORP COMMON	ONE VOTE	$17.550	$10.650	$11.010	27.43%	21.12%	32.30%	25.11%	94.81%
HEICO CORP CL A	1/10 VOTE	$14.490	$8.050	$8.640					5.19%
17 HUBBELL, INC CL A	20 VOTES	$35.000	$25.600	$29.770	(7.26%)	(6.17%)	(5.54%)	(5.90%)	76.61%
HUBBELL, INC CL B	ONE VOTE	$37.300	$27.100	$32.100					23.39%
18 IDT CORP COMMON & CL A	ONE VOTE	$23.320	$15.300	$17.650	10.80%	14.59%	16.88%	15.49%	95.73%
IDT CORP CL B	1/10 VOTE	$20.350	$13.090	$15.930					4.27%
19 JO-ANN STORES CL A	ONE VOTE	$32.350	$7.150	$30.000	28.48%	23.95%	7.52%	20.61%	100.00%
JO-ANN STORES CL B	NONVOTING	$26.100	$6.650	$23.350					0.00%
20 LIBERTY CORP CL B	10 VOTES	$15.900	$6.380	$8.690	3.95%	5.79%	3.57%	5.14%	90.57%
LIBERT MEDIA CL A	1 VOTE	$15.030	$6.160	$8.360					9.43%

Continued

STUDY OF VOTING PREMIUMS
AS OF AUGUST 31, 2002

COMPANY	PER SHARE VOTING RIGHTS	2002 HIGH	2002 LOW	August 31, 2002 PRICE	August 31, 2002 VOTING PREMIUM	HIGH VOTING PREMIUM	LOW VOTING PREMIUM	AVERAGE HI-LOW VOTING PREMIUM	PERCENT OF VOTING RIGHTS
21 MCCORMICK & CO	VOTING	$27.000	$20.500	$22.600	(2.38%)	(0.92%)	(0.97%)	(0.94%)	100.00%
MCCORMICK & CO	NONVOTING	$27.250	$20.700	$23.150					0.00%
22 MCDATA CORP CL A	ONE VOTE	$33.880	$5.700	$9.570	(1.64%)	(2.31%)	(5.00%)	(2.70%)	97.22%
MCDATA CORP CL B	1/10 VOTE	$34.680	$6.000	$9.730					2.78%
23 MCRAE IND CL B	ONE VOTE	$7.400	$5.300	$7.000	(1.13%)	(1.33%)	0.00%	(0.78%)	76.41%
MCRAE IND CL A	1/10 VOTE	$7.500	$5.300	$7.080					23.59%
24 MOLEX, INC. COMMON	ONE VOTE	$39.610	$24.640	$29.700	16.61%	17.19%	24.51%	19.89%	100.00%
MOLEX, INC. CL A	NONVOTING	$33.800	$19.790	$25.470					0.00%
25 MOOG, INC CL B	ONE VOTE	$41.000	$27.050	$34.000	6.65%	(4.38%)	26.76%	5.96%	92.08%
MOOG, INC CL A	1/10 VOTE	$42.880	$21.340	$31.880					7.92%
26 ORIOLE HOMES CL A	ONE VOTE	$4.500	$1.700	$4.250	0.00%	(1.75%)	9.68%	1.14%	94.36%
ORIOLE HOMES CL B	1/10 VOTE	$4.580	$1.550	$4.250					5.64%
27 PENN ENGR & MFG CL A	ONE VOTE	$19.200	$12.500	$13.450	1.89%	(7.47%)	6.84%	(2.31%)	100.00%
PENN ENGR COMMON	NONVOTING	$20.750	$11.700	$13.200					0.00%
28 PILGRIM'S PRIDE CL B	20 VOTES	$14.990	$8.500	$9.750	26.30%	33.24%	29.18%	31.74%	98.38%
PILGRIM'S PRIDE CL A	ONE VOTE	$11.250	$6.580	$7.720					1.62%
29 PLAYBOY ENTERPR CL A	VOTING	$15.060	$7.700	$7.960	(13.48%)	(13.94%)	(9.41%)	(12.46%)	100.00%
PLAYBOY ENTERPR CL B	NONVOTING	$17.500	$8.500	$9.200					0.00%
30 PLYMOUTH RUBBER CL A	VOTING	$2.200	$1.200	$1.200	0.00%	2.33%	84.62%	21.43%	100.00%
PLYMOUTH RUBBER CL B	NONVOTING	$2.150	$0.650	$1.200					0.00%
31 READER'S DIGEST CL B	VOTING	$30.750	$17.800	$19.990	17.04%	22.51%	24.04%	23.07%	100.00%
READER'S DIGEST CL A	NONVOTING	$25.100	$14.350	$17.080					0.00%
32 READING INTL CL B	VOTING	$4.250	$1.750	$3.700	(2.89%)	(6.59%)	6.06%	(3.23%)	100.00%
READING INTL CL A	NONVOTING	$4.550	$1.650	$3.810					0.00%
33 ROGERS COMMUN CL A	VOTING	$29.500	$11.050	$15.250	82.63%	66.48%	64.93%	66.05%	100.00%
ROGERS COMMUN CL B	NONVOTING	$17.720	$6.700	$8.350					0.00%
34 SEQUA CORP CL B	10 VOTES	$66.000	$52.250	$57.250	7.35%	0.02%	17.87%	7.19%	76.15%
SEQUA CORP CL A	ONE VOTE	$65.990	$44.330	$53.330					23.85%
35 TRAVELERS PROP & CAS CL B	7 VOTES	$19.500	$13.850	$16.290	3.63%	(7.36%)	17.87%	1.68%	93.33%
TRAVELERS PROP & CAS CL A	1 VOTE	$21.050	$11.750	$15.720					6.67%
36 VIACOM INC CL A	VOTING	$51.890	$29.790	$40.700	0.00%	0.00%	0.13%	0.05%	100.00%
VIACOM INC CL B	NONVOTING	$51.890	$29.750	$40.700					0.00%
37 WILEY SONS CL B	ONE VOTE	$27.48	$19.51	$23.15	(0.04%)	(0.54%)	1.30%	0.21%	65.51%
WILEY SONS CL A	1/10 VOTE	$27.63	$19.26	$23.16					34.49%
MEDIAN					1.89%			1.68%	
MEAN					6.52%			7.22%	

STUDY OF VOTING PREMIUMS
AS OF AUGUST 29, 2003

COMPANY	PER SHARE VOTING RIGHTS	2003 HIGH	2003 LOW	August 29, 2003 PRICE	August 29, 2003 VOTING PREMIUM	HIGH VOTING PREMIUM	LOW VOTING PREMIUM	AVERAGE HI-LOW VOTING PREMIUM	PERCENT OF VOTING RIGHTS
1 AARON RENTS CL A	VOTING	$21.66	$12.53	$19.80	(5.62%)	2.17%	10.30%	5.01%	100.00%
AARON RENTS COMMON	NONVOTING	$21.20	$11.36	$20.98					0.00%
2 ADVANTA CORP CL A	VOTING	$11.21	$5.95	$10.90	(0.18%)	(1.15%)	(13.89%)	(5.97%)	100.00%
ADVANTA CL B	NONVOTING	$11.34	$6.91	$10.92					0.00%
3 ALBERTO-CULVER CL B	ONE VOTE	$57.13	$47.08	$57.08	2.70%	2.64%	3.25%	2.91%	92.60%
ALBERTO-CULVER CL A	1/10 VOTE	$55.66	$45.60	$55.58					7.40%
4 BALDWIN & LYONS CL A	VOTING	$25.00	$18.00	$21.88	(5.40%)	(5.66%)	0.95%	(3.00%)	100.00%
BALDWIN & LYONS CL B	NONVOTING	$26.50	$17.83	$23.13					0.00%
5 BANDAG, INC COMMON	VOTING	$39.72	$28.45	$34.98	10.17%	9.42%	11.13%	10.13%	100.00%
BANDAG, INC CL A	NONVOTING	$36.30	$25.60	$31.75					0.00%
6 BEL FUSE INC CL A	VOTING	$24.70	$14.70	$23.80	(10.89%)	(8.52%)	(19.05%)	(12.75%)	100.00%
BEL FUSE INC CL B	NONVOTING	$27.00	$18.16	$26.71					0.00%
7 BIO-RAD LABS CL B	ONE VOTE	$61.00	$33.00	$51.30	0.29%	(2.94%)	(0.60%)	(2.13%)	70.62%
BIO-RAD LABS CL A	1/10 VOTE	$62.85	$33.20	$51.15					29.38%
8 BROWN-FORMAN CL A	VOTING	$84.40	$62.60	$80.86	2.30%	1.87%	3.90%	2.73%	100.00%
BROWN-FORMAN CL B	NONVOTING	$82.85	$60.25	$79.04					0.00%
9 COMCAST CLASS A	VOTING	$34.85	$23.42	$29.76	4.86%	5.61%	3.95%	4.93%	100.00%
COMCAST CLASS A SPECIAL	NONVOTING	$33.00	$22.53	$28.38					0.00%
10 CRAWFORD & CO CL B	VOTING	$6.70	$3.70	$6.22	(1.89%)	5.51%	8.82%	6.67%	100.00%
CRAWFORD & CO CL A	NONVOTING	$6.35	$3.40	$6.34					0.00%
11 FEDERAL AGRICULTURAL MTGE CL A	VOTING	$23.50	$15.50	$20.92	(28.99%)	(36.14%)	(22.89%)	(31.46%)	100.00%
FEDERAL AGRICULTURAL MTGE CL C	NONVOTING	$36.80	$20.10	$29.46					0.00%
12 FOREST CITY ENTERPRISES CLASS B	10 VOTES	$42.50	$31.25	$42.50	(0.23%)	(0.58%)	1.33%	0.22%	79.28%
FOREST CITY ENTERPRISES CL A	ONE VOTE	$42.75	$30.84	$42.60					20.72%
13 GRAY TELEVISION CL A	10 VOTES	$15.22	$10.00	$13.45	1.13%	2.15%	16.01%	7.23%	61.01%
GRAY TELEVISION CL B	ONE VOTE	$14.90	$8.62	$13.30					38.99%
14 GREIF INC CL B	VOTING	$27.90	$22.36	$27.15	6.22%	5.28%	33.49%	16.21%	100.00%
GREIF INC CL A	NONVOTING	$26.50	$16.75	$25.56					0.00%
15 HAVERTY FURN CL A	10 VOTES	$17.65	$9.75	$17.25	(0.63%)	(0.28%)	4.28%	1.29%	72.21%
HAVERTY FURN COMMON	ONE VOTE	$17.70	$9.35	$17.36					27.79%
16 HEICO CORP COMMON	ONE VOTE	$12.74	$7.35	$12.11	31.92%	34.25%	28.95%	32.26%	89.12%
HEICO CORP CL A	1/10 VOTE	$9.49	$5.70	$9.18					10.88%
17 HUBBELL INC CL A COMMON	20 VOTES	$39.15	$26.85	$38.90	(2.65%)	(2.78%)	(5.12%)	(3.75%)	79.53%
HUBBELL INC CL B	ONE VOTE	$40.27	$28.30	$39.96					20.47%
18 IDT CORP CL C	ONE VOTE	$18.33	$13.70	$17.52	(1.52%)	(0.65%)	(0.36%)	(0.53%)	86.93%
IDT CORP CL B	1/10 VOTE	$18.45	$13.75	$17.79					13.07%

Continued

COMPANY	PER SHARE VOTING RIGHTS	2003 HIGH	2003 LOW	August 29, 2003 PRICE	August 29, 2003 VOTING PREMIUM	HIGH VOTING PREMIUM	LOW VOTING PREMIUM	AVERAGE HI-LOW VOTING PREMIUM	PERCENT OF VOTING RIGHTS
19 JO-ANN STORES CL A	ONE VOTE	$30.90	$16.75	$30.20	15.27%	15.95%	19.64%	17.22%	100.00%
JO-ANN STORES CL B	NONVOTING	$26.65	$14.00	$26.20					0.00%
20 LENNAR CORP CL B	10 VOTES	$75.70	$51.45	$64.75	(3.72%)	(7.24%)	6.74%	(2.05%)	67.41%
LENNAR CORP CL A	ONE VOTE	$81.61	$48.20	$67.25					32.59%
21 MCCORMICK & CO	VOTING	$27.50	$21.50	$26.80	0.37%	(0.36%)	(0.97%)	(0.63%)	100.00%
MCCORMICK & CO	NONVOTING	$27.60	$21.71	$26.70					0.00%
22 MCDATA CORP CL A	ONE VOTE	$15.90	$6.99	$10.14	0.80%	0.70%	(0.43%)	0.35%	96.03%
MCDATA CORP CL B	1/10 VOTE	$15.79	$7.02	$10.06					3.97%
23 MCRAE IND CL B	ONE VOTE	$8.60	$6.20	$6.50	(2.69%)	(2.82%)	2.14%	(0.80%)	81.68%
MCRAE IND CL A	1/10 VOTE	$8.85	$6.07	$6.68					18.32%
24 MOLEX, INC. COMMON	ONE VOTE	$30.10	$19.98	$29.57	16.05%	16.98%	17.39%	17.15%	100.00%
MOLEX, INC. CL A	NONVOTING	$25.73	$17.02	$25.48					0.00%
25 MOOG, INC CL B	ONE VOTE	$38.25	$31.00	$38.00	0.80%	0.10%	4.91%	2.20%	62.26%
MOOG, INC CL A	LTDVOTING	$38.21	$29.55	$37.70					37.74%
26 PENN ENGR & MFG CL A	ONE VOTE	$14.00	$10.45	$13.90	(11.46%)	(12.50%)	2.45%	(6.68%)	100.00%
PENN ENGR COMMON	NONVOTING	$16.00	$10.20	$15.70					0.00%
27 PILGRIM'S PRIDE CL B	20 VOTES	$13.30	$6.90	$12.91	(0.92%)	2.07%	43.75%	13.29%	97.61%
PILGRIM'S PRIDE CL A	ONE VOTE	$13.03	$4.80	$13.03					2.39%
28 PLAYBOY ENTERPR CL A	VOTING	$13.45	$7.48	$13.28	(7.78%)	(10.03%)	(5.56%)	(8.48%)	100.00%
PLAYBOY ENTERPR CL B	NONVOTING	$14.95	$7.92	$14.40					0.00%
29 PLYMOUTH RUBBER CL A	VOTING	$1.55	$0.85	$1.35	125.00%	35.96%	174.19%	65.52%	100.00%
PLYMOUTH RUBBER CL B COMMON	NONVOTING	$1.14	$0.31	$0.60					0.00%
30 READING INTL CL B	VOTING	$6.00	$3.60	$5.90	0.68%	(4.61%)	(4.00%)	(4.38%)	100.00%
READING INTL CL A	NONVOTING	$6.29	$3.75	$5.86					0.00%
1 ROGERS COMMUN CL A CV	VOTING	$24.23	$13.07	$20.40	43.16%	46.67%	56.53%	49.98%	100.00%
ROGERS COMMUN CL B	NONVOTING	$16.52	$8.35	$14.25					0.00%
2 SEA CONTAINERS CL B	ONE VOTE	$14.50	$5.92	$14.45	0.70%	(0.96%)	7.44%	1.34%	43.75%
SEA CONTAINERS LTD CL A	1/10 VOTE	$14.64	$5.51	$14.35					56.25%
3 SEQUA CORP CL B	10 VOTES	$48.00	$35.82	$47.50	8.20%	8.35%	21.42%	13.58%	82.41%
SEQUA CORP CL A	ONE VOTE	$44.30	$29.50	$43.90					17.59%
4 TELUS CORP COMMON	VOTING	$26.85	$15.25	$25.70	51.18%	51.52%	62.75%	55.41%	100.00%
TELUS CORP NON VTG	NONVOTING	$17.72	$9.37	$17.00					0.00%
5 TRAVELERS PROP & CAS CL B	7 VOTES	$17.42	$12.98	$15.49	0.65%	(0.46%)	0.23%	(0.16%)	87.34%
TRAVELERS PROP & CAS CL A	ONE VOTE	$17.50	$12.95	$15.39					12.66%
6 VIACOM INC CL A	ONE VOTE	$48.13	$33.26	$44.99	(0.02%)	(3.26%)	0.45%	(1.77%)	100.00%
VIACOM INC CL B	NONVOTING	$49.75	$33.11	$45.00					0.00%
WILEY SONS CL B	ONE VOTE	$28.25	$21.64	$27.95	0.00%	(0.53%)	0.65%	(0.02%)	69.77%
WILEY SONS CL A	1/10 VOTE	$28.40	$21.50	$27.95					30.23%

SOURCE: September 2003 Standard & Poor's Stock Guide

	MEDIAN				0.37%			1.29%	
	MEAN				6.43%			6.51%	

445

STUDY OF VOTING PREMIUMS
AS OF AUGUST 27, 2004

COMPANY	PER SHARE VOTING RIGHTS	2004 HIGH	2004 LOW	August 27, 2004 PRICE	August 27, 2004 VOTING PREMIUM	HIGH VOTING PREMIUM	LOW VOTING PREMIUM	AVERAGE HI-LOW VOTING PREMIUM	PERCENT OF VOTING RIGHTS
1 AARON RENTS CL A	VOTING	$21.10	$12.33	$18.56	(9.64%)	(6.64%)	(8.26%)	(7.24%)	100.00%
AARON RENTS COMMON	NONVOTING	$22.60	$13.44	$20.54					0.00%
2 ADVANTA CORP CL A	VOTING	$23.21	$12.92	$22.47	(4.38%)	(3.77%)	2.87%	(1.50%)	100.00%
ADVANTA CL B	NONVOTING	$24.12	$12.56	$23.50					0.00%
3 AGERE SYSTEMS CL B	FOUR VOTES	$3.88	$0.89	$1.19	(1.65%)	(6.28%)	(11.00%)	(7.20%)	67.84%
AGERE SYSTEMS CL A	ONE VOTE	$4.14	$1.00	$1.21					32.16%
4 BALDWIN & LYONS CL A	VOTING	$29.75	$22.37	$25.06	(0.71%)	(3.03%)	0.77%	(1.44%)	100.00%
BALDWIN & LYONS CL B	NONVOTING	$30.68	$22.20	$25.24					0.00%
5 BANDAG, INC COMMON	VOTING	$51.30	$38.32	$45.76	10.00%	7.52%	8.31%	7.86%	100.00%
BANDAG, INC CL A	NONVOTING	$47.71	$35.38	$41.60					0.00%
6 BEL FUSE INC CL A	VOTING	$36.00	$24.00	$32.40	(14.44%)	(14.29%)	(16.67%)	(15.25%)	100.00%
BEL FUSE INC CL B	NONVOTING	$42.00	$28.80	$37.87					0.00%
7 BIO-RAD LABS CL B	ONE VOTE	$61.50	$50.50	$50.00	(0.68%)	(1.57%)	3.06%	0.47%	65.29%
BIO-RAD LABS CL A	1/10 VOTE	$62.48	$49.00	$50.34					34.71%
8 BROWN-FORMAN CL A	VOTING	$52.25	$45.15	$47.81	0.67%	4.50%	0.56%	2.63%	100.00%
BROWN-FORMAN CL B	NONVOTING	$50.00	$44.90	$47.49					0.00%
9 COMCAST CLASS A	VOTING	$36.50	$26.25	$28.17	1.51%	3.22%	1.39%	2.45%	100.00%
COMCAST CLASS A SPECIAL	NONVOTING	$35.36	$25.89	$27.75					0.00%
10 CRAWFORD & CO CL B	VOTING	$7.25	$4.48	$5.01	(1.76%)	1.40%	4.19%	2.45%	100.00%
CRAWFORD & CO CL A	NONVOTING	$7.15	$4.30	$5.10					0.00%
11 FEDERAL AGRICULTURAL MTGE CL A	VOTING	$23.00	$16.80	$17.52	(11.78%)	(27.90%)	1.08%	(17.97%)	100.00%
FEDERAL AGRICULTURAL MTGE CL C	NONVOTING	$31.90	$16.62	$19.86					0.00%
12 FOREST CITY ENTERPRISES CLASS B	10 VOTES	$56.80	$46.30	$56.25	1.55%	0.53%	0.11%	0.34%	73.13%
FOREST CITY ENTERPRISES CL A	ONE VOTE	$56.50	$46.25	$55.39					26.87%
13 GRAY TELEVISION CL A	10 VOTES	$15.99	$10.66	$12.85	(6.48%)	(1.42%)	(4.82%)	(2.81%)	91.88%
GRAY TELEVISION CL B	ONE VOTE	$16.22	$11.20	$13.74					8.12%
14 GREIF INC CL B	VOTING	$42.50	$34.25	$39.00	0.00%	(1.02%)	9.36%	3.35%	100.00%
GREIF INC CL A	NONVOTING	$42.94	$31.32	$39.00					0.00%
15 HAVERTY FURN CL A	10 VOTES	$23.80	$15.75	$16.75	(1.06%)	(0.75%)	(1.56%)	(1.08%)	65.79%
HAVERTY FURN COMMON	ONE VOTE	$23.98	$16.00	$16.93					34.21%
16 HEICO CORP COMMON	ONE VOTE	$18.45	$12.90	$16.31	34.24%	28.13%	29.13%	28.54%	94.41%
HEICO CORP CL A	1/10 VOTE	$14.40	$9.99	$12.15					5.59%
17 HUBBELL INC CL A COMMON	20 VOTES	$43.90	$36.90	$40.70	(5.68%)	(6.46%)	(3.20%)	(5.00%)	75.58%
HUBBELL INC CL B	ONE VOTE	$46.93	$38.12	$43.15					24.42%
18 IDT CORP CL C	ONE VOTE	$23.00	$14.18	$14.62	(2.73%)	(3.97%)	(1.46%)	(3.03%)	93.94%
IDT CORP CL B	1/10 VOTE	$23.95	$14.39	$15.03					6.06%

Continued

STUDY OF VOTING PREMIUMS
AS OF AUGUST 27, 2004

	COMPANY	PER SHARE VOTING RIGHTS	2004 HIGH	2004 LOW	August 27, 2004 PRICE	August 27, 2004 VOTING PREMIUM	HIGH VOTING PREMIUM	LOW VOTING PREMIUM	AVERAGE HI-LOW VOTING PREMIUM	PERCENT OF VOTING RIGHTS
19	K-V PHARMACEUTICAL CL B	ONE VOTE	$29.73	$16.25	$16.61	4.33%	5.95%	11.00%	7.68%	96.75%
	K-V PHARMACEUTICAL CL A	1/20 VOTE	$28.06	$14.64	$15.92					3.25%
20	LENNAR CORP CL B	10 VOTES	$53.82	$37.40	$42.42	(7.38%)	(5.55%)	(7.20%)	(6.23%)	67.58%
	LENNAR CORP CL A	ONE VOTE	$56.98	$40.30	$45.80					32.42%
21	MCCORMICK & CO	VOTING	$36.00	$28.80	$33.52	(0.09%)	(0.30%)	0.70%	0.14%	100.00%
	MCCORMICK & CO	NONVOTING	$36.11	$28.60	$33.55					0.00%
22	MCDATA CORP CL A	ONE VOTE	$10.48	$4.23	$5.16	3.61%	1.26%	4.70%	2.22%	96.92%
	MCDATA CORP CL B	1/10 VOTE	$10.35	$4.04	$4.98					3.08%
23	MCRAE IND CL B	ONE VOTE	$11.50	$8.85	$8.80	2.92%	(2.13%)	6.63%	1.50%	74.85%
	MCRAE IND CL A	1/10 VOTE	$11.75	$8.30	$8.55					25.15%
24	MOLEX, INC. COMMON	ONE VOTE	$36.10	$27.07	$28.87	15.62%	18.91%	16.18%	17.72%	100.00%
	MOLEX, INC. CL A	NONVOTING	$30.36	$23.30	$24.97					0.00%
25	MOOG, INC CL B	ONE VOTE	$38.10	$33.33	$35.75	0.56%	(0.55%)	9.14%	3.75%	51.97%
	MOOG, INC CL A	LTDVOTING	$38.31	$30.54	$35.55					48.03%
26	PENN ENGR & MFG CL A	ONE VOTE	$18.45	$12.40	$15.75	(17.54%)	(14.50%)	(11.43%)	(13.29%)	100.00%
	PENN ENGR COMMON	NONVOTING	$21.58	$14.00	$19.10					0.00%
27	PLAYBOY ENTERPR CL A	VOTING	$14.78	$7.60	$8.75	(3.74%)	(10.32%)	(5.00%)	(8.58%)	100.00%
	PLAYBOY ENTERPR CL B	NONVOTING	$16.48	$8.00	$9.09					0.00%
28	PLYMOUTH RUBBER CL A	VOTING	$2.07	$1.40	$1.71	137.50%	95.28%	460.00%	164.89%	100.00%
	PLYMOUTH RUBBER CL B COMMON	NONVOTING	$1.06	$0.25	$0.72					0.00%
29	READING INTL CL B	VOTING	$8.35	$5.80	$7.40	(4.52%)	(4.02%)	2.65%	(1.39%)	100.00%
	READING INTL CL A	NONVOTING	$8.70	$5.65	$7.75					0.00%
30	ROGERS COMMUN CL A CV	VOTING	$28.27	$22.66	$23.50	32.17%	36.18%	37.42%	36.72%	100.00%
	ROGERS COMMUN CL B	NONVOTING	$20.76	$16.49	$17.78					0.00%
31	SEA CONTAINERS CL B	ONE VOTE	$21.75	$15.00	$15.85	0.32%	(0.18%)	2.25%	0.80%	40.44%
	SEA CONTAINERS LTD CL A	1/10 VOTE	$21.79	$14.67	$15.80					59.56%
32	SEQUA CORP CL B	10 VOTES	$60.50	$48.80	$55.00	3.31%	2.14%	8.69%	4.96%	76.12%
	SEQUA CORP CL A	ONE VOTE	$59.23	$44.90	$53.24					23.88%
33	TELUS CORP COMMON	VOTING	$28.52	$20.81	$26.70	42.32%	37.38%	46.34%	41.02%	100.00%
	TELUS CORP NON VTG	NONVOTING	$20.76	$14.22	$18.76					0.00%
34	THOMAS NELSON CL B	10 VOTES	$28.75	$17.50	$19.20	1.05%	(1.17%)	1.21%	(0.28%)	40.26%
	THOMAS NELSON COMMON	ONE VOTE	$29.09	$17.29	$19.00					59.74%
35	TRIARC COS CL A	ONE VOTE	$12.29	$9.51	$10.84	(2.25%)	2.93%	(1.14%)	1.11%	78.28%
	TRIARC COS CL B	1/10 VOTE	$11.94	$9.62	$11.09					21.72%
36	VIACOM INC CL A	ONE VOTE	$45.10	$32.56	$33.86	1.65%	0.11%	8.21%	3.35%	100.00%
	VIACOM INC CL B	NONVOTING	$45.05	$30.09	$33.31					0.00%
37	WILEY SONS CL B	ONE VOTE	$33.30	$25.95	$32.12	1.29%	(0.60%)	(0.19%)	(0.42%)	64.60%
	WILEY SONS CL A	1/10 VOTE	$33.50	$26.00	$31.71					35.40%
		MEDIAN				0.00%			0.47%	
		MEAN				5.35%			6.52%	

SOURCE: September 2004 Standard & Poor's Stock Guide

STUDY OF VOTING PREMIUMS AS OF AUGUST 26, 2005

COMPANY	PER SHARE VOTING RIGHTS	2005 HIGH	2005 LOW	August 26, 2005 PRICE	August 26, 2005 VOTING PREMIUM	HIGH VOTING PREMIUM	LOW VOTING PREMIUM	AVERAGE HI-LOW VOTING PREMIUM	PERCENT OF VOTING RIGHTS
1 AARON RENTS CL A	VOTING	$23.60	$15.55	$20.16	(8.98%)	(8.28%)	(10.53%)	(9.19%)	100.00%
AARON RENTS COMMON	NONVOTING	$25.73	$17.38	$22.15					0.00%
2 ADVANTA CORP CL A	VOTING	$28.75	$20.23	$26.82	(7.04%)	(7.14%)	(7.37%)	(7.23%)	100.00%
ADVANTA CL B	NONVOTING	$30.96	$21.84	$28.85					0.00%
3 BALDWIN & LYONS CL A	VOTING	$41.00	$24.50	$26.00	0.19%	48.01%	2.08%	26.69%	100.00%
BALDWIN & LYONS CL B	NONVOTING	$27.70	$24.00	$25.95					0.00%
4 BANDAG, INC COMMON	VOTING	$50.35	$42.51	$43.30	15.10%	8.40%	14.58%	11.14%	100.00%
BANDAG, INC CL A	NONVOTING	$46.45	$37.10	$37.62					0.00%
5 BEL FUSE INC CL A	VOTING	$29.78	$21.50	$26.14	(18.74%)	(14.72%)	(15.82%)	(15.18%)	100.00%
BEL FUSE INC CL B	NONVOTING	$34.92	$25.54	$32.17					0.00%
6 BIO-RAD LABS CL B	ONE VOTE	$61.75	$47.00	$54.75	(0.82%)	(1.33%)	0.99%	(0.34%)	65.25%
BIO-RAD LABS CL A	1/10 VOTE	$62.58	$46.54	$55.20					34.75%
7 BROWN-FORMAN CL A	VOTING	$64.15	$49.56	$59.24	4.61%	4.16%	6.31%	5.08%	100.00%
BROWN-FORMAN CL B	NONVOTING	$61.59	$46.62	$56.63					0.00%
8 COMCAST CLASS A	VOTING	$34.50	$29.73	$30.74	1.89%	1.00%	2.84%	1.84%	100.00%
COMCAST CLASS A SPECIAL	NONVOTING	$34.16	$28.91	$30.17					0.00%
9 CONSTELLATION BRANDS B	10 VOTES	$31.24	$22.75	$26.58	(3.42%)	(1.14%)	1.79%	0.07%	52.10%
CONSTELLATION BRANDS A	ONE VOTE	$31.60	$22.35	$27.52					47.90%
10 CRAWFORD & CO CL B	VOTING	$7.94	$5.95	$7.35	2.65%	4.34%	(0.50%)	2.21%	100.00%
CRAWFORD & CO CL A	NONVOTING	$7.61	$5.98	$7.16					0.00%
11 FEDERAL AGRICULTURAL MTGE CL A	VOTING	$19.50	$12.89	$18.13	(22.39%)	(24.71%)	(17.00%)	(21.82%)	100.00%
FEDERAL AGRICULTURAL MTGE CL C	NONVOTING	$25.90	$15.53	$23.36					0.00%
12 FOREST CITY ENTERPRISES CLASS B	10 VOTES	$37.00	$28.06	$35.35	(0.59%)	0.35%	0.83%	0.56%	72.42%
FOREST CITY ENTERPRISES CL A	ONE VOTE	$36.87	$27.83	$35.56					27.58%
13 FREESCALE SEMCONDUCTOR CL B	5 VOTES	$26.25	$16.20	$24.08	0.84%	1.00%	2.08%	1.41%	93.75%
FREESCALE SEMCONDUCTOR CL A	ONE VOTE	$25.99	$15.87	$23.88					6.25%
14 GAMESTOP CORP CL B	10 VOTES	$33.76	$18.65	$30.14	(10.70%)	(6.66%)	0.65%	(4.19%)	95.96%
GAMESTOP CORP CL A	ONE VOTE	$36.17	$18.53	$33.75					4.04%
15 GRAY TELEVISION CL A	10 VOTES	$14.00	$10.00	$11.38	(7.48%)	(11.05%)	(5.48%)	(8.81%)	91.91%
GRAY TELEVISION CL B	ONE VOTE	$15.74	$10.58	$12.30					8.09%
16 GREIF INC CL B	VOTING	$71.00	$51.50	$57.32	(2.60%)	(7.66%)	(2.65%)	(5.62%)	100.00%
GREIF INC CL A	NONVOTING	$76.89	$52.90	$58.85					0.00%
17 HAVERTY FURN CL A	10 VOTES	$18.00	$12.38	$12.36	(0.80%)	(3.23%)	3.08%	(0.75%)	65.48%
HAVERTY FURN COMMON	ONE VOTE	$18.60	$12.01	$12.46					34.52%
18 HEICO CORP COMMON	ONE VOTE	$25.41	$18.32	$24.05	30.00%	30.91%	26.17%	28.88%	94.47%
HEICO CORP CL A	1/10 VOTE	$19.41	$14.52	$18.50					5.53%
19 HUBBELL INC CL A COMMON	20 VOTES	$49.75	$39.19	$41.46	(8.27%)	(8.21%)	(7.92%)	(8.08%)	75.48%
HUBBELL INC CL B	ONE VOTE	$54.20	$42.56	$45.20					24.52%
20 IDT CORP CL C	ONE VOTE	$15.91	$12.45	$13.03	(1.51%)	(4.10%)	(1.35%)	(2.91%)	93.27%
IDT CORP CL B	1/10 VOTE	$16.59	$12.62	$13.23					6.73%

Continued

STUDY OF VOTING PREMIUMS AS OF AUGUST 26, 2005 COMPANY	PER SHARE VOTING RIGHTS	2005 HIGH	2005 LOW	August 26, 2005 PRICE	August 26, 2005 VOTING PREMIUM	HIGH VOTING PREMIUM	LOW VOTING PREMIUM	AVERAGE HI-LOW VOTING PREMIUM	PERCENT OF VOTING RIGHTS
21 K-V PHARMACEUTICAL CL B	ONE VOTE	$25.00	$15.40	$17.12	0.35%	2.54%	(0.32%)	1.43%	96.46%
K-V PHARMACEUTICAL CL A	1/20 VOTE	$24.38	$15.45	$17.06					3.54%
22 LENNAR CORP CL B	10 VOTES	$64.00	$46.90	$57.60	(7.25%)	(7.06%)	(6.76%)	(6.93%)	67.99%
LENNAR CORP CL A	ONE VOTE	$68.86	$50.30	$62.10					32.01%
23 MCCORMICK & CO	VOTING	$39.00	$31.68	$33.75	(0.47%)	(0.36%)	1.31%	0.38%	100.00%
MCCORMICK & CO	NONVOTING	$39.14	$31.27	$33.91					0.00%
24 MCDATA CORP CL A	ONE VOTE	$6.15	$2.99	$5.37	8.05%	6.22%	5.65%	6.03%	97.64%
MCDATA CORP CL B	1/10 VOTE	$5.79	$2.83	$4.97					2.36%
25 MCRAE IND CL B	ONE VOTE	$13.25	$10.10	$12.90	4.03%	(1.78%)	(0.98%)	(1.44%)	66.10%
MCRAE IND CL A	1/10 VOTE	$13.49	$10.20	$12.40					33.90%
26 MOLEX, INC. COMMON	ONE VOTE	$30.00	$24.31	$26.70	4.71%	12.15%	13.18%	12.61%	100.00%
MOLEX, INC. CL A	NONVOTING	$26.75	$21.48	$25.50					0.00%
27 MOLSON COORS BREWING CL A	VOTING	$80.01	$62.31	$65.70	2.48%	0.03%	8.61%	3.61%	100.00%
MOLSON COORS BREWING CL B	NONVOTING	$79.99	$57.37	$64.11					0.00%
28 MOOG, INC CL B	ONE VOTE	$33.70	$26.76	$31.45	(0.19%)	(0.18%)	4.65%	1.90%	52.27%
MOOG, INC CL A	LTDVOTING	$33.76	$25.57	$31.51					47.73%
29 PLAYBOY ENTERPR CL A	VOTING	$13.55	$10.51	$12.12	(10.62%)	(8.75%)	(7.24%)	(8.10%)	100.00%
PLAYBOY ENTERPR CL B	NONVOTING	$14.85	$11.33	$13.56					0.00%
30 READING INTL CL B	VOTING	$8.20	$6.05	$7.60	(2.56%)	(3.98%)	2.37%	(1.38%)	100.00%
READING INTL CL A	NONVOTING	$8.54	$5.91	$7.80					0.00%
31 ROGERS COMMUN CL A CV	VOTING	$50.19	$31.55	$45.50	22.54%	32.71%	29.46%	31.44%	100.00%
ROGERS COMMUN CL B	NONVOTING	$37.82	$24.37	$37.13					0.00%
32 SEA CONTAINERS CL B	ONE VOTE	$21.40	$10.75	$10.90	0.93%	(0.19%)	0.09%	(0.09%)	77.98%
SEA CONTAINERS LTD CL A	1/10 VOTE	$21.44	$10.74	$10.80					22.02%
33 SEQUA CORP CL B	10 VOTES	$76.00	$48.50	$69.00	0.73%	(1.68%)	2.54%	(0.08%)	75.71%
SEQUA CORP CL A	ONE VOTE	$77.30	$47.30	$68.50					24.29%
34 TELUS CORP COMMON	VOTING	$46.55	$35.13	$45.00	21.79%	24.00%	29.39%	26.26%	100.00%
TELUS CORP NON VTG	NONVOTING	$37.54	$27.15	$36.95					0.00%
35 THOMAS NELSON CL B	10 VOTES	$24.75	$19.12	$20.50	(0.19%)	(1.39%)	2.80%	0.39%	38.11%
THOMAS NELSON COMMON	ONE VOTE	$25.10	$18.60	$20.54					61.89%
36 TRIARC COS CL A	ONE VOTE	$17.40	$12.50	$16.37	9.13%	8.75%	7.76%	8.33%	75.66%
TRIARC COS CL B	1/10 VOTE	$16.00	$11.60	$15.00					24.34%
37 VIACOM INC CL A	ONE VOTE	$39.26	$32.11	$34.08	0.26%	0.69%	0.97%	0.82%	100.00%
VIACOM INC CL B	NONVOTING	$38.99	$31.80	$33.99					0.00%
38 WILEY SONS CL B	ONE VOTE	$45.10	$33.30	$44.15	1.15%	(0.29%)	0.60%	0.09%	64.48%
WILEY SONS CL A	1/10 VOTE	$45.23	$33.10	$43.65					35.52%
	MEDIAN				0.00%			0.24%	
	MEAN				0.44%			1.82%	

SOURCE: September 2005 Standard & Poor's Stock Guide

Summary of Voting Premium Studies

	2005	2004	2003	2002	2001	2000	1999	1998	1996	1994	1993	1992
Voting Premium Year End												
Median	0.00%	0.00%	0.37%	1.89%	1.56%	2.01%	2.14%	0.00%	2.86%	0.82%	1.48%	3.54%
Mean	0.44%	5.35%	6.43%	6.52%	9.05%	9.08%	5.91%	0.57%	3.50%	5.50%	2.17%	6.65%
Voting Premium Avg Hi-Low												
Median	0.24%	0.47%	1.29%	1.68%	2.22%	1.02%	7.77%	1.42%	1.57%	2.29%	4.14%	4.51%
Mean	1.82%	6.52%	6.51%	7.22%	11.63%	8.67%	5.91%	2.19%	3.29%	5.35%	4.81%	7.68%

CHAPTER 10

Report Writing

For many analysts, the style of a written report is the culmination of many valuation engagements. In certain circumstances, particularly related to litigation, counsel in the case may request an oral report through testimony at deposition and/or trial. In certain consultation engagements, the client may request only an oral report or brief written summary. The type and format of the report to be provided may be dictated by the nature of the valuation engagement and/or the needs of the client.

The written report must answer six questions:

1. What was the analyst asked to do?
2. What standard of value was used?
3. What information did the analyst reference or utilize?
4. What procedures did the analyst perform?
5. What assumptions and limiting conditions were applicable?
6. What conclusion of value was reached?

> A full written report should provide the detail necessary to permit another qualified analyst to use similar information and to understand the work done and the valuation conclusion reached.

Particular report-writing standards are applicable in certain types of engagements. A full written report is presented as the Addendum to this chapter.

USPAP ENGAGEMENTS

The Uniform Standards of Professional Appraisal Practice (USPAP) are applicable to those who adhere to USPAP and/or where the intended user of the appraisal report is a federally insured depository institution and the intended use is a federally related transaction. There are different types of reports depending on the appraisal discipline.

Real Estate and Personal Property Reports

When USPAP is applicable, three types of written reports may be issued for real estate and personal property appraisals:

1. Self-Contained Appraisal Report
2. Summary Appraisal Report
3. Restricted Use Appraisal Report

When third-party users are involved, USPAP indicates that the Self-Contained Appraisal Report or the Summary Appraisal Report is the proper report to use. When the information is intended only for client use, the Restricted Use Appraisal Report is permitted.

The essential difference among the reports is content and depth of information. The Self-Contained Appraisal Report is the most comprehensive and complete report. The Summary Appraisal Report contains much of the same information as the Self-Contained Appraisal Report but in summary form without the same level of detail. The Restricted Use Appraisal Report is for client use and usually contains less detailed information.

Business Valuation Reports

In contrast to the three types of reports available for real estate and personal property, business valuation has only two types of reports:

1. Appraisal Report
2. Restricted Use Appraisal Report

Appraisal reports are provided when the intended users are other than the client. When the client is the intended user, a Restricted Use Appraisal Report may be provided. Generally, the main differences in the two business valuation reports are the content and level of information. See Chapter 11 for a detailed discussion of USPAP standards. Other valuation standards provide for slightly different report options. See Chapter 11 for a discussion of the alternatives.

TYPES OF VALUATION ENGAGEMENTS AND RELATED REPORTS

Valuation engagements conducted by analysts are either complete valuation engagements or other valuation engagements. Other valuation engagements encompass all engagements that are not complete valuation engagements. They could include (but are not limited to) limited scope valuation engagements, consulting valuation services, or calculations agreed to with a client. Some business valuation standards require reports except for litigation cases. (See Chapter 11.)

ValTip

Although many analysts often comply with USPAP as a general rule, many of the reports that analysts write are not conducted under the services specified by USPAP for compliance.

Analysts primarily produce two general types of valuation reports: "complete" and "other."

COMPLETE VALUATION REPORT

The complete valuation report is appropriate, when required or requested, when the analyst has been engaged to prepare a complete valuation of a business, an interest in a business, a security, or an intangible asset. It is the primary work product of the complete valuation process and should be prepared with objectivity and integrity in accordance with business valuation standards and procedures. It should describe valuation procedures in sufficient detail to enable the intended users to understand the work performed and the conclusion reached. While there is no universal format for reporting on a complete valuation, there is general consensus on the elements that can be included. A complete valuation report usually contains the following sections:

1. Valuation summary or letter of transmittal
2. Table of contents
3. Introduction
4. Sources of information
5. Analysis of the company or entity
6. Analysis of economic conditions
7. Analysis of industry conditions
8. Financial statement analysis
9. Valuation approaches and methods considered
10. Valuation approaches and methods used
11. Consideration of applicable discounts and premiums (if any)
12. Nonoperating and excess assets
13. Conclusion and reconciliation
14. Assumptions and limiting conditions
15. Certification or representation of the valuation analyst
16. Qualifications of the valuation analyst
17. Appendixes and exhibits

Each of these sections documents an important part of the analyst's thought process toward reaching the conclusion of value. In any particular engagement, this listing of sections may be added to or deleted from as the engagement circumstances dictate. If the report is to be considered a complete valuation report, most if not all sections will be appropriate and necessary.[1]

---

[1] Some business valuation standards also permit a summary report containing less detail than the complete valuation report. (See Chapter 11.)

Valuation Summary

The valuation summary usually contains the following information in summary form. It is intended to be an "executive summary" of the detailed information that follows.

Valuation Summary for Letter of Transmittal

- Identity of the client
- Purpose and intended use of the valuation
- Intended users of the valuation
- Identity of the business, business interest, security, or intangible asset being valued
- Ownership interest being valued and whether the interest has control characteristics
- Date of the valuation
- Report date
- Standard of value
- Premise of value
- Valuation conclusion

The valuation summary provides a synopsis of the entire report in just a single page or a few pages. It is intended to facilitate ease of use, not to be a substitute for the more detailed information that follows. See the sample report for an example of a valuation summary.

Introduction

The introduction section of the report should contain sufficient information to introduce the specifics of the valuation assignment and any features unique to the engagement. The introduction section may contain the following information:

- Identity of the client
- Purpose of the valuation
- Intended use and users of the valuation
- Identity of the entity being valued
- Identity of the interest being valued
- Whether the subject interest has control characteristics and its degree of marketability
- Valuation date
- Report date
- Type of report being issued
- Applicable standard of value
- Applicable premise of value
- Applicable assumptions and limiting conditions
- Restrictions or limitations in the scope of the work
- Any hypothetical conditions used in the valuation engagement
- If the work of a specialist was used, a description of how the specialist's work was included in the valuation
- Any other introductory information the analyst deems useful to enable the reader to understand the work performed
- Reference to Revenue Ruling 59-60 if applicable
- Restrictions (if any) on use of the report

The introduction section sets the stage for the detailed information that is to follow. Its purpose is to provide an overview of the engagement in greater detail than that provided in the valuation summary section. It is also the place in which the analyst sets forth any scope or other limitations in the valuation.

One particularly important element discussed in the introduction section is the standard of value to be employed. The standard of value provides the foundation for valuation decisions made during the course of the valuation work. See the sample report for an example of an introduction section.

Sources of Information

The sources of information section of the report should identify the information received and developed through the analyst's research during the course of his or her work. This information could include:

- For valuation of a business, business interest, or security, a statement as to whether or not the facilities were visited
- For valuation of an intangible asset, whether the legal registration, contractual documentation, or other tangible evidence of the asset was inspected
- Identification of the persons interviewed
- Financial statements analyzed
- Tax information analyzed
- Industry, market, and economic data analyzed
- Other company documents analyzed
- Statement as to whether or not any assurance procedures were performed on the information analyzed
- Identification of other sources researched and information obtained

> In certain engagements, such as litigation, the analyst might not be granted access to the facilities. If so, the introduction section can explain this and also what was done to obtain the knowledge normally gained during a site visit.

See the sample report for an example of the sources of information section.

Analysis of the Company or Entity

Revenue Ruling 59-60 emphasizes eight factors the analyst should consider in assessing the risk inherent in the subject entity. These include:

1. The nature of the business and the history of the entity from inception
2. The economic outlook in general and the condition and outlook of the specific industry in particular
3. The book value of the entity being valued and the financial condition of the business
4. The earnings capacity of the entity
5. The dividend-paying capacity of the entity

6. Whether the entity has goodwill or other intangible value
7. Prior sales of the entity stock and the size of the block to be valued
8. The market price of stock in corporations engaged in the same or similar lines of business whose stock is actively traded in a free and open market either on an exchange or over the counter

The "Nature of the Business and Its History from Inception" is part of the company analysis section of the report. This section should contain enough information about the company for the reader to get a sense of the risks and rewards associated with an ownership interest in the company. Information in this section of the report may include (but not be limited to):

- A description of the subject entity including form of subject organization (corporation, partnership, proprietorship, LLC, etc.) and the state of incorporation or formation
- Company history and background information
- Description of the entity's facilities
- Classes of equity ownership interests and rights attached thereto
- Description of the organizational structure and management team
- Description of the officers and directors
- Description of the key employees
- Description of the entity's products
- Description of the entity's geographic markets
- Description of the entity's industry markets
- Description of key customers and suppliers
- Description of the entity's competition
- Description of other business risks faced by the entity
- Description of the entity's strategy and future plans, if available
- Governmental or regulatory environment

As part of this company analysis, it is appropriate for the analyst to comment on the external and internal business risks faced by the subject entity. Factors suggesting greater risk might include a small group of customers, a limited management team, a small number of suppliers, marketing limitations, and a shrinking market for the entity's products. Factors suggesting lesser risk include a large homogeneous group of customers, a broad-based management team, a diversified group of suppliers, and a growing market for the entity's products. At the conclusion of this section, the overall company risk can be summarized.

See the sample report for an example of the company analysis section.

Analysis of Economic Conditions

The economic analysis describes the condition of the economy in general as of the valuation date and conditions in the regions in which the company operates. Included might be analysis of:

- Global regions
- United States or other nation's economic conditions
- State or regional economic information

- City or community economic information
- Future outlook for the major regions in which the entity operates

Typically, this section includes a macroanalysis of the overall economy and a microanalysis of the economy in the geographic region(s) in which the company operates. The purpose of the economic analysis is to assist the analyst in measuring the risk associated with the current national economy and the local economy in which the subject company operates or the international economy, if applicable.

See the sample report for an example of economic analysis.

Analysis of Industry Conditions

The analysis of industry conditions provides information about the industry or industries in which the subject entity operates. The industry conditions section may contain:

- Identity of the applicable industries
- Description of the applicable industries
- Information regarding suppliers or sources of supply
- Information regarding applicable government regulation
- Industry risks that impact the subject entity
- Future outlook for the industry or industries
- Impact of economic conditions in specific industries that will have influence on the subject entity
- Summary of the overall industry risk

This section assists the analyst in documenting the outside business forces that will influence the company's ability to compete. It fulfills one of the specific risk assessment requirements of Revenue Ruling 59-60.

See the sample report for an example of industry conditions.

Financial Statement Analysis

Financial statement analysis is an important part of the analyst's work. Typically, five years of financial statements and/or tax returns are analyzed. More or less than five years might be considered if the particular entity has a longer or shorter operating cycle. If available, the auditors' report or the accountants' report and the related footnotes may be included in the analysis. The footnotes will include important information related to the entity's accounting policies, contingent liabilities, and future debt and lease payments.

The financial statement analysis often includes:

- A side-by-side comparison of the past five years' financials (or whatever number of years the analyst deems relevant)
- Explanation of the reasoning for any adjustments the analyst deems appropriate to the balance sheet, income statement, or cash flow statement
- Comments on any unusual characteristics of the financial information
- Analysis of the common size company information and comparison with applicable industry information
- Discussion of any assets that will be treated as nonoperating or excess assets
- Any trends in margins or growth rates

Financial statement adjustments may be of two different types. Normalizing adjustments convert the statements into economic financial statements. Control adjustments reflect prerogatives of control and adjust the statement to conditions only the control interest may realize.

See the sample report for an example of financial statement analysis.

Valuation Approaches and Methods Considered

One purpose of this section is to enable the analyst to set forth the reasoning in considering the methods used to value the subject business, business interest, security, or intangible asset. The analyst also has the opportunity here to provide the reasoning for rejecting any methods considered but not used.

See the sample report for an example of valuation approaches and methods considered.

Valuation Approaches and Methods Used

In this section of the complete report, the analyst should identify the selected valuation methods and provide the rationale and supporting data for their use. The section may include, where applicable:

- Any balance sheet adjustments made by the analyst if the asset approach is used
- Identification of the work of other experts used in the asset approach, including real estate and equipment appraisers
- The representative benefit stream selected (either income or cash flow) and whether a capitalized cash flow or discounted cash flow method of the income approach is used
- A discussion of the method used in selecting or computing the discount rate or capitalization rate and the risk factors identified and utilized in arriving at the rate
- A listing of the factors considered in computing a weighted average cost of capital (WACC), if the invested capital model is used
- Identification of and detailed description of selected guideline public companies if the market approach is used with publicly traded company information
- Identification of applicable multiples utilized in the market approach and discussion of the rationale for their use
- Explanation of the basis on which guideline company transactions were chosen and the reasoning behind the selected multiples, if the market approach is used with private company transaction data
- Conclusions drawn from prior transactions in company stock, if they are taken into consideration, and the reasoning used in determining that they were representative
- A detailed computation of value using the chosen methods

See the sample report for an example of the valuation methods used.

Analysis of Risk

Many factors are taken into consideration in the analysis of risk, including most of the factors set forth in Revenue Ruling 59-60. One tool available to the analyst in risk analysis is financial ratios. The financial information of the subject company is compared to the comparable financial information of other companies in the same industry or in the same Standard Industrial Classification (SIC) or North American Industry Classification System (NAICS) codes. Industry information is often available from trade associations or industry support groups. For example, Risk Management Association publishes its *Annual Statement Studies* in which "common size" financial information is published by SIC or NAICS codes.

Comparing the subject company to others of similar size in its industry provides insight into the risk factors present. The detailed financial information can be presented in the appendix to the report. These ratios are discussed in detail in Chapter 4.

See the sample report for an example of ratios, trends, and risks.

Consideration of Applicable Discounts or Premiums

Depending on the standard of value selected for the engagement and the valuation methodology employed, the application of discounts or premiums may be appropriate. If so, the report should document the support for the selected amount and types of discount or premium. See Chapter 9 for a detailed discussion of discounts and premiums.

The discounts and premiums section of the complete valuation report should identify the discounts and premiums considered and the ones deemed applicable. Some of the significant information to be considered includes:

- The minority interest (lack of control) discount and/or the control premium, if appropriate
- The rationale and supporting evidence for the minority interest discount or control premium applied
- The relationship of valuation methodologies and financial adjustments (i.e., control) to the discounts or premiums
- The discount for lack of marketability
- The supporting evidence for the discount for lack of marketability selected
- Consideration of other discounts that may include (but not be limited to):
  - Blockage discounts
  - Key person discounts
  - Trapped-in capital gain discounts
  - Portfolio discounts
  - Transferability restriction discounts
- Consideration of other adjustments that may include (but not be limited to):
  - Adjustment in value of interests in pass-through entities

These valuation adjustments may have a significant impact on the final determination of value of the subject interest. The analyst must document the relationship between the subject entity and the supportive evidence for the adjustments.

See the sample report for an example of the discussion on discounts and premiums.

Nonoperating and Excess Assets

This is the section of the report wherein the analyst covers the treatment of any non-operating or excess assets that might be present in the entity. Examples of such assets may include:

- Assets owned by the entity not used in the trade or business or not deemed necessary to the active conduct of the business
- An operating plant building owned by the business that the analyst decides to treat as non operating (net of the related debt) and added to the value of the operating assets once that value has been estimated
- Investments in marketable securities (other than for short-term investment purposes)
- Excess assets identified by the financial statement analysis

See the sample report for an example of the discussion of nonoperating and excess assets.

Conclusion and Reconciliation

Once the analyst has made the computations of value under the methods selected, a conclusion of value must be reached and documented in the report. If more than one method was selected, the weight or reliance, either quantitative or qualitative, to be given to each method should be disclosed. The conclusion section of the complete valuation report should reconcile the valuation methods and specify the rationale for the conclusion of value.

See the sample report for a discussion of the valuation methods and the reliance afforded each one.

Appendixes

The appendixes are used to include information in the report that is not a direct part of the valuation calculation process but is an important part of the disclosures in the overall report. Information commonly found in the appendixes may include:

- Valuation representation or certification and signature of the analyst (Some business valuation standards refer to this as a certification while others refer to it as a representation.)
- Valuation assumptions and limiting conditions
- Qualifications of the analyst
- Reports of other experts, if appropriate

Valuation Representation or Certification and Signature of the Analyst

The valuation representation or certification of the analysts responsible for the valuation should include (but not be limited to) statements similar to the following:

- Statement that the analyst's work, opinions, and conclusions contained in the report are limited only by the specified assumptions and limiting conditions and are the analyst's personal analysis, opinions, and conclusions

- Statement that for data included in the valuation report that have been obtained from various printed or electronic sources, the analyst believes such sources to be reliable but has performed no corroboerating procedures to verify the validity of the data
- Statement that the engagement has been completed in conformity with the business valuation standards of the organization(s) to which the analyst must conform
- Statement that the analyst has no (or the specified) present or prospective interest in the subject property
- Statement that the analyst has no (or the specified) personal interest with respect to the parties involved
- Statement that the analyst has no bias with respect either to the property that is the subject of the valuation or to the parties involved with the engagement
- Statement that the analyst's engagement is not contingent on a predetermined result
- Statement that the analyst's compensation for the subject engagement is not contingent on a predetermined result or a direction on value that favors the cause of the client
- Statement that no one provided significant professional assistance to the person signing the report (If a person or persons did provide such assistance, they must be identified and the extent of their participation identified.)
- Statement that the analyst has no obligation to update the report or conclusion of value for information coming to his or her attention after the valuation date

Analysts usually do not audit or perform reviews or any other assurance procedures on the historical financial information provided by the entity. They typically accept the information as accurate and state this in the assumptions.

The person assuming responsibility for the valuation should sign the valuation representation or certification.

See Appendix A of the sample report for an example of a certification.

Some analysts include the assumptions and limiting conditions in the engagement letter as well.

Assumptions and Limiting Conditions

Every valuation report is based on certain assumptions and limiting conditions. One common example is a caveat on the accuracy of the entity's historical financial statements and tax returns.

The valuation report should contain a listing of the assumptions and limiting conditions the appraiser took into consideration during the valuation work.

See Appendix B of the sample valuation report for an example of assumptions and limiting conditions.

OTHER BUSINESS VALUATION REPORTS

Other business valuation reports may be prepared for a variety of purposes that are specific to the respective valuation engagements. These other valuation engagements are often lesser in scope than a complete valuation engagement. For such reports, analysts may perform a number of procedures like those in a complete valuation, but the scope is limited or the work agreed upon with the client is less than that required for the engagement to be a complete valuation. The reports prepared for such engagements may be lesser in scope and content than a complete valuation report. Summary or letter reports are also used, where appropriate, for complete appraisals.

SAMPLE REPORT

The Addendum of this chapter contains a sample detailed valuation/appraisal report. It also explains why certain topics were described and presented. Discussion areas are enclosed in a box for easy reference. This is an example for presentation purposes only. Valuation reports of individual analysts can vary greatly as to content, length, and style. This is not a standard report, but it does illustrate the concepts discussed in this chapter. It is a full written report of a complete valuation analysis that complies with USPAP and the requirements of the AICPA SSVS No. 1.

Note: Some of the numbers do not tie together due to rounding issues that resulted in preparing this report for presentation. However, these variations are minor. This sample report is used to illustrate report options only versus valuation methodologies. Economic and industry data is presented for illustration purposes only and may not tie to the quoted sources.

ADDENDUM—SAMPLE VALUATION REPORT, VALUATION OF THE COMMON STOCK OF ACME MEASUREMENT DEVICES, INC., AS OF MAY 31, 2008

March 14, 2009

Robert L. Smith, Attorney
Post Office Box 10000
Denver, Colorado 00000

Re: Fair Market Value of 16,279 Common Shares of Acme Measurement Devices, Inc., as of May 31, 2008

Dear Mr. Smith:

At your request, XYZ Appraisal Associates PLLC ("XYZ") was retained to prepare a valuation analysis and appraisal (valuation engagement and conclusion of value) and detailed/comprehensive appraisal report ("report") to assist you and your client, Mr. John J. Acme, in your determination of the fair market value of 16,279 common shares of Acme Measurement Devices, Inc. ("Acme" or the "Company"), which represents a 13.1 percent common stock interest in Acme. This 13.1 percent minority interest does not possess any elements of control (minority interest), has no readily accessible market, and is thus nonmarketable. The value conclusion is considered as a cash or cash equivalent value. The valuation date is May 31, 2008 (the "Valuation Date"). This valuation and report are to be used only as of this date and are not valid as of any other date.

We have performed a valuation engagement and present our detailed report in conformity with the "Statement of Standards for Valuation Services No. 1" (SSVS) of the American Institute of Certified Public Accountants. SSVS defines a valuation engagement as "an engagement to estimate value in which a valuation analyst determines an estimate of the value of a subject interest by performing appropriate procedures, as outlined in the AICPA Statement on Standards for Valuation Services, and is free to apply the valuation approaches and methods he or she deems appropriate in the circumstances. The valuation analyst expresses the results of the valuation engagement as a conclusion of value, which may be either a single amount or a range."[1]

SSVS addresses a detailed report as follows: "The *detailed report* is structured to provide sufficient information to permit intended users to understand the data, reasoning, and analyses underlying the valuation analyst's conclusion of value."

This valuation was performed solely to assist in the determination of the value for gift tax purposes, and the resulting estimate of value should not be used for any other purpose, or by any other party for any purpose, without our express written consent.

Our analysis and report are in conformance with the 2008–2009 Uniform Standards of Professional Appraisal Practice (USPAP) promulgated by the Appraisal Foundation,[2]

---

[1] The American Society of Appraisers uses the term estimate as part of a limited appraisal. The AICPA usage of the term is equivalent to the result of the highest scope of work specified by the ASA, which is for an appraisal.

[2] The Appraisal Standards Board (ASB) of the Appraisal Foundation develops, interprets, and amends the Uniform Standards of Professional Appraisal Practice (USPAP) on behalf of appraisers and users of appraisal services. The Appraisal Foundation is authorized by Congress as the source of appraisal standards and appraiser qualifications. USPAP uses the terms *appraisal* and *appraisal report,* which are defined in pages U-1 and U-72, respectively. SSVS uses the terms *valuation engagement* and *detailed report,* which are defined in pages 54 and 22–23, respectively. USPAP also uses the term *appraiser,* while SSVS uses the term *valuation analyst.* We use these terms interchangeably in this report.

the ethics and standards of the AICPA, American Society of Appraisers (ASA), Institute of Business Appraisers (IBA), and National Association of Certified Valuation Analysts (NACVA), and with (Internal Revenue Service) IRS business valuation development and reporting guidelines.

Our analysis is also in conformance with various revenue rulings, including Revenue Ruling 59-60, which outline the approaches, methods, and factors to be considered in valuing shares of capital stock in closely held corporations for federal tax purposes. Revenue Ruling 65-192 extended the concepts in Revenue Ruling 59-60 to income and other tax purposes, as well as to business interests of any type.

The standard of value is fair market value, defined in Revenue Ruling 59-60 as "the price at which the property would change hands between a willing buyer and a willing seller when the former is not under any compulsion to buy and the latter is not under any compulsion to sell, both parties having reasonable knowledge of relevant facts." Revenue Ruling 59-60 also defines the willing buyer and seller as hypothetical as follows: "Court decisions frequently state in addition that the hypothetical buyer and seller are assumed to be able, as well as willing, to trade and to be well informed about the property and concerning the market for such property." Furthermore, fair market value assumes that the price is transacted in cash or cash equivalents. Revenue Ruling 59-60, while used in tax valuations, is also used in many nontax valuations.

Fair market value is also defined in a similar way in the *International Glossary of Business Valuation Terms*[3] as "the price, expressed in terms of cash equivalents, at which property would change hands between a hypothetical willing and able buyer and a hypothetical willing and able seller, acting at arm's length in an open and unrestricted market, when neither is under compulsion to buy or sell and when both have reasonable knowledge of the relevant facts."

Because the standard of value is fair market value, our conclusion of value and analysis is solely based on information that was known or reasonably knowable as of the valuation date that would be taken into account by hypothetical parties to a transaction on that date. Thus, actual events taking place between the valuation date and the date of this report are not relied upon in reaching our conclusion as of May 31, 2008.

The premise of value is going concern.[4] The liquidation premise of value was considered and rejected as not applicable, as the going-concern value results in a higher value for the interest than the liquidation value, whether orderly or fixed.

In our conclusion of value, we considered the following relevant factors, which are specified in Revenue Ruling 59-60:

- The history and nature of the business
- The economic outlook of the United States and that of the specific industry in particular
- The book value of the subject company's stock and the financial condition of the business

---

[3] The *International Glossary of Business Valuation Terms* has been jointly adopted by the AICPA, ASA, Canadian Institute of Chartered Business Valuators, NACVA, and the IBA.
[4] The *International Glossary of Business Valuation Terms* defines *going concern* as "an ongoing operating business enterprise" and *going-concern value* as "the value of a business enterprise that is expected to continue to operate into the future. The intangible elements of going-concern value result from factors such as having a trained work force, an operational plant, and the necessary licenses, systems, and procedures in place."

- The earning capacity of the company
- The dividend-paying capacity of the company
- Whether the firm has goodwill or other intangible value
- Sales of the stock and size of the block of stock to be valued
- The market price of publicly traded stocks of corporations engaged in similar industries or lines of business

Our analysis included, but was not limited to, these mentioned factors.

Understanding with the Client and Scope of Work

Per SSVS No. 1, the valuation analyst should establish an understanding with the client. "The understanding with the client reduces the possibility that either the valuation analyst or the client may misinterpret the needs or expectations of the other party. The understanding should include, at a minimum, the nature, purpose, and objective of the valuation engagement, the client's responsibilities, the valuation analyst's responsibilities, the applicable assumptions and limiting conditions, the type of report to be issued, and the standard of value to be used." (para. 17)

Furthermore, "a restriction or limitation on the scope of the valuation analyst's work, or the data available for analysis, may be present and known to the valuation analyst at the outset of the valuation engagement or may arise during the course of a valuation engagement. Such a restriction or limitation should be disclosed in the valuation report (paragraphs 52[m], 68[e], and 71[n])." (para. 19)

We have established an understanding with the client to perform a valuation engagement and have complied with the requirements of SSVS as stated previously. There were no scope restrictions or limitations on the work or the data available for analysis.

In accordance with the business valuation standards promulgated by the American Society of Appraisers and the Appraisal Foundation, we have prepared an appraisal. "The objective of an appraisal is to express an unambiguous opinion as to the value of a business, business ownership interest, or security, which opinion is supported by all procedures that the appraiser deems to be relevant to the valuation."[5] It is based on all relevant information available to the appraiser as of the valuation date; the appraiser conducts appropriate procedures to collect and analyze all information expected to be relevant to the valuation, and the appraiser considers all conceptual approaches deemed to be relevant.[6]

In accordance with the Scope of Work Rule in USPAP, we must:

1. Identify the problem to be solved
2. Determine and perform the scope of work necessary to develop credible assignment results
3. Disclose the scope of work in the report[7]

---

[5] ASA Business Valuation Standards BVS-1 General Requirements for Developing a Business Valuation.
[6] Ibid.
[7] USPAP 2008-2009, p. U-12.

To gain an understanding of the operations of Acme, we reviewed Company financial information and/or operational data as detailed in the Appendix/Exhibits, interviewed Company management, and visited the Company's facility. To understand the environment in which Acme operates, we researched the status of and trends in the various industries that have an impact on it. We also studied economic conditions as of the valuation date and their impact on Acme and the industry. To understand the Company's financial condition, we analyzed its financial statements.

As discussed in this report, we considered all valuation approaches and methods and applied the most appropriate methods from the income, asset, and market approaches to value to derive a conclusion of value of the subject equity interest (13.1 percent minority, nonmarketable interest). Our conclusion of value reflects these findings, our judgment and knowledge of the marketplace, and our expertise in valuation.

The procedures employed in valuing the subject interest in Acme included such steps as we considered necessary, including (but not limited to):

- An analysis of Acme's financial statements
- An analysis of Acme management's expectations as of the Valuation Date and other information supplied by management
- Discussions with management
- A visit by one of the appraisers to the Company's administrative headquarters
- An analysis of the relevant industries for the company, including its condition and outlooks as of the Valuation Date
- An analysis of the general economic environment as of the Valuation Date, including investors' equity and debt-return expectations
- An analysis of applicable discounts, including the discounts for lack of control and lack of marketability
- An analysis of other pertinent facts and data resulting in our conclusion of value

There were no restrictions or limitations in the scope of our work or data available for analysis. XYZ staff, under the direct supervision of the lead appraiser on this engagement, assisted in performing research, populating models with data, and providing other general assistance.

Based on our analysis as described in this valuation report, and the facts and circumstances as of the Valuation Date, the estimate of value of 16,279 shares of common stock of Acme Measurement Devices, Inc., as of May 31, 2008, on a minority, nonmarketable basis was $1,106,972, or $68.00 per share. This conclusion is subject to the Statement of Assumptions and Limiting Conditions found in Appendix B of this report and to the Valuation Analyst's Representation/Certification found in Appendix A of this report. We have no obligation to update this report or our conclusion of value for information that comes to our attention after the date of this report.

Distribution of this letter and report and associated results, which are to be distributed only in their entirety, is intended and restricted to you, your client, and the relevant taxing authorities, solely to assist you and your client in your determination of the fair market value of the subject interest for gift tax purposes and is valid only as of May 31, 2008. This letter and accompanying report are not to be used with, circulated, quoted, or otherwise referred to, in whole or in part, for any other purpose, or to any other party for any purpose, without our express written consent.

We hereby grant consent for this letter and report and associated results to be provided to the Internal Revenue Service.

The approaches and methodologies used in our work did not comprise an examination or any attest service in accordance with generally accepted accounting principles, the objective of which is an expression of an opinion regarding the fair presentation of financial statements or other financial information, whether historical or prospective, presented in accordance with generally accepted accounting principles or auditing standards. We express no opinion and accept no responsibility for the accuracy and completeness of the financial information (audited, reviewed, compiled, internal, prospective, or tax returns) or other data provided to us by others, and we have not verified such information unless specifically stated in this report. We assume that the financial and other information provided to us is accurate and complete, and we have relied upon this information in performing our valuation.

If you have any questions concerning this valuation, please feel free to contact Margaret Smith.

Very truly yours,
XYZ Appraisal Associates PLLC

There is no universally approved or mandated format for a valuation report, but there is general agreement as to the elements that should be included. Additionally Statement of Standard for Valuation Services No. 1 (SSVS) specifies elements to be included but does not mandate the order of presentation. The purpose of the valuation assignment dictates the level of content and the elements addressed. In this cover letter, the appraiser introduces the reader to the content of the valuation report and identifies the client, subject of the valuation, standard of value, size and type of interest, assignment purpose, valuation date, and report date. This level of completeness is recommended to ensure that the reader understands the assignment. References are clearly made to certifications and assumptions and limiting conditions of the report. All of these points are developed more clearly in later sections of the report. Analysts differ in opinion as to whether a letter such as this should include the value conclusion. Some appraisers take the position that, if the value is given here, the reader will ignore the full content of the report and not understand the limitations of the analysis. Others stress that providing the value here gives useful information that better sets up the reader to know the destination before starting the journey of reading the report.

Table of Contents

Income Statement Overview—Unadjusted Data
Cash Flow Analysis
Summary of Financial Statement Analysis
Adjustments to Financial Data for Valuation Purposes

Valuation Approaches/Methods

Income Approach

Income Capitalization Method
Factors Affecting the Selection of a Capitalization Rate for Acme
Derivation of Normalized NCF and Capitalization Rate
CAPM
WACC
Summary of Value of a 100 Percent Minority Interest
Discounted Cash Flow Approach

Market Approach

Guideline Public Company Method
Guideline Company Transaction Method
Adjusted Net Asset Method—Going-Concern Value

Other Valuation Information

Discount for Lack of Marketability

Other Factors
Conclusion for a Discount for Lack of Marketability

Nonoperating and Excess Assets

Conclusion

Appendixes

Appendix A—Valuation Certification and Signature of the Analyst
Appendix B—Assumptions and Limiting Conditions
Appendix C—Professional Qualifications of the Analyst/Appraiser
Appendix D—Other Sources Consulted

Exhibits

Exhibit 10.15   Comparative Balance Sheets
Exhibit 10.16   Comparative Income Statements
Exhibit 10.17   Statements of Cash Flows
Exhibit 10.18   Debt-Free Working Capital Computation
Exhibit 10.19   Income Capitalization Method
Exhibit 10.20   Discount Capitalization Rate Analysis
Exhibit 10.21   Transaction Data

Valuation Summary

Report Summarized:	XYZ Appraisal Associates PLLC issued the appraisal report summarized herein, plus appendixes, on March 14, 2009. This appraisal is subject to the Statement of Assumptions and Limiting Conditions contained in this report as Appendix B.
Subject of Appraisal:	A 13.1 percent minority nonmarketable interest in Acme Measurement Devices, Inc., as of May 31, 2008. The subject common stock represents the largest minority block.
Business Activity:	Acme is a manufacturer of electronic instruments for measurement of the physical properties of engineering materials. It began operations in 1965 and was incorporated in the state of Colorado on January 10, 1965. The Company is a C-corporation.
Purpose of Appraisal:	This valuation is required for gift tax purposes.
Premise of Value:	The Company is valued on a going-concern basis, as opposed to a liquidation basis of value.
Standard of Value:	Fair market value
Basis of Value:	Closely held (nonmarketable), minority basis
Date of Value:	May 31, 2008 (Valuation Date)
Value Conclusion:	The fair market value per share of a 13.1 percent minority, nonmarketable interest in the common stock of the Company as of the Valuation Date, was approximately $68.00 or $1,106,972

> The valuation summary provides an important one-page overview of the report conclusion and the elements of the assignment. All of the information here will be covered and expanded in the sections of the report to follow. Much of the information provided here was on the cover letter, but some analysts do not provide the value conclusion on the cover letter. Is providing the information again so quickly redundant? Valuation reports always contain information that is repeated and expanded. Doing this provides clarification and helps remind the reader of the foundational elements of the assignment.

Description of Assignment

XYZ Appraisal Associates PLLC has been engaged by Robert L. Smith (Attorney) to determine the fair market value per share of a minority, nonmarketable ownership interest, on a going-concern basis, in the common stock of the Company, as of the Valuation Date, for gift tax purposes. The Attorney represents John J. Acme.

The names of the analyst and the client are clearly identified along with the size and type of the interest being valued. Valuations can be prepared for different purposes. Here, the purpose of the valuation assignment is given. The valuation should be used for no other reason or by any other users.

Standard of Value

Revenue Ruling 59-60 defines the fair market value of an item of property as "the price at which the property would change hands between a willing buyer and a willing seller, neither being under any compulsion to buy or sell, and both having reasonable knowledge of relevant facts."

Both the standard of value (definition) and, importantly, the source of the definition are provided. The standard of value provided here is applicable to all valuation assignments prepared for gift, estate, and income tax purposes. The analyst must carefully adhere to the definition in determining the relative significance of facts, the weighing of those facts, and the application of judgment to the valuation process. An analyst must guard against creating a differing standard of value by the inadvertent omission of elements or in the weighting of those elements.

Premise of Value

The Company is valued on a going-concern basis, as opposed to a liquidation basis of value.

Is this enterprise a viable going concern, or is it dead or dying? Identification of the premise provides the analyst's point of reference in reviewing future operational prospects for the business. In valuing a controlling interest (or any interest with the power to cause an asset sale), the analyst should consider whether the business would have a greater value in liquidation than as an operating entity.

Valuation Methodology

The professional standards relevant to this report require the valuation analyst to gather, analyze, and adjust relevant information to perform the valuation as appropriate to the scope of work and to select and apply appropriate valuation approaches, methods, and procedures.

Consideration was given to the factors set forth in Internal Revenue Service Ruling 59-60, which outlines appropriate considerations for the valuation of closely held equity securities, specifically:

- The nature of the business and the history of the enterprise from its inception
- The economic outlook in general and the condition and outlook of the specific industry in particular
- The book value of the stock and the financial condition of the business
- The earning capacity of the company
- The dividend-paying capacity
- Whether the enterprise has goodwill or other intangible value
- Sales of the stock and the size of the block of stock to be valued
- The market price of the stock of corporations engaged in the same or a similar line of business, having their stock actively traded in a free and open market, either on an exchange or over-the-counter

Revenue Ruling 59-60 is a foundational ruling for valuations of closely held businesses for tax purposes. Through later rulings its application was expanded to valuation of entities other than corporations, such as partnerships. Valuations prepared for tax purposes should fully address the factors listed in the ruling. These factors are critical for consideration, but the ruling acknowledges that common sense, reasonableness, and informed judgment will be an important part of the process. Since the likely reader of this report will include representatives of the Internal Revenue Service, the analyst has clearly indicated that the points they expect to see are addressed.

Sources of Information

This engagement involved an analysis of Acme's recent financial performance and its prospects in the market in which it operates. In the course of developing our findings, our work included the following:

- An on-site visit to Acme's headquarters in Denver, Colorado
- Interviews with the following:
  - Company management (which included Mr. John J. Acme, Jr., the executive vice president, and Mr. Bobby Jones, the head of the engineering department) on the issues related to the Company's current and future strategy, operations, customers and competitors, and the industry environment as of the valuation date
  - Company personnel (Mr. Rich Moss, the production manager) on topics related to the Company operations
  - The Company controller and treasurer (Mr. H. Hal Burns, CPA, controller, and treasurer of the Company) on issues related to financial analysis
- Analysis of the audited financial statements[8]

---

[8] Source: Audited statements by Smith & Smith, CPAs for years ended December 31, 2003 through 2007.

- Analysis of other relevant Company documents and outside research. We also obtained and reviewed the December 31, 1998, valuation report of the Company dated March 15, 1999, prepared by Mr. Mark Jones, Jr., of Valuation Nation, Inc.
- Research on the overall economic outlook and the specific factors pertinent to the measurement devices and construction industries, which impact Acme
- Analysis of the current and future earnings capacity of Acme

Financial and other pertinent information provided has been accepted without further verification. See Appendix B for a complete list of the assumptions and limiting conditions to which this appraisal is subject and Appendix D for a list of other sources consulted.

Because the standard of value is fair market value, our conclusion of value and analysis is solely based on information that was known or knowable as of the valuation date that would be taken into account by hypothetical parties to a transaction on that date. Thus, actual events taking place between the valuation date and the date of this report are not relied upon in reaching our conclusion as of May 31, 2008.

> Major sources of information should be identified, appropriate to the purpose of the assignment. Notice that the analyst is assigning responsibility to others for the accuracy of the information on which she is relying. The analyst is not acting as an auditor. This assignment of responsibility for the data is an important disclosure to the reader. Additionally, at the end of the valuation engagement, the analyst may ask for a "representation letter" signed by management or other responsible parties, in which they acknowledge to the best of their knowledge that the information they have provided is true and complete.

Background

Company Profile/History

Acme is a manufacturer of measurement devices for assessing the physical properties of engineering materials. It began operations in 1965 and was incorporated in the state of Colorado on January 10, 1965. The Company is a C corporation, and is currently located at 1800 Cowboy Way, in Denver, Colorado.

Acme's current product offerings include testing gauges and related equipment incidental to the use of its gauges. Acme provides full-service training and maintenance support for its product line through sales and service offices in the United States, Canada, and through over 20 distributors around the world. The Company's primary customers are companies (contractors) operating in the construction industry.

The following points document some important milestones in Acme's history:

1965: Acme was founded by Mr. John J. Acme.

1966: Mr. Acme began designing and building specialized testing equipment.

1967: Mr. Acme's efforts led to the application of cutting-edge technology to testing and measuring instruments.

1972:   The launch of its main product, the 5000 Series model. Exports account for approximately 7 percent of total revenue.

1978:   Acme moved its location to Denver where it operates today. The Company employed approximately 50 individuals.

1986 and 2003:   Acme expanded its facilities.

2004:   Model 5500 XP Compactor Machine is introduced.

2006:   The Acme Model 3500 Moisture Marker and Model 9800 XYZ Oven were introduced.

2007:   Model 6750, the Acme XP Compactor Machine was introduced. The Company employs approximately 185 individuals.

2007:   In December, the Board of Directors approved the building of a 40,000-square foot Research and Development Center.

2008:   In January, the New Hot Oven was presented to board members. The Company employs approximately 150 individuals.

Ownership

As of the Valuation Date, the Company's capital stock consisted of 124,684 shares of $1.50 par value common stock issued and outstanding.

After its incorporation in 1965, Mr. Acme raised funds by selling stock to family and associates to help finance the expected growth of the business. Over time, the initial shareholders made gifts of stock in Acme to their heirs; therefore, the actual number of shareholders increased continuously.

As of the Valuation Date, the Company had 102 shareholders. As per management, the relationship of Acme's stockholders was excellent. Various members of the Acme family hold the largest amounts of Company stock.

Exhibit 10.1 shows the five main shareholders (in terms of number of shares held) of the Company as of the Valuation Date, ranked by the voting power held by each.

Exhibit 10.1   Ownership—Ranking by Voting Power

Name	Total Shares Owned	% of Total Shares Outstanding
John J. Acme	16,279	13.1%
Leigh Acme	10,562	8.5%
John J. Acme, Jr.	9,184	7.4%
Rhonda Acme-Williams	9,184	7.4%
Chris E. Acme	9,184	7.4%

Management/Personnel

General employee relations are considered good. There is an approximate annual turnover rate at Acme of 15 percent. This percentage in turnover is due to the fact that the work availability in Denver is high.

As of the Valuation Date, the Company had a total of approximately 150 nonunion employees. Acme has employment agreements with its key employees that limit their ability to work for a competitor in a specified geographical area for a certain time.

The Company's key employees and their functions are shown in Exhibit 10.2. From their background description, it can be seen that the Company has a balanced management team comprised of individuals with extensive experience in the measuring devices industry.

Exhibit 10.2   Organizational Structure

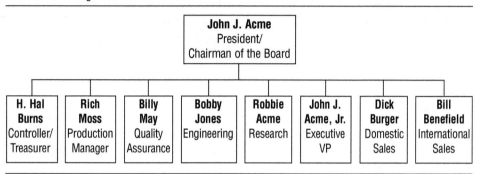

A short description of some of the key personnel follows:

John J. Acme. President of the Company and Chairman of the Board, founded Acme in 1965. Prior to that, Mr. Acme started out in the radio repair business, and later began developing testing equipment for the public and private sectors. In 1960, Mr. Acme began designing and building specialized testing equipment for clients including GE and NASA.

John J. Acme, Jr. Executive Vice President, has a B.A. degree from Colorado State University and an M.B.A. degree from the University of Colorado. His work experience began at Acme in 1986 as Sales Manager, continuing in 1989 as a Manager of Central American Sales. He has been the Executive Vice President of the Company since 1996.

H. Hal Burns, Jr., CPA. Controller and Treasurer of the Company, has a B.A. degree in Accounting from Wheaton College. His work experience includes employment with Big Eight, Ltd. from 1967 to 1992. Since 1994, Hal has been with Acme.

Bobby Jones. Head of the Engineering Department, has a Masters and a Ph.D. in Civil Engineering from the Colorado State University. Bobby has been with the company since 1995.

Rich Moss. Production Manager, has a B.S. degree in Business Administration from Central Wyoming University. Prior to coming to Acme, Rich was a Materials Manager with Big Sky Electric.

Bill Benefield. International Sales and Product Services Manager, obtained a B.A. from East Montana State University in 1970. He has been with Acme since 1983.

The table in Exhibit 10.3 shows the officers and directors of the Company, and the compensation for the officers for the year 2007.

Exhibit 10.3 Company Officers and Directors

Company's Officers and 1999 Compensation		Company's Directors
John J. Acme, President	$425,000	John J. Acme, Chairman of the Board
John J. Acme, Jr., Executive VP	$225,000	Rhonda Acme-Williams
C. Page Turner, Secretary	$ 10,000	Richard L. Hobbs
H. Hal Burns, Jr., Treasurer	$100,000	John J. Acme, Jr.
		Thomas York

Products

The products manufactured by Acme are used primarily in the construction industry. They are principally used to measure the moisture and density of certain construction materials, density of asphalt layers, and as quality control equipment in asphalt mix design.

Functionally, the Company products are designed for the following applications:

- *XP Compactor Machines.* Company's products in this area of business include Model 6750 designed for use in field labs and the Model 5500 XP Compactor Machine. These models produce a profile that is used by the designer to determine optimum aggregate mixtures.
- *Ignition Ovens.* Include the Acme New Hot Oven (NHO). The NHO combines advanced infrared technology to measure asphalt content. This produces a very clean and efficient burning of aggregate materials while limiting the aggregate degradation.
- *Moisture/Density Gauges.* Acme is a leader in the industry with its products for these applications to measure the density of aggregate construction materials.

Gauges comprise the highest percentage of revenue, with approximately 48 percent of total revenues in 2007. The compactors generated approximately 25 percent of total revenues in 2007.

The Company has been very active in research and development. In 2007, the Board of Directors approved the plan to build an advanced technology center (the Research and Development Center), which would be used for development of new products for the Company's industry. Historically, the Company spent approximately $2.8 million and $2.7 million on research and development costs in 2006 and 2007, respectively, which was approximately 10 percent of total revenues.

Company Operations/Business Risks

The Company faces a number of risks due to the nature of the technology employed. Most of the equipment manufactured by Acme utilizes a source material that emits radiation into a sample. The major product risk is related to this feature.

One risk is that of disposal of used or depleted source materials. The Company is required to track each of the sources it sells, and, when these sources are depleted, they must be returned to Acme for disposal. That places Acme in an undesirable situation, especially since there are currently no federally approved long-term nuclear waste disposal sites in the United States.

Another risk with this technology is that of public/client perception of the risks associated with the radioactive materials. Clients are required to receive training regarding the use of these instruments and must make strides to track all of their instrumentation.

Locations Maintained by the Company

The map in Exhibit 10.4 shows the locations maintained by the Company and the primary activity of each location. As shown, in the United States, the Company's headquarters and its only manufacturing facility are located in Denver, Colorado.

The Company's branches are in Dallas, Texas (the Southwestern Branch), Chicago, Illinois (the Midwestern Branch), and Sacramento, California (the Western Branch). These branches provide both sales and service of Acme equipment. All the other locations are either sales or service centers. The most recent customer service center was opened in April 2008 in Tampa, Florida. Per Company management, in the event of an increasing population of gauges, other service centers may be opened in the future.

Exhibit 10.4   Acme Sales and Service Offices in the United States

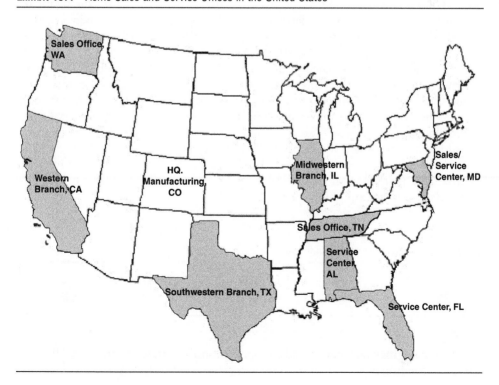

Besides the U.S. operations, the Company has international sales and service centers in Canada and Germany. The sales and service office in Canada is located in Toronto, Ontario, and the one in Germany is located in Berlin.

The Company has developed relationships with distributors all over the world. As of the Valuation Date, the Company had approximately 20 international distributors. Acme has long-term relationships with several of its distributors. The Company is continually seeking other distributors in different parts of the world.

Facilities and Space Availability/Equipment

Acme leases its headquarters facilities from Acme Owners, Ltd., which is a corporation owned by members of the president's family. The lease has an original term of 18 years, with the lease expiring October 31, 2014. The lease agreement states that the parties to the lease shall renegotiate the amount of rent every five years.

The lease agreement mentions the following:

> Landlord and tenant have studied available data on prevailing rates for commercial real estate space in Denver, and have determined that a blended rate of $15.33 per square foot for space in the building covered by the lease is somewhat below average in the area, but is reasonable and fair. The building contains 90,000 square feet on the first or main floor and 35,000 square feet in the lower or ground floor.

Lease payments for the years ended December 31, 2007 and 2006 were $1,540,000 and $1,490,300, respectively. Real estate appraisals on the Company property were not available to determine whether the rent paid approximated market rental rates, but this rate is, based on representation from management, in accordance with market rents appropriate for Denver.

At present, the work schedule at Acme is comprised of one shift. If sales grow, labor is believed to be available to add a partial second shift. One constraint that Acme faces is the floor space availability. Currently, based on demand for its products, Acme could reach a maximum capacity of production of approximately $31 million in sales. If orders increase over this amount, the Company will have to search for additional floor space for its production facility.

The Company's machinery and equipment are in very good condition. The approximate yearly capital expenditures for machinery and equipment for the past five years are shown in Exhibit 10.5.

Exhibit 10.5 Annual Capital Expenditures

2003	2004	2005	2006	2007
$809,238	$818,096	$1,036,950	$875,750	$553,260

Company management intends to spend approximately $855,000 in 2009 on capital expenditures.

Marketing and Advertising

Acme does not have a marketing department. The Company's annual budget for advertising is between $95,000 and $125,000 and is spent on participation at trade shows, direct sales calls, and visits to prospective clients.

Customers

Sales to the Company's top 10 customers ranked based on revenues generated, for the years 2003 through 2007, are presented in Exhibit 10.6.

Exhibit 10.6   Top Ten Customers

Company	2003	2004	2005	2006	2007
Twin Pines	$ 796,436	$ 447,582	$ 387,947	$ 442,361	$ 507,794
RE Materials	542,523	437,838	374,621	407,190	485,607
Hood	473,597	377,019	370,827	355,863	396,966
James & Co.	411,120	358,622	358,418	348,563	396,090
Tim Corp.	391,011	343,386	344,288	340,721	388,371
Parker, Inc.	345,882	329,336	335,234	339,837	381,296
Marathon, Inc.	342,249	324,111	301,781	326,517	366,165
Bama Boys Corp.	299,471	296,274	292,278	324,840	277,200
Rooster, Inc.	297,422	253,295	284,468	309,729	254,345
Berte, Inc.	297,333	251,450	258,911	277,706	238,008
Total	$4,197,044	$3,418,913	$3,308,773	$3,473,327	$3,691,842

As can be seen in the table, the Company has established long-term relationships with its customers. For instance, Twin Pines has been a client of the Company for more than 25 years; RE Materials, James & Co., and Tim Corp. have been clients for over 20 years. Some are one-time clients, though, as is likely to be the case of Z Corp, a Nevada company, which accounted for approximately $150,000 in revenues in 2007. The contractor declared bankruptcy in 2008.

A short description of some of the Company's main customers in 2007 follows:

- Twin Pines operates in waste management services and is a provider of environmental analysis and consulting services.
- RE Materials operates as a paving contractor in the construction services industry.
- James & Co. is part of the RaRa Corporation, one of the Southwest's largest suppliers of construction materials. RaRa provides the construction industry with a full range of aggregate products.
- Tim Corp. is an engineering services company.

The Company does not have exclusive contracts with its customers. The only exclusive contracts Acme has entered into are with some of its international distributors.

Competitors

Some of the Company's main competitors, per management, include the following companies:

- Big Instrument Company (Big) is a manufacturer of structural material testing equipment and research test equipment. Big is a provider of microprocessor-based industrial control system engineering, design, and manufacturing services for OEMs.
- Thermogo, Inc. (Thermogo) is a manufacturer of industrial ovens. Equipment produced includes bench-top ovens, incubators, power outlets, strip chart recorders, digital hot plates, stirrers, hot plates, shakers, mixers, and thermal cycles.
- Hubert Electronics Company (Hubert) is one of the nation's leading manufacturers of testing equipment for asphalt, concrete, and soil. It competes with Acme in several markets.
- Pave the World International, Inc. (PAVE) is a provider of field moisture content measurements for soils, asphalt, and concrete. It competes with Acme in the moisture device market. In the past, PAVE and Big have been very aggressive in their marketing and pricing.
- Bigger Systems, Inc. (Bigger) provides nonnuclear measurement of material density that eliminates for the customer the added cost or need for a certified nuclear technician. The product provided by Bigger has a definite appeal to the market, but the results of its measurements are questionable.

Exhibit 10.7 Acme versus the Competition—Acme Measurement Devices, Inc.

Product type	Weaknesses	Strengths
Compactor Machines	Big bought the third-ranked XP Compactor Machine manufacturer and has initiated an aggressively negative campaign about Acme's products.	Acme is responding to the negative campaign in a professional manner. Acme has excellent quality products, which are offered at competitive prices. Acme increased its service staffing and reduced its lead time to one to two weeks for delivery.
Ignition Ovens	Thermogo ignition oven is the leader in the current market.	The New Hot Oven has significant advantages over competition. It is new technology; it is relatively lightweight; it's offered in two models with different power options; and the price is competitive.
Moisture/Density Gauges	Competitors in the marketplace have improved their products, making them more comparable with Acme.	Acme is an innovator in gauge technology. There is a noticeable brand loyalty among consumers relative to Acme products.

An analysis of the strengths and weaknesses of Acme relative to its competitors is provided in the table in Exhibit 10.7.

Key Person[9]

This valuation engagement came as a result of the sudden retirement of the Company's founder, president, and chairman of the board, Mr. John J. Acme. In early May 2008, he was diagnosed with a terminal illness. His stock was gifted to his children on May 31, 2008. Mr. Acme had been actively involved in the day-to-day operations of the Company since its inception. He contributed to Company growth with his strategic judgment and long-standing contacts within the industry.

Although past normal retirement age, Mr. Acme continued to work daily until the day before his unexpected retirement. As a result, a succession plan was never put in place, and Mr. Acme made all significant management decisions until the last day he was in the office.

Mr. Acme was covered by a minimum key person life insurance policy, in the face amount of approximately $200,000, for which the Company was the beneficiary.

In adjusting for risk factors specific to Acme in Exhibit 10.20, we incorporated the estimated effect of the loss of the Company's president.

As of the Valuation Date, it was expected that Mr. Acme, Jr., would succeed Mr. Acme as president and chairman of the board of the Company.

Summary of Background Information

- The Company has a balanced management team composed of individuals with extensive experience.
- Besides its manufacturing facility and headquarters in Colorado, the Company has three other branches, three sales offices, and three service centers in the United States.
- The products manufactured by Acme are used primarily in the construction industry. The Company is the industry leader in materials testing gauges.
- The Company has established long-term relationships with several of its customers.
- The Company has been very active in research and development.
- Acme increased its service staffing, and reduced its lead time to one to two weeks for delivery.
- The New Hot Oven introduced on the market in March 2008 is a promising product; it is relatively lightweight; it is offered in two models with different power options; and the price is competitive.
- The constraints that Acme faces are those of floor space. Currently Acme has a maximum capacity of production of approximately $31 million in sales.
- The Company faces a number of risks due to the nature of the technology employed. The major risk is that of the nuclear source material, which entails a number of component risks.

---

[9] An example of a catastrophic loss of key executives was the tragic death of most of the top management of Arrow Electronics in a hotel fire in December 1980. Arrow's New York Stock Exchange–listed common stock fell approximately 20 percent after the announcement of the news. Source: *Wall Street Journal.*

- The Company is encountering many sales situations whereby a client will not buy a gauge from Acme unless it disposes of the source materials from its old gauges.
- Under current circumstances, Acme must dispose of the nuclear waste. At present in the United States there are no federally approved, long-term nuclear waste disposal sites.
- Mr. Acme was a key person in the business and kept tight control over all operations. A succession plan was never put in place, and Mr. Acme made all management decisions until the last day he was in the office.

To value the future, one must look at the past. This section of the report provides important information on the history of the business, major events, ownership, key personnel, products, marketing, customers and competitors, suppliers, and other critical factors. What has brought the Company to where it is today? Was it innovative products or excellent management? Great products can cover bad management, but only in the short term. What key risks does the company face in its market area? More important, can it continue to do in the future what it has done in the past? The level of disclosure here can be brief or lengthy, depending on circumstances and the nature of the assignment.

This section should leave the reader informed of the critical factors viewed by the analyst. After an extensive narrative, the reader is provided a bullet-point summary of what was been presented.

Industry Analysis

Acme is a manufacturer of nuclear and electronic instruments for measurement of the physical properties of construction materials. Due to the nature of the operations of Acme, we researched the Measuring and Controlling Instruments industry—which is an integral part of the Industrial and Analytical Instruments Industry—classified by the 1987 Standard Industrial Classification (SIC) manual under SIC 3829.

Since the primary source of clients for Acme products are companies operating in the highway construction industry, we researched this industry as well, which is classified under SIC 1611.

Description of the Industrial and Analytical Instruments Industry[10]

As can be seen in the table in Exhibit 10.8, the Industrial and Analytical Instruments industry encompasses three major sectors: laboratory instruments and apparatus, measuring and controlling instruments, and electrical test and measuring instruments. Of the three segments shown below, we will focus our analysis only on the Measuring and Controlling Instruments Industry.

---

[10] Source: *National Industry & Trade Outlook 2008,* Chapter 23, 1–8.
[Note: Fictitous source for illustrative purposes only.]

Exhibit 10.8 Industry Segmentation

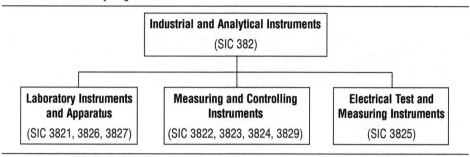

Measuring and Controlling Instruments Industry[11]

The industry main product segments include aircraft engine instruments (14 percent of industry sales for 2006), nuclear radiation detection devices (13 percent), geophysical and meteorological equipment (32 percent), and physical properties testing and inspection equipment (27 percent).

The industry was fragmented in comparison to other U.S. manufacturing sectors with an estimated 908 companies competing in 2006. The average industry participant employed 38 workers in 2006, compared to 49 for all other U.S. manufacturing firms.

Many of the products manufactured in this industry contain microprocessors that improve the speed, measurement, and process control of these instruments and systems. A recent development is the trend toward integrated products and systems. The increased use of "intelligent" products is allowing the end user—a manufacturing facility or power plant—to predict problems in advance of costly failures. U.S. companies must continue to invest in key growth technologies such as electronics and software to remain competitive in today's increasingly complex environment.

The keys to growth in today's global marketplace include acceleration of new product introductions and the globalization of the instrument business. Acquisitions, joint ventures, and strategic alliances are critical to American companies that wish to remain competitive in the global marketplace.

Nuclear Radiation Detection and Measurement Devices Industry

We employed Porter's[12] model of analysis, as shown in Exhibit 10.9, to examine more closely the nuclear radiation detection and measurement devices industry defined by SIC 3829 which is an integral part of the Measuring and Controlling Instruments Industry described in the previous section. For this analysis, we relied on sources provided by the management of Acme.

---

[11] Ibid.

[12] Michael E. Porter, *Competitive Strategy: Techniques for Analyzing Industries and Competitors* (New York: The Free Press, 1998).

Exhibit 10.9 Industry Analysis—A Classical Approach

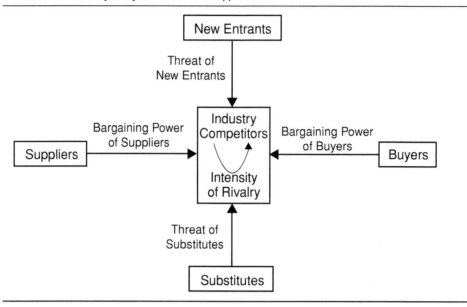

In the following paragraphs we will analyze each of the characteristics that define this industry:

- *Industry Competitors.* As mentioned in the Company Profile section of this report, competition is strong. One competitor has initiated an aggressive negative campaign about Acme's products.
- *Substitutes.* It is believed that the first company to develop a reliable and accurate product that will be capable of doing all the measurements without using radioactive isotopes will be in a significant position to capture the majority of the business in this industry. The current market trend is toward acceptance of less than reliable measurement equipment as long as it does not contain nuclear radiation materials. One competitor has developed a nonnuclear device, but the results measured are questionable. The research and development (R&D) expenditures are fairly high in the industry, between 7 and 15 percent of total revenues.
- *Buyers.* Most buyers of materials testing equipment are construction companies operating as general contractors. These contractors usually obtain their work through a bidding process that is fairly competitive; therefore, they must keep costs at a minimum. As a result, these buyers are price sensitive and tough to negotiate with. Also, the manufacturers are encountering many sales situations whereby a customer will not buy a gauge from the producer unless it disposes of the source materials from the customer's old gauges. This adds an extra cost to the manufacturer (which, due to the price sensitivity of its buyers, cannot be passed on to its customer) to dispose of the radioactive materials.

- *Suppliers.* There are very few companies in the market that supply radioactive sources; therefore, the bargaining power of suppliers is fairly high. Historically, the suppliers of radioactive materials would handle the aged products with used nuclear sources. At present, the suppliers are no longer accepting the return of these sources. Therefore, the manufacturer is put in the unenviable position of handling this nuclear waste. Currently in the United States, there are no federally approved, long-term nuclear waste disposal sites.
- *New Entrants.* Based on an analysis of this industry, the barriers to enter the market are high. A manufacturing company that decides to enter this industry must obtain and maintain specific licenses to store, use, and transport radioactive materials and must have adequate capital necessary for R&D expenditures.
- *Government Regulations.* The companies that manufacture or purchase products that contain radioactive materials must have a current radioactive materials license. Companies are required to comply with the Nuclear Regulatory Commission (NRC), State, and Department of Transportation (DOT) sets of laws.
- *Future Trends.* An examination of articles discussing the subject of nuclear waste disposal reveals that there will probably be no operational nuclear waste disposal facilities in the United States for another 15 to 20 years. The result of this is that Acme now finds itself in the business of interim nuclear disposal for its clients, which requires the Company to divert its energies from research and development, manufacturing, and marketing of its instruments to the construction and maintenance of nuclear storage and compliance with nuclear regulations.

Industry and Trade Projections[13]

Shipments by the U.S. Measuring and Controlling Instruments Industry in 2006 rose an estimated 3 percent over 2005, reaching $20.1 billion in constant dollars. The value of U.S. Measuring and Controlling Instruments Industry shipments was estimated to reach $20.7 billion in 2007, an increase of 3 percent.

U.S. industry shipments of measuring and controlling instruments are forecast to grow 3 percent to $21.2 billion in 2008.

During the five-year period ending in 2012, analysts project an annual compound growth rate of 4 percent, with total U.S. industry shipments of measuring and controlling instruments reaching $24.1 billion.

Construction Industry Overview

Due to the nature of the operations of Acme, since its primary source of clients are companies operating in the construction industry, we also researched this industry, which is classified under SIC 1611.

---

[13] *National Industry & Trade Outlook 2008.*

Results of the 2007 Construction Industry Annual Financial Survey[14]

The Economy and Competition section of the 2007 Construction Industry Annual Financial Survey indicated that the respondents to the survey were fairly optimistic regarding anticipated growth in next year's volume of contract revenue. The respondents to the 2007 survey were general members of the Construction Financial Management Association (CFMA) (i.e., contractors operating in various niches of the construction industry). The respondents projected the Heavy & Highway category with the highest growth in next year's volume.

The survey asked respondents to select from a list the three most challenging areas facing the construction industry during the next five years. Consistent with 2006, respondents selected shortage of trained help as the top challenge facing the construction industry in the future. Sources of future work and shortage of trained project managers were ranked second and third.

U.S. Construction Industry[15]

In 2007, the inflation-adjusted value of new construction put in place increased 4 percent to set an all-time record. (The 2007 current dollar value of about $700 billion is also an all-time record.)

This performance was partly the result of a small increase in the number of housing starts to 1.66 million units. Public works construction increased 5 percent, led by increases in school and road construction.

The value of new construction put in place as a percentage of gross domestic product (GDP) (about 7.8 percent in 2007) has risen slightly in recent years but is well below the post–World War II peak of 11.9 percent attained in 1966. This measure tends to understate the importance of construction in the economy because several types of construction activity that are not included in new construction data have grown rapidly in the last decade, including maintenance and repair, some commercial and industrial renovation, factory-built structures, and environmental restoration.

There were an estimated 6.3 million employees in the construction industry in 2007, about the same as the 2006 level, which was an all-time record. In addition, about 1.6 million people are self-employed in construction as proprietors and working partners, so the total number of persons employed in the industry is about 7.9 million. Construction is one of the higher-paying industries in the United States as measured by average hourly and weekly earnings.

Outlook for 2008

The constant dollar value of new construction in the year 2008 is expected to increase slightly from the 2007 level to set another record. Home building will lag behind nonresidential construction. The most promising markets are commercial buildings, educational buildings, highways, and electric utilities. The weaker construction markets will be factories, military facilities, and single-family homes.

Private, nonresidential construction will be about 2 percent higher than in 2007, with declines in factory construction offset by gains in other categories. Public works construction is expected to increase in 2008 as a result of increases in federal, state, and local construction expenditures.

---

[14] Source: The 2007 Construction Financial Management Association (CFMA) survey. [Illustration only; numbers fictitious for 2007]

[15] Source: *National Industry & Trade Outlook 2008.*

Outlook to 2012

Between 2008 and 2012, new construction is expected to increase modestly from current levels. The overall real (excluding inflation) growth rate for construction will be about 1 percent annually, compared with 2 percent for the GDP. Public works construction is expected to increase faster than is private nonresidential construction. Remodeling and repair construction is expected to increase at about the same rate as the GDP.

A key factor supporting construction during the next five years will be stable or even declining interest rates after the year 2008. This forecast assumes a very small federal deficit and modest inflation rates, which should lead to lower interest rates and a fairly good macroeconomic climate for construction.

Transportation Infrastructure

New road and bridge construction, which was at a record level in 2007, is expected to set another record in the year 2008. Expenditures for highway maintenance and repair have increased and will continue to set records as well.

About 25 percent of the value of highway construction put in place consists of bridges, overpasses, and tunnels; flatwork (primarily roads) accounts for the remaining 75 percent. Bridgework is expected to grow faster than flatwork during the next several years because of the need to replace obsolete or unsafe bridges with new bridges for the twenty-first century. According to the Federal Highway Administration's latest estimate, 23 percent of the highway bridges in the United States are structurally deficient and an additional 21 percent are functionally or structurally obsolete.

Highway maintenance and repair expenditures have grown during the last two decades as the road network has become larger and older. In 2007, the current dollar cost of highway maintenance and repair was about $31 billion, compared with $50 billion in new highway construction put in place. While some of this work consists of routine maintenance such as mowing grass, much of it is typical construction activity such as repaving roads and painting bridges. Highway maintenance and repair expenditures probably will grow more rapidly than will new construction over the next decade.

Mass transit construction was expected to decline slightly in 2007, despite the increase in new federal budget authority because of lags in the spending process. However, after 2008, mass transit construction is expected to increase sharply because of increasing federal financial support. The outlook for mass transit construction is heavily dependent on the types of funding available. Of the $235 billion in federal financial support authorized from 2006 through 2012, $35 billion has been earmarked for mass transit projects. In addition, a large share of the remaining funds can be diverted from highways to mass transit because of concern about air pollution and local development policies.

Summary of Industry Analysis

- Based on our research, there will probably be no operational nuclear waste disposal facilities in the United States for another 15 to 20 years.
- Companies operating in the nuclear radiation detection and measurement devices are required to comply with applicable Nuclear Regulatory Commission (NRC), State, and Department of Transportation (DOT) regulations.

- It is believed that the first company to develop a reliable and accurate product which will be capable of doing all the measurements without using radioactive isotopes will be in a significant position to capture the majority of the business in this industry.
- During the five-year period ending in 2012, analysts project an annual compound growth rate of 4 percent, with total U.S. industry shipments of measuring and controlling instruments reaching $24.1 billion.
- The manufacturing companies operating in the measuring and controlling devices industry find themselves in a difficult environment, being squeezed by the bargaining power of their buyers and suppliers, and also being concerned with the immediate loss of market share in the event of a discovery of substitute products that are not using radioactive materials.
- The Economy and Competition section of the 2007 Construction Industry Annual Financial Survey indicated that respondents to the survey were fairly optimistic regarding anticipated growth in next year's volume of contract revenues.
- The respondents of the 2007 CFMA survey project the heavy and highway category to have the highest growth in next year's volume.

As a result of all the factors described above, Acme finds itself in a difficult environment, being squeezed by the bargaining power of its buyers and suppliers, as well as being concerned with the immediate loss of market share in the event of a breakthrough discovery of a substitute product that does not use radioactive materials. We took this into account when determining the capitalization rate in Exhibit 10.20, as well as in determining a normalized level of revenues, expenses, and cash flow in Exhibit 10.19.

This entity manufactures highly specialized products. With such a narrow focus, the analyst believed that he or she should not only look at the production side of the industry but also see the industry status of the users of the products. Doing this often requires that more than one SIC (or NAICS) be reviewed. Often this industry analysis is presented in the back of a valuation report as an appendix. That approach is acceptable, but what can result is a "disconnect" between the industry information and its application to the subject company. Here the analyst has presented the industry information early in the report and woven it together with company information. If the analyst places the information in an appendix, care should be taken to explain its impact on the valuation process presented earlier in the report.

General Economic Overview—United States[16]

According to advance estimates released by the Department of Commerce's Bureau of Economic Analysis, real gross domestic product (GDP), the output of goods and

[16] Source: *The National Economic Review*, First Quarter, 2008, Mercer Capital (used with permission).

services produced by labor and property located in the United States, increased at an annualized rate of 0.6 percent during the first quarter of 2008. This represents the 26th consecutive positive growth rate in GDP subsequent to the 2001 recession and compares to an identical 0.6 percent increase in the fourth quarter. The 0.6 percent increase in the first quarter of 2008 was in line with economists' expectation. The increase in real GDP during the first quarter is attributed to increases in personal consumption expenditures for services, private inventory investment, exports of goods and services, and federal government spending. These factors were partially offset by negative growth in residential fixed investment and personal consumption expenditures for durable goods. Imports, a subtraction in the calculation of GDP, increased. Economists point out that the positive economic growth exhibited in the first quarter was driven largely by a rise in exports and a buildup of inventories, and, excluding those factors, the economy actually contracted during the first quarter. Consumer spending continues to be hampered by increasing energy prices, a continuing housing recession, modestly rising unemployment rates, failing consumer confidence, and tightening credit conditions related to rising delinquencies and mortgage foreclosure rates. Although many economists feel that recent governmental actions (both fiscal and monetary) will serve to buoy consumer spending for the remainder of 2008, the degree to which the economy will likely enter a sustained recessionary period is still an issue.

The 0.6 percent growth rate in real GDP in the first quarter, the same growth rate as the prior quarter, reflected an increase in inventory investment that was offset by an upturn in imports and decreases in nonresidential structures and personal consumption expenditures (PCE). Economists note that GDP grew 2.2 percent during 2007, down from a 2.9 percent growth rate in 2006. Fourth-quarter GDP growth was in line with economist expectations of approximately 0.7 percent. Economists surveyed by Briefing.com predict GDP growth on the order of 2.0 percent for the second quarter of 2008 (lower than the long-term trend but higher than the past two quarters), as consumer spending is expected to trend slightly higher (aided by the federal economic stimulus package), exports are expected to continue to grow (due, in part, to a weak dollar), and business investment in equipment and software is expected to hold steady.

Consumer Spending and Inflation

The seasonally adjusted annual rate (SAAR) of inflation for the first quarter of 2008 was 3.1 percent, compared to changes of 4.3 percent, 2.5 percent, and 6.2 percent, respectively, for the last three quarters of 2007. The index for energy rose 1.9 percent in March, following an increase of 0.7 percent in January and a decrease of 0.5 percent in February. The core rate of inflation rose at a 2.0 percent (SAAR) rate during the first quarter of 2008, following increases of 2.3 percent, 2.5 percent, and 2.6 percent for the last three quarters of 2007, respectively. The PPI increased 1.1 percent in March, after increases of 1.0 percent and 0.3 percent in January and February, respectively.

The advance estimates in percentage change in retail and food services sales for March 2008 were up 0.2 percent from the previous month and up 2.0 percent from March 2007. Real personal consumption spending increased 1.0 percent in the first quarter of 2008 compared to increases of 2.8 percent and 2.3 percent (revised), respectively, in the third and fourth quarters of 2007.

Interest Rates

The Federal Reserve's Open Market Committee (FOMC) lowered its target for the federal funds rate 200 basis points to 2.25 percent during the first quarter of 2008 at two scheduled meetings and one unscheduled meeting. These cuts follow similar cuts during the third quarter and fourth quarter of 2007, while the committee kept target rates unchanged during the third and fourth quarters of 2006 and the first and second quarters of 2007. The staff forecast prepared for the March meeting indicated that the growth in economic activity continued to decelerate during the first quarter.

Business and Manufacturing Productivity

The seasonally adjusted annual rate of nonfarm business productivity increased 2.2 percent in the first quarter, following a revised 1.8 percent increase during the fourth quarter of 2007. Productivity rose 1.9 percent for the entire business sector. Manufacturing productivity increased 4.1 percent during the quarter, as output decreased 0.3 percent and hours decreased 4.2 percent.

Industrial Production and Capacity Utilization

First-quarter 2008 production decreased at an annual rate of 0.1 percent following a revised 0.4 percent increase during the fourth quarter of 2007. Manufacturing production increased 0.1 percent in March after decreasing 0.5 percent in February. Manufacturing production is currently 1.2 percent higher than that measured in March 2007.

Capacity utilization increased 0.2 percentage points in March to 80.5 percent and was slightly below measures from a year ago (80.7 percent). For the fourth quarter, capacity utilization measured a revised 81.0 percent. First-quarter capacity remained (0.6 percentage points) above the 1972–2006 average.

Unemployment

The unemployment rate was 5.1 percent in March, higher than the February level of 4.8 percent and higher than expected by economists. Unemployment figures ranged from 4.4 percent to 4.7 percent for the first three quarters of 2007, representing the lowest levels in more than five years, while fourth-quarter 2007 unemployment figures began to trend higher. Economists had expected the unemployment rate to trend upward in the fourth quarter but believed unemployment would rise to approximately 4.9 percent by the end of the quarter. March payrolls declined by 80,000 jobs, following a revised loss of 76,000 jobs in February.

The Financial Markets

The Dow closed the first quarter at 12,262.89, down 7.6 percent for the quarter. The S&P 500 Index fell 9.9 percent during the quarter to close at 1322.70, following a 3.8 percent decline in the fourth quarter. The NASDAQ Composite Index fell 14.1 percent during the first quarter to close at 2279.10, following a 1.8 percent decline in the fourth quarter. The broad market Wilshire 5000 Index closed at 13,332.00, down 10.0 percent for the quarter. The monthly average yields-to-maturity on the 20-year Treasury bond during the first quarter of 2008 were 4.35 percent, 4.49 percent, and 4.36 percent, respectively, for January, February, and March.

Housing Starts and Building Permits

New privately owned housing starts were at a seasonally adjusted annualized rate of 947.0 thousand units in March, 11.9 percent below the revised February estimate and 36.5 percent below the revised March 2007 level. Single-family housing starts were 680.0 thousand in March, which is 5.7 percent below the February figure. Private housing units authorized by building permits were 927.0 thousand units in March, 5.8 percent below the revised February rate of 984.0 thousand units.

Economic Summary and Outlook

Due to the nature of operations, state and local economic factors are less important than those at the national level.

- Economic results related to the first quarter of 2008 were mostly negative. Housing statistics were abysmal and employment figures came in lower than expected.
- GDP growth expectations from private economists surveyed by the *Wall Street Journal* are on the order of 0.1 percent and 2.1 percent for the next two quarters of 2008, respectively, and 1.1 percent for all of 2008. This compares to GDP growth of 3.1 percent, 2.9 percent, and 2.2 percent for 2005, 2006, and 2007, respectively.
- Almost three-quarters of the polled economists foresee a recession in the near future.
- While inflation is not expected to be a major problem into 2008, should actual inflation exceed expected inflation, costs to growth could be significant.
- Rising fuel prices, which spiked toward the end of the first quarter, could be especially harmful.
- The Fed is expected to lower interest rates at least once more in April and then hold rates steady for the foreseeable future. The goal is for interest rates to be low enough to spur expansion, while keeping inflation fears low.

As can be seen in Exhibit 10.20, we approximated Acme's annual nominal growth rate with 3 percent, which is equal to the estimated inflation. The effect on the Company's value of the above economic analysis would impact primarily from the choice of a rate of growth. The effects of the above summary and outlook will be used in the development of a capitalization rate as shown in the Income Capitalization Method.

> As with the industry analysis, analysts often place the economic review in the appendixes. Here it also was presented earlier in the report. Why does the report focus on national economic issues rather than state and local conditions? From the background information, we recall that this company has locations all across the country and distributes nationally and internationally. How relevant would an extensive discussion of the local economy surrounding the home office be in this case? Carefully focus on the major economic factors affecting the company as a whole and provide your assessment of their impact on the company.

Financial Statement Analysis

Financial Statements Utilized

The Company financial statements utilized in this valuation report are the audited annual and internally prepared interim balance sheets, income statements, and statements of cash flows for the years ended December 31, 2003, through the last 12 months (LTM) ended May 31, 2008. The financial data of Acme are presented in Exhibits 10.15, 10.16, and 10.17.

Valuation in all cases is a forward-looking concept. So why are we focusing on the past? The past is often the best indicator of future expectations (Revenue Ruling 59-60). The relevant historical period to be analyzed must, however, be identified. Often it is five years (Revenue Ruling 59-60 again), but it could be longer or shorter. The prior discussions of the history and nature of the business and the status of the industry and of the economy provide information for determining the relevance of the period chosen for review. In this case, over five years are presented. The relative significance of each year to the future of the company will be determined (qualitative determination based on quantitative analysis) for utilization in our later valuation methodologies. What is the significance of audited financial statements to the financial analysis? Certainly they provide added assurance of accuracy, but often the analyst must later focus on unaudited interim information that is relevant to the valuation date. Financial analysis can be useful in determining the reasonableness of this unaudited data by comparisons to prior trends and revenue/cost relationships.

Comparative industry statistics from the 2007–2008 Risk Management Association financial statement studies were selected for NAICS 334519—"Manufacturing—other Measuring & Controlling Device Manufacturing." The comparative industry sample size included companies with revenues raging from $10 to $25 million, which was the sample closest to the Company's revenue level.

Comparisons of company performance to industry benchmarks are important. Here the analyst utilized one source of industry data. The analyst must search carefully for the best sources. More than one may be helpful. One industry source may cover different factors or provide expanded information on certain cost areas. Trade association information, one of the best sources, was not available due to the tight focus of the business. The range of revenues for the industry benchmarks was provided. Analysts also may wish to disclose the number of companies falling within that range. Is it an adequate number for comparative purposes? Analysts should also be aware of the limitations of the data on which they rely. For example, trade association data may be very detailed but out of date. Also, statistical reliability for inference to an entire industry is not assured by these sources.

Balance Sheet Overview—Unadjusted Data

Balance sheets for the Company as of December 31, 2002, through May 31, 2008, are shown in Exhibit 10.15. Below are discussions of individual assets and liabilities.

Operating Cash Balances.   As can be seen throughout the period analyzed, the cash account varied as a percent of total assets between 12.0 as of December 31, 2005 and 21.5 as of December 31, 2007. As of May 31, 2008, the cash account was $4,367,504 (17.0 percent of total assets). Besides cash, the Company had an amount of $1,128,321 (4.4 percent) in securities held to maturity. Overall, the most highly liquid assets of the Company were approximately 21.4 percent of total assets as of May 31, 2008. This is high compared to the RMA database, which shows the cash amount as a percent of total assets as 12.2 percent.

The Company management stated that the Company has been very conservative; therefore, the cash reserves were traditionally high.

Accounts Receivable.   The average number of days of sales in receivables (which measure the effectiveness of the firm's credit policies) was 38 days in 2007, which is favorable.

Acme's business is cyclical; therefore, during the winter months the amounts of accounts receivable and sales are low. These amounts are high in spring and summer. Consequently, the amount of accounts receivable was $2,795,967 as of December 31, 2007, and $4,585,083 as of May 31, 2008.

Exhibit 10.10 shows an analytical aging comparison of receivables for 2007 and 2006 for Acme.

Exhibit 10.10   Receivables Aging Comparison

	0–30 days	31–60 days	61–90 days	Over 90 Days	Allowance for Bad Debt	Total
2007	$2,045,817	$329,163	$174,793	$963,172	−$716,979	$2,795,967
2006	$2,245,242	$414,751	$279,135	$798,087	−$815,496	$2,921,720

It should be noted that this aging represents aging from invoice date. The Company is generally conservative in extending credit. While most terms are net 30 days, there are exceptions. Domestic customers are net 30 days, while the international distributors are either net 60 days or letter of credit.

Income Taxes Receivable.   There is an amount of $301,451 shown as income taxes receivable as of December 31, 2006. In that year, the Company management overestimated its deposits of estimated income tax payments, expecting a better year than the one that actually materialized.

Inventories.   Inventories include raw materials, work-in-process, and finished goods, and are valued at the lower of cost (first-in, first-out, FIFO) or market. As of May 31, 2008, total inventory accounted for $5,275,013, or 20.6

percent of total assets, which is lower than the RMA data of 28.8 percent. The typical inventory turnover at Acme is between 2.5 and 2.9 turns per year.

Usually the raw materials can be converted into a finished product in as little as two to three weeks. Historically, the inventory levels oscillated from $4,450,491 (18.4 percent) as of December 31, 2004 to $5,465,804 (22.7 percent) as of December 31, 2006. Since then the inventory levels were at approximately 21 percent of total assets. Per management, Acme has not put an emphasis on inventory control in the past.

Fixed Assets. The fixed assets consist mainly of land, building, and manufacturing equipment. Depreciation is computed on a straight-line, 150 percent declining balance basis over the estimated useful lives of the property, plant, and equipment. The estimated useful lives range from 2 to 25 years. The following lives are used for depreciation purposes:

Building	25 years
Manufacturing equipment	5 to 12 years
Office furniture and fixtures	5 to 10 years
Automobiles	3 to 5 years
Equipment leased to others	2 years

The Company leases its manufacturing facilities and office space from Acme Owners, Ltd., headed by officers of the Company. The lease has an original term of 18 years, with the lease expiring October 31, 2014. The lease agreement states that the parties to the lease shall renegotiate the amount of rent every five years.

The net fixed assets amount on the Company balance sheet as of May 31, 2008, was $7,153,778, or 27.9 percent of total assets, which was higher than the RMA data of 12.2 percent.

Other Assets. The other assets account of $2,000,984 as of May 31, 2008, is comprised of patents, officers' life insurance, other receivables, deferred taxes, and securities held to maturity. The other receivables account of $402,131 is comprised of premiums for split-dollar life insurance for John J. Acme, Jr., and Rhonda Acme-Williams. The deferred income taxes amount of $954,150 is a result of the types of temporary differences such as uniform capitalization, depreciation, capital lease, reserves for inventory obsolescence, unrealized holding gains and losses for securities available for sale, and disposal costs of certain materials.

The securities held to maturity account is comprised of U.S. Treasury bills and corporate bonds.

Accounts Payable. Throughout the period analyzed, the accounts payable amount for Acme fluctuated between $800,000 and $1,400,000. The Company's policy is to pay all its invoices within vendor's terms, which are generally 30 days.

Accrued Compensation and Related Items. This account is comprised of accrued payroll, accrued payroll taxes, and accrued profit-sharing contribution, and it was fairly constant throughout the period analyzed, at around 4 percent.

Accrued Expenses and Other Liabilities. The largest items included in this category are reserves for source disposal and reserves for warranty repairs. This account experienced a large increase in 2005, when it reached $1,566,176. The increase was due to two factors: the price of nuclear materials disposals increased and the Company had to pay to dispose of a larger than usual number of nuclear sources.

Unearned Income. Unearned income is comprised of two items: prepaid extended warranty contracts and prepaid badge monitoring services. The increase in 2007 over 2006 was due to an erroneous calculation in 2006 causing the understatement of the actual unearned income.

Obligation Under Capital Lease. The capitalized lease obligation represents the present value of future minimum lease payments for the land, building and computer equipment. As of December 31, 2007, the Company's long-term obligation under the capital lease was $7,958,802.

Stockholders' Equity. As of the Valuation Date, the Company's authorized capital stock consisted of 124,684 voting shares of $1.50 par value common stock issued and outstanding.

As of the Valuation Date, the Company had 102 shareholders who owned common stock.

An analysis by the Company of the changes during 2006 and 2007 in accumulated other comprehensive income for cumulative currency translation adjustments resulted in negative amounts of $213,684 and $219,717, respectively.

The management believes it has properly accounted for all contingent liabilities, and the Company has no material off–balance sheet liabilities.

Income Statement Overview—Unadjusted Data

Historical comparative income statement data are shown in Exhibit 10.16 for the years ended December 31, 2003 through the LTM as of May 31, 2008. Acme's total revenues had increased from $23,051,330 for the year ended December 31, 2003 to $27,577,739 as of December 31, 2004. Total revenue amount was almost flat, around $29,000,000 for the years ended 2005, 2006, 2007, and the LTM ending May 31, 2008. The compound annual growth rate for revenues over the period analyzed was approximately 5.0 percent. Historically, the net income (before adjustments) increased from a low of 1.9 percent of total revenue in 2005 to a high of 5.1 percent for the LTM ended May 31, 2008. Various components of the income statement discussed in this section were expressed as a percentage of total revenues. A more detailed analysis of the above trends is given below.

Revenues. Total revenues were almost flat at around $29 million since 2005, reaching $28,585,677 during the LTM ended May 31, 2008. As can be seen in Exhibit 10.16, historically the total revenue amounts were comprised of revenue from sale of equipment, parts and repairs, training, rentals and sales of leased equipment, and other income (comprised of interest income on investments).

For the LTM ended May 31, 2008, the highest amount of revenues came from sale of equipment (70.4 percent of total revenue) and parts and repair (19.2 percent).

Company revenues follow a cyclical pattern. Business is very good and generates high revenue in warm-weather months when most construction work is done. Business drops off significantly in the cold-weather months of November through February.

Cost of Goods Sold.   Cost of sales decreased from approximately $14.6 million (50 percent) in 2006 to approximately $13.6 million (48 percent) in 2007 and was lower than the RMA data of 56.4 percent. In 2006, the Company employed approximately 176 people. At that time, management had forecasted a high increase in orders for the Company; therefore, many people were hired. The increase in orders never materialized. As a result, as of the end of 2007, the number of people employed dropped to approximately 141, which resulted in a decrease of overhead. As of the Valuation Date, there were approximately 150 people employed.

Selling, General, and Administrative Expenses (SG&A).   The SG&A expenses followed a similar trend with cost of sales for the same reasons explained above, dropping from approximately $12.3 million (42.5 percent) in 2006 to approximately $11.3 million (39.6 percent) in 2007, and were roughly comparable to the RMA data of 33.1 percent.

The "royalty" account of the SG&A expenses encompasses royalties that Acme agreed to pay to a competitor. These expenses will no longer apply after the Valuation Date, since the Company discontinued selling the related model.

Operating Profit.   As a result of the reduced expenses mentioned in the paragraphs above, the operating profit margin—as defined by Earnings Before Interest and Taxes (EBIT)—increased after 2006 to 12.7 percent in 2007 and 14.3 percent for the LTM ended May 31, 2008.

Net Income.   Acme's net income margin displays the same pattern as that of the operating profit, rising after 2006 to 4.1 percent in 2007 and to 5.1 percent for the LTM ended May 31, 2008.

Cash Flow Analysis

The Company's cash flow statements for 2003 through 2007 are shown in Exhibit 10.17. In 2005, substantial cash had been required to build up inventory in expectation of a good year in 2006. The Company made continuous capital expenditures throughout the full period analyzed.

> The level of discussion of the financial analysis presented within the report is much less than was actually performed by the analyst. The reporting focus is on critical factors and value drivers for the business. An analyst should not just make a presentation of financial data but answer the critical question as to why this is relevant to the determination of value. Does the analysis point out unusual cost relationships that require further inquiry? Does the analysis help identify nonrecurring and potential nonoperating income and expenses? How does the company compare to its peer group (accepting the limitations of the industry data)? Does the lower current ratio indicate that the company is weaker, or perhaps more effectively managed, than the industry peer group?

Summary of Financial Statement Analysis

- The Company has adopted a very conservative strategy in the past. It maintained high cash reserves and chose not to incur interest-bearing debt.
- Average number of days receivables (which measure the effectiveness of the firm's credit policies) were 38 days in 2007, which is favorable.
- The Company's policy is to pay all its invoices within vendor's terms, which is generally 30 days.
- As of December 31, 2007, the Company's long-term obligation under the capital lease was $7,958,802.
- Total revenues were almost flat at around $29 million since 2005, reaching $28,585,677 during the LTM ending May 31, 2008.
- Company revenues follow a cyclical pattern. The business is very good and generates high revenue in warm-weather months when most construction work is done.
- In 2006, the Company employed approximately 176 people. At that time, management had forecasted a high increase in orders for the Company; therefore, many people were hired. The increase in orders never materialized.

> At the end of the financial analysis section, the appraiser has again provided a helpful list of summary points from the prior detailed analysis. These will be used in the assessment of business and financial risk to the enterprise and indications of expected future performance based on past trends. Nonoperating assets were also identified. A presentation of nonoperating assets and their impact on value is presented later in the report.

Adjustments to Financial Data for Valuation Purposes

An important part of most valuations of smaller businesses is the adjustment of the financial statements to provide an accurate portrayal of economic income and of the operating balance sheet. Adjustments were made to the reported data of Acme, as shown and detailed in Exhibit 10.19, for two purposes:

1. Remove income from excess assets and nonoperating gains. We adjust for income from excess assets and nonoperating items by removing their impact from both the balance sheet and income statement. The only items of this nature on Acme's balance sheet were cash and equivalents and investments in securities. Accordingly, the associated interest income on Acme's income statement was also adjusted in order to have a true representation of the operating condition at Acme.
2. Eliminate the effects of nonrecurring items and any other items that distort historical reported income as an indicator of normal, ongoing earning power. In this case, we adjusted for the legal expenses (expenses of $305,966 under the "Patents and Attorney" account in 2005 were normalized to $120,000 and expenses of $181,769 and $27,125 under the "Legal and Consulting" account in 2005 and 2006 were normalized to $75,000) and eliminated the related

"Oven Royalty" amounts. Other than that, no other nonrecurring expenses were detected.

> Several adjustments for nonoperating and nonrecurring items are discussed. Notice that the reasons for the adjustments are also provided. The analyst is valuing a minority interest, so controlling interest adjustments (reflecting the power to change corporate policy) are not made.

Valuation Approaches/Methods

There are three traditional valuation approaches: the cost or asset approach, the market approach, and the income approach. Practitioners differ on the classification of specific valuation methods within these three classes; however, it is generally agreed that all valuation methods can be described either as a form of one of these approaches or as a hybrid of two or more of these approaches.

Asset-based methods establish value based on the cost of reproducing or replacing the property, less depreciation from physical deterioration and functional and economic obsolescence, if present and measurable. Such approaches usually give an indication of the value of a controlling interest from which appropriate discounts may be warranted for noncontrolling interests.

Market methods are used to estimate value through analysis of recent sales of reasonably comparable property. Market-based approaches often are used to provide an indication of the value of the entire stockholders' equity or a partial interest therein, or the value of the entire invested capital (debt and equity). When used for these purposes, the market approach requires the selection of appropriate guideline companies (publicly traded or private companies); the determination of market value ratios for the guideline companies based on the market price or selling price of the security or business compared to various parameters, such as earnings, cash flow, book value, and so on; the selection of appropriate market value ratios for the subject company based on a comparison of the subject company to the guideline companies; and the determination of applicable premiums and discounts based on any differences in ownership percent, ownership rights, business ownership form, or marketability between the subject company and the guideline companies.

"Income," as used in the term "income approach," is a general term that connotes any future benefits that can be quantified in monetary terms. It does not imply that income-based approaches should be used only with projections of "income" in the accounting sense. Rather, income methods involve two general steps. The first is making a projection of the total monetary benefits expected to accrue to an investor in the property. The second step involves either discounting these monetary benefits to present worth over the entire projection period, including a terminal-year value, or capitalizing a single period amount.

Various appraisal methods combining aspects of one or more of the three basic classes of appraisal approaches can be used. In any appraisal study, all applicable methods should be considered, and the method(s) deemed most probative to valuing the appraised property will then be selected as the proper method(s) to use for that study.

> A valuation report is an educational tool designed to acquaint the reader with the process of developing the opinion and providing support for the ultimate conclusion. In this section, the analyst briefly lists the three approaches to value and what each involves. Under each approach, various methods are available. This brief logical framework better prepares the reader for the detailed analysis to follow. The analyst also indicates which approaches and methods are the most relevant for this assignment.

As a result of this process, we concluded that the Income Capitalization (Capitalized Cash Flow) Method, with a capitalization rate derived through the Weighted Average Cost of Capital[17] (WACC) formula, was the most appropriate method in this instance. We considered market methods and asset methods as correlative methodology.

> The analyst has decided to focus on the capitalization of income (Capitalized Cash Flow) utilizing a Weighted Average Cost of Capital (WACC). This method often is selected in valuing controlling interests where a change in the capital structure is likely or possible. It can, however, be used for minority interest, utilizing the existing capital structure of the company.

The resulting value from the application of the main method selected is the fair market value of the operating Company on a minority marketable basis. Since the purpose of our valuation is to determine the fair market value of a minority nonmarketable interest in the shares, the final steps in the valuation process are the subtraction of interest-bearing debt, application of a discount from the marketable value to account for the lack of marketability of the subject minority interest, and then the addition of value attributable to any nonoperating or excess assets of Acme (net of appropriate discounts).

The following sections of this report discuss the application of the above methods leading to our conclusion of value for a minority interest in the common stock of the Company.

Income Approach

Income (Capitalized Cash Flow) Capitalization Method

This method is based on the theory that the investment should yield a return sufficient to cover its initial cost and to justly compensate the investor for the inherent risks of ownership over the life of the investment. The value of closely held stock of an operating business is generally expressed as a function of its earning or cash-generating capacity, which is then capitalized or discounted at appropriate risk-adjusted rates.

---

[17] Observation: An invested capital method was used to value a minority interest by a procedure involving (first) valuing overall capital and (then) subtracting debt, the company's actual amount of debt in its capital structure. This is because it would be beyond the power of a noncontrolling stockholder to change the capital structure.

Capitalization of earnings is an income approach to valuation wherein an estimate of the next period's income is divided by a capitalization rate to arrive at the estimated fair market value of the business. The inherent assumption in applying this method is that a single earnings number, grown at a constant rate, best represents the future earnings capacity of the Company.

> The method is explained further. What are the steps involved in the application of the method? What inputs are required for the calculation and how are they developed?

The income capitalization method with a capitalization rate derived through the Weighted Average Cost of Capital (WACC) formula requires the following general steps:

1. Determination of a normalized level of income. In the case of Acme, we defined "income" as net free cash flow to overall invested capital (NCF).[18] Invested capital is all interest-bearing debt plus equity.
2. Calculation of an income capitalization rate from market rates of return, as adjusted for the specific risks of the subject company and for the type of "income" to be capitalized.
3. Capitalization of the normalized NCF into an indication of invested capital value attributable to Acme's operations, using the capitalization rate derived through the WACC formula.
4. Subtraction of Acme's total interest-bearing debt and addition (can add discounted value to discounted operating value as well) of any nonoperating assets as of May 31, 2008, to determine the value of Acme's common stock on a minority interest basis.
5. Application of appropriate discount for lack of marketability to determine the fair market value of Acme's common stock on a minority ownership interest basis.

Factors Affecting the Selection of a Capitalization Rate for Acme

An investor in Acme would consider the following quantitative factors related to Acme:

- Net revenues were almost flat at around $29 million since 2005, reaching $28,585,677 during the LTM ending May 31, 2008. Acme has exhibited an approximate 1.0 percent compounded annual growth over the last three and a half years. The Company's adjusted operating profits have risen from $1,739,378 to $3,798,117 over the same time period.

---

[18] Earnings before interest and taxes
  − Taxes on EBIT at effective tax rate
  + Depreciation
  − Capital expenditures
  ± Changes in working capital
  = Net cash flow to overall invested capital

- Acme is relatively small, based on both sales and assets. Size is generally considered inversely proportional to investment risk.
- A comparison and analysis of Acme's gross margin for the 12-month period ended May 31, 2008, with those companies that fall within SIC 3829, as previously defined, as presented in the 2008–2009 RMA studies, reveals that, at 53 percent, Acme compares favorably with the 43.6 percent margin contained by the industry data source.
- The Company's adjusted margin of 8.2 percent trails the 9.8 percent operating margin for RMA.
- At 52.5 percent, Acme's total book value of stockholders' equity (net worth) as a percentage of total assets is comparable to the 54.9 percent net worth margin as presented in the RMA studies and generally suggests that Acme has a strong balance sheet as of May 31, 2008. At 32.2 percent, Acme's total debt (comprised of obligations under capital lease) to total asset ratio indicates that Acme is moderately leveraged.

On balance, we would conclude from the above quantitative factors that Acme would be considered somewhat average in desirability as an investment compared to alternative investments in the marketplace.

In addition to the quantitative factors discussed above, an investor would consider the following factors in assessing Acme relative to the risk of alternative investments in the marketplace. Based on our market analysis, it is our opinion that potential investors in Acme would put considerable emphasis on these qualitative factors.

- Currently, the Company has a balanced management team comprised of individuals with extensive experience in the measuring devices industry.
- Key person risk—Mr. Acme made all major management decisions until the last day he was in the office. Mr. Acme is covered by a minimal key person life insurance policy, in the face amount of approximately $200,000, for which the Company is the beneficiary. The sudden loss of the services of the Company's founder, president, and chairman of the board and the fact that there were no succession plans in place for a smooth transition are negative factors.
- Acme established long-term relationships and has very good working relationships with its customers and its suppliers. The maintenance of those relationships is evidence of the resilience of these relationships.
- During the fiscal year ending December 31, 2007, approximately $3.7 million in revenues, or about 13 percent of total sales, were derived from its 10 main customers. This percentage has been fairly constant since 2004. The Company is not reliant on any of its customers to generate revenues, and the loss of any of its customers will not adversely affect its operations. This fact is a positive factor.
- Company revenues follow a cyclical pattern. Business is very good and generates high revenue in warm-weather months when most construction work is done. Business drops off significantly in the cold-weather months of November through February.
- The constraints that Acme could face are on floor space. Currently, Acme has a maximum potential capacity of production of approximately $31.0 million in sales. If orders increase over this amount, the Company management will have to search for additional floor space for its production facility. This capacity constraint is a potentially negative factor.

- Acme has well-maintained machinery and equipment. Nevertheless, capital expenditures may be required in the future for the acquisition of new equipment and for investing in its future growth. This is a potential drain on future cash flow and is a somewhat negative factor for a minority shareholder in Acme.
- Acme, which is operating in a difficult industry environment, is being squeezed by the bargaining power of its buyers and suppliers, as well as being concerned with the immediate loss of market share in the event of a breakthrough discovery of a substitute product that does not use radioactive materials.

On the basis of the above qualitative factors, we conclude that Acme would be considered of somewhat below average desirability as an investment compared to alternative investments in the marketplace.

Many valuation reports contain sections that almost seem to be stand-alone documents. There is no explanation regarding how the information presented in a separate section impacts the decisions made by the analyst in other areas of the report. Here, the analyst has taken information gathered from previous discussions in the report (qualitative and quantitative factors) and discussed its impact on the desirability of the company as an investment. Doing this takes into account a risk assessment involving financial strength, industry issues, comparisons to industry peer groups, management strength, and many other qualitative factors. It is left to the analyst to determine their ultimate significance to the assignment.

Derivation of Normalized NCF and Capitalization Rate

The quantitative and qualitative factors discussed above have a direct impact on our selection of the capitalization rate, through their incorporation into the "Adjustment for Risk Factors Specific to Acme" from Exhibit 10.20. This adjustment, the estimation of the capitalization rate as a whole, and the development of a normalized NCF are discussed in the following paragraphs.

In order to determine a normalized level of NCF for the twelve months ending May 31, 2009, we considered the following:

1. Management's 2009 budget
2. Discussions with management regarding future growth and margin expectations for Acme
3. Acme's revenues and adjusted operating performance for the years ended December 31, 2004 through LTM ended May 31, 2008

As can be seen in Exhibit 10.19, Acme's revenues stayed flat at approximately $29 million between the year ended December 31, 2004, and the LTM as of May 31, 2008. Budgeted 2009 revenues were $28 million.

Accordingly, we have estimated normalized revenues based on recent historical and budgeted revenues. We estimated normalized revenues as the average of 2009 budgeted and the 4.5-year average of 2004, 2005, 2006, 2007, and LTM ending May 31, 2008 revenues, thereby giving credence to both historical and expected future revenues. Normalized revenues were approximately $28.0 million

(($27,577,739 + 28,720,737 + 28,921,688 + 28,599,155 + 28,585,677) / (5 + 28,000,000) / 2 = $28,240,500 or $28.0 million, rounded).

Due to the fact that depreciation has greatly exceeded capital expenditures in the most current years, we also analyzed EBITDA margins (Exhibit 10.19). The five-year average margin was 14.9 percent with a range of 11.0 percent to 18.4 percent. The most recent TTM and fiscal year end EBITDA margins were 18.4 percent and 17.3 percent, respectively. For the normalized year, we assumed an EBITDA margin of 15 percent for an amount of $4,200,000. We also normalized depreciation and amortization. Normalized EBIT was $3,450,000.

Long-term normalized capital expenditures were estimated at $800,000 and normalized depreciation and amortization was estimated at $750,000. There is a period where depreciation and amortization will excel capital expenditures. This is due to the long-life assets previously acquired. The present value of this tax benefit is $1,000,000.

All the other items in the formula for computing the NCF, unless noted otherwise, were calculated using the management estimation. The working capital need was calculated by applying the 25 percent Debt-Free Working Capital (DFWC) to sales relationship (ratio developed in Exhibit 10.18) to the expected increase in sales into perpetuity.

Income taxes at an assumed 40 percent effective rate are reflected. The capitalization rate (shown on Exhibit 10.20) was developed by starting with market evidence of returns to develop a discount rate applicable to net cash flow of a typical "small" public company by using the modified capital asset pricing model (MCAPM) method.

> The development of the level of income or cash flow to be capitalized is explained in detail. Why not utilize a weighted average of past performance? Here the analyst explains the choices made. For a capitalization method, we are applying it to the next year's expected cash flow. With growth in revenue being relatively flat and expense behavior in line with past performance, the analyst is using an average of past performance for revenue and budgeted 2009 performance.

MCAPM

The MCAPM uses the beta coefficient to measure the extent to which the returns on a given investment track the stock market as a whole. Beta is a gauge of a security's volatility in comparison with the market's volatility.

Stocks whose betas are greater than 1.00 tend to have a high degree of systematic risk and a stronger sensitivity to market swings. Conversely, stocks whose betas are less than 1.00 tend to rise and fall by a lesser percentage than the market.

Since Acme is not publicly traded, a beta cannot be directly derived. In the industry section of this report we analyzed the manufacturing of measuring and controlling devices industry in which Acme conducts its business and the construction industry in which Acme's main customers operate. We felt the risk structure of the manufacturing of measuring and controlling devices industry matches closely the inherent risks associated with the operations at Acme. We obtained betas based on SIC 3829 (Measuring and Controlling Devices) and relevered with the Company's debt/equity capital structure to derive a beta of 0.90 (rounded).

The application of the MCAPM yields an expected return on equity for a large-company stock. Due to the much smaller size of the Company, a market-based size premium is added to this to obtain the expected return on the average small public company.

> Many analysts are now also using data from the Duff & Phelps, LLC, Risk Premium Report, which is published annually. These data allow for eight additional measures of size and have return and risk premium information for 25 size categories. The report also allows for comparisons based on alternative measures of risk, such as average operating margin, coefficient of variation of operating margin, and coefficient of variation of return on equity. See Chapter 6 for additional information on Duff & Phelps data.

This rate was then adjusted by four percentage points for the various risk factors specific to Acme to derive a discount rate applicable to Acme's equity net cash flow.

From the MCAPM method, an equity net cash flow discount rate of 20.95 percent was developed. This discount rate was used further in the calculation of the WACC.

> Here the analyst defines a beta coefficient and its implications on the cost of capital. Also, the analyst provides significant factors including the unlevered beta for the applicable SIC and the relevered beta (reflecting the Company's assumed capital structure). Why was the MCAPM chosen rather than the build-up approach? In this case, the analyst believed that the use of beta provided a better measure of the effect of systematic risk or industry risk on the capitalization rate. *Note:* Many analysts do not use general industry benchmark data when a search for specific guideline public companies results in no companies being found. (See Chapter 6.)

WACC

To estimate a normal debt/equity capital ratio to be used in determining Acme's WACC, we analyzed the capital structure of the Company and the industry defined by SIC 3829. This industry shows a capital structure[19] consisting of approximately 70 percent equity (at market value) and 30 percent debt. In our calculations we used the actual capital structure of Acme, since Company management specified there would not be a change in the actual capital structure in the future. These data, along with an iterative process, resulted in a capital structure of approximately 60 percent equity and 40 percent debt.

The WACC developed through this process was then applied to Acme's invested capital (or "debt-free") net cash flow. Acme's long-term expected growth rate was subtracted from the discount rate, to derive a debt-free net cash flow capitalization rate. Based on the growth outlook of 4 percent for the measuring and controlling instruments industry, and the relative flat growth in the Company's revenues, a 3.0 percent long-term growth rate was selected, which is approximately equal to the estimated inflation growth rate as described in the "General Economic Overview" section of this report.

---

[19] Source: Morningstar Cost of Capital Quarterly, 2008 Year book. [fictitious]

One of the issues of using WACC methodology is that one of the inputs is initially unknown unless a target capital structure (mix of debt and equity at market values) is utilized. In this case, we are valuing a minority interest without the power to change the capital structure to any "target." However, one of the inputs to the WACC formula is the value of equity capital. Obviously, that is not initially known. Thus, the appraiser utilized an iterative process to develop the capital structure and resulting WACC.

> The WACC developed initially is a discount rate that can be utilized to convert a stream of future cash flow into value. Because we are capitalizing a single-period income, the analyst must adjust the WACC to a capitalization rate by subtracting a factor for long-term growth (the Gordon Growth Model). Here the analyst subtracted 3 percent. Why not 5, 6, or 7 percent? Again we review past performance and the outlook for the industry. No real growth is seen, so the growth rate is equivalent to long-term expectations for inflation. The selection of the growth rate is a sensitive assumption in the development of a capitalization based on WACC. Analysts may wish to compare the cost of capital so developed to the published WACC for public companies as a test of reasonableness.

Applying the 11.0 percent WACC capitalization rate to the $1,820,000 normalized NCF (see Exhibit 10.19) derives an indicated value for the operating invested capital on a minority interest basis of Acme of approximately $16.5 million, rounded, calculated as follows:

$$\$1,820,000 / 0.11 = \$16,545,454$$

We then added $1,000,000, which was the present value of the tax shield due to the temporary difference in depreciation and amortization and capital expenditures. This results in a value of $17,545,454, or $17.5 million rounded.

To determine the value of Acme's equity on a minority interest basis, the value of any interest-bearing debt must be subtracted from the value of total invested capital and any nonoperating assets added. As of May 31, 2008, the most recent date available, Acme's interest-bearing debt totaled $8,245,866 ($7,719,261 + $526,605 = $8,245,866), which represents the total obligation of the Company under the capital lease. Subtracting this amount from the $17.5 million value of total invested capital derives a value for the operating equity of $9,254,134.

Summary of Value of a 100 Percent Minority Interest

The income approach discussed produced a minority interest indication of Acme's equity value of approximately $9,254,134 ($17,500,000 − $8,245,866 = $9,254,134), prior to application of a discount for lack of marketability and any addition for the impact of nonoperating assets.

At this point, the analyst has developed an initial indication of value for equity on a minority basis, before application of any marketability discount and before the addition of value for any nonoperating or excess assets. Some analysts may choose to apply those other factors now to fully determine the value under this particular method. Other analysts may utilize additional methods to develop additional indications of minority, nonmarketable value. Under the latter approach, a single value conclusion is reached later. The deduction for the lack of marketability discount and the addition of value for nonoperating assets then is performed in only one place in the report. When utilizing this latter approach, as illustrated in this report, care should be taken to make sure that all methods arrive at the same level of value (in this case, minority, marketable) before deduction or addition of other factors.

Discounted Cash Flow Method

The Discounted Cash Flow Method is based on the premise that the value of an asset or business enterprise is the present value of the future economic income (i.e., cash flow) to be derived by the owners of the business or asset. This method requires the analysis of revenues, expenses, capital structure, residual value, and the cost of capital (including an examination of business, financial, and systematic risk). It is most appropriate when future operating results are anticipated to be substantially different from past performance.

Based on our analysis and discussions with management, future expectations are in line with the past. No significant growth in revenue, income, or cash flow is anticipated. Therefore, while considered, we have not applied this method.

Since the value of a company is the present value of future benefits, the discounted cash flow method is theoretically preferred. However, in this case, prior discussions and analysis indicated that no unusual events were anticipated and future growth would be minimal. The analyst has provided the reasons for considering the method but chose not to apply it for this assignment.

Market Approach

Guideline Public Company Method

As a method to selecting valuation multiplies, publicly traded investment opportunities are analyzed in terms of purchase price and earnings, and are compared to the subject business on the basis of investment risk. This method is generally referred to as a price to earnings analysis, and it has application in a variety of business valuation problems.

The following steps were taken in our selection of guideline companies for the Company valuation:

- Acme manufactures instruments for measurement of the physical properties of engineering materials. In our attempt to select guideline companies, we examined companies engaged in related segments of the measuring and controlling instruments industry. We did so by referring to Edgar Online,[20] which classifies public companies by SIC-code numbers. Edgar Online is a source of descriptive and financial information covering virtually all publicly held companies in the United States. We reviewed the business descriptions of all companies engaged within the SIC codes for Measuring & Controlling Devices (SIC 3829), General Industrial Machinery (SIC 3569), Special Industry Machinery (SIC 3559), Machine Tool Accessories (SIC 3545), and Engineering Services (SIC 8711).
- Our initial selection criterion was that the company's stock be actively traded so that the quoted price of its securities provided a reliable measurement of fair market value. The quoted prices of inactively traded securities do not necessarily provide reliable indications of fair market value because they are illiquid and may be subject to manipulation. Implicit in this criterion is the public availability of company financial information as is required of SEC registrants. We established additional selection criteria that the company stock price exceeds $2.00 per share. Low-priced stocks frequently attract speculative buyers attracted to the stock because the price is seemingly low and appears to offer potential for gain. These securities often are little more than cheap speculative vehicles. Also, for a low-priced stock, even a very small price change can have a tremendous impact on the valuation multiple.
- Information on approximately 80 public companies was initially obtained. Further research on these initial public companies failed to disclose any entities that could be used as guideline companies in the valuation of Acme. Although there were several public companies that provide measuring and controlling devices, they were not similar to Acme from an operational and investment point of view. Most of the companies scrutinized derive their revenues from businesses that served many industries. The only company that was deemed similar to Acme from an operational point of view (i.e., Instron Corporation),[21] went private in 2007.

As a result of the above analysis, we did not utilize the public guideline company method in determining the value of a minority ownership interest in Acme.

> What support did the analyst provide for not utilizing this well-accepted methodology? Application of the method requires finding companies sufficiently comparable. Many companies share SICs with the subject, but further analysis was the key. The company has a narrow focus and market niche, which was not in line with the public companies. Again the analyst documents the reasons for ultimately not applying the method. Doing this helps the reader understand the unique nature of the business and why reliance must be placed on other methodologies. Analysis and judgment may have revealed companies an analyst believes to be sufficiently similar for application of this method. Going back to Revenue Ruling 59-60, we see that the use of the method is supported. We also know that the terms "same" or "similar" as they apply to publicly traded companies have been widely interpreted by the courts and by analysts.

---

[20] Source: www.edgar-online.com/bin/esearch/fullsearch.asp.
[21] Source: www.instron.com.

Guideline Company Transaction Method

The guideline company transaction method is very similar to the guideline public company method. In this method, the subject company is compared to similar companies that have recently been purchased.

We searched the following sources for information on relevant purchases of public and private companies within the above-stated SIC classifications:

- The transaction database of the Institute of Business Appraisers (IBA)
- *Pratt's Stats*
- The acquisitions database of FactSet Mergerstat, LLC
- Houlihan Lokey Howard & Zukin's *Mergerstat Review,* within the "Instruments" classifications

Our sources, which consist of transactions occurring on a national basis, located transactions within Acme's general industry group.

> The analyst documents consideration of utilizing private company transaction multiples and indicates the limitations of the method. Why were the located comparative transactions not used? They were for acquisitions of controlling interests, and synergistic considerations may be reflected in the prices. This may move the standard of value closer to "investment value" (value to a specific purchaser). We are valuing a minority interest under fair market value definition. Can we apply a minority discount to the multiples obtained from this method to develop a value for a minority, nonmarketable interest? Many analysts do so based on the level of information available about the transactions, the number of transactions available, the dates of the transactions, and other factors. The choice is made on a case-by-case basis.

As can be seen in Exhibit 10.21, the transactions were for small- to large-size companies with revenues ranging from approximately $1.1 million to $75 million. The transactions found occurred between 2003 and 2008. In addition, the transaction values ranged from $1.5 million to $85.0 million. The median Market Value to Invested Capital (MVIC) to Net Sales multiple was 1.13.

As with any analysis of this type and scale, information availability is often sketchy and incomplete. Moreover, information related to these transactions can be misleading, because economies of scale and synergies, which are considered in a buyer's analysis, are difficult to calculate based on historical public information. Also, this method is sometimes more applicable when valuing a control ownership interest in a company, since an eventual sale of the business would not be controllable by a minority shareholder.

As a result, we did not utilize the guideline company transaction method in determining the value of a minority ownership interest in Acme.

Adjusted Net Asset Method—Going-Concern Value

The adjusted net asset method gives consideration to the fair market value of the assets and liabilities of the business being valued as a starting point in the determination of the value of its equity. A current and accurate accounting of the assets and liabilities of the business can be important in obtaining an accurate indication of value.

In order to determine the fair market value of a company utilizing the adjusted net asset method, we need to adjust all assets and liabilities to reflect fair market value. In addition, any off–balance sheet assets and liabilities need to be addressed. The starting point is the financial position of the Company as set forth in its balance sheet as of May 31, 2008. As discussed in the financial review, the underlying assets of the Company are, for the most part, fairly liquid, with cash and cash equivalents, contract receivables, marketable securities, and other assets comprising approximately 50 percent of total assets. The rest is comprised of inventory and fixed assets. Liabilities similarly are very liquid, and are comprised of accounts payable and obligation under capital lease. Our analysis and discussions with management determined that all balance sheet items would remain at book value in our analysis.

In addition to the assets and liabilities stated on Acme's books as of May 31, 2008, our analysis did not determine any off–balance sheet assets (including intangible assets and goodwill) or liabilities.

Based on our analysis of the fair market value of the underlying tangible assets (making small adjustments for potential bad debts) and liabilities (adjusting for extra disposing costs for nuclear material) of the Company, we have determined the underlying net tangible asset value by subtracting the stated or estimated fair market values of the liabilities from the fair market value of the underlying tangible assets. This calculation indicated a likely value for the total equity in the Company in the range of approximately $12.45 to $12.75 million on a controlling, marketable basis. Application of discounts for lack of control and lack of marketability would result in an estimate of value of approximately $5.7 million which is below the income approach value.

The net asset value method derives an amount that the business as a whole would likely sell for and is therefore an amount that all shareholders would share in equally if it occurred. However, it is important to note that the choice to sell the business would be in the hands of a controlling interest shareholder and would not be controllable by a minority shareholder.

We did not utilize the cost approach as a primary approach in determining the value of a minority ownership interest in Acme. It was used as a reasonableness test.

> The analyst briefly considers the asset approach. Many of the company's assets are highly liquid and thus are stated at a reasonable market value. Discussions with management indicated that book value was reasonably reflective of the value of other assets. In certain types of engagements, appraisals may have been necessary. No effort was made to adjust the balance sheet for the value for any intangibles that may be present, but here the balance sheet simply was viewed as an analytical tool for gauging reasonableness of the value conclusion. We are valuing a minority interest that does not have the power to cause an asset sale and receive the value of the underlying assets. Would you have included such a discussion in your report?

Other Valuation Information

We also considered the following additional valuation information:

- We identified several transactions in the Company stock but, as per management, none occurred in the past 12 years. As a result we did not rely on the data from these transactions.

> The analyst considered prior stock transactions. Past transactions are an element for consideration under Revenue Ruling 59-60 but must be viewed with caution. Due to the dates and transaction circumstances, they were not deemed relevant to a determination of current value.

Discount Studies and Application [Illustration only]

Discount for Lack of Marketability

A discount for lack of marketability is commonly applied to the ownership capital of closely held entities to reflect the lack of a recognized market for the ownership interests and to show that such interests are not readily transferable. Investors typically prefer investments that have access to a liquid secondary market and can be readily converted into cash. All other factors being equal, ownership interests without such marketability characteristics will sell at a discount when compared to interests that include such marketability features.

To determine the discount for lack of marketability, we relied on various studies quantifying discounts for lack of marketability for closely held entities. These studies are usually based on two types of analyses. The first analyses are based on the difference between the initial public offering (IPO) price of a company and transactions of the same company's stock prior to an IPO. These analyses are referred to as IPO studies. The second set of analyses measures the difference between the private price of a restricted security and the publicly traded stock price of the same company. These analyses are referred to as restricted stock studies.

> *Note:* For summaries of the various discount studies, see James R. Hitchner, editor, *Financial Valuation: Applications and Models,* 2nd ed. (Hoboken, NJ: John Wiley & Sons, 2006), pp. 392–419.

1. IPO Studies
   a. Emory Studies
   b. Willamette Studies
   c. Valuation Advisors Pre-IPO Study
   d. Hitchner Studies[22]
   e. IPO Study Summary

The range of discounts associated with all of the IPO studies is a low of 14 percent to a high of 77 percent. The majority of the discounts in the studies are in the range of 40 percent to 60 percent. In fact, of the individual studies, many concluded median discounts of 50 percent or greater. It is important to note that this range of discounts is associated with companies that most likely knew they would go public within a short time frame. For example, in the Emory studies, all of the transactions took place within five months of the IPO. If the discount for a company going public within five months is 40 percent to 45 percent as in the Emory studies, then it is likely, all other factors being equal, that the discount would be much higher for an entity that has little or no

---

[22] James R. Hitchner, editor, *Financial Valuation: Applications and Models,* 2nd ed. (Hoboken, NJ: John Wiley & Sons, 2006), pp. 397–399.

likelihood of a public offering. The companies in the IPO studies were also not public (as opposed to the restricted stock studies) at the various transaction dates.

At the Valuation Date, Acme had no plan or expectation for going public. The subject minority interest in Acme cannot cause the Company to go public or to otherwise create liquidity for its owner. Before consideration of any mitigating factors associated with the subject interest, we would expect the discount for lack of marketability to be at least as high as the discounts on stocks of companies going public in five months.

2. Restricted Stock Studies

Another source of public information on the discount for lack of marketability is the purchase of restricted securities by investment companies. Investment companies (see Exhibit 10.11) have purchased private placements of restricted securities for years. Restricted securities are shares issued and sold by a publicly traded company without prior registration with the Securities and Exchange Commission. At the time of these studies, SEC Rule 144 guidelines imposed a minimum holding period of two years before these restricted securities could be resold.

Because of the restriction on the marketability of the securities, the investment companies purchase the securities at prices lower than the price of a registered security of the same company. The difference between the two prices represents the discount for the lack of marketability.

In the 1970s, the SEC required investment companies to make their transaction records public. The availability of the records made it possible for appraisers to determine the lack of marketability discount and use it as a comparison for the discount on closely held interests.

Exhibit 10.11 Summary of Studies of Restricted Securities Transactions

Study	Period of Study	Discount for Lack of Marketability
Securities and Exchange Commission	1966–1969	26%
Hall and Polacek	1979–1992	23%
Silber	1981–1988	33.75%
Stryker and Pittock	1978–1982	45%
Maher	1969–1973	35%
Gelman	1968–1970	33%
Moroney	1969–1973(a)	35.6%
Trout	1968–1972	33.45%
Arneson	Opinion(b)	50% or greater
Willamette	1981–1984	31.2%
Management Planning, Inc.	1980–1995	28%
FMV Opinions, Inc.	1980–1997	22%
Johnson Study	1991–1995	20%
Columbia Financial Advisors, Inc.	1996–1997	21%
Columbia Financial Advisors, Inc.(c)	1997–1998	13%

(a) Moroney did not state the exact time period of his study of restricted stocks, but it is within this time frame.
(b) The author used the 35 percent mean discount of the Maher study as a base discount. He then supports a higher discount based on his analysis of the SEC letter stock study and other SEC studies.
(c) The effect of the SEC Rule 144 change from a two-year waiting period to a one-year waiting period.
Source: James R. Hitchner, editor, *Financial Valuation: Applications and Models,* 2nd ed. (Hoboken, NJ: John Wiley & Sons, 2006), p. 404.

  a. Revenue Ruling 77-287
  b. Columbia Financial Advisors
  c. Bruce Johnson
  d. FMV Opinions
  e. Silber
  f. Willamette
  g. Standard Research Consultants/Stryker & Pittock
  h. Maher
  i. Moroney
  j. Trout
  k. Gelman
  l. Securities and Exchange Institutional Investor Studies
  m. Arneson
  n. Restricted Stock Study Summary

Revenue Ruling 77-287 amplifies Revenue Ruling 59-60 and presents guidelines for valuing restricted securities. The ruling is a good source of information concerning the characteristics of restricted stocks and the companies that issue those types of securities. The revenue ruling defines a restricted security as follows:

> These particular securities cannot lawfully be distributed to the general public until a registration statement relating to the corporation underlying the securities has been filed, and has also become effective under the rules promulgated and enforced by the United States Securities and Exchange Commission pursuant to the Federal securities laws.

The chart in Exhibit 10.12 summarizes the attributes of restricted stocks listed in Revenue Ruling 77-287 and compares them to the subject minority interest in Acme.

Exhibit 10.12 Attributes of Restricted Stocks

Common Attributes of Restricted Securities	Adjustments to a Minority Equity Interest in Acme		
	Positive	Neutral	Negative
Option to require registration at seller's expense			X
Option to require registration at buyer's expense			X
Right to receive continuous disclosure of information			X
Right to select one or more directors			X
Option to purchase additional shares of issuer's stock			X
Provision giving buyer the right to a greater voice in operations			X
Approximately 2 years for marketability			X
Underlying company is already public			X
Audited financial statements		X	

The restricted stock studies indicate a range of discounts for lack of marketability from 23 percent to 50 percent, with most indications at 30 percent to 35 percent. Based on the relatively negative characteristics of the subject interest in Acme, we would expect the discount for lack of marketability, all other factors being equal, to be at least as high as the discounts indicated in the restricted stock studies before consideration of any other mitigating factors associated with the subject interest.

3. Other Factors Influencing Marketability

When determining the discount for lack of marketability, we also considered the factors determined by the U.S. Tax Court in *Bernard Mandelbaum et al v. Commissioner* (TCM 1995-255). Factors identified by the court include financial statement analysis, dividend policy, history and outlook, management, amount of control in the transferred shares, restrictions on transferability, holding period of the shares, redemption policy, and cost associated with a public offering.

The summary table in Exhibit 10.13 considers those factors identified by the court, as well as other factors that may influence the marketability and liquidity of the subject minority interest in Acme.

Exhibit 10.13 Summary Table [Illustration only]

Marketability Adjustment Factors	Impact on Marketability Discount—Acme		
	Warrants an Above-Average Discount	Warrants an Average Discount	Warrants a Below-Average Discount
Starting point (example only)	35%	35%	35%
Accessibility and reliability of financial information		X	
Number of shareholders	X		
Concentration of control owner		X	
Number of potential buyers	X		
Access to capital marketplace	X		
Size of the business		X	
Volume of comparable private transactions		X	
Owners with adversarial relationships or an inconsistent business philosophy		X	
Desirability of the business		X	
Existence of restricted stock agreements			X
Existence of noncompete agreements			X
Yield/distribution		X	
Liquidity of control owners	X		
Quality and competence of management team			X
Existence and effect of pending litigation		X	
Size of block of stock		X	
Existence and extent of contractual restrictions			X
Degree and effect of industry regulations		X	
Effects of state law			X
Existence of swing vote characteristics		X	
Relationship between controlling and noncontrolling shareholders		X	
History and nature and outlook of the company		X	
Holding period	X		
Redemption policy	X		
Costs of IPO	X		

Source: James R. Hitchner, editor, *Financial Valuation: Applications and Models*, 2nd ed. (Hoboken, NJ: John Wiley & Sons, 2006), 423–424.

Recent Thinking Regarding the IPO Studies and Restricted Stock Studies

In recent years, some practitioners and academics have challenged the traditional studies most often used in determining discounts for lack of marketability. Other practitioners have persuasively presented the case for the continuing validity and relevance of these studies. In the following section, we briefly discuss these recent topics.

a. IPO Studies

Commentators have suggested that a 50 percent discount for lack of marketability in a transaction occurring six months before an IPO would imply a 200 percent annualized return, which would "appear to be implausibly large."[23]

Other practitioners, however, have commented that this criticism "implies that investors in pre-IPO stock can gain liquidity at the time of the IPO, which is not generally true. Most underwriters will not register selling shareholder stocks on the IPO. Those that do register it generally have an extended 'lockup' period before the existing shareholders can sell." Also, by annualizing the return, the argument "implies that a comparable investment opportunity will be available to and recognized by the investor immediately. This is almost never true."[24]

It has also been suggested that "buyers of shares prior to the IPO are likely to be insiders who provide some sort of service to the firm. . . . Thus, part of the discount may reflect equilibrium compensation for these services rather than compensation for the lack of marketability."[25]

However, several commentators have noted the lack of empirical foundation for this and substantial empirical evidence that contradicts it. For example, one author has written:

> Willamette studies attempt to eliminate insiders. The Emory and Valuation Advisors studies contain a substantial amount of arm's-length transactions, usually with institutional investors, who usually have rights that make their stock more valuable than the common stock with which it is compared at the time of the IPO. One-third to one-half of the pre-IPO transactions in recent years are convertible preferred stock, which of course is more valuable than the common stock with which its price is compared. Also, many of the institutional investors demand "put" rights. These factors would result in a downward bias in the calculated discounts.[26]

It has also been suggested that "the IPO approach is subject to a serious sample selection problem. Firms will choose to issue shares through an initial public offering

---

[23] Mukesh Bajaj, David J. Denis, Stephen P. Ferries, and Atulya Sarin, "Firm Value and Marketability Discounts," *Journal of Corporation Law,* October 2001.

[24] Shannon Pratt, "Rebuttal to Bajaj: Answers to Criticisms of Pre-IPO Studies," *Shannon Pratt's Business Valuation Update* 10, no. 6, June 2004.

[25] Mukesh Bajaj, David J. Denis, Stephen P. Ferries, and Atulya Sarin, "Firm Value and Marketability Discounts," *Journal of Corporation Law,* October 2001.

[26] Shannon Pratt, "Rebuttal to Bajaj: Answers to Criticisms of Pre-IPO Studies," *Shannon Pratt's Business Valuation Update* 10, no. 6, June 2004.

when their prospects improve. . . . Once an IPO takes place, this uncertainty is resolved and only the successful (and hence higher valued) firms issue shares."[27]

Other practitioners note, however, that "the effect of this bias is minimal. Only about 20% of companies that file for IPOs fail to have them when scheduled. Some are merely delayed, and others are acquired. Still others remain as viable private companies. Very few actually become worthless."[28]

b. Restricted Stock Studies

Regarding the restricted stock studies, it has been suggested that the observed discount between restricted stock private placements and the related freely traded public price may represent other factors in addition to lack of marketability. Because some level of discount from the public price is observed in private placements of registered unrestricted shares, some have argued that it follows that factors other than liquidity are at play in the restricted stock studies. The assumption is that such registered shares are liquid: "Registered shares can be transacted freely, and the fact that the firm was publicly traded meant there was a ready market for these shares."[29]

Practitioners have observed, however, that this assumption is faulty:

> On average, the registered shares in his [Bajaj's] study were in fact restricted under Rule 144, and had significantly limited marketability. Moreover, the study fails to examine the underlying trading volume of the private placement companies. As private placement companies, in general, are smaller and have less trading volume, it is likely that, even if the registered shares were not subject to the dribble-out provisions of Rule 144, the registered shares would not be as liquid as the typical small block sales that set the public price. In other words, the public price reflects a significantly more liquid security than the registered shares in Bajaj's private placement study.[30]

Practitioners have also noted that all restricted share blocks are not equally illiquid. Given the dribble-out provisions of Rule 144 and a particular security's trading volume, a 30 percent stock block is significantly less liquid than a 1.95 percent stock block, even though the restricted stock investments are in the same publicly traded company. "The discount accorded these two blocks must reflect the differences in their respective relative lack of liquidity."[31] Investments in closely held businesses are typically less liquid than even large blocks of restricted securities.

---

[27] Mukesh Bajaj, David J. Denis, Stephen P. Ferries, and Atulya Sarin, "Firm Value and Marketability Discounts," *Journal of Corporation Law,* October 2001.

[28] Shannon Pratt, "Rebuttal to Bajaj: Answers to Criticisms of Pre-IPO Studies," *Shannon Pratt's Business Valuation Update* 10, no. 6, June 2004.

[29] Mukesh Bajaj, David J. Denis, Stephen P. Ferries, and Atulya Sarin, "Firm Value and Marketability Discounts," *Journal of Corporation Law,* October 2001.

[30] Lance S. Hall, "Counteracting the New and Winning IRS Approach to Determine Discounts for Lack of Marketability," *Valuation Strategies,* March–April 2004.

[31] Ibid.

Bajaj and colleagues have also opined that part of the discounts in the restricted stock studies are for compensation for "1) assessing the value of the investment, 2) monitoring the investment, 3) a promise of future funding, and 4) management advice to the company" and that "it is often the case that private equity investors commit to provide the issuing firm with advice and oversight following the private placement of equity. Moreover, these investors often commit to providing capital in the future, provided that the issuing firm meets a set of predetermined goals for financial performance. Consequently, at least a portion of the price discount . . . might reflect compensation to these investors for future services rendered. . . ." Citing various academic articles, Bajaj also suggests that "discounts are required . . . to serve as compensation for the higher information and monitoring costs associated with the investments."[32]

Other practitioners have made important observations regarding these points, noting that "the very act of monitoring presupposes one can do something about the investment. In other words, if one monitors a liquid investment, and things change, the investor can decide to sell the investment and invest elsewhere. However, if one monitors an illiquid investment, and things change, that investor cannot sell the investment and the investor's alternatives are severely limited."[33]

Regarding the speculation that part of the discount is compensation for a promise of future funding, it has been noted that this assumption is unacceptable. Since a legal promise of future investment is part of the terms of a private placement purchase, such a promise should have been reported.

Finally, with regard to the thought that part of the discount is a return for advice provided to management, practitioners note that this is again speculative and without apparent foundation in the underlying data. One adds:

> It is interesting to note that this speculation has an interesting flip side. If it is assumed that advice is given by an investor, it also must be assumed that the investor expects the advice to be taken. Otherwise, there is no value to be obtained by giving it. Advice taken suggests the restricted stock investment carries with it aspects of influence or control. Accordingly, because influence and control are also valuable to an investor—especially an illiquid investment—the investor will pay more for his or her investment to exercise such influence or control. Therefore, the actual discount for lack of marketability is greater. . . . In other words, because shares with influence and control are more attractive than shares without such rights, the discount for lack of marketability for shares lacking influence and control should be greater than the discounts typically reflected by the restricted stock private placements having influence or control.[34]

In summary, while all practitioners acknowledge that neither the IPO studies nor the restricted stock studies are perfect, most practitioners continue to view these studies as valid and important data sources and embrace them as critically important parts of the body of empirical evidence supporting discounts for lack of marketability.

---

[32] Mukesh Bajaj, David J. Denis, Stephen P. Ferries, and Atulya Sarin, "Firm Value and Marketability Discounts," *Journal of Corporation Law,* October 2001.
[33] Lance S. Hall, "Counteracting the New and Winning IRS Approach to Determine Discounts for Lack of Marketability," *Valuation Strategies,* March–April 2004.
[34] Ibid.

4. Discount for Lack of Marketability Conclusion

Our analysis indicated that several characteristics of the subject minority interest in Acme would support a significant discount for lack of marketability. Acme is not required to make distributions and has not done so in the past 10 years. Management has indicated that policy will continue in the future. Other factors tended to lead toward a lower level of discount. Our overall conclusion was that the factors analyzed were neutral in relation to the overall benchmark.

Based on our analysis, we determined that a discount for lack of marketability of 35 percent should be applied to the subject interest.

The prior indication of value was developed on a minority, marketable basis. Marketability here refers to the price as if freely traded, that is, liquid. The interest in a closely held business, while clearly capable of being sold, is obviously less marketable (or less liquid) than its publicly traded counterpart. The analyst focuses on restricted stock studies for quantification of the marketability discount. Other studies (pre-IPO) are also available to assist in this process and can provide meaningful guidance. *Note:* The use of detailed restricted stock data (the FVM Restricted Stock Study), pre-IPO data (Valuation Advisors' Lack of Marketability Discount Study), the Quantitative Marketability Discount Model (QMDM), and stock-option models (Longstaff, Finnerty, etc.) are also being used by analysts.

Notice that court cases are not mentioned specifically. Such cases are relevant for issues only and not for citation as supporting a selected level of discount. Quoting cases in your report also put you on the "turf" of an attorney in a litigation engagement. Keep the issues in your "turf" based on an analysis of the specific facts and your judgment.

Nonoperating and Excess Assets

As of May 31, 2008, the total cash and equivalent account amounted to $4,367,501, or 17.0 percent of total assets, which was comprised of the following:

Cash and Equivalent

Petty cash	$ 10,725
First Commercial Bank	2,398,171
Regions Trust	698,401
Brokerage money market	379,612
Commercial checking	526,909
National Bank of Commerce	353,683
Total	$4,367,501

As of May 31, 2008, the Company had securities available for sale and securities held to maturity which amounted to $1,128,321, or 4.4 percent of total assets, as follows:

Securities

Stocks

Central Power	$ 75,187
CPC	45,657
Natural Dynamic Resources	29,437
Sterling Corp.	106,633
Lauderdale	16,405
Total stocks	273,319

Bonds

U.S. Treasury	375,000
Associates Finance	225,000
Merrill Lynch	247,500
Federal Housing Financing Agency	7,500
Total bonds	855,000
Total securities	$1,128,321

As of the Valuation Date, Acme's most liquid assets amounted to $5,495,824, or 21.4 percent of total assets, which was above the industry median (21.4 percent for Acme versus 12.2 percent 2008 RMA data). Removal of the excess cash amount aligns the Company's cash position relative to the industry median.

We concluded that the amount of $3,289,330 ($5,495,824 − $25,656,903 × 8.6% = $3,289,330) of Acme's cash and marketable securities account should be treated as a nonoperating asset. We also treated as nonoperating assets the cash surrender value of life insurance account of $86,034 and receivables accounts and other of a nonoperating nature. In addition, as of May 31, 2008, the Company had $239,583 in securities held to maturity. We believe the Company historically had high cash reserves and the seasonality would not affect our calculation.

Discussions with management indicated that there were no other nonoperating assets or liabilities on the Company's balance sheet. Therefore, the total nonoperating asset amount, as of the Valuation Date, was approximated to $4,117,078. A 10 percent discount[35] was applied to this amount to account for the fact that the minority stockholders do not have direct access to these assets. An additional 35 percent was applied for lack of marketability as previously derived. This results in a combined discount of 41.5 percent when sequentially applied.

Accordingly, we conclude that the fair market value of the total equity of the Company, on a minority, non marketable interest basis derived through the income capitalization method, is $8,423,678 {$6,015,187 + [$4,117,078 × (1 − 41.50%)]} = $8,423,678. $6,015,187 = 9,254,134 × (1 − 35%).

> A nonoperating or an excess asset is an asset that can be removed from operations and have little or no impact on the operating earnings stream of the business. Such assets can be excess cash, investments, owner toys, and the like. As such, their value is not directly captured by application of a capitalization rate to an operating cash flow, nor do several other methods capture their values.

---

[35] Based on an analysis of closed-end funds. [Illustration only.]

As indicated earlier, the analyst identified certain nonoperating or excess assets for consideration in this assignment. After his or her analysis, the analyst made an addition to value for these nonoperating items after appropriate discounts. Many analysts agree with this. Some analysts ask the following question: Why would such an addition to value be made if the minority shareholder has no power to cause an asset sale or to tap into the value of those assets? Regardless of the ultimate treatment, the presence of significant nonoperating or excess assets should generally receive consideration and discussion in the valuation report.

Reconciliation of Valuation Methods

The Company's net revenues were almost flat at around $29 million since 2005. As a result, we discarded the Discounted Cash Flow Method from our analysis and relied instead on the Income Capitalization Method.

We discarded the Guideline Public Company Method due to lack of comparability with Acme from an operational and investment point of view.

Also, we discarded the Guideline Company Transaction Method due to lack of sufficient data. The Cost Approach was used as a reasonableness check for net tangible assets.

Conclusion of Value

We have performed a valuation engagement, as that term is defined in the Statement of Standards for Valuation Services No. 1 of the American Institute of Certified Public Accountants, of 16,279 shares of common stock of Acme as of May 31, 2008, on a minority, nonmarketable basis. This valuation was performed solely to assist in your determination of the value for gift tax purposes, and the resulting estimate of value should not be used for any other purpose or by any other party for any purpose. This valuation engagement was conducted in accordance with the SSVS. The estimate of value that results from a valuation engagement is expressed as of conclusion of value.

There were no restrictions or limitations in the scope of our work or data available for analysis.

Exhibit 10.14 shows how the value indication was derived from the Income Capitalization (capitalized cash flow) Method.

Exhibit 10.14 Summary Calculation

100% Minority equity, marketable (derived from the Income Capitalization (capitalized cash flow) Method)	$9,254,134
− Marketability Discount	−35%
= 100% Equity value, on a minority interest	6,015,187
+ Nonoperating assets (cash, securities, and proceeds from life insurance of approx. $100,000) discounted by 41.5%	2,408,491
= 100% Equity minority, non marketable	8,423,678
Total number of shares	124,684
Value/share (rounded)	$ 68.00

Based on our analysis and the facts and circumstances as of the valuation date, we have concluded that the estimated fair market value of a minority, nonmarketable ownership interest, on a going-concern basis, in the common stock of Acme, as of May 31, 2000, based on 124,684 shares issued and outstanding, is approximately $68.00 per share ($8,423,678 / 124,684).

Per share value	$ 68.00
Value 16,279 shares	$1,106,972

This conclusion is subject to the Statement of Assumptions and Limiting Conditions found in Appendix A of this report and to the Valuation Analyst's Representation/Certification found in Appendix B of this report. We have no obligation to update this report or our conclusion of value for information that comes to our attention after the date of this report.

> The valuation conclusion is expressed again at the end of the report narrative. Here, a per-share calculation is presented as well as a total for the value of the subject interest. This information was carried forward in the report to the cover/transmittal letter and/or valuation summary. Thus, in keeping with good communications skills, the analyst told the company what the analyst was going to tell the company—and then did so.

Appendix A—Valuation Representation/Certification

I [we] represent/certify that, to the best of my [our] knowledge and belief:

- The statements of fact contained in this report are true and correct.
- The reported analyses, opinions, and conclusions of value are limited only by the reported assumptions and limiting conditions and are my personal, impartial, independent, unbiased, objective professional analyses, opinions, and conclusions.
- I have no present or prospective/contemplated financial or other interest in the business or property that is the subject of this report, and I have no personal financial or other interest or bias with respect to the property or the parties involved.
- My engagement in this assignment was not contingent upon developing or reporting predetermined results.
- My compensation for completing this assignment is fee-based and is not contingent upon the development or reporting of a predetermined value or direction in value that favors the cause of the client, the outcome of the valuation, the amount of the value opinion, the attainment of a stipulated result, or the occurrence of a subsequent event directly related to the intended use of this appraisal.
- The economic and industry data included in the valuation report have been obtained from various printed or electronic reference sources that the valuation analyst believes to be reliable. The valuation analyst has not performed any corroborating procedures to substantiate those data.
- My analyses, opinions, conclusions (valuation engagement), and this detailed/comprehensive appraisal report were developed in conformity with the 2008 American Institute of Certified Public Accountants Statement on Standards for Valuation Services No. 1 and the 2008–2009 Uniform Standards of Professional Appraisal Practice as promulgated by the Appraisal Foundation and [state other association standards as appropriate].
- The parties for which the information and use of the valuation report is restricted are identified; the valuation report is not intended to be and should not be used by anyone other than such parties.
- Option: The valuation analyst used the work of one or more outside specialists to assist during the valuation engagement. The specialist is Mr./Ms. _____with the firm _____. [The valuation report should include a statement identifying the level of responsibility, if any, the valuation analyst is assuming for the specialist's work.]
- The valuation analyst has no obligation to update the report or the opinion of value for information that comes to my attention after the date of the report.
- This report and analysis were prepared under the direction of Margaret Smith, CPA/ABV/CFF, ASA, CBA, CVA, with significant professional assistance from Junior B. Staffer. Ms. Smith is a certified public accountant licensed in the State of [State(s)] and is accredited in business valuation and certified in financial forensics by the American Institute of Certified Public Accountants. She is also an accredited senior appraiser with the American Society of Appraisers, a certified business appraiser with The Institute of Business Appraisers and a certified valuation analyst with the National Association of Certified Valuation Analysts.

- The American Society of Appraisers has a mandatory recertification program for its Senior Members. Ms. Smith is in compliance with that program.

Margaret Smith, CPA/ABV/CFF, ASA, CBA, CVA
XYZ Appraisal Associates PLLC

Note: If applicable, reference to NACVA and the IBA should be included for brevity. They were omitted here.

NACVA

This valuation and report were completed in accordance with the National Association of Certified Valuation Analysts Professional Standards for Conducting and Reporting on Business Valuations.

The Institute of Business Appraisers

Formal Appraisal Report
Certified Appraisal Report

That the appraiser's analyses, opinions, and conclusions were developed and that the report has been prepared in conformity with the Business Appraisal Standards of The Institute of Business Appraisers.

Appendix B—Assumptions, Limiting Conditions, and Valuation Representation/Certification

The primary assumptions and limiting conditions pertaining to the value estimate conclusion(s) stated in this detailed appraisal report ("report") are summarized below. Other assumptions are cited elsewhere in this report.

1. The conclusion of value arrived at herein is valid only for the stated purpose as of the date of the valuation.
2. Financial statements and other related information provided by Acme or its representatives, in the course of this engagement, have been accepted without any verification as fully and correctly reflecting the enterprise's business conditions and operating results for the respective periods, except as specifically noted herein. XYZ has not audited, reviewed, or compiled the financial information provided to us and, accordingly, we express no audit opinion or any other form of assurance on this information.
3. Public information and industry and statistical information have been obtained from sources we believe to be reliable. However, we make no representation as to the accuracy or completeness of such information and have performed no procedures to corroborate the information.
4. We do not provide assurance on the achievability of the results forecasted by Acme because events and circumstances frequently do not occur as expected, differences between actual and expected results may be material, and achievement of the forecasted results is dependent on actions, plans, and assumptions of management.
5. The conclusion of value arrived at herein is based on the assumption that the current level of management expertise and effectiveness would continue to be maintained and that the character and integrity of the enterprise through any sale, reorganization, exchange, or diminution of the owners' participation would not be materially or significantly changed.
6. This report and the conclusion of value arrived at herein are for the exclusive use of our client for the sole and specific purposes as noted herein. They may not be used for any other purpose or by any other party for any purpose. Furthermore, the report and conclusion of value are not intended by the author and should not be construed by the reader to be investment advice in any manner whatsoever. The conclusion of value represents the considered opinion of XYZ, based on information furnished to them by Acme and other sources.
7. Neither all nor any part of the contents of this report (especially the conclusion of value, the identity of any valuation specialist[s], or the firm with which such valuation specialists are connected or any reference to any of their professional designations) should be disseminated to the public through advertising media, public relations, news media, sales media, mail, direct transmittal, or any other means of communication, including but not limited to the Securities and Exchange Commission or other governmental agency or regulatory body, without the prior written consent and approval of XYZ.
8. Future services regarding the subject matter of this report, including but not limited to testimony or attendance in court, shall not be required of XYZ unless previous arrangements have been made in writing.
9. XYZ is not an environmental consultant or auditor, and it takes no responsibility for any actual or potential environmental liabilities. Any person entitled to rely on this report, wishing to know whether such liabilities exist or the scope

and their effect on the value of the property, is encouraged to obtain a professional environmental assessment. XYZ does not conduct or provide environmental assessments and has not performed one for the subject property.

10. XYZ has not determined independently whether Acme is subject to any present or future liability relating to environmental matters (including, but not limited to CERCLA/Superfund liability) nor the scope of any such liabilities. XYZ's valuation takes no such liabilities into account, except as they have been reported to XYZ by Acme or by an environmental consultant working for Acme, and then only to the extent that the liability was reported to us in an actual or estimated dollar amount. Such matters, if any, are noted in the report. To the extent such information has been reported to us, XYZ has relied on it without verification and offers no warranty or representation as to its accuracy or completeness.

11. XYZ has not made a specific compliance survey or analysis of the subject property to determine whether it is subject to, or in compliance with, the American Disabilities Act of 1990, and this valuation does not consider the effect, if any, of noncompliance.

12. No change of any item in this appraisal report shall be made by anyone other than XYZ, and we shall have no responsibility for any such unauthorized change.

13. Unless otherwise stated, no effort has been made to determine the possible effect, if any, on the subject business due to future federal, state, or local legislation, including any environmental or ecological matters or interpretations thereof.

14. If prospective financial information approved by management has been used in our work, we have not examined or compiled the prospective financial information and therefore do not express an audit opinion or any other form of assurance on the prospective financial information or the related assumptions. Events and circumstances frequently do not occur as expected, and there will usually be differences between prospective financial information and actual results, and those differences may be material.

15. We have conducted interviews with the current management of Acme concerning the past, present, and prospective operating results of the company.

16. Except as noted, we have relied on the representations of the owners, management, and other third parties concerning the value and useful condition of all equipment, real estate, investments used in the business, and any other assets or liabilities, except as specifically stated to the contrary in this report. We have not attempted to confirm whether all assets of the business are free and clear of liens and encumbrances or that the entity has good title to all assets.

17. The approaches and methodologies used in our work did not comprise an examination in accordance with generally accepted accounting principles, the objective of which is an expression of an opinion regarding the fair presentation of financial statements or other financial information, whether historical or prospective, presented in accordance with generally accepted accounting principles. We express no opinion and accept no responsibility for the accuracy and completeness of the financial information or other data provided to us by others. We assume that the financial and other information provided to us is accurate and complete, and we have relied on this information in performing our valuation.

18. The valuation may not be used in conjunction with any other appraisal or study. The value conclusion(s) stated in this appraisal is based on the program of utilization described in the report and may not be separated into parts. The

appraisal was prepared solely for the purpose, function, and party so identified in the report. The report may not be reproduced, in whole or in part, and the findings of the report may not be utilized by a third party for any purpose, without the express written consent of XYZ

19. Unless otherwise stated in the appraisal, the valuation of the business has not considered or incorporated the potential economic gain or loss resulting from contingent assets, liabilities, or events existing as of the valuation date.

20. All facts and data set forth in our letter report are true and accurate to the best of the Appraiser's knowledge and belief.

21. All recommendations as to fair market value are presented as the Appraiser's conclusion based on the facts and data set forth in this report.

22. During the course of the valuation, we have considered information provided by management and other third parties. We believe these sources to be reliable, but no further responsibility is assumed for their accuracy.

23. We made an on-site visit to Acme's administrative headquarters.

24. Any projections of future events described in this report represent the general expectancy concerning such events as of the evaluation date(s). These future events may or may not occur as anticipated, and actual operating results may vary from those described in our report.

25. This valuation analysis and report, which are to be distributed only in their entirety, are intended solely for use by you, your client, and your client's accountants and attorneys, solely to assist you and your client in your determination of the fair market value of the subject interests for tax purposes. It should not be used for any other purpose or distributed to third parties for any purpose, in whole or in part, without the express written consent of XYZ

26. If applicable, we have used financial projections approved by management. We have not examined the forecast data or the underlying assumptions in accordance with the standards prescribed by the American Institute of Certified Public Accountants and do not express an opinion or any other form of assurance on the forecast data and related assumptions. The future may not occur as anticipated, and actual operating results may vary from those described in our report. This would not affect our conclusion of value as of the valuation date of this valuation.

27. We have no responsibility or obligation to update this report for events or circumstances occurring subsequent to the date of this report.

28. Our report is based on historical and/or prospective financial information provided to us by management and other third parties. This information has not been audited, reviewed, or compiled by us, nor has it been subjected to any type of audit, review, or compilation procedures by us, nor have we audited, reviewed, or compiled the books and records of the subject company. Had we audited, reviewed, or compiled the underlying data, matters may have come to our attention that would have resulted in our using amounts that differ from those provided; accordingly, we take no responsibility for the underlying data presented or relied upon in this report.

29. Our valuation judgment, shown herein, pertains only to the subject business, the stated value standard (fair market value), at the stated valuation date, and only for the stated valuation purpose(s).

30. The various estimates of value presented in this report apply to the valuation report only and may not be used out of the context presented herein.

31. In all matters that may be potentially challenged by a court or other party, we do not take responsibility for the degree of reasonableness of contrary positions that others may choose to take, nor for the costs or fees that may be incurred in the defense of our recommendations against challenge(s). We will, however, retain our supporting workpapers for your matter(s) and will be available to assist in defending our professional positions taken, at our then current rates, plus direct expenses at actual, and according to our then current Standard Professional Agreement.

32. No third parties are intended to be benefited. An engagement for a different purpose, or under a different standard or basis of value, or for a different date of value, could result in a materially different opinion of value.

33. XYZ retains all exclusive rights to copyrights to the report and to control the issuance of copies by others, and the client has no right of diffusion, reproduction, distribution, or sale. The client may reproduce 10 [other] copies of the report solely for its internal use. Otherwise, the client may not reproduce the report without the prior written consent of XYZ.

34. Our report will not be used for financing or included in a private placement or other public documents and may not be relied upon by any third parties.

35. The report assumes all required licenses, certificates of occupancy, consents, or legislative or administrative authority from any local, state, or national government or private entity or organization have been or can be obtained or reviewed for any use on which the opinion contained in the report is based.

36. The obligations of XYZ are solely corporate obligations, and no officer, director, employee, agent, contractor, shareholder, owner, or controlling person shall be subject to any personal liability whatsoever to any person, nor will any such claim be asserted by or on behalf of any other party to this agreement or any person relying on the report.

37. XYZ does not consent to be "expertised" with respect to matters involving the Securities and Exchange Commission. For purposes of this report, the foregoing sentence means that XYZ shall not be referred to by name or anonymously in any filing or document. Should you breach this stipulation and refer to XYZ by name or anonymously, you will amend such filing or document upon the written request of XYZ.

38. We express no opinion for matters that require legal or other specialized expertise, investigation, or knowledge beyond that customarily employed by business appraisers.

39. Unless stated otherwise in this report, we express no opinion as to 1) the tax consequences of any transaction that may result, 2) the effect of the tax consequences of any net value received or to be received as a result of a transaction, and 3) the possible impact on the market value resulting from any need to effect a transaction to pay taxes.

Appendix C—Professional Qualifications of the Analyst/Appraiser

MARGARET SMITH, CPA/ABV/CFF, ASA, CBA, CVA
Professional Qualifications

Experience

Senior Consultant in the Business Valuation and Litigation Services group of XYZ Appraisal Associates PLLC. Ms. Smith's expertise includes both valuation and valuation-related consulting for entire business entities and business interests.

Ms. Smith specializes in financial modeling and cash flow forecasting. She has performed valuations of closely held corporations for mergers and acquisitions and gift and estate tax purposes. Ms. Smith's industry experience includes but is not limited to companies operating in the manufacturing industry, construction, automotive parts manufacturers, battery manufacturers, specialty chemical companies, investment holding companies, restaurant companies, and engineering companies.

Prior to joining the Valuation Group at XYZ Appraisal Associates PLLC, Ms. Smith spent four years with National Accounting Firm LLP. Ms. Smith's experience was predominantly in the valuation department.

Education

- M.B.A. Colorado State University (Business Strategy), (2004)
- B.A. Colorado State University (Accounting), (1998)

Membership in Professional Organizations

- American Institute of Certified Public Accountants
- Certified Public Accountant, Accredited in Business Valuation and Certified in Financial Forensics (CPA/ABV/CFF)
- American Society of Appraisers (ASA)
- Intellectual Property Owners Association
- National Association of Certified Valuation Analysts (CVA)
- Institute of Business Appraisers (IBA)

Speeches and Presentations

- Colorado State University: "Current Developments in Business Valuations" (2006)
- University of Pittsburgh: "Current Developments in Business Valuations" (2005)

Appendix D—Other Sources Consulted

Business Valuation Standards, AICPA, ASA, NACVA, and IBA.

Fishman, Pratt, Hitchner, and Griffith. *Guide to Business Valuations*, Forth Worth, TX: Practitioner's Publishing Company, 2008.

Hitchner, et al. *Financial Valuation Applications and Models*, 2nd ed., Hoboken, NJ: John Wiley & Sons, 2006.

Pratt, Shannon P. *Valuing a Business: The Analysis and Appraisal of Closely Held Companies*, 5th ed. Homewood, IL: Irwin Professional Publishing, 2008.

RMA Annual Statement Summaries. Philadelphia: Risk Management Association, annual, 2008–2009.

Standard Industrial Classification Manual. Washington, DC, 1987.

Uniform Standards of Professional Appraisal Practice. Appraisal Foundation.

Acme Measurement Devices, Inc., information including:

- Financial statements of the Company for the years ended December 31, 2003 through 2007.
- Various Company schedules of expenses, personnel, fixed assets, etc.
- Articles of incorporation, by-laws, board and stockholder meeting minutes.
- On-site visit and teleconferences with Company officers.

Exhibits

The historical financial statements in Exhibits 10.15, 10.16, and 10.17 for Acme were prepared from Company financial statements for the purpose of preparing the valuation. XYZ Appraisal Associates PLLC has not audited, reviewed, or compiled these statements and expresses no opinion or any other form of assurance on them.

Exhibit 10.15 Acme Measurement Devices, Inc.—Comparative Balance Sheets

	Audited 12/31/03	%	Audited 12/31/04	%	Audited 12/31/05	%	Audited 12/31/06	%	Audited 12/31/07	%	Internal Financials 05/31/08	%	2008–2009 RMA (a) ratios %
Assets													
CURRENT ASSETS													
Cash & cash equivalents	$3,299,826	14.9	$4,708,548	19.5	$2,976,288	12.0	$4,352,541	18.1	$5,236,842	21.5	$4,367,504	17.0	12.2
Securities													
Available for sale—													
at market value	712,058	3.2	777,762	3.2	643,511	2.6	519,198	2.2	280,821	1.2	0	0.0	
Held to maturity	587,864	2.7	669,999	2.8	179,822	0.7	0	0.0	375,000	1.5	1,128,321	4.4	
Trade accounts receivable	2,445,408	11.0	3,384,081	14.0	4,181,567	16.9	2,921,720	12.1	2,795,967	11.5	4,585,083	17.9	27.1
Income taxes receivable		0.0		0.0		0.0	301,451	1.3		0.0		0.0	
Inventories:													
Finished goods	1,348,467	6.1	1,062,243	4.4	1,699,754	6.9	1,811,675	7.5	2,167,428	8.9	1,053,000	4.1	
Work-in-process	549,150	2.5	386,700	1.6	409,521	1.7	483,375	2.0	496,500	2.0	255,000	1.0	
Materials and supplies	3,033,917	13.7	3,001,548	12.4	3,255,290	13.2	3,170,754	13.2	2,550,464	10.5	3,967,013	15.5	
Total Inventories	4,931,534	22.3	4,450,491	18.4	5,364,564	21.7	5,465,804	22.7	5,214,392	21.4	5,275,013	20.6	28.8
Deferred income taxes	440,550	2.0	493,050	2.0	796,050	3.2	994,050	4.1	951,488	3.9	951,488	3.7	
Prepaid expenses	76,350	0.3	68,454	0.3	62,517	0.3	83,286	0.3	218,220	0.9	194,735	0.8	
Total Current Assets	12,493,589	56.4	14,552,385	60.3	14,204,318	57.4	14,638,049	60.8	15,072,729	61.9	16,502,142	64.3	71.3
PROPERTY, PLANT AND EQUIPMENT, AT COST:													
Land and Building	10,447,610	47.2	10,621,832	44.0	11,421,392	46.1	11,527,878	47.9	11,540,555	47.4	11,564,268	45.1	
Manufacturing equipment	3,489,845	15.8	3,590,913	14.9	4,125,582	16.7	4,501,364	18.7	4,923,600	20.2	5,451,329	21.2	

(continues)

529

Exhibit 10.15 *continued*

	Audited 12/31/03	%	Audited 12/31/04	%	Audited 12/31/05	%	Audited 12/31/06	%	Audited 12/31/07	%	Internal Financials 05/31/08	%	2008–2009 RMA (a) ratios %
Office furniture and equipment	2,177,048	9.8	2,156,771	8.9	2,006,327	8.1	2,133,801	8.9	2,004,740	8.2	2,072,582	8.1	
Automobiles	474,515	2.1	554,291	2.3	589,812	2.4	627,471	2.6	624,156	2.6	588,827	2.3	
Equipment leased to others	302,700	1.4	317,025	1.3	346,350	1.4	412,350	1.7	355,125	1.5	310,875	1.2	
	16,891,716	76.2	17,240,831	71.4	18,489,462	74.7	19,202,864	79.7	19,448,175	79.8	19,987,880	77.9	
Less: Accumulated depreciation	8,516,358	38.4	9,233,250	38.2	10,047,561	40.6	11,333,708	47.1	12,385,041	50.8	12,834,102	50.0	
Net property, plant, and equipment	8,375,358	37.8	8,007,581	33.2	8,441,901	34.1	7,869,156	32.7	7,063,134	29.0	7,153,778	27.9	12.2
OTHER ASSETS													
Patents, less accumulated amortization	288,552	1.3	287,015	1.2	283,178	1.1	298,928	1.2	309,965	1.3	319,086	1.2	9.6
Cash surrender value of life insurance	72,464	0.3	75,939	0.3	79,367	0.3	82,739	0.3	86,034	0.4	86,034	0.3	
Other receivables	227,312	1.0	280,469	1.2	321,723	1.3	360,876	1.5	402,131	1.7	402,131	1.6	
Deferred income taxes	547,650	2.5	648,150	2.7	877,650	3.5	834,150	3.5	954,150	3.9	954,150	3.7	
Securities held to maturity	150,819	0.7	299,639	1.2	546,527	2.2		0.0	472,500	1.9	239,583	0.9	
Total other assets	1,286,796	5.8	1,591,211	6.6	2,108,444	8.5	1,576,692	6.5	2,224,779	9.1	2,000,984	7.8	16.5
Total Assets	$22,155,743	100.0	$24,151,176	100.0	$24,754,662	100.0	$24,083,897	100.0	$24,360,642	100.0	$25,656,903	100.0	100.0

Liabilities and Stockholders'
Equity

CURRENT LIABILITIES													
Accounts payable—trade	778,385	3.5	1,053,479	4.4	1,170,801	4.7	1,372,983	5.7	888,152	3.7	1,289,225	5.0	11.9
Accrued compensation and related items	937,001	4.2	1,342,259	5.6	1,116,093	4.5	819,744	3.4	837,300	3.4	969,531	3.8	
Accrued expenses and other liabilities	397,535	1.8	520,025	2.2	1,566,176	6.3	794,744	3.3	643,725	2.7	689,883	2.7	
Unearned income	290,346	1.3	274,334	1.1	281,367	1.1	350,070	1.5	480,752	2.0	505,913	2.0	
Note payable		0.0	35,787	0.1	23,384	0.1	16,697	0.1	6,710	0.0		0.0	7.3
Obligation under capital lease—current portion	176,178	0.8	323,513	1.3	250,784	1.0	362,693	1.5	480,591	2.0	526,605	2.1	
Income taxes payable	159,597	0.7	529,302	2.2	82,553	0.3	76,464	0.3	399,128	1.6	475,527	1.9	
Total Current Liabilities	2,739,041	12.4	4,078,697	16.9	4,491,156	18.1	3,793,394	15.8	3,736,356	15.4	4,456,683	17.4	36.1
OBLIGATION UNDER CAPITAL LEASE	8,628,981	38.9	8,305,469	34.4	8,801,765	35.6	8,439,072	35.0	7,958,802	32.8	7,719,261	30.1	5.0
Stockholders' Equity													
Common stock; $1.50 par value 450,000 shares authorized	197,019	0.9	196,869	0.8	189,436	0.8	188,151	0.8	112,176	0.5	187,026	0.7	
Unrealized gain on securities, net of tax	79,371	0.4	69,446	0.3	75,957	0.3	97,895	0.4	54,707	0.2	54,707	0.2	
Retained earnings	10,575,609	47.7	11,575,763	47.9	11,343,407	45.8	11,779,070	48.9	12,643,319	52.1	13,421,627	52.3	
Foreign currency translation adjustments, unrealized	(64,278)	–0.3	(75,066)	–0.3	(147,059)	–0.6	(213,684)	–0.9	(219,717)	–0.9	(182,400)	–0.7	
Total Stockholder's Equity	10,787,721	48.7	11,767,011	48.7	11,461,741	46.3	11,851,431	49.2	12,590,484	51.8	13,480,959	52.5	54.9
Total Liabilities and Stockholders' Equity	$22,155,743	100.0	$24,151,176	100.0	$24,754,662	100.0	$24,083,897	100.0	$24,285,642	100.0	$25,656,903	100.0	100.0

References:

(a) 2008-2009 RMA data for NAICS 334519 "Measuring & controlling device manufacturing, nec" with revenues between $10-25 million (used with permission). © 2009 by RMA—The Risk Management Association. All rights reserved. No part of this table may be reproduced or utilized in any form or by any means, electronic or mechanical, including photocopying, recording, or by any information storage and retrieval system without permission in writing from RMA—The Risk Management Association. Please refer to www.rmahq.org for further warranty, copyright, and use of data information.

Note: Data source is cited for illustrative purposes only. Actual dates in report will differ.

Exhibit 10.16 Acme Measurement Devices, Inc.—Comparative Income Statements

	Audited 12/31/03	%	Audited 12/31/04	%	Audited 12/31/05	%	Audited 12/31/06	%	Audited 12/31/07	%	LTM as of 05/31/08	%	2008–2009 RMA (a) ratios %
REVENUES													
Equipment	n/a		20,944,452	75.9	21,534,516	75.0	20,289,575	70.2	19,612,049	68.6	20,126,975	70.4	
Parts & repairs	n/a		4,147,502	15.0	4,386,449	15.3	5,469,996	18.9	5,763,689	20.2	5,475,587	19.2	
Training	n/a		843,693	3.1	866,817	3.0	1,011,872	3.5	1,044,042	3.7	917,651	3.2	
Other	n/a		687,122	2.5	751,631	2.6	693,132	2.4	741,018	2.6	698,804	2.4	
Net sales	21,642,206	93.9	26,622,768	96.5	27,539,412	95.9	27,464,574	95.0	27,160,797	95.0	27,219,015	95.2	
Rentals and sales of leased equipment	998,660	4.3	733,155	2.7	947,327	3.3	1,157,432	4.0	1,180,511	4.1	1,087,727	3.8	
Other income (interest income on investments)	410,465	1.8	221,816	0.8	233,999	0.8	299,682	1.0	257,847	0.9	278,936	1.0	
Total Revenue	$23,051,330	100%	$27,577,739	100%	$28,720,737	100%	$28,921,688	100%	$28,599,155	100%	$28,585,677	100%	100%
COSTS AND EXPENSES													
Cost of Goods Sold													
Materials	6,587,496	28.6	8,408,381	30.5	9,383,924	32.7	8,565,641	29.6	7,738,926	27.1	7,403,193	25.9	
Direct Labor	1,217,618	5.3	1,418,480	5.1	1,592,294	5.5	2,176,301	7.5	2,025,638	7.1	2,063,087	7.2	
Indirect Labor	661,967	2.9	674,331	2.4	834,713	2.9	1,664,589	5.8	1,565,958	5.5	1,502,237	5.3	
Payroll Taxes	140,591	0.6	155,354	0.6	180,288	0.6	285,992	1.0	269,114	0.9	267,467	0.9	
Profit Sharing	69,168	0.3	70,542	0.3	60,090	0.2	77,039	0.3	124,629	0.4	143,379	0.5	
Plant Supplies	225,365	1.0	248,571	0.9	307,887	1.1	484,310	1.7	308,285	1.1	350,028	1.2	

	Audited 12/31/03	%	Audited 12/31/04	%	Audited 12/31/05	%	Audited 12/31/06	%	Audited 12/31/07	%	LTM as of 05/31/08	%	2008–2009 RMA (a) ratios %
Repairs and maintenance	123,072	0.5	156,285	0.6	164,664	0.6	179,094	0.6	165,446	0.6	160,910	0.6	
Utilities	143,438	0.6	160,934	0.6	149,792	0.5	167,726	0.6	156,276	0.5	157,659	0.6	
Freight	88,169	0.4	92,336	0.3	127,689	0.4	131,802	0.5	107,126	0.4	126,629	0.4	
Insurance General	346,680	1.5	355,517	1.3	414,806	1.4	475,212	1.6	479,000	1.7	470,618	1.6	
Other Taxes	73,955	0.3	81,126	0.3	79,473	0.3	82,893	0.3	83,883	0.3	83,883	0.3	
Depreciation and amortization	541,712	2.4	527,657	1.9	555,750	1.9	615,084	2.1	620,613	2.2	677,382	2.4	
Telephone	22,346	0.1	18,252	0.1	25,754	0.1	24,588	0.1	16,016	0.1	16,170	0.1	
Travel	—	0.0	15,602	0.1	10,365	0.1	77,424	0.3	35,832	0.1	33,528	0.1	
Employment - Ads/Relocate	—	0.0	6,240	0.0	30,404	0.0	26,567	0.1	15,207	0.1	27,507	0.1	
Outside Labor/Services	—	0.0	95,679	0.3	204,366	0.7	126,710	0.4	35,423	0.1	45,084	0.2	
Miscellaneous Expenses	162,105	0.7	32,258	0.1	453,392	1.6	(301,626)	-1.0	106,116	0.4	50,687	0.2	
Allocated Information Resources	45,360	0.2	107,880	0.4	145,800	0.5	103,508	0.4	99,384	0.3	87,234	0.3	
Allocated Building and Grounds	(322,293)	-1.4	(331,113)	-1.2	(355,931)	-1.2	(379,026)	-1.3	(324,569)	-1.1	(320,669)	-1.1	
Total Cost of Goods Sold	**10,126,745**	**43.9**	**12,294,308**	**44.6**	**14,365,517**	**50.0**	**14,583,824**	**50.4**	**13,628,300**	**47.7**	**13,346,010**	**46.7**	**56.4**
SELLING, GENERAL, AND ADMINISTRATIVE EXPENSES (SG&A)													
Salaries and wages	5,858,048	25.4	6,560,538	23.8	6,695,264	23.3	6,736,661	23.3	6,303,152	22.0	6,210,704	21.7	
Sales commissions	178,554	0.8	77,873	0.3	86,157	0.3	68,814	0.2	75,711	0.3	51,453	0.2	
Payroll taxes	430,944	1.9	482,627	1.8	485,507	1.7	497,559	1.7	478,122	1.7	456,711	1.6	
Profit sharing & 401-K	221,319	1.0	329,345	1.2	208,257	0.7	245,036	0.8	239,966	0.8	230,490	0.8	
Outside labor	—	0.0	402,126	1.5	386,390	1.3	411,935	1.4	327,800	1.1	270,027	0.9	
Employment ads	—	0.0	31,179	0.1	64,275	0.2	86,141	0.3	54,054	0.2	68,030	0.2	
Other taxes and licenses	48,815	0.2	192,051	0.7	51,030	0.2	119,394	0.4	42,744	0.1	33,683	0.1	
Rent	186,560	0.8	184,752	0.7	187,041	0.7	195,224	0.7	193,418	0.7	228,158	0.8	

(continues)

Exhibit 10.16 *continued*

	Audited 12/31/03	%	Audited 12/31/04	%	Audited 12/31/05	%	Audited 12/31/06	%	Audited 12/31/07	%	LTM as of 05/31/08	%	2008–2009 RMA (a) ratios %
Travel and entertainment	584,660	2.5	598,113	2.2	659,990	2.3	580,998	2.0	379,589	1.3	434,316	1.5	1.5
Insurance	296,900	1.3	320,939	1.2	316,590	1.1	472,124	1.6	424,731	1.5	393,023	1.4	1.4
Telephone	140,114	0.6	148,116	0.5	182,774	0.6	187,748	0.6	136,604	0.5	136,541	0.5	0.5
Patents and attorney	157,319	0.7	192,213	0.7	305,966	1.1	103,494	0.4	118,974	0.4	116,982	0.4	0.4
Legal and consulting	99,702	0.4	100,074	0.4	181,769	0.6	27,125	0.1	73,638	0.3	67,754	0.2	0.2
Audit and accounting	88,139	0.4	140,244	0.5	164,247	0.6	136,682	0.5	174,654	0.6	180,756	0.6	0.6
Directors and shareholders meetings	15,000	0.1	15,498	0.1	21,000	0.1	21,750	0.1	15,750	0.1	8,250	0.0	0.0
Advertising	93,845	0.4	102,905	0.4	128,559	0.4	118,071	0.4	108,336	0.4	123,993	0.4	0.4
Meetings and conferences	36,371	0.2	19,736	0.1	29,496	0.1	16,289	0.1	26,147	0.1	17,142	0.1	0.1
Printing and supplies	307,724	1.3	256,358	0.9	394,443	1.4	379,310	1.3	291,671	1.0	316,965	1.1	1.1
Trade shows	—	0.0	—	0.0	—	0.0	50,937	0.2	51,159	0.2	21,776	0.1	0.1
Royalty	—	0.0	—	0.0	—	0.0	43,592	0.2	151,676	0.5	72,032	0.3	0.3
Engineering design services	134,492	0.6	102,521	0.4	138,608	0.5	108,725	0.4	94,902	0.3	94,902	0.3	0.3
Freight and postage	220,454	1.0	271,739	1.0	350,205	1.2	297,432	1.0	270,537	0.9	272,349	1.0	1.0
Dues and subscriptions	53,454	0.2	59,889	0.2	67,203	0.2	69,504	0.2	56,307	0.2	46,017	0.2	0.2
Equipment and building maintenance	91,733	0.4	59,183	0.2	64,577	0.2	44,459	0.2	50,054	0.2	56,735	0.2	0.2
Depreciation and amortization	626,759	2.7	686,661	2.5	729,153	2.5	747,125	2.6	785,616	2.7	791,096	2.8	2.8
Miscellaneous	520,712	2.3	244,493	0.9	291,972	1.0	252,881	0.9	177,398	0.6	229,301	0.8	0.8
Allocated information resources costs	(45,360)	-0.2	(107,880)	-0.4	(145,800)	-0.5	(103,508)	-0.4	(99,384)	-0.3	(87,234)	-0.3	-0.3
Allocated building and grounds costs	322,293	1.4	331,112	1.2	355,931	1.2	379,026	1.3	324,569	1.1	320,669	1.1	1.1
Total SG&A	**10,668,543**	**46.3**	**11,802,399**	**42.8**	**12,400,599**	**43.2**	**12,294,521**	**42.5**	**11,327,889**	**39.6**	**11,162,615**	**39.5**	**33.1**

	G1		G2		G3		G4		G5		G6	
Interest Expense	1,535,303	6.7	1,532,672	5.6	1,516,313	5.3	1,596,369	5.5	1,533,153	5.4	1,510,803	5.3
Other Expenses (Foreign currency translation)	402,113	1.7	224,084	0.8	162,449	0.6	76,034	0.3	199,362	0.7	213,548	0.7
TOTAL COSTS AND EXPENSES	22,732,703	98.6	25,853,462	93.7	28,444,877	99.0	28,550,747	98.7	26,688,704	93.3	26,232,975	91.8
INCOME BEFORE TAXES	**318,627**	**1.4**	**1,724,277**	**6.3**	**275,861**	**1.0**	**370,941**	**1.3**	**1,910,451**	**6.7**	**2,352,702**	**8.2**
PROVISION FOR INCOME TAXES												
Current:												
Federal	229,500	1.0	506,400	1.8	213,867	0.7	(167,937)	-0.6	679,910	2.4	n/a	
State	45,150	0.2	112,800	0.4	40,620	0.1	(25,560)	-0.1	111,735	0.4	n/a	
Deferred:												
Federal	(322,083)	-1.4	(141,764)	-0.5	(496,500)	-1.7	(141,000)	-0.5	(48,563)	-0.2	n/a	
State	(16,500)	-0.1	(10,500)	-0.0	(36,000)	-0.1	(13,500)	-0.0	(3,000)	-0.0	n/a	
Total	(63,933)	-0.3	466,937	1.7	(278,013)	-1.0	(347,997)	-1.2	740,082	2.6	886,632	3.1
NET INCOME	**$382,560**	**1.7**	**$1,257,341**	**4.6**	**$553,874**	**1.9**	**$718,938**	**2.5**	**$1,170,369**	**4.1**	**$1,466,070**	**5.1**
Operating EBIT	2,256,042	9.8	3,481,032	12.6	1,954,622	6.8	2,043,344	7.1	3,642,966	12.7	4,077,053	14.3
Total Depreciation & Amortization	1,152,008	5.0	1,214,318	4.4	1,284,903	4.5	1,453,905	5.0	1,406,625	4.9	1,468,874	5.1
EBITDA	3,408,050	14.8	4,695,350	17.0	3,239,525	11.3	3,497,249	12.1	5,049,591	17.7	5,545,926	19.4

References:

Exhibit 10.17 Acme Measurement Devices, Inc.—Statements of Cash Flows

	12/31/02	Audited 12/31/03	Audited 12/31/04	Audited 12/31/05	Audited 12/31/06	Audited 12/31/07
Operating Cash Flow						
Net profit (current earnings)		382,560	1,257,341	553,874	718,938	1,170,369
+ depreciation & amortization		1,152,008	1,214,318	1,284,903	1,453,905	1,406,625
− increase/+decrease in current assets (except cash)		(722,286)	(610,095)	(2,257,016)	961,022	172,991
+ increase/−decrease of accounts payable and other payable		(432,770)	1,156,535	503,529	(1,125,204)	136,502
Total Operating Cash Flow		379,512	3,018,098	85,290	2,008,661	2,886,486
Investing Cash Flow						
−increase/+decrease in other assets (including long term investments)		(789,107)	(818,096)	(1,036,950)	(846,470)	(553,260)
−increase/+decrease of fixed assets (cost)		1,154,858	(382,764)	371,456	822,722	(763,439)
Total Investing Cash Flow		365,751	(1,200,860)	(665,495)	(23,748)	(1,316,699)
Financing Cash Flow						
+ increase/−decrease of payments under capital lease		(223,523)	(422,265)	(490,925)	(438,935)	(596,342)
+ increase/−decrease of shareholders' equity (shares redeemed, etc.)		(753,863)	24,537	(616,623)	(103,100)	(83,112)
Total Financing Cash Flow		(977,385)	(397,728)	(1,107,548)	(542,034)	(679,454)
Effect of exchange rate changes		(43,178)	(10,788)	(44,508)	(66,626)	(6,033)
Cash increase (decrease)		(275,300)	1,408,722	(1,732,260)	1,376,253	884,301
Cash beginning of period		3,575,126	3,299,826	4,708,548	2,976,288	4,352,541
Cash the end of the period	3,575,126	3,299,826	4,708,548	2,976,288	4,352,541	5,236,842

Exhibit 10.18   Acme Measurement Devices, Inc.—Debt-Free Working Capital Computation

Industry Debt-Free Working Capital Requirements (1)

	NAICS 334519 Manufacturing - Measuring & Controlling Devices	
	All	**$10 MM - $25 MM**
As a % of Total Assets		
Current Assets	69.2%	71.3%
Less: Current Liabilities	35.5%	36.1%
Working Capital	33.7%	35.2%
Working Capital	33.7%	35.2%
Plus: Notes Payable—Short-term	8.2%	7.3%
Plus: Current Mat.—L.T.D.	2.8%	1.0%
Debt-Free Working Capital (DFWC)	44.7%	43.5%
Debt-Free Working Capital	44.7%	43.5%
Times: Total Assets ($000)	$2,232,572	$237,115
Debt-Free Working Capital ($000)	$ 997,960	$103,145
Debt-Free Working Capital ($000)	$ 997,960	$103,145
Divided by: Total Sales ($000)	$3,079,775	$388,172
DFWC/Sales	**32.4%**	**26.6%**

Subject Historical Debt-Free Working Capital Requirements

	DFWC for the Company	**DFWC/Sales**
2005, 2006 Average	$6,270,007	21.9%
Most Recent Year	$7,076,240	24.8%
Concluded Debt-Free Working Capital Requirements (2)		25.0%

Notes:
(1) 2008-2009 Risk Management Association. Used with permission. © 2009 by RMA—The Risk Management Association. All rights reserved. No part of this table may be reproduced or utilized in any form or by any means, electronic or mechanical, including photocopying, recording, or by any information storage and retrieval system without permission in writing from RMA—The Risk Management Association. Please refer to www.rmahq.org for further warranty, copyright, and use of data information.
(2) We have relied on Acme's most recent year data.

Exhibit 10.19 Acme Measurement Devices, Inc. — Income Capitalization Method

	Audited 12/31/04	%	Audited 12/31/05	%	Audited 12/31/06	%	Audited 12/31/07	%	LTM as of 05/31/08	%	2004-2008 Average	%	Normalized Expected Scenario	%
Total Revenue	27,577,739	100.0	28,720,737	100.0	28,921,688	100.0	28,599,155	100.0	28,585,677	100.0	28,480,999	100.0	28,000,000	100.0
Reported Operating Income (Loss) (EBIT)	3,481,032	12.6	1,954,622	6.8	2,043,344	7.1	3,642,966	12.7	$ 4,077,053	14.3	3,039,803	10.7	n/a	
Adjustments to operating expenses														
Minus: Other income	(221,816)	-0.8	(233,999)	-0.8	(299,682)	-1.0	(257,847)	-0.9	(278,936)	-1.0	n/a		n/a	
Plus: Oven royalty	—	0.0	—	0.0	43,592	0.2	151,676	0.5	72,032	0.3	n/a		n/a	
Plus: Patents and attorney	72,213	0.3	185,966	0.6	—	0.0	—	0.0	—	0.0	n/a		n/a	
Plus: Legal expenses	—	0.0	106,769	0.4	(47,876)	-0.2	—	0.0	—	0.0	n/a		n/a	
	(149,603)	-0.5	58,736	0.2	(303,966)	-1.1	(106,172)	-0.4	(278,936)	-1.0	n/a		n/a	
Adjusted EBITDA	4,545,748	16.5	3,298,260	11.5	3,193,283	11.0	4,943,420	17.3	5,266,991	18.4	4,249,540	14.9	4,200,000	15.0
Adjusted (EBIT)	3,331,430	12.1	2,013,357	7.0	1,739,378	6.0	3,536,795	12.4	3,798,117	13.3	2,883,815	10.1	3,450,000	12.3
Minus: Taxes on EBIT 40%	(1,332,572)	-4.8	(805,343)	-2.8	(695,751)	-2.4	(1,414,718)	-4.9	(1,519,247)	-5.3	(1,153,526)	-4.1	(1,380,000)	4.9
Plus: Depreciation & Amortization	1,214,318	4.4	1,284,903	4.5	1,453,905	5.0	1,406,625	4.9	1,468,874	5.1	1,365,725	4.8	750,000	2.7
Minus: Capital Expenditures	(818,096)	-3.0	(1,036,950)	-3.6	(875,750)	-3.0	(553,260)	-1.9	(553,260)	-1.9	(767,463)	-2.7	(800,000)	2.9
Minus increases/ Plus decreases in Working Capital	654,300	2.4	(1,511,030)	-5.3	(164,597)	-0.6	256,698	0.9	(723,935)	-2.5	(297,713)	-1.0	(204,000)[1]	0.5
Equals: Net Cash Flow to overall invested capital	3,049,380	11.1	(55,062)	-0.2	1,457,186	5.0	3,232,140	11.3	2,470,549	8.6	2,030,838	7.1	1,816,000	6.5
													Round:	1,820,000

Note:
[1] Assumes average growth of 3% per year including normalized scenario expected.

Calculation of value

Net Cash Flow to overall invested capital	1,820,000
Debt-Free Net Cash Flow Capitalization Rate	11.00%
MVIC =	16,545,454
MVIC rounded =	16,500,000
+ Present value of depreciation over capital expenditures (tax benefit)	1,000,000
– Debt (Total obligation under capital lease)	–8,245,866
= 100% Minority equity, marketable	9,254,134
– Marketability Discount –35%	3,238,947
= 100% Equity value, on a minority interest	6,015,187
+ nonoperating assets discounted by 41.5%	2,408,491
= 100% Equity minority nonmarketable	**8,423,678**

Exhibit 10.20   Acme Measurement Devices, Inc.—Discount Capitalization Rate Analysis
                 [Illustration only]

Long-term U.S. Treasury Bond Yield (1)	4.74%
Average of excess return on S&P 500 over long-term Treasury Bond income returns, 1926-2007 (2) (Large Company Stocks Equity Risk Premium)	7.10%
Beta (3)	0.90
Expected excess return on equity, large company stock	6.39%
Average of excess return of "smallest decile" public company stocks over S&P 500, 1926-1999 (4)	5.82%
Equals expected return on average "smallest decile" public company	16.95%
(Also equals the equity net cash flow discount rate for an average "smallest decile" public company.)	
Adjustment for Risk Factors Specific to ACME (5)	4.00%
Equals Equity Net Cash Flow Discount Rate Specific to ACME	20.95%
Baa debt borrowing rate as of May 30, 2008 (6)	7.06%
Ratio of normal level of equity to total invested capital (7)	60%
Preliminary WACC (8)	14.26%
Less ACME's Assumed Average Long-Term Growth (9)	3.00%
Equals Debt-Free Net Cash Flow Capitalization Rate	11.26%
Rounded	11.00%

Notes:
(1) Source: 20-year U.S. Government Bond; Federal Reserve Statistical Release.
(2) Source: Stocks, Bonds, Bills and Inflation, *2008 Yearbook*, Ibbotson Associates ("SBBI - 2008").
(3) Beta relevered with the capital structure of the Company presented on point (7) below. Source: 2000 Cost of
    Capital Quarterly; median Adj, unlevered beta for SIC 3829. (fictitious)
(4) Source: 2000 Cost SBBI - 2008. The average "small" public company earning this excess return is represented
    by companies the size of the bottom 10 percent of New York Stock Exchange companies.
(5) Based on the financial data supplied and valuation issues discussed in this report.
(6) Source: Federal Reserve Statistical Release, May 30, 2008.
(7) Source: Based on the Company's level of indebtedness (The Obligation under Capital Lease was considered debt).
(8) Also known as the Weighted Average Cost of Capital, or WACC. Assumes a 40 percent tax rate.
(9) The estimated average annual nominal growth rate is approximately 3 percent which is equal to the estimated
    inflation as described in the "General Economic Overview" section of the report.

Exhibit 10.21   Acme Measurement Devices, Inc. — Transaction Data (some dates fictitious for illustrative purposes)

	Date Announced	Date Effective	Target Name	Target Business Description	Acquiror Name	% of Shares Acq.	Value of Trans. (a) ($mil)	Target Net Sales LTM ($mil)	Target Total Assets ($mil)	Target Dep. and Amort. LTM ($mil)	Target Operating Income EBIT LTM ($mil)	Value of Trans./ Target Net Sales LTM (times)	EBIT/ Net Sales (%)	Value of Trans./ Target Operating Income EBIT LTM (times)	Target Primary SIC Code
1	09/15/1995	01/11/1996	Data Measurement Corp	Mnfr measurement systems	Measurex Corp	100.00	32.2	27.8	23.7	0.4	2.3	1.16	8.27%	14.02	3829
2	09/09/1996	10/03/1996	Mundix Control Systems Inc	Mnfr measuring devices	Sytron Inc	100.00	1.5	1.1				1.36			3829
3	07/01/1997	07/01/1997	NDC Systems	Mnfr gauging equip	Fairey Group PLC	100.00	30.0	24.2			2.5	1.24	10.33%	12.00	3829
4	07/31/1997	08/29/1997	Gems Sensors	Mnfr measuring devices	Danaher Corp	100.00	85.0	75.0				1.13			3829
5	02/17/2006	02/17/2006	Waekon Industries Inc	Mnfr testing equipment	Hickok Inc	100.00	1.7	5.0	1.4	0.1	0.4	0.33	8.00%	4.13	3829
6	06/03/2006	08/05/2006	Satec Systems Inc	Mnfr testing equipment	Instron Corp	100.00	12.8	18.0				0.71			3829
7	05/04/2006	05/04/2006	American Meter Co.	Mnfr industrial instruments for measurement	Marcum Natural Gas Services Inc	100.00	3.3	4.8				0.69			3829
8	07/08/2006	07/08/2006	Atlantic Precision Products	Mnfr precision eqmnt component	Allied Devices Corp	100.00	13.8	10.0				1.38			3829
9	12/08/2006	12/08/2006	AEA Technology PLC	Mnfr radiation detection, measuring and protection equip	Packard Bioscience Co.	100.00	11.4	14.4				0.79			3826
10	06/30/2007	07/08/2007	PK Technology	Mnfr test, measurement equip	GN Nettest (GN Great Nordic)	100.00	43.0	32.0				1.34			3829
11	01/31/2008	05/03/2008	Metrika Systems Corp	Mnfr measurement technologies	Thermo Instrument Systems Inc	100.00	14.2	72.8	112.0	2.6	6.4	0.19	8.79%	2.21	3829
					Median—All transactions		13.8	18.0				1.13		8.06	
					Range: high		85.0	75.0				1.38		14.02	
					low		1.5	1.1				0.19		2.21	

CHAPTER 11

Business Valuation Standards

HISTORY OF VALUATION STANDARDS

The history of valuation standards has both a long-term and a short-term focus. The concept of establishing value is a fundamental premise of commerce. It is the basis upon which goods and services are exchanged. Estimates of value have formed the basis for transactions in commerce since ancient times. Yet it is only since the early 1980s that the business valuation/appraisal profession as we know it has evolved.

In the early years of the business valuation profession, Mr. Ray Miles of the Institute of Business Appraisers and Dr. Shannon Pratt of Willamette Management Associates were among the first to compile the body of business valuation knowledge into a coherent form. Miles's book, *Basic Business Appraisal*, was one of the earliest texts on the subject. Pratt's book, *Valuing a Business*, was first published in 1981, when business appraising as we know it was still in its infancy. Since the publication of these two seminal texts, a host of articles, newsletters, and books have been published on a variety of valuation topics that have added to the body of knowledge about valuation theory. The evolution of business valuation theory has led to an evolution in the standards that govern the profession.

Ironically, the event which triggered the creation of national business valuation standards, was not related to business valuation but was a real estate appraisal scandal. During the savings and loan (S&L) crisis of the mid- and late 1980s, S&L's came under congressional scrutiny for having made extensive questionable loans to entities based on appraisals prepared by real estate appraisers. Many of these appraisals valued the property much higher than the realizable value of the loans against the property, causing the Savings and Loans to have substantial losses when the loans defaulted.

The Appraisal Foundation, a private nonprofit educational organization, was created in 1987 to address problems in the appraisal industry. Led by a group of entities consisting primarily of governmental agencies and real estate appraisal groups, the Foundation adopted the Uniform Standards of Professional Appraisal Practice (USPAP) on January 30, 1989. USPAP is recognized throughout the United States as one of the generally accepted standards of professional appraisal practice and will be the primary focus of this chapter.

GOVERNMENT ACTION

The Financial Institution Reform, Recovery, and Enforcement Act (FIRREA) in the late 1980s adopted USPAP as the appraisal standard to be followed for specific federally related transactions. As a result, USPAP must be followed for transactions that come under the authority of these federal agencies:

- Federal Reserve Board
- Federal Deposit Insurance Corporation
- Office of the Comptroller of the Currency
- Office of Thrift Supervision
- National Credit Union Administration

> The Internal Revenue Service has not officially adopted USPAP or any other organization's standard.

The Appraisal Foundation has a board of trustees and two distinct operating boards, the Appraiser Qualifications Board and the Appraisal Standards Board.

The function of the Appraiser Qualifications Board is to establish qualifications for state licensing of appraisers. During the early 1990s, the qualifications were established for state licensing of real estate appraisers, and these qualifications were adopted across the country. During the late 1990s, the Appraiser Qualifications Board considered establishing qualifications for state licensing of personal property appraisers. Consideration also has been given to state licensing of business valuation appraisers, but there has been considerable opposition in the business valuation community and from state administrators. It does not appear that state licensing of business valuation appraisers will occur in the foreseeable future.

The function of the Appraisal Standards Board is to establish standards under which appraisers will conduct and report their work. The Appraisal Standards Board was formed in 1989 as a successor organization to the Ad Hoc Committee on Uniform Standards that originally developed the USPAP standards in 1986–1987. The Appraisal Standards Board is continually reviewing and revising the USPAP standards. It is fair to say that these standards, together with the standards of the other organizations discussed later in this chapter, form the foundation of appraisal practice.

One of the difficulties with USPAP is that it attempts to consolidate the standards for three separate and distinct disciplines of appraising into one set of uniform standards. Real estate valuation, personal property valuation, and business valuation each has its own idiosyncrasies.

The compromises in the USPAP standards reflect the difficulties in trying to force standards for each of these disciplines into one document.

However, although there are common rules, the specific standards for each appraisal discipline are applicable only to that discipline. For example, Standard 2, Real Property Appraisal Reporting, is applicable only to real estate and not personal property or business valuation.

ValTip

Terminology used in these standards is not uniform across the professions doing appraising work. For example, USPAP Standard 3 discusses the "review" of another appraiser's work. To certified public accountants doing business valuation, the term "review" carries a meaning that is unique to the accounting profession and represents a level of service related to financial statements.

The only standard that crosses the respective lines of appraisal discipline is standard 3—Appraisal Review, Development and Reporting. Litigation cases involving the use of experts on each side have given rise to valuation review analysis of the respective experts' work. There was a need for a standard to guide this critical analysis review work. Standard 3 was originally drafted to apply only to real estate appraisal. Its jurisdiction has now been extended to personal property appraisal and to business appraisal for several years.

In an attempt to bring some uniformity to business appraising terminology, a task force was formed to develop an *International Glossary of Business Valuation Terms (International Glossary)*. The task force consisted of representatives of the major North American organizations involved in business appraising. These organizations included the American Institute of Certified Public Accountants (AICPA), the American Society of Appraisers (ASA), the Institute of Business Appraisers (IBA), the National Association of Certified Valuation Analysts (NACVA), and the Canadian Institute of Chartered Business Valuators (CICBV). The *International Glossary* is presented in Chapter 1 of this book.

It is important to note that many of the terms and definitions in the *International Glossary* are not included in the definitions section of USPAP and vice versa. The Appraisal Foundation has not adopted the *International Glossary*, and there are some differences in definitions between common terms. Analysts are encouraged to become familiar with both sets of definitions.

ORGANIZATION OF THE USPAP STANDARDS

USPAP consists of 10 standards, with supplementary information providing explanation, clarification, and guidance. The introductory section of the standards includes definitions, a preamble, and four overriding rules of conduct. These rules cover ethics, competency, scope of work, and the jurisdictional exception. As of July 1, 2006, USPAP eliminated the departure rule and replaced it with a scope of work rule. In addition to the standards and the rules, the USPAP standards include Statements on Appraisal Standards which have the full weight of a Standards Rule. They also include Advisory Opinions that provide supplemental guidance but do not establish new standards or interpret existing standards.

The USPAP standards cover all three disciplines of appraising. Standards 1 through 6 cover real estate, Standards 3, 6, 7, and 8 cover personal property, and Standards 3, 9, and 10 cover businesses and intangible assets.

USPAP BUSINESS VALUATION STANDARDS (2010/2011)

> The pertinent sections of USPAP for the business appraiser include definitions, the preamble, the ethics rule, the competency rule, the scope of work rule, the jurisdictional exception rule, the standards and standards rules, and statements on appraisal standards. Standard 9 covers development of a business appraisal, Standard 10 covers reporting, and Standard 3 covers appraisal review.

The following is a summary of the introductory sections of the Uniform Standards of Professional Appraisal Practice (2010/2011) (used with permission).

Preamble

The preamble gives the overview of the standards and their application to the appraisal process.

Ethics Rule

The ethics rule consists of four parts including Conduct, Management, Confidentiality, and Record Keeping.

Conduct

The conduct section of the ethics rule suggests that the appraiser ". . . must not perform an assignment with bias." There must be no criminal conduct by the appraiser, and assignments must be performed "with impartiality, objectivity, and independence, and without accommodation of personal interests." New in 2010 is that an appraiser must disclose to the client, including the report certification, "any service regarding the subject property performed by the appraiser within the three year period immediately preceding acceptance of the assignment, as an appraiser or in any other capacity."

Management

The management section of the ethics rule deals with the prohibition against payment of undisclosed fees, the performance of appraisals contingent upon the reporting of a predetermined value, or the attainment of a stipulated result. It also prohibits advertising that is false and misleading.

Confidentiality

The confidentiality section of the ethics rule covers the protection of the appraiser-client relationship. It suggests that the appraiser must "act in good faith with regard to the legitimate interests of the client in the use of confidential information." It also prohibits the appraiser from disclosing any confidential client information except as required by due process of law or a duly authorized peer review committee. The appraiser must also be aware of, and comply with, all confidentiality and privacy laws and regulations applicable in an assignment.

Record Keeping

The record-keeping section of the ethics rule requires that the appraiser "prepare a workfile" for each appraisal engagement and specifies that the workfile contain certain information including the name of the client and identification of any intended users, a true copy of any written report, a summary of any oral reports or testimony, and other documentation sufficient to support the appraiser's work and conclusions of value. This section further requires that the appraiser retain the workfile for a period of "five years after preparation or at least two years after final disposition of any judicial proceeding," whichever is later.

Note: Certain engagements such as deal pricing and litigation, require the analyst or appraiser to sign a nondisclosure agreement. The analyst must be comfortable that adherence to the nondisclosure agreement does not violate the record-keeping standards of USPAP.

Competency Rule

The competency rule requires that the appraiser have "the knowledge and experience to complete the assignment competently." If the appraiser does not have the knowledge or experience, the appraiser must disclose this lack of knowledge to the client before accepting the assignment, take all necessary steps to complete the assignment competently, and describe the lack of knowledge and the work done to complete the assignment competently in the report. The appraiser may have to use the services of another qualified appraiser if the assignment requires experience or knowledge the appraiser does not have.

Scope of Work

The scope of work rule requires that for each appraisal, appraisal review, and appraisal consulting assignment, an appraiser must identify the problem to be solved, determine and perform the scope of work necessary to develop credible assignment results, and disclose the scope of work in the report.

The scope of work rule was implemented July 1, 2006, and eliminated the limited appraisal and the departure rule. In essence, the scope of work rule dictates that there will be only one type of appraisal report under USPAP, and the scope of work section will describe the level of work done in completing the assignment. It is up to the reader to determine whether the scope of work is adequate for the reader's purpose. The scope of work is acceptable when it meets or exceeds the expectations of the parties who are the intended users and meets or exceeds what an appraiser's peers' actions would be in performing a similar assignment. The report must contain sufficient information to allow intended users to understand the scope of work performed.

Jurisdictional Exception Rule

The jurisdictional exception rule provides that if any part of the Uniform Standards is contrary to the law or public policy in any jurisdiction, "only that part of USPAP becomes void for that assignment." An appraiser must also "identify the law or regulation that precludes compliance with USPAP" and "cite in the report the law or regulation requiring this exception to USPAP compliance."

Standard 3—Appraisal Review, Development, and Reporting (2010/2011)

This standard has been expanded to apply to each of the three appraisal disciplines covered by USPAP. It has been further expanded into parts to cover the development and reporting of the review of the work of another appraiser. The seven rules under Standard 3 are summarized here (Note: There are many changes in the 2010/2011 edition):

Rule 3-1. Rule 3-1 documents the requirements for competency and due diligence found in the development sections of the other appraisal standards.

Rule 3-2. Rule 3-2 documents the elements necessary to properly identify the purpose of the appraisal review and to determine the scope of work needed. It discusses the client and the intended users, the intended use, the purpose, the characteristics of the work under review, the effective date of the review, and the assignment conditions.

Rule 3-3. Rule 3-3 documents the requirements for development of an appraisal review. "The reviewer is required to develop an opinion as to the completeness, accuracy, adequacy, relevance, and reasonableness in the work under review, given law, regulation, or intended user requirements applicable to the work under review." It goes on to cover the development requirements when reviewers provide their own opinion of value or review opinion.

Rule 3-4. Rule 3-4 documents the general requirements that apply to the reporting of an appraisal review assignment.

Rule 3-5. Rule 3-5 documents the specific reporting requirements for an appraisal review assignment, including identification of the minimum report content. It goes on to document the reporting requirements when reviewers provide their own opinion of value or review opinion related to the work.

Rule 3-6. Rule 3-6 documents the certification requirements for an Appraisal Review Report. These requirements are consistent with the other USPAP standards.

Rule 3-7. Rule 3-7 documents the requirements for an oral Appraisal Review Report.

Standard 9 (2010/2011)

USPAP Standard 9 covers development of the business appraisal. It requires the appraiser to take all the steps necessary to produce a credible appraisal. The five explanatory rules under Standard 9 are summarized here.

Rule 9-1. Rule 9-1 requires the appraiser to "be aware of, understand, and correctly employ those recognized methods and procedures that are necessary to produce a credible appraisal," "not commit a substantial error of omission or commission that significantly affects an appraisal," and "not render appraisal services in a careless or negligent manner."

Essentially, this rule charges the appraiser with the responsibility to know and to correctly employ the generally accepted appraisal techniques for the type of engagement being undertaken.

Rule 9-2. Rule 9-2 requires the appraiser to identify:

(a) The client and any other intended users
(b) The intended use of the appraiser's opinions and conclusions
(c) The standard (type) and definition of value and the premise of value
(d) The effective date of the appraisal
(e) The characteristics of the subject property relevant to the standard (type) and definition of value and intended use of the appraisal
(f) Any extraordinary assumptions in the assignment
(g) Any hypothetical conditions necessary in the assignment
(h) The scope of work necessary to produce credible assignment results

Rule 9-3. Rule 9-3 asks the appraiser to consider the liquidation value of the enterprise and to consider that liquidation value may be greater than the value in continued operation (as a going concern).

Rule 9-4. Rule 9-4 requires the appraiser to collect and analyze all information pertinent to the appraisal problem and to use one or more of the approaches that apply to the specific appraisal assignment. It further requires the appraiser, where relevant, to include in the analysis data regarding:

(a) The nature and history of the business or intangible asset
(b) Financial and economic conditions affecting the business enterprise or intangible asset, its industry, and the general economy
(c) Past results, current operations, and future prospects of the business enterprise
(d) Past sales of capital stock or other ownership interests in the business enterprise or intangible asset being appraised
(e) Sales of capital stock or other ownership interests in similar business enterprises
(f) Prices, terms, and conditions affecting past sales of similar ownership interests in the asset being appraised or a similar asset
(g) Economic benefit of tangible and intangible assets

An appraiser must, when necessary for credible results, analyze the effect on value, if any, of:

(a) Buy-sell and option agreements, investment letter stock restrictions, restrictive clauses, and similar features that may influence value
(b) The extent to which the interest appraised contains elements of control and is marketable and/or liquid

This rule requires the appraiser to consider issues very similar to those required by IRS Revenue Ruling 59-60.

Rule 9-5. Rule 9-5 requires the appraiser to reconcile the applicability or relevance of the various approaches, methods, and procedures used to arrive at a value as well as the quality and quantity of the data used.

Standard 10 (2010/2011)

Just as Standard 9 sets forth the requirements for developing an appraisal, Standard 10 sets forth the requirements for reporting on the appraisal assignment. The standard emphasizes that the appraiser has an obligation to communicate the results of the appraisal in a "manner that is not misleading."

The four rules under Standard 10 are summarized next.

Rule 10-1. Written or oral appraisal reports must:

(a) Clearly and accurately set forth the appraisal in a manner that will not be misleading
(b) Contain sufficient information to enable the intended user(s) to understand it
(c) Clearly and accurately disclose all assumptions and limiting conditions, extraordinary assumptions, hypothetical conditions and limiting conditions

Rule 10-2. Written valuation reports must either be an Appraisal Report or a Restricted Use Appraisal Report. Rule 10-2(a) is the rule that sets forth the minimum disclosure requirements for an Appraisal Report. Rule 10-2(b) is the rule that sets forth the minimum disclosure requirements for a Restricted Use Appraisal Report.

(a) The Appraisal Report must be consistent with the intended use of the appraisal and

  (i) State the identity of the client and any intended users by name or type
  (ii) State the intended use of the appraisal
  (iii) Summarize information sufficient to identify the entity or asset appraised
  (iv) State any elements of ownership control contained in the interest being appraised
  (v) State any elements of lack of marketability and/or liquidity
  (vi) State the standard (type) and definition of value and premise of value and sources
  (vii) State the effective date of the appraisal and the report date
  (viii) Summarize the scope of the work used to develop the appraisal
  (ix) Summarize the information analyzed, the appraisal procedures followed, and the reasoning used including exclusion of any approach
  (x) State all extraordinary assumptions and hypothetical conditions and how they affected the results
  (xi) Include a certification signed by the appraiser as described by Rule 10-3

(b) The Restricted Use Appraisal Report must be consistent with the intended use and must:
  (i) State the identity of the client by name or type and limit the report use to the client.
  (ii) State the intended use of the appraisal
  (iii) Identify the business or intangible asset and the interest appraised
  (iv) State any elements of control contained in the interest being appraised
  (v) State any elements of lack of marketability and/or liquidity
  (vi) State the standard (type) and definition of value and premise of value and source of its definition
  (vii) State the effective date of the appraisal and the report date
  (viii) State the scope of the work performed
  (ix) State the appraisal procedures followed and the value opinions and conclusions reached; reference the workfile; explain exclusion of any approach
  (x) State all extraordinary assumptions and hypothetical conditions and how they affected the results
  (xi) Include a certification signed by the appraiser according to Rule 10-3

Rule 10-3. Each written business appraisal report must contain a signed certification similar in content to the following:

I certify that, to the best of my knowledge and belief:

- The statements of fact contained in this report are true and correct.
- The reported analyses, opinions, and conclusions are limited only by the reported assumptions and limiting conditions and are my personal, impartial, and unbiased professional analyses, opinions, and conclusions.
- I have no (or the specified) present or prospective future interest in the property that is the subject of this report, and I have no (or the specified) personal interest with respect to the parties involved.
- I have no bias with respect to the property that is the subject of this report or to the parties involved with this assignment.
- My engagement in this assignment was not contingent on developing or reporting predetermined results.
- My compensation for completing this assignment is not contingent on the development or reporting of a predetermined value or direction in value that favors the cause of the client, the amount of the value opinion, the attainment of a stipulated result, or the occurrence of a subsequent event directly related to the intended use of this appraisal.
- My analyses, opinions, and conclusions were developed, and this report has been prepared, in conformity with the Uniform Standards of Professional Appraisal Practice.
- No one provided significant business valuation assistance to the person signing this certification. (If there are exceptions, the name of each must be stated.)

This certification represents a reaffirmation that the appraiser performed the work in conformity with the requirements set forth in Standard 9.

Rule 10-4. An oral business appraisal report must, at a minimum, address the substantive matters set forth in Standards Rule 10-2(a).

Summary of USPAP

Uniform Standards 9 and 10 and their related rules set forth the minimum standards that should be followed; they represent the mainstream of business valuation standards but are not intended to be all-inclusive. Standard 3, review of another appraiser's work, also applies to business valuation and should be read carefully to ensure proper compliance.

For CPAs, the word "certify" has special meaning concerning attestation of financial information. Some CPAs will add a sentence in their report that they are not certifying any financial information but are adhering to the appraisal certification requirements of USPAP. In the proposed business valuation standards of the AICPA, the word certification is replaced with representation.

Although many federal agencies have adopted USPAP as the standard for their appraisal reports, as previously stated, one of the largest users of valuation reports, the Internal Revenue Service (IRS), has not adopted these standards. The IRS has chosen to issue its own guidelines for business valuation, as described later in this chapter.

OTHER BUSINESS VALUATION STANDARDS AND CREDENTIALS

While the Appraisal Standards Board of the Appraisal Foundation was among the first to issue business valuation standards, other organizations either had or would develop their own standards and/or valuation guidelines. Among these groups are the American Society of Appraisers, the Institute of Business Appraisers, the National Association of Certified Valuation Analysts, the Canadian Institute of Chartered Business Valuators, the American Institute of Certified Public Accountants, and the Internal Revenue Service.

A brief summary of the standards and credential activity of each organization follows.

American Society of Appraisers

The American Society of Appraisers, a multidiscipline organization, was one of the early participants in formation of the Appraisal Foundation. Although its roots are primarily in the real estate appraising industry, it offers credentials in personal property appraising and in business valuation, which is its fastest-growing segment.

Membership in the American Society of Appraisers is available as an associate, candidate, or credentialed member. Credentials are available upon passing an examination and having one appraisal report approved by the credentials committee. Two credentials are available in each discipline: the Accredited Senior Appraiser (ASA) and the Accredited Member (AM). The difference between the two is that the ASA requires five years of full-time equivalent appraising experience while the AM requires only two years of full-time equivalent appraising experience.

The business valuation standards of the American Society of Appraisers date from the early 1990s. The standards provide for three types of appraisal engagements: Appraisal, Limited Appraisal, and Calculations. The calculation is similar to a consulting type of engagement and may be based on a more restrictive scope than either of the other two types of engagements.

The American Society of Appraisers business valuation standards include an explanatory preamble and nine standards. Supplemental guidance is offered through Statements of Business Valuation Standards, Advisory Opinions, and Procedural Guidelines. The American Society of Appraisers also requires adherence to USPAP in appraisal services situations.

The American Society of Appraisers can be contacted at 555 Herndon Parkway, Suite 125, Herndon, VA 20170; Phone: (703) 478-2228; Fax: (703) 742-8471; E-mail: asainfo@appraisers.org or on the Web at www.appraisers.org. There is a web site specific to business valuation at www.bvappraisers.org.

Institute of Business Appraisers

The Institute of Business Appraisers, through its founder Ray Miles, and its current CEO Howard Lewis, have been active in the business valuation community since

1978. It offers the Certified Business Appraiser (CBA) credential upon passing a proctored examination, having two business valuation reports approved by the report committee, and education and experience requirements. It also offers these certifications: Master Certified Business Appraiser (MCBA), Accredited by IBA (AIBA), Business Valuator Accredited for Litigation (BVAL), and Accredited in Business Appraisal Review (ABAR). The MCBA differs from the CBA by requiring more than 10 years as a CBA and additional experience. BVAL is for appraisers who meet requirements in expert testimony and litigation. ABAR is for appraisers who review work product performed by others.

The Institute of Business Appraisers' business valuation standards were first published in 1993 and have been revised periodically since then with the latest edition as of October 25, 2001 (a new revised version is expected in 2010/2011). The standards are somewhat unique in that in addition to preparation and written report standards, there are standards for oral appraisal reports and expert testimony.

The Institute of Business Appraisers can be contacted at P.O. Box 17410, Plantation, FL 33318; Phone (954) 584-1144. The web site is www.instbusapp.org.

Canadian Institute of Chartered Business Valuators

The Canadian Institute of Chartered Business Valuators (CICBV) is a sister organization to the Canadian Institute of Chartered Accountants (CICA). Instead of offering the credential within the CICA, the Canadian Institute decided to form a separate organization to offer the CBV credential and to issue standards.

As might be expected, the standards of the CICBV are tailored to the Canadian Securities Industry and to valuation in Canadian commerce.

The business valuation standards include standards on valuation reporting, scope of work, file documentation, and advisory and expert report disclosures. There are appendixes related to fairness opinions and other pertinent issues. The standards differentiate among a valuation report, an advisory report, and an expert report and provide the criteria for each.

The CICBV team members lent an international perspective to the Business Valuation Glossary of Terms project completed in 2000.

The Canadian Institute of Chartered Business Valuators can be reached at 277 Wellington Street West, 5th Floor, Toronto, Ontario M5V 3H2. The web site for the CICBV is http://cicbv.ca and the email contact is admin@cicbv.ca.

The National Association of Certified Valuation Analysts

The National Association of Certified Valuation Analysts (NACVA) offers a credential in business appraising as a Certified Valuation Analyst (CVA). To qualify, candidates must hold a valid CPA license, pass a half-day proctored exam, and a take home exam (report/case study). There are also educational requirements to sit for exams and for recertification.

NACVA also offers other certifications as follows: Accredited Valuation Analyst (AVA) and Certified Forensic Financial Analyst (CFFA). For valuation, the CVA differs from the AVA in that it requires a valid CPA license. The CFFA is focused on experience and knowledge in professional forensic financial litigation support services.

NACVA first published its business valuation standards in the mid-1990s with periodic updates since then. The latest version is effective January 1, 2008. The NACVA standards focus on the development of the opinion of value and on reporting.

NACVA can be reached at 1111 East Brickyard Road, Suite 200, Salt Lake City, UT, 84106-5401; Phone (801) 486-0600; Fax (801) 486-7500. The web address is www.nacva.com.

The American Institute of Certified Public Accountants

With approximately 335,000 members, the American Institute of Certified Public Accountants is one of the largest organizations of accountants in the world. Like the American Society of Appraisers, many AICPA members are in fields other than business valuation.

The AICPA is the latest of the organizations to offer a credential in business valuation. Its Accredited in Business Valuation (ABV) credential was first offered in 1997. Its credential requirements include an eight-hour proctored examination and demonstrated experience in business valuation. There are follow-up requirements for reaccreditation every three years including continuing professional education and continued involvement in additional business valuation engagements.

The AICPA currently has business valuation standards under development, and it does have more general standards that all CPAs, including those performing business valuations, must follow. These include the code of professional conduct and statement on standards for consulting services.

Because of the AICPA's close ties to the financial community rule makers and to the IRS through its members' tax services to clients, the need for specific AICPA business valuation standards was recognized, and the first of its business valuation standards was effective for engagements accepted after January 1, 2008.

The AICPA can be reached at its headquarters at 1211 Avenue of the Americas, New York, NY 10036; Phone (212) 596-2000. The web addresses are www.aicpa.org and www.cpa2biz.com.

For additional information and a discussion of the AICPA BV standards, see Addendum 1 at the end of the chapter, "Standards: A Summary of the AICPA's New BV Standards," *Financial Valuation and Litigation Expert*, Issue 8, August/ September 2007, Valuation Products and Services, LLC.

The Internal Revenue Service

The IRS is closely involved in business valuation for tax purposes. It is committed to upgrading the level of training for its business valuation team.

As a component of this improvement process, in 2001 the IRS Review Team issued its Recommendations on Internal Revenue Service Valuation Policies. This overview document provides recommendations to upgrade IRS policies in all areas of valuation. The team considered but did not recommend the adoption of USPAP for IRS purposes.

This IRS document is an encouraging step. It sends a clear signal that the IRS is closely following developments in the valuation industry. The entire profession will benefit if the IRS participates in the business valuation professional developmental process. Addendum 2 at the end of this chapter presents the current IRS Business Valuation Guidelines in the form of a checklist.

U.S. Financial Reporting Requirements

With the issuance of Statements of Financial Accounting Standards (SFAS)[1] 123(R), 141(R), 142, and 157, the Financial Accounting Standards Board (FASB) has significantly changed the rules related to accounting for goodwill and other intangible value in U.S. financial statements.

> The FASB provides guidance for how to measure fair value of financial and non financial assets and liabilities under authoritative accounting pronouncements. This fair value measurement is for financial statement purposes and is not to be confused with fair value in dissenting shareholder cases that is determined according to state laws and court decisions in the respective states.

With the requirement to demonstrate "substantial impairment" before goodwill can be written down or removed, the FASB has changed the nature of financial reporting so that reporting units of companies will have to be tested and/or revalued periodically for impairment.

As the global business environment continued to expand, demands for harmonization of U.S. and International Financial Reporting Standards (IFRS) are being heard from a number of sectors. The FASB and the International Accounting Standards Board (IASB), the developer of IFRS, are working together toward this end.

The FASB has also launched its new Accounting Standards Codification effective July 1, 2009. This document is the single source of authoritative U.S. Generally Accepted Accounting Principles (GAAP). It is believed that this document will be the basis for U.S. GAAP as it is harmonized with IFRS and the two sides work toward a unified set of accounting standards.

SUMMARY

A broad-based and highly visible national focus on valuation standards began with the Uniform Standards of Professional Appraisal Practice from the Appraisal Foundation. Business Valuation Standards have evolved into expanded publications by a number of appraisal organizations, some of which had prior standards. With increasing emphasis from the Internal Revenue Service and expanded reporting requirements imposed by the financial reporting community, valuation standards will take on increased importance as the role of the business appraiser expands in the financial reporting arena.

---

[1] New Accounting Standards Codification (ASC) is now in place.

ADDENDUM 1—STANDARDS: A SUMMARY OF THE AICPA'S NEW BV STANDARDS[2]

After almost six years of continuous writing, exposure, rewrites, and more exposures, the American Institute of Certified Public Accountants, through its Consulting Services Executive Committee, released (June 2007) the final version of its business valuation standards. Titled *Statement on Standards for Valuation Services no. 1 (SSVS 1), Valuation of a Business, Business Ownership Interest, Security, or Intangible Asset,* these standards apply to all CPAs who are members of the AICPA. The effective date was for engagements accepted after January 1, 2008, although early adoption was encouraged.[3]

It is expected that the individual state boards of accountancy will also adopt these standards, which will then become part of their rules and regulations. One interesting twist is likely to happen that will affect appraisers who do not belong to the AICPA: some accounting firms may encourage, if not require, appraisers preparing fair value appraisals for financial reporting purposes to abide by these standards, regardless of whether the appraiser is a CPA. Appraisers who are not members of the AICPA should communicate with the client and the auditors about whether compliance is desired or expected. Either way, it is probably a good idea for all appraisers to familiarize themselves with these standards. We hope to assist in that regard by providing this summary of many of the most salient provisions of *SSVS 1.* Key terms are highlighted in bold type. Most of this material was extracted and quoted verbatim from *SSVS 1.* The paragraph number from *SSVS 1* is in [brackets].

Let's start with some terminology. [2] ". . . the term **engagement to estimate value** refers to an engagement or any part of an engagement (for example, a tax, litigation, or acquisition-related engagement) that involves estimating the value of a subject interest." The estimate of value can be expressed as either a **conclusion of value** or a **calculated value.** A person who estimates value is referred to in the standards as a **valuation analyst.**

[4] ". . . the valuation analyst applies **valuation approaches** and **valuation methods** . . . and uses **professional judgment.** The use of professional judgment is an essential component of estimating value."

Exceptions

There are some exceptions. This statement is not applicable:

[5] ". . . to a member who participates in estimating the value of a subject interest as part of performing an attest engagement defined by Rule 101 of the AICPA Code of Professional Conduct (for example, as part of an audit, review, or compilation engagement)."

[6] ". . . when the value of a subject interest is provided to the member by the client or a third party, and the member does not apply valuation approaches and methods, as discussed in this Statement."

---

[2] *Financial Valuation and Litigation Expert,* Issue 8, August/September 2007, front page, Valuation Products and Services, LLC, www.valuationproducts.com, used with permission.

[3] Ed Dupke, Jim Alerding, and Jim Hitchner, *FVLE* editor, were members of the AICPA Business Valuation Standards Writing Task Force during the entire six-year process.

[7] ". . . to internal use assignments from employers to employee members not in the *practice of public accounting,* as that term is defined in the AICPA *Code of Professional Conduct* (AICPA, *Professional Standards*, Vol. 2, ET sec. 92. 25)."

[8] ". . . to engagements that are exclusively for the purpose of determining economic damages (for example, lost profits) unless those determinations include an engagement to estimate value."

[9] ". . . to **mechanical computations** that do not rise to the level of an engagement to estimate value; that is, when the member does not apply valuation approaches and methods and does not use professional judgment."

[9] ". . . when it is not practical or not reasonable to obtain or use relevant information; as a result, the member is unable to apply valuation approaches and methods that are described in this Statement."

There are also references to illustrations in Interpretation No. 1, which is attached to the Standards.

Jurisdictional Exception

[10] "If any part of this Statement differs from published governmental, judicial, or accounting authority, or such authority specifies valuation development procedures or valuation reporting procedures, then the valuation analyst should follow the applicable published authority or stated procedures with respect to that part applicable to the valuation in which the member is engaged. The other parts of this Statement continue in full force and effect."

Competency

[11] "Performing a valuation engagement with **professional competence** involves special knowledge and skill. A valuation analyst should possess a level of knowledge of valuation principles and theory and a level of skill in the application of such principles that will enable him or her to identify, gather, and analyze data, consider and apply appropriate valuation approaches and methods, and use professional judgment in developing the estimate of value (whether a single amount or a range). An in-depth discussion of valuation theory and principles, and how and when to apply them, is not within the scope of this Statement."

Objectivity and Conflict of Interest

[14] "The AICPA **Code of Professional Conduct** requires **objectivity** in the performance of all professional services, including valuation engagements. Objectivity is a state of mind. The principle of objectivity imposes the obligation to be impartial, intellectually honest, disinterested, and free from conflicts of interest. If necessary, where a potential **conflict of interest** may exist, a valuation analyst should make the disclosures and obtain consent as required under Interpretation No. 102-2, 'Conflicts of Interest,' under Rule 102, *Integrity and Objectivity* (AICPA, *Professional Standards*, Vol. 2, ET sec. 102.03)."

Independence and Valuation

[15] "If valuation services are performed for a client for which the valuation analyst or valuation analyst's firm also performs an attest engagement (defined by

Rule 101 of the AICPA *Code of Professional Conduct*), the valuation analyst should meet the requirements of Interpretation No. 101-3, 'Performance of Nonattest Services,' under Rule 101, *Independence* (AICPA, *Professional Standards*, Vol. 2, ET sec. 101.05), so as not to impair the member's independence with respect to the client."

Scope Restrictions or Limitations

[19] "A **restriction** or **limitation** on the scope of the valuation analyst's work, or the data available for analysis, may be present and known to the valuation analyst at the outset of the valuation engagement or may arise during the course of a valuation engagement. Such a restriction or limitation should be disclosed in the valuation report. . . ."

Using the Work of Specialists in the Engagement to Estimate Value

[20] "In performing an engagement to estimate value, the valuation analyst may rely on the work of a **third party specialist** (for example, a real estate or equipment appraiser). The valuation analyst should note in the **assumptions and limiting** conditions the level of responsibility, if any, being assumed by the valuation analyst for the work of the third party specialist. At the option of the valuation analyst, the written report of the third party specialist may be included in the valuation analyst's report."

Development/Types of Engagements

[21] "There are two types of engagements to estimate value—**a valuation engagement** and a **calculation engagement**. The valuation engagement requires more procedures than does the calculation engagement. The valuation engagement results in a conclusion of value. The calculation engagement results in a calculated value. The type of engagement is established in the understanding with the client. . . .
a. Valuation engagement—A valuation analyst performs a valuation engagement when 1) the engagement calls for the valuation analyst to estimate the value of a subject interest and 2) the valuation analyst estimates the value . . . and is free to apply the valuation approaches and methods he or she deems appropriate in the circumstances. The valuation analyst expresses the results of the valuation as a conclusion of value; the conclusion may be either a single amount or a range.
b. Calculation engagement—A valuation analyst performs a calculation engagement when 1) the valuation analyst and the client agree on the valuation approaches and methods the valuation analyst will use and the extent of procedures the valuation analyst will perform in the process of calculating the value of a subject interest (these procedures will be more limited than those of a valuation engagement) and 2) the valuation analyst calculates the value in compliance with the agreement. The valuation analyst expresses the results of these procedures as a calculated value. The calculated value is expressed as a range or as a single amount. A calculation engagement does not include all of the procedures required for a valuation engagement. . . ."

Hypothetical Conditions

[22] "**Hypothetical conditions** affecting the subject interest may be required in some circumstances. When a valuation analyst uses hypothetical conditions during a valuation or calculation engagement, he or she should indicate the purpose for including the hypothetical conditions and disclose these conditions in the valuation or calculation report. . . ."

Rules of Thumb

[39] "Although technically not a valuation method, some valuation analysts use **rules of thumb** or industry benchmark indicators (hereinafter collectively referred to as rules of thumb) in a valuation engagement. A rule of thumb is typically a reasonableness check against other methods used and should generally not be used as the only method to estimate the value of the subject interest."

Subsequent Events

[43] "The **valuation date** is the specific date at which the valuation analyst estimates the value of the subject interest and concludes on his or her estimation of value. Generally, the valuation analyst should consider only circumstances existing at the valuation date and events occurring up to the valuation date. An event that could affect the value may occur subsequent to the valuation date; such an occurrence is referred to as a **subsequent event.** Subsequent events are indicative of conditions that were not **known or knowable** at the valuation date, including conditions that arose subsequent to the valuation date. The valuation would not be updated to reflect those events or conditions. Moreover, the valuation report would typically not include a discussion of those events or conditions because a valuation is performed as of a point in time—the valuation date—and the events described in this subparagraph, occurring subsequent to that date, are not relevant to the value determined as of that date."

[43] "In situations in which a valuation is meaningful to the intended user beyond the valuation date, the events may be of such nature and significance as to warrant disclosure (at the option of the valuation analyst) in a separate section of the report in order to keep users informed. . . . Such disclosure should clearly indicate that information regarding the events is provided for informational purposes only and does not affect the determination of value as of the specified valuation date."

The Valuation Report

[47] "A valuation report is a **written** or **oral communication** to the client containing the conclusion of value or the calculated value of the subject interest. Reports issued for purposes of certain controversy proceedings are exempt from this reporting standard. . . ."

[48] "The three types of written reports that a valuation analyst may use to communicate the results of an engagement to estimate value are: for a valuation engagement, a **detailed report** or a **summary report;** and for a calculation engagement, a **calculation report.**"

Communicating an Estimate of Value in a Valuation Engagement

[48] "*a. Detailed Report:* This report may be used only to communicate the results of a valuation engagement (conclusion of value); it should not be used to communicate the results of a calculation engagement (calculated value). . . .
b. Summary Report: This report may be used only to communicate the results of a valuation engagement (conclusion of value); it should not be used to communicate the results of a calculation engagement (calculated value). . . .

For a valuation engagement, the determination of whether to prepare a detailed report or a summary report is based on the level of reporting detail agreed to by the valuation analyst and the client."

Communicating an Estimate of Value in a Calculation Engagement

[48] "*c. Calculation Report:* This type of report should be used only to communicate the results of a calculation engagement (calculated value); it should not be used to communicate the results of a valuation engagement (conclusion of value). . . ."

Restrictions

[49] "The valuation analyst should indicate in the valuation report the restrictions on the use of the report (which may include restrictions on the users of the report, the uses of the report by such users, or both). . . ."

Reporting Exemption for Certain Controversy Proceedings

[50] "A valuation performed for a matter before a court, an arbitrator, a mediator or other facilitator, or a matter in a governmental or administrative proceeding, is exempt from the reporting provisions of this Statement. The reporting exemption applies whether the matter proceeds to trial or settles. The exemption applies only to the reporting provisions of this Statement. . . . The provisions of the Statement . . . still apply whenever the valuation analyst expresses a conclusion of value or a calculated value. . . ."

Detailed Report

[51] "The *detailed report* is structured to provide sufficient information to permit intended users to understand the data, reasoning, and analyses underlying the valuation analyst's conclusion of value."

Financial Information Disclosures

[54] "If the financial information includes financial statements that were reported on (audit, review, compilation, or attest engagement performed under the Statements on Standards for Attestation Engagements [SSAEs]) by the valuation analyst's firm, the valuation report should disclose this fact and the type of report issued."
[54] "If the valuation analyst or the valuation analyst's firm did not audit, review, compile, or attest under the SSAEs to the financial information, the valuation analyst should so state and should also state that the valuation analyst assumes no responsibility for the financial information."

[55] "The financial information may be derived from or may include information derived from tax returns. With regard to such derived information and other tax information . . . the valuation analyst should identify the tax returns used and any existing relationship between the valuation analyst and the tax preparer."

[55] "If the valuation analyst or the valuation analyst's firm did not audit, review, compile, or attest under the SSAEs to any financial information derived from tax returns that is used during the valuation engagement, the valuation analyst should so state and should also state that the valuation analyst assumes no responsibility for that derived information."

[56] "If the financial information used was derived from financial statements prepared by management that were not the subject of an audit, review, compilation, or attest engagement performed under the SSAEs, the valuation report should:

- Identify the financial statements
- State that, as part of the valuation engagement, the valuation analyst did not audit, review, compile, or attest under the SSAEs to the financial information and assumes no responsibility for that information."

Representation of the Valuation Analyst

[65] "Each written report should contain the representation of the valuation analyst. The representation is the section of the report wherein the valuation analyst summarizes the factors that guided his or her work during the engagement.
(See Exhibit 11.1 for an example extracted from *SSVS 1*.)

Exhibit 11.1   Valuation Analyst Representation

[65] "*a.* The analyses, opinions, and conclusion of value included in the valuation report are subject to the specified assumptions and limiting conditions . . . and they are the personal analyses, opinions, and conclusion of value of the valuation analyst.

b. The economic and industry data included in the valuation report have been obtained from various printed or electronic reference sources that the valuation analyst believes to be reliable (any exceptions should be noted). The valuation analyst has not performed any corroborating procedures to substantiate that data.

c. The valuation engagement was performed in accordance with the American Institute of Certified Public Accountants Statement on Standards for Valuation Services.

d. The parties for which the information and use of the valuation report is restricted are identified; the valuation report is not intended to be and should not be used by anyone other than such parties.

e. The analyst's compensation is fee-based or is contingent on the outcome of the valuation.

f. The valuation analyst used the work of one or more outside specialists to assist during the valuation engagement. (An outside specialist is a specialist other than those employed in the valuation analyst's firm.) If the work of such a specialist was used, the specialist should be identified. The valuation report should include a statement identifying the level of responsibility, if any, the valuation analyst is assuming for the specialist's work.

g. The valuation analyst has no obligation to update the report or the opinion of value for information that comes to his or her attention after the date of the report.

h. The valuation analyst and the person(s) assuming responsibility for the valuation should sign the representation in their own name(s). The names of those providing significant professional assistance should be identified."

Representations Regarding Information Provided to the Valuation Analyst

[66] "It may be appropriate for the valuation analyst to obtain written representations regarding information that the subject entity's management provides to the valuation analyst for purposes of his or her performing the valuation engagement. The decision whether to obtain a representation letter is a matter of judgment for the valuation analyst."

Qualifications of the Valuation Analyst

[67] "The report should contain information regarding the qualifications of the valuation analyst."

Conclusion of Value

[68] "This section should present a reconciliation of the valuation analyst's estimate or various estimates of the value of the subject interest. In addition to a discussion of the rationale underlying the conclusion of value, this section should include the following or similar Statements:" (See Exhibit 11.2.)

It is anticipated that many analysts will combine the conclusion statements with the valuation analyst representation.

Summary Report

[71] "A summary report is structured to provide an abridged version of the information that would be provided in a detailed report, and therefore, need not contain the same level of detail as a detailed report." There is a minimum list of factors that should be included.

Exhibit 11.2 Conclusion Statements

[68] "a. A valuation engagement was performed, including the subject interest and the valuation date.
b. The analysis was performed solely for the purpose described in this report, and the resulting estimate of value should not be used for any other purpose.
c. The valuation engagement was conducted in accordance with the Statement(s) on Standards for Valuation Services of the American Institute of Certified Public Accountants.
d. A statement that the estimate of value resulting from a valuation engagement is expressed as a conclusion of value.
e. The scope of work or data available for analysis is explained, including any restrictions or limitations.
f. A statement describing the conclusion of value, either a single amount or a range.
g. The conclusion of value is subject to the assumptions and limiting conditions and to the valuation analyst's representation.
h. The report is signed in the name of the valuation analyst or the valuation analyst's firm.
i. The data of the valuation report is included.
j. The valuation analyst has no obligation to update the report or the conclusion of value for information that comes to his or her attention after the data of the report."

Calculation Report

[73] "The report should state that it is a calculation report. The calculation report should include the representation of the valuation analyst similar to that in paragraph 65 [detailed report], but adapted for a calculation engagement." There is a discussion of the various factors and statements that should be disclosed.

Sample Calculation Report Disclosure

[77] "In a calculation engagement, the valuation analyst and the client agree on the specific valuation approaches and valuation methods the valuation analyst will use and the extent of valuation procedures the valuation analyst will perform to estimate the value of the subject interest. A calculation engagement does not include all of the procedures required in a *valuation engagement,* as that term is defined in the SVSS. Had a valuation engagement been performed, the results might have been different."

Oral Report

[78] "An oral report may be used in a valuation engagement or a calculation engagement. An oral report should include all information the valuation analyst believes necessary to relate the scope, assumptions, limitations, and the results of the engagement so as to limit any misunderstandings between the analyst and the recipient of the oral report. The member should document in the working papers the substance of the oral report communicated to the client."

Effective Date

[79] "This Statement applies to engagements to estimate value accepted on or after January 1, 2008. Earlier application is encouraged."

[Page 55] Interpretation No. 1-01, "Scope of Applicable Services" of Statement on Standards for Valuation Services No. 1, Valuation of a Business, Business Ownership Interest, Security, or Intangible Asset

Introduction

"Through the Exposure Draft process, it was determined that the questions and answers were an integral part of the Statement and should be made authoritative. This Interpretation is part of the AICPA's continuing efforts at self-regulation of its members in valuation practice, and its desire to provide guidance to members when providing valuation services. The Interpretation does not change or elevate any level of conduct prescribed by any standard. Its goal is to clarify existing standards."

General Interpretation

"The SSVSs apply to an engagement to estimate value if, as all or as part of another engagement, a member determines the value of a business, business ownership interest, security, or intangible asset. . . In the process of estimating value, professional judgment is used to apply valuation approaches and valuation methods as described in the SSVSs. . ."

"In determining whether a particular service falls within the scope of the Statement, a member should consider those services that are specifically excluded:

- Audit, review, and compilation engagements
- Use of values provided by the client or a third party
- Internal use assignments from employers to employee members not in the *practice of public accounting*
- Engagements that are exclusively for the purpose of determining economic damages (for example, lost profits) and that do not include an engagement to estimate value
- Mechanical computations that do not rise to the level of an engagement to estimate value
- Engagements where it is not practical or reasonable to obtain or use relevant information and, therefore, the member is unable to apply valuation approaches and methods described in this Statement
- Engagements meeting the jurisdictional exception"

We hope that this summary is useful and informative. However, as with any standards, valuation analysts should read the entire document. The document has 76 pages, including a great deal of detail concerning what actually goes into a valuation analysis and what specifically goes into the reports. Good luck.

ADDENDUM 2—IRS BV GUIDELINES CHECKLIST, INTERNAL REVENUE SERVICE, ENGINEERING PROGRAM, BUSINESS VALUATION GUIDELINES 4.48.4

Business Name _____   Subject Interest _____

Valuation Date _____   Valuation Purpose _____

Standard of Value _____   Premise of Value _____

Analyst (sign and date) _____   Manager (sign and date) _____

Principal (sign and date) _____

Answering the following questions will help determine whether the development and reporting of a business valuation complies with IRS Business Valuation Guidelines. Preceding each section of questions is a reference to the section or page of the IRS BV Guidelines from which the question is drawn.

All "No" or "N/A" answers should be individually explained in the space provided on the last page of this checklist.

Yes	No	N/A	
			Purpose
❏	❏	❏	Is the Valuator aware of the [then] new IRM 4.48.4, Engineering Program, Business Valuation Guidelines dated July 1, 2006?
			Background
❏	❏	❏	Is the Valuator aware that this material is the product of the Valuation Policy Council (VPC), a cross-functional committee with executive representation from LMSB, SBSE, and Appeals?
❏	❏	❏	Is the Valuator aware that the VPC was established in 2001 to assist IRS leadership in setting direction for valuation policy that cuts across functional lines, and in identifying process improvements to improve compliance and better utilize resources?
			Nature of Materials
			1. Is the Valuator aware that this IRM provides specific guidelines for the following?
❏	❏	❏	Developing the valuation issue?
❏	❏	❏	Resolving the issue when possible?
❏	❏	❏	Preparing reports?
			2. Is the Valuator aware that this document provides specific instructions to examiners with respect to the following?
❏	❏	❏	Planning the valuation assignment?
❏	❏	❏	Analyzing relevant information?
❏	❏	❏	Preparing work papers?
❏	❏	❏	Reviewing a third-party valuation?

Yes	No	N/A	

Effect on Other Documents

| ❑ | ❑ | ❑ | Is the Valuator aware that this document has no effect on other documents? |

Audience

| ❑ | ❑ | ❑ | 1. Is the Valuator aware that the intended audience for this document is all IRS employees who provide valuation services or review the valuations and appraisals prepared by others? |

Introduction 4.48.4.1

❑	❑	❑	1. Is the Valuator aware that the purpose of this document is to provide guidelines applicable to all IRS personnel engaged in valuation practice (hereinafter referred to as "Valuators") relating to the development, resolution, and reporting of issues involving business valuations and similar valuation issues?
❑	❑	❑	If the Valuator departed from these guidelines, is he/she able to reasonably justify that departure?
❑	❑	❑	2. Is the Valuator aware that this document incorporates, by reference, the ethical and conduct provisions contained in the Office of Government Ethics (OGE) Standards of Ethical Conduct, applicable to all IRS employees?
❑	❑	❑	3. Is the Valuator aware that valuations of assets owned and/or transferred by or between controlled taxpayers (within the meaning of Treasury Regulation section 1.482-1[i][5]) may present substantive issues that are not addressed in these guidelines?

Development Guidelines, 4.48.4.2

			1. Did the Valuator successfully complete a valuation assignment by including the following:
❑	❑	❑	Planning?
❑	❑	❑	Identifying critical factors?
❑	❑	❑	Documenting specific information?
❑	❑	❑	Analyzing the relevant information?
❑	❑	❑	Are all relevant activities documented in the workpapers?
❑	❑	❑	2. Was a review appraisal the best approach to the assignment?

Development Guidelines, 4.48.4.2.1 Planning

❑	❑	❑	1. Did the Valuator adequately plan the valuation assignment?
❑	❑	❑	Did the Valuator's managers supervise the staff involved in the valuation process?
❑	❑	❑	2. Is the Valuator aware that quality planning is a continual process throughout the valuation assignment?

Yes **No** **N/A**

Development Guidelines, 4.48.4.2.2 Identifying

1. In developing a valuation conclusion, the Valuator should define the assignment and determine the scope of work necessary by identifying the following:

❑ ❑ ❑ Property to be valued?
❑ ❑ ❑ Interest to be valued?
❑ ❑ ❑ Effective valuation date?
❑ ❑ ❑ Purpose of valuation?
❑ ❑ ❑ Use of valuation?
❑ ❑ ❑ Statement of value?
❑ ❑ ❑ Standard and definition of value?
❑ ❑ ❑ Assumptions?
❑ ❑ ❑ Limiting conditions?
❑ ❑ ❑ Scope limitations?
❑ ❑ ❑ Restrictions, agreements, and other factors that may influence value?
❑ ❑ ❑ Sources of information?

Development Guidelines, 4.48.4.2.3 Analyzing

1. In developing a valuation conclusion, the Valuator should analyze the relevant information necessary to accomplish the assignment including:

❑ ❑ ❑ The nature of the business and the history of the enterprise from its inception?
❑ ❑ ❑ The economic outlook in general and the condition and outlook of the specific industry in particular?
❑ ❑ ❑ The book value of the stock or interest and the financial condition of the business?
❑ ❑ ❑ The earning capacity of the company?
❑ ❑ ❑ The dividend-paying capacity?
❑ ❑ ❑ Existence or non existence of goodwill or other intangible value?
❑ ❑ ❑ Sales of the stock or interest and the size of the block of stock to be valued?
❑ ❑ ❑ The market price of stocks or interests of corporations or entities engaged in the same or a similar line of business having their stocks or interests actively traded in a free and open market, either on an exchange or over-the-counter?
❑ ❑ ❑ Other relevant information?
❑ ❑ ❑ 2. Did the Valuator give consideration to all of the three generally accepted valuation approaches which are the asset-based approach, the market approach, and the income approach?
❑ ❑ ❑ Did the Valuator use professional judgment to select the approach(es) ultimately used and the method(s) within such approach(es) that best indicate the value of the business interest?
❑ ❑ ❑ 3. Did the Valuator analyze and, if necessary, adjust historical financial statements to reflect the appropriate asset value, income, cash flows, and/or benefit stream, as applicable, to be consistent with the valuation methodologies selected by the valuator?

Yes	No	N/A	

Development Guidelines, 4.48.4.2.3 Analyzing *(continued)*

❏	❏	❏	4. Did the Valuator select the appropriate benefit stream, such as pre tax or after-tax income and/or cash flows, and select appropriate discount rates, capitalization rates, or multiples consistent with the benefit stream selected within the relevant valuation methodology?
			5. Did the Valuator determine an appropriate discount and/or capitalization rate after taking into consideration all relevant factors such as:
❏	❏	❏	The nature of the business?
❏	❏	❏	The risk involved?
❏	❏	❏	The stability or irregularity of earnings?
❏	❏	❏	Other relevant factors?
			6. As appropriate for the assignment, and if not considered in the process of determining and weighing the indications of value provided by other procedures, the Valuator should separately consider the following factors in reaching a final conclusion of value:
❏	❏	❏	Marketability, or lack thereof, considering the nature of the business, business ownership interest or security, the effect of relevant contractual and legal restrictions, and the condition of the markets?
❏	❏	❏	Ability of the appraised interest to control the operation, sale, or liquidation of the relevant business?
❏	❏	❏	Other levels of value considerations (consistent with the standard of value in Section 4.48.4.2.2 [1] list item g) [*sic*], e.g., such as the impact of strategic or synergistic contributions to value?
❏	❏	❏	Such other factors which, in the opinion of the Valuator, are appropriate for consideration?

Development Guidelines, 4.48.4.2.4 **Workpapers**

			1. The workpapers should:
❏	❏	❏	Document the steps taken?
❏	❏	❏	Document the techniques used?
❏	❏	❏	Provide the evidence to support the facts and conclusions in the final report?
❏	❏	❏	2. Did the Valuator maintain a detailed case activity record (Form 9984, Examining Officer's Activity Record) which:
❏	❏	❏	Identifies actions taken and indicates time charged?
❏	❏	❏	Identifies contacts including name, phone number, subject, commitments, etc.?
❏	❏	❏	Documents delays in the examination?
❏	❏	❏	3. The case activity record, along with the supporting workpapers, should justify that the time spent is commensurate with work performed?

Yes **No** **N/A**

Development Guidelines, 4.48.4.2.5 Reviewing

❑ ❑ ❑ 1. In reviewing a business valuation and reporting the results of that review, the Valuator should form an opinion as to the adequacy and appropriateness of the report being reviewed?

❑ ❑ ❑ The Valuator should clearly disclose the scope of work of the review process undertaken?

2. In reviewing a business valuation, the Valuator should do the following:

Identify the:

❑ ❑ ❑ Taxpayer?
❑ ❑ ❑ Intended use of the Valuator's opinions and conclusions?
❑ ❑ ❑ The purpose of the review assignment?
❑ ❑ ❑ The report under review?
❑ ❑ ❑ The property interest being valued?
❑ ❑ ❑ The effective date of the valuation?
❑ ❑ ❑ The effective date of the review?
❑ ❑ ❑ Scope of the review process conducted?

❑ ❑ ❑ Determine the completeness of the report under review?
❑ ❑ ❑ Determine the apparent adequacy and relevance of the data and the propriety of any adjustments to the data?
❑ ❑ ❑ Determine the appropriateness of the valuation methods and techniques used and develop the reasons for any disagreement?
❑ ❑ ❑ Determine whether the analyses, opinions, and conclusions in the report under review are appropriate and reasonable, and develop the reasons for any disagreement?

❑ ❑ ❑ 3. In the event of a disagreement with the report's factual representations, underlying assumptions, methodology, or conclusions, a Valuator should conduct additional fact-finding, research and/or analyses necessary to arrive at an appropriate value for the property?

Resolution Guidelines 4.48.4.3

❑ ❑ ❑ Did the Valuator make efforts to obtain a resolution of the case after fully considering all relevant facts?

Resolution Guidelines, Objective 4.48.4.3.1

❑ ❑ ❑ 1. Is the Valuator aware that the objective is to resolve the issue as early in the examination as possible?

❑ ❑ ❑ Did the Valuator perform credible and compelling work which will facilitate resolution of issues without litigation?

❑ ❑ ❑ 2. Did the Valuator work in concert with the internal customer and taxpayer to attempt to resolve all outstanding issues?

Resolution Guidelines, Arriving at Conclusions 4.48.4.3.2

❑ ❑ ❑ 1. Once the Valuator has all the information to be considered in resolving the issue, did the Valuator use his/her professional judgment in considering this information to arrive at a conclusion?

Yes	No	N/A	

Resolution Guidelines, Arriving at Conclusions 4.48.4.3.2 *(continued)*

❑ ❑ ❑   2. If the Valuator did not have all of the information that he/she would have liked to have to definitively resolve the issue, which may happen, the Valuator should decide when he/she has substantially enough information to make a proper determination?

❑ ❑ ❑   3. Did the Valuator employ independent and objective judgment in reaching conclusions and decide all matters on their merits, free from bias, advocacy, and conflicts of interest?

Reporting Guidelines, 4.48.4.4

❑ ❑ ❑   1. The Valuator should prepare reports of his/her findings?

❑ ❑ ❑   2. Is the Valuator aware that this section requires specific information to be included or addressed in each report?

Reporting Guidelines, Overview 4.48.4.4.1

❑ ❑ ❑   1. Did the Valuator meet the primary objective of a valuation report which is to provide convincing and compelling support for the conclusions reached?

❑ ❑ ❑   2. Did the valuation report contain all the information necessary to allow a clear understanding of the valuation analyses?

❑ ❑ ❑   Did the valuation report demonstrate how the conclusions were reached?

Reporting Guidelines, Report Contents 4.48.4.4.2

❑ ❑ ❑   1. Is the Valuator aware that the extent and content of the report prepared depends on the needs of each case?

❑ ❑ ❑   2. The valuation report should clearly communicate the results and identify the information relied upon in the valuation process?

❑ ❑ ❑   The valuation report should effectively communicate the methodology and reasoning, as well as identify the supporting documentation?

❑ ❑ ❑   3. Subject to the type of report being written, valuation reports should generally contain sufficient information relating to the items in Identifying and Analyzing to ensure consistency and quality?

❑ ❑ ❑   4. If the report was written with respect to Reviewing, the report should contain, at a minimum, information relating to those items in Identifying and Analyzing necessary to support the revised assumptions, analyses, and/or conclusions of the Valuator?

Reporting Guidelines, Statement 4.48.4.4.3

                    1. The written valuation report should contain a signed statement that is similar in content to the following:

❑ ❑ ❑   To the best of my knowledge and belief:

❑ ❑ ❑   The statements of fact contained in this report are true and correct.

❑ ❑ ❑   The reported analyses, opinions, and conclusions are limited only by the reported assumptions and limiting conditions.

Yes No N/A

Reporting Guidelines, Statement 4.48.4.4.3 *(continued)*

Yes	No	N/A	
❏	❏	❏	I have no present or prospective interest in the property that is the subject of this report, and I have no personal interest with respect to the parties involved with this assignment.
❏	❏	❏	I have no bias with respect to the subject of this report or to the parties involved with this assignment.
❏	❏	❏	My compensation is not contingent on an action or event resulting from the analyses, opinions, or conclusions in, or the use of, this report.
❏	❏	❏	My analyses, opinions, and conclusions were developed, and this report has been prepared in conformity with the applicable Internal Revenue Service Valuation Guidelines.

Explain any "No" or "N/A" answers on the next page.

Explanation of "No" or "N/A" Answers

Item #   Explanation

_____

_____

_____

_____

_____

_____

_____

_____

_____

_____

_____

_____

_____

_____

_____

_____

_____

_____

_____

_____

_____

_____

_____

CHAPTER 12

Valuation of Pass-Through Entities

INTRODUCTION[1]

The appraisal profession has now continued a healthy discussion regarding the valuation of pass-through entities (PTE) for both controlling and minority interests for years, and it appears unlikely that the discussions will abate in the near future. There is now wide agreement that it is the avoidance of tax on dividends and capital gains, rather than solely an avoidance of tax on corporate income, that forms the main advantage of pass-through entities, with different views remaining about how best to measure that advantage. If there is any one thing that appraisers and analysts seem to agree on, it is that the facts and circumstances of each individual valuation need to be taken into consideration. At first this may seem noncommittal to the reader, but this simple statement is, in fact, the key to valuing these complex interests.

The topic of valuation of S corporations has produced a proliferation of writers and commentators, and these professionals have contributed great wisdom and insight to propel the discussion. Through the progression of these discussions and the many alternative scenarios and points of view presented, we see that a simple one-size-fits-all approach will simply not work in all situations. There are many issues that the analyst must consider when approaching the valuation of such an interest, and while we might prefer to have *the* answer, no such solution exists. While it is certain that it is not as simple as whether or not to tax-affect the earnings stream, neither is it an unknowable or indeterminable problem.

When reading the vast amount of literature and studies that have been published, the analyst should take care to distinguish between a controlling interest and a noncontrolling interest. Many studies discuss such interests without firmly distinguishing between the two. While not all analysts believe that minority and controlling interests in pass-through entities should be handled differently, many do.

This leads to the most significant tool for an analyst to keep in mind when valuing a pass-through entity or interest in one—it needs to make sense. Unfortunately, some of the theory and logic being discussed in this area are shrouded behind an endless loop of formulas and semantics. When considering the differences and distinctions among the theories, consider how a buyer would look at it. In the words of Chris Treharne, the author of one of the minority interest theories discussed later in this chapter, "Follow the cash."

---

[1] We would like to acknowledge the contribution to this chapter by Nancy J. Fannon who has granted permission to use much of her material, including the addendum at the end of this chapter.

This is what analysts do for any interest they are valuing; in the case of a pass-through entity, it just gets a little more interesting. To quote Roger Grabowski:

Principal value drivers are, as they should be, the amount of cash distribution the shareholders expect to receive, the expected holding period, and, most importantly, the pool of likely buyers.[2]

> The analyst should be aware that there may be differences when approaching the valuation of a controlling versus a minority interest in a pass-through entity. In some circumstances, the approach may be the same or similar, while other circumstances will dictate a different approach. After taking into consideration the rights and interests being valued, given different ownership rights, analysts may use entirely different approaches. This makes intuitive sense.

This chapter provides a framework for the questions to ask, the issues to consider, and some models that an analyst might consider applying in particular circumstances. However, it is ultimately up to the analyst to understand not only the implications of the answers relative to the company or interest being valued, but also the tools available to value such an interest.

STANDARD OF VALUE

One point that has been noticeably absent from the discussion of the valuation of pass-through entities is the effect of standard of value. Does it matter whether an analyst is valuing the company or interest for a purchase or sale, compared to estate or gift tax? What about valuing the interest in the event of a divorce or in fair value cases? The answer is *of course it matters*, just as in every other valuation issue we deal with. *Where* it matters primarily has to do with how an analyst will answer the questions that impact the valuation of such interests. If it is a sale of an

> The vast majority of the discussion of whether or not there is an "S corporation premium" is focused on the fair market value standard, within the context of estate and gift taxes. Invariably, this should be the same perspective as the marketplace, with a buyer who would consider the benefits that would flow to him or her from ownership of the interest.

[2] Roger Grabowski, "Valuation of Pass-Through Entities," AICPA 2004 National Business Valuation Conference, pp. 37–120.

interest, for example, the buyer may be known, and the standard of value is investment value. In that event, the tax position of the buyer is clearly known, as well as the benefit of the S election. The buyer and seller will negotiate, each of them knowing the tax benefits that will accrue to the buyer as a result of the election being in place. In the case of divorce, state law will likely enter in, and the issue has now been raised in a number of divorce cases. In an interesting 2007 Massachusetts case (*Bernier v. Bernier*) the Supreme Judicial Court of Massachusetts stated that in divorce, "where one of the parties will maintain, and the other will be entirely divested of, ownership of a marital asset after divorce, the judge must take particular care to treat the parties not as arm's length hypothetical buyers and sellers in a theoretical open market but as fiduciaries entitled to equitable distribution of their marital assets." This introduces to a divorce case concepts that are more typical of statutory fair value disputes between shareholders.[3]

Indeed, the court in Bernier cited with approval the PTE valuation methodology applied by the Delaware Chancery Court in a shareholder dispute. The case of *Delaware Open MRI Radiology Associates P.A. v. Kessler* is a 2006 Delaware Chancery Court decision that examined the issue in detail. In this case, the Court was presented with one expert, who simply tax-affected the S corporation's earnings, and the other expert, who simply did not. This, among other facts, led to extreme differing values. The Court rejected both experts' positions, finding that failure to tax-affect at all overstates the value, and tax-affecting at 40 percent understates the value. Citing *Adams, Heck, and Gross* of Tax Court fame, as well as a 1991 appraisal decision of the Delaware Chancery Court also titled Radiology Associates, the Court said: "Under an earnings valuation analysis, what is important to an investor is what the investor ultimately can keep in his pocket."

The specific approach applied by the Delaware Chancery Court in this case is discussed in more detail later in this chapter. We note that what distinguishes this case is that the Court recognizes that "refusing to tax-affect at all produces such a windfall." Further this case recognizes that it is not the avoidance of corporate taxes that creates value to the S corporation shareholder. It "is the avoidance of a dividend tax in addition to a tax on corporate earnings." This is the very foundation upon which the valuation theories set forth in this chapter are built.

HISTORICAL BACKDROP

This issue hit its stride in the appraisal community with the findings of the case of *Gross v. Commissioner* (TCM 1999-254, affd. 272 F 3d 333 6th Cir. 2001) and those that followed:

- *Estate of John E. Wall v. Commissioner*, TCM 2001-75
- *Estate of William G. Adams, Jr. v. Commissioner*, TCM 2002-80
- *Estate of Richie C. Heck v. Commissioner*, TCM 2002-34
- *Robert Dallas v. Commissioner*, TCM 2006-212

---

[3] In *Bernier*, the husband's expert tax-affected at 35%, asserting a purchaser would consider such taxes, and the wife's expert did not tax-affect at all, saying no sale was contemplated and S corporations pay no corporate tax. The trial court adopted the husband's expert's position. On appeal, the Supreme Judicial Court of Massachusetts cited the Delaware Chancery Court decision in *Delaware Open MRI Radiology Associates* and remanded the case.

While the Tax Court cases highlighted this issue, this was not the first time analysts' attention was focused on pass-through interests. Other occurrences in the valuation community had previously drawn attention to the valuation of S corporations.

Over the years, the selection of S corporations as a corporate entity form has become much more widespread. In 1958, Congress first established Subchapter S corporations as a means of allowing sole proprietorships to incorporate. At the time, only ten shareholders were allowed. Fueling the growth in numbers of S corporations was the liberalization of ownership restrictions, in terms of both who could own them and how many owners they could have. Likewise, as income subject to FICA/Medicare climbed, distributions, which are exempt from employment taxes, became more attractive to S corporation owners, even though they were required to draw reasonable compensation. In fact, a study submitted to Congress showed that profitable S corporations owned by single shareholders have been declaring a steadily decreasing salary as a percentage of profits every year over the period that the study was conducted.[4]

By 1985, the number of S corporations had climbed to 736,900, versus 2,432,300 C corporations. Ten years later, in 1995, the number of S corporations, 2,161,000, had grown to the equivalent number of C corporations, 2,197,000. By 2003, the number of S corporations far exceeded the number of C corporations, with 3,344,400 S corporations in comparison to 2,104,400 C corporations.

The rise of LLCs and the continued use of limited partnerships have further increased the predominance of pass-through entities. According to a 2009 study (using 2004 tax return data), in addition to 2,000,000 C corporations and 3,300,000 S corporations, there are 2,300,000 partnerships and LLCs.[5] Thus, approximately 74% of non farm businesses not organized as proprietorships are pass-through entities.

With the increase in numbers of S corporations and other pass-through entities came a corresponding increase in transactions in the market involving pass-through entities. Consequently, analysts found themselves required to value more and more such interests for various purposes, including estate, gift, divorce, and mergers and acquisitions.

Interestingly, discussions of valuing pass-through entities and the interrelationships of taxes and value have been around since the late 1980s and early 1990s, with some discussion that dates back to the late 1950s. In the appraisal community, however, this issue did not arise as a significant concern until the finding in the Gross case, and the subsequent cases that used similar methodologies applied to situations that many analysts believed to be dissimilar fact patterns. Thus, while it may have been the Tax Court cases that drove us to examine the issue, the reality of market evidence is what should drive our work.

CURRENT STATUS OF DEBATE

The discussion regarding valuation of pass-through entities and interests in them has evolved enormously in recent years. With respect to minority interests, a limited

---

[4] Statement of Russell George, Inspector General, Treasury Inspector General for Tax Administration, before the Senate Finance Committee, May 25, 2005.
[5] *Effective Federal Income Tax Rates Faced by Small Businesses in the United States*, prepared by Quatria Strategies, LLC for the U.S. SBA, April 2009.

If each model is applied diligently and with attention to the specific facts relating to the interest in mind, theoretically one should not arrive at a dramatically different conclusion no matter which model is used.

number of theories have emerged and taken prominence in much of the literature. A detailed, technical discussion of these models can be found later in this chapter. There are some significant theoretical departures between each one.

The caveat above is one of the many issues that an analyst would need to consider to reach parity among the models. This chapter will deal with the most significant of those issues.

With respect to valuation of controlling interests, there is also some theoretical departure among commentators. However, analysts now have a number of transactional studies available to draw upon. Regardless of how one interprets the studies, they provide a helpful list of specific questions to guide analysts. How the analyst interprets the answers to those questions then provides guidance for the approach and methodology in valuing the interest.

It was alarming how the so-called Gross method appeared to be adopted by the IRS, various courts, and even some in the appraisal community, despite arising from an extremely fact-specific case that had no real similarities or application to other matters. Presentations to the Tax Court need to be explicitly clear to deter analysts valuing pass-through entities from utilizing a single model that may not be relevant to the value of the subject interest.

A general trend has emerged from the models and the literature. The trend has been to value the shares from the perspective of the *investor; that is, to follow the cash all the way into the investor's pockets.* This makes intuitive sense, as we know that investors take taxes into consideration when pricing any investment.

Some valuation models, for example, stop at the corporate level, reasoning that if the cash leaves the corporation in the form of dividends to fund taxes, then it is no different from a C corporation; that is, the corporation is left in the same position. Although the corporation is left in the same position, the shareholder may not be in the same position. Most of the minority models recognize that distinction for the noncontrolling shareholder. However, other active observers and participants in the pass-through entity valuation discussion, have suggested that all of the models may be appropriately applied to both minority and controlling interests, with proper care and attention to facts and circumstances.[6]

Michael Paschall had this observation:

> The distinction made ... seems to me to be much like the distinction between merely looking at a fine meal and actually eating it ... a meal is no good unless one can have at it. Neither is a corporation any good unless one can realize the benefits through being a shareholder.[7]

There are differences between the controlling and the minority shareholder. This chapter examines some of the factors that cause these distinctions as well as circumstances where the facts might cause similar approaches to value. It is important to note that this discussion has had the benefit of literally dozens of individuals throughout the country, and we are grateful for their input.

Why Deduct Taxes from an Entity That Doesn't Incur Them?

For years, analysts have routinely been deducting taxes at either C corporation rates or personal rates in valuing pass-through entities, despite the fact that such entities do not themselves incur such taxes. And for years, analysts would have to explain why they were doing so. The explanations given in reports were many and varied and included the following:

- The analyst has to consider the whole range of buyers, most of whom are C corporations.
- The analyst has to use recognized methods of valuation, which includes taking a deduction for taxes from the income stream.
- The interest holder is at a risk that the S election could be lost.
- The income stream has to be matched to the capitalization rate, which includes consideration of corporate taxes in the income stream.
- The shareholder will have to recognize the phantom income, potentially without a receipt of equivalent cash flow, or at least potentially without enough to pay the taxes on the income he or she is allocated.
- The *IRS Appeals Officer Manual* says income taxes have to be deducted from the earnings stream.
- Tax-affecting is meant to address various costs such as the difficulty in raising or selling capital and the difficulty obtaining debt.

Some of these reasons have no applicability in some facts and circumstances. Others are integral to core valuation theory (see the fourth bullet), but nonetheless may not tell the whole story.

---

[6] See, for example, Nancy J. Fannon, "Valuing Controlling versus Minority Interests in S corporations," *Business Valuation Review* (Winter 2007), p. 111.
[7] Michael Paschall, "Some Observations on Tax Affecting," *Business Valuation Review* (March 2005), p. 25.

Exhibit 12.1 Approach Used by Expert for the Taxpayer

Tax Court Cases Dealing with S Corporation Issue

Case/Expert for the Taxpayer	Gross/McCoy	Wall/Walker	Heck/Bajaj	Adams/Shriner	Dallas/Nammacher, Oliver
Taxpayer Expert Approach	• 40% tax rate on corporate earnings • Ibbotson data used in capitalization rate	• 34% tax rate on corporate earnings • Ibbotson data used in capitalization rate	• No tax-affect • Ibbotson data used in capitalization rate	• No tax-affect • "Grossed-up" Ibbotson derived capitalization rate to pretax	• 40%, 35% tax rate on corporate earnings
Support for Approach	• Must employ recognized methods • IRS's own guide says to deduct taxes • Cites various disadvantages of being S corporation that tax-affecting is meant to address	• Potential buyers of S corporations are C corporations	• Additional risk added for S corporation	• Capitalization rate and cash flow should agree	• Would lose S corporation status in sale • Has always tax-affected • Tax-affecting widespread among appraisers and other financial professionals

Interestingly, these issues were each addressed in the Tax Court cases where the Court considered the issue of tax-affecting. Exhibits 12.1, 12.2, and 12.3 present, in summary format, the Tax Court cases that have become famous for this issue, the arguments made by the taxpayers' expert and the government's expert, and the finding of the Court in the case.

Exhibit 12.2 Approach Used by Expert for the Government

Tax Court Cases Dealing with S Corporation Issue

Case/Expert for the Government	Gross/Bajaj	Wall/Shroeder	Heck/Spiro	Adams/Spiro	Dallas/Vandervliet, Kettell
IRS Expert Approach	• 0% tax rate • Ibbotson data used in capitalization rate	• 40% tax rate • BAA Bonds/ Ibbotson data used in capitalization rate	• No tax-affect • 10% discount: cited "additional risks of S corps"	• No tax-affect • 10% premium added to discount rate in part due to S corporation status	• No tax-affect
Support for Approach	• Subject will remain an S corporation • Illogical to impute taxes when none will be paid • Virtually all earnings are distributed	• Not relied upon	• Cited restrictions impairing liquidity	• Not used	• Not relied upon

Exhibit 12.3 Finding of the Tax Court

Tax Court Cases Dealing with S Corporation Issue

Case	Gross	Wall	Heck	Adams	Dallas
The Court held:	• Tax-affecting "inappropriate under facts presented" • Judges unpersuaded by "lemmings to sea" argument (just because everyone else does it, that's no good reason to tax-affect.) • Split on appeal	• Relied on market approach • Cited Gross case in decision • Said that tax-affecting S corporations attributes no value to S status • Note both experts deducted taxes, but the Court did not	• Used Bajaj's rate of return against non-tax-affected earnings • Spiro's 10% "S Corp" discount considered in lack of control discount	• Cited Gross as authority • S corporation tax rate is zero, therefore discount rate already "matches" cash flow • Disallowed Shriner's "gross-up" of discount rate	• Cited Gross as authority • Gave little weight to claims on wide spread tax affecting because not documented • Insufficient evidence that S corp status would be lost, distributions reduced, and hypothetical buyer and seller would tax-affect

Many, if not most, of the reasons why appraisers were saying they were deducting taxes were rejected by the Tax Court. Thus, if analysts are still providing these same reasons for the deduction of income taxes in their valuation reports, then they should either examine their reasoning or better explain why they believe such logic to be well founded.

Some commentators object to the notion of a premium under any circumstance, since the S election can be made by the buyer for free. However, the election must be unanimous among the shareholders. There are benefits that may come with an election that has been in place for greater than ten years, in the avoidance of tax on built-in gains. In such cases, a buyer may be willing to pay something for such an election already in place.

CONTROLLING INTERESTS IN PASS-THROUGH ENTITIES

This section examines the market evidence and findings of various studies for controlling interests, extracting guidance for the valuations of pass-through interests. While not everyone considers these studies to be conclusive, they provide valuable insight into the issues analysts may need to consider when valuing pass-through entities. These studies include:

• Dr. Terrance Jalbert, "Pass-Through Taxation and the Value of the Firm," *American Business Review*, June 2002.

- Merle Erickson, "To Elect or Not to Elect: That Is the Tax Question," *Capital Ideas* 2, no. 4, Winter 2001.
- Merle Erickson, "Tax Benefits in Acquisitions of Privately Held Corporations," *Capital Ideas* 3, no. 3, Winter 2002.
- James Alerding, Yassir Karam, and Travis Chamberlain, "S Corporation Premiums Revisited: The Erickson-Wang Myth," *Shannon Pratt's Business Valuation Update*, January 2003.
- Michael J. Mattson, Donald S. Shannon, and David E. Upton, "Empirical Research Concludes S Corporations Values Same as C Corporations (Part I)," *Shannon Pratt's Business Valuation Upda*, November 2002.
- Michael Mattson, Donald S. Shannon, and David E. Upton, "Empirical Research Concludes S Corporation Values Same as C Corporations (Part 2)," *Shannon Pratt's Business Valuation Update*, December 2002.
- Joseph Vinso, "Distributions and Entity Form: Do They Make Any Difference in Value?" *Valuation Strategies*, September/October 2003.
- John R. Phillips, "S Corp or C Corp? M&A Deal Prices Look Alike," *Shannon Pratt's Business Valuation Update*, March 2004.

Much of the discussion regarding valuation of pass-through entities revolves around the issue of tax-affecting the earnings stream. The market data studies of transactions of pass-through entities provide a valuable framework for analysis. In reviewing the studies that have been conducted of transactions of pass-through entities, some of the issues that are raised for consideration include:

- The effect of earnings available for distribution on the value of the firm
- The possible benefits of Section 338(h)(10) and Section 754 elections, and when it is appropriate to consider such elections
- The size of the company being transacted, and impact of size on value
- The issue of basis step-up
- The impact of the company's capital structure on value
- Consideration of the structure of the deal (asset versus stock)

To approach the valuation of a pass-through entity, the analyst must initially know the base that he or she is starting *from* in order to know what he or she is making adjustments *to*. For example, using the market approach, the analyst needs to consider whether he or she is starting from the perspective of a C corporation asset sale or a C corporation stock sale. Using the income approach, an analyst should

Nearly everyone agrees that tax benefits at the corporate level can create shareholder value; however, the issue of whether tax benefits enjoyed at the election of the shareholder also create value has been the subject of more debate.

consider if he or she is starting with the value of an equivalent C corporation minority, marketable interest distributing 100 percent of its earnings or approximately 40 percent of its earnings. This starting point drives many of the adjustments for the benefits of the pass-through entity that follow.

CONTROLLING-INTEREST STUDIES

Before discussing the research that has been done comparing controlling-interest purchases in pass-through entities with C corporations (often called "double-tax firms" in this research), it is worth pausing to discuss the meaning of "control" and, more generally, the importance of considering corporate documents in pass-through entity valuation.

While the detailed models discussed later in this chapter are often referred to as "S corporation models," they are also applied to other types of pass-through entities, such as partnerships and LLCs. In applying the models to partnerships and LLCs, it is particularly important to consider the provisions of the partnership agreement or operating agreement. Many items that are allocated pro rata according to relative percentage ownership interests in an S corporation need not be, and often are not, so allocated in partnerships and LLCs. The governing agreements for these entities may specify that profits, losses, or cash distributions are allocated to partners or members in many ways. Such allocations can obviously affect the appropriate application of the "S corporation" (i.e., pass-through entity) models for a given ownership interest. Even with actual S corporations, it may be important to consider the terms of any shareholder agreements.

The nature of control in partnerships and LLCs will also often differ from S corporations. This is especially important for analysts who analyze control interests in pass-through entities differently from minority interests. Specifically, control does not automatically reside in an equity ownership percentage greater than 50 percent. In limited partnerships, most aspects of control are typically vested in one or a few general partners. The flexibility of the LLC form allows many possibilities regarding which member(s) or class of members holds control.

Several studies examine the issue of pass-through firms compared with double-tax firms. Each study helps to advance the development of the body of knowledge and the theoretical framework for the valuation of these complex interests.

Dr. Terrance Jalbert, assistant professor of finance, University of Hawaii, conducted a study that compared 94 master limited partnerships (MLPs) against samples of C corporations matched to industry and size in one control group and risk factors (using betas) in a second control group.[8] He assumes that cash flow does not grow, that it goes into perpetuity, and that all free cash flow is paid out as dividends. These assumptions, while somewhat artificial, are necessary to isolate the assumptions Jalbert tests.

Jalbert referred to several earlier studies, including Jeffrey Jaffe's 1991 study that examined the impact of capital structure on PTFs (pass-through firms). This study had the benefit of Franco Modigliani and Merton H. Miller's 1963 work entitled "Corporate Income Taxes and the Cost of Capital." Subsequent substantive

---

[8] Dr. Terrance Jalbert, "Pass-Through Taxation and the Value of the Firm," *American Business Review* (June 2002).

analysis on the subject was done by Miller and others. However, Jaffe was the first to examine the issue for PTFs. Jalbert also referred to a study by David Guenther performed in 1992, which compared PTFs and DTFs (double tax firms) and argued that while DTFs have a higher tax cost, PTFs have higher operating costs. These earlier studies are only a part of the extensive literature produced since Modigliani and Miller's work explored the interrelationship of taxes and capital structure.[9]

Jalbert's first test indicated a significant difference in the value per dollar of net operating income (NOI) of the PTFs compared to the DTFs. His second test indicated that as debt in the capital structure of the DTF rose, the valuation difference decreased. The third test indicated DTFs use more debt in their capital structure than PTFs.[10]

Jalbert concluded from this study that ". . . the method by which the firm is taxed affects the value of the firm as well as the capital structure the firm will adopt. PTFs have a higher value per dollar of NOI than DTFs. . . . The differential in value is mitigated among firms that use higher levels of debt."[11]

Thus, Jalbert found that PTFs were valued higher than DTFs. However, he found that DTFs borrowed funds, optimizing their capital structures to optimize value and offset the differential.

This study provides an indication that single-tax firms that have *distributable income* may provide a higher value than double-tax firms. It also indicates that *capital structure* ought to be considered in our analysis; for example, if we use a comparable C corporation in our market analysis that has optimized its capital structure, the valuation difference may already be mitigated (in the equity multiple).[12]

In another study, Merle Erickson, associate professor of accounting at the University of Chicago Graduate School of Business, and Shiing-wu Wang of the University of California's Leventhal School of Accounting, researched the effect of IRC Section 338(h) (10) elections on purchase price.[13] Such an election, available when the target is a subsidiary or an S corporation, allows a buyer to step up the tax basis of the assets to the purchase price, allowing valuable tax write-offs. Studying 200 subsidiary stock purchase prices between 1994 and 1998, they found:

> . . . the tax structure of the subsidiary sale affects the purchase price. Further, in a subsidiary sale, the seller should often be able to extract a purchase price premium for the tax benefits associated with the deal and the buyer should be willing to pay such a premium.[14]

The researchers commented that it was not unusual to find premiums exceeding 10 percent of the deal price.[15] However, the extent of the benefit to be gained from this tax election is very fact-specific. Further, this is a tax election that must be made

---

[9] Ibid.
[10] Ibid.
[11] Ibid.
[12] Ibid.
[13] Merle Erickson, "To Elect or Not to Elect: That Is the Tax Question," *Capital Ideas* 2, no. 4 (Winter 2001).
[14] Ibid.
[15] Merle Erickson, "Tax Benefits in Acquisitions of Privately Held Corporations," *Capital Ideas,* Vol. 3, No. 3 (Winter 2002).

at the agreement of the buyer and the seller. Clearly, a buyer would be unlikely to pay for the entire benefit, which would negate any benefit from having made the election. Thus, this issue, which affects the structure of the deal, is often one of the many factors that might enter into the negotiations regarding ultimate price.

Erickson and Wang further compared purchase prices across 77 matched pairs of taxable stock acquisitions of S and C corporations from 1994 to 2000. This study confirmed their earlier finding that purchase prices were higher by 12 to 17 percent of the deal value.[15] From these studies, Erickson found it is important to consider exit strategy when choosing organizational form, as he concluded organizational form could affect shareholder value.

The studies by Erickson and Wang indicate that the *ability to structure a deal* in a certain manner, specifically, the benefits gained by a 338(h)(10) election, have potential value. Specifically, *the buyer was a party who could use such benefits*, and thus the benefits had value to that buyer in that deal. Further, the availability of such benefits to potential buyers should be considered when choosing entity form.[16]

In this connection, it is important to note that the Section 338(h)(10) election is not available to partnerships or LLCs, and it is available with S corporations only when at least 80 percent of the equity is purchased (if less than 100 percent of the stock is purchased, the remaining minority shareholders must also consent to the election). However, with regard to basis step-up, partnerships and LLCs (but not S corporations) may benefit from a Section 754 election, which also allows the buyer to push down the purchase price to the basis of the underlying assets (i.e., step up the assets basis). The 754 election is available to partnerships (and LLCs taxed as partnerships) in sales of partial interests in the business, including minority interests, not just in control transactions.[17]

A third study was performed by Michael J. Mattson, MBA, Donald S. Shannon, PhD, CPA, and David E. Upton, PhD, CFA.[18] This study reviewed over 1,200 S and C corporations found in Pratt's Stats™ database (after eliminating those that did not distinguish). Although no distinction between asset sales and stock sales were made, this was the largest study to date on comparative prices.

This was the first of several studies of transaction multiples of privately held S versus privately held C corporations. However, in order for the analyst to put these studies in their proper context, they must understand that these studies did not address the basic question many analysts have been posing, that is, should there be a premium applied to the S corporation whose value has been determined *relative to*

---

[16] Ibid.

[17] The 754 election allows a purchasing partner or member to equalize the outside basis in the newly purchased partnership or membership interest with the inside basis in the underlying partnership assets. In partnerships or LLCs where assets have appreciated, the difference between a purchasing partner's inside basis and outside basis can cause the overstatement (and taxing) of the new partner's gains from asset distributions or prevent the new partner from realizing depreciation deductions. The 754 election remedies this by equalizing the new partner's inside and outside basis. However, while the 754 election has no immediate impact on the continuing partners, it can cause adverse tax consequences later, particularly if assets must be stepped down. This fact, and increased record-keeping burdens, may make unclear the desirability of a Section 754 election.

[18] Michael J. Mattson, Donald S. Shannon, and David E. Upton, "Empirical Research Concludes S Corporations Values Same as C Corporations: Part I," *Shannon Pratt's Business Valuation Update* (November 2002).

the publicly traded C-corporation data by which it has been valued. Comparing private C corporations to private S corporations has shed light on many interesting issues, but has not answered this question. Thus, we review them for the guidance they have offered.

The researchers selected sales as their indicator of value, due to the disparity in the data for earnings between S corporations and C corporations. This disparity is not inconsequential to the balance of this discussion, as it clearly shows that privately owned C corporations have lower profits that S corporations, likely owing to a greater desire on the part of the C-corporation owner to reduce corporate income subject to corporate income tax. S corporations were found to have a median pretax margin of 6.9 percent, but C corporations had a median pretax margin of only 2.3 percent. As indicated, they attributed this to the C corporations' motivation to bonus out earnings, lowering income subject to double taxation.[19] Segregating the data into 17 categories measured by size, determined by sales, the researchers found that on unadjusted basis, controlling only for size, C corporations sold for more than S corporations based on the mean transaction data in 16 of the 17 categories. Running a further regression on the data to hold other factors that might influence value constant, they found no statistical difference in pricing between the S corporation and the C corporation.[20]

After determining the effects of industry affiliation, asset versus stock sale, asset size, and market swings, Mattson, Shannon, and Upton began a second phase of their study. In this portion, an analysis similar to the prior study was performed, but the focus was narrowed to stock sales of S corporations and C corporations.[21] This study was in reaction to the Erickson and Wang study discussed previously.

Interestingly, of the researchers' "small-size" category (sales of $0 to $2,500,000), only 16 percent were classified as stock sales. The "medium-size" category, with sales from $2,500,000 to $10,000,000, consisted of 52 percent stock sales, and those with sales over $10,000,000 had 58 percent stock sales. The percentages of stock sales for C corporations only were significantly higher across the board, at 39 percent, 73 percent, and 73 percent, respectively.

The study found no significant evidence to support the existence of an "S" premium when stock sales were isolated and tested. However, regression results for the two largest size categories—the only size category Erickson used—show S corporations sold in a stock transaction have higher price-to-sales ratios than C corporations. When the total database is considered, no such statement can be made. In fact, in all but one category, the mean C corporation multiples were greater than the mean S corporation multiples.[22]

The findings of the Mattson, Shannon, and Upton study certainly indicate that the presumption that an S corporation is worth more than a privately held C corporation, unsupported by other evidence, is inconclusive at best. However, it also indicates that the *size of the transaction makes a difference in the deal structure*, and, at the very least, it indicates that *the enjoyment of the benefits of a Section 338(h)(10) election is not universal.*

---

[19] Ibid.

[20] Ibid.

[21] Michael J. Mattson, Donald S. Shannon, and David E. Upton, "Empirical Research Concludes S Corporations Values Same as C Corporations: Part II," *Shannon Pratt's Business Valuation Update* (December 2002).

[22] Ibid.

Moreover, as Erickson and Wang pointed out, individual circumstances dictate the extent of the benefits available. It is unlikely that such an election is a realistic consideration for many, or even most, smaller companies. Thus, the premium due to the election is a moot point in many S corporation valuations that analysts deal with. A third explanation could be that not all assets transact in the asset transactions.

The findings of Erickson and Wang were further debated by authors R. James Alerding, Yassir Karam, and Travis Chamberlain of Clifton & Gunderson.[23] They criticized the Erickson and Wang study, saying that it was based on a number of false premises, including the premise that all sales are stock sales and not asset sales. They point out that most acquirers do not want to purchase stock because of the potential for liability assumption.

Indeed, as Dr. Pratt observed, "Out of over 1,500 S corporation sales (in the Pratt's Stats database) and over 2,000 C corporation sales, 65% of S corporation sales and 42% of C corporation sales were structured as asset sales."[24]

Many of the corporations that analysts deal with are often much smaller than those that Erickson and Wang studied, where asset sales are much more common, particularly since buyers of small companies do not want to assume the liabilities of the seller.

The Erickson and Wang study, however, considered only relatively large transactions. The average purchase price in the S corporation transactions is $50.31 million, while the average C corporation sold for $46.24 million.

In summary, Alerding et al. commented, "The phenomenon that Erickson and Wang see in their matched pairs relates to the tax differences in an S corporation and a C corporation, not to a difference in the price paid to acquire the stock of each."[25]

The main point of this debate is the extent to which *tax benefits create value*. A buyer might also purchase the assets of a C corporation and get a step-up in basis. Therefore, does this mean the company is worth more simply because it's an S corporation? No. It means that a *stepped-up basis* is potentially available, allowing the corporation—whether S or C—to command a premium over the price at which it was going to sell its stock.

A further study was conducted by Joseph D. Vinso, PhD, MCBA, FIBA, ASA, of Financial Resources Management, Inc.[26] This study examined mean price-to-sales ratios for S corporations versus C corporations. It was the first study to also distinguish among limited liability partnerships, partnerships, limited liability companies, and sole proprietorships.

In analyzing the entire Business Valuation Resources database, the researchers found that based on mean and median sales multiples, C corporations are valued significantly higher than S corporations. This is generally consistent with the findings of the Mattson, Shannon, and Upton study and may be due to the same reasons

---

[23] R. James Alerding, Yassir Karam, and Travis Chamberlain, "S Corporation Premiums Revisited: The Erickson-Wang Myth," *Shannon Pratt's Business Valuation Update* (January 2003).

[24] Shannon Pratt, "Editor Attempts to Make Sense of S Versus C Corporation Debate," *Shannon Pratt's Business Valuation Update* (March 2003).

[25] R. James Alerding, Yassir Karam, and Travis Chamberlain, "S Corporation Premiums Revisited: The Erickson-Wang Myth," *Shannon Pratt's Business Valuation Update* (January 2003).

[26] Joseph Vinso, "Distributions and Entity Form: Do They Make a Difference in Value?" *Valuation Strategies* (September/October 2003).

discussed before. In fact, all pass-through entities were found to be valued lower than C corporations, based on price-to-sales ratios. Again, the comparison in this study was of private S corporations to private C corporations, and not to public C corporations such as those which provide the cost of capital data used by analysts in the income approach, for whom no S election is available, and which are widely thought to have already normalized compensation.

Vinso also performed an analysis on earnings-before-tax (EBT) multiples, again finding that C corporations are valued higher than S corporations. However, for one particular SIC that he analyzed separately, he found S corporations to be priced higher than C corporations.

We further note that many of the EBT multiples in Pratt's database, the data that were the subject of the Vinso study, in fact produce invested capital values, regardless of whether they are stock or asset sales.

C corporations have a greater incentive to bonus out earnings in order to lower their EBT relative to S corporations. For this reason, the sales multiple is the more reliable measure. Note further that C corporations generally bonus out salaries, not pay dividends. Although this ability is limited by tax regulations on excessive compensations, this contributes to the notion that double taxation is more myth than reality.

From this and other studies, it becomes apparent that the appraiser should consider that *C corporation transactional data may produce different results than S corporation transaction data*. Further, *the size of the transaction may influence the result, and even the multiple selected can impact the valuation conclusion.*

Another study was presented by John R. Phillips, CPA/ABV, CFA, of Marshall & Stevens.[27] Selecting data again from the Pratt's Stats database, Phillips stratified:

- S corporation stock versus C corporation stock sales
- S corporation asset versus C corporation asset sales

The study revealed that stock sales were priced similarly, regardless of whether they were an S or a C corporation. Additionally, Phillips found that asset sales were priced similarly, regardless of whether they were an S corporation or a C corporation. However, total asset transactions were found to be priced at a 20 percent discount compared to stock transactions.[28]

Combined with the other studies, this is indeed an interesting finding. Recall that the Mattson et al. studies, which did not distinguish between asset and stock sales, and the Vinso study, which found that C corporations were valued at prices

---

[27] John R. Phillips, "S Corp or C Corp? M&A Deal Prices Look Alike," *Shannon Pratt's Business Valuation Update* (March 2004).
[28] Ibid.

greater than S corporations. The Phillips study revealed that while 74 percent of S corporation deals were done as asset deals (in his selected dataset), only 51 percent of C corporation deals were done as asset deals.

On the whole, if asset deals are priced at a discount to stock deals, and more S corporation deals are structured as asset deals, this would cause the data to be skewed to the conclusion that C corporations are priced higher than S corporations. Once again, this data must be interpreted with the caution that all assets may not transact in asset deals.

Phillips points out that his study is consistent with the Erickson/Wang study, when limited to stock prices, as Phillip's data showed a small premium in S corporation pricing. However, Phillips characterized such data as statistically insignificant and stated that some of them could have been due to the inclusion of nontaxable stock transactions.

Roger Grabowski points out that a seller of a small C corporation or a small S corporation that is subject to built-in gains can mimic the benefits of an S election that has been in place such that it can avoid embedded gains. Buyers of small companies often allocate a portion of the sales price to noncompete agreements and employment contracts. Such allocation is deductible to the buyer and avoids the tax on embedded gains on assets in the company. This occurs both in small C corporations and in S corporations that have not had their election in place either since start-up or for longer than ten years, the amount of time necessary to avoid triggering the built-in gains tax. If one was to match the sale of 1) a C corporation with 2) an otherwise identical S corporation that was subject to built-in gains, both would be equally motivated to avoid taxes on built-in gains and would potentially seek to avoid such taxes by allocating a portion of the purchase price to employment contracts and noncompete agreements. Such allocation allows the buyer the similarity of the step-up in basis he or she may have sought on the assets by the ability to deduct these agreements.

However, if one were to match the sale of 1) a C corporation with 2) an otherwise identical S corporation that was not subject to built-in gains—that is, the S corporation had either been an S corporation since inception or the ten-year holding period had been met—then there would be no motivation for the S corporation to allocate purchase price to anything other than the assets of the corporation. The C corporation, however, would still face embedded gains issues.

Grabowski makes the argument that any comparison of "S versus C" pricing that does not take this issue of timing of the S election into consideration is missing a critical element, as an S corporation sale before the expiration of the holding period would likely transact in the same manner as a C corporation.

Various databases handle reporting of covenants not to compete and employment contracts differently, in terms of whether they are included in the acquisition price reported by the database. The Phillips, Vinso, and Mattson, Shannon, and Upton studies, each of which has been discussed previously, all relied on the Pratt's Stats database. Pratt's Stats includes noncompete agreements in the reported price, but excludes the value of any employment contracts with the seller. Thus, to the extent any value is allocated to an employment contract, it would not be included in the total purchase price.

Grabowski points out that for deals involving larger companies, allocation of purchase price to noncompete agreements and employment contracts is often a moot point, as stock ownership and management may be a totally separate issue. In larger deals that are structured as asset deals, the entire purchase price is, therefore,

ValTip

> Analysts must be careful using market data for transaction pricing for either S or C corporations without understanding the basis for the data they are using and considering, at a minimum, the following:
>
> - Asset or stock sale
> - Assets transacted
> - S or C corporation
> - Size of the transaction
> - Capital structure and liabilities assumed
>
> Failure to take these factors into consideration when using market data to value a pass-through entity could result in inappropriate valuation conclusions.

allocated to the assets, possibly without any allocation to owner agreements. This could, at least in part, explain the disparity between the small company data and the larger company data.

What else could the data mean? Perhaps that the C corporation value is enhanced by the ability to obtain better financing, or perhaps that not all assets are included in the asset transaction pricing.

While each of the studies researched the target S and C corporations, no studies examined the issue from the perspective of the buyer. This is partly because the data are not available in sufficient detail in the Pratt's Stats database to make the distinction. In other databases (e.g., Done Deals, Mergerstat), the buyers would be many public C corporations, and distinguishing results could emerge. For analysts, the issue of the most likely buyer may be an important consideration.

Additional Points Regarding Controlling Interests

In addition to the information garnered from the market transaction data studies, there are other notable omissions.

For example, while there is nothing in the market data that suggests retained net income (basis build-up of stock) has value in the marketplace—that is, that buyers are paying greater prices for their ability to build up basis in their stock because they're buying an S corporation instead of a C corporation—this doesn't suggest that the ability to build up basis is not valuable and significant to the seller upon consummating a transaction. Rather, at the time of a sale, an S corporation seller can be in a substantially better position than a C corporation seller, by virtue of having built up basis in his or her stock, leading to greater proceeds to the seller. The ability to build up such basis is an important consideration in the selection of entity formation.

However, a buyer cannot buy, and a seller cannot sell, his or her basis in the stock. What a buyer would be paying for would be the ability to build up his or her own basis in the stock in the future, achieved through undistributed net income. This is an issue that can be considered on a case-by-case basis. In order to determine the value of such basis build-up, the appraiser must determine both the amount of basis build-up and the likely timing of the exit strategy.

Some commentators also suggest that the willing buyer would consider the possibility of a 338(h)(10) election upon a future sale that may be incurred by the buyer. Such consideration is advocated by Erickson and Wang's research, and consideration of a step-up in the basis of the assets is a component of the valuation model designed by Grabowski in the minority interest discussion that follows. Recall that the premium found by Erickson and Wang occurred only in large corporations incurring 338(h)(10) elections currently. There is nothing in particular in the market data, most notably for smaller companies, that suggests that buyers are willing to pay an additional premium for the hope that they might get a step-up in the basis of assets upon a hypothetical sale somewhere down the road. However, in some circumstances, neither can one ignore the economic reality that the possibility of such step-up exists and can be significant. Therefore, it is an issue to consider in an S corporation value determination. Such factors could also come into play in the case of partnerships and LLCs via a 754 election.

In conclusion, certain fundamental questions remain for each analyst to consider: On the one hand, if S corporation minority interests command a premium but controlling interests do not, it is possible to have analyses that indicate that the value of the aggregate of minority interests exceeds the value of 100 percent control, or that the value of a large minority interest exceeds the value of a slightly larger controlling interest. On the other hand, if S corporation (or another pass-through entity) controlling interests do command a premium, then it is possible to create value merely through a free election of corporate form, which not everyone chooses to make. As the studies cited before indicate, the available empirical evidence does not lend clear support to such a view. There is a great deal of noise and interpretation in the available data, and in this connection, we reiterate once more that the studies cited previously use data from private C corporations, not from the public C corporations from which analysts draw their most detailed information about rates of return and multiples.

SUMMARY: CONTROLLING INTERESTS IN PASS-THROUGH ENTITIES

Each controlling-interest valuation is special and individual and cannot necessarily be subjected to only one set of rules. However, there are at least 12 questions to consider to help guide the valuation of such interests:

1. Who is the most likely pool of buyers?
2. Could the buyer elect "for free" on his or her own?
3. What degree of control will the buyer have, and would others make the S election anyway?
4. What is the possibility that the S election will be broken?
5. Will a buyer of a company in this industry *pay for* a corporate entity form that affords tax-advantaged distributions?
6. What is the expected distribution level?
7. What is the opportunity to build up retained net income?
8. What is the likely holding period?

9. What is the opportunity for 338(h)(10) or 754 elections (now and in the future)?
10. Is there an opportunity to step up the basis of the underlying assets?
11. What is the date of S election and is there an opportunity to avoid built-in gains tax?
12. What is the capital structure of the company, and how does the fact that it is an S corporation affect its ability to obtain capital?

This list of considerations is not all-inclusive, but it includes many of the issues analysts may consider when approaching the valuation of pass-through entities.

According to Grabowski, "Principal value drivers are, as they should be, the amount of cash distribution the shareholders expect to receive, the expected holding period, and, most importantly, the pool of likely buyers."[29]

> There is no conclusive market transactional evidence that S corporation values are different from private C corporation values on a control basis. However, if the analyst has used publicly traded C corporation data to value the S corporation, the differences between the expectations of the investor in a public C corporation and a private S corporation should be taken into consideration.

TAX RATES

One of the arguments typically raised for tax-affecting the earnings stream is to match the income stream to the capitalization rate that has been developed using Ibbotson data. Ibbotson, in turn was developed from the Center for Research in Securities Pricing Data. Many analysts mistakenly assume that the tax rate implicit in such data is at the highest marginal rate, say 40 percent. A review of the data reveals much lower actual corporate tax rates, particularly in the lowest deciles.

Many analysts value companies that fall in the tenth decile category. Therefore, many of these companies that appraisers typically deal with pay less income tax. Some commentators have concluded that these data, taken together with the market data, indicate that we should be deducting no taxes when we value pass-through entities. Others conclude that care should be taken to consider effective rather than statutory corporate tax rates.

Perhaps the most important consideration is that the rate of return we utilize is *pre–personal income taxes*. The corporate income tax expense "is whatever it is," and should be accounted for appropriately in whatever valuation model the appraiser utilizes. What is important is to match after-tax cash flow to after-tax discount and cap rates regardless of the level of tax in the public company data or the subject company.

---

[29] Roger G. Grabowski, "Valuation of Pass-Through Entities," AICPA 2004 National Business Valuation Conference, 37–120.

In discussing tax rates, it is worth pausing to note the method Delaware Chancery Court used to value a pass-through entity interest in *Delaware Open MRI Radiology Associates, P.A. v. Howard B. Kessler.* In this case, Vice Chancellor Strine of the Delaware Chancery Court showed a considerable level of sophistication in determining a hypothetical corporate tax rate to impute to the subject S corporation to produce a hypothetical prepersonal, after-corporate tax amount for purposes of discounted cash flow (DCF) analysis. His analysis treats the S corporation shareholder as receiving the entire benefit of untaxed dividends by setting the S corporation shareholder's after-tax return equal to the after-tax dividend to a C corporation shareholder. Vice Chancellor Stine "backed into" an equivalent rate corporate tax rate, reasoning that to "be consistent with Delaware law, I must tax affect Delaware Radiology's future cash flows at a lower level that recognizes the full effect of the Kessler Group's ability to receive cash dividends that are not subject to dividend taxes. In order to accurately capture the value to the Kessler Group of Delaware Radiology's S corporation status, I have estimated what an equivalent, hypothetical 'predividend' S corporation tax rate would be."

The Vice Chancellor's opinion presented a table similar to the following to illustrate the reasoning and calculation.

	C Corporation	S Corporation, Actual	S Corporation, C Equivalent for Valuation Purposes
Income before tax	$100	$100	$100
Corporate tax rate	40%	N/A	29.4%
Available earnings	$60	$100	$70.60
Dividend/personal tax rate	15%	40%	15%
After-tax distributions	$51	$60	$60

The 29.4 percent rate is thus the "backed into" rate. The Vice Chancellor's method includes certain implicit assumptions, such as that 100 percent of income is distributed in perpetuity. However, under certain circumstances, this method produces results similar to those of the models discussed later in this chapter.

On another tax-rate-related point, Nancy Fannon has argued that public market data not only reflect embedded actual effective (as opposed to statutory) corporate tax rates but also reflect embedded actual effective (i.e., not statutory) *personal* tax rates, and that effective personal rates are also generally lower than statutory rates.[30]

Should analysts measure the benefits of pass-through entities with regard to dividends and capital gains taxes at current statutory dividend and capital gains rates or at the rates embedded in public market equity returns? "Public-market returns inherently include the dividend and capital gains taxes that the public-market investor realizes."

Because public market companies' investors are diverse, many investors don't pay dividend and capital gains taxes (e.g., pension funds, retirement accounts), and many companies alter strategies for remunerating investors through, for example, stock buybacks versus dividend payments, to minimize taxes in response to tax policy; "the valuation analyst should consider that the tax rate actually embedded in the public market may not be the same as the statutory rate." Since the embedded rate is probably less, perhaps S corporation tax savings are less than statutory dividend and capital gains tax rates suggest.[31]

---

[30] Nancy Fannon, "The 'Real' S Corp Debate: Impact of Embedded Tax Rates from Public Markets," *Financial Valuation & Litigation Expert* (December 2008/January 2009). See also *Business Valuation Review*, Winter 2008.

[31] Ibid.

Much of the debate regarding pass-through entity valuation is centered on the issue of whether to deduct taxes and in what amount. An understanding of several of the valuation models reveals that while they deduct an amount for income taxes, they correspondingly recognize a benefit for dividend taxes saved. When using these models, failure to recognize the purpose and intent of all the steps in the model can lead to a great amount of confusion.

NONCONTROLLING INTERESTS IN PASS-THROUGH ENTITIES

The valuation of noncontrolling interests in pass-through entities has many of the same issues as for controlling interests, discussed in the previous sections. The obvious distinction is that the noncontrolling interest holder cannot control whether to distribute cash flows and the amount and timing of distributions. Lacking direct access to cash, the noncontrolling interest holder is at the mercy of those in control of the corporation.

Shareholders' investments, access to cash, and returns for a noncontrolling interest holder in a pass-through entity are impacted by issues such as:

- Amount and timing of distributions
- Retained net income
- Holding period and exit strategy
- Tax rates—personal versus corporate and capital gains
- Further effect of minority or marketability discounts
- Possible ability to participate in step-up-of-basis transaction

Four theories will be presented in the sections that follow: those of Chris D. Treharne, ASA, MCBA; Daniel Van Vleet, ASA, CBA; Z. Christopher Mercer, ASA, CFA; and Roger J. Grabowski, ASA.[32] Each of these noncontrolling theories for valuing pass-through entities has gained recognition in the valuation community. Each handles these issues somewhat differently, yet they largely agree on key issues. In addition, a "summary approach" that combines the key findings of the controlling interest studies with the common themes of the minority theories can be found in the Addendum at the end of this chapter.

No matter which model the analyst uses, if any, the key is to think through the foundation for the valuation model and carefully select the valuation inputs in order to reach a logical conclusion that a buyer and seller would be likely to agree upon.

ValTip

It is important to note that there are still many analysts who prefer simpler, more qualitative methods to valuing S corporations than the models presented here. Assuming a well-thought-out analysis, this is acceptable.

---

[32] We refer the reader to the Bibliography at the end of this chapter for a comprehensive listing of publications that each of these experts and others have written on the subject of S corporation valuation.

TREHARNE MODEL[33]

Treharne's model, equally relevant to all forms of pass-through entities, is a straightforward approach that relies on valuation models that appraisers are familiar with: the capitalized cash flow method or, in the alternative, it can be adapted to the discounted cash flow method. His valuation inputs reflect the minority shareholder's allocable share of cash flows. Note, however, that this would be the same result as if one were to use 100 percent of the entity's cash flows and then take a proportionate share. However, utilizing the allocable share emphasizes that the model already represents the minority shareholder's interest. Even so, the reader should not interpret this last statement as authority to use the model for controlling-interest valuations.

The model contemplates the development of capitalization rates using Ibbotson data. Ibbotson data are obtained from the Center for Research in Securities Pricing, and therefore, are developed from publicly traded stocks. Since the publicly traded stocks are C corporations, they necessarily reflect the satisfaction of C corporation tax liabilities.

Capitalization rates are developed for both the corporate income stream and the double-tax adjustment, described later in this section. The capitalization rate developed for the double-tax adjustment may be higher than the capitalization of cash flow, reflecting the greater risk associated with the ability to control distributions.

Treharne begins with the development of cash flow. He segregates cash flow into two segments: that retained by the firm, which is presented in Exhibit 12.4 through line 18 and that distributed to the investor, presented in Exhibit 12.5 through line 28. Note that the distribution to shareholder is bifurcated into two components: that which is necessary to cover the shareholder's allocable share of taxes on line 24 and "excess distributions," that is, distributions over and above the amount needed for taxes on line 25. Comparing each cash flow scenario to a non-dividend-paying C corporation, the three scenarios presented are:

- *Scenario 1a*: Reflects shareholder distributions sufficient to cover taxes associated with allocable entity income
- *Scenario 1b*: Shareholder distribution of 100 percent of net income
- *Scenario 1c*: No distributions

ValTip

> Some analysts have interpreted Treharne's articles as recommending consideration of all three scenarios for each valuation project. However, Treharne presented the three scenarios solely for the purpose of emphasizing the possible range of value conclusions attributed to the three possible input scenarios. Typically, all three scenarios do not need to be considered in each valuation project.

---

[33] This section © copyright 2006 Chris D. Treharne. All rights reserved. Used with permission.

Exhibit 12.4 begins with development of retained cash flow. In the case of the C corporation, entity taxes are deducted on line 2. For the S corporation Scenarios 1 and 2, the cash flow is still reduced for income taxes, but in the form of a distribution to the shareholder on line 12. In both scenarios, however, the cash flow has been reduced, and those earnings are no longer available for reinvestment by the entity. In Scenario 3, no distribution was made to the shareholder, and the entire balance is available to the corporation to reinvest. Treharne's position is that such reinvestment may or may not contribute to value, depending on the effectiveness of the controlling shareholder in utilizing such funds. However, the shareholder now has to fund the tax liability with his or her own money, an event that the shareholder would likely view negatively and may even move to cause an event that disqualifies the S election.

In Scenarios 1 and 3, note that the undistributed funds further contribute to the shareholder's basis. The analyst may want to consider the value of such basis build-up, if an exit strategy can be predicted with any reasonable degree of likelihood.

To calculate the retained cash flow component of value, line 22 of Treharne's model calculates the present value of net cash flow that has been retained by the corporation using discount rates derived from Ibbotson data.

Moving to Exhibit 12.6, Treharne's model identifies the steps necessary for the valuation of the investor component of value. First, on line 32, cash flow to the investor is valued similarly to the retained corporate cash flows. In Scenario 1c, the amount is negative, as the shareholder has to use personal funds to pay tax liabilities associated with entity income.

Second, the value associated with distributions in excess of tax requirements (line 13) is calculated. The benefit of such excess distributions is in the form of taxes saved—that is, the shareholder avoids paying a second tax, as he or she would for C corporation dividends, when the S corporation distributes such funds to him or her. As part of the analysis, the analyst must carefully consider the determination of excess distributions, given the past history and future reinvestment needs of the corporation.

In this calculation, the analyst also may consider using a greater discount rate than the rate used on entity retained or investor cash flows, in order to take into consideration the likelihood and associated risk of such distributions being made in the future.

Third, the fact that the S corporation shareholder has to pay taxes at a different rate than the C corporation is taken into consideration, with this amount present valued as an increment or decrement to the value determination.

As we have used minority cash flows to calculate value and have adjusted our discount rate to consider the likelihood of continuation of the distribution stream, our value determination is a minority, marketable value. A summary of the values as calculated under each scenario is presented in Exhibit 12.6.

When selecting a discount for lack of marketability to apply to the value determination reached using this model, the analyst should recognize that Treharne's model may already have considered the extent of dividends paid.

Shareholder Basis

Treharne's model assumes that the holding period is perpetuity. Using such an assumption, the value of any additions to basis through retained cash flow would be minimal. A deviation from this general principle would occur if there was reason to

Exhibit 12.4 Retained Cash Flow

		Tax Rates	C Corporation 2004	2005	2006	Present Value	Scenario 1a Distributions = Tax Liability 2004	2005	2006	Present Value	Scenario 1b Distributions = 100% of Income 2004	2005	2006	Present Value	Scenario 1c Distributions = 0% of Income 2004	2005	2006	Present Value
	Retained Cash Flow:																	
1	Pretax income		1,000	1,200	1,800		1,000	1,200	1,800		1,000	1,200	1,800		1,000	1,200	1,800	
2	Income taxes (C corp.)	40%	400	480	720													
3																		
4	Net income		600	720	1,080		1,000	1,200	1,800		1,000	1,200	1,800		1,000	1,200	1,800	
5	Noncash expenses		60	72	108		60	72	108		60	72	108		60	72	108	
6	Changes in working capital		(15)	(18)	(27)		(15)	(18)	(27)		(15)	(18)	(27)		(15)	(18)	(27)	
7	Fixed asset acquisitions		(65)	(78)	(117)		(65)	(78)	(117)		(65)	(78)	(117)		(65)	(78)	(117)	
8	Debt principal payments		(25)	(30)	(45)		(25)	(30)	(45)		(25)	(30)	(45)		(25)	(30)	(45)	
9																		
10	Net cash flow		555	666	999		955	1,146	1,719		955	1,146	1,719		955	1,146	1,719	
11	C corp. dividends paid		0	0	0													
12	S corp. tax distribution paid	41%					(410)	(492)	(738)		(410)	(492)	(738)		0	0	0	
13	S corp. excess distributions paid						0	0	0		(590)	(708)	(1,062)		0	0	0	
14																		
15	Retained cash flow		555	666	999		545	654	981		(45)	(54)	(81)		955	1,146	1,719	
16	C corp. valuation adjustment*		0	0	0		10	12	18		10	12	18		(400)	(480)	(720)	
17																		
18	Retained cash flow (C corp. basis)		555	666	999		555	666	999		(35)	(42)	(63)		555	666	999	
19	Terminal value				6,993				6,993				(441)				6,993	
20																		
21	Total		555	666	7,992		555	666	7,992		(35)	(42)	(504)		555	666	7,992	
22	Present value (retained cash flow)		463	463	4,625	5,550	463	463	4,625	5,550	(29)	(29)	(292)	(350)	463	463	4,625	5,550

*Treharne notes that previous publications and presentations of his model neglected to show the line 16 "C corp valuation adjustment" for Scenarios 1a and 1b (it was recognized in Scenario 1c). To properly value a minority interest using his model, such an adjustment (i.e., the difference between equivalent C corporation taxes and the expected personal tax liability associated with S corporation income) should be made on line 16.

Exhibit 12.5 Cash to Investor

#	Item	Tax Rates	C Corporation 2004	C Corporation 2005	C Corporation 2006	C Corporation Present Value	Scenario 1a Distributions = Tax Liability 2004	2005	2006	Present Value	Scenario 1b Distributions = 100% of Income 2004	2005	2006	Present Value	Scenario 1c Distributions = 0% of Income 2004	2005	2006	Present Value
23	**Net cash flow to investor**																	
24	S corp. tax distribution paid						410	492	738		410	492	738		0	0	0	
25	S corp. "excess distributions" paid						0	0	0		590	708	1,062		0	0	0	
26	Personal taxes on S corp. operations	41%					(410)	(492)	(738)		(410)	(492)	(738)		(410)	(492)	(738)	
27																		
28	Net cash flow to investor		0	0	0		0	0	0		590	708	1,062		(410)	(492)	(738)	
29	Terminal value			0	0				0				7,434				(5,166)	
30																		
31	Total		0	0	0		0	0	0		590	708	8,496		(410)	(492)	(5,904)	
32	Present value					0	0	0	0	0	492	492	4,917	5,900	(342)	(342)	(3,417)	(4,100)
33																		
34	**Double Taxation Adjustment**																	
35	Total S corp. distributions		0	0	0		410	492	738		1,000	1,200	1,800		0	0	0	
36	C corp entity-related taxes		0	0	0		(400)	(480)	(720)		(400)	(480)	(720)		(400)	(480)	(720)	
37																		
38	S corp. "excess distributions" paid	21%	0	0	0		10	12	18		600	720	1,080		0	0	0	
39	S corp. "excess dist" tax benefit		0	0	0		2	3	4		126	151	227		0	0	0	
40	Terminal value		0	0	0				25				1,488				0	
41																		
42	Total		0	0	0		2	3	29		126	151	1,715		0	0	0	
43	Present value (double-taxation adjustment)		0	0	0	0	2	2	16	20	104	103	968	1,176	0	0	0	0
44																		
45	**Tax-Rate Differential Adjustment**																	
46	S corp. entity-related taxes	41%	0	0	0		(410)	(492)	(738)		(410)	(492)	(738)		(410)	(492)	(738)	
47	C corp. entity-related taxes	40%	0	0	0		(400)	(480)	(720)		(400)	(480)	(720)		(400)	(480)	(720)	
48																		
49	S corp. benefit (liability)		0	0	0		(10)	(12)	(18)		(10)	(12)	(18)		(10)	(12)	(18)	
50	Terminal value			0	0				(126)				(126)				(126)	
51																		
52	Total		0	0	0		(10)	(12)	(144)		(10)	(12)	(144)		(10)	(12)	(144)	
53	Present value (tax-rate differential adjustment)		0	0	0	0	(8)	(8)	(83)	(100)	(8)	(8)	(83)	(100)	(8)	(8)	(83)	(100)
54																		
55	Present value (cash to investor)					0				(80)				6,976				(4,200)
56																		
57	**PV of retained and investor cash flows**					5,550				5,470				6,626				1,350

Exhibit 12.6 Valuation Conclusions Summary: S Corporation Minority Interests
(Minority Marketable Level)

		C Corp	S Corporation		
Scenario:			1a	1b	1c
Net cash flow for 2004		555	955	955	955
Present value (retained cash flow)		5,550	5,550	(350)	5,550
Present value (cash to investor)		0	(80)	6,976	(4,200)
		------	------	------	------
Value to investor		**5,550**	**5,470**	**6,626**	**1,350**

believe that an exit strategy was more imminent and the assumption of perpetuity
was not valid; in that instance, the appraiser should consider the facts and circumstances and value such basis build-up accordingly.

The addition of retained net income (basis) is not built into Treharne's model. It
is his position that the analyst needs to consider the facts and circumstances and the
likelihood of realizing the benefit of such basis in the future. He generally considers
such a possibility to be remote and such benefit to be negligible.

Summary of Treharne Model

Treharne's model begins with the value of an equivalent C corporation after reinvestment of all necessary cash flows. To this value determination, one makes adjustments to the equivalent C corporation value depending on:

- Distributions to the noncontrolling owner
- Tax rate differentials
- Basis build-up, if relevant

Using Treharne's model, value distinctions are made for each level of distribution.

VAN VLEET MODEL[34]

Van Vleet maintains that there is an economic mismatch between the 1) underpinnings of the empirical data typically used by analysts to value minority equity
interests in S corporations and 2) benefits actually enjoyed by shareholders of
these same S corporation equity interests. Van Vleet's model addresses differences
in the respective economic benefits enjoyed by the shareholders of C corporations
and S corporations.

The conceptual foundation for Van Vleet's model is the differences in the
income tax treatment of C corporations, S corporations, and their respective shareholders. These income tax differences can distort the value of S corporation equity
securities when empirical studies of publicly traded C corporation equity securities

---

[34] This section © copyright 2006 Daniel R. Van Vleet. All rights reserved. Used with permission.

are used in the valuation analysis. The principal income tax differences between S corporations and C corporations are as follows:

- C corporations pay taxes on corporate income at the corporate level. S corporations do not pay tax at the corporate level; instead, the shareholders recognize a pro rata share of the S corporation income on their personal income tax returns.
- C corporation shareholders pay taxes on dividends. No taxes are due when distributions are paid to S corporation shareholders. Consequently, the S corporation shareholder is subject to only a single layer of income tax.
- Income retained by the S corporation (that is, the undistributed net income) increases the income tax basis of the shareholder's stock. Conversely, the income tax basis of C corporation stock is unaffected by undistributed income.

Van Vleet's model presents a mathematical framework that conceptually addresses the relevant income tax–related differences among S corporations, C corporations, and their respective shareholders.

Business Valuation Approaches

Van Vleet maintains that his model may be used to adjust the publicly traded equivalent value of equity provided by the income, market, and asset-based approaches to business valuation.

Van Vleet begins with a premise that investment returns are separated into two components: 1) retained earnings and 2) dividends. This is consistent with fundamental capital market theory and is presented in Exhibit 12.7.

Capitalization rates (market multiples, equity rates of return, etc.) estimated from equity security transactions of publicly traded C corporations are conceptually based on expectations of both dividend and capital appreciation investment

Exhibit 12.7 Fundamental Theory of Equity Capital Markets

Capital market investors are motivated by two things:
- (1) Capital appreciation
- (2) Dividends

Capital market P/E multiples and investment rates of return are derived from the capital appreciation and dividends of publicly traded equity securities.

$$k_1 = \frac{(S_1 - S_0) + d_1}{S_0}$$

Where:

k_1	=	Rate of return during period 1
S_1	=	Stock price at end of period 1
S_0	=	Stock price at beginning of period 1
d_1	=	Dividends paid during period 1

returns. Because both sources of shareholder investment return are derived from net income, these capitalization rates necessarily reflect 1) corporate income taxes at the entity level and 2) capital gains and dividend income taxes at the shareholder level.

The S corporation shareholder recognizes only a single layer of income tax on S corporation earnings. The S corporation shareholder is also the beneficiary of an increase in the income tax basis of his or her equity ownership interest attributable to retained earnings. This treatment results in avoided capital gains taxes when the securities are sold.

Because of the significant income tax differences among S corporations, C corporations, and their respective shareholders, the use of capitalization rates derived from transactions of publicly traded equity securities of C corporations has the potential to distort the value of the S corporation equity securities, if left unadjusted.

Fundamental Underpinnings of the Van Vleet Model

Van Vleet's model has a number of fundamental assumptions that the appraiser should carefully consider:

- The capital appreciation of equity is derived solely from undistributed earnings (i.e., retained net income) on a dollar-for-dollar basis.
- Capital market investors inherently recognize the capital gains tax liability concurrent with the capital appreciation of the equity security. This is principally due to the fact that the capital appreciation investment return is liquid and can be obtained at the option of the security holder.
- Depending on relevant income tax characteristics, the net economic benefit to S corporation shareholders may be greater than, less than, or equal to the net economic benefit to C corporation shareholders, regardless of the C corporation dividend payout ratio assumed in the analysis. Under current federal income tax law, dividends and capital gains are taxed at equal rates. Consequently, the assumed dividend payout ratio of the publicly traded equity securities used in the analysis does not affect the Van Vleet Model. To the extent there is a difference in the capital gains and dividend income tax rates, the dividend payout ratio assumed in the Van Vleet Model may affect the results.
- The net economic benefit to S corporation shareholders is the same regardless of the amount of distributions the corporation is making. This is because, using the assumptions in Van Vleet's model, the shareholder recognizes value either through distributed cash or capital appreciation through retained net income. Regardless of the mix, the net value to the shareholder is the same. The Van Vleet Model essentially converts the C corporation publicly traded equivalent value into a hypothetical S corporation publicly traded equivalent value. In this hypothetical market, the S corporation capital appreciation or dividend form of investment return would be equally liquid to the investor, just as it is to the publicly traded C corporation investor.
- The net economic benefit to C corporation shareholders remains the same regardless of dividend payout ratio. This is true as long as dividends and capital appreciation are taxed at the same rate. If the tax rates on dividends and capital appreciation change in the future, the Van Vleet Model contains components that will reflect this disparate treatment.

The S Corporation Economic Adjustment

The S corporation economic adjustment (SEA) is based on mathematical equations that compare the economic benefits of C corporation shareholders to those of S corporation shareholders. On one side of the equation is the net economic benefit of the C corporation income stream (NEB$_C$); on the other side of the equation is the net economic benefit of the S corporation income stream (NEB$_S$). The SEA corrects the inequality difference between the NEB$_C$ and NEB$_S$.

Exhibit 12.8 illustrates the NEB$_C$ and the NEB$_S$. A 50 percent dividend payout ratio is assumed for both the S corporation and the C corporation. Under current tax law, the NEB$_C$ and the NEB$_S$ would not be affected by the dividend payout ratio. Using the income tax rates assumed in Exhibit 12.8, the S corporation shareholder has a greater net economic benefit than the C corporation shareholder. This is because the C corporation shareholder receives his or her cash after entity level taxes have been paid and after income taxes on dividends at the shareholder level. Further, the capital appreciation is subject to capital gains tax at the shareholder level. The S corporation shareholder, however, pays tax only on his or her pro rata share of S corporation earnings. Distributions from an S corporation are not taxable and the capital appreciation of the S corporation share is conceptually tax-free due to the increase in tax basis of the S corporation share attributable to undistributed net income.

These items form the foundation for the NEB$_C$ and the NEB$_S$ equations.

The NEB$_C$ equation is made up of two components: 1) net cash received by shareholders from dividends after the payment of a) income taxes at the entity level and b)

Exhibit 12.8 Net Economic Benefits to Shareholders

	Public C Corp.($)	Private S Corp.($)
Income before corporate income taxes	100,000	100,000
Corporate income taxes @ 35.0%	(35,000)	NM
Net income	65,000	100,000
Dividends		
Dividends paid to S corporation shareholders @ 50.0% (DPR)	NM	50,000
Income tax due by S corporation shareholders @ 35.0%	NM	(35,000)
Net cash flow benefit to S corporation shareholders	NM	**15,000**
Dividends paid to C corporation shareholders @ 50.0% (DPR)	32,500	NM
Dividend tax due by C corporation shareholders @ 15.0%	(4,875)	NM
Net cash flow benefit to C corporation shareholders	**27,625**	NM
Capital Appreciation		
Net income	65,000	100,000
Dividends paid to shareholders	(32,500)	(50,000)
Retained earnings (i.e., net capital appreciation)	32,500	50,000
Effect of retained earnings on the income tax basis of the shares	NM	(50,000)
Net taxable capital appreciation	32,500	0
Capital gains tax liability @ 15.0%	(4,875)	0
Net capital appreciation benefit to shareholders	**27,625**	**50,000**
Net Economic Benefit to shareholders		
Net cash flow benefit to shareholders	27,625	15,000
Net capital appreciation benefit to shareholders	27,625	50,000
Total Net Economic Benefit to Shareholders	**55,250**	**65,000**

Exhibit 12.9   Net Economic Benefit to C Corporation Shareholders (NEB$_C$)

Dividends + Capital Appreciation = Net Economic Benefit

$$\text{Dividends} = I_p \times (1 - t_c) \times D_p \times (1 - t_d)$$

$$+$$

$$\text{Capital Appreciation} = I_p \times (1 - t_c) \times (1 - D_p) \times (1 - t_{cg})$$

$$=$$

$$NEB_C = [I_p \times (1 - t_c) \times D_p \times (1 - t_d)] + [I_p \times (1 - t_c) \times (1 - D_p) \times (1 - t_{cg})]$$

I_p	=	Income prior to federal and state income tax ($I_p > 0$)
t_c	=	C corporation effective income tax rate
D_p	=	Dividend payout ratio
t_d	=	Income tax rate on dividends
t_{cg}	=	Income tax rate on capital gains

income taxes on dividends at the shareholder level and 2) net capital appreciation of the equity security after recognition of capital gains taxes at the shareholder level.

The equation for NEB$_C$ is shown in Exhibit 12.9.

The NEB$_S$ equation is much less complex and simply reflects the shareholder's tax on the pro rata share of S corporation net income. The equation for NEB$_S$ is shown in Exhibit 12.10.

The SEA is defined as the inequality between the NEB$_C$ and NEB$_S$ equations. This inequality arises from the difference in the net economic benefit realized by the C corporation shareholder and the S corporation shareholder, as reflected in Exhibit 12.8.

The SEA equation is presented in Exhibit 12.11.

S Corporation Equity Adjustment Multiple

Typically, appraisers use C corporation data to value S corporations. The SEA is used to calculate a multiple that may then be applied to the C corporation publicly

Exhibit 12.10   Net Economic Benefit to S Corporation Shareholders (NEB$_S$)

$$NEB_S = I_p \times (1 - t_i)$$

I_p = Reported income prior to federal and state income tax ($I_p > 0$)
t_i = Individual ordinary income tax rate

Exhibit 12.11   S Corporation Economic Adjustment (SEA)

$$NEB_c \neq NEB_s$$

$$NEB_c = NEB_s - SEA$$

$$SEA = NEB_s - NEB_c$$

$$SEA = I_p \times (t_c + t_{cg} - t_i - t_c t_{cg} + D_p t_d - D_p t_{cg} - D_p t_c t_d + D_p t_c t_{cg})$$

traded equivalent value in order to convert such value to an S corporation publicly traded equivalent value. This multiple is referred to as the *S corporation equity adjustment multiple* (SEAM).

Mathematically, the SEAM is calculated by dividing the SEA by the NEB_C and then adding that percentage to 1.0. This calculation is presented in Exhibit 12.12.

Assumptions in the Van Vleet Model

The SEAM is conceptually based on noncontrolling equity interest transactions involving publicly traded equity securities. Consequently, Van Vleet maintains it would be incorrect to apply the SEAM to a controlling interest indication of equity value. Since the SEAM is an equity adjustment model, Van Vleet also maintains that application of the SEAM to the value of total invested capital or to the value of assets is not appropriate.

Exhibit 12.12   SEAM Multiple

$$SEAM\ Multiple = 1 + \frac{SEA}{NEB_C}$$

Actual Formula

$$SEAM = 1 + \frac{[I_p \times (1 - t_i)] - \{[I_p \times (1 - t_c) \times D_p \times (1 - t_d)] + [I_p \times (1 - t_c) \times (1 - D_p) \times (1 - t_{cg})]\}}{[I_p \times (1 - t_c) \times D_p \times (1 - t_d)] + [I_p \times (1 - t_c) \times (1 - D_p) \times (1 - t_{cg})]}$$

Algebraically Simplified Version

$$SEAM = 1 + \frac{(t_c + t_{cg} - t_i - t_c t_{cg} + D_p t_d - D_p t_{cg} - D_p t_c t_d + D_p t_c t_{cg})}{(1 - t_c - t_{cg} + t_c t_{cg} - D_p t_d + D_p t_{cg} + D_p t_c t_d - D_p t_c t_{cg})}$$

The Van Vleet Model is based on several significant assumptions, which the analyst should consider in order to determine whether adjustments are warranted:

- The subject company will continue as an S corporation in perpetuity.
- Investors are indifferent between distributions and unrealized capital gains.
- Investors in publicly traded C corporations recognize the capital gains tax liability when incurred.
- Buyers are willing to pay sellers for the S corporation income tax benefits.
- The current income tax law treatment of S corporations vis-à-vis C corporations will continue into perpetuity.
- The subject S corporation will continue as a profitable venture in perpetuity.

Van Vleet recognizes that to the extent any one of these assumptions is not true, the SEAM may distort the value of the S corporation equity security.

We note that Van Vleet's model discusses only the S corporation as a form of pass-through entity. Regardless, his model may be useful in the analysis of other forms of pass-through entities as long as the initial indication of value provided by the analysis is a C corporation publicly traded equivalent value. The appraiser should be careful to consider whether there are any differences that warrant adjustment.

Example of Van Vleet Model

An example of Van Vleet's model is presented in Exhibit 12.13.

For each level of selected inputs, the SEAM is simply a mathematical calculation. At the given inputs, the calculation results in SEAMs ranging from 1.1471 to 1.2188. In Exhibit 12.12, the dividend payout ratio affects the SEAM due to the assumption that dividends and capital gains are taxed at different rates. To the extent that this is not true, the assumed dividend payout ratio will not affect the SEAM. The dividend payout ratio assumed in the analysis should be based on the publicly traded C corporations used in the analysis, not the dividend payout ratio of the subject S corporation.

Next, the SEAM is applied to the C corporation publicly traded equivalent value in Exhibit 12.14.

In Exhibit 12.13, value determinations are compared to the C corporation publicly traded equivalent value for each assumed level of dividend payout. As a final step, an appropriate discount for lack of marketability is determined and applied to each indication of value. Note that the lack of marketability discount is reduced as the dividend payout ratio increases. This is a subjective adjustment that the appraiser should quantify and support in the analysis.

Summary: Van Vleet Model

Van Vleet's model begins with the economic benefits of a C corporation equity interest, fully burdened with income tax at the corporate level, as well as dividend tax on distributions and capital gains tax on retained earnings. That benefit is compared to the S corporation economic benefit that bears only one layer of income tax. The mathematical formula that results from this difference becomes the SEAM adjustment.

The SEAM assumes that shareholders of publicly traded companies are indifferent between distributions and capital gains. This is generally true because both

Exhibit 12.13 Calculation of SEAM

SEAM Formula

$$SEAM = 1 + \frac{(t_c + t_{cg} - t_i - t_c t_{cg} + D_p t_d - D_p t_{cg} - D_p t_c t_d + D_p t_c t_{cg})}{(1 - t_c - t_{cg} + t_c t_{cg} - D_p t_d + D_p t_{cg} + D_p t_c t_d - D_p t_c t_{cg})}$$

SEAM Model Components

Federal/state blended income tax rate on C corporations	40.0%	40.0%	40.0%
Federal/state blended income tax rate on capital gains	20.0%	20.0%	20.0%
Federal/state blended income tax rate on individual ordinary income	41.5%	41.5%	41.5%
Federal/state blended income tax rate on dividends	15.0%	15.0%	15.0%
Dividend payout ratio of the guideline companies*	0.0%	50.0%	100.0%

S corporation Equity Adjustment Multiple (SEAM)	**1.2188**	**1.1818**	**1.1471**

Notes:

*Relevant only when the income tax rates on dividends and capital gains are different.

Exhibit 12.14 SEAM Applied to C Corporation Publicly Traded Equivalent Value

C Corporation Analysis

	Enterprise Value 10.0% Minority C Corporation		
	0.0%	50.0%	100.0%
Dividend payout ratio (DPR)			
Marketable, noncontrolling value	$3,750.26	$3,750.26	$3,750.26
Discount for lack of marketability	45.0%	40.0%	35.0%
Nonmarketable, noncontrolling value	$2,062.64	$2,250.16	$2,437.67

S Corporation Analysis

	Enterprise Value 10.0% Minority S Corporation		
As if a C corporation	$3,750.26	$3,750.26	$3,750.26
SEAM - DPR of guideline companies is 0.0%	1.2188		
SEAM - DPR of guideline companies is 50.0%		1.1818	
SEAM - DPR of guideline companies is 100.0%			1.1471
Indications of value	$4,570.63	$4,432.13	$4,301.77

	Discount For Lack of Marketability		
S Corporation with a DPR of 0.0%	50.0%	50.0%	50.0%
S Corporation with a DPR of 50.0%	45.0%	45.0%	45.0%
S Corporation with a DPR of 100.0%	40.0%	40.0%	40.0%

	Indications of Value		
S Corporation with a DPR of 0.0%	$2,285.32	$2,216.06	$2,150.89
S Corporation with a DPR of 50.0%	$2,513.85	$2,437.67	$2,365.97
S Corporation with a DPR of 100.0%	$2,742.38	$2,659.28	$2,581.06

forms of investment return are equally liquid to the public company shareholder. Therefore, the SEAM inherently assumes that the subject S corporation is paying 100 percent of its earnings in distributions, as this is the only way that an investment return on a privately held security can be completely liquid. Van Vleet's model recognizes that the level of distributions for the subject company can impact value and recognizes it through the extent of the discount for lack of marketability.

MERCER MODEL[35]

Mercer cites many arguments in support of tax-affecting S corporations, beginning with a number of qualitative arguments:

- The S election has no impact on the operating cash flows of a business.
- The benefits of the S election are shareholder, not corporate, benefits. Capitalization of such benefits, according to this theory, overstates the value of the firm. However, for minority interests, this theory recognizes that the economic benefits of identical S corporation and C corporation interests could be different over the expected holding periods of the investments.
- S corporations virtually always pass through a sufficient portion of their earnings to their shareholders to enable them to pay their shareholder/corporate taxes, leaving the corporation in the same position as if it were a C corporation, assuming similar rates.
- Most of the likely buyers of S corporations are C corporations or groups organized as C corporations. If there were a benefit to the S election, it would be evident in the marketplace. However, such advantage does not exist.
- The reduction of the dividend rate to 15 percent eliminated much of the relative value of the S corporation shareholders over C corporation shareholders. These rates, of course, are subject to change by Congress at any time.
- Mercer's experience in investment banking has shown that buyers will pay no more for an S corporation than they will for a C corporation.
- Finally, the buyer would be unlikely to pay for an election he or she could make for free upon consummation of the transaction.

Value versus Proceeds

Many theories cite the ability to build up basis as a reason for an increase in value of the S corporation. Clearly, to the extent that net income is retained over time and basis is increased, it can result in substantially greater proceeds to the seller, due to the elimination of capital gains tax upon the sale.

Mercer cautions not to get the issue of proceeds upon a sale confused with value. Value is equal to the future cash flow of the entity, discounted to the present. The value of an identical S corporation and C corporation will be the same, if one accepts as a practical matter:

- Equivalent or substantially equal tax rates
- No additional risks of being an S corporation at the enterprise level
- That the underlying expected growth rate is the same

---

[35] This section © copyright 2006 Mercer Capital. All rights reserved. Used with permission.

Further, the proceeds associated with selling an S corporation may be more or less than those of selling a C corporation. This is due to the build up of basis and the ability of the S corporation to sell assets and avoid embedded gain. However, when an S corporation sells its assets, its shareholders retain the tail liability for any liabilities associated with the corporation. Such tail liability has potential, and sometimes dramatic, costs that should be considered.

The conclusion is that the net proceeds of the sale of an S corporation may be greater than, equal to, or less than those of an equivalent C corporation as a result. Regardless, it does not affect value.

Assuming the S corporation distributes sufficient cash for shareholders to pay their allocable share of income taxes, the S corporation will have the same value as the C corporation at the enterprise level. This is because entity cash flows are identical and retained net income serves to increase proceeds to the seller but does not represent value to the buyer.

There is potential value in retained net income that the buyer could build up for himself or herself and therefore shelter his or her future capital gains, as opposed to that which the seller has created. This is a modest reduction to the discount determined by the Quantitative Marketability Discount Model (QMDM), discussed subsequently.

Valuation of Noncontrolling Interests

It is critical to note that, unlike Treharne and Van Vleet, when Mercer refers to "no distributions or dividends," he means no dividends *over and above* distributions needed to fund the income taxes due on the shareholder's allocable share of corporate earnings. Mercer assumes that S corporations distribute sufficient funds to pay income taxes. Therefore, "no distributions" under Mercer's model, by comparison to the other three models, means "distributions sufficient to pay income tax."

Mercer considers three alternative scenarios for the valuation of minority interest:

- No distributions (i.e., only taxes are funded)
- 50 percent distributions
- 100 percent distributions

Mercer's theory relies on two foundations, which are both valuation theories that Mercer has developed and advocated: the Integrated Theory of Business Valuation (ITBV)[36] and the QMDM. Mercer first uses ITBV to measure value at the enterprise level and then uses QMDM to measure value at the shareholder level.

ITBV holds that regardless of the level of distributions made, the value at the enterprise level will remain the same. This concept can be illustrated through a progression of illustrations.

Exhibit 12.15 reflects a corporation that has chosen to retain 100 percent of its earnings. The model reflects sufficient funds being paid out for taxes. Following that, 100 percent of net cash flow is retained by the firm; therefore, there are no interim

---

[36] Z. Christopher Mercer, *Valuing Enterprise and Shareholder Cash Flows: The Integrated Theory of Business Valuation* (Memphis: Peabody Publishing, LP, 2004), www.integratedtheory.com; *Quantifying Marketability Discounts: 2005 E-Book Edition* (Memphis: Peabody Publishing, LP, 2005), www.mercercapital.com. Mercer's E-book includes the QMDM Companion, the Excel spreadsheet/working model of QMDM, and a several-page, quick-start tutorial for the QMDM.

Exhibit 12.15   Enterprise Value—100 Percent Earnings Retained

Basic Assumptions of the Comparative Analyses

1. Uniform Operating Assumptions
   - a. Year One Sales — $ 5,000.00
   - b. Forecast for — 4 years
   - c. Enterprise Discount Rate (Reinvestment Rate) — 15.0%
   - d. Interim Earnings Growth Rate — 15.0%
   - e. Long-Term Growth Rate—terminal value — 5.0%
   - f. Pretax Margin — 12.5%
   - g. Earnings Retention Rate — 100.0%

2. Uniform Tax Rate Assumptions
   - a. C Corp Federal/State Blended Rate — 40.0%
   - b. Federal/State Blended Rate on Dividends — 15.0%
   - c. Federal/State Blended Rate on Ordinary Income — 41.5%
   - d. Federal/State Blended Rate on Capital Gains — 20.0%

Business owners have four choices each period:

1. Retain all earnings
2. Distribute all earnings
3. Combination
4. Repurchase shares (analogous to distributions)

	0	1	2	3	4	5	
Sales	$ 4,545.00	$ 5,000.00	$ 5,750.00	$ 6,612.50	$ 7,604.38	$ 8,745.03	
Pretax Margin		12.5%	12.5%	12.5%	12.5%	12.5%	
Pretax Earnings	$543.5	$625.0	$718.8	$826.6	$950.5	$1,093.1	
State Taxes	1.5%	($9.38)	($10.78)	($12.40)	($14.26)	($16.40)	
After State Taxes		$615.625	$707.969	$814.164	$936.289	$1,076.732	
Federal Taxes	39.08629%	($240.63)	($276.72)	($318.23)	($365.96)	($420.85)	
Net Income		$375.000	$431.250	$495.938	$570.328	$655.877	
Reinvestment		($375.0)	($431.3)	($495.9)	($570.3)	$0.0	
Net Cash Flow		$0.000	$0.000	$0.000	$0.000	$655.877	
Periods to Discount		1.000	2.000	3.000	4.000	4.000	
Present Value Factors	15%	0.86960	0.75610	0.65750	0.57180	0.57180	
Present Value of Interim Cash Flows		$0.00	$0.00	$0.00	$0.00	$6,558.8	Terminal Value
Present Value of Terminal Value					$3,750.31		
Enterprise Value	$3,750.3						
Multiple of Pretax	6.000						
Multiple of Net Income	10.00						

					Terminal	
Earnings Retention Rate		100.0%	100.0%	100.0%	100.0%	0.0%
Implied Dividend Payout		0.0%	0.0%	0.0%	0.0%	100.0%
Interim Interest Distributions (C Corp.)	10.00%	$0.0	$0.0	$0.0	$0.0	
Terminal Cash Flow					$655.9	
Earnings Growth Rate		15.00%	15.00%	15.00%	15.00%	15.00%
Distribution Yield		0.00%				
Total Return		15.00%				

cash flows subject to present value. The earnings growth rate, set at 15 percent, reflects the fact that the retained cash flow has been used to grow the firm. The resulting value is $3,750.

For the calculation in Exhibit 12.16, the earnings retention rate has been changed to 50 percent. The analyst must consider that now, without the benefit of 100 percent of the available funds produced by the company, the earnings growth rate will likely be less than in the previous scenario. Thus, the earnings growth rate was set at 10 percent. As a result, the same value conclusion of $3,750 was reached.

In the final scenario, presented as Exhibit 12.17, no earnings are retained by the company, resulting in significant shareholder current return. However, earnings would be expected to grow only modestly. Setting the interim growth rate at 5 percent produces the same value conclusion of $3,750.

Therefore, regardless of the level of reinvestment versus net cash flow available to shareholders, utilizing the Integrated Theory of Business Valuation model, the value is the same. This is because the sum of the interim growth rate plus the distribution yield, in all three scenarios, is equal to the same thing. See Exhibit 12.18.

From this analysis, Mercer concludes that the level of distributions causes no difference in value at the enterprise level.[37]

---

[37] The assumption is that, in accordance with basic financial theory, the shareholders' return comprises dividends plus capital appreciation. Assuming that all reinvestment occurs at the enterprise discount rate, shareholders will achieve their expected return, that is, the discount rate.

Exhibit 12.16 Enterprise Value—50 Percent Earnings Retained

Basic Assumptions of the Comparative Analyses

1. Uniform Operating Assumptions
   a. Year One Sales — $ 5,000.00
   b. Forecast for — 4 years
   c. Enterprise Discount Rate (Reinvestment Rate) — 15.0%
   d. Interim Earnings Growth Rate — 10.0%
   e. Long-Term Growth Rate—terminal value — 5.0%
   f. Pretax Margin — 12.5%
   g. Earnings Retention Rate — 50.0%

   ← Note: Value does not change with distribution/retention policy.

2. Uniform Tax Rate Assumptions
   a. C Corp. Federal/State Blended Rate — 40.0%
   b. Federal/State Blended Rate on Dividends — 15.0%
   c. Federal/State Blended Rate on Ordinary Income — 41.5%
   d. Federal/State Blended Rate on Capital Gains — 20.0%

	0	1	2	3	4	5	
Sales	$ 4,545.00	$ 5,000.00	$ 5,500.00	$ 6,050.00	$ 6,655.00	$ 7,320.50	
Pretax Margin		12.5%	12.5%	12.5%	12.5%	12.5%	
Pretax Earnings	$568.2	$625.0	$687.5	$756.3	$831.9	$915.1	
State Taxes	1.5%	($9.38)	($10.31)	($11.34)	($12.48)	($13.73)	
After State Taxes		$615.625	$677.188	$744.906	$819.397	$901.337	
Federal Taxes	39.08629%	($240.63)	($264.69)	($291.16)	($320.27)	($352.30)	
Net Income		$375.000	$412.500	$453.750	$499.125	$549.038	
Reinvestment		($187.5)	($206.3)	($226.9)	($249.6)	$0.0	
Net Cash Flow		$187.500	$206.250	$226.875	$249.563	$549.038	
Periods to Discount		1.000	2.000	3.000	4.000	4.000	
Present Value Factors	15%	0.86960	0.75610	0.65750	0.57180	0.57180	
Present Value of Interim Cash Flows		$163.05	$155.95	$149.17	$142.70	$5,490.4	Terminal Value
Present Value of Terminal Value					$3,139.40		
Enterprise Value	$3,750.3						
Multiple of Pretax	6.000						
Multiple of Net Income	10.00						

					Terminal
Earnings Retention Rate		50.0%	50.0%	50.0%	50.0%	0.0%
Implied Dividend Payout		50.0%	50.0%	50.0%	50.0%	100.0%
Interim Interest Distributions (C Corp.)	10.00%	$18.8	$20.6	$22.7	$25.0	
Terminal Cash Flow					$549.0	
Earnings Growth Rate		10.00%	10.00%	10.00%	10.00%	10.00%
Distribution Yield		5.00%				
Total Return		**15.00%**				

Exhibits 12.15, 12.16, 12.17, and 12.18 illustrate the enterprise-level value for both a C corporation and an S corporation. However, at the shareholder level, other considerations may affect the value determination.

No Distributions or Dividends

For an identical C and S corporation, in the event of no distributions beyond the tax liability, Mercer finds no differential in value between the C corporate share and the S corporate share. However, there may be incremental risks to being a shareholder in an S corporation that do not exist in a C corporation. Such risks may cause the discount rate for the S corporation to exceed the discount rate for the C corporation. If this is true, then the value for the S corporation shareholder may be less than the value for the C corporation shareholder. The use of the QMDM (discussed subsequently) validates this theory.

Economic Distributions Greater Than the Tax Liability (50 Percent and 100 Percent)

When S corporation distributions are greater than the amount necessary for taxes, the cash flow of the S corporation shareholder will be greater than that of the C corporation shareholder. Where the cash flow is greater for the S shareholder, value will be greater than for the C corporation shareholder for the expected length of the

Exhibit 12.17 Enterprise Value—0 Percent Earnings Retained

Basic Assumptions of the Comparative Analyses

1. **Uniform Operating Assumptions**
   a. Year One Sales $ 5,000.00
   b. Forecast for   4 years
   c. Enterprise Discount Rate (Reinvestment Rate)   15.0%
   d. Interim Earnings Growth Rate   5.0%
   e. Long-Term Growth Rate—terminal value   5.0%
   f. Pretax Margin   12.5%
   g. Earnings Retention Rate   0.0%

   Note: Value does not change with distribution/retention policy.

2. **Uniform Tax Rate Assumptions**
   a. C Corp Federal/State Blended Rate   40.0%
   b. Federal/State Blended Rate on Dividends   15.0%
   c. Federal/State Blended Rate on Ordinary Income   41.5%
   d. Federal/State Blended Rate on Capital Gains   20.0%

	0	1	2	3	4	5	
Sales	$ 4,545.00	$ 5,000.00	$ 5,250.00	$ 5,512.50	$ 5,788.13	$ 6,077.53	
Pretax Margin		12.5%	12.5%	12.5%	12.5%	12.5%	
Pretax Earnings	$595.2	$625.0	$656.3	$689.1	$723.5	$759.7	
State Taxes	1.5%	($9.38)	($9.84)	($10.34)	($10.85)	($11.40)	
After State Taxes		$615.625	$646.406	$678.727	$712.663	$748.296	
Federal Taxes	39.08629%	($240.63)	($252.66)	($265.29)	($278.55)	($292.48)	
Net Income		$375.000	$393.750	$413.438	$434.109	$455.815	
Reinvestment		$0.0	$0.0	$0.0	$0.0	$0.0	
Net Cash Flow		$375.000	$393.750	$413.438	$434.109	$455.815	
Periods to Discount		1.000	2.000	3.000	4.000	4.000	
Present Value Factors	15%	0.86960	0.75610	0.65750	0.57180	0.57180	
Present Value of Interim Cash Flows		$326.10	$297.71	$271.84	$248.22	$4,558.1	Terminal Value
Present Value of Terminal Value						$2,606.35	
Enterprise Value	$3,750.2						
Multiple of Pretax	6.000						
Multiple of Net Income	10.00						

					Terminal	
Earnings Retention Rate		0.0%	0.0%	0.0%	0.0%	0.0%
Implied Dividend Payout		100.0%	100.0%	100.0%	100.0%	100.0%
Interim Interest Distributions (C Corp.)	10.00%	$37.5	$39.4	$41.3	$43.4	
Terminal Cash Flow					$455.8	
Earnings Growth Rate		5.00%	5.00%	5.00%	5.00%	5.00%
Distribution Yield		10.00%				
Total Return		15.00%				

© 2004 Mercer Capital. All rights reserved. Used with permission.

Exhibit 12.18 Regardless of Distribution/Retention Policy, the Sum of Interim Growth and Distribution Yield Equals the Discount Rate of 15 Percent

Earnings Retention Rate	Interim G	Yield
0%	5%	10%
50%	10%	5%
100%	15%	0%

Z. Christopher Mercer, *Valuing Enterprise & Shareholder Cash Flows: The Integrated Theory of Business Valuation* (Memphis: Peabody Publishing, LP, 2004), www.integratedtheory.com; Z. Christopher Mercer, *Quantifying Marketability Discounts: 2004 E-Book Edition* (Memphis: Peabody Publishing, LP, 2004), www.mercercapital.com. © Mercer Capital, 2004

Exhibit 12.19 Developing Required Holding Period Returns

		C Corporation			S Corporation		
Retention %		100%	50%	0%	100%	50%	0%
DPO %		0%	50%	100%	0%	50%	100%
Expected Growth in Value	QMDM #1	15.0%	10.0%	5.0%	15.0%	10.0%	5.0%
Expected Distribution Yield	QMDM #2	0.0%	5.0%	10.0%	0.0%	5.9%	11.8%
Expected Growth in Distributions	QMDM #3	na	10.0%	5.0%	na	10.0%	5.0%
Expected Holding Period (Years)	QMDM #4	4.0	4.0	4.0	4.0	4.0	4.0
Discount Rate for Enterprise		15.0%	15.0%	15.0%	15.0%	15.0%	15.0%
Combined Shareholder Risk Factors		6.0%	5.0%	4.0%	7.0%	6.0%	5.0%
Required Holding Period Return	QMDM #5	21.0%	20.0%	19.0%	22.0%	21.0%	20.0%

Marketable Minority Value $375.0
(of 10% of the Enterprise)

QMDM Assumptions

Z. Christopher Mercer, *Valuing Enterprise and Shareholder Cash Flows: The Integrated Theory of Business Valuation* (Memphis: Peabody Publishing, LP, 2004), www.integratedtheory.com; Z. Christopher Mercer, *Quantifying Marketability Discounts: 2005 E-Book Edition* (Memphis: Peabody Publishing, LP, 2005), www.mercercapital.com. © Mercer Capital, 2004

holding period. Mercer notes that this increase in value may be offset at least in part by a higher rate of return required for the S corporation interest.

THE QUANTITATIVE MARKETABILITY DISCOUNT MODEL

Once the value of the marketable, minority interest is established, Mercer turns to the application of the Quantitative Marketability Discount Model to determine the value of the illiquid, minority interests in the S corporation.[38]

The QMDM has five inputs that must be determined by the analyst. Each of these is a consideration in the valuation process in a typical valuation.

1. The expected growth rate in value of the underlying enterprise
2. The expected dividend/distribution yield (expressed on a C corporation equivalent basis)
3. The expected growth rate of distributions or dividends
4. The required holding period rate of return, or the shareholders' discount rate
5. The expected holding period (or range of holding periods)[39]

In Exhibit 12.19, a range of assumptions for identical C corporation and S corporation interests is presented at each of the varying levels of distributions.

An examination of Exhibit 12.19 shows that each of the factors is the same for the S corporation and the C corporation, with two notable exceptions: The S corporation distribution yield is slightly higher, and the shareholder risk factors are higher. An incremental premium of 1 percent is added to reflect risks associated with being

---

[38] Z. Christopher Mercer, *Quantifying Marketability Discounts: 2005 E-Book Edition* (Memphis: Peabody Publishing, LP, 2005), www.mercercapital.com. Note that Mercer indicates in Chapter 3 of *The Integrated Theory of Business Valuation* that the QMDM is not really a separate theory but a subset of the Integrated Theory.
[39] Ibid.

Exhibit 12.20   Quantitative Marketability Discount Analysis

No Distribution Example

Base Value (Marketable Minority Interest)	$1.00

Basic Assumptions of the Model		**Reference/Brief Explanation**
1. Expected Growth Rate of Underlying Value	15.0%	1. Value grows at R because of Reinvestment
2. Expected Dividend Yield	0.0%	2. No distributions assumed
3. Expected Growth Rate of Dividend	0.0%	3. Therefore, no growth in distributions
4. Midpoint Required Return	21.0%	4. Assumed 6% premium to R for HPP
5a. Minimum Holding Period	4	5. Given in example
5b. Maximum Holding Period	4	

QMDM Modeling Assumptions

Dividends Received End of Year ("E") or Mid-year ("M")	E	
Premium (+) / Discount (−) to Marketable Minority Value at Exit	0.0%	Exit Assumed at Marketable Minority Level

Average Indicated Discounts for Selected Holding Periods (Midpoint Return +/- 1%)

Average of 2–4 Year HP	14%	Average of 5–10 Year HP	31%
Average of 5–7 Year HP	26%	Average of 10–15 Year HP	46%
Average of 8–10 Year HP	37%	Average of 15–20 Year HP	58%
Average of 10–20 Year HP	52%		

Concluded Marketability Discount	18.4%

								Assumed Holding Periods in Years								
		1	2	3	4	5	6	7	8	9	10	15	20	25	30
							Implied Marketability Discounts									
Required Holding Period Return (Annual %)	17.0%	1.7%	3.4%	5%	7%	8%	10%	11%	13%	14%	16%	23%	29%	35%	40%
	18.0%	2.5%	5.0%	7%	10%	12%	14%	16%	19%	21%	23%	32%	40%	47%	54%
	19.0%	3.4%	6.6%	10%	13%	16%	19%	21%	24%	26%	29%	40%	50%	57%	64%
	20.0%	4.2%	8.2%	12%	16%	19.2%	23%	26%	29%	32%	34.7%	47%	57%	65%	72%
	21.0%	5.0%	9.7%	14%	18.4%	22.5%	26%	30%	33%	37%	39.9%	53%	64%	72%	78%
	22.0%	5.7%	11.1%	16%	21%	25.6%	30%	34%	38%	41%	44.6%	59%	69%	77%	83%
	23.0%	6.5%	12.6%	18%	24%	28.6%	33%	38%	42%	45%	49.0%	64%	74%	81%	87%
	24.0%	7.3%	14.0%	20%	26%	31%	36%	41%	45%	49%	53%	68%	78%	85%	90%
	25.0%	8.0%	15.4%	22%	28%	34%	39%	44%	49%	53%	57%	71%	81%	88%	92%

a shareholder in an S corporation, compared to being a shareholder in a C corporation, including the risk of:

- Possible loss of the S election
- That the holding period will be shorter than anticipated, and therefore there will be less time to realize the benefit of tax-free distributions
- That there will be no distribution made with which to pay taxes on allocable earnings
- Any other relevant holding period risks

These factors are input into the QMDM model, resulting in an estimated marketability discount for the various scenarios presented in Exhibit 12.19. Exhibit 12.20 displays the output of the QMDM model for a C corporation with a four-year holding period that pays no dividends.

A marketability discount of 18.4 percent is indicated. Applying the discount rates indicated by the analysis results in the implied discounts presented in Exhibit 12.21 for the C corporation and S corporation interests with each respective level of distribution.

Mercer also recognizes that basis shelter may contribute to value. Using the same four-year holding period, Exhibit 12.22 presents the calculation of the retained net income for each of the three scenarios.

When distributions are zero, the maximum shelter is available to contribute to value. Value is calculated as the capital gains tax saved and present valued at the holding period return rate developed in the QMDM assumptions. As distributions increase, basis shelter correspondingly decreases.

Exhibit 12.21 Development of Marketability Discounts

Shareholder Cash Flows	C Corp	1	2	3	4	S Corp	1	2	3	4	S vs. C Value Diff.	
0% Distributions												
Interim Cash Flows		$0.0	$0.0	$0.0	$0.0		$0.0	$0.0	$0.0	$0.0		
Terminal Value					$655.9					$655.9		
Present Value Factors @	21.0%	0.8264	0.6830	0.5645	0.4665	22.0%	0.8197	0.6719	0.5507	0.4514		
Present Value Cash Flows	$305.97	$0.0	$0.0	$0.0	$306.0	$296.06	$0.0	$0.0	$0.0	$296.1	–3.2%	*in $ value*
Implied Marketability Discount	18.4%					21.1%					2.6%	*in points of discount*
50% Distributions												
Interim Cash Flows		$18.8	$20.6	$22.7	$25.0		$22.1	$24.3	$26.7	$29.4		
Terminal Value					$549.0					$549.0		
Present Value Factors @	20.0%	0.8333	0.6944	0.5787	0.4823	21.0%	0.8264	0.6830	0.5645	0.4665		
Present Value Cash Flows	$319.89	$15.6	$14.3	$13.1	$276.8	$319.70	$18.2	$16.6	$15.1	$269.8	–0.1%	*in $ value*
Implied Marketability Discount	14.7%					14.8%					0.1%	*in points of discount*
100% Distributions												
Interim Cash Flows		$37.5	$39.4	$41.3	$43.4		$44.1	$46.3	$48.6	$51.1		
Terminal Value					$455.8					$455.8		
Present Value Factors @	19.0%	0.8403	0.7062	0.5934	0.4987	20.0%	0.8333	0.6944	0.5787	0.4823		
Present Value Cash Flows	$332.80	$31.5	$27.8	$24.5	$248.9	$341.53	$36.8	$32.2	$28.1	$244.4	2.6%	*in $ value*
Implied Marketability Discount	11.3%					8.9%					–2.3%	*in points of discount*

The Actual Present Value Math

Z. Christopher Mercer, *Valuing Enterprise and Shareholder Cash Flows: The Integrated Theory of Business Valuation* (Memphis: Peabody Publishing, LP, 2004), www.integratedtheory.com; Z. Christopher Mercer, *Quantifying Marketability Discounts: 2004 E-Book Edition* (Memphis: Peabody Publishing, LP, 2004), www.mercercapital.com. © Mercer Capital, 2004

Exhibit 12.22 Estimating Benefit of S Corporation Basis Build-up

Relatively few nondistributing S Corporations	**Basis Shelter 0% Distributions (100% Retention)**				
	Beginning Basis (Cost)	$375.0	$412.5	$451.9	$493.2	
	Plus Addition to Basis	$37.5	$39.4	$41.3	$43.4	**Maximum Shelter**
	Ending Basis	$412.5	$451.9	$493.2	$536.7	
	Build-up of basis (Sheltered)				$161.6	
	Capital Gains Tax Avoided		20.0%		$32.33	
	Present Value of Tax Avoided at R_{hp}		22.0%		$14.6	
	Tax Avoided as Percent of Cost					
	(Potential reduction of marketability discount in %)				3.9%	

	Basis Shelter 50% Distributions				
	Beginning Basis (Cost)	$375.0	$393.8	$414.4	$437.1	
	Plus Addition to Basis	$18.8	$20.6	$22.7	$25.0	**Some Shelter**
	Ending Basis	$393.8	$414.4	$437.1	$462.0	
	Build-up of basis (Sheltered)				$87.0	
	Capital Gains Tax Avoided		20.0%		$17.40	
	Present Value of Tax Avoided at R		21.0%		$8.12	
Most S corporations are relatively heavy distributors of earnings	Tax Avoided as Percent of Cost					
	(Potential reduction of marketability discount in %)				2.2%	

	Basis Shelter 100% Distributions				
	Beginning Basis (Cost)	$375.0	$375.0	$375.0	$375.0	
	Plus Addition to Basis	$0.0	$0.0	$0.0	$0.0	
	Ending Basis	$375.0	$375.0	$375.0	$375.0	**No Shelter**
	Build-up of basis (Sheltered)				$0.0	
	Capital Gains Tax Avoided		20.0%		$0.00	
	Present Value of Tax Avoided at R		20.0%		$0.00	
	Tax Avoided as Percent of Cost				$0.0	
	(Potential reduction of marketability discount in %)				0.0%	

Summary of Mercer's Model

Mercer's model begins with the value of identical C and S corporations at the marketable minority level, which he determines to be of equivalent value, regardless of the level of distributions. He calculates the S corporation premium or discount at the shareholder level by reference to C corporation equivalent yields on distributions and employs the Quantitative Marketability Discount Model to determine the values. Such analysis can lead to a positive or negative value differential between the S and the C corporation, depending on the facts and circumstances. The issues to consider include:

- The length of the holding period that the S shareholder may continue to enjoy the benefits of the S election
- The extent of the expected distributions
- The risk of loss of benefits. Such loss may come about by changes in law, a disqualifying event, a change in the distribution policy of the firm, or any number of reasons that cause the S election benefits to diminish or cease.

Mercer estimates the differing relative values to retained earnings shelter depending on expected distribution policies.

GRABOWSKI MODEL[40]

Grabowski's model measures three benefits of ownership of a pass-through entity:

1. Income is subject to only one level of taxation at the individual shareholder level, with no double taxation, though the model adjusts for differences in income tax rates between ordinary income tax rates (on the passed-through entity income of the S corporation) and the tax rates on dividends and capital gains (on C corporation shareholder returns).
2. Retained net income provides an increase in shareholder basis, reducing capital gains tax on sale of the shareholder's interest.
3. The owner of a controling interest of an S corporation is more likely to sell assets and command a premium for his or her business, as the buyer realizes depreciation and amortization benefits. This can be accomplished by an actual sale of the assets or by a sale of the stock and corresponding 338(h)(10) election, discussed earlier in this chapter.

Recall that the Erickson and Wang study (discussed in the controlling-interest section of this chapter) attributed a 12 to 17 percent premium to the ability to participate in a 338(h)(10) election. The data they used were found to be at the highest end of the market that analysts typically obtain market data for, and, in fact, subsequent research supported the notion that S corporations were priced higher at the level of size they studied. The Phillips study, also discussed earlier, reflects that the majority of S corporations sell as actual asset transactions, increasingly so in the smallest segments of the market. However, the researchers found that asset sales were priced at a 20 percent *discount* compared to stock sales. This may be partly a function of the types of intangible

---

[40] This section © copyright 2005 Duff & Phelps, LLC. All rights reserved. Used with permission.

assets sold, for example, the ability to transfer contracts in an asset versus stock sale. While we refer the reader to the discussion in the controlling-interest section relating to possible reasons for this, clearly the appraiser needs to consider the facts and circumstances of the appraisal assignment. There may be indications that a step-up in the basis of assets or a 338(h)(10) election would be significant in the future, and a buyer would consider it; however, it is clearly a case-by-case issue.

In the case of a minority interest, the S corporation shareholder has no control over the decision of if or when to sell and, if a sale is consummated, whether to sell stock or assets. Therefore, the only thing that the minority shareholder can be assured of is single taxation and a step-up in basis that may be realized if a sale is accomplished at some date in the future.

Valuation of Minority Interests

Grabowski offers four different models for the valuation of an S corporation interest and reconciles the differences. For purposes of this analysis, we will present the Modified Traditional Method. At the close of the chapter, we will provide a brief summary of the other three methods. However, depending on the facts and circumstances, the analyst may wish to use an alternative method, which would be equally useful.

The Modified Traditional Method for valuation of minority interests begins with the value of 100 percent of an equivalent C corporation, assuming income taxes at C corporation rates, and assumes 100 percent of the net cash flow is available to be distributed (paralleling the traditional formatting most often applied to C corporation valuations).

He then proposes five adjustments to reflect the benefits described here that are available to an owner of an interest in an S corporation:

1. Present value of taxes saved as an S corporation: Calculate 100 percent of the tax savings from the avoidance of double taxation and multiply it by the dividend rate and present value the stream of savings at the same rate at which the corporate free cash flows were valued. This is added to the equivalent C corporation value.
2. The tax decrement from having to pay ordinary income taxes on the shareholder's allocable share of S corporation income, compared to the earnings being retained by a C corporation and not distributed, is recognized.
3. A downward adjustment is made for the higher tax rate paid by S corporation shareholders, who generally pay income taxes at the highest marginal personal rate, compared to C corporation shareholders, who would pay taxes on the dividend rate of an assumed 20 percent combined federal and state rate.

Once these three adjustments by Grabowski are made, note that the Treharne and Grabowski models have accomplished the same thing, with one significant distinction. Treharne makes adjustment 2 to the extent that distributions equal, exceed, or are less than C corporation taxes on total corporate net income. Since Grabowski's model begins with the assumption that 100 percent of free cash flow is available to distribute, the analyst should consider appropriate minority and lack of marketability discounts to the extent that such amounts will not be distributed. This parallels the approach often taken in valuing minority interests in C corporations.

This model goes on to present two further adjustments, each of which requires consideration of exit strategies:

4. Calculate the retained net income over free cash flow. This amount is added to basis for an assumed holding period and reduces taxes upon a sale of the subject interest. Note that this benefit is available to the interest holder upon the sale of his or her interest and is not dependent upon the sale of the entire company. At the end of the willing buyer's projected holding period, this amount is present valued and added to the value determination. This adjustment depends only upon the estimated holding period of the willing buyer.

5. Include consideration of a premium that an S corporation shareholder might receive from a sale of assets (or sale of stock with a 338[h][10] election) as opposed to stock and a carryover basis in the assets. Buyers generally pay a premium for an asset amortization benefit, as their future income taxes will be reduced. This benefit would be measured somewhere between the total benefit they stand to gain and no benefit, resulting from the negotiation between the buyer and seller. This adjustment depends on the likely holding period of the controlling shareholder(s) and may be inapplicable in circumstances where no sale of the business is likely.

Note that this latter benefit contemplates that the buyer will be someone who can use these benefits.

Example of Grabowski Model

The assumptions to be used in Grabowski's example are found in Exhibit 12.23.

Exhibit 12.23 Grabowski Example Assumptions

(1)	Growth rate	5.0%
(2)	Pretax margin	12.5%
(3)	Depreciation as a percent of sales	4.0%
(4)	Reinvestment rate	150.0%
(5)	Net working capital as a percent of sales	10.0%
(6)	Rate of return on equity	15.0%

In addition, assume an entity-level (C corporation) tax rate of 40 percent and a personal income tax rate of 41.5 percent.

For simplicity's sake, this example assumes the corporation has no debt. Further, for illustrative purposes, the assumption is made that net income exceeds free cash flow, that the expected holding period is four years, and that at the end of the holding period, the S corporation is presumed to be sold to a C corporation (to illustrate the affect of that possibility on value).

Grabowski Modified Traditional Method

The Modified Traditional Method begins with the traditional calculation of free cash flow; that is, deduct C corporation taxes from net income to arrive at free cash flow of the entity. The earnings stream and the terminal value are discounted in the same manner as the analyst would if he or she was valuing a C corporation using a traditional discounted cash flow method.

In the Modified Traditional Method, for purposes of this example, the hypothetical willing buyer is expected to have a four-year holding period, at which time an exit strategy must be evaluated.

The modification to the Traditional Method is in the adjustments that the analyst considers to the traditional calculation. Exhibit 12.24 presents an example of the Modified Traditional Method.

Exhibit 12.24 begins with the value of the entity "as if" a C corporation, which is simply the sum of the discounted cash flows on line 18 and the terminal value provided on line 23. The next step is to consider each of the issues that would cause an S corporation to be more valuable than the value that has been determined for the C corporation:

1. Add the entity-level income taxes saved during the four-year holding period. Note that the model assumes that 100 percent of free cash flow is available to be distributed. This savings arises because a deduction was taken for entity-level taxes in calculating the value of the discounted cash flow. However, in reality, those taxes would not be borne by the S corporation. The model assumes that these savings increase shareholder distributions and, thus, converts them to an equivalent C corporation dividend by dividing them by (1 – dividend rate). This amount is present valued as a benefit to the S corporation shareholder and added to the value conclusion.
2. Subtract income taxes on net income to the extent that it exceeds cash flow. The shareholder will have to pay taxes on an allocable share of net income that exceeds the cash flow he or she will receive. This is equated to a shareholder equivalent dividend using the C corporation rate, with the present value being subtracted from the value indication.
3. Subtract income taxes paid due to the higher ordinary income tax rate paid by individuals, compared to the tax rate that would be paid by the individual on dividends and capital gains. This amount is converted to its pretax equivalent cash flow at the owner's dividend tax rate and present valued using the C corporation rate.
4. Add the value of the retained net income. In this example, for the duration of the willing buyer's expected holding period, net income exceeds cash flow. The amount of the excess serves to increase the S corporation shareholder's basis in his or her stock, saving capital gains taxes upon sale of the interest. The tax savings of the added basis are converted to their pretax equivalent cash flow and present valued.
5. The value of an assumed premium upon the sale of the company in four years is added to the value determination. In instances where the willing buyer may foresee a likely sale of the business, one would add this adjustment (e.g., the controlling shareholder is 70 years old and no heirs are active in the business). This is designed to quantify the adjustment that would be necessary in those circumstances. In this example, the buyer is a C corporation able to benefit from a step up in the basis of the underlying assets by obtaining depreciation and amortization write-offs in future periods. In this particular example, it assumes that such benefit comes from intangible assets. In the real world, the analyst would need to consider what assets, if any, might be subject to such a transaction, the likelihood of a sale within a presumed time horizon, and the likelihood of a buyer paying a premium for such assets.

Exhibit 12.24 Example—Modified Traditional Method

	Assumption (from Exhibit 11.24) or Line #	Projected Fiscal Year				Stabilized as if C Corp.
		1	2	3	4	
(7) Revenue		5,000,000	5,250,000	5,512,500	5,788,125	6,077,531
(8) Income before tax	(2) × (7)	625,000	656,250	689,063	723,516	759,691
(9) Entity-level tax rate (C corp.)		40.0%	40.0%	40.0%	40.0%	40.0%
(10) Entity-level tax	(8) × (9)	(250,000)	(262,500)	(275,625)	(289,406)	(303,877)
(11) Net income	(8) − (10)	375,000	393,750	413,438	434,109	455,815
(12) Depreciation	(3) × (7)	200,000	210,000	220,500	231,525	243,101
(13) Capital expenditures	(4) × (12)	(300,000)	(315,000)	(330,750)	(347,288)	(364,652)
(14) Net working capital (increase)/decrease	(5) × (increase in 7)	(23,810)	(25,000)	(26,250)	(27,563)	(28,941)
(15) Free cash flow	Σ (11) to (14)	251,190	263,750	276,938	290,784	305,324
(16) Present value factor	15.0%	0.8696	0.7561	0.6575	0.5718	
(17) Discounted cash flows	(15) × (16)	218,427	199,433	182,091	166,257	

Exhibit 12.24 *continued*

				Box A		
(18)	Sum of discounted cash flows	Σ (17)	766,207			
(19)	Tax savings of S corp. election	(32)	917,474	Terminal value before benefit		3,053,236
			–			
(20)	Pass-through basis adjustment	(40)	76,277	Estimated % of intangible assets		50.0%
(21)	Tax on income in excess of free cash flow	(45)	(195,909)	Intangible assets		1,526,618
(22)	Taxes paid due to tax rate differential	(52)	(586,670)	Step-up factor (15-year period)(†)		118.5%
(23)	PV terminal value as if C corp.	(a)	1,745,698	Step-up value of intangible assets		1,809,693
(24)	Asset sale amortization benefit	*See Box A*	161,849	Addition to selling price		283,075
(25)	Indicated value (marketable, 100%)	Σ (18) to (24)	**2,884,925**	PV of addition to selling price (‡)		161,849

(a) Calculated as (stabilized cash flow) / (discount – growth rate) × year 4 present value factor.
(†) Calculated using a 15 percent discount rate and a 40 percent tax rate.
(‡) Applies year 4 present value factor.

			Projected Fiscal Year			
			1	2	3	4
(26)	Entity-level taxes for S corp.	Assumed 1.5% on line (8)	(9,375)	(9,844)	(10,336)	(10,853)
(27)	Entity-level taxes for C corp.	(10)	(250,000)	(262,500)	(275,625)	(289,406)
(28)	Difference in entity-level taxes	(26) – (27)	240,625	252,656	265,289	278,554
(29)	Pretax equivalent (owner-level dividend tax rate)	(28) / (1–20%)	300,781	315,820	331,611	348,192

(continues)

Exhibit 12.24 *continued*

			1	2	3	4
(30)	Present value factor	(16)	0.8696	0.7561	0.6575	0.5718
(31)	Discounted tax savings of S corp. election	(29) × (30)	261,549	238,806	218,040	199,080
(32)	**Tax savings of S corp. election**	Σ (31)	**917,474**			

			Projected Fiscal Year			
			1	2	3	4
(33)	S corp. net income	(8) – (26)	615,625	646,406	678,727	712,663
(34)	S corp. free cash flow	(33) minus cash flow adjusted	491,815	516,406	542,227	569,338
(35)	Net income less free cash flow	(33) – (34)	123,810	130,000	136,500	143,325
(36)	Sum of cash flow differential	Σ (35)	533,635			
(37)	Tax benefit of 20% (capital gains rate)	(36) × 20%	106,727			
(38)	Pretax equivalent cash flow	(37) / (1 – 20%)	133,409			
(39)	Present value factor	(16)	0.5718			
(40)	**Pass-through basis adjustment**	(38) × (39)	**76,277**			

			Projected Fiscal Year			
			1	2	3	4
(41)	Tax on income in excess of free cash flow	(35) × 41.5%	51,381	53,950	56,648	59,480
(42)	Pretax equivalent (owner-level dividend tax rate)	(41) / (1 – 20%)	64,226	67,438	70,809	74,350
(43)	Present value factor	(16)	0.8696	0.7561	0.6575	0.5718
(44)	Discounted tax adjustment	(42) × (43)	55,849	50,992	46,558	42,510

Exhibit 12.24 *continued*

		Σ (44)	**195,909**			
(45)	**Tax on income in excess of free cash flow**					

				Projected Fiscal Year		
			1	**2**	**3**	**4**
(46)	Owner-level taxes if C corp.	(15) × 20%	50,238	52,750	55,388	58,157
(47)	Owner-level taxes if S corp.	(34) × 41.5%	204,103	214,309	225,024	236,275
(48)	Income tax differential	(46) – (47)	153,865	161,559	169,637	178,118
(49)	Pretax equivalent (owner-level dividend tax rate)	(48) / (1 – 20%)	192,332	201,948	212,046	222,648
(50)	Present value factor	(16)	0.8696	0.7561	0.6575	0.5718
(51)	Discounted tax adjustment	(49) × (50)	167,245	152,702	139,423	127,300
(52)	**Tax increase due to tax rate differential**	Σ (51)	**586,670**			

Exhibit 12.25 Summary: Modified Traditional Method

(a) Sum of discounted cash flows	766,207	
(b) Tax savings of S election	917,474	Tax savings of S corporation tax burden: S corporation taxes compared to C corporation rates
(c) Pass-through basis adjustment	76,277	Increase in basis (net income > cash flow) present value year four
(d) Tax on income in excess of free cash flow (FCF)	−195,909	Tax on net income in excess of FCF: personal rate over dividend rate
(e) Tax paid–tax rate differential	−586,670	$134,895 sum of tax adjustments (sum of (b) and (d) and (e))
(f) Present value terminal value as if C corporation	1,745,698	$2,511,905 value "as if" C corporation (sum of (a) and (f))
(g) Asset sale amortization benefit	161,849	$238,126 adjustments made assuming sale year four (sum of (c) and (g))
Indicated value (marketable, 100%)	$2,884,925	

If one is valuing a minority interest and there is no likelihood that the company will be sold in the foreseeable future, the likely exit strategy for the owner is to simply sell the stock to another minority owner. In that case, no benefit from any step-up should be added to the residual. The Grabowski model can be easily adapted to other forms of pass-through entities. For example, if one adapts the model to value an interest in an LLC, the buyer of the subject minority interest will receive a step-up in basis at the valuation date (to the extent that the purchase price exceeds the tax basis of the seller), as will the next buyer of the subject minority interest at the end of the assumed holding period, even if the company is not sold.

Exhibit 12.25 provides a summary of the components of Grabowski's Modified Traditional Method. As shown in this example, the model provides a premium of $134,895 for adjustments relating to tax differentials between the S corporation and the C corporation and $238,126 for adjustments relating to benefits to be gained and realized upon a hypothetical sale in four years.

Grabowski offers three other valuation models: the Modified Gross, the C-Corporation Equivalent, and the Pretax Discount Rate methods.

The Modified Gross Method begins with the method used by the Gross case in which no income tax deduction was allowed by the Court. In this model, only taxes that the S corporation would actually bear as a corporate entity are deducted from the earnings stream in calculating entity-level value. Since the tax benefits of the S election are already incorporated into the free cash flows that have been discounted, the appraiser needs to add the preowner-level income tax equivalent adjustment for the differences in the entity-level tax rate of an S corporation and a C corporation. This amount is discounted by the C corporation discount rate. All the other adjustments remain the same, and, in particular, the terminal value is the same in this example because it assumes a sale to a C corporation where the buyer of the business will deduct C corporation entity-level taxes in valuing the business upon sale. Some analysts might prefer this since it is similar to the method used by the court in the *Gross* case.

The C Corporation Equivalent Method begins with the S corporation shareholder's equivalent C corporation dividend. Entity earnings are determined by subtracting S corporation taxes (typically any state income taxes that might apply to the subject S corporation) as well as personal taxes on the shareholder's allocable share of pass-through income. After subtracting these amounts, the net is converted to the equivalent C corporation dividend by dividing it by (1 – dividend rate). Using this method, any tax adjustments between the S corporation and the C corporation are taken into consideration. Therefore, the only other adjustments that warrant consideration are the pass-through basis adjustment and the basis step-up adjustment.

The Pretax Discount Rate Method begins with after-corporate-tax discount rates derived from returns on publicly traded securities. One converts that appropriate rate of return in turn first to its after-personal-tax equivalent and then to its pre-personal-income-tax equivalent. Entity earnings are determined by subtracting S corporation taxes (typically any state income taxes that might apply to the subject S corporation) but not personal income taxes due on the shareholder's allocable share of pass-through income. The discount rate (pre–personal tax) then matches the cash flows (pre–personal tax).[41] In this example capital expenditures exceed depreciation expense and the change in net working capital is greater than zero, making the discount rate conversions difficult and beyond the scope of this chapter.

The results of applying the Modified Traditional, Modified Gross, and C Corporation Equivalent methods to the example are compared in Exhibit 12.26.

Summary: Grabowski Method

Grabowski's modified traditional method begins with the value of a C corporation interest, fully burdened with income tax at the corporate level, adding back the savings gained by virtue of being an S corporation, and making adjustments for tax differentials on pass-through income.

The model recognizes that the distributions for the subject company can impact value. One may either alter the net cash flow available to distribute by increasing retention for reinvestment in the cash flows themselves or recognize the difference between available cash and distributions through the minority interest and/or lack of marketability discounts.

The model assumes that a willing buyer of stock in an S corporation estimates his or her expected holding period and takes into consideration the build-up of basis from retained net income over distributed cash flow. And where circumstances

---

[41] If one is valuing the business using the Gordon Growth Model and capital expenditures equal depreciation and change in net working capital equal zero, one can convert from an after-corporate, pre-personal-tax discount rate to an after-personal-tax discount rate using the following relationship: $K_{cap} = \{(K_{cbp} - g)(1 - t_{cp})\} + g$, where K_{cbp} equals the after-corporate, pre-personal-income-tax return on C corporation equity, t_{cp} equals the personal income tax rate on C corporation equity returns, and K_{cap} equals the after-corporate, after-personal return on C corporation equity. The reconversion to a pre-personal-tax discount rate can be accomplished using the following relationship: $K_{sbp} = ((K_{cap} - g) / (1 - t_{ps}) + g$ where K_{sbp} equals the pretax return on S corporation equity and t_{ps} = personal income tax rate on S corporation income.

Exhibit 12.26 Method Comparisons

	Modified Traditional Method	Modified Gross Method	C Corporation Equivalent Method
Sum of discounted cash flows	766,207 (posttax cash flow)	1,500,187 (pretax cash flow)	901,102 (pre-personal-income-tax C corporation dividend)
Tax adjusted to pretax equivalent	917,474	183,495	
Pass-through basis adjustment	76,277	76,277	76,277
Tax on income in excess of free cash flow	−195,909	−195,909	
Tax paid—rate differential	−586,670	−586,670	
Present value of terminal value as if C corp	1,745,698	1,745,698	1,745,698
Asset sale amortization benefit	161,849	161,849	161,849
Indicated value	**2,884,925**	**2,884,925**	**2,884,925**

dictate, the model considers the effect of a possible asset or stock sale with 338(h)(10) election on a sale of the business in year X.

SUMMARY: NON-CONTROLLING INTEREST IN PASS-THROUGH ENTITY THEORY

Four models for the valuation of noncontrolling interests in pass-through entities have been presented. Each of these theories has foundation in the logical issues that a noncontrolling buyer and seller would consider upon a transaction of their interest. However, to quote Daniel Van Vleet, none of these models is a black box, into which data can be thrown and meaningful results can be expected.

Each of the four theories considers the following issues:

- Amount and timing of distributions
- Retained net income
- Holding period and exit strategy
- Tax rates—personal, corporate, and capital gains
- Further effect of minority or marketability discounts
- Possible ability to participate in step-up-of-basis transaction

The analyst can carefully consider the inputs in order to get a meaningful valuation conclusion. While each of the theories treats these issues somewhat differently, if the analyst is diligent in the understanding and/or application of the model, carefully considering the inputs and output, he or she should get a logical valuation conclusion.

A review of the issues follows.

Amount and Timing of Distributions

All four models recognize that distributions impact value. Treharne's model holds that minority owners receiving distribution amounts greater than the amount needed for taxes have greater value than equivalent C corporation interests, interests in entities distributing funds sufficient to pay taxes are likely of about equivalent value to C corporation interests, and interests in entities distributing insufficient funds are likely worth less than equivalent C corporation interests. Van Vleet's model holds that the S corporation publicly traded equivalent value is not affected by the level of distributed or retained funds, just as is the case in the C corporation publicly traded equivalent value. As such, the Van Vleet model inherently assumes that the subject S corporation is distributing 100 percent of its net income. To the extent that this is not true, Van Vleet recommends that the analyst adjust the value determination through the lack of marketability discount. Mercer concludes that the amount of distributions causes no difference in value, regardless of whether the subject company is an S corporation or a C corporation, at the enterprise level. However, he goes on to make value distinctions by use of the QMDM. Grabowski's model assumes that 100 percent of net cash flow is distributed and recommends that adjustments be made through the minority interest discount to the extent that this is not true.

Retained Net Income (Build-Up in Basis of Stock)

Each of the four theories recognizes that there is potential value in retained net income as that which the buyer could build up for himself or herself and therefore shelter his or her future capital gains. Because such basis has the potential to create additional cash flow to the buyer, they say that it could create additional value. Treharne says that this value is negligible, because his model assumes that the entity is held into perpetuity. The S corporation publicly traded equivalent value provided by the Van Vleet model recognizes the impact of retained earnings immediately, just as is the case in the C corporation publicly traded equivalent value. Grabowski, as will be discussed in a following section, assumes that the willing buyer projects his or her holding period and present values such benefit from that defined point. Mercer recognizes this as a modest reduction to the discount determined by the QMDM.

Holding Period

Each model has different assumptions with respect to holding period. Treharne's model assumes that the interest is held into perpetuity; however, to the extent that is not true, such impediment can be corrected by converting the model, which is presented as a capitalization model, to a discounting model. The S corporation publicly traded equivalent value provided by the Van Vleet Model assumes the ownership interest can be liquidated at the option of the shareholder in an efficient capital market. Consequently, no holding period is inherently assumed by the Van Vleet Model. Obviously, no such capital market exists for S corporation equity interests. Therefore, Van Vleet recommends that this lack of marketability be taken into account in the lack of marketability discount. Mercer assumes a selected holding period and uses it in the QMDM to determine the lack of marketability discount. Grabowski's model considers two holding periods: The willing buyer estimates a holding period for his stock interest and, where circumstances dictate, assumes that the willing buyer estimates a time when the business may be sold.

Tax Rates—Personal versus Corporate and Capital Gains

With respect to income tax on corporate income, Treharne's, Van Vleet's, and Grabowski's models contemplate the differences in S corporation and C corporation tax rates on ordinary income. Mercer makes note that such rate differences are negligible. Regarding dividend tax, all four models consider dividend tax on C corporation dividends. On the issue of capital gain tax, Van Vleet's model contemplates the capital gains tax benefit associated with retained net income as it is earned; Grabowski calculates capital gains tax on retained net income upon an assumed sale at a selected date in the future. Treharne's model does not explicitly calculate such a tax, but Treharne says it should be considered. Mercer similarly says that basis shelter and the capital gains tax saved should be considered.

Further Effect of Minority or Marketability Discounts

Treharne states that his model produces a minority, marketable value. The analyst should consider any lack of marketability discount that would be applicable. To the extent that the analyst considers cash distributions in his or her analysis of such lack of marketability discount, he or she should consider that the cash flow stream to the minority shareholder has already been accounted for by use of his or her model. Van Vleet states that his model produces an S corporation publicly traded equivalent value. As such, the indication of value is on a minority, marketable basis. Consequently, the application of a lack of marketability discount is typically warranted. He further states that the analyst should understand the fundamental assumptions of his model and consider adjusting the lack of marketability discount to the extent that disparities exist between these assumptions and the attributes of the subject S corporation equity security. Mercer begins with the value of a minority, marketable interest, which he holds is the same for S corporation and C corporation shareholders, and recognizes the difference between the S corporation shareholder benefits and the C corporation shareholder by use of the QMDM. The inputs to that model drive the extent of the discount that is taken. Grabowski suggests that both minority interest and lack of control discounts be considered in his model—the former, presumably, if one has used control based cash flows in his model.

Possible Ability to Participate in Step-Up-of-Basis Transaction

Grabowski recognizes, as a part of his model, that a buyer may consider the ability to command a premium upon the sale of his or her interest through a step-up-in-basis transaction. Grabowski is clear that this component should not be "automatically" included but carefully considered for each valuation. Certainly, for some acquisitions, particularly of larger companies, it can be a consideration. However, for many smaller to midsized companies, it may not be. Like all components of these models, each one needs to be considered as to relevancy for the particular subject company.

> It is important to note that there are still many analysts who prefer simpler, more qualitative methods to valuing S corporations than the models presented here. Assuming a well-thought-out analysis, this is acceptable.

It is evident that the four theories agree on the factors that impact the value of S corporation interests. Each arrives at the conclusion by a different path. Analysts must understand and carefully apply whatever method is used, if any.

BIBLIOGRAPHY

R. James Alerding, Yassir Karam, and Travis Chamberlain. "S Corporation Premiums Revisited: The Erickson-Wang Myth," *Shannon Pratt's Business Valuation Update*, January 2003.

Merle Erickson. "Tax Benefits in Acquisitions of Privately Held Corporations," *Capital Ideas* 3, no. 3, Winter 2002.

Merle Erickson. "To Elect or Not to Elect: That Is the Tax Question," *Capital Ideas* 2, no. 4, Winter 2001.

Nancy Z. Fannon, Christopher Mercer, Chris Treharne, Daniel Van Vleet, and Roger G. Grabowski. "Valuation of Pass-Through Entities," *AICPA 2004 National Business Valuation Conference*, November 8, 2004.

Roger J. Grabowski. "S Corporation Valuations in a Post-Gross World-Updated," *Business Valuation Review*, September 2004.

Roger J. Grabowski. "Valuation of Pass-Through Entities," *AICPA 2004 National Business Valuation Conference*, pp. 37–120.

Roger J. Grabowski, and William McFadden. "Chapter 5: Applying the Income Approach to S Corporation and Other Pass-Through Entity Valuations," *The Handbook of Business Valuation and Intellectual Property Analysis*. New York: Reilly/Schweihs, McGraw-Hill, 2004.

James R. Hitchner, Nancy Fannon, and Chris Treharne. "Pass-Through Entities: What's All the Fuss About?" *American Institute of Certified Public Accountants Conference*, November 2003.

James R. Hitchner, Nancy Fannon, and Chris Treharne. "Valuation of Pass-Through Entities," *American Society of Appraisers Annual Conference*, October 2004.

James R. Hitchner, Nancy Fannon, and Chris Treharne. "Valuation of Pass-Through Entities," *Institute of Business Appraisers Annual Conference*, May 2004.

Terrance Jalbert. "Pass-Through Taxation and the Value of the Firm," *American Business Review*, June 2002.

Mark S. Luttrell, and William A. Duerksen. "Tax Affecting Earnings: Do Businesses Actually Pay Tax?" *The Witness Chair*, Summer 2004.

Michael J. Mattson, Donald S. Shannon, and David E. Upton. "Empirical Research Concludes S Corporations Values Same as C Corporations: Part I," *Shannon Pratt's Business Valuation Update*, November 2002.

Michael J. Mattson, Donald S. Shannon, and David E. Upton. "Empirical Research Concludes S Corporations Values Same as C Corporations: Part II," *Shannon Pratt's Business Valuation Update*, December 2002.

Z. Christopher Mercer. "Are S Corporations Worth More Than C Corporations?" *Business Valuation Review*, September 2004.

Z. Christopher Mercer. *Quantifying Marketability Discounts*. Memphis: Peabody Publishing, LP, 1997, pp. 233–239.

Z. Christopher Mercer. *Quantifying Marketability Discounts: 2005 E-Book Edition*. Peabody Publishing, LP, 2005, www.mercercapital.com. Mercer's E-book includes the QMDM Companion, the Excel spreadsheet/working model of QMDM, and a several-page, quick-start tutorial for the QMDM.

Z. Christopher Mercer. "S Corporation Versus C Corporation Values," *Shannon Pratt's Business Valuation Update*, June 2002.

Z. Christopher Mercer. *Valuing Enterprise and Shareholder Cash Flows: The Integrated Theory of Business Valuation*. Memphis: Peabody Publishing, LP, 2004, www.integratedtheory.com.

Z. Christopher Mercer, and Travis W. Harms. "S Corporation Valuation in Perspective: A Response to the Article 'S Corporation Discount Rate Adjustment,'" *AICPA ABV E-Valuation Alert*, 4, issue 7, July 2, 2002.

Michael Paschall. "Some Observations on Tax Affecting," *Business Valuation Review*, March 2005.

John R. Phillips. "S Corp or C Corp? M&A Deal Prices Look Alike," *Shannon Pratt's Business Valuation Update*, March 2004.

Shannon Pratt. "Editor Attempts to Make Sense of S Versus C Corporation Debate," *Shannon Pratt's Business Valuation Update*, March 2003.

Shannon Pratt, and David Laro. *Business Valuation and Taxes, Procedures, Law and Perspective* (Hoboken, NJ: John Wiley & Sons, 2005).

Chris D. Treharne. "Comparing Three Payout Assumptions' Impact on Values of S Versus C Corps," *Shannon Pratt's Business Valuation Update*, September 2002.

Chris D. Treharne. "Valuation of Minority Interests in Subchapter S Corporations," *Business Valuation Review*, September 2004.

Chris D. Treharne, and Nancy J. Fannon. "Valuation of Pass-Through Tax Entities: Minority and Controlling Interests," *S-Corp. Association*, February 2004, www. S-Corp.org.

Daniel Van Vleet. "Chapter 4: The S Corporation Economic Adjustment," *The Handbook of Business Valuation and Intellectual Property Analysis*. New York: Reilly/Schweihs, McGraw-Hill, 2004.

Daniel Van Vleet. "The S Corporation Economic Adjustment Model Revisited," *Willamette's Insight*, Winter 2004.

Daniel Van Vleet. "The S Corp Economic Adjustment Model," *Business Valuation Review*, September 2004.

Daniel Van Vleet. "The Valuation of S Corporation Stock: The Equity Adjustment Multiple," *Willamette's Insight*, Winter 2003.

Joseph Vinso. "Distributions and Entity Form: Do They Make a Difference in Value?" *Valuation Strategies*, September/October 2003.

Additional Updates

Nancy Fannon. "Lag Time in Date of Appraisal Results in Another S Corp Win for the IRS," *Financial Valuation and Litigation Expert*, October/November 2006.

Nancy Fannon. "Subchapter S Corporation Valuation—A Simplified View," *Business Valuation Review*, Spring 2007.

Nancy Fannon. "Avoiding S Curves: The Shortest Distance between Two Points," *Business Valuation Review*, Summer 2007.

Nancy Fannon and David Foster. "S Corporations," Business Valuation Resources, November 13, 2007, teleconference.

Lawrence J. Kasper. "S Corporation Valuations—An Analysis in Search of a Solution," *Business Valuation Review*, Winter 2007.

John Mitchell and Douglas Evan Ress. "Tax-Affecting and Beyond: *Dela. Radiology* Experts Discuss 'Landmark' Case," *Business Valuation Update*, May 2007.

Nancy Fannon. "Valuing Controlling versus Minority Interests in S Corporations," *Business Valuation Review*, Winter 2007.

Travis W. Harms and Z. Christopher Mercer. "S Corporation Model Comparisons," *Business Valuation Review*, Spring 2008.

Nancy J. Fannon. *Fannon's Guide to Subchapter S Corporation Valuation*, Business Valuation Resources, 2008.

Nancy Fannon. "The 'Real' S Corp Debate: Impact of Embedded Tax Rates from Public Markets," *Business Valuation Review*, Winter 2008.

Nancy Fannon. "The 'Real' S Corp Debate: Impact of Embedded Tax Rates from Public Markets," *Financial Valuation and Litigation Expert*, December 2008/ January 2009.

Effective Federal Income Tax Rates Faced by Small Businesses in the United States, prepared by Quantria Strategies, LLC, for the U.S. Small Business Administration, April 2009.

Daniel R. Van Vleet. "S Corporation Valuation Update," *Financial Valuation and Litigation Expert*, February/March 2007.

Daniel R. Van Vleet. "A Review and Critique of the Fannon S Corp Model," *Business Valuation Review*, Winter 2008.

ADDENDUM—A SUMMARY APPROACH TO PTE VALUATION[1]

Perhaps you're confused by the multitude of approaches to PTE valuation and now are left wondering what to do. If so, you're not alone. Since the *Gross* decision, the sheer volume of commentators offering a diverse variety of good, solid advice on the economic theory associated with PTE valuation has left many wondering just how to sort it all out. The following analysis is presented, along with grateful appreciation for the insight provided by the controlling-interest studies and S-corporation valuation theories of our colleagues as presented in this text, in an attempt to help clarify and simplify the extensive debate that has gone on regarding pass-through entity valuation.

Most valuation analysts now accept the notion that if an individual has the choice between receiving $1,000 that's subject to double taxation, or $1,000 that's subject to single taxation, they'll chose the single-tax option. Why? Because if money only has to be taxed once, the individual will keep more of it in their pocket—simple math. The problem has been that the empirical data valuation analysts rely on to value the cash flow that the investor receives that's "only taxed once"—that is, publicly traded C corporation rates of return—comes from data that are based on investors' expectations of money that is "twice taxed"—first at the corporate level, and again at the individual level.

Many analysts have attempted to cure this problem by simply not deducting taxes from the corporate-level income stream and applying the rate of return from public C corporations. In so doing, they believe that they have left the investor in the position of having been "only taxed once." However, this is not so; merely not deducting corporate-level taxes grossly overstates the value of the pass-through entity. This is because the second tax, the one that is being avoided, is not the corporate-level tax (generally represented at or near 40 percent), but rather, the dividend tax (generally at or around 20 percent for federal and state combined.)

At the other end of the spectrum, analysts who deduct corporate taxes and take no further steps fail to recognize the benefits that may inure to the investor by virtue of holding an investment through a vehicle that avoids this second level of taxation. Since the earliest days of finance, the impact of taxes on the value of an investment has been recognized; to ignore it is to ignore the economic reality of the investment).

The most significant point of this entire debate is this: The difference between valuing an S corporation and a C corporation is not about whether or not corporate-level taxes should be deducted, and it never has been. Both S corporations and C corporations bear these taxes, and whether they bear them corporately or individually makes no difference. What *does* make a difference is that rates of return on C corporations are derived from an investor's expectation of having to pay a dividend tax upon receipt of dividends from the corporation, while S corporation investors need pay no such tax. Therefore, if we are using a rate of return that reflects an investor's expectation of having to pay a tax upon receipt of dividends, as is clearly the case when we use Ibbotson data, then it is axiomatic that if we are using this same rate of return data to value a corporation where the investor will *not* have to pay such a tax, then the financial benefit of not paying a dividend tax must be taken into consideration. The need to consider this

---

[1] This section was originally prepared by Nancy J. Fannon. For additional information and updates, see *Nancy Fannon's Guide to the Valuation of Subchapter S corporations*, BV Resources, 2008 (to be updated in 2010/2011) and www.bvresources.com.

benefit is as true for a noncontrolling interest as it is for a controlling interest where the buyer will continue to receive such benefit; whether it will be realized depends on a whole host of factors.

Given this, the simplest solution to valuing a pass-through entity is to first value the entity "as if" it were a C corporation, and then to separately assess the effect on value of those benefits specific and inherent to pass-through entities and interests in them, but not available to publicly-traded C-corporation interest holders, whose data we have used to value the S corporation. The most significant benefits include the avoidance of dividend tax on distributions, discussed above, as well as the S corporation investor's opportunity to benefit from a build-up in the basis of their stock, which an investor in a C corporation cannot benefit from. This section will present just such a straightforward model and culminate in a single, simple spreadsheet adaptable for use in the valuation of any pass-through entity.

The reader will note that the starting point for most pass-through entity valuation models begin with the valuation of the company "as if" it were a C corporation. This is for a good reason: The empirical data that analysts have available to them is all from publicly traded C corporations. It is only *after* the analyst has valued the pass-through entity (PTE) "as if" it were a C corporation that we *then assess the benefits of ownership of the PTE.*

We start, then, with the assumption of a simple build-up model, using Ibbotson data, as presented in Exhibit 12.27.

Our discussion will be based on the valuation of a subject company, presented in Exhibit 12.28. This valuation relies on a three-year forecast model. To arrive at the cash flow-to-equity, an entity-level tax of 35 percent is applied to the net income before taxes. Assumed C-corporation cash flow adjustments are reflected, resulting in cash flows-to-equity of $120,000, $185,000 and $227,500.

Note that although the example presents an equity valuation, we could alternatively use an invested capital model.

The discount and capitalization rates derived in Exhibit 12.27 were applied to the forecasted after-tax cash flows using a mid-year convention. The sum of the discounted cash flows and the present value of the terminal year is $920,972. At this point, we have simply valued the company "as if" it were a C corporation. Now we must consider the relative benefits of the pass-through entity.

There are many questions and considerations for both controlling and minority interests in a PTE. While these questions are relevant for both types of interests, every valuation is case and fact specific, and the analyst's answers might differ dramatically, not only between controlling and non controlling interests, but also from one noncontrolling interest to another, or one controlling interest to

Exhibit 12.27   Discount and Capitalization Rate Build-Up (Illustration only)

Total Market Return on Small Stocks[1]	16.7%
Industry-Risk Premium	2.5%
Specific-Company Risk Premium	5.0%
Discount Rate	24.2%
Less: Long-Term Growth	-2.5%
Capitalization Rate	21.7%

[1] www.federalreserve.gov as of August 8, 2005.
© Ibbotson Associates' *Stocks, Bonds, Bills, and Inflation Valuation Edition 2005 Yearbook.*

Exhibit 12.28 Valuation

Valuation		Year 1	Year 2	Year 3
Net Income Before Tax		200,000	300,000	350,000
Entity-Level Tax @ 35%	–35%	(70,000)	(105,000)	(122,500)
Net Income After Tax		**130,000**	**195,000**	**227,500**
Adjustments:				
Depreciation		25,000	30,000	30,000
"Normal" Capital Additions		(25,000)	(30,000)	(30,000)
Less: Working Capital		(10,000)	(10,000)	–
Cash Flow to Equity		**120,000**	**185,000**	**227,500**
Present Value Rate		24.2%	24.2%	21.7%
Discounted Cash Flows		$107,676	$133,656	$1,048,387
Sum of Discounted Cash Flows	$241,333		Discount Rate	24.2%
			Present Value of	
PV Terminal Value "as if C Corp"	$679,639		Terminal Value	$679,639
Indicated Value "as if C Corp"	**$920,972**			

Note: Some figures may not foot due to rounding. In this exhibit and those that follow, terminal year PV calculation differs from what many other analysts do, not material for this illustration.

another. There are no cookie cutter formulas or set-in-stone mathematical calculations; there are, however, several important questions that, when answered, will help guide the analyst through the valuation of both controlling and noncontrolling interests:

- Who is the most likely buyer?
  - A review of market transactional data may give the analyst a good indication as to who, and what type of entity, is involved in transactions in the subject company's industry. Discussions with the subject company's management may provide further enlightenment on the subject. The old stand-by, "All of the buyers are C corporations," however, will likely not be as plausible an answer unless backed up with empirical evidence.
- What is the possibility that the S election will be broken? (not applicable to an LLC)
- What is the expected distribution level?
  - Historical distributions may be an indicator of future distribution patterns; however, they may not. In a controlling-interest valuation, assuming the cash flow includes all cash flows needed for operations including reinvestment needs, then you may conclude that 100 percent is available for distribution.
- What is the opportunity to build up retained net income, and how will that retained net income be used to build value?
  - Whatever isn't distributed doesn't just disappear, it builds value for the shareholder and should be given consideration. Depending on the likelihood of the shareholder ever realizing a benefit from the retention, the analyst may choose to recognize more, or less, of the retained net income, by making appropriate adjustments to the discount rate.
- What is a likely holding period for the interest?
  - While this may, in some instances, be nothing more than educated guesswork, many analysts agree that a reasonable terminal period should be determined. At this point the analyst might choose to recognize the benefits of the retention of earnings and the related build-up in the basis of the investor's stock.

With respect to the first two of these questions, it is often the case that there is no distinct answer. This is caused by several factors. Poor market data would give no obvious indication of who, or what form of entity, might be a likely acquirer of the company. While a buyer of a controlling interest in a small-sized company would most likely continue the pass-through entity status and it is unlikely that the S election would be broken, the company could also be acquired by a C corporation. Thus, it may be appropriate to consider the pass-through entity benefits and then weight them by the probability that the pass-through entity status will be maintained.

The valuation analyst must also consider the perspective of the pool of hypothetical buyers of the subject company. There are a variety of sources for potential buyers: individuals, including the management team; the descendents of the owner; outside buyers who would operate the Company in much the same manner as it has been run for many years; or acquisition by an existing corporation or competitor. Therefore, the make-up of the pool of hypothetical buyers for any specific case may shed light on the S or C corporation election question for that valuation.

To reflect the economic benefits of the PTE status, we start with the recognition of the benefit of the avoidance of the dividend tax. The model used is the "Double

Taxation Adjustment" of the Treharne Method[2] presented earlier in this chapter. This calculation is presented in Exhibit 12.29. For purposes of this example, we assumed a company that distributes 75 percent of its net income before tax. Note that in the exhibits in this Addendum, the particular decision points that affect the pass-through entity adjustment have been highlighted. It is on these points that the analyst needs to make decisions regarding the specific characteristics of the pass-through entity and the ownership interest which will affect the magnitude of the adjustment from the "as if C corporation" value.

Depending on the entity status chosen by the hypothetical buyer, a weighting may be placed on the present value to determine the amount added to the value indication "as if a C corporation." Assuming that the most likely buyer would maintain the pass-through entity status and that the S election would not be broken, the full amount of the premium may be added to the value indication "as if a C corporation." Alternately, with an unknown buyer/entity structure, the resulting present value is weighted. In the example, we have weighted the result 75 percent, indicating we believed it was more likely that the pass-through entity status would be continued than that it would not. This adjustment results in a final double-tax adjustment of $101,647 for our example, as shown in Exhibit 12.29.

We readily acknowledge that by making this allocation (75 percent in our example), we make an imperfect estimate, meant as a means of giving recognition to the fact that we simply do not know who the most likely buyer would be; however, recognizing some amount of premium for these purposes makes economic

Exhibit 12.29   Adjustment for Dividend Tax Avoided

A	Percent of Income Distributed Annually	Year 1	Year 2	Year 3
HIGHLIGHTED CELLS DENOTE SPECIFIC DECISION POINTS FOR THE PTE CALCULATIONS				Assumed Exit/Terminal Year
PTE Distributions (75% of income in this example; percentage depends on expected distribution stream)	75%	150,000	225,000	262,500
Total Entity Taxes (C corp—from above)		(70,000)	(105,000)	(122,500)
Equivalent C corp Dividends		80,000	120,000	140,000
State	8.5%	6,800	10,200	11,900
Federal	15.0%	12,000	18,000	21,000
Net PTE Benefit (Liability)		18,800	28,200	32,900
Terminal Value Cap Rate				21.7%
				151,613
Present Value Rate		24.2%	24.2%	24.2%
Present Value		$16,869	$20,374	$98,286
Sum of Double Taxation Adjustment Present Values				$135,529
Likelihood of Buyer Benefitting from Pass-Through Benefits (could be ZERO to 100%)				75%
Estimated Benefit				101,647

[2] David Laro and Shannon P. Pratt, *Business Valuation and Taxes: Procedure, Law, and Perspective* (Hoboken, NJ: John Wiley & Sons, 2005), 106.

Exhibit 12.30   Benefit of Build-Up in Basis

Benefit of Build-Up in Basis (retained net income)		
HIGHLIGHTED CELLS		
DENOTE SPECIFIC DECISION		
POINTS FOR THE PTE		
CALCULATIONS		
PTE Net Income Over Period		$850,000
PTE Distributions Over Period		$637,500
Income Over PTE Distributions (sum net income before tax less sum PTE distributions)		212,500
Capital Gains Tax (estimated combined federal & state)	20%	42,500
PV Rate (appropriate rate of return considering risk of realizing retained net income)		29.2%
Estimated Benefit		$25,460
Likelihood of Buyer Benefitting from Pass-Through Benefits (could be ZERO to 100%)		75%
Estimated Benefit		$19,095

sense. Note that for a controlling interest, however, if the analyst were to determine that the entire pool of hypothetical buyers was comprised of C corporations that this percentage would be zero, in effect resulting in no additional value for a pass-through entity premium. Often, however, it is a blend of C corporations and pass-through entities that makes up the pool of potential hypothetical buyers. For a minority interest, on the other hand, the analyst might be more likely to conclude that the PTE status would continue, and 100 percent of the benefit might be added.

Furthermore, as is shown in Exhibit 12.30, the opportunity to build up retained net income is a possibility for the hypothetical buyer that should not be ignored. Note that the issue of retained net income was discussed earlier in this chapter, in all four models presented. Of particular note, Roger Grabowski's model discusses this issue at some length, as does that of Daniel Van Vleet. In Grabowski's model, the retained net income is recognized at an assumed terminal (exit) period, while in Van Vleet's model capital gains are recognized immediately, as is true in the public markets; to the extent this is not true, one would make a lack of marketability adjustment against Van Vleets model. The assumptions for each of their models can be found earlier in this chapter.

In the instant case, the example presented in this section assumes that over the three-year period of the forecast the Company would have retained considerable funds and, correspondingly, the buyer would have built-up basis in his/her stock. While both a C corporation and an S corporation can retain funds, only the PTE shareholder's basis in their stock is increased by the amount of the retained funds, resulting in a lower gain upon selling their stock in the future. In our example the Company has retained 25 percent of their profits, which we have assumed will continue going forward; therefore, the opportunity for the PTE owner to build-up basis in their stock clearly exists.

There is often no way to know what that buyer's exit strategy might be or at what point in time he/she might be inclined, or even able, to sell. Note that, while our example assumed an exit in three years, in real life it will usually be a much longer time, potentially even very long. One way to take these unknowns into consideration is in the rate of return, assuming the analyst can ask questions that pro-

Exhibit 12.31   Summary of Recognized Benefits

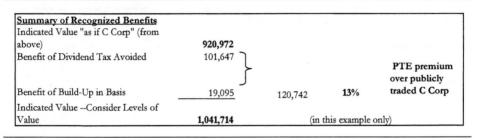

Summary of Recognized Benefits				
Indicated Value "as if C Corp" (from above)	**920,972**			
Benefit of Dividend Tax Avoided	101,647			**PTE premium over publicly traded C Corp**
Benefit of Build-Up in Basis	19,095	120,742	**13%**	
Indicated Value --Consider Levels of Value	**1,041,714**		(in this example only)	

vide a reasonable basis upon which to make adjustments to the previously determined rate. Given the unknowns regarding the timing and use of such a benefit by a hypothetical buyer, the selected rate must be appropriate to apply to the basis build-up. The resulting amount is then added to the value determination. Note that this particular example reflects an exit in only three years; for a particular valuation, an analyst might determine that such benefits are more appropriately recognized at five, ten, or fifteen years or more from the present or, alternatively, even every year, as Van Vleet's model assumes, or into perpetuity as Treharne's model assumes.

In conclusion, the total premium added for pass-through entity considerations in this example is 13 percent, including both the benefit for avoidance of dividend tax and basis build-up. This is presented in Exhibit 12.31. Note that this benefit can vary significantly, depending on the facts of the particular situation.

While this summary analysis is not an exhaustive presentation of either the benefits or detriments of pass-through entity ownership, it does present what are typically the most common and the most material issues the analyst will encounter in determining the value of such an entity. For further analysis, the reader is encouraged to study the models and assumptions that are the foundation of the theories presented in the earlier sections of this chapter.

The entire summary analysis is presented together in Exhibit 12.32. Also as mentioned before, there are still many analysts who consider these factors in a more qualitative manner, usually through the discounts applied.

Exhibit 12.32   FVG Co. Valuation

	Exhibit 6—FVG Co. Valuation			
Valuation		**Year 1**	**Year 2**	**Year 3**
Net Income Before Tax		200,000	300,000	350,000
Entity-Level Tax @ 35%	−35%	(70,000)	(105,000)	(122,500)
Net Income After Tax		**130,000**	**195,000**	**227,500**
Adjustments:				
Depreciation		25,000	30,000	30,000
"Normal" Capital Additions		(25,000)	(30,000)	(30,000)
Less: Working Capital		(10,000)	(10,000)	-
Cash Flow to Equity		**120,000**	**185,000**	**227,500**
Present Value Rate		24.2%	24.2%	21.7%
Discounted Cash Flows		**$107,676**	**$133,656**	**$1,048,387**
Sum of Discounted Cash Flows	$241,333		Discount Rate	24.2%
			Present Value of	
PV Terminal Value "as if C Corp"	$679,639		Terminal Value	**$679,639**
Indicated Value "as if C Corp"	$920,972			

Numbers in the right margin of the Valuation section:
- 850,000 Sum net income
- 637,500 Sum of Distributions

Adjustment for Dividend Tax Avoided		**Year 1**	**Year 2**	**Year 3**
HIGHLIGHTED CELLS DENOTE SPECIFIC DECISION POINTS FOR THE PTE CALCULATIONS	Percent of Income Distributed Annually			Assumed Exit/Terminal Year
PTE Distributions (75% of income in this example; percentage depends on expected distribution stream)	75%	150,000	225,000	262,500
Total Entity Taxes (C corp—from above)		(70,000)	(105,000)	(122,500)
Equivalent C corp Dividends		80,000	120,000	140,000
State	8.5%	6,800	10,200	11,900
Federal	15.0%	12,000	18,000	21,000
Net PTE Benefit (Liability)		18,800	28,200	32,900
Terminal Value Cap Rate				21.7%
				151,613
Present Value Rate		24.2%	24.2%	24.2%
Present Value		**$16,869**	**$20,374**	**$98,286**
Sum of Double Taxation Adjustment Present Values				$135,529
Likelihood of Buyer Benefitting from Pass-Through Benefits (could be ZERO to 100%)				75%
Estimated Benefit				101,647

Benefit of Build-Up in Basis (retained net income)		
HIGHLIGHTED CELLS DENOTE SPECIFIC DECISION POINTS FOR THE PTE CALCULATIONS		
PTE Net Income Over Period		$850,000
PTE Distributions Over Period		$637,500
Income Over PTE Distributions (sum net income before tax less sum PTE distributions)		212,500
Capital Gains Tax (estimated combined federal & state)	20%	42,500
PV Rate (appropriate rate of return considering risk of realizing retained net income)		29.2%
Estimated Benefit		$25,460
Likelihood of Buyer Benefitting from Pass-Through Benefits (could be ZERO to 100%)		75%
Estimated Benefit		$19,095

Summary of Recognized Benefits			
Indicated Value "as if C Corp" (from above)	920,972		
Benefit of Dividend Tax Avoided	101,647		
Benefit of Build-Up in Basis	19,095	120,742	13%
Indicated Value—Consider Levels of Value	1,041,714	(in this example only)	

PTE premium over publicly traded C Corp

CHAPTER 13

Estate, Gift, and Income Tax Valuations

Selected Internal Revenue Code Provisions, Treasury Regulations, and Revenue Rulings

In this world nothing is certain but death and taxes.
—Benjamin Franklin, American patriot, 1789

The avoidance of taxes is the only pursuit that still carries any reward.
—John Maynard Keynes, British economist, 1942

While "nothing is certain but death and taxes," one also might argue that given human nature, an additional certainty is that taxpayers will seek to minimize their taxes. For estate, gift, and income tax planning purposes, minimization of taxes is one of the primary objectives for owners of closely held businesses. This chapter presents a general overview of the guidelines for estate, gift, and income tax valuations as set forth in the Internal Revenue Code, Treasury Regulations, and Internal Revenue Service (IRS) Revenue Rulings. Detailed discussions of valuation considerations such as approaches, methods, and discounts are discussed elsewhere in the book. Chapter 15 presents a more complete discussion of relevant Tax Court cases. Detailed checklists/ready reference of Revenue Rulings 59-60, 77-287, and 93-12 that analysts can use in their valuations are presented at the end of this chapter.

VALUATIONS IN ESTATE AND GIFT TAXES

General guidelines for estate and gift valuations are primarily set forth in the Internal Revenue Code (IRC), Treasury Regulations, and Revenue Rulings (Rev. Rul.). Additional guidance is also found in the IRS positions as set forth in Technical Advice Memorandums and Private Letter Rulings. Court cases are also very useful (see Chapter 15).

SELECTED INTERNAL REVENUE CODE PROVISIONS

The Internal Revenue Code provides general guidance on the valuation of closely held companies as well as the applicable valuation dates for estate and gift taxes.

Valuation of Closely Held Companies

IRC § 2031(b) addresses the valuation of closely held companies for estate tax purposes and suggests that consideration be given to the value of publicly traded guideline company stocks when valuing the stock of a closely held business.

§ 2031(b) VALUATION OF UNLISTED STOCK AND SECURITIES

In the case of stock and securities of a corporation the value of which, by reason of their not being listed on an exchange and by reason of the absence of sales thereof, cannot be determined with reference to bid and asked prices or with reference to sales prices, the value thereof shall be determined by taking into consideration, in addition to all other factors, the value of stock or securities of corporations engaged in the same or a similar line of business which are listed on an exchange.[1]

Revenue Ruling 59-60, discussed elsewhere in this chapter, further elaborates on the use of publicly traded guideline companies to value closely held businesses.

Valuation Date

The applicable valuation date for estate taxes is defined as the date of death in IRC § 2031(a):

§ 2031(a) GENERAL

The value of the gross estate of the decedent shall be determined by including to the extent provided for in this part, the value at the time of his death of all property, real or personal, tangible or intangible, wherever situated.[2]

Further, an alternative valuation date of six months subsequent to the date of death is provided for in IRC § 2032(a).[3]

ValTip

Use of the alternative date may help to minimize estate taxes. For example, if the decedent was the key person in a closely held business, then the business's financial performance may decline during the period subsequent to death. The actual financial results will serve to support the proposition that the business was dependent on the decedent.

The valuation date for gift taxes is set forth in IRC § 2512(a) as the date of the gift:

§ 2512. VALUATION OF GIFTS

(a) If the gift is made in property, the value thereof at the date of the gift shall be considered the amount of the gift.[4]

---

[1] IRC § 2031(b).
[2] IRC § 2031(a).
[3] IRC § 2032(a).
[4] IRC § 2512(a).

Special Valuation Guidelines

Other important Internal Revenue Code sections having estate and gift tax valuation implications include Chapter 14 of the IRC, specifically § 2701-2704.[5] Chapter 14 of this book presents an overview of these sections.

SELECTED TREASURY REGULATIONS

Treasury Regulations represent the IRS's interpretation of the IRC. Key Treasury Regulations address the applicable standard of value for estate and gift taxes, guidelines for valuing closely held businesses, and disclosure requirements for gift tax returns.

Standard of Value

Treasury Regulation § 20.2031-1 defines the standard of value for estate tax matters as *fair market value:*

> § 20.2031-1 Definition of gross estate; valuation of property
> (b) *Valuation of property in general.* The value of every item of property includible in a decedent's gross estate under sections 2031 through 2044 is its fair market value at the time of the decedent's death, except that if the executor elects the alternate valuation method under section 2032, it is the fair market value thereof at the date, and with the adjustments, prescribed in that section. The fair market value is the price at which the property would change hands between a willing buyer and a willing seller, neither being under any compulsion to buy or to sell and both having reasonable knowledge of relevant facts.[6]

The corresponding regulation for gift tax valuations is found in Treasury Regulation § 25.2512-1.

Valuation of Corporate Stock

Treasury Regulation § 20.2031-2(f) addresses the valuation of corporate stock for estate tax purposes where stock prices are unavailable. This regulation also discusses certain factors to consider when valuing such securities.

> § 20.2031-2 Valuation of stocks and bonds
> (f) *Where selling prices or bid and asked prices are unavailable.* If the provisions of paragraphs (b), (c), and (d) of this section are inapplicable because actual sale prices and bona fide bid and asked prices are lacking, then the fair market value is to be determined by taking the following factors into consideration:
> (1) In the case of corporate or other bonds, the soundness of the security, the interest yield, the date of maturity, and other relevant factors; and

---

[5] IRC § 2701-2704.
[6] Treasury Regulation § 20.2031-1(b).

(2) In the case of shares of stock, the company's net worth, prospective earning power and dividend-paying capacity, and other relevant factors.

Some of the "other relevant factors" referred to in subparagraphs (1) and (2) of this paragraph are: the goodwill of the business; the economic outlook in the particular industry; the company's position in the industry and its management; the degree of control of the business represented by the block of stock to be valued; and the values of securities of corporations engaged in the same or similar lines of business which are listed on a stock exchange. However, the weight to be accorded such comparisons or any other evidentiary factors considered in the determination of a value depends upon the facts of each case. In addition to the relevant factors described above, consideration shall also be given to nonoperating assets, including proceeds of life insurance policies payable to or for the benefit of the company, to the extent such nonoperating assets have not been taken into account in the determination of net worth, prospective earning power and dividend-earning capacity. Complete financial and other data upon which the valuation is based should be submitted with the return, including copies of reports of any examinations of the company made by accountants, engineers, or any technical experts as of or near the applicable valuation date.[7]

The corresponding regulation for gift tax valuations is found in Treasury Regulation § 25.2512-2(f).

Valuation of Unincorporated Interests in Businesses

Treasury Regulation § 20.2031-3 discusses valuation of unincorporated interests in businesses for estate tax purposes. Of particular note is the regulation's emphasis on the valuation of goodwill.

§ 20.2031-3 Valuation of interests in businesses

The fair market value of any interest of a decedent in a business, whether a partnership or a proprietorship, is the net amount which a willing purchaser, whether an individual or a corporation, would pay for the interest to a willing seller, neither being under any compulsion to buy or to sell and both having reasonable knowledge of relevant facts. The net value is determined on the basis of all relevant factors including:

(a) A fair appraisal as of the applicable valuation date of all the assets of the business, tangible and intangible, including goodwill;

(b) The demonstrated earning capacity of the business; and

(c) The other factors set forth in paragraphs (f) and (h) of § 20.2031-2 relating to the valuation of corporate stock, to the extent applicable.

Special attention should be given to determining an adequate value of the goodwill of the business in all cases in which the decedent has not agreed, for an adequate and full consideration in money or money's worth, that his interest passes at his death to, for example, his surviving

---

[7] Treasury Regulation § 20.2031-2(f).

partner or partners. Complete financial and other data upon which the valuation is based should be submitted with the return, including copies of reports of examinations of the business made by accountants, engineers, or any technical experts as of or near the applicable valuation date.[8]

The corresponding regulation for gift tax valuations is found in Treasury Regulation § 25.2512-3.

Disclosure of Gifts

On December 3, 1999, the IRS issued its final regulations regarding adequate disclosure of gifts on gift tax returns. The regulations provide for a three-year statute of limitations beyond which the IRS cannot challenge the tax return provided that the gifts are adequately disclosed. These regulations are applicable to all gifts made after December 31, 1996, for which gift tax returns are filed after December 3, 1999.

Treasury Regulation § 301.6501(c)-1 sets forth the adequate disclosure requirements. Treasury Regulation § 301.6501(c)-1(f)(3)(i) lists the requirements that must be satisfied by the analyst who prepares the valuation:

§ 301.6501(c)-1(f)(3)(i)

(3) *Submission of appraisals in lieu of the information required under paragraph (f)(2)(iv) of this section.* The requirements of paragraph (f)(2)(iv) of this section will be satisfied if the donor submits an appraisal of the transferred property that meets the following requirements—

(i) The appraisal is prepared by an appraiser who satisfies all of the following requirements:

(A) The appraiser is an individual who holds himself or herself out to the public as an appraiser or performs appraisals on a regular basis.

(B) Because of the appraiser's qualifications, as described in the appraisal that details the appraiser's background, experience, education, and membership, if any, in professional appraisal associations, the appraiser is qualified to make appraisals of the type of property being valued.

(C) The appraiser is not the donor or the donee of the property or a member of the family of the donor or donee, as defined in section 2032A(e)(2), or any person employed by the donor, the donee, or a member of the family of either;[9]

Treasury Regulation § 301.6501(c)-1(f)(3)(ii) lists the information that must be disclosed in the valuation report to satisfy the adequate disclosure requirements:

§ 301.6501(c)-1(f)(3)(ii)

(ii) The appraisal contains all of the following:

(A) The date of the transfer, the date on which the transferred property was appraised, and the purpose of the appraisal.

(B) A description of the property.

(C) A description of the appraisal process employed.

---

[8] Treasury Regulation § 20.2031-3.
[9] Treasury Regulation § 301.6501(c)-1(f)(3)(i).

(D) A description of the assumptions, hypothetical conditions, and any limiting conditions and restrictions on the transferred property that affect the analyses, opinions, and conclusions.

(E) The information considered in determining the appraised value, including in the case of an ownership interest in a business, all financial data that was used in determining the value of the interest that is sufficiently detailed so that another person can replicate the process and arrive at the appraised value.

(F) The appraisal procedures followed, and the reasoning that supports the analyses, opinions, and conclusions.

(G) The valuation method utilized, the rationale for the valuation method, and the procedure used in determining the fair market value of the asset transferred.

(H) The specific basis for the valuation, such as specific comparable sales or transactions, sales of similar interests, asset-based approaches, merger-acquisition transactions, etc.[10]

SELECTED REVENUE RULINGS

Revenue rulings provide guidance for general situations not requiring a specific change in the Treasury Regulations. This section discusses key revenue rulings relating to valuations for estate and gift tax purposes, including 59-60, 77-287, and 83-120, and 93-12.

Revenue Ruling 59-60

Approach to Valuation

Revenue Ruling 59-60 is the single most important revenue ruling relating to the valuation of closely held companies for estate and gift tax purposes. It was later amplified to include valuation guidance for income tax purposes as well. While it relates primarily to valuations of closely held businesses for estate, gift, and income taxes, because of its wide acceptance by various courts and venues, the users of valuation information, and valuation analysts, it is often cited as a relevant source for other types of valuations.

Standard of Value

Revenue Ruling 59-60 cites the definition of fair market value provided in Treasury Regulations § 20.2031-1(b) and § 25.2512-1 as the applicable standard of value.

> § 20.2031-1(b) of the Estate Tax Regulations and § 25.2512-1 of the Gift Tax Regulations define fair market value, in effect, as the price at which the property would change hands between a willing buyer and a willing seller when the former is not under any compulsion to buy

---

[10] Treasury Regulation § 301.6501(c)-1(f)(3)(ii).

and the latter is not under any compulsion to sell, both parties having reasonable knowledge of relevant facts.[11]

It expands on this definition to state that the buyer and seller are presumed to be *hypothetical* buyers and sellers (as opposed to specific buyers and sellers) and also are *able* as well as willing to trade (i.e., they have the financial wherewithal and operational control to consummate the hypothetical transaction).

> Court decisions frequently state in addition that the hypothetical buyer and seller are assumed to be able, as well as willing, to trade and to be well informed about the property and concerning the market for such property.[12]

Information to Be Considered

Valuation is not an exact science; rather, the appraiser must consider all of the relevant facts and use common sense, judgment, and reasonableness in assessing those facts and determining their importance relative to the valuation of the subject company.[13]

Guidance as to the "cut-off" date for information that may be used for purposes of the valuation is provided. The valuation must be *based on the facts available at the required date of appraisal.*[14]

> Often events that would otherwise affect a subject company's value occur subsequent to the valuation date. Such events generally should not be considered for purposes of estate and gift tax valuations. The key to determining what events should be considered is what facts were known or knowable as of the valuation date.

Importance of Future Financial Performance

The ruling indicates that the valuation of securities is a *prophecy as to the future* and reflects the degree of optimism or pessimism with which investors regard the future of the subject company's prospects as of the appraisal date.[15]

Assessment of Risk and Its Relationship to Value

Revenue Ruling 59-60 specifically addresses the relationship between risk (uncertainty) and value, noting that "uncertainty as to the stability or continuity of the

---

[11] Rev. Rul. 59-60, 1959-1 CB 237, Sec. 2.02.

[12] Ibid.

[13] Ibid., Sec. 3.01.

[14] Ibid., Sec. 3.03.

[15] Ibid., Sec. 3.02–3.03.

future income from a property decreases its value by increasing the risk of loss of earnings and value in the future."[16]

Analysts must exercise judgment as to the degree of risk. This risk is reflected in the discount rate when employing an income approach (discussed in Chapter 6) or in the valuation multiple when using a market approach (discussed in Chapter 7).

> Many analysts make the mistake of focusing on a subject company's past historical performance as the primary determinant of value. The expectation of the company's future performance as of the valuation date is what determines value. Past performance is only relevant to the extent that it is indicative of the company's future performance.

Use of Market Approach for Valuing Closely Held Companies

The best measure of a stock's value is the price realized in a free and active market. However, where a stock is traded infrequently or closely held, then some other measure must be used. In many cases, the next best alternative is to use the prices of the stocks of companies in the same or similar line of business.[17]

Factors to Consider

Revenue Ruling 59-60 notes eight factors or tenets of value that should be considered when valuing the stock of closely held companies. While these factors are not all-inclusive, they do provide a good general framework for structuring analytical work. A summary of the pertinent points relating to each factor follows.

Nature and History of the Business

The history of a business provides an indication of its stability, growth, diversification of operations, and the like that provide an indication of the business's risk. Aspects of the business history that should be analyzed include the nature of the business, its products or services, operating and investment assets, capital structure, plant facilities, sales records, and management. More detailed information should be collected and analyzed for events that are near to the valuation date as they are probably more indicative of the company's future performance. Events of the past that are unlikely to recur in the future should be discounted, since value has a close relation to future expectations.[18]

Economic and Industry Outlook

A valuation must consider the current and future economic and industry conditions as of the date of the valuation in order to assess the subject company's competitive position as well as the overall competitiveness of the company's industry with other

---

[16] Ibid., Sec. 3.02.
[17] Ibid., Sec. 3.03.
[18] Ibid., Sec. 4.02(a).

industries. Chapter 3 presents a detailed discussion of external facts to be considered for valuation purposes, as well as sources for obtaining this information.

A key company-specific consideration is whether there is a "key person" upon which the success of the business depends. The loss of such an individual may have a detrimental effect on value if the company has not planned for management succession. Mitigating factors such as the existence of life insurance or the ability to hire replacement management also should be considered as these may offset some of the loss of a key person's services and the detriment to value.[19]

Book Value of the Stock and the Financial Condition of the Business

The analyst should obtain balance sheets for the company for two or more years preceding the valuation date as well as the month preceding the valuation date. In analyzing the balance sheets, the analyst should focus on liquidity, working capital, major fixed assets, long-term debt, the company's capital structure, and net worth. Analysis of this information over time will permit identification of significant events and trends, such as changes in financial position and capital structure and acquisitions. Nonoperating assets should be identified and segregated from the operating assets and restated at market value. If the company has more than one class of stock, the corporate documents should be examined to determine the rights and privileges of the various classes, including voting powers and dividend and liquidation preferences.[20] A detailed discussion of the analysis of the balance sheet is presented in Chapter 4.

Earning Capacity of the Company

> Value is dependent on investors' expectations of a company's *future* earnings capacity. If an unprofitable operation can be discontinued without adversely affecting the company's other lines of business, then the future earnings capacity (and hence the value) of the remaining lines of business may be materially greater than if the values of all operating lines were aggregated. In other words, the sum of *some* of the parts may be greater than the whole.

Income statements should be obtained for five or more years preceding the valuation date as well as the period immediately preceding the valuation date. This information will facilitate analysis of revenues by source, significant operating expenses, interest expense, depreciation and amortization, reasonableness of officers' compensation, contributions, income taxes, income available for distribution to shareholders, rates and amounts of dividends paid on each class of stock, and retained earnings. As with the balance sheet, the appraiser should segregate operating and nonoperating items. Further, the analyst should determine whether any line of business in which the company is engaged is operated consistently at a loss and might be abandoned with benefit to the company.

---

[19] Ibid., Sec. 4.02(b).
[20] Ibid., Sec. 4.02(c).

Analysis of the company's historical earnings may be indicative of future performance. Revenue Ruling 59-60 stresses that reliance on *arbitrary 5- or 10-year averages without regard to current trends or future prospects will not produce a realistic valuation.* Consideration should be given to observed trends. For example, if a company exhibits progressively increasing or decreasing earnings trends, then current earnings may be given greater weight. Common size analysis of the income statements may be beneficial in assessing risk and determining marginal performance relative to the industry.[21]

A detailed discussion of the analysis of the income statement is presented in Chapter 4.

Dividend-Paying Capacity

The capacity of the company to pay dividends to shareholders, as opposed to dividends historically paid, should be given primary consideration in determining value, recognizing that it may be necessary for a company to retain a reasonable portion of its profits to meet competition.

Revenue Ruling 59-60 further notes that payment of dividends is discretionary for a controlling interest. Such an interest may substitute compensation for dividends with the effect of reducing net income and income available for distribution as dividends. Consequently, actual payments of dividends may not be a reliable indication of value.[22]

ValTip

> The definition of dividend-paying capacity is equivalent to equity net cash flows (i.e., *those cash flows available to pay out to equity holders [in the form of dividends] after funding operations of the business*).[23]

Intangible Assets

Goodwill is based on earnings and results from the ability of a company to realize a higher value than it would otherwise realize on its tangible assets alone. Factors contributing to goodwill include a company's reputation, ownership of trade or brand names, and a history of successful operation over time in a particular location. It may not be possible to segregate the value of goodwill and other intangibles from the value of the tangible assets. However, the value of such intangibles is implicit in the value of the overall enterprise.[24]

Past Sales of Company Stock

Sales of the subject company's own stock should be considered as an indication of value. Such sales may be indicative of value if the transactions are at arm's length, and the sales did not result from force or distress.

---

[21] Ibid., Sec. 4.02(d).
[22] Rev. Rul. 59-60, 1959-1 CB 237, Sec. 4.02(e).
[23] *International Glossary of Business Valuation Terms.*
[24] Ibid., Sec. 4.02(f).

The size of the block of stock should be considered, including the impact of control and lack of marketability on value. With respect to control, Revenue Ruling 59-60 notes that "control of a corporation, either actual or in effect, representing as it does an added element of value, may justify a higher value for a specific block of stock." Regarding marketability, Revenue Ruling 59-60 acknowledges that a "minority interest in an unlisted corporation's stock is more difficult to sell than a similar block of listed stock"[25]

Market Price of Stocks of Guideline Publicly Traded Companies

Many inexperienced appraisers fail to consider the use of the market approach/guideline public company methodology because they believe that publicly traded companies are too large to be truly comparable. While the size of many public companies may eliminate them as comparables, the sizes of many public companies may approximate that of the closely held company being valued, particularly in certain industries, such as high technology, for which there have been initial public offerings for companies with relatively small market capitalizations.

Revenue Ruling 59-60 does not specifically address the use of the market approach/guideline company transaction method in valuing closely held companies, as these data have become widely available only recently. However, the guidelines relating to comparability of the business lines and consideration of other relevant factors presented in Revenue Ruling 59-60 for the application of the guideline public company method may be applicable to the guideline company transaction method as well.

Revenue Ruling 59-60 cites IRC § 2031(b), which indicates that consideration be given to the value of publicly traded guideline company stocks when valuing the stock of a closely held business. It emphasizes that the guideline public stock be actively traded, and only the stocks of comparable publicly traded companies should be considered. In defining comparability, Revenue Ruling 59-60 reiterates the provision in Treasury Regulation § 20.2031-2(f) that the companies' lines of business be the same or similar. However, it also notes that consideration should be given to other relevant factors to ensure the most valid comparable companies are identified.[26]

A more detailed discussion of the selection of publicly traded guideline companies is presented in Chapters 3 and 7.

---

[25] Ibid., Sec. 4.02(g).
[26] Ibid., Sec. 4.02(h).

Weight Accorded to Factors

In assessing all the factors, certain ones may be given more weight than others, depending on the facts and circumstances. For example, earnings may be more important when valuing companies that sell products or services, whereas the underlying assets may be more important when valuing holding companies. With respect to assets, Revenue Ruling 59-60 notes that:

> The market values of the underlying assets give due weight to potential earnings and dividends of the particular items of property underlying the stock, capitalized at rates deemed proper by the investing public at the date of appraisal. For these reasons, adjusted net worth should be accorded greater weight in valuing the stock of a closely held investment or real estate holding company, whether or not family owned, than any of the other customary yardsticks of appraisal, such as earnings and dividend-paying capacity.[27]

ValTip

Revenue Ruling 59-60 supports the use of an asset approach for valuing investment or holding companies. Therefore, use of an asset approach when valuing family limited partnerships and limited liability companies (LLCs) with similar characteristics is considered reasonable in view of this ruling.

A discussion of the valuation of family limited partnerships is presented in Chapter 14 and valuation of other pass-through entities is presented in Chapter 12.

Capitalization Rates

When using an income approach, the determination of the capitalization rate (and, by implication, a discount rate) is one of the most difficult problems in valuation. Rates of return vary widely, even for companies in the same industry, and can fluctuate from year to year depending on the prevailing economic conditions. Consequently, no standard rates can be formulated for application to a closely held company. In determining the capitalization rate, the following factors should be considered:

- Nature of the business
- Risk involved
- Stability or irregularity of earnings[28]

Determination of the discount and capitalization rates is discussed in Chapters 5 and 6.

---

[27] Ibid., Sec. 5(b).
[28] Ibid., Sec. 6.

Average of Factors

Because valuations cannot be made based on some predetermined formula, there is no means to assign mathematical weights to alternative valuation approaches and methodologies. "For this reason, no useful purpose is served by taking an average of several factors (for example, book value, capitalized earnings and capitalized dividends) and basing the valuation on the result."[29]

ValTip

> Inexperienced analysts often make the mistake of arbitrarily averaging each of the various valuation approaches/methodologies used in valuing a closely held company. For example, if three approaches are used, each approach may be assigned an equal one-third weighting. As noted in Revenue Ruling 59-60, such an approach would serve no purpose. Rather, each valuation is subject to particular facts and circumstances, and these must be considered in selecting the most appropriate approach(es) and level of reliance when determining the final estimate of value.

Restrictive Agreements

For estate tax (but not gift tax) purposes, where stock is acquired by a decedent subject to an agreement that contains an option to repurchase the stock at a specified price, that price may be accepted as the fair market value of the stock if the agreement is the result of a voluntary action by the stockholders and is binding during life as well as at death. In this instance, the agreement is a factor to be considered, along with other relevant factors, in determining the fair market value of the stock. However, if a stockholder is free to dispose of the stock during his or her life and the repurchase option becomes effective only upon the decedent's death, the fair market value is not limited to the option price. It will be necessary to consider the relationship of the parties, the relative number of shares held by the decedent, and other material facts to determine whether the agreement represents a bona fide business arrangement or is simply a device to pass the decedent's shares to heirs for less than adequate consideration.[30] See Chapter 24 for additional information on buy/sell agreements.

Section 8 of Revenue Ruling 59-60 has been superseded in certain instances by IRC § 2703. See discussion of § 2703 in Chapter 14.

> **REV-RUL, Valuation of stocks and bonds, Rev. Rul. 59-60, 1959-1 CB 237, (Jan. 01, 1959)**
> **Rev. Rul. 59-60, 1959-1 CB 237**
>
> SECTION 2031. DEFINITION OF GROSS ESTATE
> 26 CFR 20.2031-2: Valuation of stocks and bonds.

---

[29] Ibid., Sec. 7.
[30] Ibid., Sec. 8.

(Also Section 2512.)
(Also Part II, Sections 811[k], 1005, Regulations 105, Section 81.10.)

In valuing the stock of closely held corporations, or the stock of corporations where market quotations are not available, all other available financial data, as well as all relevant factors affecting the fair market value must be considered for estate tax and gift tax purposes. No general formula may be given that is applicable to the many different valuation situations arising in the valuation of such stock. However, the general approach, methods, and factors which must be considered in valuing such securities are outlined.

Revenue Ruling 54-77, C.B. 1954-1, 187, superseded.

[Text]

SECTION 1. PURPOSE.

The purpose of this Revenue Ruling is to outline and review in general the approach, methods, and factors to be considered in valuing shares of the capital stock of closely held corporations for estate tax and gift tax purposes. The methods discussed herein will apply likewise to the valuation of corporate stocks on which market quotations are either unavailable or are of such scarcity that they do not reflect the fair market value.

SEC. 2. BACKGROUND AND DEFINITIONS.

.01 All valuations must be made in accordance with the applicable provisions of the Internal Revenue Code of 1954 and the Federal Estate Tax and Gift Tax Regulations. Sections 2031(a), 2032, and 2512(a) of the 1954 Code (sections 811 and 1005 of the 1939 Code) require that the property to be included in the gross estate, or made the subject of a gift, shall be taxed on the basis of the value of the property at the time of death of the decedent, the alternate date if so elected, or the date of gift.

.02 Section 20.2031-1(b) of the Estate Tax Regulations (section 81.10 of the Estate Tax Regulations 105) and section 25.2512-1 of the Gift Tax Regulations (section 86.19 of Gift Tax Regulations 108) define fair market value, in effect, as the price at which the property would change hands between a willing buyer and a willing seller when the former is not under any compulsion to buy and the latter is not under any compulsion to sell, both parties having reasonable knowledge of relevant facts. Court decisions frequently state in addition that the hypothetical buyer and seller are assumed to be able, as well as willing, to trade and to be well informed about the property and concerning the market for such property.

.03 Closely held corporations are those corporations the shares of which are owned by a relatively limited number of stockholders. Often the entire stock issue is held by one family. The result of this situation is that little, if any, trading in the shares takes place. There is, therefore, no established market for the stock and such sales as occur at irregular intervals seldom reflect all of the elements of a representative transaction as defined by the term "fair market value."

SEC. 3. APPROACH TO VALUATION.

.01 A determination of fair market value, being a question of fact, will depend upon the circumstances in each case. No formula can be devised that will be generally applicable to the multitude of different valuation issues arising in estate and gift tax cases. Often, an appraiser will find wide differences of opinion as to the fair market value of a particular stock. In resolving such differences, he should maintain a reasonable attitude in recognition of the fact that valuation is not an exact science. A sound valuation will be based upon all the relevant facts, but the elements of common sense, informed judgment and reasonableness must enter into the process of weighing those facts and determining their aggregate significance.

.02 The fair market value of specific shares of stock will vary as general economic conditions change from "normal" to "boom" or "depression," that is, according to the degree of optimism or pessimism with which the investing public regards the future at the required date of appraisal. Uncertainty as to the stability or continuity of the future income from a property decreases its value by increasing the risk of loss of earnings and value in the future. The value of shares of stock of a company with very uncertain future prospects is highly speculative. The appraiser must exercise his judgment as to the degree of risk attaching to the business of the corporation which issued the stock, but that judgment must be related to all of the other factors affecting value.

.03 Valuation of securities is, in essence, a prophecy as to the future and must be based on facts available at the required date of appraisal. As a generalization, the prices of stocks which are traded in volume in a free and active market by informed persons best reflect the consensus of the investing public as to what the future holds for the corporations and industries represented. When a stock is closely held, is traded infrequently, or is traded in an erratic market, some other measure of value must be used. In many instances, the next best measure may be found in the prices at which the stocks of companies engaged in the same or a similar line of business are selling in a free and open market.

SEC. 4. FACTORS TO CONSIDER.

.01 It is advisable to emphasize that in the valuation of the stock of closely held corporations or the stock of corporations where market quotations are either lacking or too scarce to be recognized, all available financial data, as well as all relevant factors affecting the fair market value, should be considered. The following factors, although not all-inclusive are fundamental and require careful analysis in each case:

(a) The nature of the business and the history of the enterprise from its inception

(b) The economic outlook in general and the condition and outlook of the specific industry in particular

(c) The book value of the stock and the financial condition of the business

(d) The earning capacity of the company

(e) The dividend-paying capacity

(f) Whether or not the enterprise has goodwill or other intangible value

(g) Sales of the stock and the size of the block of stock to be valued

(h) The market price of stocks of corporations engaged in the same or a similar line of business having their stocks actively traded in a free and open market, either on an exchange or over-the-counter

.02 The following is a brief discussion of each of the foregoing factors:

(a) The history of a corporate enterprise will show its past stability or instability, its growth or lack of growth, the diversity or lack of diversity of its operations, and other facts needed to form an opinion of the degree of risk involved in the business. For an enterprise which changed its form of organization but carried on the same of closely similar operations of its predecessor, the history of the former enterprise should be considered. The detail to be considered should increase with approach to the required date of appraisal, since recent events are of greatest help in predicting the future; but a study of gross and net income, and of dividends covering a long prior period, is highly desirable. The history to be studied should include, but need not be limited to, the nature of the business, its products or services, its operating and investment assets, capital structure, plant facilities, sales records, and management, all of which should be considered as of the date of the appraisal, with due regard for recent significant changes. Events of the past that are unlikely to recur in the future should be discounted, since value has a close relation to future expectancy.

(b) A sound appraisal of a closely held stock must consider current and prospective economic conditions as of the date of appraisal, both in the national economy and in the industry or industries with which the corporation is allied. It is important to know that the company is more or less successful than its competitors in the same industry, or that it is maintaining a stable position with respect to competitors. Equal or even greater significance may attach to the ability of the industry with which the company is allied to compete with other industries. Prospective competition which has not been a factor in prior years should be given careful attention. For example, high profits due to the novelty of its product and the lack of competition often lead to increasing competition. The public's appraisal of the future prospects of competitive industries or of competitors within an industry may be indicated by price trends in the markets for commodities and for securities. The loss of the manager of a so-called "one-man" business may have a depressing effect upon the value of the stock of such business, particularly if there is a lack of trained personnel capable of succeeding to the management of the enterprise. In valuing the stock of this type of business, therefore, the effect of the loss of the manager on the future expectancy of the business, and the absence of management-succession potentialities are pertinent factors to be taken into consideration. On the other hand, there may be factors which offset, in whole or in part, the loss of the manager's services. For instance, the nature of the business and of its assets may be such that they will not be impaired by the loss of the manager. Furthermore, the loss may be adequately covered by life insurance, or competent management might be employed on the basis of the consideration paid for the former manager's services. These, or other offsetting factors, if found to exist, should be carefully weighed against the loss of the manager's services in valuing the stock of the enterprise.

(c) Balance sheets should be obtained, preferably in the form of comparative annual statements for two or more years immediately preceding the date of appraisal, together with a balance sheet at the end of the month preceding that date, if corporate accounting will permit. Any balance sheet descriptions that are not self-explanatory, and balance sheet items comprehending diverse assets or liabilities, should be clarified in essential detail by supporting supplemental schedules. These statements usually will disclose to the appraiser 1) liquid position (ratio of current assets to current liabilities); 2) gross and net book value of principal classes of fixed assets; 3) working capital; 4) long-term indebtedness; 5) capital structure; and 6) net worth. Consideration also should be given to any assets not essential to the operation of the business, such as investments in securities, real estate, and so on. In general, such non-operating assets will command a lower rate of return than do the operating assets, although in exceptional cases the reverse may be true. In computing the book value per share of stock, assets of the investment type should be revalued on the basis of their market price and the book value adjusted accordingly. Comparison of the company's balance sheets over several years may reveal, among other facts, such developments as the acquisition of additional production facilities or subsidiary companies, improvement in financial position, and details as to recapitalizations and other changes in the capital structure of the corporation. If the corporation has more than one class of stock outstanding, the charter or certificate of incorporation should be examined to ascertain the explicit rights and privileges of the various stock issues including: 1) voting powers, 2) preference as to dividends, and 3) preference as to assets in the event of liquidation.

(d) Detailed profit-and-loss statements should be obtained and considered for a representative period immediately prior to the required date of appraisal, preferably five or more years. Such statements should show 1) gross income by principal items; 2) principal deductions from gross income including major prior items of operating expenses, interest and other expense on each item of long-term debt, depreciation and depletion if such deductions are made, officers' salaries, in total if they appear to be reasonable or in detail if they seem to be excessive, contributions (whether or not deductible for tax purposes) that the nature of its business and its community position require the corporation to make, and taxes by principal items, including income and excess profits taxes; 3) net income available for dividends; 4) rates and amounts of dividends paid on each class of stock; 5) remaining amount carried to surplus; and

6) adjustments to, and reconciliation with, surplus as stated on the balance sheet. With profit and loss statements of this character available, the appraiser should be able to separate recurrent from nonrecurrent items of income and expense, to distinguish between operating income and investment income, and to ascertain whether or not any line of business in which the company is engaged is operated consistently at a loss and might be abandoned with benefit to the company. The percentage of earnings retained for business expansion should be noted when dividend-paying capacity in considered. Potential future income is a major factor in many valuations of closely-held stocks, and all information concerning past income which will be helpful in predicting the future should be secured. Prior earnings records usually are the most reliable guide as to the future expectancy, but resort to arbitrary five-or-ten-year averages without regard to current trends or future prospects will not produce a realistic valuation. If, for instance, a record of progressively increasing or decreasing net income is found, then greater weight may be accorded the most recent years' profits in estimating earning power. It will be helpful, in judging risk and the extent to which a business is a marginal operator, to consider deductions from income and net income in terms of percentage of sales. Major categories of cost and expense to be so analyzed include the consumption of raw materials and supplies in the case of manufacturers, processors, and fabricators; the cost of purchased merchandise in the case of merchants; utility services; insurance; taxes; depletion of depreciation; and interest.

(e) Primary consideration should be given to the dividend-paying capacity of the company rather than to dividends actually paid in the past. Recognition must be given to the necessity of retaining a reasonable portion of profits in a company to meet competition. Dividend-paying capacity is a factor that must be considered in an appraisal, but dividends actually paid in the past may not have any relation to dividend-paying capacity. Specifically, the dividends paid by a closely held family company may be measured by the income needs of the stockholders or by their desire to avoid taxes on dividend receipts, instead of by the ability of the company to pay dividends. Where an actual or effective controlling interest in a corporation is to be valued, the dividend factor is not a material element, since the payment of such dividends is discretionary with the controlling stockholders. The individual or group in control can substitute salaries and bonuses for dividends, thus reducing net income and understating the dividend-paying capacity of the company. It follows, therefore, that dividends are less reliable criteria of fair market value than other applicable factors.

(f) In the final analysis, goodwill is based upon earning capacity. The presence of goodwill and its value, therefore, rests upon the excess of net earnings over and above a fair return on the net tangible assets. While the element of goodwill may be based primarily on earnings, such factors as the prestige and renown of the business, the ownership of a trade or brand name, and a record of successful operation over a prolonged period in a particular locality, also may furnish support for the inclusion of intangible value. In some instances it may not be possible to make a separate appraisal of the tangible and intangible assets of the businesses. The enterprise has a value as an entity. Whatever intangible value there is, which is supportable by the facts, may be measured by the amount by which the appraised value of the tangible assets exceeds the net book value of such assets.

(g) Sales of stock of a closely held corporation should be carefully investigated to determine whether they represent transactions at arm's length. Forced or distress sales do not ordinarily reflect fair market value nor do isolated sales in small amounts necessarily control as the measure of value. This is especially true in the valuation of a controlling interest in a corporation. Since, in the case of closely held stocks, no prevailing market prices are available, there is no basis for making an adjustment for blockage. It follows, therefore, that such stocks should be valued upon a consideration of all the evidence affecting the fair market value. The size of the block of stock itself is a relevant factor to be considered. Although it is true that a minority interest in an unlisted corporation's stock is more difficult to sell than a similar block of listed stock, it is equally true that control of a corporation, either actual or in effect, representing as it does an added element of value, may justify a higher value for a specific block of stock.

(h) Section 2031(b) of the Code states, in effect, that in valuing unlisted securities the value of stock or securities of corporations engaged in the same or a similar line of business which are listed on an exchange should be taken into consideration along with all other factors. An important consideration is that the corporations to be used for comparisons have capital stocks which are actively traded by the public. In accordance with section 2031(b) of the Code, stocks listed on an exchange are to be considered first. However, if sufficient comparable companies whose stocks are listed on an exchange cannot be found, other comparable companies which have stocks actively traded on the over-the-counter market also may be used. The essential factor is that whether the stocks are sold on an exchange or over-the-counter there is evidence of an active, free public market for the stock as of the valuation date. In selecting corporations for comparative purposes, care should be taken to use only comparable companies. Although the only restrictive requirement as to comparable corporations specified in the statute is that their lines of business be the same or similar, yet it is obvious that consideration must be given to other relevant factors in order that the most valid comparison possible will be obtained. For illustration, a corporation having one or more issues of preferred stock, bonds, or debentures in addition to its common stock should not be considered to be directly comparable to one having only common stock outstanding. In like manner, a company with a declining business and decreasing markets is not comparable to one with a record of current progress and market expansion.

SEC. 5. WEIGHT TO BE ACCORDED VARIOUS FACTORS.

The valuation of closely held corporate stock entails the consideration of all relevant factors as stated in Section 4. Depending upon the circumstances in each case, certain factors may carry more weight than others because of the nature of the company's business. To illustrate:

(a) Earnings may be the most important criterion of value in some cases whereas asset value will receive primary consideration in others. In general, the appraiser will accord primary consideration to earnings when valuing stocks of companies which sell products or services to the public; conversely, in the investment or holding type of company, the appraiser may accord the greatest weight to the assets underlying the security to be valued.

(b) The value of the stock of a closely held investment or real estate holding company, whether or not family owned, is closely related to the value of the assets underlying the stock. For companies of this type the appraiser should determine the fair market values of the assets of the company. Operating expenses of such a company and the cost of liquidating it, if any, merit consideration when appraising the relative values of the stock and the underlying assets. The market values of the underlying assets give due weight to potential earnings and dividends of the particular items of property underlying the stock, capitalized at rates deemed proper by the investing public at the date of appraisal. A current appraisal by the investing public should be superior to the retrospective opinion of an individual. For these reasons, adjusted net worth should be accorded greater weight in valuing the stock of a closely held investment or real estate holding company, whether or not family owned, than any of the other customary yardsticks of appraisal, such as earnings and dividend-paying capacity.

SEC. 6. CAPITALIZATION RATES.

In the application of certain fundamental valuation factors, such as earnings and dividends, it is necessary to capitalize the average or current results at some appropriate rate. A determination of the proper capitalization rate presents one of the most difficult problems in valuation. That there is no ready or simple solution will become apparent by a cursory check of the rates of return and dividend yields in terms of the selling prices of corporate shares listed on the major exchanges of the country. Wide variations will be found even for companies in the same industry. Moreover, the ratio will fluctuate from year to year depending upon economic conditions. Thus, no standard tables of capitalization rates applicable to closely held corporations can be formulated. Among the more important factors to be taken into consideration in deciding upon a capitalization rate in a particular case are: 1) the nature of the business; 2) the risk involved; and 3) the stability or irregularity of earnings.

SEC. 7. AVERAGE OF FACTORS.

Because valuations cannot be made on the basis of a prescribed formula, there is no means whereby the various applicable factors in a particular case can be assigned mathematical weights in deriving the fair market value. For this reason, no useful purpose is served by taking an average of several factors (for example, book value, capitalized earnings and capitalized dividends) and basing the valuation on the result. Such a process excludes active consideration of other pertinent factors, and the end result cannot be supported by a realistic application of the significant facts in the case except by mere chance.

SEC. 8. RESTRICTIVE AGREEMENTS.

Frequently, in the valuation of closely held stock for estate and gift tax purposes, it will be found that the stock is subject to an agreement restricting its sale or transfer. Where shares of stock were acquired by a decedent subject to an option reserved by the issuing corporation to repurchase at a certain price, the option price is usually accepted as the fair market value for estate tax purposes. See Rev. Rul. 54-76, C.B. 1954-1, 194. However, in such case, the option price is not determinative of fair market value for gift tax purposes. Where the option, or buy and sell agreement, is the result of voluntary action by the stockholders and is binding during the life as well as at the death of the stockholders, such agreement may or may not, depending upon the circumstances of each case, fix the value for estate tax purposes. However, such agreement is a factor to be considered, with other relevant factors, in determining fair market value. Where the stockholder is free to dispose of his shares during life and the option is to become effective only upon his death, the fair market value is not limited to the option price. It is always necessary to consider the relationship of the parties, the relative number of shares held by the decedent, and other material facts, to determine whether the agreement represents a bona fide business arrangement or is a device to pass the decedent's shares to the natural objects of his bounty for less than an adequate and full consideration in money or money's worth.[31]

Revenue Ruling 77-287

Revenue Ruling 77-287 provides guidance for the valuation of restricted stock for estate and gift tax purposes. Restricted stock represents shares of stock that cannot be immediately resold because they are restricted from resale pursuant to federal securities laws. Revenue Ruling 77-287 identifies five types of such securities:

1. *Restricted Securities.* "Defined in Rule 144 adopted by the SEC as 'securities acquired directly or indirectly from the issuer thereof, or from an affiliate of such issuer, in a transaction or chain of transactions not involving any public offering.'"
2. *Unregistered Securities.* "Securities with respect to which a registration statement, providing full disclosure by the issuing corporation, has not been filed with the SEC pursuant to the Securities Act of 1933."
3. *Investment Letter Stock and Letter Stock.* "Shares of stock that have been issued by a corporation without the benefit of filing a registration statement with the

---

[31] Rev. Rul. 59-60, 1959-1 CB 237.

SEC. Such stock is subject to resale and transfer restrictions set forth in a letter agreement requested by the issuer and signed by the buyer of the stock when the stock is delivered."

4. *Control Stock.* "Shares of stock have been held or are being held by an officer, director, or other person close to the management of the corporation. These persons are subject to certain requirements pursuant to SEC rules upon resale of shares they own in such corporations."

5. *Private Placement Stock.* "Stock has been placed with an institution or other investor who will presumably hold it for a long period and ultimately arrange to have the stock registered if it is to be offered to the general public."[32]

Securities Industry Practice in Valuing Restricted Securities

The valuation of restricted stocks, as opposed to that of their unrestricted counterparts, is problematic because the restricted stocks are not actively traded on a public exchange; hence, their fair market value cannot readily be determined. Some guidance for measuring the discounts for restricted securities is provided by the results of the *Institutional Investors Study* conducted by the Securities and Exchange Commission (SEC) and published in 1971. The SEC performed the study in order to assess the effect of institutional purchases, sales, and holdings on the securities market. The study analyzed actual transactions in the marketplace for the period January 1, 1966, to June 30, 1969, and determined that the magnitude of the discounts allowed for restricted securities from the trading price of unrestricted securities was based on four factors:

1. *Earnings.* "Earnings played the major part in establishing the ultimate discounts at which these stocks were sold from the current market price. Apparently earnings patterns, rather than sales patterns, determine the degree of risk of an investment."

2. *Sales.* "The results of the study generally indicate that the companies with the lowest dollar amount of sales during the test period accounted for most of the transactions involving the highest discount rates, while they accounted for only a small portion of all transactions involving the lowest discount rates."

3. *Trading Market.* "The market in which publicly held securities are traded also reflects variances in the amount of discount that is applied to restricted securities purchases. According to the study, discount rates were greatest on restricted stocks with unrestricted counterparts traded over-the-counter, followed by those with unrestricted counterparts listed on the American Stock Exchange, while the discount rates for those stocks with unrestricted counterparts listed on the New York Stock Exchange were the smallest."

4. *Resale Agreement Provisions.* "Resale agreement provisions often affect the size of the discount. The discount from the market price provides the main incentive for a potential buyer to acquire restricted securities. In judging the opportunity cost of freezing funds, the purchaser is analyzing two separate factors. The first factor is the risk that underlying value of the stock will change in a way that, absent the restrictive provisions, would have prompted a decision to sell. The second factor is the risk that the contemplated means of legally

---

[32] Rev. Rul. 77-287, 1977-2 CB 319, Sec. 3.02.

disposing of the stock may not materialize. From the seller's point of view, a discount is justified where the seller is relieved of the expenses of registration and public distribution, as well as of the risk that the market will adversely change before the offering is completed. The ultimate agreement between buyer and seller is a reflection of these and other considerations. Relative bargaining strengths of the parties to the agreement are major considerations that influence the resale terms and consequently the size of discounts in restricted securities transactions. Certain provisions are often found in agreements between buyers and sellers that affect the size of discounts at which restricted stocks are sold."[33]

Since the completion of the SEC *Institutional Investors Study* in 1971, other restricted stock studies have been performed that considered additional factors. It is worth noting that the majority of these studies were performed prior to 1997, when the effective holding period for restricted stocks as defined in Rule 144 was a minimum of two years. On April 29, 1997, the minimum holding period was reduced to one year. Since the change in holding periods, there has been at least one additional restricted stock study performed that focused on the period subsequent to the change. Chapter 9 presents additional discussion of these studies.

Facts and Circumstances Material to Valuation of Restricted Securities

When valuing restricted stock, Revenue Ruling 77-287 indicates that the factors enumerated in Revenue Ruling 59-60 should be considered, along with the following:

(a) A copy of any declaration of trust, trust agreement, and any other agreements relating to the shares of restricted stock

(b) A copy of any document showing any offers to buy or sell or indications of interest in buying or selling the restricted shares

(c) The latest prospectus of the company

(d) Annual reports of the company for 3 to 5 years preceding the valuation date

(e) The trading prices and trading volume of the related class of traded securities one month preceding the valuation date, if they are traded on a stock exchange (if traded over-the-counter, prices may be obtained from the National Quotations Bureau, the National Association of Securities Dealers Automated Quotations [NASDAQ], or sometimes from broker-dealers making markets in the shares)

(f) The relationship of the parties to the agreements concerning the restricted stock, such as whether they are members of the immediate family or perhaps whether they are officers or directors of the company

(g) Whether the interest being valued represents a majority or minority ownership[34]

---

[33] Ibid., Sec. 4.02.
[34] Ibid., Sec. 5.02.

Weighing Facts and Circumstances Material to Restricted Stock Valuation

Like Revenue Ruling 59-60, Revenue Ruling 77-287 notes that certain of these factors may carry more weight than others. For example, earnings, net assets, and net sales should be given primary consideration in determining an appropriate discount for restricted securities. Earnings and net sales should be weighted more heavily for manufacturing, producing, and distributing companies; however, more weight should be given to net assets for investment or holding companies.

Resale provisions found in the restriction agreements also should be analyzed to determine the magnitude of any discount. Time and expense are key considerations—the longer the buyer of the shares must wait to liquidate the shares, the greater the discount. In addition, the discount also will be greater if the buyer must bear the expense of registration. However, if provisions make it possible for the buyer to "piggyback" shares at a subsequent offering, the discount will be smaller.

The relative negotiation strengths of the buyer and seller also may affect the size of the discount.

The actual trading results for freely tradable securities that are the same class as the restricted securities may be significant in determining the size of discount. The value for publicly traded stock is usually higher than that of closely held stock. In addition, the type of exchange in which the unrestricted securities are traded must be considered.

Additional discussion of the valuation of restricted stock is presented in Chapter 24.

REV-RUL, Valuation of securities restricted from immediate resale, Rev. Rul. 77-287, 1977-2 CB 319, (Jan. 01, 1977)
Rev. Rul. 77-287, 1977-2 CB 319

SECTION 2031. DEFINITION OF GROSS ESTATE
26 CFR 20.2031-2: Valuation of stocks and bonds.
(Also Sections 170, 2032, 2512; 1.170A-1, 20.2032-1, 25.2512-2.)
[IRS Headnote] Valuation of securities restricted from immediate resale.

Guidelines are set forth for the valuation, for federal tax purposes, of securities that cannot be immediately resold because they are restricted from resale pursuant to federal securities laws; Rev. Rul. 59-60 amplified.

[Text]

SECTION 1. PURPOSE.
The purpose of this Revenue Ruling is to amplify Rev. Rul. 59-60, 1959-1 C.B. 237, as modified by Rev. Rul. 65-193, 1965-2 C.B. 370, and to provide information and guidance to taxpayers, Internal Revenue Service personnel, and others concerned with the valuation, for federal tax

purposes, of securities that cannot be immediately resold because they are restricted from resale pursuant to federal securities laws. This guidance is applicable only in cases where it is not inconsistent with valuation requirements of the Internal Revenue Code of 1954 or the regulations there under. Further, this ruling does not establish the time at which property shall be valued.

SEC. 2. NATURE OF THE PROBLEM.

It frequently becomes necessary to establish the fair market value of stock that has not been registered for public trading when the issuing company has stock of the same class that is actively traded in one or more securities markets. The problem is to determine the difference in fair market value between the registered shares that are actively traded and the unregistered shares. This problem is often encountered in estate and gift tax cases. However, it is sometimes encountered when unregistered shares are issued in exchange for assets or the stock of an acquired company.

SEC. 3. BACKGROUND AND DEFINITIONS.

.01 The Service outlined and review[ed] in general the approach, methods, and factors to be considered in valuing shares of closely held corporate stock for estate and gift tax purposes in Rev. Rul. 59-60, as modified by Rev. Rul. 65-193. The provisions of Rev. Rul. 59-60, as modified, were extended to the valuation of corporate securities for income and other tax purposes by Rev. Rul. 68-609, 1968-2 C.B. 327.

.02 There are several terms currently in use in the securities industry that denote restrictions imposed on the resale and transfer of certain securities. The term frequently used to describe these securities is "restricted securities," but they are sometimes referred to as "unregistered securities," "investment letter stock," "control stock," or "private placement stock." Frequently these terms are used interchangeably. They all indicate that these particular securities cannot lawfully be distributed to the general public until a registration statement relating to the corporation underlying the securities has been filed, and has also become effective under the rules promulgated and enforced by the United States Securities and Exchange Commission pursuant to the Federal securities laws. The following represents a more refined definition of each of the following terms along with two other terms—"exempted securities" and "exempted transactions."

(a) The term "restricted securities" is defined in Rule 144 adopted by the SEC as "securities acquired directly or indirectly from the issuer thereof, or from an affiliate of such issuer, in a transaction or chain of transactions not involving any public offering."

(b) The term "unregistered securities" refers to those securities with respect to which a registration statement, providing full disclosure by the issuing corporation, has not been filed with the SEC pursuant to the Securities Act of 1933. The registration statement is a condition precedent to a public distribution of securities in interstate commerce and is aimed at providing the prospective investor with a factual basis for sound judgment in making investment decisions.

(c) The terms "investment letter stock" and "letter stock" denote shares of stock that have been issued by a corporation without the benefit of filing a registration statement with the SEC. Such stock is subject to resale and transfer restrictions set forth in a letter agreement requested by the issuer and signed by the buyer of the stock when the stock is delivered. Such stock may be found in the hands of either individual investors or institutional investors.

(d) The term "control stock" indicates that the shares of stock have been held or are being held by an officer, director, or other person close to the management of the corporation. These persons are subject to certain requirements pursuant to SEC rules upon resale of shares they own in such corporations.

(e) The term "private placement stock" indicates that the stock has been placed with an institution or other investor who will presumably hold it for a long period and ultimately arrange to have the stock registered if it is to be offered to the general public. Such stock may or may not be subject to a letter agreement. Private placements of stock are exempted from the registration and prospectus provisions of the Securities Act of 1933.

(f) The term "exempted securities" refers to those classes of securities that are expressly excluded from the registration provisions of the Securities Act of 1933 and the distribution provisions of the Securities Exchange Act of 1934.

(g) The term "exempted transactions" refers to certain sales or distributions of securities that do not involve a public offering and are excluded from the registration and prospectus provisions of the Securities Act of 1933 and distribution provisions of the Securities Exchange Act of 1934. The exempted status makes it unnecessary for issuers of securities to go through the registration process.

SEC. 4. SECURITIES INDUSTRY PRACTICE IN VALUING RESTRICTED SECURITIES.

.01 *Investment Company Valuation Practices.* The Investment Company Act of 1940 requires open-end investment companies to publish the valuation of their portfolio securities daily. Some of these companies have portfolios containing restricted securities, but also have unrestricted securities of the same class traded on a securities exchange. In recent years, the number of restricted securities in such portfolios has increased. The following methods have been used by investment companies in the valuation of such restricted securities:

(a) Current market price of the unrestricted stock less a constant percentage discount based on purchase discount

(b) Current market price of unrestricted stock less a constant percentage discount different from purchase discount

(c) Current market price of the unrestricted stock less a discount amortized over a fixed period

(d) Current market price of the unrestricted stock

(e) Cost of the restricted stock until it is registered

The SEC ruled in its Investment Company Act Release No. 5847, dated October 21, 1969, that there can be no automatic formula by which an investment company can value the restricted securities in its portfolios. Rather, the SEC has determined that it is the responsibility of the board of directors of the particular investment company to determine the "fair value" of each issue of restricted securities in good faith.

.02 *Institutional Investors Study.* Pursuant to Congressional direction, the SEC undertook an analysis of the purchasers, sales, and holding of securities by financial institutions, in order to determine the effect of institutional activity upon the securities market. The study report was published in eight volumes in March 1971. The fifth volume provides an analysis of restricted securities and deals with such items as the characteristics of the restricted securities purchasers and issuers, the size of transactions (dollars and shares), the marketability discounts on different trading markets, and the resale provisions. This research project provides some guidance for measuring the discount in that it contains information, based on the actual experience of the marketplace, showing that, during the period surveyed (January 1, 1966, through June 30, 1969), the amount of discount allowed for restricted securities from the trading price of the unrestricted securities was generally related to the following four factors.

(a) *Earnings.* Earnings and sales consistently have a significant influence on the size of restricted securities discounts according to the study. Earnings played the major part in establishing the ultimate discounts at which these stocks were sold from the current market price. Apparently earnings patterns, rather than sales patterns, determine the degree of risk of an investment.

(b) *Sales.* The dollar amount of sales of issuers' securities also has a major influence on the amount of discount at which restricted securities sell from the current market price. The results of the study generally indicate that the companies with the lowest dollar amount of sales during the test period accounted for most of the transactions involving the highest discount rates, while they accounted for only a small portion of all transactions involving the lowest discount rates.

(c) *Trading Market.* The market in which publicly held securities are traded also reflects variances in the amount of discount that is applied to restricted securities purchases. According to the study, discount rates were greatest on restricted stocks with unrestricted counterparts traded over-the-counter, followed by those with unrestricted counterparts listed on the American Stock Exchange, while the discount rates for those stocks with unrestricted counterparts listed on the New York Stock Exchange were the smallest.

(d) *Resale Agreement Provisions.* Resale agreement provisions often affect the size of the discount. The discount from the market price provides the main incentive for a potential buyer to acquire restricted securities. In judging the opportunity cost of freezing funds, the purchaser is analyzing two separate factors. The first factor is the risk that underlying value of the stock will change in a way that, absent the restrictive provisions, would have prompted a decision to sell. The second factor is the risk that the contemplated means of legally disposing of the stock may not materialize. From the seller's point of view, a discount is justified where the seller is relieved of the expenses of registration and public distribution, as well as of the risk that the market will adversely change before the offering is completed. The ultimate agreement between buyer and seller is a reflection of these and other considerations. Relative bargaining strengths of the parties to the agreement are major considerations that influence the resale terms and consequently the size of discounts in restricted securities transactions. Certain provisions are often found in agreements between buyers and sellers that affect the size of discounts at which restricted stocks are sold. Several such provisions follow, all of which, other than number (3), would tend to reduce the size of the discount:

(1) A provision giving the buyer an option to "piggyback," that is, to register restricted stock with the next registration statement, if any, filed by the issuer with the SEC

(2) A provision giving the buyer an option to require registration at the seller's expense

(3) A provision giving the buyer an option to require registration, but only at the buyer's own expense

(4) A provision giving the buyer a right to receive continuous disclosure of information about the issuer from the seller

(5) A provision giving the buyer a right to select one or more directors of the issuer

(6) A provision giving the buyer an option to purchase additional shares of the issuer's stock

(7) A provision giving the buyer the right to have a greater voice in operations of the issuer, if the issuer does not meet previously agreed upon operating standards

Institutional buyers can and often do obtain many of these rights and options from the sellers of restricted securities, and naturally, the more rights the buyer can acquire, the lower the buyer's risk is going to be, thereby reducing the buyer's discount as well. Smaller buyers may not be able to negotiate the large discounts or the rights and options that volume buyers are able to negotiate.

.03 *Summary.* A variety of methods have been used by the securities industry to value restricted securities. The SEC rejects all automatic or mechanical solutions to the valuation of restricted securities, and prefers, in the case of the valuation of investment company portfolio stocks, to rely upon good faith valuations by the board of directors of each company. The study made by the SEC found that restricted securities *generally* are issued at a discount from the market value of freely tradable securities.

SEC. 5. FACTS AND CIRCUMSTANCES MATERIAL TO VALUATION OF RESTRICTED SECURITIES.

.01 Frequently, a company has a class of stock that cannot be traded publicly. The reason such stock cannot be traded may arise from the securities statutes, as in the case of an "investment letter" restriction; it may arise from a corporate charter restriction, or perhaps from a trust agreement restriction. In such cases, certain documents and facts should be obtained for analysis.

.02 The following documents and facts, when used in conjunction with those discussed in Section 4 of Rev. Rul. 59-60, will be useful in the valuation of restricted securities:

(a) A copy of any declaration of trust, trust agreement, and any other agreements relating to the shares of restricted stock

(b) A copy of any document showing any offers to buy or sell or indications of interest in buying or selling the restricted shares

(c) The latest prospectus of the company

(d) Annual reports of the company for three to five years preceding the valuation date

(e) The trading prices and trading volume of the related class of traded securities one month preceding the valuation date, if they are traded on a stock exchange (if traded over-the-counter, prices may be obtained from the National Quotations Bureau, the National Association of Securities Dealers Automated Quotations [NASDAQ], or sometimes from broker-dealers making markets in the shares)

(f) The relationship of the parties to the agreements concerning the restricted stock, such as whether they are members of the immediate family or perhaps whether they are officers or directors of the company

(g) Whether the interest being valued represents a majority or minority ownership

SEC. 6. WEIGHING FACTS AND CIRCUMSTANCES MATERIAL TO RESTRICTED STOCK VALUATION.

All relevant facts and circumstances that bear upon the worth of restricted stock, including those set forth above in the preceding Sections 4 and 5, and those set forth in Section 4 of Rev. Rul. 59-60, must be taken into account in arriving at the fair market value of such securities. Depending on the circumstances of each case, certain factors may carry more weight than others. To illustrate:

.01 Earnings, net assets, and net sales must be given primary consideration in arriving at an appropriate discount for restricted securities from the freely traded shares. These are the elements of value that are always used by investors in making investment decisions. In some cases, one element may be more important than in other cases. In the case of manufacturing, producing, or distributing companies, primary weight must be accorded earnings and net sales; but in the case of investment or holding companies, primary weight must be given to the net assets of the company underlying the stock. In the former type of companies, value is more closely linked to past, present, and future earnings while in the latter type of companies, value is more closely linked to the existing net assets of the company. See the discussion in Section 5 of Rev. Rul. 59-60.

.02 Resale provisions found in the restriction agreements must be scrutinized and weighed to determine the amount of discount to apply to the preliminary fair market value of the company. The two elements of time and expense bear upon this discount; the longer the buyer of the shares must wait to liquidate the shares, the greater the discount. Moreover, if the provisions make it necessary for the buyer to bear the expense of registration, the greater the discount. However, if the provisions of the restricted stock agreement make it possible for the buyer to "piggyback" shares at the next offering, the discount would be smaller.

.03 The relative negotiation strengths of the buyer and seller of restricted stock may have a profound effect on the amount of discount. For example, a tight money situation may cause the buyer to have the greater balance of negotiation strength in a transaction. However, in some cases the relative strengths may tend to cancel each other out.

.04 The market experience of freely tradable securities of the same class as the restricted securities is also significant in determining the amount of discount. Whether the shares are privately held or publicly traded affects the worth of the shares to the holder. Securities traded on a public market generally are worth more to investors than those that are not traded on a public market. Moreover, the type of public market in which the unrestricted securities are traded is to be given consideration.

SEC. 7. EFFECT ON OTHER DOCUMENTS.
Rev. Rul. 59-60, as modified by Rev. Rul. 65-193, is amplified.[35]

Revenue Ruling 83-120

Revenue Ruling 83-120 expands on Revenue Ruling 59-60 by providing additional guidance for the valuation of common stock of closely held companies as well as preferred stock for estate and gift tax purposes. Valuation issues relating to preferred and common stock often result from estate planning transactions involving situations where an owner's interest in common stock is converted to both preferred and common, with the preferred having a stated par value equal to a significant portion of the fair market value. The owner then gifts the common stock to a family member with the objective of transferring potential appreciation in the stock with minimal gift tax. This is a classic "freeze" transaction.

Approach to Valuation—Preferred Stock

Generally, the most important factors to consider when valuing preferred stock are the yield, dividend coverage, and liquidation preferences.

The adequacy of the *yield* should be determined by comparing the subject company's preferred stock dividend rate with that of a high-grade publicly traded stock. For purposes of identifying comparable publicly traded preferred stock to determine the yield required on closely held stock, factors such as similarity of the line of business, assets, liquidation preferences, and voting rights are typical considerations. All other factors being equal, if the yield on the subject company's preferred stock is lower than that of the comparable publicly traded stock, then the subject company stock value would be less than par. Also, if the interest rate on debt charged by the

---

[35] Rev. Rul. 77-287, 1977-2 CB 319.

subject company's creditors is higher than the rate charged to those creditors' most creditworthy borrowers, then the yield on the subject company's preferred stock should be higher than the yield on high-quality preferred stock. A yield that is not higher reduces the value of the preferred stock. A fixed dividend rate and nonparticipation also affect the value of the preferred stock.[36]

The *coverage of dividends* by the corporation's earnings highlights the risk associated with the subject company's ability to pay the stated dividends on preferred stock on a timely basis. The dividend coverage is measured by the ratio of the sum of earnings before interest and taxes (EBIT) to the sum of the total interest to be paid and the pretax earnings needed to pay the after-tax dividends. The ratio for the subject company preferred stock should be compared with the ratios for high-quality preferred stocks to determine whether the preferred stock has adequate coverage. If the coverage ratio is inadequate, the value of preferred stock should be lower than its par value. Also, if preferred dividends are not cumulative, it is questionable whether the stated dividends will be paid, and this stock will have a lower value than a cumulative preferred stock with the same yield, liquidation preference, and dividend coverage.[37]

The ability of the subject company to pay the full *liquidation preference* at liquidation also should be considered. This risk can be measured by the ratio of the excess of the fair market value of the subject company's assets over its liabilities to the aggregate liquidation preference. The resulting ratio for the subject company should be compared with the ratios for high quality preferred stock to determine the adequacy of coverage.[38]

Other factors to be considered in valuing the preferred stock include:

- Existence of voting rights and control
- Peculiar covenants or provisions of the preferred stock that may inhibit the marketability of the stock or the power of the holder to enforce dividend or liquidation rights
- Redemption privileges[39]

Approach to Valuation—Common Stock

If the common stock has the exclusive right to the benefits of future appreciation of the value of the corporation (i.e., the preferred stock has a fixed rate of dividend and is nonparticipating), then the common stock usually has substantial value. The value of this right depends on the subject company's historical growth, the industry conditions, and economic conditions. Analysis of the other factors discussed in Revenue Ruling 59-60 will be required. In addition, the subject company's net income in excess of the stated dividends on the preferred stock at the time the preferred stock is issued will increase the value of the common stock. The value of the common stock also will be increased if the subject company reinvests its earnings.[40]

---

[36] Rev. Rul. 83-120, 1983-2 CB 170, Sec. 4.02.
[37] Ibid., Sec. 4.03.
[38] Ibid., Sec. 4.04.
[39] Ibid., Sec. 4.05-4.07.
[40] Ibid., Sec. 5.01.

If the preferred stock has voting rights, and especially if the preferred stock also has control, the value of the preferred stock could increase and the value of the common stock could decrease. This change in value may be mitigated if the rights of common stockholders are protected under state law from actions by another class of shareholders, particularly where the common shareholders possess the power to disapprove a proposal to allow preferred stock to be converted into common stock.[41] Additional discussion of preferred stock valuations is presented in Chapter 24.

REV-RUL. Valuation; stock; closely held business, Rev. Rul. 83-120, 1983-2 CB 170, (Jan. 01, 1983)
Rev. Rul. 83-120, 1983-2 CB 170

SECTION 2512.—VALUATION OF GIFTS
26 CFR 25.2512-2: Stocks and bonds.
(Also Sections 305, 351, 354, 368, 2031; 1.305-5, 1.351-1, 1.354-1, 1.368-1, 20.2031-2.)

[IRS Headnote] Valuation; stock; closely held business.—
The significant factors in deriving the fair market value of preferred and common stock received in certain corporate reorganizations are discussed. Rev. Rul. 59-60 amplified.

[Text]

SECTION 1. PURPOSE.
The purpose of this revenue ruling is to amplify Rev. Rul. 59-60, 1959-1 C.B. 237, by specifying additional factors to be considered in valuing common and preferred stock of a closely held corporation for gift tax and other purposes in a recapitalization of closely held businesses. This type of valuation problem frequently arises with respect to estate planning transactions wherein an individual receives preferred stock with a stated par value equal to all or a large portion of the fair market value of the individual's former stock interest in a corporation. The individual also receives common stock which is then transferred, usually as a gift, to a relative.

SEC. 2. BACKGROUND.
.01 One of the frequent objectives of the type of transaction mentioned above is the transfer of the potential appreciation of an individual's stock interest in a corporation to relatives at a nominal or small gift tax cost. Achievement of this objective requires preferred stock having a fair market value equal to a large part of the fair market value of the individual's former stock interest and common stock having a nominal or small fair market value. The approach and factors described in this revenue ruling are directed toward ascertaining the true fair market value of

---

[41] Ibid., Sec. 5.02.

the common and preferred stock and will usually result in the determination of a substantial fair market value for the common stock and a fair market value for the preferred stock which is substantially less than its par value.

.02 The type of transaction referred to above can arise in many different contexts. Some examples are:

(a) *A* owns 100 percent of the common stock (the only outstanding stock) of *Z* Corporation which has a fair market value of 10,500x. In a recapitalization described in section 368(a)(1)(E), *A* receives preferred stock with a par value of 10,000x and new common stock, which *A* then transfers to *A*'s son *B*.

(b) *A* owns some of the common stock of *Z* Corporation (or the stock of several corporations) the fair market value of which stock is 10,500x. *A* transfers this stock to a new corporation *X* in exchange for preferred stock of *X* corporation with a par value of 10,000x and common stock of corporation, which *A* then transfers to *A*'s son *B*.

(c) *A* owns 80 shares and his son *B* owns 20 shares of the common stock (the only stock outstanding) of *Z* Corporation. In a recapitalization described in section 368(a)(1)(E), *A* exchanges his 80 shares of common stock for 80 shares of new preferred stock of *Z* Corporation with a par value of 10,000x. *A*'s common stock had a fair market value of 10,000x.

SEC. 3. GENERAL APPROACH TO VALUATION.

Under section 25.2512-2(f)(2) of the Gift Tax Regulations, the fair market value of stock in a closely held corporation depends upon numerous factors, including the corporation's net worth, its prospective earning power, and its capacity to pay dividends. In addition, other relevant factors must be taken into account. See Rev. Rul. 59-60. The weight to be accorded any evidentiary factor depends on the circumstances of each case. See section 25.2512-2(f) of the Gift Tax Regulations.

SEC. 4. APPROACH TO VALUATION—PREFERRED STOCK.

.01 In general, the most important factors to be considered in determining the value of preferred stock are its yield, dividend coverage, and protection of its liquidation preference.

.02 Whether the yield of the preferred stock supports a valuation of the stock at par value depends in part on the adequacy of the dividend rate. The adequacy of the dividend rate should be determined by comparing its dividend rate with the dividend rate of high-grade publicly traded preferred stock. A lower yield than that of high-grade preferred stock indicates a preferred stock value of less than par. If the rate of interest charged by independent creditors to the corporation on loans is higher than the rate such independent creditors charge their most credit worthy borrowers, then the yield on the preferred stock should be correspondingly higher than the yield on high quality preferred stock. A yield which is not correspondingly higher reduces the value of the preferred stock. In addition, whether the preferred stock has a fixed dividend rate and is nonparticipating influences the value of the preferred stock. A publicly traded preferred stock for a company having a similar business and similar assets with similar liquidation preferences, voting rights and other similar terms would be the ideal comparable for determining yield required in arms length transactions for closely held stock. Such ideal comparables will frequently not exist. In such circumstances, the most comparable publicly traded issues should be selected for comparison and appropriate adjustments made for differing factors.

.03 The actual dividend rate on a preferred stock can be assumed to be its stated rate if the issuing corporation will be able to pay its stated dividends in a timely manner and will, in fact, pay such dividends. The risk that the corporation may be unable to timely pay the stated dividends on the preferred stock can be measured by the coverage of such stated dividends by the corporation's earnings. Coverage of the dividend is measured by the ratio of the sum of pretax and pre interest earnings to the sum of the total interest to be paid and the pretax earnings needed to pay the after-tax dividends. *Standard & Poor's Ratings Guide,* 58 (1979). Inadequate coverage exists where a decline in corporate profits would be likely to jeopardize the corporation's ability to pay dividends on the preferred stock. The ratio for the preferred stock in question should be compared with the ratios for high quality preferred stock to determine whether the preferred stock has adequate coverage. Prior earnings history is important in this determination. Inadequate coverage indicates that the value of preferred stock is lower than its par value. Moreover, the absence of a provision that preferred dividends are cumulative raises substantial questions concerning whether the stated dividend rate will, in fact, be paid. Accordingly, preferred stock with noncumulative dividend features will normally have a value substantially lower than a cumulative preferred stock with the same yield, liquidation preference, and dividend coverage.

.04 Whether the issuing corporation will be able to pay the full liquidation preference at liquidation must be taken into account in determining fair market value. This risk can be measured by the protection afforded by the corporation's net assets. Such protection can be measured by the ratio of the excess of the current market value of the corporation's assets over its liabilities to the aggregate liquidation preference. The protection ratio should be compared with the ratios for high quality preferred stock to determine adequacy of coverage. Inadequate asset protection exists where any unforeseen business reverses would be likely to jeopardize the corporation's ability to pay the full liquidation preference to the holders of the preferred stock.

.05 Another factor to be considered in valuing the preferred stock is whether it has voting rights and, if so, whether the preferred stock has voting control. See, however, Section 5.02 below.

.06 Peculiar covenants or provisions of the preferred stock of a type not ordinarily found in publicly traded preferred stock should be carefully evaluated to determine the effects of such covenants on the value of the preferred stock. In general, if covenants would inhibit the marketability of the stock or the power of the holder to enforce dividend or liquidation rights, such provisions will reduce the value of the preferred stock by comparison to the value of preferred stock not containing such covenants or provisions.

.07 Whether the preferred stock contains a redemption privilege is another factor to be considered in determining the value of the preferred stock. The value of a redemption privilege triggered by death of the preferred shareholder will not exceed the present value of the redemption premium payable at the preferred shareholder's death (i.e., the present value of the excess of the redemption price over the fair market value of the preferred stock upon its issuance). The value of the redemption privilege should be reduced to reflect any risk that the corporation may not possess sufficient assets to redeem its preferred stock at the stated redemption price. See .03 above.

SEC. 5. APPROACH TO VALUATION—COMMON STOCK.

.01 If the preferred stock has a fixed rate of dividend and is nonparticipating, the common stock has the exclusive right to the benefits of future appreciation of the value of the corporation. This right is valuable and usually warrants a determination that the common stock has substantial value. The actual value of this right depends upon the corporation's past growth experience, the economic condition of the industry in which the corporation operates, and general economic conditions. The factor to be used in capitalizing the corporation's prospective earnings must be determined after an analysis of numerous factors concerning the corporation and the economy as a whole. *See* Rev. Rul. 59-60, at page 243. In addition, after-tax earnings of the corporation at the time the preferred stock is issued in excess of the stated dividends on the preferred stock will increase the value of the common stock. Furthermore, a corporate policy of reinvesting earnings will also increase the value of the common stock.

.02 A factor to be considered in determining the value of the common stock is whether the preferred stock also has voting rights. Voting rights of the preferred stock, especially if the preferred stock has voting control, could under certain circumstances increase the value of the preferred stock and reduce the value of the common stock. This factor may be reduced in significance where the rights of common stockholders as a class are protected under state law from actions by another class of shareholders, see *Singer v. Magnavox Co.*, 380 A.2d 969 (Del. 1977), particularly where the common shareholders, as a class, are given the power to disapprove a proposal to allow preferred stock to be converted into common stock. See ABA-ALI Model Bus. Corp. Act, Section 60 (1969).

SEC. 6. EFFECT ON OTHER REVENUE RULINGS.

Rev. Rul. 59-60, as modified by Rev. Rul. 65-193, 1965-2 C.B. 370 and as amplified by Rev. Rul. 77-287, 1977-2 C.B. 319, and Rev. Rul. 80-213, 1980-2 C.B. 101, is further amplified.[42]

---

[42] Rev. Rul. 83-120, 1983-2 CB 170.

Revenue Ruling 93-12

Prior to 1993, the IRS took the position that that the ownership interests of family members should be aggregated for the purpose of determining whether or not a transferred interest was valued as a controlling or minority interest for gift tax purposes. This position was set forth in Revenue Ruling 81-253, which held that "ordinarily no minority discount will be allowed with respect to transfers of shares of stock among family members where, at the time of the transfer, control (either majority voting control or de facto control) of the corporation exists in the family."[43]

Petitioners often challenged this position on the basis that the definition of fair market value as defined in Treasury Regulation § 25.2512-1 and Revenue Ruling 59-60 presumes a hypothetical buyer and seller, whereas the IRS's position was based on the identity of specific individuals.

The Courts heard numerous cases on this issue, deciding in favor of the petitioners in many instances. Among these cases were *Estate of Bright v. United States,* 658 F.2d 999 (5th Cir. 1981), *Propstra v. United States,* 680 F.2d 1248 (9th Cir. 1982), *Estate of Andrews v. Commissioner,* 79 T.C. 938 (1982), and *Estate of Lee v. Commissioner,* 69 T.C. 860 (1978), *nonacq.,* 1980–2 C.B.2.

In 1993, the IRS finally acquiesced by revoking Revenue Ruling 81-253 and issuing Revenue Ruling 93-12. Citing the aforementioned cases, the IRS concluded that:

> In the case of a corporation with a single class of stock, notwithstanding the family relationship of the donor, the donee, and other shareholders, the shares of other family members will not be aggregated with the transferred shares to determine whether the transferred shares should be valued as part of a controlling interest.[44]

Revenue Ruling 93-12 was a landmark ruling in that it opened the door for use of FLPs and other pass-through entities for estate planning purposes for family-owned businesses. See Chapters 11 and 13.

> **REV-RUL, FINH ¶12,521, Estate and gift taxes: Valuation: Closely held stock: Minority shareholder discount—Revenue Ruling 93-12, 1993-1 CB 202, I.R.B. 1993-7,13, (Feb. 16, 1993)**
>
> Revenue Ruling 93-12, 1993-1 CB 202, I.R.B. 1993-7,13, February 16, 1993.1993-7 I.R.B. dated
>
> [*Code Secs. 2031 and 2512*]
>
> Estate and gift taxes: Valuation: Closely held stock: Minority shareholder discount.—Where a donor transferred 20 percent of the stock in a closely held corporation to each of the donor's five children, the factor of corporate control in the family was not considered in valuing each transferred interest for gift tax purposes. Consequently, a minority discount was not disallowed solely because the transferred interest, when aggregated with

---

[43] Rev. Rul. 81-253, 1981-2 CB 187.
[44] Rev. Rul. 93-12, 1993-1 CB 202.

interests held by family members, was part of a controlling interest. Rev. Rul. 81-253 is revoked. Acquiescence is substituted for the nonacquiescence in issue one of *E. Lee Est.*, 1980-2 C.B. 2.

ISSUE

If a donor transfers shares in a corporation to each of the donor's children, is the factor of corporate control in the family to be considered in valuing each transferred interest, for purposes of section 2512 of the Internal Revenue Code?

FACTS

P owned all of the single outstanding class of stock of *X* corporation. *P* transferred all of *P*'s shares by making simultaneous gifts of 20 percent of the shares to each of *P*'s five children, *A*, *B*, *C*, *D*, and *E*.

LAW AND ANALYSIS

Section 2512(a) of the Code provides that the value of the property at the date of the gift shall be considered the amount of the gift.

Section 25.2512-1 of the Gift Tax Regulations provides that, if a gift is made in property, its value at the date of the gift shall be considered the amount of the gift. The value of the property is the price at which the property would change hands between a willing buyer and a willing seller, neither being under any compulsion to buy or to sell, and both having reasonable knowledge of relevant facts.

Section 25.2512-2(a) of the regulations provides that the value of stocks and bonds is the fair market value per share or bond on the date of the gift. Section 25.2512-2(f) provides that the degree of control of the business represented by the block of stock to be valued is among the factors to be considered in valuing stock where there are no sales prices or bona fide bid or asked prices.

Rev. Rul. 81-253, 1981-2 C.B. 187, holds that, ordinarily, no minority shareholder discount is allowed with respect to transfers of shares of stock between family members if, based upon a composite of the family members' interests at the time of the transfer, control (either majority voting control or de facto control through family relationships) of the corporation exists in the family unit. The ruling also states that the Service will not follow the decision of the Fifth Circuit in *Estate of Bright v. United States*, 658 F.2d 999 (5th Cir. 1981).

In *Bright*, the decedent's undivided community property interest in shares of stock, together with the corresponding undivided community property interest of the decedent's surviving spouse, constituted a control block of 55 percent of the shares of a corporation. The court held that, because the community-held shares were subject to a right of partition, the decedent's own interest was equivalent to 27.5 percent of the outstanding shares and, therefore, should be valued as a minority interest, even though the shares were to be held by the decedent's surviving spouse as trustee of a testamentary trust. See also *Propstra v. United States*, 680 F.2d 1248 (9th Cir. 1982). In addition, *Estate of Andrews v. Commissioner*, 79 T.C. 938 (1982), and *Estate of Lee v. Commissioner*, 69 T.C. 860 (1978), *nonacq.*, 1980-2 C.B. 2, held that the corporation shares owned by other family members cannot be attributed to an individual family member for determining whether the individual family member's shares should be valued as the controlling interest of the corporation.

After further consideration of the position taken in Rev. Rul. 81-253, and in light of the cases noted above, the Service has concluded that, in the case of a corporation with a single class of stock, notwithstanding the family relationship of the donor, the donee, and other shareholders, the shares of other family members will not be aggregated with the transferred shares to determine whether the transferred shares should be valued as part of a controlling interest.

In the present case, the minority interests transferred to *A*, *B*, *C*, *D*, and *E* should be valued for gift tax purposes without regard to the family relationship of the parties.

HOLDING

If a donor transfers shares in a corporation to each of the donor's children, the factor of corporate control in the family is not considered in valuing each transferred interest for purposes of section 2512 of the Code. For estate and gift tax valuation purposes, the Service will follow *Bright, Propstra, Andrews,* and *Lee* in not assuming that all voting power held by family members may be aggregated for purposes of determining whether the transferred shares should be valued as part of a controlling interest. Consequently, a minority discount will not be disallowed solely because a transferred interest, when aggregated with interests held by family members, would be a part of a controlling interest. This would be the case whether the donor held 100 percent or some lesser percentage of the stock immediately before the gift.

EFFECT ON OTHER DOCUMENTS

Rev. Rul. 81-253 is revoked. Acquiescence is substituted for the nonacquiescence in issue one of *Lee,* 1980-2 C.B. 2.[45]

VALUATIONS FOR INCOME TAXES

There are many different types of valuations for income tax planning and compliance purposes. The following list presents a summary of the most common types of taxable transactions requiring valuation services.[46]

- Deduction for abandoned or donated property
  - Abandonment losses
  - Casualty losses
  - Charitable contributions of property
- Receipt of noncash distributions from a business
  - Property distributed to employees as compensation

---

[45] Ibid.

[46] Shannon P. Pratt and Alina V. Niculita, *Valuing a Business: The Analysis and Appraisal of Closely Held Companies,* 5th ed. (New York: McGraw-Hill, 2008), 725.

- • Property distributed to shareholders as dividends
- • Property distributed to shareholders as part of a liquidation
- • Employee stock options and other stock rights
- Recognition of income by a business
  - • Rents received by a business in the form of property
  - • Cancellation of indebtedness income
- Conversion of property
  - • Conversion of C to S corporations and calculation of related built-in gain taxes
  - • Taxable or tax-free exchange of properties
- Tests of reasonableness
  - • Reasonableness of compensation paid to owners
  - • Undistributed excess accumulated earnings retained in a corporation
  - • Reasonableness of transfer price for intercompany transfer of goods, services, or properties
- Determination of tax basis for assets transferred into, purchased by, or transferred out of a business
  - • Purchase price allocation
- Other
  - • Bargain purchases
  - • Basis of property
  - • "Boot" in tax-free transfer
  - • Foreclosure of mortgaged property
  - • Incorporation of a business
  - • Insolvency
  - • Recapitalization
  - • Residence converted to a rental property
  - • Stock rights
  - • Tax shelters

A more detailed discussion of selected types of income tax valuations follows. Obviously, tax laws and regulations change periodically. The reader is encouraged to research current information.

Charitable Contributions of Property

Treasury Regulation § 1.170A-13(c)(3)(ii) addresses the contribution of closely held stock or other property whose value is greater than or equal to $5,000. Such contributions must be accompanied by a "qualified appraisal." A qualified appraisal:

1. Is made not earlier than 60 days prior to the date of contribution of the appraised property nor later than the date of the donor's tax return on which the deduction is claimed
2. Is prepared, signed, and dated by a qualified appraiser
3. Includes the following information:
   a. A description of the property
   b. In the case of tangible property, the physical condition of the property
   c. The date of the contribution
   d. The terms of any agreement entered into by the donor or donee that relates to the use, sale, or other disposition of the property contributed
   e. The name, address, and the identifying number of the qualified appraiser and the firm that employs the qualified appraiser

    f.   The qualifications of the appraiser who signs the appraisal, including the appraiser's background, experience, education, and membership in professional appraisal associations

    g. A statement that the appraisal was prepared for income tax purposes

    h. The date on which the property was appraised

    i.   The appraised fair market value of the property on the date of contribution

    j.   The method of valuation used to determine the fair market value

    k. The specific basis for the valuation, such as specific comparable sales transactions[47]

A qualified appraisal must be prepared by an individual who satisfies the requirements of a "qualified appraiser" as defined in Treasury Regulation § 1.170A-13(c)(5). These requirements state:

1. The individual either holds him or herself out to the public as an appraiser or performs appraisals on a regular basis
2. The appraiser is qualified to make appraisals of the type of property being valued
3. The appraiser is not:
    a.   The donor or the taxpayer who claims a deduction for the contribution of the property that is being appraised
    b.   A party to the transaction in which the donor acquired the property being appraised unless the property is donated within two months of the date of acquisition and its appraised value does not exceed its acquisition price
    c.   The donee of the property
    d.   Any person employed by any of the foregoing persons
    e.   Any person related to any of the foregoing persons
    f.   An appraiser who is regularly used by the donor, donee, or party to the transaction and does not perform a majority of appraisals for other parties
4. The appraiser understands that an intentionally false or fraudulent overstatement of the value of the property described in the qualified appraisal or appraisal summary may subject the appraiser to a civil penalty for aiding and abetting an understatement of tax liability.[48]

Conversion of Property

Trapped-In Capital Gains Tax

A "trapped-in capital gain" refers to the excess of the fair market value of an appreciated asset over the adjusted basis of that asset. Before 1986, the General Utilities Doctrine[49] permitted a corporation to develop a liquidation plan, sell such appreciated assets, and distribute the proceeds realized from the sale without paying corporate-level taxes on the capital gain.[50]

The adoption of the Tax Reform Act of 1986 eliminated the ability of corporations to avoid paying corporate level taxes on the capital gain. IRC § 336(a) requires that the selling corporation treat the sale of the assets as if they were sold at fair

---

[47] Treasury Regulation § 1.170A-13(c)(3)(ii).

[48] Treasury Regulation § 1.170A-13(c)(5).

[49] *General Utilities & Operating Co. v. Commissioner,* 296 U.S. 200 (1935).

[50] IRC § 333 (repealed).

market value and recognize the difference between the fair market value and the adjusted basis of the asset as a capital gain or loss for tax purposes.[51] The corporation's earnings and profits are then taxable to the shareholder upon distribution or liquidation of the corporation.[52]

With the above changes resulting in a corporation having to pay capital gains tax on the sale of appreciated assets, it seems reasonable that a hypothetical seller and buyer would consider the potential tax liability when determining the fair market value of the corporation. However, until 1998, the IRS and Tax Courts rejected this position.

In 1998, the U.S. Tax Court finally acknowledged the perspective of the hypothetical seller and buyer issue regarding the trapped-in capital gain in *Estate of Davis v. Commissioner:*

> We are convinced on the record in this case, and we find, that, even though no liquidation of ADDI&C or sale of its assets was planned or contemplated on the valuation date, a hypothetical willing seller and a hypothetical willing buyer would not have agreed on that date on a price for each of the blocks of stock in question that took no account of ADDI&C's built-in capital gains tax. We are also persuaded on that record, and we find, that such a willing seller and such a willing buyer of each of the two blocks of ADDI&C stock at issue would have agreed on a price on the valuation date at which each such block would have changed hands that was less than the price that they would have agreed upon if there had been no ADDI&C's built-in capital gains tax as of that date.[53]

While recognizing the existence of a discount for the tax on the trapped-in capital gains, the amount of the discount allowed by the Tax Court was less than the full amount of the tax.

In *Eisenberg v. Commissioner,*[54] the Tax Court, relying on case precedent prior to the 1986 repeal of the *General Utilities Doctrine*, declined to recognize a discount for the trapped-in capital gains. The petitioner appealed the decision to the Second Circuit Court of Appeals. The Court of Appeals, citing the *Davis* case, vacated the Tax Court decision and remanded the case back to the Tax Court. The Tax Court ultimately recognized the trapped-in gain.[55]

The magnitude of the trapped-in gains discount was considered by the Tax Court in *Estate of Simplot v. Commissioner.*[56] In *Simplot,* the Tax Court accepted the position of the experts for the petitioner and the IRS, which stated that 100 percent of the tax on the trapped-in capital gain on an appreciated asset should be deducted.[56] The Tax Court decision was appealed and reversed on other grounds, but the decision relating to the trapped-in capital gains was left unchallenged.[57]

---

[51] IRC § 336(a).

[52] IRC § 316; IRC § 331(a).

[53] *Estate of Davis v. Commissioner,* 110 T.C. 530 (1998).

[54] *Eisenberg v. Commissioner,* 155 F.3d 50 (2d Cir. 1998).

[55] David Laro and Shannon P. Pratt, *Business Valuation and Taxes* (Hoboken, NJ: John Wiley & Sons, 2005), p. 268.

[56] *Estate of Simplot v. Commissioner,* 112 T.C. 130 (1999).

[57] Laro and Pratt, p. 268.

Since the decisions by the Tax Court in the aforementioned cases, the IRS has acquiesced on its position that there was a legal prohibition against a discount for trapped-in capital gains.[58]

Subsequent to the aforementioned decisions, there have been additional cases dealing with the treatment of trapped-in capital gains. Most recently, in *Estate of Jelke v. Commissioner*,[59] the Tax Court allowed a reduction on the trapped-in capital gain but limited the reduction to the present value of the gain based on an assumed future-sales date. The Tax Court also noted that because the built-in gain is a corporate liability, it should be treated as a reduction in the value of the assets before consideration of discounts for lack of control and marketability.

Another more recent case was *Litchfield v. Commissioner*, TCM 2009-21, January 29, 2009. The court opined as follows:

> In view of the asset valuation method employed by the parties and their experts, the highly appreciated nonoperating investment assets held by LRC and LSC as of the valuation date, and the C corporate tax liabilities to which LRC and LSC remain subject, we consider it likely that a willing buyer and a willing seller would negotiate and agree to significant discounts to net asset values relating to the estimated corporate capital gains taxes that would be due on the sale of LRC's and LSC's nonoperating assets.
>
> On the facts presented to us, we believe that, as of the valuation date, a hypothetical buyer of LRC and LSC stock would attempt to estimate this extra corporate level tax burden on holding-period asset appreciation and would include the estimated cost or present value thereof in a built-in capital gains discount that would be negotiated between the hypothetical buyer and seller.
>
> We note that in *Estate of Jelke v. Commissioner*, TCM 2005-131, the methodology used by the Court to calculate a discount for built-in capital gains taxes did not include holding-period asset appreciation. However, in *Jelke*, the Court also emphasized the factual nature of the calculation of discounts for built-in capital gains taxes in a particular case and expressly stated that a valuation methodology used in one case was not binding on the Court in another case.

The *Jelke* case was appealed, *Estate of Jelke et al. v. Commissioner*, 05-15549, U.S. Court of Appeals for the 11th Circuit, November 15, 2007. The Eleventh Circuit overturned the Tax Court and allowed the estate a dollar-for-dollar reduction in fair market value for the hypothetical tax on trapped-in gains for a C corporation minority shareholder. The Eleventh Circuit reviewed all of the prior trapped-in gains cases in the various circuits. The court discussed the lack of any plan to liquidate CCC and the inability of a minority shareholder to force liquidation, but found those factors unpersuasive.

---

[58] Laro and Pratt, pp. 268–269.
[59] *Estate of Jelke v. Commissioner*, TCM 2005-131.

The court noted:

> The rationale of the Fifth Circuit in the *Estate of Dunn* eliminates the crystal ball and the coin flip and provides certainty and finality to valuation as best it can, already a vague and shadowy undertaking. It is a welcome road map for those in the judiciary, not formally trained in the art of valuation. The *Estate of Dunn* dollar-for-dollar approach also bypasses the unnecessary expenditure of judicial resources being used to wade through a myriad of divergent expert witness testimony, based upon subjective conjecture, and divergent opinions. The *Estate of Dunn* has the virtue of simplicity and its methodology provides a practical and theoretically sound foundation as to how to address the discount issue. . . . This 100% approach settles the issue as a matter of law, and provides certainty that is typically missing in the valuation arena. We thereby follow the rationale of the Fifth Circuit in the Estate of Dunn, that allows a dollar-for-dollar, $51 million discount for contingent capital gains taxes. . . .

Additional discussion of these Tax Court cases is presented in Chapter 15.

Built-In Gains for S Corporations

The issue of trapped-in capital gains is also a consideration for S corporations as set forth in Internal Revenue Code §1374. As it relates to an S corporation, the built-in gain refers to the excess of the fair market value over the adjusted basis of an asset at the beginning of the first year a company makes an S election. It applies to C corporations that elect S status after 1986. Generally, any gain from the sale of assets that the corporation recognizes within the 10 postconversion years is taxed at the highest corporate rate as of the conversion date. The gain flows through to the shareholders, net of the corporate-level tax paid, creating a near double-level tax to the corporation and its shareholders. Any appreciation in assets that occurs after the S conversion period (including goodwill) will not be subject to the built-in gains tax.

For purposes of determining any potential tax exposure from the C to S corporation conversion, a valuation should be performed as of the date of conversion.

Appraisal Penalties for Undervaluation of Estate, Gift, and Income Tax Returns

Treasury Department Circular 230

Treasury Department Circular 230 ("Circular 230"), which was issued on September 26, 2007, provides regulations governing practitioners representing taxpayers before the IRS. Practitioners include attorneys, certified public accountants, enrolled agents, and other persons.[60] Appraisers are not specifically defined as a practitioner in Circular 230; however, Circular 230 does cover advice involving appraisals; consequently, appraisers may be subject to the provisions of Circular 230.

Practice before the IRS includes all matters connected with a presentation to the IRS relating to a taxpayer's rights, privileges, or liabilities under laws or regulations

---

[60] Treasury Circular 230, § 10.0, p. 4.

administered by the IRS. Such presentations include, but are not limited to, preparing and filing documents, communicating with the IRS, rendering written advice or other plan or arrangement having a potential for tax avoidance or evasion, and representing a client at meetings or hearings.[61]

If an appraiser is found to have knowingly prepared a valuation that improperly supports an understatement of tax liability, the appraiser may be subject to fines under IRC § 6701 for such an understatement. In addition, if the appraiser is found to have committed a violation, the appraiser may be referred the IRS's Office of Professional Responsibility and subject to proceedings to disqualify the appraiser from practicing before the IRS.[62]

Circular 230 allows a practitioner to include a disclaimer that clearly states that written advice is not intended to be relied upon by the taxpayer to avoid penalties for written advice rendered after June 20, 2005.[63] To ensure compliance with Circular 230, many appraisers include a disclaimer with language similar to the following on written communications with taxpayers:

> IRS Circular 230 Disclosure: To ensure compliance with requirements imposed by the IRS, we inform you that any tax advice contained in this communication (including any attachments) is not intended or written to be used, and cannot be used, for the purpose of i) avoiding any penalties under the Internal Revenue Code or ii) promoting, marketing or recommending to another party any transaction(s) or tax-related matter(s) addressed herein.

The 2006 Pension Protection Act

In 2006, the U.S. Congress enacted the Pension Protection Act of 2006 (PPA). The PPA restated the definition of a qualified appraisal and further defined the qualifications for appraisers preparing tax-related valuations. The PPA also imposed stricter penalties for valuation misstatements attributable to incorrect appraisals.

The PPA reiterated that the definition of a *qualified appraisal* is as set forth in the U.S. Treasury Regulations. Further, the PPA expanded on the definition of a *qualified appraiser* as used in the U.S. Treasury Regulations as follows:

> (ii) QUALIFIED APPRAISER.—Except as provided in clause (iii), the term "qualified appraiser" means an individual who—
>   (I) has earned an appraisal designation from a recognized professional appraiser organization or has otherwise met minimum education and experience requirements set forth in regulations prescribed by the Secretary,
>   (II) regularly performs appraisals for which the individual receives compensation, and
>   (III) meets such other requirements as may be prescribed by the Secretary in regulations or other guidance.

The PPA amended IRC § 6695A to provide for a monetary penalty if the following criteria were met:

---

[61] Treasury Circular 230, § 10.2 (a)(4), p. 4.
[62] Treasury Circular 230, Subpart D § 10.60, p. 30.
[63] Treasury Circular 230, § 10.35 (b)(5)(ii), pp. 22–23, 26.

(a) IMPOSITION OF PENALTY.—If—

(1) a person prepares an appraisal of the value of property and such person knows, or reasonably should have known, that the appraisal would be used in connection with a return or a claim for refund, and

(2) the claimed value of the property on a return or claim for refund which is based on such appraisal results in a substantial valuation misstatement under chapter 1 (within the meaning of section 6662[e]), or a gross valuation misstatement (within the meaning of section 6662[h]), with respect to such property, then such person shall pay a penalty in the amount determined under subsection (b).

The PPA further amended IRC § 6695A to quantify the penalties:

(b) AMOUNT OF PENALTY.—The amount of the penalty imposed under subsection (a) on any person with respect to an appraisal shall be equal to the lesser of—

(1) the greater of—

(A) 10 percent of the amount of the underpayment (as defined in section 6664[a]) attributable to the misstatement described in subsection (a)(2), or

(B) $1,000, or

(2) 125 percent of the gross income received by the person described in subsection (a)(1) from the preparation of the appraisal.

(c) EXCEPTION.—No penalty shall be imposed under subsection (a) if the person establishes to the satisfaction of the Secretary that the value established in the appraisal was more likely than not the proper value.

ADDENDUM — VALUATION CHECKLISTS/READY REFERENCE (REVENUE RULINGS 59-60, 77-287, AND 93-12)

Introduction

The Revenue Rulings addressed in this chapter provide useful guidance in various valuation situations. Revenue Ruling 59-60 is applicable to many types of valuation engagements. Revenue Ruling 77-287 applies to restricted securities, such as private placements, investment letter stock, control stock, or unregistered securities. Revenue Ruling 93-12 applies to valuing minority interests in closely held companies for intrafamily transfers.

A valuation checklist/ready reference has been created for each of these revenue rulings to assist in a quick review of its key points as well as for the practical application of these rulings to an actual valuation.

Although Revenue Ruling 59-60 and others provide excellent guidance, they are often cumbersome to apply. The checklists are designed to make it easier to apply these rulings.

Keep in mind that many valuation analysts disagree with various components of the revenue rulings. However, a thorough understanding of these revenue rulings is essential to prepare valuations for tax and other purposes.

Revenue Ruling 59-60

Revenue Ruling 59-60 contains a wealth of information. It has also stood the test of time and is often quoted in various valuation situations. However, many analysts feel that it is poorly organized and hard to follow. This checklist presents the ruling in an easy-to-follow format.

The primary information concerning discounts and premiums is highlighted by an asterisk (*).

1. *Purpose*

_____ Estate tax

_____ Gift tax

_____ Income tax (as amplified by Revenue Ruling 65-192)

_____ *Value of closely held corporations

_____ *Value of thinly traded stock

_____ Value of other business entities such as partnerships, proprietorships, and so on (as amplified by Revenue Ruling 65-192)

2. *Background Definitions*

Dates of Valuation

_____ Date of death

_____ Alternate date (6 months after date of death)

Definition of Fair Market Value

_____ "The price at which the property would change hands between a willing buyer and a willing seller when the former is not under any compulsion to buy and the latter is not under any compulsion to sell, both parties having reasonable knowledge of relevant facts."

_____ "The hypothetical buyer and seller are assumed to be able, as well as willing, to trade and to be well informed about the property and concerning the market for such property."

3. *Approach to Valuation*

_____ Facts and circumstances

_____ No general formula applicable

_____ Wide difference of opinion as to fair market value

_____ Valuation is not an exact science

_____ Sound valuation:

    _____ Relevant facts

    _____ Common sense

    _____ Informed judgment

    _____ Reasonableness

_____ Future outlook:

    _____ Value varies as general economic conditions change

    _____ Optimism versus pessimism

    _____ Uncertainty as to the stability or continuity of future income

    _____ Risk of loss of earnings and value

    _____ Highly speculative value to very uncertain future prospects

    _____ Valuation is a prophecy as to the future

_____ Use of guideline public companies

4. *Factors to Consider*

Nature of the Business and History of the Enterprise from Inception

_____ Past stability or instability

_____ Growth or lack of growth

_____ *Diversity or lack of diversity of its operations

_____ *Degree of risk in the business

_____ Study of gross and net income

_____ *Dividends history

_____ Nature of the business

_____ Products or services

_____ Operating and investment assets

_____ *Capital structure

_____ Plant facilities

_____ Sales records

_____ *Management

_____ Due regard for recent significant changes

_____ Discount events of the past that are unlikely to recur in the future

_____ Value has a close relation to future expectancy

_____ Recent events are of greatest help in predicting the future

Economic Outlook in General and Condition and Outlook of the Specific Industry in Particular

_____ Current and prospective economic conditions

_____ National economy

_____ Industry or industries

_____ More or less successful than its competitors; stable with competitors

_____ Ability of industry to compete with other industries

_____ Prospective competition

_____ Price trends in the markets for commodities and securities

_____ *Possible effects of a key person or thin management/lack of succession

_____ Effect of the loss of the manager on the future expectancy of the business

_____ *Key person life insurance could be partially offsetting

Book Value of the Stock and the Financial Condition of the Business

_____ Two historical fiscal year-end balance sheets

_____ Balance sheet as of the end of the month preceding the valuation date

_____ *Liquid position (ratio of current assets to current liabilities)

_____ Gross and net book value of principal classes of fixed assets

_____ Working capital

_____ Long-term indebtedness

_____ *Capital structure

_____ Net worth

_____ *Revalued nonoperating assets (i.e, investments in securities and real estate) on the basis of their market price

_____ Generally, nonoperating assets command lower rates of return

_____ Acquisitions of production facilities or subsidiaries

_____ Improvements in financial position

_____ *Recapitalizations

_____ *Changes in capital structure

_____ *Classes of stock

_____ *Examine charter or certificate of incorporation for rights and privileges of the various stock issues including:

    _____ Voting powers

    _____ Preference as to dividends

    _____ Preference as to assets in the event of liquidation

The Earning Capacity of the Company

_____ Preferably five or more years of detailed profit and loss statements

_____ Gross income by principal items

_____ Deductions from gross income:

    _____ Operating expenses

    _____ Interest and other expense on each item of long-term debt

    _____ Depreciation and depletion

    _____ *Officers' salaries in total if reasonable and in detail if they appear excessive

    _____ Contributions based on nature of business and its community position

    _____ Taxes

_____ *Net income available for dividends

_____ *Rates and amounts of dividends paid on each class of stock

_____ Remaining amount carried to surplus

_____ Adjustments to, and reconciliation with, surplus as stated on the balance sheet

_____ Separate recurrent from nonrecurrent items of income and expense

_____ *Distinguish between operating income and investment income

_____ Ascertain whether or not any line of business is operating consistently at a loss and might be abandoned with benefit to the company

_____ *Note percentage of earnings retained for business expansion when considering dividend-paying capacity

_____ Secure all information concerning past income that will be helpful in predicting the future (potential future income is a major factor in many valuations)

_____ Prior earnings records are usually the most reliable guide as to future earnings expectancy

_____ The use of arbitrary five- or ten-year averages without regard to current trends or future prospects will not produce a realistic valuation

_____ If a record of progressively increasing or decreasing net income is found, consider according greater weight to the most recent years' profits in estimating earning power

_____ Look at margins and percentages of sales to assess risk:

      _____ Consumption of raw materials and supplies for manufacturers, processors, and fabricators

      _____ Cost of purchased merchandise for merchants

      _____ Utility services

      _____ Insurance

      _____ Taxes

      _____ Depreciation and depletion

      _____ Interest

Dividend-Paying Capacity

_____ *Primary consideration to dividend-paying capacity rather than dividends actually paid

_____ *Recognition of the necessity of retaining a reasonable portion of profits to meet competition

_____ *When valuing a controlling interest, the dividend factor is not a material element, since the payment of such dividends is discretionary with the controlling stockholders

_____ *The individual or group in control can substitute salaries and bonuses for dividends, thus reducing net income and understating the dividend-paying capacity of the company

_____ *Dividends are a less reliable factor for valuation than dividend-paying capacity

Whether the Enterprise Has Goodwill or Other Intangible Value

_____ Goodwill is based on earning capacity

_____ Goodwill value is based on the excess of net earnings over and above a fair return on the net tangible assets

_____ Factors to consider to support intangible value:

     _____ Prestige and renown of the business

     _____ Trade or brand name

     _____ Record of success over a prolonged period in a particular locality

_____ Sometimes it may not be possible to make a separate valuation of tangible and intangible assets

_____ Intangible value can be measured by the amount that the value of the tangible assets exceeds the net book value of such assets

Sales of the Stock and the Size of the Block of Stock to Be Valued

_____ Prior sales should be arm's length

_____ Forced or distressed sales do not reflect fair market value

_____ Isolated sales in small amounts may not control as a measure of value

_____ *Blockage is not an issue since the stock is not publicly traded

_____ *Size of the block of stock is a relevant factor

_____ *A minority interest in an unlisted corporation's stock is more difficult to sell than a similar block of listed stock

_____ *Control of a corporation, either actual or in effect, may justify a higher value for a specific block of stock since it is an added element of value

Market Price of Stocks of Corporations Engaged in the Same or a Similar Line of Business Having Their Stocks Actively Traded in a Free and Open Market, Either on an Exchange or Over-the-Counter

_____ *Must be evidence of an active free public market for the stock as of the valuation date to be used as a comparable company

_____ Use only comparable companies

_____ The lines of business should be the same or similar

_____ A comparable with one or more issues of preferred stock, bonds, or debentures in addition to its common stock should not be considered to be directly comparable to one having only common stock outstanding

_____ A comparable with a declining business and decreasing markets is not comparable to one with a record of current progress and market expansion

5. *Weight to Be Accorded Various Factors*

_____ Certain factors carry more weight than others because of the nature of the company's business

_____ Earnings may be the most important criterion of value in some cases, whereas asset value will receive primary consideration in others

_____ Give primary consideration to earnings when valuing stocks of companies that sell products or services to the public

_____ Give greatest weight to the assets underlying the security to be valued for investment or holding-type companies

_____ Closely held investment or real estate holding company:

    _____ Value is closely related to the value of the assets underlying the stock

    _____ The appraiser should determine the fair market values of the assets of the company

    _____ *Operating expenses of such a company and the cost of liquidating it, if any, merit consideration

    _____ The market values of the assets give due weight to potential earnings and dividends of the particular items of property underlying the stock, capitalized at rates deemed proper by the investing public at the valuation date

    _____ Adjusted net worth should be accorded greater weight in valuing the stock of a closely held investment or real estate holding company, whether or not it is family owned, than any of the other customary yardsticks of appraisal, such as earnings and dividend-paying capacity

6. *Capitalization Rates*

_____ Capitalize the average or current results at some appropriate rate

_____ One of the most difficult problems in valuation

_____ No ready or simple solution will become apparent by a cursory check of the rates of return and dividend yields in terms of the selling price of corporate shares listed on the major exchanges

_____ Wide variations will be found even for companies in the same industry

_____ The ratio will fluctuate from year to year depending upon economic conditions

_____ No standard tables of capitalization rates applicable to closely held corporations can be formulated

_____ *Important factors to consider:

    _____ Nature of the business

    _____ Risk

    _____ Stability or irregularity of earnings

7. *Average of Factors*

_____ Valuations cannot be made on the basis of a prescribed formula

_____ There is no means whereby the various applicable factors in a particular case can be assigned mathematical weights to derive the fair market value

_____ No useful purpose is served by taking an average of several factors (e.g., book value, capitalized earnings, and capitalized dividends) and basing the valuation on the result

_____ Such a process excludes active consideration of other pertinent factors, and the end result cannot be supported by a realistic application of the significant facts in the case except by mere chance

8. *Restrictive Agreements*

_____ *Where shares of stock were acquired by a decedent subject to an option reserved by the issuing corporation to repurchase at a certain price, the option price usually is accepted as the fair market value for estate tax purposes

_____ *The option price is not determinative of fair market value for gift tax purposes

_____ *Where the option or buy and sell agreement is the result of voluntary action by the stockholders and is binding during the life as well as at the death of the stockholders, such agreement may or may not, depending on the circumstances of each case, fix the value for estate tax purposes

_____ *Such restrictive agreements are a factor to be considered, along with other relevant factors, in determining fair market value

_____ *Where the stockholder is free to dispose of his shares during life and the option is to become effective only upon his or her death, the fair market value is not limited to the option price

_____ *Determine whether the agreement represents a bona fide business arrangement or is a device to pass the decedent's shares for less than an adequate and full consideration in money or money's worth:

_____ Relationship of the parties

_____ Relative number of shares held by the decedent

_____ Other material facts

Revenue Ruling 77-287

Revenue Ruling 77-287 deals with the valuation of "restricted securities." These types of securities are also referred to as unregistered securities, investment letter stock, control stock, and private placement stock. A thorough understanding of this revenue ruling will also assist in determining Discounts for Lack of Marketability (DLOM) in closely held companies.

1. *Purpose*

_____ Amplifies Revenue Ruling 59-60

_____ Valuation of securities that cannot be resold because they are restricted from resale pursuant to federal securities laws

2. *Nature of the Problem*

_____ Valuation of stock that has not been registered for public trading when the issuing company has stock of the same class that is actively traded in the securities markets

_____ Determine the difference between the fair market value of the registered actively traded shares versus the unregistered shares of the same company

_____ For estate and gift tax as well as when unregistered shares are issued in exchange for assets or the stock of an acquired company

3. *Background and Definitions*

_____ Restricted securities cannot lawfully be distributed to the general public until a registration statement relating to the corporation underlying the securities has been filed and has become effective under the rules of the SEC and federal securities laws.

_____ *Restricted securities:* Defined in Rule 144 as "securities acquired directly or indirectly from the issuer thereof, or from an affiliate of such issuer, in a transaction or chain of transactions not involving any public offering."

_____ *Unregistered securities:* Securities where a registration statement, providing full disclosure by the issuing corporation, has not been filed with the SEC pursuant to the Securities Act of 1933. The registration statement provides the prospective investor with a factual basis on which to make an investment decision.

_____ *Investment letter stock:* Also called letter stock. Shares of stock issued without SEC registration. The stock is subject to resale and transfer restrictions set forth in a letter of agreement requested by the issuer and signed by the buyer. Such stock may be found in the hands of individual or institutional investors.

_____ *Control stock:* The stock is held by an officer, director, or other person close to corporate management. These people are subject to certain requirements pursuant to SEC rules upon resale of shares they own in such corporations.

_____ *Private placement stock:* The stock has been placed with an institution or other investor who will presumably hold it for a long period and ultimately arrange to have the stock registered if it is to be offered to the general public. This stock may or may not be subject to a letter agreement. Private placements are exempted from the registration and prospectus provisions of the Securities Act of 1933.

_____ *Exempted securities:* Expressly excluded from the registration provisions of the Securities Act of 1933 and the distribution provisions of the Securities Exchange Act of 1934.

_____ *Exempted transactions:* Certain sales or distributions that do not involve a public offering and are excluded from the registration and prospectus provisions of the 1933 and 1934 Acts. Issuers do not have to go through the registration process.

4. *Securities Industry Practice in Valuing Restricted Securities*

_____ Investment company valuation practices:

    _____ Open-end investment companies must publish the valuation of their portfolios on a regular basis

    _____ Many own restricted and unrestricted securities of the same companies

    _____ Valuation methods:

        _____ Market price of unrestricted publicly traded stock less a constant percentage discount based on purchase discount

        _____ Market price of unrestricted publicly traded stock less a constant percentage discount different from purchase discount

        _____ Market price of unrestricted publicly traded stock less a discount amortized over a fixed period

        _____ Market price of the unrestricted publicly traded stock

        _____ Cost of the restricted stock until it is registered

    _____ The SEC stated that there are no automatic formulas

    _____ The SEC has determined that it is the responsibility of the board of directors of the particular investment company to determine the "fair value" of each issue of restricted securities in good faith

_____ *Institutional Investors Study:*

    _____ The SEC undertook an analysis of the purchases, sales, and holding of securities by financial institutions

    _____ Published in March 1971

    _____ Includes an analysis of restricted securities

    _____ Period of study is January 1, 1966, through June 30, 1969

    _____ Characteristics of the restricted securities purchasers and issuers

    _____ The size of transactions in both dollars and shares

    _____ Marketability discounts on different trading markets

    _____ Resale provisions

_____ The amount of discount allowed for restricted securities from the freely traded public price of the unrestricted securities was generally related to the following factors:

Earnings

_____ Earnings and sales have significant influence on the size of the discounts

_____ Earnings patterns rather than sales patterns determine the degree of risk of an investment

Sales

_____ The dollar amount of sales of the issuers' securities also has a major influence on the amount of discounts

_____ Generally, companies with the lowest dollar amount of sales during the period accounted for most of the transactions involving the highest discounts while they accounted for the lowest number that involved the lowest discounts

Trading Market

_____ Higher discounts for over-the-counter, followed by the American Stock Exchange, then the New York Stock Exchange

Resale Agreement Provisions

_____ The discount from market price provides the main incentive for a potential buyer to acquire restricted securities

_____ Two factors are important in judging the opportunity cost of freezing funds in a restricted security:

   _____ The risk that the underlying value of the stock will change in a way that, absent the restrictive provisions, would have prompted a sale

   _____ The risk that the contemplated means of legally disposing the stock may not materialize

_____ Seller may be relieved of the expenses of registration and public distribution as well as the risk that the market will adversely change before the offering is completed

_____ Buyer and seller bargaining strengths influence the discount

_____ Most common provisions are:

   _____ Option for "piggyback" rights to register restricted stock with the next registration statement, if any, filed by the issuer with the SEC

   _____ Option to require registration at the seller's expense

   _____ Option to require registration, but only at the buyer's own expense

_____ Right to receive continuous disclosure of information about the issuer from the seller

_____ Right to select one or more directors of the issuer

_____ Option to purchase additional shares of the issuer's stock

_____ Provision given the buyer the right to have a greater voice in operations of the issuer, if the issuer does not meet previously agreed-upon operating standards

_____ Institutional buyers often obtain these rights from sellers of restricted stocks

_____ The more rights a buyer can acquire, the lower the buyer's risk, thus the lower the buyer's discount

_____ Small buyers may not be able to negotiate the large discounts or the rights and options that the volume buyers are able to negotiate

Summary

_____ A variety of methods have been used by the securities industry to value restricted securities

_____ The SEC rejects all automatic or mechanical solutions to the valuation of restricted securities

_____ The SEC prefers to rely upon good-faith valuations by the board of directors of each company

_____ An SEC study found that restricted securities generally are issued at a discount from the market value of freely traded securities

5. Facts and Circumstances Material to the Valuation of Restricted Securities

_____ Often a company's stock cannot be traded because of securities statutes as in the case of investment letter restrictions

_____ Stock may also may be restricted from trading because of a corporate charter restriction or a trust-agreement restriction

_____ The following documents and facts, when used in conjunction with those discussed in section IV of Revenue Ruling 59-60, are useful in the valuation of restricted securities:

   _____ Any declaration of trust agreement or any other agreements relating to the shares of restricted stock

   _____ Any documents showing any offers to buy or sell or indications of interest in buying or selling the restricted shares

   _____ Latest company prospectus

   _____ Three to five years of annual reports

   _____ Trading prices and trading volume and the related class of traded securities one month preceding the valuation date

_____ The relationship of the parties to the agreements concerning the restricted stocks, such as whether they are members of the immediate family or whether they are officers or directors of the company

_____ Whether the interest being valued represents a majority or minority ownership

6. _Weighing Facts and Circumstances Material to Restricted Stock Valuation_

_____ Depending on the circumstances of each case, certain factors may carry more weight than others

_____ Earnings, net assets, and net sales must be given primary consideration

_____ In some cases, one element may be more important than others

_____ For manufacturing, producing, or distributing companies, primary weight must be accorded earnings and net sales

_____ For investment or holding companies, primary weight must be given to the net assets

_____ Careful review of resale provisions found in restricted agreements

_____ The two elements of time and expense should be reflected in a discount

_____ The longer the buyer of the shares must wait to liquidate the shares, the greater the discount

_____ If certain provisions make it necessary for the buyer to bear the expense of registration, the discount is greater

_____ If the provisions of the restricted stock agreement make it possible for the buyer to "piggyback" shares of the next offering, the discount would be smaller

_____ The relative negotiating strengths of the buyer and seller of restricted stock

_____ A tight money situation may cause a buyer to have more negotiating strength

_____ In some cases, the relative strengths may tend to cancel each other

_____ The market experience of freely tradable securities of the same class as restricted securities is also significant

_____ Whether the shares are privately held or publicly traded

_____ Securities traded on a public market generally are worth more to investors than those not traded on a public market

_____ The type of public market in which the unrestricted securities are traded can be given consideration

Revenue Ruling 93-12

The IRS revoked Revenue Ruling 81-253, which applied family attribution to determine control when valuing minority interests in closely held companies. After Revenue Ruling 81-253 was issued, the IRS lost a majority of the court cases concerning family attribution.

Revenue Ruling 93-12 states that a minority discount on stock transferred to a family member will not be challenged solely because the transferred interest, when aggregated with interests held by other family members, will be a part of a controlling interest. This ruling arose from a gift tax case.

Issue

_____ If a donor transfers shares in a corporation to each of the donor's children, is the factor of corporate control in the family to be considered in valuing each transferred interest?

Facts

_____ Taxpayer owned all the shares of stock of a corporation

_____ Taxpayer made simultaneous gifts of 20 percent blocks of stock to each of five children

Law and Analysis

_____ The value of the property at the date of the gift shall be considered the amount of the gift

_____ The value of the property is the price at which the property would change hands between a willing buyer and a willing seller, neither being under any compulsion to buy or to sell, and both having reasonable knowledge of relevant facts

_____ Fair market value on the date of the gift

_____ Among the factors to be considered is the degree of control of the business being represented by the block of stock to be valued

_____ Revenue Ruling 81-253, 1981-1 C.B. 187 holds that, ordinarily, no minority shareholder discount is allowed with respect to transfers of shares of stock between family members if, based on a composite of the family members' interests at the time of the transfer, control (either majority voting control or de facto control through family relationships) of the corporation exists in the family unit

_____ Revenue Ruling 81-253 states that the Internal Revenue Service will not follow the decision in the 1981 case *Estate of Bright v. United States*

_____ In *Bright,* the court allowed a 27.5 percent interest to be valued as a minority interest, even though the shares were to be held by the decedent's surviving spouse

_____ *Propstra v. United States (1982), Estate of Andrews v. Commissioner (1982)* and *Estate of Lee v. Commissioner (1978).* These cases held that the corporations'

shares owned by other family members cannot be attributed to an individual family member for determining whether the individual family member's share should be valued as a controlling interest of the corporation

_____ The IRS has concluded, in the case of a corporation with a single class of stock, notwithstanding the family relationship of the donor, the donee, and other shareholders, the shares of other family members will not be aggregated with the transferred shares to determine whether the transferred shares should be valued as part of a controlling interest

_____ The five 20 percent interests that were gifted should be valued without regard to the family relationship of the parties

Holding

_____ If a donor transfers shares in a corporation to each of the donor's children, the factor of corporate control in the family is not considered in valuing each transferred interest

_____ The IRS will follow *Bright, Propstra, Andrews,* and *Lee* in not assuming that all voting power held by family members may be aggregated as part of a controlling interest

_____ A minority discount will not be disallowed solely because a transferred interest, when aggregated with interests held by family members, will be part of a controlling interest

_____ This will be the case whether the donor held 100 percent or some lesser percentage of the stock immediately before the gift

Effect on Other Documents

_____ Revenue Ruling 81-253 is revoked

Valuation of Family Limited Partnerships

CHAPTER 14

The family limited partnership (FLP) is a sophisticated financial planning technique that, when implemented properly, enables a family to hold and manage its wealth, including the family business, within several generations of family members as partners. Families with significant wealth increasingly establish an FLP rather than a corporation because the FLP often is better suited to achieving certain objectives.

Some background on corporations and partnerships is helpful to understanding the FLP. The profits of a C corporation are taxed at a maximum rate of 35 percent (for federal tax purposes); when the after-tax profits of the C corporation are distributed to the shareholders as dividends, those same profits are taxed a second time to the individual shareholders, up to the maximum federal statutory rate of 38.6 percent. The combined corporate and personal tax rate can easily exceed 60 percent, even before state and local income taxes are taken into account.

Alternatively, the profits of a subchapter S corporation are, in general, taxed at the shareholder level only—making the S corporation a more appealing structure than the C corporation in many instances. However, there are numerous restrictions on the qualifications for functioning as an S corporation, even after the liberalizing amendments enacted in 1996.

By comparison, a partnership is a pure "flow-through" entity, meaning that the income realized by the entity flows through and in all cases is taxable to its individual owners and not to the business per se. As a result, the limited partnership has become increasingly popular as a flexible and tax-efficient vehicle for conducting business—particularly as compared to a corporation, which is a more formal and generally a tax-inefficient means for conducting business.

Further enhancing the desirability of partnerships is the Uniform Limited Partnership Act, adopted by a large majority of states. This statute standardizes and simplifies the laws governing a limited partnership's conduct of business in more than one state.

FAMILY LIMITED PARTNERSHIP USES

In addition, FLPs may be used by families as the means:

- To provide a resolution of any disputes that may arise among the family, preserve harmony, and avoid the expense and problems of litigation
- To maintain control of the family assets

- To promote the efficient and economic management of the assets and properties under one entity
- To consolidate fractional interests in family assets
- To increase family wealth
- To make annual gifts without fractionalizing the underlying family assets
- To restrict the right of nonfamily members to acquire interests in the family assets
- To provide protection of the family assets from claims of future creditors
- To prevent the transfer of a family member's interests as a result of a failed marriage
- To provide flexibility in business planning not available through trusts, corporations, or other business entities
- To facilitate the administration and reduce the cost associated with the disability or probate of the estate of family members
- To promote the family's knowledge of and communication about the family assets

These goals can be achieved as a result of the FLP's ability to:

- Engage in the real estate business; that is to acquire, own, hold, develop, and operate real estate enterprises
- Invest funds and to raise funds to be invested in furtherance of the underlying purposes
- Invest, manage, and operate various investments including but not limited to marketable securities, stocks, bonds, gold, silver, grain, cotton, other commodities, and debt instruments

TAX ADVANTAGES

This type of entity structure also provides a vehicle to maximize the profits and yield to the family members due to two factors:

1. A partnership structure eliminates the possibility of double taxation (i.e., taxation at the entity and the individual level). This will provide higher returns to the family members by reducing their tax burden. Unlike outright gifts, this structure minimizes the possibility that any new partners could impair the value of the assets.
2. Internal Revenue Code Section 754 permits a partnership to file an election upon the death of a partner to adjust the basis under IRC Section 743(b). Again, this provides additional value to the family members.

HOW FAMILY LIMITED PARTNERSHIPS ARE FORMED

The family limited partnership usually is formed by the senior generation by transferring assets in return for general and limited partnership interests. These interests carry certain rights as to distributions, cash flows, and/or access to assets based on the state law provisions specific to the state of governance.

Assets are generally investment real estate, marketable securities, bonds, or other assets that are expected to appreciate. General partner interests usually range from 1 to 5 percent. Alternatively, limited partner interests usually range from 95 to 99 percent. Further, general partner interests are sometimes held by the senior generation or by a separate entity, whereby the senior generation retains control of the entity and the underlying assets.

Subsequently, gifts generally are made to the junior generation of limited partnership interests as a highly efficient means of transferring value and assets out of the estate of the senior generation while maximizing the use of the federal and state estate and gift tax structure. Such efficiency and tax structure benefits are made possible because federal and state laws and regulations treat an ownership interest in a limited partnership substantially differently from a direct ownership interest in particular assets.

For example, assume that a husband and his spouse own various marketable securities worth $1 million. They both transfer these assets to an FLP. Later, they transfer a 10 percent interest to their child. This transfer typically will be taxed for gift tax purposes based on the value transferred. If a 10 percent interest in the underlying assets were directly transferred, the taxable value would be $100,000 ($1,000,000 × 10 percent). However, through the use of the FLP, the taxpayers (husband and spouse) can leverage the amount of the gift. The taxable value, due to the nature of the interest transferred, would not be a pro rata interest in the underlying assets. Rather, it would be the amount that a "hypothetical buyer" would pay for a 10 percent interest in a limited partnership. This interest would consider the fact that a limited partner's interest (or an assignee's interest) cannot and does not have access to partnership assets and cannot force any distribution or effectively control the ability to receive a return on his or her investment.

As a result, the transferred interest above would be discounted for these ownership and marketability issues and might be valued as follows:

Value of underlying assets		$1,000,000
Interest transferred		× 10%
Pro rata value of interest		100,000
Discount for lack of control	25%*	− 25,000
		75,000
Discount for lack of marketability	30%*	− 22,500
Value of interest transferred		$ 52,500

*Note: For illustrative purposes only

By utilizing this type of transfer structure, the taxpayers have effectively reduced their exposure to estate and/or gift taxes by $26,125 ($100,000 pro rata value − $52,500 discounted value = $47,500 × 55 percent marginal estate/gift tax rate = $26,125) or 26.0 percent.

This type of "wealth preservation planning" technique can accomplish multiple goals with respect to an individual's assets, wealth, and estate. However, these benefits do not come without their share of issues.

OTHER CHARACTERISTICS OF FAMILY LIMITED PARTNERSHIPS

- Family limited partnerships require at least two different partners: one general partner and one limited partner
- The general partner(s) has (have) full control over the management, decisions, and day-to-day operations of the partnership affairs
- The general partner(s) is (are) responsible for all financial and legal obligations of the partnership
- The limited partner(s) is (are) viewed as a silent family member(s) with no voice in the partnership operations or management
- The limited partner(s) is (are) not responsible for any unguaranteed financial and legal obligations in excess of the investment

STATE LAW, PROPERTY RIGHTS, AND THEIR IMPORTANCE TO THE VALUATION PROCESS

To fully assess the magnitude and volatility of an investment's risks and returns, the valuation analyst needs to begin with a precise definition of the specific investment or ownership interest to be valued. The analyst's function will then be to quantify the value of the "bundle of rights" associated with the investment or specific ownership interest. The characteristics of this bundle of rights heavily impact the value of the investment and provide some indication of the risk and return associated with it. In addition, the more rights associated with the investment or ownership interest, the more valuable it is. Consequently, the analyst also must precisely define the bundle of rights associated with the subject interest, or the resulting value (although mathematically correct) may be of the wrong investment.

Rights are granted to a specific ownership interest by the underlying state laws that govern the investment to be valued. For this reason, attorneys are best qualified to opine on the characteristics of the bundle of rights associated with the subject investment. To assure accuracy of the legal assumptions on which the value opinion will be based, the analyst may want to include legal counsel in early discussions of the property being valued and the state laws and property rights associated with it.

For instance, the value on a per share basis of a 32.5 percent interest in a closely held California corporation and a 33.5 percent interest in the same California corporation are not necessarily the same. As discussed in *Estate of Luton vs. Commissioner, TCM 1994-539*, an interest in a California corporation of one-third or greater has the ability to force liquidation under certain circumstances. Accordingly, the liquidation rights associated with the 33.5 percent interest increase its value since an investor may be willing to pay more on a per-share basis for such rights.

Another case in which the result was impacted by the interest held was *Estate of Jones v. Commissioner, 116 T.C. 121*, in which a gifted limited partnership interest of greater than 80 percent needed to be valued. In that regard, a greater than 50 percent limited partner interest had the ability to remove the general partner. As a result, any adjustment for lack of control was disallowed. Conceivably, this result could have been avoided by making two separate gifts of less than 50 percent.

By way of another example, an assignee interest typically will have the lowest level of rights of any interest, which may include factors such as the following:

- A right to receive, to the extent assigned, nonliquidating distributions and liquidating distributions to which the assignor/partner would be entitled as well as a right to receive, to the extent assigned, allocations of income, gain, loss, deduction, credit, or similar item to which assignor/partner would be entitled
- No right to require any information or account of the FLP transactions
- No right to inspect the FLP books
- No right to vote on any matters that a general or limited partner would be entitled to vote
- No right to call partnership meetings
- No voice in the management of the FLP
- No ability to maintain an action (lawsuit) against a general partner for breach of fiduciary duty
- No right to withdraw from the FLP *and* receive fair value for its assignee interest prior to the expiration of the term of the partnership

FLP property rights consist of either or both: 1) an ownership interest in the partnership and 2) management rights. Both general and limited partners, as well as their assignees, have no interest in the underlying assets owned by the FLP because these assets are no longer owned directly by the contributing partners. They are now owned by the FLP. The contributing partners received interests in the partnership in exchange for their contribution of assets and surrendered their ownership interest in the underlying partnership assets.

It is important to clarify what the specific interest is that needs to be valued. Again, this interest is a legal determination and may require legal counsel to assist in the proper description of the rights, obligations, and restrictions associated with the interest. It is also important that all documentation be consistent with the interest that is to be valued, including the report and engagement letter.

Therefore, an interest in the partnership is considered intangible personal property and consists of the partner's share of FLP distributions and the allocation of income, gain, loss, deduction, credit, or similar items, irrespective of the actual physical character of the underlying partnership assets.

ValTip

Once a valuation analyst has a solid understanding of the bundle of rights, he or she is better prepared to determine how to capture their addition to or detriment from value in the subject's benefit stream, rate of return, discount applied to enterprise value, or a combination of these. Doing this will involve gaining a picture not only of the rights that exist but, more important, of those rights that do not exist.

IMPROPER FORMATION CAN CREATE PROBLEMS FOR PARTNERS

A variety of considerations regarding FLP formation have become the focus of recent Internal Revenue Service (IRS) attacks and litigation. These considerations include but are not limited to:

- Gifts on formation
- Indirect gifts
- Subsequent asset infusions
- Asset diversification
- Real property assessments

"Gift on Formation," Indirect Gifts, and Subsequent Asset Infusions

Gifts of assets on the formation of an FLP typically are transferred to the newly formed entity in return for partnership interests (limited and general). As such, it is important that these initial contributions be transferred on the date the FLP is formed and that they have been appropriately valued to provide the desired basis from which to determine the percentage of ownership to attribute to each contributing partner. The percent ownership interest received by each partner in exchange for contributed assets should be based on the relative value of those assets and should be reflected in the individual partner's capital account. Last, the partnership should be a "straight-up" pro rata partnership with respect to all allocations. Allocations of all items should be based on the partnership interest percent.

If assets are not transferred upon formation in return for the same percentage of partnership interest in relation to the assets, there can be an unintended gift of the value differential between the assets transferred and the interest received.

"Indirect" gifts typically are created through non–pro rata allocations of income or capital appreciation and/or the attribution of improper asset values to a particular partner's capital account at formation. When additional assets are transferred to the FLP after formation and the value of the subsequent assets is not attributed to the donor's capital account, an indirect gift to the nondonating partners can also occur.

Asset Diversification

When publicly traded securities are contributed to an FLP, it is important to avoid triggering the gain recognition rules under the "Investment Company" provisions of Internal Revenue Code (IRC) § 351.

IRC § 721(a) provides that, as a general rule, no gain or loss is recognized by any partner transferring property to a partnership in exchange for an interest in the partnership. However, IRC § 721(b) provides that the transfer of appreciated property to a partnership that would be treated as an investment company within the meaning of IRC § 351 (if it were incorporated) would not be a tax-free transfer under IRC § 721(a). The section further states that such a transfer would be considered taxable if:

- The transfer results, directly or indirectly, in the diversification of the transferor's interests

- The transfer is to an entity holding more than 80.0 percent of the value of its assets, excluding cash and nonconvertible debt instruments, for investment in readily marketable stocks, securities, or interests in regulated investment companies or real estate investment trusts

Real Property Reassessment

Property tax laws in the governing state are of crucial importance when valuing an FLP. Certain transfers of real property into an FLP can give rise to a reassessment of the real property for real estate tax purposes. In certain states, real property tax reassessment may not be triggered by the initial transfer of real property to the FLP but may be triggered by the subsequent transfer of the FLP interests. In many jurisdictions, the exclusions for reassessment that apply to the direct transfer of real property may not apply in the context of the transfer of FLP interests. As a result, in certain situations (usually upon the transfer of 50.0 percent or more of the FLP interests on a cumulative basis), this may result in a reassessment. In addition, some states have a transfer tax on real property exchanges.

VALUATION OF FAMILY LIMITED PARTNERSHIP INTERESTS

The valuation of an FLP interest involves a number of considerations and steps:

Preliminary Considerations

- Information required
- Analyzing the agreement
- IRC Chapter 14 considerations

The Valuation Process

- Understanding the assets, operations, and financial components of the partnership
- Data sources, comparative/benchmark information
- Valuation approaches
- Application of the data and multiples or adjustments

Each of these considerations is discussed in depth below.

Preliminary Considerations

Information Required

As with all valuation engagements, the information required to prepare the valuation of an FLP is dependent on the facts in the case. However, where available, certain information should be considered the minimum foundation to complete the assignment. This information includes:

- Final partnership agreement and all amendments and assignments associated with it
- Documentation of assets being contributed

- Appraisals of real estate and other partnership assets
- Other valuations as needed (in tiered-entity structures)
- Balance sheet as of valuation date
- Income statement as of valuation date
- Tax returns or prior filings
- Certificate of limited partnership
- Income and distribution history
- Prior valuations of the partnership
- Details of prior transfers (gift or otherwise) into or out of the partnership
- Management structure and analysis of decision-making rights
- Governing state partnership laws

Analyzing the Agreement

One of the key considerations to valuing an FLP interest is a thorough understanding of the provisions of the partnership agreement to accurately reflect them in the value estimate. Given the fact that the agreement is a legal document and most analysts are not attorneys, the analyst will want to seek the guidance of legal counsel for this task.

The provisions of the agreement, as well as governing state partnership law, will define the interest and rights associated with the particular FLP. A typical agreement will have provisions regarding capital contributions, distributions, allocations, liquidation, voting, term, withdrawal, death, transfer, and termination. Furthermore, the agreement will provide for certain rights and restrictions specific to the general partner(s) and to the limited partners.

Examples of 15 common provisions in family limited partnership agreements are provided below, using typical terminology and language structure.

1. *Term.* "The Partnership will commence upon the filing of a certificate of limited partnership in the office of the Secretary of State of Anystate and shall continue for forty years from December 1, 2002, unless sooner dissolved pursuant to the provisions of this Agreement or unless continued by unanimous consent of the Partners."

ValTip

> Term restriction is important from a valuation perspective because it defines the inability of the limited partners to receive a return on their investment prior to the completion of the partnership term.

2. *Business Purposes.* "The business purpose of the Partnership shall be to acquire, own, operate, and dispose of investment real estate property. Additional related business activities permitted by law may be engaged in by the Partnership from time to time as determined by the General Partners."

3. *Majority Vote.* "Majority vote shall mean the affirmative vote by the Limited Partners of record, which vote represents more than 50 percent of the aggregate Interests of the Limited Partners of record entitled to vote."

This type of provision provides rights for limited partners in certain circumstances that may enable them to affect some operations of the partnership. As such, the impact of this type of provision is partially dependent on the size of the limited partnership interest being valued.

4. *Transfer of Partnership Interests.*

    a. "The term 'transfer,' when used in this article with respect to a Partnership interest, shall include any sale, assignment, gift, pledge, hypothecation, mortgage, exchange, or other disposition of such Partnership interest."
    b. "No Partnership interest shall be transferred, in whole or in part, except in accordance with the terms and conditions set forth in this article. Notwithstanding the preceding sentence, if all of the Partners enter into an Agreement for the purchase of a Partner's Partnership interest, such Agreement shall be binding upon the Partners and the Partnership."

If the provisions in the agreement are anything other than fair market value between family members, it may be disregarded under § 2703.

Most partnership agreements have a clearly stated restriction on transferability of partnership interests, primarily to protect all partners from finding themselves legally bound to a partnership with individuals not of their choice. From a valuation perspective, such restrictions on transferability may have a material impact on the selection of the degree of discount for lack of control and lack of marketability. However, if other provisions modify the transferability restrictions, they may provide a mitigating effect on the depth of the discount for lack of control and lack of marketability.

5. *Capital Contribution of General Partners.* "The General Partners shall be credited with the Gross Asset Value of the property contributed by them. As of the date of such contributions, the Capital Account balance of the General Partners shall equal XX percent of the aggregate Capital Account balances of all Partners."

All contributions are to be credited to the partners' accounts to avoid the "gift on formation" issues previously discussed.

6. *General Authority and Obligations of the General Partners.* "The General Partners shall actively manage and conduct the business of the Partnership devoting such time to the management as the General Partners may deem necessary. The General Partners shall have the full and complete power to do any and all things necessary or incident to the management and conduct of the Partnership business. The General Partners shall have full power and authority to take any action they deem necessary or advisable on behalf of the Partnership and shall make all decisions affecting the business, affairs, and properties of the Partnership. No person dealing with the Partnership shall be required to inquire into the authority of the General Partners to take any action or execute any document on behalf of the Partnership. Specific powers include:

a. *Conveyances.* The General Partners shall have the authority to sell, exchange, assign, or transfer any of the property or assets of the Partnership, in furtherance of the business of the Partnership, and, in connection therewith, to execute, in the Partnership name, by agent or nominee, any and all assignments, documents, bills of sale, and other papers pertaining to the Partnership business.

b. *Authorized Acts of the General Partners.* Without limiting the generality of the provisions of this Agreement concerning general authority and obligations of the General Partners and conveyances and in furtherance of the purposes of the Partnership, but subject to any specific limitations provided in the Act or in this Agreement, the General Partners are hereby authorized to do any and all of the following:

   i.   Resolve claims of or demands against the Partnership
   ii. Pay as a Partnership expense all costs associated with the operation of the Partnership
   iii. Apply the Partnership's funds in a manner consistent with this Agreement
   iv. Make tax elections
   v.   Require in Partnership contracts that no Limited Partner have any personal liability thereon

vi.   Execute all documents or instruments of any kind that the General Partners deem appropriate for carrying out the purposes of the Partnership, except as otherwise provided herein

vii. Acquire, hold, develop, improve, maintain, operate, lease, sell, exchange, and dispose of any real property and personal property that may be necessary to the accomplishment of the Partnership's purposes

viii. Borrow money from banks or other lending institutions on behalf of the Partnership; and in connection therewith, mortgage, pledge, or create other security interests on any or all of the Partnership assets and income therefrom and secure or provide for the repayment of such borrowing or loans

ix.   Deposit Partnership funds in bank certificates of deposit, interest-bearing savings and checking accounts, prime commercial paper, or government obligations

x.   Purchase insurance, or extend the General Partners' insurance, at the Partnership's expense, to protect Partnership properties and the business of the Partnership against loss and to protect the General Partners against liability to third parties arising out of Partnership activities

xi.   Enter into any kind of activity and perform and carry out contracts of any kind necessary to the accomplishment of the purposes of the Partnership, so long as said activities and contracts may be lawfully carried on or performed by a partnership under the laws of the State of XXXXXX."

7. *Transfer by General Partners.* "If a General Partner desires to sell or transfer all or part of his partnership interest to a person or entity who is not a General Partner, such transfer shall be permitted if, and only if, i) the proposed transferee is to become a Limited Partner and shall be subject to the provisions of this Agreement having to do with the transfer of a Limited Partnership interest, or if ii) the proposed transferee is approved as an additional or successor General Partner by unanimous consent of all partners."

8. *Amendments to Be Adopted Solely by the General Partners.* "Except as otherwise provided in the following section, the General Partners may, without the consent of any Limited Partner, amend any provision of this Agreement, and execute whatever documents may be required in connection therewith."

9. *Amendments Not Allowable.* "Unless approved by the Partner affected thereby, no amendment to this Agreement shall be permitted if the effect of such amendment would be to:

a. Extend the term of the Partnership as set forth as provided in the provisions of this Agreement having to do with the term of the Partnership;

b. Amend this section;

c. Convert the interest of a Limited Partner into the interest of a General Partner;

d. Alter the interest of a Limited Partner in the Profits, Losses, or Distributions of the Partnership, except for a change which is necessary to cure any ambiguity or correct or supplement any provision contained in this Agreement which may be incomplete or inconsistent with any other provision contained herein;

e. Increase the amount of Capital Contributions payable by any Limited Partner;

f. Modify the limited liability of a Limited Partner or reduce or modify the liability of any General Partner; or

g. Otherwise increase the duties or liabilities of the General Partners or of any Limited Partner."

The provisions concerning amendments to the partnership agreement provide a substantial level of authority to the general partner with input by the limited partners. However, many partnership agreements provide for a "power of attorney" clause whereby the limited partners specifically provide the authority for the general partner to act on their behalf. In addition, a restriction on transferability provides some level of protection to the limited partners regarding possible changes in partnership management of the partnership. These restrictions as well as the general partner(s)' legally binding fiduciary responsibility toward the limited partners may allow for some level of discount for lack of control when valuing a general partner interest.

10. *Capital Contributions of the Limited Partners.* "The Limited Partners shall be credited with the Gross Asset Value of the property contributed by them. As of the date of such contribution, the Capital Account balance of the Limited Partners shall equal XX percent of the aggregate Capital Account balances of all Partners."

Like the provision for the general partner capital accounts, this provision makes it clear that all contributions are to be credited to the partners' account to avoid the "gift on formation" issues previously discussed.

11. *Limitation of Liability.* "No Limited Partner shall be liable for any debts, liabilities, contracts, or obligations of the Partnership; have any personal liability for the repayment of the Capital Contribution of any other Partner; and be required to lend any funds to the Partnership."

> One of the benefits to a limited partnership structure is the protection afforded the limited partners from the debts and obligations of the partnership or other partners.

12. *No Management Responsibility.* "No Limited Partner, when acting solely as such, shall take part in the management of the Partnership or transact any business for the Partnership. All management responsibility is hereby vested in the General Partners."

13. *No Authority to Act.* "No Limited Partner, when acting solely as such, shall have the power to sign for or bind the Partnership or transact business in the name of the Partnership. All authority to act on behalf of the Partnership is hereby vested in the General Partners."

14. *Access to Information.* "Each Limited Partner shall have the right to obtain, from time to time upon written request, for any purpose reasonably related to the Limited Partner's interest as a Limited Partner, any such requested information relating to the business of the Partnership and such other information as a limited partner has a right to obtain under the Act, provided that the Partnership may require the Limited Partners to pay the costs incurred by the Partnership in responding to any such request for information."

15. *Transfer by a Limited Partner.* "A Limited Partner may assign and transfer all or any part of such Limited Partner's Partnership interest only with the written consent of the General Partners.

    a. Any successor or transferee of a Limited Partner hereunder shall be bound by the provisions of this Agreement.

    b. Any assignee who is not a Partner at the time of the assignment shall be entitled to the allocations and distributions attributable to the interest assigned to it and to transfer and assign such interest in accordance with the terms of this Agreement; provided, however, such assignee shall not be entitled to the other rights of a Limited Partner until it becomes a substitute Limited Partner.

    c. No assignee of a Limited Partner's Partnership interest is entitled to become a substitute Limited Partner until the following have occurred:

        i.   The General Partners shall have given their prior written consent, which consent may be withheld in his absolute discretion;

        ii. The transferring Limited Partner and the transferee shall have executed and acknowledged such other instrument or instruments as the General Partners may deem necessary or desirable to effect such admission;

        iii. The transferee shall have accepted, adopted, and approved in writing all of the terms and provisions of this Agreement as the same may have been amended; and

        iv. The transferee shall pay or obligate itself to pay, as the General Partners may require, all reasonable expenses connected with its admission as a substitute Limited Partner, including but not limited to the cost of preparing appropriate amendments to this Agreement."

The above provisions are the foundation for selecting appropriate discounts for lack of control and lack of marketability for two reasons:

1. A limited partner, by definition, does not have any right to manage or control the partnership, thus eliminating his or her ability to determine the amount and timing of any distributions or asset liquidations of the partnership. This effectively eliminates some of the sources of return on the partner's investment.
2. In addition, the inability to readily transfer the interest or withdraw from the partnership eliminates the other avenue for a limited partner to receive a return on his or her investment.

Internal Revenue Code Chapter 14 Considerations

Chapter 14 (§§ 2701-2704 of the Internal Revenue Code [IRC]) was enacted by the Omnibus Budget Reconciliation Act of 1990 as a response to perceived "estate freeze" abuses by estate planning professionals and their clients. Chapter 14 focuses on the taxation of certain transfers of corporate and partnership interests (§ 2701), the impact of buy-sell agreements on such transfers (§ 2703), the effect that certain lapsing rights have on the value of property subject to such transfers (§ 2704), and the taxation of certain transfers in trust (§ 2702). Sections 2701, 2703, and 2704 can significantly affect the value of an interest in a closely held corporation and a family limited partnership. Therefore, a detailed discussion of these code sections is provided.

Section 2701. Section 2701 addresses transfers of interests in controlled entities. Subject to several definitions and qualifications, § 2701 applies to:

- A transfer of an interest in a corporation or partnership
- An applicable family member
- Where the transferor or an applicable family member retains an "applicable retained interest" after the transfer and
- Where the transferor and applicable family members control the corporation or partnership following the transfer

If § 2701 applies, special valuation rules must be used in computing the value of the interest in the corporation or partnership that is transferred to an applicable family member.

These rules require that the value of the entire corporation or partnership must be computed first. That value will *generally* be attributed to the *transferred* interests except to the extent that the retained interests have regular and fixed distribution rights that are cumulative; other rights generally will be ignored.

Section 2701 normally would apply to the typical family limited partnership arrangement but for the exception provided under § 2701(a)(2)(B) for transfers of interest that are the "same class" as the retained interest except for "nonlapsing differences with respect to management and limitations on liability." In the standard FLP, general and limited partners do have the same interests in profits and losses of the partnership based on each partner's proportionate interest in the partnership, with general partners having management rights and limited partners having limitations on liability pursuant to applicable state law. Consequently, a transfer of a limited partnership interest should not be subject to the § 2701 valuation rules if the items of income, gain, loss, deduction, and credit are allocated among all the partners, including limited partners, based on their capital accounts.

By basing partnership allocations and distributions on the partners' capital account balances (i.e., pro rata allocations and distributions), the transfer of partnership interests should *not* be subject to § 2701 and the partnership agreement does not need to contain the complex provisions of § 704(b) (dealing with the substantial economic effect test that applies to special allocations).

Section 2703. Section 2703 provides that the value of property for estate, gift, and generation-skipping transfer tax purposes is determined without regard to any restrictions on the sale or use of the property unless:

- The restriction (e.g., a buy-sell agreement) is a bona fide business arrangement
- The restriction is not a device to transfer property to family members for less than full and adequate consideration; and
- The restriction is comparable to similar arrangements entered into by persons in an arm's-length transaction

Section 2703 applies to a "right or restriction," whether explicitly fashioned as such, contained in the partnership agreement or similar document, or merely implicit in the capital structure of the entity.

If § 2703 applies, key provisions commonly found in an FLP agreement, such as restrictions against partners transferring interests in the partnership and the partners' inability to liquidate their interest until the end of a specified term of years, can be ignored.

Thus, it is important to establish that the partnership agreement:

- Is a bona fide business arrangement
- Is not a device to transfer the property to members of the decedent's family for less than full and adequate consideration in money or money's worth
- Is an arrangement with terms comparable to similar arrangements entered into by persons in arm's-length transactions

The IRS interpretation and application of § 2703 arguably is contrary to congressional intent. Specifically, the legislative history pertaining to § 2703(a) indicates that, in enacting § 2703, Congress was concerned with perceived abuses of *buy-sell agreements and options*. For example, the *Congressional Record* states that:

> [T]he committee is aware of the potential of buy-sell agreements for distorting transfer tax value. Therefore, the committee establishes rules that attempt to distinguish between arrangements designed to avoid estate taxes and those with legitimate business agreements. The rules generally disregard a buy-sell agreement that would not have been entered into by unrelated parties acting at arm's length. 136 Cong. Rec. S15681 (10/18/90).
>
> The bill does not affect minority discounts or other discounts available under present law.

In the Conference Report under the heading "Buy-Sell Agreements and Options," it is stated:

> [T]he conferees do not intend the provision governing buy-sell agreements to disregard such an agreement merely because its terms differ from those used by another similarly situated [entity] . . . H.R. Rep. 964, 101st Cong., 2d Sess. 1137 (1990).

The Senate Report statement reads that, apart from the restrictions concerning acquisition or use of the property addressed in the bill, the bill does not otherwise alter the requirements for giving weight to a buy-sell agreement. For example, it leaves intact present law rules requiring that an agreement have lifetime restrictions in order to be binding on death.

These sources of legislative history demonstrate that Congress's intent in enacting IRC § 2703 was *not* to deny the existence of valid partnerships but rather to combat potential abuses associated with certain buy-sell agreements. Thus, the IRS interpretation of the statute, as set forth in the Technical Advice Memorandums (TAMs), is contrary to Congress's intent.

The IRS interpretation of IRC § 2703(a) also is inconsistent with the Code's statutory construction. The IRS view of § 2703(a) supersedes the need for § 2704, which covers restrictions in an agreement with respect to liquidation. Under Treasury Regulation § 25.2704-2(b), any option, right to use property, or agreement covered by § 2703(a) is not covered by § 2704(b). Thus, to the extent that § 2703(a) applies to a restriction, § 2704(b) is ignored.

If the IRS interpretation of § 2703(a) is adopted and the existence of a partnership can be ignored, all restrictions affecting the rights of partners are covered by § 2703(a) and nothing remains to be addressed by § 2704(b). Taken to its logical conclusion, the IRS view assumes that Congress passed a meaningless statute in the form of § 2704(b).

The IRS interpretation also is contrary to the Treasury Department's intent and the construction of regulations under § 2703. It does not appear that Treasury intended that § 2703 could be applied to disregard a partnership when valuing property for federal transfer tax purposes. This is evident in Treasury Regulation § 25.2703-1, which states that "a right or restriction may be contained in a partnership agreement, articles of incorporation, corporate bylaws, a shareholder's agreement, or any other agreement." This language is different from "a right or restriction may be a partnership or a partnership agreement," which would be the appropriate language if Treasury had believed that legal entities established under state law should be ignored.

Additionally, if a partnership or corporation could be disregarded under § 2703, Treasury would not have stated in paragraph (b)(5) of Treasury Regulation § 25.2703-1 that:

> *[I]f property is subject to more than one right or restriction described in [section 2703(a)], the failure of a right or restriction to satisfy the requirements of [section 2703(b)] does not cause any other right or restriction to fail to satisfy those requirements if the right or restriction otherwise meets those requirements. Whether separate provisions are separate rights or restrictions, or are integral parts of a single right or restriction, depends on all the facts or circumstances.*

Logically, if a partnership can be disregarded under § 2703 as a "restriction," there is no need to elaborate on the subject of multiple restrictions. If the IRS view of § 2703 is adopted, paragraph (b)(5) is void of meaning. This could not have been Treasury's intent.

Since the IRS interpretation of IRC Code § 2703(a) is contrary to Congress's and Treasury's intent and to the statutory construction of the Code and regulations, it should be rejected, and § 2703(a) should not be applied in a manner that disregards the creation of a partnership. Nonetheless, the broad manner in which the statute and regulations are written and the lack of substantial legislative history enable the IRS to credibly argue that § 2703 can be applied to disregard a partnership for federal transfer tax valuation purposes.

Section 2704.   Section 2704 is intended to accomplish two purposes:

1. Section 2704(a) treats the lapse of certain rights as a gift by, or as includible in the estate of, the owner of the lapsed right
2. Section 2704(b) disregards certain restrictions on the ability of an entity to liquidate when determining the estate or gift tax value of the interest to which the restriction applies

Section 2704(a).   Section 2704(a) provides that, if certain control criteria exist, a lapse of any voting, liquidation, or similar right in a partnership will be treated as a transfer for gift tax purposes by, or, if applicable, will be included in the estate of, the individual who held the right immediately before the lapse. Section 2704(a) applies only if, both before and after the lapse, the individual holding the lapsed right immediately before the lapse and members of such individual's family control the partnership (§ 2704[a][1][B]).

The definition of control for partnerships is different for a general partnership than for a limited partnership. For a general partnership, control means "the holding of at least 50 percent of the capital or profit interests in the partnership" (§§ 2704[c][1] and 2701[b][2][B][i]). For a limited partnership, control means "the holding of any interest as a general partner" (§§ 2704[c][1] and 2701 [b][2][B][ii]).

Most family limited partnership agreements contain provisions that cause a general partnership interest to convert to a limited partnership interest upon the occurrence of certain triggering events (e.g., transfer, death, bankruptcy). The conversion of a general partnership interest to a limited partnership interest does constitute a lapse of voting and liquidation rights and thus will be subject to § 2704(a). As a result, the general partnership interest must be valued as if there had been no lapse in the general partner's voting and liquidation rights. This means that any lapsed rights will be assumed to have not lapsed, thus increasing the value.

> To avoid the negative impact § 2704(a) can have on the estate tax value of a limited partnership interest, it is better if the limited partner does *not* own a general interest in the partnership at death. Alternatively, the limited partner can gift all of his or her limited interest before he or she dies. The GP can also be a separate entity.

Section 2704(b).   Under § 2704(b), if a person transfers an interest in a partnership to (or for the benefit of) a family member and the transferor and members of the transferor's family control the entity immediately *before* the transfer, then the transferred interest will be valued without considering any "applicable restriction."

An "applicable restriction" means any restriction that limits the ability of a partnership to liquidate if:

- The restriction lapses, in whole or in part, after a transfer of an interest in the partnership to (or for the benefit of) a member of the transferor's family; or
- After the transfer, the transferor or any member of the transferor's family (either alone or collectively) has the right to remove the restriction in whole or in part (§ 2704[b][2]).

Section 2704(b)(3) provides two exceptions to the definition of an applicable restriction:

1. An applicable restriction does not include a commercially reasonable restriction that arises as part of any corporate or partnership financing with a person who is not related to the transferor, the transferee, or a family member of either
2. An applicable restriction does not include any restriction imposed, or required to be imposed, by federal or state law

Thus, despite the enactment of § 2704, the exceptions to § 2704 provide at least three situations where an FLP can be used to reduce the estate or gift tax value of a limited partnership interest. An FLP arrangement may generate estate and gift tax valuation discounts when:

- One or more of the general partners are not family members
- A liquidation restriction is imposed as part of a financing arrangement with an unrelated party
- A liquidation restriction is imposed under federal or state law.

A restriction that requires the unanimous consent of all of the partners to be removed should be respected notwithstanding § 2704(b), provided there is at least one unrelated general partner in the partnership and, under state law, the family members by themselves cannot have the restriction removed.

If one or more of the general partners are not family members and the liquidation restriction does not lapse in whole or in part after the transfer, the restriction should be respected because it cannot be removed by the transferor or members of his or her family either alone or collectively. However, the ability to remove the restriction is determined by reference to the state law that would apply but for a more restrictive rule in the governing instrument of the partnership.

If a general partnership interest is given to a charitable organization, for example, and the organization's consent is required, under the partnership agreement and applicable state law, to liquidate the partnership or an interest therein, arguably the provisions of § 2704(b) should not apply and the value of a limited interest in the partnership may be determined by applying valuation discounts thereto. This technique also could be used by giving a general partnership interest to a nonfamily member rather than to a charitable organization.

In summary, if an FLP violates any of the provisions of Chapter 14 (IRC § 2701, 2703, or 2704), it can be detrimental to the valuation of the FLP. It is best to avoid the application of Chapter 14.

For instance, under § 2701, if the only differences between the senior and junior equity instrument are those of management, voting, or liability, then the complex and negative impact of the code section will not apply.

Under IRC § 2703, it is important to make sure that all provisions under the three-part test are satisfied:

1. Bona fide business purpose
2. Not a device to transfer
3. Similar to other arm's-length transactions

Under IRC § 2704, it is important to make sure that none of rights in the FLP lapse upon death or transfer. The liquidation restrictions should be no more restrictive than the governing state law.

Accordingly, the underlying provisions of Chapter 14 add a substantial level of complexity and possible detrimental impact on the valuation. If these provisions are triggered, a qualified professional with a good grasp of these provisions should be consulted.

NEW DEVELOPMENTS IN CHAPTER 14

The elements of Chapter 14 of the Internal Revenue Code were being advanced in the mid- to late 1990s as a basis for the IRS to argue against family limited partnerships. During those early private letter rulings and some of the case law, the government was relatively unsuccessful in advancing these arguments. However, in a recent case, the government was successful in making a Chapter 14 argument under Internal Revenue

Code section 2703 (a)(2). This was primarily a result of some specific provisions that were put in place in the partnership agreement. The case is *Estate of Holman vs. Commissioner*, 130 T. C. No. 12, May 27, 2008.

This case involved the petitioner, Thomas H. Holman, Jr., who was employed by Dell Computer Corp. from October 1988 through November 2001. During this time Holman received substantial stock options, some of which were exercised. The petitioner's main annual gifts of the Dell stock were to three custodial accounts under the Texas Uniform Transfer to Minors Act. Initially, Holman served as custodian for the accounts until he resigned in August 1999 and was replaced by his mother. At the time of his resignation, the accounts held 10,030 shares of Dell stock.

In late 1997, after moving to St. Paul, Minnesota, from Texas, the petitioners met with an estate planning attorney to discuss estate planning and wealth management issues, including the use of FLPs. These discussions lasted for two years until an FLP was formed. Holman stated that he had four reasons for forming a family limited partnership:

- Very long-term growth
- Asset preservation
- Asset protection
- Education

He stated: "The preservation of capital is important to us. We did not want our daughters to just go blow this money. . . . We really are concerned about negatively affecting their lives with the wealth, so by creating a partnership, we can establish a vehicle that preserves the wealth and such that the kids won't go off and spend it."

Holman also said: "Long-term asset growth to us meant that we're looking at assets for the benefit of the family over decades. Preservation really meant that they wanted a vehicle where our children would be demotivated and disincentivized to spend the assets. Protection . . . we were worried that the assets that the girls would eventually come into would be sought after by third-party people, friends, spouses, potential creditors."

The partnership agreement had various provisions in them, including the following:

- The purposes of the Partnership are to make a profit, increase wealth, and provide a means for the Family to gain knowledge of, manage, and preserve Family Assets
- The General Partners shall have exclusive management and control of the business of the Partnership, and all decisions regarding the management and affairs of the Partnership shall be made by the General Partners. . . . [Specifically,] they shall have the power and authority . . . 1) to determine the investments and investment strategy of the Partnership
- No Limited Partner may withdraw from the Partnership except as may be expressly provided in this Agreement
- A Limited Partner may not, without the prior written consent of all Partners, assign/encumber his or her Interest in the Partnership, except as permitted by this Agreement
- If an assignment of a Partnership Interest occurs that is prohibited or rendered void by the terms of this Agreement, but the General Partners determine that such

assignment is nevertheless effective according to then-applicable law, the Partnership shall have the option (but not the obligation) to acquire the Interest of the assignee or transferee upon the following terms and conditions:

- The Partnership will have the option to acquire the Interest by giving written notice within 90 days
- Unless the Partnership and the transferee/assignee agree otherwise, the purchase price for the interest or any fraction to be acquired by the Partnership shall be its FMV based upon the assignee's right to share in distributions, as determined by an appraisal performed by an independent appraiser selected by the General Partners

There were various gifts of limited partnership interests made over the years. These gifts were the subject of this court case. Upon the formation of the partnership, there was no plan other than to hold the Dell shares. Dell shares were the only assets as of all dates of gifts. At no time from the formation through 2001 did the partnership have a business plan and had no annual statements. The partnership had no employees and no telephone listing in any directory.

The IRS argued provisions under Chapter 14 as follows:

> Alternatively, it is determined that the transferred interest in the Holman Limited Partnership should be valued without regard to any restriction on the right to sell or use the partnership interest within the meaning of IRC Section 2703(a)(2).

> Alternatively, it is determined that certain restrictions on liquidation of the Holman Limited Partnership interests contained in the articles of organization and operating agreement should be disregarded for valuation purposes pursuant to IRC Section 2704(b).

The court decided that Internal Revenue Code section 2703(a) does not apply if the three-part test is satisfied under Internal Revenue Code section 2703(b), which includes a bona fide business arrangement, not a device to transfer at below fair market value and comparable terms that would be negotiated in an arm's-length transaction. As such, the court turned its view to the various provisions in the partnership agreement, specifically paragraphs 9.1, 9.2, and 9.3, which governed the assignment of limited partnership units. The court stated: "The restrictions on transferability, the right of first refusal, and the payout mechanism in 9.1, 9.2, and 9.3 of the partnership agreement serve a bona fide business purpose, by preventing interests from passing to nonfamily members."

The courts found the redemption provisions and restrictions to be a device to transfer at less than fair market value to the "natural objects of the petitioner's bounty." Ultimately, because the provisions allowed the partnership the option to acquire the interest by giving written notice within 90 days at a discounted value based on the assignee's right to his or her share of distributions, the courts felt this option would always be exercised. To the extent that interests are acquired at a discount, this benefited the remaining interest holders. Accordingly, given the single holding of Dell stock, no real business operations, and the implicit restrictions in the agreement on transferability and operation, the courts found that Internal Revenue Code section 2703(a) applied.

TIERED DISCOUNTS

In recent years, there has been much discussion regarding the application of tiered discounts in a family limited partnership structure. The applicability of tiered discounts was validated in a recent court case (*Astleford v. Commissioner*—TCM 2008-128. May 5, 2008). We will summarize the case in this section as an illustration of how tiered discounts have applied. However, in any circumstance, it is important to consider the business purpose for creating nested entities beyond the impact on the discounts. As you'll see from the *Astleford* case, there were various discounts at various levels, with nested entities or interests subject to different risks and ownership.

The *Astleford* case was dealing with various gifted interests at August 1, 1996, and December 1, 1997. It also involves an interest in a general partnership that held interest in real property subject to an absorption discount, as well as an interest in a limited partnership that held the interest in the general partnership. More specifically, Mr. Astleford formed the general partnership in 1970 with an unrelated party named Pine Bend Development Company. This partnership was a 50-50 partnership. The partnership purchased 3,000 acres near St. Paul, Minnesota, including 1,187 acres of farmland in Rosemount. About February 20, 1992, Mr. Astleford and his wife created separate revocable trusts in which they transferred various interest in real property to the trusts. Mr. Astleford passed away April 1, 1995. On August 1, 1996, Mrs. Astleford formed Astleford Family Limited Partnership.

On August 1, 1996, Mrs. Astleford funded the FLP by transferring her ownership interest in an eldercare assisted living facility with a stipulated value of $870,904. Also on August 1, 1996, she gave each of her three children a 30 percent limited partnership interest in the FLP, retaining for herself a 10 percent general partnership interest. On December 1, 1997, as an additional capital contribution to the FLP, she transferred her 50 percent interest in Pine Bend, as well as her ownership interest in 14 other real estate properties located in the Minneapolis–St. Paul area.

The tiered discount element comes into play in valuing the FLP interest, since the FLP owns the 5 percent general partnership interest in Pine Bend, which in turn owns a substantial parcel of real property ultimately determined to be subject to an absorption discount. Effectively in this case, a discount was taken on the real property as part of determining the value of the Pine Bend interest. Further, a discount was taken in determining the value of the 5 percent interest in Pine Bend for both minority and marketability. This discounted general partnership interest was then used as part of the net asset value in determining the value of the FLP, which once again was discounted in determining the value of the specific FLP interest. Effectively, there were three levels of discounts in this case, first at the real property level, second at the general partnership level, and third at the FLP level. Although the government argued that the tiered discounts should not be allowed and in fact wanted no discounts applied to the Pine Bend interest at all, the courts found otherwise.

The court noted that both the court and the respondent had previously accepted and allowed tiered discounts in minority owning minority situations. They cited the following cases: *Estate of Piper v. Commissioner*, 72 T.C. 1062, 1085 (1979); *Janda v. Commissioner*, TCM 2001-24; *Gow v. Commissioner*, TCM 2000-93, affd. 19 Fed. Appx. 90 (4th Cir. 2001); *Gallun v. Commissioner*, TCM

1974-284. They also noted that the courts have rejected tiered discounts where the lower-level interest constituted a significant portion of the parent entities assets, such as in the case of *Martin v. Commissioner*, TCM 1985-424 (minority interests in subsidiaries comprised 75 percent of parent entity's assets) or where the lower-level interest was the parent entities' "principal operating subsidiary"; see *Estate of O'Connell v. Commissioner*, TCM 1978-191, affd. On this point, revd. On other issues 640 F.2d 249 (9th Cir. 1981).

In this case, the 50 percent Pine Bend interest constituted less than 16 percent of the FLP's net asset value and was only one of 15 real estate investments held by the FLP. As such, the tiered discounts were allowed.

Valuation Process

The valuation of an FLP interest carries with it many of the same considerations that exist in the valuation of other closely held investments. For instance:

- Consideration must be given to the three basic approaches to valuation (asset, income, and market)
- The approach that is given the most weight is dependent on the interest being valued as well as the facts and circumstances in a given case

The following are some of the key factors and definitions controlling FLP valuations.

Lack of an Available Public Market

Many partnerships are nontraded investment vehicles designed to be held by original family members until such time as the partnership sponsor elects to sell the underlying assets and make liquidating distributions to the partners. Unlike securities traded in the public markets, there is not a readily available reference source to assist in establishing these partnerships' fair market values. Although there exists a "secondary market" in which publicly held partnership interests are thinly traded, the transaction volume for them is insufficient to constitute a true market.

Net Asset Value

Due to the highly restrictive nature of limited partnership interests in FLPs, the right to receive distributions represents the most significant economic benefit due to the limited partners. Net asset value represents the theoretical cash distribution (net of costs) that would be available to the partners in the event of an immediate, all-cash sale of the partnership's underlying assets.

Liquidation Rights of General and Limited Partners

While the value of liquidation rights is important to family members and should be considered in the valuation of any FLP interests, the significance of these rights is reduced in instances where liquidations are neither imminent nor certain.

Individually and collectively, partners may not be able to determine the timing or amount of distributions, control the purchase or sale of assets, or set management policies. Therefore, the complete lack of liquidation rights of the limited partners may add significantly to the discount for lack of control.

Fair Market Value

The appropriate measure of value for FLP limited partnership interests is fair market value. Long-standing regulations and rulings, such as Treasury Regulation 20.2031-1(b) and Revenue Ruling 59-60, 1959-1 C.B. 237, have provided definitions for fair market value and guidelines for estate and gift tax valuations for more than 40 years and have been referenced in numerous legal cases.

If fair market value is the appropriate standard of value, factors influencing the pricing of partnership interests in secondary transactions may be considered.

Investment Factors Considered by Limited Partnership Investors

Typical considerations of investors in partnership investments where a market exists provide some foundation for understanding how an investor may look at an interest in an FLP. However, FLPs may have characteristics similar in nature but often inferior to those with some market in which to transact.

Buyers and sellers of securities (including partnership interests) express their preferences with respect to a number of investment characteristics when they evaluate buy and sell decisions. Buy/sell preferences for partnership interests are principally driven by these factors:

- Secondary market liquidity and investment control
- Cash flow and distributions
- Asset type and quality
- Management capabilities and fee structure
- Market capitalization
- Portfolio diversification
- Capital structure (debt versus equity)
- Liquidation time horizon
- Goodwill
- Recent historical performance
- Analytical complexity

Secondary Market Liquidity and Investment Control.   Due to the restrictive nature of partnership agreements and state law, a limited partner in a publicly traded partnership may be explicitly prohibited from exercising control over the operations of the partnership. Given the absence of control, often the only means of exercising choice regarding a limited partnership interest is through selling the interest on the secondary market.

The market normally applies an adjustment for absence of control. This adjustment is often smaller for partnership interests that actively transact on the secondary market (exhibit liquidity) and larger for partnership interests that seldom or never change hands in secondary transactions (are virtually illiquid). The premise underlying these adjustments is that the negative consequences associated with lack of control are decreased in instances where a relatively liquid secondary market exists and are increased when liquidation through sale of the partnership interest in a secondary transaction is not possible or is severely limited.

Cash Flow and Distributions. Partnership interest investors can receive economic benefits through distributions of current cash flow and/or the cash resulting from the sale or financing of assets. However, since individual investors in limited partnership interests have limited control over partnership distribution policies and the timing of asset sales/financings or resulting distributions, they place heavy emphasis on current cash flow distributions when making investment decisions.

Since secondary market investors express a strong preference for current distributions, partnerships that distribute amounts in excess of existing current cash flow from existing cash balances usually carry larger discounts or lower value. Some partnerships historically accumulated cash and distributed it years after it was generated. This is an indication the current distribution level cannot be sustained. Alternatively, partnerships that have strong current cash flows and distribution that are supported by current partnership operations usually will carry smaller discounts.

Asset Type and Quality. The economic benefits investors in partnership interests receive will depend on the performance of the existing partnership asset pool over the expected remaining investment-holding period. Unlike operating companies, partnerships generally do not sell or finance assets and reinvest the resulting proceeds in new assets. As a consequence, partnership investors are highly concerned with the type and quality of assets held in a partnership portfolio at the time of investment. Accordingly, adjustments to net asset value will be made for partnerships that own assets of inferior quality and/or are out of favor with investors.

Management Capabilities and Fee Structure. For a partnership expected to operate indefinitely, an evaluation of management capabilities, fee structure, and financial incentives is critical in an investor's decision to buy or sell a partnership interest.

The market can reflect premiums for partnerships operated by respected management companies, which charge reasonable fees and have adequate incentives and a demonstrated capability to create value. The market usually penalizes management that has a poor reputation.

Market Capitalization. In the markets for publicly traded securities, a security's market capitalization influences the amount of attention it receives from investors. This principle also holds true in the secondary market for partnership securities. Larger issues with significant equity receive more attention from the brokerage community and from secondary market firms than smaller partnerships with less current equity. This increase in buy-side interest increases demand for the partnership interests and results in higher prices paid by secondary market buyers.

The market usually applies a larger adjustment to net asset value to reflect the negative influence of small market capitalization on the partnership's unit price.

Portfolio Diversification. Partnerships with concentrated ownership in a single asset or in a pool of assets with very similar investment characteristics are inherently more risky than partnerships that are broadly diversified. As such, the market usually adjusts the net asset value to account for the impact of such risks on the partnership's unit price.

Capital Structure (Debt versus Equity). Financial leverage increases risk. Accordingly, larger adjustments may be appropriate in partnerships with high debt levels.

Liquidation Time Horizon. For partnerships with extended liquidation time horizons, net asset value becomes a factor of diminishing importance and operating risks become a more significant consideration. The opposite is true for partnerships expected to liquidate in the near term. The market usually applies larger adjustments to net asset value for partnerships not expected to liquidate in the near term.

Goodwill. In a few instances, investors demonstrate strong favor for certain partnership investments due to name recognition or other "intangibles." In such instances, the market applies premiums to net asset value to account for the influence of these factors on the price of the partnership interest.

Recent Historical Performance. Partnership family members are strongly influenced by recent performance trends. Recent and significant changes in partnership's distributions/cash flow or reported changes in the performance of a partnership's underlying assets will impact the pricing of a partnership interest.

Analytical Complexity. Numerous factors can complicate the analysis of a partnership investment. Such factors may include complex financial reporting, convoluted joint venture structures, inadequate disclosure by management, and ownership of difficult-to-value assets.

Partnership family members favor simplicity. Accordingly, the market usually applies larger adjustments to net asset value for partnerships that are difficult to evaluate.

Other Factors That Affect Value and Need to Be Considered

- Provisions in the partnership agreement or in the certificate of limited partnership that the partnership shall continue to exist for a definite term of years, unless dissolved or liquidated prior thereto
- The reputation, integrity and perceived competence of the partnership's management/general partner(s)
- Lack of guarantees by general partner(s) regarding the return of partner capital contributions, allocations of profits or losses, or cash distributions, including amounts to cover the tax burden
- Exclusion of limited partners from participation in management and approval rights of limited partners required for certain major decisions
- Means by which new managing general partners are elected
- Number of investors in the partnership
- Type and diversification of assets owned by the partnership

- Amount of debt in the partnership's capital structure
- Degree and reliability of the information flow to the limited partners
- General partner rights to determine distributable cash
- Current and historical amount of cash actually distributed to partners and assignees
- Underlying cash flow coverage of yearly distributions made to partners and assignees
- Capital call provisions obligating limited partners and assignees to contribute more capital
- Limitations on the voluntary and involuntary transferability of general partner limited partner, and assignee interests
- Presence of rights of first refusal for transfers
- Size of the partnership interest
- Universe of interested buyers
- Limitations such as:
  - A transferee or assignee of an interest in the partnership will not become a substituted limited partner unless approved by the consent of all partners
  - Whether the managing general partners or general partners are required to make an IRC § 754 election to step up the basis in the assets at the date of transfer. This would eliminate exposure to capital gains and increase depreciation on certain assets
  - The right of the general partner to withdraw from the partnership prior to the expiration of its stated term
  - The right of a limited partner or assignee to withdraw from the partnership prior to the expiration of its stated term
- Provisions for dissolution of the partnership that do or do not mirror the provisions of state law
- The "Default Rules" under state law. All states have partnership acts. However, not all states have the same provision language.

Evaluating and Understanding the Financial Components

The analyst needs to evaluate and understand the following financial components of a partnership at a minimum:

- Assets
- Liabilities
- Income
- Expenses
- Distributions
- Investment yield

The next sections provide an in-depth discussion of these key financial components.

Assets. The analyst needs to understand the underlying risk associated with an FLP's assets, incuding its liquidity, its ability to appreciate and generate cash flows, and its respective lives. Assets are usually some combination of closely held business interests, real estate, or marketable securities and cash, and possibly other assets, such as art collections or other valuable personal property and patents, copyrights, or other intangibles. Generally, the less risky the underlying partnership assets, the higher the value of the FLP.

> Assets within a particular category may produce different impacts on value. For instance, if an FLP is holding undeveloped land instead of an income-producing property, its value will be influenced by the inability of the undeveloped land to generate a return to partners other than through ongoing appreciation and possible liquidation of the asset.

Another reason for understanding the asset base of an FLP is that it can have an impact on the sources of data to be used in the context of the valuation. Such data sources will be discussed in another section.

Liabilities.   Liabilities are also important in the context of the valuation due to the impact they may have on the equity of the asset base as well as the cash flows generated from the underlying assets and operations. High levels of debt increase the exposure of the asset base and related cash flows to instability and other risks. The existence of debt allows fluctuations in asset value to impact and erode partnership ownership values. In addition, the existence of a debt service obligation creates a fixed-cost component that can substantially impair the FLP's ability to cover other expenses or make distributions. Other similarly value-eroding factors are future obligations, such as balloon payments on loans, deferred maintenance costs, or development costs associated with real estate assets. All of these factors negatively impact the FLP's ability to provide a return to the partners and, thus, negatively impact value.

Income, Expenses, and Distributions.   An FLP's ability to generate an income stream and provide distributions to partners is important. In some cases, the only distribution to partners comes upon liquidation of partnership assets and/or termination of the partnership. Potential investors seek ongoing liquidity and returns. Thus, FLP values are often heavily discounted due to lack of liquidity and lack of returns.

The analyst needs to understand the subject FLP's ability to generate income as well as its expense structure (including debt service) to fully assess its impact on distributions and value.

Investment Yield.   All of the above factors directly influence FLP investment yield as does the general investment rule that high-yield assets typically carry higher levels of associated risk.

In FLPs, there are two types of yields to consider:

1. Yield within the partnership (i.e., net cash flow plus appreciation generated by the partnership)
2. Distribution yield to the partners (based on actual distributions made)

These yields may be different percentages because most partnerships do not distribute 100 percent of the cash flow generated, plus the first kind of yield includes capital appreciation on assets, if any.

Valuing an FLP Using the Income Approach

In some cases, valuation professionals will try to value family limited partnerships utilizing an income approach. Although this has some appeal, it may be difficult to apply in practical circumstances for a number of reasons. These reasons include the following:

- The partnership may not be deriving a substantial amount of income from the underlying assets and may be more focused on asset appreciation versus cash flow. In such a circumstance, there is little if any benefit stream to be discounted or capitalized.
- The partnership may not be providing distributions to the investors. As such, even if the partnership is generating income, an investor is still not receiving ongoing returns from his or her investment.
- The value of the underlying investments may have been factored in the income streams generated from the investments. This would be the case, as it relates to the value of commercial real estate properties. In this regard, a commercial real estate appraiser will typically capitalize the cash flows from the real estate at the appropriate capitalization rate derived from other real estate investments and the marketplace. To utilize the same cash flows in the context of valuing the family limited partnership could potentially duplicate the efforts of the real estate appraiser. Consequently, the value of those cash flows has already been incorporated in the underlying property value and should not be reconsidered.
- The ability to derive an appropriate rate of return to use as the discount rate or capitalization rate in this context is problematic at best. Clearly, we may be able to derive what the market rate returns are for various investment vehicles. However, the majority of these returns are based upon direct ownership of the various investments, which is not the case for a limited partnership. To incorporate the lack of control and lack of marketability discounts into the rate of return may confuse the issues of investment risk, control, and marketability, which have historically been separate issues in the context of a valuation.

If it were possible to reconcile the various templates necessary to calculate the value on an income-based approach, valuing a family limited partnership would consider the following factors and resemble the following analysis:

Assume that the portfolio includes cash of $100,000, bonds of $400,000, and securities of $500,000. Accordingly, the weighting between the various asset classes would be 10 percent, 40 percent, and 50 percent respectively. This analysis will require us to find a reasonable rate of return based upon market derived information for each of the asset classes held by the partnership. These returns can be based upon current yield or historical yield of the portfolio or comparable portfolios, if available. However, it is important to consider whether the yields derived are based upon cash flows and/or distributions only, or if they include capital appreciation. Assuming that the market rate returns for the respective asset classes were 3 percent for cash, 5 percent for bonds, and 12 percent for securities, we can determine the weighted average return for the family limited partnership holdings as follows:

	Values	Percentage	Returns	Weighted Returns
Cash	$ 100,000	10.0%	3.0%	0.3%
Bonds	400,000	40.0%	5.0%	2.0%
Securities	500,000	50.0%	12.0%	6.0%
	$1,000,000	100.0%		8.3%

Accordingly, the weighted return associated with the above analysis would be 8.3 percent based upon a diversified portfolio of direct interests held in the investments. In that regard, this return would need to be adjusted upward to take into consideration the elements of control and marketability that may not exist in the interest held in a family limited partnership.[1] This adjustment would be subjective and based upon the judgment of the valuation professional and as such would be subject to more scrutiny, especially given the fact that there is no empirically derived evidence to directly support it. For the sake of illustration, let's assume that this additional adjustment in this case would be 3 percent. This would result in an overall capitalization rate of 11.3 percent. This capitalization rate would then be applied to the estimated returns expected from the investment portfolio, as follows:

	Values	Percentage Returns	Dollar Returns
Cash	$ 100,000	3.0%	$ 3,000
Bonds	400,000	5.0%	20,000
Securities	500,000	12.0%	60,000
	$1,000,000		$ 83,000
Capitalization Rate			11.3%
Partnership Value			$734,515
Resulting Discount from NAV			26.5%

Although this analysis results in a discount of 26.5 percent, it is based upon dollars and returns derived by the use of estimated percent returns, which may not be consistent with the actual returns on the portfolio or at the partners' investment level. Although it is possible to use the income approach in the valuation of the family limited partnership, it needs to be cautiously applied, and limitations need to be considered.

Sources of Information to Assist in FLP Valuations

Numerous sources of information can assist in the valuation of FLPs. Some provide empirical data as a basis to understand the difference in value from the underlying assets or cash flow to the interest to be valued. These sources include the traditional initial public offering (IPO) and restricted stock studies and the Quantitative Marketability Discount Model (QMDM) for quantifying a marketability discount, all of which have been discussed elsewhere in this book (Chapter 9).

However, other available data sources are specific to the valuation of an FLP. The specific data source used will be dictated by the underlying asset breakdown of the FLP and the facts in a given case. Next we will focus on several of the more commonly used data sources.

---

[1] If the income approach is used, some analysts may apply discounts similar to how they do so in an asset method.

Data Sources for Family Limited Partnerships Holding Marketable Securities.
An FLP holding marketable securities has many characteristics in common with a
closed-end fund. Accordingly, most practitioners utilize an analysis of closed-end
mutual funds as a foundation for determining either a discount or a multiple to be
applied to the net asset value of the FLP.

Some of the reasons that closed-end funds are useful sources of empirical data
by which to value FLP interests follow.

1. *Breadth of asset mix and size of universe.* There are literally hundreds of closed-
   end funds available, all offering numerous specialized investment options.
2. *Fund unit prices represent minority interests.* The prices paid for publicly traded
   closed-end fund units represent minority interests that are otherwise fully marketable. Therefore, if the net asset values of a closed-end fund can be found and
   compared with the freely traded price of the fund units, it can be determined
   when and under what conditions the market applies an adjustment (positive or
   negative) to the net asset value of a minority interest.

> The closed-end funds to be used should match as closely as possible the
> specific portfolio structure of the FLP. For instance, if the FLP is hold-
> ing only technology stock and some blue chips, the closed-end funds
> selected should have a similar asset mix so that they will appropriately
> reflect the market perception of risk for the type of portfolio being held
> by the FLP.

3. *Ownership restrictions.* A closed-end fund issues a fixed number of shares that
   does not change over the life of the fund. Investors desiring to own shares in the
   fund must purchase the shares from other closed-end fund shareholders, not
   from the fund itself. When the demand for units in a closed-end fund increases,
   the unit price of the fund increases. This is more consistent with an FLP with a
   specified number of units issued.

> As a point of reference, publicly traded open-end mutual funds issue
> and redeem shares directly to and from the fund itself. Consequently, if
> the demand for an open-end fund increases, the fund issues more
> shares. An open-end mutual fund normally prices unit purchases and
> redemptions at the transaction cost adjusted net asset value. Therefore,
> these types of funds will continually dilute and grow with purchases
> and shrink with sales. Typically, they do not experience the relative
> price fluctuations that closed-end funds do.

4. *Similar base for net asset values.* The net asset value of a closed-end fund is the aggregate value of the stocks and bonds owned by the fund, and the transactions in a closed-end fund take place at the current trading unit price of the fund. This trading unit price may be equal to, more than, or less than the net asset value per unit.

5. *Similar investor lack-of-control issues.* An investor in a closed-end fund does not have any ability to control, manage, or otherwise determine the nature of the investments made by the fund manager, although he or she has some assurance that the fund will continue to invest in certain types of investments based on its stated investment objectives. The investor's only choice is whether to continue as an investor in the fund or to liquidate the investment and invest in a different fund. Accordingly, ownership interests in closed-end mutual funds have many of the same lack of control characteristics and restrictions as FLP ownership interests have.

Analysis of closed-end funds with similar investment characteristics to the subject FLP can provide an indication of the adjustment to net asset value that the market would require.

6. *Abundance of data sources.* Since closed-end funds are publicly traded, numerous sources of data regarding them are available. In fact, any service that provides public market data typically can provide information related to closed-end funds.

One such source is Morningstar—Principia Pro.[2] This subscription service listing closed-end securities allows the analyst to sort over 600 closed-end funds using various search criteria including fund type, performance, risk, portfolio, and operations. Each search criteria provides a wealth of subcategories to enable the analyst to narrow the scope of the search. A sample of search results from Morningstar is included as Exhibit 14.5 later in this chapter. Morningstar provides historical and current statistics on a fund-by-fund basis as well as the trading price per unit and net asset value per unit. The analyst can evaluate such data based upon industry sectors, portfolio profile, investment objectives, investment duration, and performance to more readily determine the differences between the selected funds and the subject FLP interest.

Since closed-end funds are publicly traded, the difference between the trading price and net asset value has nothing to do with marketability. In addition, some funds are thinly traded and, as a result, are not good indicators of market dynamics.

---

[2] Morningstar Principia Pro for Closed-End Funds, Morningstar, www.morningstar.com.

Data Sources for Family Limited Partnerships Holding Real Estate. Two primary sources of information typically are utilized for valuing an FLP holding real estate: 1) data regarding transactions in real estate investment trusts (REITs), and 2) data regarding transactions in publicly held syndicated real estate limited partnerships (RELPs). Information on REITs is available through brokers who promote such investments or through the National Association of Real Estate Investment Trusts (NAREIT). Data on RELPs are available through Partnership Profiles, Inc.[3] The data from these sources need to be selected carefully to get a meaningful comparison to the subject FLP.

Ownership interests in REITs and publicly held real estate LPs are considered comparable to FLP interests because they have no:

- Control over the distribution of cash flows
- Control over the reinvestment of cash flows
- Control over the liquidation of assets
- Management control or voice

However, unlike most FLPs, REITs have required distribution of substantially all income on an annual basis. This means that they often are not considered as applicable as a source of data for FLP valuation purposes.

1. *REIT Data:* Shows various statistics and historical yields or returns for several types of REITs. These REITs are usually broken down into property type as well as REIT type. REIT data also includes:

   a. Debt structure
   b. Distribution history
   c. Property type
   d. Property diversification

2. *Partnership Profiles* (formerly *The Partnership Spectrum*, a publication of Partnership Profiles, Inc.)[4] conducts studies of secondary market transactions of publicly held real estate limited partnerships to determine the difference between the partnership trading value and the net asset value. These studies primarily sort the information by partnership type and debt structure. However, they also provide information such as distribution yield and trading price per unit versus net asset value per unit. In addition, the analyst can access a specific partnership's financial data filed with the Securities and Exchange Commission for purposes of better analyzing the fit with the subject FLP interest.

---

[3] Annual Partnership Re-Sale Discount Study, which has been replaced by the "Executive Summary Report" published by Partnership Profiles, Inc., Also, Annual Partnership Profiles Minority Interest Discount Database, www.PartnershipProfiles.com.

[4] *The Partnership Spectrum* (Annual May/June Issue). *The Partnership Spectrum* was published by Partnership Profiles, Inc., P.O Box 7938 Dallas, Texas 75209, www.Partnership Profiles.com. The web site now includes the "Minority Interest Discount Database," the "Executive Summary Report," the "Rate of Return Study," "Partnership Guideline Reports," and other information.

Valuation Approaches

The valuation of an FLP interest utilizes the same approaches that are used in the valuation of business interests. The asset, income, and market approaches can all be applicable to FLP interests. The degree of applicability is dependent on the analyst's judgment coupled with the facts and circumstances in the case.

Although there are published methods and discussions of the income approach, for many analysts, FLP valuations are not based on an income approach for two reasons:

1. Many FLPs hold assets that do not generate an ongoing income stream, making the only applicable benefit stream the cash from liquidation at some undefined time in the future
2. The individual asset valuations used in the cost or market approaches may have already incorporated the FLP's benefits streams, and valuing them using the income approach may count them twice

Double counting typically can happen when an FLP holds income-producing real estate. In this case, the underlying real estate appraisal is based on an income or market approach that includes valuing the anticipated benefits from the real estate. To use the same benefit streams again in an income approach could be a mistake. Accordingly, many FLP valuations are based on an asset and/or market approach.

Generally, the analyst will do an analysis of the assets, liabilities, income, expenses, and distributions as discussed above. He or she will do data searches to extract comparable market data from the various data sources. The resulting information will be the foundation for the discount from net asset value of the partnership using the asset approach.

Alternatively, this discount can be applied as a market multiple to net asset value in the context of a market approach. For example, if the closed-end fund analysis provided a discount from net asset value of 10 percent, this would imply a market multiple of 90 percent. The value estimate would be the same; the only difference would be in the means of presentation.

VaiTip

The derived discount from Net Asset Value (NAV) can be viewed in two ways. The first is as a discount as follows:

$$\text{NAV} \times (1 - D) = \text{Value} \quad \text{Where: } D = \text{Discount}$$

$$\$1,000,000 \times (1 - .20) = \$800,000$$

Or it can be viewed as a market multiple as follows:

$$\text{NAV} \times \text{Multiple} = \text{Value}$$

$$\$1,000,000 \times .80 = \$800,000$$

Again, some cases have successfully used a combination of a cost approach and an income approach. However, these cases typically involve FLP interests in which the FLP had the characteristic of a holding entity with regard to real estate and the characteristics of an operating entity because the real estate was a working ranch or farm. It may be less meaningful to use a combination method such as this for an FLP interest holding marketable securities.

ILLUSTRATIVE CASE STUDY

Assume that Chance Family FLP held certain assets as shown in Exhibit 14.1.

Exhibit 14.1 Asset Portfolio

	Marketable Securities:		
Asset Type	**Historical Cost**	**Value**	**% of Asset Mix**
Money Market Funds	$ 251,295	$ 251,295	8.5%
Bond—Fixed Income	265,947	290,278	9.8%
Equities	1,187,937	2,174,981	73.5%
Equity Funds	200,662	241,134	8.2%
Totals	$1,905,841	$2,957,688	100.0%

Real Estate:

Assets	Type	FMV
Property 1	Commercial	$1,125,000
Property 2	Commercial	845,000
Property 3	Commercial	238,000
Totals		$2,208,000

Other Assets: Chance Family FLP held other assets in the form of $10,000 in cash in the bank at the date of valuation. Accordingly, the total assets held by Chance Family FLP are shown in Exhibit 14.2.

Exhibit 14.2 Total Assets

Assets	**Type**	**Amount**	**% of Asset Mix**
Property 1	Commercial	$1,125,000	21.7%
Property 2	Commercial	845,000	16.3%
Property 3	Commercial	238,000	4.6%
Marketable Securities		2,957,688	57.1%
Cash		10,000	0.2%
Totals		$5,175,688	100.0%

The analysis of the historical income, expenses, and distribution is shown in Exhibit 14.3.

Exhibit 14.3 Analysis of Historical Income, Expenses, and Distributions

	20X1	20X2	20X3	20X4	20X5	20X6	Average
Income							
Taxable Interest Income	$ 1,732	$ 975	$ 982	$ 975	$ 541	—	$ 868
Tax-Exempt Income	29,657	24,101	33,473	28,509	33,644	29,238	29,770
Dividend Income	29,380	35,716	44,237	38,544	46,290	32,967	37,856
Net Rents	174,300	174,300	174,300	174,300	174,300	174,300	174,300
Net Capital Gain/(Loss)	7,829	24,563	149,899	17,523	173,850	27,762	66,904
Total Income	$242,898	$259,655	$402,891	$259,851	$428,625	$264,267	$309,698
Expenses							
Guaranteed Payments	$ 6,000	$ 6,000	$ 6,000	$ 6,000	$ 6,000	$ 5,500	$ 5,917
Accounting Fees	—	3,200	—	5,544	3,058	4,291	2,682
Other Expenses	99	238	130	130	33	80	118
Taxes	60	97	82	72	156	144	102
Total Expenses	$ 6,159	$ 9,535	$ 6,212	$ 11,746	$ 9,247	$ 10,015	$ 8,819
Net Income	$236,739	$250,120	$396,679	$248,105	$419,378	$254,252	$300,879
Distributions	—	$ 31,362	$152,617	$216,123	$ 56,650	$ 59,190	$ 85,990

	1995	1996	1997	1998	1999	2000	Average
Income							
Taxable Interest Income	0.71%	0.38%	0.24%	0.38%	0.13%	0.00%	0.28%
Tax-Exempt Income	12.21%	9.28%	8.31%	10.97%	7.85%	11.06%	9.61%
Dividend Income	12.10%	13.76%	10.98%	14.83%	10.80%	12.47%	12.22%
Net Rents	71.76%	67.13%	43.26%	67.08%	40.66%	65.96%	56.28%
Net Capital Gain/(Loss)	3.22%	9.46%	37.21%	6.74%	40.56%	10.51%	21.60%
Total Income	100.00%	100.00%	100.00%	100.00%	100.00%	100.00%	100.00%

Expenses							
Guaranteed Payments	2.47%	2.31%	1.49%	2.31%	1.40%	2.08%	1.91%
Accounting Fees	0.00%	1.23%	0.00%	2.13%	0.71%	1.62%	0.87%
Other Expenses	0.04%	0.09%	0.03%	0.05%	0.01%	0.03%	0.04%
Taxes	0.02%	0.04%	0.02%	0.03%	0.04%	0.05%	0.03%
Total Expenses	2.54%	3.67%	1.54%	4.52%	2.16%	3.79%	2.85%
Net Income	97.46%	96.33%	98.46%	95.48%	97.84%	96.21%	97.15%
Distributions	0.00%	12.08%	37.88%	83.17%	13.22%	22.40%	27.77%
Distributions/Net Income	0.00%	12.54%	38.47%	87.11%	13.51%	23.28%	28.58%
Average Total Income Yield							5.98%
Average Net Income Yield							5.81%
Average Distribution Yield							1.66%

735

As can be seen from the previous information, Chance Family FLP holds a substantial amount of assets with no debt. Approximately 50 percent of the assets are held in a liquid diversified marketable security portfolio, with the remainder held in unencumbered, income-producing real estate. Additionally, the expenses associated with the partnership are low in relation to the total income generated. However, the yields on the investments are low on a cash flow basis, resulting in a total yield of less than 6 percent. The distribution yield (amount paid to partners) is even lower and is below 2 percent.

The analysis incorporated a search of the Partnership Profiles database as well as the Morningstar database to find a portfolio of securities and real estate that is comparable to the holdings of Chance Family FLP. Our search of the Partnership Profiles data was based on finding commercial properties with no debt that are distributing partnerships. Additionally, the search was for those properties that had less than 10 properties owned. (See Exhibit 14.4.)[5]

With respect to the marketable security portfolio, the Morningstar database was searched for the funds that were considered "blue chip" and had fundamental objectives first of growth and secondarily of income. We wanted a diversified mix across various sectors but those that invested primarily in domestic equities due to the holdings of Chance Family FLP. These funds can be summarized as shown in Exhibit 14.5.[6]

Chance Family FLP's expected yield is much lower than the average yield for distributing partnerships and the funds analyzed above. The Chance Family FLP holdings are much smaller than those of the funds and partnerships. This smaller size typically provides for less diversification as well as more exposure to risk. Accordingly, an investor typically requires a higher return from this type of investment compared to the marketplace, given the additional elements of risk inherent in the nature of this investment. Typically these partnerships are more marketable and desirable than Chance Family FLP.

Based on the above information, we then apply the various discount factors to the net asset value of Chance Family FLP in the context of an asset approach as shown in Exhibit 14.6.

For illustrative purposes, we have used the average from the various studies. Some analysts compare specific partnerships and put more weight on certain ones depending on the similarities. Due to the higher risk in Chance than in the real estate partnerships and the closed-end funds, we could have increased the weighted discount from 18.2 percent to somewhere above that amount, say 22 percent. This is subjective but still is warranted since Chance is smaller and enjoys a lower yield, among other risks.

This calculation is representative of the discount for lack of control as it relates to the net asset value in an asset approach. Alternatively, the discount can be converted to a multiple of .78 to be applied to the net asset value in the context of a market approach. After this discount is applied, the resulting value is of a minority, marketable interest in Chance Family FLP.

Accordingly, the analyst needs to apply a marketability discount to obtain a value of the Chance Family FLP interest on a minority, nonmarketable basis. For illustration purposes we have applied a marketability adjustment of 30 percent, as shown in Exhibit 14.7. The analyst would have to support the use of this adjustment based on the analysis and comparisons to various marketability benchmark studies. Marketability discounts are discussed in Chapter 9 of this book.

---

[5] Ibid.
[6] Morningstar Principia Pro for Closed-End Funds, Morningstar © 1996–2001, www.morningstar.com. Used with permission.

Exhibit 14.4 Partnership Profiles

Partnership Detail	Rancon Income Fund I	Wells Real Estate Fund III-A	Wells Real Estate Fund IV-A	Wells Real Estate Fund V-A	Wells Real Estate Fund VI-A
Units Outstanding	14,555	19,635,965	1,322,909	1,556,416	2,188,724
Num. of Props.	3	6	4	5	9
Prop. Types	C, R	C, R	C, R	C	C, R
NAV Per Unit	$368.00	$1.09	$12.17	$11.77	$10.75
Price Per Unit	$263.50	$0.76	$7.70	$7.35	$ 7.50
Annualized Distribution	$ 20.00	$0.07	$0.64	$0.62	$ 0.83
Revenue	$908,000	$1,137,000	$684,000	$706,000	$1,057,000
Operating Surplus	$331,000	$1,653,000	$1,049,000	$1,192,000	$1,789,000
GCF	$22.74	$0.08	$0.79	$0.76	$0.82
NCF	$14.70	$0.08	$0.74	$0.72	$0.81
Property at Cost	$8,320,000	$15,574,000	$9,463,000	$12,178,000	$17,885,000
Cash	$1,208,000	$129,000	$46,000	$22,000	$155,000
Borrowings	—	—	—	—	—
Total NAV	$5,356,240	$21,403,202	$16,099,803	$18,319,016	$23,528,783
Invested Capital	$5,356,240	$21,403,202	$16,099,803	$18,319,016	$23,528,783
Price to NAV	0.716 : 1	0.697 : 1	0.633 : 1	0.624 : 1	0.698 : 1
Borrowings to NAV	0.00%	0.00%	0.00%	0.00%	0.00%
Yield to NAV	5.40%	6.40%	5.30%	5.30%	7.70%
Yield to Price	7.60%	9.20%	8.30%	8.40%	11.10%
Operating Surplus to NAV	6.20%	7.70%	6.50%	6.50%	7.60%
GCF to NAV	6.20%	7.70%	6.50%	6.50%	7.60%
NCF to NAV	4.00%	7.60%	6.10%	6.10%	7.50%

Partnership Detail—Summary

Units Outstanding	Num. of Props.	Prop. Types	Other
24,718,569	27	C, R	
4,943,714	5.4	<=Averages	
Average NAV Per Unit			$80.76
Average Price Per Unit			$57.36
Average Annualized Distribution			$4.43
Average Revenue			$898,400.00
Operating Surplus			$1,202,800.00
Average GCF			$5.04
Average NCF			$3.41
Average Property at Cost			$12,684,000.00
Average Cash			$312,000.00
Average Borrowings			—
Average Total NAV			$16,941,408.80
Invested Capital			$16,941,408.80
Price to NAV			0.6736
Borrowings to NAV			0.00%
Yield to NAV			6.02%
Yield to Price			8.92%
Operating Surplus to NAV			6.90%
GCF to NAV			6.90%
NCF to NAV			6.26%

Exhibit 14.5 Morningstar Blue Chip Funds (Used with Permission)

	Price	NAV	Premium/ Discount	Percent in Cash	Percent in Stocks	Percent in Bonds	Totals	Yield
Avalon Capital	18.13	18.51	−2.1%	N/A	N/A	N/A	N/A	3.2%
Bergstrom Capital	224.00	226.55	−1.1%	1.4%	96.1%	0.0%	97.5%	12.0%
Blue Chip Value	7.55	8.17	−7.6%	7.3%	92.6%	0.0%	99.9%	11.8%
Morgan Funshares	7.00	8.18	−14.4%	1.2%	93.7%	0.0%	94.9%	10.0%
Morgan Grenfell Smallcap	11.75	13.40	−12.3%	5.7%	94.3%	0.0%	100.0%	11.2%
Average	53.69	54.96	−7.5%	3.9%	94.2%	0.0%	98.1%	9.6%
Median	11.75	13.40	−7.6%	3.6%	94.0%	0.0%	98.7%	11.2%
High	224.00	226.55	−14.4%	7.3%	96.1%	0.0%	100.0%	12.0%
Low	7.00	8.17	−1.1%	1.2%	92.6%	0.0%	94.9%	3.2%

	Utilities	Financials	Cyclicals	Durables	Staples	Services	Health	Tech	Totals
Avalon Capital	0.0%	46.4%	1.7%	0.0%	29.2%	22.6%	0.0%	0.0%	99.9%
Bergstrom Capital	0.1%	7.9%	7.5%	0.2%	6.9%	13.4%	29.8%	26.9%	92.7%
Blue Chip Value	2.2%	20.0%	11.7%	2.0%	0.0%	11.1%	7.2%	28.3%	82.5%
Morgan Funshares	0.0%	0.0%	8.1%	2.7%	41.7%	25.0%	22.5%	0.0%	100.0%
Morgan Grenfell Smallcap	0.0%	9.1%	9.0%	2.3%	0.0%	22.5%	13.8%	26.5%	83.2%
Average	0.5%	16.7%	7.6%	1.4%	15.6%	18.9%	14.7%	16.3%	91.7%
Median	0.0%	9.1%	8.1%	2.0%	6.9%	22.5%	13.8%	26.5%	92.7%
High	2.2%	46.4%	11.7%	2.7%	41.7%	25.0%	29.8%	28.3%	100.0%
Low	0.0%	0.0%	1.7%	0.0%	0.0%	11.1%	0.0%	0.0%	82.5%

Exhibit 14.6 Discount Factors

Property	Amount		Average Discount From Studies	Weighted Discount
Property 1	$1,125,000	21.7%	32.64%	7.09%
Property 2	845,000	16.3%	32.64%	5.33%
Property 3	238,000	4.6%	32.64%	1.50%
Marketable Securities	2,957,688	57.1%	7.50%	4.28%
Cash	10,000	0.2%	7.50%	0.02%
Totals	$5,175,688	100.0%	Weighted Avg. =>	18.2%

Exhibit 14.7 Fair Market Value of a 10 percent LP Interest (Illustration only)

Assets

Cash	$ 10,000
Securities	2,957,688
Real Property	2,208,000
Other Assets	—
Total Assets	$5,175,688
Total Liabilities	—
Adjusted Net Assets	$5,175,688
Interest Being Valued	10.0%
Pro rata Enterprise Value	$ 517,569
Valuation Adjustments (22%—Lack of control)	113,865
Adjusted Net Assets (noncontrolling, marketable basis)	$ 403,704
Valuation Adjustments (30.0%—Lack of marketability)	121,111
Fair Market Value of a Ten Percent (10.0%) Limited Partnership Interest (on a noncontrolling, nonmarketable basis)	$ 282,593
Fair Market Value of a Ten Percent (10.0%) Limited Partnership Interest (on a noncontrolling, nonmarketable basis)—rounded	$ 283,000

Many of the marketability discount studies show discounts in the range of 30 percent to 45 percent. We selected 30 percent to reflect the lower discount attributable to the real estate portion (Equity/Net Assets) of the analysis. There is some limited liquidity in sales of interests of partnerships from Partnership Profiles, whereas there is practically instant marketability for sales of interests in the publicly traded closed-end funds. Some analysts will separate the two components (real estate and marketable securities) and apply the discounts separately. For example, the net asset discount for the real estate may have been 15 percent and the securities 40 percent. This would produce a weighted discount for lack of marketability (DLOM) of 30 percent as follows:

$$
\left(\begin{array}{c} \text{Real Estate} \\ \text{FMV} \\ \text{as a \%} \\ \text{of total} \\ \text{asset mix} \end{array}\right) \left(\text{DLOM}\right) + \left(\begin{array}{c} \text{Securities} \\ \text{FMV} \\ \text{as a \% of} \\ \text{total asset} \\ \text{mix} \end{array}\right) \left(\text{DLOM}\right) = \begin{array}{c} \text{WEIGHTED} \\ \text{DLOM} \end{array}
$$

$$
(.427) \qquad (15\%) \quad + \qquad (.573) \qquad (40\%) \quad = 29\%, \text{ say } 30\%
$$

The above case was presented for illustration purposes only relative to the use of the specific data. The numbers, discounts, level of discounts, and the presentations can vary considerably depending on the situation. This example illustrates a technique in a specific presentation style and may not be appropriate in a specific engagement. However, as stated earlier, it is important to describe the factors associated with a specific engagement, and their impact on value, including but not limited to:

- Partnership agreement
- Ownership structure
- State law provisions
- Interest being valued
- Standard of value
- Discount analysis
- IPO studies
- Restricted stock studies
- Other empirical evidence

Although many analysts believe that valuing FLPs is a simple task, at times it can prove to be time consuming and difficult.

Beware of IRC § 2036

Although Internal Revenue Code Section 2036 does not deal with valuation issues, it certainly deals with FLPs. It has become one of the strongest methods used by the Internal Revenue Service in unraveling an FLP structure. Accordingly, it is important that we understand the underpinnings of Section 2036 and that clients know the problems, pitfalls, and concerns.

A number of court decisions have upheld the IRS's position that the entire value of the assets initially transferred by a decedent should be included in his or her estate for death-tax purposes under Section 2036(a) of the Code. Section 2036(a) generally includes the value of any assets transferred during lifetime in the decedent's estate if the decedent retained for his or her life either:

1. The possession, enjoyment, or right to income from the property transferred, or
2. The right, either alone or in conjunction with any person, to designate the person or persons who shall possess or enjoy the property so transferred or the income therefrom.

Both subsections look at whether the transferor actually departed with domin-ion and control of the assets when the assets were transferred to the FLP. If either § 2036(a)(1) or § 2036(a)(2) applies to a transferred asset, then the full fair market value of the asset as of the decedent's date of death, rather than the value of the FLP interest, is included in his or her estate for death-tax purposes. Section 2036(a) specifically does not apply to any assets transferred by a decedent in a *bona fide sale* for *adequate and full consideration* in money or money's worth, including bona fide transfers to an FLP for an interest therein.

To qualify as a bona fide sale, the courts now look at whether a taxpayer has a valid business purpose (other than tax benefits) for forming the FLP. A valid business purpose may include:

- Creating, preserving, and increasing family wealth
- Lowering administrative costs and providing for coordinated, active management of family assets
- Providing a mechanism for continuity of management, including active involve-ment of younger family members
- Legal protection from creditors
- Keeping wealth in the family by restricting non-family-members' rights to acquire interests, including provisions for retaining interests in the event of a divorce
- Providing a mechanism for facilitating gifts to family members without fraction-alizing individual assets
- Promoting family harmony and including formal dispute resolution provisions in the event of a disagreement

Further, it is important to follow the agreement and use appropriate business practices including the following:

- All of the legal formalities in forming the FLP under state law must be observed
- All of the family members should also participate in the formation process, includ-ing the right to retain separate counsel and to comment on the formal governing documents
- Each family member should transfer assets (or valuable services) to the entity in exchange for a pro rata interest therein, and such contributions should be cred-ited to each partner's or member's capital account at full fair market value in accordance with regular partnership accounting rules
- Family members should not transfer too many assets such that they would then own insufficient assets outside the FLP to independently provide for their support
- Personal and partnership assets must not be commingled; that is, separate bank-ing and brokerage accounts must be maintained at all times. In particular, it is not advisable for a principal residence to be transferred to the FLP or FLLC. Last, keep liquid assets outside the FLP to allow for a continuance of lifestyle without the need to invade the corpus of the FLP
- Gifts and other transfers of interests (other than a sale for full and adequate con-sideration) should not occur contemporaneously with the formation of the entity.
- Distributions from the FLP should be made on a pro rata basis to all of the part-ners or members, and all decisions regarding whether to make a distribution should be properly documented, including the reasons for such decision

CHAPTER 15

Summary of Tax Court Cases Issues

This chapter discusses tax cases that affect business valuations. The discussion focuses on tax cases, since these are more general in application and often contain detailed information on valuations. Civil cases vary by jurisdiction and are very often inconsistent between jurisdictions. Absent are court cases in marital dissolution since they can vary so dramatically from jurisdiction to jurisdiction. Some of these cases are discussed in Chapters 2, 16, 18, 19, and 20 on Standards of Value, Shareholder Disputes, Divorce, Small Businesses, and Professional Practices.

Almost all the cases referenced here are from 1999 to 2009. Although knowledge of older court cases can be important and relevant (see Chapter 9), the cases from the last few years, particularly in the tax area, have dealt with many of the controversial issues faced by analysts today.

In the first two editions of this book, we organized the cases according to major valuation issues; for example, discounts, built-in gains tax, weighted average cost of capital (WACC) and capital asset pricing model (CAPM). These cases convey a strong sense of the direction of the courts. The format for these cases is brief but relevant bullets allow for easy access to important information and the general direction of recent court decisions concerning important valuation topics. However, it is recommended that analysts read the cases to absorb the full context of the issues. Some of the cases will appear more than once since they address several topics. Furthermore, the case information is presented basically as written in the court opinions, including divergent views of various experts.

Newer cases are in the website Addendum—Current Tax Court Cases of Interest found at www.wiley.com/go/FVAM3E. These are summaries of the salient factors.

TAX CASES[1]

Tax cases generally spring from the United States Tax Court, the United States Courts of Appeal, or various state courts. Tax disputes can be litigated in state courts only after the disputed tax has been paid. Since the payment of taxes is not required to litigate in United States Tax Court (Tax Court), it is often the venue of choice. Cases heard in Tax Court may be appealed to the United States Court of Appeals for

---

[1] The full texts of Tax Court opinion and memorandum cases from 9/25/95 forward are available at www.ustaxcourt.gov. Full texts of most cases discussed in this chapter are also available for free at www.fairmarketvalue.com.

the district in which the taxpayer resides. The various Courts of Appeal often have different precedential law, and analysts would be wise to study the case law for the Court of Appeals to which their client might appeal a Tax Court decision. It is common for the Tax Court to discuss the case law for the Court of Appeals, which would have jurisdiction over the case if the taxpayer were to appeal the Tax Court decision.

In its weekly *Internal Revenue Bulletins,* the Internal Revenue Service (IRS) announces its positions via an Action on Decision for selected cases with the following description:

> *The recommendation in every Action on Decision will be summarized as acquiescence, acquiescence in result only, or nonacquiescence. Both "acquiescence" and "acquiescence in result only" mean that the Service accepts the holding of the court in a case and the Service will follow it in disposing of cases with the same controlling facts. However "acquiescence" indicates neither approval nor disapproval of the reasons assigned by the court for its conclusions; whereas "acquiescence in result only" indicates disagreement or concern with some or all of those reasons. Nonacquiescence signifies that the Service does not agree with the holding of the court and, generally will not follow the decision in disposing of cases involving other taxpayers. In reference to an opinion of a circuit court of appeals, a nonacquiescence indicates that the Service will not follow the holding on a nationwide basis. However, the Service will recognize the precedential impact of the opinion on cases arising within the venue of the deciding circuit.[2]*

In addition to understanding case law, analysts should study the statutes and case law that apply for the relevant state jurisdiction and consult with an attorney familiar with case law in the jurisdiction. For example, different state statutes regarding the rights of partners or limited liability company members can cause different values for otherwise identical entities. Again, readers are advised to read the full text of any court case for a more complete understanding of the facts and circumstances particular to each issue within each case.

Use of Previous Tax Court Cases as Support for Valuations

While it is important and useful to understand Tax Court decisions, practitioners should not rely on them in arriving at fair market value since each valuation must rely on its own unique facts and circumstances. Some cases have also been appealed.

Estate of Berg[3]

- The taxpayer expert relied on judicial precedent to arrive at the discounts for lack of control and lack of marketability.
- The Court said, "The fact that petitioner found several cases which approve discounts approximately equal to those claimed in the instant case is irrelevant. Therefore, in deciding the appropriate discounts in the instant case we will take

---

[2] *Internal Revenue Bulletin.*
[3] *Estate of Edgar A. Berg v. Commissioner,* TCM 1991-279 (June 20, 1991).

into account all relevant facts and circumstances of petitioner's interest in [the company], and do not consider the amount of discount applied in other cases cited by petitioner as persuasive."

- The IRS expert relied on empirical data and adjusted for the specific circumstances of the subject company, and the Court accepted this.

Estate of Foote[4]

- The taxpayer expert arrived at a blockage discount of 22.5 percent by selecting 18 Tax Court cases dealing with blockage discounts that were "factually similar to the matter under discussion." The blockage discounts allowed in these cases ranged from 8.1 percent to 52.9 percent with a mean of 26 percent and a median of 19 percent. The appraiser averaged the mean and the median blockage discounts to arrive at the 22.5 percent.
- The Tax Court was highly critical of this approach and accepted the report of the IRS expert.

Discounts for Lack of Control and Marketability

The most commonly discussed valuation issues in court cases relate to discounts for lack of control and marketability. Since together these discounts can reduce the entity-level value by 50 percent or more and their derivation is subject to significant levels of professional judgment, they are fertile ground for dispute.

Estate of Lea K. Hillgren[5]

- This was primarily a bad facts § 2036 case.
- Subject was a real estate limited partnership with seven properties.
- Four of the seven properties in the partnership were subject to a 1994 business loan agreement (BLA) between decedent and her brother Mark. Under the terms of the BLA, Mark had the sole right to determine whether underlying property could be sold.
- For one of the BLA-encumbered properties, Mark was entitled to 25 percent of any net cash proceeds from the sale or refinancing of the property (lender interest).
- The IRS argued that the disregarded partnership (taxpayer lost on § 2036 argument) should supersede the BLA, while the estate argued that the subject matter of each agreement was separate. The Tax Court concluded that the BLA, ". . . had apparent business purpose. Moreover, a hypothetical buyer would not disregard or ignore the BLA."
- The appraiser used by the estate for preparing the return took the BLA into account in determining discounts to be applied to the partnership interest, although the terms of the BLA were considered incorrectly as a result of faulty instructions by the estate's attorney.
- The estate used a different appraiser for trial.
- For the single property subject to the 25 percent lender interest described previously, the estate's trial appraiser first reduced fair market value by 25 percent. The

---

[4] *Estate of Dorothy B. Foote v. Commissioner*, TCM 1999-37 (February 5, 1999).

[5] *Estate of Lea K. Hillgren*, TCM 2004-46 (March 3, 2004).

taxpayer's appraiser then analyzed median discounts to net asset value for *comparable* publicly registered limited partnerships based on revenues, debt to equity, and distributions. After this analysis, the appraiser arrived at a 50 percent combined discount for lack of control and marketability.
- The significant discount was due in part to the high level of debt on this property.
- The IRS appraiser also determined a 35 percent marketability discount based on restricted stock studies.
- On brief, the estate pointed out that the IRS appraisal contained incorrect assumptions about cash flow and the effect of the BLA.
- The Court said that the taxpayer expert's "opinion on discounts is reasonable and is not contradicted by reliable evidence. Thus we adopt it."
- For the three other properties not subject to the 25 percent interest, the estate's appraiser did a similar analysis, arriving at combined discounts for lack of control and marketability of 35, 35, and 40 percent. The IRS appraiser arrived at discounts of 30, 30, and 40 percent. Because the difference was *"insubstantial,"* the Tax Court adopted the estate's discount.

Estate of Trompeter[6]

- Remand from Ninth Circuit with instructions to Judge Laro to explain his original 1998 fair market value calculation.
- No discount for lack of marketability for preferred stock since Judge Laro's calculation was not the freely traded value.
- No explanation why calculated value was not freely traded value.

Estate of Mildred Green[7]

- Subject was a single bank holding company.
- Taxpayer claimed 40 percent DLOM; IRS claimed 25 percent.
- Both appraisers relied on restricted stock studies.
- Taxpayer appraiser also relied on pre-IPO studies.
- IRS expert used *Mandelbaum* analysis.
- IRS expert *"placed considerable reliance"* on Management Planning Study.
- Tax Court criticism of IRS expert:
  - Disagreed with using "rock bottom" of Management Planning Study
    - *"Furthermore we question his 24-percent lower range limit. He himself states that most of the restricted stock studies showed median marketability discounts in a range from 30 to 35 percent."*
    - During cross-examination, the IRS expert admitted that he was unfamiliar with transactions identified by the taxpayer expert that were smaller, more like RBI, and smaller transactions had higher discounts. The IRS expert said, *"I can look that up. I would like to see that."*
  - *"[The IRS expert] cites only two studies that he says indicate median discounts of 24 percent or lower. One of those studies is the Securities and Exchange Comn. Institutional Investor Study. [citation omitted] On cross-examination, however, [the IRS expert] was unable to respond satisfactorily to the estate's*

[6] *Estate of Trompeter*, TCM 2004-27 (February 4, 2004).
[7] *Estate of Mildred Green*, TCM 2003-348 (December 29, 2003).

contention that the SEC study describes various categories of sales transactions, and that the category for nonreporting over-the-counter companies, which are most comparable to smaller businesses like RBI, shows a median price discount of 32.6 percent.

- "[The IRS expert] also relied on the 'Hall/Polacek study' which, in his opinion, indicated a mean discount of 23 percent. [citation omitted] The Hall/Polacek study also indicates, however, that 'Lack of marketability discounts appear to increase as the capitalization of the corporation decreases below $50 million (30%–40%) compared to corporations with capitalizations in excess of $100 million (10%–20%).' Because RBI's capitalization was below $50 million, the Hall/Polacek study would appear to indicate a higher discount (30 to 40 percent) than the mean discount of 23 percent upon which [the IRS expert] relied." Taxpayer appraiser determined his discount for lack of control using Mergerstat data.

- For the discount for lack of control, the IRS expert relied on an analysis of Mergerstat data in Mercer's *Quantifying Marketability Discounts* that showed a mean and median discount of 19 percent, and in addition conducted his own study that resulted in a median discount of 18.4 percent and a mean discount of 19.6 percent.

- The IRS expert then compared the characteristics of the decedent's interest in RBI with his study to determine whether there were differences that should result in a higher or lower discount.

- The Tax Court found his comparative analysis flawed on several fronts, including, "[The IRS appraiser] claims that decedent's 5.09 percent interest in RBI is 'a substantially larger interest than typical minority interests in publicly traded shares in banks and this would result in a minority interest discount which would tend to be somewhat lower than' the indicated range of 18.4 to 19.6 percent for banking interest. [The appraiser] offers no independent evidence or empirical data to verify these conclusions, and we are unpersuaded that he appropriately relied on this factor in his discount analysis."

- The Court also thought the taxpayer expert had not adequately supported his 17 percent discount, but ultimately accepted it anyway.

Peter S. Peracchio[8]

- Partnership held only cash and marketable securities.
- At trial, the taxpayer offered two experts and the IRS one.
- For the discount for lack of marketability, both of the taxpayer experts started with a benchmark rate and used the Mandelbaum factors (*Estate of Mandelbaum v. Commissioner*, TCM 1995-255) to determine whether the subject's discount should be higher or lower than the benchmark. The Court said, "*Because we are unpersuaded by either expert's determination of the appropriate benchmark (starting point), we give little weight to their respective analysis.*"
- One of the appraisers simply used the benchmark in *Mandelbaum* as a starting point, to which the Court said, "*To the extent [the appraiser] believes that the benchmark range of discounts we used in* Mandelbaum *[citations omitted] is controlling in this or any other case, he is mistaken.*"

---

[8] *Peter S. Peracchio*, TCM 2003-280 (September 25, 2003).

- The other taxpayer appraiser started with a 30 percent discount based on the private placement studies. The Court said, "*While restricted stock studies certainly have some probative value in the context of marketability discount analysis, see, for example,* Estate of McCord v. Commissioner, *120 T.C. at 390-393, [the expert] makes no attempt whatsoever to analyze the data from those studies as they relate to the transferred interests. Rather, he simply lists the average discounts observed in several such studies, effectively asking us to accept on faith the premise that the approximate average of those results provides a reliable benchmark for the transferred interests. Absent any analytical support, we are unable to accept that premise, particularly in light of the fundamental differences between an investment company holding easily valued assets (such as the partnership) and the operating companies that are the subject of the restricted stock studies.*"
- The IRS expert did not fare much better in the Court's analysis. He started with a judgmentally determined benchmark range of 5 to 25 percent and offered a brief analysis of six factors that may influence the size of the marketability discount within that range. The Court said, "*. . . we are not persuaded by his opinion that the appropriate range of marketability discounts is 5 to 25 percent. We are even less impressed by his arbitrary selection of the midpoint of that range (15 percent as his suggested discount).*"
- Ultimately, the Court selected a 25 percent discount for lack of marketability, treating the 25 percent upper end of the range determined by the IRS expert as a concession and concluding the taxpayer did not meet his burden of proof to arrive at a higher discount.
- For the minority discount, all of the experts used closed-end mutual funds. The minority discount analysis of the second taxpayer expert was dismissed by the Court because, "*. . . his methodology is comparatively both imprecise (his 5-percent discount is not statistically derived from observed discounts) and incomplete (he considers only domestic equity funds).*"
- The Court was clearly not pleased with the analyses of the other two experts either but did use their calculations to some degree.
- For the cash portion of the investments, the remaining taxpayer expert applied a 5 percent discount and the IRS expert used 2 percent.
  - Both appraisers lacked any empirical data for their discount.
  - The Tax Court found neither expert persuasive but allowed a 2 percent discount since this amount was conceded by the IRS, and the taxpayer did not meet the burden of proof for a higher amount.
- For the marketable securities, the main dispute was the selection of closed-end funds to include in the discount calculation.
- The taxpayer expert eliminated what he believed were "outliers" from his analysis.
- To determine the discount from the selected funds, the taxpayer expert used the median discount while the IRS expert used the mean (average) discount.
  - The Court was puzzled why the median was appropriate since the outliers had already been removed.
- The taxpayer expert was also unable to articulate at trial why the median was superior and the Court elected to use the mean.
- The Court made its own calculation using 6.9 percent for U.S. government bond funds, 3.5 percent for state and local bonds, 3.4 percent for national municipal bond funds, 9.6 percent for domestic equities, and 13.8 percent for foreign

equities, arriving at a 6 percent weighted average minority discount for all of the cash and marketable securities.

Clarissa W. Lappo[9]

- FLP with marketable securities (mostly municipal bonds) and real estate.
- The taxpayer expert relied on restricted stock data assembled by his firm for the lack of marketability discount. The Tax Court found that 13 of the 39 companies relied upon were high-tech companies and not comparable to the partnership. Removing these companies from the average resulted in a 19.45 percent discount before further adjustments.
- The IRS expert relied on the Bajaj study that showed the portion of private placement discounts attributable solely to impaired marketability was 7.2 percent. The Tax Court noted that it preferred this private placement approach to the taxpayer expert's restricted stock approach, but concluded, *"Absent further explication of the Bajaj study by [IRS expert], however, and without the benefit of other empirical studies that would tend to validate the conclusions of the Bajaj study, we are unpersuaded that a 7.2% discount is an appropriate quantitative starting point . . ."*
- The Tax Court looked to the raw data in the Bajaj study that had an average discount of 22.21 percent and the Herztel & Smith study cited by Bajaj that had a 20.14 percent average discount. The Court averaged these two and arrived at 21 percent as the discount prior to adjustments specific to the partnership.
- Both experts made adjustments to the data from the studies to reflect the particular circumstances of the partnership. The Tax Court reviewed the various considerations raised by the two appraisers and concluded a 3 percent upward revision was appropriate, arriving at a final marketability discount of 24 percent.
- The taxpayer expert concluded that a 7.5 percent minority discount should be applied to the marketable securities and a 35 percent minority discount should be applied to the real estate.
- The IRS expert applied an 8.5 percent minority discount.
- The parties engaged in a little horse trading and a slight increase in asset values by the IRS was offset by applying the higher IRS 8.5 percent minority discount to the marketable securities.
- Taxpayer and IRS experts agreed that publicly traded real estate investment trusts (REITs) were the appropriate starting point for the minority interest discount.
- The taxpayer expert used a sample of only seven comparable companies out of a population of over 400 REITs. The Court believed the small number of companies in the sample was insufficient to negate comparability issues between the seven companies and the partnership.
- The IRS expert had a sample of 52 companies and the Court concluded that, *". . . [the] sample was sufficiently large to make tolerable any dissimilarities between the partnership and the REITs in his guideline group."*
- Both experts made adjustments to their REIT sample averages to arrive at an appropriate discount for the partnership.
- The Court was troubled by the taxpayer expert's *"terse"* explanation for his adjustments and concluded that his *". . . upward adjustments are, to some*

---

[9] *Clarissa W. Lappo*, TCM 2003-258 (September 3, 2003).

extent, plug numbers used to justify his ultimate, very round minority interest discount figures . . ."

- The IRS expert adjusted his REIT data based on the study by Bajaj, concluding that a 7.5 percent liquidity adjustment should be made to the REIT discount.
- The Tax Court was hesitant to rely on a single academic study, particularly one in which the IRS expert did not participate in preparing and could not elaborate upon firsthand.
- The Tax Court did find that there were similarities between the Bajaj study and the Wruck study and Hertzel & Smith study cited by Bajaj.
- The Tax Court ultimately averaged the *"average discount observed in unregistered private placements"* in each of the three studies, arriving at an illiquidity discount of 17.6 percent.
- The Court added this to the REIT discount and rounded to a 19 percent discount for the real estate.

Johann and Johanna Hess[10]

- The taxpayer expert used a 30 percent discount for lack of marketability, while the IRS expert used 25 percent. Based on wording in the taxpayer expert's report, the Tax Court concluded there was an overlap between the discounts for lack of control and marketability that had not been properly taken into account: *"Minority interest shares are significantly less marketable and liquid than controlling interest shares because few investors are interested in minority interest investments in closely held companies."*
- The Court termed the IRS expert's 25 percent "reasonable" and accepted it as the proper amount.

Estate of Helen A. Deputy[11]

- The taxpayer expert arrived at a 44 percent combined discount for lack of control and marketability using a matrix his firm constructed. This matrix assigned a numeric amount to:
  - Information availability and reliability
  - Investment size
  - Company outlook, management, and growth potential
  - Ability to control
  - Any restrictions on transferability, anticipated holding period, and company's redemption policy
  - Dividend payout history and outlook
- The Tax Court said, *"The divergent valuation approaches by the parties' experts force the Court to choose one method over the other without necessarily fully accepting that method or approach."*
- The Court used the taxpayer experts' matrix, *"merely as a guide to assist in our analysis of the facts presented in the record . . ."*
- Using the matrix, the Court ultimately concluded a 30 percent combined discount for lack of control and marketability was appropriate.

---

[10] *Johann and Johanna Hess*, TCM 2003-251 (August 20, 2003).
[11] *Estate of Helen A. Deputy*, TCM 2003-176 (June 13, 2003).

Charles T. McCord, Jr., and Mary S. McCord[12]

- Both IRS and taxpayer appraisers agreed that a discount for lack of marketability is appropriate and that the calculation is done on a composite basis and not on an asset-by-asset basis.
- They further agreed that empirical studies of the marketability discount fall into two major categories, the pre-IPO studies and the restricted stock studies.
- The taxpayer expert said he relied on the restricted stock studies but contended that the IPO studies also supported his 35 percent marketability discount.
- The IRS expert relied on a variant of the restricted stock approach termed the "private placement approach" by the Tax Court and arrived at a 7 percent marketability discount.
- Rejection of IPO approach
  - The IRS expert argued that the IPO approach is "flawed both in concept and in application." His principal criticism was that the IPO premium might reflect more than just the availability of a ready market. He cited several other criticisms and concluded that "[T]*he IPO approach probably generates inflated estimates of the marketability discount. Consequently, it is of limited use in estimating the value of closely held firms.*"
  - The Court noted that the taxpayer expert failed to offer any criticism of this assertion in his rebuttal testimony. The taxpayer expert did cite the Willamette Management Associates, Inc., studies in his rebuttal, noting, "*The evidence from the Willamette study was quite compelling and offered strong support for the hypothesis that the fair market values of minority interests in privately held companies were and should be greatly discounted from their publicly traded counterparts.*"
  - The IRS expert's rebuttal testimony offered what the Tax Court termed "*a compelling criticism*" of both the Willamette studies and another series of studies conducted by John Emory of Robert W. Baird and Co.
  - This expert said the latest study conducted by Emory was biased because it did not adequately take into account the highest sale prices in pre-IPO transactions and the Willamette study did not disclose enough data to reveal whether it suffered from a similar bias.
  - The Tax Court concluded, "[*The IRS expert*] *has convinced us to reject as unreliable* [*the taxpayer expert's*] *opinion to the extent it is based on the IPO approach.*"
- Restricted stock and private placement analysis
  - The taxpayer expert relied on four restricted stock studies plus the Willamette studies and attempted to infer a marketability discount based on a comparison of revenue, income, NAV, and the size of the gifted interest. The Tax Court was critical of this analysis and concluded that, "*. . . we give little weight to* [*the taxpayer expert's*] *restricted stock analysis.*"
  - The IRS expert believed that the discounts observed in the restricted stock studies are attributable in part to factors other than impaired marketability.
  - He asserted that part of the discount in these studies is due to the cost of "assessing the quality of the firm and for the anticipated cost of monitoring the future decisions of its managers."

---

[12] *Charles T. McCord, Jr., and Mary S. McCord*, T.C. No. 13 (May 14, 2003). On appeal to Fifth Circuit.

- He listed four factors that influence the assessment and monitoring costs and attempted to isolate the impact of those factors using a statistical analysis.
  - The size of the private placement relative to the issuer's total shares outstanding
  - The volatility of the issuer's recent economic performance
  - The overall financial health of the issuer
  - The size of the private placement in terms of total proceeds
- *"Dr. Bajaj posits that the additional discount observed in unregistered issues could be attributable solely to impaired marketability only if those four additional factors were present in equal measure among both registered and unregistered private placements."*
- After concluding that factors unrelated to impaired marketability play a variable role in the total discounts observed in private placement transactions, Dr. Bajaj attempted to isolate the impaired marketability portion of the total discount.
- Using a multivariate statistical analysis for 1990 to 1995, he concluded that a private issue that was registered would require a discount of 7.23 percent more than an otherwise unregistered issue.
- He then considered an additional adjustment for the long-term impaired marketability of an assignee interest in the partnership compared to the restricted stock studies and concluded no adjustment was required. *"His rejection is based primarily on the opinion, supported by the economic analysis of others, that the level of discount does not continue to increase with the time period of impaired marketability, because investors with long-term time horizons would provide a natural clientele for holding illiquid assets and would compete to purchase all of a portion of a gifted interest."*
- He rounded the 7.23 percent to a final marketability discount of 7 percent.
- The taxpayer expert's rebuttal criticized the IRS expert for focusing on liquidity at the expense of negative characteristics of small closely held entities that contribute to lack of marketability.
- The Tax Court said the IRS expert was helpful in focusing their attention on the distinction between liquidity and other factors that contribute to private placement discounts, but said, *"However, his apparent confusion regarding the nature of the discount for lack of marketability (i.e., whether other factors may be involved) is troubling . . . Therefore, while we are impressed by portions of [the IRS expert's] analysis, he has not convinced us that the appropriate marketability discount in this case can be inferred from the illiquidity cost associated with the private placements."*
- Even though they rejected the IRS expert's quantification of the appropriate discount for lack of marketability, the Court relied on his private placement study. They did this believing that assessment and monitoring costs are high in unregistered private placements and a sample consisting entirely of unregistered private placements would be inappropriately skewed.
- The Court also noted that this study was the only one that covered the period from 1990 through 1995, which immediately preceded the valuation date.
- The Court looked to the middle group of private placements in this study with an average discount of 20.36 percent. Believing that they could not *"refine that figure any more to incorporate the characteristics specific to [the partnership],"* they concluded a 20 percent discount for lack of marketability was appropriate.

- Taxpayer and IRS appraisers both agreed that each asset class was subject to its own minority interest discount and that the overall discount would be the weighted average of each of the asset classes' separate minority discounts. The Tax Court determined a weighted average minority discount of 15 percent based on the following analysis.
- Equity portfolio
  - Both appraisers determined the minority discount using closed-end mutual funds.
  - They disagreed on which funds should be included in their data set and the factors that should be considered in arriving at a partnership discount either higher or lower than the average closed-end fund discount in their respective data sets.
  - The Tax Court was troubled that the taxpayer appraiser used January 11, 1996, trading prices and December 26, 1995, net asset values for the January 12, 1996, valuation date.
  - One interesting argument raised by the IRS expert was that the partnership was akin to a new investment fund that would generally trade at lower discounts to net asset value than mature funds.
  - The Tax Court noted that the partners had held the equity portfolio for a number of years and ignored this argument.
  - Each expert had various arguments why the partnership's discount should be higher or lower than the average, but the Court found flaws in both of their arguments and used the average discount of 10 percent.
- Bond portfolio
  - The analysis and arguments here were similar to the equity portfolio analysis.
  - The taxpayer appraiser excluded single-state bond funds, but since the bond portfolio included 75 percent Louisiana bonds, the Court concluded the data set should include only single-state bond funds.
  - The Court had issues with both analyses and arrived at a 10 percent discount based on the average discount to net asset value for 62 single-state bond funds.
- Real estate partnerships
  - The IRS appraiser used real estate investment trusts to determine the level of discount.
  - The taxpayer expert criticized this since REITs "*are primarily priced on a current yield basis because REITs are required by law to annually pay out a large portion of earnings to shareholders.*"
  - The Tax Court did not accept this criticism since the investment funds used by the taxpayer expert in his equity portfolio and bond portfolio analyses are also required to distribute substantially all of their income each year in order to maintain their tax-favored status as regulated investment companies under IRC § 852(a)(1).
  - The taxpayer expert relied on only three public companies to determine his discount, and these were found not to be sufficiently comparable to allow reliance on such a small sample.
  - According to the IRS expert, the difference between NAV and trading price for a REIT is composed of a positive amount for the liquidity premium and a negative amount for the minority discount.
  - The Court adjusted the numbers used by the IRS expert and combined a 22 percent liquidity premium with the 1.3 percent discount to NAV and arrived at 23.3 percent discount for lack of control.

Jeffrey L. Okerlund et al. v. United States, U.S. Court of Federal Claims[13]

- Both experts relied on restricted stock and pre-IPO studies, with the taxpayer expert concluding a 45 percent discount was appropriate and the IRS expert concluding a 30 percent discount was justified.
- The Court noted the taxpayer expert's report contained a far more detailed analysis of the studies. [Author's note—The case contains a good analysis of the factors the experts considered in their determination of the discount.]
- The Court found the taxpayer expert's analysis to be more persuasive, including his higher reliance on the pre-IPO studies.
- The Court reduced the discount for the 1992 valuation from 45 percent to 40 percent because some of the factors considered were based on the estate plan of Marvin Schwan, whose death was unanticipated in 1992.
- For a 1994 charitable donation, the IRS did not present expert testimony to support its challenge to the value on the taxpayers' individual income tax return. The Court accepted the value calculated by the taxpayer expert, including a 45 percent discount for lack of marketability and a 5 percent discount for lack of voting rights.

Estate of Bailey v. Commissioner[14]

- Lewis Bailey died in 1995, owning a 25 percent interest in C&L Bailey, Inc. (C&L), which owned and operated a motel in Arkansas and one in California.
- On the original estate tax return, the value of the C&L stock was based on the "liquidation value" of the two motels net of liabilities, reduced by 50 percent for "Key Man, Minority Ownership, Lack of Market Discount."
- In his original appraisal, the IRS appraiser subtracted only a 25 percent discount for lack of marketability from this to arrive at fair market value. In the notice of deficiency, the IRS increased the total discount to 50 percent, matching the discount taken on the original estate tax return.
- The taxpayer appraiser deducted a 20 percent discount for lack of control and a 40 percent discount for lack of marketability based on the pre-IPO studies.
- The Tax Court was "unpersuaded that [the taxpayer expert] appropriately relied on these studies in deriving his recommended 40-percent marketability discount."
- The Tax Court agreed with the IRS expert and determined a 50 percent combined discount for lack of control and marketability was proper, as claimed in the original estate tax return.

Estate of William G. Adams, Jr. v. Commissioner[15]

- The taxpayer expert claimed a discount of 20 percent.
- The IRS expert claimed a 35 percent discount, but changed this to between 40 and 45 percent at trial because of litigation he did not know about before trial.
- The Tax Court applied a 35 percent discount.

---

[13] *Jeffrey L. Okerlund et al. v. United States,* U.S. Court of Federal Claims, Consolidated Numbers 99-133T and 99-134T (August 23, 2002).
[14] *Estate of Bailey v. Commissioner,* TCM 2002-152 (June 17, 2002).
[15] *Estate of William G. Adams, Jr. v. Commissioner,* TCM 2002-80 (March 28, 2002).

Estate of Heck v. Commissioner[16]

- The IRS expert subtracted a 15 percent "liquidity discount" and a 10 percent discount for "additional risks associated with S corporations," including "the potential loss of S corporation status and shareholder liability for income taxes on S corporation income, regardless of the level of distribution" to arrive at the operating value.
- The IRS expert added the value of excess land and excess cash. He applied a 25 percent minority discount and a 25 percent liquidity discount to the excess land and a 25 percent liquidity discount to the excess cash.
- The taxpayer expert applied a 25 percent marketability discount and a 10 percent discount "to reflect the negative impact of a right of first refusal and what [the expert] refers to as 'agency problems' (the inability of a purchaser of decedent's minority interest to influence dividend distributions, which would be at the discretion of the controlling shareholder . . ."
- The Tax Court was critical of the IRS expert's 15 percent marketability discount, noting that the expert had conceded that average discounts were often in excess of 35 percent. The Tax Court further said that the IRS expert failed to make clear why his concluded discount was at the low end of the range for acceptable discounts. In oral testimony, this expert set forth a theory that there was "a group of purchasers who would value the shares on other than an investment basis" and would pay a higher price for the shares. The Tax Court rejected this argument and accepted the 25 percent marketability discount used by the taxpayer expert.
- The Court allowed a 10 percent discount for lack of control. The Court believed that the 10 percent "agency discount" included by the taxpayer expert as part of the discount for lack of marketability was really a discount for lack of control and was similar to the S corporation discount included by the IRS expert.
- The Tax Court combined the 25 percent discount for lack of marketability and the 10 percent discount for lack of control into a 35 percent total discount that it applied to the operating assets and nonoperating assets, net of debt.

Mandelbaum v. Commissioner[17]

- The Court used restricted stock and pre-initial public offering (IPO) studies as a starting point.
- The Court compared [the company] to these studies in the following areas:
  - Private versus public sales of the stock
  - Financial statement analysis
  - Company's dividend policy
  - Nature of the company, its history, its position in the industry, and its economic outlook
  - Company's management
  - Amount of control in transferred shares
  - Restrictions on transferability of stock
  - Holding period for stock
  - Company's redemption policy
  - Costs associated with making a public offering

---

[16] *Estate of Heck v. Commissioner,* TCM 2003-34 (February 5, 2002).
[17] *Mandelbaum v. Commissioner,* TCM 1995-255 (June 12, 1995).

- Based on the comparison of the subject company to these factors, the Court arrived at a 30 percent marketability discount.

Robert T. and Kay F. Gow v. Commissioner[18]

- The case is important because of "nested" discounts.
- Despite ignoring the entity value calculated by taxpayer expert, the Court adopted this expert's lack of control and marketability discounts as presented.
- Taxpayer owned a noncontrolling interest in Williamsburg Vacations, Inc. (WVI), which in turn owned beneficial one-third interest in a joint venture partnership, Powhatan Plantation (Powhatan).
- A 15 percent discount for lack of control and 30 percent discount for lack of marketability were allowed on Powhatan.
- A 20 percent discount for lack of control and 30 percent discount for lack of marketability were allowed on one valuation date and a 30 percent discount for lack of control and 30 percent discount for lack of marketability allowed on a second valuation date for WVI.

Estate of Beatrice Ellen Jones Dunn v. Commissioner[19]

- The decedent owned 62.96 percent of Dunn Equipment, a Texas C corporation.
- The Tax Court allowed the estate to average the income and asset valuation approaches but weighed the income approach at 35 percent, not the 50 percent used by the estate.
- After averaging the two approaches, the Court allowed application of the 15 percent marketability discount, which was undisputed by the experts.
- The Court then allowed a discount of 7.5 percent for lack of supermajority control, as claimed in the original tax return's appraisal, despite the taxpayer's argument on brief that the discount should be 10 percent.

Estate of Frank A. Branson v. Commissioner[20]
The case is regarding the Savings Bank of Mendocino County (Savings) and Bank of Willits:

- The decedent owned 12.89 percent of the outstanding shares and two other family members owned 16.72 percent and 17.35 percent, respectively.
- The remaining 53.04 percent was widely distributed with many of the shareholders owning less than 3 percent.
- The company's stock was not traded on any established exchange or over the counter, but the investment department of Savings maintained an informal list of people who were interested in buying shares of its stock.
- The parties agreed that the best indication of the "market value" of Savings stock was the actual sale price of the shares.

[18] *Robert T. and Kay F. Gow v. Commissioner*, TCM 2000-93 (March 20, 2000).
[19] *Estate of Beatrice Ellen Jones Dunn v. Commissioner*, TCM 2000-12 (January 12, 2000). Appealed August 1, 2002, reversed and remanded.
[20] *Estate of Frank A. Branson v. Commissioner*, TCM 199-231 (July 13, 1999).

- The taxpayer argued that the actual sales price was "just the starting point for deciding fair market value—that discounts should be applied to the sale price for minority interest, lack of marketability, and blockage."
- The IRS argued that the actual sale price was already reflective of the discounts for lack of control and marketability.
- The taxpayer expert relied on the pre-IPO and restricted stock studies.
- The Court faulted the taxpayer expert's use of the restricted stock studies, and found his

> *. . . reliance on the restricted stock studies for the size of the discount factor to be misplaced, since the studies analyzed only restricted stock that had a holding period of 2 years. The Savings shares were not restricted either by law or by agreement. The fact that Savings maintained a waiting list of willing buyers is evidence that the stock's history of low trading volume is due to the shareholder's preference to hold Savings shares for investment rather than for sale. As the investment time horizon of an investor in Savings stock evidently is long term, we do not believe that marketability concerns rise to the same level as a security with a short-term holding period like a restricted stock. Therefore, we find no persuasive evidence in the record to support reliance on the restricted stock studies in determining an appropriate marketability discount.*

- The Court further rejected the use of pre-IPO studies, noting that the amount received by the decedent in the sale shortly before his death is more likely "40 to 45 percent less, rather than more, than the price at which the same shares would sell in an IPO."
- The IRS expert relied on restricted stock and pre-IPO studies and 19 opinions of the Tax Court decided after 1983 where there was a discount separately and specifically identified for either lack of marketability or restrictions on transfer.
- The discounts in the studies and the cases ranged from 10 percent to 45 percent, and the appraiser concluded that a 20 percent discount was appropriate.
- The Court disallowed all discounts for lack of control and marketability but allowed a 10 percent blockage discount.

Bank of Willits (Willits)

- At the date of death, there were 48 Willits shareholders, with decedent owning 6.25 percent of the outstanding shares.
- The taxpayer expert applied a 45 percent discount for lack of marketability based on the "usual restricted stock and IPO studies."
- As in Savings, the judge rejected the use of these studies and gave little weight to that portion of the expert's opinion.
- The IRS expert used the same studies as in Savings and concluded a 25 percent discount for lack of marketability.
- Again, the judge found no persuasive evidence to rely on the restricted stock and pre-IPO studies but allowed a 20 percent blockage discount.

Estate of Harriet R. Mellinger v. Commissioner[21]

- The sole valuation dispute was the discounts to apply.
- One of the two taxpayer experts determined the appropriate marketability discount was 32 percent and the other 31 percent.
- The expert for the IRS determined that a 15 percent "blockage" discount was appropriate.
- The IRS expert was criticized for relying on a single study in determining the discount, ignoring an entire body of restricted stock studies.
- The Court noted "each expert excluded information that contradicted his result" and was generally critical of all of the appraisal experts.
- The Court concluded that none of the experts was correct and a 25 percent marketability discount was appropriate. (The Court's opinion also referred to this as a blockage discount.)

Estate of William J. Desmond v. Commissioner[22]

- The taxpayer's expert calculated fair market value under the asset, discounted cash flow, and market approaches.
- Under the market approach, he added a 25 percent control premium to bring the minority value determined by this approach to the control value owned by the decedent.
- The expert analyzed a range of discounts for lack of marketability and concluded that a range of 25 to 45 percent was appropriate.
- After considering 10 factors, including the potential environmental liabilities, the expert concluded that a 25 percent marketability discount was appropriate.
- The IRS expert's engagement was limited to determining the appropriate marketability discount.
- The expert determined the appropriate discount for lack of marketability was between 0 and 5 percent.
- Because of the limitations imposed by the IRS on its expert, the Court totally rejected that expert's report.
- The IRS argued that applying a discount for potential environmental liabilities was improper because these discounts were implicit in the unadjusted value calculation under the income method and the market method.
- The court agreed that this was true with the market method, but not for the income method.
- The court analyzed six factors that favored a high marketability discount:

  1. Lack of public market
  2. Profit margins below industry averages
  3. Right of first refusal by other shareholders for stock sales to outsiders
  4. Lack of prospects for a public offering
  5. The large size of the interest valued
  6. Environmental liabilities not already considered

---

[21] *Estate of Harriet R. Mellinger v. Commissioner*, 112 T.C. No. 4 (January 26, 1999).
[22] *Estate of William J. Desmond v. Commissioner*, TCM 1999-76 (March 10, 1999).

- The only factor favoring a lower marketability discount was the company's past practice of distributing most of the company's profit to shareholders through higher than market compensation.
- The Court concluded that a 30 percent lack of marketability discount was appropriate, which included 10 percent for environmental liabilities. The Court applied this 30 percent discount only to the income approach and used 20 percent under the market approach since the Court had concluded that environmental liabilities are implicit in this latter approach.
- The Court determined that the petitioner should have taken into account a control premium under the income approach since this method "assumed the continuation of Deft's [the company] present policies and did not account for a change in control."
- The Court accepted the 25 percent control premium used by the taxpayer under the market method and applied that same percent to the income approach unadjusted value.

Estate of Helen Bolton Jameson v. Commissioner[23]

- One of the taxpayer experts claimed a 10 percent marketability discount for the existence of a minority shareholder, which the Tax Court called a "nuisance discount."
- The Tax Court rejected the "nuisance discount," but did recognize the existence of a marketability discount, which it allowed at 3 percent.
- The Tax Court further ruled that a hypothetical purchaser would not liquidate the company, and based on that, disallowed selling costs.

Estate of Etta Weinberg v. Commissioner[24]

- The decedent held a general power of appointment over a marital deduction trust that owned a 25.235 percent limited partnership interest.
- The taxpayer expert subtracted a 35 percent marketability discount "based on market studies of illiquid securities," particularly the Securities and Exchange Commission (SEC) study.
- The IRS expert calculated a 15 percent marketability discount using the Quantitative Marketability Discount Model (QMDM).
- The Court first calculated the implied minority discount. Since both experts had started with a minority income stream, this discount was implicit in the capitalized income value.
- Based on a comparison of the net asset value to the fair market value before the marketability adjustments determined by each expert, the Court determined a 42.7 percent minority discount had been taken by the taxpayer and 20.1 percent by the IRS.
- The judge then calculated that the total discounts taken were 62.7 percent by the taxpayer and 32.1 percent by the IRS.

---

[23] *Estate of Helen Bolton Jameson v. Commissioner,* TCM 1999-43 (February 9, 1999).
[24] *Estate of Etta Weinberg v. Commissioner*, TCM 2000-51 (February 15, 2000).

- The Court disagreed with the use of the QMDM analysis because "slight variations in the assumptions used in the model produce dramatic differences in the results." The Court's analysis showed how changes in the QMDM assumptions would double the marketability discount calculated by the model and concluded, "Because the assumptions are not based on hard data and a range of data may be reasonable, we did not find the QMDM helpful in this case."
- The taxpayer expert's marketability discount was likewise rejected because the expert did not take into account certain characteristics of the subject limited partnership: 1) consistent dividends, 2) the nature of the underlying assets, and 3) the low degree of financial leverage.
- The Court determined a 20 percent marketability discount was appropriate.

Janda v. Commissioner[25]

- Both experts agreed on the marketable minority value, which included a 10 percent minority discount.
- The taxpayer expert used the Quantitative Marketability Discount Model to arrive at a 65.77 percent discount for lack of marketability.
- The IRS appraiser relied largely on prior Tax Court cases to arrive at a 20 percent marketability discount.
- The Tax Court did not agree with either appraiser, concluding a 40 percent combined discount for lack of control and marketability was appropriate.
- Regarding QMDM, the Court expressed "grave doubts about the reliability of the QMDM model to produce reasonable discounts, given the generated discount of over 65 percent."

Other Cases (Discussed in Other Sections of This Chapter)

- *Estate of Dorothy B. Foote v. Commissioner,* TCM 1999-37 (February 5, 1999).
- *Estate of Richard R. Simplot v. Commissioner,* United States Court of Appeals for the Ninth Circuit, 249 F.3d 1191 (May 14, 2001).
  - *Estate of Richard R. Simplot v. Commissioner,* 112 T.C. No. 13 (March 22, 1995).
- *Estate of H.A. True Jr. et al. v. Commissioner,* TCM 2001-167 (July 6, 2001).
- *Estate of Jones v. Commissioner,* 116 T.C. No. 11 (March 6, 2001).
- *Knight v. Commissioner,* 115 T.C. No. 36 (November 30, 2000).
- *Estate of Artemus D. Davis v. Commissioner,* 110 T.C. 530 (June 30, 1998).
- *Estate of Paul Mitchell v. Commissioner,* 87 AFTR2d (May 2, 2001).
  - *Estate of Paul Mitchell v. Commissioner,* TCM 1997-461 (October 9, 1997).

Built-In Gains Tax

Built-in gains arise when the tax basis of assets inside of an entity are lower than their fair market values. This is most significant in a C corporation but can also be a

---

[25] *Janda v. Commissioner,* TCM 2001-24 (February 2, 2001).

factor in S corporations, partnerships, and limited liability companies. Prior to the repeal of the *General Utilities* doctrine[26] in 1986, taxpayers could avoid paying tax on the sale of appreciated assets at both the C corporation and shareholder level. With the repeal of *General Utilities,* C corporation gains are taxed both at the shareholder and corporation level.

Estate of Beatrice Ellen Jones Dunn v. Commissioner[27]

- The Tax Court (*Estate of Beatrice Ellen Jones dunn v. Commissioner,* TCM 2000-12 [January 12, 2000]) valued Dunn Equipment by assigning only a 35 percent weight to the value determined using the income approach, a value that was lower than that resulting from the use of the asset approach.
- The remaining 65 percent of value was determined under the asset approach, including a reduction for only 5 percent of the trapped-in taxable gain based on the probability of liquidation of the assets.
- In Tax Court, the IRS argued that no discount should be allowed for the trapped-in gains and no weight should be assigned to the lower income approach value. The Fifth Circuit said,

> *Yet, instead of supporting his own higher values (for which he had the burden of proof) by proffering professional expert valuation testimony during the trial, the Commissioner merely engaged in guerilla warfare, presenting only an accounting expert to snipe at the methodology of the Estate's valuation expert. The use of such trial tactics might be legitimate when merely contesting values proposed by the party opposite, but they can never suffice as support for a higher value affirmatively asserted by the party employing such a trial strategy. This is particularly true when, as here, that party is the Commissioner, who has the burden of proving the expanded value asserted in his amended answer . . .*
>
> *Consequently, the Commissioner's insistence at trial that the value of the subject stock in Dunn Equipment be determined exclusively on the basis of the market value of its assets, undiminished by their inherent tax liability—coupled with his failure to adduce affirmative testimony of a valuation expert—was so incongruous as to call his motivation into question. It can only be seen as one aimed at achieving maximum revenue at any cost, here seeking to gain leverage against the taxpayer in the hope of garnering a split-the-difference settlement—or, failing that, then a compromise judgment—somewhere between the value returned by the taxpayer (which, by virtue of the Commissioner's eleventh-hour deficiency notice, could not effectively be revised downward) and the unsupportedly excessive value eventually proposed by the Commissioner. And, that is precisely the result that the Commissioner obtained in the Tax Court.*

---

[26] *General Utilities & Operating Co. v. Helvering,* 16 AFTR 1126 (December 9, 1935).

[27] *Estate of Beatrice Ellen Jones Dunn v. Commissioner,* U.S. Court of Appeals for the Fifth Circuit, No. 00-60614 (August 1, 2002).

- The Tax Court accepted a 34 percent tax rate on the trapped-in gain, but followed the IRS "no imminent liquidation" argument, allowing only 5 percent of the trapped-in gains as a reduction to the net asset value. The Fifth Circuit termed this a "red herring" and said,

> We are satisfied that the hypothetical willing buyer of the Decedent's block of Dunn Equipment stock would demand a reduction in price for the built-in gains tax liability of the Corporation's assets at essentially 100 cents on the dollar, regardless of his subjective desires or intentions regarding use or disposition of the assets. Here, that reduction would be 34%. This is true "in spades" when, for purposes of computing the asset-based value of the Corporation, we assume (as we must) that the willing buyer is purchasing the stock to get the assets, whether in or out of corporate solution. We hold as a matter of law that the built-in gains tax liability of this particular business's assets must be considered as a dollar-for-dollar reduction when calculating the asset-based value of the Corporation, just as, conversely, built-in gains tax liability would have no place in the calculation of the Corporation's earnings-based value.

- While criticizing the likelihood of liquidation concept in determining the reduction in value for trapped-in capital gains, the Fifth Circuit said this concept does play a key role in assigning relative weights to the income and asset approaches. The lesser the likelihood of liquidation, the greater the weight that must be assigned to the income approach.
- The Fifth Circuit called the Tax Court's assignment of a 35 percent weight to the income approach a "legal, logical, and economic non sequitur."
- The Fifth Circuit determined that 85 percent of the final value should be determined using the income approach.
- In its conclusion, the Fifth Circuit cited the IRS commissioner's "extreme and unjustifiable trial position in advocating a valuation based entirely on asset value (with no reduction for built-in tax liability and no weight given to income-based value), exacerbated by his failure to adduce expert appraisal testimony in support of his own exorbitant proposed value" and told the Tax Court to entertain any claim that the taxpayer might make under IRC § 7430, which awards certain costs and fees to the taxpayer.

Raymond J. Martin et al., Plaintiffs v. Martin Bros. Container & Timber Products Corp. et al., Defendants, U.S. District Court for the Northern District of Ohio, Western Division[28]

- Case is Ohio shareholder dispute.
- The plaintiff and defendant each had an appraiser plus there was a joint appraiser.
- All three appraisers agreed that the fair market value of the corporation was properly calculated by the asset-based approach.
- The plaintiff expert concluded the built-in gains tax discount should be the present value of the tax assuming the assets would be sold at the end of 30 years.

---

[28] *Raymond J. Martin et al., Plaintiffs v. Martin Bros. Container and Timber Products Corp. et al., Defendants*, U.S. District Court for the Northern District of Ohio, Western Division, Case No. 3:00CV7642.

- The defendant expert and the joint expert both calculated the built-in gains tax discount assuming the tax would be incurred on the valuation date.
- The court cited *Estate of Pauline Welch v. C.I.R.*, 208 F.3d 213, 2000 WL 263309, **4 (6th Cir. 2000) (unpublished disposition)*, and *Eisenberg v. Commissioner*, 155 F.3d 50, 57 (2d Cir. 1998) and disagreed with all three appraisers.
- The court acknowledged that some discount was appropriate, noting that *". . . the tax-reduction or avoidance tactics referenced by the plaintiffs' expert (i.e., conversion from a C to an S corporation) are not a realistic means of getting out from underneath, or even significantly reducing, the built-in capital gains tax liability."*
- Ultimately, the court determined various future sales dates for the underlying assets, with the last sale being December 31, 2012, and instructed the parties to prepare a revised valuation taking the assumed sales dates into account.

Estate of Artemus D. Davis v. Commissioner[29]

- This is the first post-*General Utilities* repeal Tax Court case to allow reduction in fair market value for built-in gains.
- One taxpayer expert and the IRS expert took 15 percent additional marketability discount (about $9 million) to account for built-in gains tax.
- One taxpayer expert reduced net asset value by approximately $25 million in built-in gains tax.
- Tax Court allowed $9 million in built-in gains tax as a reduction in arriving at fair market value.

Eisenberg v. Commissioner[30]

- The Second Circuit overturned a Tax Court decision that disallowed consideration of the built-in gains tax in determining fair market value.
- The remanded case was settled without trial.
- The IRS "acquiesced" in this case.[31]

Estate of Richard R. Simplot v. Commissioner[32]

- The company owned a sizable holding in Micron Technology, a nonoperating asset.
- The taxpayer expert subtracted selling costs, 5 percent for blockage, and a 6 percent minority discount in arriving at the Micron fair market value.
- The taxpayer expert also reduced the publicly traded value of the Micron stock for 100 percent of the tax on the difference between the value of the stock and the underlying tax basis.
- The IRS expert assumed that any blockage discount on the Micron stock would be offset by a premium on the sale of the stock.
- The IRS expert subtracted a 3.825 percent discount for underwriting costs.

---

[29] *Estate of Artemus D. Davis v. Commissioner*, 110 T.C. 530 (June 30, 1998).

[30] *Eisenberg v. Commissioner*, 155 F.3d 50, 57 (2d Cir. 1998).

[31] *Internal Revenue Bulletin 1999-4* (January 25, 1999).

[32] *Estate of Richard R. Simplot v. Commissioner*, 112 T.C. No. 13 (March 22, 1999).

- This expert also deducted the entire built-in gains tax on the appreciation of the Micron stock above its tax basis.
- The Tax Court adopted the position of the IRS expert.

Estate of Helen Bolton Jameson v. Commissioner[33]

- The taxpayer owned 97 percent of a company owning appreciated timber property.
- The taxpayer experts deducted the built-in gains tax in arriving at fair market value.
- The IRS expert disagreed with the reduction in value for the built-in gains tax, arguing that it "is founded on a counter intuitive premise; that is, a hypothetical and instantaneous sale of the same assets which the willing buyer has just purchased."
- In dealing with the built-in gains tax discount, the Tax Court said:

> *While it may still be possible after the repeal of the* General Utilities *doctrine to avoid recognition of built-in capital gains, respondent has failed to convince us that any viable options for avoidance would exist for a hypothetical buyer of decedent's Johnco stock. The tax strategies suggested by [taxpayer's expert], who is not an expert in taxation, can at best defer the recognition of built-in capital gains, but only by deferring income and ultimately cash-flow, and suggest the work of an advocate rather than a disinterested expert witness. Perhaps anticipating that the avoidance strategies offered by his expert do not withstand scrutiny, respondent argues on brief that petitioner could "hire some creative and resourceful tax practitioner" and since "someone might think of a way to avoid the tax effect of an immediate liquidation," the tax on built-in capital gains is only speculative. Contrary to respondent, we do not think [respondent's expert] has demonstrated any real possibilities for avoidance of the built-in capital gains tax by Johnco, let alone done so in a manner sufficient to prevent petitioner from being able to carry its burden of final persuasion, as respondent asserts.*

Estate of Jones v. Commissioner[34]

- The fair market value of the partnership assets substantially exceeded their tax bases.
- The taxpayer expert claimed a discount for this excess while the IRS appraiser said no discount should be applied.
- The estate, the IRS, and both experts agreed that tax on the built-in gain could be avoided by a § 754 election. The only situation identified where a § 754 election would not be made was the taxpayer expert's example of a syndicated partnership with "lots of partners . . . and lots of assets" where the administrative burden would be great.

---

[33] *Estate of Helen Bolton Jameson v. Commissioner,* TCM 1999-43 (February 9, 1999).

[34] *Estate of Jones v. Commissioner,* 116 T.C. No. 11 (March 6, 2001).

- The Court allowed no discount, concluding "the buyer and seller of the partnership interest would negotiate with the understanding that an election would be made and the price agreed upon would not reflect a discount for built-in gains."

Estate of H.A. True, Jr. et al. v. Commissioner[35]

- The taxpayer expert valued one of the companies assets by consulting auction guides, trade magazines, and new and used equipment dealers.
- The Court said, "This suggests an active market for these types of assets. However, Black Hills Trucking's fixed assets had a low tax basis relative to their resale value, which would trigger a tax liability on sale. Also, a willing seller would incur other transaction costs to dispose of the company's assets either on a bulk sale or an item-by-item basis."
- The built-in gains issue was one of the items considered in arriving at a 20 percent discount for lack of marketability for a controlling interest discussed supra.

Buy-Sell Agreements

Determining whether a buy-sell agreement fixes a value for estate and gift purposes can be a difficult situation. Analysts are advised to review this with the client's attorney. Agreements that represent testamentary devices must be ignored not only in setting value but also in the consideration of that agreement in determining other potential discounts such as for lack of marketability.

Okerlund et al. v. United States Federal Circuit[36]

- The Court of Federal Claims valued the nonvoting stock of SSE gifted by Marvin Schwan at December 31, 1992. Schwan died unexpectedly on May 9, 1993, and in accordance with his estate plan, a charitable foundation received two-thirds of the outstanding SSE stock. SSE redeemed the foundation's shares pursuant to a February 4, 1993, redemption agreement.
- On appeal, the taxpayers contended that the potential triggering of the redemption agreement was not properly taken into account.
- As to the redemption agreement being triggered, the Court of Appeals agreed with the Court of Federal Claims conclusion that "... *in 1992 the estate plan provisions, although in place, had neither been triggered nor anticipated in the immediate future. In other words, they were prospective concerns rather than actual concerns as of the 1992 valuation date.*"

Johann and Johanna Hess[37]

- HII was a holding company for subsidiaries engaged primarily in manufacturing specialty machines and tools and dies, mostly for the automotive industry.
- In 1995, HII retired a key employee's stock as part of a transaction that included an eight-year covenant not to compete and a three-year employment agreement.

---

[35] *Estate of H.A. True, Jr. et al. v. Commissioner,* TCM 2001-167) (July 6, 2001).

[36] *Okerlund et al. v. United States Federal Circuit,* U.S. Court of Appeals for the Federal Circuit (April 9, 2004).

[37] *Johann and Johanna Hess,* TCM 2003-251 (August 20, 2003).

- The shareholder agreement that had been in place was not followed and was terminated as part of the transaction.
- The retiring shareholder was paid $4 million for his 20 shares and the two agreements.
- The Tax Court agreed with the taxpayer that the terminated-shareholder agreement was not determinative of fair market value. The judge did consider the value under the agreement but gave it *"relatively little weight."*

Estate of George A. Blount v. Commissioner[38]

- Decedent and his brother-in-law, as sole shareholders of Blount Construction Co. (BCC), signed a buy-sell agreement in 1981.
- This agreement was controlling for all purposes and specified book value as the price to be paid for the shares.
- In 1992, the company formed an ESOP, which became a shareholder in BCC. Decedent's brother-in-law died in 1996, and his shares were redeemed under the 1981 agreement based on a book value of about $8 million.
- In 1996, shortly after decedent was diagnosed with terminal cancer, he entered into a buy-sell agreement with the company for his 83.2 percent ownership.
- He signed the agreement both as the shareholder and on behalf of the company. The ESOP was not a signatory to the agreement.
- The agreement specified a fixed value of $4 million as a lump sum payment for the shares and was controlling only at death.
- The Tax Court determined the modified buy-sell agreement did not comply with Chapter 14 of the Internal Revenue Code and disregarded it in determining fair market value.
- The Court found that decedent had the unilateral ability to modify the agreement, rendering the agreement not binding during his lifetime, as required by Section 20.2031-2(h), Estate Tax Regs.
- Also, IRC Section 2703, applied to the modified agreement because the 1996 modification, which occurred after the effective date of IRC Section 2703, was a substantial modification.
- The modified agreement was also disregarded under IRC Section 2703(a), because it failed to satisfy IRC Section 2703(b)(3), which required that the terms of the agreement be comparable to similar arrangements entered into by persons in an arm's-length transaction.
- The Tax Court selected a value very close to the IRS expert's value.

Estate of H.A. True, Jr., et al. v. Commissioner[39]

- The analysis focused on the factors in *Estate of Lauder v. Commissioner*[40] (Lauder II).
- There are four parts to the Lauder II test:

  1. Is the offering price fixed and determinable under the agreement?
  2. Are the agreements binding during life and at death?

[38] *Estate of George A. Blount v. Commissioner,* TCM 2004-116 (May 12, 2004), appealed October 31, 2005, affirmed in part, reversed in part.
[39] *Estate of H.A. True, Jr., et al. v. Commissioner*, TCM 2001-167) (July 6, 2001).
[40] *Estate of Lauder v. Commissioner*, TCM 1992-736.

3. Are agreements entered into for bona fide business reasons?
4. Are agreements substitutes for testamentary dispositions?

- For number 4 above, the testamentary purpose test, the Court considered the following:
  - What was the condition of decedent's health when he entered into the agreement?
  - Was there negotiation of buy-sell agreement terms?
  - Was there consistent enforcement of buy-sell provisions?
  - Did the parties seek significant professional advice in selecting the formula price? On this issue the Court said,

  > We reject any notion that [the accountant] was qualified to opine on the reasonableness of using the tax book value in the True family buy-sell agreements. [The accountant] was closely associated with the True family; his objectivity was questionable. More importantly, he had no technical training or practical experience in valuing closely held businesses. The record shows no technical basis (in the form of comparables, valuation studies, projections) for [the accountant's] assertion that tax book value represented the price at which property would change hands between unrelated parties.

  - Did the parties obtain or rely on appraisals in selecting formula price?
  - Were significant assets excluded from the formula price?
  - Was there periodic review of formula price?
  - Did the business arrangements with True children fulfill Dave True's testamentary intent?
  - Was there adequate consideration?
- The Court concluded the buy-sell agreements were testamentary devices that did not set the value for estate and gift purposes.

Voting versus Nonvoting Stock

Voting shares of stock may be considered to have a higher fair market value than otherwise identical nonvoting shares.

Jeffrey L. Okerlund et al. v. United States[41]

- The taxpayer expert cited studies showing that discounts for lack of voting rights ranged between 3 and 10 percent, while the IRS expert cited studies where the discount ranged from 4 to 5.44 percent.
- Both experts concluded a 5 percent discount was appropriate, and the Tax Court accepted this.

Estate of Richard R. Simplot v. Commissioner[42]

- The Tax Court assigned a 3 percent premium to 18 shares of Class A voting stock in J.R. Simplot Co.

---

[41] *Jeffrey L. Okerlund et al. v. United States,* U.S. Court of Federal Claims, Consolidated Nos. 99-133T and 99-134T (August 23, 2002).

[42] *Estate of Richard R. Simplot v. Commissioner,* United States Court of Appeals for the Ninth Circuit, 249 F.3d 1191 (May 14, 2001); *Estate of Richard R. Simplot v. Commissioner,* 112 T.C. No. 13 (March 22, 1999).

- The Court calculated the premium based on the entire net worth of the company, saying, "a hypothetical buyer" of the shares "would gain access to the 'inner circle' of J.R. Simplot Co., and by having a seat at the Class A shareholder's table, over time, the hypothetical buyer potentially could position itself to play a role in the Company."

- The Tax Court considered "the characteristics of the hypothetical buyer" and supposed the buyer could be a Simplot, a competitor, a customer, a supplier, or an investor.

- The Tax Court also assumed that a buyer "would probably be well-financed, with a long-term investment horizon and no expectations of near-term benefits." The Tax Court went on to envisage the day when the hypothetical buyer of the 18 shares would hold the largest block because the three other Simplot children had died and their shares had been divided among their descendants.

- The Ninth Circuit determined that the Tax Court erred in three areas:

  1. *Hypothetical Willing Buyer.* The Tax Court departed from the hypothetical willing buyer standard because the Tax Court believed that "the hypothetical sale should not be constructed in a vacuum isolated from the actual facts that affect value." The Ninth Circuit believed the Tax Court relied on "imagined facts" and said, "In violation of the law the Tax Court constructed particular possible purchasers."

  2. *Error in Valuing All Voting Shares.* The Tax Court's premium calculation was incorrect. The Tax Court calculated the premium that all the Class A shares as a block would command and then divided this premium by the number of Class A shares. The Ninth Circuit said, "The Tax Court valued an asset not before it—all the Class A stock representing complete control. There was no basis for supposing that whatever value attached to complete control a proportionate share of that value attached to each fraction of the whole."

  3. *Lack of an Increased Economic Advantage.* Even a controlling block of stock should not be valued at a premium for estate tax purposes, unless the IRS can show that a purchaser would be able to use the control in a manner that assured an increased economic advantage worth paying a premium for. The Ninth Circuit noted that, "'No seat at the table' was assured by this minority interest; it could not elect a director. The Commissioner points out that Class A shareholders had formed businesses that did business with Simplot. If these businesses enjoyed special advantages, the Class A shareholders would have been liable for breach of their fiduciary duty to the Class B shareholders" (citations omitted).

- The Ninth Circuit said that much of the IRS argument was devoted to speculation as to what might happen after the valuation date, noting, "Speculation is easy but not a proper way to value the transfer at the time of the decedent's death. In Richard Simplot's hands at the time of transfer his stock was worth what a willing buyer would have paid for the economic benefits presently attached to the stock. By this standard, a minority holding Class A share was worth no more than a Class B share"(citation omitted).

- The Tax Court's decision was reversed and remanded for entry of a judgment in favor of the estate.

- One judge dissented to this opinion, believing the Tax Court was correct.

Wall v. Commissioner[43]

- This case concerns a dispute over the value of nonvoting shares.
- After noting that this was a case that should have settled without resorting to Tax Court, the Court accepted the IRS valuation, including a 40 percent discount for lack of marketability and a 2 percent discount for nonvoting stock.

Capital Asset Pricing Model, Discount Rate, and Weighted Average Cost of Capital

The Tax Court has generally not viewed the use of CAPM favorably because of its reliance on beta. It also has generally not been supportive in the use of WACC. However, this may have more to do with faulty application than the models themselves.

Estate of Thompson[44]

- The estates arrived at a 30.5 percent capitalization rate, including an "Internet and Management" risk of 12 percent and a 0 percent growth rate.
- In its calculation, the Tax Court used the capitalization of income method with an 18.5 percent capitalization rate (still without any adjustment for growth).

Estate of Trompeter[45]

- In the original case (*Trompeter* I), the Court determined the fair market value of the cumulative preferred stock using a 4 percent discount rate compounded daily. Upon remand (*Trompeter* II), the Court explained the calculation of present value but concluded that annual compounding was more appropriate since the dividends were compounded annually.
- The Ninth Circuit questioned whether a 4 percent discount rate adequately reflected the risk that the preferred stock would not be redeemed as provided by agreement. Judge Laro noted that the 4 percent did not reflect the risk that the stock would not be redeemed as required, but rather only the time value of money, noting, "As to the risk that Sterling would not meet its contractual obligation to redeem its series A preferred stock, we believe that a hypothetical buyer would have demanded minimal additional compensation to accept such a risk under the facts herein."
- In *Trompeter* II, Judge Laro did conclude that the 4 percent did not take into account the risk that "Sterling would not redeem its series A preferred stock for the contractual amount . . . but would redeem those shares at a lesser amount." Based on that, Judge Laro increased the 4 percent discount in *Trompeter* I to 12.5 percent in *Trompeter* II.

Estate of Hoffman v. Commissioner[46]

- The IRS expert used CAPM.
- He determined a 7.5 percent risk-free rate of return based on 30-year Treasury bonds and a 7.2 percent equity risk premium based on Ibbotson data.

[43] *Wall v. Commissioner*, TCM 2001-75 (March 27, 2001).
[44] *Estate of Thompson*, TCM 2004-174 (July 26, 2004).
[45] *Estate of Trompeter*, TCM 2004-27 (February 4, 2004).
[46] *Estate of Hoffman v. Commissioner*, TCM 2001-109 (May 9, 2001).

- The expert used a beta of 1 because "he could not obtain a reliable estimate of beta from comparable publicly traded stocks."
- He also used Ibbotson data to arrive at a 5.3 percent premium for "unsystematic risk to account for investment in a small company stock."
- Subtracting a 3 percent growth rate, he arrived at a final capitalization rate of 17 percent.
- The Tax Court disagreed with using CAPM for a small, closely held company, terming the failure to calculate beta a "significant shortcoming in the use of the CAPM to value a closely held corporation."
- The Court said, "[The IRS expert] has failed to provide the evidence necessary for us to determine whether use of CAPM was appropriate, and whether the figures used in his calculation were reliable."
- The Court was also critical of the expert's use of the 5.3 percent small stock premium without explaining why "such a figure is appropriate for WLI [company] specifically."

Estate of Emily F. Klauss v. Commissioner[47]

- The IRS expert used CAPM to determine the discount rate, while the taxpayer expert used the build-up method.
- The IRS expert chose a beta of 0.7 to estimate Green Light's [company] systematic risk.
- The Court disagreed, noting, "Green Light was a small, regional company, had customer concentrations, faced litigation and environmental claims, had inadequate insurance, was not publicly traded, and had never paid a dividend. A beta cannot be correctly calculated for the stock in a closely held corporation; it can only be correctly estimated on the basis of the betas of comparable publicly traded companies."
- The Court also concluded that the CAPM method was not appropriate because Green Light had little possibility of going public.
- The Court accepted the small company stock premium using Ibbotson Associates data.

Estate of Mary D. Maggos v. Commissioner[48]

- Both taxpayer and IRS experts used the discounted cash flow (DCF) method.
- The Tax Court expressed concern with the inherent difficulty of determining the residual value, which was "neither minimal nor easily calculated."
- The Court expressed further concern with the use of the Capital Asset Pricing Model and the weighted average cost of capital in valuing closely held small companies by citing a previous case as follows: "We do not believe that CAPM and WACC are the proper analytical tools to value a small, closely held corporation with little possibility of going public."
- The IRS expert used a 0.76 beta; however the Tax Court was not persuaded that the guideline companies used in this analysis were appropriate.

---

[47] *Estate of Emily F. Klauss v. Commissioner*, TCM 2000-191 (June 27, 2000).
[48] *Estate of Mary D. Maggos v. Commissioner*, TCM 2000-129 (April 11, 2000).

- The Tax Court did not believe an interest rate less than 2 percent above the government bond rate was appropriate in the WACC calculation for borrowed funds.
- The Tax Court concluded a 17 percent discount rate was appropriate rather than the 12 percent used by the IRS expert and the 22.24 percent used by one of the taxpayer experts.

Gow v. Commissioner[49]

- The taxpayer expert used a 32 percent discount rate, using the build-up method, including a 9.02 percent small-stock premium and a 10 percent company-specific risk premium.
- The IRS used two employees as experts, a real estate appraiser and a business appraiser.
- The IRS real estate appraiser valued the inventory of unsold timeshare units and the undeveloped land owned by Powhatan.
- This appraiser used a discounted cash flow method to value the unsold timeshare units, utilizing a 25 percent discount rate using "the band of investment" method, which is a "synthesis of mortgage and equity [yield] rates, which market data discloses as applicable to comparable properties."
- In arriving at the 25 percent discount rate, she combined the safe rate of return from the 10-year U.S. Treasury bond (9.17 percent and 8.47 percent on the two valuation dates) and the equity rate expected by land and real estate developers (between 15 and 30 percent).
- The IRS business appraiser then used the net asset approach using the real estate values determined by the real estate appraiser.
- The Tax Court found the testimony of the IRS experts "more persuasive."
- The Court agreed with the IRS experts that that taxpayer expert's report contained "fatal errors":
  - Understating the income stream
  - Overstating the discount rate
  - Applying a 15-percent contingency discount
- The Court adopted the prediscount valuation of the IRS experts.

Gross v. Commissioner[50]

- Subject company was an S corporation.
- One taxpayer expert arrived at a 19 percent cost of equity capital, stating "The required rate of return is determined by comparison to rates of return on investments of similar risk." He then ranked various investments by quality, as of December 1991, beginning with long-term Government bonds and ending with the category "extreme risk." One ranking consists of CC Bond and "Very Small Cap. Companies," which showed "Yield to Maturity" of "18+." The next higher ranking, "CCC Bond" and "Small Cap. Companies" showed a "Yield to Maturity" of 21+.

---

[49] *Robert T. and Kay F. Gow v. Commissioner*, TCM 2000-93 (March 20, 2000).
[50] *Walter L. Gross, Jr. et ux., et al. v. Commissioner*, TCM 1999-254 (July 29, 1999).

- This expert testified that he chose 19 percent because it fell within the range of yields for very small capitalization companies.
- He checked this conclusion by building the rate of return from Ibbotson data as follows:
  - A 2.1 percent risk-free rate (which he had reduced by 4 percent for inflation)
  - A 7 percent equity risk premium
  - A 1 percent company-specific risk
  - A 4.8 percent small-company risk premium, for a total (rounded) of 19 percent
- At trial, he admitted that he used Ibbotson Associates data for the small-company risk premium but that G&J [company] did not fall into the Ibbotson definition of a small company.
- The IRS expert calculated a 15.5 percent cost of equity capital.
- He arrived at this using CAPM by adding a 7.46 percent risk-free rate of return and a 7.4 percent equity risk premium increased for a beta coefficient of 1.09. (7.46 + [7.4% × 1.09] = 15.5%)
- The Court accepted 15.5 percent as the cost of equity capital.
- The Court allowed a 14.4 percent WACC to be used.
- The Court believed that it was significant that the expert applied a "pretax" discount rate to pretax earnings, although it is not apparent from the opinion why the discount rate was considered "pretax."
- See discussion infra regarding tax-affecting S corporation earnings.

Estate of William J. Desmond v. Commissioner[51]

- The taxpayer expert used CAPM.
- The IRS claimed that the higher betas in this industry compared to others was due to the potential environmental liabilities facing the subject company.
- The Court disagreed with this assertion based on a lack of evidence presented by the IRS at trial and concluded an additional discount was necessary for environmental liabilities under the income method.

Estate of James Waldo Hendrickson v. Commissioner[52]

- For the cost of capital used in the DCF method, the IRS expert used the WACC and calculated the cost of equity capital using CAPM.
- To calculate beta, the IRS expert used only large multilocation publicly traded banks compared to the relatively small single-location subject.
- The IRS expert determined a beta of 1.
- The Court noted that the IRS expert had significant shortcomings in his application of CAPM.
- The Court expressed doubts over the appropriateness of CAPM in the valuation of small, closely held companies, especially those with little prospect of going public.
- The Court pointed out a number of the problems with applying CAPM, including the accuracy of beta.

---

[51] *Estate of William J. Desmond v. Commissioner*, TCM 1999-76 (March 10, 1999).
[52] *Estate of James Waldo Hendrickson v. Commissioner*, TCM 1999-278 (August 23, 1999).

- Further, the Court faulted the IRS expert for ignoring the small-stock risk premium as a crucial part of determining cost of capital.

Furman v. Commissioner[53]

- The IRS valuation engineer used CAPM and WACC.
- The Tax Court said:

> *We do not believe that CAPM and WACC are the proper analytical tools to value a small, closely held corporation with little possibility of going public. CAPM is a financial model intended to explain the behavior of publicly traded securities that has been subjected to empirical validation using only historical data of the two largest U.S. stock markets. . . . Contrary to the assumptions of CAPM, the market for stock in a closely held corporation like FIC (the company) is not efficient, is subject to substantial transaction costs, and does not offer liquidity. . . . Because the calculation of beta requires historical pricing data, beta cannot be calculated for stock in a closely held corporation. The inability to calculate beta is a significant shortcoming in the use of CAPM to value a closely held corporation. . . .*

Tax-Affecting S Corporation Earnings

Estate of Heck v. Commissioner[54]

- Richie C. Heck died on February 15, 1995, owning 39.62 percent of the common shares of F. Korbel & Bros, Inc. (Korbel), a California S corporation.
- The IRS expert used a 10 percent discount for "additional risks associated with S corporations," including "the potential loss of S corporation status and shareholder liability for income taxes on S corporation income, regardless of the level of distribution" to arrive at the operating value.
- The IRS and taxpayer experts agreed on the applicability of the discounted cash flow method of the income approach, but they disagreed on the computation of the cash flow.
- The Court reviewed the assumptions used by the experts and adopted portions of each expert's analysis, but it primarily adopted the taxpayer expert's cash flow assumptions. Neither expert deducted imputed federal income taxes in arriving at the S corporation's cash flow.

Estate of William G. Adams v. Commissioner[55]

- Valuation of a 61.59 percent interest in an insurance agency.
- Taxpayer expert grossed up the 20.5 percent after-tax rate to 31.9 percent to match the pre tax S corporation cash flow stream to which it was applied.
- Tax court did not allow this rate of return adjustment.

---

[53] *Maude G. Furman et al. v. Commissioner*, TCM, 1998-157 (April 30, 1998).
[54] *Estate of Heck v. Commissioner*, TCM 2002-34 (February 5, 2002).
[55] *Estate of William G. Adams, Jr. v. Commissioner*, TCM 2002-80 (March 28, 2002).

Gross v. Commissioner[56]

- The taxpayer expert tax-affected S corporation earnings in the income approach while the IRS expert did not.
- The taxpayers introduced two IRS documents to support their approach: "A Valuation Guide for Income Estate and Gift Taxes" (the Guide) and "Examination Technique Handbook for Estate Tax Examiners" (the Handbook).
- One excerpt from the Guide noted "S corporations are treated similarly to partnerships for tax purposes. S corporations lend themselves readily to valuation approaches comparable to those used in valuing closely held corporations. You need only to adjust the earnings from the business to reflect estimated corporate income taxes that would have been payable had the Subchapter S election not been made."
- The Court read the excerpt as "neither requiring tax effecting nor laying the basis for a claim of detrimental reliance."
- Further, the Court noted that the taxpayers "have failed to prove that they relied on either the Guide or the Handbook in any way" and the IRS was not stopped "from disregarding a fictitious tax when valuing an S corporation."
- The taxpayer expert presented a list of costs or trade-offs shareholders incur because of electing S corporation status.
  - The first argument that the subject company might not make actual distributions sufficient to cover the shareholders' tax obligations was dismissed by the Court as an unreasonable assumption.
  - The second argument that the S corporation might lose its favorable tax status was similarly dismissed by the Court.
  - The final argument that S corporations have a disadvantage in raising capital was also dismissed since the Court believed this argument was appropriately addressed in the cost of capital rather than in the tax affecting of earnings.
- The Court concluded, "the principal benefit that shareholders expect from an S corporation election is a reduction in the total tax burden imposed on the enterprise. The owners expect to save money, and we see no reason why that savings ought to be ignored as a matter of course in valuing the S corporation."

Wall v. Commissioner[57]

- The Tax Court completely ignored the income approach calculation of both experts, citing the inability of the company to make projections.
- Even though this approach was ignored, the Tax Court's analysis made several comments about imputing income taxes to the earnings of an S corporation, saying that the tax-affected cash flow used by both appraisers was incorrect.
- The Court said, "Because this methodology attributes no value to Demco's S corporation status, we believe it is likely to result in an undervaluation of Demco's stock."

Blockage Discounts

Blockage discounts arise in both tangible asset appraisals and business appraisals. In business appraisals, the discount is mostly for publicly traded stock where the sale of

[56] *Walter L. Gross Jr. et ux., et al. v. Commissioner*, TCM 1999-254 (July 29, 1999).
[57] *Wall v. Commissioner*, TCM 2001-75 (March 27, 2001).

the subject shares in a short period of time could depress the public market. For real estate entities, the discount arises from the dollar amount or other size factor of the properties appraised compared to the amount of similar properties in the relevant market.

Estate of Foote[58]

- The decedent owned 280,507 (2.2 percent of the total) outstanding shares of Applied Power, Inc., which traded on the New York Stock Exchange.
- As part of the original return, the estate claimed a 5.24 percent blockage discount without appraisal.
- In connection with an IRS examination, the estate obtained two appraisals, one claiming an 8 percent blockage discount and the other claiming 22.5 percent.
- The IRS appraiser opined that the market was free of abnormal factors and influences and that the trading prices for the Applied Power stock were representative of the stock's fair market value.
- The appraiser tabulated trading statistics for eight days where more than 50,000 shares were traded and compared the closing price with the previous day's close. He also noted that 240,000 of the 280,507 shares were sold within 90 days after death at prices that did not depress the previous day's trading prices for the stock.
- On rebuttal, the estate's expert argued against the use of the subsequent events.
- In the Court's ruling, the judge, while mindful of the general rule that only facts known on the valuation date should be considered, said, "Here, we believe the three sales . . . within 3½ months of the decedent's death to be relevant and reasonably proximate to the valuation date."
- The Tax Court allowed the 3.3 percent discount claimed by the IRS expert.

Fractional Interest Discounts

Fractional interest discounts primarily apply to undivided interests in real property. Readers are advised to consider the differences between community property states and equitable distribution states when considering this discount when the co-owners are married. We have presented a few representative cases for reference purposes.

Estate of Augusta Porter Forbes v. Commissioner[59]

- A QTIP trust owned a 42 percent interest in one property and a 42.9 percent interest in another.
- The original estate tax return claimed a 30 percent fractional interest discount.
- The first taxpayer expert was unable to find comparable sales for similar fractional interests but found that real estate brokers had applied fractional interest discounts of 10 to 30 percent in liquidation partnerships.
- Based on this information and considering possible intrafamily conflicts and other factors adversely affecting the marketability of the undivided interests, the expert concluded a 30 percent discount was appropriate.

---

[58] *Estate of Dorothy B. Foote v. Commissioner*, TCM 1999-37 (February 5, 1999).
[59] *Estate of Augusta Porter Forbes v. Commissioner*, TCM 2001-72 (March 23, 2001).

- The second taxpayer expert determined that a 36 percent discount was appropriate utilizing the present value of annual income streams based on hypothetical partitions or forced sales of the properties under various scenarios.
    - The Tax Court was critical of this expert's approach, noting the present value calculations were inadequately explained, particularly the 14 percent equity discount rate he used.
- According to the Tax Court, the IRS expert "purported to use a comparable sales approach to determine an appropriate valuation discount." The appraiser used three "appropriate examples" that had fractional interest discounts ranging from 25 to 64 percent.
- The Court said that, with little explanation, the IRS appraiser concluded that based on the examples and "other market oriented research completed by this appraiser," the appropriate discount rate was 18 percent.
- The Tax Court concluded:

> *We are unpersuaded that the "examples" on which [the appraiser] bases his comparable sales analysis actually represent comparable sales. Even if they did, we find no adequate justification for his selection of an 18-percent discount rate—a rate that is well below the smallest discount indicated by [the appraiser's] own "comparables." Consequently, we do not rely on [the expert's] report. See Rule 143(f)(1). We are unsatisfied that any of the parties' experts have adequately justified their recommended discount rates—a shortcoming that might be attributable in part to a lack of available empirical data. Given that the parties agree that some valuation discount is appropriate, however, and lacking any firm basis on which we might independently derive one, we accept [the taxpayer expert's] recommended 30-percent valuation discount as being the most reasonably justified of the opinions presented to us.*

Estate of Rebecca A. Wineman v. Commissioner[60]

- The IRS expert examined sales of 21 partial interests and concluded that "an inverse relationship existed between the size of the pro rata interest and the amount of the adjustment." Smaller fractional interests would lead to larger discounts.
- He took a 10 percent discount for parcels in which the decedent owned 51 percent interests and a 15 percent discount for a parcel in which the decedent owned a 50 percent interest.
- The Tax Court was critical of some of the comparable partial interest sales used by the IRS appraiser since these transactions resulted in the buyer owning 100 percent. The Court said, "A buyer consolidating all the fractional interests is likely to pay a premium for those interests. Such a sale does not indicate the appropriate discount applicable between the hypothetical willing buyer and willing seller for a partial interest."
- The taxpayer expert examined six sales of partial interests and concluded a 15 percent discount would be appropriate for the decedent's 50 percent and 51 percent interests and a 20 percent discount would be appropriate for a 25 percent interest.

---

[60] *Estate of Rebecca A. Wineman v. Commissioner*, TCM 2000-193 (June 28, 2000).

- The Tax Court found this analysis "helpful," and allowed a 15 percent discount for the 50 percent and 51 percent owned parcels.

J. C. Shepherd v. Commissioner[61]

- The IRS argued that the discount for an undivided interest should be limited to the cost to partition.
- This argument was rejected by the Court, which noted that this approach failed to give adequate consideration to other factors, such as lack of control in managing and disposing of the property.
- The court allowed a 15 percent undivided interest discount.

Estate of William Busch v. Commissioner[62]

- The decedent owned a one-half interest in real estate.
- The decedent's appraiser discounted the value by 40 percent to account for the decedent's partial interest.
- The IRS appraiser valued the one-half interest with no discount for partial ownership.
- The Court allowed only a 10 percent discount based primarily on the cost to partition.

Internal Revenue Code Section 2036

IRC Section 2036 is designed to include transfers of assets that were testamentary in nature in a deceased taxpayer's gross estate. If an asset transfer is not a bona fide sale for adequate and full consideration, and if the decedent retained certain rights in the property, the full value of the property will be included in the gross estate. In other words, any entity created would be ignored and valuation discounts eliminated. By the time an appraiser is engaged, the Section 2036 may or may not already exist. The IRS has had some success attacking estate valuations under Section 2036. Following are some recent cases:

Estate of Bongard v. Commissioner, 124 T.C. No. 8 (March 15, 2005)

Estate of Bigelow v. Commissioner, TCM 2005-65 (March 30, 2005)

Estate of Lea K. Hillgren, TCM 2004-46 (March 3, 2004)

Estate of Ida Abraham, TCM 2004-39 (February 18, 2004)

Betsy T. Turner, Executrix of the Estate of Theodore Thompson, Deceased v. Commissioner (No. 03-3173) (U.S. Court of Appeals for the Third Circuit) (September 1, 2004)

Kimbell v. United States, U.S. Court of Appeals for the Fifth Circuit (May 20, 2004)

Estate of Eugene E. Stone III, TCM 2003-309 (November 7, 2003)

Estate of Albert Strangi, TCM 2003-145 (May 20, 2003) (on appeal to Fifth Circuit)

---

[61] *J. C. Shepherd v. Commissioner,* 115 T.C. No. 30 (October 26, 2000).

[62] *Estate of William Busch v. Commissioner,* TCM 2000-3 (January 15, 2000).

Asset Approach

Estate of Trompeter[63]

- The Ninth Circuit vacated and remanded TCM 1998-35 with instructions to explain the basis for arriving at the $4.5 million fair market value of assets fraudulently omitted from the estate.
- The $4.5 million of omitted assets included diamonds, jade, rugs, coins, cash, and similar assets.
- The opinion discusses the manner in which the fair market value of such assets is determined (i.e., based on the market in which the decedent would purchase the asset).
- For example, an individual would purchase estate jewelry at retail from a dealer, while the dealer would buy that jewelry at auction.
- This means the same jewelry item would have different fair market values for estate purposes, depending on whether the decedent was a dealer or a consumer.

Market Approach

Johann and Johanna Hess[64]

- HII was a holding company for subsidiaries engaged primarily in manufacturing specialty machines and tools and dies, mostly for the automotive industry.
- The taxpayer's expert criticized the IRS expert's guideline public companies approach calculation since the expert relied solely on price/earnings (P/E) ratios.
- The Court found the IRS expert's explanations to be thorough and complete, and the taxpayers failed to explain how considering only P/E ratios impacted the valuation results.
- There was also some dispute about the periods of time used in the analysis. The Court decided that the calculation did not necessarily overstate the fair market value of HII stock, however the Court, "... *recognize[ed] this possibility and [we] consider[ed] it in reaching our conclusion.*"
- The IRS and taxpayer appraisers both used a 15 percent minority discount.

Income Approach

Johann and Johanna Hess[65]

- HII was a holding company for subsidiaries engaged primarily in manufacturing specialty machines and tools and dies, mostly for the automotive industry.
- HII was a very cyclical business and had great difficulty in making profit projections with any accuracy.
- The taxpayer expert used the discounted cash flow approach and the market approach.
- Even though the Tax Court found the DCF analysis flawed, it was accorded some weight because the analysis was thorough and the appraiser made a site visit and interviewed personnel.

---

[63] *Estate of Trompeter*, TCM 2004-27 (February 4, 2004).
[64] *Johann and Johanna Hess*, TCM 2003-251 (August 20, 2003).
[65] Ibid.

- The IRS appraiser did not use the DCF method because he concluded that, "*relatively small changes in certain assumptions which were used resulted in large changes to the indicated value of the company.*"
- The Tax Court disagreed saying, "*It is axiomatic that even small changes in certain assumptions in a valuation analysis can result in dramatic changes in the value derived.*"

Noncompete Agreements

Johann and Johanna Hess[66]

- HII was a holding company for subsidiaries engaged primarily in manufacturing specialty machines and tools and dies, mostly for the automotive industry.
- In 1995, HII retired a key employee's stock as part of a transaction that included an eight-year covenant not to compete and a three-year employment agreement.
- The shareholder agreement that had been in place was not followed and was terminated as part of the transaction.
- The retiring shareholder was paid $4 million for his 20 shares and the two agreements.
- There was no allocation made among the share purchase, the employment agreement, and the covenant not to compete, although all parties filed tax returns that treated the entire amount as attributable to the value of the shares.
- The IRS appraiser determined that the values of the noncompete agreement and the employment agreement were "immaterial" in applying the prior transaction method.
- The taxpayer expert prepared supplemental reports that calculated the portion of the $4 million transaction that should be attributed to the noncompete and employment agreements.
- The Tax Court decided that the IRS expert overstated the stock value by not considering the other agreements but that the taxpayer expert's analysis overstated the agreements' value.

Weighting of Methods

Johann and Johanna Hess[67]

- The IRS expert based his value on a weighting of net asset value (10 percent), the prior stock transaction (40 percent), the shareholder agreement (10 percent), and the guideline public company method (40 percent).
- The taxpayers argued that the net asset approach (which resulted in a low value) should be weighted at more than 10 percent (apparently notwithstanding that their expert did not use this approach at all).
- The Tax Court concluded that since HII was an operating company and not a holding company, and because the asset approach ignored significant intangible value, only a small weight was justified.

---

[66] Ibid.
[67] Ibid.

Subsequent Events

Estate of Trompeter[68]

- On remand from the Ninth Circuit, Judge Laro explained how he calculated fair market value in TCM 1998-35 and made some adjustments to that original calculation.
- The Court also ". . . noted but [did] not rely upon . . ." the fact that the preferred shares were subsequently redeemed at a reduced price.

Estate of Helen M. Noble v. Commissioner[69]

- Decedent died on September 2, 1996, owning 116 shares (an 11.6 percent interest) of Glenwood State Bank (Glenwood Bank). Glenwood Bancorporation (Bancorporation) owned the remaining 88.4 percent.
- During the 15 months prior to decedent's death, Bancorporation purchased two blocks of Glenwood Bank shares: in June 1995, a block of 10 shares (1 percent) for $1,000 per share and in July 1996, a block of 7 shares (0.7 percent) for $1,500 per share.
- After decedent's death, the majority shareholder in Bancorporation tried to purchase decedent's shares. The appraisal obtained for the attempted purchase determined a fair market value of $878,004 ($7,569 per share), including a 29 percent discount for lack of control and a 35 percent discount for lack of marketability. The estate declined to sell its shares at this price. On October 24, 1997, some 14 months after death, the estate sold the shares for $1.1 million ($9,483 per share).
- The taxpayer asserted that the share sales prior to death were representative of fair market value.
- The Court said, "We disagree that the two prior sales of 10 shares and 7 shares, either separately or together, are an accurate measure of the applicable fair market value of decedent's 116 shares . . . we are also unpersuaded that either of those sales was made by a knowledgeable seller who was not compelled to sell or was made at arm's length."
- The Court noted that these two sellers did not sell their stock for the amount set forth in an appraisal, but in fact for much less than the amount determined in later appraisals, while the estate sold its stock after the appraisal for more than appraised value.
- The two prior sales were 1 percent and 0.7 percent interests that the Court contrasted with decedent's 11.6 percent interest.
- One of the estate experts testified that since the remaining 11.6 percent was the only interest not owned by Bancorporation, it was reasonably foreseeable that Bancorporation would eventually want to buy that interest, and this added a special value to the interest.
- As the Court said, "Our hypothetical seller would have known the same at the time of the hypothetical sale and as part of the hypothetical sale would have demanded compensation for this special value so as otherwise to not equate selling price for 10 shares and 7 shares with the hypothetical selling price of decedent's 116 shares."

---

[68] *Estate of Trompeter*, TCM 2004-27 (February 4, 2004).
[69] *Estate of Helen M. Noble v. Commissioner*, TCM 2005-2 (January 6, 2005).

- The major disagreement in the case was whether the subsequent sale of the 116 shares should have been used to determine fair market value.
- The Tax Court referenced the Court of Appeals for the Eighth Circuit's (the most likely court to which an appeal would be made), holding that "In determining the value of unlisted stocks, actual sales made in reasonable amounts at arm's length, in the normal course of business, within a reasonable time before or after the basic date, are the best criterion of market value."
- The Tax Court acknowledged that a valuation is generally made without any regard to any event happening after that date. The Court noted, however, that a subsequent event is not necessarily irrelevant if it was reasonably foreseeable at the valuation date.
- The Court went on to add, "An event occurring after a valuation date, even if unforeseeable as of the valuation date, also may be probative of the earlier valuation to the extent that it is relevant to establishing the amount a hypothetical willing buyer would have paid a hypothetical willing seller for the subject property as of the valuation date." [citations omitted]
- The taxpayers argued that the subsequent sale was a strategic sale at higher than fair market value.
- The IRS argued that it was simply an arm's-length sale.
- The Court agreed with the IRS, saying, "Although petitioners observe correctly that an actual purchase of stock by a strategic buyer may not necessarily represent the price that a hypothetical buyer would pay for similar shares, the third sale was not a sale of similar shares; it was a sale of the exact shares that are now before us for valuation."
- The Court was "unpersuaded by the evidence at hand that Glenwood [sic] was a strategic buyer that in the third sale paid a premium for the 116 shares. The third sale was consummated by unrelated parties (the estate and Bancorporation) and was prima facie at arm's length."
- In relying on the subsequent sale, the court noted that the record (i.e., trial testimony and exhibits) did not reveal any material change in circumstances that occurred between the valuation date and the subsequent sale.
- The Court reiterated the "on the basis of the record" comment several times in concluding that the only adjustment to be made to the $1.1 million sale price was for inflation.
- The Court's research found that inflation was slightly less than 3 percent and adjusted the subsequent sale by that 3 percent to arrive at a fair market value of $1,067,000.

Okerlund et al. v. United States[70]

- The Court of Federal Claims valued the nonvoting stock of SSE gifted by Marvin Schwan at December 31, 1992. Schwan died unexpectedly on May 9, 1993.
- On appeal, the taxpayers contended that in the December 31, 1992, valuation the Court of Federal Claims failed to consider SSE's actual earnings results in 1993 and 1994.
- The 1992 valuation report of the taxpayers' expert discussed several risk factors for SSE, including, "*1) reliance on a home delivery route system; 2) thin management ranks; 3) reliance on a key management figure, Marvin Schwan;*

---

[70] *Okerlund et al. v. United States,* U.S. Court of Appeals for the Federal Circuit (April 9, 2004).

> 4) *the risk of food contamination; 5) the competitors' greater human resources; 6) SSE's inability to invest in a national advertising campaign, based on its lack of a nationally recognizable brand name and the demographics of its customer base; 7) less diversity in product offerings than the guideline companies; and 8) the relatively small size of SSE's Board of Directors."*

- By the end of 1994, at least two of these risks had materialized: Marvin Schwan died and an outbreak of salmonella in October 1994 led to a product recall, a plant closure, and a class action lawsuit.
- The taxpayers argued that the actual occurrence of these events meant that the IRS appraiser "*. . . underestimated their ex ante probability in his 1992 valuation . . .*"
- The taxpayers also challenged the IRS expert's assertion that considering actual 1993 and 1994 revenues when determining a 1992 valuation would have been "*inappropriate appraisal practice.*"
- As to the 1993 and 1994 events and the market approach, the Court concluded, "*Valuation must always be made as of the donative date relying primarily on ex ante information; ex post data should be used sparingly. As with all evidentiary submissions, however, the critical question is relevance. The closer the profile of the later-date company to that of the valuation-date company, the more likely ex post data are to be relevant (though even in some cases, they may not be). The greater the significance of exogenous or unforeseen events occurring between the valuation date and the date of the proffered evidence, the less likely ex post evidence is to be relevant—even as a sanity check on the assumptions underlying a valuation model.*"

Johann and Johanna Hess[71]

- In his DCF analysis, the expert relied in part on an adjustment for errors in 1995 reserves for machine construction projects, discovered in 1997.
- The Tax Court did not accept this adjustment, saying, "*We cannot conclude from the evidence presented that a hypothetical buyer or seller would have discovered, or even considered, the understatement of reserves in 1995 . . . we are not convinced that the discovery of the alleged understatement was reasonably foreseeable on the gift date.*"

Estate of Natalie M. Leichter[72]

- Harlee was a California S corporation that imported and distributed water beds and futons.
- Approximately four years after the return was filed, the appraiser was called to meet with the estate's attorneys during the IRS examination of the estate.
- Shortly after the meeting, the estate appraiser informed the estate that, as a result of information received during the meeting, he discovered he had made errors in the appraisal.
- Placed in the position of discrediting its original appraiser, the estate argued that the appraiser's work was incorrect, citing several errors in the report.
- The Court noted that "*. . . most of the errors complained of by the estate are orthographic. While they might reflect that [the appraiser's] report needed proofreading, they do not show that the value is erroneous.*"

---

[71] *Johann and Johanna Hess*, TCM 2003-251 (August 20, 2003).
[72] *Estate of Natalie M. Leichter*, TCM 2003-66 (March 6, 2003).

Gift of Future Interest

Albert and Christine Hackl v. Commissioner[73]

- In *Hackl* I, the Tax Court determined that gifts of LLC interests were gifts of future interests and did not qualify for the annual gift tax exclusion.
- The Tax Court based its decision primarily on the terms of the LLC operating agreement.
- In *Hackl* II, the Seventh Circuit seemed to have modest concern for Hackl's economic motives, saying, "*Most post-retirement hobbies don't involve multi-million dollar companies or land retirees in hot water with the IRS, but these are the circumstances in this case. . . . Our story begins with A. J. Hackl's retirement and subsequent search for a hobby that would allow him to keep his hand in the business world, diversify his investments, and provide a long-term investment for his family.*"
- The Hackls' argument on appeal was that the gift tax does not apply to a transfer if the donors give up all of their legal rights.
- The Hackls also argued that their position reflected the meaning of "future interest" in the statute and the Tax Court's reliance on materials outside the statute (such as Treasury regulations and case law) was wrong.
- In what the Seventh Circuit called "hedging their bet," the Hackls also argued that the Treasury regulations support the conclusion that giving up all legal rights makes their gift a present interest.
- The Seventh Circuit noted that even though the voting shares that the Hackls gave away had the same legal rights as those they retained, the LLC operating agreement restrictions on transferability of the shares meant that they were essentially without immediate value to the donees.
- The Hackls argued that their LLC was the same as any other LLC, and the restrictions on share transfers are common in closely held companies.
- The Seventh Circuit said, "*While this may be true, the fact that other companies operate this way does not mean that shares in such companies should automatically be considered present interests for purposes of the gift tax exclusion.*"
- The Seventh Circuit concluded, "*The onus is on the taxpayers to show that their transfers qualify for the gift tax exclusion, a burden the Hackls have not met.*"

Key Employee Discount

Estate of Natalie M. Leichter[74]

- Harlee was a California S corporation that imported and distributed water beds and futons.
- Decedent's husband, who died in July 1995, was a key Harlee employee, accounting for 80 to 90 percent of all sales.
- Her son, Steven, worked at Harlee for 13 years prior to being fired in June 1994.
- Steven had been disinherited by decedent in a codicil to her will one week before she died. However, shortly after her death, he returned to Harlee and assumed responsibility for day-to-day operations.

---

[73] *Albert and Christine Hackl v. Commissioner,* U.S. Court of Appeals for the Seventh Circuit (July 11, 2003) (Hackl II).

[74] *Estate of Natalie M. Leichter,* TCM 2003-66 (March 6, 2003).

- The appraiser discounted the results of the various appraisal approaches for the loss of Leichter as a key employee.
- The appraiser also deducted a discount for lack of marketability, which the Court considered to be double-counting the key employee issue.
- The Court ultimately questioned whether this appraiser's report could be relied upon.

Valuation Date

Estate of Natalie M. Leichter[75]

- One of the taxpayer's appraisers valued Harlee two months after the date of death and "... *merely states that 'this date is appropriate.'*"
- The Court concluded, "*We accord no weight to [the appraiser's] report because of the lack of adequate explanations in support of his conclusions.*"

Preferred Stock

Estate of Trompeter[76]

- On remand from the Ninth Circuit, Judge Laro explained how he calculated fair market value in TCM 1998-35 and made some adjustments to that original calculation.
- In the original case (*Trompeter* I), the Court determined the fair market value of the cumulative preferred stock using a 4 percent discount rate compounded daily.
- Upon remand (*Trompeter* II), the Court explained the calculation of present value, but concluded that annual compounding was more appropriate since the dividends were compounded annually.
- The Ninth Circuit questioned whether a 4 percent discount rate adequately reflected the risk that the preferred stock would not be redeemed as provided by agreement.
- Judge Laro noted that the 4 percent did not reflect the risk that the stock would not be redeemed as required, but rather only the time value of money, noting, "*As to the risk that Sterling would not meet its contractual obligation to redeem its series A preferred stock, we believe that a hypothetical buyer would have demanded minimal additional compensation to accept such a risk under the facts herein.*"
- In *Trompeter* II, Judge Laro concluded that the 4 percent did not take into account the risk that, "*Sterling would not redeem its series A preferred stock for the contractual amount . . . but would redeem those shares at a lesser amount.*"
- Based on that, Judge Laro increased the 4 percent discount in *Trompeter* I to 12.5 percent in *Trompeter* II.
- The Court also "... *noted but [did] not rely upon . . .*" the fact that the preferred shares were subsequently redeemed at a reduced price.
- Also on remand, the estate argued that the value of preferred stock should be reduced by a discount for lack of marketability.
- Judge Laro disagreed, noting that his calculation of fair market value for the preferred shares was not the freely traded value of those shares, so a discount was not appropriate.

---

[75] Ibid.
[76] *Estate of Trompeter*, TCM 2004-27 (February 4, 2004).

• The opinion does not explain why the value determined was not a freely traded value.

Concluding Observations—Tax Court Cases

• The Tax Court is increasingly critical of experts who appear to be hired guns.
• The Tax Court wants the data relied on by experts in reaching their opinions to be related directly to the company being valued, particularly in the area of discounts for lack of marketability. This will continue to pose problems for appraisers. For example, in *Janda* the Tax Court criticized one expert for using general marketability studies instead of industry specific marketability studies (which do not exist). In the same case the Court criticized another expert for using the Quantitative Marketability Discount Model which utilizes other assumptions.
• The IRS has lost some key family limited partnership cases dealing with the formation of those partnerships. This leaves attacks on discounts for lack of control and marketability as the main concern on the value of these entities.
• Some Courts of Appeal cases (particularly the Ninth Circuit) have been critical of the Tax Court for not accepting either expert's analysis and arriving at their own conclusion without adequate analysis.

Daubert Challenges

In 1923, the federal courts first articulated and applied a test against which expert opinions would be compared to determine whether experts should be allowed to testify and the opinion admitted into evidence. This was known as the "Frye Test" (*Frye v. United States,* 293 F. 1013 [D.C. Cir. 1923]). In 1993, *Frye* was superseded in the federal courts by *Daubert v. Merrell Dow Pharmaceuticals, Inc.* 509 U.S. 579 (1993). There are two later cases that expanded upon the *Daubert* gatekeeping function, *General Electric Co. v. Joiner,* 522 U.S. 136 (1997) and *Kumho Tire Co. v. Carmichael,* 526 U.S. 137 (1999). In common usage, a "*Daubert* challenge" or "*Daubert* test" refers to this trilogy of cases.

Most states have adopted the *Daubert* rule, but some still adhere to the *Frye* rule. Readers must determine which rule applies in the state in which they are providing expert testimony. While this chapter summarizes a few cases, more current information can be found at www.dauberttracker.com (fee-based, hourly, or by annual subscription) and www.daubertontheweb.com (free).

Tax Cases

Gross v. Commissioner of Internal Revenue[77]

The taxpayer made a motion in limine to exclude the IRS expert, arguing his opinion was derived from the application of scientifically unreliable methodologies. The Court accepted its role as a gatekeeper but denied the taxpayer's motion, thus admitting the IRS expert.

---

[77] *Gross v. Commissioner of Internal Revenue,* 272 F.3d 333 (6th Cir. 2001) cert. denied, 537 U.S. 827 (2002).

Robertson v. Commissioner of Internal Revenue[78] (unpublished)

The Tax Court concluded that a computer sale leaseback was a sham transaction and assessed penalties for negligence. It excluded the taxpayer equipment appraiser, finding his appraisal a "summary of conclusory assertions" and "not a document worthy of reliance." The Ninth Circuit affirmed the expert's exclusion.

Estate of Helen M. Noble v. Commissioner[79]

The Tax Court was not persuaded that the work of the IRS expert was his own and his report was excluded. The Court also cited *Daubert* and Fed. R. Evid. 401 in considering the relevance of subsequent event.

Michael T. Caracci and Cindy W. Caracci et al. v. Commissioner[80]

The Court denied the taxpayer's *Daubert* challenge, noting, "These contentions are nonsensical and border on the frivolous."

Seagate Technology, Inc. v. Commissioner[81]

The taxpayer challenged the IRS expert's opinion as unreliable as part a motion for summary judgment. The Court denied the motion, noting, "Our conclusion that there remains a genuine dispute about a material fact does not presume that respondent's expert(s) is qualified or that the opinion(s) is necessarily helpful or admissible, but that such questions cannot be decided in the context of this summary judgment motion."

Brewer Quality Homes, Inc.[82]

The Court said, "Each expert does a much better job of explaining why the other side is wrong than why his or her analysis is correct. . . . To put it another way, the experts have provided substantial assistance to the trier of fact [citation omitted] in identifying and winnowing out the chaff; they have provided far less assistance in identifying and keeping the wheat." All three experts were admitted.

Bank One Corporation v. Commissioner of Internal Revenue[83]

The IRS argued that the work of the taxpayer expert was tainted by the significant participation of the taxpayer's attorney. The taxpayer's expert did not convince the Court that the work was his own, and his rebuttal report was excluded from evidence.

---

[78] *Robertson v. Commissioner of Internal Revenue,* No. 99-71368 (9th Cir. 2001) (unpublished).
[79] *Estate of Helen M. Noble v. Commissioner,* TCM 2005-2 (January 6, 2005).
[80] *Michael T. Caracci and Cindy W. Caracci, et al. v. Commissioner,* 118 T.C. No. 25 (May 22, 2002).
[81] *Seagate Technology, Inc. v. Commissioner,* TCM 2000-388 (December 22, 2000).
[82] *Brewer Quality Homes, Inc.* TCM 2003-200 (July 10, 2003).
[83] *Bank One Corporation v. Commissioner of Internal Revenue,* T.C. No. 11 (May 2, 2003).

WEB ADDENDUM 1—CURRENT TAX COURT CASES OF INTEREST AT www.wiley.com/go/FVAM3E

These Tax Court summaries were written by John Gilbert of The Financial Valuation Group in Montana or Chris Treharne, John Walker, and Fawntel Romero of Gibraltar Business Appraisals in Colorado. These are not all inclusive, but do contain some of the most important Tax Court cases since the last edition of this book.

CHAPTER 16

Shareholder Disputes

The valuation analyst must know and understand the nuances and subtleties associated with valuations being performed for a specific purpose. In the shareholder dispute arena, the analyst must begin with an understanding of the various actions that cause these types of suits. In addition, the analyst must understand the statutes and case law in this area, as these factors often control how the assignment is performed. These factors include the appropriate standard of value, the use of the various appraisal methodologies, and the appropriateness of valuation adjustments (discounts and premiums).

> State statutes and judicial precedent control this area of valuation. Although analysts should not be acting as attorneys, it is important that they become generally familiar with the statutes and case law in the jurisdiction in which the lawsuit has been filed.

In some jurisdictions, there may not be relevant case law, in which case the valuation analyst should speak with legal counsel regarding the appropriate case law guidance for that particular matter.[1]

This chapter discusses the various issues that arise in stockholder dispute actions, particularly those lawsuits that are filed by minority shareholders who believe that they have been treated unfairly.

HISTORY OF SHAREHOLDER DISPUTES

Prior to the twentieth century, most states' common law required a unanimous vote for significant corporate actions. As a result, there was no need for state statutes that protected minority shareholders, as their votes could control a corporate action. Over time, states began to change their statutes and provided companies with the ability to go forward with significant corporate transactions based on a majority

---

[1] Those states that do not have case law in this area often look to other states whose statutes are similar. The attorney working on the case should be able to provide the valuation analyst with the appropriate case law for the jurisdiction that the case was originated in.

vote. As a result, states began to adopt statutes that provided protection for the minority shareholders. Many states have adopted the Revised Model Business Corporation Act. This act includes a definition of fair value, which is the statutory standard of value used in these types of actions. "Fair value" means the value of the corporation's shares determined:

(i)   Immediately before the effectuation of the corporate action to which the shareholder objects;
(ii) Using customary and current valuation concepts and techniques generally employed for similar businesses in the context of the transaction requiring appraisal; and
(iii) Without discounting for lack of marketability or minority status except, if appropriate, for amendments to the article pursuant to Section 13.02(a)(5).[2]

Although this defines the standard of value, it does not define the methods by which the value should be calculated.

CAUSES OF ACTION

> Shareholder dispute cases typically arise under two different state statutes, dissenting shareholder actions and minority oppression (dissolution) actions.

All states have dissenting shareholder statutes. These actions arise when a minority shareholder believes that a proposed action of the corporation (known as a triggering event) will adversely affect him or her. Under state statute, the minority shareholder must "perfect" the action by performing specific steps as laid out in the statute. In New Jersey, for example,[3] the shareholder must take two steps:

1. Before the vote on the triggering event, the minority shareholder must notify the company that if the proposed event is approved, he or she will ask the company to purchase his or her shares.
2. Next, within 20 days of the date the company mailed notices to each shareholder advising that the proposed event was approved, the minority shareholder must make a written demand for payment (N.J.S.A. § 14A: 11-2). When written demand is made, the minority shareholder becomes a "dissenting shareholder" and forfeits all shareholder rights, except the right to be paid the fair value of his or her shares (N.J.S.A. § 14A: 11-3[2]).[4]

---

[2] Model Business Corporation Act, Section 13.01(4) (2002).
[3] Although there are variations in the states' statutes, New Jersey's statutes are typical of many other states as it relates to dissenting shareholder issues.
[4] Jay E. Fishman, Shannon P. Pratt, et al., *Guide to Business Valuation*, 12th ed. (Fort Worth, TX: Practitioners Publishing Co., 2009), ¶ 1501.11.

Following the shareholder's demand, the company must then take certain steps as defined by statute, including the provision of financial statements. The company may also make an offer to buy the dissenting shareholder's shares at fair value at this time. If no agreement is reached as to fair value, the dissenting shareholder will file an action to determine fair value. This is known as the stockholder's appraisal right or appraisal remedy.

Each state statute lists specific triggering events. These events include all or some of the following: merger, sale, exchange or other disposition of all or some of the company's stock, and, in some cases, the disposition of some or all of the company's assets. "Oppression has come to include conduct by the majority that breaches fiduciary duty, denies the minority shareholder his or her reasonable expectations in acquiring shares and entering into a shareholder agreement, or is burdensome, harsh, and wrongful to minority shareholder interests."[5] If a dissenting event occurs, the shareholder has the right to call for judicial dissolution.

An oppressed shareholder dispute resembles a "corporate divorce." These types of actions generally are triggered when a minority shareholder in a closely held company has expectations that are not met. In these instances, the minority shareholder "seeks a remedy for the majority shareholder's fraud, illegality, mismanagement, oppression, or similar reasons."[6]

Although a handful of states have not enacted judicial dissolution statutes, the remainder either have statutes or allow for dissolution based on majority behavior that is illegal, unfair, or fraudulent in some way. In many of the statutes, the minority shareholder must prove oppression, fraud, illegality, or mismanagement before the Court orders a remedy. Although there are similarities between oppression and dissenting shareholder disputes, there are differences as well. Dissension suits are the result of a corporate action, while oppression suits are generally more personal in nature. Therefore, it is sometimes difficult to determine if oppression has occurred.

Three of the facts the courts look for to determine oppression are:

1. Breach of reasonable expectations
2. Breach of fiduciary duty (obligation owned to minority shareholders by the majority
3. Heavy-handed and arbitrary or overbearing conduct[7]

In general, the remedy in a dissenting shareholder case is for the minority shareholder to be bought out. In an oppression case, however, there are three possible remedies available:

1. Requiring the company to purchase the shares, which is the most common remedy
2. Requiring the company to be liquidated and the proceeds equitably distributed
3. Finding there has been no oppression and maintaining status quo[8]

---

[5] Jay E. Fishman, Shannon P. Pratt, and William J. Morrison. *Standards of Value: Theory and Applications* (Hoboken, NJ: John Wiley & Sons, 2007), p. 101.

[6] Anne E. Singer and Jay Fishman, "Fair Value for Oppressed and Dissenting Shareholders," in *Advanced Business Valuation*, Robert Reilly and Robert Schweihs, eds. (New York: McGraw-Hill, 1999), p. 299.

[7] Ibid., 110–115.

[8] Fishman, Pratt, et al., *Guide to Business Valuation*, ¶ 1501.18.

However, judges are often given wide latitude. In one case, the Court allowed the minority shareholder to buy out the controlling shareholders.[9]

STANDARD OF VALUE

To proceed with any valuation assignment, the analyst must clearly define and understand the appropriate standard of value and apply it properly.

> In both dissenting and oppressed shareholder disputes, the statutes are clear—the standard of value is *fair value* in almost all states.

Judicial precedent also agrees on this issue. As previously mentioned, in most jurisdictions, fair value is defined as in the Revised Model Business Corporation Act as "the value of the shares immediately before the effectuation of the corporate action to which the dissenter objects, excluding any appreciation or depreciation in anticipation of the corporate action unless exclusion would be inequitable."[10]

Some jurisdictions have varied this definition by excluding the phrase "unless exclusion would be inequitable." Other jurisdictions have included the consideration of "all relevant factors." Finally, some statutes use different terminology, such as "fair cash value" and "value."

Although the definition of fair value leaves the interpretation of its meaning open, the judicial interpretation of this definition indicates that fair value is not fair market value, which is defined as "the amount at which the property would change hands between a willing buyer and a willing seller when the former is not under compulsion to buy and the latter is not under any compulsion to sell, both parties having reasonable knowledge of relevant facts."[11]

Exhibit 16.1 illustrates the differences between the two standards of value.

In *Financial Valuation: Businesses and Business Interests*, under standard of value, the author indicates:

> Although there is no precise legal definition of the term fair value, current jurisprudence suggests that fair value is not fair market value. In essence, "fair value" appears to be a legal concept separate and distinct from "fair market value," which is an appraisal concept.
>
> In order to better understand the subtle distinctions between fair value and fair market value, a review of the definition of fair market value is in order. The IRS's Revenue Ruling 59-60 defines fair market value as "the price at which the property would change hands between a willing buyer and a willing seller when the former is not under any compulsion

---

[9] *Muellenberg v. Bikon Corp.*, 143 NJ 168, 183, 669 A.2d 1382 (1996).
[10] Model Business Corporation Act.
[11] Revenue Ruling 59-60.

Exhibit 16.1   Differences Between Fair Market Value and Fair Value[12]

Fair Market Value	Fair Value
1. Willing buyer	1. *Not always a* willing buyer
2. Willing seller	2. *Not* a willing seller
3. Neither under compulsion	3. Buyer *not always* compelled; seller *under compulsion*
4. Assumes a typical *hypothetical* buyer and seller	4. The impact of the proposed transaction not considered; the concept of *fairness to the seller a possible consideration*
5. A *price equitable to both*	5. A concept of "fairness" *to the seller,* considering the inability to keep the stock
6. Assumes both buyer and seller have *equal knowledge*	6. No *such assumption*
7. Assumes *reasonable knowledge* of both parties	7. No *such assumption*
8. Applicable to *controlling interests or minority blocks*	8. Applicable to *minority* blocks
9. Applies to *all federal tax valuations*	9. The most common value standard in *state dissenting and oppressed shareholder statutes*

to buy and the latter is not under any compulsion to sell, both parties having reasonable knowledge of relevant facts." Further, the word "fair" in fair market value modifies the word market, perhaps implying an open and active market. On the other hand, the word "fair" in fair value modifies the word value, perhaps suggesting a just and equitable value.[13]

ValTip

Not only is the standard of value important in determining the methodology that will be performed and the discounts and premiums that will or will not be applied, but the courts have also shown that they do not equate fair value and fair market value.

---

[12] Gary R. Trugman, *Understanding Business Valuation: A Practical Guide to Valuing Small to Medium-Sized Businesses,* 3rd ed. (New York: American Institute of Certified Public Accountants, 2008) p. 97. Reprinted with permission, copyright © 2008 by American Institute of Certified Public Accountants, Inc.

[13] James H. Zukin, ed. *Financial Valuation: Businesses and Business Interests* (New York: Maxwell Macmillan Professional and Business Reference Division of Macmillan Information Company, Inc., 1990), pp. 9–37.

In the *Matter of Slant/Fin. Corp. v. the Chicago Corp.*, a New York Court stated:

> Because the petitioner's expert . . . in its valuation report (on title page) and
> on 15 occasions refers to its valuation to be based on Fair Market Value,
> and the Business Corporation Law only uses the term Fair Value . . . the
> Court considers it a threshold question as to whether Fair Value and Fair
> Market Value are synonymous.
>
> The Standard upon which [the company's expert's] valuation was
> based was Market Value . . . the statutory standard is much broader . . .
> The Court may give no weight to market value if the facts of the case so
> require.[14]

In fact, the Court rejected the report that was based on fair market value.

In another case, *LeBeau v. M.G. Bancorporation, Inc.*,[15] "the investment banker
had issued a fairness opinion on a squeeze-out merger based on fair market value
rather than on fair value. The Delaware Court of Chancery stated that this was 'legally
flawed' as evidence regarding fair value."[16] The Court stated, "No weight was given
to that opinion in the appraisal, as [the expert] had determined only the 'fair market
value' of MGB's minority shares rather than their pro rata share of enterprise value."

This is complicated by the fact that the courts sometimes do not differentiate
between fair value and fair market value. In a Florida corporate dissolution case, the
Court stated, "'fair value' rests on determining what a willing purchaser in an arm's-
length transaction would offer for an interest in the subject business."[17] The Court
also noted that the value should be based on an offer for the corporation. However,
in rendering its decision, the value was derived based on an offer for 50 percent of the
common stock, which appears to be a fair market value determination.

These are examples of the importance of understanding and utilizing the proper
standard of value when preparing reports for dissenting and oppressed shareholder
disputes. As stated in one valuation treatise:

> When appraising the fair value of a block of stock for a dissenting share-
> holder dispute, it is recommended that the appraiser consider the legal
> precedents for the applicable jurisdiction. Also, the opinion of counsel
> should be obtained regarding the interpretation of fair value in the juris-
> diction in which the case originates. *One should not assume that there is a
> clear and concise conceptual definition of fair value.* [Emphasis added.][18]

As previously stated, this area of valuation is driven by state statute and judicial
interpretation. Therefore, the valuation analyst must be prepared to perform the
appraisal in conjunction with these guidelines.

---

[14] *Matter of Slant/Fin. Corp. v. The Chicago Corp.* (NY Sup. Ct. Oct. 5, 1995), *aff'd* 236
A.D.2d 547, 654 N.Y.S.2d 627 (NY App. Div. Feb. 18, 1997).

[15] *LeBeau v. M.G. Bancorporation, Inc.*, No. Civ. A. 13414, 1998 WL 44993 (Del. Ch.
Jan. 29, 1998).

[16] Shannon P. Pratt, and Anita Niculita, *Valuing a Business*, 5th ed. (New York: McGraw-Hill,
2008), p. 918.

[17] *G&G Fashion Design, Inc. v. Enrique Garcia*, (2004 Fla. App LEXIS 1349).

[18] Richard C. May, and Loren B. Garruto, eds. *Financial Valuation: Businesses and Business
Interests*, 2000 Update (New York: Warren, Gorham & Lamont, 2000), U9A-7.

VALUATION DATE

When preparing a fair value analysis, the valuation analyst should consult the attorney on the engagement who will consider the state statute and case law to establish the valuation date.

In general, in dissenting shareholder lawsuits, the value is determined as of the day before the shareholders' meeting where the transaction being dissented from was proposed. In this way, the value is derived without the effects (either positive or negative) of the transaction, and the stockholder does not benefit or suffer the results of the proposed transaction. This does not mean that the appraiser ignores the future in determining value; it just means that the appraiser ignores the effects of the proposed transaction (merger, acquisition, etc.). In an oppressed shareholder case, the date of the valuation is usually the date of the filing of the complaint.

As in a fair market value appraisal, the valuation analyst should be considering those facts that were "known or knowable" as of the valuation date. In *Tri-Continental v. Battye*, the Court stated that the appraiser and the courts must consider any facts that are known or could be ascertained as of the date of the merger, as these are essential in determining value.[19] Therefore, the selection of the valuation date is important, so that the appraiser can determine what information can be utilized in the analysis and preparation of the report.

FUTURE APPRECIATION OR DEPRECIATION

The fair value standard excludes any appreciation or depreciation that occurs due to the transaction that the shareholder is dissenting from, unless the exclusion is inequitable. "Primarily, appreciation in value due to the normal course of business can be included, but the exclusion provision suggests that if the action was unfair or self-dealing by the majority having enriched themselves at the expense of the dissenter, those acts may be considered in the determination of fair value."[20]

ENTIRE FAIRNESS

As previously discussed, fair value cases arise because minority shareholders disagree with a company's actions or a company's management, and the result is generally the purchase of the minority shareholder's stock at fair value. In theory, fair value is supposed to be "fair" to both parties, and some courts look at a concept known as "entire fairness," which requires not only a "fair" price but also a fair procedure in determining that price. To comply with "entire fairness," a company must show

---

[19] 74 A.2d (Del. 1950).
[20] *Standards of Value,* 122.

consideration in the form of absolute and relative fairness. Absolute fairness addresses whether the consideration received by the shareholders was adequate relative to the value of the interest that was given up. Relative fairness addresses whether the consideration received was fair in comparison with what other stockholders received.[21]

In essence, what the courts are looking for is the fair treatment of the minority shareholders from the beginning of the process, such as having a valuation performed for the company, independent of the controlling interests. Although the usual remedy in a fair value case is the purchase of the minority shareholder's stock, if a court determines that "entire fairness" was lacking, judges have awarded greater amounts to compensate for the lack of fairness exhibited.

In the case of *Ryan v. Tad's Enterprises, Inc.*, Vice Chancellor Jacobs stated:

> The absence of any adequate independent representative for the minority shareholders, and of any arm's-length negotiation over the Merger terms, precludes a finding that the merger was a product of fair dealing. . . . [The defendants'] desire to minimize transaction costs . . . cannot relieve the corporate fiduciaries from their duty to assure that the interests of minority shareholders in a self-dealing transaction are adequately protected. . . . The defendants . . . are liable to the plaintiffs for breaching their fiduciary duty of loyalty. The question then becomes: what is the extent of that liability? . . . *The measure of damages for breach of fiduciary duty is not limited to the corporation's fair value as determined in an appraisal.*[22] [Citations omitted, emphasis added.]

Although this is a legal issue rather than a valuation issue, it is imperative that analysts remember that they are advocates for their opinion only. Although the analysts may be working for one side or the other, they must remember to remain objective and independent with respect to the client, so as not to be perceived as a hired gun and not be the cause of the Court determining a lack of fairness in the valuation.

In one decision, the judge stated:

> Typically both sides in an appraisal proceeding present expert opinions on the fair value of the petitioner's shares. In theory, these opinions facilitate judicial fact finding and conclusions by wrapping the experts' factual assumptions in complicated financial models with which they, and usually not the court, are conversant. One might expect the experts' desire to convince the Court of the reasonableness and validity of their assumptions and financial models would produce a somewhat narrow range of values, clearly and concisely supported, despite the individual parties' obvious conflicting incentives. Unfortunately, as this case and other cases most decidedly illustrate, one should not put much faith in that expectation, at least when faced with appraisal experts in this Court.

---

[21] Shannon P. Pratt. *Valuing a Business*, 5th ed. (New York: McGraw Hill, 2008), p. 905.
[22] *Ryan v. Tad's Enterprises, Inc.*, 709 A.2d 682, 693, 697 (Del.Ch., 1996), as quoted in an article by Shannon P. Pratt, "Shareholder Suit Valuation Criteria Vary from State to State," *Valuation Strategies* 2, no. 3 (January/February 1999), p. 14.

This clear tendency of experts to provide an extreme value most favorable for their client encourages disagreement in every area of the proceeding. Weighing of these numerous minor areas of conflict, and not necessarily the interpretation of financial models, is perhaps the best reason for this Court to consider appointing an independent expert to sort through the clutter submitted.[23]

The judge continued to make other comments regarding the experts that clearly showed his displeasure in their "hired gun" valuations. Despite this, the judge took both reports into consideration. He accepted certain portions of each analyst's analysis and determined his own conclusion of value.

ValTip

Courts look to the valuation analyst to provide a well-reasoned, objective valuation to aid them in their findings. To do so requires that analysts maintain objectivity and independence.

VALUATION METHODOLOGY

Since many large U.S. corporations are incorporated in the State of Delaware, much of the judicial precedent in dissenting shareholder suits comes out of the Delaware Chancery courts. Prior to 1983, the methodology that was ordinarily applied in these cases was known as the Delaware Block Method. It utilized various methods that resulted in three values: investment value, market value, and asset value. Once these values were derived, mathematical weightings were assigned to each value, and a weighted average was calculated to determine the final value. The weightings for a category could be zero, resulting in a final value that might be based on one or two of the three rather than on some average of the three values.

The definitions of value utilized in the Delaware Block Method were different from the definitions of value utilized in business valuation today. Investment value was a value derived from earnings or dividends, and the capitalization and discount rates used could be derived from the build up or capital asset pricing model or from market approach methods. Essentially, investment value was derived from a combination of what is currently known as the income and market approach methods. Market value under the Delaware Block Method was derived from prior transactions in the company's own stock. Asset value was based on the current value of the company's assets.

---

[23] *MPM Enterprises, Inc. v. Gilbert*, No. 14416, 709 A.2d 663; 1997 Del. Ch. Lexis 141 (September 29, 1997).

In 1983, the Delaware Supreme Court decided the case of *Weinberger v. UOP, Inc.*[24] In this case, the Court ruled that the Delaware Block Method alone was not sufficient; instead "all relevant factors" should be considered. The Court ruled that the Delaware Block Method was "clearly outmoded" because other valuation methods were being utilized in the financial community that were not considered in the method. This case did not eliminate the use of the Delaware Block Method; rather, it provided the analyst with the ability to use additional methodologies as well—in this particular case, the discounted cash flow method.

> Currently, the three approaches to value—market, income, and asset—are all acceptable in the shareholder dispute arena, although it is important to confer with the attorney in the particular jurisdiction. Methodologies (or preferred methods) vary from one jurisdiction to the other.

The courts will accept the use of various methodologies in fair value cases. However, like the Tax Courts, they look for proper utilization of the methodologies and will disregard a method if it is determined that it was not applied properly.

The Delaware Chancery Court has stated that the discounted cash flow method is "increasingly the model of choice for valuations in this Court."[25] Although different courts accept different methodologies, many states look to the Delaware courts for guidance. Therefore, it would not be surprising to find other courts accepting the discounted cash flow model in these types of cases in the future.

> Various courts interpret the methodologies differently and refer to commonly known methods by other names.

For this reason, it is wise for analysts to become generally familiar with case law as well. For example, one court defined asset value as a market multiple times book value, which most analysts would consider to be a market-derived value. If an analyst was going to provide expert testimony in that jurisdiction, it would be

---

[24] *Weinberger v. UOP, Inc.*, 457 A.2d 701 (Del. 1983).
[25] *Charles L. Grimes v. Vitalink Communications Corporation*, No. C.A. 12334, 1997 WL 538676 (Del. Ch. Aug 28, 1997), *aff'd* No. 425, 1997 (Del. Apr. 1, 1998).

helpful to understand the knowledge and direction of the court to help make a more persuasive and convincing argument.

VALUATION ADJUSTMENTS

When a valuation analyst is retained to determine the fair market value of a subject interest, conventional wisdom would have the analyst apply appropriate discounts and premiums. In these valuations, the question is not whether the discount or premium be applied; the question becomes how large or small should the discount or premium be.

Although these questions arise in fair value analysis, there is much less consensus among attorneys and the courts as to the answers. As previously explained, although fair value is defined in the state statutes, there is no clear-cut explanation of how to apply this definition to individual facts and circumstances. As a result, the analyst, along with the attorney, might consider applicable case law for guidance. Treatments vary from one state to another. Some states:

- Disallow both the discount for lack of control and the discount for lack of marketability
- Allow both the discount for lack of control and the discount for lack of marketability
- Allow a discount for lack of control but no discount for lack of marketability
- Allow a discount for lack of marketability but not a discount for lack of control

An issue also arises as to whether this discount should be applied at the entity or the shareholder level. Fishman et al. state:

> If the statutes were created to protect the shareholder from the controlling shareholders, a minority discount would be contrary to logic, as the majority shareholders would obviously benefit from a reduction in the amount they would have to pay the minority. With respect to marketability discounts, one could argue that the statute proposes that the judicial proceeding itself creates a market for the shares, and therefore, no marketability discount can be taken at the shareholder level. Alternatively, if indeed the minority investor is losing a pro rata proportion of the corporation in having to sell his or her shares, the application of discounts may be viewed as encouraging bad behavior by the majority, as they receive a premium for mistreating the minority.[26]

As if this is not confusing enough, some states have decided that the applicability of discounts should be decided on a case-by-case basis. As a result, these states have conflicting judicial decisions. Although the issue of control premiums does not arise often, there is case law on the subject, and some states have allowed control premiums in certain circumstances.

It cannot be reiterated enough how important the general understanding of the appropriate case law is when practicing in this arena. In some instances, what appears to be conflicting case law is, in fact, not. The next excerpt discusses two

---

[26] *Standards of Value,* 130.

cases handed down by the New Jersey Supreme Court in July 1999. At first glance, it appears that the court contradicted itself . . . but read on.

> In July 1999, the Supreme Court of New Jersey ruled on two fair value cases. One of these cases was filed as a dissenting shareholder action, while the other was filed under the New Jersey Oppressed Shareholder Statute. Although there were several issues on appeal in each case, the commonality between them was the issue of a Discount for Lack of Marketability (DLOM). These cases highlight the differences that can arise under the same standard of value.
>
> The *Lawson Mardon Wheaton, Inc. v. Smith* (A-63/64-98) case deals with a family-owned business. After a number of shares of this family-owned business were sold or conditionally sold to a British company, the Board of Directors approved a plan to restructure the corporation. The reason for this restructuring was to keep the stock in the family by restricting future public sales of the company's stock. When the plan was approved in 1991, those stockholders who did not approve were notified of their right to demand payment of the fair value of their shares under N.J.S.A. 14A:11-1 to -11, also known as The Appraisal Statute. Twenty-six shareholders owning approximately 15 percent of the shares dissented and demanded payment for their shares. The corporation offered $41.50 per share, which included the deduction of a 25 percent DLOM. This discount was based on the belief that there was a limited market of potential buyers for this stock. When the dissenters rejected this offer, this action was instituted.
>
> Both the trial court and the appellate court determined the price of the stock after considering a DLOM finding that there were extraordinary circumstances in this situation that gave rise to the applicability of this discount. The Supreme Court disagreed.
>
> The Supreme Court's opinion stresses the nature of the term fair value and states, "Courts must take fairness and equity in account in deciding to apply a discount to the value of the dissenting shareholders' stock in an appraisal action." The Court goes on to say:

Indeed, equitable considerations have led the majority of states and commentators to conclude that marketability and minority discounts should not be applied when determining fair value of dissenting shareholders' stock in an appraisal action. Although there is no clear consensus, the use of a fair value standard, combined with application of equitable principles, has resulted in a majority of jurisdictions holding that a dissenting shareholder is entitled to her proportional share of the fair market value of the corporation. The value of the shares will not be discounted on the ground that the shares are a minority interest or on the related grounds of a lack of liquidity or marketability.

In addressing the issue of extraordinary circumstances, the Supreme Court disagreed with the lower courts. According to the decision, extraordinary circumstances exist when a dissenting shareholder holds out in order to benefit him- or herself by doing so. In this case, the Court felt that disagreeing (dissenting) to a corporate change was not extraordinary, but rather an ordinary business matter.

In light of the issue of fairness and the fact that extraordinary circumstances did not appear to exist, the Supreme Court overturned the lower courts on these issues and held that a discount for lack of marketability was not applicable in this case.

On the same date, the Court ruled in the opposite direction in *Emanuel Balsamides, Sr., et. al. v. Protameen Chemicals, Inc., et. al.* (A-27-1998), which was an action brought under the New Jersey Oppressed Shareholder Statute (N.J.S.A. 14A: 12-7).

In this case, Balsamides and Perle were equal partners in a manufacturing business. After many years of jointly running the business, the partners began having trouble working together. Over a number of years, this relationship deteriorated. Balsamides sought relief as an oppressed shareholder. Under this statute, if the Court finds the plaintiff to be oppressed, the Court "may appoint a custodian, appoint a provisional director, order a sale of the corporations stock [as provided below], or enter a judgement dissolving the corporation. . . ." After a 19-day trial, the Court found that Balsamides was oppressed, that Perle had conducted himself in such a way as to harm the business, and concluded that Balsamides should purchase Perle's share of the business. The trial court determined the purchase price of these shares of stock after the deduction of a 35 percent DLOM.

The case was appealed to the appellate division, which overturned the trial court's decision relating to this discount. The appellate court "concluded that such a discount was not appropriate in this case because there was no sale of Perle's stock to the public, nor was Balsamides buying an interest that might result in the later sale of that interest to the public."

The case was then appealed to the Supreme Court, which overturned the appellate division on the issue of the discount for lack of marketability. The decision stated:

> The position of the Appellate Division ignores the reality that Balsamides is buying a company that will remain illiquid because it is not publicly traded and public information about it is not widely disseminated. Protameen will continue to have a small base of available purchasers. If it is resold in the future, Balsamides will receive a lower purchase price because of the company's closely held nature.
>
> If Perle and Balsamides sold Protameen together, the price they received would reflect Protameen's illiquidity. They would split the price and also share that detriment. Similarly, if Balsamides pays Perle a discounted price, Perle suffers half the lack-of-marketability now; Balsamides suffers the other half when he eventually sells his closely held business. Conversely, if Perle is not required to sell his shares at a price that reflects Protameen's lack of marketability, Balsamides will suffer the full effect of Protameen's lack of marketability at the time he sells.

In the *Balsamides* decision, the Supreme Court distinguishes the two cases. In summary, the cases are distinct based on the facts and on the different statutes under which these cases arise. Regarding *Wheaton,* the Court states, "It would be unfair and inequitable to apply a marketability discount. To allow the major shareholders to buy out the minority dissenters at a discount would penalize the minority for exercising their statutory rights. Moreover, it would create the wrong incentives for shareholders." Regarding the *Balsamides* decision, the Court states:

> In cases where the oppressing shareholder instigates the problems, as in this case, fairness dictates that the oppressing shareholder should not

benefit at the expense of the oppressed. The statute does not allow the oppressor to harm his partner and the company and be rewarded with the right to buy out that partner at a discount. We do not want to afford a shareholder any incentive to oppress other shareholders.

Despite the differences that appear to exist in the cases, the bottom line appears to be that the Court is looking for all shareholders to be treated fairly, regardless of the circumstances.[27]

This is a fairly obvious example of the case law in the shareholder dispute area. On the first reading of the cases, the reaction is that the Supreme Court of New Jersey contradicted itself. However, one of the major differences in these cases is that they arose from different causes of action. As a result, the judges' decisions were different. Another issue that becomes clear is the Court's attempt to be "fair" to both sides, which is one of the underlying themes of fair value.

Since the issues before the courts are numerous and case specific, a discussion of individual states' specific decisions has not been included. However, for very detailed state-by-state information, we refer the reader to Jay E. Fishman, Shannon P. Pratt, William S. Morrison, *Standards of Value: Theory and Applications* (Hoboken, NJ: John Wiley and Sons, 2007).

For another view of discounts or premiums, see the article in the Web Addendum, Gilbert E. Matthews, CFA, and Michelle Patterson, JD, PhD, "Testing for 'an Implied Minority Discount' in Guideline Company Prices," *Financial Valuation and Litigation Expert*, Issue 19, June/July 2009 at www.wiley.com/go/FVAM3E.

RECENT COURT CASE

In 2006, the Delaware Court of Chancery ruled on *Delaware Open MRI Radiology Associates, P.A. v. Howard B. Kessler, et al.*[28] This case is widely known in the valuation community because Vice Chancellor Strine opined on the issue of tax-affecting an S corporation's earnings. However, as stated in the decision, "the key question is whether the minority shareholders of Delaware Open MRI Radiology Associates, P.A. received fair value in a squeeze-out merger with an acquisition vehicle of the majority stockholders, Delaware Open Acquisition, P.A."

In the 85-page decision, Judge Strine discusses a number of issues related to fair value and its interpretation. For a detailed description of the judge's analysis, it is recommended that the analyst read the case in its entirety. A brief summary follows.

What started as an eight-person radiology practice ended up as the Broder Group with five doctors and the Kessler Group with three. The physicians originally shared the radiology "reads" equally, but over time, more and more reads went to the Broder Group until the time came when the Kessler Group (which owned 37.5 percent of Delaware Radiology) was receiving no reads at all. In addition, the Broder Group set up a new entity and effectuated a merger that squeezed out the Kessler Group. The Kessler Group was offered $16,228.55 per share.

---

[27] Excerpted from *Valuation Trends,* the newsletter of Trugman Valuation Associates, Inc. (used with permission).
[28] CA. No. 275-N.

Judge Strine ruled that the merger price was not fair and that the Kessler Group was entitled to $33,232.26 per share, or the pro rata of Delaware Radiology's appraisal value on the date of the merger. The first 20 pages of the decision discuss the background of the situation and how the lawsuit came to be. The judge then goes on to discuss the legal nature of the case. He states:

> The resolution of this case is complicated by the presence of both an equi-table entire fairness claim and a statutory appraisal claim. The key issues relevant to each type of claim are common and the differing rubrics have relatively little influence on the bottom line outcome of the case, which turns on whether the merger was financially fair.

To determine if the merger was financially fair, the judge would have to look at the company as a going concern on the merger date and consider all "relevant, non-speculative data." This included an analysis of the valuations performed by both sides' experts, which were considerably far apart in value.

The judge goes on to state the following:

> Unlike a statutory appraisal action, the success of an equitable action premised on the assertion that a conflicted merger is unfair ultimately turns on whether the court concludes that the conflicted fiduciaries breached their duties. Here, there is no question that the merger implicates the entire fairness doctrine, as the Broder Group comprised all members of the Delaware Radiology board and the acquiring company's board, and used its majority control to vote through the merger. Nor did the Broder Group use any of the procedure devices that could temper (or in some contexts, eliminate) the application of the entire fairness standard, such as a special negotiating committee of disinterested and independent directors or a majority of the minority stockholder vote provision.
>
> Therefore, the Broder Group bears the burden to prove that the merger was entirely fair. That burden has been said to require that the proponents of a conflicted merger demonstrate that they proceeded in a manner that was both procedurally and substantively fair. This is more than a bit of a misnomer, as the overriding consideration is whether the substantive terms of the transaction were fair. Thus, it has been said that the two-part fairness test is not a bifurcated one; rather, all aspects of the transaction are examined as a whole in order to aid in coming to the bottom-line conclusion of whether the transaction was fair. In a non-fraudulent transaction, therefore, price may be the preponderant consid-eration outweighing other features of the merger.

Most of the remainder of the case discusses the various experts' valuations and the judge's ultimate conclusions regarding what he perceived as errors in their processes. The three major issues as they related to the valuations were:

1. Reading and management fees. An issue arose regarding the fairness of the read-ing and management fees that were being paid by the majority shareholders to entities that they were involved in. The majority's appraiser accepted the fees as being at fair market rents. Based on the court's analysis, it was determined that

both the read fees and management fees were too high, and the fees were reduced to the judge's determination of the fair market rates.

2. Should the merger include the company's expansion plans? At the time of the filing of the complaint, two MRI centers were operating, and there were plans to open three more. The majority's expert excluded all three centers because they were not open at the date of the merger. The judge stated, "It never really occurred to him that there was any value there at all," and added, "if that is true, he has a jarringly novel view of corporate finance, in which the value of McDonald's does not include the revenues it expects to make from the new franchises it will open." Ultimately, the judge included value for all three of the centers that were being discussed at the valuation date.

3. Should the earnings of the corporation be tax-effected? Much has been written on this aspect of the case. In summary, the majority's expert tax-effected by 40 percent and the minority's expert did not tax-effect at all. The judge determined that the earnings should be tax-effected and used Chris Treharne's model to determine the appropriate tax rate.

In reading the case, it becomes very clear that the judge's goal was to determine the "fairness" of the transaction and to make sure that the appraisal petitioner "be paid for that which has been taken from him." In his conclusion, he stated, "I find that the merger was unfair and that the Kessler Group therefore prevails on its fiduciary duty claim."

COURT CASE CAVEATS

The last section of this chapter discussed the seemingly contradictory decisions that were not; the decisions were based on the statutes under which the cases were filed. But this is not the only problem that can occur when reading cases.

In some cases, there is a very specific issue before the Court. Readers who do not carefully analyze the case can be misled and apply a ruling to an incorrect set of circumstances.

> For example, the Supreme Court of Kansas recently ruled against both minority and marketability discounts in *Arnaud v. Stockgrowers Bank of Ashland* (1999 Kan. Lexis 645 [Nov. 5, 1999]). However, the ruling was in response to the question, "Is it proper for a corporation to determine fair value of a fractional share, pursuant to K.S.A. § 17-6405 by applying minority and marketability discounts when the fractional share resulted from a reverse stock split intended to eliminate the minority shareholder's interest in the corporation?"[29]

The decision in this case specifically related to this question, not to other questions regarding fair value. Therefore, unless the facts and circumstances of a case are similar to this, the ruling in this case may not be extended to other fair value cases.

---

[29] Fishman, Pratt, et al, *Guide to Business Valuation,* section 1502.11.

In another case, the Minnesota appellate court relied on the two New Jersey cases discussed in the last section to disallow a discount for lack of marketability.[30] The problem with this decision is that the *Balsamides* and *Wheaton* cases reached opposite conclusions.

Finally, courts have reversed previous decisions,[31] so it is important to coordinate with the attorney on the applicable law.

CONCLUSION

Preparing valuation analyses and reports in the shareholder dispute arena can be fraught with uncertainty for the valuation analyst who has not done his or her homework. In conjunction with the attorney, the analyst must become generally knowledgeable about the statutes and case law in the jurisdiction where the lawsuit will take place to ensure that the proper methodology is followed to derive a supportable conclusion of value that will be accepted by the courts.

---

[30] Ibid., section 1502.12.
[31] *Hansen v. 75 Ranch Company,* 1998 MT 77, 957 P.2d 32 (April 9, 1998).

CHAPTER 17

Employee Stock Ownership Plans

A fair-haired child of Congress and rightfully so.

Valuations of closely held securities held by employee stock ownership plans (ESOPs) differ from other types of closely held company valuations. It is important that the analyst understand these differences, especially the restrictions placed on ESOP shares. This chapter explores and defines these various differences, evaluates their individual and cumulative effect on the valuation process, and reconciles the findings. The focus here is to offer practical advice for the valuation of ESOP shares.

INTRODUCTION TO EMPLOYEE STOCK OWNERSHIP PLANS

Employee stock ownership plans or trusts, often referred to as ESOPs or ESOTs, have been in existence since the enactment of the Employee Retirement Income Security Act (ERISA) in 1974. ERISA was enacted by Congress to provide incentives to encourage ESOP usage by spreading the wealth of equity ownership to participating employees. An employee stock ownership plan is a qualified employee benefit plan subject to the provisions of ERISA.

An integral component of an ESOP is its qualified status as an ERISA defined-contribution plan. An ESOP is designed to invest primarily in employer securities of a sponsoring corporation. Corporations can sponsor ESOPs whether the shares are traded on a public market or privately held. Companies that sponsor ESOPs generally have a business culture that allows employees to think and act like owners. Basically, an ESOP is an enhanced qualified profit-sharing retirement plan that makes the employees the beneficial owners of the stock of the sponsoring company.

Parties with the legal responsibility for the operation and safety of a qualified retirement plan are termed fiduciaries. To assure that ERISA-qualified plan rules are met, ESOPs must appoint a plan trustee(s) to act as the plan fiduciary. Trustees direct and manage the ESOP to fiduciary standards promulgated by ERISA. These standards require that trustees act solely in the interest of the participants and beneficiaries with the care, skill, prudence, and diligence a reasonable and prudent person familiar with the circumstances would use.

There are a number of reasons for the popularity of employee stock ownership plans. ESOPs provide attractive tax benefits to the sponsoring company and to existing shareholders. They allow sponsoring companies to borrow money (exempt from Prohibited Transaction Rules) and repay it in pretax dollars. ESOPs provide a way for owners of closely held businesses to sell all or part of their interests and, if properly structured and under special circumstances, defer taxation on any gain. They also make it possible for companies to provide an employee benefit by contributing common stock on a tax-deductible basis to the plan.

NEED FOR VALUATION SERVICES

At a minimum, all ESOP transactions are based on an annual financial valuation estimating the fair market value of its shares. With public companies, the fair market value is the public trading price. In contrast, private, closely held companies and some thinly traded publicly held companies are appraised by an independent appraiser/valuation analyst ("analyst"). The appraisal serves many individuals and entities that require an ESOP valuation:

- Plan trustee
- Plan participants
- Existing shareholders
- Sponsoring company
- Internal Revenue Service
- Department of Labor

The ultimate responsibility in a financial valuation engagement of a closely held company resides with the plan trustee. Thus the ESOP plan trustee engages an analyst, and the analyst issues the written valuation report to the trustee. Payment of the analyst's fee can come from the ESOP or, more commonly, the sponsoring company. Either method of payment is acceptable and creates no conflict with the analyst's independence.

An annual valuation of the shares held in the ESOP of the sponsoring company is required in accordance with the Tax Reform Act of 1986. A valuation is also required when the ESOP makes its first acquisition of stock, if the ESOP sells out its stock position, and whenever there is a transaction with a controlling stockholder or member of a control group. These valuations are valid up to a year after the valuation date. Every valuation an analyst performs must adhere to regulations promulgated by the Internal Revenue Service (IRS) and the Department of Labor (DOL).

The trustee or named fiduciary is required to act in good faith, having arrived at a determination of fair market value through a prudent investigation of circumstances prevailing at the time of the valuation and with the application of sound valuation principles. The fiduciary preparing the valuation must also be independent of all parties to the transaction or relying on the report of an analyst who is independent of all parties to the transaction. The IRS put forth a similar set of valuation considerations; however, they focus on the federal income tax aspects of ESOP valuation. The IRS's concern is that fair market value is used in the valuation of non–publicly traded stock in the acquisition, sale, or noncash contribution of the sponsoring company's stock.

The process of valuing ESOP stock involves more steps than a typical non-ESOP engagement. As part of the valuation process, the analyst should obtain all the necessary data relevant to the ESOP as well as the sponsoring company. The checklist of items should include the ESOP plan documents and estimates of contribution levels to the plan. If leveraged, the checklist should also include a copy of all loan documents, an amortization schedule, and the terms and conditions of the debt. Additionally, at a minimum, the analyst should obtain a copy of the ESOP plan financial statement(s), minutes of the company's board of directors dealing specifically with the ESOP, and the stock record book.

FEASIBILITY OF AN ESOP

Often, difficulties occur when there is insufficient planning before an ESOP is initiated. One solution is a feasibility study. This analysis can be simple or multifaceted. A financial advisor to the plan often provides the plan trustees with financial modeling on deal points, interest rates, taxation, and cash flow analysis that assess the sponsoring company's operating ability to underwrite the ESOP. A well-crafted feasibility study incorporates short-, intermediate-, and long-term horizons. There are a number of aspects considered in a feasibility study:

1. Entity status ("C" or "S" taxation)
2. Estimated share transaction pricing (sometimes a calculation engagement)
3. Cash flow available to the ESOP for debt repayment or retirement of participants
4. Financial capacity to meet the ESOP's and the sponsoring company's ongoing operational requirements
5. Sufficient qualifying salary base to support required plan contributions
6. Estimated repurchase obligation, including plan design and other related issues

HOW ESOPs ARE USED

The ESOP can buy both new and existing shares of the sponsoring company, for a variety of purposes:

- ESOPs can be used in the succession planning of a company's ownership in buying the shares of a retiring shareholder. Among other considerations and requirements, in a C taxpayer environment the owners can defer tax on the gain made from the sale if the ESOP holds more than 30 percent of the company's stock after the transaction is complete. Additionally, the ESOPs share purchases are made, in most cases, with tax-deductible or tax incentive dollars.
- ESOPs are used to divest or acquire subsidiaries, to buy back outstanding shares in the market, or restructure an existing benefit plan by replacing existing benefit contributions with an ESOP.
- ESOPs are used to buy newly issued shares in the sponsoring company. The sponsoring company can use the proceeds of the funds for business purposes. For example, in a leveraged ESOP scenario, the sponsoring company can, in effect, finance growth or acquisitions with tax-deductible debt repayments, and this simultaneously sets up a qualified employee benefit plan.

These uses generally involve borrowing money by or through the sponsoring company of the ESOP. However, a company can contribute new shares of stock to an ESOP, or cash to buy existing shares, as a means of creating an employee benefit plan. The usage of ESOPs is becoming more prevalent as companies attempt to instill an employee ownership culture.

SECURITY LAWS AND THE ESOP

At the federal level, the Securities Exchange Commission (SEC) has the responsibility to regulate securities. At the state level, securities boards or commissions offer direction to businesses for limited and private securities offering exemptions to the various rules and regulations. Each securities commission provides information for the security laws of that jurisdiction. Thus, exemptions in one state may not apply to another. An analyst should be familiar with the state security laws of the subject company's state of incorporation and, in particular, the exemptions to that state's blue sky laws.

If a private company uses its equity as an incentive to enhance or compensate its employees or consultants, the rules generally allow for some form of exception or exemption from registration. This is particularly true of those securities offered to the ESOP.

A major factor of the ESOP is that it is considered a single shareholder for purposes of compliance with all security and tax laws. Additionally, the trustee has the responsibility of voting the shares as a block in most circumstances (see Voting and Other Rights of the ESOP Shareholders).

TAX ADVANTAGES OF ESOPs

There are several tax advantages to having an ESOP over other employee incentives. A company can deduct contributions up to 25 percent of covered payroll, plus, in a C corporation, any dividends on ESOP stock. In a C corporation, when an ESOP securities acquisition loan is used to purchase stock, the cash dividends can be deducted, as long as the dividends are passed through to the employees. Dividends paid on leveraged ESOP stock can be deducted when the dividends are used to reduce the principal or pay the interest on the loan used to purchase the stock. There are three primary ways in which C corporation employers can deduct dividends paid on ESOP-held stock:

1. Cash to ESOP participants
2. Applied to the leveraged ESOP loan
3. Dividends that are voluntarily reinvested

For additional S corporation tax advantages, see "Differences in Entity Structure."

DIFFERENCES IN ENTITY STRUCTURE

ESOPs can own stock in subchapter C or S corporations. While S corporation ESOPs operate under most of the same rules that C corporations do, there are five important differences.

1. Unlike C corporations, interest payments on ESOP loans count toward the annual plan contribution limits.
2. Certain flow-through dividends on ESOP shares distributed to participants are deductible to a C corporation and are not deductible to an S corporation.
3. Sellers to an ESOP in an S corporation do not qualify for the tax-deferred rollover treatment (see Internal Revenue Code section 1042).

4. There is no difference in the contribution limitations used by an S or C corporation.

5. An S corporation ESOP is unique, as neither it nor the sponsoring company pays federal income tax and, in some states, does not pay state income or franchise tax on any profits attributable to its allocation of income.

These differences can make converting to an S corporation very enticing when a C corporation ESOP owns a significant portion of the sponsoring company's stock.

As with all S corporations, shareholders receive pro rata distributions when, and if, dividends are paid. Accordingly, the ESOP proportionately participates in the dividend with other stockholders. The ESOP can apply dividend distributions to purchase additional outstanding or new-issue shares, to create a fund for future repurchase requirements, and/or to invest as additions to individual participant accounts.

Where cash dividend payments are made by an S corporation, the distributions are generally made to meet the personal tax obligations of the non-ESOP shareholders. These payments flow directly to the shareholder and, in the case of the ESOP, to the ESOP trust. In both scenarios, the cash is no longer available to the company for investment in the operations of the enterprise. With some restrictions, the ESOP can use dividend distributions to lower company contributions to the plan, pay down existing debt, purchase or repurchase shares, and/or pay plan benefits.

In the case of an S corporation that is owned 100 percent by an ESOP, the cash retention to the company can be significant, as no payments are required for federal income taxes. Therefore, the company annually realizes a cash savings equal to the dollar amount of the taxes the company would have paid if it were a C corporation.

Most incentive tax advantages accrue only to the shares while they reside as an asset of the ESOP. Based on the sponsoring company's entity structure, the absence or reduction of income taxes and the deductibility from taxable income of loan principal represents true and substantial cash savings to the sponsoring company.

Often, in an S corporation environment, the company's cash savings must be put to productive operating use in order to reflect enhancements in the enterprise value. When reduction in cash flow occurs as a result of paying out dividends, the owner of the common stock may earn a portion of its total return in the form of dividends above the amount needed to pay taxes.

IMPORTANT DIFFERENCES IN SHARE OWNERSHIP (ESOP VERSUS OTHER)

As a shareholder, the ESOP is different in a number of respects from the characteristics of direct equity ownership. The participants are beneficial owners within a tax-exempt qualified ERISA retirement plan. Significant differences include the following:

- The ESOP is considered a single shareholder of outstanding shares of the sponsoring company's stock, and the retirement plan participants do not have direct title to their shares. Rather, the shares are owned according to a pooled plan allocation, and the participants are not at will to transact.
- Except in specific extraordinary instances, the ESOP shares are voted as one shareholding by the plan trustee, unless specifically provided by a plan design that says the shares' voting rights are granted on all voting issues.

- An ESOP is primarily designed to own one class of the sponsoring company stock; thus there is no diversification available to the plan or its participants (except certain age-related diversification requirements under ERISA).
- Plan participants are not only subject to ownership as a beneficial interest but also subject to retirement plan vesting, termination, and forfeiture rules that differ from those of outright ownership.
- Often, where there is acquisition debt associated with a leveraged ESOP transaction, the ability to sell those associated plan shares is impaired by plan restrictions that require all plan debt on all acquisition shares be paid in full before any payout to departing ESOP participants.
- Departing ESOP participants have requirements restricting them from freely selling the shares.
- Plan designs allow the ability for the distribution of retirement plan benefits by providing a secured note with the sponsoring company to purchase the shares over an extended period of time with interest. In contrast, collection of the proceeds from the sale of publicly traded shares, trading in an active market place, occurs in a relatively shorter period of time (within three business days).

Identifying these differences provides the analyst a better understanding in assessing the liquidity of the share interests and the participant's ability to transact the shares.

ADEQUATE CONSIDERATION: HOW AND WHY IT WORKS

Adequate consideration, as defined by the DOL, has a very specific meaning in the valuation of ESOPs. Adequate consideration is the fair market value of the asset as determined in good faith by the trustee or named fiduciary pursuant to the terms of the plan and in accordance with regulations promulgated by the Secretary of Labor. It means the trustee is responsible to employee participants to ensure they are neither disadvantaged by what the plan pays for sponsoring company shares nor disadvantaged by what they receive upon their termination from the plan. Thus, the ESOP cannot pay more than adequate consideration in a purchase of shares and must pay fair market value in the case of participant termination (receipt of benefits from the shares). As an example, the plan trustee accepts the analyst's valuation as reasonable at $20 per share for purposes of adequate consideration. A non-ESOP shareholder is selling shares, and the plan has an interest and purchases them for $19 per share. Obviously, the ESOP has not paid more than adequate consideration and is well within the prudent rules and intent of DOL. In contrast, an ESOP participant terminates the plan and tenders shares, and, for the sake of this illustration, the ESOP purchases the shares. In this instance, the trustee will pay $20, the fair market value for the ESOP shares, as is required and does not disadvantage the ESOP participant. Paying more than fair market value would be greater than adequate consideration and not be in compliance with the adequate consideration provisions.

Expounding on the DOL adequate consideration requirement, the ESOP cannot pay more than fair market value for its shares. The Internal Revenue Service, in its July 24, 2009 UILC (Uniform Issue List Code) 4975.04-00 release, acknowledged that "adequate consideration" is of "particular importance to the establishment and maintenance of ESOPs. . . ." This UILC goes on to confer ". . . the determination of adequate consideration is a central safeguard in many statutory exemptions applicable to plan transactions with the plan sponsor." The fair market value standard of valuation imposes a willing buyer, willing seller concept, where the buyers and sellers are both hypothetical. While the difference is subtle, the DOL adequate consideration requirement provides only for the purchase of shares and rightly so, because in an ERISA plan, the acquisition is paramount.

ESOPs AND PLAN CONTRIBUTIONS

ESOP contributions are expenses to a corporation that are unique in several respects as compared to those of other qualified plan counterparts. Shares of sponsoring company stock at their then fair market value and/or cash can be used as a qualified plan contribution with differing financial impact to the cash flow of the sponsoring company. Yet, they both achieve a tax-deductible charge against income. In the instance of contributing sponsoring company stock to the ESOP, there is a corresponding but not always proportionate dilution, as newly issued shares and/or treasury stocks now become outstanding shares. The share dilution is disproportionate because of the tax consequences (savings) of the contribution.

Valuation considerations center on the analyst's determination of how the different types of contributions (cash or stock) affect the sponsoring company's earnings and cash flow and, thus, the value conclusion of the stock. In this regard, two valuation considerations surface with ESOPs:

1. How do the benefit plan contributions to the subject company compare to those of comparable companies?
2. What effect does the contribution have on a pretax basis to the sponsoring company?

The analyst should consider the tax benefit derived by the contribution of shares of stock, as this method of employee benefit reflects a positive cash flow in much the same way as amortized expenses. This positive cash flow is derived as the sponsoring company obtains a tax deduction for the fair market value of the shares contributed. This employee benefit does not require an outlay of cash. In this instance, consideration is also given to the cash flow generated, reflective of the tax benefit achieved by such method of contribution. The probability of this method of contribution on an ongoing basis should be carefully studied. Future projections should be weighed carefully for the dilution impact on outstanding shares.

GENERAL CONSIDERATIONS FOR ESOP LOANS

The ESOP can borrow money from virtually anyone, such as commercial lenders, sellers of their stock, and the sponsoring company. The proceeds can be used to make acquisitions of the sponsoring company stock. This leverage is generally obtained by the plan in one of three ways:

1. A direct loan to the ESOP from a third-party lender, which generally requires the guarantee of the sponsoring company

2. Through an indirect loan, often termed a mirror loan, made to the sponsoring company by a third-party lender, then in a mirror loan, with identical terms and conditions, to the ESOP
3. Through an employer loan to the ESOP with no assistance from a third-party lender

Typically, a lender will make a loan to the company, while the company lends the money to the ESOP in a second loan. The primary reasons for these mirror loans center on the lender's ability to secure the loan with company assets. In most leveraged transactions, lenders require a second step in the loan process of making the loan to the company instead of the trust. The sponsoring company then lends the proceeds to the ESOP. The ESOP then uses the loan proceeds to buy new or treasury shares of stock or existing shares owned by other shareholders. Thus, loan proceeds from treasury or newly issued stock are available for operations, which differ from loan proceeds used to purchase shares from outside shareholders.

Any loan to an ESOP must meet several requirements. The loan must have reasonable rates (risk adjusted) and terms, and the loan must be repaid only from employer contributions, dividends on unallocated shares, and earnings from other investments in the trust contributed by the employer. There are no limitations on the terms of an ESOP loan other than what lenders will accept. Loans typically amortize over five to seven years.

When the ESOP uses debt to acquire company stock, the encumbered collateral company shares in the plan are held in a suspense account as unallocated shares. As the loan is repaid, these suspense shares are released and allocated to the individual accounts of plan participants, based on the original cost of the company shares.

ESOPs THAT INCLUDE DEBT

ESOPs are unique among benefit plans as they can borrow money to make acquisitions of the sponsoring company's stock. The most complicated incentive transactions involve the ESOP borrowing money to acquire stock of the sponsoring company.

In a leveraged ESOP, the ESOP or its corporate sponsor borrows money from a qualified lender, the specific shareholder, or both. The proceeds from the loan(s) can be used to buy stock from one or more existing owners and/or from the sponsoring company. The lender will require the corporation to offer surety and guarantees for the repayment of the loan. The sponsoring company makes annual tax-deductible cash contributions to the ESOP that repays the loan over the amortized loan period.

Tax incentives make borrowing through an ESOP extremely attractive to companies that might otherwise never consider financing their employees' acquisition of stock. Since ESOP contributions are tax deductible, a corporation that repays an ESOP loan in effect gets to deduct principal as well as interest from taxable income. This deductibility can significantly reduce the cost of financing to the company by reducing the number of pretax dollars needed to repay the principal (depending on the company's graduated income tax rates).

Proceeds from the loan can be used for any business purpose, including acquiring shares from existing shareholders. The acquired stock is placed into a suspense account, from which it is released to individual participant accounts as the loan is repaid. By making the loan through the ESOP, the company gets a number of unique tax benefits.

One benefit, subject to certain payroll-based limitations, is that the company deducts the entire loan payment as an ESOP contribution. In a C corporation, the company, within limitations, can deduct the interest and principal of the loan. Additionally, a C corporation can deduct dividends paid on the shares acquired with the proceeds of the loan that are used to repay the loan itself or paid through to employees.

Not only can the ESOP be funded directly by discretionary corporate contributions of cash but also it can make contributions at fair market value. These cash or sponsoring company stock contributions are tax deductible.

A thorough evaluation of investor risk and valuation methodologies is needed to correlate the relevant effects of ESOP debt, required plan contributions, and the value of the ESOP shareholders' equity. Based on company-specific factors, additional risk is generally associated with companies that are more highly leveraged. This additional risk is reflected in the analysis of overall risk of the sponsoring company. A different and additional risk premium is generally needed for the use of ESOP debt when the proceeds are for nonoperating purposes, such as the purchase of existing shares from existing shareholders of the sponsoring company. Conversely, given the same ESOP debt, when the proceeds are used for operating purposes and the ESOP buys shares from the sponsoring company (via its treasury stock or newly issued shares and the proceeds are used to expand the business, acquire a subsidiary, or replace existing debt of the company), the value may not require a different or additional risk premium. Also, an additional risk premium may not be necessary, as an investor may see the incentives of deductible note principal as advantageous, although, in this instance, there will be a dilutive effect due to the increase in the number of shares outstanding. The risk factors will be adjusted accordingly as the ESOP debt is repaid over the amortization period.

In valuation and economic theory, the value of a stock is what an investor perceives as the risk-adjusted present value of anticipated future benefits generated from the investment. Of paramount importance in a leveraged ESOP valuation is an analysis of the sponsoring company's forecasted earnings and free cash flow. This is generally achieved by using acceptable methodologies that develop valuation models on either a debt-free or net cash flow basis. In a leveraged ESOP, it is necessary to consider using a weighted average cost of capital in the income approach and comparability with guideline public companies by assessing the invested capital of the subject company. These total invested capital methods provide a better basis for assessing the characteristics of their debt and tax consequences.

Discounting the projected free cash flow at an appropriate risk-adjusted discount rate is essential. All debt considered to be long-term debt with inclusion of the routinely renewed working capital and line of credit debt, net of any federal income tax benefits that may accrue to the ESOP portion of the debt, is then deducted from the present value of the discounted free cash flow to establish an indication of value.

Additionally, when guideline companies and other market data are used, the difference in capital and debt structure should be considered, and those considerations should include the debt-free earnings and cash flow of the guideline and sponsoring company.

ACCOUNTING STANDARDS AND ESOPs WITH DEBT

The American Institute of Certified Public Accountants (AICPA) issued Statement of Position (SOP) 93-6, *Employers' Accounting for Employee Stock Ownership Plans* with an effective date for financial statement presentation of accounting years beginning after December 15, 1993. (Existing ESOPs will apply this approach to all new ESOPs and all new acquisitions of shares but not to refinancing old acquisitions, as prior ESOP transactions are allowed to retain their prior accounting treatment.)

Balance Sheet Issues and the Leveraged ESOP

Under SOP 93-6, direct and indirect loan arrangements of the company for the ESOP loan should be shown as an obligation (liability) of the company with a contra account as a reduction in the equity section termed "Unearned ESOP Shares," known as suspense shares representing the pledged ESOP shares. As the ESOP debt is repaid, the suspense shares are released. Shares are allocated and may not necessarily be proportionate to the debt reduction. Dividends on allocated and released and unallocated shares are charged to retained earnings. In cases where there has been an increase in the market value of the stock over that of suspense shares, the increase is added to paid-in-capital. There is no financial statement consideration given to the future tax benefits derived by the income tax deductibility associated with the repayment of the ESOP debt principal.

The ESOP buys shares of stock from treasury stock, from newly issued stock of the sponsoring company, from existing shareholder(s), or in any combination of these three. Loan repayments typically are made quarterly. The sponsoring company makes repayment of the loan to the ESOP as a tax-deductible plan contribution. In the case of a direct loan, the plan pays the lender directly from the funds received by the sponsoring company. If the loan repayment is part of an indirect loan arrangement, the company pays the lender directly and generally accounts for the transaction as a plan contribution. By paying directly, the company eliminates the need to contribute to the plan. Then the plan pays the sponsoring company, which in turn pays the lender under the original installment note agreement.

Under SOP 93-6, accounting for the direct and indirect loan arrangements requires several steps and creates an interesting financial statement presentation that requires the analyst's good faith interpretation and probable valuation adjustment. SOP 93-6 requires, in the case of either a direct or indirect loan used to purchase stocks held by shareholders in the open market, the sponsoring company to record the transaction as a treasury stock acquisition. Then the accountant must record a subsequent issue of the shares to the ESOP, by relieving the treasury stock account of the acquired shares and creating the contra equity account unearned ESOP shares. Should the ESOP acquire new issue (unissued) shares from the company, the company will increase the common stock account at the current value of the shares with a corresponding entry to the unearned ESOP shares account.

Earnings per Share Issues

Dividends on released common shares constitute an exchange of ESOP shares for compensated services (earned). As such, they are considered outstanding for earnings per share calculations. However, shares that are not to be released (suspense shares) are not considered earned and are not outstanding in the earnings per share calculations.

Dividends on convertible preferred stock issued to an ESOP will affect earnings per share (EPS) calculations as dividends can be paid on allocated or unallocated shares and, accordingly, are recorded differently by the company on leveraged ESOP shares, depending on that allocation. In essence, the sponsoring company has control of dividends on the unallocated shares. Thus, when dividends paid on unallocated shares are used for debt service, the liability for the debt or accrued interest is charged, and, if added to participant accounts, they are charged as compensation expense. Thus, in both instances, payment of dividends on unallocated shares requires no accounting adjustment to net income in the earnings per share calculation.

Dividends paid on allocated shares added to participant accounts are no different than any other dividend on convertible stock and are included in the EPS calculation by using the "if converted" method. If the dividends on the allocated shares are used for debt service, net income in the EPS calculation may need reduction.

Statement of Income Issues for the Leveraged ESOP

There are two primary issues relative to income statement presentation: the measurement of compensation expense associated with an ESOP plan and the period in which that expense is to be associated. Under the measurement of compensation, each accounting period has a different compensation expense, which fluctuates with the market price of the shares to be released. The company measures compensation expense on the basis of the fair value (an accounting term considered here similar with fair market value) of the shares to be released. In these instances, a dramatic impact will result where share values fluctuate and compensation costs will be different and vary with these fluctuations. The average value for the year is used, as the stock is considered earned throughout the year. This treatment differs in the nonleveraged plans accounting, as the expense is equal to the cash paid for the shares committed at the date of the commitment.

Dividends and the Leveraged ESOP

For financial statement purposes, dividends are chargeable to retained earnings and not compensation expense, with one exception. In the case where dividends were paid on unallocated shares arising from repayment of debt, these dividends will be treated as compensation expense. The accounting theory suggests that these dividends can be used to satisfy an obligation of the plan rather than accruing to the participants' accounts, thus losing their character as a dividend.

Valuation Impact

Financial statement presentation for leveraged ESOPs under SOP 93-6 remains controversial. While the underlying accounting theory in SOP 93-6 attempts to address financial reporting inconsistencies with leveraged and nonleveraged plans under the superseded SOP 76-3, it does not create a clear picture for valuation purposes and presents several issues that must be reconciled. Analytically and for valuation purposes, the impact will be addressed for each of the points in the accounting in the categories that follow.

For valuation purposes, there are no GAAP accounting differences or analytical valuation adjustments warranted with a nonleveraged ESOP, as the superseded SOP 76-3 and the SOP 93-6 handle these plans similarly. However, for a leveraged ESOP, the difference in financial reporting is significant.

Prior to enactment of SOP 93-6, there were neither suspense shares nor fair value compensation expense that required differentiation of the proper accounting period for the allocation of shares. This GAAP treatment results in fluctuation of compensation expense based entirely on estimates of a nonexistent market where hypothetical willing buyers and sellers are used to match employee earned services with an estimated value of shares. Additionally, prior to SOP 93-6, the number of shares outstanding did not depend on whether shares had been released as allocated as debt was repaid. Instead, it followed an economic rationale of ownership, with debt as collateral rather than a debt controlling the ownership relationship.

Armed with a clear understanding of the financial presentation requirements of GAAP, the analyst may find it difficult to support certain provisions of SOP 93-6 in the valuation of leveraged ESOPs without economic and monetary adjustment. By not considering adjustments, the value indication could result in a material misstatement that could go beyond the parameters of a supportable valuation conclusion and border on breaching the definition of adequate consideration to be used in the valuation as promulgated by the DOL.

In a leveraged ESOP valuation, while the loan is typically made with the company as guarantor or the maker of the ESOP loan, the economic realities of the transaction cannot be ignored. In most leveraged transactions involving ESOPs, the plan pledges the sponsoring company shares that come from the purchase from shareholders. It is typical for lenders to require as collateral the ESOP shares acquired from the seller. When proceeds are used by the sponsoring company to acquire outside shareholder stock, the sponsoring company's assets are still typically encumbered as a condition of the loan, and the loan ordinarily requires a personal guarantee of an officer and/or the selling shareholder.

If a leveraged ESOP were buying newly issued stock of the sponsoring company, the company would be the recipient of the proceeds of the loan, thereby increasing the assets of the company and increasing the cash flow accordingly for future business enhancement.

In essence, valuation adjustments should consider the following:

- All shares owned by the ESOP should be considered outstanding, including those that may be carried as convertible preferred
- Fluctuating compensation expenses based on unallocated suspense shares as period charges using estimated fair values should be adjusted to their original cost and allocated as an expense at that time and as the principal of the debt is reduced
- All shares of stock owned by the ESOP, whether held as suspense shares, unallocated, or as allocated shares, should be considered outstanding to fully capture the dilutive effect

SECTION 415 LIMITS

Employer securities held by a leveraged ESOP are released from the suspense account and allocated to participants' accounts as principal is reduced. If stock has been acquired in an exempt loan, annual additions under IRC section 415(c) can be calculated under either of two methods. The annual additions can be determined with respect to either 1) the amount of the employer contributions to the ESOP used to repay a loan or 2) the value of the employer securities allocated to participants. Plan terms should specify the method used.

CRITERIA FOR VALUING ESOP SHARES

The level of value for all ESOP transactions of employer securities, where no public market exists for the shares, is that of a nonmarketable, noncontrolling interest or a nonmarketable controlling interest. (Special consideration is given for the put rights; see Adjustments for Lack of Marketability. Additionally, special consideration is given to extraordinary liquidations, sales, or mergers of the company, which are outside the discussion in this chapter.)

END-OF-YEAR AND MID-YEAR CONVENTIONS

For most closely held businesses, analysts use discounted cash flow models to provide indicated values. These cash flow models are based on a present-value computation estimating annual cash flows that are received throughout the forecasted period and are available to equity owners. Cash flow estimates are always forward-looking and generally span a number of years, with each year representing a forecasted period. Using the end-of-year convention, computation of cash flow present value presupposes that forecasted cash flows will be available to equity owners at the end of each forecasted period. Mid-year convention presupposes that forecasted cash flows will be available to the equity owners at a midpoint, or halfway into the forecasted period. By the design of these conventions, the mid-year conventions for profitable companies will always produce a higher value indication than end-of-year conventions because cash flow is forecasted to equity holders more rapidly. In most private companies, management adopts a "wait until we see how the year goes" style of making available cash returns to equity holders because business and economic conditions often tender an environment of intermittent and varying cash flows over the forecasted periods. It is important to differentiate these conventions because company-specific realities may be considered in adopting the appropriate convention model. In an ESOP environment, the default convention may be end-of-year.

CONSIDERATIONS IN THE CALCULATION OF THE TERMINAL VALUE

Many fact-laden decisions are made in developing the final forecast period in discounted cash flow models. The estimate that produces the terminal value generated during this final period is often the chief component of the value indication using the discounted cash flow method. An ESOP is an ERISA-defined contribution plan with provisions allowing it to invest primarily in employer securities. By plan design, contributions are generally allowed to be made only by the sponsoring company. These retirement plan contributions are voluntary unless leverage is involved in ESOP share acquisitions or the plan is under a contractual multistage shareholder purchase agreement. Voluntary retirement plan contributions are choices that typically reflect, among other things, the directives of management—operational results of the company, effort made by employees, compensation plans, and contemplated future expenditures. When plan contributions are required, the term and amounts of their requirements on future forecasted periods are identified. However, once the obligations are met, there may be no assurance that voluntary contributions will continue or, if they do, will continue at the same level. In developing the terminal forecast cash flow period, the analyst should consider the ongoing benefits of the voluntary-involuntary nature of plan contributions and their impact on the benefit stream to equity shareholders, capitalized into perpetuity.

ADJUSTMENTS FOR LACK OF MARKETABILITY

Marketability adjustments are intended to reflect hypothetical buyers' concerns regarding the absence of a ready and available market when they decide to sell. In contrast to shares of stock in public companies that have an active market, ownership interests in closely held companies are typically not readily marketable. Therefore, it is often appropriate to apply an adjustment in the form of a discount to the value of closely held shares to reflect the reduction in value due to lack of marketability. A greater or lesser discount is measured on the basis of the impact of ESOP factors such as:

- Restrictions on transfer
- Buy-sell or bylaw agreement
- Prospect of a public offering or sale of the company
- Viability and strength of the put option
- The market available that may be interested in purchasing shares
- Dividend yields in distributions

When referencing publicly traded securities in valuing a minority position in a closely held corporation, note that an adjustment for the lack of marketability of the privately held interest is required, as the shareholders have no access to an active public market for their investment. Further, shareholders cannot force registration to create marketability. Without market access, an investor's ability to control the timing of potential gains, to avoid losses, and to minimize the opportunity cost associated with alternative investments is impaired. Given two investment instruments identical in all other respects, the market will accord a considerable premium to one that can be liquidated into cash quickly, especially without risk of loss in value. For this reason, an investment in a privately held company usually is adjusted to a lesser stock price than an otherwise comparable investment in a publicly traded entity. The ESOP is subjected to much the same lack of market as non-ESOP shares. The only difference is the required put provisions for private stocks.

Two types of empirical studies—restricted stock transactions and pre-IPO studies—have been undertaken that provide indications of the adjustment for marketability to investors. These studies compare the discounted prices paid for equity securities subject to trading restrictions with market prices for similar securities that are freely tradable without such restrictions. Both types of studies can be considered for their guidance as to the appropriate lack of marketability adjustment to apply to ESOP share interests. There are other studies, data, and models that can also be used. See Chapter 9. Even with the put provisions in private companies, adjustments are warranted for the time delay in transacting the shares due to time delays converting the securities to cash.

ADJUSTMENTS FOR CONTROL OR LACK OF CONTROL— MINORITY INTEREST

The ESOP valuation level of value is that of a noncontrolling minority interest, unless compelling requisite relevant factors, empirical evidence, and support in both form and substance are available. The expansion of 100 percent owned S corporation ESOPs has additional valuation considerations.

The DOL proposed regulation on adequate consideration states that an ESOP may pay a control premium only if the plan obtains control "both in form and in substance" and that the premium must be consistent with what a third party would pay. There is a certain amount of controversy as to whether an ESOP can have control "in substance," although it may have it "in form," by a percentage of votes. Each analyst must take added precaution when consulting on or estimating if and/or the amount of control premium and should include all the circumstances unique to each case when making such a determination. Many analysts take the cautionary measure of providing in the appraisal report an explanation as to the analysis and likely implementation of obtaining control.

Determining the degree and extent of control purchased by the ESOP is a significant factor in the classification of minority or control interest in the valuation. The Department of Labor considers control as determined not only by the size of the block of shares held by the ESOP but also by the prerogatives of control that may attach to those shares.

In an ESOP environment, the trustee as a fiduciary has the obligation to consider all the relevant facts and circumstances as to whether payment of a control premium is warranted. A control premium is warranted only where the plan obtains both voting control and control in fact.

The DOL makes a clear distinction between numerical and actual control when valuation issues center on the ESOP owning (or can reasonably expect to own) more than 50 percent of the sponsoring company's common stock. While the DOL acknowledges that a control premium may be applicable in certain instances, it stresses that there must be compelling evidence of actual control in addition to numerical control that must or will pass to the ESOP and that this control will not dissipate over time.

Value of a minority interest differs from that of a controlling interest because of the lack of prerogatives of control inherent to the minority shareholder, which can warrant an adjustment for the lack of actual power in form to that of a control shareholder. In a private company setting, a minority interest adjustment is generally illustrated as a discount from control value of the sponsoring company or reflected in the cash flows. In virtually all cases, the minority interest is worth less than its proportionate share of the value of all the outstanding shares at a control value. The magnitude of a minority interest adjustment depends on the shareholder's inability to exercise any or all of the rights typically associated with ownership of the shares.

This adjustment should take into account the full definition of fair market value, including the assumption of a hypothetical buyer and seller outside the setting of the ESOP. The philosophy behind and quantification of a minority interest adjustment is important in the valuation of closely held stock for purposes of ESOP transactions of the sponsoring company shares. A minority interest discount can be reflected in the cash flows or a reduction to the initial indicated value on account of a lack of control prerogatives, such as declaring dividends, liquidating the company, going public, issuing or buying stock, directing management, setting management salaries, and so on. Quantifying the amount of minority interest adjustment rests with the good faith interpretation of the facts and circumstances of the engagement.

When valuing a minority block of stock of a closely held corporation, there is no range of discounts that will universally be applicable in any given circumstance.

While the ESOP may transact a larger block of stock as a percentage of the company, the participants generally transact small holdings of minority interest. The analyst should search for verifiable exchanges or sales of the sponsoring company stock within a reasonable period of time prior to the valuation date. Each approach in estimating the minority interest adjustment constitutes only a factor in the overall consideration.

VOTING AND OTHER RIGHTS OF THE ESOP SHAREHOLDERS

Voting rights are passed through to the ESOP participants only on issues that require majority stockholder votes. In public companies, voting rights are passed through to plan participants as with other shareholders. In private companies, an ESOP participant must be able to direct the trustee on the voting of his or her allocated shares for the sale of all or substantially all of the company's assets or for a merger, liquidation, recapitulation, reclassification, dissolution, or consolidation. In these cases where a vote pass-through is required, appropriate information on the issues must be provided, just as it would be to other shareholders.

Participants in an ESOP do not have rights to the sponsoring company's financial statements, stock record books, or salary information. Disclosures of these items are at the complete discretion of the sponsoring company. However, as a practical matter, summary financial information is often made available to the plan trustee.

REPURCHASE REQUIREMENT, THE PUT RIGHT—WHAT AND HOW TO DEAL WITH IT?

The ESOP repurchase requirement can be defined as a right for a claim, called the put right, to be made by a plan participant, obligating the sponsoring company to convert their vested ESOP shares to cash upon their departure from the plan. A put right is a legal right, and not the requirement of a departing plan participant, to convert their sponsoring company stock. There is no accounting standard requirement to record an estimated repurchase liability for the ESOP plan shares on sponsoring company financial statements for this obligation. For publicly traded shares with active public markets, shares typically transact at market values.

Under the IRS Tax Code, the ESOP participant who has terminated by reason of death, disability, or retirement has two 60-day windows for the company to repurchase its ESOP shares. Those two 60-day window periods are:

- First, immediately after the distribution
- Second, one year later, allowing for the next valuation of the shares to have taken place

For participants who leave the plan for reasons other than death, disability, or retirement, the repurchase obligation at the trustee's option can be delayed until the end of the fifth year following the year the participant terminates the plan. The funding of the repurchase can be a lump sum or paid out over an extended period of time and is based on the shares' fair market value at the time of distribution.

The majority of ESOP shares tend to be repurchased by the sponsoring company in a lump sum, either as treasury stock or by making contributions to the plan. The ESOP uses its available funds to make the acquisition.

There are essentially three ways for shares of the sponsoring company stock to be purchased, according to the dictates found in most ESOP trust agreements:

1. The ESOP will purchase the shares using pooled funds inside in the plan
2. If the ESOP does not have available funds, the sponsoring company can make a cash contribution to the plan to acquire the shares from the participant as a plan asset
3. The sponsoring company may purchase the stock as treasury shares, and the number of shares outstanding and the amount of cash expended in the transaction will be reduced proportionately to the value of the overall company on an aggregate basis

It is important to note that special situations apply to S corporation repurchases of shares. The federal tax-exempt status of an ESOP owning S corporation shares does not continue with the shares after they are transferred to a participant at their departure from the plan. Thus, the exempt status provides no share value enhancement. As S corporations are pass-through entities, the pro rata share of ownership earnings and profits passed through to an ESOP is not subject to income tax and dividend distributions received by an ESOP on allocated shares and is considered plan earnings that are allocated to participants based on accumulated account balances. When dividend plan earnings are used to repurchase shares from departing ESOP participants, those shares will be proportionately allocated to those participants who received the dividend. This differs from using company contributions where allocation is based on eligible annual compensation.

The size of the repurchase obligation changes due to vesting, underlying stock value, age of participants, age and size of the plan, debt, personnel turnover, and other factors. Estimating repurchase liability is difficult, and plan provisions are essential. An important consideration is the percentage of outstanding shares of the sponsoring company held by the ESOP, as the repurchase obligation is proportionately reduced to the percentage ownership of the ESOP.

The materiality of the sponsoring company's obligation depends on several factors. These factors include the ability of the company to borrow money and the probability of continued operating income sufficient to meet the normal attrition of participants. Additional factors include an analysis of the adequacy of cash reserves within the sponsoring company that could be used to fund the purchase rights of the departing participants. There is no dilutive impact on the per-share value to the remaining shareholders as a result of the redemption as long as the transaction occurs at fair market value. The contemplated liquidation or sale of the sponsoring company or the termination of the ESOP itself would be considered extraordinary and are not factors in a typical repurchase obligation study.

Promissory notes can be used to meet the requirements of the put right, as long as the following conditions are met:

- The note provides for substantially equal periodic payments that begin within 30 days and end no longer than five years from the exercise of the put option
- There is adequate security for the note
- The note bears a reasonable interest rate

Promissory notes require collateral, and the sponsoring company must determine what type of collateral will be used. It is imperative that collateral be sufficient so that the participant is not harmed in the event of default.

In instances where repurchase amounts can be reasonably estimated, an economic adjustment may be warranted to reflect the obligation as a liability of the sponsoring company. The analyst should consider the ESOP's ability to meet the obligation with ESOP funds before such an adjustment is warranted. An adjustment may extend to the sponsoring company's balance sheet and cash flow, if necessary.

In most cases, the put right acts to reduce the amount of adjustment for lack of marketability since the put provision provides a limited market for the ESOP shares. The put right may not eliminate a marketability adjustment and in some extreme instances may have little effect on the need for and consideration of a liquidity adjustment for the sponsoring company shares of the ESOP.

The repurchase obligation of an ESOP company is a compensation decision and should be viewed in relation to the compensation levels that are prevalent in the company's industry. An understanding of the differences in the methods of redeeming ESOP shares and recognition of the impact of the repurchase obligation on the value of the company are essential.

PENALTIES FOR AN IMPROPER VALUATION

The DOL and the IRS are continuing to raise the penalties for overvaluing and undervaluing stock. The Pension Protection Act of 2006 applies to analysts and imposes substantial penalties when a substantial and gross misstatement of value is recognized.

VALUATION CONCLUSION: WRITING A CONCLUSION

The valuation process is not complete until a written report is furnished to the trustee. In order to comply with the requirements of the Department of Labor, the analyst(s)' conclusion of fair market value must be reflected in a written document of valuation. The DOL describes or implies that the valuation report must contain:

- Full description of the asset being valued
- Statement(s) of conclusion of the assets' value
- Statement(s) of the purpose of the valuation
- Statement(s) of the effective date of the valuation
- Statement(s) of the approaches and methods considered
- Statement(s) of the relevance of each methodology employed
- Statement(s) of any restrictions or other limiting condition(s)
- Statement(s) of the factors considered in the formulation of the conclusion of value
- A written assessment of all relevant factors, which must include those factors cited in Internal Revenue Service Revenue Ruling No. 59-60
- A statement that all rules of the proposed DOL regulations have been met
- A written assessment of all relevant factors detailing any marketability adjustment(s) and stating that the put option rights were considered
- A written assessment of all relevant factors detailing any control or minority interest adjustment(s)
- A summary of the qualifications of the analyst(s)
- Signatures of the analyst(s) and the date the report was signed

It is a requirement that the trustee supply a copy of the report prepared by the independent analyst, accompanying the annual retirement plan information tax return. At a minimum, the valuation report should include the value of the company as an aggregate company value on a nonmarketable, noncontrolling, or controlling basis, as the case may be. This allows for computations of the proportionate effect of dilution when additional shares of stock are purchased, contributed, and optioned. A per share value can be determined by dividing the outstanding shares of the company into the appropriate aggregate company value.

An example to consider in determining the number of shares outstanding is the following. For financial statement purposes, an accrual was made for the ESOP contribution at fiscal year end. It is not known on the date if the contribution will be made in the form of cash, new issue or treasury stock, or a combination of the two. Is the per-share value affected? There would be a dilutive effect with newly issued shares that would on its face reduce the per-share equivalent value. There would also be a cash flow savings equal to the cash expended net of its federal income tax impact. Using shares of stock actually increases cash flow as the shares generate a tax deduction. However, the new shares create a new fully diluted share total, thereby diluting the per-share value, but less than proportionately since the tax savings and cash flow increase.

In summary, the report should be written to the plan trustee. It is not a requirement for the trustee to use the analyst's value estimate; rather, it is the plan trustee's responsibility to render the final conclusion. The analyst's task is to offer to the trustee a professional estimate of the ESOP shares' fair market value.

Additional Information

For more detailed information on ESOP valuation issues, see Larry R. Cook, *Financial Valuation of Employee Stock Ownership Plan Shares* (Hoboken, NJ: John Wiley & Sons, 2005).

INFORMATION SOURCES

IRC § 401(a)(14)

IRC § 401(a)(28)(B)

IRC § 404(a)(9)(A)-(B)

IRC § 404

IRC § 409(h)(1)(B)

IRC § 409(h)(4)

IRC § 409(h)(5)

IRC § 409(o)(A)

IRC § 409(o)(1)(B)

IRC § 409(p)

IRC § 411(a)

IRC § 411(d)(6)(I)

IRC § 415 (c)

IRC § 501

IRC § 512

IRC § 1042

IRC § 1361

IRC § 4975

Revenue Ruling 59-60

Revenue Ruling 77-287

Priv. Ltr. Rul. 8644024 (August 1, 1986)

Priv. Ltr. Rul. 19934006 (May 21, 1999)

Priv. Ltr. Rul. 9619065 (February 12, 1996)

Priv. Ltr. Rul. 9821022 (February 17, 1998)

Priv. Ltr. Rul. 9846015 (November 13, 1998)

Priv. Ltr. Rul. 9852004 (December 24, 1998)

Priv. Ltr. Rul. 199938052 (July 2, 1999)

Treas. Reg. § 1.1042-1T

Treas. Reg. § 54.4975-7(b)(5)(iii)

Department of the Treasury, Internal Revenue Service, "2000 Instructions for Forms 1120 and 1120-A," pp. 1–23

Department of the Treasury, Internal Revenue Service, "2000 Instructions for Forms 1120S," pp. 1–31

Department of the Treasury, Internal Revenue Service, "2000 Instructions for Form 5500, Annual Return/Report of Employee Benefit Plan," pp. 1–62

Tax Reform Act of 1984

Tax Reform Act 1986

Tax Act 2001

Department of Labor, Proposed Regulation, 29CFR, Part 2510.3-1, 2510.3-2, 2510.3-3, 2510.3-21, 2510.3-37, 2510.3-101. 2550-408(b)-3(1)

Section 3(18)(B) of The Employee Retirement Income Security Act of 1974 (ERISA)

29 USC Section 1002(21)(A) of the Employee Retirement Income Security Act (ERISA)

Section 8477 (a)(2)(B) of the Federal Employees' Retirement System Act of 1986 (FERSA)

American Institute of Certified Public Accountants, Statement of Position 93-6

Business Appraisal Standards, pub. No. P-311a (Institute of Business Analysts, Inc., 1993)

Employers' Accounting for Employee Stock Ownership Plans (November 22, 1993)

The National Center for Employee Ownership. *ESOP Valuation: Expert Guidance for Companies, Consultants and Analysts,* 2nd ed. (Oakland, CA), 1–203

The National Center for Employee Ownership. *Leveraged ESOPs and Employee Buyouts,* 4th ed. (Oakland, CA), pp. 1–259

Principles of Appraisal Practice and Code of Ethics, rev. ed. (Washington, DC: The American Society of Analysts, 1994)

Standards Board of the Appraisal Foundation. *Uniform Standards of Professional Appraisal Practice,* 2003 ed. (Washington, DC: The Appraisal Foundation, 2003)

www.dol.gov

www.irs.gov

www.nceo.org

http://www.esopassociation.org/

www.nceo.org

www.the-esop-emplowner.org

TAM 9438002

Larry R. Cook, *Financial Valuation of Employee Stock Ownership Plan Shares* (Hoboken, NJ: John Wiley & Sons, 2005)

CHAPTER 18

Valuation in the Divorce Setting

Divorce valuations are completely state-specific and are dependent on the specific facts and circumstances of each case. This chapter presents some general but important concepts and also references certain state-specific cases where an important issue was addressed. For additional information on some of these issues, see Chapter 19, Valuation Issues in Small Businesses, and Chapter 20, Valuation Issues in Professional Practices.

STANDARDS OF VALUE IN DIVORCE

It is incumbent on the analyst to know what standard of value is appropriate in the valuation of a business or business interest in a divorce. Since this may vary from state to state and from jurisdiction to jurisdiction, the analyst should be aware of the terminology used in the jurisdiction and how that terminology is defined within that jurisdiction. Most often, case law within the jurisdiction is the appropriate source for defining the standard of value. Furthermore, the definitions of the standard of value for divorce may differ from the traditional definitions for other areas of valuation, which are discussed in Chapters 1 and 2.

Value or Fair Value

Some state marital dissolution statutes refer to "value" or "fair value." Fair value is a statutorily or judicially defined standard of value. Historically, fair value has been used primarily in litigation matters involving a marital dissolution or with dissenting minority interest shareholders. When valuing a business using the standard of fair value, the analyst normally considers all elements of a business's value (e.g., income or cash flows, risk-adjusted rates of return, or value of assets in place) with the possible exception of its investment value in the actual marketplace. However, state statutes and case law may affect normal valuation procedures. For example, in certain states, when valuing a closely held business for purposes of a marital dissolution, case law specifically disallows any discounts for lack of control and/or lack of marketability. "Fair value" and "value" are really only legal terms that must be further defined for the analyst to determine a value for divorce purposes.

ValTip

> The analyst must know the specific definition of value that is to be used in determining a value in a divorce setting. Failure to do so could result in the valuation being excluded, discounted, or ignored by the judge if challenged. The attorney should provide guidance on the law to the analyst.

Fair Market Value

Fair market value is another often used standard of value in divorce cases. However, as with fair value, what is called "fair market value" for divorce purposes by a state or jurisdiction often may not be pure fair market value as used for other valuation purposes, such as tax reasons. The analyst should not assume that fair market value is the standard. Furthermore, if it is the standard, don't assume its definition without getting clarification from the attorney and/or a colleague in that state.

Family law courts generally seek to establish equitable valuations and division of marital assets. As such, they often make determinations of value that might seem odd to the analyst who is used to making determinations of pure "fair market value." As previously mentioned, many state dissolution statutes refer to "value" and "fair value" rather than "fair market value." Since "value" and "fair value" are generally legal standards, the courts are given a high level of discretion in the determination of value. Appellate and supreme courts generally are reluctant to overturn valuation decisions of trial courts unless there is a clear abuse of judicial discretion or, more commonly, a valuation issue (such as personal versus entity goodwill) that has been handled inappropriately.

Another issue related to fair market value that often arises in divorce valuation decisions is whether or not the valuation of a business interest assumes a "sale" of the business interest. Some states have determined that a sale is not assumed in valuing the interest. This results in a value that more represents an investment value standard than a fair market value standard (see investment value section that follows). The result of this assumption usually is that personal goodwill ends up being computed as part of the value of the business interest. In this regard, the assumption that no sale has occurred is the antithesis of the exclusion of personal goodwill as a marital asset. In at least one state, there are multiple decisions that both exclude the assumption of a sale, but also exclude the inclusion of personal goodwill (separate decisions).

Investment Value in Divorce

Investment value is the value of a business to a specific buyer as opposed to the hypothetical buyer assumed in fair market value. When valuing a closely held business using the standard of investment value, the appraiser should consider the specific synergies, cost savings, and other buyer-specific attributes of the target buyer. It is rarely used in a marital matter. However, a "hybrid" investment value is used in some divorce situations. In these cases, an "investment value" standard might be applied to capture the personal goodwill attributable to the owner(s) of the business in the value of the business and in the marital estate. For example, in valuing a medical practice, the analyst might adjust actual physician compensation to the average for the particular specialty, thereby increasing anticipated cash flows. However, the value so determined is not likely to be a fair market value, because a hypothetical buyer may not adjust compensation this way. Some states still might use this hybrid investment value to determine the value of a business for divorce purposes, but the trend is away from this and toward a bifurcation of personal and entity goodwill.

As more and more states exclude personal goodwill from the marital assets, investment value is used less and less. However, it might still be used as the starting point for determining the amount of personal goodwill existing in a particular business or business interest.

Intrinsic Value in Divorce

Intrinsic value is a standard of value that is used often in reference to publicly traded securities. It might refer to the "pure" value of the security as opposed to its traded value. It might also refer to a breakup value or an underlying asset value. In a divorce setting, this standard, in its defined form, would not be used. However, as in the case of the investment value standard, a hybrid form of the intrinsic value standard might be found in a divorce setting.

PREMISE OF VALUE—GOING CONCERN

Analysts and courts sometimes confuse the "premise of value" with the "standard of value." The two most commonly used premises of value are the *going-concern* and the *liquidation* premise of value. When a business is a going concern it will continue to operate in the foreseeable future and not cease operations and liquidate.

The *International Glossary of Business Valuation Terms* defines going-concern value as follows:

1. The value of a business enterprise that is expected to continue to operate into the future.
2. The intangible elements of going-concern value result from factors such as having a trained workforce, an operational plant, and the necessary licenses, systems, and procedures in place.

Notice that the going-concern premise may include intangible assets in the calculation of value, whereas liquidation value may or may not include it. Most divorce courts also will recognize the inclusion of goodwill in the value, but elements of goodwill might be eliminated from inclusion in the marital estate. Therefore, divorce valuations will be made more often under a going-concern premise but the conclusion of value might not include all elements of going-concern value or goodwill value.

PREMISE OF VALUE—LIQUIDATION

The *orderly* liquidation premise of value assumes that ongoing operations have ceased and that the business's assets will be sold on a piecemeal basis in an orderly manner to obtain the highest possible price. *Forced* liquidation value assumes that the assets will be sold as quickly as possible (i.e., at auction) and almost always

832   FINANCIAL VALUATION

results in a lower value than that achieved under an orderly liquidation. Therefore, if liquidation value is used in a divorce setting, the analyst should clearly state whether it is an orderly or a forced liquidation.

A liquidation premise of value would make sense in a divorce setting only in the same instances it would make sense in a nondivorce setting—that is, when the business is actually in a liquidation mode or when the liquidation value of the assets is greater than the income and market approach values for a controlling interest. Since most states intend to provide equity in the determination of the marital estate, the liquidation premise would not usually provide an equitable solution.

GOODWILL—THE BATTLEGROUND FOR DIVORCE VALUATIONS

Goodwill has become the battleground for divorce valuations. How much and what goodwill will be included in a divorce valuation often has a material impact on the total value of the marital estate. Since many marital estates have few assets as valuable as the business or business interest of one of the spouses, the amount of goodwill included in the value of this business/business interest can be critical in determining the total value of the marital estate as well as the relative economic position of the spouses after the divorce. The business is the primary source of funds (i.e., cash) for shifting value from the business-owner spouse to the non-business-owner spouse. Overvaluation of the business interest can result in an inequitable shift of value to the non-business owner, with possible bankruptcy for the business owner. Undervaluation of the interest can result in an inequitable shift of value to the business owner. Goodwill is the determining factor in most of these situations.

DEFINING GOODWILL

Goodwill is a generic term that sometimes is used to include a bundle of intangible assets and sometimes is used only as a single intangible asset (calculated as a residual value) within a bundle of intangible assets.

The *International Glossary of Business Valuation Terms* defines intangible assets as "non physical assets (such as franchises, trademarks, copyrights, goodwill, equities, mineral rights, securities, and contracts as distinguished from physical assets) that grant rights, privileges, and have economic benefits for the owner." It defines goodwill as "that intangible asset arising as a result of name, reputation, customer loyalty, location, products, and similar factors not separately identified."

ValTip

The various definitions and components of goodwill often cause confusion. It is important to fully understand the term's meaning in the context it is being used.

STATE INTERPRETATIONS ON INCLUDING GOODWILL IN THE MARITAL ESTATE

How goodwill is handled in a divorce setting depends on the particular jurisdiction. Some courts never include any goodwill as a divisible marital asset. Wisconsin, for example, in *Holbrook v. Holbrook*, 309 N.W.2d 343,345 (Wis. Ct. App. 1981), held that professional goodwill is too difficult to distinguish from future earning capacity to be marital property.[1]

Other courts always include goodwill as a divisible marital asset, regardless of the nature of the goodwill. In *Dugan v. Dugan*, 457 A.2d 1 (N.J. 1983), the New Jersey Supreme Court held that all goodwill, whether personal or entity, is marital property because it would be inequitable to ignore the nonpropertied spouse's contributions to the development of that economic resource.[2]

Many states, however, differentiate between "enterprise goodwill" (entity goodwill), which is considered to be a divisible marital asset, and "personal goodwill," which is not.[3]

This emphasizes again the importance of the expert knowing the applicable decisions in the jurisdiction in which he or she is testifying. Some states are equitable distribution states that have alimony; some are equitable distribution states with no alimony; and some are community property states with or without alimony. In some cases, the courts might have been influenced by trying to provide equity under their particular state law, and in other cases, the courts might simply have looked to the decisions in other states to guide their own conclusions. It is clear that the system, as constituted, leads to wide variations of divisions of marital assets across the various states and jurisdictions. Many of the differences result from the basic state law (e.g., community property versus equitable distribution). Other differences result from interpretations of state law.

ValTip

> Since state laws are so diverse, the analyst must constantly be alert to not only the espoused standard of value in a particular jurisdiction, but also the variations imposed by judicial decisions. Consultation with an attorney is advised.

PERSONAL VERSUS ENTITY (ENTERPRISE) GOODWILL

Personal goodwill has burst onto the scene over the past few years. It is not a new concept but one that seems to have "caught on" recently in many areas. The most

---

[1] See also *Sorenson v. Sorenson*, 839 P.2d 774 (Utah, 1992); *Travis v. Travis*, 795 P.2d 96 (Okla. 1990); *Hickum v. Hickum*, 463 S.E.2d 321 (S.C. Ct. App. 1995).

[2] See also *Prahinski v. Prahinski*, 582 A.2d 784 (Md. 1990); *Powell v. Powell*, 648 P.2d 218 (Kan. 1982).

[3] See *Yoon v. Yoon*, 711 N.E.2d 1265 (Ind. 1999); *Hanson v. Hanson*, 738 S.W.2d 429, 434 (Mo. 1987); *Taylor v. Taylor*, 386 N.W.2d 851 (Neb. 1986); *Beasley v. Beasley*, 518 A.2d 545 (Pa. Super. Ct. 1986).

visible emergence is in the divorce arena. A number of states, such as Indiana, Minnesota, and Virginia (to name a few and there are many others), have had decisions dealing with the exclusion of personal goodwill from the marital estate.

Personal goodwill is that goodwill that attaches to the persona and the personal efforts of the individual. It is generally considered to be difficult to transfer, if at all. Entity goodwill is the goodwill that attaches to the business enterprise.

An individual may not be able to easily transfer his or her personal goodwill to someone else or "take" entity goodwill for him- or herself.

While numerous cases discuss goodwill, very few analyze the methodologies used to distinguish between personal and enterprise goodwill. However, there seems to be consensus that how to divide goodwill is entirely dependent on the facts of each case and the magnitude of the financial impact the hypothetical departure of the propertied spouse will have on the business.

In *Howell v. Howell*, 523 S.E.2d 514 (Va. App. 2000), the husband, a tax law attorney, appealed the trial court's valuation decision of his interest in a law firm, Hunton & Williams. The husband argued that the firm's partnership agreement defined the value of the partnership interest upon termination or death by entitling the partner to receive only the balance of his capital account and his share of the net income. In this case, the two items amounted to $85,614. The husband maintained that the agreement fixed the value of his partnership interest for equitable distribution purposes, and therefore it precluded consideration of whether his interest had additional goodwill value. The trial court, on the other hand, ruled that his partnership interest had goodwill because the firm's agreement made no provision for goodwill. In affirming the trial court's decision, the Virginia Court of Appeals held the following:

- Neither the existence of goodwill nor the method of its valuation is fixed as a matter of law; rather, both are functions of the facts of the particular case.
- The trial court accepted the methodology of the wife's expert, the excess earnings method. In the absence of plain error by the trial court, its finding must be upheld.

In *Moretti v. Moretti*, 766 A.2d 925 (R.I. 2001), the trial court held, in part, that the value of the landscaping business owned by the husband included goodwill. The husband appealed the decision, arguing that the trial court erred in its finding that goodwill is included in the value of the business. The Supreme Court of Rhode Island remanded the case in order for the trial court to distinguish between enterprise goodwill and personal goodwill.

In *Yoon v. Yoon*, 711 N.E.2d 1265 (Ind. 1999), the Indiana Supreme Court held that goodwill attributable to the business enterprise is divisible property, but to the extent that goodwill is personal, it is not divisible property. Two important points were addressed in this case:

1. The goodwill that depends on the continued presence of a particular individual is a personal asset.
2. The use of the market approach, more specifically the transaction method, might be an appropriate methodology to determine enterprise goodwill.

DIVIDING GOODWILL INTO PERSONAL AND ENTITY COMPONENTS

There are no generally "accepted" methodologies to divide goodwill into its personal and entity components. There are, however, methods that can be used to calculate personal goodwill, which may depend on the particular case or jurisdiction.

One method was implied by the Indiana Supreme Court in its *Yoon* decision, where the court ruled that if the practice (or business) could be "sold or transferred" in a market transaction, that might indicate a value that included only entity goodwill. However, just because an entity is salable, there should not be a presumption that the goodwill embedded in the sales price is 100 percent entity goodwill and 0 percent personal goodwill. Depending on the jurisdiction, this distinction may be affected if the selling owner executes a noncompete agreement.

Another method is to analyze the various factors that pertain to entity versus personal goodwill and then use those to allocate total goodwill into the appropriate proportions of each. The most widely cited case that indicates the factors to be considered when valuing professional (i.e., personal) goodwill is *Lopez v. Lopez*.[4] The factors determining the amount of personal goodwill were:

- Age and health of the professional
- Professional's demonstrated earning power
- Professional's reputation in the community for judgment, skill, and knowledge
- Professional's comparative professional success
- Nature and duration of the professional's practice, either as a sole proprietor or as a contributing member of a partnership or professional corporation

In addition, these factors can be relevant in determining personal goodwill and thus in allocating the goodwill between personal and entity goodwill:[5]

- Marketability of the practice
- Types of clients and services
- Location and demographics
- How the fees are billed
- Source of new clients
- Individual practitioner's amount of production

---

[4] In re: *Lopez v. Lopez*, 113 Cal. Rptr. 58 (38 Cal. App. 3d 1044 (1974)).
[5] Robert E. Kleeman, Jr., R. James Alerding, and Benjamin D. Miller, *The Handbook for Divorce Valuations* (New York: John Wiley & Sons, 1999), p. 79.

- Workforce and length of service
- Number of other professionals in the community competing in the same service or specialty

Even though this method is subjective, it still presents a practical solution to the allocation of goodwill problem. No empirical studies provide a baseline against which specific goodwill might be measured. If the valuation analyst presents his or her case well and supports the allocations with sound logic, the result should be a reasonable approximation of the personal versus entity goodwill. There is no "average" percentage that can be assumed to be either personal or entity goodwill.

If analysts present their case well and support the allocations with sound logic, the court will be more likely to accept their value conclusions as a reasonable approximation of the personal versus entity goodwill.

APPLYING THE FACTORS TO SEPARATE GOODWILL

Age and Health of Professional

The age and health of the practitioner are important issues in the determination of goodwill. Practitioners close to retirement may have lower personal goodwill because their expected future earnings will not continue much longer. If practitioners have health problems that hamper their performance, personal goodwill is lower.

Earning Power

Another consideration is the expected future earnings of the practitioner and the practice. Demonstrated past earning power can be an important part of expected future earnings. If supposed goodwill elements (e.g., a recognizable practice name or a good business reputation) do not result in future earnings, then there may be no goodwill value. The higher the future earnings, the higher the possible goodwill value. The key to assessing the amount of goodwill is to determine the factors generating the future earnings that also might be related to goodwill. For example, if the level of earnings is due to the fact that the practitioner works substantially more hours than similar practitioners, then the goodwill value derived likely will be personal and not entity goodwill. If the future earnings will be a result of the fact that the practice is the only one of its kind in a 50-mile radius, then the goodwill may be more entity goodwill.

Reputation

A practitioner's reputation for judgment, skill, and knowledge is vital to goodwill. The background, education, and skills of the practitioner play a large part in assessing the level of goodwill. These qualities are what keep clients coming back and referring new clients.

Comparative Success

Another means of assessing reputation/goodwill is to analyze the success of the professional and the practice in light of the success of other similar professionals and practices. "Success" usually is measured by earnings of the practice, but other factors, such as hours worked, clients/patients seen, and standards of living, also play a role. Surveys of earnings also can be considered.

Duration

The duration of the practice is important to consider as well. The length of time the practice has been in operation has an effect on the goodwill because goodwill is built over time.

Marketability

The marketability of the practice is another factor that can help determine the existence of entity and personal goodwill. Demand for the practice determines marketability, although market demand may not be as much for the specific practice as for the type of practice specialties it represents. For example, if there is a entity wanting to purchase a large number of medical practices, then the market demand for these practices is going to rise and the entity goodwill of specific firms will increase, perhaps beyond the level warranted under more normal circumstances. Another factor, ease of entry into a particular field, may lower the level of entity goodwill. If everyone can do it, then it is replaceable, not unique.

Types of Clients and Services

The types of patients and clients also play a role in the valuation of goodwill. For example, in a medical practice, how does each patient pay for services? Do most use some form of insurance? Are some of the patients involved in Medicare or Medicaid? All of these issues could play a part in the bifurcation of personal and entity goodwill.

Location and Demographics

The location of the practice plays a vital role in goodwill determination. Some locations are more desirable than others. If a practice is located within a short travel distance for clients, it may have higher practice goodwill than a practice located an hour away. The demographics of the area where the practice is located are important as well. The people who live in the area, the health of those people (in the case of a physician practice), and the quality of life are all important factors.

As in most valuation situations, nothing is as simple as it seems and everything depends on the facts and circumstances of the engagement. For example, let's say a physician in his early forties died suddenly. He had been in a solo primary care practice but had shared office space with three other physicians. His practice was in a very

Location of the client might not be as important for law and accounting practices except in smaller communities.

high-income, high-growth area with many other primary care physicians in the area. Ordinarily, the deceased physician's practice might have a high entity goodwill because of location and demographics. In fact, the opposite was true. Because he shared offices with three other physicians, and because the area was growing so rapidly and had a high per-capita income, the practice could not be sold at any price. The physicians who shared offices with the deceased physician simply took over the patients. Therefore, any goodwill that had existed in that practice was personal goodwill. Even though this was not a divorce case, and certainly the death of the physician had some impact on the ability to transfer value, it is a clear example of how factors such as location and demographics can be deceiving with regard to their impact on personal versus entity goodwill.

Fees

Another factor to consider is the fee schedule of the practice. How does the practice charge its clients, by procedure performed or by amount of time spent on each client? Other considerations may include the impact of the increase or decrease of fees on the practice. Would clients leave or stay if the fees were changed? Are clients willing to pay high hourly fees because of the practitioner/owner providing the service?

Source of New Clients

The referral base, as a steady source of new business, is one of the most important considerations in the valuation of goodwill. If the referrals of the practice are coming from a large number of current clients, the practice may have more entity goodwill than one that relies on referrals from a small client base or from other professionals. If referrals generally are made to individuals within a practice instead of to the practice as a whole, personal goodwill is likely to be higher. For example, in valuation practices, especially those with a high level of litigation cases, the referral sources might refer to the particular analyst because of his or her ability to testify. If that individual is no longer with the practice, the goodwill relating to those referrals is likely to leave with him or her. Additionally, if the particular "expert" retires or signs a noncompete agreement, the goodwill related to that expert's business may still not be able to be transferred to the entity.

Production

The practitioner's work habits are also important. How many hours a week does the practitioner work? Does the practitioner spend a lot of time with each patient or client, or does he or she work on several patients or clients at a time? A practitioner who spends more personal time with patients is likely to increase his or her personal goodwill, but the practice goodwill may decrease due to the time spent on each patient as opposed to other patients. In addition, a practitioner who works more than the "average" schedule for the practice specialty may accrue a higher level of personal goodwill.

Workforce

The workforce of the practice also should be considered. When a professional practice sells to a new buyer, repeat customers want to see the familiar faces of the support staff.

Nonowner professionals who are involved in the practice also may hold the goodwill of some clients. If they were to leave the practice, the clients might leave with them.

Analysts should consider the number of employees, the job titles and job descriptions, the pay scale, and the length of service.

The impact of nonowner professionals on the base value is a consideration of value prior to the bifurcation of goodwill. Such issues as noncompete agreements and their enforceability (with the nonowner professionals) are considerations in determining the base fair market value of the professional practice.

The issue of nonowner professionals and their impact on value is one that moves beyond the issue of separation of personal and entity goodwill. In determining the fair market value of a professional practice, the issue of control of clients, patients, and customers is one that relates to the transferable value of the practice without just the consideration of personal and entity goodwill of the owner.

Competition

The degree of competition, such as the number of other professionals with similar specialties in the same geographical location, the reputation of the competition, and the number of patients/clients seen by the competition, will affect the levels and types of goodwill present.

ROLE OF NONCOMPETE AGREEMENTS IN DETERMINING PERSONAL VERSUS ENTITY GOODWILL

Some would argue that valuing a noncompete agreement would result in the proxy value of personal goodwill. The purpose of a noncompete agreement is to prevent the covenantor from exercising his or her personal skills to generate value to any entity other than the current one. The value of the entity that is left after deducting the value of a noncompete agreement is the value a buyer would pay in the marketplace for the entity without the skills of the covenantor and with the covenantor competing. As in all other issues dealing with personal goodwill, using a noncompete agreement is not a perfect solution but it may provide some guidance.

A practical methodology for valuing a noncompete agreement in a professional practice consists of determining the probability of competition on a yearly basis over a certain period of time and identifying the profits attributable to the seller. In constructing the forecasts of these profits and taking into account the probability of competition, the analyst needs to consider the elapsed time before competition starts, the potential buyer's response, and the adjustment of years after year 1 for the multiplicative effect of the probability.[6]

Another method of determining the value of a noncompete agreement is to examine factors considered by the courts in determining the economic reality of a covenant and using those factors to construct a model to determine covenant value. In *Thompson v. Commissioner,* TCM 1997-287 (June 24, 1997), the Tax Court concluded to the value of a noncompete agreement, using an 11-factor "economic reality test." These factors included probability of competition, length of the covenant, and ability of the individual to compete. They were used in tandem with estimates of the amount of revenue and income the departure of the covenantor could impact to determine the value of the noncompete agreement. Unfortunately, this method is still subjective, and some of the factors may fail adequately to measure the full impact of personal goodwill. For example, one of the assumptions, the length of the covenant, might result in some personal goodwill value being excluded if the covenantor will compete successfully *after* the covenant period has expired. See Chapter 21 for a more detailed explanation and example of the value of a covenant not to compete.

In valuing personal goodwill, the analyst should look into whether the individual has executed a noncompete agreement (stand-alone or within an employment agreement) with the business entity and his or her ability to change such an agreement. Some analysts consider the execution of a noncompete agreement to be equivalent to the individual having "transferred" his or her personal goodwill to the entity. To date, this theory has not been fully tested in court.

PERSONAL GOODWILL IN COMMERCIAL BUSINESSES

A controversy has emerged in some jurisdictions regarding the measurement of personal goodwill for a commercial business owner compared to a professional practice owner. Traditionally, the issue of personal goodwill arose almost exclusively in the context of the professional practice owner. However, some analysts and attorneys have presented this concept in the nonprofessional arena. There is no doubt that

---

[6] Ibid., p. 10.

there is substantial personal goodwill in a professional practice, particularly in one- or few-owner professional practices. In a commercial business, more investigation is needed to determine whether personal goodwill exists. In some commercial businesses, there is likely little or no personal goodwill. In others, however, the personal goodwill might be substantial.

An example of where there was little or no goodwill occurred in *Frazier v. Frazier*, 737 N.E.2d 1220 (Ind. App. 2000). The business being valued was a single-location retail furniture store. While the propertied spouse's attorneys claimed that most of the goodwill was personal, the facts were that very little of the value, if any, could be attributed to the owner. He did not have any special relationship with the customers who came from the general public, and he had no special relationships with suppliers. While a buyer would insist on a noncompete agreement, it would really have value only to keep the owner from a "suicidal" attempt to compete in a nearby location. In this case there was no real personal value to the business.

An example of where there can be substantial personal goodwill in a commercial business can be gleaned from the well-known tax case, *Martin Ice Cream v. Commissioner*, 110T.C.189 (1998). The issue was over the split-off of a subsidiary, Strassberg Ice Cream Distributors, Inc. (SIC). Martin Strassberg developed personal relationships with customers over the previous 25 years, and was instrumental in the design of new ice cream packaging and marketing techniques. He was responsible for the introduction of Häagen-Dazs products into high-volume retail stores in New Jersey. There was an oral agreement with Häagen-Dazs for Strassberg to distribute products in New Jersey. Strassberg sold the assets of SIC to Häagen-Dazs in 1988. The Tax Court ruled that the oral contract and personal relationships were never assets of Martin Ice Cream, but owned solely by Strassberg as an individual. Upon the sale of those assets to Häagen-Dazs, Strassberg received capital gains treatment. This is a clear case where a commercial enterprise had a significant element of personal goodwill.

ValTip

The arguments set forth by proponents of a personal goodwill element for commercial businesses sound similar to a key-person discount.

VALUATION OF THE S CORPORATION AND OTHER PASS-THROUGH ENTITIES IN DIVORCE VALUATIONS

The issue of whether to tax an S corporation or other pass-through entity in a divorce case has found its way into the divorce setting. One of the most noted cases on this matter is *Bernier v. Bernier* (Mass SJC-09836, 2007). In that case, the Massachusetts Supreme Judicial Court decided that a control interest in an S corporation should be tax-affected (at an adjusted tax rate) in determining the value of a 100 percent control interest in two S corporations owned half each by the parties. Each S corporation operated a supermarket on Martha's Vineyard. In part, it based its decision on a Delaware Chancery Court case (which was not a divorce case) *MRI*

Radiology Assocs. v Kessler, 898 A.2d 290, 327 (Del. Ct. Ch. 2006) (*Kessler*). See Web Addendum 1, "Divorce Valuation: A Tale of Two States—Massachusetts, Supermarkets, and Tax Affecting S Corporations," *Financial Valuation and Litigation Expert*, Issue 9, October/November 2007 at www.wiley.com/go/FVAM3E.

RESTRICTIONS ON DATA

In certain situations, the analyst may find that access to some company data and company management is restricted in some manner. In determining which valuation approach is most applicable, the analyst must keep in mind the unavailable data and what impact it could have on the conclusion of value. This situation occurs often in divorce situations, especially where the business-owner spouse is purposely uncooperative.

RANGE VERSUS SPECIFICITY

Generally, divorce decrees specify amounts of marital assets (identified in dollars) allocated to each spouse. The amounts are specific (as indicated) instead of a range of amounts. Therefore, the valuer in a divorce situation will normally be asked to determine a specific amount of value instead of a range of value.

PROFESSIONAL STANDARDS IN A DIVORCE SETTLEMENT

The role of professional standards in divorce valuations is increasing in importance as judges and attorneys become more sophisticated and knowledgeable about the business valuation profession. Experienced attorneys often look for accredited valuation analysts, and many judges give more credibility to their opinions than to those who are not accredited. Additionally, analysts have a responsibility to avoid conflicts of interest and to remain independent in order to render their expert opinion. With the advent of the AICPA Statement on Standards for Valuation Services No. 1 (SSVS), it is likely that courts will pay more attention to the process followed by the analyst. This should help improve the quality of valuations in the divorce arena. However, analysts need to avoid potential conflicts of interest. See the Web Addendum 2 "Potential Conflicts of Interest in a Divorce Setting for CPAs," by Scott R. Saltzman, CPA, CVA, ASA, CFFA at www.wiley.com/go/FVAM3E.

ROLE OF STANDARDS

The Uniform Standards of Professional Appraisal Practice (USPAP) and the SSVS are discussed in Chapter 11. The purpose here is to explain the role of these and other business valuation standards in a divorce setting. They are used in divorce valuations generally only in relation to the analyst presenting the case in the divorce matter. If the analyst is a member of an organization that requires compliance with USPAP, SSVS, or other standards, then he or she should prepare a valuation that complies with the appropriate standards. However, marital courts generally do not make USPAP (or any other business valuation standards) mandatory for acceptance in the determination of a value conclusion. The analysts might be challenged by the ethics committee of the organization requiring compliance where USPAP is not followed, but it may not change the decision of the court. Noncompliance is not generally an issue on which an appeal of a value may be based.

Notwithstanding the fact that compliance with USPAP is not a requirement for an acceptable value for divorce purposes, the cross-examining attorney can nevertheless use noncompliance as a tool for impeachment.

STATEMENT ON STANDARDS FOR VALUATION SERVICES NO. 1 (AICPA)

In June of 2007, effective for engagements accepted on or after Jan. 1, 2008, the AICPA promulgated the Statement on Standards for Valuation Services No. 1. The Statement establishes standards for AICPA members who are engaged to (or as part of another engagement) estimate the value of a business, business ownership interest, security, or intangible asset. This means that any CPA in public or private practice who is a member of the AICPA or, if not a member, practices in a state where the State Board of Accountancy adopts the AICPA standards, must adhere to the Statement. See Chapter 11 for additional information on standards.

OTHER STANDARDS

The American Society of Appraisers (ASA), Institute of Business Appraisers (IBA), and the National Association of Certified Valuation Analysts (NACVA) have all developed standards to be followed by their members. The ASA standards are detailed enhancements to USPAP, which the ASA had previously adopted as a requirement for their members. Therefore, a member of ASA offering an analysis or report of value in a divorce litigation will often comply with both USPAP and the ASA separate business valuation standards.

The IBA and NACVA also have developed business valuation standards that require compliance from their members. See Chapter 11 for additional information on standards.

Noncompliance to standards does not necessarily invalidate the valuation report for the court (that decision is up to the judge), but it can provide fodder for cross-examination.

DAUBERT CHALLENGES IN DIVORCE

The *Daubert* type challenge for impeaching expert witnesses has not yet become widespread in divorce litigation, probably, in part, because the challenging attorney might be challenging an expert used in the past or one who might be used again in the future. In many locales, family law attorneys are a close community, and they tend to use a smaller group of analysts. If they begin presenting *Daubert* challenges against these experts and succeeding, their pool of experts will diminish. It took a long time for *Daubert* to become an accepted concept in commercial litigation. While it might take a while longer, *Daubert* challenges will most likely find their way into divorce litigation as well. See Chapters 15 and 23 for additional information on *Daubert*.

VALUATION METHODOLOGY AND THE APPLICATION OF DISCOUNTS IN DIVORCE VALUATIONS

Generally, and depending on state laws or judicial precedent, once the analyst has determined the appropriate value before discounts, the discounts to be applied and the method of applying them is determined as in any other valuation. Therefore, if a minority interest is being valued in a divorce setting, the analyst likely would determine a minority marketable value (depending on the valuation method) first and then apply a discount for lack of marketability. In arriving at the minority value using the income approach, the analyst might use the minority cash flows to determine the minority value, as in any other valuation. When using the asset approach, the analyst might have to determine and apply a minority interest discount to arrive at the minority marketable value. Again, the level of the discount is normally arrived at as it would be in any other valuation.

AVOID DOUBLE COUNTING

Because of the unique aspects of divorce valuations in some jurisdictions, the possibility of double (or more) discounting arises. For example, in a jurisdiction where personal goodwill is excluded from the value of a business interest, whether or not to take an additional discount for marketability may be a double-counting issue. In other jurisdictions, when an intrinsic value is used and includes all personal and entity goodwill, a marketability and/or minority discount might not be appropriate under the particular definition of intrinsic value. The analyst should consult with the attorney about the proper application of the law.

Another double-counting issue revolves around the compensation adjustment that is often used in determining a control value of a business interest. The compensation is often adjusted downward, thereby increasing the value of the business. However, the actual compensation is usually used in determining alimony. In effect, this results in a higher value for the business but also higher alimony, thus a possible double-counting effect.

WHEN AN INTEREST IS CONSIDERED CONTROL IN A DIVORCE SETTING

As is true in so many other issues in divorce valuation, whether an interest is control in a divorce setting is often an issue of jurisdiction. In most jurisdictions, the interests of both spouses are aggregated to determine whether the interest should be valued as a control or a minority interest. For example, if the husband owns 40 percent of a business and the wife owns another 20 percent of the same business, most jurisdictions will merge the two and include the value of a 60 percent interest in the marital estate. The primary reason for this is that the courts generally consider marital assets, including business interests, to be fungible (i.e., one asset can be freely substituted for another). Furthermore, the entire business interest included in a marital estate usually is given to one spouse or the other. The spouse not receiving the business interest receives an equivalent value (stated in dollars) of other marital assets. Thus, in the example, if the wife is the active party in the business and receives the entire 60 percent interest owned by the marital estate, she is receiving a control interest. To value those interests as two minority interests of 40 percent and 20 percent and apply minority and related lack of marketability discounts would understate the value of those interests and result in the non–business owner spouse (in this case the husband) receiving a less than equivalent share of other assets in the division of the marital estate.

If the judge decides for a variety of reasons to give one spouse, say, 25 percent and the other spouse 35 percent, then a question of whether to use a control or a minority value does arise. It may be appropriate in such a case to use a minority value for the spouse not active in the business. As to the spouse remaining active in the business, the most likely scenario may also be to use a minority value. However, the facts of the situation should be examined to see if the active spouse has effective control.

FAMILY AGGREGATIONS IN DIVORCE SETTINGS

There is often no rationale for aggregating family interests in a divorce valuation setting to determine whether an interest is a control or a minority interest. For example, if the business owner spouse is a 25 percent owner in a company in which he or she is active along with his or her three siblings, should the interest of the divorcing spouse be considered a control interest because of the ownership of the other interests by siblings? In the tax valuation arena, despite years of trying to aggregate these family interests, the IRS finally acquiesced and agreed that they should not be aggregated since the standard of fair market value would not contemplate such aggregation. (See IRS Rev. Rul. 93-12.)

Notwithstanding, many divorce courts have taken the position that family interests should be aggregated. This decision usually is grounded in the theory of "equity" that maintains that the non–business owner spouse is at a disadvantage by not being part of the family that owns and operates the business asset and needs additional consideration.

PARTNERSHIPS, LLCs, LLPs, AND FAMILY ENTITIES IN A DIVORCE SETTING

Minority interests in pass-through entities often are found in marital estates. Often the other interests are not owned by family members but by nonrelated parties or by business partners. Again, some marital courts may look at the interest as a control interest when the other interests are owned by business partners of the owner-spouse. The equity theory once again comes into play because some courts believe that business partners would tend to "take care of" each other. Again, the analyst should consult with the lawyer and/or a resident colleague on the appropriate application.

The interests that the courts consider controlling by aggregation are often in entities that hold the real estate used by the company owned by the same individuals. While the court may look at the corporate interest as a minority interest, it may turn the underlying real estate interest into a control value. In such a case, the analyst should stick to the principles of the standard of value to be used in the jurisdiction.

In many instances, the pass-through entity being valued is a family entity such as a family limited partnership (FLP). A minority holder in such an entity usually has no control over distributions and no rights to the underlying assets. If that person is not a controlling general partner, the realities are that he or she truly has no control. Some courts tend to take the approach that such family entities are established for the purpose of limiting or reducing the value for tax or marital purposes. However, that does not change the facts of the situation, that a minority interest in the entity simply has no ability to exercise any control elements.

Not to apply the same discounts that would be applied in a nondivorce situation ignores the legal and economic realities of the situation. However, courts sometimes ignore such realities and make determinations that can cause severe financial problems to both parties in the divorce. Unless the jurisdiction has determined specifically that the interest should be valued as a control interest, the analyst should consider applying discounts to the extent they would be applied (based on the specific facts) in any other valuation situation. Furthermore, absent a requirement in the FLP agreement, since family members do not have a legal obligation to "transfer" part of their value in the FLP to the spouse being divorced by a family member partner, there may not be a reason to apply a lower level of discount due to the family relationships.

LIQUIDITY MYTH IN PASS-THROUGH ENTITIES

Marital courts sometimes stress equity instead of economic reality in judging the value of an interest in a pass-through entity. The resulting overvaluation of the interest creates the liquidity myth, that is, the spouse left holding the entity does not have sufficient liquid assets to satisfy the award of the court in dividing the supposed value of the marital assets. The result is a disservice to both spouses since often the court's decision will have to be modified to resolve the disparity between the parties.

The theory espoused by some courts, that the family or business partner interests should be aggregated in determining value, feeds into the liquidity myth. As previously indicated, neither family nor business partners are under any obligation to provide liquidity from the pass-through entities. As a result, the spouse holding the pass-through entity interest will not have either cash flow or sale value of the interest sufficient to satisfy the obligations of the dissolution. It is the analyst's responsibility to determine the proper value of these entities in accordance with the standards for business valuation and the local law. (See Chapter 12 for more information.)

DIVORCE VALUATION AND BANKRUPTCY

Because of the liquidity myth, business interests valued in a divorce setting sometimes end up being valued again in a bankruptcy court. This section deals with the correlation between value in the divorce proceeding and a possible later valuation in the bankruptcy court.

Liquidity Myth Revisited

The lack of liquidity to a spouse who owns the interests in pass-through entities can result in that spouse filing for bankruptcy. Once that happens, the interest might be valued again in that court. At the very least, the interest might be offered for sale by the trustee in bankruptcy, where the economic realities surrounding the interest are more likely to be recognized than in the marital courts.

Valuing Pass-Through Entities in a Bankruptcy Court

An interest in a pass-through entity (including a family limited partnership) is not immune to the claims of creditors in a bankruptcy estate, subject to the rules and restrictions of the Bankruptcy Code and state law.

The Bankruptcy Code exempts payments to a former spouse for alimony or maintenance from discharge. The challenge is determining what is alimony and maintenance and what is property division. If the bankruptcy court determines that an obligation resulting from a divorce decree is for alimony or maintenance, it could refuse to discharge the obligation. The result could be that the cycle is repeated. If the bankrupt spouse comes out of the bankruptcy still holding the pass-through entity but not being able to discharge the obligation to the former spouse, he or she might still be trapped in the liquidity myth and end up back in bankruptcy court at a future date.

SUMMARY

Divorce valuations are very state-specific. However, we have presented many general nuances particular to valuations prepared in a divorce setting. For further information see *The Handbook for Divorce Valuation* by Kleeman, Alerding, and Miller (New York: John Wiley & Sons, 1999), which was used with permission as part of this chapter.

CHAPTER 19

Valuation Issues in Small Businesses

WHAT IS A SMALL BUSINESS?

A small business is frequently defined as a business with less than $5 million in revenue. Such businesses usually are owned by individuals, family members, or employees, and are likely to be highly dependent on the owner/manager. They also tend to have lower-quality financial statements and less access to capital than larger businesses. Buyers of small businesses often expect to be involved in day-to-day management of the business and are very concerned with lifestyle issues. Higher risks are associated with these small businesses.

Lack of Management Depth

Small businesses often have a high degree of reliance on one or more key owner/managers. In extreme cases, the business may rely on a single person for sales, technical expertise, and/or personal contacts and may not be able to survive without that person. Professional middle managers are a luxury that small businesses seldom can afford. To be profitable, small businesses must operate with a very thin management group. In addition, leaders of small businesses frequently are entrepreneurs who are not comfortable with delegation of management duties to others and may not work well with middle managers.

Small companies are apt to have a board of directors composed of insiders—members of the owner's family and/or employees. Thus they lack the diverse expertise and perspective outsiders can bring to a board of directors.

Lower-Quality Financial Statements

Small businesses tend to have lower-quality financial statements that are less likely to have been prepared by an outside accountant. Their statements tend to be tax-oriented rather than oriented to stockholder disclosure, as in larger companies.

If an outside accountant prepares the subject company's financial statements, the quality of the financial statements will depend on the extent of the work done by the accountant. The reliability and completeness of accounting information often decreases as one goes from audited to reviewed to compiled financial information. In an audit, the accountant has done extensive analysis and testing and has prepared footnote disclosures and a complete set of financial statements. Likewise, in an audit, the accountant expresses an opinion or disclaims an opinion on the fairness with which the financial statements represent the financial position, the results of operations, and the changes in financial position.

In a review, on the other hand, the accountant has performed fewer procedures and offers less assurance, indicating only that no material modifications need to be made to the financial statements for them to be in conformity with generally accepted accounting principles (GAAP). In a compilation, the accountant pulls together financial information for the subject company, does no testing or analysis of the financial information, and may not prepare footnote disclosures. Compiled financial statements are management's representations and the outside accountant provides no assurance on the statements. Small, closely-held companies often do not have a reason to go to the expense of having an audit or a review. If the subject company has compiled financial statements, the analyst should make more inquiries and do more analysis to ascertain the reliability of the financial information. In addition, it is likely that adjustments may be necessary to bring the financial statements closer into conformity with generally accepted accounting principles or to derive normalized cash flow.

When subject company financial statements are prepared internally, it may be important to inquire about the qualifications of the person responsible for preparing them. Some internal accountants have a strong background in accounting and prepare reliable financial statements on a timely basis. Others have no background in accounting. Overall, small companies usually have less internal accounting expertise than large companies.

Whereas large companies usually keep separate records for the preparation of tax returns and generally accepted accounting principles financial statements, small businesses that have no outside owners often have no reason to go to the expense of maintaining separate records for tax and book purposes. Thus, their financial statements may tend to reflect a bias toward minimizing income and taxes. The statements are often not in accordance with GAAP and are not applied on a consistent basis. Accruals of such items as wage-related expenses and warranties may be missing. Cut-off of sales and expenses may not provide for proper matching of revenues and expenses in the same period. Many small businesses utilize cash-basis rather than accrual-basis accounting. As a result, financial statements may not include accounts receivable, accounts payable, and various GAAP accruals. Finally, small companies are likely to have a number of related-party transactions, and owner discretionary expenses may be high. These characteristics of small business financial statements may increase the number of adjustments necessary in the valuation process.

For valuation assignments, where necessary, adjustments from cash-basis accounting to a more accrual-basis accounting can be made among the smallest companies.

Less Access to Capital

Small businesses have less access to capital than larger companies and often must rely on capital infusions from the owner family and/or owner employees. Access to debt capital is also more limited because of the higher risk of smaller businesses. The cost of borrowing is higher, and the owner usually must personally guarantee debt. Many small businesses operate with little or no debt, reflecting their limited access to debt capital and a frequent reluctance of owners to take on the risk of substantial debt. Many small business owners minimize debt to reduce risk during economic downturns and to increase the probability of keeping the business in the family.

If an entrepreneur owns interests in more than one entity, it is fairly common for one entity that may be more profitable to lend funds to another entity that may need them. In addition, owners of small businesses frequently make shareholder loans as a means of self-financing. Sometimes, these so-called loans are actually disguised infusions of equity, especially if they do not pay interest and have been on the books for a long time. Related party funding is sometimes used in lieu of, or in addition to, bank debt.

From a valuation perspective, it may be necessary to ensure that intercompany accounts are reconciled among several companies under common ownership. This sometimes involves an assessment of whether the borrower has the ability to repay a loan to the related party lender.

Other Operational Characteristics

Small businesses can lack diversity in products, markets, and geographic location. Frequently they are dependent on a few key customers, as when a small manufacturing company primarily produces parts for a single automobile manufacturer. They also may be dependent on a key supplier, as when a manufacturer's key raw material is a by-product of a single large local manufacturer.

Small businesses may have difficulty competing for employees. They may not be able to offer competitive benefit packages and may be in less desirable locations. Good managers may perceive less opportunity for promotions because of the company's small size and the owning family's dominance of top management positions.

Small businesses can be less informed about their market and competition. They are seldom in a position to pay for sophisticated market studies. Knowledge of markets and competition must come from the experience of a relatively limited number of managers—quite often the experience of a single person. Trade associations supplement this personal knowledge of the market. Thus small businesses operating in industries in which the trade associations are strong may be at less of a disadvantage.

In small companies, the portfolio of operations or products frequently reflects the interests and contacts of a particular owner. Sometimes these operations or products have few synergies, and the portfolio may have little appeal to potential buyers.

ValTip

The characteristics of small businesses tend to result in overall higher risk than is found in larger businesses. These characteristics can be extreme in the smallest of small businesses. Risk tends to increase as size decreases.

FINANCIAL STATEMENT ADJUSTMENTS

Financial statement adjustments are an important part of the valuation process with any company (see Chapter 4). These adjustments may include:

- Adjustments of the financial statements to GAAP basis accounting, including adjustment from cash basis to accrual basis
- Adjustments for unreported cash revenues
- Normalization adjustments to eliminate nonrecurring revenues and expenses from the financial statements
- Adjustments for unrecorded assets and liabilities
- Adjustments to make the subject company more comparable to others and itself over time to facilitate financial analysis
- Adjustments for nonoperating assets and/or liabilities and related revenues and expenses
- Adjustments for discretionary owner items

Small business financial statements tend to require more adjustments during the valuation process, especially for GAAP-type issues and for owner-discretionary items. It is important to consider the impact of adjustments on both the income statement and the balance sheet. As adjustments are made, it is also important to consider the possible tax effect of the adjustment, if warranted or applicable. Some types of adjustments apply when valuing either control or minority interests. Other types of adjustments apply only when valuing control interests.

GAAP Adjustments

Common GAAP balance sheet adjustments include adjusting receivables for collectibility, inventory for obsolescence, and fixed asset depreciation from accelerated tax methods to economic depreciation. Some analysts adjust fixed assets to appraised value. GAAP income statement adjustments include adjusting revenue and expenses for proper cutoff.

GAAP adjustments may also include converting from cash-basis accounting to accrual-basis accounting. Cash-to-accrual adjustments to the income statement require recording revenue when earned rather than when the cash is collected and recording expenses when incurred rather than when paid in cash. Cash-to-accrual adjustments to the balance sheet may include recording accrued assets and liabilities not found on a cash-basis balance sheet—accounts receivable, prepaid expenses, accounts payable, and other accrued assets or liabilities.

Unreported Cash Revenues

In some small businesses, there may be a greater likelihood that a portion of its revenue is not reported. This may occur where some customers pay their bills in cash.

Sometimes, the analyst may identify source documentation that can be used to quantify the amount of the unreported cash. For example, some medical practices keep an informal log of cash payments (which are often insurance copays) that are received by the office receptionist. These could be summarized and compared with bank deposit slips to determine the amount of cash that was, or was not, deposited into the business bank account. Often bank deposits are what constitute reported revenue for a practice, so assuming the analyst can cross-check what went into reported cash receipts, it may be possible to quantify any cash that did not get reported as revenue.

However, it is usually very difficult to identify and fully quantify the amount of unreported cash revenue for a business. In matrimonial proceedings where this is an issue, analysts may compare the lifestyle for the parties to their reported income; if their lifestyle expenditures exceed income, it may be because they are living off savings, funding lifestyle with debt (both of which, at least in theory, can be confirmed by a review of books and records), or using unreported cash to supplement their income.

Normalization Adjustments

Normalization adjustments include the removal of nonrecurring revenue and expenses to get a better understanding of the earnings expected in the future. Common nonrecurring items that may require adjustment include:

- Gains and losses on disposal of assets
- Income and losses from discontinued operations on the income statement and the related assets and liabilities on the balance sheet
- Settlements and payments due to lawsuits
- Losses due to an unusual natural disaster, such as flood damages not covered by insurance
- Funding of the retirement of a longtime owner/manager, which reflects a lump-sum payment for past service (it may be appropriate not to eliminate this item but to spread the expense over a period of years)

Unrecorded Assets

As discussed previously, when the subject business uses cash-basis accounting, there may be a number of unrecorded assets. In companies that use accrual-basis accounting, off–balance sheet assets may include favorable judgments in lawsuits against others. They may also include intangible assets—the customer list, an assembled workforce, technical expertise, trademarks, goodwill, and the like.

Analysts often adjust the balance sheet only to net tangible asset value, omitting intangible assets. The reason for this is that, to determine intangible asset value, one can first compare the expected future earnings of the business with the expected return on its net tangible assets to determine if the business has any intangible assets. Then one can determine what intangible assets exist and value each intangible asset separately. If the analyst concludes that intangible assets exist and the objective of the valuation is to value an ownership interest in the business as a whole, the analyst usually will turn to an earnings or a market method to value the tangible and intangible assets of a business together. In such situations, it is usually not cost effective to identify and value each intangible asset. Usually it is worthwhile to value individual intangible assets only when the purpose of the valuation is to determine the value of individual assets, such as in a purchase price allocation.

Unrecorded Liabilities

Unrecorded liabilities include cash-to-accrual basis adjustments, such as recording accounts payable and various accruals. Even businesses using accrual-basis accounting can require adjustments to record accruals for items such as warranty expense for products and vacation expense for employees. Accruals also may be necessary to comply with governmental regulations, such as environmental remediation actions and modifications to the workplace environment to meet requirements of the Occupational Safety and Health Administration (OSHA). Unrecorded liabilities may also include contingent liabilities.

Adjustments to Improve Comparability

It may be necessary to make certain adjustments to improve comparability of the subject company to industry norms, publicly traded companies, or companies involved in market transactions considered in the valuation process.

For example, if the subject company uses last-in, first-out (LIFO) accounting and the industry standard is first-in, first-out (FIFO) accounting, both the subject's inventory on the balance sheet and cost of goods sold on the income statement may be adjusted to FIFO before comparison to industry norms. Adjustments to improve industry comparability may just require some reclassifications or changes in presentation of the financial data. For example, comparisons of engineering and architectural firms to the industry may require presentation of both gross revenue and net revenue, after subcontractor revenues are deducted. Profitability for engineering and architectural firms may be analyzed by review of profit before taxes and bonuses; this is divided by either gross or net revenue to analyze profit margins over time.[1]

Adjustments also may be necessary to compare trends within the company if accounting methods changed during the period analyzed.

Nonoperating Assets and Liabilities

Small businesses frequently have nonoperating assets and liabilities. Owners often retain cash or other forms of working capital in excess of business needs, have investments in securities or land within the business, or purchase assets in the pursuit of a personal interest (e.g., antique cars or art). Items such as excess cash and investments reflect the aversion of the small business owner to financial risk, the desire to minimize taxes, and the frequent lack of perception of a line of demarcation between business and personal assets. When adjusting for nonoperating items, it is important to consider both their balance sheet and income statement impact. For example, when adjusting for a nonoperating item such as a vacation home, it is important to adjust for related expenses (e.g., insurance and maintenance) and related income (e.g., rental income).

---

[1] See, for example, the 2009 *Zweig White Financial Performance Survey of Architecture, Engineering, Planning & Environmental Consulting Firms* (Natick, MA: Zweig White, 2009).

Discretionary Owner Items

The small business may also pay higher than market rate compensation to the owners and family members. The business may pay discretionary personal expenses for things like country club dues and vacation homes for the owner(s). Transactions with related parties, such as leases, may be at rates above or below market. High owners' compensation and perquisites are not necessary to the operation of the business, and cost savings on related party transactions would not be available to another owner.

When valuing a control interest in a small business, it is appropriate to adjust for discretionary items. When valuing a minority interest, it may not be appropriate to adjust for discretionary items because the owner of a minority interest is not in a position to change these items. However, a minority shareholder may be in a position to force an adjustment as an oppressed shareholder.

QUALITATIVE FACTORS AFFECTING VALUE

Qualitative factors such as management depth, stability of the workforce, and expertise affect the value of any business. Certain qualitative factors are specific to small businesses. In reality, the buyers of such businesses may be buying themselves a job and a family lifestyle. Therefore, they may evaluate the attractiveness of a business differently from buyers of larger businesses who may be concerned only with return on investment. For example, a retail store in a downtown area that is open only on weekdays may sell for a higher price than a similar business in a mall that is open seven days a week and evenings. The price difference is due to the impact of these hours on the owner's personal and family life. Other very small businesses, such as bait shops, may sell for higher multiples of earnings because buyers perceive an opportunity to convert a hobby into a job.

Small businesses requiring strong technical expertise may sell at lower prices because few potential buyers have the requisite skills. Where there is a large pool of potential buyers, prices tend to be higher. There tends to be a large pool of buyers for manufacturing companies, because they can be more stable than service businesses and have substantial tangible assets that can be financed. This relatively large potential pool of buyers tends to increase prices.

Business brokers can provide insight into the qualitative factors being considered in a particular market.

VALUATION METHODS

Accepted methods for valuing closely held companies include asset, income, and market approaches. Theoretically, the value of a company is the present value of expected future benefits—usually earnings, cash flow, dividends, or capital appreciation to be realized at a later date—that will accrue to the owners. Valuation methods are discussed in detail in other chapters, and the basic principles remain the same when valuing small businesses. The characteristics of small businesses affect the application and relevance of these methods to small businesses. One method—using owners' discretionary cash flow—is usually relevant only for small businesses.

Asset Approach Valuation Methods

Overall, small businesses have a high failure rate, and many existing businesses may be in precarious shape. For small businesses with low earnings or losses, net tangible asset value—the market value of assets minus the market value of liabilities—may be the best indication of value (see Chapter 8).

It is important to define the premise of value. Is the business expected to continue operations, with going concern being the appropriate premise of value, or is the business likely to be terminated, making orderly liquidation or forced liquidation the appropriate premise of value? If real property or machinery and equipment appraisals are used in the valuation of the business, it is important to be sure that these appraisals use the same premise of value.

Although the book value of real estate is often less than its market value, other assets of small businesses may have book values significantly greater than market value in liquidation. The market value of computers and software drops precipitously after purchase. Other assets commonly held by small businesses—such as certain used equipment and office furniture—are available in abundance in some areas of the country, and this oversupply may result in very low values in liquidation. Thus the value of a struggling small business may well be less than book value.

Income Approach Valuation Methods

Income approach methods, particularly capitalized cash flow or earnings and discounted future cash flow or earnings, are just as important in valuing small businesses as in valuing large businesses (see Chapters 5 and 6). Small businesses are less likely to have reliable projections because of a lack of financial expertise. Buyers tend to be more skeptical of their earnings' projections because of lower-quality historical financial statements. When using projected future earnings, the analyst must consider whether projected revenue and earnings represent a fantasy as to how the owners of the company think it ought to perform or how they expect the actual company to perform. If the company has a record of meeting budgets and projecting accurately in the past, more reliance can be placed on projections in the valuation process. Since most small businesses have little or no budgeting experience, it may be difficult to get good projections.

Buyers of very small mom-and-pop businesses also expect future earnings to be the result of their own efforts and often are unwilling to pay a price based on projections that they have to make happen.

Earnings in the latest 12 months and average earnings in recent years tend to be given the most weight in establishing prices for these smallest businesses. Capitalization of earnings/cash flow is often an appropriate method for valuing these small businesses.

Manufacturing companies and other small businesses at the larger end of the spectrum of small businesses are more likely to be sold based on projections of future earnings than the smaller mom-and-pop operations. They are more likely to have some financial expertise and are usually more stable. Buyers are more willing to place reliance on their financial projections. Thus the discounted future cash flow or earnings method, which involves discounting a projected stream of future cash flow or earnings, can be an appropriate valuation method for these small businesses.

Market Approach Valuation Methods

This approach (see Chapter 7) requires the appraiser to research available sources of information to find similar investments. It can be very difficult to obtain sufficient reliable data concerning transfers of business ownership interests in the private marketplace. Analysts generally consider three types of market transactions:

1. Transactions involving minority interests in publicly traded companies (guideline public companies)
2. Merger and acquisition transactions involving publicly traded or privately held companies (guideline company transactions)
3. Transactions in the subject company's stock

Guideline Public Company Method

Guideline public companies can provide a reasonable basis for comparison to the relevant investment characteristics of the company being valued. Ideal guideline public companies are in the same industry as the company being valued; if there is insufficient transaction evidence available in the same industry, it may be necessary to consider companies in related industries with an underlying similarity of relevant investment characteristics, such as markets, products, growth, and cyclical variability. Guideline public companies should be evaluated by size, capital structure, and trend of sales and earnings. To fully reflect public market analysis and valuation, its stock should be actively traded, whether on an exchange or over the counter. The analyst must often exercise a great deal of judgment in determining which companies are similar enough to be used as guideline companies.

Many analysts assume that the guideline public company method is never applicable to small businesses. For the mom-and-pop very small business, this is often a safe assumption. For other small businesses, this assumption is not always safe. There are a large number of publicly traded companies with market capitalization less than $50 million, putting them within reasonable range for some small businesses.

Before Internet resources became readily available, doing a preliminary search for guideline public companies could be burdensome. With Internet resources, it is possible to do an efficient preliminary search for guideline public companies and avoid the danger of overlooking reasonably good ones. In many cases, no guideline public companies will be found for a small business because of differences in size, diversity, and management depth among the small business being valued and the publicly traded companies. Nevertheless, sometimes reasonably comparable public companies can be found for small businesses. Even if the analyst decides that the potential guideline public companies are not sufficiently comparable to use as a basis for calculating value, their disclosure documents—such as Form 10-K, 10-Q, and 8-K—may contain valuable information concerning opportunities and threats in the subject company's industry or transaction information from acquisitions.

Even the compensation paid to top officers of the business, which can be found in its annual proxy filings, may provide useful data on what top executives are paid in the industry.

Guideline Company Transactions Method

Merger and acquisition activity within the industry may give insight into the value of the stock of a closely held company. Such transactions are an indication of the investing attitude of the public toward the industry. However, reliable data regarding M&A transactions, particularly involving closely held companies, are difficult to find for many industries. Often the information concerning such transactions is too incomplete to be used in calculations of value for a subject company; however, it may be useful as a reasonableness test of the value conclusion. When information concerning transactions is available, it can provide objective evidence of the value placed on guideline companies by the market.

There are currently four small business transaction databases:

1. *Pratt's Stats*™ and *Public Stats*™ are published by Business Valuation Resources LLC®, 1000 SW Broadway, Suite 1200, Portland, OR 97205 (phone 1-888-287-8258) and are available online from www.BVMarketData.com.
2. The *Bizcomps*® database is published by Jack Sanders, Managing Director of Spectrum Corporate Resources, LLC, PO Box 97757, Las Vegas, NV 89193 (phone 702-454-0072) and is available online from www.BVMarketData.com or on disk from www.bizcomps.com.

3. The *IBA Market Database* is published by The Institute of Business Appraisers (IBA), PO Box 17410, Plantation, FL 33318 (phone 954-584-1144) and is made available to IBA members.
4. The *DoneDeals®* database is published by Thomson Reuters, and is available online from www.donedeals.com.

The information available in these databases has expanded tremendously in recent years. The *IBA Market Database* has the largest number of transactions. *Pratt's Stats* usually has the most detailed information on each transaction. The information in *DoneDeals* is derived from public documents rather than business brokers. Where available, *DoneDeals* and *Pratt's Stats* disclose the name of the companies involved in the transactions. All four databases disclose different information on terms of the deal. These terms may have a large impact on the multiples paid. Data limitations need to be considered when making comparisons between the transactions and the subject company.

> The analyst must exercise caution in using transaction databases because they define variables in different ways.

DoneDeals and *Pratt's Stats* include inventory in the deal price, but *Bizcomps* excludes inventory. *Bizcomps* uses the term "seller's discretionary cash flow" and *Pratt's Stats* uses the term "discretionary earnings" to describe earnings before taxes, interest, compensation to one owner, and noncash charges. The *IBA Market Database* uses the term "annual earnings" but includes noncash charges.

> Revenue and discretionary earnings are two of the most common multiples used in the guideline company transaction method.

Deal values reported by *IBA* and *Bizcomps* are asset sales but exclude certain assets like real property. *Pratt's Stats* now reports all multiples based on the market value of invested capital (MVIC). *DoneDeals* discloses which deals are for stock and which are for assets within each individual transaction record. However, all multiples are based on the reported "price" (price to assets, price to stockholder's equity, price to net income, price to EBITDA, etc.), regardless of whether they are for stock or invested capital.

Revenue multiples are used most often for service businesses or when reliable data on earnings is not available. Using this multiple implies that the subject company and the acquired companies have similar asset ratios and similar profit margins.

Discretionary earnings reflect the cash available to service acquisition debt and to pay the owner a salary. When this multiple is used, the method reflects a cash payback concept. The transaction databases provide information concerning multiples to be used to arrive at an indication of value. Business brokers commonly use this method to determine prices for small businesses.

When a guideline company transaction multiple is used to determine value, the result will, depending on what transaction databases are used, not include adjustments for an excess or a shortage of working capital, real estate, long-term debt, noncompete agreements, and so on. For example, multiples derived from the *Bizcomps* database do not include inventory. These items must be added to or subtracted from the initial result to determine the value of the enterprise.

The majority of the individual transaction data in *DoneDeals, Pratt's Stats, Bizcomps*, and the *IBA* do not contain enough information for use as a primary valuation method. See Web Addendum 1 to Chapter 7 for the article "Transaction Databases: Useful or Not?" (*Financial Valuation and Litigation Expert* journal, Issue 21, October/November 2009) at www.wiley.com/go/FVAM3E. If public disclosures and/or additional supporting details are available, transactions, often with adjustments, can be used as a part of a primary valuation method. See Chapter 7 for additional information on the databases.

> Value indications derived from the guideline company transaction method are on a control basis.

Past Transactions in the Company's Stock

One of the best market approach methods to value involves analysis of recent transactions in the subject company's own stock. There is generally no active market for closely held common stock, but if some transactions have occurred, a market value sometimes can be derived and used as an element in the determination of fair market value. It is important that these transactions be arm's length. Even if only limited transactions have occurred at arm's length, the analyst sometimes can draw inferences about fair market value based on these transactions.

Rules of Thumb

There are many rules of thumb for valuing small businesses in various industries. They are often widely discussed in a particular industry, and business brokers may refer to them. As an analyst, it is important to be aware of these rules of thumb and

> Although rules of thumb may provide insight on the value of a business, it is usually better to use them for reasonableness tests of the value conclusion.

to be able to discuss why the value conclusion for the subject company falls at the top or bottom or even outside of the range indicated by rules of thumb. They do not address important factors influencing the value of a particular company or terms of deals. Rules of thumb purport to reflect average multiples paid in transactions but are not traceable to specific transactions. Thus, transaction databases can provide better, more objective information on multiples.

Sources on rules of thumb are covered in Chapter 20, "Valuation Issues in Professional Practices."

Excess Cash Flow (Earnings) Method

The excess cash flow/earnings method is a hybrid method, combining aspects of both the asset and income approach.

> The excess earnings/cash flow method is widely used for small businesses, but analysts frequently misuse it.

Four general steps are involved:

1. Determine the market value of the net tangible assets of the business.
2. Determine the normalized or representative cash flow/earnings of the business.
3. Determine appropriate rates of return on both the net tangible and intangible business assets. Multiply the value of net tangible assets by the required rate of return for net tangible assets to determine the return on net tangible assets, then subtract that return from normalized earnings to derive "excess earnings." Divide these excess earnings by the required rate of return (cap rate) on intangible assets to determine the value of intangible assets.
4. Add the value of the net tangible assets to the value of intangible assets to arrive at a value for the business.

Although this method appears easy, a number of subjective judgments are involved, the most difficult being determination of an appropriate rate of return/cap rate for excess earnings/cash flow. This determination is a largely subjective process and requires substantial analyst judgment. See Chapter 5 for a more detailed example on the application of this valuation method.

REASONABLENESS TESTS

After arriving at a preliminary conclusion of value for a small business, it is important to step back from the process and consider the reasonableness of the conclusion. One of the tests of the reasonableness of the value conclusion is to consider the feasibility of financing a transaction at the concluded value. Although there are variations, for a small business, typical financing assumptions might include:

- Down payment of 25 to 30 percent[2]
- Repayment period of three to five years
- Market rate of interest rate considering the risk of a small business
- Seller financing

For larger small businesses with strong earnings and substantial assets, better terms might be:

- Down payment of 20 percent
- Repayment period as long as seven to ten years
- Possible bank financing

The business should be able to generate adequate cash flow to provide reasonable compensation to the owner and make its debt payments.

Other reasonableness tests include:

- Considering the range of value implied by rules of thumb and the strength of the subject company relative to others in the industry
- Developing a capitalization rate using the build-up method and comparing it to the overall rate implied by the excess cash flow/earnings method, if used
- Considering the reasonableness of the magnitude of goodwill implied by any cash flow/earnings and market methods used

SUMMARY

Small businesses are usually owned by individuals, family members, or employees. They are likely to be highly dependent on the owner/manager. They also tend to have lower-quality financial statements and less access to capital than larger businesses. Buyers of small businesses expect to be involved in day-to-day management of the business and are concerned with lifestyle issues. These characteristics of small businesses influence the adjustments appropriate in the valuation process and influence the choice of valuation methods.

---

[2] See, for example, the "Business Owner's Toolkit" which indicates down payments of 25 to 30 percent are often necessary to satisfy commercial lenders (Toolkit Media Group at www.toolkit.com/small_business_guide/sbg.aspx?nid=P11_2422).

CHAPTER 20

Valuation Issues in Professional Practices

Professional practice valuation follows the same principles as the valuation of other businesses. Many of the concerns in valuing professional practices are similar to valuing small businesses, such as the likelihood that a practice is highly dependent on a single individual or a few individuals and that it often uses cash-basis accounting. Professional practices are service businesses and usually have few tangible assets. The success of professional practices is dependent on relationships with clients or patients and the reputation of the professionals in the community.

Many professional practices obtain most of their patients or clients through referrals, based on the reputation of specific professionals.

Professional practices, especially medical practices, may have contractual relationships with third-party payers. Professionals are required to meet specific educational requirements and most must obtain professional licenses. These characteristics of professional practices influence their valuations.

In some jurisdictions, an important issue in valuing professional practices is distinguishing between the goodwill that is solely attributable to the professional (and difficult to transfer) and the goodwill that is attributable to the practice.

Case law, regulatory concerns, and rapidly changing economic circumstances also influence the valuation of professional practices. The complexity of valuing professional practices has led some analysts to specialize in valuing professional practices or even in valuing specific kinds of professional practices, especially medical practices, for which the market has been very active.

TYPES OF PRACTICES

There are many different types of professional practices. However, from a valuation perspective, most analysts are involved in the following practices: medical, dental, law, accounting, architecture, and engineering. Often a differentiating factor between professional practices and service businesses is that in the former, a license to practice is required.

Medical Practices

The medical practice environment is rapidly changing, complex, and highly regulated. A description of some major trends in the medical practice environment that influence value follows:

- The healthcare sector in the United States generates more than $1 trillion in annual revenue. Physician services on an outpatient basis make up about 20 percent of this sector.[1]
- There are more than 200,000 physician offices in the United States, according to First Research,[2] and U.S. consumption rates for physician services are estimated to increase at a compound annual rate of 7 percent between 2008 and 2013. The Bureau of Labor Statistics estimated that in 2006, there were 468,000 physicians and surgeons in the United States, and that there would be employment growth of 17.1% total over the 10-year period from 2006 to 2016.[3]
- Healthcare providers can be highly dependent on reimbursement rates by third-party insurers, managed care organizations, Medicare, and Medicaid. Insurers often follow trends set by Medicare in establishing rates from year to year. While growth in reimbursement rates each year may be modest, operational costs for medical practices have continued to increase faster, especially for malpractice coverage.
- As of the date of this writing, the outlook for the industry was clouded somewhat because of the possibility that some kind of comprehensive healthcare reform might be enacted by the U.S. government.
- Consumer medical expenses have been growing at such a rapid rate that it has led to the general public perception that medical costs are out of control.
- Managed care organizations designed to control costs have emerged as a major market force. The growth of managed care organizations has led to growth in capitation or reimbursement based on the number of covered patients served rather than on the specific services rendered.

---

[1] First Research, Inc., "Industry Profile: Healthcare Sector" (Quarterly Update 6/22/2009).
[2] Ibid.
[3] Bureau of Labor Statistics, U.S. Department of Labor, *Career Guide to Industries, 2008–9 Edition: Health Care* (Updated 3/12/2008).

- There has been a shift from individual physician practices to corporate-like medicine in recent years. This shift is a response to growing physician numbers, an ever-increasing administrative and regulatory burden, and the emergence of managed care. This shift from sole practitioner physician practices includes:
  - Growth in group medical practices
  - Growth in vertically integrated delivery systems with hospitals acquiring physician practices
  - The appearance (and sometimes demise) of publicly traded, practice management companies
- Vertically integrated delivery systems have sometimes been disappointing in their profitability, and some acquired medical practices have been spun off.
- Publicly traded practice management companies provide medical practices with access to capital markets, strong management, and managed care expertise. However, many of these entities have suffered financial hardships.
- Complex regulation affects the healthcare industry. The federal government provides constant oversight of healthcare transactions. Increased scrutiny of the Internal Revenue Code § 501(c)3 status of tax-exempt organizations has affected the market for selling medical practices to charitable institutions. The primary concern about these transactions is that they should not result in any private benefit or private inurement to certain insiders of a tax-exempt organization. Almost every year there are new guidelines to prevent healthcare fraud. Analysts valuing medical practices must keep up with changes in the regulatory environment. Buyers unaware of the illegality of activities of a medical practice may be liable for penalties for violations.[4] In his *Medical Practice Valuation Guidebook 2001/2002*, Mark Dietrich states the following: "I cannot overemphasize the importance (or associated difficulty) of a good working knowledge of the Stark, Fraud and Abuse, and similar state regulations of healthcare transactions when doing valuations."[5]

Valuing Medical Practices for Acquisition by Hospitals

A critical issue for analysts when valuing medical practices for acquisition by hospitals is the treatment of physician compensation. Hospitals that pay more than fair market value for medical practices are at risk of running afoul of various healthcare regulations. In these transactions, hospitals will commonly retain and employ the in-place physicians under various employment agreements with contractual compensation arrangements.

When applying the income approach, the analysts should keep in mind the inverse relationship of the level of planned future physician compensation and the fair market value of the medical practice and advise the parties accordingly (i.e., the greater the compensation that is paid to the physicians under the employment agreements post-transaction, the lower the net cash flow to the hospital-owner of the medical practice, thereby resulting in a lower fair market value).

---

[4] Mark O. Dietrich, *Medical Practice Valuation Guidebook 2001/2002* (San Diego, CA: Windsor Professional Information, 2001), pp. 327–363.
[5] Ibid. p. 328.

The hospital-client should also be advised that the compensation arrangements (including both base and incentive pay) used in the valuation analysis should be consistent with the contractual compensation per the physician employment agreements. Failure to do so may result in the hospital overpaying for the medical practice in instances where the valuation assumed a lower compensation arrangement than what is actually put in place.

Finally, the hospital-client providing the future physician compensation arrangement to the analysts should ensure that the compensation represents a fair market value rate based on the physician services to be provided and that it is commercially reasonable.[6]

For further information on medical practices, see Chapter 25.

Dental Practices

The Bureau of Labor Statistics estimated that in 2006, there were 96,000 dentists in the United States, with that number estimated to grow by 7.5% total from 2006 to 2016.[7] First Research estimates that there are about 120,000 dentists in the United States, most of whom are sole practitioners; the average revenue per year is about $600,000 per office.[8] Demographics play into the success of a dental practice, with children and the elderly often needing the most dental care.

Law Practices

In the past, state laws and legal ethics forbidding the sale of client files and goodwill have hampered transactions in legal practices. In recent years, state laws concerning the sale of law practices have relaxed, but there is still little market information concerning the value of legal practices.

Law practices span many sizes, from sole proprietorships to multinational law firms with hundreds of partners and well over a thousand attorneys. Particularly in divorce valuations, the amount of information made available for the valuation of a small law firm may greatly outweigh the volume of documents voluntarily produced by a large law firm. Larger law firms are often reluctant to provide much, if any, information on partners, other than the one whose interest is being valued. The valuation analyst may find that otherwise basic information, such as financial statements and specifics on buy-in and buyout transactions, is often not produced voluntarily.

In addition, partners with very small interests in large firms often have little influence or ability to control the amount of total compensation paid to them. While the level of their billable hours and fee generation is obviously performance-driven, often a compensation committee (consisting of a small group of attorneys at the firm)

[6] Don Barbo, "The Anatomy of a Medical Practice Valuation: Valuation Strategies for Medical Practices," presentation to the Financial Consulting Group Annual Fall Advanced Business Valuation Conference, Houston, TX (September 12, 2004).
[7] Bureau of Labor Statistics, U.S. Department of Labor, *Career Guide to Industries, 2008–9 Edition: Health Care* (Updated 3/12/2008).
[8] First Research, Inc., "Industry Profile: Dentists Offices & Clinics" (Quarterly Update 6/22/2009).

may set the level of profit to be allocated to each partner at the firm. In contrast, partners in small law firms or sole proprietors may have significant ability to determine the amount of their total compensation (based on fee generation and revenues earned/received, net of expenses). These differences may affect the assumptions made by the analyst in the course of a valuation.

Contingent fee–based law firms can be especially challenging from a valuation perspective, because earning fees is dependent on the successful resolution of a case. Therefore, the amount of work in process at any given time for a contingent fee–based practice may be difficult to estimate.

Accounting Practices

Accounting practices tend to have few tangible assets, and their value arises primarily from professional relationships with clients. The terms of the sale of accounting practices generally include a noncompete agreement and an earnout or a guarantee of revenue or client retention. These terms reflect the importance of client retention to the value of the practice. In addition, due to the risk of client loss and the lack of tangible assets, the sale of an accounting practice is frequently seller-financed. Banks tend to prefer loans to be backed by tangible assets. Seller financing tends to increase the seller's motivation to help with client retention. Finally, because accounting practices have simple cost structures and few tangible assets, often they are sold at a multiple of revenue.

Architecture and Engineering Firms

Architectural and engineering firms are sometimes viewed as mixed discipline, in that firms may employ professionals who are architects, engineers, environmental consultants, or a combination of each. Single-discipline firms often employ subcontractors to assist in completion of their projects, whose fees are merely a pass-through on the firm's income statement and therefore have no net impact on profit.

For financial statement purposes, service revenues are usually presented both gross (including subcontractors) and net (excluding subcontractor revenues). Engineers and architects are often compensated through a base salary plus a bonus. Profitability is sometimes analyzed through consideration of profit before taxes and bonuses.[9]

As with law firms, companies in this segment may be small or very large; some of the biggest firms are publicly traded. The number of employees may be more prone to upswings when the economy and the industry are growing, and to layoffs with declines in employment in a recession.

The 2009 Zweig White *Merger & Acquisition Survey* surveyed 49 firms about their recent acquisitions. There were more asset purchases than stock sales. The respondents' latest acquisitions were priced at multiples of 62.5% of price to net service revenue and 4.0x predistribution EBITDA; both are the medians reported.[10]

---

[9] Zweig White, *Financial Performance Survey of Architecture, Engineering, Planning & Environmental Consulting Firms* (Natick, MA: Zweig White, 2009), pp. 44–45, 48–49.

[10] Zweig White, *Merger & Acquisition Survey of Architecture, Engineering, Planning & Environmental Consulting Firms* (Natick, MA: Zweig White, 2009), p. 37. Note: Be careful in relying on general pricing multiples without the underlying supporting detail.

PURPOSE OF VALUATION

> Although professional practices are valued for the same reasons as other types of businesses, litigation (including disputes among principals and marital dissolutions) and transactions (including the sale of a practice, an associate buying in, and buy-sell formulas) account for a large portion of the valuation work.

In addition to acquisitions, partnership buyouts, and divorce, succession planning is another reason why professional practices may require appraisal, as older partners contemplate selling interests to new and/or younger partners.

PROFESSIONAL GOODWILL AND PRACTICE GOODWILL

Goodwill is defined in the valuation industry as "that intangible asset arising as a result of name, reputation, customer loyalty, location, products, and similar factors not separately identified."[11]

Other insights into goodwill can be obtained by reviewing the California Code of Civil Procedure. Within the meaning of this article, goodwill is:

> . . . the benefits that accrue to a business as a result of its location, reputation for dependability, skill or quality, and any other circumstances resulting in probable retention of old or acquisition of new patronage.[12]

A large portion of the value of a professional practice may be attributable to intangible assets. Many professional practices, such as accounting and law practices, have relatively few tangible assets. Other professional practices, such as dental and optical practices, have considerable tangible assets—dental practices with a substantial investment in equipment and some inventory and optical practices with a substantial investment in inventory.

> Goodwill may be the primary intangible asset found in professional practices, but the definition of goodwill differs in different scenarios.

---

[11] *International Glossary of Business Valuation Terms* by American Institute of Certified Public Accountants American Society of Appraisers, Canadian Institute of Chartered Business Valuators National Association of Certified Valuation Analysts, The Institute of Business Appraisers, Copyright © 2001 Business Valuation Resources.

[12] California Code of Civil Procedure, Chapter 9, Article 6, paragraph 1263.510.

In the legal community (and case law), goodwill often represents all asset value above tangible assets. In the world of accounting and appraisal, goodwill represents asset value that has not been identified as related to a specific tangible or intangible asset.

In many states' professional practice case law, goodwill is composed of a "practice" or "enterprise" goodwill component that is attributable to the practice entity and a "personal" or "professional" goodwill component that is attributable to professional practitioners personally.

The intangible value or goodwill of a professional practice can be difficult to measure and can be difficult to preserve in a transaction. Much of the value of a professional practice consists of professional goodwill. Although a sizable part of personal goodwill may not be able to be transferred to another professional, there is often some transferability to a qualified buyer with careful planning and cooperation between the seller and the buyer. The selling practitioner can transfer some client trust by introducing clients to the buying practitioner and by bringing the buyer into the practice as an associate, providing a transition period. A noncompete agreement between the buyer and seller can help ensure the successful transfer of clients; and the buyer usually is willing to pay an additional amount for this further assurance of the transfer of clients.

When a professional practice is being valued for transaction or litigation purposes, it may be important to identify professional and practice goodwill separately and to discuss the likelihood that a portion of the professional goodwill can be transferred in a transaction.

For marital dissolution purposes, the analyst generally needs to know applicable state law and precedent concerning personal goodwill. Courts in several states have ruled that personal goodwill is a marital asset to be valued and divided between the divorcing spouses along with other property. In these states, the practice is valued on a going-concern basis assuming that the practitioner will continue in an active capacity for a reasonable period of time, depending on the age, health, and work habits of the professional. Little or no weight may be given to the difficulty of transferring a professional practice that is dependent on referral sources. In other words, no transaction is actually contemplated.

Conversely, in states where personal goodwill is excluded from the marital estate, the underlying assumption is that a hypothetical transaction is contemplated. The theory is that in a sale, a seller would not remain with the business, so his or her continued work efforts should not be included in value, as they are not transferable to the buyer. Therefore, only "enterprise" or "practice" goodwill is included in value.

SELECT CASE LAW FOR MARITAL DISSOLUTION

Case law related to personal goodwill as property subject to distribution generally falls into two camps: included (value to the holder) or excluded (value in exchange). One California court defined the value to the holder concept as follows:

[I]n a matrimonial matter, the practice of the sole practitioner husband will continue, with the same intangible value as it had during the marriage. Under the principles of community property law, the wife, by virtue of her position of wife, made to that value the same contribution as does a wife to any of the husband's earnings and accumulations during marriage. She is as much entitled to be recompensed for that contribution as if it were represented by the increased value of stock in a family business.[13]

In New Jersey, fair value is the standard of value following the ruling in *Brown v. Brown*.[14] However, the *Dugan* and *Piscopo* rulings include discussion of concepts relating to the investment value standard. As stated in the *Dugan v. Dugan* decision, involving the valuation of a sole practitioner's interest in a law practice:

Future earnings capacity per se is not goodwill. However, when that future earning capacity has been enhanced because reputation leads to probable future patronage from existing and potential clients, goodwill may exist and have value. When that occurs the resulting goodwill is property subject to equitable distribution. . . . As matters now stand limitations on the sale of a law practice with its goodwill may have an adverse effect upon its value. However, as previously observed, goodwill may be of significant value irrespective of these limitations.[15]

In their book *Standards of Value: Theory and Applications*, Jay Fishman, Shannon Pratt, and Bill Morrison identify 10 states where, in their words, "some version of a value to the holder premise" is used.[16] As previously suggested, California is one of those states; others include Washington and North Carolina. New Jersey is considered a "hybrid" state, given existing case law.[17]

An alternate view of this issue is discussed in the Illinois ruling in the *Zells* matter. As noted later, the court excluded personal goodwill from the marital estate and adopted a value in exchange premise as follows:

Although many businesses possess this intangible known as goodwill, the concept is unique in a professional business. The concept of professional goodwill is the sole asset of the professional. If goodwill is that aspect of a business which maintains the clientele, then the goodwill in a professional

---

[13] *Golden v. Golden*, 75 Cal. Rptr. 735 (Ct. App. 1969) at 738. As quoted in Ronald L. Brown, *Valuing Professional Practices and Licenses*, 3rd ed. (New York: Aspen Publishers, 2008), Section 1.03[b].

[14] *Brown v. Brown*, 348 N.J. Super. 466; 792 A.2d 463.

[15] *Dugan v. Dugan*, 92 N.J. 423; 457 A.2d 1; 1983 N.J. Lexis 2351. Note that New Jersey also has a Supreme Court ruling, *Stern v. Stern*, where the provisions of the buy-sell agreement were relied upon. See 66 N.J. 340; 331 A.2d 257; 1975.

[16] Jay E. Fishman, Shannon P. Pratt, and William J. Morrison, *Standards of Value: Theory and Applications* (Hoboken, NJ: John Wiley & Sons, 2007), p. 242.

[17] Ibid., p. 199.

business is the skill, the expertise, and the reputation of the professional. It is these qualities which would keep patients returning to a doctor and which would make those patients refer others to him. The bottom line is that this is reflected in the doctor's income-generating ability. . . .

Although goodwill was not considered in the court's valuation of the business itself, it was a factor in examining [the husband's] income potential. To figure goodwill in both facets of the practice would be to double count and reach an erroneous valuation.[18]

The book *Standards of Value: Theory and Applications* identifies 34 states where the "value in exchange" concept has been used in family law case matters.[19] In other words, the relative transferability of the interest is considered in the valuation. Examples of states that fall under this category include Pennsylvania, Connecticut, and Illinois (as the previously mentioned *Zells* decision suggests).

Some states exclude professional goodwill in an even more defined way, by consideration of a walk-away doctrine. This concept implies that an owner could sell his or her business without a noncompete agreement and then walk across the street and open a similar business that could in theory immediately compete with the business that had been sold. Therefore, the value of the business should be determined by excluding any value attributable to a noncompete agreement. Under that scenario, what would the value of the owner's former business be, assuming he or she could fully complete from day one?

Several decisions in Florida address this concept. The *Thompson* decision stated that:

If goodwill depends on the continued presence of a particular individual, such goodwill, by definition, is not a marketable asset distinct from the individual. Any value which attaches to the entity solely as a result of personal goodwill represents nothing more than probable future earnings capacity, which, although relevant in determining alimony, is not a proper consideration in dividing marital property in a dissolution proceeding.[20]

The *Weinstock* decision indicated the following:

The purest form of comparable in the sale of any business would be a sale in which, on the day of closing, the seller simply picks up the sales proceeds and retires or moves out of the area, thus eliminating any further personal influence the seller could have on the business.[21]

---

[18] In re: *Marriage of Zells*, 572 N.E. 2d at 946 (quoting In re: *Marriage of Courtwright*, 507 N.E. 2d 891 [Ill. App. 1987]).

[19] Jay E. Fishman, Shannon P. Pratt, and William J. Morrison, *Standards of Value: Theory and Applications* (Hoboken, NJ: John Wiley & Sons, 2007), p. 226.

[20] *Thompson v. Thompson*, 576 So. 2d 267; 1991 Fla. Lexis 69; 16 Fla. L. Weekly S 73.

[21] *Weinstock v. Weinstock*, 634 So. 2d 775; 1994 Fla. App. Lexis 3065; 19 Fla. L. Weekly D 724.

The *Held* ruling further refined discussion of the issue, as follows:

> The trial court's valuation of enterprise goodwill turned on the assumption that in "any sale of enterprise goodwill," the husband would be precluded from doing business with the company's 60 clients. The judge attempted to distinguish a "non solicitation/non piracy agreement" from a broader covenant not to compete, which, as we ruled in *Walton*, was attributable to the personal reputation of the seller/husband and not to the enterprise goodwill of the business. [However] For the purpose of distinguishing enterprise goodwill from personal goodwill in the valuation of a business, there is no distinction between a "non solicitation/non piracy agreement" and a covenant not to compete. Both limit a putative seller's ability to do business with existing clients of the business. In this case, the husband's personal relationship with his clients allowed him to obtain their repeat business.[22]

FACTORS AFFECTING VALUE

A number of factors influence the value of a professional practice and the allocation of goodwill between personal and enterprise goodwill:

- Level and stability of practice earnings and/or cash flow
- Qualifications and work habits of the professionals
- Age and health of the professional
- Specialty and fee schedule including fees earned compared to others in the specialty
- Trained and assembled workforce
- Reliance on referrals
- Type of clients or patients served and contractual relationships with third-party payers
- Geographic location
- Supply of professionals and competition
- Previously demonstrated ability to transfer clients/patients

Earnings and/or Cash Flow

The expected future earnings and/or cash flow of a professional practice are a primary determinant of value. Professional practices usually pay out all their earnings to their principals as compensation and benefits. Thus, the analyst generally should focus on the economic income of the professional practice—earnings before compensation and benefits are paid to the practice principals—as a measure of earnings. If earnings are highly volatile, as they are for a law firm with large contingent-fee cases, value tends to be lower based on earnings' riskiness. However, consistently high earnings do not necessarily indicate a high practice value. A professional with an outstanding reputation may attract many referrals, but the resulting high earnings in the practice may reflect personal goodwill, not enterprise goodwill. A professional may work much longer than normal hours, but the resulting high earnings may not increase the value of the practice.

---

[22] *Held v. Held*, 912 So. 2d 637 (Fla. 4th DCA 2003)

Qualifications and Work Habits of the Professionals

The analyst should consider the professional qualifications and work habits of practice professionals. To assess the extent to which a practice professional is receiving higher than average compensation and benefits, the analyst may obtain information concerning the education, licenses, additional qualifications, personal skills, special training, age, and years of experience of that professional and the other professionals in the practice. This information can be used to compare the professional's compensation and/or the practice's economic income with averages for professionals of the same age and with the same specialty in the same market.

ValTip

It is important to be sure the professional's earnings and/or the practice's economic income have been calculated in the same manner as the comparative compensation data.

The analyst also should inquire about the work habits of the professionals—asking about the number of hours worked each week and the amount of time spent away from work each year for vacation and continuing education. If professionals are spending more than normal time on professional duties, it may decrease value relative to practice earnings because a buyer, who is a professional, might not be willing to work more than normal hours. If the extra time spent at work is spent handling administrative matters that could be handled by nonprofessional staff members, the negative impact may be less.

Age and Health of the Professional

The age of the practitioner may be an important factor in determining average compensation for similar professionals in the market area. Age, along with the health and work habits of the practitioner, provide indications of the expected future work life of the practitioner. Health also provides an indication of the practitioner's ability to sustain the current workload.

Specialty and Fees Schedule

The type of services provided and the efficiency of the practitioner influence practice earnings and practitioner compensation. Fee schedules, in comparison with community standards, provide an indication of the professional's reputation and skills. If the fee schedule is above-average and the practice retains a large number of clients, it is an indication of above-average professional skills.

Trained and Assembled Workforce

A trained and assembled workforce in place contributes to the value of a professional practice. A trained administrative staff following established management systems is an asset to a professional practice. If clients or patients have ongoing relationships with paraprofessionals, such as dental assistants, who handle many client services, these employees can enhance practice value. If nonowner professionals have strong relationships with clients or patients, it is important to determine if such key professionals have employment agreements with the practice. If employment agreements are in place, it may support or enhance value; if not, it may detract from value.

The value of a trained and assembled workforce is sometimes broken out in matrimonial appraisals as a separate component of intangible value related to the enterprise. However, this is not permitted in valuations performed for financial reporting purposes, as it is considered an element of goodwill that should not be separately allocated.

> In a small professional practice, value may be greater if a successor for the key professional is in place. Bringing in an associate and introducing the associate to clients or patients may facilitate the transfer of some "professional goodwill" and may increase the price received by the exiting professional.

Reliance on Referrals and Client Persistence

In certain types of professional practices, the professionals and staff develop strong relationships with clients or patients. Clients or patients become accustomed to coming to a specific location or dialing a specific phone number for professional services. If such client relationships are persistent, it tends to increase the value of the professional practice.

In other types of professional practices, clients or patients are referred to professionals because of their reputation and skills. Reliance on referrals tends to decrease the value of a practice because such a practice relies on the personal reputation of the professional, which is difficult to transfer to another party.

Thus, general dentistry practices, pediatric practices, and some larger accounting practices may have value in the form of enterprise goodwill—patient or client relationships that may be able to be transferred with careful planning. On the other hand, orthodontist practices, orthopedic surgeon practices, and business valuation practices may have less enterprise goodwill because of their dependence on referrals.

Types of Clients or Patients

The client base of the practice should be analyzed. The volume and quality of client records, the demographics of the client group, and payer source affect the value of the practice. For example, medical practices may receive reimbursement directly from the patient ("private pay") or from various third-party payers, including traditional insurance plans, health maintenance organizations, Medicare, and Medicaid. Practices with more private-pay patients and traditional insurance plan patients tend to be worth more than practices with substantial dependence on Medicare and Medicaid patients.

In many markets, contractual relationships with various third-party payers control access to patients and influence the value of medical practices. If a high proportion of clients are from health maintenance contracts that cannot be transferred, the value of the practice is less in a "value in exchange" assumption. The analyst needs to understand the local market and inquire about the composition of the patient/client pool of a practice.

In an accounting or law practice, there should be an analysis of which clients are *recurring*, *nonrecurring*, or *recurring nonrecurring*. *Recurring* clients need services each year, as in an annual audit or tax return service. *Nonrecurring* clients show up only once, as in a personal injury case for a plaintiff represented by a law firm. *Recurring nonrecurring* clients appear once in a while but not in a predictable manner, as in damage cases for a larger corporation or an accounting firm.

Location

Professional practices located in attractive neighborhoods in cities with strong economies, good schools, recreational opportunities, and cultural amenities have greater appeal to professionals and their families than less attractive locations. Thus, an attractive location may increase practice value.

Supply of Professionals and Competition

Existing professional practices become more attractive and more valuable when the supply of professionals in that particular field is high. If there is a shortage of professionals in a field, it can be relatively easy to hang up one's "shingle" and go into business for oneself. If there is a strong supply of professionals in a particular field, the barriers to entry for a new practice increase, and buying an established practice becomes more attractive.

Previously Demonstrated Ability to Transfer Clients/Patients

During the course of an engagement, the analyst may identify circumstances in which professionals at a practice have historically shown an ability to transfer client or patient relationships. For example, if one were to track patient referrals over time at a group practice, could it be shown that referrals from an outside physician gradually switched from an older physician to a younger one? Is there a history of shareholders leaving the practice and the remaining owners picking up their business without a loss in the existing client or patient base—even if the departing owner is now competing for business? These are factors that may point to the ability of the practitioners to transfer relationships.

Summary

Value factors such as the qualifications, skills, age, and work habits of the professional relate primarily to personal goodwill. Other factors such as an assembled workforce, geographic location, type of clients or patients and contractual relationships with third-party payers, and supply of professionals relate primarily to enterprise goodwill. Reliance on referrals tends to increase the importance of the professional's qualifications and the reliance of the practice on the continued presence of the practitioner.

The analyst usually obtains the answers to these and other pertinent questions during a management interview. Several general and supplemental questionnaires have been developed to assist with organizing the information. See Addendums 1–3 at the end of this chapter.

FINANCIAL STATEMENT ADJUSTMENTS

> When valuing professional practices, it is important to analyze and make appropriate adjustments to the financial statements. The widespread use of cash-basis accounting may require a number of adjustments.

In a cash-basis entity, there is frequently substantial value in unrecorded assets, such as accounts receivable, inventory, prepaid expenses, and leasehold improvements. In addition, the practice may have fully depreciated assets that are still in use. There may also be unrecorded liabilities, such as accounts payable, accrued wages and vacation time, and accrued taxes. Determining appropriate cash to accrual adjustments (if applicable) is relatively simple if the valuation date is current but tends to be more difficult when the valuation date is in the past. When the valuation date is in the past, estimates are often based on inquiries and an analysis of the historical timing of cash inflows and outflows.

Some professional practices may have nonoperating assets, such as excess cash and art collections. Such nonoperating assets and any related income or expenses must be considered when making adjustments. Finally, the analyst should inquire about and consider any possible contingent liabilities, particularly lawsuits. See Chapters 4 and 5 for further information on financial statement adjustments.

Accounts Receivable

As many professional practices report on a cash basis, accounts receivable are not recorded on their balance sheets. The analyst can determine the accounts receivable balance as of the valuation date by obtaining computer printouts of accounts receivable or examining the manual accounts receivable journal, provided the valuation date is reasonably current. When the valuation date is in the past, it may be more difficult to determine the accounts receivable balance. Sometimes the accounting system of the professional practice does not provide historical receivables information. Then it is necessary to estimate receivables based on cash collections after the valuation date and to make inquiries about the collection cycle of the practice.

It is also important to obtain an accounts receivable aging schedule and make inquiries about the collectibility of older receivables to determine what may ultimately be realized. This analysis will include accounts that have been turned over to collection agencies. Although the value of such accounts is usually small after the agency's collection fee, it will need to be considered along with other receivables. After considering the collection history of the practice and any trends upward or downward, older accounts usually should be discounted for the time value of money and the risk that they may never be collected.

Inventory

Another asset often not recorded on the balance sheet is inventory, both supplies and unbilled accounts receivable (work-in-process inventory). Supplies may be immaterial in an accounting or legal practice but may be material in some professional practices, such as dental or optometric practices. If the valuation date is in the past, supplies can be estimated from subsequent cash expenditures and discussions with management.

Professional practices that bill on an hourly basis or on a percentage-of-completion basis have unrecorded assets for work they have done but have not billed. For past valuation dates, the analyst may estimate unbilled receivables at the valuation date based on subsequent billings and inquire about how often billing is done and the historical level of write-offs of chargeable hours.

Equipment

Many professional practices have little equipment other than office furniture, computers, and computer peripherals. These may quickly become economically obsolescent and may not require adjustment. Some professional practices, such as dental practices, may have a substantial investment in specialized equipment. In such cases, the analyst should judge if it is necessary to have the equipment appraised by a machinery and equipment appraiser and to adjust the value recorded on the balance sheet.

Other Unrecorded Assets

Other unrecorded assets might include prepaid expenses, leasehold improvements, and fully depreciated assets still in use. Rent and insurance are often prepaid and may represent significant assets as of the valuation date, especially if there have been recent payments for extended future periods. For example, annual malpractice insurance premiums, if paid two months before the valuation date, would result in a prepaid asset for 10 months of insurance premiums.

If the analyst notes during the management interview that the office is in good condition but leasehold improvements have been fully depreciated on the practice's depreciation schedule, it may be appropriate to adjust the value of the leasehold improvements. Any such adjustment should reflect the expected remaining life of the improvements and the remaining term of the lease.

A number of other practice assets, such as library resources, normally are expensed as acquired and commonly are not recorded on the books. Adjustments can be made to reflect the value of such assets on the balance sheet.

Appraisals by a qualified personal property appraiser should be considered if such nonoperating assets are to be retained by the practice.

> If the practice owns material amounts of nonoperating assets, such as art collections and antiques in excess of what is customary in the decor of comparable offices, it may be necessary to value these assets separately from practice operations.

Accounts Payable and Accruals

Cash-basis balance sheets usually do not include accounts payable. If the valuation date is current, the analyst can simply list unpaid invoices to determine the accounts payable. If the valuation date is historical, the analyst can estimate accounts payable based on a review of canceled checks and the associated invoices. If the practice's expenses are incurred evenly throughout the year and paid on a regular basis (e.g., weekly or monthly), it may be possible to estimate accounts payable as of the valuation date by dividing annual expenses (adjusted for expenses not included in accounts payable, i.e., payroll expenses) by the payment cycle (e.g., 52 weeks, 12 months).

Cash-basis balance sheets do not included accrued liabilities. Most of the accrued liabilities of a service business are related to employees, such as wages, payroll taxes, and accrued vacation and sick leave. These accrued liabilities can be estimated based on total payroll, the payroll cycle, and inquiries about accrued vacation and sick leave.

Deferred Liabilities

The deferred liabilities of a professional practice include unearned income and deferred expenses. Law practices and consulting firms frequently collect retainers before providing any client service. Certain medical bills also are collected in advance of rendering the service. Until the practitioner actually performs the professional service, the firm has a liability payable to the client.

Deferred taxes reflect timing differences in the recognition of certain revenue and expenses between tax returns and financial statements. For example, equipment may be depreciated over shorter lives, and the depreciation expense may be higher for tax purposes in early years than for financial statement purposes. Thus financial statement income may be higher than tax return income. Deferred taxes on the financial statements reflect a tax liability to cover the anticipated higher financial statement income. In addition, as valuation adjustments are made to the financial statements, the deferred taxes related to these adjustments may be recorded, if material. Some analysts use tax depreciation in place of book depreciation for assets instead of a deferred tax adjustment.

Long-Term Debt

Long-term debt in a professional practice usually arises from equipment purchases or from past transactions in practice ownership interests. In either case, the existence of long-term debt highlights the possibility that accrued interest expense may need to be recorded. If the long-term debt arose from a past transaction, the analyst should inquire about the terms of the transaction, when it occurred, and whether the price was negotiated on an arm's-length basis (in case the transaction might qualify as an indication of practice value).

The practice also may have lease obligations that should be recorded on the balance sheet or should be adjusted to market value. The analyst should inquire as to whether the lease involves related parties and whether the lease rate is a market rate. If the lease is not at a market rate, an adjustment may be indicated.

Contingent Liabilities

The analyst needs to inquire about contingent liabilities that may be reasonably estimated. Possible contingent liabilities of a professional practice include malpractice lawsuits, disputes about past billings, and owner retirement obligations. These and other questions should be addressed during the management interview.

VALUATION METHODS

The three basic valuation approaches—asset, income, and market—include methods that may be applicable to the valuation of a professional practice.

Asset Approach

The asset approach attempts to place a value on each asset and each liability of a business or professional practice as a means of determining the net asset value of the business or practice. One difficulty of this method arises in the valuation of the individual intangible assets, which in professional practices can account for most of the value of the practice. The valuation of individual intangibles, including client records and goodwill, usually requires use of an income, cost, or a market method. (See Chapter 21.) The asset method, which includes the value of individual intangible assets, is usually not applied in the valuation of professional practices because this total asset method is time consuming, expensive, and often unnecessary. (Note that the excess earnings method, a hybrid of the asset and income approaches, is discussed later in this chapter.)

Income Approach

The income approach determines a value indication for a professional practice by converting anticipated future economic benefits, such as earnings or cash flow, to a present value using a discount rate or capitalization rate. This approach to valuing a professional practice requires the analyst to determine normalized future income or cash flow. It is possible that recent trends may be more of a predictor of future performance than results several years prior, such as changes in the healthcare industry. The economic benefit measure that best reflects the future economic benefits stream available to the professional practice varies. Economic benefits measures often considered in valuing a professional practice include:

- Net cash flow—the Internal Revenue Service prefers the discounted net cash flow method when appraising the fair market value of medical practice entities under Internal Revenue Code Section 501(c)3[23]
- Pretax earnings after a market rate salary to the owner or practitioner
- Economic income or total pretax earnings, including the owner's or practitioner's salary and benefits
- After-tax earnings

---

[23] Robert J. Cimasi, "The Valuation of Healthcare Entities in a Changing Regulatory and Reimbursement Environment," proceedings of the ASA Advanced Business Valuation Conference (October 1999), 25. American Society of Appraisers, Herndon, VA.

The discount rate to be applied to the economic benefits stream is calculated using the build-up method or, if applicable, the modified capital asset pricing model (MCAPM). A discount rate is the total expected rate of return, stated as a percentage, that a willing buyer/investor would require on the purchase price of an ownership interest in an asset (i.e., an ownership interest in a professional practice) given the risk inherent in that ownership interest. This required rate of return varies over time—even for the same investment—due to differences in prevailing interest rates and in returns available on alternate investments. It also varies due to changes in the general economy and in investor perceptions about equity markets. It reflects not only risks in equity markets as a whole but also risks that are specific to the professional practice being appraised. To obtain a capitalization rate, growth is subtracted from the discount rate. See Chapter 6 for more detailed information on discount and capitalization rates.

> If the economic benefits stream being discounted or capitalized is pretax earnings or pretax earnings plus owners' compensation and benefits, the discount rate or the capitalization rate should be higher than if the benefits stream is net cash flow—after tax.

Discounted future benefits methods apply a discount rate to economic benefits projected for a period of years. Discounted future benefits methods are most useful when future operations are expected to be substantially different from current operations and growth is not expected to be stable—as when high growth rates are expected in the near term and lower growth rates are expected in the long term.

Capitalized future economic benefits methods apply a capitalization rate to the economic benefits expected in the next year (frequently based on historical performance). The capitalized future economic benefits method is most useful when current operations are indicative of future operations and stable growth is expected in the future. See Chapter 5 for more detailed information on the income approach.

If a practice has nonoperating assets, these nonoperating assets must be valued separately (with appropriate income and expense adjustment) from practice operations and added back to obtain total practice value. These income methods result in value indications for the professional practice as a whole, including goodwill.

Market Approach

The market approach applied to the valuation of professional practices typically includes guideline company transactions and past transactions in the subject practice. Guideline company transactions can provide objective evidence of the value of a professional practice when adequate information concerning the transactions is available. However, information concerning the terms of guideline company transactions and the nature of the practices involved is sometimes too incomplete to provide a basis for calculating a value indication.

It may be possible to obtain sufficient data on medical practice transactions because of the large volume of recent transactions in most specialties. Nevertheless, the analyst must exercise caution because of the complexity of the transactions and because of rapid changes in the market for medical practices.

> Guideline company transactions sometimes are used as a reasonableness test for values obtained by other methods.

Market information concerning the value of intangibles in medical and dental practices may be found in several publications, including the *Goodwill Registry*, published annually by the Health Care Group in Plymouth Meeting, Pennsylvania. The *Goodwill Registry* reports all practice intangibles under the label of goodwill. Reported values for intangibles are not adjusted to cash equivalent value and other factors. In addition, reported values are not all derived from arm's-length transactions; some are derived from appraisals for divorce and other purposes and arbitrary allocations are made between tangible and intangible assets. For these reasons and because of the incompleteness of the data, information from the *Goodwill Registry* is useful only for very general reasonableness tests of values for intangibles obtained using other methods.

Although in recent years state laws prohibiting the sale of law practices have started to change, often sufficient market transaction data are not available to provide indications of value. In valuing an interest in a large law firm, the valuation analyst may more likely obtain transactional data within the firm itself, or confirm that prior transactions were in accordance with the terms of the partnership agreement. In valuations for matrimonial interests, the analyst should be aware of relevant case law that relates to rulings on the possible relevance of the terms of prior transactions and a firm's partnership agreement.

In accounting practices, business brokers or other intermediaries sometimes provide useful information. See Chapter 7 for more information on transaction databases.

Past transactions in ownership interests in the professional practice may provide objective evidence of the value of a professional practice, depending on whether they were negotiated at arm's length and on how much time has elapsed between the transaction date and the valuation date.

> The usefulness of past transactions in the subject company often is limited by the way the transactions are structured. A substantial portion of the practice value transferred may be included through salary differentials, and it may be difficult to distinguish that portion of the salary differential attributable to the buyout of a practitioner. Prior transactions also sometimes reflect a punishment to the exiting practitioner for early withdrawal of capital and the practitioner's professional services.

Excess Cash Flow/Earnings Method

The excess cash flow/earnings method combines an asset approach and an income approach in valuing a business. This method determines the value of the net tangible assets using a net asset method and determines the value of the intangibles by capitalizing "excess earnings." The method provides a basis for estimating the value of intangibles by first determining the "excess" portion of a practice's earnings over and above an adjustment for the market replacement cost of the owning practitioner's compensation and after a reasonable rate of return on the tangible assets of the practice. The method requires subjective judgments concerning appropriate rates of return for the tangible and the intangible assets of the professional practice. While family law courts in certain states may expect to see professional practices valued using the excess earnings method, the Internal Revenue Service normally prefers other valuation methods when available. See Chapter 5 for a more detailed discussion of this method.

Rules of Thumb

There are rules of thumb for valuing professional practices. It may be helpful to be aware of these rules of thumb and to be able to discuss why the value conclusion for the subject professional practice falls at the top or bottom or even outside of the range indicated by rules of thumb.

Rules of thumb do not address important factors influencing the value of a specific professional practice. Rules of thumb purport to reflect average revenue multiples paid in transactions but are not traceable to specific transactions. They can be particularly misleading when valuing medical practices, the economics of which and the market for which have been changing so rapidly in recent years. As such, many valuation analysts may only use rules of thumb as a check on value.

ValTip

> Although rules of thumb may provide insight on the value of a professional practice, it is usually appropriate to use them only for reasonableness tests of the value conclusion.

Three common sources of rules of thumb are:

1. *The 2009 Business Reference Guide: The Essential Guide to Pricing Businesses and Franchises*, by Thomas L. West (Business Brokerage Press, 2009).
2. *Handbook of Business Valuation*, 2nd ed., edited by Thomas L. West and Jeffrey D. Jones (New York: John Wiley & Sons, 1999).
3. *Handbook of Small Business Valuation Formulas and Rules of Thumb*, 3rd ed., by Glenn M. Desmond, et al. (Camden, ME: Valuation Press, 1993).

SUMMARY

Many of the concerns in valuing professional practices are similar to concerns in valuing small businesses, but the analyst must understand the differences specific to professional practices. Distinguishing between the goodwill that is attributable solely to the professional (difficult to transfer) and the goodwill that is attributable to the practice can be critical. In addition, regulatory concerns and rapidly changing economic circumstances influence the valuation of professional practices. The complexity of valuing professional practices has led some analysts to specialize in valuing professional practices or in valuing specific kinds of professional practices.

Exhibit 20.1   Professional Practice Assets, Returns, and Income (Illustration Only—State Specific)

When professional goodwill is included as a marital asset in the division of property, care must be taken not to double count the professional's earnings capacity by also considering it when setting any alimony payments, as may be required by local law.

Column 1 demonstrates that tangible assets provide the floor to any business. On top of this floor come the intangible or soft assets. Although soft, these assets are nonetheless real and very often the primary assets. To the degree that a rate of return on all assets exceeds a reasonable rate of return for each of the tangible and intangible assets, such rate of return must come from residual goodwill. Thus, residual goodwill is the softest of all assets. As Column 2 demonstrates, tangible assets for all comparable practitioners (similar geographic region, similar training, similar experience) result in an expected or normal salary overall. To the degree that an individual practitioner has abnormal salary, it must come from something. The task of the analyst is to identify what that something is.

Since a fundamental financial cornerstone is that the higher the risk the higher the return demanded, the rate of return on these softer, more risky intangible assets, including residual goodwill, must be higher than the more fundamental, less risky assets. Column 3 demonstrates this. For example, if a professional practice has an overall rate of return of a certain percent, then some assets (the tangible less risky ones) will have a lower return forcing the softer, more risky intangible assets to have a higher rate of return. Only in this way can all assets, thus the practice, average the overall rate of return.

It is this higher rate of return which forms the capitalization factor necessary to value the goodwill of a professional practice. Column 4 demonstrates this. To the degree that the abnormal salary is capitalized by the appropriate higher rate of return, this portion of actual salary cannot be considered for other periodic distributions. That is, if a practitioner has a total salary of $150,000 (expected to continue in the foreseeable future) and if $50,000 is determined to result from (and therefore capitalized back into) goodwill, the Court must consider only $100,000 as the basis for periodic alimony. To use the $150,000 as the basis for capitalized goodwill and as the basis for periodic alimony would be double dipping by $50,000, one-third of the salary.

1 ASSETS	2 CASH FLOW To Get to Take Home Pay	3 RATES OF RETURN	4 AVAILABLE FOR EQUITABLE DISTRIBUTION
GOODWILL Professional, Nontransferrable Practice, Transferrable		Highest ROR	
INTANGIBLES Contracts in Force Client Lists Patents/Trademarks/Copyrights Medical Charts Patient Histories Other	ABNORMAL SALARY	Higher ROR	LUMP SUM (Included in Fair Market Value)
TANGIBLES Other Tangibles Accounts Receivable (Billed and Unbilled) Equipment Land and Building Cash and Securities Deposits and Prepaids	NORMAL SALARY	Lower ROR	PERIODIC (Excluded from Fair Market Value)

ADDENDUM 1—MANAGEMENT INTERVIEW MEDICAL PRACTICE (SAMPLE)[24]

Date:_____

Exact Practice Name: _____

Address: _____

_____

Phone: _____

Interviewer: _____

The objective of this management interview is to provide us with operational information that will aid us in the valuation of your business. We will keep the information confidential. Describe the following information to the best of your ability on a separate sheet of paper, with reference to each item number. If some items are not applicable, please indicate N/A.

1. **Interviewee(s)**

Name	Title
(a) _____	_____
(b) _____	_____
(c) _____	_____
(d) _____	_____

2. **Description of the Business**

    (a) Full name of the practice

    (b) Date the practice was established

    (c) Discuss the history of the practice, from founding to present, including past physicians, important dates, past locations, etc.

3. **Name, Address, and Telephone Number of the Practice's Attorney(s)**

4. **Name, Address, and Telephone Number of the Practice's Accountant(s)**

5. **Physicians**

    (a) For all doctors, provide

        (1) Name

        (2) Age

---

[24] For expanded and additional checklists see James R. Hitchner, Michael J. Mard, *Financial Valuation Workbook*, 3rd ed., (Hoboken, NJ: John Wiley & Sons, 2011).

    (3)   Education background

    (4)   Special license requirements

    (5)   Board certification

    (6)   Number of years experience

    (7)   Articles written

    (8)   Lectures delivered

    (9)   General health (excellent, good, or poor)

(b)   Describe life insurance in which the practice is the beneficiary

(c)   Describe the typical work week for each doctor, including

    (1)   Average number of patients per day

    (2)   Nature of treatment

    (3)   Average time per patient/treatment

    (4)   Hours worked per day

    (5)   Time spent in

        (i)   Office visits/treatments

        (ii)   Surgery—hospital

        (iii)   Surgery—in office

        (iv)   Administration

        (v)   Promotion

        (vi)   Civic affairs

6. Personnel

(a)   Provide a current organizational chart

(b)   Provide a list of employees, other than physicians, at year-end for last year including current employee classifications, general wage scales, and approximate rate (distinguish full-time and part-time)

(c)   List management personnel with title, length of service, age, and annual compensation (including bonuses) for the current year and past two years

	Name	Title	LOS	Age	Compensation
(1)	_____	_____	___	___	_____
(2)	_____	_____	___	___	_____
(3)	_____	_____	___	___	_____
(4)	_____	_____	___	___	_____
(5)	_____	_____	___	___	_____

(d) List board of directors by name and title, including occupation for outside members

7. **The Practice**

   (a) Type of marketing

      (1) Professional referral

      (2) Patient referral

      (3) Direct mail

      (4) Yellow pages

      (5) Other

   (b) Provide list of competition

      (1) Specialized

      (2) General

      (3) Mini-hospitals

   (c) Discuss growth trends, revenue, operating capacity, and equity

      (1) Past

      (2) Projected

      (3) Limiting factors

      (4) New products/services being considered

      (5) Any recent sales of stock (or interests) or offers to buy (or sell)

      (6) Any comparable sales of similar practices

8. **Property and Equipment**

   (a) Describe your office facilities

      (1) Square feet

      (2) Number of examining rooms

      (3) Number of operating rooms

      (4) Number of X-ray rooms

      (5) If owned, provide

         (i) Age and condition

         (ii) Assessed value

         (iii) Fair market value, if known

      (6) If leased, amount of monthly payment

    (b) Discuss specialized equipment

        (1) If owned, provide

            (i)   Age and condition

            (ii)   Assessed value

            (iii) Fair market value, if known

        (2) If leased, provide amount of monthly payment

    (c) List and discuss company-owned vehicles

    (d) Describe the library

        (1) Original cost

        (2) Replacement cost

        (3) Unique volumes

9. General Outlook (if not covered elsewhere)

10. Other Pertinent Information About the Practice

ADDENDUM 2—MANAGEMENT INTERVIEW LAW PRACTICE (SAMPLE)

Date:_____

Exact Business Name:_____

Address: _____

_____

Phone: _____

Analyst/Interviewer: _____

The objective of this management interview is to provide us with operational information that will aid us in the valuation of your business. We will keep the information confidential. Describe the following to the best of your ability on a separate sheet of paper, with reference to each item number. If some items are not applicable, please indicate N/A.

1.   Interviewee(s)

	Name	Title
(a)	_____	_____
(b)	_____	_____
(c)	_____	_____
(d)	_____	_____

2.   Attorneys

(a)   List key personnel with title, and approximate annual compensation (with bonuses listed separately)

	Name	Title	Compensation	Bonus
(1)	_____	_____	_____	
(2)	_____	_____	_____	_____
(3)	_____	_____	_____	_____
(4)	_____	_____	_____	_____
(5)	_____	_____	_____	_____
(6)	_____	_____	_____	_____
(7)	_____	_____	_____	_____
(8)	_____	_____	_____	_____
(9)	_____	_____	_____	_____
(10)	_____	_____	_____	_____

(b) Provide an abbreviated curriculum vitae of each attorney, including age, education, board certification, and unusual experience

(c) Describe any limitations of each attorney due to health

(d) Describe life insurance in which the firm is the beneficiary

(e) Describe a typical week for the average partner, including the percentage of time spent in the following areas:

    (1) Directly billable

    (2) Administrative

    (3) Promotion

    (4) Civic affairs

3. **The Firm**

(a) If not correct above, exact name of the firm.

(b) Provide a brief history of the development of the firm, including date firm was established, past partners, important dates, previous locations, etc.

(c) Provide a current organizational chart. Describe the management team including current title, age, length of service, background, the annual salary, and bonus of each person for the current year and the last two years.

(d) Attach a list of all personnel (other than attorneys and the management team) stating the title/function and compensation of each.

(e) List board of directors by name and title, including occupation for outside members.

(f) Describe the growth trends, revenue, and operating capacity (billable hours).

(g) Describe changes in legal services offered that are being considered.

(h) Describe firm responsiveness to seasonal fluctuations. (For instance, does the firm have a disproportionate estate practice susceptible to northern residents?)

(i) Previous and future marketing and advertising plans.

(j) Please describe the office facilities including:

    (1) Any land owned

        (i) Acreage

        (ii) Original cost

        (iii) Approximate fair market value

    (2) Buildings owned

        (i) Age and condition

        (ii) Original cost

        (iii) Approximate fair market value

        (iv)   Fire insurance amount

        (v)   Square feet

    (3)   Furniture, fixtures and equipment (FF&E). (Since the FF&E schedule has been requested in our valuation information request, there will be no need to duplicate the listing here. What is requested is a discussion of the future plans for significant purchases of FF&E.)

    (4)   Library

        (i)   Description by major service and/or groups of works

        (ii)   Original cost

        (iii)   Replacement cost

        (iv)   Unique volumes, if any

4.   Other Pertinent Information About the Firm

    (a)   Any information that will add to (or detract from) the reputation of the firm or the individual practitioners will have a similar effect on the valuation.

ADDENDUM 3—MANAGEMENT INTERVIEW ACCOUNTING PRACTICE (SAMPLE)

Date:_____

Exact Business Name:_____

Address: _____

_____

Phone:_____

Analyst/Interviewer: _____

The objective of this management interview is to provide us with operational information that will aid us in the valuation of your business. We will keep the information confidential. Describe the following to the best of your ability on a separate sheet of paper, with reference to each item number. If some items are not applicable, please indicate N/A.

1. **Interviewee(s)**

	Name	Title
(a)	_____	_____
(b)	_____	_____
(c)	_____	_____

2. **Accountants**

    (a) List key personnel with title, and approximate annual compensation (with bonuses listed separately)

	Name	Title	Compensation	Bonus
(1)	_____	_____	_____	_____
(2)	_____	_____	_____	_____
(3)	_____	_____	_____	_____
(4)	_____	_____	_____	_____
(5)	_____	_____	_____	_____

    (b) Abbreviated curriculum vitae of each accountant, including age, education, specialty certification, and unusual experience

    (c) Accountant limitations due to health, if any

    (d) Life insurance in which the practice is the beneficiary

(e) Typical week for the average partner, including the percentage of time spent in the following areas

    (1) Directly billable

    (2) Administrative

    (3) Promotion

    (4) Civic affairs

3. **The Practice**

(a) If not correct above, exact name of the practice

(b) Date practice established

(c) Brief history of the development of the practice, including past partners, important dates, previous locations, etc.

(d) Current organizational chart

(e) List the management team including current title, age, length of service, background, annual salary, and bonus of each person for the current year and the last two years

(f) List all personnel (other than accountants and the management team), stating the title/function and compensation of each

(g) List board of directors by name and title, including occupation for outside members

(h) Growth trends, revenue, and operating capacity (billable hours) by service line, e.g., audit, tax

(i) Changes in accounting services being considered

(j) Practice sensitivity to seasonal fluctuations (e.g., does the practice have a disproportionate tax practice)

(k) Sales and marketing strategy

(l) Office facilities, including

    (1) Any land owned

        (i) Acreage

        (ii) Original cost

        (iii) Approximate fair market value

    (2) Buildings owned

        (i) Age and condition

        (ii) Original cost

        (iii) Approximate fair market value

        (iv) Fire insurance amount

        (v) Square feet

      (3)   Furniture, fixtures, and equipment (FF&E). (Since the FF&E schedule has been requested in our valuation information request, there will be no need to duplicate the listing here. What is requested is a discussion of the future plans for significant purchases of FF&E.)

      (4)   Library

            (i)   Description by major service and/or groups of works

            (ii)   Original cost

            (iii)   Replacement cost

            (iv)   Unique volumes, if any

4. Other Pertinent Information About the Practice

CHAPTER 21

Valuation of Intangible Assets

INTRODUCTION

Business combinations are among the largest transactions undertaken by entities. They are often global transactions where having converged guidance is essential— the only way to level the financial playing field. Beginning January 1, 2009, the guidance for fair value measurements (ASC Topic 820) and for business combinations (ASC Topic 805), including noncontrolling interests (ASC Topic 810) for calendar-year companies, will be required for generally accepted accounting principles (GAAP) financial statements for all companies, public and private.

This regulatory change reflected the Financial Accounting Standards Board (FASB)'s recognition of the need for international comparability of accounting standards (i.e., to bring U.S. accounting standards more in line with worldwide GAAP). As a result of capitalizing intangible assets and goodwill, the income statement bears additional amortization reflecting the write-off of these capitalized assets.

This chapter discusses changes in regulatory requirements leading to the identification and measurement of intangibles. It discusses at length the FASB's Accounting Standards Codification (ASC or Codification), which incorporates SFAS 141R and SFAS 142, and the treatment of in-process research and development (IPR&D). For more information related to fair value beyond this chapter, see Michael Mard, Jim Hitchner, and Steve Hyden, *Valuation for Financial Reporting: Fair Value, Business Combinations, Intangible Assets, Goodwill and Impairment Analysis*, 3rd edition (John Wiley & Sons, 2011). Various checklists are provided in the companion *Financial Valuation Workbook,* Third Edition, that will aid the valuation analyst in the identification and measurement of intangible assets. The purpose of this chapter is to provide a theoretical and practical overview of intangible assets and their valuation. It also presents a detailed case study on a business combination accounted for using the acquisition method, including the valuation of intangible assets and goodwill.

WHAT ARE INTANGIBLE ASSETS?

The Report of the Brookings Task Force on Intangibles defined intangibles as:

> ... nonphysical factors that contribute to or are used in producing goods or providing services, or that are expected to generate future productive benefits for the individuals or firms that control the use of those factors.[1]

---

[1] Margaret Blair and Steven Wallman, *Unseen Wealth: Report of the Brookings Task Force on Intangibles* (Washington, DC: Brookings Institution Press, 2001), 3.

The International Valuation Standards Council was, perhaps, a bit more precise in their definition of intangible assets:

> . . . assets that manifest themselves by their economic properties; they do not have physical substance; they grant rights and privileges to their owner; and usually generate income for their owner. Intangible assets can be categorized as arising from: Rights; Relationships; Grouped Intangibles; or Intellectual Property.[2]

This was revised in March 2010 to the following:

> . . . a non monetary asset that manifests itself by its economic properties. It does not have physical substance but grants rights and economic benefits to its owner or the holder of an interest.[3]

The International Valuation Standards Council goes on to define each of those categories.

Probably the briefest definition is provided by the FASB:

> Assets (not including financial assets) that lack physical substance.[4]

According to the FASB, intangible assets are distinguished from goodwill. The FASB provides specific guidance for the identification of intangible assets such that any asset not so identified would fall into the catchall category of goodwill.

Each of these definitions is correct and, in its venue, appropriate, but the nature of intangible assets requires more explanation. Some intangible assets are a subset of human capital, which is a collection of the education, experience, and skill of a company's employees. Structural capital is distinguished from human capital but also includes intangible assets such as process documentation and the organizational structure itself, which is the supportive infrastructure provided for human capital and encourages human capital to create and leverage its knowledge. Intangible assets are the codified physical descriptions of specific knowledge that can be owned and readily traded. Separability and transferability are fundamental prerequisites to the meaningful recognition and measurement of intangible assets.

> Intangible assets receiving legal protection become intellectual property, which is generally categorized into five types: patents, copyrights, trade name (trademarks and trade dress), trade secrets, and know-how.

WHY INTANGIBLE ASSETS ARE DIFFICULT TO MEASURE

The Brookings Task Force succinctly described measurement difficulties when it said:

> Because one cannot see, or touch, or weigh intangibles, one cannot measure them directly but must instead rely on proxies, or indirect measures

---

[2] International Valuation Standards Council, International Valuation Guidance Note No. 4, *Valuation of Intangible Assets* (2006), at 3.15.
[3] International Valuation Standards Council, International Valuation Guidance Note 4, *Valuation of Intangible Assets* (2010), at 2.3.
[4] Financial Accounting Standards Board, Accounting Standards Codification (2009), Glossary.

to say something about their impact on some other variable that can be measured.[5]

Over the years, the FASB has sought to change the historical cost focus of measurement. In fact, the FASB has increasingly required fair value determination as applicable to specific accounting standards (see Addendum 1 at the end of this chapter).

THE NATURE OF INTANGIBLE ASSETS

Opportunity cost is a fundamental concept of finance and can be defined as the cost of something in terms of an opportunity forgone. Many finance courses focus on the opportunities available to utilize tangible assets, with the goal of applying those tangible assets to the opportunity with the highest return. Opportunities not selected can be viewed as returns forgone. The physical reality is that tangible assets can only be in only one place at one time. Professor Baruch Lev of New York University looked at the physical, human, and financial assets (all considered tangible) as competing for the opportunity. In a sense, these assets are rival or scarce assets "in which the scarcity is reflected by the cost of using the assets (the opportunity forgone)."[6]

Such assets distinguish themselves from intangible assets in that intangible assets do not rival each other for incremental returns. In fact, intangible assets can be applied to multiple uses for multiple returns. As Professor Lev says:

> The non rivalry (or non scarcity) attribute of intangibles—the ability to use such assets in simultaneous and repetitive applications without diminishing their usefulness—is a major value driver at the business enterprise level as well as at the national level. Whereas physical and financial assets can be leveraged to a limited degree by exploiting economies of scale or scope in production (a plant can be used for at most three shifts a day), the leveraging of intangibles to generate benefits—the scalability of these assets—is generally limited only by the size of the market. The usefulness of the ideas, knowledge, and research embedded in a new drug or a computer operating system is not limited by the diminishing returns to scale typical of physical assets (as production expands from two to three shifts, returns decrease due, for example, to the wage premium paid for the third shift and to employee fatigue). In fact, intangibles are often characterized by increasing returns to scale. An investment in the development of a drug or a financial instrument (a risk-hedging mechanism, for example), is often leveraged in the development of successor drugs and financial instruments. Information is cumulative, goes the saying.[7]

IDENTIFICATION AND CLASSIFICATION OF INTANGIBLE ASSETS

Identification of intangible assets is a broad endeavor. There are the well-accepted intangibles such as customer base, in-process research and development, and technology, as well as intellectual property such as patents, copyrights, trademarks, trade

[5] Blair and Wallman, *Unseen Wealth*, 15.
[6] Baruch Lev, *Intangibles: Management, Measurement, and Reporting* (Washington, DC: Brookings Institution Press, 2001), p. 22.
[7] Ibid., p. 23.

secrets, and know-how. The value of such assets typically accounts for most of an enterprise's total intangible value. There are also unique intangible assets peculiar to an industry or enterprise, such as bank deposits.

In an attempt to provide some structure to the recognition of intangible assets and to enhance the longevity of its financial model, the FASB has classified intangibles into five categories:

1. Marketing-related intangible assets
2. Customer-related intangible assets
3. Artistic-related intangible assets
4. Contract-based intangible assets
5. Technology-based intangible assets[8]

The FASB provides an explanation and examples for each of the categories. Notably, the assembled workforce is excluded because FASB believes it fails the separability and transferability tests. A company may have excellent employees who contribute mightily to the success of an organization, but they have no value if separated from the business. Further, the FASB was not confident of the reliability of the measurement tools most often used for the assembled workforce and its associated intellectual capital. The FASB instead chose to categorize the assembled workforce within the components of goodwill.[9]

MEASUREMENT OF INTANGIBLE ASSETS

The theoretical and practical framework for the cost approach, the income approach, and the market approach (the three basic valuation approaches) are covered elsewhere in this book.

Since return requirements increase as risk increases and since intangible assets are usually more risky for a company than are tangible assets, it is reasonable to conclude that the returns expected on intangible assets typically will be at or above the average rate of return (discount rate) for the company as a whole.

A key fundamental underlying the valuation of intangible assets is the concept of the tension between risk and return. As Professor Lev states:

Assuredly, all investments and assets are risky in an uncertain business environment. Yet the riskiness of intangibles is, in general, substantially higher than that of physical and even financial assets. For one, the prospects of a total loss common to many innovative activities, such as a new drug development or an Internet initiative, are very rare for physical or financial assets.

---

[8] Financial Accounting Standards Board, Accounting Standards Codification (2009), at 805-20-55-13.
[9] Financial Accounting Standards Board, Statement of Financial Accounting Standards No. 141R, *Business Combinations* (December 2007, superseded in 2009 by Accounting Standards Codification), at B178.

Even highly risky physical projects, such as commercial property, rarely end up as a loss. A comparative study of the uncertainty associated with R&D and that of property, plant, and equipment confirms the large risk differentials: The earnings volatility (a measurement of risk) associated with R&D is, on average, three times larger than the earnings volatility associated with physical investment.[10]

A fundamental tenet of economics holds that return requirements increase as risk increases, with many intangible assets being inherently more risky than tangible assets. It is reasonable to conclude that the returns expected on many intangible assets typically will be at or above the average rate of return (discount rate) for the company as a whole.[11] The relationship of the amount of return, the rate of return (including risk), and the value of the asset creates a mathematical formula used in analysis. Typically, two of three elements are known or can be computed, thus leading to a solution for the third element.

$$\text{If} \qquad \frac{\$ \text{ Return}}{\text{Rate of return}} = \text{Value (for an intangible asset)}$$

$$\text{Then} \qquad \frac{\$ \text{ Return}}{\text{Value}} = \text{Rate of return}$$

$$\text{And} \quad \text{Rate of return} \times \text{Value} = \$ \text{ Return}$$

BUSINESS COMBINATIONS

In December 2007, FASB revised Statement of Financial Accounting Standards (SFAS) 141. The new statement, SFAS 141R, was subsequently superseded by the Accounting Standards Codification (ASC), recognized assets acquired and liabilities assumed using a new process called the *acquisition method*. Prior to issuance of the revised statement, the cost accumulation and allocation of cost to assets and liabilities (purchase method) was the basis for the determination of fair values.

ValTip

A *business combination* is a transaction or other event in which an acquirer obtains control of one or more businesses.[12]

Control means a controlling financial interest. The acquirer is the entity that obtains control over the other business (the acquiree) and consolidates the acquiree. Various examples of GAAP literature provide guidance for determining when control has been achieved and consolidation is required.

With the issuance in 2001 of SFAS 141, *Business Combinations*, the use of the pooling of interests method to account for a business combination was immediately

---

[10] Lev, *Intangibles*, p. 39.

[11] Note, however, that the returns expected on some intangible assets may be below the company average such as a service business that has mostly intangible assets.

[12] Financial Accounting Standards Board, Accounting Standards Codification (2009), Glossary.

Exhibit 21.1   Changes between SFAS 141R and SFAS 141

(New) SFAS 141R	(Old) SFAS 141
The *acquirer* is specifically defined as "the entity that obtains control of the acquiree."	Acquirer was not defined.
Acquirer must recognize the assets acquired, liabilities assumed, and any noncontrolling interest in the acquiree as specified in 141R (more at fair value).	Cost allocation process.
Acquisition-related costs are accounted for separately.	Acquisition-related costs were included in the cost of the acquisition and were allocated to the assets acquired and liabilities assumed.
Restructuring costs that the acquirer expects but is not obligated to incur are to be accounted for separately.	Restructuring costs were recognized as a liability assumed at the acquisition date if certain criteria were met.
In a business combination achieved in stages, the identifiable assets and liabilities, as well as the noncontrolling interest in the acquiree, are recognized at their full amounts.	In a business combination achieved in stages, the cost of each investment was allocated.
Requires the acquirer to recognize contingent consideration at the acquisition date, measured at its fair value.	Contingent consideration was usually not recognized until resolved and issued or became issuable.
In situations where there is a *bargain purchase* (where the excess of the fair value of the identifiable net assets acquired exceeds the fair value of the consideration transferred plus any noncontrolling interest in the acquiree), the excess is required to be recognized in earnings as a gain attributable to the acquirer.	The excess, or "negative goodwill," was required to be allocated as a pro rata reduction of amounts that otherwise would have been assigned to assets acquired.
Acquired research and development assets will be recognized at their acquisition-date fair value separately as identifiable assets.	Acquired research and development assets were measured at their acquisition-date fair values and immediately charged to expense.

prohibited and was replaced by the purchase method, which required identification of all assets of the acquiring enterprise, both tangible and intangible. Any excess of the cost of an acquired entity over the net amounts assigned to the tangible and intangible assets acquired and liabilities assumed is classified as goodwill.[13] When FASB revised SFAS 141 in December 2007 (SFAS 141R), the purchase method was replaced with the acquisition method.[14]

In addition, SFAS 141R included additional guidance in several key areas. Exhibit 21.1 lists some of the additional prominent changes between the two documents. These changes are incorporated into the ASC.

The FASB revised its definition of a business. According to the Codification, a *business* is "an integrated set of activities and assets that is capable of being conducted

---

[13] Financial Accounting Standards Board, Statement of Financial Accounting Standards No. 141, *Business Combinations* (2001), at 13–14.
[14] Financial Accounting Standards Board, Accounting Standards Codification (2009), at 805-10-25-1.

and managed for the purpose of providing a return in the form of dividends, lower costs, or other economic benefits directly to investors or other owners, members, or participants."[15] A business can be another company or a part of another company (such as a subsidiary, segment, division, or smaller unit).

Determining What Is Part of a Business Combination

When parts of the combination or transactions of the acquiree are done for the benefit of the acquirer or the combined entity, these actions should be accounted for separately from the business combination transaction. For example:

- A preexisting relationship or arrangement is settled.
- Compensation for future services is provided.
- Hidden acquisition costs are identified.

Look to 1) the reason for the transaction, 2) the party(ies) who initiated the transaction, and 3) the timing of the transaction to determine what should be accounted for separately.

Transactions that are similar to a business combination but don't meet the requirements to be accounted for as a business combination are excluded from the guidance in ASC Topic 805, *Business Combinations*. These include the following; however, the reader is encouraged to read the ASC for specific guidance:

- Formations of joint ventures
- Combinations in which the assets acquired do not constitute a business
- Combinations involving entities under common control
- Certain transactions by not-for-profit organizations[16]

THE ACQUISITION METHOD

Application of the acquisition method requires several key steps, as follows:

1. *Identifying the Acquirer*—The acquirer is the entity that obtains control of the Acquiree.[17]
2. *Determining the Acquisition Date*—The Acquisition Date is the date on which the acquirer obtains control of the acquiree.[18] Usually, this is the closing date for a combination—the date the consideration is transferred to the prior owners of the acquiree. However, if control occurs other than on the closing date by contract, the control date is the Acquisition Date.
3. *Recognition and Measurement*
   - *Recognition principle*—To qualify for recognition under the acquisition method, the identifiable assets acquired and liabilities assumed must meet the definitions of assets and liabilities in FASB's Statement of Financial Accounting Concepts No. 6, *Elements of Financial Statements*. A brief list of example assets and liabilities is shown in Exhibit 21.2.

---

[15] Financial Accounting Standards Board, Accounting Standards Codification (2009), Glossary.
[16] Financial Accounting Standards Board, Accounting Standards Codification (2009), at 805-10-15-4.
[17] Ibid., at 805-10-25-4 to 805-10-25-5.
[18] Ibid., at 805-10-25-6 to 805-10-25-7.

- *Measurement principle*—The acquirer shall measure the identifiable assets acquired, the liabilities assumed, and any noncontrolling interest in the acquiree at their acquisition-date fair values, with certain exceptions.[19]

4. *Recognition of Goodwill or Gain from a Bargain Purchase.*[20]

Exhibit 21.2 Examples of Acquired Assets and Assumed Liabilities Initially Recognized at Fair Value

---

Assets
Financial Instruments
Cash
Accounts receivable
Notes receivable
Investments in equity securities
Investments in debt securities
Investments in entities to be carried on the equity method
Interest rate swaps and other derivatives in an asset position
Tangible Assets
Inventory
  Finished goods
  Work in process
  Raw materials
Property, plant, and equipment
  Land
  Buildings
  Machinery and equipment
Other Assets
Prepaid expenses
Intangible Assets
See separate section for examples, and remember that the acquirer may recognize intangible
  assets not recognized by the acquiree

Liabilities
Financial Instruments
Assets payable
Loans payable
Bonds payable
Other Liabilities
Asset retirement obligations
Warranty obligations

The accounting for the acquired assets and assumed liabilities that are initially recorded at their acquisition-date fair values follows regular GAAP subsequently except as specified in the ASC. See ASC Section 805-10-35 for examples of GAAP that are followed after recording the business combination.

Sometimes the acquirer acquires an asset that it does not plan to use or to sell, or the use of the asset is not the asset's highest and best use that is used to determine the asset's fair value. Such assets are to be recorded at fair value, which is measured as value to "market participants" regardless of the acquirer's plans for the asset.

For example, an acquirer may acquire an acquiree's technology for a product that competes with the acquirer's product. For competitive reasons, the acquirer decides

---

[19] Ibid., at 805-20-30-1.
[20] Ibid., at 805-20-30-2.

not to sell or use the acquired technology. In this case, the acquirer records an asset for the technology at its fair value at the acquisition date.

Recognition of Intangible Assets

As stated earlier, the definition of intangible assets includes current and noncurrent assets (not including financial instruments) that lack physical substance. An acquired intangible asset shall be recognized apart from goodwill if that asset arises from contractual or other legal rights. If an intangible asset does not arise from contractual or other legal rights, it shall be recognized apart from goodwill only if it is separable. That is, it must be capable of being separated or divided from the acquired enterprise and sold, transferred, licensed, rented, or exchanged (regardless of whether there is an intent to do so). An intangible asset that cannot be sold, transferred, licensed, rented, or exchanged individually is still considered separable if it can be paired with a related contract, asset, or liability and be sold, transferred, licensed, rented, or exchanged.

An important exception to the individual recognition of intangible assets is the value of an assembled workforce of "at-will" employees. Thus, a group of employees acquired in a business combination who are not bound by an employment agreement will be recorded as goodwill regardless of whether the asset meets the criteria for recognition apart from goodwill.[21] However, the assembled workforce still needs to be valued as a contributory asset (discussed later).

The foregoing discussion prompts an obvious question: Customer relationships (at least those that are noncontractual) are not separable; why are they not lumped into goodwill? In the real world, companies move in and out of noncontractual customer relationships as business dictates, with matters of supply, demand, quality, and competition, to name just a few, dictating whether the customer relationship will continue in the future. However, customer relationships that are noncontractual and not separable are not recognized. Emerging Issues Task Force (EITF) 02-17 clarified that if the relationship had ever been covered by a contract, it meets the contractual criterion. If it is capable of being separated, it qualifies. However, if it is not capable of being separated and was never contractual, it is not recognized.

INTANGIBLE ASSET VALUATION ISSUES

In-Process Research and Development

In this age of technology, as research and development (R&D) activities become an increasingly large part of industrial activity, the financial reporting of assets to be used in R&D activities, especially specific in-process research and development (IPR&D) projects, has become critically important. Under purchase accounting, amounts assigned to IPR&D often accounted for over half of the total acquisition value.

The FASB has addressed this issue by referencing "the multiperiod excess earnings method, which is used to measure the fair value of certain intangible assets." This is referenced in SFAS No. 157, paragraph 18, which is then documented by footnote 10, which references the IPR&D Practice Aid. The IPR&D Practice Aid states, "This Practice Aid identifies what the Task Force members perceive as best practices related to defining and accounting for, disclosing, valuing, and auditing assets acquired to be used in R&D activities, including specific

---

[21] Ibid., at 805-20-55-6.

IPR&D projects.[22] All practitioners working in the area of fair value/intangible assets should be very familiar with the IPR&D Practice Aid. The reader should note that the IPR&D Practice Aid is no longer in print. However, a revised edition is expected to be released in 2010/2011, but as of this writing it has not been issued.

In-process research and development can be generally defined as an R&D project that has not yet been completed. Acquired IPR&D is a subset of an intangible asset to be used in R&D activities. Costs to be allocated to assets acquired to be used in R&D activities should possess the characteristics of control and expected economic benefit, with fair value being estimable with reasonable reliability. If an asset to be used in R&D activities is a specific IPR&D project, that project should have both substance and be incomplete.[23]

> Under the acquisition method, IPR&D is capitalized if it is acquired as part of a business combination, rather than expensed at the acquisition date as required by prior guidance.

R&D assets (tangible and intangible) are recorded at their acquisition-date fair value separately from goodwill. The prior requirement that the asset be completed or have an alternative future use is eliminated.

- The fair value of R&D assets is to be based on market participant assumptions assuming the asset's highest and best use even if the acquirer does not intend to use the asset in that manner.
- R&D costs incurred after recording the business combinations that are related to a recognized IPR&D asset are expensed as incurred.

Tax Effects

Intangible assets are valued after tax. This means that the valuation analyst needs to provide for income taxes in any forecast of cash flow, include in normalized financial statements the tax amortization of intangible assets over a 15-year period per Internal Revenue Code Section 197, and capture in the fair value of that intangible asset the associated amortization benefit (i.e., the incremental value attributable to an intangible by virtue of its tax deductibility).

> Including such tax effects in the valuation process is more common in the income and cost approaches, but is not typical in the market approach, since any tax benefit should be factored into the quoted market price.

---

[22] Randy J. Larson et al., *Assets Acquired in a Business Combination to Be Used in Research and Development Activities: A Focus on Software, Electronic Devices, and Pharmaceutical Industries* (New York: AICPA, 2001), Introduction.
[23] Ibid., p. 20.

Amortization Benefit

Residual value may factor into determining the amount of an intangible asset to be amortized. It is defined as the estimated fair value of an intangible asset at the end of its useful life, less any disposal costs. A recognized intangible asset with an indefinite useful life should not be amortized until its life is determined to be no longer indefinite. If no legal, regulatory, contractual, competitive, economic, or other factors limit the useful life of an intangible asset, the useful life of that asset should not be considered indefinite.[24] The term *indefinite* does not mean infinite. A recognized intangible asset that is not amortized must be tested for impairment annually, and on an interim basis if an event or circumstance occurs between annual tests indicating that the asset might be impaired.[25]

As stated, the valuation of an intangible asset includes the tax benefits resulting from the amortization of that intangible asset for income tax purposes (amortization benefit).[26]

In the IPR&D Practice Aid, the American Institute of Certified Public Accountants (AICPA) explains that the logic of the amortization benefit is supported by SFAS 109, *Accounting for Income Taxes* (issued February 1992). SFAS 109 prohibited the net-of-tax approach, to which the AICPA adds:

> When the business combination is structured as an asset sale for tax purposes (as opposed to a stock sale), practice typically includes the associated tax benefits in the valuation of the assets acquired because it is assumed that the assets acquired will be amortized for both book and tax purposes. When a stock sale occurs without a corresponding change in the bases of assets acquired and liabilities assumed for tax purposes, some have argued that no tax benefit should be included in the valuation of the intangible assets acquired because the buyer will not amortize the intangible assets acquired for income tax reporting purposes.[27]

Before SFAS 96 and SFAS 109, *Accounting for Income Taxes*, the net-of-tax approach was used in assigning values to assets acquired and liabilities assumed in a business combination. Under the net-of-tax approach, the future tax effects of differences between fair values and tax bases and timing of those tax effects (i.e., discounting) were considered in assigning values to assets acquired and liabilities assumed. Consequently, deferred tax assets and liabilities were not recognized in a business combination.[28] SFAS 109 "prohibit[ed] the net-of-tax approach and require[d] assets acquired and liabilities assumed to be recorded at their 'gross' fair value."[29]

---

[24] Financial Accounting Standards Board, Statement of Financial Accounting Standards No. 142, *Goodwill and Other Intangible Assets* (June 2001), at 11–14.

[25] Ibid., at 17.

[26] As noted in paragraph 41 of FASB's Statement of Financial Accounting Concepts No. 7, *Using Cash Flow Information and Present Value in Accounting Measurements*, "interest rates used to discount cash flows should reflect assumptions that are consistent with those inherent in the estimated cash flows." That is, assumptions about taxes and discount rates should not result in double-counting their efforts.

[27] Larson et al., *Assets Acquired in a Business Combination*, at 5.3.99.

[28] See Emerging Issues Task Force (EITF) No. 96-7, *Accounting for Deferred Taxes on In-Process Research and Development Activities Acquired in a Purchase Business Combination*.

[29] Larson et al., *Assets Acquired in a Business Combination*, at 5.3.100.

Thus, fair value must include the amortization benefit:

> The task force believes that the fair value of an intangible asset would include the value of the tax benefit resulting from the amortization of that asset because FASB Statement No. 109 requires that the cost assigned to an acquired intangible asset be the same whether the asset is acquired piecemeal or in a nontaxable business combination in which the asset had no corresponding tax basis. If the value of the tax benefit resulting from the amortization of that asset were not included in the fair value of the intangible asset, it would have the impact of stating that asset on the balance sheet "net of tax."[30]

And thus:

> However, the value of tax amortization benefits associated with intangible assets, including IPR&D assets, should be recognized when the purpose of the valuation is to estimate fair value as that term is defined under U.S. generally accepted accounting practices, including for transactions where the buyer will not be allowed to gross up and amortize the value of purchased intangible assets for income tax purposes (that is, nontaxable business combinations rather than asset purchases). FASB Statement No. 109, Accounting for Income Taxes, prohibits the net-of-tax approach and requires assets acquired and liabilities assumed to be recorded at their "gross" fair value.[31]

In accordance with paragraph 5.3.102 of the AICPA Practice Aid, the fair value of the intangible assets includes the value of the tax benefit resulting from the amortization of those assets. The benefits of amortizing the values of the assets are added to the values previously determined.

ValTip

> The amortization benefit is calculated as the present value of the tax savings resulting from the 15-year amortization of the asset.

The formula for calculating the amortization benefit is presented in the case study later in this chapter.

Returns on and of Contributory Assets

As will be demonstrated in the case study later in this chapter, major intangible assets for which it is possible to isolate discrete income streams are often valued using the income approach—multiperiod excess earnings method (MPEEM). This method honors the concept that the fair value of an identifiable intangible asset is equal to the present value of the net cash flows attributable to that asset and recognizes the notion that the net cash flows attributable to the subject asset must recognize the support of many other assets, tangible and intangible, that contribute to the realization of the cash flows.

---

[30] Ibid., at 5.3.102.
[31] Ibid., at 5.3.100.

In applying the MPEEM to an intangible asset, after-tax cash flows attributable to the intangible assets are charged amounts representing a "return on" and a "return of" the contributory assets. The return *on* the asset refers to a hypothetical assumption whereby the project pays the owner of the contributory assets a fair return on the fair value of the hypothetically rented assets (i.e., return *on* is the payment for using the asset—an economic rent). For self-developed assets (e.g., the assembled workforce or customer relationships), the annual cost to replace these assets should be factored into cash flow projections as part of the operating cost structure. Similarly, the return *of* fixed assets is included in the cost structure as depreciation. Return *of* is the cost to replace the asset and is deducted from the subject revenues.

Present Value Considerations for Intangible Assets

The FASB concludes that fair value is the objective when using present value in measurements at the initial recognition and fresh start measurements of assets. Two techniques are specifically recognized: the discount rate adjustment technique and the expected present value technique. The expected present value technique focuses on the variations in the amount and timing of estimating cash flows and their relative probability of occurrence, whereas the discount rate adjustment technique attempts to capture those same factors by focusing on the selection of a return rate that is commensurate with the risk. There are five elements of a present value measurement that, taken together, capture the economic differences among assets:

1. An estimate of the future cash flow or, in more complex cases, series of future cash flows at different times
2. Expectations about possible variations in the amount or timing of those cash flows
3. The time value of money, represented by the risk-free rate of interest
4. The price for bearing the uncertainty inherent in the asset or liability
5. Other sometimes unidentifiable factors, including illiquidity and market imperfections[32]

Estimates of future cash flows for intangibles are subject to a variety of risks and uncertainties, such as the following. This is especially true of new product launches.

- The time it takes to bring the product to market
- The market and customer acceptance
- The viability of the technology
- Regulatory approval
- Competitor response
- The price and performance characteristics of the product[33]

ValTip

The risk premium assessed to a new product launch should decrease as a project successfully proceeds through its continuum of development because the uncertainty related to each subsequent stage typically diminishes.

---

[32] Financial Accounting Standards Board, Concepts Statement No. 7, *Using Cash Flow Information and Present Value in Accounting Measurements,* (February 2000), at 39.
[33] Larson et al., *Assets Acquired in a Business Combination,* at 5.3.83.

NATURE OF GOODWILL

The definition of goodwill warrants repeating: Goodwill is the excess of the cost of an acquired entity over the net of amounts assigned to assets acquired and liabilities assumed.[34] For GAAP purposes, goodwill includes all amounts that fail the criteria of an identified intangible asset. Importantly, the practitioner must understand that the nature of goodwill for financial reporting is different from that used in a legal setting. Such "legal goodwill" is generally considered to be all value above tangible asset value. For financial reporting, it helps to consider the elements of goodwill as follows:

- The excess of the fair values over the book values of the acquired entity's net assets at the date of acquisition.
- The fair values of other net assets that had not been recognized by the acquired entity at the date of acquisition.
- The fair value of the "going-concern" element of the acquired entity's existing business.
- The fair value of the expected synergies and other benefits from combining the acquiring entity's and acquired entity's net assets and businesses. Those synergies and other benefits are unique to each combination, and different combinations would produce different synergies and, hence, different values.
- Overvaluation of the consideration paid by the acquiring entity stemming from errors in valuing the consideration tendered.
- Overpayment or underpayment by the acquiring entity. Overpayment might occur, for example, if the price is driven up in the course of bidding for the acquired entity, while underpayment may occur in the case of a distress sale or fire sale.[35]

Goodwill Calculation in a 100 Percent Acquisition

The following example illustrates the calculation of goodwill in a 100 percent acquisition:

Consideration transferred:	
Cash	$ 1,000,000
Common stock (fair value at acquisition date)	9,000,000
Contingent consideration arrangement	1,500,000
Total consideration transferred	11,500,000
Net assets recognized (selected types):	
Other than selected types	9,800,000
Contingent liability	(500,000)
Defensive intangible assets (per ASC 360-30-55-1)	400,000
Restructuring liability	0
Total net assets recognized	9,700,000
Goodwill	$ 1,800,000

---

[34] Financial Accounting Standards Board, Accounting Standards Codification (2009), Glossary.

[35] Financial Accounting Standards Board, Statement of Financial Accounting Standards No. 141, *Business Combinations* (2001), at B102.

Goodwill Calculation in a Full Acquisition (Acquirer Has an Existing Investment)

The accounting for a 100 percent acquisition and a full acquisition (the acquirer owned a noncontrolling interest before the business combination, but 100 percent is owned by the acquirer at the completion of the transaction) is the same except for the accounting for the preexisting noncontrolling investment.

The acquirer adjusts the carrying amount of its existing investment in the acquiree to its acquisition-date fair value and recognizes a gain or loss in earnings. If the acquirer accounts for the investment as a "held for sale" security, the unrealized gain or loss is recognized as realized at the acquisition date.[36]

Assume in this instance that the acquirer 1) owned a minority interest whose acquisition-date fair value has been determined to be $500,000, and 2) paid a total consideration of $11 million for the remaining interest. Using the same facts as in the 100 percent acquisition shown in the previous section except for these, goodwill is calculated as follows:

Consideration transferred	$11,000,000
Acquisition-date fair value of existing investment	500,000
Total consideration transferred	11,500,000
Net assets recognized	9,700,000
Goodwill	$ 1,800,000

Calculation of Goodwill in a Partial Acquisition and Recording Noncontrolling Interest

The accounting for the acquisition of a *controlling interest* in an acquiree, but not a 100 percent or full interest, is substantially the same as a 100 percent or full acquisition except for the acquiree's noncontrolling interest (previously called the minority interest). However, the accounting for a partial acquisition is substantially different from the accounting for a full acquisition.

Because the acquirer has control, the assets acquired and liabilities assumed in the business combination are measured and reported in the same manner as if the business combination were a 100 percent acquisition. However, because the consideration transferred and liabilities assumed represent less than a 100 percent acquisition, the noncontrolling interest must be recognized on the acquirer's books at fair value.

Previously, the amounts reported for the assets/liabilities were a combination of value at the acquisition date and a carryforward of the acquiree's book value. For example, if the acquirer acquired an 80 percent interest in the acquiree, the reported amounts reflected an acquisition-date fair value amount for 80 percent and a carryforward amount of 20 percent. Accordingly, the noncontrolling interest (minority interest) was recorded at the 20 percent carryforward amount. Also, goodwill was calculated only on the 80 percent acquired even though the acquirer controlled all of the goodwill.

Under the ASC, the partial acquirer who nonetheless obtains control reports the assets acquired and liabilities assumed in the same manner as if the acquisition were a 100 percent acquisition. The noncontrolling interest in the subsidiary that is not acquired by the acquirer is recorded at its acquisition-date fair value. The fair values

---

[36] Financial Accounting Standards Board, Accounting Standards Codification (2009), at 805-10-25-10.

of the acquirer's interest and the noncontrolling interest in a subsidiary may be different on a per-share basis because of control premiums or a noncontrol discount.

Using similar facts as in the 100 percent acquisition shown in a previous section, except for an adjustment of the consideration transferred and the recognition of the noncontrolling interest assuming an acquisition of 80 percent of the acquiree, goodwill would be calculated as follows:

Consideration transferred	$ 9,200,000
Noncontrolling interest at acquisition-date fair value	2,000,000
Total consideration transferred	11,200,000
Net assets recognized	9,700,000
Goodwill	$ 1,500,000

Gain from a Bargain Purchase

Occasionally, the consideration transferred by an acquirer (and the fair value of the acquirer's existing investment in the acquiree or the fair value of the noncontrolling interest) may be less than the amounts recognized for the net assets acquired (assets acquired less liabilities assumed). This is called a bargain purchase. Under the original SFAS 141, which used an allocation of the purchase price approach for recording a business combination, the excess of net assets over the purchase price was eliminated by reducing the amounts assigned to certain assets, or in very unusual circumstances recognizing a gain. ASC Topic 805 now requires that the acquisition method be applied for all business combinations. Assuming the acquirer and acquiree are independent of each other, a bargain purchase event is unlikely. The ASC requires the acquirer to account for the excess by recognizing such excess in income.

It is important to point out that before a gain on a bargain purchase is recognized, the acquirer is required to reassess whether it had correctly identified all of the assets acquired and liabilities assumed and shall recognize any additional assets or liabilities that are identified in that review.[37] This reassessment requires procedures used to measure fair value of the identifiable assets acquired and liabilities assumed, the noncontrolling interest in the acquiree (for a business combination achieved in stages), the acquirer's previously held equity interest in the acquiree, and the consideration transferred.[38]

Note that ultimately the accounting for a bargain purchase under old SFAS 141 also resulted in the acquirer reporting a gain, but this gain (the result of understating the amortization or write-off of the arbitrarily reduced amounts recognized for assets acquired) was not transparent, and interfered with the reporting of financial activity in periods after the acquisition.

Goodwill, Intangible Assets, and the Impairment Test

The ASC mandates that goodwill shall not be amortized over a defined period; rather, goodwill must be tested for impairment at least annually at the "reporting unit" level.[39] All goodwill reported in the financial statements of a subsidiary is to be tested for impairment as if the subsidiary were a stand-alone entity. A reporting unit is defined as an operating segment or one level below an operating segment (called a component). A component of an operating segment is a reporting unit if the component constitutes

[37] Ibid., at 805-30-25-4.
[38] Ibid., at 805-30-30-5.
[39] Ibid., at 805-20-35-1.

a business for which discrete financial information is available and segment management regularly reviews the operating results of that component. Goodwill must be defined and allocated at this component level. Entities that are not required to report segment information are nevertheless required to test goodwill for impairment at the reporting unit level.[40]

Goodwill is the excess of cost over the assets acquired and liabilities assumed, but this statement requires clarification. The amount of goodwill allocated to a reporting unit is contingent upon the expected benefits of the combination to the reporting unit. This goodwill allocation is required even though other assets or liabilities of the acquired entity may not be assigned to that reporting unit; that is, they may be assigned to other reporting units.[41]

A relative fair value allocation approach similar to that used when a portion of a reporting unit is disposed of should be used to determine how goodwill should be allocated when an entity reorganizes its reporting structure in a manner that changes the composition of one or more of its reporting units. However, goodwill is ultimately tested for impairment.

The measurement of the fair value of intangibles and goodwill can be performed at any time during the fiscal year as long as it is consistently applied from year to year. Although different measurement dates can be used for different reporting units, whichever date is selected for a subject reporting unit must be consistent from year to year.

A detailed determination of the fair value of a reporting unit may be carried forward from one year to the next if all of the following criteria have been met:

- The assets and liabilities that comprise the reporting unit have not changed significantly since the most recent fair value determination
- The most recent fair value determination results in an amount that exceeds the carrying amount of the reporting unit by a substantial margin
- Based on an analysis of events, it is determined that the possibility is remote that a fair value determination will be less than the current carrying amount of the reporting unit[42]

Goodwill of a reporting unit should be tested for impairment on an interim basis if an event occurs that would more likely than not reduce the fair value of a reporting unit below its carrying value. Examples of such events are:

- A significant adverse change in legal factors or in the business climate
- An adverse action or assessment by a regulator
- Unanticipated competition
- A loss of key personnel
- A more-likely-than-not expectation that a reporting unit or a significant portion of a reporting unit will be sold or otherwise disposed of
- The testing for recoverability under SFAS 144 of a significant asset group within a reporting unit
- Recognition of a goodwill impairment loss in the financial statements of a subsidiary that is a component of a reporting unit[43]

---

[40] Ibid., at 350-20-35-34 to 350-20-35-38.

[41] Ibid., at 350-20-35-41.

[42] Ibid., at 350-20-35-29.

[43] Ibid., at 350-20-35-30.

The impairment test is a two-step process. In the first step, the fair value of the reporting unit is determined and compared with the carrying amount of the reporting unit, including goodwill.

> Goodwill impairment potentially exists when the carrying value of the reporting unit, including goodwill, exceeds the fair value of the reporting unit.

The fair value of a reporting unit refers to the amount at which the unit as a whole could be bought or sold in a current transaction between willing parties. Quoted market prices in active markets are considered the best evidence of fair value and should be used as the basis for the measurement, if available. However, the market price of an individual share of stock (and thus the market capitalization of a reporting unit with publicly traded stock) may not be representative of the fair value of the reporting unit as a whole.[44] Therefore, the quoted market price of an individual share of stock is not required to be the only basis of measurement of the fair value of a reporting unit. If a quoted market price of the shares of a reporting unit is not available, the estimate of fair value should be based on the best information available, including prices for similar assets and liabilities and the results of other valuation techniques.

See Addendum 1, *Fair Value*, at the end of this chapter regarding the implementation of fair value measurement. The following comments relate to traditional valuation methods.

A valuation technique based on multiples of earnings, revenue, or a similar performance measure may be used to estimate the fair value of a reporting unit if that technique is consistent with the objective of measuring fair value. Such measures may be appropriate, for example, when the fair value of an entity that has comparable operations and economic characteristics is observable and the relevant multiples of a comparable entity are known. Conversely, use of multiples would not be appropriate in situations in which the operations or activities of an entity for which the multiples are known are not comparable in nature, scope, or size to the reporting unit for which fair value is being estimated.[45]

> A present value technique is often the best available technique with which to estimate the fair value of a group of assets (such as a reporting unit).

If a present value technique is used to measure fair value, estimates of future cash flows should be consistent with the objective of measuring fair value. Those cash flow estimates should incorporate assumptions that marketplace participants would use in their estimates of fair value whenever that information is available without undue cost and effort. Otherwise, an entity may use its own assumptions. Such cash flow estimates should be based on reasonable and supportable assumptions and

---

[44] Ibid., at 350-20-35-22.
[45] Ibid., at 350-20-35-24.

should consider all available evidence. The weight given to the evidence should be commensurate with the extent to which the evidence can be verified objectively. If a range is estimated for the amounts or timing of possible cash flows, the likelihood of possible outcomes should be considered.

The second step of the goodwill impairment test requires determining the amount of goodwill impairment associated with the impairment of the fair value of the reporting unit.[46] All long-lived assets must be tested for impairment before the goodwill impairment test. In addition, intangible assets not subject to amortization are to be tested for impairment at least annually.[47]

> The second step of the goodwill impairment test is triggered if the carrying value of the reporting unit, including goodwill, exceeds the fair value of the reporting unit.

> The second step requires performing what amounts to a new purchase price allocation—as though a business combination were consummated on the date of the impairment test.

The allocation includes determining the new fair values of both the originally recognized assets and new assets that may have been unrecognized at the valuation date but were developed between the acquisition date and the test date. The fair values of the assets at the test date are deducted from the fair value of the reporting unit to determine the *implied fair value of goodwill* at the test date. If the implied fair value of goodwill at the test date is lower than its carrying amount, goodwill impairment is indicated and goodwill is written down to its implied fair value.[48] Performing the new asset allocation answers the implied question, "What, exactly, is impaired—specifically identifiable tangible assets, specifically identifiable intangible assets, or goodwill?"

The ASC requires that assets (or asset groups) other than goodwill be tested for impairment before goodwill. Consequently, if the asset (or asset group) was impaired, the impairment loss would be recognized prior to goodwill being tested for impairment in step one.[49] This means that impairment of other assets must also be recognized. For example, assume a company has a reporting unit with a fair value of $80 million, including goodwill of $35 million. The relative fair values of the assets have been estimated and recorded on the books of the acquirer as follows:

Recognized tangible assets	$15,000,000
Recognized identifiable intangible assets (with defined life)	30,000,000
Goodwill	35,000,000
Fair value of reporting unit	$80,000,000

---

[46] Ibid., at 350-20-35-9.
[47] Ibid., at 350-30-35-18.
[48] Ibid., at 350-20-35-9 to 350-20-35-17.
[49] Ibid., at 350-20-35-31.

After one year, assume the carrying amounts of certain assets after amortization are:

Recognized tangible assets	$12,000,000
Recognized identifiable intangible assets (with defined life)	25,000,000

Now assume an impairment test is performed at this time one year later and the fair value of the reporting unit is $70 million. This decline in value indicates impairment but not necessarily a goodwill impairment charge of $10 million. A contemporaneous asset allocation must be performed to determine the new goodwill amount. The assumptions of the fair values as of the date of the impairment test are:

Fair value of:

Recognized tangible assets	$13,000,000
Unrecognized tangible assets*	1,000,000
Recognized identifiable intangible assets	20,000,000
Unrecognized identifiable intangible assets*	7,000,000
Goodwill	29,000,000
Fair value of reporting unit	$70,000,000

*Assets acquired or developed after the acquisition date

The step two results are:

	Net Carrying Amount	Fair Value	Impairment Amount
Recognized tangible assets	$12,000,000	$13,000,000	$0
Unrecognized tangible assets	0	1,000,000	0
Recognized identifiable intangible assets (with a defined life)	25,000,000	20,000,000	5,000,000*
Unrecognized identifiable intangible assets	0	7,000,000	0
Goodwill	35,000,000	29,000,000	6,000,000
Fair value of reporting unit	$72,000,000	$70,000,000	$11,000,000

*It is assumed that impairment is indicated under the applicable statement.

In this example, step one would fail by $2 million (total carrying amount of $72 million less fair value of $70 million), but the step two analysis shows an impairment charge of $11 million.

Of course, if the impairment test finds that the fair value of the reporting unit has not declined materially, no further analysis is required. Increases in the fair value of goodwill are never recognized.

Reporting Units and Annual Impairment Testing

An entity must establish its reporting units using its current reporting structure and the reporting unit guidance from the ASC. Recognized net assets, excluding goodwill, should be assigned to those reporting units. Recognized assets and liabilities that do not relate to a reporting unit, such as an environmental liability for an operation previously disposed of, need not be assigned to a reporting unit. All goodwill recognized in an entity's statement of financial position should be assigned to one or more reporting units based on a reasonable and supportable analysis. Goodwill in each reporting unit should be tested for impairment annually and between annual tests in the event circumstances arise that would more likely than not reduce the fair value of a reporting unit below its carrying amount.[50]

FINANCIAL REPORTING DISCLOSURES—SELECTED DISCLOSURE REQUIREMENTS

A number of the new business combination disclosure requirements relate to the significant changes made to the accounting for an acquisition. The following are some of the disclosures that are required.

- Because financial assets are recorded at fair value without a carryforward of the acquiree's allowance for loan losses or bad debts, information about the acquired receivables by major classes:
  - Fair value of the acquired receivables
  - Gross contractual amount of the receivables
  - Best estimate at the acquisition date of the contractual cash flows that are *not* expected to be collected
- More information about assets/liabilities arising from acquired contingencies:
  - Amounts recognized or an explanation of why no amount was recognized
  - The nature of recognized and unrecognized contingencies
  - An estimate of the range of outcomes (undiscounted) of recognized or unrecognized contingencies or why a range cannot be estimated
- Information about changes to provisional amounts, contingent considerations, and assets and liabilities for recognized contingencies in periods subsequent to the acquisition
- Information about transactions recognized separately:
  - Description of each transaction
  - How each transaction was accounted for
  - The amount and line item for each transaction
  - If the transaction is a settlement amount, how it was determined
- How the amounts and where acquisition-related costs are accounted for
- Bargain purchase gain amount and line item and why the transaction was a bargain purchase
- The amount and how the fair value of noncontrolling interest was determined
- The fair value and any gain or loss recognized (and line item) to adjust a previously owned investment in the acquiree
- For public companies, information about the impact of the acquisition on the consolidated financial statements, if practicable:
  - Revenue and earnings included subsequent to the acquisition
  - Various supplemental pro forma information

Disclosure is more involved when an impairment loss is recognized. In such a situation, the following disclosures are required:

- A description of the facts and circumstances leading to the impairment
- The amount of the impairment loss and the method of determining the fair value of the associated reporting unit (whether based on quoted market prices, prices of comparable businesses, or a present value or other valuation technique)

---

[50] Ibid., at 350-20-35-28 to 350-20-35-30.

- If a recognized impairment loss is an estimate that has not yet been finalized, that fact and the reasons for it should be disclosed. Further, in subsequent periods, the nature and amounts of any significant adjustments made to the initial estimate of the impairment loss must be disclosed.[51]

The valuation analysts must make sure their report and work papers provide the client and auditor the information necessary for these disclosures.

CASE STUDY: DETERMINING THE VALUE OF GOODWILL AND OTHER INTANGIBLE ASSETS IN A BUSINESS COMBINATION

For continuity of presentation, we present the case study here in its entirety. It is an acquisition of 100 percent of the assets of a company (the acquiree or the company) by a larger public company (the acquirer). Exhibits referenced in the case study text are presented at the end of the case study. For simplicity of presentation, we have deliberately limited the number of nonintangible assets owned and liabilities owed by the acquiree. In reality, there may be a significant number of such items that may exist for a given acquiree. In practice, one may find assets such as various other types of investments and securities, and liabilities such as pension plan liabilities, asset retirement obligations, warranty obligations and contingencies, to name but a few. There are also assets and liabilities not reported at fair value according to the ASC.

> Under GAAP, an acquiring company must record a business combination by applying the acquisition method described previously.

The acquisition method comprises four elements:

1. Identifying the acquirer
2. Determining the acquisition date
3. Recognizing and measuring the identifiable assets acquired, the liabilities assumed, and any noncontrolling interest in the acquiree
4. Recognizing and measuring goodwill or gain from a bargain purchase

The acquisition method requires numerous measurements, most of which will probably be under the fair value standard. However, certain assets and liabilities are recorded under guidance that results in an other-than-fair-value measurement, such as share-based payment awards. This case study presents an example of the application of the acquisition method to a business combination.

The last step of the acquisition method concerns goodwill. ASC Subtopic 805-30 describes the measurement of goodwill or gain from a bargain purchase:

> The Acquirer shall recognize goodwill as of the acquisition date, measured as the excess of (a) over (b) below:
>
> (a) The aggregate of the following:
>   (1)   The consideration transferred measured in accordance with this Section, which generally requires acquisition-date fair value

---

[51] Ibid., at 350-20-50-2.

(2)   The fair value of any noncontrolling interest in the Acquiree

(3)   In a business combination achieved in stages, the acquisition-date fair value of the Acquirer's previously held equity interest in the Acquiree

(b)   The net of the acquisition-date amounts of the identifiable assets acquired and the liabilities assumed measured in accordance with this Statement.[52]

Occasionally, an Acquirer will make a bargain purchase, which is a business combination in which the amount in paragraph 805-30-30-1(b) exceeds the aggregate of the amounts specified in (a) in that paragraph. If that excess remains after applying the requirements in paragraph 805-30-25-4, the Acquirer shall recognize the resulting gain in earnings on the acquisition date. The gain shall be attributed to the Acquirer.[53]

The example that follows is of an acquisition of the assets of a privately held corporation, and may differ in the treatment of certain issues compared with an acquisition of stock or public company acquisition. Although the numerous steps and processes are presented sequentially, in practice the various activities are performed simultaneously over a period of weeks, often by a staff of several analysts.

Consideration and Calculation of the Total of Intangible Assets and Goodwill

In business combination accounting, the consideration transferred must be measured in order to ultimately determine the fair value of goodwill or whether a bargain purchase has occurred. This measurement is made with reference to payments in cash and/or securities, fair values of assets distributed as consideration, and the fair values of liabilities assumed by an acquiring entity, including contingencies. In our example, the total consideration is $474,570,000 based on the following assumptions:

Payments:	
Cash	$100,000,000
Stock (at acquisition-date fair value)	325,600,000
Contingent consideration (assumed acquisition-date fair value—earn-out)	48,970,000
Total consideration transferred	$474,570,000

Let us further assume the following liabilities (stated at acquisition-date fair value):

Current liabilities (excluding debt)	$ 48,000,000
Current maturities of long-term debt	14,000,000
Long-term debt	95,000,000
Total liabilities	$157,000,000

A valuation concept that may be useful to the practitioner is the total cost of assets acquired. The total consideration transferred plus the fair value of all liabilities assumed equates to the total paid for all of the acquired company's assets, which here is calculated to be $631,570,000. It is important to distinguish this amount

---

[52] Ibid., at 805-30-30-1.
[53] Ibid., at 805-30-25-2.

from the invested capital concept, which is defined as the sum of debt and equity in an enterprise on a long-term basis, shown here as $583,570,000 ($474,570,000 plus $14,000,000 plus $95,000,000) in terms of cost.

At this point, it may be useful for the analyst to grasp the overall magnitude of the intangible assets. This can be easily achieved by taking the sum of the consideration transferred and subtracting the estimated net amount of identifiable current, fixed, and other tangible assets acquired and liabilities assumed. Note that this is a practical tip, not to be confused with the determination of goodwill. As stated previously, goodwill is the excess of the consideration transferred over the net of all assets, tangible and intangible, and liabilities assumed. At this stage of the case study, we are merely reworking the arithmetic to solve for the gross magnitude of only the intangible assets.

An analysis of the company's balance sheet and asset records as of the *valuation date* reveals that the aggregate recorded or carrying amounts of the assets is $204,000,000:

Cash	$ 8,000,000
Marketable securities	9,000,000
Accounts receivable	48,000,000
Inventory	27,000,000
Prepaid expenses	10,000,000
Land and building, net	22,000,000
Machinery and equipment, net	53,000,000
Organization costs and goodwill	27,000,000
Total assets	$204,000,000

The next step is to adjust recorded values to their *acquisition-date* fair values. In practice, depending on materiality, separate valuations may be undertaken of certain tangible assets. For example, a machinery and equipment analyst may be brought in to independently value the fixed assets if it is determined that 1) the fixed assets are material, and 2) the book values do not reasonably represent fair value. Similarly, the fair values of receivables and other current assets may not be reflected by their carrying amounts and may require adjustment. For purposes of this analysis, it is assumed that adjustments are required to certain asset accounts and that the fair values of cash and prepaid expenses are equal to their carrying amounts. After the adjustments, the fair values of the tangible assets are as follows:

	Carrying Amount	Fair Value	
Cash	$ 8,000,000	$ 8,000,000	
Marketable securities	9,000,000	18,000,000	(a)
Accounts receivable	48,000,000	40,000,000	(b)
Inventory	27,000,000	30,000,000	(c)
Prepaid expenses	10,000,000	10,000,000	
Land and building, net	22,000,000	36,000,000	(d)
Machinery and equipment, net	53,000,000	85,000,000	(e)
Organization costs and goodwill	27,000,000	0	(f)
Total assets	$204,000,000	$227,000,000	

(a) Fair value of marketable securities, as marked to market. These were carried by the acquiree at cost.
(b) To record a fair value measurement that includes a current assessment of the risk of uncollectibles.

(c) To record a fair value measurement that reflects the value added to inventory by the requisition and manufacturing processes that have occurred as of the acquisition date.

(d) Fair value per real estate appraisal.

(e) Fair value per machinery and equipment appraisal.

(f) Written off (see "Valuation of Tangible Assets" and "Valuation of Intangible Assets" sections later in this case study).

It should be noted that in our case study, the identified current, fixed, and tangible assets are recognized and recorded at fair value pursuant to the ASC. However, there are a number of potential acquired assets that are recognized or measured at other than fair value. These exceptions are:

- Exceptions to the Recognition Principle:
  - Assets and liabilities from contingencies
  - Income taxes
  - Employee benefits (multiple statements)
  - Indemnification assets
- Exceptions to the Measurement Principle:
  - Reacquired rights
  - Share-based payments
  - Assets held for sale
  - Income taxes (SFAS 109)
  - Employee benefits (multiple statements)
  - Indemnification assets
  - Certain assets and liabilities from contingencies

Nonetheless, a majority of recognized assets are measured at fair value, and such measurements still must follow the requirements of the ASC. That is, the preparer must make cogent judgments for each tangible asset for the following:

- Unit of account
- Principal or most advantageous market
- Highest and best use on an in-use or in-exchange basis
- Assumptions of market participants (often hypothetical market participants), including specific risk/uncertainty premiums.

We address the application of the ASC to the tangible assets later in this case study.

The fair value of the assets is $227,000,000 and the fair value of the liabilities is $157,000,000 (as shown earlier), so the estimated preliminary fair value of net assets acquired is $70,000,000. Subtracting this amount from the total consideration of $474,500,000 leaves a "gap" available for the aggregate fair value of all intangible assets of $404,570,000 (consideration of $474,570,000 minus the estimated preliminary fair value of net assets acquired of $70,000,000). A simple way of presenting the interrelationship of these categories is in the form of a schematic presented in Exhibit 21.3, which sets forth the foregoing in the form of a box, where the left side represents the assets, and the right side represents the consideration and liabilities.

Exhibit 21.4 depicts the aggregate amounts to be recorded, assuming no bargain purchase.

In our example, we established that the fair value of the consideration transferred and liabilities assumed is $631,570,000. Exhibit 21.4 reveals that this equates

Exhibit 21.3   General Formula Based on Fair Values

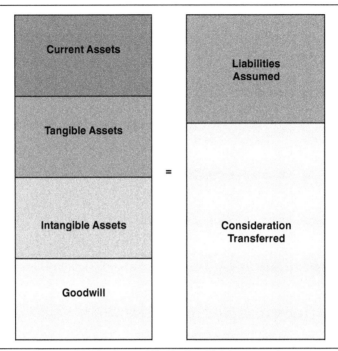

Exhibit 21.4   Acquiree Schematic

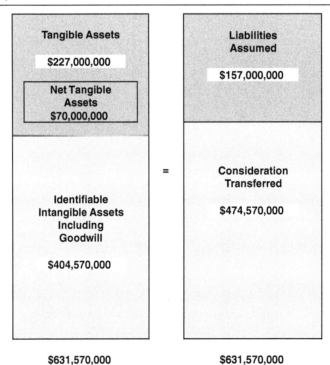

to a total asset value, including goodwill, of $631,570,000 and that the total fair value of the identifiable intangible assets and goodwill is $404,570,000.

Said another way, the amount of intangible assets and goodwill can be determined by comparing the consideration exchanged of $474,570,000 to the net assets acquired of $70,000,000, or $404,570,000. Alternatively, calculating the difference between the fair value of consideration and liabilities assumed ($474,500,000 + $157,000,000 = $631,570,000) and the total assets acquired of $227,000,000 provides the total fair value of intangible assets and goodwill of $404,570,000. In its discussion of calculating goodwill, the ASC uses the former approach.

Identifying Intangible Assets

Appropriate due diligence to obtain substantial competent evidence through adequate data gathering and management interviews is important. Assume that an investigation of the acquiree and its operations has been conducted, and it has been determined that, in accordance with the guidance contained in the ASC, there are six identifiable intangible assets that are subject to being valued, plus assembled workforce (an element of goodwill) and goodwill.

The intangibles are set forth as follows:

Intangible Asset	Type
Software	Technology-based
Trade name	Marketing-related
Noncompete agreements	Contract-based
Technology	Technology-based
In-process research and development	Technology-based
Customer relationships	Customer-related

The fair value of each of these intangible assets must be determined according to the guidance contained in the ASC. Consistent with determining the fair value measurement for tangible assets, the same considerations must be taken into account for each intangible asset:

- Unit of account
- Principal or most advantageous market
- Highest and best use on an in-use or in-exchange basis
- Assumptions of market participants (often hypothetical market participants), including specific risk/uncertainty premiums

Each intangible asset will be analyzed and the most appropriate technique(s) will be employed. As will be seen, the valuation of the intangible assets of the acquiree will typically be performed using a combination of the cost and income approaches, with an element of market approach in selecting the royalty rate used for the trade name valuation. Royalty rates are also used to test the reasonableness of the technology and in-process research and development valuations. We have chosen to omit detailed explanations of the three approaches, but such may be found in other chapters of this book. The multiperiod excess earnings method of the income approach will typically be used to value the customer relationships. However, the other assets must be valued first (aside from goodwill, which is valued using a residual method, where the value of all identified assets is subtracted from the total consideration). This is because in the multiperiod excess earnings method there is a deduction representing returns or contributory charges on the fair values of the other assets employed in the business.

After each intangible asset is valued, the degree of observable inputs must be considered to determine the appropriate fair value hierarchy for disclosure purposes. In actual practice, the analyst will be hard-pressed to find observable Level 1 or Level 2 inputs for valuing most intangible assets.

Remaining Useful Life Analysis

Identifiable assets must be analyzed to determine whether the asset has a finite or indefinite useful life. This subject is addressed in ASC Subtopic 350-30:

> The accounting for a recognized intangible asset is based on its useful life to the reporting entity. An intangible asset with a finite useful life is amortized; an intangible asset with an indefinite useful life is not amortized.[54]

The useful life of an intangible asset to an entity is the period over which the asset is expected to contribute directly or indirectly to the future cash flows of that entity.[55]

The ASC mentions several pertinent factors that should be taken into account:

- Expected use of the asset
- Expected use of similar assets
- Legal, regulatory, and contractual provisions that may limit the useful life or enable renewal or extension
- The effects of obsolescence, demand, competition, and other economic factors
- Required future maintenance expenditures

Analysts often rely on management's estimates of lives, decay rates, survivorship, and so on. Analysts also rely on statistically based predictions of future behavior by developing survivor curves, sometimes using tools such as Iowa-type curves or Weibull distributions. The subject of "lifing" is very complex and beyond the scope of this chapter. However, there is no shortage of writings on the subject; for a start, try Chapter 11 of *Valuing Intangible Assets* by Robert F. Reilly and Robert P. Schweihs (McGraw-Hill, 1998). Further clarification is provided in the ASC, which addresses factors that should be considered in developing renewal or extension assumptions for the estimation of a remaining useful amortization life.

In our case study, we assume that various analyses and techniques have been performed to determine the remaining useful lives of the amortizable intangible assets, but we do not describe those complexities.

Business Enterprise Analysis

Our analysis will proceed with the development of a business enterprise analysis (BEA) using a discounted cash flow (DCF) methodology. Performing a business enterprise analysis using the discounted cash flow method is important in several major respects. First, it requires an in-depth review of the industry and of the acquiree's operations and results, both historical and projected—critical tasks for an analyst. Second, it provides

---

[54] Ibid., at 350-30-35-1.
[55] Ibid., at 350-30-35-2.

the analyst with a reasonableness test of the fair value of the enterprise (and rate of return) and thus its assets and liabilities, pursuant to the acquisition method. In addition, in performing a BEA, revenue, earnings, and cash flow streams are forecasted, which may be helpful for valuing certain assets by the income approach. Keep in mind that fair value measurement is driven by market participant behavior, not entity-specific behavior. In keeping with the ASC, an analyst will seek to model market participant cash flows—that is, enterprise cash flows that might be expected from market participant investors. These cash flows may or may not be appropriate to use in valuing individual intangible assets, as market participants for those assets may have different expectations than market participants for the enterprise.

The DCF method requires a number of assumptions, including sales and operating expense projections, taxes, working capital, and capital outlay expenditure requirements. The nature and underlying rationales for these assumptions are discussed throughout the chapter.

Discounted Cash Flow Method

In the discounted cash flow method of the income approach, a pro forma analysis consistent with market participant inputs is made of the subject company to estimate future available cash flows. Available cash flow is the amount that could be paid out to providers of capital without impairment of business operations.

Annual projected available cash flows are then discounted to indicate a present value. The sum of the annual present values, including the present value of any estimated residual value, equals the capitalized earnings of the business. When performed on a debt-free basis (this is an appraisal term for a DCF model that reflects returns to debt and equity stakeholders, i.e., before an interest expense deduction), the business's capitalized earnings equates to invested capital, defined as the sum of equity value plus the value of all interest-bearing debt. This value is often called the firm's business enterprise value.

It should be noted that an acquirer's financial projections may include results of synergies between the acquirer and the acquiree. While it is an axiom that buyers do not like to pay for their own synergies, in fact it is frequently done. Also, many acquisitions fail to earn a return on the new investment equal to the acquirer's cost of capital.

Nevertheless, while the projections used by a buyer most likely include synergies and thus help explain a purchase price, buyer-specific synergies are specifically excluded from the cash flows used to value intangibles. Only *market-participant* synergies should be included to comport with the definition of fair value. Thus, an analyst initially provided with projections that include buyer-specific synergies may have to obtain or help prepare a second set of projections with buyer-specific synergies removed, thus representing an estimate of market participant projections. The removal of buyer-specific synergies will reduce the value of certain identifiable intangible assets and increase goodwill, compared with what the calculated value of those asset groups would have been using projections that include buyer-specific synergies. Said another way, buyer-specific synergies wind up in goodwill. Such is the intent of FASB guidance.

In our example, and as presented in Exhibit 21.5, principal assumptions utilized in developing the estimates of enterprise cash flow are as follows:

- Sales are projected to increase from $500,000,000 in 2009 to $575,000,000 in 2010, growth of 15 percent, due to growing the number of new customers and

Exhibit 21.5 Acquiree: Business Enterprise Value—Assumptions as of December 31, 2009

	ACTUAL 2009	2010	2011	2012	2013	2014 FORECAST	2015	2016	2017	2018	2019
SALES											
Sales Growth Percentage		15.0%	15.0%	12.5%	10.0%	10.0%	7.5%	7.5%	7.5%	7.5%	7.5%
Net Sales	$500,000	$575,000	$661,250	$743,906	$818,297	$900,127	$967,636	$1,040,209	$1,118,224	$1,202,091	$1,292,248
EXPENSES											
Cost of Sales Percentage	50.0%	50.0%	49.0%	49.0%	49.0%	49.0%	49.0%	49.0%	49.0%	49.0%	49.0%
Cost of Sales	$250,000	$287,500	$324,013	$364,514	$400,965	$441,062	$474,142	$509,702	$547,930	$589,025	$633,202
Operating Expenses Percentage	38.0%	38.0%	37.0%	37.0%	37.0%	37.0%	37.0%	37.0%	37.0%	37.0%	37.0%
Operating Expenses	$190,000	$218,500	$244,663	$275,245	$302,770	$333,047	$358,025	$384,877	$413,743	$444,774	$478,132
(1) Depreciation (MACRS)	$7,057	$13,158	$22,967	$18,008	$14,646	$12,434	$13,284	$14,191	$11,165	$10,008	$12,922
Amortization		26,971	26,971	26,971	26,971	26,971	26,971	26,971	26,971	26,971	26,971
Other Income (Expense), Net Percentage	0.0%	0.0%	0.0%	0.0%	0.0%	0.0%	0.0%	0.0%	0.0%	0.0%	0.0%
CASH FLOW											
Capital Expenditures Percentage	1.0%	1.0%	1.0%	1.0%	1.0%	1.0%	1.0%	1.0%	1.0%	1.0%	1.0%
Capital Expenditures		$5,750	$6,613	$7,439	$8,183	$9,001	$9,676	$10,402	$11,182	$12,021	$12,922
Projected Working Capital as Percent of Sales	15.0%	15.0%	15.0%	15.0%	15.0%	15.0%	15.0%	15.0%	15.0%	15.0%	15.0%
(2) Projected Working Capital Balance	$58,000	$86,250	$99,188	$111,586	$122,745	$135,019	$145,145	$156,031	$167,734	$180,314	$193,837
Projected Working Capital Requirement		28,250	12,938	12,398	11,159	12,274	10,126	10,886	11,702	12,580	13,524
OTHER											
Effective Tax Rate	40.0%										
Required Rate of Return	15.0%										
Terminal Growth Rate	5.0%										

Footnotes:
(1) 2018 and 2019 estimated.
(2) Balance at December 31, 2009 stated at fair value. After MACRS period.

Note: Some totals may not foot due to rounding.

price increases. The overall increase is based largely on estimated growth of 20 percent in one key market. However, the growth rate of the key market is expected to decline after 2011. The 10-year compound annual growth rate is 9.41 percent.

- Cost of sales (50 percent in 2010, improving to 49 percent thereafter) and operating expenses (38 percent in 2010, improving to 37 percent thereafter) excluding depreciation (tax basis—separately forecast using IRS Modified Accelerated Cost Recovery System [MACRS] tables) and amortization are also forecast. The prospective financial information (PFI) is in line with the acquiree's historical averages and with management's expectations at the time of the acquisition, and were felt to represent the best estimate of these costs consistent with market participants. These assumptions are also in line with growth rates and margins expected by similar products from similar companies in the marketplace.
- Working capital requirements (debt free) were forecast at 15 percent of sales, based on the company's historical working capital position, expected needs, and industry benchmarks.
- Capital expenditures are projected at 1 percent of net sales. This level of capital expenditures is considered adequate to support future levels of sales.
- Tax amortization of total intangible asset value is based on Section 197 of the Internal Revenue Code, which provides for such amortization over a 15-year period. The amortization acts as a tax shield and is added back to cash flow. Annual amortization is $26,971,000 ($404,570,000 ÷ 15). The reader should note that this example is an asset purchase. In a stock purchase, the intangible assets generally are not amortizable for tax purposes absent a Section 338 election. However, market participants in a business combination, namely the buyer for purposes of this discussion, are generally assumed to be enterprises qualifying for Section 197 tax treatment, and in such a case an amortization benefit will apply.
- Other assumptions (illustration purposes only):
  - Required rate of return (discount rate)*   15.00%
  - Terminal growth rate   5.00%
  - Tax rate   40.00%

  *Discussed more fully in the next section, "Discount Rate."

Assumptions are summarized in Exhibit 21.5. Exhibit 21.6 presents the prospective financial information for a period of 10 years.

Cash flows in year 11 are increased by the terminal growth rate and then capitalized into perpetuity by dividing by the capitalization rate, defined as the difference between the discount rate and the terminal growth rate. This terminal value is then discounted to present value to provide the net present value of the terminal cash flow. The terminal cash flow represents the expected cash flow for years 11 to perpetuity.

Because the Section 197 amortization has a finite amortization period of 15 years, the terminal calculation must be adjusted so the amortization is not capitalized into perpetuity. First, the annual amortization of $26,971,000 is added back to year 10 cash flow. Thus, cash flow to be capitalized ignores any amortization benefit after year 10. After accounting for taxes at 40 percent, the present value of the remaining five years of tax amortization is added to the terminal calculation. This amount is $9,586,000. After the adjustment, the amortization of intangibles reflects

Exhibit 21.6 Acquiree: Business Enterprise Value—Cash Flow Forecast as of December 31, 2009

	ACTUAL 2009	FORECAST 2010	2011	2012	2013	2014	2015	2016	2017	2018	2019
Sales Growth Percentage		15.0%	15.0%	12.5%	10.0%	10.0%	7.5%	7.5%	7.5%	7.5%	7.5%
Net Sales	$ 500,000	$ 575,000	$ 661,250	$ 743,906	$ 818,297	$ 900,127	$ 967,636	$ 1,040,209	$ 1,118,224	$ 1,202,091	$ 1,292,248
Cost of Sales	(250,000)	(287,500)	(324,013)	(364,514)	(400,965)	(441,062)	(474,142)	(509,702)	(547,930)	(589,025)	(633,202)
Gross Profit	250,000	287,500	337,238	379,392	417,331	459,065	493,494	530,506	570,294	613,067	659,047
Operating Expenses	(190,000)	(218,500)	(244,663)	(275,245)	(302,770)	(333,047)	(358,025)	(384,877)	(413,743)	(444,774)	(478,132)
Depreciation (MACRS)	($ 7,067)	(13,158)	(22,967)	(18,008)	(14,646)	(12,434)	(13,284)	(14,191)	(11,165)	(10,008)	(12,922)
(1) Amortization of Intangibles (Pretax)	-	(26,971)	(26,971)	(26,971)	(26,971)	(26,971)	(26,971)	(26,971)	(26,971)	(26,971)	(26,971)
Total Operating Expenses	(197,067)	(258,629)	(294,601)	(320,224)	(344,387)	(372,452)	(398,280)	(426,039)	(451,879)	(481,753)	(518,025)
Taxable Income	52,933	28,871	42,637	59,168	72,945	86,613	95,214	104,467	118,415	131,314	141,021
Income Taxes 40.0%	(21,173)	(11,548)	(17,055)	(23,667)	(29,178)	(34,645)	(38,086)	(41,787)	(47,366)	(52,526)	(56,409)
Net Income	$ 31,760	$ 17,323	$ 25,582	$ 35,501	$ 43,767	$ 51,968	$ 57,128	$ 62,680	$ 71,049	$ 78,788	$ 84,612
Net Cash Flow											
Net Income		$ 17,323	$ 25,582	$ 35,501	$ 43,767	$ 51,968	$ 57,128	$ 62,680	$ 71,049	$ 78,788	$ 84,612
Capital Expenditures		(5,750)	(6,613)	(7,439)	(8,183)	(9,001)	(9,676)	(10,402)	(11,182)	(12,021)	(12,922)
Change in Working Capital		(28,250)	(12,938)	(12,398)	(11,159)	(12,274)	(10,126)	(10,886)	(11,702)	(12,580)	(13,524)
Depreciation		13,158	22,967	18,008	14,646	12,434	13,284	14,191	11,165	10,008	12,922
(1) Amortization of Intangibles (Pretax)		26,971	26,971	26,971	26,971	26,971	26,971	26,971	26,971	26,971	26,971
Net Cash Flow		$ 23,452	$ 55,970	$ 60,642	$ 66,042	$ 70,097	$ 77,580	$ 82,554	$ 86,301	$ 91,166	$ 98,060
(2) Present Value Factor at Discount Rate 15.0%		0.9325	0.8109	0.7051	0.6131	0.5332	0.4636	0.4031	0.3506	0.3048	0.2651
Present Value of Net Cash Flow		$ 21,869	$ 45,386	$ 42,759	$ 40,490	$ 37,376	$ 35,966	$ 33,278	$ 30,257	$ 27,787	$ 25,996

		FORECAST			
	2020	2021	2022	2023	2024
(1) Amortization Tax Benefit, Years 2020–2024					
Amortization of Intangibles (Pretax)	$ 26,971	$26,971	$26,971	$26,971	$26,971
40.0% Tax Benefit of Amortization	$ 10,788	$10,788	$10,788	$10,788	$10,788
(2) 15.0% Present Value Factor at Discount Rate	0.2305	0.2004	0.1743	0.1516	0.1318
Present Value of Tax Benefit	$ 2,487	$ 2,162	$ 1,880	$ 1,635	$ 1,422
Present Value of Tax Benefit, 2020–2024	$ 9,586				
Invested Capital					
2019 Taxable Income	$141,021				
Intangible Asset Amortization	26,971				
2019 Adjusted Taxable Income	167,992				
40.0% Income Taxes	(67,197)				
2019 Adjusted Net Income	$100,795				
5.0% 2020 Adjusted Net Income, Growth	$105,835				
15.0% 2020 Working Capital Provision	(9,692)				
2020 Adjusted Cash Flow	$ 96,143				
(3) Terminal Capitalization Rate, Perpetual Growth	10.0%				
2020 Terminal Value	$961,431				
15.0% Present Value Factor at Discount Rate	0.2651				
Present Value of Terminal Cash Flow	$254,875				
Present Value of Net Cash Flow, 2010–2019	$341,164				
Present Value of Terminal Cash Flow	254,875				
Present Value of Tax Benefit, 2020–2024	9,586				
Total Invested Capital, Rounded	$605,625				

Footnotes:

(1) See Amortization Benefit section in Case Study text.

(2) Based on mid-period assumption at Company's weighted average cost of capital.

(3) Calculated by subtracting the Growth Rate of 5.0% from the Discount Rate of 15.0%.

Note: Some totals may not foot due to rounding.

a benefit period of 15 years. The present value of the enterprise's net cash flows, plus the present value of the terminal period, provides total capitalized cash flow. The BEA is presented in Exhibit 21.6.

Discount Rate

> In most applications, the appropriate rate of return for determining the business enterprise value is the weighted average cost of capital (WACC). The WACC is the weighted average of the return on equity capital and the return on debt capital. The rate must be a rate that market participants would use in discounting enterprise cash flows.

Analysts often determine the debt and equity weights with reference to the anticipated long-term industry average leverage position (i.e., average amount of debt capital to equity capital; this assumes that the industry average can be used as a surrogate for market participants, which is often but not always the case). The rate of return on debt capital is adjusted to reflect the fact that interest payments are tax deductible to the corporation.

The WACC is expressed in the following formula:

$$\text{WACC} = (ke \times We) + (kp \times Wp) + (kd(pt)[1 - t] \times Wd)$$

Where

WACC = Weighted average cost of capital

ke   = Cost of common equity capital

We   = Percentage of common equity in the capital structure, at market value

kp   = Cost of preferred equity capital

Wp   = Percentage of preferred equity in the capital structure, at market value

kd(pt) = Cost of debt (pretax)

t   = Tax rate

Wd   = Percentage of debt in the capital structure, at market value

The WACC represents the average rate of earnings investors require to induce them to supply all forms of long-term capital (debt and equity) to a company.

It is beyond the scope of this example to provide a detailed explanation of rates of return, and the reader is encouraged to refer to Chapter 6. For this case (for illustration purposes only), assume an equity discount rate (which in a corporate acquisition is often calculated using the capital asset pricing model) of 19 percent and a pretax cost of debt of 5.25 percent (the assumed prime rate plus 200 basis points, perhaps based on the average credit rating of the market participant buyers). Further, assume a capital structure of 25 percent debt and 75 percent equity. Theoretically, an optimal capital structure based on how the valuation analyst would expect market participants to behave should be used to estimate a company's WACC in the case of an acquisition. Analysts often, where appropriate, rely on the capital structures of public companies as a proxy for what market participants would do. A target capital structure of approximately 25 percent debt and 75 percent equity was estimated for the acquiree, based on a review of guideline publicly traded companies. The acquiree has no preferred equity. Substituting these values into the WACC formula described previously provides the following:

$$
\begin{aligned}
\text{WACC} &= (19.00\% \times 75.00\%) + [5.25\% \ (1 - 40.00\%) \times 25.00\%] \\
&= (14.25\%) + (3.15\% \times 25.00\%) \\
&= (14.25\%) + (0.79\%) \\
&= 15.04\% \\
&= 15\% \text{ rounded}
\end{aligned}
$$

Applying the WACC to cash flows estimated earlier indicates the fair value of the invested capital of the acquiree on the valuation date was (rounded) $605,625,000 (Exhibit 21.6). The actual amount paid for the acquiree's invested capital was $583,570,000 (consideration transferred plus the fair value of long-term liabilities assumed), so we are confident that the DCF model reasonably reflects what was paid for the business.

But what was paid doesn't necessarily reflect the fair value of the enterprise. As a reasonableness test of enterprise fair value, one might consider using a market approach to further test the DCF conclusion. It is important that the analyst gain as much comfort as possible that the DCF represents the fair value of the enterprise to market participants. We have already noted that in many cases market participant cash flows used to value individual assets may differ from enterprise cash flows. In such cases, the sum of the fair values of assets acquired will not reconcile to enterprise fair value. As noted earlier, in practice the purchase price can exceed the BEA, especially if there has been competitive bidding among two or more potential buyers. For the purposes of this case study, we are assuming that the projections include market participant but not buyer-specific synergies, and that the deal was priced accordingly.

Valuation of Tangible Assets

For purposes of this case study, all of the assets acquired are assets to be measured at fair value. Although this may be unrealistic in that many acquirees will possess assets recorded at other than fair value under the ASC, the focus of this case study is the valuation of the *intangible assets* acquired.

The guidance of the ASC has been described in depth earlier. In this case study, the acquiree owns a number of assets for which fair value must be determined. For each of these assets, the overriding principle is, of course, to comply with the guidance of the ASC. While we will not present an in-depth valuation of each of these assets, keep in mind the following for each asset class.

Marketable Securities

It bears repeating that fair value is an exit price. The ASC states:

> When an asset is acquired or a liability is assumed in an exchange transaction for that asset or liability, the transaction price represents the price paid to acquire the asset or received to assume the liability (an entry

price). In contrast, the fair value of the asset or liability represents the price that would be received to sell the asset or paid to transfer the liability (an exit price). Conceptually, entry prices and exit prices are different.

In many cases, the transaction price will equal the exit price and, therefore, represent the fair value of the asset or liability at initial recognition.[56]

Thus, the analyst may look to transaction prices to determine whether such prices represent an exit price to market participants, bearing in mind the principal or most advantageous market for such assets, which are generally valued in exchange. Pricing may be based on an observable and active market for an identical asset, and thus disclosure may be a Level 1 asset. Further note that transaction costs are excluded from the fair value measurement.

Accounts Receivable

Short-term receivables have traditionally been reported at the net realizable value (NRV), which is the gross amount of accounts receivable less an allowance for uncollectible accounts. In determining the fair value of such an asset, however, there are a number of other considerations:

- In positing an exit price, one must at a minimum identify a hypothetical buyer (the market participant). For receivables, this might be a factor.
- A factor purchases receivables at a discount and assumes the risk of collection. Thus, a discount must be assessed, and this discount will depend largely on the age of the receivable. Some receivables may not be factorable. The discount considers the uncertainty of collection. Thus, as pointed out previously, this fair value measurement does not include a separate allowance for uncollectible amounts.

Inventory

Although the carrying amount of inventory, as set forth in ASC Topic 330, is not covered by the fair value requirement, the initial recognition amount of acquired inventory in a business combination is a fair value measurement. ASC 820-10-55-21 provides a discussion of determining fair value for "finished goods inventory at retail outlet"; all acquired inventory is to be recorded at fair value. In most situations, the fair value of an acquiree's inventory (raw materials, work in process, or finished goods) will be greater than the acquiree's carrying amount, as value is added through the requisition and manufacturing process.

Prepaid Expenses

This is one asset for which it would be difficult to posit an in-exchange premise—that is, prepaids have value within the context of a going concern—thus, their value lies in use. It would seem that a discounted cash flow of benefits would capture the value of prepaids, with the only risk being that of whether the company will be around long enough to enjoy the benefits. While greater than zero, in most cases in

---

[56] Ibid., at 820-10-30-2 to 820-10-30-3.

a business combination this risk is minimal, and for purposes of this case we are assuming that the measurement is equal to the carrying amount. In some cases, it will be possible to obtain pricing information for the service and the period over which these services will be rendered after the acquisition date.

Land and Building

The key question in the case of land is: What is the highest and best use? In the ASC, the choice is between 1) the value of the land as used currently for industrial use (in-use value) versus 2) the value of the land as a vacant site (in-exchange value). The building normally would be valued in-use or in-exchange as well, once it is determined what the premise is for the land. In most cases, the highest and best use of the building will follow that of the land. However, a preparer may deem that a market participant will render different conclusions regarding the highest and best use of the building and the land, which may be different from the entity's actual use. Facts and circumstances will dictate.

Machinery and Equipment

Similar to the previous example, the first major judgment is to determine whether the highest and best use of the asset is in-use or in-exchange. In most cases, machinery and equipment in an industrial context will be valued in-use. At this point, the preparer will choose the appropriate valuation techniques. An example of this is presented in ASC 820-10-55-38, with the cost and market approaches employed and the income approach rejected due to the inability to identify an income stream from which to develop reliable cash flow estimates.[57]

Organization Cost and Existing Goodwill

The acquiree's organization costs and existing goodwill amounts do not meet the definition of an asset once the acquiree is acquired by the acquirer. Thus, the amounts that had been recognized by the acquiree are not recognized by the acquirer.

Summary of Values

We have attempted to describe some of the issues that must be dealt with in determining the measurement of the current, fixed, and other tangible assets. However, since the focus of this case study is on the determination of fair value of the acquired intangible assets, an in-depth discussion of the assets listed is beyond the scope of the case (see Chapter 8). Our assumptions of values are:

Cash	$ 8,000,000
Marketable securities	18,000,000
Accounts receivable	40,000,000
Inventory	30,000,000
Prepaid expenses	10,000,000
Land and building, net	36,000,000
Machinery and equipment, net	85,000,000
Organization costs and goodwill	0
Total assets	$227,000,000

---

[57] Ibid., at 820-10-55-37.

Valuation of Intangible Assets

In determining the fair value of the intangible assets acquired in a business combination, the same principles apply as for the tangibles. For each intangible asset, the analyst must determine answers for these questions, among others:

- What is the unit of account for the asset or asset group?
- What is the highest and best use? Is that use in-use or in-exchange?
- What is the principal or most advantageous market?
- Who are the market participants?
- Based on the preceding criteria, are there observable Level 1 or Level 2 inputs from which one could draw conclusions as to fair value?
- What is the appropriate risk/uncertainty premium for each asset (since the income or discounted cash flow is often used)?

In actual practice, there will be only a limited number of instances where observable inputs (Level 1 or Level 2) will be found for intangibles. Unlike tangible assets, there are not many transactions involving intangibles. For example, companies rarely if ever sell their internal software.[58] Customer relationships cannot be sold, either.[59] Trademarks and other types of intellectual property are often licensed, and licensing terms can be extrapolated to help one determine value, but Level 1 inputs are rare and a comparability problem can limit their use as Level 2 inputs.

The foregoing applies to most, if not all, intangibles. Thus, in valuing intangible assets we usually find ourselves applying Level 3 valuation techniques, which are techniques based on unobservable market participant inputs. As we illustrate the valuation of intangible assets, we will revisit these criteria as they apply to each asset class.

Rates of Return

For each asset valued in the following sections, a rate of return, or discount rate, must be selected. For assets valued using the Income Approach, the discount rate is used to reduce future benefit streams to present value. For those assets as well as for assets valued using the cost approach, the discount rate is an important input for calculating the amortization benefit (see "Present Value Considerations for Intangible Assets" section presented previously in this chapter). The rate is selected on an asset-by-asset basis consistent with those rates of return expected from market participants.

Our assumptions (illustration only) for the rates for the intangible assets are:

Acquired software	16%
Assembled workforce	15%
Trade name	15%
Noncompete agreement	15%
Existing technology	18%
In-process research and development	24%
Customer relationships	17%

---

[58] By internal software we mean operations software used in the company's business, as distinguished from a software product that directly generates revenues.

[59] The term *customer relationships* refers to a company's ongoing contact with its customers, which features the customer purchasing goods or services and thereby providing a revenue stream. This definition is in contrast with a customer list, which is a compendium of names and information that can be sold.

Exhibit 21.7   Valuation of Acquired Software (as of December 31, 2009)

IN PLACE	LINES OF CODE	(1) PRODUCTIVITY ASSESSMENT	RATE	HOURS TO RECREATE
Modules Rated **Easiest** to Program	367,000	1	4.0	91,750
Modules Rated **Moderate** to Program	442,000	2	3.0	147,333
Modules Rated **Difficult** to Program	577,000	3	2.0	288,500
Total Number of Lines	1,386,000			
Total Number of Hours to Recreate				527,583
Blended Hourly Rate				$ 154
Reproduction Cost				$ 81,247,782
Less: Taxes		40.0%		(32,499,113)
After Tax Reproduction Cost				48,748,669
(2) Obsolescence		20.0%		(9,749,734)
Replacement Cost				38,998,935
Amortization Benefit				
Discount Rate		16.0%		
Tax Rate		40.0%		
Tax Amortization Period (Years)		15		
Amortization Benefit				7,435,666
Fair Value of Software, Rounded				**$ 46,000,000**

Software Development Costs—Estimated Project Team

Function	Number	Burdened Hourly Rate	Function Hourly Rate
Project Manager	1	$350.00	$ 350.00
Assistant Project Manager	1	250.00	250.00
Systems Analysts	4	250.00	1,000.00
Technical Writers	4	175.00	700.00
Programmers	10	135.00	1,350.00
Support	6	60.00	360.00
Totals	26		$4,010.00
Blended Hourly Rate, Rounded			$ 154.00

Footnotes:
(1) Lines of code per hour, based on productivity assessment for average module of programming.
(2) Estimate based on number of lines of redundant/extraneous code, effective age, and remaining economic life of system. Remaining life of this asset is four years.

Source: Director of Product Development, Target Company

Note: Some totals may not foot due to rounding.

The discount rates shown here are for illustrative purposes only. Actual rates must be selected based on consideration of the facts and circumstances related to each asset as seen through the prism of market participants.

Acquired Software

The acquiree employs a sophisticated array of computer programs to manage its product and production processes (see Exhibit 21.7). Operational software was developed in-house and is not commercially available. The unit of account for this asset is the proprietary operational software package in its entirety.

The highest and best use is in-use. There is no principal market for the asset, and the software utility is not replaceable by publicly available packages. The most advantageous market is the universe of potential buyers of the acquiree, as we have determined that the asset has no market on a stand-alone basis. There are no Level 1 or Level 2 inputs available for this asset; thus, we will employ market participant inputs (Level 3).

A cost approach was applied to value the software, because this asset is a supporting or contributory asset with no directly attributable revenue or income streams. However, if a revenue or income stream could be attributed to this asset, and if the software had salable commercial applications, an income approach would have been considered.

The company's software system comprises numerous modules, each in turn made up of a number of programs written in a sophisticated programming language. To apply this form of the cost approach, it is necessary to obtain a reliable indication of the cost to re-create the programs. A line count (a management report detailing the number of lines of code per program and/or module) was obtained.

Next, it is necessary to determine the productivity with which the hypothetical re-creation effort would take place. The modules were arranged in three groups, with management assessing productivity ratings of 1 to 3, noting that software rated 1 could be programmed at four lines of code per hour; software rated at 2 could be programmed at three lines of code per hour; and software rated 3, the most complex and difficult, could be programmed at two lines of code per hour. The coding rates encompass completely debugged program statements, including requirements definition, systems design, debugging and documentation, testing, and so forth. In performing an analysis in this manner, it is important that management has maintained detailed records of programmer productivity.

By dividing the lines of code for each module by the coding rate, the number of hours to re-create the programs was calculated, totaling 527,583 hours for the entire system. The sum of hours was then multiplied by the blended hourly rate of $154 per hour. In estimating the hourly rate, it was hypothesized that if the software were to be re-created today, a project team of 26 individuals would be assembled. The team would include one project manager, one assistant project manager, four systems analysts, four technical writers, ten programmers, and six support persons. Using their fully burdened rates, the weighted average rate of $154 per hour was calculated for the team. The rates include employee benefits and facilities and overhead charges and approximate the rates that would be charged by a software consulting firm.

Reproduction cost of the software system was determined by multiplying the total number of hours to re-create by the blended hourly rate. In *Valuing Intangible Assets*, Robert Reilly and Robert Schweihs define reproduction cost as:

> the estimated cost to construct, at current prices as of the date of the analysis, an exact duplicate or replica of the subject intangible asset, using the same materials, production standards, design, layout, and quality of workmanship as the subject intangible asset. The reproduction intangible asset will include the same inadequacies, superadequacies, and obsolescence as the subject intangible asset.[60]

In this example, reproduction cost before the tax effect totals $81,247,782. The after-tax reproduction cost is $48,748,669. Because reproduction cost equates to brand-new software, an obsolescence factor is applied to recognize the fact that the acquired software is not brand-new. Rather, it may have redundant or extraneous code, likely has been patched over the years, and contains other inefficiencies that brand-new software presumably would not have. For this application, after discussing

---

[60] Robert F. Reilly and Robert P. Schweihs, *Valuing Intangible Assets* (New York: McGraw-Hill, 1998), p. 122.

the capabilities of the software with the information technology (IT) department, it was estimated that an obsolescence factor of 20 percent was warranted, reducing the reproduction cost to its replacement cost of $38,998,935.

Replacement cost (not reproduction) is defined by Reilly and Schweihs as:

> the estimated cost to construct, at current prices as of the date of the analysis, an intangible asset with equivalent utility to the subject intangible, using modern materials, production standards, design, layout, and quality of workmanship. The replacement intangible asset will exclude all curable inadequacies, superadequacies, and obsolescence that are present in the subject intangible asset.[61]

After adding an amortization benefit (see next section), the fair value of the acquired software is $46,000,000 (rounded) as of December 31, 2009 (see Exhibit 21.7). The remaining useful life is four years.

Amortization Benefit

Added to the replacement cost is an amortization benefit, which reflects the additional value accruing to an asset brought about by the ability under the Internal Revenue Code to deduct the amortization of the asset over its 15-year tax life. The amortization benefit is an element of the fair value of all intangible assets that are deductible for tax purposes.

The amortization benefit represents the present value of the tax savings resulting from amortizing the asset for tax purposes. A spreadsheet presentation of the calculation of the amortization benefit is adapted from the presentation found in the IPR&D Practice Aid.[62] The calculation, using the acquired software asset, is shown in Exhibit 21.8.

The amortization benefit calculation may also be expressed in the following formula:

$$AB = PVCF \times (n/(n - ((PV(Dr,n, - 1) \times (1 + Dr) ^ 0.5) \times T)) - 1)$$

Where

AB	= Amortization benefit
PVCF	= Present value of cash flows from the asset
N	= 15-year amortization period
Dr	= Discount rate
PV(Dr,n,−1) × (1 + Dr) ^ 0.5	= Present value of an annuity of $1 over 15 years, at the discount rate, using a mid-year convention
T	= Tax rate

[61] Ibid.
[62] Larson et al., *Assets Acquired in a Business Combination*, at Exhibit 5.2F. The authors remind the reader that this publication is no longer in print. It is currently being revised by the AICPA.

Exhibit 21.8   Amortization Benefit—The Long Way

Year	Midpoint	Annual Amortization	16.0% PV Factor	40.0% Tax Rate	PV Tax Benefits
1	0.5	6.66667%	0.92848	40.0%	2.47594%
2	1.5	6.66667%	0.80041	40.0%	2.13443%
3	2.5	6.66667%	0.69001	40.0%	1.84003%
4	3.5	6.66667%	0.59484	40.0%	1.58623%
5	4.5	6.66667%	0.51279	40.0%	1.36744%
6	5.5	6.66667%	0.44206	40.0%	1.17883%
7	6.5	6.66667%	0.38109	40.0%	1.01623%
8	7.5	6.66667%	0.32852	40.0%	0.87606%
9	8.5	6.66667%	0.28321	40.0%	0.75522%
10	9.5	6.66667%	0.24415	40.0%	0.65106%
11	10.5	6.66667%	0.21047	40.0%	0.56125%
12	11.5	6.66667%	0.18144	40.0%	0.48384%
13	12.5	6.66667%	0.15641	40.0%	0.41710%
14	13.5	6.66667%	0.13484	40.0%	0.35957%
15	14.5	6.66667%	0.11624	40.0%	0.30998%
		100.00000%			16.01320%

Acquired Software asset used in the following example:

Indicated Value	Discount Rate	PV Tax Benefits	Tax Benefits	Fair Value
$38,998,935	16.0%	16.01320%	$7,435,666	$46,435,000

Note: (FV = Indicated Value ÷ (I − PV Tax Benefits)) Some totals may not foot due to rounding.

Discount Rate for Amortization Benefit

The authors believe that the majority of analysts use the same discount rate for calculating the amortization benefit as is used for the particular asset. The calculations in this case study follow that protocol. It is important to remember that the application of an amortization benefit to measure fair value must be made from the perspective of the market participant.

Some analysts, however, argue the amortization schedule under Section 197 is set as of a moment in time (i.e., the acquisition date), and therefore the risk of the particular asset is not relevant. These analysts argue that the risk to the entity or market participant as a whole, of enjoying the amortization benefits, contrasted with the risks of achieving the cash flows for individual assets, is related to overall risk (as represented by the WACC for the market participant). A few even argue that the rate should be a risk-free rate, inasmuch as the amortization is regulatory. As of this writing, the latter view is being presented by certain academics and has not found much traction among analysts.

Controversy—When to Apply

In keeping with the ASC, an analysis of the (hypothetical) market participant motivations is appropriate to determine when or whether the amortization benefit should be applied. There is a good argument for not applying this factor if it is determined that the market participant buyer would not be able to amortize the asset under Section 197. This might be the case in a stock acquisition where the premise is in-use and Section 197 is unavailable. Other analysts believe that the amortization benefit should be applied in all cases; this position is based on viewing the hypothetical transaction that gives rise to the fair value of the asset as involving an individual asset, where the amortization benefit would typically be available, rather than in the context of an entity acquisition, where the benefit may or may not be available. In any event, it is important to remain current on views espoused by other analysts, regulators, standard setters, and auditors.

Assembled Workforce

The buyer of the acquiree obtained an assembled and trained workforce. Considerable expenditures for recruiting, selecting, and training would be required to replace these employees with individuals of comparable skills and expertise. By acquiring fully trained personnel, the buyer avoided the expenditure required to hire and train equivalent personnel. The unit of account for this asset is all personnel acquired, although, as will be seen, the methodology (unit of valuation) segments the various levels of personnel.

> The ASC specifically prohibits the recognition of the assembled workforce as an intangible asset apart from goodwill.

However, in the application of the multiperiod excess earnings method, which is used to value the company's customer relationships, contributory charges are taken on the fair values of all of the contributory assets acquired in the acquisition. The value of the assembled workforce is calculated so that a contributory charge on that asset may be recognized. However, its fair value is included in goodwill and is not separately recognized.

The highest and best use is in-use. There is no principal market for the asset. The most advantageous market is the universe of potential buyers of the acquiree, as we have determined that the asset has no market on a stand-alone basis. There are no Level 1 or Level 2 inputs available for this asset; thus, we will employ Level 3 inputs.

> The value of the assembled workforce is represented by the assemblage cost avoided. Therefore, the cost approach is the most appropriate valuation technique to value this asset.

Using this approach, the costs associated with employee recruitment, selection, and training provide the measurement of value. The valuation of the acquired assembled workforce is shown in Exhibit 21.9.

Recruiting costs are incurred to obtain a new employee, who may be either untrained or previously trained. The major components of recruiting costs are employment agency fees, advertising, and other recruitment-related expenses. In order to hire most professional-level employees with similar skill sets, an employment agency may be used, which would typically charge a fee based on the starting salary. For the level of employees employed by the company, it is estimated the recruiting costs will run between 20 percent and 30 percent of starting salary, depending on the position. For purposes of this case study, it was assumed that all of the staff and support positions would require the services of a recruiter.

Exhibit 21.9 Valuation of Assembled Workforce (as of December 31, 2009)

NO.	JOB TITLE	STATED PER EMPLOYEE AVERAGE SALARY	20.0% BENEFITS	TOTAL	(1) TRAIN. PER. CLASS	YEARS	33.3% COST	(2) RECRUITING RATE	$	INTERVIEW & H.R.	TOTAL
1	Chief Executive Officer	$500,000	$100,000	$600,000	1	0.167	$ 33,367	30.0%	$ 150,000	$ 1,500	$ 184,867
1	Chief Operating Officer	400,000	80,000	480,000	1	0.167	26,693	30.0%	120,000	1,500	148,193
1	Chief Financial Officer	350,000	70,000	420,000	1	0.167	23,357	30.0%	105,000	1,500	129,857
1	Chief Information Officer	350,000	70,000	420,000	1	0.167	23,357	30.0%	105,000	1,500	129,857
	Department Heads										
1	Sales & Marketing	275,000	55,000	330,000	2	0.250	27,473	30.0%	82,500	750	110,723
1	Engineering/R&D	275,000	55,000	330,000	2	0.250	27,473	30.0%	82,500	750	110,723
1	Human Resources	275,000	55,000	330,000	2	0.250	27,473	30.0%	82,500	750	110,723
1	Finance & Accounting	275,000	55,000	330,000	2	0.250	27,473	30.0%	82,500	750	110,723
	Vice Presidents										
8	Sales & Marketing	150,000	30,000	180,000	2	0.250	119,880	30.0%	360,000	6,000	485,880
4	Engineering/R&D	125,000	25,000	150,000	2	0.250	49,950	30.0%	150,000	3,000	202,950
3	Administration	100,000	20,000	120,000	2	0.250	29,970	30.0%	90,000	2,250	122,220
3	Finance & Accounting	100,000	20,000	120,000	2	0.250	29,970	30.0%	90,000	2,250	122,220
	Staff										
36	Sales & Marketing	60,000	12,000	72,000	1	0.167	144,144	25.0%	540,000	54,000	738,144
18	Engineering/R&D	75,000	15,000	90,000	1	0.167	90,090	25.0%	337,500	27,000	454,590
12	Human Resources	60,000	12,000	72,000	1	0.167	48,048	25.0%	180,000	18,000	246,048
42	Administration	50,000	10,000	60,000	1	0.167	140,140	25.0%	525,000	63,000	728,140
28	Finance & Accounting	75,000	15,000	90,000	1	0.167	140,140	25.0%	525,000	42,000	707,140
	Support										
20	Sales & Marketing	50,000	10,000	60,000	3	0.083	33,167	20.0%	200,000	7,500	240,667
6	Engineering/R&D	50,000	10,000	60,000	3	0.083	9,950	20.0%	60,000	2,250	72,200
8	Human Resources	50,000	10,000	60,000	3	0.083	13,267	20.0%	80,000	3,000	96,267
32	Administration	50,000	10,000	60,000	3	0.083	53,067	20.0%	320,000	12,000	385,067
12	Finance & Accounting	50,000	10,000	60,000	3	0.083	19,900	20.0%	120,000	4,500	144,400
240	Total						$1,138,349		$4,387,500	$255,750	$5,781,599

Replacement Cost of Assembled Workforce	$5,781,599
Less: Taxes 40.0%	(2,312,640)
After Tax Replacement Cost	$3,468,959
Amortization Benefit	
Rate of Return 15.0%	
Tax Rate 40.0%	
Tax Amortization Period (Years) 15	
Amortization Benefit	696,538
Fair Value of Assembled Workforce, Rounded	**$4,000,000**

Footnotes:

(1) Qualified Replacement Training

Class	Training Period	Hours	Interview & H.R. Rate	Amount
1 = 2 months	0.167	20	$75.00	$1,500.00
2 = 3 months	0.250	10	75.00	$ 750.00
3 = 1 month	0.083	5	75.00	$ 375.00

(2) Per Recruiter. Assumes entire Staff and Support are hired through recruiting firms.

Note: Some totals may not foot due to rounding.

Training costs are incurred to train employees and bring them to the level of performance normally expected of an individual in a given position. The training costs of an employee reflect the amount of time inefficiently used by a new employee (inefficiency training cost) and the time inefficiently used by a training supervisor (direct training cost) during the first few months on the job. Training and supervisory costs were estimated by multiplying the fully burdened weekly salary of the employee by the average amount of inefficiency incurred during the training period. The inefficiency estimate used here for training and supervisory costs is 33.3 percent, or one-third of the time. This can vary, depending on the business. Interview costs are estimated based on average hours per employee class, as follows:

Class	Hours
1	20
2	10
3	5

The average fully burdened interview rate is $75 per hour.

The summation of the hiring and training costs results in the total cost to replace the assembled workforce, as shown in Exhibit 21.9. Based on the cost approach, and after adjusting for taxes at 40 percent and adding the amortization tax benefit, the fair value of the assembled workforce is estimated to be approximately $4,000,000 (rounded) as of December 31, 2009. No obsolescence is recognized for this asset in this example.

Trade Name

In this example, the acquiree has one valuable trade name. However, a company may have many trademarks/trade names, some with indefinite lives and some with finite lives. Depending on the purpose and scope of the valuation, each name or mark may be valued separately.

All of the company's products and services are sold under the company trade name, and each major product is identified by this trade name. Upon acquiring the acquiree's assets, the buyer gained and paid for the right to use this trade name. The

ValTip

Trade names and trademarks must be considered individually to determine their remaining useful life. Trade names and trademarks that are associated with a company name or logo (e.g., McDonald's) typically have indefinite lives. Many product trade names and trademarks also will have an indefinite life if no reasonable estimate can be made of the end of the product life (e.g., Coca-Cola). However, the analyst must be careful to find out whether there is a planned phaseout of a product or ascertain whether it can be estimated with reasonable certainty that a name will lose value or be abandoned over time. In such a case, a finite life is suggested and, therefore, an amortization period is warranted. Remember, for tax purposes, generally all intangibles are amortizable over a 15-year life.

name valued in this section enjoys great recognition and prestige in the acquiree's markets. The trade name is recognized as representing the premier company in the industry. In most cases, the trade name identifies the top products available in the marketplace. The use of this trade name is considered critical to the continued success of the company and provides for a seamless and invisible ownership change by maintaining continuity in the minds of customers.

The unit of account for this asset is each trade name. The highest and best use is in-use. There is no principal market for the asset. The most advantageous market is the universe of potential buyers of the acquiree, as we have determined that the asset has no market on a stand-alone basis. There are no Level 1 or Level 2 inputs available for this asset; thus, we will employ market participant inputs (generally Level 3).

To value the trade name, the cost approach and the market approach were both considered but determined not to be feasible valuation techniques here. It can be difficult to accurately identify all of the costs related to re-creating the trade name and building recognition, a factor required to use the cost approach. Trademarks and trade names rarely sell separately in the marketplace; thus, information required to perform a market approach valuation is rarely available. A comprehensive method to value the name is a variant of the income approach known as the relief from royalty method. The premise of this valuation methodology is the assumption that an owner/operator of a company would be compelled to pay the rightful owner of the intangible asset (such as a trade name) if the owner/operator did not have the legal right to utilize the subject intellectual property. Because ownership of a trade name relieves a company from making such payments (royalties), the financial performance of the firm is enhanced to the extent that these royalty payments are avoided. The royalty is typically expressed as a pretax percentage of revenues.

ValTip

The relief from royalty method relies on two general types of inputs—the royalty rate and the revenue forecast.

The rate could be a Level 1 or more likely a Level 2 input, but the forecast is Level 3. Because the forecast is a significant input, the measurement will be a Level 3 measurement.

The relief from royalty method equates the value of a trademark or trade name to the portion of the company's earnings that represents the pretax royalty that may have been paid for using the trade name. For the name valued, we have determined that a royalty rate of 1 percent is applicable, stated as a percentage of sales (see Exhibit 21.10).

This pretax royalty rate was selected based on observed royalty rates in the market (market participants) and on an analysis of the rate that the company's margins could support. We observed market data in our own proprietary database documenting the range of royalty rates for trademarks to be 1 percent to 10 percent, with the median at 4 percent. Addendum 2 "Intellectual Property" at the end of this chapter presents a summary of licensing databases and royalty rates and the use of that data.

Thus, based largely on our review of publicly available data on trademark/trade name licensing transactions and a comparison of the name recognition between the trade name and the guideline royalties, a 1 percent average royalty rate was selected to value the trade name. The BEA (shown in Exhibit 21.6) indicates that there are ample earnings to allow for this level of royalty payments and still earn a fair return on sales. That is, the acquiree could easily pay these royalties if it did not own the right to use the trade name.

The rights to use the trade name transfer to the buyer in perpetuity, giving it an indefinite life. The fair value of the trade name is the present value of the royalties projected for the 10-year period 2010–2019, plus the present value of the terminal at the end of the 10-year period, plus the amortization tax benefit. It is important to note that not all trade names will be indefinitely lived. A 15 percent rate of return was chosen to reflect a risk assessment that the trade name was approximately as risky as the business overall.

Based on our analysis as presented in Exhibit 21.10, the aggregate fair value of the trade name as of the valuation date was $59,000,000 (rounded).

Noncompete Agreement

The purchase agreement identifies a separate agreement not to compete. The purchase agreement specifies that, for a period of three years commencing at the date of the purchase transaction, the sellers will not engage in any activity that competes with the acquired company. The unit of account for this asset is each noncompete agreement. Our case study demonstrates one.

The highest and best use is in-use. There is no principal market for the asset. The most advantageous market is the universe of potential buyers of the acquiree, as we have determined that the asset has no market on a stand-alone basis. There are no Level 1 or Level 2 inputs available for this asset; thus, we will employ market participant inputs (Level 3).

The valuation of noncompete agreements is typically performed by preparing two discounted cash flow models—one that is based on the market participant BEA and assumes a noncompete agreement is in place and a second that assumes that the noncompete agreement is not in place.

Presumably, in the absence of such an agreement, the sellers would be free to compete and take business away from the acquired company, and perhaps cause the company to spend more to defend its market position, thus reducing its margins. The value of having the noncompete agreement, then, is the difference in the present value of two cash flow projections, one whose underlying assumptions reflect competition from the covenantees, and one that assumes no competition, as shown in Exhibit 21.11.

Compared with the cash flow scenario representing the status quo and that mirrors the BEA (i.e., with a noncompete agreement in place), the cash flow scenario under the assumption that there is no agreement results in reduced cash flows due to the effects of competition. Under the assumption of competition, the seller could negatively impact the acquiree, affecting the growth of sales (i.e., the seller, if not under a noncompete agreement, could theoretically go to work for a competitor or start a new company and cause the acquired company to grow more slowly than

Exhibit 21.10 Valuation of Trade Name (as of December 31, 2009)

				FORECAST		
		2010	**2011**	**2012**	**2013**	**2014**
(1) Net Sales		$575,000	$ 661,250	$ 743,906	$ 818,297	$ 900,127
Pretax Relief from Royalty	1.0%	$ 5,750	$ 6,613	$ 7,439	$ 8,183	$ 9,001
Income Tax Liability	40.0%	(2,300)	(2,645)	(2,976)	(3,273)	(3,600)
After-tax Royalty		$ 3,450	$ 3,968	$ 4,463	$ 4,910	$ 5,401
(2) Present Value Factor at Discount Rate	15.0%	0.9325	0.8109	0.7051	0.6131	0.5332
Present Value of Royalties Avoided		$ 3,217	$ 3,218	$ 3,147	$ 3,010	$ 2,880

				FORECAST		
		2015	**2016**	**2017**	**2018**	**2019**
(1) Net Sales		$967,636	$1,040,209	$1,118,224	$1,202,091	$1,292,248
Pretax Relief from Royalty	1.0%	$ 9,676	$ 10,402	$ 11,182	$ 12,021	$ 12,922
Income Tax Liability	40.0%	(3,870)	(4,161)	(4,473)	(4,808)	(5,169)
After-tax Royalty		$ 5,806	$ 6,241	$ 6,709	$ 7,213	$ 7,753
(2) Present Value Factor at Discount Rate	15.0%	0.4636	0.4031	0.3506	0.3048	0.2651
Present Value of Royalties Avoided		$ 2,692	$ 2,516	$ 2,352	$ 2,199	$ 2,055

Sum of Present Value of Royalties Avoided: 2010–2019	$ 27,286

Terminal Calculation:

2019 After-tax Royalty		$ 7,753
2020 After-tax Royalty, Assuming Growth of	5.0%	8,141
(3) Terminal Capitalization Rate, Perpetual Growth		10.0%
2020 Terminal Value		$ 81,410
Present Value Factor at 2019		0.2651
Fair Market Value of Terminal		
Present Value of Trade Name Royalty Flows		21,582
		48,868
Amortization Benefit		
Discount Rate	15.0%	
Tax Rate	40.0%	
Tax Amortization Period (Years)	15	
Amortization Benefit		9,812
Fair Value of Trade Name, Rounded		**$ 59,000**

Footnotes:
(1) See Business Enterprise Analysis—Cash Flow Forecast (Exhibit 21.6).
(2) Based on mid-period assumption. Discount rate for this asset determined to be 15.0%.
(3) Calculated by subtracting the Growth Rate of 5.0% from the Discount Rate of 15.0%.

Note: Some totals may not foot due to rounding.

Exhibit 21.11 Valuation of Noncompete Agreement (as of December 31, 2009)

Comparison: Scenario I and Scenario II			FORECAST			
		2010	2011	2012	2013	2014
Debt-free Net Cash Flow						
(1) With Restrictive Covenant		$40,452	$55,970	$60,642	$66,042	$70,097
(2) Without Restrictive Covenant		45,009	55,615	45,683	54,884	70,097
(3) Reduction in Debt-free Net Cash Flow		($ 4,557)	$ 355	$14,959	$11,158	($ 0)
(4) Present Value Factor at Discount Rate	15.0%	0.9325	0.8109	0.7051	0.6131	0.5332
Present Value of Cash Flow		($ 4,249)	$ 288	$10,548	$ 6,841	$ 0
Sum, Present Value of Cash Flows		$13,428				
Amortization Benefit						
Discount Rate	15.0%					
Tax Rate	40.0%					
Tax Amortization Period (Years)	15					
Amortization Benefit		2,696				
Raw Value of Noncompete Agreement		$16,124				
(5) Probability of Competing		50.0%				
Fair Value of Noncompete Agreement, Rounded		**$ 8,000**				

Footnotes:

(1) See Projected Cash Flows Over Competitive Time Horizon, Scenario I: With Noncompete Agreement with Seller In Place (Exhibit 21.12).

(2) See Projected Cash Flows Over Competitive Time Horizon, Scenario II: Without Noncompete Agreement with Seller In Place (Exhibit 21.13).

(3) Although this asset has a life of three years, there is a reduction in debt-free net cash flow in year four to account for the additional amount of Incremental Working Capital required to fund the working capital balance to meet projections.

(4) Based on mid-period assumption. Discount rate for this asset determined to be 15.0%.

(5) Per Management.

Note: Some totals may not foot due to rounding.

otherwise projected). The acquiree would then incur more marketing and other expenses. Thus, the net sales under the changed assumptions are:

Net Sales	With Noncompete Agreement in Place (Exhibit 21.12)	Without Noncompete Agreement in Place (Exhibit 21.13)
2010	$575,000,000	$517,500,000
2011	661,250,000	529,000,000
2012	743,906,000	669,515,000
2013	818,297,000	818,297,000
2014	900,127,000	900,127,000

Variable expense percentages are assumed to be the same under both scenarios (Illustration purposes only; see Exhibits 21.12 and 21.13).

Net cash flows with and without the noncompete agreement in place are presented in Exhibit 21.11. The present value of the cash flows, including amortization benefit, is $16,124,000. This amount is multiplied by a factor that takes into account the covenantee's perceived likelihood of competing, if the company hypothetically were not so constrained (in acquisitions where potential competition is a real risk, it is rare that a seller would not be required to agree to a noncompete contract). Factors to consider in assessing this issue include age of covenantee, health, resources, ability, and desire to compete. Here, we estimate the factor at 50 percent. Thus, the fair value of the noncompete agreement is determined to be (rounded) $8,000,000.

Technology (Existing and In-Process) and Customer Relationships

The company's technology, both existing and in-process, and its customer relationships are the critical value drivers, with the other assets playing a supporting role. The units of account for these assets are each category of technology and customers. In our case study, we assume two major technologies and one type of customer relationship.

ValTip

> The valuation method known as the multiperiod excess earnings method (MPEEM) is generally reserved for the value drivers, the intangibles with the most direct relationship to the revenue and cash flow streams of an enterprise.

But what is the analyst to do when it is not clear which of the value drivers are preeminent?

Here, the technology, both existing and in-process, can lay claim to being the assets with the most direct relationship to revenues and cash flows. However, an equally compelling argument can be made on behalf of the customer relationships—that group of loyal patrons who, year after year (albeit with some annual attrition), purchase the company's products and services and provide its lifeblood.

A controversial aspect of the MPEEM occurs when there are two value drivers and the MPEEM is used to value both. There is diversity of practice, and many valuation specialists have heretofore used simultaneous MPEEMs. In its newly released *Best Practices for Valuations in Financial Reporting: The Identification of Contributory*

Exhibit 21.12 Projected Cash Flows over Competitive Time Horizon: Scenario 1

			FORECAST		
	2010	2011	2012	2013	2014
(1) Total Revenues	$ 575,000	$ 661,250	$ 743,906	$ 818,297	$ 900,127
(1) Cost of Goods Sold	(287,500)	(324,013)	(364,514)	(400,965)	(441,062)
(1) Operating Expenses	(218,500)	(244,663)	(275,245)	(302,770)	(333,047)
EBITDA	$ 69,000	$ 92,575	$ 104,147	$ 114,562	$ 126,018
EBITDA Margin	*12.0%*	*14.0%*	*14.0%*	*14.0%*	*14.0%*
(1) Depreciation (MACRS)	($ 13,158)	($ 22,967)	($ 18,008)	($ 14,646)	($ 12,434)
(2) Amortization of Intangibles (Tax)	(26,971)	(26,971)	(26,971)	(26,971)	(26,971)
EBIT	$ 28,871	$ 42,637	$ 59,168	$ 72,945	$ 86,613
EBIT Margin	*5.0%*	*6.4%*	*8.0%*	*8.9%*	*9.6%*
Income Taxes 40.0%	($ 11,548)	($ 17,055)	($ 23,667)	($ 29,178)	($ 34,645)
Debt-free Net Income	$ 17,323	$ 25,582	$ 35,501	$ 43,767	$ 51,968
Debt-free Net Income Margin	*3.0%*	*3.9%*	*4.8%*	*5.3%*	*5.8%*
Net Cash Flow					
Depreciation	$ 13,158	$ 22,967	$ 18,008	$ 14,646	$ 12,434
Amortization	26,971	26,971	26,971	26,971	26,971
(1) Capital Expenditures	(5,750)	(6,613)	(7,439)	(8,183)	(9,001)
(3) Incremental Working Capital	(11,250)	(12,938)	(12,398)	(11,159)	(12,274)
Debt-free Net Cash Flow	$ 40,452	$ 55,970	$ 60,642	$ 66,042	$ 70,097

Footnotes:
(1) See Business Enterprise Analysis—Assumptions (Exhibit 21.5).
(2) See Business Enterprise Analysis—Cash Flow Forecast (Exhibit 21.6).
(3) Incremental Working Capital in 2010 reflects a lower provision than shown in the Business Enterprise Analysis—Cash Flow Forecast (Exhibit 21.6) (BEA) because the BEA provision normalizes from an actual balance, while the provision for the noncompete agreement only accounts for the incremental amount necessary based on the growth of revenues.

Note: Some totals may not foot due to rounding.

Assets and the Calculation of Economic Rents, the Intangible Asset Working Group of the Appraisal Foundation says:

> The Working Group recognizes that there has been diversity in practice as to whether two subject intangible assets that are each valued using a MPEEM should reflect a cross charge against one another as a contributory asset. For example, both customer-related assets and technology assets are often simultaneously valued using this method with such cross charges reflecting an attempt to adjust for overlapping revenues/cash flows. Commentary by respondents to the discussion draft which preceded this document varied widely on the applicability of a method incorporating such simultaneous cross charges.
>
> The Working Group strongly believes that the use of simultaneous application of the MPEEM to two intangible assets should be avoided whenever possible. The best method for avoiding overlapping revenues/cash flows would be to "revenue/cash flow split" the PFI related to the two subject intangible assets such that their analyses are mutually exclusive. In such a case neither subject intangible asset should be charged for the other.
>
> When it is not possible to revenue/cash flow split the PFI, the Working Group believes that the next best alternative is to value one subject intangible asset using the MPEEM and the other asset using an alternative method (e.g., relief from royalty, cost approach, Greenfield method). In this case, the asset valued using the MPEEM would be charged for the other asset to the extent that the other asset is contributory or to the extent that the other asset's value is derived from overlapping revenues/cash flows.
>
> When a simultaneous application of the MPEEM cannot be avoided, the Working Group believes that one asset should be treated as the "primary" asset due to its high level of importance in generating the cash flows of the entity. The second subject intangible asset should be treated as the "secondary" asset, due to being of lesser importance. The "primary" asset should not be charged for the secondary asset. However, the secondary asset should be charged for the primary asset. This approach, while not perfect, avoids the potential for double counting the charge and improperly estimating the value of one or the other subject intangible asset. The designation of subject intangible assets as being either primary or secondary should be based on a qualitative consideration of the relative importance of one or the other of the subject intangible assets to the entity.
>
> The Working Group believes that application of simultaneous cross charges results in more than one solution to MPEEM calculation, rendering them inappropriate for use in estimating fair value.[63]

Where data is available to enable reasonably supportable forecasts, some analysts might employ an analysis where projected cash flows are segmented into four areas:

1. Current customers buying new technology (value falls to customer relationships)
2. New customers buying existing technology (technology)

---

[63] The Appraisal Foundation, *Best Practices for Valuations in Financial Reporting: The Identification of Contributory Assets and the Calculation of Economic Rents,* Intangible Asset Working Group, Exposure Draft (February 25, 2009) at 3.5.05–3.5.09.

Exhibit 21.13 Projected Cash Flows over Competitive Time Horizion: Scenario 2

				FORECAST		
		2010	2011	2012	2013	2014
(1)	Total Revenues	$ 575,000	$ 661,250	$ 743,906	$ 818,297	$ 900,127
	Decline in Revenues Caused by Competition of Seller	10.0%	20.0%	10.0%	0.0%	0.0%
	Decline in Revenues	$ 57,500	$ 132,250	$ 74,391	$ 0	$ 0
	Adjusted Base Revenues	517,500	529,000	669,515	818,297	900,127
(2)	Cost of Goods Sold	(258,750)	(259,210)	(328,062)	(400,965)	(441,062)
(3)	Operating Expenses	(196,650)	(195,730)	(247,721)	(302,770)	(333,047)
	EBITDA	$ 62,100	$ 74,060	$ 93,732	$ 114,562	$ 126,018
	EBITDA Margin	*12.0%*	*14.0%*	*14.0%*	*14.0%*	*14.0%*
(4)	Depreciation	($ 11,903)	($ 18,515)	($ 16,068)	($ 14,646)	($ 12,434)
(5)	Amortization of Intangibles (Tax)	(26,971)	(26,971)	(26,971)	(26,971)	(26,971)
	EBIT	$ 23,227	$ 28,574	$ 50,693	$ 72,945	$ 86,613
	EBIT Margin	*4.0%*	*4.3%*	*6.8%*	*8.9%*	*9.6%*
	Income Taxes 40.0%	($ 9,291)	($ 11,430)	($ 20,277)	($ 29,178)	($ 34,645)
	Debt-free Net Income	$ 13,936	$ 17,144	$ 30,416	$ 43,767	$ 51,968
	Debt-free Net Income Margin	*2.7%*	*3.2%*	*4.5%*	*5.3%*	*5.8%*

Net Cash Flow

Depreciation	$11,903	$18,515	$16,068	$14,646	$12,434
Amortization	26,971	26,971	26,971	26,971	26,971
(6) Capital Expenditures	(5,175)	(5,290)	(6,695)	(8,183)	(9,001)
(7) Incremental Working Capital	(2,625)	(1,725)	(21,077)	(22,317)	(12,274)
Debt-free Net Cash Flow	$45,009	$55,615	$45,683	$54,884	$70,097

Footnotes:

(1) See Business Enterprise Analysis—Assumptions [Exhibit 21.5].

(2) Calculated at Cost of Sales Percentage (see Business Enterprise Analysis—Assumptions [Exhibit 21.5]) for Adjusted Base Revenues.

(3) Calculated at Operating Expenses Percentage (see Business Enterprise Analysis - Assumptions [Exhibit 21.5]) for Adjusted Base Revenues.

(4) Depreciation gives effect to an estimated reduction due to reduced net sales, which it is assumed would result in reduced capital expenditures.

(5) See Business Enterprise Analysis—Cash Flow Forecast (Exhibit 21.6).

(6) Calculated at Capital Expenditures Percentage (see Business Enterprise Analysis - Assumptions [Exhibit 21.5]) for Adjusted Base Revenues.

(7) Incremental Working Capital in 2010 reflects a lower provision than shown in the Business Enterprise Analysis—Cash Flow Forecast (Exhibit 21.6) (BEA) because the BEA provision normalizes from an actual balance, while the provision for the noncompete agreement only accounts for the incremental amount necessary based on the growth of revenues. Incremental Working Capital in other years reflects different amounts than shown in the BEA in order to fund working capital balances based on different revenue projections.

Note: Some totals may not foot due to rounding.

Net cash flows with and without the noncompete agreement in place are presented in Exhibit 21.11. The present value of the cash flows, including amortization benefit, is $16,124. This amount is multiplied by a factor that takes into account the covenantee's perceived likelihood of competing, if the company hypothetically was not so constrained. (It is rare that a seller would not be required to agree to a noncompete contract.) Factors to consider in assessing this issue include age of covenantee, health, resources, ability, and desire to compete. Here, we estimate the factor at 50 percent. Thus, the fair value of the noncompete agreement is determined to be (rounded) $8,000,000.

3. Current customers buying existing technology (percent to customer relationships, percent to technology)
4. New customers buying new technology (goodwill)

The advantage of this method is that discrete cash flows are developed for each asset, but at the cost of additional judgement. Also, in-process research and development would get shortchanged here, as there is no provision for allocating cash flows to that asset (the first and last area would have to provide for that allocation).

Thus, as with many appraisal issues, the analyst must make an informed judgment based on facts and circumstances. In this case study, the acquired company's customers are its lifeblood and over time have been loyal to the company through many iterations of technology and platforms. For purposes of this analysis, we have determined that the company's customer relationships are the primary value driver, and while technology, both existing and in-process, supports the product and service lines, this asset group is subservient to the customer relationships.

Therefore, we will employ the MPEEM to value the customer relationships, but not the two technology assets (existing technology and IPR&D). The technology assets will be valued using a relief from royalty method.

Existing Technology

As with the trade name, we have employed a relief from royalty method to value the existing technology. The unit of account for this asset is the technology in its entirety. The highest and best use is in-use. There is no principal market for the asset. The most advantageous market is the universe of potential buyers of the acquiree, as we have determined that the asset has no market on a stand-alone basis.

Again, the premise of this valuation methodology is the assumption that an owner/operator of a company would be compelled to pay the rightful owner of the intangible asset if the owner/operator did not have the legal right to utilize the subject asset. Because ownership of the existing technology relieves the company from making such payments (royalties), the financial performance of the company is enhanced to the extent that such royalty payments are avoided. The royalty is typically expressed as a pretax percentage of revenues.

The relief from royalty method relies on two general types of inputs—the royalty rate and the revenue forecast. The rate could be a Level 1 or more likely a Level 2 input, but the forecast is Level 3. Because the forecast is a significant input, the measurement will be a Level 3 measurement.

The relief from royalty method equates the value of technology to the portion of the company's earnings that represents the pretax royalty that may have been paid for using the technology. For the existing technology valued, we have determined that a royalty rate of 10 percent is applicable, stated as a percentage of sales.

This pretax royalty rate was selected based on observed royalty rates in the market (market participants) and on an analysis of the rate that the company's margins could support. We observed market data in our own proprietary database documenting the range of royalty rates for technology up to 35 percent, with the median at 10 percent.

Thus, based largely on our review of publicly available data on technology licensing transactions and a comparison of the existing technology to the guideline royalties, a 10 percent average royalty rate was selected to value the existing technology. A probability analysis (not shown) indicates that there are ample earnings to allow for this level of royalty payments and still earn a fair return on sales once adjustments are made to the income stream to remove expenses not associated with the existing technology. That is, the acquiree could easily pay these royalties if it did not own the right to use the existing technology.

The rights to use the existing technology transfer to the buyer in perpetuity, but the life of the asset is limited in that the existing technology is expected to produce revenues only through 2014. The fair value of the existing technology is the present value of the royalties projected for the five-year period 2010–2014, plus the amortization benefit. The discount rate of 18 percent reflects the higher relative risk of this asset compared with the business overall and the other intangibles.

Based on our analysis, we concluded that the fair value of the acquired technology on the valuation date was $75,000,000 (rounded), as shown in Exhibit 21.14. As with the other intangible assets, the value is determined after deducting an income tax charge and adding an amortization tax benefit. The asset's remaining useful life is five years, but the indicated survivor curve provides a potential means to record future amortization consistent with the contribution to cash flows in each year, rather than by the straight-line method.

In-Process Research and Development

The value of in-process research and development (IPR&D) was also estimated using a relief from royalty method. The unit of account for this asset is the IPR&D project. The highest and best use is in-use. There is no principal market for the asset. The most advantageous market is the universe of potential buyers of the acquiree, as we have determined that the asset has no market on a stand-alone basis. There are no Level 1 or Level 2 inputs available for this asset; thus, we will employ market participant inputs (Level 3).

Similarly to our methodology for valuing the technology, a relief from royalty model was constructed, starting with expected sales based on the technology that was in-process at the valuation date (see Exhibit 21.15). For simplicity, we are assuming that the IPR&D will be completed in early 2010 at no material additional cost. After completion, the IPR&D will be classified to technology. It is projected to produce sales of $60,000,000 in 2010. Sales are further projected to increase in 2011, then decline over time. Similar to the technology valuation, a royalty rate of 10 percent was applied.

It is assumed for purposes of this example that the IPR&D is a brand-new, stand-alone technology not supported by the base or core technology, defined as technology that has value through its use or continued reuse within a product family. If an IPR&D project is supported by a core or base technology, a contributory charge must be assessed. We selected a market participant discount rate of 24 percent to reflect the additional risk of the unproven technology. A six-year remaining useful life was estimated. After accounting for the amortization tax benefit, we concluded that the fair value of the IPR&D as of December 31, 2009, was $18,000,000 (see Exhibit 21.15).

Multiperiod Excess Earnings Method

ValTip

The MPEEM measures the present value of the future earnings to be generated during the remaining lives of the subject assets.

Exhibit 21.14 Calculation of Existing Technology (as of December 31, 2009)

		FORECAST				
		2010	2011	2012	2013	2014
(1) Net Sales — Existing Technology		$515,000	$318,270	$273,182	$196,964	$115,928
Pretax Relief from Royalty	10.0%	51,500	31,827	27,318	19,696	11,593
Income Tax Liability	40.0%	(20,600)	(12,731)	(10,927)	(7,878)	(4,637)
After-tax Royalty		30,900	19,096	16,391	11,818	6,956
(2) Present Value Factor at Discount Rate	18.0%	0.9206	0.7801	0.6611	0.5603	0.4748
Present Value of Royalties Avoided		$ 28,447	$ 14,897	$ 10,836	$ 6,622	$ 3,303
Sum of Present Values, 2010–2014		$ 64,105				
Amortization Benefit						
Discount Rate	18.0%					
Tax Rate	40.0%					
Tax Amortization Period (Years)	15					
Amortization Benefit		11,091				
Fair Value of Technology, Rounded		**$ 75,000**				

Footnotes:
(1) Based on management's forecast. Sales attributable to the existing technology, which are 100.0% of company sales in 2009, are projected to decline over time as the technology becomes obsolete and competitors increasingly impact sales.

(2) Based on mid-period assumption. Discount rate for this asset determined to be 18.0%.

Note: Some totals may not foot due to rounding.

Exhibit 21.15 Valuation of IPR&D (as of December 31, 2009)

				FORECAST			
		2010	2011	2012	2013	2014	2015
(1) Net Sales—In-process Research and Development		$60,000	$104,640	$98,771	$89,440	$64,098	$37,061
Pretax Relief from Royalty	10.0%	6,000	10,464	9,877	8,944	6,410	3,706
Income Tax Liability	40.0%	(2,400)	(4,186)	(3,951)	(3,578)	(2,564)	(1,482)
After-tax Royalty		3,600	6,278	5,926	5,366	3,846	2,224
(2) Present Value Factor at Discount Rate	24.0%	0.8980	0.7242	0.584	0.471	0.3798	0.3063
Present Value of Royalties Avoided		$ 3,233	$ 4,547	$ 3,461	$ 2,527	$ 1,461	$ 681
Sum of Present Values, 2010–2015		$15,910					
Amortization Benefit							
Discount Rate	24.0%						
Tax Rate	40.0%						
Tax Amortization Period (Years)	15						
Amortization Benefit		2,145					
Fair Value of IPR&D, Rounded		**$18,000**					

Footnotes:
(1) Based on management's forecast.
(2) Based on mid-period assumption. Discount rate for this asset determined to be 24.0%.

Note: Some totals may not foot due to rounding.

Using the market participant BEA as a starting point, we calculate pretax cash flows attributable to the acquired asset(s) as of the valuation date. As with the BEA, deductions are made for cost of goods sold and operating expenses. We then take contributory charges on the other identified assets.

As already noted, returns on and of contributory asset charges represent charges for the use of contributory assets employed to support the subject assets and help generate revenue. The cash flows from the subject assets must support charges for replacement of assets employed and provide a fair return to the owners of capital. The respective rates of return, while based on judgement, are directly related to the analyst's assessment of the risk inherent in each asset.

The following list from the IPR&D Practice Aid[64] provides examples of assets typically treated as contributory assets, and suggested bases for determining the fair return. Generally, it is presumed that the return of the asset (reflecting the "using up" of the asset) is reflected in operating costs when applicable (e.g., depreciation expense). The contributory asset charge is "the product of the asset's fair value and the required rate of return on the asset."

Asset	Basis of Charge
Working capital	Short-term lending rates for market participants (e.g., working capital lines or short-term revolver rates).
Fixed assets (e.g., property, plant, and equipment)	Financing rates for similar assets for market participants (e.g., terms offered by vendor financing), or rates implied by operating leases, capital leases, or both, typically segregated between returns of (i.e., recapture of investment) and returns on assets.
Workforce (which is not recognized separately from goodwill), customer lists, trademarks, and trade names	Weighted average cost of capital for young, single-product companies (may be lower than the discount rate applicable to a particular project).
Patents	WACC for young, single-product companies (may be lower than discount rate applicable to a particular project). In cases where risk of realizing economic value of patent is close to or the same as risk of realizing a project, rates would be equivalent to that of the project.
Other intangibles, including base (or core) technology	Rates appropriate to the risk of the subject intangible. When market evidence is available, it should be used. In other cases, rates should be consistent with the relative risk of other assets in the analysis and should be higher for riskier assets.

It is important to note that the assumed fair value of the contributory asset is not necessarily static over time. Working capital and tangible assets may fluctuate throughout the forecast period, and contributory asset charges (CACs) are typically taken on estimated average balances in each year. Average balances of tangible assets, subject to accelerated depreciation (as is the case here), may decline as the depreciation outstrips capital expenditures in the early years of the forecast. While the carrying value of amortizable intangible assets declines over time, there is a presumption that such assets are replenished each year, so the contributory asset charge usually takes the form of a fixed charge each year. An exception to this rule is a noncompete agreement, which is not replenished and does not function as a supporting asset past its expiration period.

---

[64] Larson et al., *Assets Acquired in a Business Combination*, at 5.3.64.

The return requirements used here are after-tax and are:

Contributory Asset Charges	Rate
Working capital	4.0%
Land and building, net	6.5%
Machinery and equipment, net	7.5%
Software	16.0%
Assembled workforce	15.0%
Noncompete agreement	15.0%

The discount rates shown here are for illustrative purposes only and represent general relationships among assets. Actual rates must be selected based on consideration of the facts and circumstances related to each category of asset as determined based on market participants. The CAC calculations are shown in Exhibit 21.16.

For those assets valued using a relief from royalty methodology, the CAC is calculated by applying the royalty rate to revenues projected for the subject assets:

Contributory Asset Charge	Rate
Trade name	1.0%
Technology (existing and IPR&D)	10.0%

Required returns were deducted from the cash flows. Returns on working capital and fixed assets are taken on the average balances for each year in the projection period, as determined in the development of the BEA. The return of assets is satisfied through the replenishment of the assets through ongoing expenditures. Contributory charges on the intangible assets are taken on the fair values at acquisition. The returns of these assets are satisfied by that portion of operating expenses that relate to the replenishment of the various intangibles.

Customer Relationships

The customer relationships were judged to be the critical value driver, and the MPEEM was employed to value this asset. The unit of account for this asset is total customers. The highest and best use is in-use. There is no principal market for the asset. The most advantageous market is the universe of potential buyers of the acquiree, as we have determined that the asset has no market on a stand-alone basis. There are no Level 1 or Level 2 inputs available for this asset; thus, we will employ market participant inputs (Level 3). In applying the MPEEM to the valuation of the company's customer relationships, we employed as a starting point a projection of future revenues attributable to existing customers. As part of the cash flow projection, a remaining useful life was estimated to be seven years, based on an analysis of sales statistics over a five-year historical period and conversations with management. The seven-year life produces a survivor curve whose survivorship is forecast to decline on a straight-line basis (illustration purposes only).

Using a discount rate of 17 percent, and after adding the amortization tax benefit, the fair value of this asset was determined to be $93,000,000 (rounded) (see Exhibit 21.17).

Exhibit 21.16 Valuation of Customer Relationships (as of December 31, 2009)

I. Asset Balances

				FORECAST			
	2010	2011	2012	2013	2014	2015	2016
Contributory Assets Customer Relationships							
Net Working Capital	$ 72,125	$ 92,719	$105,387	$117,165	$128,882	$140,082	$ 150,588
Land and Building, Net	36,644	38,029	39,605	41,357	43,277	45,349	47,555
Machinery and Equipment, Net	80,652	67,386	52,348	42,080	35,212	29,620	23,716
Acquired Software	46,000	46,000	46,000	46,000	46,000	46,000	46,000
Assembled Workforce	4,000	4,000	4,000	4,000	4,000	4,000	4,000
Noncompete Agreement	8,000	8,000	8,000	0	0	0	0

II. CAC Based on Asset Balances

	Rate				FORECAST			
		2010	2011	2012	2013	2014	2015	2016
Net Working Capital	4.0%	$ 2,885	$ 3,709	$ 4,215	$ 4,687	$ 5,155	$ 5,603	$ 6,024
Land and Building, Net	6.5%	2,382	2,472	2,574	2,688	2,813	2,948	3,091
Machinery and Equipment, Net	7.5%	6,049	5,054	3,926	3,156	2,641	2,222	1,779
Acquired Software	16.0%	7,360	7,360	7,360	7,360	7,360	7,360	7,360
Assembled Workforce	15.0%	600	600	600	600	600	600	600
Noncompete Agreement	15.0%	1,200	1,200	1,200	0	0	0	0
CAC Based on Asset Balances		$ 20,476	$ 20,395	$ 19,875	$ 18,491	$ 18,569	$ 18,733	$ 18,854
Total BEV Revenues		$575,000	$661,250	$743,906	$818,297	$900,127	$967,636	$1,040,209
CAC % of Revenues		3.60%	3.10%	2.70%	2.30%	2.10%	1.90%	1.80%
Customer Relationships		2010	2011	2012	2013	2014	2015	2016
Revenue Forecast (Exhibit 21.17)	A	$487,725	$433,283	$372,177	$303,877	$227,817	$143,390	49,952
Total CAC % of Revenues for Customers	B	3.60%	3.10%	2.70%	2.30%	2.10%	1.90%	1.80%
CAC—Customers	A × B	$ 17,558	$ 13,432	$ 10,049	$ 6,989	$ 4,784	$ 2,724	$ 899

Exhibit 21.17 Valuation of Customer Relationships (as of December 31, 2009)

		ACTUAL	FORECAST						
		2009	2010	2011	2012	2013	2014	2015	2016
(1) Net Sales - Surviving Existing Customer Relationships			$ 487,725	$ 433,283	$ 372,177	$ 303,877	$ 227,817	$ 143,390	$ 49,952
(2) Cost of Sales		($250,000)	(243,863)	(212,309)	(182,367)	(148,900)	(111,630)	(70,261)	(24,476)
Gross Profit		250,000	243,862	220,974	189,810	154,977	116,187	73,129	25,476
(3) Operating Expenses	10.0%	(160,000)	(121,931)	(103,988)	(89,322)	(72,930)	(54,676)	(34,414)	(11,988)
(4) Depreciation (MACRS), Allocated		(7,067)	(5,580)	(7,524)	(4,506)	(2,720)	(1,573)	(984)	(341)
Technology Royalty	1.0%		(48,773)	(43,328)	(37,218)	(30,388)	(22,782)	(14,339)	(4,995)
Trade Name Royalty			(4,877)	(4,333)	(3,722)	(3,039)	(2,278)	(1,434)	(500)
Total Expenses		(167,067)	(181,161)	(159,173)	(134,768)	(109,077)	(81,309)	(51,171)	(17,824)
Taxable Income		82,933	62,701	61,801	55,042	45,900	34,878	21,958	7,652
Income Taxes	40.0%	(33,173)	(25,080)	(24,720)	(22,017)	(18,360)	(13,951)	(8,783)	(3,061)
Net Income		$ 49,760	$ 37,621	$ 37,081	$ 33,025	$ 27,540	$ 20,927	$ 13,175	$ 4,591
(5) Cash Flow Attributable to Existing Customer Relationships									
Contributory Asset Charges			$ 37,621	$ 37,081	$ 33,025	$ 27,540	$ 20,927	$ 13,175	$ 4,591
			17,558	13,432	10,049	6,989	4,784	2,724	899
After-tax Cash Flow			$ 20,063	$ 23,649	$ 22,976	$ 20,551	$ 16,143	$ 10,451	$ 3,692
(6) Present Value Factor at Discount Rate	17.0%		0.9245	0.7902	0.6754	0.5772	0.4934	0.4217	0.3604
Present Value of Cash Flows			$ 18,548	$ 18,687	$ 15,518	$ 1 1,862	$ 7,965	$ 4,407	$ 1,331
Sum of Present Values, 2010-2016			$ 78,318						
Amortization Benefit									
Discount Rate	17.0%								
Tax Rate	40.0%								
Tax Amortization Period (Years)	15								
Amortization Benefit			14,210						
Fair Value of Customer Relationships, Rounded			**$ 93,000**						

Footnotes:

(1) Assumes sales to existing customers will increase at a rate of 5.0% (to account for inflation and some real growth), before considering attrition.

(2) Calculated at Cost of Sales Percentage (see Business Enterprise Analysis—Assumptions [Exhibit 21.5]) for Net Sales—Existing Customer Relationships.

(3) Calculated at Operating Expenses Percentage (see Business Enterprise Analysis—Assumptions [Exhibit 21.5]) for Net Sales—Existing Customer Relationships, excluding expenses of a) 6.0% for the solicitation of potential new customers to reflect that existing customers should not be burdened by the expense of developing new customers and b) 7.0% to remove new technology development expenses to avoid double counting the contributory asset charge, as the charge is calculated on a constant, non-amortizing balance, which effectively recognizes the cost of developing new technology.

(4) See Business Enterprise Analysis—Assumptions (Exhibit 21.5).

(5) See Calculation of Contributory Asset Charges (Exhibit 21.16).

(6) Based on mid-period assumption. Discount rate for this asset determined to be 17.0%.

Note: Some totals may not foot due to rounding.

Valuation of Goodwill

In the valuation of a successful business enterprise, there are often intangible assets that cannot be separately identified. These intangible assets are generally referred to as goodwill. The term *goodwill*, however, is sometimes used to describe the aggregate of all of the intangible assets of a business (such as for tax purposes).

For financial reporting purposes, included in the goodwill value is the fair value of the assembled workforce of $4,000,000. Based on our analysis, we concluded that the value to be assigned to goodwill on December 31, 2009, was $105,570,000 (see Exhibit 21.18).

In summary, goodwill is calculated as follows:

Consideration transferred		$474,570,000
Fair value of noncontrolling interest		0
Previously held interest		0 $474,570,000
Assets acquired	$227,000,000	
Identifiable intangible assets	299,000,000	
Identifiable assets acquired		$526,000,000
Liabilities assumed		157,000,000
Net assets acquired and recognized separately		369,000,000
Goodwill*		$105,570,000

*Including the value of the assembled workforce. If the goodwill amount calculated is negative, a bargain purchase is deemed to have been made and the amount is recorded as income.

Exhibit 21.18 Valuation of Goodwill (as of December 31, 2009)

Consideration Transferred			$474,570
Identifiable Assets Acquired			
Fair Value of Current Assets		$106,000	
Fair Value of Tangible Assets		121,000	
Fair Value of Intangible Assets			
Acquired Software	$46,000		
Trade Name	59,000		
Noncompete Agreement	8,000		
Technology	75,000		
In-process Research and Development	18,000		
Customer Relationships	93,000	299,000	
		526,000	
Liabilities Assumed			
Debt-free Current Liabilities	48,000		
Current Maturities of Long-term Debt	14,000		
Long-term Debt	95,000	157,000	369,000
(1) **Residual Goodwill**			$105,570

Footnote:
(1) Residual Goodwill includes the value of Assembled Workforce of $4 million.

Note: Some totals may not foot due to rounding.

Exhibit 21.19 Acquiree's Summary of Values (Illustration only)

ASSET NAME	EXHIBIT	FAIR VALUE	RETURN	PERCENT TO PURCHASE PRICE	WEIGHTED RETURN
Current Assets	na	$106,000			
Debt-free Current Liabilities	na	(48,000)			
Net Working Capital		58,000	4.0%	9.9%	0.40%
Land and Buildings	na	36,000	6.5%	6.2%	0.40%
Machinery and Equipment, Net	na	85,000	7.5%	14.6%	1.10%
TOTAL NET WORKING CAPITAL AND TANGIBLE ASSETS		179,000			
Acquired Software	21.7	46,000	16.0%	7.9%	1.26%
Assembled Workforce	21.9	4,000	15.0%	0.7%	0.11%
Trade Name	21.1	59,000	15.0%	10.1%	1.52%
Noncompete Agreement	21.11	8,000	15.0%	1.4%	0.21%
Technology	21.14	75,000	18.0%	12.9%	2.32%
In-process Research and Development	21.15	18,000	24.0%	3.1%	0.74%
Customer Relationships	21.17	93,000	17.0%	15.9%	2.70%
TOTAL INTANGIBLE ASSETS		303,000			
(1) GOODWILL (excluding Assembled Workforce)	21.18	101,570	25.0%	17.4%	4.35%
TOTAL		$583,570			15.11%

Footnote:
(1) For financial reporting purposes, the fair value of goodwill includes the fair value of assembled workforce for a total fair value of residual goodwill of $105.57 million. Note: The goodwill return can, and often will, be substantially higher than the other returns (illustration only).

Note: Some totals may not foot due to rounding.

Weighted Average Return on Assets

The summary of values is presented in Exhibit 21.19. In this exhibit, the valuation conclusions are separated into the following groups: elements of net working capital; property, plant, and equipment; intangible assets; and goodwill. Individual asset valuations are presented within each group.

In addition to presenting the summary of values, this schedule provides a sanity check in the form of a weighted return calculation (illustration only).

ValTip

> The weighted average return on assets (WARA) calculation employs the rate of return for each asset weighted according to its fair value relative to the whole. The WARA should approximate the overall WACC for the business.

The analyst should take care and not rely blindly on the results of this exercise. Since the hypothetical buyer of each asset (or group of assets) is a separate and distinct market participant, the rates of return used for each asset may not equate or be reconcilable to the WACC for the acquiree. The WARA can be a useful sanity check, however.

The returns for each asset are those actually used in the foregoing valuation methodology (i.e., for tangible assets and contributory intangible assets). For contributory intangible assets that were valued using a form of the income approach (trade name, noncompete agreement, and the technology assets), the return is equal to the discount rate used to value that asset. Finally, the return for the assets valued under the multiperiod excess earnings method is also their discount rate.

It should be clear that the one asset that does not have a return is goodwill, and, admittedly, the return assigned is determined by trial and error. Essentially, the goodwill return is imputed based on determination of the overall weighted return needed to equal the WACC.

ValTip

By its nature, goodwill is the riskiest asset of the group, and therefore should require a return much higher than the overall business return.

Thus, in this calculation, the goodwill return of 25 percent suggests that goodwill is substantially riskier than all of the other assets, but, at a return of 25 percent, it is still well within reason for a proven going concern. At a goodwill return of 30%, the WACC would be 16%, still very close to the WACC calculated here of 15%. Thus, we are satisfied that the returns chosen for each asset are reasonable.

ADDENDUM 1—FAIR VALUE

Fair value is here to stay, and fair value measurements are becoming a pillar of accounting and auditing. The accounting model has changed. No longer is accounting based solely on historical cost; in fact, it never was. It has always been a mixed-attribute system: a little historical cost here and a little fair value there. The more pronounced change, however, has been from hierarchal guidance, predominately rules-based to principles-based. Accounting has always been regulatory driven. Up to now, professionals could cite a specific rule to document compliance, a "one size fits all" rule. Now, though, the citations must be principles driven; "do what's right given the circumstances."

Fair Value Measurements

The Financial Accounting Standards Board is the U.S. accounting standard setter for anyone reporting under generally accepted accounting principles. It is the standard setter because the U.S. Securities and Exchange Commission (SEC) effectively recognizes the FASB for establishing GAAP applicable to publicly registered companies (subject to additional SEC requirements). Therefore, the fair value accounting literature issued by the FASB is effectively a regulatory accounting standard.

The FASB continues to move ahead with an agenda that includes fair value accounting. In 2006, it issued Statement of Financial Accounting Standards No. 157, *Fair Value Measurements* (SFAS 157) to take effect for financial statements issued for fiscal years beginning after November 15, 2007, and interim periods within those fiscal years. In 2009, this statement was incorporated into the FASB's Accounting Standards Codification (ASC or Codification). The changes brought about by SFAS 157 are discussed in the following pages.

Scope

The fair value measurement standard establishes a framework for making fair value measurements and requires additional disclosures about the measurements. The pronouncement does not establish any new areas in financial reporting where fair value accounting is required. Rather, it interacts with other accounting literature (in fact, it is woven throughout the ASC) that requires or permits fair value measurements.

Fair Value

For financial reporting, the ASC provides a single authoritative definition of *fair value*:

> Fair value is the price that would be received to sell an asset or paid to transfer a liability in an orderly transaction between market participants at the measurement date.[65]

An important distinction with the FASB definition is that fair value may not consider synergies and attributes of a *specific* buyer and a *specific* seller, but may consider synergies available to *market participants*.

---

[65] Financial Accounting Standards Board, Accounting Standards Codification (2009), Glossary.

Fair value for financial reporting is not quite the same as fair market value as used with the IRS and other purposes. Characteristics of fair value in business combinations under GAAP include:

- Valuation methodologies specified in accounting literature and/or acceptable to the auditors
- Values are generally established on an asset-by-asset and a situation-by-situation basis
- Typically a control value, but more specifically driven by the unit of account
- The fair values of individual assets do not include a specific buyer's unique synergies unless such synergies are also those of market participants
- The additional purchase price paid in a business combination due to a synergistic component is recorded as goodwill and subsequently is subject to impairment testing
- In the absence of quoted market prices, the technique used to estimate fair value is the method producing a fair value best approximating quoted market prices
- Typically includes tax amortization benefits for individual assets in a business combination
- Transaction costs are not an attribute of the asset or liability, and thus the purchase price is not adjusted
- Considers the highest and best use of market participants in the principal (or most advantageous) market to establish the valuation premise (in-use or in-exchange)
- Considers a reporting entity's credit standing, or the credit standing of the creditor in the case of liabilities
- Requires the use of market participant assumptions in assessing management's prospective financial information (projections)

Fair Value Hierarchy

The FASB has specified a hierarchical approach to determining fair value. The ASC defines a hierarchy[66] in the development of fair value measurements as follows:

- *Level 1*. Inputs are observable market inputs that reflect quoted prices for identical assets or liabilities in active markets that the reporting entity has the ability to access at the measurement date.
- *Level 2*. Inputs are observable market inputs other than quoted prices for identical assets or liabilities in active markets that the reporting entity has the ability to access at the measurement date. Level 2 inputs include the following:
  - Quoted prices for similar assets or liabilities in active markets.
  - Quoted prices for identical or similar assets or liabilities in markets that are not active; that is, a market in which there are few transactions for the asset or liability, the prices are not current, or price quotations vary substantially either over time or among market makers (e.g., some brokered markets) or in which little information is released publicly (e.g., a principal-to-principal market).
  - Market inputs other than quoted prices that are directly observable for the asset or liability; for example, interest rates, yield curves, volatilities, and default rates that are observable at the commonly quoted intervals.

---

[66] Ibid., at 820-10-35-40, 820-10-35-47, and 820-10-35-48.

- Market inputs that are not directly observable for the asset or liability but that are derived principally from or corroborated by other observable market data through correlation or by other means (market-corroborated inputs); for example, inputs derived through extrapolation or interpolation that are corroborated by other observable market data.
- *Level 3.* Inputs are unobservable market inputs; for example, inputs derived through extrapolation or interpolation that are not able to be corroborated by observable market data. Unobservable market inputs shall be used to measure fair value if observable market inputs are not available, thereby allowing for situations in which there is little, if any, market activity for the asset or liability. However, the fair value measurement objective remains the same—that is, an exit price from the perspective of a market participant (seller). Therefore, a fair value measurement using unobservable market inputs within Level 3 shall consider the assumptions that market participants would use in pricing the asset or liability, including assumptions about the amount a market participant (buyer) would demand to assume the risk related to the unobservable market inputs used to measure fair value. The reporting entity's own data used to develop the inputs shall be adjusted to exclude factors specific to the reporting entity if information is available that indicates that market participants would use different assumptions.

Level 1 and Level 2 inputs are sometimes called mark-to-market inputs, while Level 3 inputs are sometimes called mark-to-model inputs.

Entry Price versus Exit Price

Fair value is defined from the perspective of an exit (sale) price rather than an entry (purchase) price. The price is determined based on the amount required to exchange the asset or liability in an orderly transaction between market participants. *Exchange* means to sell the asset or transfer the liability at the measurement date. An orderly transaction assumes exposure to the market for a period prior to the measurement date to allow for marketing activities that are usual and customary. An exit price is based on a hypothetical transaction from the perspective of a market participant who holds the asset or owes the liability. Therefore, the objective is to determine the price that would be received to sell the asset or paid to transfer the liability at the measurement date, which makes it an exit price.

Although the idea that an exit price can be different from an entry price is something that was featured in deliberations and pronouncements by both the FASB and the International Accounting Standards Board (IASB), the experience of the International Valuation Standards Board (IVSB) is that most valuers do not consider this to be a meaningful or valid distinction.[67] If fair value is supposed to represent the price in a sale or a transfer, that price is simultaneously an exit for the seller and an entry for the buyer. Confusion is sometimes caused by people looking for the supposed difference and imagining unstated assumptions. For example, some consider that "exit" implies a liquidation or breakup; others consider that "entry" implies consideration of entity-specific requirements.

---

[67] The IVSB is currently working on an exposure draft of the revised International Valuation Standards (IVS).

Principal (or Most Advantageous) Market

The exit price is to be considered from the perspective of market participants in the principal (or most advantageous) market for the asset or liability.[68] A fair value measurement is based on a transaction assumed to occur in the principal market for the asset or liability. The principal market is the market with the greatest volume and level of activity for the asset or liability. The most advantageous market is the market that would provide the highest price for an asset and the lowest for a liability. The principal market trumps the most advantageous market and is considered by the FASB to be a more expedient, relevant, and consistent metric for the preparer. If for whatever reason the principal market cannot be defined, the preparer may default to an advantageous market. If there is a principal market for the asset or liability, the fair value measurement shall represent the price in that market (whether that price is directly observable or otherwise determined using a valuation technique), even if the price in a different market is potentially more advantageous at the measurement date. For more on markets, see the later section titled "Active Market."

Transaction Costs

Transaction costs are specific to the transaction and represent the incremental direct costs to sell the asset or transfer the liability; thus, the price should not be adjusted for transaction costs, because they are not an attribute of the asset or liability. However, transportation costs are included in the fair value measurement of an asset measured on an in-use basis.[69]

Market Participants

Market participants are defined for purposes of fair value measurements.[70] They are buyers and sellers in the most advantageous market for the asset or liability. Market participants are also:

- Independent of the reporting entity.
- Knowledgeable (having all relevant information, including obtaining information through usual and customary due diligence).
- Able to transact.
- Willing to transact (motivated but not compelled).

Highest and Best Use of an Asset

A fair value measurement of an asset assumes the highest and best use of the asset from the perspective of market participants, regardless of how the company actually intends to use it.[71] It also requires considering that the use of the asset is:

- Physically possible
- Legally permissible
- Financially feasible

---

[68] Financial Accounting Standards Board, Accounting Standards Codification (2009), at 820-10-35-5.
[69] Ibid., at 820-10-35-7.
[70] Ibid., Glossary.
[71] Ibid., at 820-10-35-10 to 820-10-35-13.

Highest and best use is based on the use of the asset and generally results in maximizing the value. As such, the valuation premise may be either:

- *In-use,* which would provide maximum value through its use in combination with other assets as a group. As early practice has evolved, the in-use premise most often applies (and may only apply) to nonfinancial assets.
- *In-exchange,* which would provide maximum value on a stand-alone basis, such as some financial assets.

Importantly, the fair value of an asset in-use is determined based on the use of the asset together with other assets as a group (consistent with its highest and best use from the perspective of market participants), even if the asset that is the subject of the measurement is aggregated (or disaggregated) at a different level for purposes of applying other accounting pronouncements. This requirement may result in different aggregation assumptions from those used for impairment analyses.

Applicability to Liabilities

For a liability, a fair value measurement assumes a transfer of the liability to market participants. For the determination of price related to the transfer of a liability, nonperformance risk must be considered and must be the same before and after the assumed transfer. Nonperformance risk is the risk of not fulfilling the obligation and includes (but may not be limited to) the reporting entity's own credit risk.[72]

Initial Recognition

When an asset is acquired or a liability is assumed in an exchange transaction, the transaction price represents an *entry price* to acquire or assume. By contrast, fair value measurement after acquisition or assumption is a function of the hypothetical price to sell the asset or paid to transfer the liability and is thus an *exit price.*[73]

Valuation Approaches: Market, Income, and Cost

Fair value measurement also calls for valuation techniques used to measure fair value that are consistent with the market approach, income approach, and cost approach.[74] The measurement objective is to use a valuation technique (or a combination of techniques) appropriate for the circumstances but maximizing the use of market inputs.[75]

Fundamentally, value is a function of economics and is based on the return on assets. The cost approach represents the things owned or borrowed. The income approach quantifies the return these assets can be expected to produce. The market approach merely reflects the market's perceptions of the things owned and borrowed or their expected returns.

---

[72] Ibid., at 820-10-35-16.
[73] Ibid., Glossary
[74] Ibid., at 820-10-35-28 to 820-10-35-35.
[75] Ibid., at 820-10-35-36.

For the determination of fair value measurement, the *cost approach* is based on the current replacement cost—the amount that at the measurement date would be required to replace the service capacity of the asset. It is based on the cost to a market participant to acquire or construct a substitute asset of comparable utility, adjusted for obsolescence, whether physical, functional, or economic.

The *income approach* uses valuation techniques to convert future amounts to a single present amount and is based on the value indicated by current market expectations about those future amounts. This approach includes present value techniques such as option-pricing models, binomial models, and the multiperiod excess earnings method.[76] Importantly, present value techniques originally presented by the FASB in Statement of Financial Accounting Concepts No. 7 are now Level A GAAP.[77] These techniques include:

- *Discount rate adjustment technique*, which is the traditional method whereby the denominator incorporates all risk elements related to the single cash flow being discounted.[78]
- *Expected present value technique*, which is a function of the probability-weighted average of all possible cash flows discounted at a risk-free rate. There are two methods:
  1. Adjusting the expected cash flows for systematic (or market) risk
  2. Not adjusting the expected cash flows for systematic risk, but instead including the risk adjustment in the discount rate[79]

The *market approach* uses prices of market transactions involving identical or similar assets or liabilities. Remember here the fair value hierarchy: Level 1 is identical assets or liabilities and Level 2 is similar assets or liabilities. Therefore, the market approach may be either a Level 1 or Level 2 determination. Further, matrix pricing is considered consistent with the market approach. This applies to debt securities that do not rely exclusively on quoted prices for the specific securities, but rather rely on the securities' relationship to other benchmark quoted securities. Because people often confuse the term *market approach* with *market value*, the forthcoming exposure draft of the revised International Valuation Standards (IVS) uses the term *direct market comparison approach* rather than *market approach*.

Inputs: Observable and Unobservable

Inputs refer broadly to the assumptions that market participants would use in pricing the asset or liability and can be of two types:

1. *Observable inputs* are based on assumptions that market participants would use and be independent of the reporting entity
2. *Unobservable inputs* are based on the entity's own assumptions about the assumptions market participants would use based on the best available information[80]

---

[76] Ibid., at 820-10-35-33.

[77] Accounting standard setters have classified accounting pronouncements into a hierarchy (or levels).

[78] Financial Accounting Standards Board, Accounting Standards Codification (2009), at 820-10-55-4.

[79] Ibid.

[80] Ibid., at 820-10-35-36.

Fair value measurements require maximizing observable inputs and minimizing unobservable inputs.

Active Market

The FASB has provided the following rather vague definition of *active market*:

> An active market for an asset or liability is a market in which transactions for the asset or liability occur with sufficient frequency and volume to provide pricing information on an ongoing basis.[81]

As stated previously, Level 1 inputs are observable market inputs that reflect quoted prices for identical assets or liabilities in active markets. In explaining its reasoning for referencing quoted market prices, the FASB cited paragraph 57 of SFAS No. 107:

> The Board concluded that quoted market prices provide the most reliable measure of fair value. Quoted market prices are easy to obtain and are reliable and verifiable. They are used and relied upon regularly and are well understood by investors, creditors, and other users of financial information. In recent years, new markets have developed and some existing markets have evolved from thin to active markets, thereby increasing the ready availability of reliable fair value information.[82]

Further, the FASB affirmed:

> that its intent was not to preclude adjustments to a quoted price if that price is not readily available or representative of fair value, noting that in those situations, the market for the particular asset or liability might not be active. To convey its intent more clearly, the Board clarified that, in those situations, the fair value of the asset or liability should be measured using the quoted price, as adjusted, but within a lower level of the fair value hierarchy.[83]

The FASB recognizes the distinction between a thin and an active market. The ASC essentially calls for a process to determine whether a market may not be active and a transaction is not distressed.[84] First, a preparer of a company's financial statements should analyze factors that indicate a market is not active, including:

- Few recent transactions (based on volume and level of activity in the market). Thus, there is not sufficient frequency and volume to provide pricing information on an ongoing basis.
- Price quotations are not based on current information.
- Price quotations vary substantially either over time or among market makers (for example, some brokered markets).

---

[81] Ibid., Section 820-10-20.

[82] Financial Accounting Standards Board, Statement of Financial Accounting Standards No. 157, *Fair Value Measurements* (2006), at C166.

[83] Ibid., at C68.

[84] Financial Accounting Standards Board, Accounting Standards Codification (2009), at 820-10-35-51a.

- Indexes that previously were highly correlated with the fair values of the asset are demonstrably uncorrelated with recent indications of fair value for that asset or liability.
- Abnormal (or significant increases in) liquidity risk premiums or implied yields for quoted prices when compared with reasonable estimates (using realistic assumptions) of credit and other nonperformance risk for the asset class.
- Abnormally wide bid-ask spread or significant increases in the bid-ask spread.
- A significant decline or absence of a market for new issuances (i.e., a primary market).
- Little information is released publicly (for example, a principal-to-principal market).

After evaluating all factors and considering the significance and relevance of each factor, the reporting entity shall use its judgment in determining whether the market is active. If the reporting entity concludes that the market for the asset is not active, then the transactions or quoted prices available may be distorted and not indicative of fair value. In such a case, the reporting entity must develop further analysis and may determine that a significant adjustment is necessary to the transaction or quoted price. Such analysis may include whether there was sufficient time before the measurement date to allow for usual and customary marketing activities for the asset and whether there were multiple bidders for the asset.

Mark-to-Market Accounting

On March 12, 2009, FASB Chairman Robert Herz testified about mark-to-market accounting before the U.S. House of Representatives Subcommittee on Capital Markets, Insurance, and Government Sponsored Enterprises. Herz appeared at a hearing convened by Congressman and Committee Chairman Paul E. Kanjorski (D-PA) on "Mark-to-Market Accounting: Practices and Implications."

> Many investors have made it clear that, in their view, fair value accounting allows companies to report amounts that are more relevant, timely, and comparable than amounts that would be reported under alternative accounting approaches, even during extreme market conditions.[85]
>
> The fact that fair value measures have been difficult to determine for some illiquid instruments is not a cause of current problems but rather a symptom of the many problems that have contributed to the global crisis—including lax and fraudulent lending, excess leverage, the creation of complex and risky investments through securitization and derivatives, the global distribution of such investments across rapidly growing unregulated and opaque markets lacking a proper infrastructure for clearing mechanisms and price discovery, faulty ratings, and the absence of appropriate risk management and valuation processes at many financial institutions.[86]

---

[85] Testimony of Robert H. Herz, chairman, Financial Accounting Standards Board, before the U.S. House of Representatives Financial Services Subcommittee on Capital Markets, Insurance, and Government Sponsored Entities, March 12, 2009, 8.
[86] Ibid.

Statement 157 is a principles-based standard that requires the application of sound judgment in determining fair value estimates. Judgment is not new in accounting; however, the increased attention on fair value estimates and principles-based standards has increased focus on the use of judgment. In its final report to the SEC, CIFiR [Advisory Committee on Improvements to Financial Reporting] recommended that the SEC issue a statement of policy articulating how it evaluates the reasonableness of accounting judgments, including the factors that it considers when making this evaluation. That recommendation also included a suggestion that the PCAOB [Public Company Accounting Oversight Board] should adopt a similar approach with respect to auditing judgments.[87]

The reality is that the standard setters, like FASB, can only set the standards. Others, principally the SEC, must enforce them. The newly appointed chairman of the SEC, Mary Schapiro, recently announced additional funding to bolster the enforcement division of the SEC. It's all a simple formula, really. The FASB establishes the standards, the preparers (companies) implement them into financial statements, and the SEC and others are the cops to make sure the laws are followed. Chairman Herz was more elegant when he stated:

The primary roles of accounting standard setters and prudential regulators are fundamentally different. Accounting standard setters focus on developing accounting standards that help provide transparency in general-purpose financial statements of reporting enterprises that are used by investors and others to make capital resource allocation decisions. The information needs of those parties often differ from that of regulators, who are largely concerned with safety and soundness and financial stability. Accounting standard setters stress the importance of having the information in general purpose financial statements be neutral, that is, free from bias. The goal is to provide information useful to users of financial statements in their decision making. Such users include present and potential investors, lenders, suppliers, and other trade creditors, customers, employees, governments and their agencies, and the public. Primacy is given to the informational needs of investors (both equity and debt security holders).

The focus of financial reports is on the communication of information to investors and the capital markets to facilitate informed investment decisions, without which markets do not function well. This focus informs the structure and purpose of the financial accounting and standard-setting process and the resultant standards.

A paramount goal of the federal government has been to ensure the stability of the financial system. A principal policy tool used to achieve this goal has been the prudential regulation and supervision of financial institutions, which is designed to remove or lessen the threat of systemic instability, as well as, in the case of commercial banks and other deposit-taking institutions, to protect customer deposits.[88] (Footnotes omitted.)

---

[87] Ibid., 14.
[88] Ibid., 4.

Fair value, including mark-to-market accounting, requires orderly transactions. Sometimes the market is wrong, not orderly, like now [2009/2010]. In these instances, preparers, auditors, valuators, regulators, and users of financial statements all have a responsibility to use judgment—the judgment to present reasonable estimates based on an efficient, balanced, and stable market. To do otherwise creates a bias that harms everyone.

ADDENDUM 2—INTELLECTUAL PROPERTY

One of the major difficulties in valuing intellectual property is determining value in the context of licensor/licensee negotiations. All too often this context is assumed or simplified, resulting in market royalty rates being applied out of context. Most valuation analysts traditionally develop royalty rates from any of four traditional sources:

1. Negotiated licensing agreements.
2. Surveys performed by various professionals, generally in cooperation with trade associations.
3. Judicial opinions, which vary greatly depending on individual fact patterns.
4. Databases of licensing agreements extracted from publicly available sources. Such direct market data is some of the most compelling evidence available to determine the appropriate royalty rate in a valuation.

The market guideline–transaction method initially has four steps to derive an overall value estimate: 1) research the appropriate market for guideline intellectual property transactions; 2) verify, where possible, the information by confirming that the market data obtained is factually accurate and that the license exchange transactions reflect arm's-length market considerations; 3) compare and apply the guideline license transactions' financial and operational aspects with the subject intellectual property; and 4) reconcile the various value indications into a single value indication or range of values.

Empirical Research and Verification of Royalty Rates

Proprietary research of intangible assets and intellectual properties is important in business valuation. The value the market perceives in intellectual property–intensive companies is associated with their intangible assets and intellectual properties. Valuation of such companies may often be an exercise in intangible asset valuation methods rather than traditional business valuation methods. Emphasis can be placed on proprietary studies (industry research, industry pricing metrics, and comparable intellectual property transactions). Research and verification of guideline data can be a time-consuming process. Recently, advances in information technology and the availability of online public records have made research of intellectual property transactions a more realistic endeavor.

Databases that gather and organize guideline intellectual property transactions are rapidly becoming the tool of the future to those analysts who specialize or practice in intellectual property valuation. At the time of publication, five known Internet sites have collated data or provide information for a fee:

1. BV Resources (www.bvresources.com)
2. Consor (www.consor.com)
3. ktMINE (http://ktmine.com)
4. RoyaltySource (www.royaltysource.com)
5. The Financial Valuation Group (www.fvgfl.com)

Comparing and Applying the Data

Intellectual property transactions should be compared to the subject company using the following guidelines:

- The legal rights of intellectual property ownership conveyed in the guideline transaction
- The existence of any special financing terms or other arrangements
- Whether the elements of arm's length existed for the sale or license conditions
- The economic conditions that existed in the appropriate secondary market at the time of the sale or license transaction
- The industry in which the guideline intellectual property was or will be used
- The financial and operational characteristics of the guideline properties compared with the company's intellectual property

Reconciliation

The last phase of the market approach valuation analysis is the reconciliation. The strengths and weaknesses of each guideline transaction are considered; the reliability and appropriateness of the market data are examined, including the analytical techniques applied. After considerable review, transactions selected should be reasonably comparative to the company transaction and then synthesized into a reasonable range.

Detailed Example of an Intellectual Property Database

The intellectual property transactions database of The Financial Valuation Group is based on publicly available data. It includes approximately 40 fields consisting of the names of the licensor and licensee; both the Standard Industrial Classification (SIC) and the North American Industry Classification System (NAICS) numbers for the licensor and the licensee; the type of agreement (i.e., trademark, patent, copyright); the industry name; the remuneration structure; royalty percentages (base rate, the low end and high end of variable rates); royalty dollars (base flat fee, annual and variable fees); a description of the product or service; and so on. Custom searches of the database (using keywords, SIC/NAICS numbers, or both) can be performed to obtain market guideline data.

Searches of "all transactions" in The Financial Valuation Group database at the publication date revealed the following.

Transactions by Industry (Sample)

Industry groups as represented by the first two digits of the U.S. government SIC codes are represented in transactions in the database as shown in Exhibit 21.20.

Intellectual Property Typically Licensed (Sample)

While there are approximately 90 distinctly different intangible assets, the majority of assets licensed are intellectual property assets, which can be grouped within categories shown in Exhibit 21.21. Patents tend to be the most licensed intellectual property, with trademarks, products, and technology following.

Exhibit 21.20   Intellectual Property Transactions Database: Transactions by Two-Digit SIC Industry

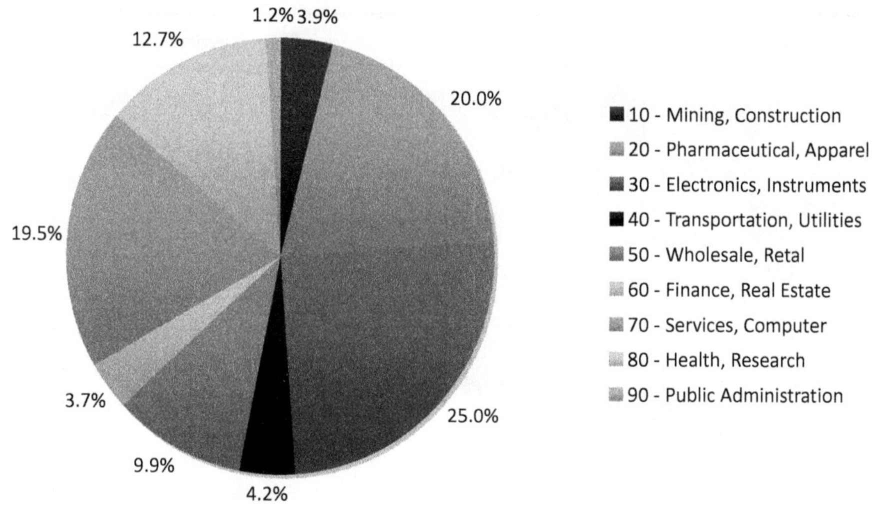

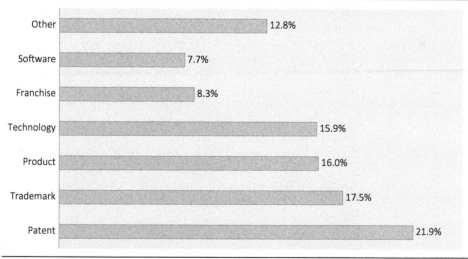

© Copyright 2009 by The Financial Valuation Group of Florida, Inc. All rights reserved.

Payment Structures of Intellectual Property Transactions (Sample)

A comparison of the royalty payment structures disclosed in each transaction reveals that approximately half of the licensing agreements are based on a set percentage or set dollar amount. Many transactions involve high/low payments, which are usually based on performance, sales, or both. Annual fee and monthly fee agreements tend to be set at a fixed amount paid on a regular basis throughout the life of the agreement. Exhibit 21.22 shows the various royalty rate payment structures by the reported transactions analyzed.

Exhibit 21.21   Intellectual Property Transactions Database: Database Percentages for Types of Transactions

© Copyright 2009 by The Financial Valuation Group of Florida, Inc. All rights reserved.

Exhibit 21.22   Intellectual Property Transactions Database: Payment Structures of Database Transactions

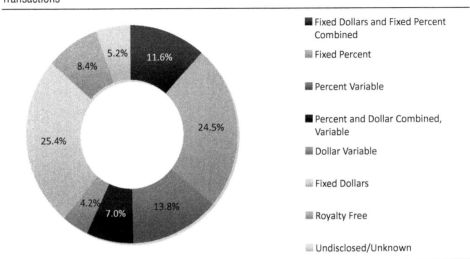

- Fixed Dollars and Fixed Percent Combined
- Fixed Percent
- Percent Variable
- Percent and Dollar Combined, Variable
- Dollar Variable
- Fixed Dollars
- Royalty Free
- Undisclosed/Unknown

Reasons to Use the Database

The database is used to support:

- Damages in an intellectual property litigation case
- Reasonable royalty percentage rates
- Accurate valuation conclusions
- Rebuttal of unreasonable value estimates put forth by others
- Transfer pricing opinions

Royalty rates derived from transactions take many economic structures. Analysis of licensing transactions similar to a particular fact situation would be necessary to determine a market royalty rate applicable to that situation. The analyst with requisite skill, knowledge, education, experience, and training will be able to draw upon the data to form better-founded and defensible conclusions and opinions.

CHAPTER **22**

Marketing, Managing, and Making Money in a Valuation Services Group

PURPOSE AND OVERVIEW[1]

In addition to providing intellectually challenging work projects with almost endless variety, the field of business valuation offers potential for good compensation. However, it is possible to win an engagement and provide quality client service but fail to bill and collect a fair fee and/or incur sizable cost overruns due to poor practice management. Optimizing the potential of a business valuation practice is not accidental, nor is it the natural result of merely "doing good work." It involves developing a strong skill set in nontechnical areas such as marketing and practice management.

For the purposes of this chapter, the term "good economics" will be used to indicate a business valuation practice that has optimized its potential, given such practice characteristics as the types of clients, the geographic market served, type of services offered, staff size and quality, and age of the practice. This chapter explores the key determinants of good economics for a given business valuation practice, summarized as:

- The qualifications of the practice professionals to provide the particular services offered by the firm
- The existence of niche valuation services that the firm can serve profitably
- The temperament suitability of the practitioners, especially the leadership, for the type of engagements undertaken
- The practice's acceptance criteria for engagements and its adherence to these criteria
- The management/operating practices of the firm

When the three Ms—marketing, managing, and money—are all properly synchronized, business valuation in a professional services firm can be a rewarding career.

It is important to note that these very broad and informal engagement and practice guidelines outline suggested goals that may not be achievable, depending on the nature and type of practice. They are also more applicable to a group practice.

---

[1] See James R. Hitchner and Michael J. Mard, *Financial Valuation Workbook, Third Edition,* 2011, John Wiley and Sons, for an expanded discussion and tools to better manage a practice.

WHAT GOOD ECONOMICS LOOKS LIKE

Record Maintenance and Analysis

To attain good economics, a practice should set realistic goals for operational results and analyze unfavorable variances to determine the changes that should be made to achieve specified goals. Management should keep complete and timely records of key practice results and analyze the results against previous periods and against budgets and goals.

> Some practices whose revenues are based primarily on fixed fees make the mistake of failing to maintain or to evaluate time records and other information about efficiency and profitability that would indicate problem areas that need corrective action.

Higher Billing Rates

Until a practice's reputation is established in the marketplace, it may not be able to command top fees. However, practices should attempt to exit a market or type of service that will not allow for higher rates over time, unless there are compelling reasons to remain in that market or offer that service, such as a high volume of engagements, to gain experience or because of the type of marketplace.

Realization and Productivity

If the practice's rate structure (hourly or fixed fees) is appropriate for its skill sets and marketplace, and engagements are managed for top efficiency, then the realization percentage should be more than 90 percent.

> It is desirable that staff chargeable hours for engagements should, on average, result in billings equal to 90 percent or more of the recorded hours.

Most practices count standard hours as 2,000 or 2,080 a year, or the number of hours a professional is available. Obviously, to attain a healthy average, the less experienced people should be 90 percent or more productive and the professionals with leadership and sales responsibilities should be less productive. Unless the practice fields a large team, say more than 8 people, then the practice leader(s) should be productive for 40 to 50 percent of standard hours, since the practice's highest billing rates are charged by its leadership and leadership is involved in marketing and other critical, nonbillable work.

> On average, a group practice should be charging billable hours to engagements for more than 70 percent of the standard hours available for them to work.

Few Uncollectible Accounts

Unfortunately, bad debts and postengagement fee adjustments are unavoidable. Many practitioners view them as a cost of doing business. With appropriate engagement acceptance processes, including collecting significant retainers that are held as deposits, and close engagement management, uncollectible receivables can be minimized. Since uncollectible accounts and billing adjustments occur on a client-by-client basis, there does not seem to be a minimum or "acceptable" range for which to strive.

Profit Margin Greater Than 40 percent

Before any compensation charges for the practice leaders, but after all other expenses, the profit margin of the practice can be at least 40 percent. It usually should not be below 30 percent. A well managed and efficient, highly productive practice can maintain a 50 percent or more profit margin. Obviously this has a lot to do with the type of services offered and the percentage of fixed fee competitive work.

Right Fit

Practices often start their life taking whatever type of valuation services they can get, or whatever the leader is accustomed to performing or comfortable delivering. Over time, practices may evolve to other lines of services and may become entrenched in one or more specific service niches. To attain good economics, the practice leader(s) and key senior professionals must become highly qualified in a particular service line and be temperamentally well suited for the requirements of the service. For example, not everyone is comfortable with or interested in the requirements of dispute resolution work.

> In spite of the higher profits offered by litigation services, some practitioners find that being an expert witness is disruptive to the processes needed to direct a practice that must deliver valuation reports on a regular basis.

Each practice should frequently evaluate the services it offers and consider these questions for possible action:

- Which services are more profitable than the others and should be encouraged, and which ones are below the acceptable range of profitability?
- Which services are susceptible to the practice adjusting its pricing and operational approaches to attain more profitability?
- Which lines of valuation services really suit the skill sets, the temperaments, and career goals of the practice team and its leader(s)?

OPERATIONAL KEYS FOR GOOD ECONOMICS

Certain key attitudes and habitual actions in operating a business valuation practice are important to the attainment of good economics.

Proactivity

Successful and profitable engagements do not result from sitting back and waiting for information to come from clients, third parties, or the practice engagement team. Practice leaders can establish a clearly documented schedule for each engagement and anticipate in advance changes in client needs or the ability of the practice to deliver that schedule. Close monitoring and communication with the engagement team and, for some matters, with the client must be a key component of each engagement. This is particularly applicable to litigation services engagements because of the many stops, starts, and long delays involved and because most of the general engagement direction and delivery dates are determined by third parties, such as the client's attorney.

ValTip

Since a business valuation engagement is a consulting project, proactive planning and control is key to maximization of the efficiency, quality, and profitability of the work process and product.

Continual Marketing Activities and Sales Results

Since the profitability of a professional practice is dependent on a high level of productivity, there must be an order input rate that consistently is greater than the output rate. In other words, the practice cannot run out of work for any significant period of time. Some fortunate practices have a steady supply of work, but even those fortunate ones recognize that maintaining ongoing activities is a critical factor for future sales. When practice rainmakers are busy with client work, marketing often takes a backseat. Good economics require marketing and sales results to be fairly constant to maintain an order input rate greater than the output rate. In some practices, that may require the leader to hire a seasoned or more experienced professional. Doing this will free up time to market and sell.

Planning and Communication

Certified Public Accountants are familiar with the General Standard of the American Institute of Certified Public Accountants that work is to be planned and adequately supervised. This standard not only promotes the delivery of quality professional service, but is also key to superior profits. When practical, the profitable practitioner must develop continuous and timely planning for engagements and other aspects of the practice, and for communication of those plans to other professionals in the practice.

Flexible Resources, Especially Staffing

In spite of the best marketing activities and planning for engagements, fluctuations in the workflow will occur. These range from having too little work available to keep the present staff busy to having more work than the staff can accomplish on time. Therefore, the practice must strive for resource flexibility, especially its most costly resource, the professional staff.

> Resource flexibility is a rich area for practice leaders to explore as they seek to smooth the peaks and valleys of the workflow.

Any practice that operates in a competitive marketplace can form alliances with other practices to share staff during slow times and can cultivate part-time professionals to pick up the slack during times of high activity.

Another smoothing methodology, particularly for high-volume engagement practices, is to parcel out segments of an engagement for various professionals to perform. For instance, one person performs the economic and industry research while another performs the valuation approaches for the same subject company. Some practices, particularly those that produce a significant volume of reports, believe this method promotes quality and efficiency. In addition, some professional staff prefer to perform one part of an engagement rather than another, and these preferences also can result in superior quality and efficiency. Again, this depends on the type of practice and the complexity of the work.

Resource flexibility calls for a practice to look ahead to the nonhuman resources that it may need and planning for economical ways to attain those resources quickly. These resources include new databases, software, and other time-saving and quality-enhancing resources.

Quality Results and Client Value

If a practice does not have a culture of providing quality results and client value in its engagements, then the work product may not meet client expectations, may result in unpaid rework or reduction in fees, and could damage the practice's reputation.

Unless the practice has a culture toward quality and client value, there is less chance for good economics, at least for any sustained period of time.

An often overlooked element of quality results and client value is the opportunity to collaborate with other qualified business analysts on some aspects of a particular engagement. The input of other qualified professionals can enhance the quality of the information utilized, the methods selected and implemented, and the professional judgments used throughout the valuation.

Training and Quality Improvement

All business valuation practitioners are "practicing" their craft and seek, like other professions, to constantly improve their performance. A practice aspiring to good economics must invest in regular training and improvement of its staff's and leadership's abilities to provide quality services.

KEY ENGAGEMENT PRINCIPLES

An organized and disciplined approach is required for engagements with several team members to coordinate the tasks required for the completion of the project.

Litigation services engagements in particular need an organized and disciplined approach because so often the engagement criteria identified at the start are augmented and revised over the life of the project. It is not unusual at the start of some litigation service engagements that the engagement criteria is vague and specific tasks are undefined.

Practices that aspire to good economics are advised to develop their own uniform but flexible processes for engagement organization and control. These processes may take the form of checklists, reporting deadlines, schedules for client communication, team meetings, and other means to promote disciplined engagement activities.

Some practices have developed some written "guidelines" for appropriate engagement processes and procedures that also allow flexibility for the particular needs of an engagement that are resolved by professional judgment. Some practices do not have written guidelines but rely more on training and culture. A "guideline approach" to engagement organization and control would address suggested procedures for these areas:

- Engagement acceptance process
- Terms and objectives of the engagement approach, resources, work plan, budget, fees and collections
- Engagement control
- Achievement of quality and client value
- Litigation services' engagements

ENGAGEMENT ACCEPTANCE PROCESS

Guidelines that assist professionals in the engagement acceptance process can prevent the acceptance of an unprofitable engagement as well as properly establish the requirements and environment for a profitable engagement.

Profile of Acceptable Engagements

An important element of the guidelines for the acceptance process is a profile of acceptable clients and engagement types for the practice or, in the alternative, a profile of unacceptable engagements. For example, a practice may not be willing to accept engagements for valuations for marital dissolution or for employee stock ownership plans.

The profile should be well known and adhered to with discipline unless the practice leader makes an exception. Discipline is particularly important when the practice has a low backlog of work, for it is easy to rationalize that "any work is better than no work." The fallacy of this rationalization is that any given engagement can result in the loss of time that could be used more profitably for marketing, training or vacation, or performing an engagement later that is more profitable.

ValTip

> A practice may not want to accept engagements for individuals (as opposed to companies) as clients without receiving substantial retainers.

Questionable Opportunities

The acceptance process should include consideration of the ability of the practice to obtain needed resources to perform the engagement and other matters that would qualify the unit to accept a given opportunity. Sometimes the best engagement of the year is the one that was declined and/or referred to another firm.

Guidelines for acceptance should include procedures to identify the characteristics of a potential client that contribute to a profitable engagement. This includes the willingness of the client to assist in the engagement, for example, internal data gathering, and to agree on a reasonable delivery schedule. An important client characteristic to search for in the acceptance process is whether the client is both willing and able to pay for the anticipated services.

Relationship Checking Process

The firm also may want to construct a database of prior relationships with potential clients and third parties. The database can be used to research the desirability of the potential client prior to accepting an engagement. Such a database also can be used to determine if relationships exist with opposing clients or attorneys from either side. Such a database should be kept current.

Client Expectations

The acceptance process should include communications with the client representative before work begins to explain how the engagement process works and what the terms of the engagement will be for such matters as fees and payment, client assistance, and deliverables. To maximize the opportunity for good economics, clients should know at the outset the expectations for their role and the anticipated economics and contractual terms of the engagement.

FEES, RETAINERS, BILLING, AND COLLECTION

Engagement guidelines will include procedures for setting fees, retainers, and client billings and collections. These items should be discussed during the acceptance process with the potential client. The decisions as to whether to accept the engagement and how to structure the terms of the engagement must consider any balking by the potential client about the practice's guidelines.

Determining the Fee Schedule

Hourly rates charged and fixed-fee minimums should be fair for the market and the qualifications of the practice and practice leader(s) and fit the risk and complexity of the engagement. This can mean different rates and fees for different engagements and analysts. The practice should monitor rates of its competitors frequently. Given its own reputation, portfolio of services and clients, it should examine rate schedules periodically to adjust to market rates, costs of the practice, and changing trends in the industry. On a given engagement, the rate schedule should not be an issue with the client, although the overall fee may be an issue regardless of the rates.

Retainers—By All Means

The firm should strive to obtain a retainer in advance of starting work on each engagement, often held as a deposit until final bills are paid. Retainers are collected to insure against future or unknown problems beyond the control of the analyst. The amount received should cover a reasonable portion of the total engagement and, depending on the size of the engagement and the type of client, may be 50 percent or more of anticipated fees. It is not usually wise to start working on an engagement until the retainer is received. There are obviously exceptions to this rule, such as working with known clients or attorneys who have good reputations regarding payment of fees.

Retainers also serve as a client qualification tool. Beware of the potential client, particularly the new client who refuses to pay a retainer, or who wants to heavily reduce the requested retainer or continues to decline to remit the agreed-upon retainer. These are warning signals of a potential client who is not willing to pay fees and are a precursor to future fee problems. These traits can be included in the profile for unacceptable engagements.

> In most situations, if you are good enough to be engaged, you are good enough to be paid a portion of the fee in advance.

Work Plans and Budgets

A sensible approach to engagement planning and control and to engagement economics, and where appropriate and applicable, is to prepare a work plan and budget for some engagements. This can be very general or more specific. In some instances, it is desirable to obtain approval from the client and client's attorney for the work plan and budget. These can be orally conveyed or written.

The budget may need to be revised during the course of the engagement. For this reason, it is important to discuss with the client as soon as possible why additional work must be done and to arrange a fee increase. Clients are usually understanding about fair compensation for needed changes but do not want to be surprised about an increase in fees.

> Work plans and budgets, where appropriate, can be valuable tools that aid in the supervision and control of the engagement team, and can help in obtaining efficiency on the job. These can be detailed or general and in writing or oral.

Prompt and Frequent Billings

Guidelines should include procedures for prompt and frequent billings on engagements. Analysts should explain to clients during the engagement acceptance process how billings work, and what expectations are for prompt payment. Include specific payment terms in the engagement letter, including the provision that valuation reports will not be issued, nor will expert witness reports be issued or testimony in deposition or trial be provided, unless outstanding bills are paid. Develop a process for fixed fee engagements that results in bills being accepted and paid at fixed intervals of time or engagement performance.

Collecting Fees

Monitor compliance with payment schedules and follow up as necessary with calls to the client decision maker. Slow payment of billings may indicate an unspoken problem with the engagement, so troubleshoot all laggards. Send reminder notices of unpaid accounts on a regular basis.

ENGAGEMENT CONTROL

Becoming more efficient and increasing the practice's realization are functions of exercising engagement control. Part of this control involves managing client expectations and setting timetables, but most of it lies primarily with the ability of the engagement leader(s) to be knowledgeable of the engagement details and to make critical judgments and, if necessary, take prompt corrective action. Unless the leader knows what is going on, corrective action can be delayed and the result can be an expensive "redo."

Sometimes the best approach to take with an engagement that is floundering economically is to take the practice's best people and put them on the job to finish it up.

Many engagement leaders are reluctant to get into the smallest details or tasks of the engagement; after all, they worked hard and learned their craft in order to delegate work to others. But the profits are in the details, and depending on the type of engagements, the leader may plan and monitor the work and manage time devoted by the team to the engagement at a level of detail necessary for that engagement.

The old adage "People do what you inspect, not what you expect" applies to valuation engagements, for team members may not know or admit on a timely basis that they are off track about the direction their work is headed.

The key is to review the status of each team member on a timely basis to avoid misdirection of his or her efforts. This principle can also apply to the engagement leader. The reason for the universal application of this principle is that performing business valuations and consulting engagements requires the exercising of a considerable degree of sequential and overall judgment. Anyone can "get off track" somewhere within the planning, framework, and conclusions of an engagement. Everyone can benefit from collaboration with another professional, if appropriate and applicable.

> A very general rule of thumb for frequency of inspection by a practice leader or engagement manager is that the work of juniors/novices should be reviewed every two hours or so. The work of all other professionals should be inspected on a time interval of three hours or so for each year of their experience. This is particularly affected by the type and complexity of the engagement, the staff person, and the practice leader. Some senior staff need only periodic discussions of the engagement progress and issues.

LITIGATION SERVICES' ENGAGEMENTS

Litigation services present significant differences from typical business valuation engagements, even though the engagement may entail only performing a business valuation or evaluating the work of another analyst. Some of the reasons for the differences between typical valuation assignments and litigation services are:

- The uncertainty of the nature, scope, and timing of dispute resolution work
- The fact that dispute resolution engagements can and often do end abruptly, with unbilled work in process and unpaid billings
- Third-party involvement, especially the client's attorney and an adversary expert
- High stress on the analyst due to many reasons, including an emotional client
- Some of the work may have to be done alone or with less-experienced staff
- Written reports, required by U.S. District Courts, that may not be typical valuation reports
- Disruption to normal nondispute work flow, including time lost while waiting to testify or obtain guidance

Planning and Communication

Because of the consulting nature of dispute work, an organized problem-solving approach should be used in the planning stages and as the engagement progresses. One such approach is commonly called the "look-back" approach due to its technique of visualizing all the elements needed at various stages of delivery and then looking back to plan in reverse all the tasks that are needed to reach the delivery point on time.

The analyst's qualifications for the potential engagement are considered carefully because someone else may challenge the work product, especially if the engagement is for expert witness testimony or court-appointed valuations. Depending on the type of engagement, practitioners may be well advised to collaborate with another experienced practitioner on dispute resolution engagements, especially less experienced expert witnesses.

Timing of Work

Because disputes begin with a number of key unknowns about data to be used and tasks that are needed, and because disputes are prone to end abruptly due to settlement, the scope of work assigned to the analyst at the outset often changes significantly. Due to this factor, anticipated revenue flow may terminate prematurely. When work is assigned, it should be completed as soon as possible within the schedule agreed on with the client or the attorney. This may help an attorney in the settlement process. Also due to the shifting nature of the tasks within the scope of a dispute engagement, when the completion date for a task is delayed but not canceled, a timely completion of this task according to the original schedule will mean it will not have to be completed at a later date, possibly under more stressful conditions.

Work Plans, Budgets, Billings, and Collections

Again, the nature of disputes—with their uncertain scope of work and propensity for an abrupt ending—requires an even greater awareness and attention to the principles needed to attain good economics.

ValTip

> Preparing a work plan and budget (whether written or oral) for known tasks and obtaining approval aids the client and the attorney to understand the likely fee levels required.

Additional work plans and budgets may be used as the engagement progresses. Prompt and frequent billings and payments are important, all of which should be explained in the acceptance process and insisted on during the engagement. In a high-fee engagement, billing should occur more frequently than monthly, perhaps weekly or every two weeks. Determine at the outset the billing format desired by the client and the attorney. Plan the scope of written reports as soon as possible, and budget liberally for time to prepare the reports and review them with the client and attorney. The cost to prepare written reports, especially Rule 26 reports for U.S. District Courts, can be a great surprise.

Supervision and Engagement Control

The engagement leader is often involved in certain details of litigation services tasks, regardless of whether he or she is to be a consultant or expert witness. Three major reasons for this are:

1. The consulting role calls for the analyst to provide a wide range of ideas and problem-solving advice

2. The testifying expert must know the details of the work plan that provide the foundation for opinions
3. Other than the preparation of the business valuation aspects of dispute engagements, some of the tasks to be performed may be unique, and staff may not be as experienced with this type of work

Working with the Client's Attorney

In litigation engagements, the client's attorney is likely to be directly involved with the analyst, and the client may have little or no involvement. For good economics and other reasons, the analyst needs to communicate proactively, clearly, and often with the attorney on many aspects of the engagement. The client's attorney is also very likely to be the go-between for all client communications, which places a premium on clear understanding with the attorney about retainers, fees, payment of invoices, and any action required by the client.

Do not assume anything without frequent and clear communication with the client and the client's attorney.

CONCLUSION

Professionals in service firms, particularly the leaders, need to practice the three Ms (marketing, managing, and making money) to ensure a rewarding and fulfilling career and successful practice. The disciplines of planning and supervision will greatly assist in the achievement of the desired goals of the practice and its professionals.

CHAPTER 23

Business Damages

This chapter discusses legal principles and quantitative issues and methods related to determining business damages in litigation matters. It illustrates the differences between the estimation of value for a business valuation and the calculation of lost profit damages. The theory and practice described apply to both testifying experts (professionals who expect to testify as expert witnesses) and consulting experts (professionals who do not expect to testify but who will serve as consultants to attorneys). Only compensatory damages (lost profits and diminution of value) are discussed in this chapter. Benefit-of-the-bargain, recovery of out-of-pocket expenses, punitive damages, and other types of recovery allowable under the law are not discussed, nor are areas of the law with specific criteria for determining recoverable damages (such as patent infringement cases) addressed.

ROLE OF THE LAW AND FINANCIAL EXPERTS

The law drives all litigation matters, including damage issues. Case law and statutory law are the most important areas of the law that apply to financial experts.

> Although financial experts are usually not attorneys and are not expected by their professional standards to know the law, attorneys frequently choose experts who have some knowledge of the law that applies to a particular litigation matter.

As a practical matter, the financial expert may want to become familiar with important cases and statutory law in the jurisdiction in which a particular matter will be tried.

Financial professionals who serve as testifying experts will be retained by the plaintiff or defendant (or the respective attorney) or will work as a jointly retained or court-appointed expert. In business damage cases, the plaintiff's expert will present an opinion of the amount of damages and the basis for the opinion. The defendant's expert will either critique the plaintiff's damage claim and/or offer an alternative damage calculation.

LEGAL PRINCIPLES GOVERNING DAMAGES

For the plaintiff to be awarded damages in business litigation, he or she must prove two things:

1. The defendant was liable (e.g., it breached the contract or its product was defective).
2. The plaintiff suffered damages as a result of the defendant's actions.

In most business litigation, the financial expert is not involved in the liability portion of the case (with some exceptions, e.g., proving accounting malpractice). Therefore, only legal principles most relevant to the financial expert are discussed in the following sections.

Reasonable Certainty

The plaintiff must prove that the damages claimed are *reasonably certain,* that is, it is reasonably certain that the plaintiff would have earned the amount of claimed lost profits or the company would have been worth the specified business value.

Belleville Toyota, Inc. v. Toyota Motor Sales U.S.A., Inc. 199 Ill. 2d 325,770 N.E. 2d 177 (2002) states that "the law does not require that lost profits be proven with absolute certainly. Rather, the evidence need only afford a reasonable basis for the computation of damages which, with a reasonable degree of certainty, can be traced to the defendants' wrongful conduct. Defendants should not be permitted to escape liability entirely because the amount of the damage they have caused is uncertain. To do so would be to immunize defendants from the consequences of their wrongful act."

> Establishing reasonable certainty involves rigorous analysis, of which the identification and testing of key assumptions may be an important part. Some of these key assumptions are commonly based on client representations.

Accountants who compile financial statements (as opposed to audited and reviewed financial statements) and who prepare tax returns are accustomed to accepting client representations without independent verification or testing. However, in a litigation setting, similar blanket acceptance of key client representations should generally not be done unless they are considered reasonable by the expert. Critical assumptions that have not been evaluated for reasonableness may not be accepted by the trier-of-fact (e.g., jury, judge, arbitrator) and may render the expert's damage opinion invalid. Therefore, it is important for the financial expert to evaluate the key assumptions to the damage opinion, including those provided by the client.

Business plans (or litigant's financial projections) sometimes are used as a foundation for damage calculations because business plans and projections created prior to the wrongful actions are independent of the litigation motives of the parties. However, since some courts have ruled that unproven business plans and financial projections are not adequate to provide the base assumptions for damages calculations, the expert should consider evaluating the business plan or projection.

Exclusions Based on Insufficient Facts and Data—Failure to Provide Independent Analysis

Ellipsis, Inc. v. The Color Works, Inc. 428 F. Supp. 2nd 752, 760 (WD. Tenn. 2006)

- "Courts must consider the factual basis of an expert's testimony when considering its reliability."
- The expert relied exclusively on data provided by the plaintiff, made an estimate of growth rate without any basis, made an assumption of a comparable market, and failed to analyze other factors regarding the sale of the product in question.

Proximate Cause

The plaintiff also must prove *proximate cause,* that is, that damages have been proximately (directly) caused by the defendant's wrongful conduct. Sometimes *proximate cause* is simply referred to as *causation.* Under the principle of proximate cause, only that portion of the decline in plaintiff profits attributable to defendant's wrongful actions is recoverable. For example, loss of profits due to a slowdown in the economy is not recoverable.

Use of Hindsight in Causation

In assessing cause, the expert should consider other possible causes for the plaintiff's financial results, including general economic factors such as inflation, growth, or market demand.

Penn Mart Supermarkets, Inc. v. New Castle Shopping, LLC. No. 20405=NC (Del. Chan. 2005)

The court found three "separate and distinct causes" that contributed to plaintiff's loss of sales and that it did not account for in its damages calculation: 1) increased competition, 2) the bankruptcy of a primary supplier, and 3) a major construction project near the entrance to its store.

ValTip

Attorneys sometimes request that financial experts offer opinions on causation. The expert should evaluate whether he or she has the qualifications and foundation to render such an opinion.

Foreseeability

Another legal principle applicable to contract claims but not torts is *foreseeability,* that is, "whether and to what extent . . . damages, to be recoverable, must have been foreseeable as a natural and probable result of a breach of contract at the time the contract was made."[1] In other words, the plaintiff must show that, at the time the contract was made, the claimed lost profits were a foreseeable result of the defendant's wrongful actions. Damages that actually may have occurred but were not foreseen as a probable result of a hypothetical breach during the making of the contract by the parties are not recoverable.

Example: A parts manufacturer was delinquent in delivering goods to an automotive plant according to the schedule specified in the contract. This delay at one plant had a compounding effect and caused three other plants to be shut down. Based on the foreseeability principle, the plaintiff recovered its losses at all four plants because both parties, during the making of the contract, had contemplated and understood the compounding effect of a scheduling delinquency.

ADMISSIBILITY OF EXPERT OPINIONS

In the 1990s, several court cases raised the standards for the admissibility of expert testimony in federal jurisdictions. The most notable is *Daubert v. Merrell Dow Pharmaceuticals, Inc.* (113 S. Ct. 2786, 125 C. Ed., 2d 469 [1993]). This case established trial judges as "gatekeepers" over the admissibility of expert testimony at trial.

> Although *Daubert* involved a scientific expert, the court set forth four criteria by which a trial judge could evaluate the reliability of all expert testimony.

The *Daubert* factors are enumerated in Supreme Court of the United States No. 92-102, *William Daubert, et ux, etc., et al., Petitioners v. Merrell Dow Pharmaceuticals, Inc.*:

- ". . . whether a theory or technique . . . can be (and has been) tested."
- ". . . whether the theory or technique has been subjected to peer review and publication."
- ". . . the known or potential rate of error . . . and the existence and maintenance of standards controlling the technique's operation."
- ". . . explicit identification of a relevant scientific community and an express determination of a particular degree of acceptance within that community."

Since the Court stated that these factors should be applied flexibly and that other factors also may be considered, the *Daubert* factors are not necessarily applied literally.

---

[1] R. Dunn, *Recovery of Damages for Lost Profits,* 5th ed. (Westport, CT: Lawpress Corporation, 1998), § 1.8.

Congruent with *Daubert*, Federal Rule of Evidence 702, "Testimony by Experts," states that an expert witness may testify "if 1) the testimony is based upon sufficient facts or data, 2) the testimony is the product of reliable principles and methods, and 3) the witness has applied the principles and methods reliably to the facts of the case."

Daubert and Rule 702 emphasize that expert witnesses must apply accepted methods in the proper context and should expect to defend such methods not only through *ipse dixit* ("because I said so") but also through various external proofs. Since the 1993 *Daubert* case, the federal courts have been moving resolutely toward excluding "junk" testimony. In addition, some state courts have adopted stricter criteria for the admissibility of expert testimony.

What does this mean for the financial expert providing testimony? The expert should be prepared to prove that the methods and damage theory being used are generally accepted in the professional community. The expert should know the relevant professional standards and apply them properly. The expert should be knowledgeable of and be prepared to reference the appropriate professional literature for generally accepted methods. Furthermore, critical underlying data and assumptions should be reasonable and applied appropriately.

MEASURE OF DAMAGES: DIMINUTION OF VALUE OR LOST PROFITS

Business damages commonly are measured by one of two approaches: lost profits or diminution of value. When is each of these measures appropriate? The following scenarios will provide general guidance from which to answer this question.

Scenario 1: Temporary Impairment

The defendant breached a five-year contract to purchase merchandise from the plaintiff. These lost revenues represented only a portion of the plaintiff's entire business. The company mitigated its damages by eventually replacing the lost sales, and the business continued to operate. The results of the breach are illustrated in Exhibit 23.1. The measure of damages for a temporary impairment is considered lost profits.

Exhibit 23.1 Temporary Impairment

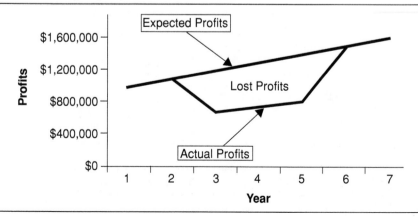

Scenario 2: Immediate Destruction of Business

The defendant breached a five-year contract to purchase merchandise from the plaintiff. These lost revenues represented substantially all of the plaintiff's revenues, and the remaining customer revenues did not cover the business's fixed costs. As a result, the plaintiff went out of business soon after the breach. The results of the breach for this example are illustrated in Exhibit 23.2.

Exhibit 23.2   Immediate Destruction of Business
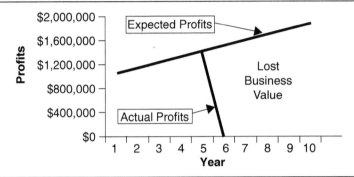

Where an immediate destruction of the business occurs, diminution of value generally would be indicated as the most appropriate measure of damages. Under the income approach of valuation, the present value of the future earnings or cash-flow is the value of the company under the discounted future earnings/cash flow method using the business's cost of capital as the discount rate. However, some experts believe a lost-profits analysis may be a better measure of the plaintiff's actual damages to make it whole in some circumstances.

Scenario 3: Slow Death of Business

The defendant breached a five-year contract to purchase merchandise from the plaintiff. These lost revenues represented a substantial portion of the plaintiff's revenues. The company struggled to stay in business for a few years before it eventually closed due to the breach. The results of the breach for this example are illustrated in Exhibit 23.3.

Exhibit 23.3   Slow Death of Business
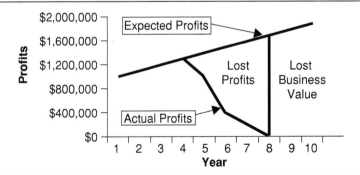

The slow death of a business, as presented above, might use a combination of the two measures. For the period after the breach in which the business still operated, a lost-profits calculation could be done. When the business ceased its operations, a value for the business might be established *as of that date,* using the diminution of value measure.

Reasonable certainty and proximate cause also would have to be demonstrated to prove damages by any measure.

DIFFERENCES BETWEEN DAMAGE COMPUTATIONS AND BUSINESS VALUATIONS

The differences between the assumptions and methodologies used in commercial damage calculations and those used in business valuations are slight in some regards and great in others. The most common differences between business valuations and lost profit calculations are summarized in Exhibit 23.4. Several of these differences are discussed in depth.

Level of Scrutiny

The level of scrutiny of a business valuation in a litigation setting is significantly higher than valuations done for other reasons. Often, opposing counsel will ask a series of questions designed to attack the expert's credibility and destroy his or her testimony. In most nonlitigation situations, however, the distribution of the valuation professional's report is limited, as is scrutiny of report details, underlying data, and the valuation professional's qualifications.

ValTip

> In litigation, the financial expert can expect to be challenged regarding qualifications, the proper application of valuation theory, and the appropriateness of the underlying assumptions and facts.

Period of Recovery

The period of recovery is sometimes called the damage period or period of loss. In a lost-profits model, the damage calculation is made for a specific time period (e.g., from the date of injury to date of trial plus three years), implying a time limitation for recoverable lost profits.

ValTip

> One of the most challenging aspects of a lost-profits calculation is determining how far into the future to project ongoing lost profits. The period of recovery largely depends on the facts and circumstances of the case and on the consideration of reasonable certainty and proximate cause.

Exhibit 23.4   Common Differences Between Lost-Profit Calculations and Business Valuations (FMV)

Issue	Lost-Profit Calculations	Business Valuations
Level of Scrutiny	High	Typically low outside of litigation, otherwise high
Period of Recovery	Damages calculated for a fixed period and meet the test of reasonable certainty	Valuation done as of specific date and company usually assumed to continue in perpetuity
Protagonist	Actual, specific litigant–may be unwilling buyer/seller	Hypothetical willing buyer and seller
Incremental Costs	Need to calculate costs that would have been incurred, had plaintiff made projected lost revenues	Not applicable
Pre-judgment Interest	Often required to calculate interest payable to plaintiff between date of injury and date of trial	Typically not done by appraiser
Discount Rates	Often based on what would make the plaintiff whole under the circumstances	Based on company's cost of capital
Benefit Stream	Either income or cash flow	Typically cash flow
Tax Considerations	Use after-tax discount rate on pre tax lost profits (or after-tax discount rate on after-tax lost profits and gross up for taxes on damages)	Matching of after-tax discount rate with after-tax benefit stream
Subsequent Events	Usually information through date of trial considered *(ex post)*	Usually information considered up to valuation date *(ex ante)*

For example, if a defendant has breached a long-term contract with 20 years of the term remaining, can a lost-profits calculation for 20 years in the future pass the test of reasonable certainty? What economic or industry factors might affect a 20-year lost-profits projection and, thus, create a problem with the test of proximate cause? Due to the uncertainty in such long-term projections, many courts and experts believe that, in most situations, lost business profits can be projected three or more years into the future and still pass the tests for reasonable certainty and proximate cause.[2] In any

---

[2] For example, see B. Brinig et al., PPC's *Guide to Litigation Support Services*, 9th ed. (Fort Worth, TX: Practitioner Publishing Company, 2004), ¶ 303.39 and Dunn, *Recovery of Damages*, § 6.19.

event, the damage period will not extend beyond a reasonable time for the plaintiff to fully recover from the injury inflicted by the defendant.

Business valuations are based on a value estimate as of a single, specific date and usually assume the business will operate into perpetuity.

Protagonist—Litigant versus Hypothetical Willing Buyer/Seller

In business litigation, the objective of compensatory damages is to make the plaintiff whole. Doing this requires the consideration of a specific plaintiff's unique facts and circumstances. In many situations, this may not fit the standards established by the business valuation profession for fair market value.

In business valuation, not only do the fair market value standards exclude specific buyers and sellers in favor of the "hypothetical" buyer/seller, but they also require that the hypothetical buyer/seller be willing and fully informed. In business litigation, depending upon venue and circumstances, none of these requirements for buyer and seller may exist.

Incremental Costs

Incremental costs are those expenses that, due to lost sales, the plaintiff does not incur. In damage calculations for businesses that have been partially impaired, the incremental costs associated with lost revenues will be used to reduce those lost revenues and arrive at an estimate of lost profits.

Example: If a tire factory lost a contract order for $1 million in sales, the costs of manufacturing and selling those tires will be deducted as incremental costs, as illustrated in the following formula:

$$\text{Lost Revenues} - \text{Incremental Costs} = \text{Lost Profits}$$

Since business valuations typically focus on valuing the company's normalized earnings or cash flow, all the company's expenses are usually considered in the computations.

Prejudgment Interest

In business litigation, the financial expert may be required to calculate damages at some date in the past and then provide an additional damage calculation, called prejudgment interest, from the date of injury up to the date of trial.

ValTip

In many jurisdictions, the law mandates the treatment of prejudgment interest, often by prescribing a statutory interest rate, generally based on simple rather than compound interest calculations.

If the law is silent regarding prejudgment interest, the expert will want to examine judicial practice in the jurisdiction of the trial and ask the attorney whether the court or the expert will perform prejudgment interest calculations. If there is no legal guidance available, the expert will have to select and apply a rate of return he or she believes is appropriate, taking into account that a discount rate to be used with past lost profits may need to be different from that to be used with future lost profits.

Prejudgment interest is not normally calculated as part of a traditional business valuation.

Discount Rates

The discussion in this section uses "nominal" currency amounts and rates of return that include the effects of inflation rather than "real" currency amounts and rates of return where the effects of inflation have been eliminated.[3]

Discount rates are used in lost-profit calculations for determining the present value of lost future income. The selection of the discount rate has a significant effect on the present value of the future lost profits and, thus, on the amount of the damages awarded to the plaintiff. Exhibit 23.5 provides an example of the magnitude of this effect.

Exhibit 23.5   Effect of Discount Rates on Lost Profits (Mid-Year Convention)

Total Lost Profits for 3 Years into the Future	
($100,000 + 110,000 + 120,000)	$330,000
Present Value of $330,000 at 5%	$306,048
Present Value of $330,000 at 10%	$285,251
Present Value of $330,000 at 20%	$251,040

In addition, the determination of an appropriate discount rate to use in calculating business damages involves a fundamental legal presumption.

ValTip

The purpose of compensatory damages is to make the plaintiff whole. That is, the plaintiff should receive no more or no less than is necessary to make it whole.

---

[3] Nominal amounts are the actual currency amounts or rates of return including inflation. Real amounts are inflation-adjusted currency amounts or rates of return. Some economists present rates of return in damage calculations as real rates, or inflation-adjusted rates. A 5 percent normal rate of return for a safe investment would be reduced by inflation of, say, 3 percent, to result in a real return of 2 percent.

While it is common for the courts to award damages to make the plaintiff whole, there may be situations where damages are limited as a matter of law. In other situations, the law might allow the plaintiff to recover more than its lost profits, as in cases that disgorge the defendant of its profits (unjust enrichment). This chapter discusses the concept of making the plaintiff whole as a matter of fact rather than exceptions as a matter of law.

There is little guidance in finance literature or case law to direct the expert in selecting the appropriate discount rate for future lost-profit damages. In a few business damage cases, a risk-free rate has been specified as a matter of law. However, most courts favor the discount rate as a question of fact instead of a matter of law. Financial experts generally have viewed the appropriate discount rate for lost-profit damages in three ways:

1. Use a risky projection of future lost profits and apply a higher discount rate to consider the higher level of risk.[4]
2. Use a low-risk (conservative) projection and apply a low-risk discount rate.
3. Use a discount rate based on how the plaintiff will invest the damage award and apply it to a projection of future lost profits that is "reasonably certain."

The first and second approaches of determining a discount rate are analogous to the determination of the cost of capital in the discounted cash flow (DCF) methodology in business valuations. Both use a risk-adjusted discount rate. The third approach focuses on the plaintiff's investment return on the damage award.

The third approach suggests the consideration of how the plaintiff can be expected to reasonably "invest" the portion of a court award related to future lost profits. Using the table in Exhibit 23.5, if the plaintiff reasonably expects to invest a court award received today at a rate of return of 10 percent, then it would receive $285,251 from a court award today and invest it at 10 percent to compensate it for the $330,000 of profits it would have received over the next three years. An award based on a 5 percent discount rate but actually invested at 10 percent would overcompensate the plaintiff. An award based on a 20 percent discount rate but actually invested at 10 percent would undercompensate the plaintiff.

Several benchmarks that could be used to assist in selecting appropriate discount rates include:

- Return on a conservative investment
- Return on an investment portfolio
- The company's cost of debt
- The company's weighted average cost of capital
- The company's cost of equity
- Return on an investment similar to the destroyed business

The facts and circumstances necessary to select one (or a blend) of these will vary from case to case. The selection of a discount rate in any specific lawsuit may depend on matters of fact and matters of law. For example, the requirement of a

---

[4] The case that is often cited is *Jones & Laughlin Steel Co. v. Pfeifer*, 462 U.S. 538 (1983), which discussed parity in risk, parity in inflation, and parity in income taxes. However, this case was related to personal injury.

risk-free discount rate might be a matter of law mandated by a prior case in the jurisdiction. Matters of fact might include consideration of these types of questions:

- Are the lost profit projections reasonable?
- If a plaintiff is partially impaired, does the plaintiff have the ability to reinvest a damage award in the company?
- If the plaintiff is totally destroyed, should it be assumed that the plaintiff should invest a damage award in another investment similar to the destroyed business?

Some practitioners believe the discount rate also should factor in the risks associated with achieving projected future lost profits, as is commonly done in business valuations. However, some courts have rejected this approach.[5] As previously mentioned, in determining the discount rate, there is little consistent guidance from case law regarding what factors to consider.[6]

The following cases address the discount rate in future lost-profit damages.

Purina Mills, LLC v. Less[7]

The plaintiff had a contract with Less requiring the defendant to purchase a set number of livestock at a fixed price over a period of several years. The defendant failed to make the required livestock purchases. The damages were based on the number of livestock specified in the contract and the stated price per head. The court found the appropriate discount rate to be applied to future damages should be the corresponding Treasury rate, which ranged from 1.24 percent (one-year Treasury) to 3.17 percent (five-year Treasury) in this situation. These discount rates represent a risk-free rate.

Energy Capital Corp. v. The United States[8]

The plaintiff had a contract with the U.S. government to originate $200 million in loans related to government-assisted housing. The contract was breached approximately five and one-half months after it was signed and before the plaintiff had completed the process of originating any loans. The plaintiff claimed damages for lost profits.

The appellate court said that the appropriate discount rate on future lost profits is a question of fact rather than a matter of law. It found that a risk-free rate as a matter of law found by the trial court was not appropriate. The appellate court said, "The purpose of the lost profits damages calculation is to put Energy Capital in as good a position as [it] would have been had the contract been performed." It adopted a risk-adjusted discount rate of 10.5 percent based on the average yield on mortgage REITs of 8.5 percent plus a 2 percent adjustment. It rejected a 25 percent risk-adjusted discount rate presented by the defendant's expert.

---

[5] See *American List Corp. v. U.S. News & World Report, Inc.*, 75 N.Y.2d 38, 550 N.Y.S.2d 590 (1989). In this case, the trial court found a higher discount rate (18 percent) should be used to factor in the risk the plaintiff would not be able to perform the contract in the future. The appellate court rejected the higher discount rate.

[6] Dunn, *Recovery of Damages*, p. 504.

[7] 295 F. supp. 2d 1017 (N.D. Iowa 2003).

[8] 302 F. 3d 1314; 2002 U.S. App. Lexis 16447.

Munters Corporation v. Swissco-Young Industries, Inc.[9]

Swissco went bankrupt after equipment supplied by Munters failed to meet specifications. Swissco had purchased and installed the equipment at its customer's site. Swissco's customer then refused to pay Swissco because of the equipment problems, which resulted in the bankruptcy. Lost profits were claimed by Swissco against Munters over a ten-year period plus a terminal value for the company. The court affirmed the trial court's use of a 10 percent discount rate used by the plaintiff's expert and rejected the defendant's expert, who opined the discount rate should be at least 20 percent.

Burger King Corporation v. Barnes[10]

In this case, Barnes had operated a franchised fast-food restaurant for 29 months. The court allowed Burger King Corporation's damages related to future lost royalties to be projected for 210 months (17.5 years) into the future over the remaining term of the franchise agreement based on the amount of the restaurant's historical sales. The opinion indicates that neither inflation nor any other increase in profits was projected above the actual historic sales. The future lost profits were discounted at a 9 percent discount rate. Therefore, the 9 percent is a real rate of return rather than a nominal rate.

Knox v. Taylor[11]

The appellate court did not overturn the use of a 7 percent risk-free discount rate in a lost-profit damage calculation as a matter of law.

Olson v. Neiman's, Ltd.[12]

The appellate court allowed the expert's damage opinion for the plaintiff that used a 19.4 percent discount rate based on a 14.4 percent normal return for public companies plus a 5 percent premium for risk. The discount rate was applied to lost patent royalty income.

Tax Considerations

Business damages are subject to taxation under the Internal Revenue Code.[13] Therefore, the Internal Revenue Service will tax a court award or settlement, and taxes should be considered in the damage calculation. The thought process and calculation go as follows:

Had the plaintiff remained in its original condition before the injury, it would have earned certain profits and paid the associated income taxes. Exhibit 23.6 demonstrates the expected profits of the plaintiff, XYZ Inc., "but-for" the defendant's

---

[9] 100 S.W. 3d 292; 2002 TX App (1st) 511.

[10] *Burger King Corporation v. Barnes,* 1 F. Supp 2d 1367 (S.D. Fla. 1998).

[11] *Knox v. Taylor,* 992 S.W.2d 40 (Tex. App. 1999).

[12] *Olson v. Neiman's, Ltd.,* 579 N.W.2d 299 (Iowa 1998).

[13] Only compensatory damages related to personal physical injury or sickness are excluded from taxable income. See Internal Revenue Code § 104(a)(2).

actions, for three years into the future. Year 0 represents the current base year used in projecting future profits for years 1 to 3. Assume that XYZ Inc. has a constant tax rate of 40 percent.

Exhibit 23.6   XYZ Inc.: Expected Future Income But-For the Defendant's Actions

	Year			
	0	**1**	**2**	**3**
Income before taxes	$100,000	$110,000	$121,000	$133,100
Income taxes at 40%	(40,000)	(44,000)	(48,400)	(53,240)
Net Income	$ 60,000	$ 66,000	$ 72,600	$ 79,860

Exhibit 23.7 demonstrates a calculation of damages, based on discounting XYZ's pretax income at its after-tax weighted average cost of capital (WACC) of 12 percent and using the mid-year discounting convention.

Exhibit 23.7   XYZ Inc.: Calculation of Damages for Future Lost Profits

Year	Future Lost Profits (pre tax)	Present Value
1	$110,000	$103,940
2	121,000	102,084
3	133,100	100,261
	Damages	$306,285

In a court award, XYZ would receive $306,285 as full compensation for future lost profits. After a 40 percent tax hit, XYZ would have $183,772, which it could reinvest at its WACC of 12 percent.

Exhibit 23.8 presents the calculations for determining how much XYZ Inc. expects to have at the end of a three-year period during which it has reinvested the net-of-tax damage award of $183,772 at its WACC of 12 percent.

Exhibit 23.8   Reinvestment of Damage Award Net of Taxes

	Annual Earnings (12%)	Amount at End of Year
Damages awards after taxes are paid		$183,772
Year 1	$22,053	205,825
Year 2	24,699	230,524
Year 3	27,663	258,186

How does this amount in Exhibit 23.8 compare to what it would have received "but-for" the defendant's actions, as determined in Exhibit 23.6? Exhibit 23.9 presents

Exhibit 23.9   But-For Net Income Plus Accumulated Earnings Through the End of Year 3

Year	But-For Net Income*	No. of Years to End of Yr. 3	Future Value at 12%
1	$66,000	2.5	$ 87,617
2	72,600	1.5	86,053
3	79,860	0.5	84,516
Total			$258,186

*See Exhibit 23.6

the plaintiff's position at the end of year 3, using the "but-for" net income data from Exhibit 23.6.

VaITip

This section demonstrates the concept of discounting future *pretax* earnings by the appropriate *after-tax* discount rate in calculating damages.

The results of both calculations (Exhibits 23.8 and 23.9) are identical.

An alternative presentation with the same result is to apply the after-tax income to the WACC of 12 percent to arrive at a present value and then "gross up" the result by the 40 percent tax factor.

Were the effective tax rate to vary rather than remain constant over the projection period, a different analysis might be necessary.

In contrast to this treatment of taxes in damages calculations, in a business valuation income approach, discount rates are developed from market data that typically are based on after-corporate-tax rates of returns for investments in public companies. Once a valuation professional has determined the appropriate discount rate using this market data, it is applied to the subject company's after-tax earnings, applying an *after-tax* discount rate with *after-tax* earnings. Theoretically, an after-tax discount rate could be adjusted to a pretax discount rate and applied to the subject company's pretax earnings to arrive at the same value. However, in many situations, this is not a common business valuation practice.

For a more detailed quantitative analysis on taxes and discount rates, see G. Hallman and M. Wagner, "Tax Effects of Discount Rates in Taxable Damage Awards," *CPA Expert* (New York: American Institute of Certified Public Accountants, Winter 1999), 1–5.

Subsequent Events and Measurement Date

Compensatory damages in litigation seek to make the plaintiff whole usually at the time the trier-of-fact renders its decision (e.g., the date of trial). Therefore, damage computations usually consider events through the date of trial, including events subsequent to the date of injury (i.e., date of valuation).

A business valuation determines the fair market value of a business on a specific date (i.e., the valuation date) by contemplating what a hypothetical willing buyer would pay for it on that date. Only the information that was known or knowable to the hypothetical buyer and seller on that date is usually considered. Events that occur subsequent to the valuation date usually are not considered because they are unknowable to the hypothetical buyer and seller.

Example: Sample Corp. was destroyed in September 2005 by a hurricane. If a financial expert were asked to calculate Sample Corp.'s lost-profits damages for an injury that impaired the business in August 2004, and the trial occurred in October, 2006, the expert would typically need to include the effect of the hurricane in the calculations to ensure that Sample Corp. was not going to be made more than whole (this would not be true if the law did not allow consideration of the hurricane).

However, if the same financial expert were asked to value Sample Corp. for tax purposes as of August 31, 2004, the expert may not include the effect of the hurricane in the calculations since it was unknowable on the date of the valuation (e.g., August 31, 2004).

The measurement date for damages should be determined through discussions with the attorney. The two concepts are *ex ante* and *ex post* measurements. An *ex ante* damage measurement typically results in a measurement as of the date of injury. Most business valuations are prepared on this basis. An *ex post* damage measurement typically considers information through the date of trial (or the closest practical date). Most lost-profits computations are prepared on this basis.

CAN BUSINESS DAMAGES EXCEED THE FAIR MARKET VALUE OF THE BUSINESS?

There is no general legal guidance for an expert in determining whether lost profit damages can exceed the value of a business. Since the expert does not have any matter of law as a guide, the matters of fact in each specific case determine the answer. Business damages could exceed the fair market value of the business for two reasons:

1. The facts and circumstances of the case
2. The differences between lost-profit damage calculations and the business valuation fair market value standard

Since the goal of awarding compensatory damages is to make the plaintiff whole, there are valid facts and circumstances under which a damage award for the fair market value of the business might not achieve that goal.

Example: A governmental entity decided to widen a public road and condemned part of the land owned by a franchised fast-food restaurant. As a result of taking away the land, the restaurant lost one-third of its parking and could no longer operate profitably from that location. Due to limited availability of other restaurant sites and possible infringement on the territories of other franchisees, the restaurant could not relocate. The restaurant was forced to cease operations and had no opportunity to mitigate its losses. Should damages be limited to the fair market value of the fast-food restaurant?

Assuming the restaurant's cost of equity was 25 percent, and assuming damages were limited to the fair market value of the business, an award would have been made based on the theory that the plaintiff would put the award into an investment yielding a 25 percent rate of return for the future. In reality, however, there were no conventional investments that would generate a consistent 25 percent rate of return.

Although the argument might be made that the plaintiff could use the award to buy another comparable business yielding a 25 percent rate of return, from a legal standpoint should the plaintiff be forced to undergo the risks and effort involved in a search for such a hypothetical business, which may not actually exist? In addition, suppose the plaintiff was a passive owner, 60 years of age, and in poor health. What if the plaintiff only had skills in operating a fast-food restaurant? How should these specific facts be considered in computing the plaintiff's damages?

In this example, it is clear that a damage award limited to the fair market value of the business may not make the plaintiff whole.

Therefore, it is important to consider the unique facts and circumstances of the case when determining the best approach to measure the plaintiff's damages. Each case is different, and the plaintiff's situation should be considered. In addition, local law should be taken into account.

CONCLUSION

Business damages are part of a lawsuit and are subject to statutes, case law, local judicial practice, and legal interpretations. The expert should look to the attorney to give direction in these areas. Matters of law in a particular case are outside of a financial expert's expertise and should be explained by the attorney on how they affect damages. Legal matters may have a substantial effect on the amount of damages that are recoverable. On the other hand, matters of fact are not legal in nature; therefore, they are the subject of the opinion of experts and others or on other evidence.

CHAPTER 24

Other Valuation Services Areas

This chapter presents limited and general information on other valuation services areas that analysts sometimes encounter. The following sections only provide an overview of each topic. Future editions of this book may expand on these areas.

A: Valuation for Public Companies and/or Financial Reporting
B: Valuation Issues in Buy-Sell Agreements
C: Valuing Debt
D: Valuation Issues in Preferred Stock
E: Restricted Stock Valuation
F: Valuation of Early-Stage Technology Companies
G: Valuation Issues Related to Stock Options and Other Share-Based Compensation
H: Real Option Valuations
I: Maximizing Shareholder Value

A: VALUATIONS FOR PUBLIC COMPANIES AND/OR FINANCIAL REPORTING

The Changing Face of Public Company Valuations

There are over 10,000 publicly traded companies in the United States. Whether driven by financial reporting requirements, tax planning and compliance, transactions, management planning, or litigation services, these companies represent potential clients for business valuation analysts. Asset price volatility and the proliferation of derivatives and other financial instruments similarly result in more valuation opportunities.

ValTip

> The increasing importance of intangible assets and intellectual property to public companies' financial positions and strategic profiles also increases the need for valuation services.

In the 1990s, independent auditors assisted at will with fair value determination and other valuation assignments either directly or through in-house experts. Beginning with the Independence Standards Board's (ISB) Interpretation 99-1, however, auditor independence came under scrutiny when the auditor was found to be auditing his or her own work. Much of the ISB's work was incorporated into the SEC's auditor independence rules, which were adopted in November 2000. The SEC adopted additional amendments to its auditor independence requirements in January 2003. These amendments incorporate the requirements found in the Sarbanes-Oxley Act (SOX) of 2002. Among other things, SOX identified nine categories of services that cannot be provided by the auditor without impairing the auditor's independence. Included in the nine categories are "appraisal or valuation services, fairness opinions, or contribution-in-kind reports."

As a result of legislation and Standards Board pronouncements, greater attention is paid to management's reliance on independent valuation experts. Valuation groups within accounting firms are increasingly relied upon by audit teams to evaluate the reliability and quality of work done by independent valuation experts. It is therefore critical for independent valuation analysts to stay current with relevant accounting and auditing pronouncements and practices.

Major Reasons for Public Company Valuations

Financial Reporting Requirements

Unlike most other valuation assignments, the need for public company valuation services is often dictated by generally accepted accounting principles (GAAP).

The GAAP pronouncements state what type of assets and liabilities need to be valued, when they need to be valued, the standard of value to be utilized, and even, for certain assets/liabilities, the valuation procedures to be applied.

The standard of value used most often in financial reporting valuations is fair value. This is different from the "fair value" used in shareholder disputes.

SFAS No. 157, Fair Value Measurements (now ASC 820 Fair Value Measurements and Disclosures), established a consistent definition of fair value for GAAP purposes:

Fair value is the price that would be received to sell an asset or paid to transfer a liability in an orderly transaction between market participants at the measurement date.

This definition contains a number of important concepts:

- The "price that would be received . . . or paid" refers to an *exit value*, or value in exchange. This means that the price paid for an asset (an *entry value*) is not necessarily equivalent to fair value.
- An "orderly transaction" (fair value) is differentiated from a distressed transaction (not necessarily fair value).
- The "market participants" concept means that fair value is determined by reference to the hypothetical buyer, and thus excludes any synergies that would be unique to the current owner.

SFAS No. 157 establishes and/or clarifies a number of other concepts, including:

- Principal (or most advantageous) market
- Valuation techniques (market, income, cost)
- Observable versus unobservable inputs; observable inputs are preferable
- A three-level hierarchy for classifying inputs and resulting values

SFAS No. 157 also excludes from its scope certain types of assets, including:

- Share-based compensation under SFAS No. 123R
- Vendor-specific objective evidence (VSOE) provisions

This does not require a fair value estimate to be prepared by an independent valuation analyst. The specialized knowledge that an independent valuation analyst provides, however, can help management meet its business prudence requirement and keep corporate resources focused on managing the company.

ValTip

> When engaged to provide an opinion regarding the fair value of a particular public company's assets or liabilities, it is important to confirm with the company's auditor the exact definition (and interpretation) of fair value to be utilized and to clearly identify which items are to be valued.

Exhibit 24.1 lists the classifications of engagements that may be performed for GAAP-related purposes and some of the major applicable pronouncements.

Exhibit 24.2 identifies the relevant sections of this book that discuss further the factors to consider and the methodologies to use in the valuation of these various assets (or liabilities).

The need for GAAP-driven valuation work is expected to continue to increase.

Exhibit 24.1   Accounting Pronouncements

Type of Engagement	Major Pronouncements
Purchase Price Allocations	SFAS No. 2
	SFAS No. 86
	SFAS No. 141
	FASB Technical Bulletin 84-1
	FASB Interpretation No. 4
	FASB Interpretation No. 6
	SOP 98-1
	EITF 02-17
	SFAC No. 7
Options and Derivative Instruments	SFAS No. 133
	SFAS No. 137
	SFAS No. 138
Employee Stock Options and ESOPs	SFAS No. 123(R)
	SOP 93-6
	APB Opinion No. 25
Nonmonetary Transactions and Contributions-in-Kind	APB Opinion No. 29
	FASB Technical Bulletin 85-1
Asset Impairment	SFAS No. 144
	SFAS No. 142
	EITF 02-13 Deferred Income Tax
Quasi-reorganizations	APB No. 43
Transfers and Servicing of Financial Assets	SFAS No. 140

Source data: *Financial Accounting Standards Board.* (This table does not include a complete list of related pronouncements and does not reflect the new accounting standards codification system.)

Tax Planning and Compliance

One of the most common business appraisal assignments results from federal or state income or capital gains tax planning or compliance and includes:

- Transfer pricing analyses
- Employee stock option valuations
- Purchase price allocations
- Built-in gains analyses

Exhibit 24.2   Types of Assets

Asset	Chapter
Intangible assets	21
Real estate	8
Machinery and equipment	8
Common stock	Various
Preferred stock	24D
Debt	24C
Stock options and warrants	24G

The tax valuation needs of an entity, whether public or private, normally are centered on tax compliance, deferral, or minimization. Regardless of which of these is the primary focus, often independent and objective business valuation services are an integral part of achieving the client's goal.

Transfer pricing analyses are governed by § 482 of the Internal Revenue Code (IRC). Specifically, transfers relating to intangible assets require the expertise of a valuation analyst to analyze the nature of the intangible assets and determine the most appropriate valuation methodology. Chapter 21 of this book briefly addresses intercompany transfer pricing, including the relevant valuation methods.

Employee stock option valuations are as necessary for IRS purposes as they are for financial reporting purposes. Section G in this chapter gives a detailed description of the different types of employee stock options, when they need to be valued, and the methods for valuing each type.

ValTip

> While a public corporation's traded stock has a readily determinable value and the company may have publicly traded options, distinct differences between employee stock options and publicly traded stock options influence their value. Also, corporations may grant employee stock options on shares that are not publicly traded, including shares in subsidiaries and shares with voting rights different from those of the publicly traded stock.

Tax-related purchase price allocations made up a large portion of the valuation engagements performed prior to 1993. Then came the Omnibus Budget Reconciliation Act of 1993, which introduced § 197 to the Internal Revenue Code. Instead of allocating the purchase price among various assets and asset categories and depreciating the value of the identifiable intangible assets over a demonstrated limited life, the Act reclassified most intangible assets as § 197 assets, which are written off over 15 years. This, however, did not eliminate the need for purchase price allocations for tax purposes. IRC § 1060 still requires that the seller and purchaser each allocate the consideration paid or received in a transaction among the assets bought/sold in the same manner as amounts are allocated under IRC § 338. Section 338 identifies seven general asset allocation classes:

Class I. Cash and cash equivalents
Class II. Actively traded personal property as defined in IRC § 1092(d)(1)
Class III. Accounts receivable, mortgages, and credit card receivables that arise in the ordinary course of business
Class IV. Stock-in-trade of the taxpayer or other property of the kind that would properly be included in the inventory of the taxpayer if on hand at the close of the tax year, or property held by the taxpayer primarily for sale to customers in the ordinary course of business
Class V. All assets not in Class I, II, III, IV, VI, or VII

Class VI. All IRC § 197 intangibles, except those in the nature of goodwill and
   going-concern value
Class VII. Goodwill and going-concern value

> In certain businesses, the lines are blurred between the intangible assets
> and income-producing real estate. Some examples include hotels, motels,
> hospitals, and skilled nursing centers. By performing a purchase price
> allocation, the analyst can separate intangible assets from the real prop-
> erty and the client can then amortize them over a much shorter life.

A corporate built-in gains analysis is a specialized valuation focused on
determining the built-in gains in a company that has been acquired. Built-in gains
can be associated with any asset, including intangible assets or investments in private companies. Built-in gains valuations are performed pursuant to IRC § 382,
which allows a corporation to maximize its use of any net operating loss carry-
forwards acquired. In general, § 382 limits the use of net operating loss carryfor-
wards and certain built-in losses following ownership change. The general
limitation is that the net operating loss carryforward cannot exceed the value of
the old corporation multiplied by the long-term tax-exempt rate. Any net unrealized built-in gain from the old corporation allows the new company to increase
the § 382 limitation by the recognized built-in gain from that year. The analysis
and execution of this type of engagement requires careful coordination with the
company's tax advisors.

Management Consulting Engagements

The specialized knowledge and experience of a valuation analyst is also useful to
corporate management in its general decision-making process. Often these consulting engagements use standards of value that differ from the traditional tax and
accounting standards. For instance, investment value and intrinsic value may be relevant standards of value in management consulting engagements.

> Clients typically are not versed in the differences among standards of
> value, so early communication and active listening are the keys to a suc-
> cessful engagement.

Exhibit 24.3 outlines some of the various types of engagements that could be
performed for management consulting purposes and the chapters of this book that
discuss these engagements.

Exhibit 24.3   Valuations for Management Consulting

Engagement	Standard of Value	Typical Valuation Method or Approach	Chapter
Economic value added analysis	Investment value or FMV	DCF	24
Solvency opinion*	N/A	Numerous	N/A
Royalty rate, fee analysis	Investment value or FMV	DCF, Transactions and Licensing	21

*The AICPA has restrictions on these services for CPAs.

Litigation Services

Public corporations, due to their widespread operations, high visibility, and perceived "deep pockets," are targets for various forms of litigation. Many of these cases require valuation analysis as well as expert testimony. Among the potential sources of litigation are business interruption, wrongful termination, breach of contract, infringement of intellectual property rights, and wrongful death. Chapter 23 discusses litigation services engagements in further detail.

Summary

There are myriad reasons why public companies may require the services of a qualified business appraiser. Auditor independence issues and general business and economic trends both tend to increase the demand for these services. The business appraiser, when performing valuations for financial reporting purposes, should rely on the relevant GAAP pronouncements. These pronouncements typically state the standard of value to be applied (fair value) and may even provide an outline of the valuation procedures to be followed. Tax valuations are all at fair market value. Other valuation engagements may require the use of other standards of value (i.e., investment or intrinsic value). For these valuations, the valuation professional must communicate early and often with management to ensure that the proper standard of value is used and that management realizes the effect the valuation standard may have on the conclusion reached.

B: VALUATION ISSUES IN BUY-SELL AGREEMENTS

The Importance of Buy-Sell Agreements

Buy-sell agreements are relevant to a discussion of valuation for two reasons:

1. Valuation analysts are uniquely qualified to assist clients and attorneys on constructing these agreements
2. The existence of such an agreement may have an impact on the value determined in a valuation engagement

Every closely held business owner should have a buy-sell agreement with his or her business partners/shareholders.

It is surprising how many business owners fail to draft such an agreement when things are going well and their partners/shareholders are "in the mood" to reach an amicable agreement. Furthermore, many owners who do have an agreement drafted may not understand the implications of the agreement that they have signed.

This becomes apparent when some highly stressful circumstance triggers the mechanisms provided in their agreements and they find they are negotiating stock buy-outs and prices or struggling over terms of the agreement that each owner thought they understood. These stressful circumstances might include:

- Owner in-fighting, that leads to one or more deciding to leave and wishing to be bought out
- Owner disability, and consequent need to be cashed out
- Owner death, and surviving owner needs to buy the stock from the estate
- Owner divorce, where the spouse, who is awarded half the stock, is demanding to be paid

The battles that accompany these agreements often occur at a time when the company needs most to be projecting assurances to its employees and customers. This can disrupt operations and ultimately, serve to reduce the very value over which the owners are at odds.

Analysts are uniquely qualified to consult with clients and their attorneys before the buy/sell agreements are written. They can help the attorney understand valuation provisions and walk the business owner and the attorney through some of the land-mines for the unwary, of which there are many.

Provisions of Typical Buy-Sell Agreements

A properly drafted buy-sell agreement that is clearly understood by all parties can be a critical tool in assuring the continuity of the company in the event of circumstances occurring like those mentioned previously. The agreement should establish the ground rules for the transition of ownership interests, including to whom the ownership interests can be sold, and how a price is to be determined. In many cases, this effectively provides a market for what might otherwise be an unmarketable asset. However, in most cases, such an agreement restricts the market for the stock to the company, other shareholders, bloodline relatives, and sometimes only to those who wouldn't jeopardize the company's S corporation election, if applicable.

The buy-sell agreement may deal with how the sale of the stock is to be funded and paid for, thereby relieving financial pressure on the company or other parties buying the stock and providing a selling shareholder or estate of the decedent a mechanism for getting his or her money.

Buy-sell agreements often contain employment clauses, requiring the selling shareholder to work for some period of time after sale of his or her ownership interest. They may also include noncompete clauses, which are designed to prevent the departing shareholders from competing with the company for a specified period after they leave.

The agreement may address continuity of management in the event that a shareholder is to leave, providing for the smooth, continued care of the company and its operations during the transition period.

The agreement may address specific management issues, such as control over various decision-making responsibilities, and authority and intentions regarding distributions to shareholders. Such clauses are particularly important to noncontrolling shareholders who may have no input over such matters.

Many agreements set forth a mechanism for the resolution of disputes among the parties. There has been an increasing trend toward the use of arbitration or mandatory mediation, both of which can serve to significantly reduce costs and provide a framework for a more mutually agreeable solution to the dispute.

> A buy-sell agreement can set the ground rules for any matter the owners want to include. For this reason, there is no "one size fits all" when it comes to shareholder agreements. An owner who signs a "cookie-cutter" buy-sell agreement is practically assured of disagreement and misunderstanding down the road. If you have seen one buy-sell agreement, you have seen one buy-sell agreement.

Valuation Aspects of Buy-Sell Agreements

Types of Agreements

There are three types of commonly used buy-sell agreements:

1. Repurchase agreements, in which the company redeems the stock of the departing shareholder
2. Cross-purchase agreements, in which the remaining shareholders are given the option to buy the stock of the withdrawing party
3. Hybrid agreements, in which either the company or the other shareholders are offered the stock of the departing shareholder first, and the other party has a second option on the stock

Most agreements are structured as hybrids, leaving the shareholders more flexibility in how they structure the deal at the time of the triggering event. The option chosen will be influenced by considerations such as how the payment will be funded, the number of parties to the agreement, and tax issues.

The various selling provisions can be either exercised at the option of the purchaser, or be binding (i.e., a "put" option). The greater the selling restrictions, the greater the possible impact on any lack of marketability discount and/or lack of control discount. If the provisions provide for a purchase at the option of the buyer, (the company or the other shareholders), and the buyer declines, then the shareholder is generally permitted to find an outside buyer who meets various criteria and restrictions established in the agreement. In fact, many agreements require a shareholder wishing to sell to find an outside buyer first, and then offer the stock to the company or other shareholders at the same price that the outside buyer is willing to pay. Unfortunately, this often serves to severely restrict the chances of a sale, and the price that might be paid, since few serious investors are willing to go through the exercise of due diligence and preparing an offer with the knowledge that their offer will likely be usurped by another party.

Valuation Clauses

Perhaps nothing is as great a surprise to many shareholders as it is to realize the implications of the valuation clauses in their agreement, particularly if this realization occurs during a triggering event. For instance, a selling shareholder may suddenly realize that the payment he or she is to receive is far less than anticipated, or a buying shareholder may find that the acquisition price may appear unreasonable because it is far in excess of their expectations and what they think the cash flow of the business can support.

> Most disputes that arise as a result of a triggering event do so because the agreement is either unclear or misunderstood by the parties involved. Unfortunately, this is also the worst time to try to resolve such a dispute; it's better to be in the position of making these decisions when the parties are amicable.

Such mishaps are often the result of neglecting to meticulously craft the valuation section of the agreement. Again, the valuation analyst is ideally suited to assist the attorney and client in understanding this all-important topic.

Standard of Value

Perhaps nothing is as important in the valuation section as it is to clearly define the standard of value to be used in the agreement. This single item is perhaps the most overlooked aspect of drafting the agreement, yet it is fraught with the greatest dangers for the parties involved.

The parties can agree to the use of any standard of value they wish. However, the failure to clearly define the standard of value can create some serious problems. Consider the following examples:

- Shareholder A is ready to cash in a $^1/_3$ interest in the business. All the shareholders agree that the company is worth $1,000,000, so Shareholder A believes he is due a payment of $333,333. What Shareholder A has failed to realize is that the standard of value for company stock is the "fair market value" of the interest. The interest will need a fair market valuation that may include a discount for minority interest and/or lack of marketability. This will yield a much smaller payment than Shareholder A had expected.
- Shareholder B owns 50 percent of a business that is in a rapidly growing industry. Shareholder B wants to sell out to Shareholder A, and the terms of the buy-sell agreement specify that the stock is to be offered in a cross-purchase arrangement for "value." Shareholder B knows that consolidators have been paying 3 times revenues for comparable businesses and expects the price for the shares to be calculated using the same multiple, since they believe it is representative of "value." However, Shareholder A knows that the only way the company's cash flow could support such payment is if the entire company is sold, which he does not want to do.

Both of these examples are common scenarios that inevitably lead to conflict and disruption of the business. Both situations could have been avoided if the parties had realized the meaning of the terminology used in the agreement, or had avoided using ambiguous terminology, such as "value." The standard of value should be both named and defined in the agreement to prevent a misunderstanding among the parties at a later time.

Analysts are well equipped to explain the alternatives and meanings of the different standards of value. By helping the shareholders through the process of deciding what their intentions are with respect to one another, analysts can help them select the standard of value that meets those intentions, and that will be financially feasible should a triggering event occur.

Approaches to Valuation

Value under a buy-sell agreement is typically determined one of three ways:

1. By use of a formula
2. By a process that is defined in the agreement
3. By negotiation among the parties

Formula Approaches. Formula approaches are often used, but seldom appropriate. Agreements often contain formulas that were developed because the parties thought they were easy to understand and use.

Rarely do formulas result in "easy" solutions when the time comes to put them into practice.

A formula that produces a fair valuation at the time an agreement is put in place will probably not result in a fair valuation two, five, ten, or twenty years down the road. Factors about the company, the industry, competition, suppliers, the economy and general market conditions rarely stay static, and a static valuation formula may fail to capture those changing conditions.

Process Defined in the Agreement.   A far better alternative is for the parties to agree on a process by which the value will be determined. This is really the only way that the parties can be assured that the valuation will take into consideration the current value of the stock using whatever standard of value the parties have agreed to.

Some buy-sell agreements require the company to obtain an annual appraisal so that the parties are kept aware of the value of their holdings. Although ideal, it is a costly alternative. A reasonable solution for some companies is to have a complete valuation done only periodically, with update letter reports done in-between.

Problems occur with such arrangements when the company fails to obtain the annual valuation and a triggering event occurs. Unfortunately this is an all-too-common scenario. However, it can be avoided if the agreement includes a "fall back" provision directing the shareholders to obtain a valuation as of the date of the triggering event. In fact, some buy-sell agreements require the valuation to be done only at the time of a triggering event.

The agreement should also include a mechanism for choosing a valuation analyst. It might stipulate a particular analyst to be retained by the company. An alternate should be named as well in the event that the first choice is not available.

Alternatively, the agreement might require the selling shareholder to obtain a valuation, and the company or acquiring shareholder to do the same. If this is the case, then a mechanism needs to be put in place to deal with differences in the two valuations. This might involve shareholder negotiations, or hiring a third analyst to review the first two valuations. Some agreements stipulate that the results be averaged, but this may not be a good alternative if the parties desire to reach a meaningful representation of value.

Finally, the agreement might require the departing shareholders to obtain a valuation at their expense. However, the agreement also will need to provide a means to handle potential disagreement by the company over the departing shareholder's valuation conclusion. Some agreements require the valuation to be done by the company's CPA firm. Although this might initially make sense to the shareholders, the CPA firm may not necessarily be qualified to perform valuation services.

Negotiation.   If the agreement does not provide any mechanism for valuation, an acceptable alternative may be an annual documented negotiation between the parties. If negotiation is left until a triggering event, it may be harder to reach a satisfactory conclusion.

Another method of negotiation is a "show-down" clause. This type of clause requires shareholders who want to withdraw to offer their stock to the other shareholders for a specified payment and term arrangement. The shareholders to whom it is offered then have the opportunity to either buy or sell the stock at the same payment arrangement proposed by the departing shareholder. Supposedly, this assures fairness since the departing shareholders do not know if they will be selling or buying shares.

Show-down clauses need to be structured with great care because they can create unfairness, which they are supposed to avoid. For example, if the selling shareholder is an insider who owns 80 percent of the stock, and the remaining shareholder is an outsider who owns the other 20 percent, the insider stockholder probably has better knowledge of the company and possibly greater financial means to consummate the buyout of the remaining shareholder. The outsider has neither knowledge of the company, nor the means to buy a large majority interest. In this case, the show-down clause may amount to little more than a squeeze-out of the minority shareholder.

Whatever the valuation arrangement, clarity up front can save long, costly battles that only serve to hurt the parties and the very company that the agreement is designed to preserve.

Terms. Just as an effective buy-sell agreement must call for an appropriate manner of valuing the stock, it must also address the issue of terms. Just like any stock deal, terms can be anything the shareholders agree to.

The buyer of the stock, be it the company or the other shareholders, will typically prefer a payment stream over a number of years to help with their ongoing cash flow. The departing shareholder, on the other hand, often would like to get all the cash up front. A deferred payment arrangement necessarily leaves them subject to some risk that the company or the other shareholders will perform and be able to make good on the payment arrangement.

To the extent that payments are deferred, the selling shareholder will usually require some form of collateral, either in the form of the stock that is the subject of the sale, other assets of the company, or assets of the acquiring party. Personal guarantees may be required as well. In a deferred payment arrangement, the selling shareholder is being put in the place of a creditor. As such, the seller will likely require similar assurances that banks or other outside creditors would require. Typically, when collateral is assigned, the departing shareholder will be in a position second to the bank.

The buyer and seller will also need to agree to the allocation of the price to be paid. For example, the payment might be only for the stock, or a portion of the price might be allocated to a covenant not to compete, or perhaps to an employment or ongoing consulting arrangement.

Whatever the payment terms, there are varying tax implications to both the buyer and the seller. All parties to the agreement should understand the tax implications of the agreement.

Financing. All of the good efforts and intentions stated by the shareholders in the buy-sell agreement will be wasted if a realistic funding plan has not been addressed. Many times, shareholders believe that because they have the right of first refusal and the corporation has second (or vice versa) before a shareholder who wishes to depart can sell the shares to an outsider, that they are "safe" from allowing such outsiders in the company. However, if the buyout cannot be consummated by the corporation or the other shareholders because of lack of funding, then that protection the shareholders relied on is lost. Funding can come from any number of sources, including operations or borrowings against corporate or personal assets.

Many agreements require the parties to carry life insurance to fund the purchase upon the death of a stockholder. If it is a redemption agreement, the corporation will hold life insurance on the lives of the shareholders. If it is a cross-purchase agreement, the shareholders will hold policies on each other's lives. However, in cases where there are multiple shareholders, cross-purchase insurance can become cumbersome and costly. Such considerations may cause the parties to more carefully consider a redemption agreement instead.

Occasionally, the parties carefully structure a buy-sell as a cross-purchase arrangement, or leave the option open for either a cross-purchase or a redemption, but then unwittingly buy a corporate policy on the lives of the shareholders. The company then ends up receiving the insurance proceeds, but it is the shareholders who need the money. This can end up being a costly mistake or cause the manner in which the insurance is held to be the driving factor in the decision of whether to accomplish the buyout via a redemption or a cross purchase. The parties should be advised by both their tax and insurance consultants on the issues relative to each type of insurance.

Section 2703 of the Internal Revenue Code

Section 2703 of the Internal Revenue Code sets forth rules that apply generally to transfers of family owned businesses among family members, occurring after October 8, 1990. A business is considered a family business if family members control 50 percent or more of the vote or value of the business. Section 2703(a) states that a shareholder agreement among family members that allows for the acquisition or transfer of property at a price that is less than fair market value will be ignored for purposes of mitigating estate and gift taxes.

With respect to buy-sell agreements, Section 2703 provide that such agreements will be ignored unless they meet three tests:

1. They are bona fide business arrangements.
2. They are not devices to transfer property to family for less than full and adequate consideration.
3. The terms of the agreement are comparable to similar arrangements entered into by persons in an arm's-length transaction.

If a buy-sell agreement entered into after October 8, 1990, contains a clause that would value the stock at less than fair market value, it will be disregarded for tax purposes.

Agreements that were drafted before October 8, 1990, and have not been substantially modified since that date are considered exempt from the application of Section 2703(a). Such agreements are subject to the old rules.

"Substantial modification" is considered to be any discretionary modification of a right or restriction that results in anything other than a de minimis change to the quality, value, or timing of the rights of any party subject to the agreement, and includes all family members below the lowest generation that is already a party to the agreement.

Impact of Buy-Sell Agreement on Valuation

The existence of a buy-sell agreement may have an impact on the value of the company. The magnitude of the impact will depend on the terms of the agreement, including transferability restrictions that may affect a lack of marketability discount for a minority interest, and possibly, whether it is a control interest.

The magnitude of the impact of a buy-sell agreement on the valuation may also depend on the purpose of the valuation. For example, whether or not a buy-sell agreement will be controlling for purposes of divorce valuation depends on the statute and case law of each state. Some states consider the buy-sell value controlling, while others disregard it entirely.

> Shareholders who have signed agreements that value the company's stock at something less than fair market value may find themselves in the unfortunate position of having transferred the stock for the price set by the agreement only to find that the IRS values it at something greater. This may result in an unexpected tax liability.

When preparing an appraisal for estate or gift tax purposes, the analyst needs to consider whether a buy-sell agreement exists, when it was drafted, if it was drafted before October 8, 1990, whether it has been substantially modified, and whether it meets the related requirements.

Summary

Buy-sell agreements present both planning opportunities for analysts and an area that needs to be considered for its valuation impact. Analysts are in a unique position to provide consulting services that go beyond the preparation of the valuation, by providing valuable advice on the shareholders' agreement while it is being drafted.

For more information see Addendum 2, "An Expert's," *Financial Valuation and Litigation Expert,* Issue 3, October/November, 2006, Valuation Products and Services, LLC, pp. 16–18, at www.wiley.com/go/FVAM3E.

C: VALUING DEBT

Introduction

Generally defined, a fixed income security (e.g., debt and preferred stock) is a financial obligation of a borrower to repay a specified sum of money at a predetermined future date to a lender. The terms and characteristics of such obligations, particularly debt obligations, vary greatly based on the lender's (creditor's) and borrower's (issuer's) respective expectations and needs.

Features of Debt Securities: Basic Overview

Types of Debt

Debt obligations include bank loans, bonds, accounts payable, mortgage-backed securities, asset-backed securities, and unsecured promissory notes. Bank loans are the most common form of debt taken on by closely held companies. As methods of financing corporate activity evolve, companies are entering into increasingly diverse forms of debt contracts.

Covenants

The covenants of a debt contract are clearly outlined in the loan agreement, also known as the indenture. Affirmative covenants are promises the borrower agrees to keep. The most common example of an affirmative covenant is the promise of the borrower to make principal and interest payments to the lender on a timely basis.

Other affirmative covenants include: preparing audited or reviewed financial statements, complying with tax regulations, keeping current with all taxes, and the like. Negative covenants are restrictions and limitations on the borrower's activities. Negative covenants include prohibiting the borrower from altering his or her capital structure by taking on new debt, outside of certain parameters. Limitations on shareholders' compensation, dividends, and loans are also common negative covenants.

Par Value

Also known as the face value or maturity value, the par value of a debt security (bond) is the amount that the borrower promises to repay the lender by the maturity date. Bonds can carry any par value, and the current market value of the bond is quoted as a percentage of its par value. For example, if a bond with a par value of $1,000 is selling for $975, it is said to be "selling at 97.5." This bond is trading at a discount since it is selling below its par value. Conversely, a bond selling above par value is said to be trading at a premium.

Maturity

The term to maturity, the number of years over which the borrower has promised to meet its obligation, is critical to the valuation of debt securities for three primary reasons.[1]

1. The term to maturity indicates the point in time at which the borrower must have the full principal amount paid and indicates the time over which the borrower can expect to make interest payments. This information provides a basis for preparing forecasts for using the income approach.
2. The term to maturity has an influence on the offered yield on a debt security. If a borrower desires a longer payoff period, it is likely that the borrower will have to pay a higher rate of interest, which also will have an impact on cash flow.
3. Finally, the volatility of the price of a debt security often depends on its term to maturity. Long term to maturity periods result in greater interest rate risk and greater exposure to default risk. These two items combine to increase the volatility of the debt's value.

---

[1] Frank J. Fabozzi, *Fixed Income Analysis for the Chartered Financial Analyst® Program* (New Hope, PA: Frank J. Fabozzi Associates, 2000), p. 5.

The maturity date, the predetermined date that the debt obligation will be paid in full, determines the term to maturity.

Yield to Maturity

Yield to maturity is the rate of interest that will make the present value of the cash flows from a debt security equal to the market price at the date of purchase.

Example: An investor purchases a $1,000 par, 6 percent, four-year bond for $950. The issuer makes payments semi annually. What is the yield to maturity? The investor will receive 8 payments of $30 and then receive the par value of $1,000 at the end of the term to maturity. The yield to maturity is the interest rate that makes the market price of $950 equal to the present value of the cash receipts from this investment, here, 7.47 percent.

Coupon Rate

The coupon rate, or nominal rate, is the interest rate the issuer promises to pay on the par value.

Call Provisions

A call provision enables the issuer to repay the debt prior to its maturity date. The issuer usually pays a premium in exchange for the benefits received from the early retirement of debt (i.e., reduced interest payments). A call provision typically cannot be exercised for a period specified in the indenture agreement. If the interest rate on the debt is higher than market rates, the valuation analyst should focus on yield-to-call data (the information available at the date the call can be exercised) rather than yield to maturity.[2]

Put Provisions

A put provision enables the lender to force the borrower to pay the debt back early at a specified price and on designated dates. A bond is usually putable at par if it is issued at or close to par value.[3] This gives the lender the flexibility to cash in on its lower-yielding investment in times of rising market rates and issue new, higher-rate debt securities.

Conversion Options

A conversion option grants the bondholder the right to convert the bond into a specified number of shares of the issuing corporation's common stock. The terms of a convertible security usually are structured so that there is no immediate benefit

VarTip

The value of a convertible bond is a function of the value of the bond as a straight debt instrument plus the value of the conversion feature.

---

[2] Shannon P. Pratt and Alina Niculita, *Valuing a Business: The Analysis and Appraisal of Closely Held Companies*, 5th ed. (New York: McGraw-Hill, 2008), p. 557.
[3] Frank J. Fabozzi, *Fixed Income Analysis for the Chartered Financial Analyst® Program*, p. 20.

available from a conversion. For example, it is unlikely that a bondholder would convert a bond with a par value of $1,000, convertible into 25 shares of common stock, if the market price per share was $38. However, if the common share price were to rise above $40, conversion would be considered.

Since an observable market price per share is usually not readily available for the convertible debt securities of closely held companies, valuation analysis for these securities is problematic compared to that of debt securities of publicly held corporations. The simplest way to deal with this issue is to determine the value of the straight, nonconvertible debt and the value of the conversion option separately.[4]

Sinking Fund Provision

A sinking fund provision requires the issuer to repay periodically a predetermined amount of debt principal prior to maturity. This reduces the amount due by the issuer at maturity and subsequently reduces default risk to the investor.

Collaterized Debt

Collaterized debt is a debt security that is backed up with a specific asset. The floor value of collaterized debt is usually the liquidation value of the underlying asset. Conversely, uncollaterized debt, or a debenture, is not secured by a specific asset so there is no mitigation of default risk. It subsequently requires a higher yield to maturity than an identical collaterized debt security.

Zero-Coupon Debt

A zero-coupon debt security is unique in that there are no coupon payments made to the investor. The entire par value is paid to the investor at the date of maturity. However, interest is paid implicitly because the security is sold to the investor at a deep discount. Bondholders who hold zero-coupon debt are exposed to greater interest rate risk than those who hold bonds yielding regular cash payments. For this reason, zero-coupon bonds typically sell at higher yields to maturity.

Tax Status

Interest earned on debt is typically subject to federal and state income taxation. However, most interest associated with government debt issues (e.g., U.S. Treasury securities and state and municipal bonds) is often exempt from federal and/or state taxation. This is reflected in the yield to maturity. All things being equal (usually not the case), a municipal bond should have a similar yield to maturity as a debt security after taxes are taken into consideration.

Valuation of Closely Held Debt Securities Using the Discounted Cash Flow Method

Formula

The fair market value of a simple debt security is equal to the present value of the future cash payments, discounted back to the present using a discount rate that embodies the risk associated with the investment.

---

[4] Shannon P. Pratt and Alina Niculita, *Valuing a Business: The Analysis and Appraisal of Closely Held Companies,* 5th ed., p. 559.

Since a bond with a long period until maturity is more volatile than a bond that will mature in the near future, the bond with the longer term to maturity usually has a higher discount rate than the bond with the shorter term to maturity. Inverted yield curves (i.e., where short-term interest rates are higher than longer-term rates) can occur, though.

This formula approximates the value of a debt security:

$$\text{Present Value} = \frac{PMT_1}{(1 + k_d)^1} + \frac{PMT_2}{(1 + k_d)^2} + \frac{PMT_3}{(1 + k_d)^3} + \frac{PMT_n}{(1 + k_d)^n} + \frac{\text{Face Value}}{(1 + k_d)^n}$$

Where k_d = market discount rate on debt

Example: A bond with three years to maturity has a par value of $1,000. The coupon rate is 8 percent, and the issuer makes coupon payments annually. The current market discount rate for this kind of security is 10 percent. What is the present value (PV)?

$$PV = \frac{\$80}{(1.10)^1} + \frac{\$80}{(1.10)^2} + \frac{\$80}{(1.10)^3} + \frac{\$1,000}{(1.10)^3} = \$950.26$$

One must know the amount and timing of future payments and the appropriate discount rate, or yield to maturity, to calculate the price of a debt security.

The current market price is equal to the present value of the future cash flows discounted back using the market determined yield to maturity. The yield to maturity should embody the risk associated with the particular debt security, including the financial strength and qualitative characteristics of the issuing company and the terms of the specific security. Debt securities are typically subject to less risk than equity securities since bondholders, as creditors of the company, usually have payback priority in the event of company failure.

Determinants of Market Interest Rates[5]

In general, the nominal (or stated) interest rate on a debt security, k, is composed of a real risk-free rate of interest, k*, plus several premiums that reflect inflation, the riskiness of the security, and the security's marketability (or liquidity). This relationship can be expressed as follows:

$$\text{Market Interest Rate} = k = k^* + IP + DRP + LP + MRP$$

[5] Eugene F. Brigham and Louis C. Gapenski, *Financial Management—Theory and Practice*, 6th ed. (Dryden Press, 1991), 78.

and if we combine k* and IP and let this sum equal k_{RF}, then we have this expression:

$$k = k_{RF} + DRP + LP + MRP$$

Here

k = the nominal, or stated, rate of interest on a given security.[6] There are many different securities, hence many different stated interest rates.

k* = the real risk-free rate of interest; k* is pronounced "k-star", and it is the rate that would exist on a riskless security if zero inflation were expected.

k_{RF} = the nominal risk-free rate of interest. This is the stated interest rate on a security such as a U.S. Treasury bill, which is very liquid and free of most risks. Note that k_{RF} does include a premium for expected inflation, so k_{RF} = k* + IP.

IP = inflation premium. IP is equal to the average expected inflation rate over the life of the security.

DRP = default risk premium. This premium reflects the possibility that the issuer will not pay interest or principal on a security at the stated time and in the stated amount.

LP = liquidity premium. This is a premium charged by lenders to reflect the fact that some securities cannot be converted to cash on short notice at a reasonable price.

MRP = maturity risk premium. Longer-term bonds are exposed to significant risk of price declines, and a maturity premium is charged by lenders to reflect this risk.

The yield to maturity of a closely held company's debt security must be estimated, rather than calculated directly from the market, and thus is more subjective.

> Since there are significant public trading markets for debt securities, it is easy to determine the present value of a publicly traded debt security.

Developing a Yield to Maturity

A guideline public company analysis allows the valuation analyst to quantify a closely held debt security's risk by using the market-determined yields to maturity of similar debt securities from publicly traded companies.

---

[6] The term *nominal* as it is used here means the stated rate as opposed to the real rate, which is adjusted to remove the effects of inflation. If you bought a 10-year Treasury bond in January 1990, the stated, or nominal, rate would be about 8 percent; but if inflation averages 5 percent over the next 10 years, the real rate would be about 8% – 5% = 3%.

> The best method to estimate the yield to maturity of a debt security of a closely held company is a guideline public company analysis.

Assessing Risk

Due to the inverse relationship between bond prices and the market interest rate, the trading price of the bond issue will decline if market interest rates increase beyond the bond's original issue rate.

Interest Rate Risk

Due to the inverse relationship between bond price and the market interest rate, the value of a debt security is subject to interest rate risk. If market rates are higher than the interest rate of a particular bond issue, the trading price of the bond issue will decline.

Prepayment/Call Risk and Reinvestment Risk

In periods of declining interest rates, issuers tend to prepay debts and/or refinance. Similarly, issuers of callable bonds are likely to call parts of the security prior to the maturity date. From the perspective of the investor, risk is increased as the expected cash flow of future interest payments is disrupted. These are called prepayment risk and call risk. In addition, the investor is now forced to reinvest the principal amount at a lower interest rate. This is called reinvestment risk.

Default Risk

An investor in debt securities assumes the risk that the borrower will fail to meet the obligations set forth in the covenant regarding the timely repayment of principal and interest. This is called default risk, or credit risk. To properly assess default risk, the valuation analyst should examine the financial position of the company and the specific collateral to determine whether the issuer is creditworthy.

Summary

Debt security valuations are needed for various reasons. Whether the valuation is for an investor or a borrower, the valuation process includes an analysis of the terms of the agreement, the amount and timing of the payments, and a consideration of the various risk factors that may be applicable to the security.

D: VALUATION ISSUES IN PREFERRED STOCK

Introduction

Direct equity ownership of a corporate entity comes in the form of either common stock or preferred stock. There may be multiple classes of common and preferred stock with different rights and privileges.

Preferred stock is a "hybrid" security with features similar to both common stock and bonds. Like common stock, it represents equity ownership and much like a bond (debt holder) it can receive fixed income distributions and preferential treatment.

In general, preferred shareholders have preferential rights over common shareholders when it comes to dividends, liquidation rights, and other considerations. In early stage companies, the most common and important preference is the liquidation preference. In late stage entities, it is a dividend guarantee.

Preferred Stock Features

Dividend Rate

The dividend rate is the predetermined rate an issuer promises to pay the preferred shareholder.

This rate is typically stated as a percentage of a share's par value. For example, a share of preferred stock with a par value of $100 and a dividend rate of 12 percent will pay a dividend of $12 to the shareholder.

The dividend rate is usually fixed or adjustable following the movement of market interest rates. Adjustable-rate dividends typically present the investor with less pricing risk since they adjust to the current market climate and trade near par. Another advantage of adjustable rate preferred stocks (ARPs) for corporate investors is that only 30 percent of the dividends are taxable to corporations.[7]

Cumulative versus Noncumulative

A company that has issued preferred stock with cumulative dividend terms has an obligation to make all accumulated dividend payments to the preferred stockholders before declaring and paying a dividend on common stock.

---

[7] Eugene F. Brigham and Joel F. Houston, *Fundamentals of Financial Management*, 8th ed. (Fort Worth: The Dryden Press, 1998), p. 770.

For example, one share of cumulative preferred stock of Company ABC has a par value of $50 and a dividend rate of 8 percent. As such, a shareholder of 1 share of ABC is entitled to receive a dividend payment of $4 every year. Company ABC has failed to make the dividend payments for the past two years. If Company ABC were to want to declare and pay a dividend to common shareholders, the company is first obligated to pay preferred shareholders $8 for the prior two years accumulated dividend and $4 for the current year.

Cumulative preferred stock has a lower level of risk because the shareholder is assured, to the extent available, of receiving all dividend income. Liquidation coverage can become more important than dividend coverage since a preferred shareholder is entitled to all dividends in arrears in addition to priority over common shareholders when it comes to the liquidation of the issuing company's assets.

Shares of preferred stock with noncumulative features do not carry a guarantee of dividend payments and carry more risk as a result.

However, if a company with noncumulative shares has a history of making payments each period and appears to have the intention and ability to do so in the future, an analyst might decrease risk for these shares.

Redeemable versus Nonredeemable

Redeemable preferred stock is very similar to a callable security in that it has a contractual redemption provision that can be exercised at the discretion of the issuing company. In general, preferred stock is redeemable under one of the following sets of terms:[8]

- The issuing company has the option to redeem the issue in its entirety at a predetermined price over a specified time period. The price paid for the security is usually par value. This type of issue is typically referred to as *callable*.
- The issuing company has the option to redeem the issue in its entirety at a predetermined price contingent upon a certain event, such as a change in ownership, the death of a majority shareholder, or issuance of other securities.
- The issuing company is obliged to redeem the issue according to a specific schedule with funds set aside by the issuer for this purpose. This is referred to as a *sinking fund preferred* since it has similar provisions to a bond that is retired on a regular schedule up to its maturity date.

Voting versus Nonvoting

Preferred shares often come with voting rights or other attributes of control which can increase the value to the shareholder.

---

[8] Shannon P. Pratt and Alina Niculita, *Valuing a Business: The Analysis and Appraisal of Closely Held Companies,* 5th ed. (New York: McGraw-Hill, 2008), p. 570.

Minority and Control

The data typically used to compute control premiums for common stock is not as directly applicable to preferred stock. This is due to the income component of the preferred return and to the specific features a given preferred stock may possess.

Participating versus Nonparticipating

With participating preferred stock, the shareholder has the right to share in earnings of the company over and above stated dividend amounts. Conversely, a shareholder of nonparticipating stock only has access to the dividend payments stated in the initial agreement.

Similarly, upon liquidation, the preferred may just receive the face value of the preferred plus unpaid dividends (nonparticipating) or may also participate with the common shareholders in any value exceeding the preferred liquidation preference.

Convertible versus Nonconvertible

> Convertible preferred stock gives the investor the option to exchange the security for common stock giving the shareholder more flexibility.

Put Options

A put option grants the shareholder the right to sell the share back to the issuing company at a predetermined price, often its par value. This, of course, assumes the entity has the financial wherewithal to perform under the put.

Liquidation Preference

Another significant advantage a preferred equity owner has over a common equity owner is the first right, after all creditors have received what is owed, to the issuing company's assets in the event of liquidation. The liquidation preference of preferred stock is most often equivalent to the initial investment made by the preferred shareholders plus any dividends in arrears owed to the shareholder.

Valuation Methods

Revenue Ruling 83-120

> Revenue Ruling 83-120 is intended to amplify Revenue Ruling 59-60 and set out other considerations regarding the valuation of preferred and common stock for gift tax and recapitalization of private companies.

As with any asset valuation, understanding the specific rights and obligations conveyed by the security is an important first step. Often, the most important factors to consider when valuing preferred stock are its yield, dividend coverage, and protection of its liquidation preference.

- Quoting RR 83-120, "The adequacy of the dividend rate should be determined by comparing its dividend rate to the dividend rate of high-grade publicly traded stock." The conclusion of this assessment should then be used to determine whether or not the subject company's preferred stock yield supports a valuation of the stock at par value.
- Dividend Coverage: Is the issuing company able to pay this? Is it likely that the issuing company will pay it?
- Protection of the stock's liquidation preference.
- Other
  - Power granted to the shareholder(s) through voting rights
  - Unique provisions and covenants that may have an impact on the fair market value of the preferred stock
  - Redemption privileges included in the provisions

Dividend Discount Model

> For later stage, dividend-dependent preferred stock, the fair market value of the stock is equal to the present value of the future cash payments, discounted back to the present value using a discount rate that embodies the risk associated with the investment.

The formula for doing so is as follows:

$$P_0 = \frac{D}{k_p}$$

P_0 = Price of stock
D = Annual dividend
k_p = Investors' required rate of return for preferred stock

(This formula is easily converted to a discrete cash flow discounting if a redemption date for the preferred is known.)

Example: A share of preferred stock has a par value of $100 and a stated rate of 12 percent. What is the current price of the share if the required rate of return (yield) is 8 percent?

$$
\begin{aligned}
D &= .12 \times \$100 = \$12 \\
P_0 &= 12/.08 \\
P_0 &= \$150
\end{aligned}
$$

Although this valuation model is simple, determining the value of preferred share of stock of a closely held private company is complex due to the challenges involved in determining an appropriate discount or yield rate. The financial strength and qualitative characteristics of the issuing company and the terms of the specific security must be evaluated. Two critical factors that must be evaluated are:

1. The dividend rate, which is the key to calculating cash flow to the investor
2. Liquidation coverage, indicating the company's ability to pay the full liquidation preference

One of the best measures for determining dividend payment risk is the company's fixed charge ratio, which is required by Revenue Ruling 83-120 for valuations involving income taxes, federal gift, or estate taxes.

$$\text{Fixed Charge Coverage Ratio} = \frac{\text{Earnings Before Interest and Taxes (EBIT)}}{\text{Interest Expense + Preferred Dividends Adjusted for Taxes}}$$

The higher this ratio is, the easier it is for the issuing company to pay its preferred dividends, thus, the lower the rate of return that should be required by the investor.

According to Revenue Ruling 83-120, the issuing company's ability to pay the full liquidation preference must be taken into consideration when determining the fair market value of preferred stock. The ruling states that the risk to a shareholder can be measured by the "protection ratio" or liquidation coverage ratio, a measure that calculates the protection afforded by a company's net assets.

$$\text{Liquidation Coverage Ratio} = \frac{\text{Fair Market Value of Assets–Fair Market Value of Liabilities}}{\text{Liquidation Preference of Preferred Stock}}$$

This ratio can be compared to the ratios of publicly traded preferred stocks and should be greater than 1.0, indicating that the total liquidation preference can be covered.

One of the best methods to estimate the appropriate yield to apply to a share of preferred stock of a closely held company is through a guideline public company analysis. With this method, one can obtain an understanding of a closely held company's preferred stock risk level by comparing it to public preferred securities.

Other Issues

Valuing Preferred Stock with Redemption and/or Put Options

When valuing preferred stock with redemption options the analyst must consider the length of time before redemption is permissible and the call out price. Consideration must be given to an issuing company's plan for financing the redemption of preferred stock, and the discount rate must be adjusted accordingly.

A sinking fund preferred stock has a specified redemption schedule and will be valued based on the number of dividend payments expected to be received in addition to the terminal value of the security.

Valuing Participating Preferred

The value of a participating share is determined by assessing the potential amount of additional earnings above and beyond the stated dividend rate and the likelihood that these earnings will be realized.

Valuing Convertible Preferred

The value of a convertible share of preferred stock is determined by assessing the value of the underlying common security as well as the guaranteed future cash flows that are offered by the preferred share.

Marketability

To a shareholder in a late-stage, dividend-paying company, the value of a nonconvertible preferred stock primarily lies in the dividend cash flow received, whereas the value of common stock comes from dividends if paid, growth in the share price, and a subsequent sale of the security. It is clear, then, that marketability is more critical to a shareholder of common stock than to an owner of preferred stock of a relatively mature private company. As such, an identical Lack of Marketability Discount typically cannot be applied to seemingly comparable shares of preferred stock and common stock of the same corporation. It is critical that a valuation professional examines each situation and makes an LOM discount conclusion on an individual basis.

Summary

When valuing preferred stock, it is imperative that the valuation professional consider, above all else, the issuing company's ability to meet the terms of a preferred stock issue (its dividend obligation) and protect the preferred shareholders in the event of liquidation. As such, a preferred shareholder should be in a lower-risk, income receiving investment position. Special features can also greatly affect value.

Preferred Stock Valuation of Yaboo, Inc. (Illustration Only)

The following example illustrates the types of data utilized in valuing preferred stock of closely held companies. Yaboo, Inc. is a private real estate investment trust (REIT). The purpose of the valuation is estate tax.

The analysis of yields and preferred returns follows the guidelines contained in IRS Revenue Ruling 83-120 pertaining to the valuation of preferred stocks for gift tax and other purposes. According to this revenue ruling, the most important factors to consider when determining the value of a preferred stock are:

- Its dividend yield
- Its dividend coverage, or the amount of pretax, preinterest earnings available to pay interest and dividends
- Its liquidation protection, or the difference between the company's assets and liabilities
- Its voting rights
- The existence of any peculiar covenants or provisions not normally found on publicly traded preferred stocks
- Whether it has any redemption privileges

The Company has issued shares of preferred stock. Preferred shareholders receive a dividend of $60.00 per share.

In order to estimate the fair market value of Yaboo's preferred stock, it is necessary to develop a comparable group of publicly traded preferred stocks. Three grades of publicly traded nonconvertible preferred stocks, speculative grade, investment grade, and unrated, were examined. These classifications were selected in order to compare their respective yields with that of the Company's preferred stock. A total of 47 publicly traded REIT preferred stocks were examined.

The speculative grade and unrated preferred stocks are generally of low investment quality with moderate earnings and asset protection. The assurance of dividend payments over time is uncertain. The investment grade preferred stocks are high-quality investments with good earnings and asset coverage. Dividend payment is more certain than that of the speculative grade.

A group of publicly traded preferred stocks was identified and analyzed in relationship to Yaboo's preferred stock in several dimensions. These dimensions include the stated dividend rates, the coverage of the dividend (fixed charge coverage ratio), the liquidation coverage (a measure of the Company's ability to pay the preferred stock's liquidation preference), and other dimensions, including other financial ratios, voting rights, and redemption privileges. See Exhibit 24.4.

Due to Yaboo's lower debt, its coverage ratios exceeded those of even the highest rated issues. However, its pretax return on capital is lower than all but the most speculative issues. And, while the subject REIT is comparable in size to the publicly traded ones, its shares of stock are not readily marketable. Given all of these considerations, we have estimated the appropriate yield for Yaboo's preferred stock to be 7.5 percent, which falls between average yields of the higher and lower investment grade REIT preferred stocks.

The calculations for the coverage ratios of the comparative publicly traded companies are presented in Exhibit 24.4. Based on a market yield of 7.5 percent, the indicated fair market value of a share of Yaboo preferred stock is $800 as follows $60/.075 = $800.

Early Stage Companies

Many early stage companies are financed with preferred stock. For these companies, the preferred stock's most important features are associated with its:

- Liquidation preference
- Common conversion rights
- Put/call rights
- Control features

Often, these early stage company shares are not as dividend-dependent as preferred stock issued by more mature companies.

E: RESTRICTED STOCK VALUATION

Introduction

The valuation of restricted stock is not just about understanding the restricted stock studies used in estimating lack of marketability discounts (Chapter 9). The stock's price volatility, applicable trading restrictions, and the cost of hedging instruments or other strategies can all play a significant role in its valuation.

Exhibit 24.4 Yaboo, Inc., Preferred Stock Analysis of Publicly Traded REIT Companies as of December 31, 2001

	COMPANY	Company Ticker	Preferred Stock Ticker	Convertible?	Rating	Price / Share	Div. / Share	Preferred Div. Yield	Price / Share	First Call Date	EBIT # MM	Cash Dividends -Preferred $ MM	Interest Expense $ MM
1	Weingarten Realty Series C	WRI	WRIPrC	No	A-	$49.950	$3.52	7.05%	$50.00	03/14/04	120.307	20.040	47.394
2	Kimco Realty	KIM	KIMPrC	No	BBB+	$25.050	$2.08	8.30%	$25.00	04/14/01	295.217	26.328	92.100
3	Public Storage	PSA	PSAPrK	No	BBB+	$25.300	$2.08	8.22%	$25.00	01/18/04	334.951	111.180	13.071
4	Archstone Communities Tr.		ASNPrC	No	BBB	$25.350	$2.16	8.52%	$25.00	08/19/02			
5	AvalonBay Communities	AVB	AVBPrH	No	BBB	$26.740	$2.16	8.08%	$25.00	10/14/08	255.342	39.779	101.937
6	Duke-Weeks Realty	DRE	DREPrF	No	BBB	$24.960	$2.00	8.01%	$25.00	10/09/02	381.417	48.981	166.948
7	Equity Office Properties Trust		EOPPrC	No	BBB	$25.500	$2.16	8.47%	$25.00	12/07/03	1,038.401	45.924	535.533
8	Equity Residential Prop.Trust	EQR	EQRPrD	No	BBB	$25.950	$2.16	8.32%	$25.00	07/14/07	786.665	100.854	388.419
9	Equity Residential Prop.Trust		EQRPrL	No	BBB	$24.420	$1.92	7.86%	$25.00	02/12/03			
10	Healthcare Prop. Investment	HCP	HCPPrC	No	BBB	$25.000	$2.16	8.64%	$25.00	10/26/02	216.213	24.900	86.747
11	Post Properties	PPS	PPSPrB	No	BBB	$24.320	$1.92	7.89%	$25.00	10/27/07	174.212	11.875	51.939
12	Prologis Trust		PLDPrD	No	BBB	$23.710	$2.00	8.44%	$25.00	04/12/03	413.998	56.763	190.691
13	BRE Properties	BRE	BREPrA	No	BBB-	$25.210	$2.12	8.41%	$25.00	01/28/04	127.156	4.569	61.462
14	Highwood Properties	HIW	HIWPrD	No	BBB-	$23.340	$2.00	8.57%	$25.00	04/23/03	265.357	32.580	136.496
15	Liberty Property	LRY	LRYPrA	No	BBB-	$25.100	$2.20	8.76%	$25.00	07/29/02	271.492	11.000	126.095
16	Vornado Realty		VNOPrB	No	BBB-	$25.150	$2.12	8.43%	$25.00	03/16/04	496.798	38.690	182.542
17	Vornado Realty		VNOPrC	No	BBB-	$25.050	$2.12	8.46%	$25.00	05/16/04			
18	Develp Div Rlty Dep-	DDR	DDRPrC	No	BBB-	$24.350	$2.08	8.54%	$25.00	07/06/03	174.016	27.262	95.230
19	Develp Div Rlty Dep.		DDRPrD	No	BBB-	$25.000	$2.16	8.64%	$25.00	08/19/03			
20	Fed'l Realty Investment Trust	FRT	FRTPrA	No	BBB-	$24.100	$2.00	8.30%	$25.00	10/05/02	129.804	7.950	79.718
21	Shurgard Storage	SHU	SHUPrC	No	BBB-	$25.760	$2.16	8.39%	$25.00	12/07/03	80.437	8.750	40.011
22	Colonial Prop. Trust	CLP	CLPPrA	No	BB+	$25.100	$2.20	8.76%	$25.00	11/05/02	143.083	10.940	81.455
23	Hospitality Prop Tr.	HPT	HPTPrA	No	BB+	$25.620	$2.36	9.21%	$25.00	04/11/04	163.953	7.125	37.682
24	Realty Income	O	OPrB	No	BB+	$25.750	$2.36	9.17%	$25.00	05/24/04	79.623	9.712	32.547
25	PS Business Parks	PSB	PSBPrA	No	BB+	$25.300	$2.32	9.17%	$25.00	04/29/04	71.298	5.088	2.896
26	United Dominion Realty Trust	UDR	UDRPrB	No	BB+	$25.450	$2.16	8.49%	$25.00	05/28/07	207.460	36.891	159.640
27	Apartment Investment & Mgt.		AIVPrG	No	B+	$25.250	$2.36	9.35%	$25.00	07/14/08	357.080	63.183	279.104
28	iStar Financial	SFI	SFIPrD	No	B+	$21.350	$2.00	9.37%	$25.00	10/07/02	389.429	36.908	174.404
29	FelCor Lodging		FCHPrB	No	B	$23.390	$2.24	9.58%	$25.00	05/06/03	291.058	24.682	160.620
30	Host Marriott	HMT	HMTPrA	No	B	$24.910	$2.52	10.12%	$25.00	08/02/04	805.000	20.000	473.000
31	Host Marriott		HMTPrB	No	B	$24.910	$2.52	10.12%	$25.00	04/28/05			

(continues)

Exhibit 24.4 *continued*

	COMPANY	Pretax Income $ MM	Total Taxes $ MM	Tax Rate	Total Assets $ MM	Debt-Total $ MM	Total Liabilities $ MM	Total Stockholders' Equity $ MM	Preferred Stock Liqui. Value $ MM	Fixed Charge Coverage	Liquidation Coverage	Capitalization Ratio	Pretax Return On Capital
1	Weingarten Realty Series C	81.649	0.000	0.000	1,517.581	792.353	887.714	629.867	0.277	1.784	2,273.888	0.557	9.07%
2	Kimco Realty	207.079	—	0.0%	3,171.348	1,325.663	1,467.009	1,704.339	329.564	2.493	5.171	0.546	9.87%
3	Public Storage	335.444	—	0.0%	4,513.941	156.003	789.824	3,724.117	1,155.150	2.696	3.224	0.338	8.98%
4	Archstone Communities Tr.												
5	AvalonBay Communities	212.512	—	0.0%	4,397.225	1,729.924	1,954.732	2,442.493	458.068	1.802	5.332	0.524	7.54%
6	Duke-Weeks Realty	304.563	—	0.0%	5,460.036	1,973.215	2,747.146	2,712.890	608.874	1.766	4.456	0.551	10.06%
7	Equity Office Properties Trust	538.881	—	0.0%	18,794.254	8,802.994	10,723.058	8,071.195	613.923	1.786	13.147	0.558	6.37%
8	Equity Residential Prop.Trust	596.672	—	0.0%	12,263.966	5,706.152	6,644.419	5,619.547	1,183.136	1.608	4.750	0.608	8.70%
9	Equity Residential Prop.Trust												
10	Healthcare Prop. Investment	139.222	—	0.0%	2,398.703	1,158.928	1,254.148	1,144.555	274.487	1.937	4.170	0.622	9.81%
11	Post Properties	116.116	—	0.0%	2,551.237	1,213.309	1,522.627	1,028.610	0.150	2.730	6,857.400	0.541	7.50%
12	Prologis Trust	225.194	5.130	2.278	5,946.334	2,677.736	3,018.963	2,927.371	691.403	2.830	4.234	0.601	7.42%
13	BRE Properties	46.435	—	0.0%	1,718.129	825.253	917.013	801.116	53.750	1.926	14.904	0.540	6.63%
14	Highwood Properties	157.189	—	0.0%	3,701.602	1,587.019	1,910.057	1,791.545	397.500	1.569	4.507	0.587	8.69%
15	Liberty Property	181.583	—	0.0%	3,396.355	1,703.896	2,075.550	1,320.805	125.000	1.980	10.566	0.605	10.17%
16	Vornado Realty	337.490	—	0.0%	6,370.314	2,656.897	4,291.594	2,078.720	489.462	2.246	4.247	0.664	10.98%
17	Vornado Realty												
18	Develp Div Rlty Dep.	120.426	—	0.0%	2,332.021	1,227.575	1,548.271	783.750	303.750	1.421	2.580	0.761	10.72%
19	Develp Div Rlty Dep.												
20	Fed'l Realty Investment Trust	67.067	—	0.0%	1,621.079	1,034.446	1,153.425	467.654	100.000	1.481	4.677	0.755	9.77%
21	Shurgard Storage	49.026	—	0.0%	1,239.157	495.354	598.592	640.565	100.000	1.650	6.406	0.524	7.84%
22	Colonial Prop. Trust	79.393	—	0.0%	1,944.099	1,179.095	1,490.273	453.826	0.050	1.549	9,076.521	0.722	9.85%
23	Hospitality Prop Tr.	126.271	—	0.0%	2,220.909	464.748	737.969	1,482.940	75.000	3.659	19.773	0.277	8.42%
24	Realty Income	54.788	—	0.0%	934.766	404.000	419.197	515.569	99.368	1.884	5.188	0.547	9.50%
25	PS Business Parks	77.922	—	0.0%	930.756	30.971	366.413	564.343	55.000	8.930	10.261	0.144	13.58%
26	United Dominion Realty Trust	80.170	—	0.0%	3,453.957	1,992.330	2,235.065	1,218.892	435.206	1.056	2.801	0.756	7.47%
27	Apartment Investment & Mgt.	113.589	—	0.0%	7,699.874	4,392.445	5,198.217	2,501.657	837.717	1.043	2.986	0.759	5.70%
28	iStar Financial	218.486	—	0.0%	4,034.775	2,131.967	2,246.890	1,787.885	402.500	1.843	4.442	0.647	10.02%
29	FelCor Lodging	73.826	—	0.0%	4,103.603	1,838.241	2,269.498	1,834.105	293.265	1.571	6.254	0.580	6.38%
30	Host Marriott	133.000	(98.00)	0.0%	8,396.000	5,797.000	6,975.000	1,421.000	205.000	1.633	6.932	0.832	8.40%
31	Host Marriott												

	COMPANY	Company Ticker	Preferred Stock Ticker	Conver-tible?	Rating	Price / Share	Div. / Share	Preferred Div. Yield	Price / Share	First Call Date	EBIT # MM	Cash Dividends -Preferrered $ MM	Interest Expense $ MM
32	Equity Inns	ENN	ENNPrA	No	B-	$22.240	$2.36	10.61%	$25.00	06/24/03	54.065	6.531	34.072
33	Associated Estates Realty	AEC	AECPrA	No	B-	$24.900	$2.44	9.80%	$25.00	N/A	41.470	5.484	43.640
34	JDN Realty	JDN	JDNPrA	No	B-	$24.770	$2.36	9.53%	$25.00	09/14/03	58.299	4.688	48.873
35	Omega Healthcare Investors	OHI	OHIPrB	No	D	$18.900	Div. Susp. 02/01/01	N/A	$25.00	6/30/03	(12.481)%	16.928	42.400
36	Alexandria RE Equities	ARE	AREPrA	No	NR	$27.370	$2.36	8.6%	$25.00	6/10/04	51.800	3.666	33.501
37	CBL & Associates Properties	CBL	CBLPrA	No	NR	$25.200	$2.24	8.9%	$25.00	6/30/03	174.742	6.468	94.597
38	Corporate Office Trust	OFC	OFCPrB	No	NR	$25.780	$2.52	9.8%	$25.00	7/14/04	55.604	3.802	35.725
39	Corrections Corp. of America	CXW	CXWPrA	No	NR	$18.600	Div. Omitted 06/23/00	N/A	$25.00	1/29/03	10.522	13.526	153.345
40	Crown America Realty Trust	CWN	CWNPrA	No	NR	$51.700	$5.52	10.7%	$52.50	7/30/07	64.817	13.695	59.062
41	Eastgroup Properties	EGP	EGPPrA	No	NR	$25.500	$2.24	8.8%	$ 5.00	6/18/03	46.688	10.008	20.630
42	G&L Realty	GLR	GLRPrB	No	NR	$17.350	$2.40	13.8%	$25.00	12/31/01	14.831	7.164	13.819
43	Great Lakes REIT	GL	GLPrA	No	NR	$25.990	$2.44	9.4%	$25.00	12/15/03	38.330	3.656	15.193
44	LTC Properties	LTC	LTCPrB	No	NR	$20.700	$2.28	11.0%	$25.00	12/31/01	65.877	15.087	27.426
45	Parkway Properties	PKY	PKYPrA	No	NR	$24.620	$2.20	8.9%	$25.00	4/22/03	48.727	5.797	23.818
46	Prime Group Realty	PGE	PGEPrB	No	NR	$17.400	$2.24	12.9%	$25.00	6/4/03	81.001	12.147	69.988
47	Sovran Self Storage	SSS	SSSPrB	No	NR	$26.500	$2.48	9.4%	$25.00	7/29/04	45.227	2.955	17.497

MEDIAN FOR ALL COMPANIES

	Div. / Rating	Yield
	8.76%	
MEDIAN FOR RATING OF	AA / AA-	NA
MEDIAN FOR RATING OF	A+ / A / A-	7.05%
MEDIAN FOR RATING OF	BBB+ / BBB / BBB-	8.42%
MEDIAN FOR RATING OF	BB+ / BB / BB-	9.17%
MEDIAN FOR RATING OF	B+/B/B-	9.69%
MEDIAN FOR RATING OF	D	N/A
MEDIAN FOR RATING OF	NR	9.39%

Selected Yield 7.50%

Yaboo, Inc.	35.459	0.060	0.000

(continues)

1037

Exhibit 24.4 *continued*

1038

	COMPANY	Pretax Income $ MM	Total Taxes $ MM	Tax Rate	Total Assets $ MM	Debt-Total $ MM	Total Liabilities $ MM	Total Stockholders' Equity $ MM	Preferred Stock Liqui. Value $ MM	Fixed Charge Coverage	Liquidation Coverage	Capitalization Ratio	Pretax Return On Capital
32	Equity Inns	16.677	—	0.0%	801.743	383.403	417.957	383.786	68.750	1.332	5.582	0.589	6.61%
33	Associated Estates Realty	5.342	—	0.0%	819.559	568.243	623.103	196.456	56.250	0.844	3.493	0.817	6.41%
34	JDN Realty	23.719	—	0.0%	1,083.963	574.141	597.354	486.609	50.000	1.088	9.732	0.588	6.84%
35	Omega Healthcare Investors	(49.557)	—	0.0%	948.451	451.392	484.138	464.313	207.500	(0.210)	2.238	0.720	-0.78%
36	Alexandria RE Equities	26.009	—	0.0%	780.984	431.256	461.832	319.152	38.588	1.394	8.271	0.626	7.93%
37	CBL & Associates Properties	96.134	—	0.0%	2,115.565	1,424.337	1,680.740	434.825	0.029	1.729	14,993.964	0.766	10.26%
38	Corporate Office Trust	23.875	—	0.0%	794.837	474.349	601.109	193.728	31.250	1.407	6.199	0.757	8.92%
39	Corrections Corp. of America	(778.909)	(48.00)	0.0%	2,176.992	1,152.570	1,488.977	688.015	188.142	0.063	3.657	0.728	-33.99%
40	Crown America Realty Trust	6.886	—	0.0%	855.501	725.248	758.929	96.572	0.025	0.891	3,862.878	0.883	8.02%
41	Eastgroup Properties	36.889	—	0.0%	666.205	270.709	290.813	375.392	113.125	1.524	3.318	0.594	8.90%
42	G&L Realty	1.029	—	0.0%	205.466	158.942	165.575	39.891	0.072	0.707	554.042	0.800	7.47%
43	Great Lakes REIT	34.271	—	0.0%	431.610	190.911	212.537	219.073	37.500	2.034	5.842	0.557	12.06%
44	LTC Properties	32.619	—	0.0%	676.585	262.560	282.458	394.127	165.500	1.550	2.381	0.652	9.14%
45	Parkway Properties	34.900	—	0.0%	655.237	307.352	329.488	325.749	66.250	1.645	4.917	0.590	9.27%
46	Prime Group Realty	21.472	—	0.0%	1,439.093	799.171	1,077.330	361.763	39.890	0.986	9.069	0.723	7.88%
47	Sovran Self Storage	27.730	—	0.0%	547.139	231.223	269.741	277.398	30.000	2.211	9.247	0.514	8.89%
	MEDIAN FOR ALL COMPANIES									1.639	5.457	0.603	8.7%
	MEDIAN FOR RATING OF AA / AA–									NA	NA	NA	NA
	MEDIAN FOR RATING OF A+ / A / A–									1.784	2,273.888	0.557	9.07%
	MEDIAN FOR RATING OF BBB+ / BBB / BBB–									1.864	4.713	0.573	8.84%
	MEDIAN FOR RATING OF BB+ / BB / BB–									1.884	10.261	0.547	9.50%
	MEDIAN FOR RATING OF B+/B/B–									1.332	5.582	0.647	6.61%
	MEDIAN FOR RATING OF D									(0.210)	2.238	0.720	(0.78%)
	MEDIAN FOR RATING OF NR									1.465	7.235	0.687	8.90%
	Yaboo, Inc.	35.459	—	0.0%	518.673	—	0.025	518.648	0.001	590.988	518,647,590	0.000	6.84%

Sources: Standard & Poor's Stock Guide December 2001, S&P's Research Insight (Database), and MSN Money Central (Online).

Definition and Types of Restricted Stock

VaITip

> Restricted stock is stock of a publicly traded corporation that is restricted from public trading for a specified period of time. Restricted stock is often identical to its publicly traded counterpart, except that it is not freely tradeable.

VaITip

> The seminal revenue ruling in this area, Revenue Ruling 77-287, provides guidance for the valuation of restricted stock.

Revenue Ruling 77-287 recognizes that a discount from the freely traded price is applicable in the valuation of its restricted counterpart. In the valuation of restricted stock, the ruling notes:

> In judging the opportunity cost of freezing funds, the purchaser is analyzing two separate factors. The first factor is the risk that the underlying value of the stock will change in a way that, absent the restrictive provisions, would have prompted a decision to sell. The second factor is the risk that the contemplated means of legally disposing of the stock may not materialize. From the seller's point of view, a discount is justified where the seller is relieved of the expenses of registration and the public distribution, as well as of the risk that the market will adversely change before the offering is completed.

Revenue Ruling 77-287 identifies five types of restricted securities:

1. *Restricted Securities.* Defined in SEC Rule 144 as "securities acquired directly or indirectly from the issuer thereof, or from an affiliate of such issuer in a transaction or chain of transactions not involving any public offering."
2. *Unregistered Securities.* "Those securities to which a registration statement, providing full disclosure by the issuing corporation, has not been filed with the SEC [Securities and Exchange Commision] pursuant to the Securities Act of 1933."
3. *Investment Letter Stock or Letter Stock.* "Shares of stock that have been issued by a corporation without the benefit of filing a registration statement with the SEC. Such stock is subject to resale and transfer restrictions set forth in a letter agreement requested by the issuer and signed by the buyer of the stock when the stock is delivered."
4. *Control Stock.* "Shares of stock that have been held or are being held by an officer, director, or other person close to the management of the corporation. These

persons are subject to certain requirements pursuant to SEC rules upon resale of shares they own in such corporations."

5. *Private Placement Stock.* "Stock that has been placed with an institution or other investor who will presumably hold it for a long period and ultimately arrange to have the stock registered if it is to be offered to the general public."

Two other types of restrictions that result in a restricted security include:

1. *Underwriter Imposed Lock-up.* This agreement places restrictions on the sale of stock following an underwriter assisted equity offering. The restricted time period can vary with each offering; the agreement usually contains a provision allowing the underwriter to lift the restriction prior to the end of the restriction term.
2. *Company Imposed.* The company often imposes blackout periods restricting the sale of shares by particular shareholders (board members, management, or in some cases all employees) around certain dates or key events to avoid running afoul of insider trading laws.

Rule 144 Restrictions

Rule 144 is designed to prohibit the creation of public markets in securities of [companies on] which adequate current information is not available to the public. At the same time, when adequate current information concerning the issuer is available to the public, the rule permits the public sale . . . of limited amounts of securities owned by persons controlling, controlled by, or under common control with the issuer and by persons who have acquired restricted securities of the issuer.[9]

Rule 144 imposes two types of restrictions:

1. *Holding Period.* Prior to 1997, Rule 144 stated that "a minimum of two years must elapse between the later of the date of acquisition of the securities from the issuer or from an affiliate of the issuer, and if the acquirer takes the securities by purchase, the two year holding period shall not begin until the full purchase price or other consideration is paid or given."[10]

   Effective April 29, 1997, this holding period was reduced to one year.
2. *Volume Limitations.* Even after the holding period lapses, the shares are subject to additional volume limitations. These volume limitations lapse after a holding period of two years for nonaffiliates but continue indefinitely for affiliates. An affiliate is defined in Rule 144 as "any person or entity who has the direct or indirect power to direct or cause the direction of management and management policies, whether through the ownership of voting securities, by contract or otherwise." The volume limitations are:

   - A holder of restricted stock cannot sell more than 1.0 percent of the outstanding shares of stock during any three-month period

---

[9] Z. Christopher Mercer, *Quantifying Marketability Discounts* (Peabody Publishing, LP, 1997), pp. 40–41.
[10] Ibid.

- A holder of restricted stock cannot sell more stock in a three-month period than the average weekly market trading volume in such securities during the four calendar weeks preceding any such sale

Restricted Stock Studies

Revenue Ruling 77-287 references the SEC *Institutional Investors Study* published in March 1971. Since that time, other restricted stock studies have been completed. Most of these studies were completed before the holding period for Rule 144 stock was changed from two years to one year. The average price discount from these studies generally ranged from 20 to 36 percent. One study completed by Standard Research Consultants arrived at a median price discount of 45 percent.

At least two studies have been completed since the Rule 144 holding period was reduced to one year. Kathryn A. Aschwald of Columbia Financial Advisors published a study of restricted stock sales between January 1, 1997, and December 31, 1998. This study resulted in 15 transactions with an average discount of 13 percent and a median of 9 percent. The discounts ranged from 0 to 30 percent.[11]

The second study was performed by Lance S. Hall of FMV Opinions, Inc., who published the results of his study in September 2003. The FMV Opinions study analyzed 182 restricted stock transactions occurring between 1997 and 2000.[12] This study addressed stock with a Rule 144 one-year holding period. The study then compared the results observed in this study with the FMV Opinions pre-1997 restricted stock study. Since the Rule 144 holding period was reduced from two years to one year in May 1997, the two studies, which followed a similar protocol, can be compared to examine the impact of the holding period on lack of marketability. The most important aspect of the most recent FMV Opinion study, however, is that it helps isolate the effect of the volatility of a company's stock price on the magnitude of the observed discount.

Please refer to Chapter 9 for a thorough review of the restricted stock studies.

Typical Reasons for Restricted Stock Valuations

Perhaps the most dominant reason to value restricted stock is for compliance purposes. Financial reporting requirements (typically the fair value disclosure requirements) have been and should continue to be a major reason why restricted stock needs to be valued. Demand for restricted stock valuation services also arises from the Internal Revenue Service income, gift, and estate tax compliance. The fair market value of restricted securities can be needed to support a business's compensation deduction, a giftor's gift of restricted securities, or the donation of same to a charitable organization, or to assist in the valuation of a decedent's gross estate. With the increase in initial public offerings (IPOs) in the late 1990s, restricted stock transactions became more prevalent, as did the need for the

---

[11] Kathryn F. Aschwald, "Restricted Stock Discounts Decline as a Result of One-Year Holding Period," *Shannon Pratt's Business Valuation Update* (May 2000), p. 1.

[12] Lance S. Hall, "Why Are Restricted Stock Discounts Actually Larger for One-Year Holding Periods?" *Business Valuation Update* (September 2003), pp. 1–4.

compliance valuations discussed earlier. As the bottom fell out of the technology market in 2000, litigation (including disputes between companies and their employees) rose in prominence and created another reason why restricted stock needed to be valued.

Documents to Review and Factors to Consider in the Valuation Process

Revenue Ruling 77-287 lists data and documents to be considered in the valuation of restricted stock. These 12 items are discussed below and are in addition to the eight general factors discussed in Revenue Ruling 59-60. (See Chapter 12 for a discussion of Revenue Ruling 59-60.) All references to "the study" refer to the SEC *Institutional Investors Study* published in 1971.

1. *Earnings.* "Earnings played a major part in establishing the ultimate discounts at which these stocks were sold from the current market price. Apparently earnings patterns . . . determine the degree of risk of the investment."
2. *Sales.* "The dollar amount of sales of issuer's securities. The results of the study generally indicate that the companies with the lowest dollar amount of sales accounted for most of the transactions involving the highest discount rates, while they accounted for only a small portion of all transactions involving the lowest discount rates."
3. *Trading Market.* "According to the study, discount rates were greatest on restricted stocks with unrestricted counterparts traded over-the-counter followed by those with unrestricted counterparts listed on the American Stock Exchange, while discounts for . . . those stocks with unrestricted counterparts listed on the New York Stock Exchange were the smallest."
4. *Resale Agreement Provisions.* "Certain provisions are often found in agreements between buyers and sellers that affect the size of discounts at which restricted stocks are sold." These provisions may include piggyback registration rights, option to require registration at either the buyer's or seller's expense, or provisions giving the buyer the right to receive continuous disclosure information.
5. Trading prices and trading volume of the related class of traded securities one month preceding the valuation date.
6. Copy of any declaration of trust, trust agreement, and any other agreements related to the shares of restricted stock.
7. Copy of any document showing any offers to buy or sell or indications of interest in buying or selling the restricted shares.
8. Latest prospectus of the company.
9. Annual reports of the company for three to five years preceding the valuation date.
10. The relationship of the parties to the agreements concerning the restricted stock, such as whether they are members of the immediate family or officers or directors of the company.
11. The relative negotiating strengths of the buyer and seller of restricted stock may have a profound effect on the amount of the discount. For example a tight money situation may cause the buyer to have more negotiating strength in a transaction.
12. Whether the interest being valued represents a majority ownership.

The following five additional factors are believed to have an impact on the fair market value of restricted securities:

1. *Trading Volume and Bid/Ask Spread.* "Companies with a history of thin trading volumes and high bid/ask spreads may be subject to greater liquidation risk and therefore command a higher discount for lack of liquidity."[13]
2. *Dividend History and Policy* (also noted in Revenue Ruling 59-60). "Companies with a history of high-yield dividends may be considered less risky investments than companies with little or no dividend history. Therefore, such companies command a lower discount for lack of liquidity."[14]
3. *Brokerage House Analysts' Buy/Sell Recommendations.*[15] How many analysts follow the stock, and are there recent changes in recommendations?
4. *History of Stock Repurchases by the Issuing Company.* "Occasionally, companies will announce stock repurchases. Typically, this occurs when the company believes the market price of the subject stock is undervalued. It is necessary to review the history of company stock repurchases in the analysis of restricted stocks to determine if a future company repurchase is likely."[16]
5. *Ability and Cost to Construct a Hedge Position* using publicly traded derivative securities: These factors help estimate the lack of marketability discount for restricted stock, stock option grants where the underlying stock is publicly traded and for large blocks of publicly traded securities.[17]

Valuation Methodologies

One of the first tasks facing the analyst during the valuation of restricted securities is framing the issue in an understandable context. This involves:

- Clearly and completely identifying and discussing the material restrictions to which the security is subject
- Examining relevant restricted stock studies' findings and conclusions
- Performing independent research into recent restricted stock transactions

Once the framework has been constructed and the need for a discount from the freely traded value of the security is established, the analyst can concentrate on estimating the magnitude of the discount. In addition to comparisons using the previously mentioned restricted stock studies, the analyst can use:

- Option-pricing analysis
- The cost of registering or monetizing the stock

---

[13] Daniel R. Van Vleet and Frank D. Gerber, "Valuation Analysis of Restricted Stocks of Public Companies," *Insights Quarterly* (Willamette Management Associates, 1999).
[14] Ibid.
[15] J. Michael Julius, "Delayed Liquidity for Sellers Receiving Restricted Shares," *Mergers & Acquisitions* (January–February 1997), p. 36.
[16] Daniel R. Van Vleet and Frank D. Gerber, "Valuation Analysis of Restricted Stocks of Public Companies," *Insights Quarterly* (Willamette Management Associates, 1999).
[17] Les Barenbaum and Walter Schubert, "Modern Financial Engineering and Discounts: the Collar Message," *Business Valuation Review* (June 2004), pp. 69–73.

Option-Pricing Analysis

Three "hedge" opportunities may be available to holders of restricted stock. If these hedging opportunities were available, the cost to implement the strategy would be equivalent to the lack of marketability/restricted stock discount appropriate for the subject security.

1. *Open Market Hedge.* If the restricted stocks' publicly traded counterpart has put and call options associated with it, a hedge can be constructed that locks in the market price of the stock as of the valuation date. This type of hedge is referred to as "a collar." The cost of establishing the collar represents the lack of marketability/restricted stock discount.
2. *Structured Hedge.* Certain brokerage firms and investment banks offer an investment strategy designed to manage the risk associated with holding large blocks of restricted securities. The complexity of these strategies and related requirements may preclude their use by certain investors. Where feasible, however, they transfer the risk of fluctuating market prices to the investment/brokerage house and away from the holder of the restricted securities. The fees to implement the strategies represent the lack of marketability/restricted stock discount.
3. *Black-Scholes Hedge.* If there are no traded options associated with the restricted security's public counterpart, the Black-Scholes Option Pricing Method (BSOPM) can be used to estimate the cost of a put option and the proceeds from a call option.

Numerous articles discuss hedging strategies:

- J. Michael Julius, "Delayed Liquidity for Sellers Receiving Restricted Shares," *Mergers & Acquisitions* (January-February 1997), p. 36.
- David B. H. Chaffe, III, "Option Pricing as a Proxy for Discount for Lack of Marketability in Private Company Valuations," *Business Valuation Review* (December 1993), pp. 182–185
- Kasim L. Alli and Donald J. Thompson, II, "The Value of the Resale Limitation on Restricted Stock: An Option Theory Approach," *Valuation* (March 1991), pp. 22–33.
- Les Barenbaum and Walter Schubert, "Modern Financial Engineering and Discounts: the Collar Message," *Business Valuation Review* (June 2004), pp. 69–73.
- David Tabak, "Hedging and the Estimation of Marketability Discounts," *Business Valuation Update* (August 2003), pp. 1–5.
- Mukesh Bajaj, David J. Denis, Stephen P. Ferris, and Atulya Sarin, "Firm Value and Marketability Discounts," *Journal of Corporation Law* (Fall 2001), pp. 89–115.

The articles by Julius, Chaffe, and Alli et al. suggest only purchasing a put. This strategy may not lock in the market price as of the valuation date and may overestimate the lack of liquidity discount. To lock in the market price as of the valuation date, an investor needs to construct a collar. The proceeds from the sale of the call would offset a portion of the cost of purchasing a put, thereby reducing the net cost of the hedge.

Cost of Registering or Monetizing the Stock

If the restricted stock in question conveys "demand rights" (i.e., can demand that the company register the shares), "piggyback rights" (i.e., can follow along when the company registers other shares), or represents a controlling interest, the registration of the shares may be a viable option. In such cases, the cost (including the time value of money) to register and sell the shares may be an appropriate proxy for the lack of marketability/restricted stock discount.

The cost of registering and selling the stock may include such items as the market price impact of introducing a new large block of shares into the market, the underwriter's fee, and other selling concessions and out-of-pocket fees like legal and accounting fees.

Monetizing a restricted stock position is simply borrowing against the stock to achieve some percentage of liquidity. The loan-to-value ratio may be as low as 25 percent, and the interest rate is often prime plus a few hundred basis points. This strategy is a partial answer at best. Perhaps the best use of the loan proceeds is to fund the cost of constructing a collar and in this way potentially reduce the effective cost of the collar.

Dribble-Out Period

As discussed earlier, Rule 144 imposes volume-trading restrictions on the restricted stockholder *after* the initial holding period lapses. The effect the dribble-out provisions have on value may be estimated in a couple of ways. The first begins with estimating how long it would take to liquidate the restricted stock position without running afoul of the dribble-out restrictions. This is done by reviewing the publicly traded stock's daily volume history over a relevant period of time and deciding how quickly the stock can be liquidated without affecting the public stock price and without violating the dribble-out restrictions. The particular length of trading history to examine is a judgment call but should be long enough to reflect the market conditions likely to be encountered during the dribble-out period. On occasion, market-makers or knowledgeable stock brokers can be interviewed to help ascertain the amount of shares that can be sold without affecting the stock price. Next, the present value of the sales proceeds is computed and compared to the freely traded value of the stock; the difference is an estimate of the lack of marketability/restricted stock discount.

Another way to estimate the effect of volume trading restrictions on value is to consider their impact on the effective holding period. This approach also begins with estimating the time needed to fully liquidate the restricted stock position. Rather than estimating the sales proceeds and computing present value, the weighted-average time to complete the dribble-out is added to the initial holding period. Then the hedge strategies discussed earlier are implemented to hedge the position over the longer effective holding period. The cost of the hedge reflects the lack of marketability/ restricted stock discount covering both the initial holding period and the weighted average dribble-out period.

Effect of Stock Price Volatility on Restricted Stock Discounts

In the Black-Scholes world, volatility is the option holder's friend. An increase in volatility implies a greater chance that the option will be in-the-money before it expires. For holders of restricted stock, however, volatility is the enemy. Without the ability to time the sale of the security, the holder is subject to the downside risks but may not be able to capture the potential upside benefits. Frances A. Longstaff published an article in the *Journal of Finance* in 1995 that utilized option-pricing concepts to calculate estimates of lack of marketability discounts for restricted stock based upon two factors: the length of the marketability restriction period and the volatility in the returns of the subject security's publicly traded counterpart.[18] The results of the article were consistent with the existing stock studies and provided a framework for evaluating the effect of restriction periods that are either longer or shorter than the restriction periods measured by the restricted stock studies. The article includes calculations of the maximum percentage restricted stock discounts for periods ranging from one day to five years at three different measures of volatility.

A limitation to Longstaff's analysis is that it considers only three different measures of volatility (10, 20, and 30 percent). If the subject shares have a higher volatility (as many technology stocks do), Longstaff's conclusions cannot be easily extrapolated to these more volatile shares.

> The Longstaff analysis indicates that the greater the volatility, the greater the discount and that the marketability discount is not a linear function of time because the greatest risks, and therefore the largest increases in percentage discount, occur early in the restriction period.

For example, one effect of volatility could be: A stock with an annual volatility of 20 percent has an estimated discount of 24.6 percent if the restriction period is two years. A 50.0 percent reduction in the restriction period to one year produces only a 31 percent reduction in the discount (from 24.6 to 17 percent). A further 50 percent reduction to six months again reduces the discount by only 31 to 11.7 percent. Thus, a six-month restriction period would imply a discount almost half as large as that resulting for a 24-month period.

As Longstaff notes, the methodology utilized provides an estimate of the upper bounds of the discount for lack of marketability. He compares this to the restricted stock studies in which "the empirical estimates of the discount for lack of marketability closely approximate the upper bound," implying that the analytical results of his research actually may provide useful approximations of the value of marketability rather than just serving as its upper bound.

Conclusion

To perform restricted stock valuations, the appraiser should fully understand the material restrictions placed on the stock and understand the factors affecting restricted stock discounts. The published restricted stock studies and articles can be reviewed to help identify the need for and the relative magnitude of the appropriate lack of marketability discount. Each particular security comes with its own facts and circumstances. Accordingly, each restricted stock analysis should stand on its own merit. Option pricing and hedge analyses often are used to estimate the cost to "cure" the lack of marketability and, by extension, the magnitude of the appropriate discount.

---

[18] Frances A. Longstaff, "How Much Can Marketability Affect Security Values?" *Journal of Finance* 1, no. 5 (December 1995), pp. 1767–1774.

F: VALUATION OF EARLY-STAGE TECHNOLOGY COMPANIES

Introduction

Early stage technology companies have many characteristics that separate them from more traditional, "old-economy" companies. These characteristics make early stage companies challenging for valuation analysts, security analysts, and the investing public to value.

Characteristics of Early Stage Technology Companies

Exhibit 24.5 lists the unique characteristics of these companies and the impact each has on the valuation process.

Reasons Why Early Stage Technology Companies Need Valuation Services

Early stage technology companies need valuation services for a variety of reasons. The most common reasons are discussed below.

Share-Based Compensation

Share-based compensation is an important piece of the attract-and-retain-employees puzzle. Stock options, restricted stock, or similar securities are granted to employees as part of their compensation package.

> To avoid excess compensation charges, companies are required to set the grant price equal to or greater than the underlying common stock's fair market value at the time of issuance.

The American Jobs Creation Act (2004) substantively changed the way in which nonqualified deferred compensation, including stock options, is designed, administered, and taxed. Analysts should be familiar with the provisions of Section 409A of this act.

Prior to an initial public offering, the Securities and Exchange Commission will closely scrutinize whether the grant price equals fair market value or whether the company must restate (i.e., increase) its compensation expense in the year its options were issued. The review process typically covers a 12- to 18-month look-back period. Management (often at the insistence of its auditors or legal counsel) will engage valuation analysts to assist it in estimating the fair market value of its option grants.

Financial Statement Disclosure

The Financial Accounting Standards Board has issued a number of pronouncements whereby the fair value of certain assets, options, and securities needs to be estimated for financial statement disclosure purposes.

Exhibit 24.5   Characteristics of Early Stage Technology Companies

Characteristic	Impact on Valuation Process
1. Expectation for rapid and longer term "abnormally high growth" in revenue and earnings	This feature is the primary and most pervasive aspect of early stage companies. A company's growth rate affects the amount, timing, and realization of cash flow, an item of paramount importance to investors and valuation analysts.
2. Large potential market/significant untapped markets	To compensate investors for the enormous risk associated with investing in these companies, the entities must be able to demonstrate large potential returns. A large potential market is often necessary to attain large investor returns for known products.
3. New, often innovative products and services	By definition, these companies need to offer a product or service that is new or innovative. As a result, the time to develop the product or service, the ultimate cost structure achieved, the pricing of the product or service, and the market's acceptance of same are unknown.
4. Unproven business plan and management team	For the first few years of an early stage company's existence, the valuation analyst may only have management's projections available when attempting to estimate the value of the company's equity securities. The business plan on which the projections are based, and management's ability to execute same, are two of the greatest risks valuation analysts must assess.
5. Complex capital structures	Securing current and future capital is critical to the success of these companies. Capital is often raised by issuing preferred stock, convertible debt, options, and warrants. Each of these senior or dilutive securities must be addressed before the value of common equity can be estimated.
6. Existence of off–balance sheet assets	Technology companies' assets are often intangible in nature and tied to a particular technology and/or labor force. This makes estimating even a "floor value" for these companies quite difficult.

Obtaining Capital

Obtaining capital is critical to the success of early stage technology companies. At each financing event, the value of the company and/or the specific securities issued must be negotiated. While the value agreed upon is often a matter of negotiating power and skill, management may require valuation assistance and consulting to help set a reasonable negotiating range.

Estate Planning

It is most employees' and investors' fervent hope that the value of their technology shares experience dramatic future appreciation. The goal of most estate plans is to remove the most rapidly appreciating assets from the estate. Accordingly, early stage technology securities often are selected to be gifted to family or friends. Valuation analysts are often needed to estimate the fair market value of the gifted securities for transfer purposes.

Litigation

Shareholder disputes, employment-related disputes, contract disputes, intangible asset infringement disputes, and marriage dissolutions are just some of the litigation-related matters for which valuation assistance may be needed. When the market turns south, shareholder and investor litigation usually increases as former company values are tested.

Valuation Approaches

As with all potentially income-producing assets, there are three general approaches available to estimate the value of early stage technology companies: asset, market, and income. Early stage technology companies pose unique problems in implementing each of these general approaches. A good general reference on the valuation of privately held companies, including early stage companies, is AICPA's Audit and Accounting Practice Aid Series publication, "Valuation of Privately Held Equity Securities Issued as Compensation." This publication is currently undergoing a complete update and should be ready by 2010/2011.

Asset Approach

The asset approach is the least often used approach when valuing other than the most early stage technology companies. Most often this approach is used in liquidation scenarios, down rounds, asset impairment studies, or before the entity has achieved any meaningful milestones.

ValTip

> The analyst may need to focus on when the company expects to achieve sustainable profit margins and work backward to the valuation date.

Research and development expenses, programmers' wages, and other similar expenses may need to be referenced when implementing the asset approach. Determining whether these expenditures have any present or future value is perhaps the most difficult aspect of using the asset approach. Technical obsolescence, inefficient use of resources, or simply the hit-or-miss nature of start-up and early stage activities all complicate the question of whether dollars spent equates to value built.

Market Approach

Three general methods are used when implementing the market approach to value early stage technology companies:

1. Guideline public company method
2. Guideline company transaction method
3. Common or preferred stock investments in the subject company

Refer to Chapter 7 for a more complete discussion of the market approach methods.

Guideline Public Company Method. This method involves identifying publicly traded companies that are sufficiently comparable to the subject company and using their pricing metrics as guidelines for valuing the subject company's securities. Ascertaining where the subject company is in its management, product, and market evolution (i.e., where it is in its life cycle) vis-à-vis any of the deemed guideline companies is an important first step in properly performing this method. The other issues to consider are:

- If one company is public and the other isn't, they are unlikely to be in the same stage of product and market development.
- There is likely to be a wide dispersion among the guideline companies' valuation multiples. Identifying why this dispersion is present and adjusting for it regarding the subject company is difficult.
- The subject company may lack traditional pricing metrics; it may not have revenue, earnings, or debt-free cash flow. Alternative metrics like eyeballs, clicks, users, miles of cable laid, and population service area may be poor proxies for cash flow and may contain little information about when or if sustainable cash flow will be realized for a particular subject company.

> The analyst may need to focus on when the company will attain sustainable profit margins and work backward to the valuation date.

- The presence of preferred stock in the subject's capital structure can complicate the valuation. Usually, when a technology company goes public, its preferred stock is converted into common stock. The subject company, however, may have four or five separate preferred stock issues outstanding at the valuation date. Furthermore, each issue may have redemption, conversion, liquidation preference, and voting right features different from the others. An invested capital approach (rather than direct-to-common equity) may initially help to bypass this issue. If the ultimate goal is to value the subject company's common equity, however, invested capital will need to be allocated among debt capital and preferred and common equity. (Refer to AICPA's Practice Aid, "Valuation of Privately Held Company Equity Securities Issued as Compensation," or *Valuing Early Stage and*

Venture–Backed Companies, written by Neil Beaton and published by John Wiley & Sons in 2010.)

- The potential future dilution of earnings per share (from the exercise of warrants, options, and convertible securities) may be substantially different for the subject and guideline companies.

Guideline Company Transaction Method. In addition to the issues discussed under the guideline public company method, the complexities present in the guideline company transaction method with technology companies include:

- *Stock-funded acquisitions.* Here the acquirer pays the acquiree in its stock, typically based on an exchange ratio. Relative value may have been established by this, but not necessarily absolute value. Also, lock-up agreements, trading restrictions, and blockage issues all may affect the fair market value of the consideration received.
- *Presence of royalty, earn-out, or other agreements.* These agreements may result in value being dependent on future events. The calculation of the fair market value of the consideration paid is more difficult when these types of agreements are included.
- *Presence of employment and noncompetition agreements.* A portion of the total purchase price may be allocated to these "personal" rather than "enterprise" assets. In those cases, understanding the economic rationale for the allocation of value to these assets is important.

> As with more traditional companies, the largest impediment to properly using this method in the technology arena is lack of information. Information on what bundle of assets and liabilities were acquired, what the true price and terms were, and whether strategic considerations were present is difficult to obtain.

Common or Preferred Stock Investment in the Subject Company. Often employee option grants occur at or near an external financing, and such financing can be used (with appropriate adjustment) to help estimate common stock fair market value through a proper allocation model. Even if such a transaction is present, the analyst must be aware of:

> This is the preferred market approach method if the analyst is fortunate enough to have a contemporaneous or fairly recent transaction in the subject company's securities.

- *The presence of value-creating events that occurred between the investment and the valuation date.* Key additions to the management team, successful completion of a product's beta test, or entering into a key strategic alliance not previously contemplated are examples of events that could cause a technology company's value to increase (or decrease under other circumstances) in a relatively short period of time.
- *A transaction in the company's preferred stock as the base for estimating the value of its common stock.* It is common for pre-IPO investments in technology companies to result in the issuance of preferred rather than common stock. Before using a preferred stock investment to value common stock, the analyst must adjust for differences in the respective securities' rights and restrictions. Typical preferred stock will have:

  - Antidilution provisions
  - Redemption rights
  - Conversion features
  - Dividend and liquidation preference
  - Voting rights or other control attributes

  Consideration also should be given to the investment round, the investor board representation, or other control features and differences in marketability between the investment and the subject securities.

  A rule of thumb used to be that, in the early financing rounds such as series A, common stock had a value of 10 percent of the preferred stock's value. In later rounds, the value of the preferred and common securities would begin to converge so that by the IPO, they were closer in value. While this general progression has intuitive appeal, it does not necessarily represent reality. Instead, the company's ability to execute its business plan as well as the specific features of the preferred stock tend to dictate whether value rests in a company's preferred or its common stock.

  The bankruptcy-predicting Z-score also can be used with option pricing methodology to estimate the difference in value between the common and preferred stock arising from the liquidation preference,[19] but this methodology is not common in practice.

- *The effects of certain rights or restrictions on the security being valued.*

> Simultaneous gifts made by the same donor in the same security can have different fair market values.

---

[19] Gregory A. Barber, "Valuing Common Stock in Development-Stage Companies," *Valuation Strategies* (September/October 2000).

For example, a gift of stock that is subject to Rule 144 or underwriter-instituted restrictions will have trading restrictions if made to someone defined as an affiliate and have no trading restrictions if gifted to a nonaffiliate. Consequently, each gift may have a different fair market value. Does this violate the hypothetical willing buyer/seller assumption that is such a key part of fair market value, or is it the attribute of the gifted security that is the ultimate decision maker? Unless a particular characteristic follows the gifted security, it may not affect fair market value.

Income Approach

The expanded view of the income approach generally includes the following methods:

- Capitalization of cash flow
- Discounted future cash flow
- Contingent claims analysis, such as real options analysis and decision (tree) analysis.

A number of authors and valuation analysts believe that the more a company's future outcomes become dependent on contingent future events, the less appropriate a discounted cash flow method is and the more appropriate a contingent-claims analysis becomes. This relationship is displayed in Exhibit 24.6.

Exhibit 24.6   Valuation Tools Matched to the Type of Growth Opportunity[20]

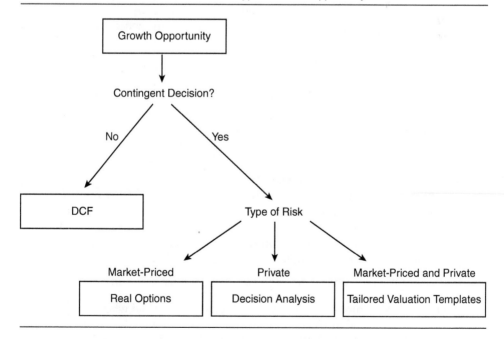

---

[20] Martha Amram, *Value Sweep—Mapping Corporate Growth Opportunities* (Cambridge, MA: Harvard Business School Press, pp. 2002).

Please refer to Sections H and G in this chapter for a further discussion of real option analyses. The remainder of this section will focus on the discounted cash-flow approach.

> Due to the potential for abnormally high growth in operations, revenue, and cash flows, the discounted cash flow method is the income approach method of choice when valuing early stage technology companies that have achieved some semblance of product or technical feasibility.

Cash flow to invested capital (rather than to common equity) is typically the economic measure selected because of the heavy presence of preferred stock in the capital structures of many technology companies. The presence of "senior securities" (whether debt or more typically preferred stock) often indicates that the valuation needs to be oriented toward invested capital.

Discounted Cash Flow.   This section addresses the special considerations associated with performing a discounted cash flow (DCF) method for early-stage technology companies. Please refer to Chapter 5 for a thorough discussion of the income approach.

The starting point for most DCF analyses is the company's business plan and accompanying financial projections. These projections are generally prepared by management to aid in securing financing and thus may be overly optimistic. Furthermore, many ventures are unique; it is difficult to assess the product's or service's cost structure, selling price, market acceptance, or even viability.

> One of the first decisions the valuation analyst will face in implementing the income approach is whether to accept management projections as representing the most likely potential outcome or whether multiple scenarios should be projected and a probability of occurrence assigned to each. In theory, the latter approach is best, but, due to practical considerations, most often projection risk is addressed in the discount rate and not through multiple outcome scenarios.

Management has more control over how much it spends and when it is spent than it does over if, when, and in what amount revenue and profits will be generated. This fact argues for "losses" being discounted with a rate lower than profits. Another major decision is how to estimate terminal value. Most likely management's projections will not extend beyond 5 to 10 years. The prospects for continually high growth, however, may extend far past the forecast period. Should a multiple or "staged" DCF

Forecast losses that result from prerevenue-phase expenditures (e.g., R&D and brand building) can be discounted at a rate different from the profits.

model be used? Again, theory says yes, but in the real world there is often little objective data to support forecast assumptions beyond five years or so. This is especially true of early stage companies. The terminal value often (due to interim losses) represents 100 percent or more of a technology company's present value. Whether the terminal value is estimated using an EBITDA, or other, market-based multiple, or whether some variation of the Gordon growth model is used, may have a material effect on the concluded value. Many practitioners believe that if terminal value is estimated using a market-based multiple, the entire DCF process is converted from an income approach to a market approach. As with the market approach, potential future dilution in per-share economic measures should be considered.

Discount Rates.   Discount rates for early stage technology companies are generally determined in the same manner as other companies' discount rates except for higher premiums for risks. Rates of return used in venture capital (VC) often are used to quantify this additional risk.

The use of decision tree analyses and/or real options methods helps bring these "losses" into focus. They are both discretionary and contingent on the continued success of management in achieving its milestones.

If venture capital rates of returns, however, are referenced in selecting an appropriate discount rate, the valuation analyst may need to adjust the lack of marketability discount applied later on because many VC discount rates are predicated on investments in nonmarketable securities.

Exhibit 24.7   Discount Rate Considerations

	Enhances Value	Detracts from Value
Quality of story/business plan	Easily understood and credible	Convoluted/Questionable
Management/Board of Directors	Strong and experienced	Incomplete or inexperienced
Size of market	Large and/or growing	Small or flat
Barriers to entry	High	Low
Competitors	Few	Many
Proprietary technology	Yes	No
Achieve plan and financial milestones	Performance as promised	Late or fail to achieve

Refer to Chapter 6 for a discussion of the discount rates synthesis process. Exhibit 24.7 lists certain factors more peculiar to technology-company risk assessment and the general effect that items have on the discount rate.

Two publications provide guidance about the rates of return sought by venture capital investors at various stages of the subject company's development:

- *QED Report on Venture Capital Financial Analysis* by James Plummer (currently being updated)
- *A Method for Valuing High-Risk, Long-Term Investments: The Venture Capital Method* by Daniel Scherlis and William Sahlman

Venture Capital Rates of Return

Stage of Development	Plummer	Scherlis and Sahlman
Start-up	50%–70%	50%–70%
First stage or "early development"	40%–60%	40%–60%
Second stage or "expansion"	35%–50%	30%–50%
Bridge/IPO	25%–35%	20%–35%

These returns relate to investor expectations for an individual investment. The *2000 Investment Benchmark's Report on Venture Capital* issued by Venture Economics includes data on portfolio returns earned by 869 venture capital private partnerships formed between 1969 and 1999. (See Addendum 1 at the end of this chapter for additional sources of venture capital returns.)

Allocation of Enterprise/Invested Capital Value

The presence of preferred stock in the subject company's capital structure can complicate the valuation if the ultimate goal is to value the subject company's common equity. As noted earlier, when a technology company goes public, its preferred stock is converted into common stock. However, before an IPO, the preferred stock will have different attributes, also as noted previously. Therefore, once the subject company's invested capital has been determined using one or more of the three approaches to value (i.e., cost, market, and income approaches), the next step in arriving at a value for the subject company's common equity is to allocate the invested capital value among the various classes of preferred stock, with the residual going to the common stock.

As discussed in *Valuation of Privately Held Company Equity Securities Issued as Compensation*, published by the AICPA as part of their Practice Aid Series (and currently under revision), three common methodologies are employed in such an allocation:

1. The current value method
2. The option pricing method
3. The probability-weighted expected return method

The Current Value Method

The current value method is based on the allocation theory that shareholders with senior stock rights would attempt to maximize the value of their holdings based solely on the senior stock's underlying liquidation preference, participation rights, and an imminent liquidity event. The current value method may not be appropriate in many instances, however, as it is limited by the assumption of an imminent liquidity event in the form of an acquisition or dissolution of the company. If an imminent liquidity event is not expected, the option pricing and probability-weighted expected return methods are typically more appropriate value allocation methods.

The Option Pricing Method

The option method relies on financial option theory to allocate value among different classes of stock based upon a future "claim" on value. Essentially, the equity claim of the common shareholders are equivalent to a call option on the common stocks' participation in the value of the subject company above the respective preferred shareholders' liquidation preferences. Thus, the common stock can be valued by estimating the value of its share in each of these call option rights using the Black-Scholes option pricing (or other) model at a series of exercise prices that coincide with the liquidation and conversion preferences of the preferred shareholders.

The option pricing method is limited, however, under the two following situations:

1. If the subject company's equity securities contain an escalating participation provision for the preferred stock, the implementation of a closed form option pricing method may not be a viable method with which to allocate value.
2. If the subject company has a more-probable-than-not opportunity to either go public or be acquired at a premium in the near future, the option pricing method does not capture the potential discontinuity in value.

The Probability-Weighted Expected Return Method

Under a probability-weighted expected return method, the value of the subject company's common stock is estimated based on an analysis of future values for the entire enterprise, assuming various future outcomes. Share value is based upon the probability-weighted present value of these expected outcomes, as well as the rights of each class of preferred and common stock.

This method involves a forward-looking analysis of the following:

- Possible future outcomes available to the subject company (e.g., an initial public offering, a strategic merger or sale, dissolution, or continued operation as a viable private enterprise)
- The estimation of future and present value under each outcome
- The application of a probability factor to each outcome as of the valuation date

The steps in applying this method to a company's enterprise value are as follows:

1. For each possible future event, future values of the subject company's invested capital are estimated at certain future points in time.
2. For each event value and date, the rights and preferences of each shareholder class are considered in order to determine the appropriate allocation value between the share classes.

3. For each possible event, an expected future value is calculated for each share class. This future value is then discounted to a present value using an appropriate risk-adjusted discount rate.
4. A probability is estimated for each possible event based on the facts and circumstances as of the valuation date.
5. Based on the probabilities estimated for the possible events, a probability-weighted return, expressed in terms of a per-share value, is then determined for each share class.

   Critical assumptions required to perform the probability-weighted expected return method include the following:

Valuations. Expected valuations under each future event scenario are estimated based upon management's future revenue estimates and current industry pricing multiples.
Timing. Expected dates of each event are estimated based upon discussion with the subject company's management and analysis of market conditions.
Discount rates. Risk-adjusted rates of return are selected under each event scenario.
Discounts. Appropriate lack of control or lack of marketability discounts, if any, required to estimate the common share value under each scenario are applied.
Event probabilities. Estimates of the probability of occurrence of each event are assigned based on discussions with the subject company's management and an analysis of market conditions.

While each of the preceding allocation methods should be considered, only one, or at most two, of the three methods would generally be used in a typical allocation assignment.

Summary

Traditional valuation approaches can and are used to value early-stage technology companies. Special consideration is needed, however, to address the unique factors associated with these high-growth, intangible-intensive entities. Exhibit 24.8 summarizes the available valuation methodologies and lists the more important factors to consider in their implementation.

G: VALUATION ISSUES RELATED TO STOCK OPTIONS AND OTHER SHARE-BASED COMPENSATION

Introduction

A key trend over the past two decades has been the increased importance of intangible assets to the overall value of a company. In the old asset-based economy, tangible assets such as land, buildings, and machinery dominated the value of companies. The ability of a company to generate sales and earnings was mostly a function of the amount of capital equipment and labor available for production. However, as the economy moved from being asset based to being information based, tangible assets became less important. Instead, intangible assets like trademarks,

Exhibit 24.8 Valuation Approach/Method

Valuation Approach/Method	Factors to Consider
Asset Approach (Chapter 8)	• Possibly the least relevant of approaches for other than nascent early stage entities • Difficult to identify and value off–balance sheet, intangible assets
Market Approach (Chapter 7)	• Analysis of stage of life cycle critical in determining comparability • Lack of traditional pricing metrics complicates process; nontraditional/nonfinancial metrics may not correlate to cash flow prospects • Complex capital structures indicate an invested capital approach may be most appropriate • Stock swaps, earn-outs, and other noncash items affect value of consideration received under the similar transaction method • Differences between the security invested in and the subject security, as well as differences in the actual investors and the hypothetical willing-buyers, must be addressed in the direct investment method.
Income Approach (Chapters 5 and 6)	• Reliance on management forecasts • Use of multiple scenarios or management's best estimate • Different discount rates for "losses" vs. "profits" • Terminal value often comprises 100+ percent of present value
Real Options (1) (Section 24H)	• One of most theoretically sound approaches • Extends financial option theory to valuation of management or "real" options • Difficult to identify and model potential outcome of real options

(1) Option and contingent claims analysis are subsets of the income approach.

goodwill, and patents, that reflect the "knowledge capital" of a business, became dominant. Since most intangible assets are not capitalized on a company's books unless acquired from a third party, a company's true value is not reflected on its balance sheet. Examples of this intangible value abound in the stock market where it is not uncommon to see companies trading at multiples of their net asset values.

The human intelligence, skill, and leadership embodied in a company's workforce are integral components in maintaining and supporting its intangible assets. Incentive compensation plans have evolved to reward activities that increase the value of a company's stock and to promote employee retention. The most direct of these plans use the company's stock or the rights to acquire that stock as a form of compensation.

Both intangible assets and share-based compensation have become integral components in the wealth makeup of companies and individuals. Valuing these assets and liabilities is undertaken for a variety of purposes, including financial reporting, tax reporting, litigation, transactions, and strategic planning.

Option valuation techniques is one of the fastest-growing areas of financial theory and application. Option models allow for enhanced flexibility in decision making and in analyzing contingent events. These models are not only applicable to the valuation of stock options but are used to value capital investments, intangible assets, and entire divisions or companies.

Before these valuation techniques are introduced, it is important to understand the characteristics of stock options and the terminology used in describing them. The following paragraphs review those key issues and create the foundation for the work that follows.

Employee stock options (ESOs) can be attractive given the fact that cash is not normally involved. Vesting rights often are embedded in these ESOs to promote employee retention by rewarding longevity.

Definitions

1. *American option.* An option that can be exercised at any time during its life.
2. *Asian option.* An option whose payoff is dependent on the average price of the underlying asset during a specified period. European options are paid off based on the end-of-period value of the underlying asset.
3. *Binomial option pricing model.* An option pricing model based on the assumption that stock prices can move only to two values over a short period of time.
4. *Black-Scholes model.* A model used to calculate the value of a European call option. Developed in 1973 by Fisher Black and Myron Scholes, it uses the stock price, strike price, expiration date, risk-free return, and the standard deviation (volatility) of the stock's return to estimate the value of the option.
5. *Call option.* A provision that gives the holder the right, but not the obligation, to buy a stock, bond, commodity, or other instrument at a specified price within a specific time period.
6. *Carrying value.* Also known as "book value," it is a) a carrying value of total equity or b) total assets minus non–interest bearing debt (carrying value of invested capital).
7. *Employee stock option.* Stock options granted to specified employees of a company. These options carry the right but not the obligation to buy a certain amount of shares in the company at a predetermined price.
8. *European option.* An option that can be exercised only at the end of its life.
9. *Incentive stock option (ISO).* A type of employee stock option with various tax benefits granted under Section 422 of the Internal Revenue Code of 1986. These options may be granted only to individuals who are employees of the granting

company or a parent or subsidiary of the granting company. A number of restrictions under Section 422 may disqualify an ISO, in which case it becomes a nonqualified stock option.

10. *Long-term equity anticipation securities (LEAPS)*. An options contract that has an original maturity ranging from nine months to two years.
11. *Nonqualified stock option (NSO)*. A type of employee stock option which is less advantageous for the employer from a tax standpoint than an ISO, but which is less restrictive and generally easier to set up and administer. Any stock option granted to an employee that is not an incentive stock option is, by default, an NSO.
12. *Put option*. A provision giving the holder the right, but not the obligation, to sell a stock, bond, commodity, or other instrument at a specified price within a specific time period.
13. *Strike price*. The stated price per share for which underlying stock may be purchased (for a call) or sold (for a put) by the option holder upon exercise of the option contract.

Option Basics

Stock options generally grant the holder the right, but not the obligation, to acquire stock in a corporation. The lack of an obligatory purchase requirement distinguishes stock options from forward or future contracts where final purchase is mandatory. When granted, stock options usually carry an exercise price and a stated option term.

ValTip

Employee stock options are classified as either incentive stock options or nonqualified stock options.

Stock option plans usually are set up to promote the long-term success of the company granting the options by attracting and retaining employees, outside directors, and consultants. Options encourage these individuals to focus on the company's long-range goals by granting them an ownership interest in the company.

Most stock options can be characterized as call options where the holder possesses the right to buy the underlying stock at a specified price and date. In contrast, a put option allows the holder to sell the underlying stock at a specified price and date. Many employee stock ownership plans (ESOPs) contain put provisions (not options) for stock owned by employees of the company.

ValTip

Options that can be exercised during and up to the expiration date are known as American options. Options that can be exercised only upon the expiration date are known as European options.

The strike price, also known as the exercise price, is a fixed price at which the holder may purchase the underlying stock. The exercise price is set upon the granting of the specific option and, under most circumstances, cannot be changed without triggering somewhat onerous reporting requirements.

Most stock options lapse after a certain time period. Incentive stock options cannot have an expiration date more than 10 years after the granting date. However, publicly traded options generally have expiration dates that are measured in months rather than years.

Contract

The purchaser of an option typically is referred to as the option holder. Sellers of options typically are referred to as option writers, since they "write" the option contract. In exchange for the contract, the option holder pays a premium to the option writer. There are seven items specified in the option contract:

1. *Underlying instrument.* The instrument that may be bought or sold.
2. *Contract size.* The number of shares of underlying stock that the contract involves.
3. *Exercise price (or strike price).* The price at which the underlying stock will transact if the option is exercised.
4. *Settlement date.* The date on which money is received for the contract.
5. *Expiration date (expiry).* The date that the option expires.
6. *Style.* The ability to exercise prior to expiry (i.e., American or European).
7. *Premium.* Price paid for the contract.

While options on stock indices, foreign exchange, agricultural commodities, precious metals, futures, and interest rates exist, the discussion in this chapter is limited to stock options granted to employees of the issuing corporation.

Option parameters specify how the option can be exercised. The most common styles are American and European options. American options can be exercised at any time on or before the expiration date. European options can be exercised only on the expiration date. There is a third type of option that is exercisable only on predetermined dates, such as every month, or every quarter. They are referred to as Bermuda options.

ValTip

If not exercised before the expiration date, the option simply expires with no value.

Most publicly traded options have expiration dates of less than a year, but the Chicago Board Options Exchange (CBOE) now lists longer-term options on several blue-chip stocks. Known as long-term equity anticipation securities, or LEAPS for short, these options have longer-term expiration dates. In contrast, ISOs normally have a 10-year life.

Descriptive Terminology

Options have a particular vocabulary, especially in describing their status. The following are some of most common terms and definitions related to options.

At the money. The term used when the exercise price and the underlying price are equal.

In the money. The term used when an option's strike price is less than the current price of the underlying stock.

Out of the money. The term used when an option's strike price is greater than the underlying stock price.

Warrants

A warrant is a particular type of call option issued by the company itself. When the warrant is settled, the company issues additional shares, increasing the number of shares outstanding; in contrast, a call option is settled with the delivery of previously issued shares. In addition, the cash flows of the company increase with the exercise of a warrant since the exercise price is paid to the company. Therefore, the dilution created by the issuance of stock is partially offset by the cash received.

As a result of dilution, the value of a warrant may vary somewhat from the value of a call option with identical terms.

Options Trading

Standardized options contracts were first traded on a national exchange in 1973, when the Chicago Board Options Exchange began listing call options. Option contracts now are traded on a number of exchanges, including the CBOE, Philadelphia Stock Exchange, American Stock Exchange, New York Stock Exchange, and Pacific Exchange. Some options trade in the over-the-counter (OTC) markets as well. Over-the-counter stocks do not have standardized terms but are customized for each transaction. Due to the customization, the market is limited, thus increasing the cost of establishing an OTC option contract. Most public option trading occurs on organized exchanges.

Components of Value

Two basic components make up the price paid for an option: intrinsic value and time value. The most obvious component of an option's value is its intrinsic value. This intrinsic value is the amount of money available from the immediate exercise of the option, or the amount the option is in the money. For a call option, this amount reflects the value of the stock less the exercise price.

Volatility is the expected standard deviation of the underlying stock. As volatility increases, so does the probability that the stock will increase (calls) or decrease (puts) by a large enough magnitude to allow the option to be "in the money" before it expires.

To illustrate this concept, consider the holder of a call option. The holder of a call option is not exposed to the downside risk of the stock. The holder's loss if the stock price declines is limited to the price paid for the call option, no matter what the likelihood that the stock price will decline. However, the more a stock's price can increase over a given period, the higher the option holder's potential profit. This makes the option holder prefer high volatility since it increases the chance that the stock's price will increase above the exercise price.

Even without being in the money, an option may have value. This value is created by the possibility that the option could be exercised profitably in the future. Three factors determine time value:

1. Volatility of the stock underlying the option
2. Risk-free rate of interest over the option period
3. Length of time before the option expires

The final determinant of an options price is the risk-free rate. The risk-free rate represents the interest rate that could be earned by investing the exercise price over the time period from option purchase to exercise. Assuming a call option holder had perfect knowledge that the stock price would increase, the holder would, in effect, be getting a risk-free loan for the length of the option. For a put option, it is just the opposite, since the option holder gives up the potential to invest.

The length of time before an option expires is a fairly straightforward concept. The longer the period until expiration, the greater the chance the option will end up above or below the exercise price of the underlying stock.

Exhibit 24.9 summarizes the effects that a change in one variable has on the value of an underlying call or put option, all else being equal.

Exhibit 24.9   Effect of an Increase in Variable on Option Value

Variable	Call Option	Put Option
Market value of stock	+	−
Exercise price	−	+
Volatility	+	+
Risk-free rate	+	−
Expiration date*	+	+

*For European options on dividend-paying stocks, value may not increase with time due to the dividend effect.

The Dividend Effect

Dividends represent a cash return to the investors. A company has the choice of either paying dividends or reinvesting that money in the business. The reinvestment of that cash could allow the business to earn more in the future, thus increasing its stock price. Paying out the dividend effectively reduces the stock price by the dividend amount on the ex-dividend date (the date that the shareholders of record are determined for dividend payment). By reducing the stock price on the ex-dividend date, the value of a call option decreases and the value of a put option increases.

Valuation Tools

With the introduction of stock options and the components that drive their value, tools have been developed to calculate their value. The following models were designed to value publicly traded options. Each has its own virtues and limitations. Understanding those limitations and adjusting for them is the key to valuing a wide variety of options.

A discussion of the complex mathematical assumptions used to derive these formulas is beyond the scope of this chapter. Software programs of option models are available from numerous sources or can be modeled using the provided equation. The focus here is on the benefits of each model and the selection of appropriate inputs for the option valuation models.

Black-Scholes Model

The most widely recognized option-pricing model is known as the Black-Scholes model. Developed by Fisher Black and Myron Scholes in 1973, the Black-Scholes model was the first model used to calculate a theoretical call price (ignoring dividends paid during the life of the option). The model (shown in Exhibit 24.10) uses the five key determinants of an option's price:

1. Underlying stock price
2. Exercise price
3. Volatility of the underlying stock
4. Time to expiration
5. Short-term (risk-free) interest rate

While advanced mathematical techniques were used to develop the Black-Scholes model, it is not necessary to understand the formula's derivation in order to use it.

Normally, each component of the formula is readily available. The stock price is based on the closing price of the stock as of the day of valuation or, when the stock is restricted (and the restriction period lasts longer than the option term) or in a private company, on the estimated price of the stock.

The *exercise price* is given in the contract.

The *time remaining until expiration* can be expressed as a percentage of a year for options with expirations of less than a year or in years for those options with expiries greater than a year.

The *risk-free rate* is approximated by using rates paid for U.S. Treasury bills, matching the length of the option maturity to the U.S. Treasury bill period.

Exhibit 24.10   Black-Scholes Option Pricing Model

The original formula for calculating the theoretical call option price is as follows:

$$C = S \times N(d_1) - Xe^{-rt} \times N(d_2)$$

Where:

$$d_1 = \frac{\ln\left[\dfrac{S}{x}\right] + \left[r + \dfrac{\sigma^2}{2}\right]T}{\sigma\sqrt{T}}$$

$$d_2 = d_1 - \sigma\sqrt{T}$$

C	=	Call price
S	=	Stock price
X	=	Exercise price
T	=	Time remaining until expiration
r	=	Current risk-free interest rate
σ	=	Expected annual volatility of stock price
ln	=	Natural logarithm
N(x)	=	Standard normal cumulative distribution function
e	=	Exponential function

Volatility is the expected volatility of the underlying stock. Historical volatility is measured using the annualized standard deviation of the underlying stock price movements adjusted for dividends. Generally, the expected volatility can be calculated from the historical volatility in the stock or the implied volatility from publicly traded stock options.

When using historical volatility, it is generally best to review the latest 12-month period although longer or shorter periods are sometimes used. When long-term options exist or nonrecurring events have occurred, adjustments may be made to reflect expectations of future performance.

When the stock is lightly traded or not publicly traded, it may be necessary to use an average of the historical volatilities of similar stocks in the marketplace as a proxy for anticipated volatility. It is important to average the volatilities and not calculate volatility based on the standard deviation of a portfolio of these guideline stocks, since diversification among the stocks will lower volatility and not be reflective of the anticipated volatility of an individual stock. Industry volatilities also can be used.

Implied volatility is calculated for publicly traded options by adjusting the Black-Scholes formula to solve for volatility. Assuming identical options, this implied volatility should represent the market's indication of expected volatility.

As with historical volatility, when the stock is lightly traded, it may be necessary to use an average of the implied volatilities of similar stocks in the marketplace.

The *natural logarithm*, the *standard normal cumulative distribution function* and the *exponential function* are all mathematical constants.

The Black-Scholes model also gives a reasonable price for an American call. Earlier, we introduced the two components to option value, intrinsic value, and time

A key limitation of the Black-Scholes model is that it was developed to price European call options in the absence of dividends.

value. The early exercise of an American option would forfeit the time value component.

Adjusting Black-Scholes for European Puts. The Black-Scholes formula can be adjusted to calculate the value of a European put option by applying the put-call parity theorem. The concept of put-call parity is that the payoff for a put could be replicated using a combination of call options, shorting stock, and borrowing. A general formulation of put-call parity is:

$$P = C - S + Xe^{-rt}$$

Applying this to the Black-Scholes option pricing formula and simplifying the equation, the formula for valuing a put option is:

$$P = S \times N(-d_1) + Xe^{-rt} \times N(-d_2)$$

While this formula adjusts the basic Black-Scholes formula for a European put, it does not address the value of an American put. Refer to Exhibit 24.11. One of the components of time value is the risk-free rate. The risk-free rate has a negative value effect on a put option. So there is the possibility that an American put option will have negative time value, thus making early exercise valuable.

Adjusting Black-Scholes for Dividends. As previously discussed, the Black-Scholes model assumes that dividends are not paid. Since some stocks do pay dividends, the model needs adjustment to properly value the options on these stocks. To understand this adjustment, one needs to review the effect of dividends on stock price.

Basic valuation theory states that a stock is worth the present value of its future cash flows. Cash flows retained in the business are reinvested, creating higher potential future cash flows. When dividends are paid, the stockholder receives the cash and can determine whether to reinvest it in the company or in other ventures. The stockholder is equally well off in either case, but cash has come out of the company, reducing its value directly in line with the amount of dividend paid.

When valuing a longer-lived option, the Black-Scholes model can be adjusted for the expected long-term dividend yield of the stock. The formulas in Exhibit 24.11 show the Black-Scholes model adjusted for dividends.

While the formulas adjust the Black-Scholes model to estimate the value of European options in the presence of dividends, American options are not specifically addressed. The ability to exercise early and avoid the lost value of the stock due to dividends (calls) or take advantage of the decline (puts) has additional value over and above the European option.

Adjusting Black-Scholes to Price Warrants. The difference between a warrant and a call option is the dilution created by the warrant, which gives the warrant a

Exhibit 24.11 Dividend Adjusted Black-Scholes Option Pricing Model

The original formula for calculating the theoretical call option price is as follows:

$$C = S_a e^{-bT} \times N(d_1) - X e^{-bT} \times N(d_2)$$

$$P = -S_a e^{-bT} \times N(-d_1) + X e^{-bT} \times N(-d_2)$$

Where:

$$d_1 = \frac{\ln\left[\dfrac{s}{x}\right] + \left[b + \dfrac{\sigma^2}{2}\right]T}{\sigma\sqrt{T}}$$

$$d_2 = d_1 - \sigma\sqrt{T}$$

S = Stock price
X = Exercise price
T = Time remaining until expiration
b = Cost of carry (the risk-free rate minus the dividend yield)
σ = Expected annual volatility of stock price
ln = Natural logarithm
N(x) = Standard normal cumulative distribution function
e = Exponential function

---

lower value than an option with the same terms. The effect of dilution can be calculated to derive the value of the warrant. The formula is:

$$\text{Warrant Value} = \frac{1}{\left[1 + \dfrac{\text{Number of Warrants}}{\text{Number of Shares}}\right]} \times \text{Value of Option Equivalent}$$

The option equivalent is the value of an option with the same terms as the warrant.

The Binomial Model

The Black-Scholes model allows for the rapid calculation of option value. In most instances, with the proper adjustments, it yields a fairly accurate estimate of value for standardized stock options. However, its accuracy is more limited in certain situations, the most notable of which is an American put option. A more robust option valuation model was created in 1979 by John Cox, Stephen Ross, and Mark Rubinstein, when they developed a binomial model for pricing stock options. The binomial model breaks down the time to expiration into time intervals, or steps. At each step, the stock price will either move up or down. How much the stock will move up or down is related to the stock's volatility and the option's time to expiration. Charting these possible movements at each step produces a binomial tree representing all of the possible paths the stock price could take during the life of the option. This makes the binomial model more rigorous to apply than the Black-Scholes model.

Exhibit 24.12 Binomial Tree

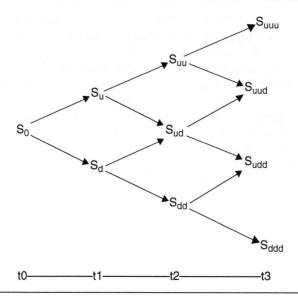

$$t0 \text{——————} t1 \text{——————} t2 \text{——————} t3$$

The option prices are calculated at each step of the tree, working from expiration to the present. The option prices at each step are calculated using the option prices from the previous step of the tree using the probabilities of the stock prices moving up or down, the risk-free rate and the time interval of each step. Any adjustments are put into the model as needed to reflect ex-dividend dates or the optimal

Exhibit 24.13 Binomial Model Formulas

Cox-Ross-Rubinstein approach

$$p = \frac{e^{r_f \Delta t} - d}{u - d}$$

$$u = e^{\sigma \sqrt{\Delta t}}$$

$$d = \frac{1}{u}$$

Equal Probability approach

$$p = 0.5$$

$$u = \frac{2e^{r_f \sigma t + 2s\sqrt{\sigma t}}}{e^{2s\sqrt{\sigma t}} + 1}$$

$$d = \frac{2e^{r_f \sigma t}}{e^{2s\sqrt{\sigma t}} + 1}$$

The variables are:

t   = Total time in years
n   = Number of periods
Δt = Length of time period in years = t/n
σ = Estimated annual volatility
r_f = Current risk-free interest rate
u   = Up ratio
d   = Down ratio

exercise for American options. Exhibit 24.12 is a pictorial representation of the binomial tree with the stock price from time 0 through time 3.

At each time period, there is either an upside or downside movement to the stock. At time 1, there are two possibilities: The stock price either went up or down. At each subsequent time, the number of possibilities increases.

The inputs into the binomial model are the same as for the Black-Scholes model. The volatility input is used to calculate both the upside and downside movement and the transitional probability in the Cox-Ross-Rubinstein approach. This approach does not work when volatility is low and interest rates are high since the calculation can lead to transitional probabilities greater than 100 percent. The binomial model overcomes this problem by assuming the transitional probability is 50 percent. Exhibit 24.13 shows the general formulas for determining the upside and downside movement and transitional probability with each approach.

Minicase: Black-Scholes v. Binomial Model

Both the Black-Scholes and binomial models are based on the same underlying concepts:

- The value of the underlying asset, and thus of the option, is known with certainty at expiry
- The possible values of the underlying asset, and thus of the option, at expiry are a function of the asset's volatility
- The option holder can avoid all outcomes in which the exercise price exceeds the value of the underlying asset
- The option holder is allowed to defer the cost of exercise until expiry

Consequently, the value of a plain-vanilla option may be calculated with either model and the results will be similar. In fact, as we increase the number of time steps per period in the binomial model, the results will exactly converge. To illustrate, assume the following option parameters:

Value of underlying stock	$25.00
Exercise price	$25.00
Volatility	50%
Maturity	2 years
Interest rate	4.0%
Dividends	N/A

Applying these inputs to a standard Black-Scholes model, we arrive at a value of $7.64 per option. To calculate the value with a binomial model, we are faced with a single decision: How many time steps should be chosen? To keep the illustration simple, 12 periods per year are selected. The binomial solution, which appears in Exhibit 24.14, is developed as follows:

- The expected evolution of the underlying asset is modeled. In this case, the stock price begins at $25.00. In each future time step, it is assumed to either rise or fall, with the magnitude of each up/down move based on its volatility.

Exhibit 24.14 Binomial Solution

Binomial Template
Two-year call, 12 periods per year

Standard deviation	50%		Rf	1.003
Per period	0.1443		p	0.4755
Up movement	1.1553		1 – p	0.5245
Down movement	0.8656			

Evolution of Expected Stock Price

Period	0	1	2	3	4	5	6	7	8	9	10	11	12	13	14	15	16	17	18	19	20
Value of underlying equity	25	29	33	39	45	51	59	69	79	92	106	122	141	163	189	218	252	291	336	388	448
		22	25	29	33	39	45	51	59	69	79	92	106	122	141	163	189	218	252	291	336
			19	22	25	29	33	39	45	51	59	69	79	92	106	122	141	163	189	218	252
				16	19	22	25	29	33	39	45	51	59	69	79	92	106	122	141	163	189
					14	16	19	22	25	29	33	39	45	51	59	69	79	92	106	122	141
						12	14	16	19	22	25	29	33	39	45	51	59	69	79	92	106
							11	12	14	16	19	22	25	29	33	39	45	51	59	69	79
								9	11	12	14	16	19	22	25	29	33	39	45	51	59
									8	9	11	12	14	16	19	22	25	29	33	39	45
										7	8	9	11	12	14	16	19	22	25	29	33
											6	7	8	9	11	12	14	16	19	22	25
												5	6	7	8	9	11	12	14	16	19
													4	5	6	7	8	9	11	12	14
														4	4	5	6	7	8	9	11
															3	4	4	5	6	7	8
																3	3	4	4	5	6
																	2	3	3	4	4
																		2	2	3	3
																			2	2	2
																				2	2
																					1

(continues)

Exhibit 24.14 (*Continued*)

Strike price	25																				
Value of European option	7.58																				
	10	13	18	23	29	36	45	56	68	82	98	117	139	164	194	227	266	311	364	424	
	5	7	10	13	17	22	29	36	45	56	68	82	98	117	139	164	193	227	266	311	
		4	5	7	9	13	17	22	28	36	45	55	68	82	98	117	139	164	193	227	
			2	3	5	7	9	12	16	22	28	36	45	55	67	82	98	117	139	164	
				1	2	3	4	6	9	12	16	21	28	35	44	55	67	81	98	117	
					1	1	2	3	4	6	8	11	16	21	27	35	44	55	67	81	
						0	1	2	2	4	5	8	11	15	21	27	35	44	55	55	
							0	0	1	1	2	5	8	11	15	21	27	35	44	35	
								0	0	1	1	2	3	5	7	10	15	20	27	20	
									0	0	0	1	1	2	3	4	7	10	14	9	
										0	0	0	1	0	1	2	4	6	6	3	
											0	0	0	0	0	0	1	2	2	0	
												0	0	0	0	0	0	0	0	0	
													0	0	0	0	0	0	0	0	
														0	0	0	0	0	0	0	
															0	0	0	0	0	0	
																0	0	0	0	0	
																	0	0	0	0	
																		0	0	0	
																			0	0	
																				0	

- At expiry (period 24 in our two-year model) the stock price is expected to be in the range of $1 (24 down moves) to $799 (24 up moves). Based on these end values, the option value at expiry is then calculated.
- These potential option values at expiry are then brought to present value by adjusting for the probability of each outcome, and discounting it at the risk-free rate.

The end result, $7.58, is within 1 percent of the Black-Scholes value. Greater precision can be obtained by modeling more time steps per year. It is important to note that option pricing models are conceptually similar to discounted cash flow methods (i.e., expected future cash flows are brought to present value). The major difference is that option pricing methods separate the probability of each outcome from the time value of money, whereas DCF methods combine these two processes into a single, risk-adjusted discount rate.

Privately Held Stock Options

Privately held stock options typically take the form of warrants that are issued or sold to third parties or employee stock options.

Warrants

Warrants can be given to creditors as incentive for the restructuring of debt, sold with other equity in units, or sold individually to raise capital. In some cases, the company will structure the warrants so they can be publicly traded. More often, warrants are structured to the specific desires of the purchaser, or their transfer is restricted.

> Warrants often are sold in connection with other financial instruments as a "sweetener" to enhance the attractiveness of the placement of the financial instrument they are bundled with or to get favorable terms on another financial instrument.

Employee Stock Options

Employee stock options have become a common part of employee and executive compensation, especially in high-technology firms that are usually short on cash but long on promise. Unlike publicly traded options, ESOs typically have a much longer life. Additionally, ESOs typically have a number of provisions that restrict their transfer, exercise, and ownership rights.

Benefits of Employee Stock Options

Employee stock options have a number of benefits for the corporation. They help the company recruit and retain employees by providing financial incentive while not requiring an initial outlay of cash. For start-up firms, this is a highly attractive feature. Also, ESOs can be used as part of the compensation strategy for senior executives. The Revenue Reconciliation Act of 1993 limited the deductibility of cash salaries above $1 million. Stock options, however, qualify as "objectively determined performance-based compensation." Properly structured, the company can deduct the intrinsic value of the option in the year it is exercised, thus avoiding the limitation on cash compensation. Finally, ESOs are intuitively appealing in that they reward employees based on the performance that stockholders are most interested in, the appreciation in the stock itself.

Incentive Stock Options versus Nonqualified Stock Options

> ESOs are characterized as incentive stock options or nonqualified stock options.

An incentive stock option is an option granted to an employee of a company to purchase company stock at a specified price for a specified period of time that qualifies for favorable tax treatment under § 422 of the Internal Revenue Code. A nonqualified stock option (NSO) is any option that does not qualify for favorable tax treatment under IRC § 422.

With an ISO, there are restrictions on how the option is structured and how it can be transferred. Generally, with an ISO, there are no tax consequences upon the receipt or exercise of the option, although the difference between the fair market value of the stock and the exercise price are alternative minimum tax adjustments. Upon the sale of the underlying stock, the employee will generally record tax based on the capital gain. The company cannot take a tax deduction for any related compensation expense so long as the ISO is disposed of in a qualifying disposition.

Requirements for ISOs include:

- The stock option may be granted only to an employee who must exercise the option while employed or no later than three months after termination of employment (one year if the employee is disabled).
- The stock option must be an option to purchase stock of the employer corporation or the stock of a parent or subsidiary corporation.
- The stock may be capital stock of any class of the corporation, including voting and nonvoting common or preferred stock. Special classes of stock exclusively issued to and held by employees is permissible.
- The option must be granted under a written plan, the ISO agreement, specifying the total number of shares that may be issued and which employees are eligible to receive the options.
- The plan must be approved in a manner that complies with the charter, bylaws, and state laws that regulate stockholders' approval within 12 months before or after plan adoption.

- Each stock option issued under the ISO agreement must be written and must list the restrictions placed on its exercise. It must set forth an offer to sell the stock at the option price and the period of time that the option will remain open.
- The option must be granted within 10 years of the date of adoption or shareholder approval, whichever date is earlier.
- The option must be exercisable only within the 10-year period after grant.
- The stock option exercise price must equal or exceed the fair market value of the underlying stock at the date of the grant.
- The employee may not own more than 10 percent of the voting power of all stock outstanding at the time of the grant unless the exercise price is at least 110 percent of the fair market value of the stock and the option is not exercisable more than five years from the time of the grant.
- The ISO agreement must specify in writing that the ISO cannot be transferred by the option holder other than by will or by the laws of decedent and cannot be exercised by anyone other than the option holder.
- The aggregate fair market value of the stock bought by exercising the ISOs that are exercisable for the first time cannot exceed $100,000 in a calendar year.

To qualify for favorable tax status, the stock cannot be disposed of until the expiry of the statutory holding period. The ISO statutory holding period is the later of two years from the date of granting of the ISO or one year from the date the options were exercised. If the disposition qualifies, an employee receiving an ISO recognizes no income upon its receipt or exercise. In the case of a disqualifying disposition of an ISO, the employee recognizes ordinary income in the amount the fair market value of the stock exceeds the option price. The employee also realizes a capital gain which is the difference between the fair market value of the stock on the date of exercise and the disposition proceeds.

In contrast, the employer does not receive a deduction with respect to the granting of the ISO; if a disqualifying disposition occurs, the employer will be able to deduct the amount realized by the employee as ordinary income. The employer is not subject to any withholding requirement for the amount of ordinary income recognized from the disqualifying disposition. In addition, that ordinary income is not considered taxable income for FICA or FUTA purposes.

An NSO may have no restrictions on its structure or transfer. An NSO is taxable to the employee on grant if:

- The option is publicly traded or is transferable by the optionee.
- The option is exercisable immediately in full by the optionee.
- Neither the option nor the underlying property is subject to any restrictions that have a significant effect on the option's value.
- The purchase fair market value of the option privilege is readily ascertainable.

Generally, options on stock that is not actively traded will be deemed not to have a readily ascertainable value. If the NSO meets these requirements, ordinary income is recognized based on the value of the option less any amount paid for the option. Any further tax is generally paid at capital gains rates, and is based on the selling price of the stock (less any amount paid for the exercise of the stock), and any amount included in income upon the option's grant. If the fair market value of the option is not readily ascertainable upon grant, no tax consequences are recognized until the exercise of the option. At that point, the difference between the amount paid for the stock and the fair market value of the stock received is reported as compensation income. The company takes a deduction for ordinary income equal to the ordinary income realized by the employee.

The American Jobs Creation Act ("Act"), passed in 2004, substantively changed the way nonqualified deferred compensation plans, including stock options, are designed, administered, and taxed. Section 409A of this act addresses "Discounted Options," which are defined as stock options whose exercise price is lower than the fair market value of the underlying stock at the date of grant of the option. Among other provisions, section 409A requires that the employee may not receive a distribution from the plan (e.g., the receipt of stock or cash from exercise of the option) until the earlier of:

- Separation from service to the employer
- Disability or death of the option holder
- A fixed date or series of fixed dates in the future
- A change in control or ownership of the assets of the company
- The occurrence of an unforeseeable emergency

The Act applies to compensation deferred in taxable years beginning after December 31, 2004, and any amounts not vested as of December 31, 2004. Further, the new rules extend to any deferred compensation in a plan "materially modified" after October 3, 2004.

Vesting

Employee stock options typically have vesting rules associated with them. Under vesting, employees gain an increasing right to the stock option awards granted to them based on their seniority or, occasionally, a performance factor. The four most common types of vesting include:

1. Equal annual vesting
2. Cliff vesting
3. Variable annual vesting
4. Hybrid annual/other vesting

In equal annual vesting, the most common type of vesting, an employee's options become exercisable at a fixed percentage each year. Under cliff vesting, all of an employee's options from a grant become exercisable at one specific date. In variable annual vesting, an employee's options become exercisable each year based on some individual formula. Finally, if an employee's options first vest after one year and then vest on a more frequent schedule, this is characterized as hybrid annual/other vesting.

Valuation Considerations

Significant differences in the terms and rights underlying nonpublic stock options versus their publicly traded counterparts can materially affect the value. In many cases, determining value puts the analyst in a theoretical world, since many of these options cannot be sold based on the terms of the options contract itself. In other cases, a sale may have significant disincentives that would make a willing seller unwilling to sell the option.

Despite the inability to sell the instrument itself, there are benefits to holding the option. Many times it is necessary to value the benefits under the assumption that the benefits could be exchanged.

Before discussing valuation issues related to ESOs, as with any valuation, the analyst must appropriately define the assignment:

- Follow valuation procedures to define the assignment appropriately so that the right level/standard of value, valuation date, and procedures are used
- Gather appropriate support
- Analyze the data in a meaningful and appropriate manner before arriving at a conclusion and writing the report

Reasons for Valuing

For publicly traded options, like publicly traded stock, a valuation is not necessary when the publicly traded price accurately reflects value. However, in some situations there are sufficient differences between the publicly traded instrument and the instrument being valued to necessitate a valuation. For instance, when a corporate insider, a person in a position to control the business affairs of the corporation or who has access to inside information, holds an option, the stock that is associated with the option may be restricted, thus affecting the stock's value as well as the option's. In other cases, there may be no public market for the options and/or the stock, such as ESOs in private firms.

ValTip

The causes driving the need for a valuation are fairly universal: litigation/divorce, management planning, tax oriented (gift or estate), transaction oriented, or financial reporting.

One reason ESOs are valued is for financial reporting purposes according to FAS 123R (now ASC 718). Employee stock options valued for FAS 123R purposes apply a fair-value-based measurement standard that may not result in the same conclusions as an analysis applying a fair market value standard. For example, the fair-value-based measurement in FAS 123R excludes conditions related to vesting and performance that may apply in a tax analysis. Black-Scholes, binomial, and Monte Carlo simulation models can be used to value options for FAS 123R.

Of the seven option model inputs for closely held stock discussed earlier, the three that require the most appraiser judgment are:

1. Underlying stock price (estimated with standard valuation procedures)
2. Volatility (see later section for additional comments):
   - Implied volatility—only for public stocks with long-term traded options
   - Historical volatility—again, only if stock is publicly traded
   - Comparable company volatility—like the market approach in business valuation

3. Expected term/life of the option.

The following should be analyzed as part of the expected term analysis:

- Stock option grantee's propensity to voluntarily exercise early. ESOs are American options that can be exercised before the end of their term. This is called suboptimal exercise
- Grantee's option weighted propensity to terminate employment after vesting
- Weighted average life of option grants
- Employee behavior

During the transition period of adoption of FAS 123R, the SEC allowed for shortcut methods in certain circumstances. These procedures are described in SAB 107 and SAB 110.

Volatility

As noted earlier, volatility is based on the anticipated return of an underlying stock. This volatility can be estimated from the historical or anticipated volatility of a public stock. For an option that is not publicly traded but where the company has publicly traded options with different terms, the implied volatility of those other options can be used to estimate the volatility of the private option. For instance, in valuing an option with five months remaining to expiration, the average of the implied volatility of a four-month option and six-month option may be appropriate.

> If the underlying stock is lightly traded or not publicly traded, volatility can be estimated using a representative sampling of guideline companies or an industry benchmark.

As discussed earlier, it is important to average the volatility calculations of these guideline companies as opposed to creating an index of the companies and calculating the volatility of that index. The diversification of the index will smooth the standard deviation and result in a volatility measure that may not represent the anticipated volatility of an individual stock.

When using guideline companies to calculate volatility, begin by selecting a group of companies using factors similar to those used in selecting guideline companies for pricing multiples. If the stock is not publicly traded but has been valued using the market approach, the guideline companies used in that analysis would be a good starting point for volatility analysis.

When selecting guideline companies in a market approach valuation analysis, it is important to be familiar with the operations and markets of the subject company, its size, growth prospects, liquidity, and profitability. Two other important considerations when selecting guideline companies are stage of maturity and degree of financial leverage. When selecting guideline companies for volatility estimation, it is also important to know the history of the price movements and any intervening events that may have affected those movements.

> If an intervening event is identified in the analysis, it may be appropriate to exclude it from the volatility.

It also can be useful to compare how volatility has changed from one time period to the next, especially when industries or companies are in flux or evolving rapidly. Trends in volatility, including growth, decline, seasonality, and cyclicality, can materially affect the expectations of future volatility.

Finally, it may be necessary to adjust the analysis for the anticipation of events, such as a public offering of the stock. Clearly, a consideration of the chance of going public and the potential option payoffs for going public versus remaining private must be key among the factors considered.

In arriving at a conclusion of the volatility to apply, as when arriving at a conclusion of value, it is necessary to weigh all the evidence and the strengths and weaknesses of each part of the analysis to reach a reasonable conclusion. Since volatility has the greatest potential effect on the price of an option, it is important to give significant attention to the development of this variable.

Marketability

Marketability has two potential effects on the value of stock options.

1. There are marketability issues if the underlying stock that the option is based on is either not marketable or if its marketability is restricted beyond the vesting period. Leverage is a vital consideration. Other factors aside, the volatility of a company's equity increases with leverage. Therefore, adjustments for differences in leverage should be considered before using observed guideline company volatility.
2. There may be a reduction in value due to the lack of marketability if the option itself is not marketable.

In the first situation, there is the lack of marketability of the underlying stock. The current value of the stock is an input in both the Black-Scholes and binomial option pricing models. Being a derivative, the option is tied to that stock's value on an as-if-publicly-traded basis or a discounted value reflecting the lack of marketability. If there is a way to structure the transaction to avoid the lack of marketability and allow the option holder to receive unrestricted, publicly traded shares, then the as-if-publicly-traded value of the stock is the appropriate input. If there is not a way for the holder to receive unrestricted shares, then the discounted stock price may be the appropriate input.

> The final consideration is the marketability of the option itself. There
> are no studies available regarding the lack of marketability of closely
> held stock options.

In the end, the consideration of an appropriate discount for the lack of marketability is a matter of the analyst's informed judgment. In arriving at an estimate,
it is important to take into account the value components of an option, its terms,
and the characteristics of the markets for publicly traded options. The value of an
option is made up of both an intrinsic value and time value, and since the option
can be exercised to receive the underlying stock, the intrinsic value may not be as
affected by the lack of marketability of the option itself, (assuming the options are
vested). Therefore, the marketability analysis may focus more on the time value
component.

Vesting

One of the last components to consider in valuing ESOs can be one of the most
important. Vesting determines the ability to gain the rights to the stock option
awards. If the terms of the vesting agreement are not met, then the employee will
never receive ESOs subject to vesting.

There are two general schools of thought on vesting:

1. The option does not exist until the vesting requirements have been met
2. An unvested option is an asset just as future pension proceeds are deemed an
   asset

By reviewing the facts and circumstances of each case, the likelihood that the
option will vest can be established and adjustments made to reflect the current value
of the option. For valuing individual grants, this leads to a probability-weighted
approach to valuation. When valuing the pool of options that a company has given,
it is also possible to look at the historical ratio of options granted to options vested
to estimate the number of stock options that will vest for the entire pool of options.
FAS 123R requires that an estimate of the number of options expected to vest must
be made at the time of the grant in order to calculate compensation expense. However, while vesting restrictions are factored into the number of options counted as
compensation expense, the value of the options is not impacted by vesting for 123R
purposes.

H: REAL OPTION VALUATIONS

Introduction

It has been said that the only certainty is that nothing is certain. For financial executives and managers, uncertainty is a way of life. Today's fast-paced business

environment has created even greater uncertainty among financial executives and has challenged some of the traditional economic theory of business valuation and securities analysis. The fact is, financial executives must negotiate business realities and make capital investment decisions filled with uncertainty on a regular basis. These investment decisions can be challenging, especially when they involve capital requirements and cannot be easily reversed. Making the wrong decision can be costly.

Traditional theory has led financial executives and investors to evaluate investment decisions or strategic initiatives using a discounted cash flow or net present value approach. Typically, executives develop a model for a particular investment. They predict the amount of capital necessary, predict the amount it will return each year, and discount the net amount based on the company's cost of capital. Some executives will perform a sensitivity analysis—altering various components of the model—while other executives apply some probability to the potential outcomes. The decision for investments using a traditional DCF lies in the net present value rule. Management will accept the project when the discounted cash flow analysis indicates a positive net present value and will reject the project when the discounted cash flow analysis indicates a negative net present value.

Limitations of the DCF

Because the DCF is a static model, there may be limitations in applying this methodology to many investment decisions. Each investment decision or strategic initiative can incorporate a significant amount of uncertainty or volatility. Financial executives must adjust to these uncertainties throughout the project's economic life. The application of a traditional DCF model does not directly incorporate uncertainty into its assumptions. A discount rate is applied in a traditional DCF model to determine the present value of the uncertain expected cash flows. This risk-adjusted discount rate, however, may not reflect the changing economic environment or changes specific to the project's risk profile that occur throughout a project's economic life.

The business reality is that management will have the choice or flexibility to address uncertainties over the economic life of the investment. The traditional DCF model ignores that flexibility. It assumes that a project will proceed as planned even if future expectations are not met, and it does not incorporate the flexibility a manager has to alter strategic decisions over the project's economic life. "To accurately analyze and model flexibility, you must be able to describe specific decisions managers could take in response to future events, including the cash flow implications of those decisions."[21]

In these instances, the traditional DCF model fails to capture the value of management's flexibility ("real option") in responding to uncertainty in investment decisions. Management's discretion, however, may have real value. The real options theory reflects the reality of business decisions and captures the value of management's flexibility to expand, defer, abandon, reduce, or even switch an investment decision.

---

[21] Tim Koller, Marc Goedhart, and David Wessels, McKinsey and Co. Inc., *Valuation: Measuring and Managing the Value of Companies,* 4th ed. (Hoboken, NJ: John Wiley & Sons, 2005), 543.

Uncertainty

If *certainty* implies knowing with high probability what the return on an investment decision will be in the future, *uncertainty* implies the amount or percentage difference the actual return will be from the expected return of an investment decision. Uncertainty has two aspects: the high side and the low side. In other words, uncertainty means that the actual return can be higher or lower than the expected return. Hence, the uncertainty of an investment decision can also be referred to as the volatility of an investment decision.

In a traditional DCF model, the volatility within an investment decision is characterized as risk. Projected cash flows inherently contain a certain amount of risk (actual values that might differ from expected values). As such, the discount rate, usually the cost of capital that is used to discount these cash flows, requires the addition of a risk premium. This generalized application of a risk premium, however, is not without its limitations.

The application of a risk premium in a DCF model acknowledges that the deviations from the expected cash flow can vary in either a positive or negative manner. This generalized application may not distinguish the distortion or slant between the positive or negative variances. The level of the positive or negative variance can be important, especially to the extent that a particular investment decision carries with it a large downside risk.

In addition, if not done carefully, the broad-paintbrush approach of adding a single risk premium to the discount rate may fail to effectively capture the potential multiple sources of uncertainty, including the following risks:

- Currency
- Inflation
- Economic
- Liquidity
- Market
- Interest rate
- Credit
- Business
- Competitive
- Technological
- Regulatory
- Financing

Uncertainty in a traditional DCF comes in the form of a discount rate. The higher the risk premium applied to the discount rate, the lower the present value of the expected cash flows. This application, unfortunately, may not give financial executives the potential cash flow ranges that an investment decision could generate.

Flexibility

A principal example of this shortcoming is where a company has chosen to defer a particular investment for a period of time due to uncertainty in the market place. The company would perform additional analyses to accumulate the necessary information before restarting that particular investment. When using a traditional DCF model to identify the net present value of the expected cash flows associated with this investment, the traditional DCF model may often provide an indication of a

The traditional DCF model may also fail to capture the existence of any flexibility that a financial executive maintains as the decision maker of a project or strategic initiative. Once an investment decision is initiated, a financial executive may expand it, shut it down, defer additional work until later and then restart it, or even switch the investment entirely into another strategic purpose.

value of zero. Alternatively, the application of a real option analysis would likely capture the company's flexibility and apply some indication of value to the investment's potential.

The benefit of real option analysis is its ability to apply a positive indication of value to uncertainty or volatility. Financial executives have many options in reacting to changes throughout the investment's economic life by adapting or revising their decisions in response to unexpected developments. This flexibility clearly provides companies with value, and the real option analysis assesses the value of this flexibility.

Real Options Defined

Real option theory is a strategic planning tool that applies financial option theory to real investment decisions, such as IT or R&D investments, plant expansions, or oil exploration. The most widely recognized form is the Black-Scholes model. Similar to financial option theory, the real option framework gives analysts the tools to capture the value of flexibility in an uncertain environment.

The analysis behind real option theory is the valuation of opportunities associated with management's flexibility and is derived from the relationship connecting the methods in valuing financial options and the methods in valuing flexibility.

Similar to a financial option—one that gives its owner the right, but not the obligation, to purchase or sell a security at a given price—a real option gives a company or its financial executives the right, but not the obligation, to make value-added investment decisions. Investment decisions applying a traditional DCF model may overlook the value identified in real option analysis—again, the most notable being flexibility.

Financial Options

A *financial option* provides the owner/investor with the right, but not the obligation, to purchase or sell an asset or security at a given price within a specified period of time. A *call option* is the right to purchase a security. A *put option* is the right to sell a security.

For example, a call option would allow the owner of that option to buy one share of stock of Company A at $100 on or before a specified expiration date. The decision to exercise that option is dependent upon whether the stock price of Company A exceeds the $100 exercise price on or before the exercise date.

Most investment decisions are similar to call options in that they provide the financial executive the right to make an investment in a particular project. Most investment decisions, however, are not necessarily a now-or-never opportunity. As rapidly changing economic environments generate volatility, a project's value fluctuates. A financial executive will exercise the option of an investment decision only if the project's expected cash flow is sufficiently high, or *in the money*.

The value of a financial option is generally driven by six variables:

1. Value of underlying asset (stock price)
2. Strike or exercise price
3. Time to expiration
4. Variance in value of asset (volatility)
5. Risk-free rate
6. Expected dividends

The values of each of these variables, as well as the significance of the differences between these variables, influence the price of the financial option—most notably, the spread between the stock price and the exercise price, the period of time until the expiration of the option, and the volatility of the underlying asset.

Stock Price vs. Exercise Price

In determining the value of a financial option, the first identified variable (value of underlying asset or stock price) is generally known. The strike price, which is the exercise price at which the asset can be purchased by the owner at some point in the future, is also known. The greater the excess of the exercise price over the stock price, the less valuable the call option becomes, because only a significant change could cause the value of the stock price to increase above the exercise price, rewarding the owner of the option. Small movements in the stock price are much more likely to occur than significant changes. Conversely, the lower the excess of the exercise price over the stock price, the more valuable the call option becomes, because there does not necessarily need to be much change in the market for the value of the stock price to increase in value above the exercise price.

Period of Time

The longer the period of time the option has until expiration, the greater the chance for the value of the stock price to exceed the value of the exercise price. Hence, the longer the period of time to expiration, the greater the chance for the owner of the option to make a profit and the greater the value of the option.

Volatility

Also encompassed in the price of the option is the volatility (all else equal) in the value of the underlying asset. The greater the volatility in the value of the underlying asset, the higher the value of the option will be. This is because it is more likely that the stock price will rise above the exercise price, putting the owner of the option in a profitable position, or in the money. Alternatively, the more certain the cash flow or the less volatile the underlying asset, the less valuable the option will be. The impact of asset volatility on the value of an option differs significantly from its impact in a traditional DCF analysis. In a typical DCF framework, as volatility increases, the risk-adjusted discount rate also increases, resulting in a decrease in the asset value, all else constant. Of course, the impact of asset volatility on the discount rate varies, due to issues such as the correlation between the asset's and the market's volatility. Thus, volatility impacts the value of the underlying asset on which the option is based; like traditional DCF analyses, high volatility generally decreases the value of the underlying asset. However, the same volatility that reduced the value of the underlying asset works to increase the value of an option on that underlying asset, for the reasons just discussed. The net impact of an increase in asset volatility, therefore, is complex—it generally produces a decrease in the value of the underlying asset, along with an increase in the option value.

Risk-Free Rate

The risk-free rate is known and the appropriate rate to use is the risk-free rate over an interval corresponding to the exercise time. One of the key reasons that options are valuable is because the investment (or exercise price) can be deferred until more information is available. Therefore, one component of the value of a one-year option with an exercise price of $100, for example, is the ability to defer making the $100 payment for one year. In effect, the holder of the option is able to invest this amount for the one-year period. The value of this deferral is based on the risk-free rate applicable over this expected one-year period; the higher the risk-free rate, the more valuable the ability to defer the expenditure.

Linking Financial Options to Real Options

Several economic variables are applied in the financial option formula to determine value; these correspond directly to economic variables in real options theory. Exhibit 24.15 shows how the financial options variables correspond directly to those in real options theory.

Exhibit 24.15   Relationship in Financial Option Theory and Real Options Theory

Financial Option Theory	Real Options Theory
Stock price	Present value of expected cash flow
Strike or exercise price	Present value of fixed costs
Time to expiration	Period of time decision may be deferred
Risk-free interest rate	Risk-free interest rate
Variance in value of asset (volatility)	Uncertainty of investment's value
Dividends	Value of cash flow lost

The comparison between financial option theory and real option theory, however, is not as simple as Exhibit 24.15 indicates. The most widely recognized model used to value options, the Black-Scholes formula, does have its limitations. The formula is based on a European option, which allows for the option to be exercised only at the date of expiration. An American-style option allows the owner to exercise the option at any time prior to its expiration date.

Other contrasts between the financial options theory and real options theory are the differences between the stock price, expiration date, and exercise price. In the case of financial options, most (if not all) of these variables are known. Volatility in most cases can be determined using historical data. From the perspective of the real world, or real options, the present value of expected cash flows and fixed costs can be difficult to estimate, and the period of time to defer a decision has uncertainty.

Despite these limitations, the Black-Scholes formula can provide an adequate initial indication of value for simple real options, and applying a real options analysis can make a difference in the valuation of a project compared to the traditional DCF model. Using a real options analysis emphasizes the importance of a financial executive having the choice or option to change his or her strategic decisions based on unexpected developments.

Other Techniques Used in Valuing Real Options

The Monte Carlo approach is another technique that can be applied in valuing real options. This approach does allow for integrating multiple sources of uncertainty without the restrictions on distribution. The limitation of the Monte Carlo approach, however, is similar to the Black-Scholes formula in that it is not as well suited to value American-style real options.

A more generic approach to value real options is the binomial model. This approach allows for changing levels of volatility because the binomial model breaks down the time to expiration in time intervals. At each time interval, the underlying asset value can move up or down, based on its volatility. Charting the possible up or down movement at each time interval creates a binomial lattice.

Real Options Valuation

Real options valuations give financial executives the flexibility to address uncertainty and to employ certain strategies in improving the value of the option before management exercises that option. Hence, there are a few steps to undertake before proceeding with the valuation of real options.

ValTip

Real options exist in most businesses and may be more representative of the manner in which businesses operate, although they are not always very readily identifiable.

The financial executive must first start with the identification of any real options that might be embedded in a given investment decision and then decide how the company will value the real options. Almost all investment decisions contain real options, as almost all cash flows are uncertain. Managers and financial executives must be aware of the primary uncertainties facing the investment decision.

In analyzing uncertainty and a financial executive's flexibility, options can generally be segmented into four mutually exclusive categories: option to defer investment, abandonment option, follow-on options, and option to adjust production.[22]

Option to Defer Investment

The option to defer an investment is similar to a call option in that it requires waiting until the value of the underlying asset exceeds the strike price before exercising. There are opportunity costs to consider, however, in deferring an investment.

Abandonment Options

An option to abandon an investment decision is similar to a put option. If the investment decision has produced results lower than expected, management may decide to abandon the entire project and sell at a liquidation value. "A project that can be liquidated is worth more than a similar project with the possibility of abandonment."[23]

Follow-On Option

An investment that allows the financial executive to undertake a follow-on investment at a later time based on new information is considered a follow-on option, or growth option. This type of option is best represented by a staged investment in which each stage of the investment is contingent upon the preceding investment. A very general example would be the production of a motion picture and the production of a sequel to the original movie.

Option to Adjust Production

A financial executive's option to adjust production includes expanding, contracting, extending, shortening, or switching the investment decision altogether. For example, if the outcome of a particular investment is more favorable than expected, management can choose to expand the scope of the investment or project. Similarly, if the outcome of a particular investment is less favorable than expected, management may contract the scale of the investment.

SUMMARY

The traditional DCF model may be unable to capture the value of the flexibility inherent in many businesses today. Uncertainty lies in almost every investment decision. Real-option analysis adds flexibility of management in addressing these uncertainties in investment decisions and adds to the analysis the importance of strategic and financial issues.

---

[22] Tim Koller, Marc Goldhart, David Wessels, McKinsey & Co. Inc., *Valuation: Measuring and Managing the Value of Companies,* 4th ed. (Hoboken, NJ: John Wiley & Sons, 2005), pp. 550–552.
[23] Ibid., p. 550.

Real-option analysis can become an important measurement tool in management's strategic decision making. Although many analysts still predominantly use DCF, real-option analysis, as it becomes better understood and properly applied, may be more prevalent in the future.

I: MAXIMIZING SHAREHOLDER VALUE[24]

Introduction

One of the most fundamental goals of corporate executives is to maximize shareholder value and increase the value of their business. That is, executives must be able to identify measurable performance criteria throughout all levels of their business, obtain favorable financing or capital, and invest that capital in profitable strategic business decisions. Historically, corporate executives would chase continued growth in revenue and earnings, asserting that shareholder value would be a natural consequence.

Measuring shareholder value, however, has become more complex as the analysis of identifying and tracking a company's performance has become increasingly sophisticated. What is shareholder value, and what creates shareholder value? Each individual shareholder would likely respond with his or her own characterization of whether the management of a company has provided shareholder value.

Shareholder value, then, is created when the cash flow that is left over exceeds the return shareholders require for the use of their money or cost of capital. A shareholder's required rate of return is focused on the nature of the company itself—the industry in which it operates, the operational and financial risk inherent in that company, and other prevailing factors. In the easiest of terms, value is added when a company's equity returns exceed a shareholder's required rate of return. But this simple idea has become a not-so-simple concept and has created a growing industry of professionals, consultants, and professors who are developing various techniques to measure value creation.

The most notable metric that has attempted to better measure value creation and has become increasingly accepted by analysts is the concept popularized by Stern Stewart & Company: Economic Value Added (EVA).

Economic Value Added (EVA)

Measuring earnings or value has routinely been established through financial statements: the net amount after all costs and expenditures associated with production

---

[24] Many of the concepts explained here are from the book by Tim Koller, Marc Goldhart, David Wessels, McKinsey & Co. Inc., *Valuation: Measuring and Managing the Value of Companies,* 4th ed. (Hoboken, NJ: John Wiley & Sons, 2005).

have been paid. These expenses include items from cost of goods sold to selling, general and administrative items to interest charges, and even the government's piece of the pie. The remaining amount after all expenses is the income that belongs to the shareholders of the corporation, or equity holders.

Similar to any other factor in the production process, such as interest payments that represent the charge on debt capital, equity capital should also have a charge or an opportunity cost. Financial statements, however, do not directly account for this opportunity cost of equity capital.

> The EVA concept, which is a value-driven financial performance measure, attempts to charge earnings with an expense for the cost of capital employed. In other words, it is simply a measure of what is left to the shareholders over the cost of capital.

The EVA metric can be defined as the net operating profit of a company before interest, less taxes paid, less a charge for debt and equity tied up in the business. The remaining amount then is a measure of the company's performance after satisfying the opportunity cost of all resources employed by the company.

> The principle behind the EVA concept is that if a corporation's net income is positive after applying a charge for the cost of capital employed, the corporation has added shareholder value. If a corporation's net income is negative after applying a charge for the cost of capital employed, the corporation has destroyed shareholder value.

The formula for calculating EVA is as follows:

$$\text{EVA} = \text{net operating profit after taxes} - (\text{weighted average cost of capital} \times \text{invested capital})$$

Net operating profit after taxes (NOPAT) can be determined by deducting taxes from operating profit (before interest and other nonoperating gains and losses).

The formula for calculating NOPAT is as follows:

$$\text{NOPAT} = \text{Adjusted Operating Profits before Taxes} - \text{Cash Operating Taxes}$$

The formula can be further broken down as follows:

> Operating profit (EBIT)
> + Interest on operating leases
> + Increase in LIFO reserve
> + Research and development expenses
> = Adjusted operating profits before taxes

> Income tax expense
> + Decrease in interest expense
> + Tax benefit from interest expense
> + Tax benefit from interest on leases
> − Taxes on nonoperating income (expense)
> = Cash operating taxes

Invested capital (IC) is typically determined by deducting all non-interest-bearing liabilities from total liabilities and equity.

An alternative for calculating invested capital when calculating EVA is as follows:

> Debt-free net working capital
> + LIFO reserve
> + Net plant, property, and equipment
> + Other assets, including intangible assets
> + Goodwill
> + Present value of operating leases
> = Invested capital

Weighted average cost of capital (WACC) is a percentage that represents the weighted average after-tax cost of debt plus the weighted average cost of equity. In general terms, it is the return expected by lenders and investors.

As seen in the preceding formulas, it is important for NOPAT and IC to be adjusted from accrual-based generally accepted accounting principles to cash-based accounting. The following are the most common adjustments, but the list is not all-inclusive:

- *Research and development expenses.* As these expenses represent an investment in the future of the firm, they should be capitalized and amortized, and thus added back to earnings to derive NOPAT.
- *LIFO reserve.* Any inventory LIFO reserve should be added back to invested capital, and any increase in the LIFO reserve should be added back to earnings to derive NOPAT.
- *Operating leases.* Similar to research and development expenses, operating leases should be capitalized and the interest should be added back to earnings to derive NOPAT.
- *Deferred taxes.* Deferred taxes should be eliminated and thereby only cash taxes are expensed.

The EVA metric, as one of the most widely recognized shareholder value creation concepts, has gained acceptance as a measure that aligns management decision making with shareholder value creation.

For growth companies, divisions, or projects where significant investments in infrastructure (i.e., research and development, capital expenditures, acquisitions) have occurred or are planned, the EVA metric may be an inappropriate measure of value creation. This is especially true when the investments in infrastructure have long gestation periods, such as for pharmaceutical industries.

When IC is difficult to measure and leverage cannot be easily changed due to regulatory requirements (i.e., financial institutions, utilities), the EVA metric can be transformed in equity terms. The formula for calculating equity EVA is as follows:

$$\text{Equity EVA} = (\text{Return on Equity} - \text{Cost of Equity}) \times \text{Equity Invested}$$

Equity invested is typically determined by the book value of equity, with adjustments similar to those previously mentioned.

Return on equity is determined by dividing the adjusted net income by the adjusted book value of equity.

Cost of equity is the risk-adjusted measure for the cost of equity for the company, division, or project for which equity EVA is being measured.

ValTip

Similar models such as market value added (MVA), return on invested capital (ROIC), and cash flow return on investment (CFROI) are also value-based concepts that claim to parallel the interests of shareholders with management.

Accounting Measures of Value

The accounting measure of shareholder value can be dissected into the income statement measures and the balance sheet measures. A primary balance sheet measure that is a commonly mistaken concept is that increasing capital through retained earnings is a value driver. The reality, however, is that retaining a company's earnings and pumping that money back into the company does not necessarily increase the value of the company. The reason is that book value of equity does not equal the fair market value of equity. The fair market value of equity in many cases is higher than the book value due to the book value not being able to capture the intangible asset value of a company. Conversely, the fair market value of equity may be less than the book value due to poor operating margins or poor managerial investment decisions.

A similarly mistaken measure of creating value, and sometimes a more destructive use of capital, is investing in assets. From the public market standpoint, asset size is one of the criteria used in ranking the Fortune 500. As such, management has given great credence to the theory of increasing the assets as a means of building a financially stronger company. This strategy, unfortunately, can be disastrous from an investor's standpoint. Accumulating assets for size without sound investment decisions that yield an appropriate return can destroy shareholder value.

A common theory for creating value is also an income statement measure: increased sales. This fundamental can appear to have the most direct influence on the profitability of the company. However, as many companies have learned, a direct increase in revenues does not necessarily translate to higher profits. The simplest reason could be that a company has poor operating margins. What is most often overlooked when aiming for higher revenue is how to get there. Increased revenue can come at a price (cost of expansion, increased working capital, etc.). These increased costs, however, can actually lower shareholder value.

Arguably the most popular measure of value is profits. Some executives might even take offense at the idea that there could be a more comprehensive performance measurement than profitability or earnings. Using profitability as a measurement tool, a company's earnings can be applied to the number of shares outstanding, common stockholder's equity, and to net assets or capital. These measurements are known as *earnings per share* (EPS), *return on equity* (ROE), and *return on assets* (ROA). While these measurements can sometimes provide a good indication of a healthy bottom line and are considered by many as the driving force behind share price, they each rely on financial statements that are prepared in accordance with generally accepted accounting principles. As we all know, the financial statement is not a clear representation of the true amount of cash available to shareholders. At the end of the day, cash is what company management and investors alike should be most concerned with. Financial statements prepared in accordance with GAAP provide general guidelines in determining a company's financial performance and help protect outside investors' interests (albeit some Enron investors might strongly disagree).

Doing More for Less

Consider the following information and determine which company would be most attractive.

	Company ABC	Company XYZ
Profit	$10,000,000	$ 10,000,000
Employees	100	300
Fixed assets	$20,000,000	$100,000,000

Although both companies have generated the same level of profits, Company ABC has been able to create the same amount with less. Methods such as EVA may better capture this information, and it may not be just total profits that determine whether a business has created value or destroyed value.

Driving Shareholder Wealth

First, managers must understand what drives value. The term *value driver* is an expression that has been coined to quantify those economic characteristics of a company that, when implemented, allow it to maximize its cash flow and create value. These are characteristics that can reduce risk and improve profitability.

Value drivers can be identified in almost any company. Some of the more widely recognized value drivers are:

- Sales growth
- Key people
- Optimal profit margins
- Effective capital controls
- Broad and varied customer base
- Optimal cash flow

Value drivers can also be industry-specific. For example, companies in various high-tech industries may have proprietary technology that is protected from competition, thus providing them the opportunity to maintain customer loyalty and higher pricing. Another example might be companies involved in distribution. A likely value driver for these companies would be the manufacturers that they represent.

Creating shareholder value takes initiative, planning, and time. To create shareholder value, executives should do the following:

Think differently. How do managers identify what value drivers are within their own organization? It has been said that standing on the outside and looking in can create an entirely new perspective. Executives must encourage their organizations to think from the perspective of the buyer or the investor. What would a buyer be willing to pay for their company? What does their company have that would generate top dollar? What does their company have or what does it lack that would cause a buyer to pay less? When looking in, managers must identify those characteristics that are a primer to creating shareholder value.

Establish goals. Creating value means being aware of the goals that you are striving for and establishing those goals. Setting goals should not be a matter of how you are going to get there, but what you are doing to do to get there. By establishing which resources are necessary and what level of risk the organization is willing to accept, executives can establish appropriate yet ambitious goals.

Develop strategies. Corporate executives need to understand how developing various strategies translates into shareholder value. Talented and committed people are the driving force of almost any company. Executives must learn to assign responsibility and delegate authority. They must encourage their employees to maintain focus and ensure the strategies work by rewarding behavior that creates value.

Improve cash flow. Generally, executives can tackle easy projects with lower operating costs before attacking high-risk, capital-intensive projects.

SUMMARY

A corporate executive's fundamental obligation to shareholders is to create value. In the early days, the metrics that measured shareholder value were earnings or discounted cash flow models. Years of rapidly changing economic conditions have necessitated the need for more sophisticated measures, as the analysis of identifying and tracking a company's performance has become difficult. One of the greatest challenges facing corporate executives is that standard accounting measures, without adjustments, may not adequately determine value creation. One of the basic shortcomings is that a company's value today takes the form of intellectual capital, which is not readily identifiable on the balance sheet. In addition, accounting measures have many variables that impact profitability but do not provide an appropriate indication of the cash available to shareholders. The requirements involved in reporting financial information has become almost overwhelming, and sometimes lost in the process is the focus on what drives the value of a company. In the most general terms, accounting measures may fail to incorporate a return to shareholders after applying an opportunity cost of capital. See Chapters 4 and 5 for additional information.

ADDENDUM 1—RATES OF RETURN FOR HIGHER-RISK COMPANIES

Eva Lang, CPA/ABV, ASA, Financial Consulting Group
  —(Taken from *Valuation Products and Services Q&A*, Issue 2, March 2008.)

Question: What information is out there for rates of return for higher-risk businesses, including venture capital return data?

Answer from Eva Lang and Jim Hitchner: One of the most well known and often cited data sources is the *1987 QED Report on Venture Capital Financial Analysis* by James L. Plummer. It is dated and hard to find but is still relevant. Professor Josh Lerner at Harvard Business School has compiled one of the most current, comprehensive bibliographies on venture capital as well as private equity analysis, available at www.people.hbs.edu/jlerner/bib.html. Professor Lerner also offers that the new textbook by Wharton's Andrew Metrick, *Venture Capital and the Finance of Innovation* (John Wiley & Sons, 2006) is definitely worth checking out, as it covers the relationship between risk and return in venture capital, historical statistics on VC investment performance, total and partial valuation methods and data, and more (available at www.amazon.com and most online sellers).

The HVA/VentureOne study examines private venture capital financing of high-tech (electronic, semiconductor, software, and communications) and life sciences (biotechnology and medical devices) companies that went public from January 1993 to June 1997 (*The Pricing of Successful Venture Capital Backed High Tech and Life Sciences Companies*, Houlihan Valuation Advisors/VentureOne Study, San Francisco, California, www.cogentvaluation.com/pdf/JournalofBusinessVenturing_VentureOne.pdf).

William A. Sahlman and Daniel R. Scherlis wrote *A Method for Valuing High-Risk, Long-Term Investments: The Venture Capital Method*, 1987, revised 2003 (www.harvardbusinessonline). Jeffry Timmons, a professor at Babson College, and Stephen Spinelli wrote *New Venture Creation: Entrepreneurship in the 21st Century*, 7th ed. (McGraw-Hill/Irwin, 2006). There is *Classic Venture Capital in the Next Millennium*, 1997, by William D. Bygrave, also of Babson College (www.babson.edu). Tim Maio and William Pittock of Ernst & Young presented "Valuing Early Stage Life Sciences and Biotechnology" at the Fifth Annual Joint ASA CICBV Advanced Business Valuation Conference in Orlando in October 2002 (www.bvappraisers.org/contentdocs/Conference/Maio_Biotech_Final.pdf).

Eva Lang, CPA/ABV, ASA, of the Financial Consulting Group (Memphis), is coauthor of *The Best Websites for Financial Professionals, Business Appraisers, and Accountants* (John Wiley & Sons; www.gofcg.org). Jim Hitchner, CPA/ABV, ASA, Valuation Products and Services and Financial Valuation Advisors (Ventnor City, NJ).

CHAPTER 25

Valuation of Healthcare Service Businesses

Performing valuations of healthcare service businesses and interests in those businesses requires fundamental business valuation expertise. It also requires special knowledge of the key economic drivers, trends, healthcare niche issues, and unique regulatory environment prevalent in the healthcare industry. This chapter provides insight into how these unique characteristics impact the valuation of healthcare businesses. We do not focus on the fundamental mechanics of performing a valuation but rather on the unique considerations that must be made in healthcare valuation. We also provide two detailed case studies to illustrate these nuances at the end of this chapter: an ambulatory surgery center (Addendum 1) and a hospital (Addendum 2). These case studies are only general examples since the procedures, methods and amount of detailed analysis can differ from engagement to engagement depending on the purpose and scope of the engagement.

The healthcare industry has its own language. Exhibit 25.1 contains a glossary of terms that may be reviewed to provide a foundation for understanding the healthcare industry.

Exhibit 25.1   Glossary of Terms

501(c)(3)—Refers to Section 501(c)(3) of the United States Internal Revenue Code of 1954. This section deals with nonprofit organizations that are exempt from federal income taxes (i.e., charitable, religious, scientific, and educational institutions).

Acute Care Hospital—A hospital caring for patients with serious debilitating illnesses and injuries; generally, the illnesses and diseases have an average length of stay of 30 days or less; commonly referred to as a short-term hospital.

Ambulatory Surgery Center (ASC)—A facility where physician surgeons perform outpatient surgeries. Generally, the patient is admitted and discharged within a 24-hour period. It is not uncommon for an ASC to perform the following services: Anesthesia, Dental, ENT, General Surgery, Orthopedics, Ophthalmology, Plastic, Podiatry, and Urology.

Ambulatory Payment Classification (APCs)—A prospective payment system for hospital outpatient services. APCs refer to a service classification system designed to explain the amount and type of resources used in an outpatient encounter.

(continues)

Exhibit 25.1   *Continued*

Average Length of Stay (ALOS)—The total average number of days between the time a patient is admitted and discharged from a healthcare facility.

Balanced Budget Act of 1997—This revolutionary act, enacted in August of 1997, contained significant changes in Medicare reimbursement for certain areas including skilled nursing services, home health services, and inpatient rehabilitation. Unlike the former reimbursement system whereby reimbursement rates were derived from cost reports subject to review by government agencies, the new Prospective Payment System (PPS) is based on established federal discharge diagnosis rates for a host of services. This new law required that the new PPS be phased in over a three-year cost-reporting period, beginning with those cost reports on or after January 1, 1999.

Capitation—A flat, periodic payment whereby a physician, hospital, healthcare facility, or healthcare system is compensated on a per-person per-month basis. Under the terms of these agreements, the provider assumes the risk that the fixed monthly payment will cover the costs associated with treating the patient.

Certificate of Need (CON)—A certificate, traditionally issued by a government (i.e., state agency), approving a healthcare facility's request for a specific service or function. In most cases, a CON is required to build, purchase, or occupy a service.

Computed Tomograph (CT)—Refers to a technique for making detailed X-rays of a predetermined section of a solid object while blurring out the images of other planes.

Cost-Plus Reimbursement—A type of reimbursement in which the recipient receives compensation for the costs associated with providing a service plus an additional amount as a fee or profit.

Designated Health Services (DHS)—Health services designated by the Stark Laws that are prohibited from physician self-referrals. Those services subject to the referral restrictions include: clinical lab services; physical therapy, occupational therapy, and speech-language pathology services; radiology and other imaging services (including nuclear medicine); radiation therapy services; durable medical equipment; prosthetics, orthotics, and prosthetic devices; home health services; outpatient prescription drugs; inpatient hospital services; outpatient hospital services; and parental and enteral nutrients, associated equipment, and supplies.

End-Stage Renal Disease (ESRD)—The clinical term for kidney failure. This disease can be caused by a number of conditions, including: diabetes, sickle cell disease, hypertension, and congenital renal disease. Individuals with this condition must rely on kidney dialysis to survive.

Frees-standing Outpatient Surgery Center (FOSC)—A facility providing surgeries on an outpatient basis. Although a hospital may own one of these facilities, it is not a physical part of the hospital. In theory, FOSCs can be more profitable than inpatient surgery centers in hospitals since it is not subject to the same cost structures.

Healthcare Fraud and Abuse—A number of federal statutes address fraud and abuse in federally funded healthcare programs, including Medicare and Medicaid. These statutes include the False Claims Act, the antikickback statute, the Stark law, as well as additional program-related penalties and exclusions. Federal penalties for fraudulent activities in healthcare include civil and criminal penalties as well as permissive and mandatory exclusions from federal healthcare programs. The basic Medicare and Medicaid program-related antifraud provisions are generally found in Title XI of the Social Security Act, 42 U.S.C. §§ 1320a-7 et seq. Under Section 1128A of the Social Security Act (42 U.S.C. § 1320a-7a), the Office of the Inspector General (OIG) at the Department of Health and Human Services is authorized to impose civil penalties on any person, organization, agency, or other entity that knowingly presents or causes to be presented to a federal or state employee or agent certain false or fraudulent claims. Monetary penalties of up to $10,000 for each item or service claimed, up to $50,000 under certain

Exhibit 25.1   *Continued*

additional circumstances, as well as treble damages apply to this section. Section 1128B of the Social Security Act (42 U.S.C. § 1320a-7b) provides for criminal penalties involving federal healthcare programs. Under this section, certain false statements and representations, made knowingly and willfully, are criminal offenses. Persons who have violated the statute and have furnished an item or service under which payment could be made under a federal health program may be guilty of a felony, punishable by a fine of up to $25,000, up to five years' imprisonment, or both. The False Claims Act (FCA), a law of general applicability, is invoked frequently in the healthcare context. Under the FCA, and person who "knowingly presents or causes to be presented . . . a false or fraudulent claim for payment or approval" to the U.S. government may be subject to civil penalties. Healthcare program false claims often arise in terms of billing, including billing for services not rendered, billing for unnecessary medical services, double billing for the same service or equipment, or billing for services at a higher rate than provided. Penalties under the FCA include treble damages, plus an additional penalty of $5,500 to $11,000 for each false claim filed. Estimates project that billions of dollars are lost to healthcare fraud and abuse on an annual basis. These losses lead to increased healthcare costs and potential increased costs for coverage.[A]

Health Maintenance Organization (HMO or Health Plan)—A type of managed care organization (MCO) that provides a form of health insurance coverage that is fulfilled through hospitals, doctors, and other providers with which the HMO has a contract. Unlike traditional indemnity insurance, care provided through an HMO generally follows a set of guidelines set for the HMO's network of providers. Under this model, providers contract with an HMO to receive more patients and in return usually agree to provide services at a discount. This arrangement allows the HMO to charge a lower monthly premium, which is an advantage over indemnity insurance, provided that its members are willing to abide by the additional restrictions.

Joint Venture (JV)—A contractual business undertaking between two or more parties. Individuals or companies choose to enter joint ventures in order to share strengths, minimize risks, and increase competitive advantages in the marketplace. Joint ventures can be distinct business units (a new business entity may be created for the joint venture) or collaborations between businesses.

Magnetic Resonance Imaging (MRI)—A special technique that images the internal soft tissue features of the human body. Generally, MRIs are superior in quality to traditional X-ray images.

Managed Care Organization (MCO)—A term applied to those organizations that provide management services for the reduction or control of healthcare costs. Generally, MCOs offer their services to corporations and insurers. Health Maintenance Organizations (HMOs) also fall under this category.

Medicaid—Founded in 1965, this federal program provides healthcare to indigent persons and those individuals with certain illnesses or diseases. The Medicaid program is administered by the states.

Medicare—Also established in 1965, this federal program provides healthcare to those individuals 65 years and older and to others entitled to Social Security benefits. The Medicare program is administered at the federal level.

Medicare, Part A: Medicare Part A refers to the hospital care portion of this program. Eligible enrollees are: i) 65 years of age or older, ii) under 65 years of age but have been eligible for disability for more than 2 years, or iii) qualify for End Stage Renal Disease (ESRD).

Medicare, Part B: Medicare Part B refers to the part of Medicare whereby individuals who qualify for Part A obtain assistance with the payment for physician services.

Medicare Prescription Drug, Improvement, and Modernization Act (MMA)—A law passed in 2003 that produced the largest overhaul of Medicare in its history. After nearly six years of debate and negotiation in Congress, it was signed by President George W. Bush on December 8, 2003.

Exhibit 25.1   *Continued*

Ophthalmology—The subset of medicine that is concerned with the anatomy and treatment of the eye.

Physician Practice Management (PPM)—Refers to the industry that flourished in the early to mid-1990s. Companies using this model purchased independent physician practices and then provided these practices with the necessary business functions (i.e., accounting, human resources, etc.) based on a percentage of the businesses' revenue or cash flow stream.

Preferred Provider Organization (PPO)—A managed care organization (MCO) of medical doctors, hospitals, and other healthcare providers who have covenanted with an insurer or a third-party administrator to provide health care at reduced rates to the insurer's or administrator's clients.

Prospective Payment System (PPS)—The name given to the current pricing system for Medicare services. Under this system, patients are grouped under a diagnostic-related group (DRG) for which prices are negotiated and imposed on the healthcare facility.

Stark Laws—Stark law (Section 1877 of the Social Security Act—42 U.S.C. § 1395nn) was created by the Omnibus Budget Reconciliation Act of 1989, P. 101-239, 103 Stat. 2423 (1989). Stark law barred self-referrals for clinical laboratory services under the Medicare program, effective January 1, 1992. The Omnibus Budget Reconciliation Act of 1993, P.L. 103-66, §13562, 107 Stat. 312 (1993) expanded the restriction to a range of additional health services and applied it to both Medicare and Medicaid; this legislation, known as "Stark II," also contained clarifications and modifications to the exceptions in the original law. Regulations for Stark II have been issued by the Centers for Medicare and Medicaid Services (CMS) in three phases. Phase III regulations of Stark II went into effect in January 2008.

Tertiary Care—Medical care that is highly specialized in nature. Typically, these types of services are provided in an educational setting, such as a university medical school or hospital.

TRICARE—A healthcare program for active duty and retired uniformed services members and their families (formerly known as the Civilian Health and Medical Program of the Uniformed Services, or CHAMPUS).

Universal Healthcare (UH)—Healthcare coverage that is extended to all eligible residents of a governmental region. Universal healthcare programs vary widely in their structure and funding mechanisms, particularly the degree to which they are publicly funded. Typically, most healthcare costs are met by the population via compulsory health insurance or taxation, or a combination of both. Universal healthcare systems require government involvement, typically in the forms of enacting legislation, mandates, and regulation. In some cases, government involvement also includes directly managing the healthcare system, but many countries use mixed public-private systems to deliver universal healthcare.

[A] "CRS Report for Congress—Health Care Fraud and Abuse Laws Covering Medicare and Medicaid: An Overview." October 24, 2007. Jennifer Starman.

INDUSTRY BACKGROUND AND TRANSITION

From 1990 through 1998, transactions in the industry were driven primarily by the development of integrated delivery systems, the consolidation of health systems, and the consolidation of the physician practice management industry. The mergers and acquisition (M&A) market in the healthcare industry was very active during that period.

At the heart of the M&A activity in healthcare during the 1990s was an incredible number of transactions involving physician practices. A new company called Phycor emerged in 1989 with a new business model, which was the beginning of the Physician Practice Management (PPM) industry. By 1997, the PPM industry had became a public market segment with over 30 public companies and $13 billion in public market capitalization. The PPM industry consisted of companies that were created and grown by acquisitions. This segment illustrated a classic rollup or consolidation strategy with public companies being priced based on their acquisition growth, then using the publicly traded stock as currency to continue acquiring physician groups.

In addition to PPMs, hospitals and healthcare systems sought to defensively secure patient volumes by owning primary care practices and other referring physicians. As the PPM segment was actively "rolling up" physician practices, hospitals also were competing for physician practices as part of their planned integrated delivery systems.

The rampant market consolidation of physician practices in the 1990s slowed dramatically with the failure of the PPM business model in late 1997 and the financial distress of hospitals and healthcare systems brought on by changes in reimbursement in early 1998 due to the Balanced Budget Act of 1997 (BBA97). The BBA97 fundamentally changed Medicare reimbursement to hospitals and health systems. The federal government had previously reimbursed hospitals based on their cost to provide services (cost plus reimbursement). The BBA97 converted many cost-based payments to a prospective payment system or a specific fee for service. There was a significant reduction in payments to hospitals for the provision of services to Medicare patients. Although the hospital market expected those changes from the federal government, hospital management did not adapt quickly, resulting in financial difficulty during 1998 and 1999. In addition, all but several unique PPM companies failed and healthcare systems moved away from the integrated delivery system development strategy.

Another driving force in the M&A market during the 1990s was the consolidation of hospitals and healthcare systems. Columbia HCA Healthcare Corporation (Columbia HCA), a public company, was at the forefront of this consolidation. It was formed in 1994 when Columbia Healthcare Corporation was merged with HCA. Columbia HCA was intent on consolidating the hospital segment through acquisitions. By 1997, it had a portfolio of over 300 hospitals and 120 ambulatory surgery center partnerships. Columbia HCA and other public hospital corporations such as Tenet Healthcare stayed on the acquisition trail throughout much of the 1990s. This acquisition activity caused many health systems, including not-for-profit systems, to seek defensive mergers with other systems. However, the hospital M&A market slowed dramatically in 1998 with the introduction of the BBA97 and the fraud investigation of Columbia HCA brought by the federal government. Because of these financial difficulties, many public and private health systems greatly reduced their acquisition activity.

The late 1990s and the early 2000s were characterized by the proliferation of various healthcare joint venture strategies. In the midst of the federal government's investigation into HCA's billing practices, HCA began a series of divestitures, which included spinning off two hospital groups from its portfolio—LifePont Hospitals, Inc., and Triad Hospitals, Inc. In addition, HCA divested many physician groups that it had acquired during the 1990s, stemming losses from ownership in those groups. A majority of not-for-profit and for-profit hospital chains followed suit and moved away from the physician practice ownership structure that exploded in the early and mid-1990s. With the number of market players expanded, the healthcare industry began shifting to new joint venture arrangements involving outpatient services, which were not outlawed by Stark law regulations. Stark laws prohibited physicians from owning certain designated health services unless the business was in effect within the physicians' group practice. Hospitals developed joint ventures with physicians in de novo and existing business lines, including outpatient surgery, outpatient cancer treatment, diagnostic imaging, whole hospitals, specialty hospitals, and other ancillary healthcare businesses. One of the most significant areas of joint venture development occurred in the ambulatory or outpatient surgery center segment.

In 1999, there were approximately 2,900 licensed freestanding surgery center partnerships in the United States. From 2000 to 2005, freestanding surgery center partnerships experienced 12.2 percent compounded annual growth. That growth slowed beginning in 2005 to 2.5 percent compounded annually. By the end of 2007, there were more than 5,300 licensed freestanding surgery centers in the United States. Ambulatory surgery refers to lower-acuity, planned surgical procedures that can be performed on an outpatient basis and typically require less than a 24-hour stay. These surgeries can be performed in either a hospital outpatient surgery unit or in a nonhospital site such as a freestanding ambulatory surgery center (ASC). ASCs are touted as being more efficient and productive environments than traditional acute-care hospitals since doctors can maintain their schedules without being interrupted by emergencies that can delay scheduled surgeries in the hospital setting. Likewise, patients may prefer the less institutionalized environment of an ASC. ASCs also provide a setting for surgical procedures to be performed at a considerable discount, in terms of cost, compared to a hospital setting. These joint ventures, along with joint ventures in other areas such as diagnostic imaging, cancer treatment (radiation), dialysis, specialty hospitals, and whole hospitals, allowed physician providers to form strategic alliances that benefit both parties.

The hospital and healthcare system transaction market continued to be robust from 2000 to 2008. In 2005, private equity and venture capital firms began funding the development of new private proprietary hospital companies. The M&A market continued its upward trend in 2006, effectively shaking off any remains from the negative impact that the capital markets had experienced during the years previous to 2005 and filling the M&A market with available capital. However, activity slowed in 2007. The decline was attributed in part to the financial crisis that began midsummer involving the subprime mortgage market, which then expanded into other areas of the credit markets and into the overall economy. Since then, the uncertainty in the credit markets prompted a number of buyers, especially financial buyers such as private equity groups, to withdraw wholly or partially from the M&A market. There were similarities, however, between the 2007 M&A market and 2006, being that in both years very large, multihospital transactions occurred. In 2006 a consortium of private equity companies privatized HCA, Inc., in a deal worth $33.0 billion, while in 2007, Community Health Systems paid $6.8 billion to acquire Triad Hospitals and its facilities. The reshuffling of portfolios to create stronger regional networks and to cast off financially and strategically marginal outlying facilities within the healthcare market, which began in 2005, continued into 2006 and 2007. Going forward, the continued absence of financial buyers from the market should encourage the entry of more strategic buyers into the market, help deflate transaction pricing, and encourage additional strategic transactions.

During the first decade of this century there has been a common theme of increased healthcare costs fueled by the baby boomers consuming more and more resources from the system, and the increasing number of uninsured Americans (voluntary and involuntary). As the new Obama administration was sworn into office in early 2009, healthcare reform has become the centerpiece of desired legislation. With complicated problems in place, successful legislation solving those problems has proven elusive. With as much as 18 percent of the gross domestic product (GDP) at stake, the special interest groups representing health plans, hospitals, physicians, and pharmaceuticals have continued to fight hard to protect their pieces of the pie. Without credible reform and problem-solving ideas coming forth, change or reform may be a difficult proposition for the new administration. That being said, regardless of the outcome, healthcare will continue to be collaboration between doctors, hospitals, patients/employers, insurers, pharmaceutical device manufacturers, and the government. All of those participants, save pharmaceutical and the federal government, are highly fragmented. Absent a government takeover of healthcare, those participants will continue to find legal structures allowing for a collaborative and strategic venture to provide care to Americans. Therefore, transactions and valuations of those transactions will continue to be an important aspect of healthcare services.

ValTip

In the mergers and acquisition marketplace, the demand for business valuation services has shifted away from transactions involving physician practices toward various types of joint venture deals.

HEALTHCARE INDUSTRY'S UNIQUE ATTRIBUTES

The healthcare industry is unique because of the following major factors:

- Size
- Fragmentation
- Aging population and healthcare cost containment trends
- Physician factor
- Healthcare regulatory environment

Size

The healthcare services industry remains the largest component of the U.S. economy, accounting for approximately 17 percent, or $2.4 trillion, of the nation's gross domestic product.[1] The healthcare dollar accounts for approximately one out of every six dollars spent in America.

---

[1] "Health Insurance Costs: Facts on the Cost of Health Insurance and Health Care." National Coalition of Health Care, www.nchc.org/facts.

The source of healthcare consumer dollars are "payers," which can be broken down into two major components:

1. Federal/state government
2. Employers (insurance companies)/private payers

The federal government is the largest single payer of healthcare services in the United States through the Medicare, Medicaid, and TRICARE programs. The Medicare program insures those citizens 65 years or older. Medicaid provides reimbursements to those who meet certain economic need criteria. TRICARE insures those individuals who are current or eligible retired members of the U.S. armed forces. The federal government spends approximately $760 billion per year for healthcare services through the Medicare and Medicaid programs. On the private payer side, employers typically purchase health insurance and offer those plans to employees at a discounted rate as part of employee benefit packages.

The provision of healthcare begins with the physician who directs patient care, treats patients, orders diagnostic tests, and performs surgeries. According to the American Medical Association, there were approximately 920,000 physicians in the United States in 2003.[2] According to the Centers for Medicare and Medicaid Services (CMS), these physicians represent an estimated revenue stream of approximately $480 billion.[3] Those physicians represent the starting point or referral source of substantially all of the revenue generated in the healthcare services industry. The remaining expenditures are for hospital care, pharmaceuticals, postacute care, ancillary services, and the like. Physician participation in the healthcare service industry is a unique and very important characteristic of the healthcare industry and will be stressed throughout this chapter.

Fragmentation

The major segments of the industry include:

- Physician services
- Acute care hospital services
- Postacute care
- Ancillary outpatient care (surgery, diagnostic imaging, laboratories, cancer centers, dialysis facilities, etc.)

Within each of these segments there are large multiple niches. The following is a list of segments and niches with their annual estimated expenditures:

---

[2] *Physician Characteristics and Distribution in the US,* 2008 Edition. American Medical Association.

[3] "Table 2: National Health Expenditures Aggregate Amounts and Average Annual Percent Change, by Type of Expenditure: Selected Calendar Years 1960–2007." Centers for Medicare & Medicaid Services, www.cms.hhs.gov/statistics/nhe/historical/.

Healthcare Niche	Estimated Annual Expenditures
Physician practices and clinics	$479 billion[a]
Acute care hospitals	$697 billion[a]
Nursing home care	$131 billion[a]
Home health care	$ 59 billion[a]
Assisted living facilities	$ 35 billion[b]
Ambulatory surgery centers	$ 9 billion[c]
Cancer treatment centers	$ 72 billion[d]
Clinical laboratories	$ 52 billion[e]
Dialysis centers	$ 31 billion[f]
Durable medical equipment	$ 25 billion[a]

NOTES:

[a] "National Health Expenditures Aggregate Amounts and Average Annual Percent Change, by Type of Expenditure: Selected Calendar Years 1960–2007." Office of the Actuary, Centers for Medicare and Medicaid Services.

[b] "SBDCNet Connections Issue 51: Assisted Living Facilities" (July 2009). Jesse Ortiz.

[c] "The Outpatient Surgical Center Industry in the U.S. Is Highly Fragmented with the Largest Operators Holding Only about 30 Percent of the Market" (March 24, 2006). Red Orbit News.

[d] "Cancer Trends Progress Report—2007 Update: Costs of Cancer Care." National Cancer Institute, www.cancer.gov.

[e] Laboratory Corporation of America Holdings 10K as of December 31, 2008, www.sec.gov.

[f] Dialysis Corporation of America 10-K as of December 31, 2008, www.sec.gov.

The two largest segments, physician services and acute care hospitals, clearly illustrate the fragmented nature of the healthcare services industry. This is discussed below.

Physician Services

The majority of the estimated 920,000 physicians operate in small group practices or as sole practitioners. As previously mentioned, large-scale consolidation of physician practices has proven to be unsuccessful; physician practices have proven much more difficult to organize than other nonprofessional components of healthcare.

Acute Care Hospitals

According to the American Hospital Association, the acute care hospital segment in the United States consists of 5,708 hospitals. Only 873 hospitals operate as investor-owned for-profit facilities, some of which are part of publicly traded hospital corporations. In addition, approximately 2,913 are community not-for-profit, 1,111 are state and local government community hospitals, 213 are federal government hospitals, 136 are long-term care hospitals, and 18 facilities are units of institutions (prisons, college, etc.). Approximately 85 percent of the hospital market consists of not-for-profit or tax-exempt hospital facilities.[4]

---

[4] American Hospital Association, www.aha.org.

Aging Population and Cost Containment Trends

The United States population is getting older. Seniors over the age of 65 are the fastest growing segment of our population. The baby boomers in the United States, those born between 1946 and 1964, will cause that trend to continue. According to the U.S. Census Bureau, there were approximately 38 million people over the age of 65 in 2008 comprising 12.8 percent of the total population. The Census Bureau also estimates that by 2010, this segment will exceed 40 million people. By the year 2030, when all of the baby boomers have reached the age of 65, the senior population is estimated to be 72 million, or approximately 19 percent of the total population.[5] As a result, the demand for healthcare services over the next 25 years will increase not only with population growth but also by way of greater per-capita utilization as the largest group of our population enters their senior years. The projected cost of that care to the federal government has been the topic of heated political debate.

Over the last 20 years, employers and the federal government have looked to health insurers to provide solutions to these escalating costs. During that time, managed care organizations (MCOs) were developed by insurers to reduce and/or control escalating healthcare costs. A significant shift in the economics and the operations of the healthcare industry came with the development of insurance products provided through health maintenance organizations (HMO) and preferred provider organizations (PPO).

HMO insurance products were introduced as an option to control the cost of care to employers and employees. The HMO product is a fixed-fee premium product that has very minimal additional costs (copays) to patients as they utilize healthcare services. However, by accepting the larger insurance risk, the insurers (MCOs) have stepped in to control this risk by dictating to physicians the conditions under which referrals are made and services rendered. As a result, many consumers, attorneys, and physicians have argued that insurance companies illegally dictate how care is to be given, that is, illegally practice medicine.

PPOs are another form of product that is offered by commercial insurance companies. The difference between HMOs and PPOs is economic in nature, with PPO premiums higher than HMO premiums. In addition, there are additional costs associated with deductibles and copayments for services rendered. The offset to the higher cost in PPO products is greater choice of physicians and healthcare facilities. PPO products also allow patients to receive care out of the PPO network for an additional fee that is not as onerous as receiving care out of network in an HMO.

The federal government has embraced the HMO concept through the development of senior HMO risk products. By allowing MCOs to accept a fixed or capitated rate for services, the federal government shifts the risk to the insurance company. Many insurance companies have discontinued their Medicare risk programs because they are unprofitable. The difficulty stems from the high utilization of services by seniors who typically utilize healthcare services at a rate that is three to five times higher than the average nonsenior.

The federal government passed the Balanced Budget Act of 1997 in part to address escalating healthcare costs. The result of BBA97 was a significant reduction

---

[5] "Table 3: Percent Distribution of the Projected Population by Selected Age Groups and Sex for the United States: 2010 to 2050." U.S. Census Bureau, www.census.gov.

in reimbursement of healthcare services for Medicare-eligible patients. It shifted reimbursement of many hospital services from a cost plus reimbursement methodology to a prospective pay system (PPS). The change in reimbursement placed many hospitals and health systems in financial distress. Many hospitals eliminated or reduced the provision of certain hospital services, such as skilled nursing units, home healthcare, and physical therapy, because of an inability to generate reasonable profits. In addition, many companies participating in the long-term care segment were forced to file bankruptcy. The federal government, through legislative action, is requiring health service providers to operate more efficiently. There will no longer be any financial incentive or reward to have high cost-of-care services.

As the aging population continues to grow and further tax the healthcare system, the federal government and commercial insurers will continue to implement cost-cutting measures. These cost-cutting measures will most likely take the form of reduced reimbursement. In addition, there will be pressure to move healthcare services from higher cost-of-care settings to lower cost-of-care settings, such as ambulatory surgery centers (ASCs).

Reimbursement is a critical assumption in the financial projections of healthcare organizations. Many analysts make the inaccurate assumption that reimbursement will continue to increase at the national inflation rates. Analysts must first understand the payer mix of the business being valued, including how specific payers reimburse for services and the prospect for future changes in that reimbursement.

Analysts can utilize the *Federal Register* to understand Medicare reimbursement for specific types of procedures or care provided by facility type. Changes in Medicare reimbursement typically are published in advance on implication by the federal government. For example, on July 1, 2009, the CMS published a Proposed Rule detailing planned changes to the reimbursement rates for Medicare hospital outpatient services paid under the prospective payment system. The proposed changes would be applicable to services furnished on or after January 1, 2010. The government controls approximately one-third of healthcare spending and has the ability to change reimbursements, especially given the state of the current Medicare program and pending healthcare reform.

In many situations, the reimbursement for specific procedures can vary over time. As part of the Medicare Modernization Act of 2003 (MMA), the General Accountability Office (GAO) was required to study the relative cost of services provided in ASCs and hospital outpatient departments and determine whether the outpatient PPS procedure groups reflected ASC procedures. Based on the GAO study, effective January 1, 2008, CMS revised the payment system for services provided in ASCs. The new system fixed payment for procedures based on a percentage of the payments to hospital outpatient departments pursuant to the hospital outpatient prospective payment system. The new payment system called for a scheduled phasing in of the revised rates over four years, beginning January 1, 2008. Following the full phasing in of the new payment system, ASCs have planned annual increases in reimbursement to ASC rates beginning in 2010 based on the consumer price index (CPI).

President Barack Obama and Congress are working together to pass comprehensive healthcare reform in order to control rising healthcare costs in the United States, guarantee choice of doctor, and assure high-quality, affordable healthcare for all Americans. The President's effort to change healthcare began with the stimulus bill passed in 2008, which directed money toward the computerization of health records and research on the effectiveness of medical procedures. While the degree of the discussed healthcare reform is yet to be determined, analysts should be aware that extensive changes to the U.S. healthcare system are expected to be experienced within the next few years.

> The volatility of reimbursement for individual procedures can be very high. It is important to consider prospective reimbursement changes when performing the valuation analysis.

Physician Factor

The single largest factor impacting the valuation of healthcare organizations is the recognition that a physician and only a physician can perform surgery, admit a patient to a hospital, order a diagnostic imaging test, perform a cardiac catheterization procedure, and so on. The starting point for understanding and ultimately valuing any healthcare service organization is to understand how physician practice patterns impact risks and ultimately the cash flow of the subject healthcare business.

> Individual physicians exert a significant amount of control over the direction of patient referrals to healthcare service providers.

Example: A single-specialty ophthalmology outpatient surgery center is performing over 6,000 ophthalmic surgery cases per year, generating $6.0 million in net service revenue (the net revenue of the surgery center net of contractual allowances-GAAP [generally accepted accounting principles] accrual net revenue) and $2.7 million in earnings before interest, taxes, depreciation, and amortization (EBITDA). The center has exhibited a 10-year track record of profitability and growth. However, one ophthalmologist represents 80 percent of the volume.

This same ophthalmologist sold his surgery center to the current owners five years ago and simultaneously entered into a five-year covenant not to compete (relating to competition in the outpatient surgery business). That covenant not to compete will expire during the first year following the valuation date. In addition, the barriers to entry in the surgery center business are very low. There are no requirements for a certificate of need (CON) and the cost of the project can be financed primarily with debt. Therefore, the shareholders of the center are at risk of experiencing major loss of revenue if the key ophthalmologist:

- Decides to move out of the service area
- Is disabled and can no longer perform surgery
- Dies
- Retires
- Decides to compete

If any of these events occurs, the surgery center may lose 100 percent of its intangible asset value. Many valuation analysts do not properly identify this risk. A common mistake is to assume that the key ophthalmologist is replaced at similar volume levels. The replacement of a physician and the related revenues may be difficult in a community where the physician previously has built significant professional goodwill. As a result, this assumption may be erroneous and could lead to an overvaluation.

The actual results of operations of the opthalmic practice in the example were that the key physician left and volume deteriorated to a run rate of 1,000 cases per year from a run rate of 6,000 cases per year in a period of one month. The EBITDA in the surgery center went from $2.7 million annually to a net operating loss over the same period of time.

The opposite end of the physician factor spectrum would be a very large 450-bed tertiary care acute care hospital that exhibits the following characteristics:

- Very large barriers to entry—capital costs in excess of $200 million
- Revenue stream in excess of $250 million
- EBITDA of $50 million
- 250 physicians on staff, multiple specialties and subspecialties
- No single physician represents more than 5 percent of the net revenue of the hospital
- Very strong managed care contracts
- Long history in the community

The physician-factor risk profile of the hospital compared to that of a single-specialty ophthalmology center is very different. However, some valuation analysts might attempt to value both businesses using the same rules of thumb (e.g., x times EBITDA). Failure to understand the underlying risk/reward relationship in the valuation of healthcare firms can result in erroneous opinions of value.

Understanding how the "physician factor" impacts the volume of patients in a subject healthcare business is one of the very first steps that should be performed in valuation. Exhibit 25.2 presents several questions that should be answered as part of the valuation process for a healthcare business.

Exhibit 25.2   Physician Factor Evaluation

In order to properly evaluate the physician factor, the following questions must be answered and understood by the valuation analyst.

1. Does a physician dictate volume in a particular healthcare service entity? (in most cases, the answer is yes)
2. Which physicians are primarily responsible for the current patient volume?
3. Are there any physicians that represent a significant percentage of the volume?
4. What is the age and expected remaining professional practice term of each physician?
5. What competition exists for the subject entity in the immediate service area?
6. Which key physicians might have compelling reasons to leave the subject entity and what might these reasons be?
7. Are there any barriers to exit or entry that would deter a departing physician from competing with the subject entity?
8. What capital costs are associated with the development of a new business?

Healthcare Regulatory Environment

The federal government has not overlooked the importance of the "physician factor" to the economics of health care. As a result, healthcare service providers are subject to an array of federal and state regulations that address the relationship between physicians and healthcare services businesses. In addition, the dominance of tax-exempt organizations in the healthcare industry has created heavy involvement by the Internal Revenue Service (IRS) in the operations, structure, and transactions of healthcare organizations.

The following laws are an important part of the healthcare regulatory environment:

- Federal antikickback laws (fraud and abuse law and regulations)
- Stark laws and regulations
- IRS private inurement regulations (impacting tax exempt organizations)
- State antikickback and self-referral laws

Federal Antikickback Laws

The most notable of the Medicare/Medicaid fraud and abuse provisions of the Social Security Law is 42 USC 1320a-7b(b), which is commonly referred to as the antikickback law. The antikickback law makes it a felony to offer, pay, accept or solicit payment for the referral of, or the arranging for the referral of, items, services, or patients reimbursed by any federal or state healthcare program. Specifically, the law prohibits the willful and knowing offer, solicitation, or receipt of any remuneration (including any kickback, bribe, or rebate), directly or indirectly, overtly or covertly, in cash or in kind, for 1) referring an individual for an item or service reimbursed by a federal or state healthcare program; or 2) purchasing, leasing, ordering, arranging for, or recommending the purchase, lease, or order of any good, facility, service, or item covered under any state or federal healthcare program.

Violations of the antikickback law are treated as felonies and are punished by up to five years' imprisonment per violation and/or a criminal fine of up to $25,000 per violation. The Balanced Budget Act of 1997 also added a civil penalty of up to $50,000 per violation plus up to three times the remuneration offered. In addition, civil sanctions include exclusion from participation in federal and state healthcare programs.

Safe Harbors to the Antikickback Statute

Because the statutory language prohibiting kickbacks is so broad, many potentially harmless (and, in some cases, even beneficial) commercial arrangements could be prohibited by the antikickback law. Therefore, the Office of Inspector General (OIG) has issued several sets of regulations designating specific safe harbors for various payment and business practices that, while arguably prohibited by the law, would not be subject to criminal and civil prosecution enforcement under the statute. The safe harbors seek to protect various sorts of payment and business practices that Congress or the OIG have determined present little risk of fraud and abuse. In order to qualify for protection under a safe harbor, the arrangement must meet the precise terms and conditions of the safe harbor. It is important to note that failure to comply with a safe harbor provision does not mean that an arrangement is illegal. An investment that does not meet all the requirements within a safe harbor provision may still be perfectly lawful if there is no intent to generate remuneration for referral of Medicare or Medicaid patients.

The first regulatory safe harbors were published in 1991 in a final rule by the OIG (56 *Federal Register* 35952, July 29, 1991). The 1991 final rule established safe harbors in ten broad areas: investment interests, space rental, equipment rental, personal services and management contracts, sale of practices, referral services, warranties, discounts, employees, and group purchasing organizations. In 1999, the OIG published a final rule, establishing new safe harbor provisions and clarifying or modifying six of the original ten safe harbors published in 1991 (64 *Federal Register* 63518, November 19, 1999). The new safe harbor regulations included the following areas: investment interests in underserved areas, ambulatory surgical centers, investment interests in group practices, practitioner recruitment, obstetrical malpractice insurance subsidies, referral agreements for specialty services, and cooperative hospital service organizations. Additionally, the OIG established two new safe harbors to provide protection for certain managed care arrangements (64 *Federal Register* 63504, November 19, 1999). Since then, the OIG has issued another final rule in 2001 pertaining to ambulance restocking (66 *Federal Register* 62979, December 4, 2001). The OIG continually reviews suggestions for new and modified safe harbors, as Congress intended for the regulations to be evolving rules that would be updated periodically to reflect changing business practices and technologies in the healthcare industry.

Valuation analysts should understand that the level of scrutiny may be very high when providing opinions of fair market value that could be subject to the antikickback laws. A significant number of transactions are subject to the antikickback regulations.

A significant number of healthcare business valuations are required as a result of the antikickback statutes. If the following fact pattern exists, the valuation will be subject to the criteria of the fraud and abuse regulations:

- Subject healthcare business receives reimbursement from a federal program (Medicare, Medicaid, TRICARE).
- There is a referral relationship involved between the parties involved in a transaction—for example, a physician/hospital joint venture of an ambulatory surgery center.

It is important to identify applicable situations and possibly seek advice from healthcare attorneys as to the fraud and abuse implication of valuations performed in the healthcare services industry.

Stark Laws

Section 1877 to the Social Security Act, commonly referred to as the "Stark Law," addresses the general issue of physician self-referral. It prohibits a physician from making referrals for certain designated health services payable by Medicare or Medicaid to an entity with which the physician or an immediate family member has a financial relationship, unless an exception applies. In addition, no entity may submit a claim to Medicare or bill any individual or entity for services furnished pursuant to a prohibited referral, and no payment may be made by the Medicare program for such services. Finally, the Stark Law requires entities that furnish Medicare-covered designated health services to submit reports on their financial relationships with physicians.

The Omnibus Budget Reconciliation Act of 1989 (OBRA 1989) added section 1877 to the Social Security Act and initially applied only to clinical laboratory services. Numerous modifications and refinements were made over the next several years. For example, in 1993 the Stark Law was amended to cover 10 additional designated health services, including physical therapy services; occupational therapy services; radiology services; radiation therapy services; durable medical equipment; parenteral and enteral nutrients, equipment, and supplies; prosthetics, orthotics, and prosthetic devices; home health services; outpatient prescription drugs; and inpatient and outpatient hospital services. Additional legislative changes to Section 1877, for example, including Medicaid as well as Medicare, led to the further development of Stark regulations. These were issued in phases. Phase I was published in the *Federal Register* in 2001 (66 *Federal Register* 856, January 4, 2001), Phase II regulations were published in 2004 (69 *Federal Register* 16054, March 26, 2004), and Phase III regulations were published in 2007 (72 *Federal Register* 51012, September 7, 2007).

Services rendered pursuant to a prohibited referral are not payable by Medicare, and anyone submitting claims to Medicare or billing any entity for such services has an obligation to make a prompt refund. Submission of such claims or failure to promptly refund payments is punishable by civil monetary penalties of up to $15,000 per service and, potentially, exclusion from the Medicare program. Failure to meet reporting requirements can result in a civil monetary penalty of up to $10,000 per day.

It is important to note that violations of the antikickback law are subject to criminal fines and possible imprisonment, whereas violations of the Stark Law are punishable only by civil penalties at this time.

The intent of the Stark regulations is not only to prohibit referring physicians from owning an interest in businesses to which they refer but also to require that contractual relationships between referring physicians and parties to which they refer are consummated at fair market value. The Stark regulations actually define a valuation term called "fair market value," which requires emphasis on commercially reasonable standards and cannot be based on the value or volume of referrals from a particular physician as defined.

Exceptions to the Stark regulations allow physicians to own interests in certain entities included in the designated health services list. Two key exceptions are 1) the whole hospital exception and 2) the group practice exception. Physicians are permitted to own interests in whole hospital facilities that include designated health services. They also are permitted to own and provide designated health services as a component of their group practice. As with all healthcare regulations, detailed components to each set of laws may require an analyst to consult with a qualified healthcare regulatory attorney to understand the complex nuances of each set of regulations.

Appropriately factoring the regulatory environment into the valuation is important when valuing healthcare businesses.

IRS Private Inurement and Private Benefit

A hospital or healthcare organization that is exempt from tax must be operated exclusively for charitable purposes. No part of an exempt hospital's net earnings may inure to the benefit of a private shareholder or individual. The primary purpose of the exempt hospital must remain to serve the public interest rather than a private interest. Revenue Ruling 69-545, 1969-2 C.B. 117, establishes the community benefit standard for the exemption of healthcare providers. It focuses on a number of factors, indicating that the operation of a tax-exempt entity such as a hospital benefits the community rather than serving private interests. An organization cannot be operated exclusively for charitable purposes unless it serves a public rather than a private interest. Thus, to meet the requirements of IRC 501(c)(3) as a tax-exempt entity, an organization must establish that it is not organized or operated for the benefit of private interests. Private inurement generally involves persons who, because of their relationship with an organization, can control or influence its activities. As such, the payment for businesses that exceed fair market value may cause an organization to lose its tax-exempt 501(c)(3) status.

> It may be necessary to consult a qualified tax lawyer to understand how to appropriately consider the tax laws when valuing a business that involves a tax-exempt enterprise.

Regulatory Environment and the Standard of Value

As a result of the fraud and abuse regulations, Stark Laws, and private inurement requirements, many healthcare transactions are required to be consummated at fair market value. Fair market value is defined in the tax regulations as "the price at which property would change hands between a willing buyer and a willing seller when the former is not under any compulsion to buy and the latter is not under any compulsion to sell, both parties having reasonable knowledge of the relevant facts." The most notable transactions are between physicians and hospitals or any party to which they refer, where the physician might gain a prohibited economic benefit.

> If a valuation is being performed as a result of regulatory requirements, the valuation must apply the fair market value standard of value.

The following types of transactions are subject to the state and federal fraud and abuse regulations. To the extent that a transaction between a physician and a hospital exhibits one of the following characteristics, the federal government will take the position that referrals were being purchased or, in the case of a tax-exempt organization, that the tax exemption was being inured to the benefit of the non–tax-exempt organization.

- Physician sells surgery center to hospital for greater than fair market value
- Physician buys interest in surgery center for less than fair market value
- Physician buys interest in a hospital for less than fair market value
- Physician sells interest to hospital for greater than fair market value

Investment Value

There are several differences between fair market value and investment value. Investment value can be defined as the related value of a particular asset or service to a particular individual or entity. In other words, the investment value of a particular piece of property differs from buyer to buyer. Hence, investment value takes into consideration a specific buyer and seller. Fair market value does not assume a specified buyer or seller, but rather the hypothetical buyer(s)/seller(s) in the marketplace. See Chapters 1 and 2 for a more detailed discussion concerning standards of value.

The federal government takes the position that if a buyer (subject to the regulations) purchases a business or business interest from a potential referral source at greater than fair market value, there has been a monetary inducement for referrals. As a result, investment value transactions are less common. Publicly traded or proprietary healthcare companies sometimes enter into transactions that exhibit investment value. This should be noted and considered when analyzing publicly available transaction data.

OVERVIEW OF CONSIDERATIONS FOR VALUING HEALTHCARE ENTITIES

Understanding the Market and Economic Drivers for the Industry Niche

Performing a healthcare valuation requires that the valuation analyst have a thorough understanding of the market in which the subject healthcare entity operates as well as the economic drivers for each specific healthcare niche. These factors will affect the volume of service and the risk associated with that volume.

Understanding the Impact of Healthcare Laws and Regulations

Prior to accepting the engagement, the valuation analyst should have an understanding of the healthcare laws and regulations that might impact the valuation process. For example, the engagement might involve a fair market value opinion of a diagnostic imaging center partnership that has individual referring physician ownership. Since diagnostic imaging is a designated health service as defined by Stark regulations and cannot have referring physician ownership, the analyst may be unable to provide the fair market value of an entity that has been illegally structured. In fact, if there is any question about the legality of a business structure, a regulatory attorney should be consulted.

Understanding the Motivations and Economic Drivers of the "Typical Buyer" in the Marketplace

Two groups most commonly represent the typical buyer in the healthcare marketplace:

1. Local and regional not-for-profit healthcare systems
2. National or regional for-profit specialty healthcare service firms

The motivations and economic drivers for these two potential buyers are widely divergent. The not-for-profit healthcare system is driven by the requirement to serve the local community's healthcare service needs and generally reinvests significant levels of capital back into the community health system. The not-for-profit healthcare organization always must be cognizant of the regulations necessary to maintain its tax-exempt status. The board of directors of the tax-exempt hospital typically will require that third-party appraisers are engaged to determine the fair market value of a prospective entity for the purposes of supporting the price of a transaction.

The national or regional for-profit healthcare provider is driven by two factors:

1. Providing high quality services that successfully compete with the not-for-profit providers
2. Generating a return to the equity investors of the corporation

These factors will definitely change the dynamics of and motivations for transactions. The standard of value may shift from fair market value (the standard for not-for-profits) to investment value if the regulatory environment allows. This difference in standards of value can create an uneven playing field as not-for-profit entities compete with for-profit entities.

Understanding the Types of Revenues Generated by Healthcare Entities

There are two types of revenue in healthcare services, "technical" and "professional." The technical revenues in healthcare represent the reimbursement levels related to the facility, equipment, supplies, other operating expenses, and capital costs associated with the provision of care. For example, a hospital is reimbursed a technical fee for the services associated with a surgical procedure. Surgery requires a licensed hospital or outpatient facility, operating room, supplies, staff, and other operating and capital expenses to perform the procedure. The technical fee represents the cost of services excluding the physician's professional fee. The physician's professional fee is called the professional component of reimbursement. A combination of technical fees and professional fees is known as a global fee.

It is important to understand what is included in the revenue stream of the subject entity since professional versus technical revenue generation can involve different valuation dynamics.

VALUATION PROCESS

Fundamental Understanding

The valuation process should begin with a discussion with the client pertaining to:

- Standard of value
- Date of valuation
- Purpose and use of the valuation
- Specific business or interest to be valued

These fundamental factors set the foundation for the remaining steps of the engagement:

- Information gathering
- Valuation approaches and methods
- Income approach

Information Gathering

The information-gathering process can be challenging and time consuming for health-care valuations. Many entities operate on a cash basis and do not have audited financial statements. In addition, many are small and do not have the administrative resources needed to facilitate information gathering. As a result, the quality of information obtained may vary widely and careful attention must be paid to anomalies. If the analyst does not have healthcare expertise, an industry expert may need to be consulted.

Valuation Approaches and Methods

Similar to any other business valuation, the three primary approaches to value—income, market, and asset—should be considered. Selecting the appropriate valuation methodology, as always, depends on the facts and circumstances of the subject business being valued. However, most healthcare services businesses that are going concerns are valued with heavy reliance on the income approach due to the nature of service businesses. The market approach has less applicability due to limitations on the quantity and supportability of the underlying data. Under the asset approach, the value of the underlying net tangible assets of healthcare organizations is typically less than the overall value of the organization such that the intangible component of value can be the largest percentage of the overall value. The primary exception to this rule is in the valuation of some acute-care hospitals that have significant investment in land, buildings, improvements, equipment, and working capital.

Income Approach

For transaction-based valuations, the discounted cash flow (DCF) method of the income approach is typically one of the primary methods that is used to value healthcare service businesses. The DCF allows the analyst to work with detailed assumptions regarding volumes, reimbursement, payer mix, growth, staffing levels, staffing costs, medical supply costs, occupancy costs, other operating expenses, capital expenditures, and working capital. When analyzing projections, it is important to consider these components:

- Net patient revenue
- Operating expenses
- Working capital requirements
- Capital expenditures

Net Patient Revenue. Net patient revenue is the product of volume and charges (gross patient revenue) less contractual allowances. The contractual allowance is the difference between the charges and the amount that payers are contractually obligated to reimburse the provider for services.

Obtaining a concrete picture of the volume of patient flows and the charges associated with the types of procedures being performed by the subject entity will help quantify gross patient revenue. Since volumes are dependent on physician activity, the following information will be useful when analyzing current volumes and developing volume projections for the subject entity:

- The source of volume at the physician and physician specialty level
- Changing practice patterns of utilizing physicians

- Competition in the service area that could impact existing volume
- Population growth and demographic changes in the service area

The final component of the projection of net revenue is the reimbursement to be received on patient charges. However, this is not a straightforward issue since the payer mix will determine the anticipated amount of reimbursement to be received. The analyst must understand the subject company's payer mix for various services/procedures, and, if necessary, tie this to the Medicare reimbursement schedules in the *Federal Register*, and use these data to evaluate reimbursements used in the net revenue projections.

A negative reimbursement trend for certain healthcare services is not uncommon. It may be erroneous to assume, without performing a reimbursement analysis, that reimbursement will increase at inflationary rates.

Operating Expenses.

- **Salaries, Wages, and Benefits.** This is typically the largest expense for healthcare service businesses. It is appropriate to analyze the staffing patterns and projected staffing as a function of patient or procedure volume in the business.
- **Medical Supply Costs.** Supply costs are a significant cost for most healthcare service businesses. Supply costs should also be analyzed and projected based upon volume.
- **Occupancy Costs.** These costs are relevant if the company rents its property. Typically, occupancy costs include utility costs.
- **Insurance.** Liability insurance can be a significant cost.
- **Bad Debt.** This expense can change significantly from year to year and can be benchmarked against other facilities to consider the reasonableness of the expense.
- **General and Administrative.** This category includes telephone, postage, office expenses, travel, entertainment, marketing, management fees, and other administrative costs.

One of the erroneous assumptions sometimes made in healthcare valuations is that variable expenses are always solely a function of revenue.

As in other industries, the operating expenses of a healthcare firm are both fixed and variable. Most of the variable expenses, although related to revenue, are really a function of volume.

Salaries and medical supplies vary with the number of procedures performed rather than the net revenue of the business. Even when reimbursement revenues are flat or declining, staffing and medical supplies continue to be affected by volume. If volumes continue to grow, staffing and supplies must keep up. Over the last five years, profit margins of some healthcare services businesses have declined because reimbursement has been flat or, in some cases, declined, while volumes continued to grow, increasing the costs associated with employees and supplies.

The net result of volatile reimbursement levels for some healthcare entities is declining margins. Valuation professionals must carefully track variable costs.

Working Capital Requirements. Working capital for a typical healthcare service business includes cash, accounts receivable, inventory, and prepaid expenses, less vendor payables and other current liabilities. Accounts receivable is usually the most significant component of working capital. Working capital costs often are based on a reasonable level of working capital in the business as compared to similar businesses. It is common for normal working capital requirements to be between 10 and 25 percent of net revenue for healthcare services firms.

Capital Expenditures. Depending on the type of healthcare entity, capital expenditure assumptions can have a dramatic impact on the valuation. Issues that must be considered include age and condition of equipment, technological obsolescence, historical capital expenditures, and plans for any nonroutine capital expenditures.

Income Approach Discounted Cash Flow Method: Developing a Discount Rate

The next step in a DCF analysis is the development of a discount rate. Although direct equity methods can be used, the invested capital method of the income approach, using the weighted average cost of capital (WACC), is more common in the acquisitions area. Both direct equity and invested capital models are used in other areas such as tax and litigation.

To derive the equity return within the WACC, analysts can use the build-up method or the Modified Capital Asset Pricing Model (MCAPM). One of the most challenging issues in using the MCAPM to develop a discount rate for a healthcare entity is the selection of beta. The healthcare industry has been less volatile than the rest of the stock market for several years. The extreme volatility in the stock market has forced the current beta for the healthcare services industry to be significantly less than one. Using MCAPM with low betas (0.2 to 0.4) can cause the equity return to be much lower than other industries. Analysts must consider the reasonableness of a low beta and whether it applies to the subject business.

Income Approach Discounted Cash Flow Method: Estimate of Value

If performed properly, the DCF typically yields a valuation that most effectively considers the facts, circumstances, and risk of the cash flow of a particular business. See Chapter 5 (Income Approach) and Chapter 6 (Cost of Capital/Rates of Return) for more detailed information.

Market Approach

Two accepted methodologies may be considered in the valuation of healthcare businesses utilizing the market approach:

1. Guideline public company method
2. Guideline company transactions method

Guideline Public Company Method

The guideline public company method uses similar publicly traded companies (if available) as sources for market multiples that are used to determine the value of the subject entity. Market multiples may include:

- Invested capital/sales
- Invested capital/EBITDA
- Invested capital/EBIT
- Price/net income

Based on the comparability of the public companies, adjustments are made to the market multiples that are then applied to the subject company. See Chapter 6 for a more detailed discussion of the guideline public company method.

Information on public healthcare companies can provide an analyst with an overview regarding financial characteristics of companies engaged in the same niche as the subject company. However, utilizing publicly traded company valuation data is very difficult. In the healthcare industry, publicly traded companies are valued based on such characteristics as size, diversification, growth (acquisitions), access to capital, and so forth, factors that simply are not present in most single-location or single-market healthcare businesses. For example, publicly traded hospitals sometimes trade above nine times EBITDA. However, individual hospitals often are priced in the range of five to eight times EBITDA, which is higher than historical multiples for individual hospitals due to the demand the private equity market placed on the hospital market prior to 2007. As a result, publicly traded comparable company multiples are often not applicable.

Historically, public healthcare companies have been acquisitive and have had high valuation multiples. As a result, the multiples generated by public companies are generally not comparable to those of small private businesses.

Guideline Company Transactions Method

The guideline company transactions method involves developing the pricing multiples from tranactions of similar companies in the marketplace and applying these multiples to the subject company. The information is synthesized through a number of different sources including Securities and Exchange Commission 8-K reports, Irving Levin and Associates Healthcare M&A report, *Mergerstat Review*, *DoneDeals,* and *Pratt's Stats*. The benefit in utilizing individual transaction data is that the companies often are more similar in size and may be affected by similar economic factors.

The drawbacks to utilizing these data include:

- Lack of disclosure of all transaction terms
- Facts and circumstances that may differ dramatically between the target company being analyzed and the subject company

The information needed to appropriately analyze market transactions include:

- Terms of purchase agreement
- Historical financial and operational information of target company
- Facts, circumstances, history, and outlook of the target company

Detailed private transaction data such as that listed above is rarely made available to the public. The details of a purchase agreement include price, consideration paid, assets and liabilities included, assets and liabilities excluded, postclosing adjustments, conditions, and warranties of the transaction. Publicly available information such as transaction announcements typically exclude the data necessary to perform a reasonable guideline transaction analysis. Without thoroughly analyzing the data, it is very difficult to develop reasonable pricing multiples.

Many analysts try to force the use of guideline company transaction multiples. This can increase the risk of a flawed valuation. Unfortunately, rarely is the information at the level of detail necessary to perform a supportive primary guideline company transaction analysis. However, they can sometimes be used as a general reasonableness test depending on the situation.

If the valuation analyst follows the industry closely and develops relationships with those responsible for buying and selling healthcare businesses in each niche, he or she can develop general ranges of market multiples for transaction pricing and use them as a test for reasonableness.

Asset Approach

The asset approach is applicable in those situations in which the value of the underlying assets of the business are greater than the values derived from the income and market approaches. Underperforming healthcare entities sometimes experience this situation.

The asset approach begins with proper identification of the tangible and intangible assets of the entity. A typical asset base can include:

Tangible Assets

- Working capital
- Furniture
- Leasehold improvements
- Medical and other equipment
- Real estate

Intangible Assets

- Trained workforce
- Customer contracts
- Trade name
- Covenants not to compete
- Managed care relationships
- Customer/patient relationships
- Leasehold interests
- Proprietary software

If the analysis requires significant fixed assets or real estate valuation, a qualified appraiser in each area may be engaged. If the underlying profitability of a healthcare entity decreases significantly because of systematic changes in the industry, such as reimbursement, the underlying assets of the business may experience economic obsolescence. The assets may no longer be able to generate an adequate rate of return over their remaining economic useful lives. Many assets in healthcare, such as buildings, improvements, and equipment, are single purpose by nature. As the economics of the industry change, so can the underlying value of the tangible assets. Obsolescence of assets should be considered when performing an asset approach to value. See Chapter 8, Addendum 2 (Understanding Real Estate Appraisals) and Addendum 3 (Understanding Machinery and Equipment Appraisals) for more details on tangible asset valuations.

CONTROL PREMIUMS AND MINORITY DISCOUNTS

When performing a healthcare valuation, it is important to consider the appropriate level of value. Generally, there are four basic levels (sometimes five) of value applicable to a business or business interest (see Chapter 9):

1. *Control strategic*—The value of the enterprise including synergies
2. *Controlling interest*—The value of the enterprise as a whole
3. *Marketable minority interest*—The value of a minority interest lacking control but enjoying the benefit of market liquidity
4. *Nonmarketable minority interest*—The value of a minority interest lacking both control and market liquidity

Control interests are usually more valuable than minority interests on a pro rata basis. Although the issue of control is very broad and may encompass several factors, some common prerogatives of control are:

- Appointment of management and the determination of their compensation
- Setting business policy and control of the day-to-day operations
- Control of dividends, distributions, and contributions
- Inclusion of buy/sell provisions in a partnership or corporation agreement
- Acquisition or liquidation of assets
- Acquisition of other companies or the sale of the company itself
- Selection of customers
- Acquisition or sale of treasury shares
- Change or amendment of the articles of incorporation
- Dilution or constriction of ownership

To determine whether a discount or premium is warranted, the analyst must consider the valuation method used and whether the cash flows are on a minority or control basis. Some valuation methods result in a control level of value. If one of those methods is used to value a minority interest, a discount may be warranted. But if a valuation method yields a minority interest level of value, then the base value already reflects the minority owner's lack of control, and a further discount would not necessarily be appropriate.

One of the differences in minority discounts for healthcare businesses is that many healthcare joint ventures and partnerships are structured to minimize the disadvantages of minority ownership. Healthcare partnerships are typically structured to be favorable to the minority shareholder in terms of distributions, buy-sell provisions, and participation in management. Partnerships that involve physician ownership include surgical hospitals, ambulatory surgery centers, diagnostic imaging centers, cardiac cath labs, and other ancillary businesses. A common feature of a healthcare partnership is a provision for regular (quarterly and semiannual) distributions based on a formula or protocol. The resulting marketability that these partnerships exhibit is significant. This fact should always be considered in the development of minority and marketability discounts.

Minority partners (physicians) in most healthcare partnerships are also customers of the business. Management in hospitals and ancillary healthcare businesses, such as surgery centers, typically provide utilizing physicians very high levels of input in the day-to-day operations of the business. In addition, physician owner/customers usually are asked to provide input related to clinical policies and practices. If the physician owner/customer is not satisfied with management of the operations, they typically do not practice at that location. The underlying operating agreements and specific facts and circumstances should be considered carefully before applying a minority discount.

Many minority interests in healthcare partnerships do not exhibit the general characteristics that would require the magnitude of discounts in other closely held businesses.

DISCOUNTS FOR LACK OF MARKETABILITY

Marketability relates to the ability of an investor to convert the ownership interest to cash quickly, incur minimal transaction and administrative costs, and enjoy a relatively high degree of certainty of realizing the expected amount of net proceeds (see Chapter 9). Although the issue of marketability discounts is very broad and may encompass several factors, the key areas considered are:

- Restrictions on transfer of shares
- Availability of a ready market
- Approach and method of value

As with minority discounts, many healthcare partnerships are structured with provisions that minimize the issues associated with lack of marketability:

- Regular distributions typically are paid, making the interest more desirable
- The qualified buyers of a partnership are peers (i.e., surgeons/customers), which creates a built-in market
- Many operating or partnership agreements provide buy/sell provisions that often define the calculation of value or require a value analysis in advance of the sale of an ownership interest

The analyst should read the operating and/or partnership agreement to determine the level of minority or marketability discount.

VALUATION ISSUES FOR SPECIFIC HEALTHCARE INDUSTRY NICHES

The next section provides insight into the unique issues associated with the valuation of healthcare services organizations that operate in specific niches of the industry. Healthcare organizations in specific market niches are subject to the pressures and trends of the healthcare industry as a whole. However, each niche presents unique economic and operations issues of its own that impact the valuation of those organizations. This section identifies the key issues to consider when valuing entities in the following industry niches:

- Hospitals and health systems
- Physician and physician group practices
- Ambulatory surgery centers
- Diagnostic imaging centers
- Dialysis centers

> The regulatory and legal issues discussed earlier in this chapter may pertain to the valuation of entities in many industry niches.

Hospitals and Health Systems

Background

Hospitals and health systems make up a large segment of the healthcare industry. Not-for-profit hospitals make up 85 percent of the 5,708 hospitals in the United States. Only 873 investor-owned hospitals are operated in the United States. Hospitals and health systems are one of the largest employers in most cities and urban areas. Although the hospital market has gone through a rapid consolidation process over the last 10 years, it still remains considerably fragmented.

Based on Irving Levin's healthcare transaction data, the 2007 hospital M&A market resembled 2006 in that both years could boast very large, multihospital transactions that tended to skew statistics. Unlike the period of 2004–2006, financial buyers such as private equity groups were largely absent in 2007. Only one deal, involving the acquisition of a portfolio of long-term acute care hospitals, was carried out by a private equity firm; the rest were strategic buyers. Another feature that characterized the hospital M&A market for 2007, as it did in 2004–2006, is a reshuffling of portfolios to create stronger regional networks and cast off financially, strategically, and geographically marginal outlying facilities.[6]

Regulatory Issues

Federal antikickback statutes, Stark regulations, and IRS private inurement are all potentially relevant in a hospital valuation. The antikickback statutes will be important in transactions that involve physician ownership. The Stark regulations define the exceptions that allow physicians to own interests in hospitals and health systems, called the whole-hospital exception of the Stark regulations. The IRS regulations are important to the extent that the buyer or seller of a hospital is a tax-exempt organization.

---

[6] "The Health Care Acquisition Report," 14th ed. (2008). Irving Levin Associates, Inc.

Typical Purpose of Valuation

Valuations typically are performed prior to hospital sale or purchase, hospital partnership interest sale or purchase, and financing associated with a hospital transaction. In addition, in some situations the value of a hospital is contested and litigated among shareholders.

Investment value is usually not the required standard of value except certain situations where two proprietary hospital companies negotiate the sale/purchase of a facility.

Valuation Methodologies

In most situations, the *income approach,* more specifically the discounted cash flow method, is used. This method captures the facts, circumstances, risks, and ultimately the cash flow of the hospital in an ever-changing environment.

The *market approach* has several deficiencies that make it difficult to apply to hospitals:

- Individual hospitals are typically not purchased/sold at the same values as publicly traded health systems
- Transactions are difficult to use because of the lack of detailed information regarding the hospital purchased as well as the terms of the transaction
- Popular price-per-bed multiples often do not reflect the economics of a hospital, resulting in unreasonable values

The guideline company transactions method can be used as long as the appropriate data regarding the transaction and the sellers' financial statements and operations have been provided. Care should be taken to analyze each transaction.

A common oversimplification is utilizing limited market transaction data without understanding the transactions, a situation that can lead to faulty conclusions. They can be used as a reasonableness test.

The *asset approach* to value may be considered in situations where the income approach to value produces a valuation that is similar to or less than the underlying value of the net tangible assets of a hospital. However, because hospitals are single-use facilities, impairment of the asset base should be considered if the asset value exceeds the income approach value.

Specific Issues to Address

- Analyze the top 20 admitters and top 20 surgeons on staff of the hospital, including any risks associated with key physicians.
- Understand where medical patient admissions and surgical patient admissions originate.
- Understand the services provided by the facility on an inpatient and outpatient basis.
- Understand the facility's case and payer mix.

- Understand the commercial insurance reimbursement environment.
- Analyze the staff and supplies expenses and benchmark the subject hospital to peer groups to understand the efficiency of the hospital. Common benchmarks are full-time equivalent (FTE) per adjusted occupied bed and supply cost per adjusted patient day.
- Review annual capital expenditures for replacement of the depreciating capital base, and review any potential one-time capital expenditures for new programs or new facilities.

Physician and Physician Group Practices

Background

The M&A market associated with physician practices has declined dramatically from the activity levels associated with the early to mid-1990s. Hospitals are no longer purchasing large numbers of physician practices as part of their strategic growth, and the PPM market segment proved to be a strategic failure.

Regulatory Issues

Antikickback statues, Stark regulations, and IRS private inurement are involved.

Typical Purpose of the Valuation

Valuations typically are performed prior to a new partner's buy-in, sale of practice by retiring physician, shareholder disputes, divorce, merger, sale to a strategic buyer, or sale to a hospital.

Valuation Methodologies

In the application of the *income approach,* the most important consideration is physician compensation. It is common for physicians to retain 100 percent of the earnings as compensation. Since this leaves no earnings in the practice to value, the income approach can result in zero value. Many valuation analysts use published data to overlay comparable median or average physician compensation. This assumption may be arbitrary since an individual physician generating a certain compensation stream may not take a pay cut and continue to produce the same amount of revenue. The PPM industry overwhelmingly demonstrated that physician pay cuts create an unsustainable relationship (even when the physician was paid consideration for taking the pay cut).

Without making an assumption concerning a lower level of physician compensation, the income approach may not produce value. An exception to this occurs when the practice uses physician extenders such as physician assistants or nurse practitioners. There also can be value in a growing practice that employs younger physicians at lower compensation levels.

In the *market approach,* the availability of accurate market transaction data is very limited. Several sources of information are published, such as the *Goodwill Registry* and transactions reported by publicly traded companies. The difficulty with all these sources is twofold: accuracy and completeness of terms. As discussed previously, to understand the economics of the transaction one must understand the terms of the transaction. For example, the same physician practice could have significantly different valuations if two different physician compensation models were assumed on a posttransaction basis. The Physician Practice Management Companies created an economic model that proved to be unsustainable. As a result, the transaction market for physician practices has changed dramatically. Physicians no longer have the opportunity to sell their practices to third-party management companies. The market that remains is composed primarily of junior employed physicians buying into an existing physician practice. Valuation analysts must fully understand historical transaction data before using it to develop a transaction method to value.

The *asset approach* is used to determine the aggregate value of all tangible and intangible assets, including practice and professional goodwill. This determination is often unnecessary, as this value is captured in the income approach. The tangible assets sometimes are valued when there are nominal earnings in the practice and the practice is worth only its net fixed asset value.

Specific Issues to Address

The valuation of a physician practice is significantly different from that performed for any other healthcare entity. Since a single or group physician practice is a professional practice, most of the entity value is based on underlying intangible assets commonly referred to as professional goodwill and practice goodwill. The separation of professional goodwill from practice goodwill is arguably the most difficult analysis that analysts are required to do in healthcare valuation. How much of the intangible value of the practice walks out of the office everyday in the form of a single physician?

Separating "professional compensation" from "practice earnings" may be one way to quantify an answer to this question. However, this may be challenging to accomplish, depending on the facts of the valuation.

Under yet another scenario, certain physician practices do not generate profits based on the professional goodwill of the physicians but, rather, based on contractual relationships with hospitals. Hospital-based physicians in specialties such as emergency room care, anesthesiology, radiology, and pathology may have exclusive contracts to provide their services to a hospital. As a result, the intangible value—professional goodwill—of these physicians is partially converted into a corporate-owned intangible asset (i.e., a contract). See Chapter 20 for more details on the valuation of professional practices.

Ambulatory Surgery Centers

Background

The development of outpatient or ambulatory surgery centers has been one of the most active areas in the healthcare services industry over the last seven to ten years. The trend has been driven by two factors:

1. The desire of surgical or procedural specialists to own an interest in the outpatient surgery centers where they work and to be more involved in management of those centers.
2. The movement of outpatient surgical cases into lower cost-of-care settings out of higher-cost acute-care hospitals.

Currently, there are two pure-play public surgery center companies: AmSurg and Novamed. However, because of attractive public multiples and the natural movement to outpatient surgery, many venture capital-backed ambulatory surgery center companies have started recently. There are at least 20 private surgery center management companies, some of which probably will be taken public or acquired by public companies over the next several years.

Regulatory Issues

These issues include antikickback statutes, Stark regulations, and IRS private inurement.

The regulatory environment is crucial to determining who is allowed to own an interest in a surgery center and under what terms. On November 19, 1999, the Office of the Inspector General published the "Clarification of the Initial OIG Safe Harbor Provisions Under the Anti Kickback Statute." These regulations created new safe harbor provisions which protect arrangements from prosecution under the anti-kickback statute, which prohibits anyone from knowingly and willfully offering, paying, soliciting, or receiving payment or remuneration to induce volumes reimbursable under the federal or state healthcare programs. Within the safe harbors, the federal government created an ambulatory surgery center safe harbor. The basic theme of this safe harbor is the extension of the practice theory. The safe harbor allows those physicians for whom outpatient surgery or outpatient procedures represent a significant percentage of their practice and practice income to own interests in outpatient surgery centers. The federal government views the surgery center as an extension of those physicians' practices. As a result, they do not receive remuneration for making a referral but rather make additional returns on procedures that are a normal part of their everyday practice.

Typical Purpose of Valuation

- Sale of controlling interest in surgery center
- Minority interest of a partnership
- Disputes

Valuation Methodologies

The discounted cash flow method of the *income approach* often is used and should consider, by specialty, patient volume, reimbursement changes, and physician practice pattern changes. In addition, the underlying cost structure of the surgery center should be considered, as should routine capital expenditures since ambulatory surgery centers must constantly replace and/or purchase new surgical equipment.

The guideline public company method of the *market approach* usually is not appropriate since usually there are no public companies whose multiples can be applied to the typical ambulatory surgery center. If the guideline company transaction method of the market approach is used, detailed data concerning private transactions should be considered carefully. These data include:

- Purchase price
- Considerations paid (cash or stock)
- Percentage interest of ambulatory surgery center
- Assets and liabilities purchased
- Assets and liabilities excluded
- Specialty case mix
- Payer mix
- Volume growth or contraction
- Utilizing surgeon analysis
- Unique capital expenditure requirements in facility
- Terms of any underlying covenants not to compete
- Terms of shareholder agreements or partnership documents

- Certificate of need in place
- Competition in the subject service area
- Post-closing purchase price adjustments

Each transaction is unique. If the detailed components of a reported transaction are not fully understood, the results are less reliable.

An *asset approach* should be considered to the extent that the subject surgery center does not generate sufficient profitability.

Specific Issues to Address

In most cases, the structure of the ambulatory surgery center is a partnership (limited liability partnership, S corporation, limited liability corporation, limited partnership). Ownership includes physicians, physicians and hospitals, and physicians and ambulatory surgery center management companies.

Ambulatory surgery center regulatory safe harbors dictate who the shareholders of the surgery center can be. The only physicians who are allowed to own an interest in a surgery center are surgeons and proceduralists (gastrointestinal doctors and anesthesiologists). The physician owner of a surgery center is by definition a shareholder and a customer. The surgery center will operate in the manner that the customer or physician shareholder desires, or the customer will find another location to perform cases. This is an important issue when analyzing minority and lack of marketability discounts. In general, operating agreements in surgery center partnerships are designed to minimize the issues associated with discounts.

Reimbursement in ambulatory surgery centers has recently been revised and as a result has become a very important factor to address in valuation. The new system proposed in 2007 outlined a system in which payments to ambulatory surgery centers are to be fixed by procedures based on a percentage of the payments experienced by hospital outpatient departments for the same procedures pursuant to the hospital outpatient prospective payment system (HOPPS). The revised rates under the new payment system began their four-year phasing in on January 1, 2008. This change is an important factor to be aware of when performing ambulatory surgery center valuations, as each individual surgery center will be affected differently.

Addendum 1 to this chapter presents a case study for the valuation of an ambulatory surgery center.

Diagnostic Imaging Centers

Background

The outpatient diagnostic imaging center is a business that is named in the Stark regulations as a designated health service. As a result, ownership is limited to physicians. The in-office ancillary services exception to the Stark regulations exempts services personally provided by a physician member of the same group practice as the referring physician or personally by individuals who are directly supervised by the referring physician or another physician in the same office. As a result of this exception, the only way a referring physician may own an interest in an imaging center would be to operate the business within the group practice exception of Stark. By definition, this would not be a freestanding outpatient imaging center but rather a component of a group practice.

Radiologists are not considered referring physicians (much like surgeons in a surgery center), since the federal government views a diagnostic imaging center as an extension of the practice of radiology. Therefore, radiologists are not prohibited from owning an interest in a freestanding outpatient imaging center. The typical imaging center valuation consists of a partnership between radiologists and a hospital or health system. Radiologists perform procedures in hospitals, so the same regulatory requirements exist for radiology joint ventures.

Regulatory Issues

The issues involved are antikickback statutes, Stark, and IRS private inurement.

Typical Purpose of the Valuation

- Sales of Center
- Minority interest in joint venture
- Disputes

Valuation Methodologies

The discounted cash flow method of the *income approach* typically is used as it captures estimates of future volume, reimbursement, revenue, expenses, and capital cost assumptions.

The guideline transaction method of the *market approach* often is not reliable because the following information is usually not available:

- Assets and liabilities purchased (excluded assets such as working capital not reported)
- Consideration (cash versus stock in the buyers company)
- Modality and volume mix of the imaging center (MRI, CT, ultrasound, fluoroscopy, mammography, X-ray, bone density, nuclear, etc.) as some modalities are far more profitable than others
- Volume growth
- Competition in service area
- Payer mix
- Global fee revenue versus technical fee only
- Radiology relationship and/or contract
- Maintenance agreement
- Equipment manufacturer, age, and condition
- Available capacity in the center
- Need for large capital reinvestment

The *asset approach* can be applied if the valuation of the business on an income approach is similar to or less than the estimated net asset value. Engagement of specialized equipment appraisers is probably necessary given the unique type and use of the assets.

Specific Issues to Address

Capital expenditures as a percent of operating earnings for diagnostic imaging centers is higher than in other healthcare businesses. Equipment in a diagnostic imaging facility is very expensive: MRI machines can cost $0.6 million to $2.5 million, and CT machines can cost $0.3 million to $1.2 million. In addition, the technological obsolescence in imaging technology is very rapid, resulting in more frequent equipment purchases. Reimbursement in diagnostic imaging centers is also an important issue to be addressed. Like ambulatory surgery cents, diagnostic imaging reimbursement has experienced recent changes. Signed into law by President George W. Bush in February 2006, the Deficit Reduction Act (DRA) of 2005 outlined a $39 billion decrease in federal spending, of which approximately $2.8 billion was allocated to reimbursement cuts in diagnostic imaging reimbursement. The DRA effectively outlined a plan to equalize Medicare reimbursement for outpatient and hospital imaging procedures by providing capped reimbursement for the technical component of physician office imaging to the lesser of the hospital outpatient prospective payment system or the Medicare Physician Fee Schedule (MPFS). These major economic influences result in valuation multiples that are often lower than those in other healthcare businesses.

Dialysis Centers

Background

Patients who suffer from end-stage renal disease (ESRD) are required to have dialysis treatments approximately 12 to 13 times per month. Regardless of age, patient ESRD is the only program that is reimbursed by the Medicare program. Patients who are diagnosed with ESRD qualify for the Medicare program 24 months after having been diagnosed. As a result, Medicare is always a very large payer for dialysis services.

Medicare's heavy participation in the dialysis business creates the risk that CMS will change reimbursement levels for a significant percentage of the business. With the government as a major payer, the regulatory requirements in the business are significant.

Purpose of the Valuation

- Sales and buy-ins
- Disputes
- Regulatory issues
- Antikickback statutes, Stark, IRS private inurement

Valuation Methodologies

The DCF method of the *income approach* typically is used, as it captures estimates of future volume, reimbursement, revenue, expenses, and capital cost assumptions.

The guideline transactions method of the *market approach* can be utilized in the valuation of dialysis facilities, unlike most other healthcare entities. The uniformity of utilization (volume by patient) and payer mix (Medicare) allows careful use of transaction data. Price per patient can be used very carefully as a check on the results established in the income approach. The quality and depth of information is also important. Availability of total purchase price, consideration paid, assets and liabilities included, number of patients, and payer mix are desirable to rely on this approach. In some cases, those data can be found in the Irvin Levin Healthcare M&A database and public company SEC reports.

Typically the *asset approach* to value is not relied on in the valuation of a dialysis facility unless the facility is financially underperforming. Each dialysis machine costs between $20,000 and $30,000, so for a 30-station facility, the machines could cost almost $1 million. In addition, special water purification systems used in the dialysis process must be installed in each facility. The underlying cost of the facility, including equipment, tenant improvements, working capital, and other intangible assets, should be considered during the valuation process. To the extent that the valuation under an income and market approach falls below that of the asset approach, the underlying net assets should be considered as an appropriate indication of value.

Specific Issues to Address

The volume of patient treatments is very predictable based on the number of patients treated at the dialysis center. However, the risk associated with competition from the patient's primary physician (the nephrologist) is very high. Nephrologists who are responsible for the patients in a dialysis center can direct patients from center to center. As a result, nephrologists typically are subject to medical directorship agreements that include strong covenants not to compete. The lack of covenants not to compete with the nephrologists treating patients in a dialysis center would increase the risk of the cash flow stream dramatically. The medical directorship payment should also be evaluated.

ValTip

Understanding the dialysis center's relationship with the nephrologist is critical in assessing risk.

PUBLIC AND PRIVATE HEALTHCARE SERVICES COMPANIES BY NICHE

The following healthcare entities are some of the best known within their niche. Public information about these companies and information disclosed in their public filings can assist the analyst in understanding the dynamics influencing the economic performance of the particular niche. (*Note:* This list is not meant to be all-inclusive, nor does it address medical device or pharmaceutical companies.)

Niche	Public Companies	Private Companies
Behavioral Health Companies	Horizon Health Corporation Magellan Health Services, Inc. Psychiatric Solutions, Inc. Res-Care, Inc.	NextHealth, Inc.
Cancer Treatment (Radiation and Medical Oncology)		Alliance Oncology Oncure Medical Corp. 21st Century Oncology U.S. Oncology, Inc. Vantage Oncology, Inc.
Dental Services	American Dental Partners, Inc. Birner Dental Management Services, Inc.	Bright Now! Dental, Inc. InterDent, Inc.

Niche	Public Companies	Private Companies

Diagnostic Imaging	Alliance Health Services, Inc.
	Insight Health Services Holding
	   Corporation
	Radnet, Inc.
		American Radiology Services, Inc.
		Diagnostic Health Services (formerly
		   HealthSouth)
		MQ Associates, Inc.
		Raytel Medical Corporation

Dialysis Providers	DaVita, Inc. Dialysis Corporation of America Fresenius Medical Care Corporation	Dialysis Clinic, Inc. Renal Care Group, Inc. U.S. Renal Care, Inc.
Disease Management	Curative Health Services, Inc. Healthways, Inc.	

Home Healthcare	Allied Healthcare International, Inc.
	   (formerly Transworld
	   HealthCare, Inc.
	Almost Family, Inc. (formerly
	   Caretenders Health Corp.)
	Amedisys, Inc.
	American HomePatient, Inc.
	Arcadia Resources, Inc.
	Chemed Corporation
	Gentiva Health Services, Inc.
	LHC Group, Inc.
	Lincare Holdings, Inc.
	New York Health Care, Inc.
	PHC, Inc.
		Apria Healthcare Group, Inc.
		Cambridge Home Health Care, Inc.
		Coram Healthcare Corporation
		Guardian Home Care Holdings, Inc.
		LifeCare Solutions, Inc.
		National Home Health Care
		   Corporation
		Trinity HomeCare, LLC

Hospices	Odyssey Healthcare, Inc. VITAS Healthcare Corp. (subsidiary of Chemed)	
Hospitals	Community Health Systems, Inc. Health Management Associates, Inc. Lifepoint Hospitals, Inc. Tenet Healthcare Corporation Universal Health Services, Inc.	Ardent Health Services, LLC Capella Healthcare Essent Healthcare, Inc. HCA Inc. Iasis Healthcare Corporation Vanguard Health Systems, Inc.

Lab Companies	Bio-Reference Laboratories, Inc.
	Genzyme Corporation
	Laboratory Corporation of America
	   Holdings
	Quest Diagnostics Incorporated
		AmeriPath, Inc.
		Caris Diagnostics
		Pathology Associates (subsidiary of
		   Bourget Health Services, Inc.)
		Specialty Laboratories, Inc.
		Spectrum Laboratory Network

Lithotripsy	HealthTronics, Inc.	American Kidney Stone Management, Ltd.
LTACHs	Kindred Healthcare, Inc. LHC Group, Inc.	LifeCare Hospitals Promise Healthcare, Inc. Select Medical Corporation Triumph Healthcare

Niche	Public Companies	Private Companies
Outpatient Rehabilitation/ Physical Therapy	Rehab Care Group, Inc. US Physical Therapy, Inc.	Genesis Healthcare Horizon Health Corp. Physiotherapy Associates (Benchmark Medical, Inc.) Select Medical Corporation
Pharmacy Benefit Management	Caremark RX, Inc. Express Scripts	Medco Health Solutions, Inc.
Physician Organizations	IPC Hospitalists Mednax, Inc.	US Oncology, Inc.

Postacute Care	Advocat, Inc.
	Beverly Enterprises, Inc.
	CabelTel International Corporation
	  (formerly Greenbriar Corp.)
	Capital Senior Living Corporation
	Emeritus Corporation
	Extendicare, Inc.
	Five Star Quality Care, Inc.
	Genesis Healthcare Corporation
	InterWest Medical Corporation
	Manor Care, Inc.
	National HealthCare Corporation
	Salem Senior Housing, Inc. (formerly
	  Diversified Senior Services)
	Sun Healthcare Group, Inc.
	Sunrise Senior Living, Inc. (formerly
	  Sunrise Assisted Living, Inc.)
		Alterra Healthcare Corporation
		Altria Senior Living Group
		Balanced Care Corporation
		Hearthstone Management, Inc.
		Leisure Care, LLC
		Merrill Gardens, LLC
		Regent Assisted Living, Inc.
		Sava Senior Care, LLC
		Southern Assisted Living, Inc.

Rehabilitation Hospitals	HealthSouth Corporation RehabCare Group, Inc.	Centerre Healthcare Horizon Health Corporation Reliant Hospital Partners, LLC Select Medical Corporation
Specialty Hospital Companies	MedCath Corporation	National Surgical Hospitals

Surgery Center Companies	Amsurg Corp.
	NovaMed, Inc.
		Ambulatory Surgical Centers of
		  America
		Foundation Surgery Affiliates
		Meridian Surgical Partners
		National Surgical Care, Inc.
		Nueterra Healthcare, LLC
		Regent Surgical Health, LLC
		Surgical Care Affiliates (formerly
		  HealthSouth)
		Symbion, Inc.
		Titan Health Corporation
		United Surgical Partners
		  International, Inc.
		Woodrum Ambulatory Systems
		  Development

ADDENDUM 1—ROCKY SURGERY CENTER, LP

The Engagement

Background

It is early 2009. Rocky Surgery Center (Rocky or center), LP is a freestanding, multi-specialty surgery center located in a metropolitan area in the southern part of the United States. The center has three operating rooms and two procedure rooms and accommodates the following specialties: ear, nose, and throat; general surgery; gastrointestinal; gynecology; neurology; orthopedic; pain management; plastic; podiatry; urology; and vascular surgery. Over the past three years, Rocky Surgery Center has increased its total volume from 2,038 cases in 2006 to 6,038 total cases in 2008. As a result, the partnership has almost tripled its EBITDA from approximately $500,000 to $1.4 million.

The center is not reliant on a hospital network or affiliation for its case volumes. It is heavily reliant on the individual surgeons currently performing the cases at the center. Hence external forces, such as the development of a new center, can cannibalize these cases when surgeons perform their cases elsewhere.

A new competing surgery center Apollo Surgery Center (Apollo) is in the final phase of construction approximately two blocks away. Apollo will have four operating rooms, two treatment rooms, and will immediately become a serious competitor. Some of the physicians currently utilizing Rocky own an interest in Apollo. Apollo has attracted some of the Rocky Surgery Center's younger, nonshareholder surgeons to perform their cases at the new facility upon completion. In addition, two of the Rocky's surgeons have informed the center's administrator, John Adrian, of their intentions to retire next year. John Adrian has engaged Mission Critical Valuation (MCVal) to provide a fair market value opinion of a 1 percent limited partnership interest in the center so that the partnership can transact limited partnership interests in the surgery center for the purpose of purchasing the two retiring surgeon's interests and offering units to other younger incoming surgeons.

Note: **Some of the numbers do not foot or tie due to rounding.**

Exhibit 25.3 Case Facts

Name of Center:	Rocky Surgery Center, LP
Purpose of Valuation:	Rocky is planning on a sale of 1 percent limited partnership units to young surgeon investors and buying out the interests of two retiring surgeons.
Standard of Value:	Fair market value
Valuation Date:	12/31/2008

Information Request

As with most valuation consulting engagements, time is of the essence. To expedite the information-gathering process, MCVal used a preliminary information request form that included the following:

- Descriptions of all of the competing surgery centers, including exact location, number of operating rooms, estimated number of cases performed, reputation in the community, hospital affiliations, etc.

- Annual financial statements (income statements and balance sheets) for the last three fiscal years, 2006 through 2008
- A summary of Rocky's history, including dates of formation, growth record, and addition of specialties
- Operational reports, by specialty and physician, for the three years prior to the valuation date and the most recent year-to-date period, including:
  - Cases performed by specialty (and physician if available)
  - Charges and net revenues by specialty
  - Top 10 cases by specialty
  - Top 10 payers by charges
  - Copies of actual bills associated with the top 10 cases along with their respective explanation of benefits (EOBs) for each of the last four months and a sampling of five bills per month over the last 12 months
- Information regarding the current and projected status of physician-surgeons using the facility
- Managed care contracts and an overall discussion of payer mix by volume (Medicare, Medicaid, private insurance, and managed care)
- Information regarding the average insurance reimbursement as a percentage of Medicare
- A list and description of the outstanding accounts receivable as of the valuation date, including an aged accounts receivable report
- A list and description of prior stock transactions and details of any offers to buy assets or interests in the center
- A list of employees:
  - Name
  - Compensation
  - Average hours worked per week
  - Benefits
  - Responsibility/position description
  - Tenure
- Detailed information concerning facility leases including:
  - Square footage
  - Rental rates
  - Terms of lease
- A detailed list of fixed assets including:
  - Original acquisition cost
  - Date of acquisition
  - Depreciation (if available)
- A summary of any outstanding contingencies or liabilities not described in the financial statements
- A copy of the partnership agreement and/or operating agreement
- List of the current shareholders and number of shares owned
- A copy of the center's relevant accreditation and licensing information (or summary)
- A copy of any market research or demographic data for the center's service area
- A copy of documents related to any future expansion plans, expected capital expenditures, anticipated staffing changes, or other significant change in the operations of the center

Information Receipt

Upon receipt of the requested information, often it is found that information is missing or incomplete. Consider this example of incomplete or unusable data. (*Note:* It is only one of many possible examples.) The gross charges, adjustments, and net charges for Rocky Surgery Center (see Exhibit 25.4) are not broken out by specialty but are grouped together for the center.

Exhibit 25.4   Rocky Surgery Center Net Charges

	2006	2007	2008
Gross Charges	$5,461,021	$6,714,955	$7,031,506
Adjustments	($3,429,500)	($2,788,081)	($2,895,326)
Net Charges	$2,031,521	$3,926,874	$4,136,180

Since the information is needed by specialty to accurately project the net revenues per case for each respective specialty, MCVal contacted John Adrian and requested the additional breakdown of data, as shown in Exhibit 25.5.

Exhibit 25.5   Rocky Surgery Center: FYE 2008

Specialty	Gross Charges	Adjustments	Net Receipt
GI	2,059,354	864,227	1,195,127
ENT	1,669,127	714,745	954,382
General	481,836	195,463	286,373
GY	2,330	966	1,364
Neurology	135,977	62,348	73,629
Orthopedic	299,047	118,282	180,765
Pain Management	864,540	337,539	527,001
Plastic	244,342	115,820	128,522
Podiatry	175,427	84,631	90,796
Urology	960,976	340,599	620,377
Vascular	138,550	60,706	77,844
Total	7,031,506	2,895,326	4,136,180

All of the other articles of information were received as requested. MCVal reviewed the partnership agreement (Exhibit 25.6) next to get a more complete understanding of Rocky's operations.

Choice of Valuation Approach

On first glance at the center's profit and loss statement, it appears that the income approach was the preferred valuation method. However, MCVal considered the benefits and determinants of each of the three approaches to value before making a final selection.

Exhibit 25.6   Rocky Surgery Center Partnership Agreement Clauses

Term: The term of the partnership agreement is effective from September 24, 20XX, to September 24, 20XX, unless extended or sooner liquidated in accordance with the Agreement.

Name of Partnership: Rocky Surgery Center, LP a limited partnership.

Status of General Partner: The General Partner, a Hospital Corporation, has the exclusive authority to manage the operations of the business of the Partnership under state law. The Partnership has entered into a Management Agreement with John Adrian in which Adrian manages the day-to-day operations of the Center for 5.0 percent of gross operating revenues less allowances.

Status of Limited Partners: No limited partner is granted the right to participate in the management or control of the Partnership's business. These powers and/or rights are reserved for the General Partner. Consequently, no Limited Partner will have any personal liability, to the Partnership, another Partner or to the creditors of the Partnership.

Distributions: Except otherwise noted, available cash is distributed on a quarterly basis to the Partners according to the percentage ownership of each Partner. Available cash is defined as the excess cash, or profit, remaining after all overhead costs have been paid.

Buy/Sell Agreements: Except as otherwise provided in the agreement, no Limited Partner has the right to sell or transfer units without the consent of the General Partner. Before any such unit is sold or transferred, the General Partner has the first right of refusal to acquire the interest. Any Limited Partner may sell his/her units to the General Partner at a price and terms agreed-upon by both parties. The purchase price for these units shall be payable in cash to seller, or to the holder of a promissory note if one is available.

Agreed-Upon Value of Partnership Interests: The agreed upon value of an interest in the Partnership will be determined based on a formulaic approach equaling trailing 12 months EBITDA multiplied by 4.0 less interest-bearing debt. If the General Partner determines that a third-party valuation is required for regulatory purposes because of dramatic changes in the financial performance of the business, they may elect to engage a third-party valuation firm.

Reminder

The asset approach considers the cost of replicating a comparable asset, security, or service with the same level of utility. In a general sense, the asset approach is considered when the value derived exceeds the value generated from the income or market approach. To the extent that the asset approach value does not exceed either of the other two approaches, it is not heavily relied upon.

The market approach estimates value by comparing the value of similar assets, securities, or services (hereinafter collectively referred to as the guidelines) traded or transacted in a free and open market. The value of the subject can be estimated by adjusting the market value of the guidelines for qualitative and quantitative differences.

The income approach estimates value by analyzing the historical financial information and estimating the future level of cash flows to be generated by the subject company. Once an appropriate rate of return is estimated for the subject company, its benefit stream is discounted or capitalized back to present value, which represents value to an investor in the subject.

Ambulatory Surgery Center Industry

An ambulatory surgery center is usually established as a freestanding independent surgery center or as a hospital-owned facility where outpatient surgery is performed. ASCs are also referred to as freestanding outpatient surgery centers (FOSCs) or surgicenters.

Several factors differentiate ASCs from other businesses in the healthcare field. ASCs provide the physician and patient a location outside the hospital setting for surgical procedures to be performed at a considerable discount. As a result, Medicare, Medicaid, and private insurers now allow over 3,300 procedures to be performed in an ASC setting.

The fact that healthcare costs have increased at rates in excess of inflation is considered the primary factor in the development and increased utilization of surgery centers. Procedures performed on an outpatient basis generally cost between 30 percent and 60 percent less than the same procedures in a hospital setting. A study done by Blue Cross/Blue Shield of (certain state) demonstrated that a 47 percent drop in surgery costs is attributable to ASCs.

While cost containment was the initial driver in the growth of ASCs, current growth in the industry also is driven by advantages to both patients and physicians. In a survey completed by the U.S. Department of Health and Human Services Office of the Inspector General, those Medicare beneficiaries who underwent procedures in ASCs strongly preferred ASCs over hospitals. Reasons cited include less paperwork, lower cost, more convenient location, better parking, less waiting time, better organization, and friendlier staff. The study also determined that the ASC provides an environment that is as safe as a hospital and that postoperative care is also comparable to a hospital. In addition to increased patient satisfaction, physicians prefer performing surgeries in an ASC because they are able to achieve larger volumes and greater economies of scale. Typically, ASCs provide faster operating room turnover time, and cases do not get transferred to emergency rooms as often as they do in acute-care hospitals.

Technological advances also have contributed to substantial growth in the ASC segment. Advances such as laser, endoscopy, and arthroscopic procedures have allowed for less invasive procedures that fit well in an ASC setting. Medicare reimbursement rates for freestanding ASCs have recently undergone significant changes. The new payment system is similar to the old Medicare payment system in that CMS pays ASCs a facility fee intended to cover the technical costs associated with providing a surgical procedure. But instead of categorizing payments into one of nine groups, the new payment is based on one of 201 ambulatory payment classifications (APCs). Medicare uses the same APCs for ASCs and Hospital Outpatient Departments (HOPDs). Each procedure performed is assigned a common procedural terminology (CPT) code, which in turn cross-walks to an APC, and each APC has a specific payment rate.

Though ASCs and HOPDs both use APCs, payment rates vary between the two. The rate paid to an HOPD for each APC is based on relative weight, a measurement that ranks the costs to perform the procedures in one APC compared to the costs of those in another. CMS determines the relative weight for each APC using hospital cost reports. The relative weight is then multiplied by a uniform dollar conversion factor to get the national HOPD payment rate. ASCs payment is a percentage of the national HOPD rate. Based on the new system, some ASC procedures will be positively impacted whereas others will experience a decrease in reimbursement rates.

Site Visit

By now, MCVal had gained a solid understanding of the nature of the business, the industry, and the center's financial and operating history. A site visit came next. Fifteen of the key issues MCVal was seeking to better understand were:

1. The facility's hours of operations to analyze scheduling issues and capacity levels
2. Major competitors
3. Reasons why case volumes/revenues by specialty increased so dramatically over the past two years
4. Historical and future physician practice volume patterns
5. Anticipated changes in the center's overall payer mix (i.e., managed care contract changes, etc.)
6. New employee hires in the past year
7. Anticipated staffing level changes over the next year
8. Details regarding:
   a. Equipment lease costs
   b. Contract services costs
   c. Other operating expenses
9. Recent purchases of partnership interests by new surgeons
10. Types of services provided through the management fee
11. Copy of the management agreement
12. Estimated capital expenditures in the near future
13. Types of equipment, quantities, manufacturers' names, manufacturers' ID numbers, and the dates of purchase
14. Whether to engage a machinery and equipment appraiser
15. Overall condition of the building and status of the current equipment

Interviews are conducted with the top surgeons to understand their utilization intentions in the future and to uncover key pieces of information (e.g., retirement) that might have gone undetected during document review. After the visit, the information is synthesized and used in the valuation model(s). In all likelihood, some other issues may have surfaced during the site visit that may need extra clarification. It is not uncommon for the analyst to phone the administrator to ask additional questions after the site visit has taken place.

Performing the Valuation

Income Approach—Preparatory Analyses

At this point, MCVal had determined that the discounted cash flow method of the income approach was the appropriate method to use to value Rocky Surgery Center. MCVal performed the following important analyses as preparation for applying the DCF to Rocky.

- *Analysis of Specialty (Volume) Mix.* What specialties make up Rocky's case mix? Has the total specialty mix noticeably changed over the past several years? Are the cases, on a percentage basis, consistent with the historical case figures? Does the ASC perform pain case procedures? How many cases per day are performed per operating room? (See Exhibit 25.7.)

Exhibit 25.7   Rocky Surgery Center, Case Volume, Mix, and Percent

	2006	2007	2008	2006	2007	2008
GI	1,255	2,274	2,571	46.6%	45.9%	42.6%
ENT	365	716	750	13.5%	14.4%	12.4%
General	86	265	359	3.2%	5.3%	5.9%
GYN	—	1	2	0.0%	0.0%	0.0%
Neurology	47	67	90	1.7%	1.4%	1.5%
Orthopedic	52	143	158	1.9%	2.9%	2.6%
Pain Management	322	451	1,163	11.9%	9.1%	19.3%
Plastic	130	249	237	4.8%	5.0%	3.9%
Podiatry	14	103	75	0.5%	2.1%	1.2%
Urology	369	495	498	13.7%	10.0%	8.3%
Vascular	55	192	131	2.0%	3.9%	2.2%
Totals	2,695	4,956	6,034	100.0%	100.0%	100.0%

The total case volume for Rocky has increased 49.6 percent (compounded annually) from 2,695 cases in 2006 to 6,034 cases in 2008. Gastrointestinal (GI) and pain cases account for 3,734 (or 61.9 percent) of the total 2008 case volumes. GI and pain cases are procedurally oriented and do not require an operating room. These procedures are performed in a procedure room.

It is important to understand the underlying components in the case mix, since the reimbursement rates for each specialty are not homogenous.

Based on 250 work days per year, the center performs 24.1 cases per day, or 8.1 cases per day per room. The average surgery case (excluding pain and GI cases) takes approximately 45 minutes to one hour to perform. As a result, a surgery center open nine hours per day (8 A.M. to 5 P.M.) can perform, on average, 8 to 10 cases per day per operating room. Based on a nine-hour day, it would appear as if Rocky had excess capacity.

- *Analysis of Caseloads of Top 10 Surgeons.* It is not uncommon for the top 10 surgeons in an ambulatory surgery center to account for a large percentage of the center's caseload. The top 10 Rocky surgeons account for 73 percent of the total FYE 2008 caseload (see Exhibit 25.8).

The analysis must ascertain the likelihood that the top 10 surgeons will continue to perform cases at a center, which affects the specialty growth rates used in the projections.

Exhibit 25.8 Top Ten Physicians—2008

Name	Specialty	2008	%	Year 1 Growth	Cases Year 1	Comments
Capor	GI	1,239	21%	2%	1,264	Reaching capacity; moderate growth projected
Harpert	GI	731	12%	3%	753	Moderate growth in the future
Peters	Pain	468	8%	3%	482	Moderate growth in the future
Roberts	Urologist	524	9%	−100%	0	Retiring
Shazo	ENT	360	6%	3%	371	Moderate growth in the future
Fossey	ENT	50	1%	15%	58	Started performing cases in December 2008
Wilson	GI	247	4%	−100%	0	Retiring
Keter	ENT	115	2%	10%	127	Started performing cases in August 2008
Bryan	General	283	5%	3%	291	Moderate growth in the future
Dallas	Pain	375	6%	−50%	188	Performing cases at new surgery center
Top Ten		4,392	73%	−25%	3,533	
Total Cases		6,034	100%	−21%	6,062	

This analysis provides insight into the productivity of the top 10 physicians at Rocky. As Exhibit 25.8 indicates, Roberts and Wilson have shown declining case volumes over the past two years and have indicated their interest in retiring in 2009. As a result, John Adrian has begun to consider ways to replace their lost case volumes. In the interview, Adrian indicated that Rocky did not have the capability to replace the lost urology case volumes immediately. Therefore, MCVal decreased total urology case volumes 50 percent for year 1 of the projection period. In addition, physicians who will invest in Apollo Surgery Center will also negatively affect case volumes.

• *Payer Mix Analysis.* What percentage of the center's business is associated with Medicare? Medicaid? Managed care? Self-pay? Other? Answers to such questions provided the data by which MCVal estimated future net revenue per case. (See Exhibit 25.9.)

Exhibit 25.9 Rocky Surgery Center Payer Mix Analysis—Expressed as a Percentage of Net Revenue

	2006	2007	2008
Medicare	47.0%	48.0%	49.0%
Commercial	18.0%	20.0%	8.0%
Blue	10.0%	11.0%	13.0%
HMO	9.0%	10.0%	14.0%
Medicaid	6.0%	5.0%	3.0%
PPO	3.0%	3.0%	11.0%
Worker's	2.0%	2.0%	1.0%
Champus	1.0%	1.0%	1.0%
Other	4.0%	0.0%	0.0%
Total	100	100	100

Analysts can obtain a sampling of the surgery center's explanation of benefits from the most recent surgical cases to understand the dynamics of the payer mix. An adequate sampling of 25 to 30 EOBs with the associated gross and net charges for that procedure will provide an understanding of the main procedures performed under each specialty as well as help assess the reasonableness of the facility's overall charge rates.

Medicare accounts for approximately half (49 percent) of the center's payer mix. For this reason, Medicare reimbursement rates may be a good starting point for a reasonableness check of the net Rocky revenue per case amounts.

Exhibit 25.10 provides an example of the detailed information extracted from 3 EOBs of Rocky Surgery Center.

Exhibit 25.10   Procedure Codes and Charges

Procedure Code	Specialty	Gross Charge	Adjustment	Net Charge
66984	Oph	$1,828.00	$1,100.00	$728.00
66984	Oph	$1,795.00	$1,125.00	$670.00
69400	ENT	$2,150.00	$1,250.00	$900.00

MCVal did a payer mix analysis and a charge and collection analysis to identify any risk associated with potential future changes in reimbursement. Based on the new ASC payment system, MCVal determined that Rocky Surgery Center could be faced with challenges associated with lowered reimbursement based on its current case volume mix.

- *Staffing Roster Analysis.* Since employee salaries and wages are the largest controllable expense allocation for any medical practice, MCVal re-created an employee salaries and wages schedule from the staffing roster to benchmark it against reported historical data as of the valuation date. The staffing roster included such things as names, rates of pay, hire/termination dates, and estimated (FTE) status (see Exhibit 25.11).

Exhibit 25.11   Rocky Surgery Center Salary and FTE Breakdown

	Est. Annual Salary	Estimated FTEs	Average Salary/FTE
Nursing Staff	$450,152	13.07	$34,442
Tech Staff	$152,822	5.98	$25,550
Administrative Staff	$238,346	8.07	$29,528
Total Staff	$841,320	27.12	$89,520

FTE is the acronym for "full-time equivalent." 1.0 FTE represents a single individual working 40 hours per week (full time).

a. *Nurse FTEs.* There are different classes of Nursing FTEs: PRNs (Latin, meaning "pro re nata," or "as matters are needed"), LPNs (licensed practical nurses), and RNs (registered nurse). Typically, Nurse PRNs act as "floating FTEs" and either work on a part-time or as-needed basis. As a result, PRNs are not each represented by 1.0 FTE. LPNs and RNs typically are hired on a full-time basis and are each represented by 1.0. Generally, total estimated nursing FTEs increase as cases (procedures) increase, although this is not necessarily a linear relationship. FTEs tend to be variable with case volumes.

b. *Technical FTEs.* In today's surgery centers, there is a high demand for the use of sophisticated equipment and the medical and technician staff to operate it. Typically, the ratio of technical FTEs to medical FTEs in any given ASC is approximately 1:3. Generally, total estimated technical FTEs increase as cases (procedures) increase, but this is not necessarily a linear relationship. FTEs tend to be variable with case volumes.

c. *Administrative FTEs.* Administrative FTEs consist of employees such as administrative assistant, billing office manager, receptionist, secretary, and so on. Unlike nursing and technical FTEs, the number of administrative FTEs is not tied directly to case volumes. However, once certain case/physician volume thresholds are met, additional administrative FTEs may need to be added.

d. *Employee Benefits Analysis.* The industry standard benefit package is approximately 8.0 and 13.0 percent for payroll taxes and employee benefits, respectively. However, since each ASC has a different benefit structure, MCVal visited with John Adrian in order to prepare an accurate employee benefit analysis.

- *Medical Supplies Analysis.* Aside from employee salaries and wages, medical supply expenses are probably the most important expense allocation for a per-case rate. The medical supply rate will need to be adjusted to volume changes during the projection period (see Exhibit 25.12).

Exhibit 25.12 Rocky Surgery Center Medical Supplies Analysis

Medical Supplies	Restated 2007	Restated 2008	Normalized Base Year	Projections Year 1
Total Cases	4,956	6,034	6,034	6,062
Estimated Supply Cost per Case*	$ 104.98	$ 47.84	$ 47.84	$ 49.27
Total Medical Supplies	$520,263	$288,652	$288,652	$298,692
*Excludes Associated Drug Costs				

The medical supply costs per case (excluding associated drug costs) is approximately $48 in FYE 2008. The decrease in medical supply per-case rate is due to the addition of pain cases. The related medical supplies associated with pain cases can be as much as 50 to 75 percent lower than the typical surgery case. This medical supply case rate is multiplied by the forecasted case volumes to arrive at estimated medical supply expenses for year 1 of the projection period. The medical supply case rates increased at CPI, or 3.0 percent, from the normalized base year to year 1 to accommodate for inflation.

- *Facility Expense Analysis.* Does the facility own the building or pay a specified rental expense related to a facility lease agreement? If the ASC does pay a rent expense, the analyst can get a copy of the lease agreement from ASC management. By reading the lease agreement, the analyst will understand if expenses such as utilities and janitorial are included in the lease rates. Doing this will prevent the analyst from double counting any of these expenses in the projections.
- *General and Administrative Expense Analysis.* Typically, general and administrative expenses account for the third largest expense allocation in the operating expense profile. General and administrative expenses include items such as advertising, office expenses, legal and professional fees, and the like. The analyst should take note of the expenses included in the G&A operating profile to pinpoint key expense levels. Typically, bad debt expenses are included in G&A costs. High bad debt expenses affect the ASC's ability to collect fees, thus, negatively affecting the ASC's value.
- *Trends Analysis—Income Statement.* After the analyst has understood the dynamics of each operating expense segment, it is important to understand the overall operating expense profile (see Exhibit 25.13).

Exhibit 25.13 Major Operational Expenses and Percent of Revenue (2006–2008)

	2006	**2007**	**2008**	**2006**	**2007**	**2008**
Net Revenues	$2,031,321	$3,926,874	$4,136,180	100%	100%	100%
Total Cases	2,695	4,956	6,034	N/A	N/A	N/A
Net Revenue/Case	$ 753.74	$ 792.35	$ 685.48	N/A	N/A	N/A
Major Operating Expenses:						
Employee Salaries & Wages	467,656	901,230	1,056,796	23.0%	23.0%	25.6%
Employee Benefits	144,244	21,620	61,131	7.1%	0.6%	1.5%
Occupancy Costs	66,048	77,779	83,986	3.3%	2.0%	2.0%
Drugs & Medical Supplies	492,040	702,362	514,075	24.2%	17.9%	12.4%
Other Medical Costs	34,799	62,717	67,896	1.7%	1.6%	1.6%
Insurance	16,391	26,295	38,541	0.8%	0.7%	0.9%
General & Administrative	322,738	818,733	883,694	15.9%	20.8%	21.4%
Total	1,543,916	2,610,737	2,706,118	76.0%	66.5%	65.4%
EBITDA	$ 487,405	$1,316,137	$1,430,062	24.0%	33.5%	34.6%

The total net revenues for Rocky have increased 42.7 percent (compounded annually) from $2.03 million in 2006 to $4.13 million for 2008. The primary determinant of this revenue increase is a 49.6 percent compounded annual increase in total case volumes from 2,695 to 6,034 cases for 2006 and 2008, respectively. Total expenses, as a percentage of net revenues, actually have decreased from 76.0 percent in 2006 to 65.4 percent as of FYE 2008, due primarily to the 49.6 percent compounded annual increase in case volumes from 2,695 cases in 2006 to 6,034 cases by 2008. The 14 percent decline in the net revenue per case figures from 2007 to 2008 is primarily due to the large increase in pain volumes from 451 to 1,163 cases over the same time frame. In addition, through interviews with some of the utilizing surgeons, MCVal has learned that over the past two years, the surgeons have become more cognizant of their own medical supply per case rates and have opted to use more cost-effective supplies and instruments.

- *Trend Analysis—Balance Sheet* (see Exhibit 25.14). Have total assets increased or decreased based on the historical information? Total liabilities? Total interest-bearing debt? Working capital (current assets − current liabilities)? Does the net income as reported on the balance sheet *equal* the net income as reported on the income statement(s)?

Does the ASC own the physical assets (i.e., building and equipment) or lease these items from a third party?

The total asset base has stayed the same with $3.97 million and $3.94 million for FYE 2006 and FYE 2008. The total net working capital has decreased from $1.16 million in 2006 to $660 thousand by 2008. Total net fixed assets have decreased slightly from $1.99 million to $1.88 million over the same time frames.

Total liabilities actually have increased from $1.71 million to $2.09 million over the same time periods. The increase in total liabilities is due primarily to increases in accrued expenses.

Exhibit 25.14 Balance Sheet

	Fiscal Year Ended December 31		
	2006	**2007**	**2008**
Current Assets	$1,986,079	$2,024,409	$2,051,545
Net Fixed Assets	$1,987,930	$2,023,082	$1,884,813
Total Assets	$3,974,009	$4,047,491	$3,936,358
Current Liabilities	$ 826,215	$ 774,261	$1,392,463
Long-Term Debt	$ 879,512	$ 793,660	$ 698,760
Total Equity	$2,268,282	$2,479,570	$1,845,135
Liabilities and Shareholder's Equity	$3,974,009	$4,047,491	$3,936,358

Income Approach—Developing the Normalized Base Year

The normalized base year is developed by adjusting the selected income statement to reflect Rocky's true operational profile for the projection period. During the site visit, MCVal discussed proposed adjustments with John Adrian to assess their likelihood.

Some of the adjustments made to Rocky include:

- *Employee Salaries and Wages:* Historically, the center's accounting system included associated contract labor costs (i.e., PRNs, etc.) with employee salaries and wages. MCVal attempted to reconcile the estimated contract labor costs with historical contract labor costs based on the employee staffing roster and discussions with management.
- *Employee Benefits.* Based upon conversation with Adrian regarding future benefits, payroll taxes and employee benefits were adjusted at industry norms of 8.0 percent and 13.0 percent respectively, of employee salaries and wages.
- *Facility Rent.* The center does not currently own the facility. The estimated facility rent costs for Rocky are based on the total square footage multiplied by the contracted dollar per square foot cost with a CPI adjustment (3.0 percent per annum) included. The CPI adjustment is added in the projection period and is based on the analyst's understanding of the lease agreement.
- *Interest Expense.* Since MCVal is using the invested capital method of the DCF, the interest expense was eliminated to derive debt-free operations.
- *Income Taxes.* A blended federal and state income tax rate was calculated.

Income Approach: Development of a Discount Rate [Illustration Only]. The discount rate is often the most contested part of the income approach (Chapter 6). The weighted average cost of capital model for estimating the discount rate is a highly regarded method of estimating an appropriate discount rate, although direct equity methods can be used as well. The discount rate needs to incorporate two factors related to the projected cash flow stream:

1. *Financial risk.* The risk inherent in the subject entity's financial structure (i.e., the utilization of debt versus equity financing).
2. *Business risk.* The uncertainty associated with the economy, industry, and inherent risk profile of the subject entity.

Some of the risks associated with Rocky Surgery Center include:

- *Top 10 Physicians.* A total of 10 physicians account for almost 75 percent of the center's total case volumes. There are 18 investing surgeon shareholders in the ASC. Drs. Capor and Harpert account for 33 percent of the ASC's caseload. Therefore, a significant amount of the ASC's value (risk) is related to these physicians. Extenuating circumstances (i.e., development of new center that lures physician utilizers away) can affect the ASC's value. Failure to recognize this risk could cause an overvaluation.
- *New competition.* Rocky has not been reliant on a hospital network or affiliation for its case volumes. Instead, it is heavily reliant on the individual surgeons currently performing the cases. Hence, external forces, such as the development of a new center, can tempt these surgeons to perform their cases elsewhere. Apollo Surgery Center will be completed within the next calendar year and has already started to prey on Rocky's current surgeon base. The discount rate should incorporate some factor for the risk this introduces into the center's projected revenue stream.

MCVal used the weighted average cost of capital for this valuation. The basic formula for computing the WACC is:

$$WACC = (Ke) \times (We) + (Kd(pt)[1-t] \times Wd)$$

Where:

WACC	=	Weighted average cost of capital
Ke	=	Company's cost of common equity capital
Kd(pt)	=	Company's cost of debt capital (pretax)
We	=	Percentage of equity capital in the capital structure
Wd	=	Percentage of debt capital in the capital structure
t	=	Tax rate

The equity portion of the WACC was calculated by using the build-up model. The basic formula is:

$$Ke = Rf + RPm + RPs + RPu$$

Where:

Ke	=	Expected rate of return on the subject security
Rf	=	Rate of return on a risk free security
RPm	=	Risk premium associated with the market
RPs	=	Risk premium associated with a small company
RPu	=	Risk premium associated with Rocky

MCVal used the 20-year Treasury bond rate as of the valuation date for its risk-free rate. The long-term market equity risk premium and small stock premiums (10th decile) were reported in the 2008 *Valuation Yearbook—Market Results for Stocks, Bonds, Bills, and Inflation 1926–2008*, published by Morningstar. *Note:* Many analysts are also now relying on Duff & Phelps risk premium data. See Chapter 6.

A specific risk premium of 8 percent was selected for Rocky to compensate for the risks associated with the departure of the urology surgeons, the potential risk posed by Apollo Surgery Center as a new competitor, their reliance on a smaller number of physicians and the state of the economy.

The equity component of the WACC is as follows:

Ke	=	3.1% + 7.1% + 5.82% + 8%
Ke	=	24.00%

The capital structure used in the calculation came from a review of the average of similar companies in the industry and the center's current capital structure. This is estimated at 25 percent debt and 75 percent equity. The cost of debt is based upon available financing terms which was 7 percent.

The WACC is as follows:

$$\text{WACC} = (24.00\%)(.75) + [7\% (1 - .39)(.25)]$$

$$\text{WACC} = 19.1\%$$

Based on the procedures described above, a WACC of 19 percent was applied to the cash flows.

Income Approach—DCF

The top three specialties performed at Rocky are GI, pain, and ear, nose, and throat (ENT) respectively. GI and pain account for 62 percent of the total case volume. The center's medical supply costs per case are significantly lower than industry averages of $175 to $200 per case, due to the lower medical supply costs associated with GI and pain cases.

Due to the retiring urologist, cash flow projections reflect a loss in urology volume in year 1 of the projection period. Management has indicated that the urologist will be hard to replace immediately; however, management believes that the development of the new competing surgery center (resulting in attracting more physicians to the area) will assist it in recruiting a replacement urologist to the area by year 2. *Note:* The loss in surgeon volumes accounts for only a 4 percent decrease in total net revenues since the departure of their cases opens up the related time slots for other specialties to perform their cases. Exhibit 25.15 presents the projected cash flows for Rocky Surgery Center for years 1 to 5, the terminal year of the projection period, as well as the final estimate of value of the invested capital for Rocky.

Future growth was estimated at 3 percent. Terminal year income was adjusted for normalized depreciation.

The exhibit illustrates the results of the 4.1 percent decrease in total net operating revenues from $4.14 million in the normalized base year to $3.97 million in year 1 of the projection period. This is primarily due to the loss in urology cases due to the retiring surgeon.

DCF Analysis. After all of these steps have been performed, the final value created may/may not need to be adjusted for applicable discounts (see later in report). In addition, the value created is invested capital (total equity + interest-bearing debt). Depending on the agreed-on value, the related interest-bearing debt may/may not need to be removed from invested capital value. In the case of Rocky, the agreed-on value was equity. As a result, the analyst would need to deduct debt from total invested capital.

Value Indication

Traditionally, the fair market value of the invested capital of ASCs has ranged from a multiple of 3.5 to 7.0 times EBITDA. This range assumes moderate growth, reasonable capital expenditures, and moderate working capital needs. In the case of Rocky Surgery Center, the value conclusion falls within the low end of the range due to the substantial loss in urology volumes and related net revenues and other risk factors noted.

Exhibit 25.15   Projected Cash Flows and DCF Value

	Year 1	Year 2	Year 3	Year 4	Year 5	Terminal Year
Earnings After Income Taxes	351,118	354,628	358,479	362,098	365,907	523,165*
Cash Flow Adjustments:						
Plus: Depreciation & Amortization	291,125	312,553	333,982	355,411	376,839	150,000
Less: Required Annual Capital Expenditures	(150,000)	(150,000)	(150,000)	(150,000)	(150,000)	(150,000)
Less: Incremental Working Capital Requirements	21,824	(20,687)	(21,599)	(22,387)	(23,375)	(18,118)
Net Discretionary Cash Flow	514,067	496,494	520,862	545,122	569,371	505,047
Terminal Value						3,156,543
	0.5	1.5	2.5	3.5	4.5	4.5
Present Value Factor (Mid-Point Convention)	0.916698	0.770335	0.647340	0.543983	0.457129	0.457129
Present Value of Cash Flows	471,245	382,467	337,175	296,537	260,276	1,442,948
Sum of Present Values (Year 1 to Year 5)	1,747,700					
Present Value of Terminal	1,442,948					
Fair Market Value Indication (Total Invested Capital Level)	3,190,648					

*Excess depreciation runs out.

The value conclusion is shown in Exhibit 25.16.

Market Approach: Guideline Public Company Method

The guideline public company method relies on similar publicly traded companies as a source of market multiples. Market multiples include:

- Invested capital/sales
- Invested capital/EBITDA
- Invested capital/EBIT
- Price/net income

In the healthcare services market, publicly traded companies typically trade on very different financial dynamics from individual businesses such as Rocky.

MCVal found four potential companies that offered outpatient surgery. However, only two were pure-play, public multispecialty ambulatory surgery center companies. These companies were selected as guideline companies. All of the companies had total revenues in excess of $350 million, which substantially exceeds Rocky's. Similarly, the total EBITDA levels greatly exceed Rocky's. Other discrepancies are related primarily to company size, acquisition growth, access to capital, diversification, and the like. Because the public healthcare services companies are not comparable in business description and/or size to Rocky, MCVal decided that the guideline public company method was not applicable to value Rocky.

Exhibit 25.16   Value Conclusion

	Year 1	Year 2	Year 3	Year 4	Year 5	Terminal Year
Earnings After Income Taxes	351,118	354,628	358,479	362,098	365,907	523,165
Cash Flow Adjustments:						
Plus: Depreciation & Amortization	291,125	312,553	333,982	355,411	376,839	150,000
Less: Required Annual Capital Expenditures	(150,000)	(150,000)	(150,000)	(150,000)	(150,000)	(150,000)
Less: Incremental Working Capital Requirements	21,824	(20,687)	(21,599)	(22,387)	(23,375)	(18,118)
Net Discretionary Cash Flow	514,067	496,494	520,862	545,122	569,371	505,047
Terminal Value						3,156,543
	0.5	1.5	2.5	3.5	4.5	4.5
Present Value Factor (Mid-Point Convention)	0.916698	0.770335	0.647340	0.543983	0.457129	0.457129
Present Value of Cash Flows	471,245	382,467	337,175	296,537	260,276	1,442,948
Sum of Present Values (Year 1 to Year 5)	1,747,700					
Present Value of Terminal	1,442,948					
Fair Market Value Indication (Total Invested Capital Level)	3,190,648	3.7 × year 1 EBITDA				
Less: Long-Term Debt	698,760					
Fair Market Value Indication (Equity Level)	2,491,888					
Fair Market Value Indication (per Unit Assuming 225 Units)	$ 11,075					

Market Approach: Guideline Company Transaction Method

The guideline company transaction method involves the selection of pricing multiples of individual transactions in similar companies in the marketplace. Information on these transactions and their multiples is obtained using sources such as Irvin Levin and Associates and *Pratt's Stats*. If comparable data and multiples can be found, they are applied, where appropriate, to the subject company.

To apply a "reasonableness check" for the income approach value, multiples presented in Exhibit 25.17 were applied to Rocky's year 1 net operating revenue and EBITDA. These multiples were based on 10 private surgery center transactions that occurred over the past 12 months. It is important to obtain recent pricing multiples to account for changes in the marketplace (i.e., government-imposed regulations). The use of old, or "stale," data can cause an erroneous conclusion.

The range of values generally yielded a higher value than the income approach did. Note that these multiples should be taken only at face value since they do not consider the internal dynamics of the center (e.g., the departure of key surgeons). By multiplying the related year 1 revenues and EBITDA figures with their corresponding multiples, the analyst arrived at a value range of $2.8 million to $4.8 million. (*Note:* Multiples are typically applied against historical revenue and income. However, this would misrepresent Rocky.)

Exhibit 25.17 Guideline Company Transactions

Transaction Scenarios		Transaction Multiples		Value Indication (TIC)	
		High	Low	High	Low
Revenues, Year 1	3,968,301	1.2	0.7	$4,800,000	$2,800,000
EBITDA, Year 1	862,745	5.5	3.5	$4,700,000	$3,000,000

The income approach yielded a value of $3.2 million, which is at the very low end of the range. Although there are very limited data concerning the other surgery center transactions, this figure does provide some minimum comfort since the risks of the potential loss revenues from the departing surgeons and other risks would put the value of the center on the low side.

Asset Approach

The book value of the equity portion of the business is $1.845 million. To the extent that the income approach value and the cost approach value are similar, the analyst should consider using the cost approach. MCVal performed an analysis estimating the underlying tangible assets of the business and has determined that the book value reasonably reflects fair market value. As a result, the *asset* approach is deemed relevant and MCVal considered this approach in the valuation as a "floor" value.

Reconciliation

While we have considered each of the three approaches to value Rocky, we have primarily relied on the income approach to value the surgery center. Based on the facts, circumstances, and limiting conditions of the engagement, the value indication at the equity level is $2.49 million (TIC of $3,190,648 minus $698,760 in total debt). MCVal was engaged to perform a fair market value opinion of a 1 percent limited interest in the Rocky Surgery Center, LP As a result, assuming 225 partnership units, the analyst has arrived at an equity level, before any applicable discounts, of *$11,075 per unit* ($2.49 million divided by 225 units). However, the analyst must consider the following discounts and decide their applicability to Rocky.

Discounts

Depending on the standard of value agreed on for the valuation, at times it is necessary to consider the usage of minority and marketability discounts. Each of the following paragraphs briefly describes the rationale associated with each discount and whether the discount was deemed applicable in this valuation.

Minority Discount

In determining the fair market value of the equity of Rocky Surgery Center, MCVal considered the applicability of a minority discount to the estimate of value based on the following key control factors:

- Lack of control over day-to-day operations
- Lack of control over dividends and distribution

Lack of Control Over Day-to-Day Operations. Per the operating agreement, the business, property, and affairs of the company shall be managed by or under the direction of the management board. The management board consists of 11 center members who supplied regular input to John Adrian and the rest of his staff regarding management and operational issues. They are also considered the center's "customers." This is a key issue when determining control issues related to the ASC. Since the physician-investors are free to use other ASCs in the immediate area, it is in the best interests of the ASC to consider the physician-investor's input regarding management and operational issues. As a customer and shareholder, a physician's lack of management control is often mitigated.

Lack of Control over Dividends and Distributions. Per the operating agreement, distributions of distributable cash and accumulated cash shall be made quarterly. It is the board's decision and intention to pay quarterly distributions to the extent of available cash. In addition, Rocky has had a long history of paying distributions to its shareholders. Available cash is defined as EBITDA less estimated capital expenditures in the next quarter, less a reasonable and defined working capital reserve. The potential consequence of failure to make regular distributions could result in the physician choosing to sell back the units to the ASC and/or choosing to use other ASCs.

Based on our consideration of the factors regarding the facts and circumstances regarding the partnership agreement, it is our opinion that a discount related to a minority ownership interest is not applicable.

Marketability Discount

A marketability discount deals with an investor's ability to convert ownership interests into cash proceeds in a minimal amount of time. Some of the key factors considered are:

- Restrictions on transfer of shares
- Availability of a ready market
- Determination of pricing

Restrictions on Transfer of Shares. The general partner shall have the first option to purchase all or any portion of the ASC interests of the selling owner. If the ASC and then the other limited partners do not elect to acquire all of the units offered, the remaining portions may be offered to a qualified owner at a predetermined buyout price of approximately four times EBITDA. For regulatory purposes, the board must have an independent third party perform the valuation of the ASC before any shares are transferred or resyndicated.

Availability of a Ready Market. MCVal also considered who the most likely investor for these units would be: another physician-surgeon, who would generally satisfy the criteria noted in the above paragraph, the company itself, or a third-party investor (company in the surgery facility business). MCVal concluded that a reasonable population of likely investors does exist.

In addition, Rocky has an interest in being the market maker in its own units in order to attract future investors and provide a ready exit for disgruntled physician-investors who could potentially harm its operations and relations with the physician community.

Determination of Pricing. The operating agreement states that the center will have the option to purchase all or any portion of the interest of the selling member at an agreed-upon purchase price related to a "triggering event," such as ceasing to practice medicine. The provision also allows for the pricing of the units at 100 percent of the value upon certain "triggering events," such as the death or retirement of the member.

Conclusion on Discounts

Based on all of the above factors, MCVal concluded that a discount for lack of marketability was not applicable to the fair market value estimate of the equity of Rocky Surgery Center. This opinion could be materially different if the nature of Rocky Surgery Center's business changes or if other facts and circumstances discussed above change. (*Note:* Some analysts would apply some discounts here to reflect the risk of future changes.)

Final Value

Exhibit 25.18 Rocky Surgery Center Final Indication of Value

FMV of Invested Capital Total Enterprise, Minority Level	$3,190,648
Less: FMV of Debt	$ 698,760
Equals: FMV of Equity Total Enterprise, Minority Level	$2,491,888
FMV of Equity per Unit (Assuming 225 Partnership Units)	$ 11,075

ADDENDUM 2—VALUATION OF PAULIE HOSPITAL

The Engagement

Background

It is March 15, 2009. Paulie Hospital (Paulie or Hospital) is a 225-bed acute-care hospital located in an urban area in (certain state). A regional health system, Drago Hospital (Drago), has communicated an interest in acquiring Paulie to expand its network and gain access to the community. The board of directors of Drago has engaged Mission Critical Valuations (MCVal) to provide a fair market value analysis of Paulie. The board has indicated that the facility will be acquired in an asset purchase transaction and that certain nonoperating assets will be excluded. No interest-bearing debt will be included.

Exhibit 25.19　Case Facts

Name of Hospital:	Paulie Hospital, a private not-for-profit or 501(c)(3) hospital
Purpose of Valuation:	The valuation will be used by Drago Board of Directors and Management in assessing the potential acquisition of Paulie
Standard of Value:	Fair market value
Valuation Date:	03/15/2009

Information Request: MCVal provided a written information request for the following data:

- Annual financial statements (audited or compiled income statements and balance sheets) for the last five fiscal years, 2004 through 2008
- Interim financial statements, year-to-date 2009 and same period 2008
- Operational reports for the last four years and the most recent year-to-date period detailing:
  - Inpatient admissions
  - Outpatient volume
  - Patient days
  - Adjusted patient days
  - Other operating data for the facility
- Detailed financial statements and operational reports for the hospital
- Detailed discussion regarding services provided at the hospital
- Any detailed operating and capital budgets for the hospital
- A list and description of the outstanding accounts receivable as of the valuation date, including an aged accounts receivable report
- A list and description of prior stock transactions and details of any offers to buy assets or interests in the hospital
- A listing of employees:
  - Name
  - Compensation
  - Average hours worked per week
  - Benefits
  - Responsibility
  - Tenure

- A summary of any outstanding contingencies or liabilities not described in the financial statements provided, including all outstanding litigation
- A historical summary of the company including actual dates of formation and a discussion of the hospital's growth
- Development projects in place
- Company budget and projections
- Company capital structure detail: debt, equity, and preferred equity
- Detailed information concerning facility leases including:
  - Square footage
  - Rental rates
  - Terms of lease
- Details related to physician partnerships
- Service area demographic data

To gain a basic understanding as to the profitability and underlying assets and liabilities of the Hospital, MCVal reviewed the latest 12-month income statement ending December 31, 2008, as well as the balance sheet dated December 31, 2008. The subject hospital generated approximately $112.7 million in net operating revenue and approximately $12.9 million of EBITDA. The balance sheet as of December 31, 2008, shows that Paulie has approximately $20.1 million in assets limited as to use, $20.2 million in cash and investments, approximately $16.6 million of operating working capital, $3.1 million of other assets, and approximately $50.5 million in net plant, property, and equipment. Assets limited as to use, cash, and marketable securities are nonoperating assets, and as a result will not be included in this valuation. The net book value of the hospital prior to subtracting debt obligations and excluding nonoperating assets is approximately $70.2 million. Based upon a preliminary analysis of the financial statements and a basic knowledge of the hospital operations, it appears that the valuation will utilize each of the three approaches to value.

Reminder

The asset approach takes into consideration the cost of replicating a comparable asset, security, or service with the same level of utility. In a general sense, the asset approach typically is considered in healthcare valuations when the value derived exceeds the value generated from the income or market approach. To the extent that the asset approach value is significantly below that of the market and income approaches, it may not be heavily relied on in healthcare valuations.

The market approach estimates value by comparing the value of similar assets, securities, or services (hereinafter collectively referred to as the guidelines) traded or transacted in a free and open market. The value of the subject can be estimated by adjusting the value of the guidelines for qualitative and quantitative differences.

The income approach estimates value by analyzing the historical financial information and to estimating the future level of cash flows to be generated by the subject company. Once an appropriate rate of return is estimated for the subject company, the cash flow stream is discounted or capitalized back to present value, which represents value to an investor.

Understanding the Industry

- The healthcare industry faces the challenge of continuing to provide quality patient care while dealing with rising costs, strong competition for patients, and a general reduction of reimbursement rates by both private and government payers. In many areas, both private and government payers have reduced the scope of what may be reimbursed and have reduced reimbursement levels for what is covered. Changes in medical technology, population demographics, existing and future legislation, and competitive contracting for provider services by private and government payers may require changes in healthcare facilities, equipment, personnel, or services in the future.

- Although the business outlook for hospitals has significantly improved over the last year, the industry continues to face significant challenges. Inpatient utilization, average lengths of stay, and average occupancy rates continue to be negatively affected by payer-required preadmission authorization, utilization review, and payer pressure to maximize outpatient and alternative healthcare delivery services for less acutely ill patients. Increased competition, admissions constraints, and payer pressures are expected to continue. To meet these challenges, the industry has expanded many of its facilities to include outpatient centers and upgraded facilities and equipment, and has offered new programs and services. Positive industry dynamics include increased admissions growth driven by positive demographic shifts, increased government reimbursement, and decreased negotiating power of managed care companies.

- Over the past several years, for-profit hospitals have begun to represent a sizable portion of the market. This was due to the consolidation of or the closing of weak not-for-profit hospitals.

- The negative effects of a rising number of uninsured patients and higher insurance copayments are expected to continue to moderate after trending higher in the early 2000s.

- Industry analysts expect low-volume growth, mid-to-high, single-digit price increases from managed care, and higher Medicare reimbursement rates to contribute to revenue growth.

Site Visit

MCVal is ready to perform the site visit. Much like the ASC valuation from Addendum 1, MCVal, if possible, should have a solid understanding of the nature of the business, the industry, and the facility's financial operating history before the site visit. Similarly, MCVal should formulate a list of pertinent questions to pose to the hospital management team before the meeting day. Nine key concepts to understand to perform the valuation are:

1. Major competitors
2. Reasons why admissions (and subsequently revenues) increased over the past two years
3. Top 10 physicians in terms of both admissions and surgical cases
4. Anticipated changes in the hospital's overall payer mix (i.e., managed care contract changes, etc.)
5. New employees hired in the past year
6. Staffing level changes over the next year
7. Reasons for increases/decreases in medical supplies

8. Estimated capital expenditures over the next three to five years
9. Types of equipment, quantities, manufacturer's name and ID number, and date of purchase

Performing the Valuation

Income Approach—Preparatory Analysis

At this point, MCVal has determined that the income approach using a DCF method on an invested capital basis is most likely the primary method to value Paulie Hospital. (See Chapter 5 for more detail on the DCF method.) MCVal must understand certain information (Exhibit 25.20) and follow several basic yet key steps in performing an income approach analysis on the hospital.

Exhibit 25.20   Paulie Hospital Data

	FYE 2007	FYE 2008	Normalized Base Year
Census Data:			
Beds in Service	225	225	225
Inpatient Admissions	9,076	9,423	9,423
Inpatient Days	45,932	50,199	50,199
Avg. Daily Census—Inpatient	125.8	137.6	137.6
Percent of Occupancy—Inpatient	56%	61%	61%
Discharge Data:			
Discharges	9,076	9,423	9,423
Discharge Days	45,932	50,199	50,199
Avg. Length of Stay (ALOS)—days	5.06	5.33	5.33

Analyst Conclusions.   Inpatient admissions increased 4 percent from FYE 2007 to FYE 2008. Similarly, the average length of stay (ALOS) increased 5 percent over the same respective time frame due to the addition of the Heart Center.

Payer Mix. It is important that MCVal understands the components of the hospital's payer mix and the related revenues associated with each payer class: that is, what percentage of the hospital's business is associated with Medicare, Medicaid, managed care, self-pay, or other? (See Exhibit 25.21.) Understanding this concept also will allow MCVal to estimate future net revenue per patient day figures.

Exhibit 25.21   Paulie Hospital Payer Mix Percentages—Expressed as a Percentage of Net Revenue

	FYE 2007	FYE 2008
Self-Pay	5.8%	6.1%
Commercial	4.5%	4.8%
Medicare	51.5%	52.9%
Medicaid	10.8%	11.3%
Managed Care	23.4%	23.3%
Other	4.0%	1.6%
	100%	100%

Preparation of Exhibit 25.21 provides the valuation analyst with a framework for understanding the payer mix. Medicare accounts for approximately half (53 percent) of the hospital's payer mix and managed care and commercial payers make up approximately 28.1 percent of the payer mix. The payer mix expressed as a percentage of charges yields a different result because of different payer reimbursement rates. Medicare and Medicaid typically reimburse hospitals for services at lower rates than managed care and commercial payers. Over 64 percent of the hospital's net revenue comes from the federal government through Medicare and Medicaid reimbursement. A reasonable question to ask management is how this breakdown would look based on overall gross charges.

Staffing Roster. The analyst may review the following key components of the hospital's staffing roster: name, rate of pay, date of hire, and estimated full-time equivalent status. Since employee salaries and wages are the largest controllable expense allocation for any hospital, MCVal may review the internal dynamics of the staffing roster to benchmark the staffing ratios to the reported historicals as of a current date. Then the analyst will be able to understand the recent changes in staffing levels of the hospital (i.e., department overstaffing, etc.)

An analysis of the hospital's staffing roster (Exhibit 25.22) allows MCVal to make assessments and groupings. An FTE designates the work status of a particular individual, whereby 1.0 FTE is the equivalent of an individual working 40 hours per week. An analysis of staffing based on activity levels in the hospital can also be performed. The standard ratio used in the hospital market is FTE per adjusted occupied bed or hours worked per adjusted patient day. The inpatient days in the hospital are adjusted to take into consideration outpatient services provided by the hospital. This determines adjusted bed occupancy or adjusted patient days in a hospital facility. The key driver of revenue in any healthcare facility is volume. For hospitals, the volume is described in terms of adjusted daily census or adjusted patient days.

According to the staffing roster, the hospital employed a total of 1,015 FTEs. Although it would not prove time-efficient to diagram and assess each and every

Exhibit 25.22 Paulie Hospital FTE by Department

Code	Department	FTEs	% of Total
6120	ICU-CCU	61.38	6.0%
8050	Nutrition and Food Service	52.59	5.2%
8090	Housekeeping	51.29	5.1%
6230	Emergency Service	51.23	5.0%
7181	Medical Information Services	50.87	5.0%
7010	Lab Services	47.89	4.7%
6124	Progressive Care Unit	44.56	4.4%
6027	Unit 16	44.25	4.4%
6023	Unit 3	43.71	4.3%
	Total Displayed	447.76	44.1%
	Total FTEs	1,015	100%

employee's location within the hospital, it would be important to pinpoint those departments that employ the largest number of individuals. Exhibit 25.22 summarizes this information.

Employee Benefits. MCVal must obtain the appropriate benefit structure from management for projection purposes. The industry standard benefit package for a hospital like Paulie is approximately 7.0 and 12.0 percent for payroll taxes and employee benefits, respectively. However, each hospital is different. It is important to understand the nature of this concept to accurately portray total employee compensation figures.

Gross Revenue. Exhibit 25.23 summarizes gross charge data. Gross charges in a hospital can be over two times the actual net revenue of the facility. As a result, gross charges are used in an analysis to determine the percentage writeoff of contractual allowances (the amount of gross charges that Medicare and other payers do not reimburse for a particular procedure). For example, the gross revenue of the subject hospital during fiscal year 2008 was approximately $230.5 million, while contractual allowances and charity care for that same period were approximately $117.8 million, leaving net revenue of $112.7 million. Other operating income was approximately $1.8 million. The total net revenue for Paulie for the year ended December 31, 2008, was $114.5 million. MCVal should notice that the pharmacy department accounted for the largest gross revenues (15.5 percent of revenues, or $13.8 million) of any department in the hospital.

Trend Analysis—Income Statement. The valuation analyst must analyze net revenue and operating expenses (Exhibit 25.24). The total net revenues for the hospital have increased 8 percent, from $105.8 million in 2007 to $114.5 million for 2008. The primary determinant of this revenue increase is a 7 percent increase in adjusted patient days from 70,700 to 75,336 days. The net revenue per adjusted patient day was relatively flat from year to year. Total expenses, as a percentage of net revenues, have

Exhibit 25.23 Paulie Hospital Gross Revenue Analysis (FYE 2008)

Code	Department	% of Revenue
707	Pharmacy	15.5%
701	Lab Services	10.4%
621	Surgical Services	9.5%
625	Central Services	8.3%
703	Cardiology	6.7%
623	Emergency Services	6.0%
617	Respiratory Services	5.2%
706	CT	5.1%
704	Radiology-Diagnostic	3.5%
612	ICU-CCU	3.2%
705	MRI	3.0%
	Total Displayed	76.5%
	Total Gross Revenue	100%

1162

Exhibit 25.24 Paulie Hospital Revenue and Expenses

	FYE 2007	FYE 2008	FYE 2007	FYE 2008
Total Net Operating Revenues	$105,843,828	$114,488,780	100%	100%
Adj. Patient Days (includes OP)	70,700	75,336	N/A	N/A
Net Revenue per Adj. Patient Day	1,497	1,520	N/A	N/A
Major Operating Expenses:				
Salaries	34,923,060	40,073,310	33.0%	35.0%
Contract Labor	2,951,846	4,312,173	2.8%	3.8%
Employee Benefits	6,245,180	6,645,852	5.9%	5.8%
Professional Fees	3,534,247	3,937,569	3.3%	3.4%
Purchased Services	4,473,889	5,986,923	4.2%	5.2%
Drugs	2,941,417	3,554,613	2.8%	3.1%
Supplies	9,930,106	10,891,296	9.4%	9.5%
Utilities	1,604,097	1,690,860	1.5%	1.5%
Other Operating Expenses	11,709,831	10,986,135	11.1%	9.6%
Bad Debts	13,898,947	13,448,703	13.1%	11.7%
Total	$ 92,212,620	$101,527,434	87.1%	88.7%

increased from 87 percent in 2007 to 89 percent as of 2008. This is primarily due to the increases in staffing costs over the same respective time frames.

Trend Analysis—Balance Sheet. Have total assets increased or decreased based on the historical information? Total liabilities? Total interest-bearing debt? Working capital? Does the net income as reported on the balance sheet equal the net income as reported on the income statement(s)? (See Exhibit 25.25.)

Analyst Conclusions.   The total asset base has increased from $118.0 million to $122.4 million for FYE 2007 to FYE 2008. The primary reason for the increase in the total asset base is due to investments.

Exhibit 25.25 Paulie Hospital Balance Sheet

	As of 12/31/07	As of 12/31/08
Total Current Assets	$ 39,126,085	$ 39,338,153
Net Assets, Limited as to Use	18,579,788	17,317,078
Net Property, Plant, and Equipment	50,155,773	50,530,326
Investments	6,314,859	12,191,622
Other Assets	3,838,604	3,046,641
Total Assets	118,015,109	122,423,820
Total Current Liabilities	10,154,491	11,882,748
Long-Term Debt	52,367,154	47,817,509
Total Liabilities	62,521,645	59,700,257
Net Assets	55,493,464	62,723,563
Total Liabilities & Restricted Assets	$118,015,109	$122,423,820

Total liabilities actually have decreased from $62.5 million to $59.7 million over the same time period. The decrease in total liabilities is due primarily to decreases in long-term debts.

> *Assets limited as to use* and *investments* are considered here "excess assets" and are added back to the resulting DCF value to arrive at the total value. "Assets limited as to use" refers to those assets earmarked for specific activities (i.e., related future capital expenditures, etc.). "Investments" refers to cash/marketable securities.

Normalized Base Year. The purpose of the normalized base year is to adjust the most recent income statement, or the ones MCVal utilizes, to reflect the hospital's true operational profile for the projection period. During the site visit, the analyst should discuss these adjustments with hospital management to understand their likelihood. In addition, any related interest expense also should be removed to calculate the entity's debt-free cash flow, the type of cash flow utilized here. In addition, an appropriate income tax rate, incorporating both state and federal taxes, should be calculated.

Some of the adjustments made to Paulie Hospital include ones for:

- *Bad Debts.* Bad debt expenses were adjusted to reflect the historical averages for the facility, per conversations with management.
- *Employee Benefits.* Payroll taxes and employee benefits were adjusted at 7.0 percent and 12.0 percent respectively, per industry norms. This is also based on conversations with management regarding future benefit offerings.
- *Interest Expense.* Interest expense was eliminated to derive debt-free cash flow.
- *Income Taxes.* A blended federal and state income tax rate was calculated.

DCF Assumptions. The assumptions related to the discounted cash flow model can be projected to arrive at a value. The analyst applies acquired knowledge of the operations from the previous steps to a five-year projection of cash flow typically prepared by, or in some cases with, management.

As mentioned previously, the hospital has experienced substantial growth over the past year (Exhibit 25.24); however, a new center, Lang Center, will soon be completed approximately one mile away from the hospital. According to management, it is likely the new surgery center will result in lost outpatient surgical cases.

Exhibit 25.26 illustrates a 3.7 percent increase in total net operating revenues, from $112.7 million in the normalized base year to $116.9 million in year 1 of the projection period. These projections are based on discussions with management based on the opening of the new surgery center. As a result, total outpatient cases decrease 5 and 3 percent respectively in years 1 and 2 and are flat in year 3 before reaching standard growth levels by year 4 of the projection period. The exhibit illustrates the projection period for years 1 to 3 of the projection.

Exhibit 25.26   Paulie Hospital Revenue Assumptions

	Normalized Base Year	Projections		
		Year 1	Year 2	Year 3
Inpatient Admissions	9,423	9,894	10,191	10,497
Annual Growth %		2.0%	2.0%	2.0%
Outpatient Days	25,137	23,880	23,164	23,164
Annual Growth %		-5.0%	-3.0%	0.0%
ALOS	5.33	5.33	5.33	5.33
Patient Days	50,199	52,709	54,290	55,919
Adjusted Patient Days (IP & OP)	75,336	76,589	77,454	79,083
Net Revenue Per Adj. Patient Day	$ 1,495.86	$ 1,525.77	$ 1,541.03	$ 1,556.44
Annual Growth %		1.0%	1.0%	1.0%
Net Operating Revenues Growth	$112,691,832	$116,857,615	$119,358,974	$123,087,550
Other Operating Revenue	1,796,949	1,796,949	1,796,949	1,796,949
Net Revenues	114,488,781	118,654,564	121,155,923	124,884,499

Inpatient Admissions. According to conversations with hospital management, inpatient admissions are expected to increase at approximately 2.0 percent into the near future. As a reasonableness check, this assumption is confirmed by analyzing current capacity levels (i.e. current occupancy rate) as well as demographic projections for the next three to five years. According to demographics, the population growth estimates for the local area are approximately 2 percent. As a result, the 2 percent inpatient admission growth rate does not seem unreasonable.

Outpatient Days. Total outpatient days for the hospital are expected to decrease in year 1 due to the opening of Lang Center in the immediate area. According to management, it is expected that approximately 5 percent of its outpatient surgical caseload will depart to this new center in the upcoming year. After year 1, outpatient days decrease 3 percent and remain flat in year 2 and 3, respectively. By year 4, management expects that the total outpatient caseload will increase by 2 percent thereafter.

Simply adding inpatient days plus outpatient cases would be erroneous since patients who are treated on an outpatient basis in the hospital are not measured in terms of days. As a result, the hospital applies an outpatient conversion factor to convert the outpatient cases into outpatient days. This is necessary to arrive at adjusted patient days, the term for measuring a hospital's occupancy rate and capacity.

An example of the conversion factor for adjusted patient days follows: The hypothetical calculation states that every outpatient case in the Hospital accounts for 75 percent or 0.75 of every inpatient day.

Total Outpatient Cases × Outpatient Conversion Factor =
Total Outpatient Days [33,516 × .75 = 25,137 Inpatient Days]

Adjusted Patient Days. Total patient days are the sum of inpatient days and the provided (computed) outpatient days. Adjusted patient days are the driving force behind a hospital's core value.

Average Length of Stay (ALOS). With increasing technologies and decreasing reimbursements, it is not uncommon for a hospital's ALOS to decrease or, more conservatively, remain flat. Such is the case with Paulie. According to conversations with management, ALOS has been projected to be flat in the projection period.

Net Revenue per Adjusted Patient Day. This is calculated by dividing the hospital's net operating revenues by the adjusted patient day total provided by management. This calculation, coupled with adjusted patient days, drives the value under the discounted cash flow methodology.

DCF Analysis. After all of these steps have been performed, the final value created is the Total Invested Capital (total equity + interest-bearing debt). Depending on the deal, the related interest-bearing debt may/may not need to be removed from the total invested capital value indication.

Discount Rate [Illustration Only]. The discount rate is often the most contested part of the income approach (Chapter 6). The weighted average cost of capital is a highly regarded method for estimating an appropriate discount rate, although the direct equity method can be used as well. Two factors must be considered in estimating the present value of any projected cash flow stream:

1. *Financial Risk.* The risk inherent in an entity's financial structure (i.e., the utilization of debt versus equity financing)
2. *Business Risk.* The uncertainty associated with the economy, industry, and the inherent risk profile of the subject entity

The discount rate utilized for a hospital must appropriately encapsulate the risks associated with that hospital. Some of the risks associated with Paulie include:

- *New surgery center.* As management indicated, a new free-standing ambulatory surgery center, Lang Center (the ASC), will be completed within the next calendar year. Management has also indicated that the new ASC has already started to recruit surgeons from the hospital pool. As a result, the analyst should assume that some of the current case volumes will depart to the ASC and the discount rate and/or projections should incorporate this inherent risk.
- *Nature of business.* The hospital is heavily reliant upon the individual surgeons at the facility. External forces, such as the development of other new centers, can tempt these surgeons to perform their cases elsewhere. As a result, the discount rate should incorporate some factor to mitigate the risks associated with the business.

In estimating the WACC, we relied on the following formula:

$$WACC = (Ke \times We) + (Kd(pt) \times [1 - t] \times Wd)$$

Where:

WACC = Weighted average cost of capital

Ke   = Company's cost of common equity capital

Kd(pt) = Company's cost of debt capital (pre tax)

We   = Percentage of equity capital in the capital structure

Wd   = Percentage of debt capital in the capital structure

t   = Tax rate

The equity portion of the WACC was calculated by using the Build Up model. The basic formula is as follows:

$$Ke = Rf + RPm + RPs + Rpu$$

Where:

Ke   = Expected rate of return on the subject security

Rf   = Rate of return on a risk free security

RPm   = Risk premium associated with the market

RPs   = Risk premium associated with a small company

RPu   = Risk premium associated with Paulie

The risk-free rate used in the calculation came from the yield of 20-year Treasury bonds as of the valuation date. The long-term market equity risk premium and the small stock premium were reported in the *2009 Valuation Yearbook—Market Results for Stocks, Bonds, Bills, and Inflation 1926–2008*, published by Morningstar. *Note:* Many analysts are now relying on Duff & Phelps risk premium data. See Chapter 6. A risk premium of 2 percent was added for Paulie due to increased competition which many other hospitals are also experiencing.

The equity component of the WACC is as follows:

Ke = 3.8% + 7.1% + 5.82% + 3.0%

Ke = 19.72%

The capital structure is based on an industry standard which is 25 percent debt and 75 percent equity. The cost of debt is based upon available financing terms and was 7 percent.

The WACC is as follows:

WACC = (19.72%) (.75) + [7% (1−.40) (.25)]

WACC = 15.8%

Based on the procedures described above, a WACC of 16 percent was applied to the cash flows.

Value Indication

The value indication is shown in Exhibit 25.27.

Value indications should incorporate the related excess assets, if applicable. Failure to recognize these assets would result in an erroneous value indication. However, in this case the valuation has been performed exclusive of excess assets. As a result, the fair market value indication at the enterprise or total invested capital level based on the DCF is approximately $77 million.

Market Approach: Guideline Public Company Method

The guideline public company method relies on similar publicly traded companies as a source of market multiples. Market multiples include:

- Invested capital/sales
- Invested capital/EBITDA
- Invested capital/EBIT
- Price/net income

In the healthcare services market, publicly traded companies typically trade on very different financial dynamics from individual businesses. MCVal has found seven publicly traded hospital companies to evaluate.

These companies had total revenues ranging from $200 million to $24 billion, which substantially exceeds the net revenues for Paulie. Typically, hospital companies trade based on their ability to grow earnings and cash flow in their business (as most companies are valued). However, public hospital companies make use of their more accessible capital to grow by acquisition in addition to same-facility growth. Historically, the for-profit or proprietary hospital market has acted as a consolidator of a very large and very fragmented business. As a result, hospital companies tend to trade at multiples that reflect that acquisition growth. Publicly traded hospitals have traded at invested capital to EBITDA multiples above 9. As a result of acquisition growth opportunities, size diversification, geographic diversification, and the overall lack of comparability with the subject hospital, the guideline public company method of the market approach has not been utilized in the valuation of Paulie Hospital.

Market Approach: Guideline Company Transaction Method

The guideline company transaction method includes pricing multiplies from individual transactions of similar companies in the marketplace. Information is developed through various sources, such as Irvin Levin and Associates, *Pratt's Stats*, and

Exhibit 25.27 Paulie Hospital: Invested Capital Value

	Normalized Base Year	Year 1	Year 2	Year 3	Year 4	Year 5	Terminal
Net Income	3,942,119	5,677,070	5,885,506	6,268,380	6,782,215	7,331,443	10,699,192*
Cash Flow Adjustments:							
Plus: Depreciation		5,353,033	5,653,033	5,953,033	6,253,033	6,553,033	1,500,000
Less: Incremental Working Capital		(596,273)	(250,136)	(372,858)	(459,629)	(477,053)	(402,754)
Less: Capital Expenditures		(1,500,000)	(1,500,000)	(1,500,000)	(1,500,000)	(1,500,000)	(1,500,000)
Net Discretionary Cash Flow		8,933,829	9,788,403	10,348,555	11,075,618	11,907,423	10,296,438
Terminal Value (Gordon Growth)							79,203,369
		0.50	1.50	2.50	3.50	4.50	4.50
Present Value Factor		0.9285	0.8004	0.6900	0.5948	0.5128	0.5128
Present Value of Cash Flows		8,295,060	7,834,745	7,140,600	6,588,173	6,106,000	40,615,488

Sum of Present Values (Years 1–5)	$35,964,371
Present Value of Terminal (Gordon Growth)	$40,615,488
Total Present Value of Cash Flows	$76,579,859

5.2 × Yr 1 EBITDA

*Excess depreciation runs out (normalized income).

Mergerstat Review. The data are then applied, where appropriate, to the subject company. (See Exhibit 25.28.)

Exhibit 25.28   Paulie Hospital: Company Transactions

Transaction Scenarios	(Rounded)	Transaction Multiples		Value Indication (TIC)	
		High	Low	High	Low
Normalized Revenue	$114,000,000	1.5	0.5	$171,000,000	$57,000,000
Normalized EBITDA	$ 13,000,000	8.0	5.0	$104,000,000	$65,000,000

Ten hospital transactions were utilized in the analysis. In each of the 10 transactions, the actual purchase terms were not included; actual historical financial statements of the targets were also unavailable. The result is that the information reflects a purchase price in which there is no way to accurately determine assets included or excluded in the transaction. For example, was working capital part of the deal? Many transactions exclude working capital.

In addition, there is no way to:

- Determine the impact of special terms in the transactions including the form of consideration paid for the deal
- Accurately perform any financial analysis of the target hospital
- Determine overall profitability, payer mix, services provided by the target hospital or the trends in those areas over the last three to four years

Facts and circumstances surrounding an individual hospital facility are typically disparate. Payers in various parts of the country reimburse for services at different levels. Staffing costs in various parts of the country are different as are many other operating costs. As a result, there is less reliability of the results of the market transactions. Based on many years of research and close relationships with buyers and sellers, MCVal understands the basic range of valuation multiples that are typically paid for hospitals. As a result, the guideline company transaction method is utilized in the valuation. However, it is given less consideration and used only as a sanity check.

Asset Approach

The asset approach is based on the principle of substitution, where it is assumed that a buyer will not pay more for a particular investment than the costs to obtain an investment of equal worth. In most cases, the asset approach assumes that the business will no longer be fully operational or is not considered a going-concern business. Hence, we have encountered the following difficulties upon considering the asset approach to value Paulie Hospital. It does not consider the identifiable intangible assets and unidentifiable intangible assets of the business—goodwill, without considerable effort and time.

The net book value of Paulie Hospital prior to subtraction of debt, excluding assets limited as to use, and marketable securities, was approximately $71.7 million. This compares with the $76.6 million under the income approach to value. To provide a measure of accuracy to the asset approach, third-party equipment and real estate appraisers were engaged. The results of that analysis indicated that book value was 5 percent higher than the value of all assets of the facility as determined by the appraisers.

Based on the cost approach to value, the fair market value of Paulie Hospital excluding assets limited to use, cash, and marketable securities was approximately $68 million.

Reconciliation

While we have considered each of the three approaches to value, we have relied primarily on the income approach and, more particularly, the DCF method. Based on the facts, circumstances, and limiting conditions of the engagement, the fair market value of Paulie Hospital, as of March 15, 2009, is $77 million (rounded). This excludes the related excess assets and interest-bearing debt. This value is also within the range of the guideline transactions method results and includes $9 million of goodwill over the net asset value, which seems reasonable in this valuation.

CHAPTER 26

Special Industry Valuations

A: CONSTRUCTION

Introduction

Construction contractors range from small, sole proprietorships to large, publicly traded, multibillion-dollar corporations. However, the vast majority are small entities. According to the Bureau of Labor Statistics, about 80 percent of construction companies employ fewer than ten people.[1] IRS statistics indicate that approximately 75 percent of construction contractors are sole proprietorships, approximately 5 percent are partnerships, and approximately 20 percent are corporations.[2]

> The U.S. market for construction contractors is approximately $500 billion. About 6,000 firms have revenues exceeding $10 million, just over 100 firms have revenues exceeding $500 million, and only a handful of firms have revenues in the billions of dollars.

Types of Contractors

Construction contractors are generally separated into two categories: general contractors and subcontractors. General contractors are engaged by property owners and developers to coordinate and oversee construction projects. They hire subcontractors to perform the specialized tasks required for the project. More and more general contractors are engaging in design/build and construction management services. Design/build services are when the construction contractor not only coordinates the construction process but also oversees the design of the structures to be built. Construction management is the oversight of all aspects of a construction process, which may include site selection and acquisition, required zoning changes, architecture, engineering, and construction. The idea behind construction management services is to provide a turnkey product to the client.

---

[1] "Industry at a Glance, Construction," Bureau of Labor Statistics, www.bls.gov/oco/cg/cgs003. htm.
[2] "Business Tax Statistics," Internal Revenue Service, www.irs.gov/taxstats/bustaxstats/index.html.

Subcontractors perform specialized tasks including concrete, framers, roofers, plumbers, electricians, HVAC, drywall and plastering, finish carpenters, painters, carpet layers, landscapers, and others.

The wide spectrum of tasks performed by construction contractors makes the industry highly diverse. This diversity can be seen in the number of SIC and NAICS codes established for construction contractors. These codes are listed in Exhibit 26.1.

Exhibit 26.1   NAICS and SIC Codes

Description	NAICS	SIC
Single Family Housing Construction	233210	1521, 1531
Multifamily Housing Construction	233220	1522, 1531
Manufacturing and Industrial Building Construction	233310	1531, 1541
Commercial and Institutional Building Construction	233320	1522,1531,1541
Highway and Street Construction	234110	1611
Bridge and Tunnel Construction	234120	1622
Water, Sewer, and Pipeline Construction	234910	1623
Power and Communication Transmission		
Line Construction	234920	1623
Industrial Non-Building Structure Construction	234930	1629
All Other Heavy Construction	234990	1629
Plumbing, Heating, and Air-Conditioning Contractors	235110	1711
Painting and Wall Covering Contractors	235210	1721
Electrical Contractors	235310	1731
Masonry and Stone Contractors	235410	1741
Drywall, Plastering, Acoustical,		
and Insulation Contractors	235420	1742
Tile, Marble, Terrazzo, and Mosaic Contractors	235430	1743
Carpentry Contractors	235510	1751
Floor Laying and Other Floor Contractors	235520	1752
Roofing, Siding, and Sheet Metal Contractors	235610	1761
Concrete Contractors	235710	1771
Water Well Drilling Contractors	235810	1781
Structural Steel Erection Contractors	235910	1791
Glass and Glazing Contractors	235920	1793,1799
Excavation Contractors	235930	1794
Wrecking and Demolition Contractors	235940	1795
Building Equipment and Other Machinery		
Installation Contractors	235950	1796
All Other Special Trade Contractors	235990	1799

Construction contractors can engage in several different types of contracts that differ in the manner in which the contactor is compensated and the level of risk assumed. These contracts include fixed-price contracts, time-and-materials contracts, and unit-price contracts.

Types of Contracts

Under a fixed-price contract, sometimes called a lump-sum contract, a contractor is paid a predetermined price to complete a project. The contractor assumes the risk of completing the contract in a profitable manner.

Under a time-and-materials contract, sometimes called a cost-plus contract, the contractor is reimbursed for time and materials and is paid a fixed gross profit amount. This type of contract minimizes the risk of financial loss to the contractor.

Under a unit-price contract, the contractor receives a fixed amount for each unit installed or constructed (linear feet of sidewalk and curbing, cubit feet of concrete or excavation, etc.). This type of contract can mitigate some of the risk to the contractor.

Accounting Issues

The most significant accounting issue for construction contractors is the method of accounting for long-term contracts.

> The three most common methods of accounting are the cash-basis method, the completed-contract method, and the percentage-of-completion method.

Cash-Basis Method

Many construction contractors are small businesses. Like all small businesses, use of cash-basis accounting is common. Under cash-basis accounting, earnings are recognized when cash is received from customers, and expenses are recognized when cash is paid to vendors.

Completed-Contract Method

Under the completed-contract method, revenues and related costs are recognized in the period in which the contract is completed. General and administrative expenses not allocated to a particular project are recognized as incurred. This method can be useful for contractors who have projects lasting less than a year.

Percentage-of-Completion Method

Under the percentage-of-completion method, revenues and costs of each project are tracked separately. The actual costs incurred are compared to the estimated cost to develop a percentage of completion, which is then applied to the total contracted revenues to determine the amount of revenue to recognize. This method is useful for construction contractors who engage in projects that span a year or more. The following example demonstrates how this is done.

Example

Assume an $800,000 project is expected to span three reporting periods. The estimated total cost is $600,000, with an estimated gross profit of 25 percent. During the first year, $120,000 in costs was incurred. The computation of the amount of revenue to be recorded in the first year is as follows:

Total Cost Incurred	$120,000
Divided by Total Estimated Costs	600,000
Equals Percent Complete	20%
Multiplied by Total Contract Revenue	800,000
Revenue Earned	$160,000

The amount of revenue recognized in the first year would be $160,000. The gross profit on the project in the first year would be $40,000 ($160,000 earned revenue less $120,000 cost incurred).

During the second year, an additional $460,000 in costs was *incurred*. The computation of how much revenue is recognized in the second year is as follows:

Costs Incurred:	
First Year	120,000
Second Year	460,000
Costs Incurred since Inception	580,000
Divided by Total Estimated Costs	600,000
Equals Percent Complete	97%
Multiplied by Total Contract Revenue	800,000
Revenue Earned since Inception	776,000
Less Revenue Recognized in Year 1	(160,000)
Revenue Recognized in Year 2	$616,000

The amount of revenue recognized in the second year would be $616,000. The gross profit in the second year would be $156,000 ($616,000 earned revenue less $460,000 cost incurred).

In order to make the example more true to life, we modify some of the assumptions for year 2. We will assume that change orders were approved, increasing the contract amount by $100,000 to $900,000. The total estimated cost increased by $165,000 to $765,000. Based on these amounts, the estimated gross profit decreases to 15 percent. Under these new assumptions, the computation of the amount of revenue to recognize in the second year is as follows:

Costs Incurred:	
First Year	$120,000
Second Year	460,000
Costs Incurred from Inception	580,000
Divided by Total Estimated Costs	765,000
Equals Percent Complete	76%
Multiplied by Total Contract Revenue	900,000

Revenue Earned from Inception	684,000
Less Revenue Recognized in Year 1	(160,000)
Revenue Recognized in Year 2	$524,000

To continue the example, we assume that the project was completed in the third year. We will also assume that the cost for the third year totaled $140,000, bringing the total cost of the project to $720,000. At this point we recognize any amount remaining on the total contract amount not previously recognized as revenue. The computation of the revenue to be recognized in the third year and the total gross profit percentage for the project are as follows:

Total Contract Amount	$900,000
Less Revenue Recognized Previously	(684,000)
Revenue to be Recognized in Year 3	$216,000

Total Contract Amount	$900,000
Less Actual Costs	720,000
Gross Profit	$180,000
Gross Profit Percentage	20%

From this example, we see that the total gross profit for the project as a whole was $180,000, and the total gross profit percentage was 20 percent.

Underbillings and Overbillings

The amount a contractor bills to a client rarely matches the amount that should be recognized based on the percentage-of-completion method. This disparity happens because billing cycles do not always match the reporting periods, the process of getting a change order approved may delay the change order getting billed, and billing policies may be more or less aggressive than is needed to match the percentage-of-completion method. These disparities are called *costs and estimated earnings in excess of billings* (or commonly, underbillings) and *billings in excess of costs and estimated earnings* (or commonly, overbillings). Underbillings are presented on the balance sheet as a current asset, and overbillings are presented on the balance sheet as a current liability.

An example of the balance sheet presentation of underbillings is shown in Exhibit 26.2. An example of the balance sheet presentation of overbillings is shown in Exhibit 26.3.

Retention

Another accounting issue for construction contractors is retentions. Retentions are amounts held back, or *retained* by the customer from each billing until completion of the project. In the case of a general contractor, the owner of a project will hold back retention from the general contractor. In the case of a subcontractor, the general contractor will hold back retention from the subcontractors.

An example of balance sheet presentation of retentions is shown in Exhibit 26.4.

The amount of retention is typically between 5 percent and 10 percent of each billing. Once a project is complete to the satisfaction of the customer, the retention will be released. The purpose of the retention is to provide an incentive to the contractor to complete a project to the satisfaction of the customer.

Exhibit 26.2   Granite Construction Incorporated Consolidated Balance Sheets (Underbillings)

	December 31,	
	2008	**2009**
	(In thousands, except share and per-share data)	
ASSETS		
Current Assets		
Cash and cash equivalents	$ 69,919	$ 52,032
Short-term marketable securities	90,869	96,900
Accounts receivable, net	288,210	265,896
Costs and estimated earnings in excess of billings	**31,189**	**42,966**
Inventories	29,878	29,984
Deferred income taxes	22,421	23,056
Equity in construction joint ventures	42,250	24,329
Other current assets	43,915	12,732
Total current assets	$618,651	$547,895

Exhibit 26.3   Granite Construction Incorporated Consolidated Balance Sheets (Overbillings)

	December 31,	
	2008	**2009**
	(In thousands, except share and per-share data)	
LIABILITIES AND STOCKHOLDERS' EQUITY		
Current Liabilities		
Current maturities of long-term debt	$ 8,182	$ 8,640
Accounts payable	135,468	118,813
Billings in excess of costs and estimated earnings	**99,337**	**105,725**
Accrued expenses and other current liabilities	105,717	94,321
Total current liabilities	$248,704	$327,499

Job Schedule

The financial statements of a privately held construction contractor will typically include a *job schedule*. Publicly traded construction contractors typically will not include a job schedule with the financial statements. The job schedule is a listing of projects that the contractor completed during the reporting period and a list of the

Exhibit 26.4 Rock Corporation Consolidated Balance Sheets (Retentions)

	December 31, 2008	2009
	(In thousands, except share data)	
Assets		
Current Assets		
Cash, including cash equivalents of $60,462 and $30,042 (Note 1)	$ 67,823	$ 47,031
Accounts receivable, including retainage of $86,273 and $66,284	328,025	218,172
Unbilled work (Note 1)	116,572	112,563
Deferred tax asset (Note 5)	10,844	—
Other current assets	2,479	4,165
Total current assets	$525,743	$381,931
(Share and per-share data)		
Liabilities And Stockholders' Equity		
Current Liabilities		
Current maturities of long-term debt	$ 8,182	$ 8,640
Accounts payable	135,468	118,813
Billings in excess of costs and estimated earnings	99,337	105,725
Accrued expenses and other current liabilities	105,717	94,321
Total current liabilities	$248,704	$327,499

ValTip

> Recomputing the job schedule using historical gross profits can be a useful analysis tool in assessing the accuracy of current job estimates.

projects that the contractor has in progress during the reporting period. Exhibits 26.5 and 26.6 are examples of job schedules.

The Current Jobs in Progress section of the job schedule lists the projects that a contractor has started but remain uncompleted. The reserve of uncompleted projects is called *backlog*. Backlog includes not only uncompleted projects but also projects not yet started.

Income Tax Issues

Completed-Contract Method

The completed-contract method may be used for tax purposes but only under a limited set of circumstances (see Reg. 1.451-3[d][5]).

Look-Back Method for Percentage of Completion

The tax code requires those using the percentage-of-completion method to recompute the prior year's taxes based on actual costs if the contractor estimates of costs

Exhibit 26.5 Completed Contracts (for Year Ended December 31, 2009)

	Contract Totals			Before January 1, 2009			During the Year Ended December 31, 2009		
	Revenues Earned	Cost of Revenues	Gross Profit	Revenues Earned	Cost of Revenues	Gross Profit	Revenues Earned	Cost of Revenues	Gross Profit
Job 1	$2,156,626	$2,061,360	$ 95,266	$1,607,243	$1,539,859	$ 67,384	$ 549,383	$ 521,501	$ 27,882
Job 2	1,935,425	1,806,768	128,657	1,907,341	1,780,200	127,141	28,084	26,568	1,516
Job 3	1,053,897	967,478	86,419	526,640	489,291	37,349	527,257	478,187	49,070
Job 4	587,023	619,906	(32,883)	—	—	—	587,023	619,906	(32,883)
Job 5	353,707	277,313	75,894	—	—	—	353,707	277,813	75,894
Total Completed Contracts	**$6,086,678**	**$5,733,325**	**$353,353**	**$4,041,224**	**$3,809,350**	**$231,874**	**$2,045,454**	**$1,923,975**	**$121,479**

Exhibit 26.6 Contracts in Progress (for Year Ended December 31, 2009)

	Total Contract		From Inception to December 31, 2009					Before January 1, 2009			Year Ended December 31, 2009			At December 31, 2009		Percent Complete
	Revenues	Estimated Gross Profit	Contract Revenues Earned	Cost of Revenues Earned	Gross Profit	Billed to Date	Estimated Cost to Complete	Contract Revenues Earned	Cost of Revenues Earned	Gross Profit	Contract Revenues Earned	Cost of Revenues Earned	Gross Profits	Costs and Estimated Earnings in Excess of Billings	Billings in Excess of Costs and Estimated Earnings	
Job 6	$ 500,568	$ 51,622	$495,793	$444,663	$ 51,130	$500,568	$ 4,283	$—	$—	$—	$495,793	$444,663	$ 51,130	$ —	$ 4,775	99.0%
Job 7	899,116	224,779	159,472	119,604	39,868	145,102	554,733	—	—	—	159,472	119,604	39,868	14,370	—	17.7%
Job 8	606,450	40,000	37,011	34,570	2,441	37,528	531,880	—	—	—	37,011	34,570	2,441	—	517	6.1%
Job 9	317,115	66,403	212,070	167,663	44,407	220,590	83,049	—	—	—	212,070	167,663	44,407	—	8,520	66.9%
Total Contracts in Progress	**$2,323,249**	**$382,804**	**$904,346**	**$766,500**	**$137,846**	**$903,788**	**$1,173,945**	**$—**	**$—**	**$—**	**$904,346**	**$766,500**	**$137,846**	**$14,370**	**$13,812**	

were incorrect. A contractor may elect out of the look-back rule if the tax using estimated cost is within 10 percent of the tax using the actual costs. This rule does not apply to small contractors whose average annual gross receipts for the three tax years does not exceed $10 million or for contracts that are expected to be completed within two years.

Homebuilders

For income tax purposes, homebuilders treat their spec homes as inventory. Homebuilders are also subject to the uniform capitalization rules. However, "small" contractors are exempt. Homebuilders are prevented from using the percentage-of-completion method under the tax code.

Types of Assets

Equipment

The types of assets held by construction contractors can vary widely. Those in the heavy construction trades, such as excavating, highway construction, bridge building, and others, require significant capital investment in heavy equipment. This equipment, such as earthmoving equipment, cranes, concrete pumpers, and the like, is expensive to purchase and maintain.

Others, like many general contractors, can operate with minimal amounts of heavy equipment. If they have a temporary need for some of the more common types of equipment, such as backhoes, they can avoid making a capital expenditure by renting such equipment.

Goodwill

Many construction contractors have little, if any, goodwill value. This stems from the low margins that result from the competitive bidding process. Those with goodwill tend to have more negotiated contracts and may have a good reputation or good relationship with customers.

Nonoperating Assets

Construction contractors frequently maintain levels of working capital and debt capacity that would be considered in excess of operating needs in other industries. Excess working capital and excess debt capacity enhance the amount of bonding credit a contractor can secure, and the more bonding credit a contractor can secure, the more the contractor's business can grow. Accordingly, excess working capital and excess debt capacity need to be evaluated in light of a construction contractor's bonding credit needs.

Valuation Approaches and Methods

Cost Approach

The competitive bidding environment drives profit margins down to the point that values are frequently near net asset value. Contractors, particularly smaller ones, are often sold at or near book value because barriers to entry are minimal, causing many to start their own business rather than purchase an existing contractor.

Market Approach

Publicly Traded Guideline Companies
Most publicly traded construction companies are diversified, offering engineering and other products and services. Most of the publicly traded homebuilders also offer mortgage services. A list of publicly traded companies and homebuilders can be found at Yahoo! Finance's Industry Center.

Private Transactions
The private transaction databases also contain information on construction contractors. These databases are difficult to use to actually derive a value because they provide only limited information. Additionally, the valuation analyst often cannot determine how comparable the transactions are because the motivations of the buyer and the seller are not known, and those providing the information to the databases may not report the data correctly.

Income Approach

Discounted Future Cash Flow
One advantage to using the discounted future cash flow method with construction contractors who use the percentage-of-completions method is that cash-flow forecasts and estimating accuracy can be checked by:

- Comparing individual completed projects to prior period job schedules to determine how accurate the estimating has been historically
- Analyzing backlog (both projects in process and projects not yet started) to determine viability of forecasts

Capitalized Cash Flow
The capitalized cash-flow method assumes that growth will be constant into the future. A contractor's level of backlog can help the valuation professional support or dispute the constant growth assumption of the capitalized cash-flow method.

Major Risk Issues

There are many risks inherent in the construction industry. These risks include:

- *Cyclical industry.* The construction industry is cyclical. Demand for construction services is highly dependent on the health of the economy and can be affected by many outside forces such as interest rates, governmental spending, and corporate growth.

- *Losses from projects.* Construction contractors can experience losses from issues out of their control, such as weather delays, poor workmanship of a sub-contractor, or unforeseen difficulties during the construction process. Profit margins are so thin that losses from a single job can cause an entire construction company to be unprofitable and can even lead to bankruptcy.
- *Personnel.* Many construction contractors rely on highly skilled craftspeople such as estimators, heavy equipment operators, plumbers, and electricians. A contractor's profitability and quality of work relates directly to such employees. Contractors also use unskilled workers. Undocumented immigrants may be an area of potential liability for contractors. Contractors who hire illegal immigrants risk fines and other penalties, while others may unwittingly hire illegal immigrants who present false identification.
- *Employee safety.* The construction industry has the largest share of fatalities of any industry. Contractors can face significant liability in the event of the injury or death of an employee.
- *Insurance costs.* The inherent risks in the construction industry cause contractors to pay higher premiums for all types of insurance. The areas that cause most concern are construction defects, inexperienced employees, and poor bookkeeping.
- *Supplies and materials.* Materials used in construction are either commodities or near commodities, such as lumber products, steel, concrete, wall board, and so on. Fuel prices can also have significant impact on construction contractors, especially those who operate heavy equipment. Fluctuations in commodity prices can make estimating costs difficult and can impact profitability.

Operational and Industry Issues

Estimating

Estimators compute the contractor's cost of completing a project. If the estimates are too high, the contractors' bids will be too high and they will not secure new projects. If the estimates are too low, it could lead to financial losses. Accuracy in estimating is vital to the success of a contractor, and a good estimating staff can be invaluable.

Some of the common errors in construction cost estimating are:

- Arithmetic errors
- Incorrect measurement
- Incorrect labor rates
- Incorrect pricing of materials
- Not performing a site visit
- Overlooking haulage costs
- Failure to review building codes
- Omitting items considered minor
- Failure to carefully review bids of subcontractors
- Inadequate consideration of overhead charges

Bonding

A surety bond is a guarantee to the owner of a project on the performance of the contractor. Project owners typically require the contractor to have a surety bond. Contractors purchase surety bonds from a surety company, and the bond covers the projects the contractor builds.

> There are three types of surety bonds, as follows:
>
> *Bid bond.* Provides a financial guarantee that the bid has been submitted in good faith and that the bidder intends on entering into the contract at the bid price.
>
> *Performance bond.* Protects the owner of a project from financial losses if the contractor should fail to perform under the contract.
>
> *Payment bond.* Guarantees that the contractor will pay subcontractors.

The amount of bonding credit extended is a multiple of working capital and/or net worth, usually 5 to 20 times. The premium on the surety bond is approximately 1 percent to 1.5 percent of total contract revenue. Because the surety relies on a contractor's financial statements in determining the amout of bonding credit to extend, the contractor is often required to provide reviewed or audited financial statements. To determine working capital and net worth, surety agents, in general, look at the balance sheet as follows (Exhibit 26.7):

Exhibit 26.7 Balance Sheet Assessment

Balance Sheet Item	Included in Working Capital?	Included in Net Worth?
Assets:		
Cash	Included in full	Allowed in full
Marketable Securities	Included in full	Allowed in full
A/R	Under 90 days included	Over 90 days considered
Retention	Included	Allowed
Underbillings	Included	Included
Inventory	Included 50% to 80%	Allowed 50% to 80%
Prepaid expenses	Not included	Allowcd
Cash value of life insurance	Included	Allowed
Fixed assets	Not included	Allowed per books
Shareholder receivable	Not included	Not allowed
Goodwill	Not included	Not allowed
Intangible assets		
Liabilities:		
Liabilities	Generally as booked	Generally as booked
Overbillings	Included	Included

Even though overbillings are a liability, they are generally looked upon favorably by the surety. Overbillings indicate that the contractor is aggressive in his or her billing policies and that the project owner is "financing" the project, not the contractor. However, going into *job borrow* is viewed unfavorably. Job borrow is when overbillings exceed the estimated gross profit on a project.

A reduction in the amount of bonding credit can have a devastating financial effect on a contractor. In order to maximize the amount of bonding credit, contractors tend to have high current ratios and low levels of debt.

Competitive Bidding

Most contractors secure work through the competitive bidding process. A project owner invites construction contractors to bid on a project then awards the project to the contractor with the best bid. Sometimes the lowest bid is not always the best bid, but the amount of the bid is always an important factor. This process can be a two-edged sword for the contractor. Bids must be low enough to be attractive to the project owner, but high enough to complete the project in a profitable fashion.

Valuation Nuances

- Underbillings and overbillings are included in working capital for valuation purposes.
- If an analyst is using historical cash flows to arrive at a value for a construction contractor, no adjustment needs to be made based on the look-back method. The adjustments based on the look-back method would change not only the amount of revenue to recognize, but also the underbillings and overbillings. The change in revenue and the changes in underbillings and overbillings would offset, and the resulting cash flows would remain the same.
- Excess assets and excess debt capacity may be needed to maintain bonding credit amounts.
- Estimated future growth rates need to be considered in light of bonding credit levels and the company's ability to increase those levels.

RULES OF THUMB

General rules of thumb:

- Book value
- Book value plus a multiple of backlog
- 10 to 30 percent of annual revenues
- 2 to 3.5 times cash flows

General contractors would tend to be on the low end. Specialty contractors would tend to be on the high end. Variations based on region, name recognition, financial strength, and other reasons can occur.

These rules of thumb are provided as a very general benchmark from which reasonableness *may* be assessed. The facts and circumstances of each individual company should be considered in determining the value of that particular company.

Information Sources

Trade Associations

CFMA (Construction Financial Management Association)
Associated General Contractors of America (AGC)
Associated Builders and Contractors (ABC)
Construction Management Association of America (CMMA)
National Association of Women in Construction (NAWIC)
Women Contractors Association
National Association of Homebuilders

Industry News and Information

Zweig White, www.zweigwhite.com
Valuation Survey of Construction Companies
Merger & Acquisition Survey of Design & Construction Firms
McGraw-Hill
Engineering News Record, www.enr.com
McGraw-Hill Construction, www.construction.com
F.W. Dodge Report, fwdodge.construction.com

B: RADIO

Introduction

Radio stations are a part of the broadcasting industry. Individual stations either create their own programs or purchase the rights to broadcast radio programs produced by others. Stations typically broadcast a number of different programs, including:

- Local talk shows
- Syndicated talk shows
- National news
- Local news
- Music programs
- Sports programs

As indicated earlier, stations internally produce some of their programming. This programming would include local news programs and some music programs. Much of the programming, however, is produced outside of the station by other companies in the broadcasting industry.

Commercial radio station revenue is generated largely from the sale of advertising time. A particular station's advertising rates are dictated by the demographics of the station's listening audience, including gender, age, and average income. Radio stations that are owned and/or managed by religious organizations, educational systems, or public broadcasting entities generate their revenue primarily from various donations.

Radio broadcasting is subject to the jurisdiction of the Federal Communications Commission under the Communications Act of 1934. The Communications Act prohibits the operation of a radio or television broadcasting station except under a license issued by the FCC and empowers the FCC, among other things, to:

- Issue, renew, revoke, and modify broadcasting licenses
- Assign frequency bands
- Determine stations' frequencies, locations, and power
- Regulate the equipment used by stations
- Adopt other regulations to carry out the provisions of the Communications Act
- Impose penalties for violation of such regulations
- Impose fees for processing applications and other administrative functions

> The Communications Act prohibits the assignment of a license or the transfer of control of a licensee without prior approval of the FCC.

Regulation

Radio broadcasting is regulated by the federal government under the doctrine that the airwaves belong to the public. The first set of regulations was the Communications Act of 1934, referred to previously. Federal laws also regulate the broadcast of indecent and obscene content and impose monetary penalties for violations of these regulations.

Over the past decade, the FCC has significantly reduced its regulation of broadcast stations, including elimination of formal ascertainment requirements and guidelines concerning amounts of certain types of programming and commercial matter that may be broadcast; however, there are still statutes, rules, and policies of the FCC and other federal agencies that regulate matters such as network-affiliate relations, the ability of stations to obtain exclusive rights to air syndicated programming, cable and satellite systems' carriage of syndicated and network programming on distant stations, political advertising practices, obscenity and indecency in broadcast programming, application procedures, and other areas affecting the business or operations of broadcast stations.

The Telecommunications Act of 1996 brought about a comprehensive overhaul of the country's telecommunications laws. The 1996 act changed both the process for renewal of broadcast station licenses and the broadcast ownership rules. The 1996 act established a two-step renewal process that limited the FCC's discretion to consider applications filed in competition with an incumbent's renewal application. The 1996 act also liberalized the national broadcast ownership rules, eliminating the national radio limits.

The 1996 act mandated significant revisions to radio ownership rules. With respect to radio licensees, the 1996 act directed the FCC to eliminate the national ownership restriction, allowing one entity to own nationally any number of AM or FM broadcast stations. Other FCC rules mandated by the 1996 act greatly eased local radio ownership restrictions.

The maximum allowable number of radio stations that may be commonly owned in a market varies depending on the total number of radio stations in that market, as determined using a method prescribed by the FCC. In markets with 45 or more stations, one company may own, operate, or control 8 stations, with no more than 5 in any one service (AM or FM). In markets with 30 to 44 stations, one company may own 7 stations, with no more than 4 in any one service. In markets with 15 to 29 stations, one entity may own 6 stations, with no more than 4 in any one service. In markets with 14 stations or less, one company may own up to 5 stations or 50 percent of all of the stations, whichever is less, with no more than 3 in any one service.

These new rules permit common ownership of more stations in the same market than did the FCC's prior rules, which at most allowed ownership of no more than two AM stations and two FM stations, even in the largest markets.

The result of the relaxed ownership regulations is that individual broadcast stations have been consolidated into large networks. It is important to note that Congress and the FCC from time to time consider, and may in the future adopt, new laws, regulations, and policies regarding a wide variety of other matters that could affect, directly or indirectly, the operation, ownership, and valuation of radio stations.

State of the Industry

The radio broadcasting industry has been in a state of consolidation and is concentrated, with the top four companies earning approximately 45 percent of total industry revenues. Large media groups that own many stations have the advantages of consolidated back office administration, better negotiating positions with advertisers, and dominant presence if they control a large number of stations in a particular market. Smaller operators can effectively compete with specialized programming or by broadcasting syndicated programs that attract large audiences. The primary barriers to entry are securing a broadcast license from the FCC, which is a low hurdle to overcome, and capital to purchase the necessary transmission equipment. Substitutes include other forms of broadcast media and entertainment, including Internet sites, but the most significant substitute is subscription satellite radio.

Radio broadcasters operate with two customer bases in a symbiotic relationship. The first are the listeners. Radio broadcasters must present entertainment content that will attract listeners. The second are the advertisers that pay the radio broadcasters to pitch their products and services to the listeners. Without listeners, advertisers would not pay for air time. But without advertisers, stations would not have the revenue to present programming that attracts listeners.

Accounting/Financial Presentation Issues

As previously stated, most of the revenue generated by a radio station is from advertising. The majority of the advertising done on any given radio station is local. Advertising rates can fluctuate significantly and depend on a number of factors, such as size of the market, the station's ranking within the market, demographics of the market, demographics of the listenership (which is impacted by the programming format), time of day, time of year, programming format, and current economic conditions. Prices can range from hundreds of dollars per minute to thousands of dollars per minute. The industry has developed formulas to compute "cost per rating point" and "cost per thousand impressions," which also affect advertising rates.

Types of Assets

The radio broadcasting industry requires capital investments in transmission equipment. If a broadcaster produces its own programs, recording studios and related equipment are also needed. In many cases, the radio station also owns real estate, either directly or in a related entity. Because of accelerated depreciation methods, the fixed assets are generally worth more than the book value.

Intangible assets can take several forms. Radio personalities can draw sizable listenership, especially during morning and afternoon commute times. These personalities can be part of the station's internal programming or nationally syndicated programming. Other intangible assets can include the longevity and familiarity of a well-established call sign, a contract to broadcast nationally syndicated shows, the frequency on which the station broadcasts, and its license with the FCC.

Every commercial radio station is required to have a license from the FCC in order to operate. This license represents the station's primary intangible asset. The station may also have purchased goodwill, due in large part to the significant number of acquisitions that have occurred in the industry.

Valuation Approaches and Methods

As with any business, there are a number of factors that can impact value. These factors include:

- Degree of risk associated with the recurrence of the historical level of revenue
- Operating profit margins on historical and projected levels of revenue and operating expenses
- Market demographics
- The terms and conditions of the station's licenses
- The difficulty associated with obtaining a new license for a similar market
- The size of the geographic market served
- The level of competition in the market
- The reputation and abilities of key personnel, such as management and on-air personalities
- Well-established and recognized call letters

Radio broadcasting companies are valued by means of one or more of the following approaches:

The Income Approach

As with the valuation of other businesses, the income approach for a radio station includes the determination of an appropriate adjusted cash flow stream and a related discount and capitalization rate. The selection of an appropriate cash flow stream, representative of a station's expected performance, is very important.

Some of the issues that should be considered in selecting an appropriate cash flow stream are as follows:

- Advertising revenue is somewhat seasonal, with greater demand for advertising toward the end of the year and lower demand during the summer months.
- Advertising revenues are sensitive to local economic conditions, as advertising budgets tend to decline during economic downturns.
- The demographics of the listener base can change over time, which can change expectations of future programming and advertising revenue.
- Contract terms and the potential of renewal of contracts for personalities or syndicated programs.
- Proposed or new regulations and their impact on future revenues or expenses.

Determination of an Appropriate Discount and Capitalization Rate

As with any other business valuation, the various risks faced by a radio station should be incorporated as risk adjustments within a discount and capitalization rate. Following is a list of some of the risk factors to be considered and reflected in the risk of a radio station discount or capitalization rate:

- *Industry forecast.* The outlook for the radio broadcasting industry can change significantly from one year to the next. For instance, the impact of technological changes can significantly change the industry outlook.
- *National economy.* The national economic outlook can significantly impact a particular radio station.
- *Local economy and demographics.* The local economic outlook and demographics can significantly impact a particular radio station. Musical tastes can vary significantly based on the median age and gender of the target audience for a particular station.

The Market Approach

While the market approach can be used to value almost any business, it can be particularly effective when valuing radio stations. Using the market approach, the analyst determines a radio station's value based on private sales of other radio stations and/or the market prices of publicly traded broadcasting companies.

ValTip

As with any business valuation, it is desirable to obtain detailed financial information for the acquired business, the motives for the acquisition, the price and terms of the sale, information on the buyer, and other important qualitative information relating to the sale, in order to perform a meaningful market analysis and comparison.

The motives for the acquisition are important to consider, as they can impact the price paid for a particular radio station. A radio station may have been acquired to take advantage of market synergies, to increase market share, or to expand into a particular geographic market.

Because of the high volume of transactions in the radio broadcasting industry subsequent to the adoption of the 1996 act, and the fact that there are a large number of publicly traded radio companies, there is a sufficient amount of relevant industry transactional data to be able to use the guideline company method in most engagements. In addition, as radio broadcasting industry transactions are subject to regulatory approval, it is relatively straightforward to obtain relevant transaction documents.

Using this information, the analyst determines various valuation multiples, adjusted appropriately for differences between the data and the subject radio station.

The analyst should consider the following factors, among others, in adjusting the derived market multiples:

- *Large markets versus small markets.* Large markets generally yield much higher advertising revenue for radio broadcasters than small markets. On the other hand, competition is generally much stiffer in a larger market.
- *The station's ranking within the market.*
- *Existence of other types of media.* Radio broadcasters typically face significant competition for advertising clients from television, magazines, newspapers, outdoor advertising, and others.
- *FM versus AM stations.* FM stations typically command a higher multiple, as they have a more reliable broadcast signal.

The Asset-Based Approach

The asset-based approach is based on the economic principle of substitution. When properly applied, methods within the asset-based approach are some of the more complex and rigorous valuation analyses.

However, the theoretical underpinning of this approach is simple: The value of the business enterprise is the market value of all of the subject business's assets (both tangible and intangible) less the market value of the subject business's liabilities (both recorded and contingent).

When an asset-based method is used to value a radio station, certain adjustments need to be considered to reflect the market values of the underlying assets. The adjustments include:

- *Nonoperating assets.* Radio stations often own the real estate upon which they operate. Because the real estate has typically appreciated and the property may have been depreciated on an accelerated basis, the book values are often much lower than market values. If so, then the analyst may rely on an appraisal of all land, buildings, and improvements. A radio station may own airplanes, condominiums, and similar assets that should be adjusted to market values.
- *Intangible assets* may not be recorded on the balance sheet but could have a significant impact on a radio station. As previously stated, these assets can take the form of well established call sign, well liked personalities, contracts to broadcast syndicated programs, and other intangible assets.
- *Contingent liabilities.* It may be appropriate to adjust for certain contingent liabilities, such as environmental cleanup liabilities.

In addition to these adjustments and other similar balance sheet adjustments, an adjustment may need to be made to reflect the potential deferred tax liability related to the difference between the book values and the market values of a radio station's underlying assets.

Risk Issues

In any business valuation, the analyst should consider the key risk areas of the subject company. The risk areas of radio stations include:

- *Regulatory environment.* Because radio stations operate in a regulated environment, their operations can be impacted significantly. When a radio station is acquired, and its license is transferred, there are numerous requirements for the new owner to satisfy for the license to be transferred.
- *Changing demographics.* A radio station can be effectively forced to make significant changes in programming formats in order to respond to changing demographics.

Information Sources

The following publications and associations provide excellent sources of information in valuing radio stations:

Standard & Poor's Industry Surveys, semiannual publication of Standard & Poor's Corporation, 25 Broadway, New York, NY 20004, 800-221-5277.
National Association of Broadcasters, 1771 N Street, NW, Washington, DC 20036, 202-429-4199.
Radio Advertising Bureau, 1320 Greenway Drive, Suite 500, Irving, TX 75038, 800-232-3131
Radio & Television Business Report, 2050 Old Bridge Road, Suite B-01, Lake Ridge, VA 22192, 703-492-8191
Kagan Research, LLC, One Lower Ragsdale Drive, Building One, Suite 130, Monterey, CA 93940, 831-624-1536.

C: CABLE TV

Introduction

Cable television originated in 1948 as an alternative for households where reception of standard over-the-air TV signals was poor. Since then, it has expanded into a multibillion-dollar industry, serving over 67 percent of U.S. television households. It was originally viewed simply as a conveyer of video programming. Now, however, cable's broadband infrastructure provides an excellent platform for delivery of advanced services, including digital networks, video-on-demand, interactive television, high-speed Internet access, and telephone.

Cable television is a service that delivers multiple channels of television programming to subscribers who pay a monthly fee for the services they receive. Television signals are received over-the-air, by coaxial or fiber-optic transport or via satellite delivery by antennas, microwave relay stations, and satellite earth stations. These are modulated, amplified, and distributed over a network of coaxial and fiber optic cable to the subscribers' television sets. Cable television systems typically are constructed and operated pursuant to nonexclusive franchises awarded by local and state governmental authorities for specified periods of time.

Cable television is subject to the jurisdiction of the Federal Communications Commission under the Communications Act of 1934. The Communications Act prohibits the operation of a radio or television broadcasting station except under a license issued by the FCC and empowers the FCC, among other things, to:

- Issue, renew, revoke, and modify broadcasting licenses
- Regulate the equipment used by stations
- Adopt other regulations to carry out the provisions of the Communications Act
- Impose penalties for violation of such regulations
- Impose fees for processing applications and other administrative functions

> The Communications Act prohibits the assignment of a license or the transfer of control of a licensee without prior approval of the FCC.

Regulation

The cable television industry continues to be impacted by regulatory and technological changes. The FCC and Congress have been particularly interested in specifically increasing competition in the cable television industry. The 1996 Telecommunications Act altered the regulatory structure governing the nation's communications providers. It removed barriers to competition in both the cable television market and the local telephone market. In addition, the FCC has pursued spectrum-licensing options designed to increase competition to the cable industry by wireless multichannel video programming distributors.

There are a number of other areas where the FCC has impacted cable television operators, including the following:

Cable Rate Regulation

The FCC has regulated cable industry rates for more than a decade. Current regulations restrict the prices that cable systems charge for basic service and associated equipment. However, all other cable services are exempt from current rate regulation. Although rate regulation operates pursuant to a federal formula, local governments, commonly referred to as local franchising authorities, are primarily responsible for administering this regulation. Federal rate regulations also require cable operators to maintain a "geographically uniform" rate within each community, except in those communities facing effective competition.

Must Carry/Retransmission Consent

Current federal law includes "must carry" regulations, requiring cable systems to carry certain local broadcast television stations that the cable operator would not voluntarily select. As an alternative, widely watched commercial television stations can prohibit cable carriage unless the cable operator first negotiates for "retransmission consent," which may be conditioned on significant payments or other concessions.

If cable systems were required to simultaneously carry both the analog and the digital signals of each television station (known as *dual carriage*) while the industry moves from an analog to a digital format, the costs could be significant.

Ownership Restrictions

Historically, federal regulation of the communications industry included a number of ownership restrictions, limiting the size and ability to enter into competing enterprises for certain entities. Through a series of legislative, regulatory, and judicial actions, most of these restrictions recently were eliminated or substantially relaxed. For instance, traditional restrictions on local exchange carriers offering cable service within their telephone service area no longer exist.

In the past, the FCC adopted regulations prohibiting a particular cable operator from serving greater than 30 percent of all domestic multichannel video subscribers and from dedicating more than 40 percent of the activated channel capacity of any cable system to the carriage of affiliated national video programming services. Because various courts nullified these ownership restrictions, the FCC is currently considering adoption of replacement regulations.

Digital TV Transition

In 2005, Congress passed the Digital Transition and Public Safety Act of 2005, mandating that on February 17, 2009, television programming be transmitted digitally, ending all analog television transmission in the United States. Early in 2009, Congress enacted the DTV Delay Act, changing the date for conversion to digital signals to June 12, 2009. The transition to digital signals had little impact on cable TV subscribers.

Universal Service Fund

The Universal Service Fund (USF) was mandated by Congress to help telecommunications companies provide service to rural areas that may not otherwise receive telecommunications services. Since many cable TV providers also provide telephone services, they are affected by the USF. The FCC requires all providers of voice services, including cable telephone and VoIP, to contribute to the USF based on the revenues they generate on interstate voice services. However, only common carrier providers receive USF funding. This affects cable TV companies providing voice services in two ways: First, the required contributions decrease earnings; second, USF funding can provide common carrier providers a competitive advantage.

Alternative Delivery Systems

Direct Broadcast Service (Satellite TV)

Satellite TV delivers television programming directly to subscribers via satellite transmission. It requires each subscriber to have a satellite dish to capture the signal and a receiver to descramble the signal and, if needed, convert the signal to work with an analog television. The largest providers of satellite TV services at the end of 2008 were DirecTV, with approximately 17.6 million subscribers, and DISH Network, with approximately 13.6 subscribers.[3] The digital signal, video compression technology, and high-powered satellites allow satellite TV providers to offer more than 200 digital channels of programming from a single transponder satellite.

Internet Protocol Television (IPTV)

In an IPTV system, digital television signals are delivered over a broadband Internet connection. Several advantages are available with IPTV, including the ability to bundle Internet, television, and telephone services over a single Internet connection. Video on demand can also be provided, where users can begin a television program on their schedule and pause the program as desired. IPTV can also provide picture-in-picture, allowing one to channel-surf in a separate "window" on the television while maintaining the original program on the screen. Limitations to IPTV include its need for large bandwidth capacity and its sensitivities to data reliability.

Industry Statistics

The industry generated more than $86 billion in revenue during 2008,[4] among 1,212 cable TV operators.[5] During the same period, these operators invested approximately $14.6 billion in capital expenditures.[6]

Approximately 63.7 million basic video customers subscribed to cable TV, with Comcast by far the largest provider, with more than 24 million basic video subscribers, and Time Warner Cable a distant second, with approximately 13 million basic video subscribers. Cox Communications and Charter Communications are third and fourth, respectively, each with approximately 5 million basic video subscribers.[7]

---

[3] www.Tvbythenumbers.com and MediaBiz Competitive Intelligence.
[4] SNL Kagan.
[5] Nielsen Focus.
[6] NCTA.com.
[7] SNL Kagan.

Accounting/Financial Presentation Issues

> Cable systems are generally operated in accordance with nonexclusive franchises granted by a municipality or other state or local government entity in order to cross public rights-of-way. Cable franchises are generally granted for fixed terms and in many cases include monetary penalties for noncompliance. They may be terminable if the franchisee fails to comply with material provisions.

The specific terms and conditions of cable franchises can vary materially among jurisdictions. Generally, each franchise includes provisions governing cable operations, franchise fees, system construction, maintenance, technical performance, and customer service standards. A number of states subject cable systems to the jurisdiction of centralized state government agencies, such as public utility commissons.

Local franchising authorities have substantial discretion in establishing franchise terms. However, there are certain federal protections. For instance, federal law caps local franchise fees and includes renewal procedures designed to protect incumbent franchisees from arbitrary denials of renewal. Even if a franchise is renewed, however, the local franchising authority may seek to impose new and more onerous requirements as a condition of renewal. Similarly, if a local franchising authority's consent is required for the purchase or sale of a cable system, the local franchising authority may attempt to impose more burdensome requirements as a condition for providing its consent.

The cable TV industry is capital intensive, requiring significant investments in technology and infrastructure. As a result, fixed assets usually constitute a large portion of cable TV providers' balance sheets. It is common for cable TV providers to have negative working capital (current liabilities exceeding current assets).

Types of Assets

A cable television operator's fixed assets generally include transmission equipment, furniture, and office equipment. In many cases, the operator will also own the related real estate, either directly or in a related entity. Because of accelerated depreciation methods, the fixed assets are generally worth more than the book value.

> Significant intangible assets include FCC licenses, call letters, account lists, and audience growth potential. Accounting for license cost often includes the direct cost plus permits, as well as other costs to obtain permits for construction and expansion. This license represents the station's primary intangible asset.

Valuation Approaches and Methods

As with any business, there are a number of factors that can impact the value. These factors include:

- Degree of risk associated with the recurrence of the historical level of revenue
- Operating profit margins on historical and projected levels of revenue and operating expenses
- Market demographics
- The terms and conditions of the operator's licenses
- The difficulty associated with obtaining a new license for a similar market
- The size of the geographic market served
- The level of competition in the market
- The reputation and abilities of key personnel, such as management

Cable television companies are valued by means of one or more of the following approaches:

The Income Approach

As with the valuation of other businesses, the income approach for a cable television operator includes the determination of an appropriate adjusted earnings stream and a related discount and capitalization rate. The selection of an appropriate earnings/cash flow stream, representative of a company's expected performance, is very important.

Once an appropriate earnings/cash flow stream is selected, normalizing adjustments should be made. Some of the common income statement adjustments are as follows:

- *Owner's compensation.* An adjustment may be necessary in order to normalize owner's compensation expense. The analyst analyzes and compares owner's compensation with similar positions in the industry within a similar geographic region. Industry compensation measures are available from the Risk Management Association (RMA) *Annual Statement Studies,* Integra Information, and First Research Industry Profiles. Payroll taxes should be also be adjusted to reflect the corresponding change in taxes resulting from a change in compensation, and vice versa.
- *Discretionary expenses.* The analyst should adjust discretionary expenses to reflect market comparability. For instance, any difference between actual rent expense and fair market rents should typically be adjusted. In addition, the operator may pay for an owner's country club dues and similar items.
- *Discontinued operations.* Adjustments should be made to remove historical revenue or expenses attributable to discontinued operations.
- *Prospective contract changes.* Any broadcast or advertising contracts that may, in the foreseeable future, expire or possibly be renegotiated should be converted to an appropriate forward-looking level.

Determination of an Appropriate Discount and Capitalization Rate

As with any other business valuation, the various risks faced by a cable television operator should be incorporated as risk adjustments within a discount and capitalization rate. Following is a list of some of the risk factors to be considered and reflected in the risk of a cable television operator discount or capitalization rate.

- *Industry forecast.* The outlook for the telecommunications industry can change significantly from one year to the next. For instance, the impact of technological changes can significantly change the industry outlook.
- *National economy.* The national economic outlook can significantly impact a particular operator.
- *Local economy and demographics.* The local economic outlook and demographics can significantly impact a particular operator.

The Market Approach

Using the market approach, the analyst determines a cable television company's value based on private sales of other similar companies and/or the market prices of publicly traded broadcasting companies.

As with any business valuation, it is desirable to obtain detailed financial information for the acquired business, the motives for the acquisition, the price and terms of the sale, information on the buyer, and other important qualitative information relating to the sale, in order to perform a meaningful market analysis and comparison.

The motives for the acquisition are important to consider, as they can impact the price paid for a particular cable television company. A company may have been acquired to take advantage of market synergies, to increase market share, or to expand into a particular geographic market.

There are a large number of publicly traded cable TV companies, and thus, there is a sufficient amount of relevant industry transactional data to be able to use the guideline company method in most engagements. In addition, as the telecommunications industry transactions are subject to regulatory approval, it is relatively straightforward to obtain relevant transaction documents.

Using this information, the analyst determines various valuation multiples, adjusted appropriately for differences between the data and the subject cable television company.

The Asset-Based Approach

The asset-based approach is based on the economic principle of substitution. When properly applied, methods within the asset-based approach are some of the more complex and rigorous valuation analyses.

However, the theoretical underpinning of this approach is simple: The value of the business enterprise is the market value of all of the subject business's assets (both tangible and intangible) less the market value of the subject business's liabilities (both recorded and contingent).

When an asset-based method is used to value a cable television operator, certain adjustments may be required to reflect the market values of the underlying assets. The adjustments include:

- *Nonoperating assets.* Cable television operators often own the real estate upon which they operate. Because the real estate has typically appreciated and the property may have been depreciated on an accelerated basis, the book values are often much lower than the market values. If so, then the analyst may rely on an appraisal of all land, buildings, and improvements. An operator may own airplanes, condominiums, and similar assets that should be adjusted to market values.
- *Contingent liabilities.* It may be appropriate to adjust for certain contingent liabilities, such as environmental cleanup liabilities.

In addition to these adjustments and other similar balance sheet adjustments, an adjustment may need to be made to reflect the potential deferred tax liability related to the difference between the book values and the market values of an operator's underlying assets.

Risk Issues

In any business valuation, the valuator should consider the key risk areas of the subject company.

The risk areas of cable television companies include:

- *Regulatory environment.* Because cable television companies operate in a regulated environment, their operations can be impacted significantly. When a cable television company is acquired, and its license is transferred, there are numerous requirements for the new owner to satisfy for the license to be transferred.
- *Changing demographics.* An operator can be effectively forced to make significant changes in programming in order to respond to changing demographics.
- *Quality of equipment.* Depending on the age of the equipment, the company may have to make significant expenditures to update and upgrade existing equipment. Potential purchasers understand that a cable operator's system should generally operate with state-of-the-art equipment.
- *Revenue per subscriber/number of subscribers.* The average monthly billings, cancellation rates, and mix of basic/premium subscribers are important factors to consider.
- *Type of franchise.* In addition to required FCC licenses, cable also typically requires franchise agreements, usually with local governing bodies. The agreements set forth the terms of the cable operation and usually outline some guideline on pricing. As such, they should be analyzed in order to understand the impact of the terms on the value of the company.

Industry Nuances

The cable television industry uses a unique terminology. Following is a list of some of the more common terms that are used, compiled from the National Cable and Telecommunications Association.

Access channels. Channels set aside by the cable operator for use by the public, educational institutions, municipal government, or for lease on a nondiscriminatory basis.

Access network. The part of the carrier network that touches the customer's premises. The access network is also referred to as the local drop, local loop, or last mile.

Ad avails. Advertising spots available to a cable operator to insert local advertising on a cable network.

Allocations. The assignments of frequencies by the FCC for various communications uses (television, radio, land-mobile, defense, microwave, etc.) to achieve fair division of the available spectrum and minimize interference among users.

Alternative access provider. A telecommunications firm, other than the local telephone company, that provides a connection between a customer's premises to a point of presence of the long-distance carrier.

Antisiphoning. FCC rules that prevent cable systems from siphoning off programming for pay cable channels that otherwise would be seen on conventional broadcast TV. Antisiphoning rules state that only movies no older than three years and sports events not ordinarily seen on television can be cablecast.

Average revenue per unit (ARPU). Commonly used as a financial benchmark in the cable industry to measure average revenue per cable subscriber.

Bandwidth. 1) A measure of spectrum (frequency) use or capacity. For instance, a voice transmission by telephone requires a bandwidth of about 3,000 cycles per second (3 KHz). A TV channel occupies a bandwidth of 6 million cycles per second (6 MHz). Cable system bandwidth occupies 50 to 300 MHz on the electromagnetic spectrum. 2) Measure of capacity of a transmission channel, or the difference between the highest and lowest frequency levels. Information-carrying capacity of a communication channel. The amount of transmission capacity possessed by a system or a specific location in a system.

Basic cable. The basic program services distributed by a cable system for a basic monthly fee. These include one or more local broadcast stations, distant broadcast stations, nonpay networks, and local origination programming.

Broadband. A transmission medium that allows transmission of voice, data, and video simultaneously at rates of 1.544 Mbps or higher. Broadband transmission media generally can carry multiple channels—each at a different frequency or specific time slot.

Broadband communications system. Frequently used as a synonym for cable television. It can describe any system capable of delivering wideband channels and services.

Broadcast. A service that is delivered to all customers. Each customer may select a particular broadcast channel out of many.

Broadcaster's service area. Geographical area encompassed by a station's signal.

Broadcasting. The dissemination of any form of radio electric communications by means of Hertzian waves intended to be received by the public. Transmission of over-the-air signals for public use.

Cable network. Refers to the cable television plant that would typically be used to transmit data over cable services. Such plants generally employ a downstream path in the range of 54 MHz on the low end to a high end in the 440 to 750 MHz range and an upstream path in the range of 5 to 42 MHz. Customers share a common communication path for upstream and a separate common path for downstream (i.e., effectively a pair of unidirectional buses).

Cable system. Facility that provides cable service in a given geographic area comprising one or more headends.

Cable TV. A communications system that distributes broadcast programs and original programs and services by means of coaxial cable.

Cablecasting. Originating programming over a cable system. Includes public access programming.

Certificate of compliance. The approval of the FCC that must be obtained before a cable system can carry television broadcast signals.

Channel. A transmission path between two points. The term channel may refer to a one-way path or, when paths in the two directions of transmission are always associated, to a two-way path. It is usually the smallest subdivision of a transmission system by means of which a single type of communication service is provided, that is, a voice channel, teletypewriter channel, or data channel.

Channel capacity. The number of channels available for current or future use on a cable system.

Customer premises equipment (CPE). Equipment at the end user's premises; *may* be provided by the end user or the service provider.

Digital. 1) In communications and computer technology, *digital* refers to a method of encoding information using a binary system made up of zeroes and ones. In communications technology, this takes the form of two very different electrical voltages, several volts positive and negative, to represent the two values. This substantial difference in voltages for each state makes it unlikely that minor fluctuations in voltage due to electromagnetic interference will change the way a signal is interpreted when received. 2) Information that is encoded into bits and bytes, or packets (0s and 1s, computer binary language). Generally perceived to be an advanced communication form offering clearer signals and increased transmission capacity.

Digital subscriber line (DSL). High-speed technology to transfer data over an existing twisted-pair copper telephone line. Asynchronous technology (ADSL) provides data transmission rates up to 7 Mbps in one direction, generally within approximately three miles from a telephone central office. See also HDSL and VDSL.

Distribution hub. A location in a cable television network that performs the functions of a headend for customers in its immediate area and that receives some or all of its television program material from a master headend in the same metropolitan or regional area.

Distribution plant. The hardware of a cable system, amplifiers, trunk cable, and feeder lines, attached to utility poles or fed through underground conduits like telephone and electric wires.

Downstream. Flow of signals from the cable system control center through the distribution network to the customer. For communication purposes, associated with transmission (down) to the end user. Or in cable television, the direction of transmission from the headend to the subscriber.

Enhanced TV services. Services that enable viewers to access further information about the television programs and advertising they're watching (including how to purchase an item). They may also allow consumers to play along with game shows, participate in opinion polls, and obtain up-to-the-minute news and weather.

Equal access. The offering of access to local exchange facilities on a nondiscriminatory basis.

Exclusivity. The provision in a commercial television film contract that grants exclusive playback rights for the film or episode to a broadcast station in the market it serves. Under the FCC's rules, cable operators cannot carry distant signals that violate local television stations' exclusivity agreements.

Franchising authority. Governmental body responsible for awarding a franchise, specifying the terms of a franchise, and regulating its operation. While the franchise authority is usually a local city or county body, some areas are regulated exclusively on the state level.

Frequency. The number of times a complete electromagnetic wave cycle occurs in a fixed unit of time, usually one second. The rate at which a current alternates, measured in hertz on a telecommunications medium.

Fully integrated system. A cable television system designed to take advantage of the optimum amplifier-cable relationship for highest performance at lowest cost. Such a system is also suited to the fully automated cable television system concept.

Government channel. FCC rules require cable systems in the top 100 markets to set aside one channel for local government use, to be available without cost for the "developmental period." That period runs for five years from the time that subscriber service began, or until five years after the completion of the basic trunk line.

Headend. The control center of a cable television system, where incoming signals are amplified, converted, processed, and combined into a common cable, along with any original cablecasting, for transmission to subscribers. The system usually includes antennas, preamplifiers, frequency converters, demodulators, modulators, processors, and other related equipment.

High-definition television (HDTV). A television signal with greater detail and fidelity than the current TV systems used. The United States currently uses a system called NTSC. HDTV provides a picture with twice the visual resolution of NTSC as well as CD-quality audio.

Homes passed. Total number of homes that have the potential for being hooked up to the cable system.

Institutional network. A network that is operated in conjunction with a cable TV system and is designed to satisfy the needs of schools, businesses, or government.

Leapfrogging. Cable television operators' practice of skipping over one or more of the nearest TV stations to bring in a farther signal for more program diversity. FCC rules establish priority for carrying stations that lie outside the cable systems' service area.

Miles of plant. The number of cable plant miles laid or strung by a cable system.

Pay cable. Cable programming services for which subscribers pay an additional fee above the basic cable service charge. Also called *premium cable*.

Pay cable unit. Each premium service to which a household subscribes is counted as one unit.

Pay per view (PPV). Pay television programming for which cable subscribers pay a separate fee for each program viewed.

Pay programming. Movies, sports, and made-for-cable specials that are available to the cable customer for a charge in addition to the basic fee.

Premium cable. Cable programming services for which subscribers pay an additional fee above the basic cable service charge. Also called *pay cable.*

Syndicated exclusivity. Requirement by which cable systems must black out significant portions of their distant signals in order to protect syndicated programming offered by local television broadcasters under an exclusive contract. The FCC eliminated this requirement in 1980 and reimposed it in 1990.

Take rate. The ratio of homes that pay for a cable service to homes passed.

Tiered programming. A group of programs for which the customer is charged a fee. For example, most cable systems offer a satellite programming tier.

Viewers Per Viewing Household (VPVH). A demographic percentage that indicates how many persons per 100 or per 1,000 households are viewing. For example, a VPVH of 80 K2–11 means that for every 100 households viewing, there are an estimated 80 children ages 2 to 11.

Information Sources

The following associations provide sources of information when valuing cable television companies:

National Cable & Telecommunications Association
1724 Massachusetts Avenue, NW
Washington, DC 20036
202-775-3550

The National Association of Telecommunications Officers and Advisors
1800 Diagonal Road, Suite 495
Alexandria, VA 22314
703-519-8035

Federal Communications Commission
445 12th Street, SW
Washington, DC 20554
888-225-5322

National Telecommunications and Information Administration
U.S. Department of Commerce
1401 Constitution Ave., NW
Washington, DC 20230
202-482-7002

National Cable Television Institute
8022 Southpark Circle, Suite 100
Littleton, CO 80120-5658
303-797-9393

National Cable Television Cooperative
11200 Corporate Ave.
Lenexa, KS 66219-1392
913-599-5900

Kagan Research, LLC,
One Lower Ragsdale Drive
Building One Suite 130
Monterey, CA 93940
831-624-1536

D: RESTAURANTS

Introduction

Restaurants are a reflection of our American culture and one of the fun, great pleasures of life. Providing valuations of restaurants can be just as much fun as the dining experience itself.

> At first glance, restaurants appear similar and seemingly could all be treated the same. But in reality, each one is different and requires individual analysis.

Each restaurant is a small factory that uses skilled labor to assemble raw products, which must be ordered, inventoried, and controlled. Pricing, marketing, promotion, menu design, accounting, décor or theme, uniforms, and human resources must support the factory. The kitchen workers, waitstaff, and management staff must be trained and supervised. The small factory must be opened, different breakfast-lunch-dinner shifts and product lines must be scheduled and produced, and at the end of the business day the factory must be cleaned and prepared for yet another day. In the restaurant industry, this breakfast-lunch-dinner shift change might occur three times a day, seven times a week.

> A successful restaurant can make its owners wealthy; however, managing a restaurant is complex, and the failure rate is higher than most other businesses.

What makes a restaurant successful? What makes a restaurant fail? An insider quotation alerts the valuator:

Why would anyone who has worked hard, saved money, and often been successful in other fields want to pump his hard-earned cash down a hole that statistically, at least, will almost surely prove dry? Why venture into an industry with large fixed expenses (rent, electricity, gas, water, linen, maintenance, insurance, license fees, trash removal, etc.), with a notoriously transient and unstable workforce and highly perishable inventory of assets? The chances of ever seeing a return on your investment are about one in five. What insidious spongiform bacterium so riddles the brains of men and women that they stand there on the tracks, watching the lights of the oncoming locomotive, knowing full well it will eventually run them over? After all these years in the business, I still don't know.[8]

Current State of the Industry and Its Outlook

The restaurant industry has undergone dramatic and significant changes due to the economic downturn currently in progress. *Nation's Restaurant News* reported in its annual 2009 Outlook (January 5, 2009, *Nation's Restaurant News,* p. 29 and following) that "the year ahead is expected to be another tough one for the restaurant industry as the US recession continues to curtail consumer spending. Operators, however, are a tenacious bunch."

For the second edition of *Financial Valuation* published in 2006, restaurant sales were projected to be $476 billion. Sales in 2009 are projected to be $516 billion, which is still a 2.5 percent increase over the 2008 results. You can see the growth in the industry in three short years. Full-service restaurants are projected to have sales of $183 billion, compared with sales at limited-service restaurants of $164 billion. This reflects a 4 percent increase for limited-service restaurants (QSR), compared with a 1 percent increase for full-service restaurants. Overall, the report projects a 3.6 percent menu price inflation, which means that the average restaurant expects to slip a little more than 1 percent (2.5 percent–3.6 percent) during 2009.

Restaurants are reinventing their menus and reorganizing their specials and promotions on a rapid basis to retain their current customers and attract new customers. The mid to upscale restaurant sector has probably been hit the hardest as consumers cut back their discretionary spending. Conversely, although the quick-service restaurant sector is also struggling with the recession, the fallback from the mid to upscale restaurant sector has actually, in some cases, resulted in increased sales. This is clearly reflected in the projection increases discussed previously.

Competition continues to be fierce as restaurant expansion slows and as many weaker restaurant locations close their doors. Restaurant management must constantly watch wholesale food prices and gasoline and diesel transportation cost increases in order to adjust their menu prices, if possible, to keep their operations income stable. If this isn't a daunting task, obtaining restaurant financing has been difficult or impossible. Although interest rates are at all-time lows, financing, even from established restaurant industry financing sources, has been generally unavailable.

That higher-than-usual failure rate is in itself reason enough to research the industry in depth. A careful analysis of the state of industry trends is crucial. Trends can change the restaurant landscape rapidly; however, a broad-brush approach can

---

[8] Anthony Bourdain, *Kitchen Confidential: Adventures in the Culinary Underbelly* (New York: The Ecco Press, 2000), 84.

color the appraiser's painting. Currently, inventive and bargain pricing on regular menu items, specials, and combinations overshadow all other trends in the restaurant industry. This, of course, reflects the state of the consumer economy. However, restaurant owners cannot take their eyes off upgrading their facilities and technology (registers, ordering devices, automated cooking equipment, QSR call centers, and the like).

Food safety concerns have again surfaced, as one *E. coli* event after another seems to hit the packaged foods segment. As a sign of the times, comfort food seems to have overpowered the healthy food focus, although the "greening" of America continues to expand into the daily operations and packaging of the industry. Successful restaurants must keep up with industry trends. The valuation should consider these trends. Analysts must take the national economic environment into consideration. There is little doubt that restaurant sales are linked to a strong economy. Attention should be given to interest rates and wholesale food prices.

The restaurant outlook is tied to the economic outlook, nationally and regionally.

- As previously mentioned, the entire restaurant financing industry has undergone massive changes. Many lenders that were very active in the industry have dramatically cut back their influence. For some lenders, their ability to put together material lending packages has been either seriously delayed or even curtailed. Federal interest rates have remained low; however, lenders have asked for an increased spread over their cost of funds, reflecting the increased risk of the current recession and its effect on the restaurant industry. Covenants and restrictions have generally increased.
- Wholesale food prices have continued to move erratically on their own. Additional fluctuations are linked to the price of gasoline and diesel. The "Green" philosophy has resulted in searches for closer food and produce (possibly organic) suppliers as smart restaurateurs take advantage of these new trends.
- Seasonality interacts with economics differently for each region of the country. For example, Cape Cod restaurant sales in the winter are a fraction of the summer sales. Similarly, these regions exhibit different population increase or decline metrics. For example, people are leaving the Northeast and moving to North Carolina and Florida.

One must look at the industry trends nationally, but not forget the factors of each particular area where a restaurant location is being considered.

Accounting/Financial Presentation Issues

Every restaurant accounting system can be different, even though the National Restaurant Association publishes a "standard chart of accounts." Some financial statements are extremely detailed but lack the overall benchmarks (total administrative, for example). Other financial statements are simple and straightforward but lack the detail to analyze problem areas.

Franchisor or parent company requirements shape the individual look of their financial statements. Difficulties are encountered when the analyst tries to compare these custom statements to industry databases. For example, Risk Management Association might show labor in "Cost of Goods Sold" while the franchisor requires that it appear under "Controllable Expenses." Needless to say, a ratio comparison without adjustment might be totally misleading. On the flip side, an adjustment for industry comparison might make a franchise comparison impossible or misleading.

Other potential problem areas are as follows:

- Does the restaurant lease equipment and is that cost shown properly on the balance sheet? Operating leases can be hidden in depreciation or other accounts when they should have been capitalized. Leases are normally three to five years with a bargain purchase. Missed lease indebtedness can hide a debt coverage problem. Are the leases assumable to a buyer?
- The restaurant may take partial, infrequent, or inaccurate inventories, causing strange variations in COGS, year-end results of operations, or analysis. Analysts may question this aspect. Operating supplies and paper products might not be inventoried, although they should be. Inventories are normally at-cost, which usually approximates fair market value.
- Restaurants may utilize management companies, which may alter administration expenses either up or down inaccurately.
- Full-service restaurants have complex tip-reporting requirements and tax credits. While a valuation is certainly not an audit, an understanding of this area can provide insight into the management of the restaurant.
- Unreported sales and missing inventory issues may need to be considered.
- Could there be deferred gift certificate or frequent diner club obligations not illustrated on the balance sheet? These considerations may be material.

Types of Assets (Tangible and Intangible)

The tangible and intangible assets of the restaurant can be categorized from the company's depreciation schedule, if properly maintained. Rapid tax write-offs and removal of assets for minimizing property tax often understate the assets of the restaurant. Small wares, such as dishware, cooking utensils, and the like, are often directly expensed and therefore also hidden.

The right questions need to be asked during management interviews. Who owns the land? Who owns the building? What are the lease or rent terms? Are there any escalations? Who owns the leasehold improvements? Do they revert to the landlord upon sale? Although a franchise intangible might be written off ($27,500 original over 20 years, for example), could the franchise intangible be worth hundreds of thousands of dollars? If a franchise, when does it renew? What are the risks of non-renewal? What does a renewal cost? Could proprietary and protected menus not be illustrated on the balance sheet?

The tangible assets include the restaurant equipment, attached décor, theme play areas, signage, furniture, and fixtures. They are normally depreciated for tax purposes over five or seven years. They may have been rapidly expensed using IRS provisions. While their book value might be zero, their useful lives might be ten or more years. Historical capital expenditure averages might not accurately reflect restaurant capital expenditures going forward. Restaurant capital expenditures are highly irregular and erratic in cost. Analysts should carefully question management during their interviews to establish what reinvestment is planned in the coming years. Also, consider that restaurant equipment may be worth ten cents on the dollar to a dealer in used restaurant equipment; however, in place, calibrated, and in use, this equipment is worth more. An old nautical décor might be fully depreciated, yet in a harbor tourist setting, its customer value and allure might be high. A Spanish courtyard, if properly maintained, might have a useful life of over 40 years, since it is practically a timeless draw for customers.

Valuation Approaches and Methods

All the standard valuation approaches apply to the restaurant industry; however, the discounted cash flow (DCF) is probably the most popular. The purpose of the valuation and the standard of value intersect, as always, to determine the analyst's toolbox. For example, buy-sells, which are common, may dictate investment value and DCF. Often rents or franchise fees are laddered, showing increases at several intervals. Land leases and rents will normally have renewal provisions, subject to defined parameters. Service fees (if franchised) may increase from historical levels if sold and franchise renewals may be required in the near future. The DCF handles these future events properly.

In a divorce, gift, or estate situation, where there is a normalized cash flow and growth, the capitalization-of-earnings/cash flow method may be relied upon, depending on the circumstances.

Market-approach methods, when used, are often done so as a reasonable test or as a corroborating method. Transaction information is plentiful, but, like other indicators, the values are influenced by factors that are not known and are private. The guideline public company method can be used for larger restaurant valuations. There are hundreds of publicly traded restaurant companies, many of which are small. However, the analyst must be careful to make sure the stock is not too thinly traded.

Asset methods are rarely used. One restaurant might be valued at its book value (tax depreciation adjusted for actual useful life on a straight-line basis). If land and buildings are involved, the issue becomes more difficult because of highest and "best use"; perhaps the land is worth more than the taco franchise currently occupying the building. If a marginal restaurant is stuck in an ironclad lease with big penalties for early termination, the solution becomes more complex. The hypothetical seller will not allow the hypothetical buyer to exclude negative cash flow. All must be purchased. What is known for certain is that the loss restaurant should not be priced at $0.00. In a package purchase, the negative cash flow must be included. Internal controllers and business brokers may present this dilemma to the analyst.

Major Risk Issues

Take, for example, a McDonald's restaurant that finds out a new Wendy's is opening virtually across the street, just weeks after the purchase. There is little doubt that its value foundation has been rudely shaken. Page after page of these situations can be documented, and a high-volume restaurant is often the prime target.

> A major risk in restaurant valuation is the "risk of the unknown." Topping the list of unknowns is the risk of a competitor arriving shortly after a purchase.

Warren D. Miller states, "Few valuation analysts seem to focus much on competitors: Who they are, where they are, how big they are, what they believe, how they compete, what their strengths and weaknesses are, and what they believe should be of a prime valuation interest."[9] Situations in mature markets, with competitors in place, are an easier valuation assignment. The subjective company risk premium in this area should be addressed.

> Another potential unknown risk is the major reinvestment surprise.

Restaurants are never static; they are always redefining themselves if they are to stay successful. Sellers present that no reinvestment is needed. Buyers' egos blind them to careful assessment. If franchised, throw into the equation the agreement rewrite or changing operational requirements. Costs exceeding the million-dollar range and beyond can be encountered.

Remember the factory analogy from the Introduction? Factories wear out. Capital expenditures (cap ex) are not just the average of five years' depreciation schedule purchases. Research is necessary to address this area. Reinvestment should spur sales improvements or halt sales declines if properly designed.

Projections, while often appropriate, come with additional risk. Won't property taxes increase after a sale? And replacement cost insurance might also increase. Will the new company be able to utilize a mature experience rate in workers' compensation insurance and employee unemployment? If the franchise renewal costs $45,000 two years in the future, will this be considered? If the restaurant is a franchise, what assurance or statistical facts support the renewal process? Everyone expects a franchise to be renewed, yet sometimes it is denied. The questions are numerous.

Industry Nuances

Each industry has its own menu of fixed and variable costs. Basic accounting or finance theory presents the concept of breakeven. Once crossing this point, increased profits are the reward, because all that must be covered is the variable expenses. This is the secret formula driving restaurant valuation. Perhaps a more useful formula is

> Few restaurant managers know their breakeven point, by year, by month, or by day.

---

[9] Warren D. Miller, *Three Peas in the Business Valuation Pod: The Resource Based View of the Firm, Value Creation, and Strategy,* in Robert F. Reilly and Robert P. Schweihs, eds. *Handbook of Business Valuation and Intellectual Property Analysis* (New York: McGraw-Hill, 2004), p. 311.

the contribution margin or the percentage of profits the restaurant owner keeps after crossing breakeven. The relationship among growth, current sales, food specials, seasonal changing sales, and menu pricing is high stakes.

A yearly calculation may miss the four winter months when fixed costs drive losses. Resignation by management to always increase sales over the same comparable period last year clouds the breakeven lesson.

For example, perhaps a huge advertising expenditure is planned for the traditionally lean winter months. Assume the campaign is successful and sales are increased 15 percent. However, the restaurant is still below breakeven. Perhaps the campaign should have targeted the busy summer, when the contribution margin kicks profits into the door.

How does this concept affect our valuations? Valuations tend to be static and normalized. Maybe the DCF growth rate changes the profit equation two years out. What if the calculation of numbers missed this? For example, the analyst may use a transaction database, finding restaurants in the $500,000 to $800,000 sales range determining a $0.35-per-$1-of-sale relationship. The subject restaurant has sales of $1,200,000, so the value is $420,000. However, the $1,200,000 restaurant is worth more because it is past breakeven further into the rich contribution percentage. The $800,000 restaurant comparison may no longer be valid.

This is the second secret of restaurant valuation. Variable expenses can fall dramatically as volume increases.

Interesting things happen to a restaurant's profitability as sales increase. In addition to the contribution margin effect, efficiencies of scale kick into play, but only to a point. A busy restaurant will have less waste, raw and completed, because the food moves out quickly, while staying hot and fresh. An individual employee (remember the factory analogy) can assemble 10 salads an hour or 30, if pushed. Consider the same wage rate per hour for increased productivity.

The percentage of cost of goods sold can actually fall and not remain constant as volume increases year by year in a projection. What if the hypothetical salad maker needs a helper to make 31 salads? Now the restaurant has two salad makers, one making 15 and one making 16. This is where the system and management enter.

How competent is the management team? Two restaurants with the same sales in the same franchise, for example, will exhibit two different levels of profits. Figuring out the reasons why may be difficult. How long has the management been in place? What training has the management team had? These types of questions must be asked.

Management is the third secret of restaurant valuation.

Valuation Issues

Analysts typically normalize or stabilize profit projections to best represent the future of the restaurant we are valuing. They look at historical results, develop a current snapshot, and capitalize the cash flows. They project sales into the future using averages from the past and discount the cash flows. They know that terminal value is typically always a larger percentage of the answer. What issue presents the most difficulty to these standard methods?

Increasing debt linked to original restaurant acquisition and reinvestment complicates the valuation processes. The classic classroom problem offers a company with $100 million in sales with $20 million in debt linked to raw material, work in progress, and accounts receivable turnover. Sales increase to $120 million and debt moves to $24 million. This model does not work as well for the restaurant industry.

Consider an existing QSR restaurant, purchased for $1,500,000. Assume the debt package (approved by the franchisor) allows a seven-year amortization. The principal changes year by year as interest decreases. In seven years, debt is zero, or is it? Next, assume that in year four, a major reinvestment to the lobby and exterior begins with $400,000, an amount borrowed for another seven years. Assume in year five, new grills, frying stations, and cash registers are replaced for $125,000, exceeding the normal capital expenditures of $20,000. The assumptions can be numerous.

Several things seem clear: Debt may not reach zero, reinvestment is needed in uncertain and increasing increments, and major repairs and maintenance occur at random times. Aesthetic obsolescence may occur before functional obsolescence. Franchise renewals may dictate reinvestment sooner than expected obsolescence.

These issues complicate the classic, historically based capitalization of cash flow. The past may not be representative of an aging restaurant's future. A normalized year may differ from the historical past, especially in interest and principal projections.

Another important decision is whether to use the Ibbotson Industry Risk Rates if using a build-up method. The restaurant industry seems to land between −1 and −3 percent. Essentially, the industry beta or volatility is below one. Volatility means risk, and less risk and volatility are a good thing, all other things being equal. While restaurant stocks may not exhibit the excitement of biotech or hot technology, they do seem to grow somewhat predictably in a mature cycle of same-store sales and the like.

There does, however, appear to be a logical challenge for the industry risk premium. Certainly the restaurant industry, particularly in local and regional locations, is a risky business venture, generally perceived as such in relation to other industries. Ease of entry, large egos, readily available suppliers, and changing trends tempt the inexperienced. How can a negative 1 to 3 percent risk premium be logical? Before answering, consider a national franchise opening on a prime real estate spot in a high-growth, soccer-mom neighborhood. There probably have not been many that have closed in the past few years. The answer is that there is, dependent on the specific circumstances, a range of risks. Either choice would be tempered with the valuator's individual judgmental risk premium.

Generally, franchise restaurants are worth more than stand-alone restaurants. Franchises seem easier to transfer from one owner to the next, enhancing their value considerably. The embedded training and operational systems import value in a successful venture. In the final analysis, what is the sustainability of a $200,000 cash flow from a new McDonald's versus a new, trendy, one-chef French restaurant? No easy or absolute answers are ever available.

Valuation Nuances

In this industry, averages are often available. However, those seasonal sales patterns, changing sales growth, and many other variables complicate the search for the optimum range of values. Also, it is difficult to predict where a restaurant will fall in a range of performance statistics.

Should a group of restaurants be valued individually or as a group? The answer depends primarily upon the intended use of the valuation. Perhaps each one will be sold individually. Alternately, an analyst will often look at a group together, because all the restaurants will be sold as a group. A negative-cash-flow restaurant is seldom worth $0.00. The main reason to value restaurants as a group is to reflect economies of administration, food costs, human resources, and the like. Simply stated, a single restaurant from a group of restaurants cannot be as efficient as the group, normally. Administration is not linear; it stair-steps up with sections of significant efficiency. In a multiple situation, a restaurant can sometimes be added with lesser additional administration.

Rules of Thumb

Every restaurateur has a memorized rule of thumb. They are all different. They seldom are correct. Readers of most valuation texts are certainly aware of all the problems, limitations, and flaws in the rule-of-thumb approach, if it can even be called that.

However, the analyst must become aware of the owner's expectations. The reason is that you will have to carefully explain to your client why your result is higher, lower, or equal to his or her rule-of-thumb expectation. The restaurateur will listen intently to your explanation and logic so that this can later be recounted with authority to a potential buyer, for example. "Although your cash flow is excellent, your restaurant is worth less because of its age. Major reinvestment will be required by the buyer in order to ensure that the cash flow continues."

It is not uncommon to have owners show rule-of-thumb valuations incorrectly calculated. Even if the rule of thumb was right on the mark, the correct line items from the P&L must be selected. Some rules of thumbs are promulgated by franchisors. At first glance, they seem to have some magic higher power. They do not. For example, a formula that says a pizza restaurant doing $800,000 in yearly sales is worth $400,000 may be correct for one location. Perhaps the valuation is for an eight-store operator. Because of the administration efficiencies mentioned in the previous section, it is probable that this patch of stores will be worth more than 8 × $400,000. The multiple operator will have supervisors, training facilities, vacation coverage, accounting systems, food shortage coverage, and the like, not available to the single-store operator. The multiple operator should be able, therefore, to produce a higher resultant cash flow.

Some rules of thumb have historical precedent, perhaps even valid at one time, but not today. The classic "cents per trailing twelve" has been around for 50 years. Early franchises, for example, had constant rent percentages. As years went by, rents classically went up, sometimes 5 or 6 percent as land costs increased. Obviously, the old rule of thumb based on 8½ percent rent does not work with a rent of 13 percent. Would anyone make this mistake? It happens every day and can result in disappointed sellers and confused buyers. It makes no sense to avoid getting a valuation to save several thousand dollars when hundreds of thousands are at stake. Yet it is done everyday.

Pitfalls to Avoid

- Some restaurants use a 12-month accounting cycle and some use a 13-period accounting cycle. Spreadsheet models that annualize sales and expenses may need adjustment.
- Articles have been written about the terminal-year depreciation not exceeding the cap ex. This usually makes sense. However, the financial statements are often unsophisticated and may lump franchise amortization into the depreciation line. Franchises can run, with renewals, easily into 40 or more years. Amortization can be separated, or if included in the D&A line, the total can exceed the cap ex total.
- Changing debt was discussed at length earlier. Franchise debt amortization should normally not exceed franchisor requirements. A valuation utilizing a ten-year amortization may be flawed if the franchisor will approve only seven years.
- Lending ratios are not the only benchmarks. Franchisor requirements will normally take precedence over lending ratios. However, lending ratios may be stricter.
- Sit-down restaurants often trade food for advertising—significant food for significant advertising. It seems to be common knowledge among advertising executives that this is the key to obtaining free lunches. This procedure can throw off the P&L line items and percentages.
- Employee and manager meals may not be recorded for sales tax purposes.
- Owners may take family food and expensive wine home. The *IRS Audit Manual for Restaurants* and review may provide insight.
- Equipment dealers can provide information on replacement cost of restaurant equipment. Industry leaders can do the same (Taylor Equipment, Inc., for example).
- "Possible competitors coming" is always a big worry. Discuss. Maybe that is why your seller is selling. Disclaim.
- That new Hummer is not needed to transfer food product between restaurants.
- Employee theft can drastically alter P&L percentages. "A couple of nights a week, the chef would back cases of beer, sides of bacon into the cargo area."[10] Industry comparisons can be important and work best by type of menu offered (Mexican, Italian, steakhouse, etc.) if possible and/or available.
- Prior to your site visit, you should research the subject restaurant's food safety scoring with the applicable state or county inspector's office. Normally, this can be done with an Internet search. Food safety is such a critical component of

---

[10] Bourdain, *Kitchen Confidential*, p. 22.

today's restaurant environment. You should specifically discuss restaurant procedures relative to food safety with a manager or supervisor during your interviews. Although an analyst cannot be expected to be a food safety expert, the analyst should carefully document actual safety performance and restaurant procedures. This is an important component of the restaurant's risk premium.

Information Sources

An excellent source of a variety of restaurant information can be found at the National Restaurant Association site, www.restaurant.org, or call 800-424-5156. Once a year, the organization publishes a "Restaurant Industry Operations Report" with lots of useful statistics.

Because of the trend, menu, and technological changes, current publications are a good source of information:

Restaurant Hospitality, www.restaurant_hospitality.com, 216-696-7000
Restaurant Business, www.restaurantbiz.com, 646-654-7720
QSR, www.qsrmagazine.com, 919-489-1916
Nation's Restaurant News, www.nrn.com, 800-944-4676

The Cornell School of Hotel and Restaurant Administration has lots of publications and reference material: www.hotelschool.cornell.edu.

Edward Moran. *BVR's Guide to Restaurant Valuation,* Business Valuation Resources, 2009.
Zagat Survey of 2008 America's Top Restaurants, New York, NY, www.zagat.com, 212-977-9760.
Tom West. 2009 *Business Reference Guide: The Essential Guide to Pricing Businesses and Franchises,* 19th ed., Business Brokerage Press, 2009.
Lynda Andrews. *The Food Service Professional Guide To: Buying & Selling a Restaurant Business for Maximum Profit,* Atlantic Publishing Group, Inc., Ocala, FL, 2003.
Charles Bernstein and Ron Paul. *Winning the Chain Restaurant Game: Eight Key Strategies,* John Wiley & Sons, New York, NY, 1994.
Noah Gordon, Linda Kruschke, Alina Niculita, Shannon Pratt, and Doug Twitchell, and guest author Charles M. Perkins. *Industry Valuation Update Volume Two: Eating & Drinking Places,* Business Valuation Resources, LLC, Portland, OR, 2004, www.BVResources.com.
The Official Used Restaurant Equipment Guide, David Marketing Group, LLC, Duluth, GA, 770-497-8090.
AICPA National Restaurants Conference, normally offered in June of each year in one specific city.
The Stanford Video Guide to Financial Statements, "A Tale of Two Restaurants," Kantola Productions, 55 Sunnyside Avenue, Mill Valley, CA 94941.
The Food Channel, www.foodchannel.com/: links, food trends and publications.

Each state has a restaurant association that usually offers a website and useful information. Try typing "*State Name* Restaurant Association" in Google. Some sites are ".com" and some are ".org."

E: BARS AND NIGHTCLUBS

Introduction

This is a separate industry from restaurants; however, most bars, taverns, and night-clubs normally offer food from a menu. Perhaps the menu is limited by choice or by lunch-dinner. Readers are referred to the restaurant section first, since this shorter section will focus only on the liquor and other unique aspects of this industry.

Taverns that serve beer, wine, and liquor have been around for thousands of years. Today the names *tavern* and *bar* have been modified to reflect modern merchandising concepts. The interior ambiance of these establishments have been updated to reflect a youthful society. Exciting gaming areas, giant television screens, comfortable booths, and a dramatic array of foods being served are in vogue today to attract customers. Bands, disc jockeys, karaoke, fashion shows, and a host of other entertainment features are used to draw clientele. Business names such as "sports grill," "nightclub," and "brew factory" are vividly lit up on neon signs to reflect modern times.

Analysts need to be aware of another important nonfinancial driving force behind bar and nightclub sales and purchases. Jerry Ross, franchisor and founder of Famous Sam's Franchise Corporation sports bar, says:

> The bottom line is that beer and liquor are the products sold in all these businesses for "fun and profit." But, keep in mind, profit in this industry is only 50% of the reason that attracts people to buy or invest in this type of business. The other 50% is ego. Why in the world would million dollar sport figures and movie stars seem to gravitate to having their names linked to sport grills and restaurants? Why do they invest millions and lose millions in this business? It's ego. Ask Sylvester Stallone and Bruce Willis about their Planet Hollywood fiasco. Celebrities seem to enjoy associating themselves with the hospitality industry regardless of the fact they know nothing about the business!

Current State of the Industry and its Outlook

Federal and state legislation on drinking and driving has brought change to this industry. Health trends have also affected the industry, changing the taste norms toward light beers and lighter wines. America has become more sophisticated in wine selections and purchase, partially due to the popularity of cooking shows on numerous television channels.

Drinking establishments include:

- Neighborhood bars
- Sports bars
- Brewpubs
- Wine bars
- Nightclubs
- Gentlemen's clubs

Accounting/Financial Presentation Issues

Clear division of food-, beverage-, and alcohol-related sales is a desired goal for the analyst. Since alcohol sales are very profitable, both restaurants and bars/nightclubs should be separating components of sales and costs in these areas. This is not always the case, however. Bottom-line cash flow is what it is, yet analysis of alcohol profitability may be essential to the valuation. The nonalcoholic drinks should be separate from the alcohol drinks. Additionally, beer, wine, and hard-drink sales and costs should be detailed. Labor components (bartenders, servers, etc.) should be subscheduled under major labor headings. The overall goal is to separate the restaurant component of sales and costs, analyzing this section as discussed in the restaurant industry section.

Types of Assets

Once again, the assets will be similar to the basic restaurant. Two important distinctions deserve special analysis. First, inventory of wine, beer, and spirits can be substantial. An international wine inventory can easily approach six figures. A full bar might have several hundred expensive bottles of specialty liquor. How is it inventoried? How often is it inventoried? Is this system computerized? Are there pouring controls in place? A system in place that carefully controls the beer, wine, and hard-liquor inventory is more valuable and should be of interest to the analyst.

Second, brewpubs may have expensive equipment supporting their operations. An experienced brewmeister carefully tends to the entire process on a daily basis. Depending on the size of the tanks and the number of specialty brew systems operating at one time, several hundred thousand dollars can be involved. Given that they may be written off rapidly with accelerated tax depreciation, book value might be very low. The analyst must be alert for this situation. If appropriate, specialty equipment appraisers may have to be consulted in this area in order to reflect an accurate asset value. If the brewpub is doing poorly, the asset value of the equipment and its potential resale capability may become even more important.

Valuation Approaches and Methods

The methods are the same as detailed in the restaurant section. It is not necessary to value the restaurant separately from the drinking part of this establishment. The income approach methods will flexibly respond. However, individual comparison of alcohol consumption profitability and food profitability will affect that company's subjective risk premium. As discussed in the restaurant section, an investigation of a minimal liquor control system and below-average alcohol performance percentage-wise may mean a higher risk to a potential buyer.

Major Risk Issues

Unresolved theft or unreported income issues are clearly the major risk area in this type of valuation. Are the P&L numbers the real numbers? Is the analyst valuing a real company or a hypothetical company? Certainly, normalization entries can be made.

> "We split up the pool table money among the cooks."
> "How much would you estimate?"
> "About $100 a week."

Ignoring CPA firm income tax issues, an entry could be made to increase income by $5,200. Of course, what if it is only $50 a week? What if there are additional problem areas? What if the income is material—say, $500 per week?

Anthony Bourdain gives insight into this in his book, *Kitchen Confidential*:

> Earlier, I rashly implied that all bartenders are thieves. This is not entirely accurate, though of all restaurant workers, it's the bartender who has the greatest and most varied opportunities for chicanery. The bartenders control the register. They can collude with waiters on dinner checks, they can sell drinks out of their own bottles—I've even heard of a bartender who brought in his own register, ringing a third of the drinks there and simply carrying the whole thing home at night. But the most common bartender hustle is simply the "buy-back," when he gives out free drinks every second or third round to an appreciative customer. If you're drinking single malt all night long and only paying for half of them, that's a significant saving. An extra ten- or twenty-dollar tip to the generous barkeep is still a bargain.[11]

Each analyst must be comfortable with these types of situations.

Industry Nuances

For alcohol inventory, the industry has inventory specialists who arrive after closing and take inventory on microscales connected to computers. The computer knows the cost of Stolichnaya, for example; knows the number of ounces, knows the weight per ounce; and can automatically determine the value of the remaining vodka. Computer systems can report sales of liquor by brand for comparison sampling. Normally, bartending staff does not take the inventories.

Certain automated beverage systems dispense precise amounts of liquor per drink as a control measure. The popularity of these systems is cyclical, appearing everywhere and then disappearing. National chains are normally more systems-oriented than smaller taverns and pubs.

Sanity checks on P&L percentages can be performed by finding the cost of a bottle of beer, on average, and comparing it to the sales price.

Just as in the restaurant industry, sports pubs can be franchised with food and beverage systems. These franchises can be regional.

Valuation Issues

Again, once the alcohol control and inventory systems are evaluated, the valuation issues are the same as for the restaurant industry.

In referring to the theft/unreported income issues, rules of thumb seem more prominent at the smaller-size tavern. Perhaps they more gracefully tiptoe around these touchy issues. For example, cents per trailing 12 in the lower 40s seem to be referenced (most recent 12 month sales of $600,000 yields $240,000 to $275,000).

The lease quality with renewals (5 + 5 + 5) is a critical element that may be investigated. What are possible or scheduled increases? A right of assignment is necessary for sale. Terms with less than five years remaining might prohibit a sale to a knowledgeable buyer, rendering formal valuation methods less meaningful. The

---

[11] Bourdain, *Kitchen Confidential*, pp. 231–232.

liquor license must also be researched. Every state has different laws, prohibitions, and restrictions. Availability of insurance, possible large increases, inability to get assault and battery coverage, and deductible levels can negate a sale or transfer. Better to find out about a problem early in the company subjective risk process.

Minimum wage laws are a bit different for tipped employees who can use tips to cover a portion of their minimum wage. Tip reporting, if not being properly accomplished with IRS filings, can be a headache for a new owner.

Nightclubs have a different set of valuation issues. Patrons are often loyal to the performers rather than to the club. Competition in the technology area is expensive (TVs to plasma screens, for example). Cap Ex may not be just a historical average but a complete technology or décor change. Financial statement quality may be low. Based on previous discussions, it is usually prudent to obtain supporting tax returns. Local business brokers using the newspapers are constantly buying or selling taverns. Consult with this resource in your area if appropriate.

Rules of Thumb

An excellent source of rules of thumb (refer to discussion for caveats under "Restaurants") can be found in *Business Reference Guide* (NAR, 2006) written and edited by Tom West.

Information Sources

Please refer to the "Restaurants" section.

CHAPTER 27

Valuation Views and Controversial Issues: An Illustration

The purpose of this chapter is to highlight and discuss important concepts and views including numerous controversial issues that permeate business valuation. The following case presents selected excerpts from a business valuation report that was originally, in its entirety, in full compliance with the American Institute of Certified Public Accountants Statement on Standards for Valuation Services No. 1 and the Uniform Standards of Professional Appraisal Practice. The excerpts from the report presented here are only to form the structure to present various topics. As presented, it is not a detailed or comprehensive valuation report and should be viewed only as a teaching tool to present the various issues. Several sections of the report were purposely eliminated or truncated. At various points throughout the modified report we will stop and present Valuation Views (VV) that explain various concepts, as well as controversial issues.

This report format is one of many that analysts can use in presenting business valuations. All schedules have been omitted as they are not necessary for explaining the VVs. Some of the terms, numbers, sources and other data have been changed for ease of presentation. Furthermore, the initial view presented may not always be the best view in a particular valuation.

THE REPORT

Mr. Tom Profit
LEGGO Construction, Inc.
123 Builders Drive
Anycity, Anystate 54321

Dear Mr. Profit:

The objective of this valuation is to estimate the fair market value of 100 percent of the common stock in LEGGO Construction, Inc., ("LEGGO" or the "Company"), on a marketable, control interest basis, as of December 31, 20X5, for management purposes and internal planning. (A more informative term could be marketable illiquid. See Chapter 9.)

| VV | **Is There Such a Thing as a Marketable vs. Nonmarketable Controlling Interest?** |

Most analysts believe that there is no such thing as a "nonmarketable" controlling interest. Their point is that a 100 percent controlling interest is as marketable as any company of like kind that wants to be sold by the owners, thus the term "marketable, control." Others say that it can be nonmarketable depending on the underlying valuation methodologies used. For example, when using either the capitalized cash flow (CCF) or discounted cash flow (DCF) method in the income approach, analysts often rely upon Ibbotson or Duff & Phelps data to develop their discount and cap rates. These rates are based on public company rates of return that can include the almost instant liquidity of the stock. Even a 100 percent controlling interest in a closely held company lacks this level of liquidity. Therefore, some analysts will take a discount to adjust for this difference. An entire company cannot be sold in just a few days as public stock can be. This would be a discount for lack of liquidity (DLOL) vs. a discount for lack of marketability (DLOM). See Chapter 9.

Our conclusion of the fair market value of 100 percent of the common stock in LEGGO Construction, Inc., on a marketable, control basis, as of December 31, 20X5, for management purposes, is (rounded):

$$\$6,300,000$$

The standard of value used in this valuation report is fair market value. *Fair market value* is defined as follows:

> The price at which property would change hands between a willing buyer and a willing seller when the former is not under any compulsion to buy and the latter is not under any compulsion to sell, both having reasonable knowledge of the relevant facts.[1]

| VV | **Fair Market Value to Whom?** |

The standard of value here is fair market value. The question then is fair market value to whom? The standard answer is to a "hypothetical buyer." Furthermore, the seller is not LEGGO's current owner but a "hypothetical seller" of the shares. However, on a practical basis, it may be hard to ignore whom the seller is, since it is the client who operates the company as they see fit. The company may want the value to reflect the results of its management goals and philosophies. Assuming a "typical" hypothetical management team would operate the company in a similar manner, then the value is fair market value. However, if the company operated differently from others, then investment value may be the more appropriate standard of value.

Valuation is not an exact science subject to a precise formula. Rather, it is based on relevant facts, elements of common sense, informed judgment, and reasonableness. Our

---

[1] Treas. Reg. Sec. 25.2512-1 (Gift Tax Regulations).

scope was unrestricted and our methodology and analysis complied with the American Institute of Certified Accountants Statement on Standards for Valuation Services No. 1 and the Uniform Standards of Professional Appraisal Practice by the Appraisal Foundation. In addition, this valuation report and the values determined herein cannot be used or relied on for any purpose other than for internal management planning.

VV	**Restrictions on the Use of the Valuation Purpose**

Valuation analysts usually put restrictions on the use of the valuation. Values can differ depending on the purpose of the valuation. LEGGO management wants to know the value of the whole company to do internal planning. This value is on a stand-alone basis, reflecting the results of how the current management team runs the company. The valuation could have been for another purpose such as sale to a strategic buyer, minority gifts for tax purposes, an ESOP, or a dissenting rights case. Each of these probably would result in different values. For instance, there might be a synergistic control premium for the strategic buyer; the gifts of minority interests might have large discounts for lack of control and for lack of marketability; the ESOP value may have a higher value than the gift value but lower than the stand-alone value and much lower than the strategic value; and the dissenting rights value would differ depending on how that particular state treats discounts. The same company can have quite different values under differing circumstances and standards of value.

The enclosed narrative valuation report and exhibits, as well as all documents in our files, constitute the basis on which our opinion of fair market value was determined. Statements of fact contained in this valuation report are, to the best of our knowledge and belief, true and correct. In the event that facts or other representations relied on in the attached valuation report are revised or otherwise changed, our conclusion as to the fair market value of the common stock of the Company may require updating. However, Valking LLP has no obligation to update our conclusion of the fair market value of the common stock of the Company for information that comes to our attention after the date of this report.

No partner or employee of Valking LLP has any current or contemplated future interest in the Company or any other interest that might tend to prevent them from making a fair and unbiased conclusion of fair market value. Compensation to Valking LLP is not contingent on the conclusion reached in this appraisal report.

Very truly yours,

Val Dude, CPA/ABV/CFF, ASA, CBA, CVA
VALKING LLP

INTRODUCTION

Description of the Assignment

Valking LLP, was retained by Mr. Tom Profit to determine the fair market value of 100 percent of the common stock in LEGGO Construction, Inc., (the Company) on a marketable, control basis, as of December 31, 20X5, for management purposes and internal planning.

Summary Description and Brief History of the Company

The Company was incorporated in 1978 in the State of Anystate. The Company is a closely held subcontractor whose revenues are predominately earned from sewer and waterline construction, primarily in southern Anystate. The Company is now structured as an S corporation.

VV   **Tax-Affecting S Corporations?**

The valuation of S corporations and other pass-through entities has been one of the most controversial issue in business valuation. The main issue was whether to tax-affect S corporation income and then whether to further adjust the value.

The tax court has dealt with the matter of tax-affecting S corporations in several court cases (*Robert Dallas v. Commissioner, TCM* 2006-212; *Adams v. Commissioner*, TCM 2002-80; *Heck v. Commissioner*, TCM 2001-34; *Wall v. Commissioner,* TCM 2001-75; and *Gross v. Commissioner,* TCM 1999-254, *affd.* 276 F.3d 333 [6th Cir. 2002]). The most famous is *Gross v. Commissioner,* where the Court opined that taxes should not be assumed in valuing the shares of the company. The value of the shares was much higher since pretax income was essentially capitalized at what appeared to be after-tax discount rates.

It is important to remember that a court case decision is based on the facts and circumstances of that particular case. In addition, court decisions are ultimately the result of the legal strategy employed, decisions by the taxpayer and the quality of the attorneys and experts.

Today, most valuation analysts agree that the starting point for valuing a pass-through entity is to tax-affect the income, usually at a corporate equivalent rate. However, this is not the only adjustment that is made. Once the income is tax-affected, there is often an additional adjustment, whether upward or downward in the value, based on a variety of factors, including:

- Type of entity
- Amount and timing of distributions
- Retained net income
- Holding period and exit strategy
- Tax rates—personal versus corporate and capital gains
- Further effect of minority or marketability discounts
- Possible ability to participate in step-up-of-basis transaction
- Control versus minority interest

Many analysts also now rely on published models to value pass-through entities, including those developed by:

- Nancy Fannon
- Roger Grabowski
- Chris Mercer
- Chris Treharne
- Dan Van Vleet

See Chapter 12, "Valuation of Pass-Through Entities," for further information and detail concerning this topic.

The Company's customers generally consist of area contractors, developers, and local governments. The Company obtains most of its business through bidding competitively with other general contractors. The Company's management believes that customers contract with the Company due to its solid reputation and its competitive bids. The two largest customers of the Company include Brazen General Contractors and the City of Anycity, Anystate.

Employee relations have been harmonious with minimal turnover. All employees of the Company are unionized with the exception of several office workers. Currently, the economic climate in the market and industry are good. The Company has five to six competitors that are similar in size and nature.

Ownership and Capital Structure of the Company

The Company is legally structured as a closely held S corporation. As of the date of valuation, there were 5,000 shares of common stock outstanding structured as follows:

Name	Shares Owned	Percentage of Ownership
Tom Profit	4,250	85%
Gary Profit	250	5%
Susan Profit	250	5%
Michelle Profit	250	5%
Total	5,000	100%

VV　　　　　　　　**Discounts and Ownership Interests**

We are valuing 100 percent of the common shares in LEGGO. The percentage ownership of individual shareholders is not an issue here. However, let us assume that we are valuing the 85 percent interest of Tom Profit, or the 5 percent interest of Susan Profit. First the 85 percent interest: Would the "pro rata" value be different from 85 percent of the entire value of the company? The answer is yes, it would be different. Although Tom still controls the corporation with his 85 percent interest, there is the possibility of a nuisance value attributable to the other three 5 percent interests. Tom doesn't have complete control and could, at some time in the future, be exposed to a dissenting rights action or a shareholder oppression action. Although Tom has a great deal of power, it is not absolute.

As to Susan's 5 percent ownership interest, the "pro rata" value would typically be lower than 5 percent of the value of the entire company. To the extent that Tom is taking out "excess" compensation or perquisites, the value to Susan and the other two 5 percent owners would be diminished. There is less cash flow, thus less value. This is the discount for lack of control implicit in the reduction of cash flows due to Tom's personal motivations.

However, there are exceptions. What if Tom ran the company totally "clean"? What if his compensation and perks were normal and at market rates? What then is the discount for lack of control? Some analysts would argue that there should be no minority discount since the controlling shareholder is running the company to the benefit of all shareholders in proportion to their individual ownership. In this situation and at the current time in the

(continues)

company, there is little argument that control value and minority value are the same. This is completely predicated on "business as usual." It assumes that Tom or any other hypothetical controlling stockholder will keep the current policies forever. Well, forever is a very long time. What if Tom gets into personal financial trouble and needs more cash or Tom dies and someone else steps into his ownership interest? Will that new control owner continue the current policies of the company? No one can answer that question since we do not know who the new owner may be or what his or her motivations are. This creates uncertainty and uncertainty increases risk, which increases the discount rate, which decreases value. As such, many analysts will argue for some level of discount, albeit a lesser amount than if the controlling owner was taking monies out of the business for personal gain.

Standard of Value

The standard of value used in this report is fair market value. Fair market value is defined as:

> The price at which property would change hands between a willing buyer and a willing seller when the former is not under any compulsion to buy and the latter is not under any compulsion to sell, both having reasonable knowledge of the relevant facts.[2]

Among other factors, this valuation report considers elements of valuation listed in the Internal Revenue Service's Revenue Ruling 59-60, which "outlines and reviews in general the approach, methods, and factors to be considered in valuing shares of the capital stock of closely held corporations . . ."[3] Specifically, Revenue Ruling 59-60 states that the following eight factors should be carefully considered in a valuation of closely held stock:[4]

1. *The nature of the business and history of the enterprise from its inception.* The Company was incorporated in 1978. The Company is engaged primarily as a sewage and waterline subcontractor. The Company has grown since its inception, and its customers have remained loyal.
2. *The economic outlook in general and condition and outlook of the specific industry in particular.* The consideration of the economic outlook on both national and regional and local levels is important in performing a valuation. How the economy is performing has a bearing on how the Company performs. Overall, the outlook is positive.
3. *The book value of the stock and the financial condition of the business.* The Company has a relatively strong balance sheet with a majority of its assets in three categories: cash, contract receivables, and fixed assets. The fixed assets consist primarily of construction equipment and vehicles.

---

[2] Ibid.
[3] Internal Revenue Service, Revenue Ruling 59-60.
[4] Ibid.

4. *The earning capacity of the company*. The Company's compound growth rate from 20X1 to 20X5 was approximately 4 percent measured in revenues. The Company has demonstrated a good ability to generate profits.
5. *The dividend-paying capacity*. The Company has made distributions equal to the amount of the shareholders' respective tax liabilities in the recent past and likely will continue this trend into the future.
6. *Whether or not the enterprise has goodwill or other intangible value*. It is generally acknowledged that goodwill often is measured by the earnings ability of an enterprise being valued. Intangible assets can include customer relationships, trade names/trademarks, assembled workforce, and so on.
7. *Sales of the stock and size of the block to be valued*. There have been no recent sales of stock of the Company that would provide an indication of value during the period being analyzed.
8. *The market prices of stock of corporations engaged in the same or a similar line of business having their stocks actively traded in a free and open market, either on an exchange or over the counter*. The market approach was considered in this valuation. A search for guideline companies that are similar in nature and size to the Company was performed.

VV	**Reliance on Guideline Public Companies**

There are two choices in regard to the Guideline Public Company Method (GPCM) of the Market Approach:

1. Use it
2. Do not use it

Some analysts believe that you should use the GPCM in almost every valuation. If there are no direct comparable companies, or guideline companies that are somewhat similar, they will use companies from other industries that possess similar investment characteristics and risks. Others believe that the GPCM should be used only when there are reasonably similar guideline public companies. Revenue Ruling 59-60 states that it should be "considered," not necessarily applied, in all valuations. The current consensus is to always consider the GPCM and to use it in situations where the public companies are reasonably similar.

Sources of Information

Ten sources of information used in this appraisal include the following:

1. Audited financial statements for the years ended March 31, 20X1 through December 31, 20X5.
2. *Ibbotson SBBI, Valuation Yearbook*, published by Morningtar.
3. Duff & Phelps Risk Premium Report.
4. *The Federal Reserve Bank* for the 20-year maturity rate on 30-year bonds as of December 31, 20X5.

5. 20X1 to 20X5 Editions of *Benchmark Statistics and Ratios* (Fictitious).
6. *The National Economic Review* published by Mercer Capital Management, Inc., for the fourth quarter of 20X5.
7. *The Beige Book* published by the Federal Reserve Bank.
8. www.xls.com website for public company information.
9. www.hoovers.com website for public company information.
10. *Pratt's Stats* Online Comparable Transactions Database.
11. IBA Comparable Transactions Database.

Valking LLP has relied on the above sources but has not provided attest services in regard to any of the sources. Val Dude, a financial analyst with Valking LLP, interviewed management of the Company and made a site visit.

NATIONAL ECONOMIC OUTLOOK[5]

VV	**Using National Economic Data**

While it may seem that the national economic outlook is applicable only to companies that operate nationally, the national economic outlook should be analyzed and reviewed in all business valuations. In many industries, conditions at the national level will influence regional and local economies to some degree. There are exceptions to this rule and each valuation can be different but it is incumbent on the analyst to consider why national economic conditions are not a factor if that is the case.

Understandably, a review of national economic conditions can be lengthy and broad. The purpose of an analysis of the national economy in a valuation report is not to present an exhaustive study, but to identify those items having an affect on the value. For example, anticipated changes in inflation and anticipated changes in the Gross Domestic Product (GDP) are two important areas. Changes in GDP can affect demand and changes in inflation can affect pricing as well as interest rates. These items affect almost all industries and can be critical in some industries. For example, interest rates are an important consideration in the residential construction industry because higher interest rates preclude certain potential homeowners from buying homes. The overall conclusion for LEGGO is that the national economy appears to be performing well and is conducive to continued growth in their industry.

In conjunction with the preparation of our opinion of fair market value, we have reviewed and analyzed economic conditions around the December 31, 20X5, date of valuation. The following are summary discussions and analyses of the national economy for the fourth quarter of 20X5. These discussions are based on a review of economic statistics, articles in the financial press, and economic reviews found in business periodicals contemporaneous to the valuation date. The purpose of the review is to provide a representative "consensus" review of the condition of the national economy and its general outlook at the end of the fourth quarter of 20X5.

---

[5] See Sources of Information #5.

General Economic Overview

According to preliminary estimates released by the Department of Commerce's Bureau of Economic Analysis (BEA), real Gross Domestic Product (GDP), the output of goods and services produced by labor and property located in the United States, increased at an annualized rate of 5.8 percent during the fourth quarter of 20X5. Revised growth in GDP for the third quarter of 20X5 was 5.7 percent, which is higher than the preliminary estimated annualized growth rate of 4.8 percent. Increases in personal consumption expenditures, government spending, inventory investment, and exports were major contributors to the increase in GDP. These components were partially offset by an increase in imports. Annual growth in GDP for 20X5 was 4.0 percent, modestly lower than the 4.3 percent growth rate reported for 20X4. The U.S. economy is expected to continue expanding in the year 20X6 at approximately a 3 percent to 4 percent growth rate.

The Composite Index of Leading Economic Indicators, the government's primary forecasting gauge, increased 0.4 percent in December after rising 0.1 percent in October and 0.3 percent in November. The index attempts to gauge economic activity six to nine months in advance. Multiple consecutive moves in the same direction are said to be indicative of the general direction of the economy. In December, nine of the ten leading economic indicators rose. The most significant increases were money supply, interest rate spread, manufacturers' new orders of nondefense capital goods, stock prices, and manufacturers' new orders of consumer goods and materials. During the six-month span through December, the leading index rose 0.9 percent and seven of the ten components advanced. According to The Conference Board's report, "the leading indicators point to a continuation of the [economic] expansion during 20X6."

Stock markets ended the year at record levels. Broad market and blue chip stock indices turned in 20 percent to 25 percent annual gains, while the NASDAQ gained an unprecedented 85.6 percent during 20X5. The Federal Reserve (the "Fed") increased the federal funds rate in mid-November in an effort to slow economic growth and thus curb inflation. The Fed is attempting to cool the robust economic engine before it produces excessive inflationary pressure. Additional rate tightening is expected during the early part of 20X6. Despite a mid-quarter respite in bond price declines, bond yields reached their highest levels of the year in December, with the 30-year Treasury bond averaging a yield to maturity of 6.35 percent.

Inflation results for 20X5 reflect very low core price growth but high growth in energy prices. The Consumer Price Index (CPI) rose 2.7 percent for the year. Tight labor markets and strong economic activity are feared to be producing inflationary pressures. However, pricing data continues to suggest that gains in productivity and limited pricing power are keeping inflation in check. The inflation rate is expected to continue at approximately 2.5 percent to 3.0 percent in the first half of the year 20X6, but increasing fuel prices are posing a significant threat to future price stability.

Construction, Housing, and Real Estate

Home building is generally representative of overall economic activity because new home construction stimulates a broad range of industrial, commercial, and consumer spending and investment. According to the U.S. Commerce Department's Bureau of the Census, new privately owned housing starts were at a seasonally adjusted annualized rate of 1.712 million units in December, 7 percent above the revised November estimate of 1.598 million units, but 2 percent below the December 20X4 rate. Single-family housing starts in December were 1.402 million, 8 percent higher than the November level of 1.299 million units. An estimated 1.663 million privately owned housing units were started in 20X5, 3 percent above the 20X4 figure of 1.617 million.

The seasonally adjusted annual rate of new housing building permits (considered the best indicator of future housing starts) was 1.611 million units in December, similar to the revised November rate of 1.612 million and 6 percent below the December 20X4 estimate of 1.708 million.

Summary and Outlook

Economic growth, as measured by growth in GDP, accelerated to 5.8 percent in the fourth quarter of 20X5, after registering a revised 5.7 percent annualized rate in the third quarter. Annual growth in GDP for 20X5 was 4.0 percent. Stock markets finished the year at record levels. Both the DJIA and S&P 500 experienced double-digit growth for the fifth straight year, while the NASDAQ posted an 85.6 percent gain in 20X5. Bond prices have generally declined throughout the year but showed particular weakness on rising yields late in the fourth quarter. Fourth-quarter inflation reflected a seasonally adjusted annualized rate of 2.2 percent, representing a decrease from the third quarter rate of 4.2 percent. The rate of inflation for 20X5 was 2.7 percent, higher than the 1.6 percent rate of 20X4. After leaving interest rates unchanged at its prior meeting, the Federal Reserve's Open Markets Committee raised interest rates by a quarter of a percentage point. No change was made at the most recent meeting. Economic growth is expected to moderate somewhat from recent levels, but should remain historically favorable with GDP growing at 3 percent to 4 percent. Inflation is expected to remain relatively mild at below 3 percent, but increasing fuel prices are posing a significant threat to future price stability.

National Economic Impact on Valuation

Analyzing the national economy is an important step in performing a valuation because it helps to identify any risk that the economy may have in relation to the Company. In this case, the economy appears to be performing well.

REGIONAL ECONOMIC DATA (AS OF DECEMBER 8, 20X5)[6]

VV	**Regional Economic Data**

It is not unusual for regional and local economic data to differ from the national economy, even on a long-term basis. However, analysts must ascertain whether anticipated changes in the national economy may filter down to the regional and local economy. In the case of LEGGO, the regional and local economies are more important than the overall national economy (with the exception of interest rates), given the fact that it is a construction company that operates only in a certain geographic area. Some analysts make the mistake of reviewing just national economic data without considering regional and local data. Doing this can lead to different assumptions affecting the ultimate conclusion.

---

[6] See Sources of Information #6.

The regional economy remained strong in October and early November but was expanding more slowly than earlier in the year. Reports on consumer spending were mixed, with some noting strong sales growth for the first weekend of the 20X5 holiday shopping season.

Construction activity generally was strong. Overall manufacturing output remained strong, but conditions were varied across industry segments. The region's labor markets remained much tighter than the rest of the nation, and seasonal demand put additional strain on some sectors of the market. The fall harvest was complete, as was the planting of winter wheat. A survey of agricultural bankers indicated that slow farm loan repayments continued to be a problem.

Construction and Real Estate

Overall real estate and construction activity was robust, but softer than earlier in the year. Demand for both new and existing homes continued to ease in October and early November, but most reports described the market as strong. Those realtors contacted indicated that sales in October and early November were down about 10 percent from very strong results a year earlier. Homebuilders' reports appeared to be more positive than realtors' reports, with most reports indicating new home sales were unchanged or down slightly. Conditions in the nonresidential sector remained strong and steady for the most part, according to most reports.

Development of light industrial space was steady to down slightly, as was the development of infrastructure projects. A report from one of the largest metro areas suggested that a few large office projects that had recently broken ground might be the last of the current downtown office expansion. Some contractors noted that many customers had changed strategies, preferring to hire the contractor viewed as most likely to complete the job on schedule rather than going with the low bidder.

Regional Economic Impact on Valuation

The regional economy should also be analyzed in performing a valuation to help determine specific risks associated with the particular region that the Company operates in. In this instance, the regional economy is performing very well in many areas.

LOCAL ECONOMY

VV   **Local Economic Data**

For the valuation of smaller businesses such as LEGGO, conditions in the local economy are more relevant than regional or national economic data. It is important for the analyst to ascertain whether the activities of the company and the sales/revenue of the company were derived more from a local, regional, or national area perspective. The classic example of this would be a local hardware store. Operations of such a store would be influenced heavily by local activities as opposed to a national chain such as Home Depot, which would be affected more by national factors.

Local conditions that could have a deleterious effect on business operations include plant closings, changes in staffing of military or other government facilities, restrictive zoning ordinances, and dependence on a single industry as a primary employer.

Anycity, Anystate, was founded in 1810. It has an estimated population of 670,000 citizens and is approximately 326 square miles in area. The economy is made up primarily of trade, services, and manufacturing. Anycity has the 12th strongest economy in the nation, according to a 20X4 economic analysis. The analysis studied factors such as employment, per-capita personal income and construction, and retail employment.

According to another 20X4 study, Anycity was one of the top 10 metropolitan areas in the nation as a hot spot for starting and growing young companies. The survey measured the number of significant start-up firms created during the last 10 years and the number of 10-year-old firms that grew substantially during the last four years. Also, in November of 20X3, a national magazine named Anycity one of the top 10 "most improved cities" for business in the United States. Anycity was ranked seventh based on cost of living, educational opportunities, quality of life, and business issues. Construction activity also remained good.

Local Economic Impact on Valuation

The local economy is another important aspect to consider when performing a business valuation. The local economy represents the immediate environment that the Company operates in and thus, is vital to analyze. The economy of Anycity, Anystate, in doing very well. Thus, in our opinion, there is little risk associated with the local economy that will affect the Company.

INDUSTRY OUTLOOK

VV	**Reliance on Industry Data**

To the extent possible, the industry outlook should tie to the assumptions used in the valuation, particularly to growth rates, profit margins, and risk factors. Industry conditions can have a large effect on value. A poor or inadequate industry assessment can discredit a valuation. It is not the only deciding factor in supporting valuation assumptions, but it is an important one.

Water and Sewer Systems

Water supply construction increased 5 percent in 20X4, while sewerage construction was about the same as the level in 20X3. Both of these construction categories did well in the mid-2XXX, reflecting high levels of building construction as well as work on long-deferred projects. The strong construction market expected in 20X0 will help both categories do well. In the longer term, waterworks probably will be one of the more rapidly growing categories of public construction. The aqueduct systems of most older cities are so old that extensive replacement work must be done each year. The current level of construction in the United States is much lower than that needed to replace waterworks every 50 years, which is the recommended practice. Most water utilities are in a good position to raise the needed capital, so a steady increase in replacement construction is likely through 20X6.

The Safe Drinking Water Act requires numerous upgrades and replacements of water supply facilities. The Water Resources Act has expanded the role of the federal government in municipal water supply and appears to have facilitated increased federal funding for water supply construction. After 20X5 sewerage construction probably will continue to increase, although at a growth rate lower than that of the overall economy. Federal spending may not keep up with inflation, but the state and local share will increase steadily. A growing market factor is the need to repair, modernize, and replace the sewage treatment plants that were built during the boom of the 1970s. The sustained recovery in building construction also will support sewerage construction.

Industry Outlook Impact on Valuation

The outlook for this industry is good. The Company is a subcontractor that does mainly waterline and sewer work. The water and sewer portion of the construction sector appears to be growing and is expected to grow in the next few years. The fact that there is a need of repairs and modernization of sewage treatment plants that were built a few decades ago also provides a positive outlook for the Company.

FINANCIAL ANALYSIS OF THE COMPANY

 Presentation of Financial Data

There are two schools of thought in presenting financial information. One is to put all the financial information in tables throughout the report. For example, five years of spread financial statements would be in a table or exhibit that would be within the text. Others believe that such information should be in exhibits in an appendix to the report. The style used in this report puts the detail in the appendix and puts the summary information in the body of the report.

Historical Overview and Analysis

Financial statement amounts labeled "Dec-X4" represent the nine-month period April 1, 20X4 through December 31, 20X4, due to a change of year end.

 Relevance of Historical Financial Data

Some analysts believe that reviews of historical information have limited, if any, relevance. They support this idea by stating that valuation is a forward-looking exercise. Other analysts rely completely on historical information for formulating their opinions about the outlook and anticipated performance of a company. An analysis of the company's historical operating performance is an important component of a valuation. It indicates how well the management team is performing overall and can lead to information concerning trends.

(continues)

It is also true that history may not repeat itself and/or history may not be indicative of future performance. For example, the company may not have performed well in the past due to factors such as loss of a key person, litigation, or other such items. That company's problems may be behind it, and the effect of those factors on the financial performance of the company may no longer be negative. If the historical information (without adjustment) is then used to capitalize future income or cash flow, the company's value may be understated. In those situations, it may be better to prepare a pro forma analysis of the anticipated performance of the company. However, analysis of the historic performance of the company still would be important since it could indicate problem areas.

The historic performance of the company also should be viewed in light of the economy and industry performance during the historical period. For example, you may see an historical trend where a company's growth rate was seven percent. That may lead to a conclusion that the company is enjoying a fairly healthy growth rate. However, one may find that the company's competitors and peers in the industry were growing at 10 percent or higher during that period and that the company being valued is actually a laggard and could have problems competing. Alternatively, one could have a company that for the last 5 years has been decreasing its revenues and profits 5 percent each year indicating that it is a problem company. However, there may be a situation where an industry review indicates that everyone else was decreasing at 10 percent or 15 percent a year and the company you are valuing has less risk and is managing its resources better than its competitors during a difficult time. The analysis of the historic information should be made with respect to the local economy, the regional economy, the national economy, and the industry outlook. Doing this will give some indication as to how well the company has performed and, more important, is expected to perform.

Income Statements

Revenues

Revenues are generally the first component to be reviewed by financial analysts. All other things being equal, trends in revenues will translate into trends in profit margins, as well as the Company's ultimate fate. Increases in revenues should lead to higher profitability as the Company's fixed costs are spread over a wider revenue base leading to lower fixed costs per dollar of revenue. The following table represents the actual revenues of the Company for each year and the growth trend associated with each year.

	Mar-X1	Mar-X2	Mar-X3	Mar-X4	Dec-X4	Dec-X5
Revenues	$12,198,433	$11,345,938	$10,726,214	$11,558,858	$12,278,556	$14,819,373
% Change		−7.0%	−5.5%	7.8%	N/A	20.7%

As can be seen above, the Company's revenues have increased toward the latter part of the period analyzed. The revenues for the nine-month period December

20X4 were higher than any of the previous twelve-month periods. Over the period 20X1–20X5, the compound growth rate in revenues was approximately 4 percent.

Cost of Goods Sold

The Company's cost of goods sold were as follows:

	Mar-X1	Mar-X2	Mar-X3	Mar-X4	Dec-X4	Dec-X5
Cost of Goods Sold	$9,774,937	$9,301,970	$8,193,650	$8,804,580	$8,868,450	$11,676,380
% of Sales	80.1%	82.0%	76.4%	76.2%	72.2%	78.8%

To compare the Company to the industry, we used Benchmark studies (fictitious) 20X5. We believe that the appropriate industry classification for the Company is Standard Industrial Classification (SIC) Code 1623: Construction—General—Water, Sewer, Pipeline, Communication & Power Line Construction. According to the Benchmark study, the cost of goods sold averaged 78.2 percent in 20X5. As presented above, the Company's cost of goods sold as a percentage of revenue was 78.8 percent in 20X5, which is comparable to the industry average.

Operating Expenses

The Company's operating expenses were as follows:

	Mar-X1	Mar-X2	Mar-X3	Mar-X4	Dec-X4	Dec-X5
Operating Expenses	$1,135,984	$818,233	$1,213,537	$1,563,721	$872,841	$1,202,237
% of Sales	9.3%	7.2%	11.3%	13.5%	7.1%	8.1%

According to the Benchmark studies, operating expenses as a percentage of sales for companies in this industry were approximately 14.2 percent in 20X5. As presented in the table above, the Company's ratio was approximately 8.1 percent in 20X5, significantly lower than the industry average.

Balance Sheets

Current Assets

Current assets usually consist of cash and cash equivalents, accounts receivable, inventory, and other current assets, such as prepaid expenses.

Asset Mix

Over the period, the majority of the Company's assets has been in fixed assets and contract receivables. The following table illustrates the Company's asset mix as a percentage of total assets.

	Mar-X1	Mar-X2	Mar-X3	Mar-X4	Dec-X4	Dec-X5	Benchmark
Cash and Equivalents	13.8%	9.0%	10.2%	10.5%	1.7%	4.6%	11.2%
Contract Receivables	19.6%	15.8%	12.6%	10.1%	39.3%	34.3%	39.9%
Inventories	0.2%	0.2%	0.3%	0.2%	0.1%	0.6%	1.0%
Other Current Assets	5.8%	8.9%	14.2%	22.3%	9.7%	5.9%	7.7%
Net Fixed Assets	54.4%	58.8%	59.6%	55.3%	47.9%	53.3%	33.5%
Other Assets	6.2%	7.1%	3.3%	1.6%	1.3%	1.3%	6.7%

As presented in the table above, the Company's asset mix was stable for the most part. The contract receivables increased significantly in 20X4 and 20X5 due to the change in the reporting periods. The contract receivables tend to be higher at the December 31 year-end than they were at the March 31 year-end. The Company also has a much higher percentage of net fixed assets than the industry. The Company maintained a lower cash balance than the industry in the past few years, but that again is mainly due to the change in year-ends.

Liabilities

The highest percentage of liabilities consisted of long-term debt and the current portion of long-term debt. The following table illustrates the Company's liabilities mix as a percentage of total liabilities and stockholder's equity:

	Mar-X1	Mar-X2	Mar-X3	Mar-X4	Dec-X4	Dec-X5	Benchmark
Short-Term Notes	2.2%	2.5%	2.4%	2.9%	8.7%	2.9%	3.4%
Current Portion of LTD	0.0%	0.0%	0.0%	0.0%	3.9%	6.8%	4.8%
Accounts Payable	3.2%	7.4%	3.1%	4.3%	6.3%	7.7%	15.2%
Other Current Liabilities	12.9%	6.2%	4.1%	15.9%	4.3%	5.9%	12.8%
Long-Term Debt	10.4%	12.6%	14.5%	13.4%	6.7%	4.1%	12.9%
Equity	71.3%	71.3%	75.9%	63.5%	70.0%	72.6%	50.9%

The largest liabilities were accounts payable and long-term debt. The equity as a percent is much higher than the industry average.

Equity

Stockholder's equity refers to the difference between the book value of a company's assets and its liabilities. The stockholder's equity increased each year over the period analyzed. During the entire period 20X1 to 20X5, the stockholder's equity grew 109.8 percent.

Financial Ratio Analysis

VV   **Relevance of Benchmark Financial Ratios**

Analysts often value companies, particularly smaller ones, by comparing their historic financial performance with benchmark data available in the marketplace. These benchmarks are typically segregated by SIC or NAICS code and present aggregated information based on the ratios of the companies. Benchmark ratios include profit margins, returns on equity and assets, asset turnover ratios, liquidity ratios, and leverage ratios.

Some analysts believe that these types of comparisons are meaningless because none of the information can be directly tied to a valuation discount or capitalization rate. However, other analysts believe that this information can give a reasonable indication as to how well the company is performing against its peers within the benchmark industry group. They use it to assess risk. For example, in the valuation of LEGGO, the analyst made an extensive comparison of LEGGO's various ratios to the ratios in a national benchmark database. Although this indicates that LEGGO is performing better or worse in various areas, there are no direct links to any valuation pricing data.

When several guideline public companies are used in the guideline public company method (GPCM) of the market approach, their ratios can be tied to such pricing ratios as price to earnings, invested capital to EBITDA, and so on. The analyst can take a look at how the subject company compares to the various ratios of the public companies and then make adjustments to the public company multiples to reflect those differences. This cannot be done when using published benchmark data, which have no direct reference or tie to valuation multiples.

The information used in some of the benchmarks has not been verified and checked and/or is not time sensitive. Furthermore, much of the data may be in a format where items may be classified differently depending on how the particular company prepares its books.

A common mistake made by analysts is to use several different benchmark sources for ratios and then compare them to the ratios of the subject company without understanding how those ratios were calculated. For example, some ratios are calculated based on end-of-year balance-sheet amounts whereas others are calculated based on an average of beginning and end-of-year balance-sheet amounts. It is important that the subject company ratios are calculated in the same way as the benchmark ratios. Otherwise, inaccurate comparisons will result. In general, the use of benchmark data can be useful for risk assessments but cannot be heavily relied upon because they are not directly tied to any specific valuation multiples or cap rates.

Ratios for the nine-month period ending December 31, 20X4 are not presented.

The industry statistics used in the ratio analysis were taken from Benchmark Studies (fictitious). The median statistics used are for businesses whose primary Standard Industrial Classification code is 1623: Construction—General—Water, Sewer, Pipeline, Communication & Power Line Construction.

Ratios are divided into four groups, each representing an important aspect of the Company's financial position. The groups are liquidity, activity, leverage, and profitability.

Liquidity Ratios

Liquidity analysis assesses the risk level and ability of a company to meet its current obligations. It represents the availability of cash and the company's ability to eventually convert other assets into cash.

Current Ratio. The current ratio compares current assets to current liabilities. It measures the margin of safety a company has for paying short-term debts in the event of a reduction in current assets. It also gives an idea of a company's ability to meet day-to-day payment obligations. A higher ratio is better.

	Mar-X1	Mar-X2	Mar-X3	Mar-X4	Dec-X5
Company	2.3	2.1	3.9	1.9	2.0
Industry	1.4	1.2	1.2	1.5	1.5

The Company's current ratio was constantly above the industry average over the period. The Company's ratio is higher than the industry due to lower current liabilities.

Quick Ratio. The quick ratio adds accounts receivable to cash and short-term investments and compares the sum to current liabilities. The resulting ratio measures a company's ability to cover its current liabilities without having to convert inventory to cash. Generally, a higher ratio is better.

	Mar-X1	Mar-X2	Mar-X3	Mar-X4	Dec-X5
Company	1.9	1.5	2.4	0.9	1.7
Industry	1.1	1.0	1.0	1.2	1.2

The Company's ratios fluctuated over the period. The basic difference between the current and quick ratio is that the quick ratio includes only cash and receivables as the numerator. Thus, inventory is not included. As can be seen from the table, the industry averages contained a larger inventory base as indicated by the lower ratio. In 20X4, the Company's ratio was lower than the industry average due to a large increase in current liabilities in that year. Other than that year, the Company has been very liquid and could easily cover its current maturities.

Conclusion of Liquidity Ratios. The Company appears to have lower risk than that of the industry. The current ratio and the quick ratio are above the industry average for the most part. Thus, the Company would have little difficulty covering its obligations when compared to other companies within the industry.

Activity Ratios

Activity ratios, also known as efficiency ratios, describe the relationship between the Company's level of operations and the assets needed to sustain the activity. Generally, the higher the ratio, the more efficient the Company's operations, as relatively fewer assets are required to maintain a given level of operations. Although these ratios do not measure profitability or liquidity directly, ultimately they are important factors affecting those performance indicators.

Collection Period Ratio. The collection period ratio, also known as the days' sales in receivables, multiplies accounts receivable at year-end by 365, then divides the result by net sales for the year. This ratio measures how much control a company has over its accounts receivable. This ratio also indicates how many days, on average, it takes the company to convert accounts receivable to cash. Generally, the smaller the number of days, the better.

	Mar-X1	Mar-X2	Mar-X3	Mar-X4	Dec-X5
Company	19	19	16	16	58
Industry	55	54	59	63	60

Compared to the industry, the Company was better at collecting receivables. For four of the five years represented in the above table, the Company converted its accounts receivable to cash more quickly than the other companies within the industry. The Company's collection period ratio was higher than the industry in 20X5 due to two contracts that paid very late.

Fixed Assets Activity Ratio. The fixed assets activity ratio compares net sales to fixed assets. It indicates a company's ability to generate net sales from the use of its fixed assets. Largely depreciated fixed assets, leased assets or a labor-intensive operation may cause a distortion of this ratio. Generally, a higher ratio is better.

	Mar-X1	Mar-X2	Mar-X3	Mar-X4	Dec-X5
Company	6.9	5.2	4.7	4.1	4.1
Industry	5.8	6.2	6.1	6.9	6.4

The Company appears worse than the industry average during most of the period. The Company appears to have not utilized its fixed assets in generating revenues as effectively as the industry. However, the Company owns all of its equipment and machinery rather than renting. Thus, the higher amount of fixed assets causes the ratio to be low as opposed to the industry figures. Most companies of this nature do not own all of their equipment. The industry averages most likely represent companies that both rent and own their respective equipment and machinery.

Asset Management Ratio. The asset management ratio compares net sales to total assets. It measures a company's ability to generate sales volume using all of its assets. It is useful in comparing companies within specific industry groups on their effective employment of assets. Generally, a higher ratio is better.

	Mar-X1	Mar-X2	Mar-X3	Mar-X4	Dec-X5
Company	3.7	3.0	2.8	2.3	2.2
Industry	2.1	2.0	1.9	2.4	2.2

The Company's ratio decreased each year, and its trend was equal to or slightly less than the industry in the most recent two years. The Company is not generating sales volume using its assets as effectively as in the past but is comparable to other companies in the industry. Again, this may be the effect of the large level of owned fixed assets.

Conclusion of Activity Ratios. The Company seems to be doing better and worse than the industry in this category. The Company generally collects its receivables more quickly than other companies within the industry. However, the Company is not as effective as other companies within the industry with fixed assets, but this may be the effect of the large level of owned fixed assets.

Leverage Ratios

Leverage ratios measure the relative exposure of a business's creditors versus its shareholders. Leveraged companies accrue excess returns to their shareholders as long as the rate of return on the investments financed by debt is greater than the cost of debt. However, financial leverage brings additional risks primarily in the form of fixed costs that would adversely affect profitability if revenues decline. Additionally, the priority of interest and debt can have a severe negative effect on a company when adversity strikes. The inability to meet these obligations may lead to default and possibly bankruptcy.

Net Fixed Assets to Equity. The net fixed assets to equity ratio divides net fixed assets by a company's equity. It measures a company's ability to support the acquisition of fixed assets by using the original investment plus retained earnings. Generally, a low ratio is better.

	Mar-X1	Mar-X2	Mar-X3	Mar-X4	Dec-X5
Company	0.8	0.8	0.8	0.9	0.7
Industry	0.7	0.8	0.7	0.8	0.6

Overall, the Company is close to the industry averages. The Company's ratios were also pretty stable over the period. The Company would have no problem supporting the acquisition of fixed assets with retained earnings.

Total Debt-to-Equity Ratio. The debt-to-equity ratio compares a company's total liabilities to its net worth. It expresses the degree of protection provided by the owners for the creditors. Generally, a lower ratio is better from a risk perspective but could also indicate less than optimal use of debt.

	Mar-X1	Mar-X2	Mar-X3	Mar-X4	Dec-X5
Company	0.4	0.4	0.3	0.6	0.4
Industry	1.3	1.2	1.0	1.1	1.0

The Company's ratio has been better than the industry averages for every year. A lower ratio indicates less debt in relation to equity. As presented above, the Company had less debt than the industry.

Conclusion-of-Leverage Ratios. The Company is leveraged and contains some debt and related interest expense, but its debt is still not as high as the industry averages. The Company should have little trouble supporting the purchase of fixed assets with retained earnings or additional debt.

Profitability Ratios

Profitability ratios measure the ability of a company to generate returns for its stockholders.

Return on Equity.   The return-on-equity ratio compares the pretax income to equity. It measures a company's ability to generate a profit on the owner's investment. Generally, a higher ratio is better.

	Mar-X1	Mar-X2	Mar-X3	Mar-X4	Dec-X5
Company	54.9%	47.3%	46.8%	41.4%	40.3%
Industry	30.5%	32.7%	31.9%	28.8%	31.2%

Although the Company's return-on-equity ratio has deteriorated during the analysis period, it is still higher than the industry averages each year.

Return-on-Assets Ratio.   The return-on-assets ratio is calculated by dividing pretax income by total assets. This ratio expresses the pretax return on total assets and measures the effectiveness of management in employing the resources available to it. Generally, a higher ratio is better.

	Mar-X1	Mar-X2	Mar-X3	Mar-X4	Dec-X5
Company	39.7%	33.7%	35.5%	26.3%	29.3%
Industry	21.2%	26.2%	19.8%	23.2%	19.9%

The Company's ratios were better than the industry each year.

Conclusion-of-Profitability Ratios.   The Company is profitable and appears to be outperforming the industry although there is a recent decrease in the margins.

APPRAISAL OF FAIR MARKET VALUE

Valuation Approaches

Conventional appraisal theory provides three approaches for valuing closely held businesses: asset, income, and market. Asset approach methods look to an enterprise's underlying assets in terms of its net going concern or liquidation value. Income approach methods look at an enterprise's ongoing cash flows or earnings and apply appropriate capitalization or discounting techniques. Finally, market approach methods derive value multiples from guideline company data or transactions.

Asset Approach

Adjusted Book Value Method

This method consists of determining the fair market value of a company's assets and subtracting the fair market value of its liabilities to arrive at the fair market value of the equity. Both tangible and intangible assets are supposed to be valued. Appraisals are used to value certain assets and the remaining assets and liabilities are often included at book value, which is often assumed to approximate fair market value. This method does not provide a strong measure of value for goodwill or other intangible assets, which are more reasonably supported through the company's income stream. In this case, the value under the adjusted book value method (net tangible assets) was less than the values calculated under the income and market approaches. Thus, this method was not utilized in the determination of a conclusion of value for the Company.

VV	**Is the Asset Approach Always Necessary?**

Some analysts argue that all three approaches, including the asset approach, should be used if appropriate data are available. They often value just the tangible net assets of the business. However, other analysts argue that individual intangible assets also must be valued to implement this approach properly. Intangible assets in LEGGO include assembled workforce, trade name, customer relationships, backlog, contracts, goodwill, and going concern.

Most analysts do not use the full cost approach because increases in the accuracy of the appraisal, if any, are not worth the time and expense of having all of the assets valued. Furthermore, the aggregate value of all intangible assets is included in the values derived from the income and market approaches. The value of net tangible assets can be used to see the relationship to other approaches and methods and to generally estimate of the value of the aggregate intangible assets.

Excess Cash Flow Method

This method, which is sometimes referred to as the excess earnings or the formula method, is based on the "excess" cash flow or earnings available after a percentage return on the value of the net tangible assets used in a business has been subtracted. This residual amount of cash flow is capitalized at a percentage return for intangible assets of the business to derive the intangible asset value. Sometimes this method is used for very small businesses and in marital dissolution proceedings. The Internal Revenues Service's position on this method is that it should only be used when no better method exists.[7] It was not used in the valuation of LEGGO since better methods were available.

VV	**Use of the Excess Cash Flow Method**

Some analysts use this method when valuing a company or professional practice in a divorce setting. They use this method because the court in that jurisdiction is familiar with it and it would be perceived as an omission if excluded. Yet the IRS clearly states that it should be used only when no better method is available. Since the income approach, and often the market approach, can be used in valuations of most operating entities, other better methods often are available.

---

[7] Revenue Ruling 68-609.

The excess earnings method is often explained as a residual approach to valuation. Because of that, most analysts do not view it as a preferred method when valuing a company. However, there are occasions when the excess earnings method is the best indicator of value, such as with certain unique intangible assets. This would support why many analysts continue to use the method in appraising professional practices where there are often very few tangible assets contributing to value. Of course, there are also certain courts that expect to see the excess earnings approach because it is perceived as an omission if excluded.

Income Approach

Capitalized Cash Flow Method (Predebt Invested Capital Basis)

This method determines the value of a company as the present value of all of the future cash flows that the business can generate to infinity. An appropriate cash flow is determined and then divided by a risk-adjusted capitalization rate, here the weighted average cost of capital (WACC). In this instance, control cash flows were used. The following paragraphs describe the steps that were taken to determine the Company's indicated value from this method. The value is stated on a marketable, control interest basis.

VV   **Why, When, and Where Should Invested Capital (Predebt or Debt-Free) Methods Be Used?**

There is much debate in the valuation community about whether to use direct equity methods of valuation, in which interest expense and debt principal are included as uses of cash, or to use invested capital methods, where interest expense and debt are excluded as uses of cash. Theoretically, the use of both models should give a similar result. Both methods can be used in most valuations. However, in certain circumstances, one method may be better than the other. For example, the invested capital method may be used more in control valuations where the capital structure of the company is anticipated to change. Alternatively, in minority valuations, some analysts believe that the direct equity method is more appropriate since the minority shareholder cannot change the capital structure of the company. However the invested capital method can also be used assuming the existing level of debt.

There is also controversy surrounding whether, in a control valuation, the analyst should use an optimal capital structure that an outside buyer may employ or whether to use the existing capital structure of the company. The choice also can be affected by the ability of the current owners to obtain financing versus the hypothetical buyer's ability to get different financing. Under a fair market value standard of value, many analysts will use the existing capital structure of the company on a control basis. This would be control stand-alone value, which is the value to the current owners. Any additional value attributable to new buyers may be more akin to investment value and/or synergistic value. Other analysts will use an optimal capital

(continues)

---

structure if they believe the "typical" hypothetical buyer would employ that structure.

When using the invested capital method, the capital structure must be selected—what percent of total invested capital is debt versus equity? However, when using direct equity methods you cannot get away from a capital structure assumption, a misconception that some analysts have. Every return on equity should reflect the amount of debt used by the company. The potential increased rate of return requirements for equity holders must be reflected when increasing the debt levels of a company. Analysts can do this mathematically under the capital asset pricing model (CAPM) by unlevering and relevering the beta based on different capital structures. It is more difficult to adjust for debt when using a build-up method, which may be more judgemental. The capital structure of the company is explicitly recognized in the invested capital method through the weighted average cost of capital model, whereas it is more implicit in the direct equity method where the rate of return is derived through either the build-up model or the CAPM.

One potential problem with using the direct equity method is that the definition of cash flow includes new principal in as well as principal paid back out. If the new principal in the current year's cash flow that is being capitalized is higher than the principal being paid out, there is a disconnect in the amount of cash flows, creating an overvaluation. For example, in using the capitalized cash flow method, where the company added one million dollars of debt last year but did not pay any existing debt down, the implication when we capitalize the cash flow into perpetuity would be that a bank would give the company one million dollars per year every year without having to pay any money back. This is obviously a false assumption. In a direct equity method, when deriving cash flow, there needs to be an assumption of a normalized level of cash flow that would be capitalized into perpetuity. This includes a normalized level of debt, meaning that a debt assumption is actually made in the direct equity method.

Some analysts tend to take a practical approach and say that the use of invested capital methods is more complicated, more difficult to explain, and, as such, more difficult to support. Although the invested capital method may entail more steps than direct equity and it may appear upon first view to be more complicated, this is not a good reason to dismiss this method since it may be more appropriate to use it in various circumstances.

Determination of Appropriate Control Cash Flow. Under the capitalization of cash flows method, we used a predebt/invested capital basis for our calculation. This is due, in part, to the fact that the interest being valued is on a control interest basis. This control interest can influence the amount of debt held by the Company. We began our analysis with the adjusted pretax earnings at the date of valuation and for the five years prior to the date of valuation. The adjustments that were made to arrive at adjusted pretax earnings include an adjustment to officers' compensation, a control adjustment. We then made adjustments for interest expense, nonrecurring items, and for items that are not reflective of operations to the pretax earnings.

| **VV** | **Control versus Minority Cash Flows** |

The cash flows of a company determine whether the company is being valued on a minority or a control basis under the income approach. Many analysts also believe this for the market approach. If the owner of a company is taking out excess compensation, like Tom Profit in LEGGO, and the resulting lower income is capitalized without adjustment, that would produce a minority value indication. Adding back the owners' excess compensation and then capitalizing the higher income would indicate a control value. This is just one example of a control-type adjustment. Most analysts agree with this concept.

What if one values a company that doesn't have any control adjustments? What if the company is run for the benefit of all shareholders without any shareholder taking out any cash flow over and above what he or she is entitled to? If we have no adjustments to make, is the value control or minority? The answer is yes and yes! The value would clearly be control stand-alone since the capitalized cash flow is the cash flows of the entire company. Since the current owners of the company are operating it to the benefit of all shareholders, it becomes the minority value as well. However, it is only the minority value to the extent that the current owners continue their policy. Policies can change and/or new owners can come in. This is an additional risk factor for minority owners that could indicate that a discount for a lack of control may be appropriate. Just because the owners are operating in a certain favorable way currently, does not mean that will not change in the future. When capitalizing income we are capitalizing that income into perpetuity. The assumption is that the current owners would continue the current favorable policies forever. Consequently, an adjustment for lack of control may be appropriate to reflect the risk of potential future changes in cash flows to the minority owner from a change in management or the policies or both.

After compensation, the next adjustment was to add back the depreciation expense. This noncash expense should be added back to arrive at an appropriate level of cash flow. The adjustment for the gains and losses on the sale of marketable securities was made because the marketable securities are considered to be an excess/nonoperating asset. All income and expenses related to excess/nonoperating assets are taken out of the income stream because the total value of the asset is added to the indicated value of operations. The reason for the adjustments to dividend income and unrealized gains on marketable securities is the same. These assets relate to excess/nonoperating assets and must be taken out of the income stream. The other adjustment that was made was an adjustment to the interest income.

| **VV** | **Treatment of Nonoperating/Excess Assets** |

In valuing a controlling interest of a corporation, most analysts agree that the income and expenses of nonoperating and/or excess assets of the business must be removed from the operating earnings and the asset values added to the value

(continues)

of the operations. There should also be adjustments made to the P&L for related expense and income items associated with the nonoperating assets.

The difference of opinion occurs when valuing a minority interest. Some analysts believe that the same methodology should be employed as in valuing a controlling interest—that is, value the nonoperating or excess assets separately and make the related adjustments to earnings. They would then take a discount for lack of control and a discount for lack of marketability from the nonoperating asset values before or after they added it to the company's discounted operating value. Other analysts believe that a minority stockholder has no access to these types of assets. Therefore, the P&L should remain as is, reflecting the way the company operates. The assets are not separately valued and added back. This obviously creates a situation where the value of the nonoperating/excess assets may be $0.

Depending on the nature of the assets, either approach may be applicable. For example, if the nonoperating/excess assets are cash and that cash is for a bonus to the controlling shareholder within three months, then the minority shareholder can do nothing about it and the value of that asset to the minority interest is $0. However, in the situation where nonoperating assets are more long term in nature, such as excess land or buildings, then the former approach of removing the asset and discounting it, then adding that back to the discounted operating value, may be more appropriate.

In applying the first method, how do you discount the nonoperating assets? Typically nonoperating assets consist of real estate, marketable securities and/or cash. Depending on the materiality of the nonoperating assets, an approach not dissimilar to valuations of family limited partnerships may be appropriate. In some situations, there may be different discounts for lack of control and marketability for the nonoperating assets than there are for the operating value of the company.

The resulting amount, adjusted income before income tax, for each year was then averaged. We believe a straight average is appropriate due to the cyclical nature of the Company. However, the Company changed year-ends in 20X4. Since we have nine months of data at December 31, 20X4, this period was adjusted appropriately.

VV   Capitalizing Historical Income/Cash Flow

There are many different methods for taking historic income statements and projecting an anticipated future economic benefit to be capitalized. Those methods include: prior year, straight historical average, weighted historical average, trend line analysis, budgeted, and others. Generally, analysts will use a straight historical average when the earnings and cash flows are more volatile and are expected to continue so. The other methods are often more appropriate where there is more of a trend in the historical results.

The next step was to deduct an estimated ongoing depreciation expense in order to calculate state and federal taxes. In this instance, the ongoing depreciation expense was estimated to be $650,000, based on estimated future capital expenditures. After the ongoing depreciation was deducted, state and federal taxes were calculated at a combined rate of 40 percent and deducted. The amount that resulted was adjusted income predebt and after tax.

VV	**Normalizing Depreciation and Capital Expenditures**

A common mistake made in business valuation is to capitalize a cash flow figure into perpetuity where the depreciation greatly exceeds the future capital expenditure requirements. This is obviously an impossible situation since future capital expenditures have to be made to generate future depreciation. Many analysts will normalize depreciation and capital expenditures by making them equal or similar. This equalization process is a simplifying assumption, since capital expenditures will usually exceed depreciation due to inflationary pressure in a stable business. However, this simplification usually, but not always, has a nominal effect on the value.

There are situations in which depreciation can exceed capital expenditures for extended periods of time. These situations occur when there is a previous purchase of a large long-life asset such as a building, or where goodwill and other intangible assets are amortized over a longer period of time. In those situations, it may be appropriate to have depreciation exceed capital expenditures.

In the normalization process, the depreciation should be adjusted to the level of anticipated capital expenditures; capital expenditures should not be adjusted to depreciation. The future depreciation will be generated by future capital expenditures. Again, the concept is to normalize the cash flows of the business. The normalization process for depreciation should happen in two steps. It needs to be removed from the expenses in the income statement, with the new capital expenditure inserted. To calculate cash flow, depreciation is added back and capital expenditures are subtracted out, which can net to zero.

VV	**Methods for Calculating Taxes**

The normalized tax expense also was deducted in this valuation. We have already discussed the different views concerning tax affecting S corporations and other pass-through entities (Chapter 12). Assuming taxes are to be deducted, there are choices to be made in the method of the tax adjustments. Some analysts will go back and compute taxes in each of the years that are used in the average income as opposed to making all the adjustments on a pretax basis, calculating the average, and then adjusting for the taxes. When the tax rates are the same, this will not have an effect. However, in C corporations, where tax expenses may differ for each year due to certain types of planning, an average of five years after-tax income may be different from the average of five

(continues)

year pretax income, which is then aggregated with one tax amount applied to it. There may also be years when the taxes would be less than the marginal rate. Some analysts believe that an average of the effective rate is more appropriate. Other analysts believe that eventually the company will end up paying close to the marginal rate into perpetuity, and that would be the more appropriate rate.

Three further adjustments were then made to the predebt and after-tax income. The ongoing depreciation that was deducted to calculate taxes was added back because it is not a cash expense. The estimated future capital expenditures were then deducted. In this case, it was estimated that future capital expenditures would approximate $650,000 per year based on historical trends. The final adjustment was a working capital adjustment. This adjustment is based on industry data based on an industry working capital to revenue ratio. After making these final three adjustments, predebt and after-tax cash flow was $1,000,964. We believe that this is the cash flow that is representative of future operations. The cash flow was then divided by a risk-adjusted cap rate using the weighted average cost of capital and an anticipated long-term average growth rate to derive a value of the operations.

VV **Cash Flow versus Income**

There is continuing debate in the valuation industry concerning the use of either cash flow or income when performing discounted cash flow methods or capitalized cash flow methods. Cash is indeed king, and cash flow should be used in most situations. When depreciation and capital expenditures are equalized, the only other real adjustment would be incremental working capital. Not all businesses require incremental working capital, particularly cash businesses or businesses in which receivables are turned quickly. Particularly in small businesses, cash flow and income may be equal or similar. However, many businesses require working capital to fund growth. In those situations, working capital should be considered as a use of cash. Cash flow in a growing business typically would be less than income in those businesses that have working capital needs. Debt also would have to be normalized in terms of debt principal in and debt principal out.

Determination of Weighted Average Cost of Capital

VV **Direct Equity Method versus Invested Capital Method**

LEGGO was valued using a capitalized cash flow method relying on adjusted and normalized historical income, where each year was equally weighted. In the application of the income approach, it is also possible to use a discounted cash flow method. However, it was unnecessary in this valuation as the projected average growth rate applied to average cash flow was sufficient to estimate future earnings.

Under each one of the two main methods of the income approach, analysts can use either the direct equity method or the invested capital method. The direct equity method includes cash flows direct to equity, which are discounted to present value or capitalized using a capitalization rate based on the company's cost of equity. In an invested capital model, the cash flows would be preinterest and predebt and would be those cash flows available to both debt and equity holders. In an invested capital model, the rate of return would be a weighted average cost of capital that would include the cost of debt and equity. There is some diversity of opinion concerning when to use the invested capital method and when to use the direct equity method.

Often, one of the reasons given for using direct equity is that the analyst can avoid making assumptions of capital structure, e.g., what percent debt and what percent equity a company will use. However, in a direct equity method, there needs to be assumptions of the debt principal paid out and the new debt principal received on a normalized basis. Anytime an analyst normalizes the amount of debt that is used in a company, he or she is explicitly assuming a capital structure. Therefore, debt is a consideration in using the direct equity method.

In this valuation, the analyst used an invested capital method using the company's weighted average cost of capital. Again, it is often used in control valuations. However, each method can be used in minority and control valuations if applied properly. It is often a matter of preference.

There are a number of steps involved in calculating the weighted average cost of capital. These steps involve calculating the cost of equity, the cost of debt and the determining of an optimal capital structure for the Company, using industry benchmarks. The WACC formula is as follow:

$$\text{WACC} = \text{We (Ke)} + \text{Wd} (K_{dpt}) (1 - t)$$

Cost of Equity

We used a build-up method to calculate the cost equity. The formula is:

$$\text{Ke} = \text{Rf} + \text{RPm} + \text{RPs} + \text{RPu}$$

MCAPM versus Build-Up Model
Income Rates or Cash Flow Rates
Minority Rates or Control Rates

There is controversy in the valuation industry about whether the MCAPM should be used to value small businesses. Some analysts even believe that MCAPM or CAPM should not be used to value even larger businesses. The only difference between the MCAPM and the build-up method is the use of beta. It is often difficult to find betas for small publicly traded companies that could be applicable to small private companies. There are many different sources of

(continues)

beta and many different ways to calculate beta. Betas can differ even for the same public company at the same point in time. Sometimes analysts reject the guideline public company method of the market approach because they believe there are no similar companies. However, they may use those same rejected guideline public companies to derive betas. We believe that this is an inconsistency.

Betas are sometimes available that could be used in the MCAPM when valuing small companies. In some industries, there are large numbers of publicly traded small companies where betas may be available. If there are no reasonably similar companies whose betas could be used as a proxy for the small closely held company, then the build-up model may be the best method to use. However, if the betas are reasonable and can be used, then a capital asset pricing model may be considered. Also, there are situations where there may be indications of industry risk based on somewhat similar publicly traded companies or industry data. These may be used to increase the specific risk premium that is used in a build-up model. Each of these situations is dependent on the facts and circumstances and can differ depending on the type of company, the industry in which the company operates, and the size of the company.

Another controversy is whether the rates of return determined by the build-up model and MCAPM should be applied to income or cash flow. The current consensus is that these are cash flow rates of return. They are also rates of return after corporate tax but before personal investor tax. The rates of return are based on dividends and capital appreciation. Dividends are paid after corporate tax by public companies and capital appreciation is also after corporate tax due to retained earnings used to grow the business. However, these rates of return are before taxes to the individual investor. Morningstar/Ibbotson and Duff & Phelps, who publish risk premium data, agree that traditional rates of return derived using their data should be applied to after-tax cash flows.

There is also some discussion concerning whether the rates of returns derived using risk premium data are minority rates of return or control rates of return. Ibbotson is very clear in stating that it believes that they are neutral, not minority returns. The returns are neutral. Most analysts today believe that any control or minority features are in the company's cash flows instead of the discount rate itself. The Ibbotson and Duff & Phelps data are based on returns of shares of stock that are on a minority basis. However, Ibbotson believes that a controlling shareholder would not necessarily be able to maximize or increase the return and that the boards of directors of publicly traded companies must maximize returns for all shareholders, regardless of how the company is held, supporting the concept of a neutral return.

The first step was to begin with the risk-free rate of return (Rf) based on long-term (20-year) U.S. Treasury coupon bonds with a yield of 4.5 percent, as reported in the *Federal Reserve Bulletin* at the date of valuation.

| VV | **Proper Risk-Free Rate** |

Most analysts use a 20-year risk-free rate of return from a U.S. Treasury Bond because that is the basis from which Ibbotson and Duff & Phelps derive their risk premium data. There is no such thing as an original-issue 20-year bond. What analysts use are 30-year Treasury Bonds that have 20 years remaining to maturity. Ibbotson states that 20-year bonds are used because information on them has been available since 1926.

The next steps are to add the common stock equity risk premium (ERP or RPm) and the size risk premium (RPs). The Ibbotson information presents these two risk premiums separately. The Duff & Phelps data presents them in aggregate for use in the build-up model and separately as well for use in either the build-up model or the modified CAPM. In the past several years the Ibbotson ERP (from 1926) has been around 7 percent and the Duff & Phelps ERP (since 1963) has been around 5 percent. Furthermore, the Ibbotson tenth decile size risk premium (market value of equity capital) has been approximately 6 percent. The Duff & Phelps 24th and 25th size categories' size risk premium (market value of equity capital; Duff & Phelps has eight measures of size including market value of equity capital) has been approximately 6 percent and 7 percent, respectively. The Duff & Phelps combined risk premium for the 24th and 25th size categories (ERP and size; market value of equity capital) has been approximately 12 percent and 14 percent, respectively. Please note that some of the risk premium data was lower than other recent years in the 2009 publications.

| VV | **Equity Risk and Size Premium Choices** |

Most analysts agree that the proper equity risk premium to apply to the valuation of closely held businesses should be a long-term equity risk premium rather than short-term. Ibbotson goes back to 1926 and Duff & Phelps goes back to 1963.

In the selection of the size risk premium, there are more differences of opinion. Some analysts use the tenth decile of Ibbotson while others will use the microcap strata (the ninth and tenth deciles). As mentioned in Chapter 6, there are also differences of opinion as to which small stock risk premiums to use based on the type of beta when using MCAPM. It could be monthly betas, annual betas, or sum betas. In the valuation of LEGGO, the small stock risk premium selected was based on data from the 10th decile of Ibbotson and the 25 size-ranked categories of Duff & Phelps. For Ibbotson it was derived from the size premium return in excess of CAPM for the tenth decile. For Duff & Phelps it was taken in excess of CAPM and in excess of the risk free rate.

There have been several studies on equity risk premiums, with many of them arriving at lower rates than those published by Ibbotson. However, many analysts still choose to utilize the Ibbotson data as published until now. In the 2004 edition of *Ibbotson's Stocks, Bonds, Bills, and Inflation*, Roger Ibbotson and Peng Chen

(continues)

published a study covering the periods 1926–2000 that stated, "We estimated the equity risk premium to be 3.97% in geometric terms and 5.90% on an arithmetic basis. These estimates are about 1.25 percentage points lower than the historical estimates." More recent methods of calculating the supply-side equity risk premium in the past few years have resulted in a difference of only 0.8 percent to 0.9 percent (*Note:* In the 2010 edition, the difference was 1.5%). These new findings have convinced many analysts to reduce the long-term arithmetic average equity risk premium based on this new supply-side equity risk premium. However, the data and application are still being debated. See Chapter 6.

For the size risk premium, some analysts use the microcap risk premium because the average includes more companies. The microcap size risk premium includes the ninth and 10th deciles and has historically been less than the 10th decile. Ibbotson also reports the 10th decile split into two size categories, 10a and 10b (in 2010 they went to 10W, 10X, 10Y, 10Z). The size premium from 10b has historically been much higher than the 10th decile alone. When valuing small companies there is continuing debate about whether to use the tenth decile, microcap, or 10b strata as the measure of the size risk premium. However, many analysts are uncomfortable with using 10b data as this category includes many large companies that have a low market value of equity, often because they are distressed.

In the Duff & Phelps study and data, Roger Grabowski and, formerly, David King, take the discussion a step further in their analysis of equity risk premiums. They recommend that analysts consider alternative sources of information when estimating equity risk premiums. One alternative is to examine the historical returns over varying time periods other than 1926–present to better reflect the period of analysis. This includes the data from the risk premium report that goes back to 1963. They also recommend using alternative measures of size. The risk premium report measures size by eight categories, including market value of equity, market value of invested capital, revenues, and so on. Also, they segment the data into 25 size categories and remove distressed companies. They also have risk premium data based on fundamental measures of risk other than size, including average operating margin, coefficient of variation of operating margin, and coefficient of variation of return on equity. In 2009 and 2010, Duff & Phelps has also constructed a new, more flexible tool to value troubled or potentially troubled companies using Altman's Z-score. This new tool is called *Risk Premium Report—High Financial Risk Company Data.*

Another alternative is that analysts consider the use of forward-looking estimates, such as those implied from projections of future prices, dividends, and earnings. Grabowski's findings on published equity risk premiums and subsequent recommendations have led many analysts to further investigate their own estimates. See Chapter 6 for Duff & Phelps discussion.

The final step is to add a company-specific premium (RPu) that takes into account additional risks that are specific to the Company. These additional risks include the following:

- *Company's depth of management.* The Company appears to have sufficient depth of management.
- *Importance of key personnel to the Company.* The Company does have several key employees whose loss would have a negative effect on the Company.
- *Growth potential in the Company's market.* The water and sewer portion of the construction sector appears to be growing and is expected to grow in the next few years. (See earlier discussion on the industry outlook.)
- *Stability of the Company's earnings and gross profits.* The Company has a consistent history of generating profits.
- *Company's bidding success rates.* The Company has had good bidding success. In addition, the Company has maintained good profit margins. This indicates that the Company's bidding success is not due to underpricing contracts.
- *Financial structure of the Company.* The Company is financially sound.
- *Geographic location of the Company.* The Company is located in Anycity, Anystate. (See earlier discussion on the local economy.)
- *Company's order backlogs.* The Company has a sufficient amount of contract backlogs.
- *The diversification of the Company's customer base.* The majority of the Company's revenues is generated from only a few customers. The Company could be negatively affected should any of these customers be lost.

After considering the financial ratio analysis and the above risk factors, plus the size of the company as compared to the Ibbotson companies, it is our opinion that a company-specific premium of 4 percent is appropriate for the Company.

VV Specific Risk Premium Presentations

As illustrated in Chapter 6, there are many methods for determining the specific risk premium. All of them require judgement. For LEGGO, the analysts decided to list those items they thought were the most important in indicating how the company was performing. They then made a selection of an aggregate 4 percent risk premium. This is a common method of selecting specific risk premiums.

Some analysts argue that there should be some type of numerical system placed on the categories, for example, -3, -2, -1, 0, 1, 2, 3. Doing this implies precision that does not exist. It can also be difficult to defend in a litigation setting. Think of the following type of possible cross-examination.

Question: Mr. Dude, I notice that you concluded on a 4 percent specific risk premium based on the 9 categories. I notice that you used a system of negative 3 all the way up to positive 3 for each one of the categories. I would like to ask you a question. Is it possible that, in each one of those categories, the specific amount could have differed by, let's say, half a percent? For example in category 2, I noticed that you used a 2 percent risk premium. Is it possible that could be 1.5 percent?

Dude: Probably, yes, since no one is that precise.

Next question: Mr. Dude, assume for me if you will, that each one of the categories was a half point less. Please indicate how that would change the specific risk.

(continues)

> *Answer:* It would reduce the specific risk by 4.5 percent, and would result in a negative 0.5 percent risk premium.
>
> As you can see, this could be a difficult presentation to defend. Let us go back to the presentation that the analyst made in LEGGO. If the question is asked: Mr. Dude, could the 4 percent risk premium have been 4.5 or 3.5? The answer could still be the same, yes. However, the effect would be much less.

We prepared several calculations of the cost of equity based on the build-up model and data from Ibbotson and Duff & Phelps. This resulted in a range of equity returns of 20 percent to 22 percent. We also calculated the cost of equity using the Duff & Phelps risk premiums based on three measures of risk: five-year average operating margin, coefficient of variation of operating margin, and coefficient of variation of return on equity. We selected 21 percent.

$\boxed{VV}$ **Calculating Cost of Equity**

Many analysts will calculate several indications of cost of equity based on the data from both Ibbotson and Duff & Phelps. That was done here. Other analysts will calculate only one cost of equity based on selected data from both Ibbotson and Duff & Phelps. For example, they may look at the ERP from both sources, but pick only one as opposed to using both in separate calculations. Generally, both methods should result in a similar selected or calculated cost of equity.

Some analysts still rely only on Ibbotson. If that is the choice, it is recommended that the analyst at least become familiar with Duff & Phelps, particularly since its use is growing rapidly.

Cost of Debt

Next, we determined the cost of debt. To calculate this rate, we began by determining the Company's actual borrowing rate at the date of valuation. We believe the borrowing rate of the Company at the date of valuation should be 8 percent. A 40 percent tax rate is deducted. The result is the cost of debt, net of the estimated tax benefit, of 4.8 percent.

Weighted Average Cost of Capital

Finally, we determined the weighted average cost of capital using the debt and equity rates that were already calculated. The equity discount rate is multiplied by an equity percentage and the debt discount rate is multiplied by a debt percentage as determined based on the average capital structure for a company in this industry. In this instance, an 80 percent equity weight and a 20 percent debt weight were determined from industry averages (illustration only). The percentages were then multiplied by the equity and debt discount rates calculated earlier and then summed to arrive at the weighted average cost of capital discount rate. This rate was calculated to be 17.8 percent as follows:

$$17.8\% = .80\ (21\%) + .20\ (4.8\%)$$

VV	**Weights in the WACC**

There is some controversy concerning the selection of the weights to be used for debt and equity in the weighted average cost of capital. Most analysts agree that the existing capital structure of the company should be used without adjustment when valuing a minority interest. The calculation can be done iteratively, meaning that you choose a capital structure to value the company, then determine the percent of debt based on that value using the actual debt of the company. If it is different, then you redo the capital structure until it resolves to the proper capital structure that is in existence. This is easily accomplished with the use of spreadsheets. As you change the capital structure of the company through this iterative process, increases in debt may increase the rates of return on equity as well. This can be reflected directly through the use of CAPM by levering and unlevering betas. If a build-up model is used it is more subjective.

When valuing a controlling interest in a company, there is controversy about whether to use an optimal capital structure based on guideline public companies and/or industry benchmark data, or to use the current capital structure if that is what is anticipated to be employed by the owners of the company. This depends on the type of valuation being prepared. The valuation could be from the prospective of a sale to an owner that could employ a different capital structure. The valuation could also be done on a stand-alone basis, with the owners wanting to know the company's value on an ongoing basis using the existing capital structure. In the valuation of LEGGO the company is going to change to its optimal capital structure, so that was used here.

From this amount, a 3 percent growth factor is deducted to arrive at a net cash flow capitalization rate for the next year that is 14.8 percent. The 3 percent growth factor is a long-term inflationary component used to adjust the capitalization rate. It was also based on management's projection of growth. The rate derived after deducting the 3 percent was divided by one plus the growth rate to arrive at a net cash flow capitalization rate for the current year. In this instance, the rate amounts to 14.4 percent or 14 percent (rounded).

VV	**Common Capitalized Cash Flow Method**

Another common method for capitalizing cash flow is to take the indicated amount of cash flow, here estimated based on a straight historical average of normalized earnings, adjusted to cash flow; grow that amount by the anticipated long-term average growth rate, here 3 percent; then capitalize that amount one year out at the capitalization rate, here 14.8 percent or 15 percent (rounded).

> ## $\boxed{VV}$ Supporting Growth Rates
>
> The selection of the sustainable long-term average growth rate can have a large effect on the value conclusion. Price multiples and, therefore, values are very sensitive to growth. When applicable, some analysts use the inflation rate, or something close to it, as the perpetual growth rate in the capitalized cash flow method, as is used for LEGGO. When applicable, others use the average nominal (real and inflation) growth of the Gross Domestic Product of the United States, which has been 6 to 6.5 percent when measured from 1926 to the present. Others use what they believe to be the anticipated or long-term industry growth rate. Economic and industry information can be helpful in supporting the growth rate. The company's historical growth is also a consideration.
>
> Some analysts will use a growth rate into perpetuity that exceeds the nominal growth rate for the GDP of the United States. If that assumption is made, at some point in time in the future, perhaps several hundred years, the company's value will be greater than the GDP of the United States. In a competitive capitalistic society, it is difficult for a single company to outperform the general economy over the long term. This presentation can be difficult to defend. However, there are several circumstances where the growth rate can be higher than nominal GDP. If there will be a high growth rate for the company in the next several years and then a stabilization of the company at the GDP or some other lower rate, a blended rate may be used. A hybrid growth rate or average could be employed that would reflect the high growth rate over the next several years versus a later stabilized growth rate such as GDP. This presentation is used sometimes when the valuation is taking place in a venue where discounted cash flow is not accepted.

Capitalized Cash Flow Method Conclusion of Value on a Marketable, Control Interest Basis

The indicated value of the Company's invested capital determined under this method was $7,149,743, which was stated on a marketable, control interest basis. The final step was to add any nonoperating/excess assets and subtract any interest-bearing debt that the Company possessed at the date of valuation. In this instance, the Company possessed excess/nonoperating assets of $388,580. These assets consist mostly of marketable securities. The Company also held interest-bearing debt of $918,121. Thus, after adding the nonoperating assets to the value of the operations, a value of $6,620,202 is derived as follows:

Invested capital	$7,149,743
Plus: Nonoperating/excess assets	388,580
Less: Interest-bearing debt	918,121
Equity value	$6,620,202

Discounted Cash Flow Method

This method is a multiple-period valuation model that converts a future series of "cash flow" into value by reducing it to present worth at a rate of return (discount rate) that reflects the risk inherent therein and matches the cash flows. The "cash flow" might be pretax, after-tax, debt-free, free cash flow, or some other measure deemed appropriate by and as adjusted by the analyst. Future income or cash flow is typically determined through projections provided by the Company. However, given the trends and growth prospects of the company, the Capitalized Cash Flow (CCF) method of the income approach was deemed more appropriate. Furthermore, no such projections were available or attainable.

VV	DCF versus CCF

In a company that anticipates growing at a steady rate in the future, it is often unnecessary to prepare a discounted cash flow method. A capitalized cash flow method, as used here in the valuation of LEGGO, is sufficient. Discounted cash flow methods typically are used when short-term growth is anticipated to be different from long-term growth and/or the company's cash flow has not reached a stabilized or normalized period that can be capitalized into perpetuity.

In situations where the discounted cash flow method would be typically used, some analysts will reject it if projections are not provided by the client. Most often the client will prepare projections in situations where a DCF is more appropriate. For LEGGO there were no projections available for the company. However, again, this is a moot point because the company was anticipated to grow over the long term at the approximate average rate of inflation. In circumstances where the client will not or cannot prepare projections, some analysts will prepare them. If CPAs are performing the valuation, they must consider whether the rules on prospective financial information apply. Some CPAs or analysts provide the clients with the tools to prepare the projections. These tools can include structured questions to the client on anticipated growth rates in revenues and anticipated profit margins. The analysts can then be a conduit for that information and put it in its appropriate format for valuation. However, ultimately those projections would be management's, and may necessitate a representation letter from the company's management to the analyst.

Market Approach

Guideline Company Transactions Method

This method values a company by finding acquisitions of guideline companies in the marketplace and applying the multiples that those companies sold at to the subject company data to derive a value. In this instance, we researched various databases and found applicable transactions in two databases. These databases include *Pratt's Stats* and IBA (Institute of Business Appraisers). The transactions discovered within these databases are considered in the valuation, but only to a limited degree due to lack of detailed information.

VV	**Transaction Database Differences**

There are several databases that are commonly used for locating transactions. They are *BizComps, DoneDeals, Pratt's Stats, MergerStat*, and one created by the Institute of Business Appraisers (IBA). There are many other resources, including some that have a specific industry focus. Some analysts subscribe to all of the databases to obtain as much information as possible; others subscribe to only a few. In this valuation, the analyst reviewed and used information from IBA and *Pratt's Stats*.

One of the common mistakes made in the application of transaction multiples is to aggregate the transactions from the different databases. This will result in an inaccurate valuation since each one of the databases collects and presents its data in a different format. For example, some of the databases use invested capital multiples, some use equity multiples, some include working capital, some include debt, some include inventory, and so on. When using these databases, it is recommended that information from each database be used and applied separately to the subject company's revenue and earnings parameters. This will avoid any possible inaccuracies.

Pratt's Stats Database.   This database provides a list of transactions of companies in various industry sectors. In this instance, we researched the water, sewer, and pipeline construction sector and found transactions that took place prior to the date of valuation. The list of transactions includes sales from 20X3 to the present and includes nine transactions. Using this database, we have calculated values based on revenues and EBITDA. The values calculated using this database are presented below.

	Equity Values Calculated
Invested Capital to Revenue	$6,915,495
Invested Capital to EBITDA	$6,974,419
Average Value (illustration only) on Marketable, Control Interest Basis	$6,944,957

Note: Interest-bearing debt was subtracted to obtain equity value.

IBA Database.   This database also provides a list of transactions of companies in various industry sectors. In this instance, we researched the water, sewer, and pipeline construction sector and found a list of transactions that took place prior to the date of valuation. The list of transactions includes sales from 20X3 to the present time and includes four transactions. Using this database, we have calculated values based on gross revenues and discretionary cash flows. To each value, however, we added and deducted some balance sheet items. The multiples derived from the IBA database apply only to the value of fixed assets, inventory, and intangibles. Thus, to obtain a total entity value, all current assets must be added and all liabilities must be deducted. The values using this database are presented in the following table.

	Equity Values Calculated
Sales Price to Gross Revenue	$4,630,801
Sales Price to Discretionary Cash Flows	$3,267,016
Average (illustration only)	$3,948,908
Add: Current Assets (Less Inventory and Less Nonoperating Assets)	$3,090,597
Less: Total Liabilities	($1,864,359)
Value on Marketable, Control Interest Basis	$5,175,146

The following table presents the conclusions of value for each database after adding the nonoperating assets that the Company possesses.

	Pratt's Stats	IBA
Nonmarketable, Control Interest Value	$6,944,957	$5,175,146
Add: Nonoperating Assets	$388,580	$388,580
Total Indicated Value of LEGGO Construction, Inc., on a Marketable, Control Basis	$7,333,537	$5,563,726

VV   **Is a Controlling Interest Nonmarketable?**

The analyst in this valuation concludes that the result of the transaction method is a marketable control basis value. These analysts believe that the term nonmarketable as it applies to a control interest is inappropriate. However, the price of the transaction should reflect some reasonable amount of time to sell the company such that liquidity issues are in the value. A controlling interest may be marketable, but it is not liquid, that is, instant sale and cash within three days. See Chapter 9.

VV   **Reliability of Transaction Data**

Most of the transaction databases used to value closely held businesses lack sufficient details about the transactions. It is often the case that there is uncertainty about what specific assets were purchased and what liabilities were assumed. The motivations of the buyers and sellers are unknown, as are historical and anticipated growth rates. Some of the financial data are stale and do not coincide with the date of the deal. These are just a few of the problems with transaction data. As a result of these problems, many analysts will then dismiss this method as unreliable or unsupportable, or, at best, use it as a secondary or corroborating method, but not as a primary method.

However, there are transactions where information is available. This happens when either the buyer or the seller or both are public companies and there is disclosure of facts and data about the deal. Many analysts will then use this data as part of a primary method. For additional information see Chapter 7, Web Addendum 1 at www.wiley.com/go/FVAM3E.

Guideline Public Company Method

A market approach using guideline public companies requires estimates of a multiple derived from publicly traded guideline companies and ongoing earnings (or a variation thereof such as EBITDA) for the subject entity.

Search for Guideline Public Companies. Guideline public companies should provide a reasonable basis for comparison to the relevant investment characteristics of a company being valued. Guideline companies are most often publicly traded companies in the same or similar business as the valuation subject. Guideline companies are used as a basis to develop valuation conclusions with respect to a subject company under the presumption that a similar market may exist for the subject company as exists for the guideline companies.

Ideal guideline companies are in the same or similar business as the company being valued. However, if there is insufficient evidence in the same or similar business an option may be to consider companies with an underlying similarity of relevant investment characteristics, such as markets, products, growth, cyclical variability, and other salient factors. (*Note:* The selection of businesses in a completely different area may be difficult to support).

Our procedure for deriving guideline companies involved five steps:

1. Identify the industry in which the Company operates
2. Identify the Standard Industrial Classification Code and/or NAICS for the industry in which the Company operates
3. Using Internet search tools, search filings with the SEC for businesses that are similar to the Company
4. Screen the initial group of companies to eliminate those that have negative earnings, those with a negative long-term debt to equity ratio, and those companies for which the price of their stock could not be obtained
5. Review in detail the financial and operational aspects of the remaining potential guideline companies and eliminate those whose services differ from the Company.

Based on the above criteria, our search identified two publicly traded companies that we believe are similar to the Company. The companies selected were:

1. Kaneb Services, Inc.: Headquartered in Richardson, Texas, this company provides on-site services such as sealing underpressure leaks for chemical plants, pipelines, and power companies.
2. Infracorps, Inc.: Headquartered in Richmond, Virginia, this company specializes in the installation and renovation of water, wastewater, and gas utility pipelines. The company is now focusing on trenchless technology for the repair of subsurface pipelines.

VV	**Selecting Guideline Public Companies**

Kaneb's revenue is 30 times as large as LEGGO, whereas Infracorps is twice as large. Some analysts would eliminate Kaneb or adjust its multiples downward, because it is much larger than LEGGO. Furthermore, it does not operate in exactly the same industry. Infracorps seems to be a better fit in terms of size as well as the types of construction services it provides. Some analysts would have eliminated Kaneb and relied only on Infracorps. That would result in reliance on only one guideline public company, a presentation that may be more difficult to defend. Other analysts would completely reject the guideline public company method as it applies to LEGGO. Given the lack of good guideline companies, the analyst here decided to use the guideline public company method only as a reasonableness test for the income approach.

Some analysts believe that guideline public companies typically are not applicable to smaller businesses, such as LEGGO. However, some of these analysts are often surprised by the number of publicly traded companies that are similar in size to private companies in certain industries. At the very least, in valuing a small business, a review of public companies should be undertaken to determine whether there are any similar companies.

Some analysts believe that the selection process for guideline public companies can be expanded outside the particular industry in which the company operates. They will look for similar investment characteristics, such as growth, return on equity, profit margin, and the like. Their belief is that a prudent investor would invest in companies that have similar characteristics regardless of its industry. Generally, the courts have been reluctant to accept companies outside the subject companies industry that are not at least somewhat similar by product, market, and so on.

We have chosen to use five multiples (illustration only) to value the Company.

1. Earnings before interest, taxes, depreciation and amortization (EBITDA)
2. Earnings before interest and taxes (EBIT)
3. Revenues
4. Assets
5. Equity

We believe that the asset and equity multiples are appropriate because construction companies tend to be asset-intensive. We also believe that the EBITDA, EBIT, and revenue multiples are appropriate because the Company has a strong income statement and is profitable. We have calculated both one-year and three-year multiples due to the cyclical nature of the industry. No adjustments have been made to the financial statements of the guideline companies, as we believe none are necessary.

Selecting Guideline Company Valuation Multiples
Minority versus Control

A variety of multiples can be used to value a company. In this situation, the analyst used invested capital to EBITDA, invested capital to EBIT, invested capital to revenues, invested capital to assets, and price to equity. Other multiples that could have been considered are invested capital to debt-free net income and invested

(continues)

capital to debt-free cash flow. This is an area of judgement, and the analyst should consider all potential multiples and decide which ones may be the best fit.

Some recent controversy has emerged due to the recent volatility of the stock market. Since stock prices and P/E multiples can change so rapidly, some analysts believe that some type of average stock price or P/E multiple should be used as opposed to a P/E multiple based on a particular point in time. Traditional valuation theory holds that the value should be as of a single point in time, typically as of a single day. Some analysts believe that the stock price on the date of valuation should be used. Other analysts feel the stock price is affected by factors that have occurred recently, that are not yet affecting the company's earnings. They believe that some type of adjustment and/or averaging technique should be used. In addition to using historical P/E type multiples, which has traditionally been price divided by some historical income figure, some analysts use price to projected income figures. They believe this is a better fit of the price of the stock versus the anticipated performance of the company.

There is also some controversy about whether the application of the market approach results in a minority value or a control value. Those who believe it is a minority value argue that the underlying public stocks are minority interests, such that the application of a valuation multiple would result in a minority value. Others argue that the valuation multiples are nothing more than the inverse of capitalization rates derived from the public market. Consequently, they believe that the underlying theory about minority/control being in the cash flows for the income approach should also apply to the market approach. Also, the management of a public company is supposed to do their best to maximize earnings, cash flow, and value to all shareholders regardless of the number of shares they own.

We performed a ratio analysis of the guideline companies to determine which company was more comparable to the Company. Each company compared reasonably well to the Company by the different ratios. Thus, we have selected the average multiples.

VV   **Applying Guideline Public Company Valuation Multiples**

Some analysts use an average of the multiples to derive a value. Some use an arithmetic average (mean). That is the sum of the indications divided by the number of indications. Others believe that the median average is a better fit because it is less affected by outliers and is the midpoint. Some use the harmonic mean which is calculated by averaging the reciprocal of the data points. Other analysts believe that they should look at each guideline company multiple separately, decide which ones are the most comparable, and rely on those multiples rather than an average of the multiples. Other analysts use some average and then take a "fundamental discount" from that average to reflect the fact that the subject company may be different from the public companies making up the average. This fundamental discount often is used to adjust for size as well.

> There is also some discussion about whether the multiples used from publicly traded companies should be the most recent multiples, typically based on annual, fiscal year-end or four-quarter trailing figures or a multiple of some average earnings, such as a three-year average. If it is believed that if an average multiple would be more indicative of future performance of a company, then that may be more appropriate. Many analysts use both, the most recent period and a historical period, and weight them according to what they think would be most indicative of the future value and performance of the company.

Based on the comparisons and analysis we have not applied any size premiums to the Company or fundamental discounts to the guideline company multiples in this case. We also put more weight on the income measures of value. As mentioned previously, we must add the nonoperating assets to the value to arrive at a total indicated value. Applying these selected multiples to the one- and three-year average parameter (illustration only) of the Company's EBITDA, EBIT, revenues, assets, and equity provides the following values.

1-Year Value

	Values
Selected Value	$5,000,000
Add: Nonoperating Assets	$ 388,580
Value on Marketable, Control Interest Basis	$5,388,580

3-Year Value

	Values
Selected Value	$6,000,000
Add: Nonoperating Assets	$ 388,580
Value on Marketable, Control Interest Basis	$6,388,580

LACK OF MARKETABILITY DISCOUNT

> **VV** **DLOMs Applied to Control Interests**
>
> There is continuing controversy about whether discounts for lack of marketability or liquidity should be applied to a controlling interest, particularly a 100 percent controlling interest, as we have with LEGGO. Many analysts believe that a 100 percent interest is marketable and no discount would apply. Other analysts believe that it depends on the underlying methodology used to derive the prediscount value. For example, when using valuation multiples and rates of return derived from public company data, the rates of return and multiples reflect the fact that the public stocks can be sold in a very short amount of time, often instantly, with cash received within three days. A private company cannot be sold for cash within three days. Some analysts believe that the underlying method assumes such liquidity,
>
> *(continues)*

which does not exist in a controlling interest in a private company. Thus some level of discount may be appropriate. However, there are no known widely accepted empirical studies to determine discounts for lack of liquidity of a 100 percent controlling interest in a business. Furthermore, the direct application of a lack of liquidity discount is not often seen in actual transactions. If applicable, some analysts rely on discount for lack of marketability studies for minority interests and reduce the discount to reflect the 100 percent control.

The analyst here is reviewing a 100 percent interest in LEGGO. However, what if it were a 50 percent interest with one other 50 percent owner? Would a discount for lack of control and/or a discount for lack of marketability be appropriate? A 50 percent interest with another 50 percent interest essentially grants the 50 percent owner veto power in most states. That is a better position to be in than a minority position with one other controlling shareholder. Based on specific facts and circumstances, and adjustments to cash flows, some discount for lack of control may be applicable. A discount for lack of marketability would be appropriate, but probably not as great as in a minority situation.

Selection of Applicable Discount for Lack of Marketability/Liquidity

To quantify the discount for lack of marketability/liquidity applicable to the control ownership interest in the Company, we considered these factors to have an impact on the magnitude of the discount.

- Liquidity implied in underlying valuation methodology
- Uncertain time horizon to complete the offering or sale
- Cost to prepare for and execute the offering or sale
- Risk concerning eventual sale price
- Noncash and deferred transaction proceeds

Based on analysis of the factors we believe affect the lack of liquidity discount, it is our opinion that the appropriate discount for lack of liquidity is 5 percent (illustration only; based on facts and circumstances; not all analysts agree) for a control interest.

CORRELATION OF VALUES

To reach a final conclusion for the value of the stockholders' equity on a marketable, control basis, we considered all methods, each of which was weighed according to its merits as an indicator of value. In this instance, we believe that the CCF method gave the best indication of value because of the discernible trends of the company. This value is supported by the other methods. The guideline company transaction method (GCTM) was not chosen as the best indication of value due to the age of some of the transactions and the lack of detailed knowledge of the terms of the transactions. The guideline public company method was also not chosen as the best indication of value since there were only two companies and one of them was much larger and not as good a fit based on the industry description.

Method	Marketable, Control Basis	Discount for Lack of Liquidity	Marketable, Control Basis
Capitalized Cash Flow Method	$6,620,202	5%	$6,289,192
GCTM Pratt's Stats Database			$7,333,537
GCTM IBA Database			$5,563,726
GPCM—1 Year	$5,388,580	5%	$5,119,151
GPCM—3 Year	$6,388,580	5%	$6,069,151
Selected Value on Marketable, Control Interest Basis (Rounded)			$6,300,000

| VV | **Reconciling Values** |

In correlating and reconciling values, many analysts use a simple arithmetic average of all the indications of value. What this may imply is that each method has equal weight, equal validity, and equal accuracy. This is seldom the case in a business valuation. Other analysts assign weights to each of the methods, such as 0.5 to the income approach, 0.3 to the guideline public company approach, and 0.2 to transactions. However, again, this may imply precision that does not exist. Also, if you are only putting a 20 percent weight on a method, you may be indicating that method may not be very accurate or reliable.

Many analysts, including the one who valued LEGGO, will look at each one of the methodologies and decide which ones they believe result in the most valid answer and then pick a value based on that qualitative judgment.

TOTAL CONCLUSION OF VALUE ON A MARKETABLE, CONTROL BASIS

Our conclusion of the fair market value of 100 percent of the common stock of LEGGO Construction, Inc., on a marketable, control basis as of December 31, 20X5 for management purposes is approximately (rounded):

$6,300,000

Index